THE ENGLISH MISSAL

MISSALE ANGLICANUM

THE
ENGLISH MISSAL

This fifth edition of the Altar missal was published by
W. Knott & Son in 1958

Reissued in 2001 by The Canterbury Press Norwich
(a publishing imprint of Hymns Ancient & Modern Limited
a registered charity)
St Mary's Works, St Mary's Plain
Norwich, Norfolk, NR3 3BH
[by permission of the copyright holders Tufton Books
(a Church Union imprint) Tufton Street, London]

All rights reserved. No part of this publication which is
copyright may be reproduced, stored in a retrieval
system, or transmitted, in any form or by any means,
electronic, mechanical, photocopying, recording or
otherwise, without the prior permission of the publisher.

A catalogue record of this book is available
from the British Library

ISBN 1-85311-421-9

Printed in Great Britain by
Biddles Ltd, Guildford and King's Lynn

INTRODUCTION

A priest, enthusiastic about the reappearance of *The English Missal*, wryly remarked to me that if this reissue were to be subtitled 'a valuable resource book' it would enjoy even wider appeal.

Of course, *The English Missal* was born in an age which was the very antithesis of the age of the 'resource book'; when holiness and the pious worshipping of God in the most seemly way were emphasized. *The English Missal* was truly ecumenical in the sense that the Catholic Anglican parish was now able to use the Roman Rite, a rite largely that of the pre-Reformation English Church, in a book specifically published for use in the Anglican Church. Perhaps until recently that attitude to worship was considered to be dangerously old-fashioned, and to be fervently discouraged along with the eastward-facing celebrant.

In the second half of the twentieth century, the Church has allowed itself to be 'evangelized' by society and society's values have tended to become the Church's values. Perhaps now there are signs that the Church realizes its imprudence of recent years. Certainly in the Roman Church there is *officially* a greater tolerance towards the eastward mass, and Rome has generously provided for those former Anglican parishes in America, now in the embrace of Rome, by making Catholic the Book of Common Prayer and by providing and permitting the use of the English translation of the Roman Canon attributed to Miles Coverdale. (I thought it appropriate – at the suggestion of Fr. Hunwicke of Lancing College – to include such a beautiful consecration prayer after this Introduction.) And even within the Anglican Church, certain parts of the new publication *Common Worship* do nudge the Church of England towards a more Catholic mass.

But *The English Missal* is not reissued as a curiosity or out of sentiment and nostalgia for halcyon days. It is still a treasury (indeed, a well-packed 'resource book'!) of Collects and Propers for public and private prayer and meditation in the Roman and Anglican Churches; it will be of interest and use to those former Anglican parishes in American mentioned above and to the 'Continuing' Anglican Churches throughout the world; and it will be a great relief to theological librarians who will be able to replace their much-thumbed copies.

This edition is a reissue of the fifth and last edition (1958) of the Altar missal and, therefore, it contains much more material than the layman's third edition of the same year. In addition it provides a fresh table of moveable feasts to the year 2030. However, the size of this edition is a compromise between the two missals and will be appropriate either for the missal stand or for personal devotional use.

The English Missal was in use for well over half the century: may its use continue with the provision of this new edition.

Julien Chilcott-Monk
Epiphany, 2001

THE CANON OF THE MASS

(A translation attributed to Miles Coverdale)

Most merciful Father, we humbly pray thee, through Jesus Christ thy Son our Lord,
And we ask, that thou accept and bless these gifts, these presents, these holy and unspoiled sacrifices. We offer them unto thee, first, for thy holy catholic Church; that thou vouchsafe to keep it in peace, to guard, unite, and govern it throughout the whole world, together with they servant *N*, our Pope and *N*, our Bishop and all the faithful guardians of the catholic and apostolic faith.
Remember, O Lord, thy servants and handmaids *N* and *N* and all who here around us stand, whose faith is known unto thee and their steadfastness manifest, on whose behalf we offer unto thee, or who themselves offer unto thee, this sacrifice of praise, for themselves, and for all who are theirs; for the redemption of their souls, for the hope of their salvation and safety; and who offer their prayers unto thee, the eternal God, the living and the true.
United in one communion, we venerate the memory, first of the glorious ever Virgin Mary, Mother of our God and Lord Jesus Christ, of Joseph her spouse; as also of the blessed Apostles and Martyrs, Peter and Paul, Andrew, James, John, Thomas, James, Philip, Bartholomew, Matthew, Simon and Thaddaeus; Linus, Cletus, Clement, Xystus, Cornelius, Cyprian, Lawrence, Chrysogonus, John and Paul, Cosmas and Damian and of all thy Saints: grant that by their merits and prayers we may in all things be defended with the help of thy protection, through the same Christ our Lord. Amen.

We beseech thee then, O Lord, graciously to accept this oblation from us thy servants, and from thy whole family: order thou our days in thy peace, and bid us to be delivered from eternal damnation, and to be numbered in the fold of thine elect, Through Christ our Lord, Amen.

Vouchsafe, O God, we beseech thee, in all things to make this oblation blessed, approved and accepted, a perfect and worthy offering; that it may become for us the Body and Blood of thy dearly beloved Son, Jesus Christ.
Who the day before he suffered took bread into his holy and venerable hands, and with eyes lifted up to heaven, unto thee, God, his almighty Father, giving thanks to thee, he blessed, broke and gave it to his disciples saying:

TAKE THIS, ALL OF YOU, AND EAT IT: THIS IS MY BODY WHICH WILL BE GIVEN UP FOR YOU.

Likewise, after supper, taking also this goodly chalice into his holy and venerable hands, again giving thanks to thee, he blessed, and gave it to his disciples, saying:

TAKE THIS, ALL OF YOU, AND DRINK FROM IT: THIS IS THE CUP OF MY BLOOD, THE BLOOD OF THE NEW AND EVERLASTING COVENANT. IT WILL BE SHED FOR YOU AND FOR ALL SO THAT SINS MAY BE FORGIVEN.

DO THIS IN MEMORY OF ME.

Wherefore, O Lord, we thy servants, and thy holy people also, remembering the blessed passion of the same Christ thy Son our Lord, as also his resurrection from the dead, and his glorious ascension into heaven; do offer unto thine excellent majesty of thine own gifts and bounty, the pure victim, the holy victim, the immaculate victim, the holy Bread of eternal life, and the Chalice of everlasting salvation.

Vouchsafe to look upon them with a merciful and pleasant countenance; and to accept them, even as thou didst vouchsafe to accept the gifts of thy servant Abel the Righteous, and the sacrifice of our Patriarch Abraham; and the holy sacrifice the immaculate victim, which thy high priest Melchisedech offered unto thee.

We humbly beseech thee, almighty God, command these offerings to be brought by thy hands of thy holy Angel to thine altar on high, in sight of thy divine majesty; that all we who at this partaking of the altar shall receive the most sacred Body and Blood of thy Son may be fulfilled with all heavenly benediction and grace, Through the same Christ our Lord. Amen.

Remember also, O Lord, thy servants *N*, and *N*, who have gone before us sealed with the seal of faith, and who sleep the sleep of peace. To them, O Lord, and to all that rest in Christ, we beseech thee to grant the abode of refreshing, of light, and of peace. Through the same Christ our Lord. Amen.

To us sinners also, thy servants, who hope in the multitude of thy mercies, vouchsafe to grant some part and fellowship with thy holy Apostles and Martyrs; with John, Stephen, Matthias, Barnabas, Ignatius, Alexander, Marcellinus, Peter, Felicitas, Perpetua, Agatha, Lucy, Agnes, Cecilia, Anastasia and with all thy Saints, within whose fellowship, we beseech thee, admit us, not weighing our merit, but granting us forgiveness; through Jesus Christ our Lord, through whom, O Lord, thou dost ever create all these good things, dost sanctify, quicken, bless, and bestow them upon us; By whom, and with whom, and in whom, in the unity of the Holy Ghost, all honour and glory be unto thee, O Father Almighty, world with end. Amen.

TABLE OF MOVEABLE FEASTS

Year	Septuagesima	Ash Wednesday	EASTER DAY	Ascension	Pentecost	Corpus Christi	Advent Sunday
2001	11 February	28 February	15 April	24 May	3 June	14 June	2 December
2002	27 January	13 February	31 March	9 May	19 May	30 May	1 December
2003	16 February	5 March	20 April	29 May	8 June	19 June	30 November
2004	8 February	25 February	11 April	20 May	30 May	10 June	28 November
2005	23 January	9 February	27 March	5 May	15 May	26 May	27 November
2006	12 February	1 March	16 April	25 May	4 June	15 June	3 December
2007	4 February	21 February	8 April	17 May	27 May	7 June	2 December
2008	20 January	6 February	23 March	1 May	11 May	22 May	30 November
2009	8 February	25 February	12 April	21 May	31 May	11 June	29 November
2010	31 January	17 February	4 April	13 May	23 May	3 June	28 November
2011	20 February	9 March	24 April	2 June	12 June	23 June	27 November
2012	5 February	22 February	8 April	17 May	27 May	7 June	2 December
2013	27 January	13 February	31 March	9 May	19 May	30 May	1 December
2014	16 February	5 March	20 April	29 May	8 June	19 June	30 November
2015	1 February	18 February	5 April	14 May	24 May	4 June	29 November
2016	24 January	10 February	27 March	5 May	15 May	26 May	27 November
2017	12 February	1 March	16 April	25 May	4 June	15 June	3 December
2018	28 January	14 February	1 April	10 May	20 May	31 May	2 December
2019	17 February	6 March	21 April	30 May	9 June	20 June	1 December
2020	9 February	26 February	12 April	21 May	31 May	11 June	29 November
2021	31 January	17 February	4 April	13 May	23 May	3 June	28 November
2022	13 February	2 March	17 April	26 May	5 June	16 June	27 November
2023	5 February	22 February	9 April	18 May	28 May	8 June	3 December
2024	28 January	14 February	31 March	9 May	19 May	30 May	1 December
2025	16 February	5 March	20 April	29 May	8 June	19 June	30 November
2026	1 February	18 February	5 April	14 May	24 May	4 June	29 November
2027	24 January	10 February	28 March	6 May	16 May	27 May	28 November
2028	13 February	1 March	16 April	25 May	9 June	15 June	3 December
2029	28 January	14 February	1 April	10 May	20 May	31 May	2 December
2030	17 February	6 March	21 April	30 May	9 June	20 June	1 December

The Kalendar of the Universal Church

JANUARY

1. CIRCUMCISION OF THE LORD and Octave of the Nativity, double II class.
   Sunday between the Circumcision and the Epiphany—THE MOST HOLY NAME OF JESUS double II class.
2.
3.
4.
5. Com. St. Telesphorus, Pope and Martyr.
6. EPIPHANY OF THE LORD, double I class.
   Sunday after the Epiphany. THE HOLY FAMILY, JESUS, MARY, JOSEPH, greater double. Com. Sunday.
7.
8.
9.
10.
11. Com. St. Hyginus, Pope and Martyr.
12.
13. COMMEMORATION OF THE BAPTISM OF O L.J. CHRIST, greater double.
14. St. Hilary, Bp., Conf. and Doctor of the Church, double. Com. St. Felix, Priest and Martyr. (*Scotland: St. Kentigern, Bp. and Conf.*)
15. St. Paul the first Hermit, Conf., double. Com. St. Maurus, Ab.
16. St. Marcellus I, Pope and Martyr, simple.
17. St. Antony, Abbot, double.
18. CHAIR OF ST. PETER, AP., AT ROME, greater double. Com. St. Paul, Ap., and St. Prisca, Virgin and Martyr.
19. Com. SS. Marius, Martha, Audifax and Abachum, MM., and St. Canute, King, Martyr.
20. SS. Fabian, Pope, and Sebastian, MM., double.
21. St. Agnes, Virgin and Martyr, double.
22. SS. Vincent and Anastase, MM., simple.
23. St. Raymund de Peñafort, Conf., simple.
24. St. Timothy, Bp. and Martyr, double.
25. CONVERSION OF ST. PAUL, AP., greater double. Com. St. Peter, Ap.
26. St. Polycarp, Bp. and Martyr, double.
27. St. John Chrysostom, Bp., Conf. and Doctor of the Church, double.
28. St. Peter Nolasco, Conf., double. Com. St. Agnes, Virgin and Martyr, second.
29. St. Francis de Sales, Bp , Conf. and Doctor of the Church, double.
30. St. Martina, Virgin and Martyr, simple.
31. St. John Bosco. Conf., double.

FEBRUARY

1. St. Ignatius, Bp. and Martyr, double.
2. PURIFICATION OF THE B.V. MARY, double II class.
3. Com. St. Blasius, Bp. and Martyr.
4. St. Andrew Corsini, Bp. and Conf., double.
5. St. Agatha, Virgin and Martyr, double.
6. St. Titus, Bp. and Conf., double. Com. St. Dorothy, Virgin and Martyr.
7. St. Romuald Ab., double.
8. St. John de Matha, Conf., double.
9. St. Cyril, Bp. of Alexandria, Conf. and Doctor of the Church, double. Com. St. Apollonia, Virgin and Martyr.
10. St. Scholastica, Virgin, double.
11. APPEARING OF THE B.V. MARY IMMACULATE, greater double.
12. SS. Seven Founders of the Order of the Servants B.V.M., CC., double.
13.
14. Com. St. Valentine, Priest and Martyr.
15. Com. SS. Faustinus and Jovita, MM.
16.
17.
18. Com. St. Simeon, Bp. and Martyr.
19.
20.
21.
22. CHAIR OF ST. PETER, AP., AT ANTIOCH, greater double. Com. St. Paul, Ap.
23. St. Peter Damian, Bp., Conf. and Doctor of the Church, double.
24. ST. MATTHIAS, APOSTLE, double II class.
25.
26.
27. St. Gabriel of the Sorrowful Virgin, Conf., double.
28. In leap year the month of February has 29 days and the Feast of St. Matthias is celebrated on the 25th and the feast of St. Gabriel of the Sorrowful Virgin on the 28th February.

The Kalendar

MARCH

1 (*Wales:* ST. DAVID, BP. AND CONF., PRINCIPAL PATRON, double I class.)
2 (In Lent simple Feasts are only commemorated.)
3
4 St. Casimir, Conf., simple. Com. St. Lucius I, Pope and Martyr.
5
6 SS. Perpetua and Felicity, MM., double.
7 St. Thomas Aquinas, Conf. and Doctor of the Church, double.
8 St. John of God, Conf., double.
9 St. Frances of Rome, Widow, double.
10 The Holy Forty Martyrs, simple.
  (*Scotland: Blessed John Ogilvie, Martyr,* greater double.)
11
12 St. Gregory I, Pope, Conf. and Doctor of the Church, double.
13
14
15
16
17 St. Patrick, Bp. and Conf., double. (*Scotland:* greater double).
18 St. Cyril, Bp. of Jerusalem, Conf. and Doctor of the Church. double.
19 ST. JOSEPH, SPOUSE OF THE B.V. MARY, CONF., PATRON OF THE UNIVERSAL CHURCH, double I class.
20
21 ST. BENEDICT, ABBOT, greater double.
22
23
24 ST. GABRIEL, ARCHANGEL, greater double.
25 ANNUNCIATION OF THE B.V. MARY, double I class.
26
27 St. John Damascene, Conf. and Doctor of the Church, double.
28 St. John of Capistrano, Conf., simple.
29
30
31
  Friday after the first Sunday in Passion Tide: SEVEN SORROWS OF THE B.V. MARY, greater double. Com. feria.

APRIL

1
2 St. Francis de Paula, Conf., double.
3
4 St. Isidore Bp., Conf. and Doctor of the Church, double.
5 St. Vincent Ferrer, Conf., double.
6
7
8
9
10
11 St. Leo I, Pope, Conf. and Doctor of the Church, double.
12
13 St. Hermenegild, Martyr, simple.
14 St. Justin, Martyr, double. Com. SS. Tiburtius, Valerian and Maximus, MM.
15
16
17 Com. St. Anicetus, Pope and Martyr.
18
19
20
21 St. Anselm, Bp., Conf. and Doctor of the Church, double.
22 SS. Soter and Caius, PP. and MM., simple.
23 St. George, Martyr, simple. (*England:* PRINCIPAL PATRON, double I class. *Wales:* greater double.)
24 St. Fidelis of Sigmaringa, Martyr, double.
25 ST. MARK, EVANGELIST, double II class.
26 SS. Cletus and Marcellinus, PP. and MM., simple.
27 St. Peter Canisius, Conf. and Doctor of the Church, double.
28 St. Paul of the Cross, Conf., double. Com. St. Vitalis, Martyr.
29 St. Peter, Martyr, double.
30 St. Catherine of Siena, Virgin, double.

The Kalendar

MAY

1. St. Joseph, Spouse of the B.V.M., Worker. double I class.
2. St. Athanasius, Bp., Conf. and Doctor of the Church, double.
3. Invention of the Holy Cross, double II class. Com. SS. Alexander I, Pope, Eventius and Theodulus, MM., and Juvenal, Bp. and Conf.
4. St. Monica, Widow, double. (*England and Wales: Bl. Martyrs of England and Wales*, greater double.)
5. St. Pius V, Pope and Conf., double.
6. St. John Ap. and Ev., ante Portam Latinam, greater double.
7. St. Stanislas, Bp. and Martyr, double.
8. Appearing of St. Michael, Archangel, greater double.
9. St. Gregory Nazianzen, Bp., Conf. and Doctor of the Church, double.
10. St. Antoninus, Bp. and Conf., double. Com. SS. Gordian and Epimachus, MM.
11. SS. Philip and James, App., double II class.
12. SS. Nereus, Achilles and Domitilla, Virgin, and Pancras, MM., simple.
13. St. Robert Bellarmine, Bp., Conf. and Doctor of the Church, double.
14. Com. St. Boniface, Martyr.
15. St. John Baptist de la Salle, Conf., double
16. St. Ubald, Bp. and Conf., simple.
17. St. Paschal Baylon, Conf., double.
18. St. Venantius, Martyr, double.
19. St. Peter Celestine, Pope and Conf., double. Com. St. Pudentiana, Virgin.
20. St. Bernardine of Siena, Conf., simple.
21.
22.
23.
24.
25. St. Gregory VII, Pope and Conf., double. Com. St. Urban I, Pope and Martyr.
26. St. Philip Neri, Conf., double. Com. St. Eleutherius, Pope and Martyr. (*England and Wales:* St. Augustine, Bp. and Conf., Apostle of the English, double II class.)
27. St. Venerable Bede, Conf., and Doctor of the Church, double. Com. St. John I, Pope and Martyr.
28. *Outside England and Wales:* St. Augustine, Bp. and Conf., double.
29. St. Mary Magdalen de Pazzis, Virgin., simple.
30. Com. St. Felix I, Pope and Martyr.
31. B.V. Mary, Queen, double II class. Com. St. Petronilla, Virgin.

JUNE

1. St. Angela Merici, Virgin, double.
2. Com. SS. Marcellinus, Peter and Erasmus, Bp., MM.
3.
4. St. Francis Caracciolo, Conf., double.
5. St. Boniface, Bp. and Martyr, double.
6. St. Norbert, Bp. and Conf., double.
7.
8.
9. Com. SS. Primus and Felician, MM., (*Scotland: St. Columba, Abb.*, double.)
10. St. Margaret, Queen Widow, simple. (*Scotland: November 16.*)
11. St. Barnabas, Apostle, greater double.
12. St. John of St. Fagondez, Conf., double. Com. SS. Basilides, Cyrinus, Nabor and Nazaris, MM.
13. St. Antony of Padua, Conf. and Doctor of the Church, double.
14. St. Basil the Great, Bp., Conf. and Doctor of the Church, double.
15. Com. SS. Vitus, Modestus and Crescentia, MM.
16.
17.
18. St. Ephraem of Syria, Deacon, Conf. and Doctor of the Church, double. Com. SS. Mark and Marcellianus, MM.
19. St. Juliana de Falconeri, Virgin, double. Com. SS. Gervase and Protase MM.
20. Com. St. Silverius, Pope and Martyr.
21. St. Aloysius Gonzaga, Conf., double.
22. St. Paulinus, Bp. and Conf., double. (*England and Wales: St. Alban, Protomartyr of Britain*, greater double.)
23. Vigil.
24. Nativity of St. John Baptist, double I class.
25. St. William, Abbot, double.
26. SS. John and Paul, MM., double.
27.
28. St. Irenaeus, Bp. and Martyr, double. Com. Vigil.
29. SS. Peter and Paul, Apostles, double I class.
30. Commemoration of St. Paul, Apostle, greater double. Com. St. Peter, Ap.

(12)

The Kalendar

JULY	AUGUST
1 Most Precious Blood of O.L.J.C., double I class.	1 St. Peter, Ap., ad Vincula, greater double. Com. St. Paul, Ap., and SS. Maccabees, MM.
2 Visitation of the B.V. Mary, double II class. Com. SS. Processus and Martinian, MM.	2 St. Alphonsus de Liguori, Bp., Conf., and Doctor of the Church, double. Com. St. Stephen I, Pope and Martyr.
3 St. Leo II, Pope and Conf., simple.	3 Finding of St. Stephen, Protomartyr, simple.
4	4 St. Dominic, Conf., greater double.
5 St. Antony Mary Zaccaria, Conf., double.	5 Dedication of St. Mary of the Snow, greater double.
6	6 Transfiguration of O.L.J.C., double II class. Com. SS. Xystus II, Pope, Felicissimus and Agapitus, MM.
7 SS. Cyril and Methodius, Bpp. and Cc., double.	
8 St. Elizabeth, Queen, Widow, simple.	7 St. Cajetan, Conf., double. Com. St. Donatus, Bp. and Martyr.
9 (England and Wales: SS. John Fisher, Bp., and Thomas More, MM., double I class.)	8 SS. Cyriacus, Largus and Smaragdus, MM. simple.
10 SS. Seven Brethren, Martyrs, and SS. Rufina and Secunda, VV. and MM., simple.	9 St. John Mary Vianney, Conf., double. Com. Vigil and St. Romanus, Martyr.
11 Com. St. Pius I, Pope and Martyr.	10 St. Lawrence, Martyr, double II class.
12 St. John Gualbert, Abb., double. Com. SS. Nabor and Felix, MM.	11 Com. SS. Tiburtius and Susanna, Virgin, MM.
13 St. Anacletus, Pope and Martyr, simple.	12 St. Clare, Virgin, double.
14 St. Bonaventura, Bp., Conf. and Doctor of the Church, double.	13 Com. SS. Hippolytus and Cassian, MM.
15 St. Henry, Emperor, Conf., simple.	14 Vigil. Com. St. Eusebius, Conf.
16 Commemoration of B.V. Mary of Mount Carmel, greater double.	15 Assumption of the B.V. Mary, double I class.
17 St. Alexius, Conf., simple.	16 St. Joachim, Father of the B.V.M., Conf., double II class.
18 St. Camillus de Lellis, Conf., double. Com. SS. Symphorosa and her seven Sons, MM.	17 St. Hyacinth, Conf., double.
19 St. Vincent de Paul, Conf., double.	18 Com. St. Agapitus, Martyr.
20 St. Jerome Aemilian, Conf., double. Com. St. Margaret, Virgin and Martyr.	19 St. John Eudes, Conf., double.
21 Com. St. Praxedes, Virgin.	20 St. Bernard, Abb., Conf. and Doctor of the Church, double.
22 St. Mary Magdalen, Penitent, double.	21 St. Jane Frances Fremiot de Chantal, Widow, double.
23 St. Apollinaris, Bp. and Martyr, double. Com. St. Liborius, Bp. and Conf.	22 Immaculate Heart of the B.V. Mary, double II class. Com. SS. Timothy, Hippolytus, Bp., and Symphorian, MM.
24 Com. St. Christina, Virgin and Martyr.	
25 St. James, Apostle, double II class.	23 St. Philip Benizi, Conf., double.
26 St. Anne, Mother of the B.V.M., double II class.	24 St. Bartholomew, Apostle, double II class.
27 Com. St. Pantaleon, Martyr.	25 St. Louis, King, Conf., simple.
28 SS. Nazarius and Celsus, MM., Victor I, Pope and Martyr, and Innocent I, Pope and Conf., simple.	26 Com. St. Zephyrinus, Pope and Martyr.
	27 St. Joseph of Calasanz, Conf., double.
29 St. Martha, Virgin, simple. Com. SS. Felix II, Pope, Simplicius, Faustinus and Beatrice. MM.	28 St. Augustine, Bp., Conf. and Doctor of the Church, double. Com. St. Hermes, Martyr.
	29 Beheading of St. John Baptist, greater double.
30 Com. SS. Abdon and Sennen, MM.	30 St. Rose of St. Mary, Virgin, of Lima, double. Com. SS. Felix and Adauctus, MM.
31 St. Ignatius, Conf., greater double.	31 St. Raymund Nonnatus, Conf., double.

(13)

The Kalendar

SEPTEMBER

1. Com. St. Giles, Abb., and SS. Twelve Brethren, MM.
2. St. Stephen, King, Conf., simple.
3. St. Pius X, Pope, Conf., double.
4.
5. St. Lawrence Justinian, Bp. and Conf., simple.
6.
7.
8. NATIVITY OF THE B.V. MARY, double II class. Com. St. Hadrian, Martyr.
9. Com. St. Gorgonius, Martyr.
10. St. Nicholas of Tolentino, Conf., double.
11. Com. SS. Protus and Hyacinth, MM.
12. THE MOST HOLY NAME OF MARY, greater double.
13.
14. EXALTATION OF THE HOLY CROSS, greater double.
15. SEVEN SORROWS OF THE B.V. MARY, double II class. Com. St. Nicomede, Martyr.
16. SS. Cornelius, Pope, and Cyprian Bp., MM., simple. Com. SS. Euphemia, Virgin, Lucy and Geminian, MM. (*Scotland:* St. Ninian, *Bp. and Conf.*, double).
17. Impression of the sacred Stigmata of St. Francis, Conf., double.
18. St. Joseph of Cupertino, Conf., double.
19. SS. Januarius and Comp., MM., double.
20. SS. Eustace and Comp., MM., double.
21. ST. MATTHEW, APOSTLE AND EVANGELIST, double II class.
22. St. Thomas of Villanova, Bp. and Conf., double. Com. SS. Maurice and Comp., MM.
23. St. Linus, Pope and Martyr, simple. Com. St. Thecla, Virgin and Martyr.
24. B.V. MARY OF RANSOM, greater double.
25.
26. Com. SS. Cyprian and Justina, Virgin, MM.
27. SS. Cosmas and Damian, MM., simple.
28. St. Wenceslas, Duke, Martyr, simple.
29. DEDICATION OF ST. MICHAEL, ARCHANGEL, double I class.
30. St. Jerome, Priest, Conf. and Doctor of the Church, double.

OCTOBER

1. Com. St. Remigius, Bp. and Conf.
2. HOLY GUARDIAN ANGELS, greater double.
3. St. Teresa of the Infant Jesus, Virgin, double.
4. ST. FRANCIS, CONF., greater double.
5. Com. SS. Placid and Comp., MM.
6. St. Bruno, Conf., double.
7. MOST SACRED ROSARY OF THE B.V. MARY, double II class. Com. St. Mark, Pope and Conf.
8. St. Bridget, Widow, double.
9. St. John Leonardi, Conf., double. Com. SS. Denys, Bp., Rusticus and Eleutherius, MM.
10. St. Francis Borgia, Conf., simple.
11. MOTHERHOOD OF THE B.V. MARY, double II class.
12.
13. St. Edward, King, Conf., simple.
14. St. Callistus I, Pope and Martyr, double.
15. St. Teresa, Virgin, double.
16. St. Hedwig, Widow, simple.
17. St. Margaret Mary Alacoque, Virgin, double.
18. ST. LUKE, EVANGELIST, double II class.
19. St. Peter of Alcantara, Conf., double.
20. St. John Cantius, Conf., double.
21. Com. St. Hilarion, Abb., and SS. Ursula and Companions, VV. and MM.
22.
23.
24. ST. RAPHAEL, ARCHANGEL, greater double. Last Sunday of October—FEAST OF O.L. JESUS CHRIST THE KING, double I class.
25. Com. SS. Chrysanthus and Daria, MM.
26. Com. St. Evaristus, Pope and Martyr.
27.
28. SS. SIMON AND JUDE, APP., double II class.
29.
30.
31.

The Kalendar

NOVEMBER

1. ALL SAINTS, double I class.
2. COMMEMORATION OF ALL THE FAITHFUL DEPARTED, double.
3.
4. St. Charles, Bp. and Conf., double. Com. SS. Vitalis and Agricola, MM.
5.
6.
7.
8. Com. SS. Four Crowned Martyrs.
9. DEDICATION OF THE ARCHBASILICA OF THE MOST HOLY SAVIOUR, double II class. Com. St. Theodore, Martyr.
10. St. Andrew Avellini, Conf., double. Com. SS. Tryphon, Respicius and Nympha, Virgin, MM.
11. St. Martin, Bp. and Conf., double. Com. St. Mennas, Martyr.
12. St. Martin I, Pope and Martyr, simple.
13. St. Didacus, Conf., simple.
14. St. Josaphat, Bp. and Martyr, double.
15. St. Albert the Great, Bp., Conf. and Doctor of the Church, double.
16. St. Gertrude, Virgin, double. (*Scotland:* St. Margaret, Queen and Widow, Secondary Patron, double II class.)
17. St. Gregory Thaumaturgus, Bp. and Conf., simple.
18. DEDICATION OF THE BASILICAS OF SS. PETER AND PAUL, APP., greater double.
19. St. Elizabeth, Widow, double. Com. St. Pontian, Pope and Martyr.
20. St. Felix de Valois, Conf., double.
21. PRESENTATION OF THE B.V. MARY, greater double.
22. St. Cecilia, Virgin and Martyr, double.
23. St. Clement I, Pope and Martyr, double. Com. St. Felicity, Martyr.
24. St. John of the Cross, Conf., double. Com St. Chrysogonus, Martyr.
25. St. Catherine, Virgin and Martyr, double.
26. St. Silvester, Abb., double. Com. St. Peter of Alexandria, Bp. and Martyr.
28.
29. Com. St. Saturninus, Martyr.
30. ST. ANDREW, APOSTLE, double II class. (*Scotland:* PRINCIPAL PATRON, double I class.)

DECEMBER

1. (In Advent simple Feasts are only commemorated.)
2. St. Bibiana, Virgin and Martyr, simple.
3. ST. FRANCIS XAVIER, CONF., greater double.
4. St. Peter Chrysologus, Bp., Conf. and Doctor of the Church, double. Com. St. Barbara, Virgin and Martyr.
5. Com. St. Sabbas, Abb.
6. St. Nicholas, Bp. and Conf., double.
7. St. Ambrose, Bp., Conf. and Doctor of the Church, double.
8. IMMACULATE CONCEPTION OF THE B.V. MARY, double I class.
9.
10. Com. St. Melchiades, Pope and Martyr.
11. St. Damasus I, Pope and Conf., simple.
12.
13. St. Lucy, Virgin and Martyr, double.
14.
15.
16. St. Eusebius, Bp. and Martyr, simple.
17.
18.
19.
20.
21. ST. THOMAS, APOSTLE, double II class.
22.
23.
24. Vigil.
25. NATIVITY OF O.L.J.C., double I class with Octave.
26. ST. STEPHEN, PROTOMARTYR, Com. Octave Nativity. double II class.
27. ST. JOHN, APOSTLE AND EVANGELIST, double II class. Com. Octave Nativity.
28. HOLY INNOCENTS, MARTYRS, Com. Octave Nativity. double II class.
29. St. Thomas, Bp. and Martyr, double. Com. Octave Nativity. (*England and Wales:* double II class.)
30. Of the 6th day within Octave of the Nativity, double.
31. St. Silvester I, Pope and Conf., double. Com. Octave of the Nativity.

(15)

THE ORDER OF THE CENSING OF THE OBLATIONS

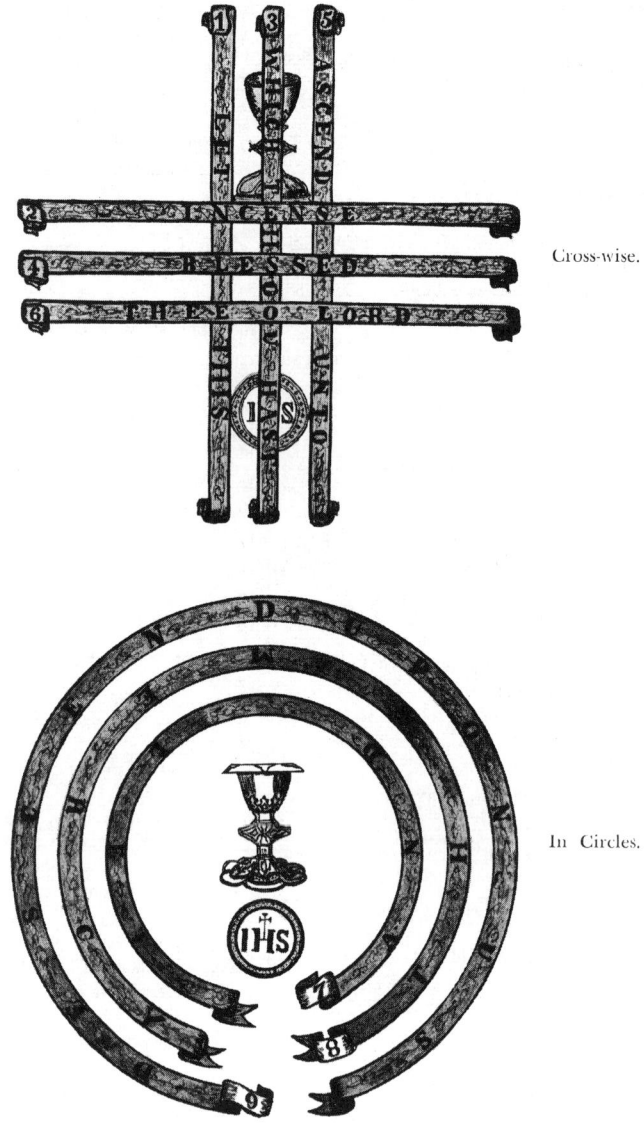

Cross-wise.

In Circles.

THE ORDER OF THE CENSING OF THE ALTAR

If there are no relics or images of Saints on the Altar, the Censing of these is omitted, and, the Cross having been Censed, the Censing of the Altar begins at once in the order 8, 9 and to 29.

THE PROPER OF THE SEASON

1. When alternative Collects, Epistles or Gospels are given, the former of the two is that appointed in the Book of Common Prayer.

2. **In Epistles and Gospels:**

   * = the Epistle or Gospel ends here, according to the Missal, but continues, according to the Book of Common Prayer.

   † = The Epistle or Gospel ends here, according to the Book of Common Prayer, but continues, according to the Missal.

The First Sunday in Advent

1st class. Double of 1st class.

Station at St. Mary Major.

Introit. Ps. 25, 1-3. Ad te levavi.

UNTO thee lift I up my soul: my God in thee have I trusted, let me not be confounded: neither let mine enemies triumph over me: for all they that look for thee shall not be ashamed. Ps. ibid., 4. Shew me thy ways, O Lord: and teach me thy paths.

℣. Glory be to the Father, and to the Son, and to the Holy Ghost. As it was in the beginning, is now, and ever shall be, world without end. Amen.

Repeat Unto thee as far as the Psalm.

¶ This manner of repeating the Introit is observed throughout the year.

¶ Glória in excélsis is not said in Masses of the Season from this Sunday until the Vigil of the Nativity of the Lord inclusive.

Let us pray. *Collect.*

ALMIGHTY God, give us grace that we may cast away the works of darkness, and put upon us the armour of light, now in the time of this mortal life, in which thy Son Jesus Christ came to visit us in great humility: that in the last day, when he shall come again in his glorious Majesty to judge both the quick and the dead, we may rise to the life immortal. Through him who liveth and reigneth with thee and the Holy Ghost, now and ever. ℟. Amen.

Or, Collect.

O LORD, raise up, we pray thee, thy power and come among us: that whereas through our sins and wickedness we are sore beset by many and great dangers; we may be found worthy to be defended from the same by thy protection, and preserved by thy deliverance: Who livest and reignest with God the Father in the unity of the Holy Ghost: ever one God, world without end. ℟. Amen.

The Lesson from the Epistle of blessed Paul the Apostle to the Romans.

Rom. 13, 8-14.

BRETHREN: Owe no man anything, but to love one another: for he that loveth another hath fulfilled the law. For this: Thou shalt not commit adultery: Thou shalt not kill; Thou shalt not steal; Thou shalt not bear false witness; Thou shalt not covet; and if there be any other commandment, it is briefly comprehended in this saying, namely: Thou shalt love thy neighbour as thyself: Love worketh no ill to his neighbour. Therefore love is the fulfilling of the law. And that knowing the time, that now it is high time to awake out of sleep. For now is our salvation nearer than when we believed. The night is far spent, the day is at hand. Let us therefore cast off the works of darkness, and let us put on the armour of light. Let us walk honestly as in the day: not in rioting and drunkenness, not in chambering and wantonness, not in strife and envying: but put ye on the Lord Jesus Christ, and make not provision for the flesh, to fulfil the lusts thereof.

Or

The Lesson from the Epistle of blessed Paul the Apostle to the Romans.
Rom. 13, 11-14.

BRETHREN: Knowing that now it is high time for us to awake out of sleep. For now is our salvation nearer than when we believed. The night is far spent, the day is at hand. Let us therefore cast off the works of darkness, and let us put on the armour of light. Let us walk honestly as in the day: not in rioting and drunkenness, not in chambering and wantonness, not in strife and envying: but put ye on the Lord Jesus Christ.

Gradual. Ps. 25, 3-4. All they that look for thee shall not be ashamed, O Lord. ℣. Shew me thy ways, O Lord: and teach me thy paths.

Alleluia, alleluia. ℣. Ps. 85, 8. Shew us thy mercy, O Lord: and grant us thy salvation. Alleluia.

¶ On Ferias of Advent when, during the week, the Mass of Sunday is resumed, Alleluia is not said nor the following Verse, but only the Gradual.

✠ The Continuation of the holy Gospel according to Matthew.
Matt. 21, 1-9.

AT that time: When they drew nigh unto Jerusalem, and were come to Bethphage, unto the mount of Olives: then sent Jesus two disciples, saying unto them: Go into the village over against you, and straightway ye shall find an ass tied, and a colt with her: loose them, and bring them unto me: and if any man say ought unto you, ye shall say, The Lord hath need of them, and straightway he will send them. All this was done, that it might be fulfilled which was spoken by the Prophet, saying: Tell ye the daughter of Sion: Behold, thy King cometh unto thee, meek, and sitting upon an ass, and a colt the foal of an ass. And the disciples went, and did as Jesus commanded them. And brought the ass, and the colt: and put on them their clothes, and they set him thereon. And a very great multitude spread their garments in the way: others cut down branches from the trees, and strawed them in the way: and the multitudes that went before, and that followed, cried, saying: Hosanna to the Son of David: blessed is he that cometh in the name of the Lord: Hosanna in the highest. And when he was come into Jerusalem all the city was moved, saying: Who is this? And the multitude said: This is Jesus the Prophet of Nazareth of Galilee. And Jesu went into the temple of God, and cast out all them that sold and bought in the temple: and overthrew the tables of the money-changers, and the seats of them that sold doves: and said unto them: It is written: My house shall be called the house of prayer: but ye have made it a den of thieves.

Or Gospel, There shall be signs, p. 4.

The Creed, which is said on all Sundays throughout the year. But it is not said on ferial days, when the Mass of the preceding Sunday is resumed.

Offertory. Ps. 25, 1-3. Unto thee lift I up my soul: my God in thee have I trusted, let me not be confounded: neither let mine enemies triumph over me: for all they that look for thee shall not be ashamed.

Secret.

LET these sacred mysteries, O Lord, so cleanse us by their mighty power, that we, growing in purity, may attain unto thee who art the author of the same. Through.

¶ The Preface of the most Holy Trinity: which is said on Sundays, if they have no proper Preface, according to the Rubrics; but not on ferial days, when the Mass of Sunday is resumed, for then is said the Common Preface.
In Masses of the Season of Advent, the Preface of the B.V.Mary is never said.

Communion. Ps. 85, 13. The Lord shall shew lovingkindness: and our land shall give her increase.

Postcommunion.

LET us wait, O Lord, for thy lovingkindness in the midst of thy temple: that with due honour we may hail the coming feast of our redemption. Through.

¶ Let us bless the Lord is said. And so always when Glória in excélsis has been omitted: otherwise Ite, Missa est is said.

¶ Throughout the year, if the Mass of the Feria is to be said during the week, the Mass of the preceding Sunday is resumed, unless there be a proper Mass. And in the same way, the Prayers of Sunday are taken, when according to the Rubrics a Commemoration is to be made of a Feria which has not a proper Mass.

¶ When in the Seasons of Advent, of Lent from Ash Wednesday until Saturday after Passion Sunday inclusive, on Ember Days, Vigils, and the greater and lesser Litanies, Mass is said of any Festival, or a Votive Mass, a Commemoration of the Feria is always made, outside the conventual or sung Mass: which is also done in conventual and sung Masses unless another Mass also conventual or sung is said of the Feria.

The Second Sunday in Advent

1st class.   Double of 1st class.

Station of St. Cross in Jerusalem.

Introit. Is. 30, 30. Populus Sion.

PEOPLE of Sion, behold, the Lord is nigh at hand to redeem the nations: and in the gladness of your heart the Lord shall cause his glorious voice to be heard. Ps. 79, 2. Hear, O thou Shepherd of Israel: thou that leadest Joseph like a sheep. ℣.Glory.

Collect.

BLESSED Lord, who hast caused all holy Scriptures to be written for our learning: grant that we may in such wise hear them, read, mark, learn, and inwardly digest them; that by patience, and comfort of thy holy Word, we may embrace, and ever hold fast the blessed hope of everlasting life, which thou hast given us in our Saviour Jesus Christ: Who liveth.

Or, Collect.

STIR up our hearts, O Lord, to prepare the way of thine only-begotten Son: that through his advent we may be cleansed from our offences, and may serve thee with a ready mind: Who liveth.

The Lesson from the Epistle of blessed Paul the Apostle to the Romans.

Rom. 15, 4-13.

BRETHREN: Whatsoever things were written aforetime, were written for our learning: that we through patience,

The Second Sunday in Advent

and comfort of the Scriptures, might have hope. Now the God of patience and consolation grant you to be like-minded one towards another, according to Christ Jesus: that ye may with one mind and one mouth glorify God, even the Father of our Lord Jesus Christ. Wherefore receive ye one another, as Christ also received us, to the glory of God. Now I say, that Jesus Christ was a minister of the circumcision for the truth of God to confirm the promises made unto the fathers: and that the Gentiles might glorify God for his mercy, as it is written: For this cause I will confess to thee among the Gentiles, and sing unto thy name. And again he saith: Rejoice, ye Gentiles, with his people. And again: Praise the Lord, all ye Gentiles: and laud him, all ye people. And again, Esaias saith: There shall be a root of Jesse, and he that shall rise to reign over the Gentiles, in him shall the Gentiles trust. Now the God of hope fill you with all joy and peace in believing: that ye may abound in hope, through the power of the Holy Ghost.

Gradual. Ps. 50, 2-3 and 5. Out of Sion hath God appeared: in perfect beauty. ℣. Gather my saints together unto me, those that have made a covenant with me with sacrifice.

¶ The following Alleluia with the Verse is said on Sunday only, on Ferias it is omitted.

Alleluia, alleluia. ℣. Ps. 122, 1. I was glad when they said unto me: we will go into the house of the Lord. Alleluia.

✠ The Continuation of the holy Gospel according to Luke.

Luke 21, 25-33.

AT that time: Jesus said unto his disciples: There shall be signs in the sun, and in the moon, and in the stars, and upon the earth distress of nations, with perplexity, the sea and the waves roaring: men's hearts failing them for fear, and for looking after those things which are coming on the earth: for the powers of heaven shall be shaken. And then shall they see the Son of man coming in a cloud with power and great glory. And when these things begin to come to pass, then look up, and lift up your heads: for your redemption draweth nigh. And he spake to them a parable: Behold the fig-tree, and all the trees: when they now shoot forth, ye see and know of your own selves that summer is now nigh at hand. So likewise ye, when ye see these things come to pass, know ye that the kingdom of God is nigh at hand. Verily I say unto you, This generation shall not pass away, till all be fulfilled. Heaven and earth shall pass away: but my words shall not pass away. Creed.

Or Gospel, When John had heard, p. 6.

Offertory. Ps. 85, 7-8. Wilt thou not turn again, O God, and quicken us, that thy people may rejoice in thee: shew us thy mercy, O Lord, and grant us thy salvation.

Secret.

WE beseech thee, O Lord, mercifully to accept the prayers and sacrifices of thy humble servants: that we, who cannot of our own prayers and merits help ourselves, may be defended by thy succour. Through.

Preface of the Most Holy Trinity.

Communion. Baruch, 5, 5; 4, 36. Arise, O Jerusalem, and stand on high, and behold the joy that cometh unto thee from thy God.

Postcommunion.

O LORD, who hast fulfilled us with spiritual food and sustenance, we humbly beseech thee: that through the partaking of these holy mysteries thou wouldest teach us to despise things earthly, and to love the things that are heavenly. Through.

The Third Sunday in Advent

1st class.   Double of 1st class.

Station at St. Peter.

Introit. Phil. 4, 4-6. Gaudete.

REJOICE in the Lord alway: and again I say, rejoice. Let your moderation be known unto all men: for the Lord is at hand. Be careful for nothing: but in every thing by prayer let your requests be made known unto God. Ps. 85, 1. Lord, thou art become gracious unto thy land: thou hast turned away the captivity of Jacob. ℣. Glory.

Collect.

O LORD Jesu Christ, who at thy first coming didst send thy messenger to prepare thy way before thee: grant that the ministers and stewards of thy mysteries may likewise so prepare and make ready thy way, by turning the hearts of the disobedient to the wisdom of the just; that at thy second coming to judge the world we may be found an acceptable people in thy sight: Who livest and reignest with the Father and the Holy Spirit, ever one God world without end. ℟. Amen.

Or, Collect.

LORD, we beseech thee, give ear to our prayers: and by thy gracious visitation lighten the darkness of our heart: Who livest and reignest with God the Father.

The Lesson from the Epistle of blessed Paul the Apostle to the Corinthians.

I Cor. 4, 1-5.

BRETHREN: Let a man so account of us, as of the ministers of Christ, and stewards of the mysteries of God. Moreover, it is required in stewards, that a man be found faithful. But with me it is a very small thing that I should be judged of you, or of man's judgment: yea, I judge not mine own self. For I know nothing by myself: yet am I not hereby justified: but he that judgeth me is the Lord. Therefore judge nothing before the time, until the Lord come: who both will bring to light the hidden things of darkness, and will make manifest the counsels of the hearts: and then shall every man have praise of God.

Or

The Lesson from the Epistle of blessed Paul the Apostle to the Philippians.

Phil. 4, 4-7.

BRETHREN: Rejoice in the Lord alway: and again I say, Rejoice. Let your moderation be known unto all men: the Lord is at hand. Be careful for nothing: but in every thing, by prayer and supplication with thanksgiving, let your requests be made known unto God. And the peace of God, which passeth all understanding, shall keep your hearts and minds in Christ Jesu our Lord.

Gradual. Ps. 80, 2, 3 and 2. Thou that sittest upon the Cherubim, stir up thy strength, O Lord, and come. ℣. Hear, O thou Shepherd of Israel: thou that leadest Joseph like a sheep.

¶ The following Alleluia with the Verse is said on Sunday only, on Ferias it is omitted.

Alleluia, alleluia. ℣. Stir up thy strength, O Lord, and come and help us. Alleluia,

✠ The Continuation of the holy Gospel according to Matthew.

Matt. 11, 2-10.

AT that time: When John had heard in the prison the works of Christ, he sent two of his disciples, and said unto him: Art thou he that should come, or do we look for another? Jesus answered and said unto them: Go and shew John again those things which ye do hear and see. The blind receive their sight, and the lame walk, the lepers are cleansed, and the deaf hear, the dead are raised up, and the poor have the Gospel preached to them: and blessed is he whosoever shall not be offended in me. And as they departed, Jesus began to say unto the multitudes concerning John: What went ye out into the wilderness to see? a reed shaken with the wind? But what went ye out for to see? a man clothed in soft raiment? Behold, they that wear soft clothing are in kings' houses. But what went ye out for to see? a Prophet? Yea, I say unto you, and more than a Prophet. For this is he of whom it is written: Behold, I send my messenger before thy face, which shall prepare thy way before thee.

Or

✠ The Continuation of the holy Gospel according to John.

John 1, 19-28.

AT that time: The Jews sent priests and levites from Jerusalem to John, to ask him: Who art thou? And he confessed, and denied not: but confessed: I am not the Christ. And they asked him: What then? Art thou Elias? And he saith: I am not. Art thou that Prophet? And he answered: No. Then said they unto him: Who art thou, that we may give an answer to them that sent us? What sayest thou of thyself? He said: I am the voice of one crying in the wilderness: Make straight the way of the Lord, as said the Prophet Esaias. And they which were sent were of the Pharisees. And they asked him, and said unto him: Why baptizest thou then, if thou be not that Christ, nor Elias, neither that Prophet? John answered them saying: I baptize with water but there standeth one among you, whom ye know not. He it is who coming after me is preferred before me: whose shoe's latchet I am not worthy to unloose. These things were done in Bethabara beyond Jordan, where John was baptizing. Creed.

Offertory. Ps. 85, 2. Lord, thou art become gracious unto thy land: thou hast turned away the captivity of Jacob: thou hast forgiven the offence of thy people.

Secret.

WE beseech thee, O Lord, that the continual offering of this sacrifice of our bounden duty: may fulfil thine institution of this sacred mystery, and may accomplish in us the wondrous work of thy salvation. Through.

Preface of the Most Holy Trinity.

Communion. Is. 35, 4. Say to them that are of a fearful heart: be strong, fear not: behold, our God will come and save us.

Postcommunion.

HAVE mercy upon us, O Lord, we beseech thee: and grant that these means of heavenly grace may so cleanse us from our iniquities, that we may be made ready to keep thy coming festival. Through.

Ember Wednesday in Advent

Station at St. Mary Major.

Introit. Is. 45, 8. Rorate.

DROP down, ye heavens, from above, and let the skies pour down righteousness: let the earth open, and bring forth the Saviour. Ps. 19, 1.

Ember Wednesday in Advent

The heavens declare the glory of God: and the firmament sheweth his handywork. ℣. Glory.

After Kýrie, eléison is said immediately:

Let us pray. Let us bow the knee.
℟. Arise.

Collect.

GRANT, we beseech thee, almighty God: that the coming solemnity of our redemption may bestow on us thy succour in this present life, and win for us the rewards of everlasting felicity. Through.

The Lesson from the Prophet Isaiah.

Is. 2, 2-5.

IN those days: Said Isaiah the Prophet: It shall come to pass in the last days, that the mountain of the Lord's house shall be established in the top of the mountains, and shall be exalted above the hills, and all nations shall flow unto it. And many people shall go and say: Come ye, and let us go up to the mountain of the Lord, to the house of the God of Jacob, and he will teach us of his ways, and we will walk in his paths: for out of Sion shall go forth the law, and the word of the Lord from Jerusalem. And he shall judge among the nations, and shall rebuke many people: and they shall beat their swords into plowshares, and their spears into pruninghooks. Nation shall not lift up sword against nation: neither shall they learn war any more. O house of Jacob, come ye, and let us walk in the light of the Lord our God.

Gradual. Ps. 24, 7, 3 and 4. Lift up your heads, O ye gates: and be ye lift up, ye everlasting doors: and the King of glory shall come in. ℣. Who shall ascend into the hill of the Lord? or who shall rise up in his holy place? Even he that hath clean hands, and a pure heart.

Here is said ℣. The Lord be with you, without Let us bow the knee.

Let us pray. Collect.

O LORD, make haste, we pray thee, tarry not, and bestow on us the succour of thy heavenly might: that they who put their trust in thy mercy may by the consolations of thine advent be relieved: Who livest and reignest.

The Lesson from the Prophet Isaiah.

Is. 7, 10-15.

IN those days: The Lord spake unto Ahaz, saying: Ask thee a sign of the Lord thy God, ask it either in the depth, or in the height above. But Ahaz said: I will not ask, neither will I tempt the Lord. And he said: Hear ye now, O house of David: Is it a small thing for you to weary men, but will ye weary my God also? Therefore the Lord himself shall give you a sign. Behold, a Virgin shall conceive, and bear a son, and shall call his name Emmanuel. Butter and honey shall he eat, that he may know to refuse the evil, and choose the good.

Gradual. Ps. 145, 18 and 21. The Lord is nigh unto all them that call upon him: yea, all such as call upon him faithfully. ℣. My mouth shall speak the praise of the Lord: and let all flesh give thanks unto his holy name.

✠ The Continuation of the holy Gospel according to Luke.

Luke 1, 26-38.

AT that time: The Angel Gabriel was sent from God unto a city of Galilee, named Nazareth, to a Virgin espoused to a man whose name was Joseph, of the house of David, and the Virgin's name was Mary. And the Angel came in unto her, and said: Hail, full of grace; the Lord is with thee: blessed art thou among women. And when she saw him, she was troubled at his saying: and cast in her mind what manner of salutation this should be. And the Angel said unto her: Fear not, Mary, for thou hast found favour with God: and, behold, thou shalt conceive in thy womb, and bring forth a son, and shalt call his name Jesus. He shall be great, and shall be called the Son of the Highest, and the Lord God shall give unto him the throne of his father David: and he shall reign over the house of Jacob for ever, and of his kingdom there shall be no end. Then said Mary unto the Angel: How shall this be, seeing I know not a man? And the Angel answered and said unto her: The Holy Ghost shall come upon thee, and the power of the Highest shall overshadow thee. Therefore also that Holy Thing which shall be born of thee shall be called the Son of God. And, behold, thy cousin Elisabeth, she hath also conceived a son in her old age: and this is the sixth month with her, who was called barren: for with God nothing shall be impossible. And Mary said: Behold the handmaid of the Lord, be it unto me according to thy word.

Offertory. Is. 35, 4. Be strong, fear not: behold, our God will come with vengeance, even God with a recompence: he will come and save us.

Secret.

WE beseech thee, O Lord, that this our fast may be acceptable in thy sight: that we, being cleansed thereby and made worthy of thy grace, may attain unto thine everlasting promises. Through.

Communion. Is. 7, 14. Behold, a Virgin shall conceive, and bear a son: and his name shall be called Emmanuel.

Postcommunion.

O LORD, who hast satisfied us with the healing gifts of thy bounty, we humbly beseech thee: that as we do rejoice in the partaking of the same, so they may be profitable to the renewing of our souls. Through.

Ember Friday in Advent

Station at the twelve Holy Apostles.

Introit. Ps. 119, 151-152. Prope es tu.

BE thou nigh at hand, O Lord, for all thy commandments are true: as concerning thy testimonies, I have known long since, that thou art from everlasting. Ps. ibid., 1. Blessed are those that are undefiled in the way: and walk in the law of the Lord. ℣. Glory.

Collect.

STIR up, we beseech thee, O Lord, thy power, and come among us: that they who put their confidence in thy goodness may speedily be delivered from all adversity: Who livest.

The Lesson from the Prophet Isaiah.

Is. 11, 1-5.

THUS saith the Lord God: There shall come forth a rod out of the stem of Jesse, and a branch shall grow out of his roots. And the spirit of the Lord shall rest upon him: the spirit of wisdom and understanding, the spirit of counsel and might, the spirit of knowledge and of the fear of the Lord; and shall make him of quick understanding in the fear of the Lord. And he shall not judge after the sight of his eyes: neither reprove after the hearing of his ears: but with righteousness shall he judge the poor, and reprove with equity for the meek of the earth: and he shall smite the earth with the rod of his mouth, and with the breath of his lips shall he slay the wicked. And righteousness shall be the girdle of his loins: and faithfulness the girdle of his reins.

Gradual. Ps. 85, 8 and 2. Shew us thy mercy, O Lord: and grant us thy salvation. ℣. Lord, thou art become gracious unto thy land: thou hast turned away the captivity of Jacob.

☩ The Continuation of the holy Gospel according to Luke.

Luke 1, 39-47.

AT that time: Mary arose, and went into the hill country with haste, into a city of Juda: and entered into the house of Zacharias, and saluted Elisabeth. And it came to pass, that, when Elisabeth heard the salutation of Mary, the babe leaped in her womb: and Elisabeth was filled with the Holy Ghost, and she spake out with a loud voice, and said: Blessed art thou among women, and blessed is the fruit of thy womb. And whence is this to me, that the Mother of my Lord should come to me? For, lo, as soon as the voice of thy salutation sounded in mine ears, the babe leaped in my womb for joy. And blessed is she that believed, for there shall be a performance of those things which were told her from the Lord. And Mary said: My soul doth magnify the Lord: and my spirit hath rejoiced in God my Saviour.

Offertory. Ps. 85, 7-8. Wilt thou not turn again, and quicken us, O God, that thy people may rejoice in thee: shew us thy mercy, O Lord, and grant us thy salvation.

Secret.

WE beseech thee, O Lord, to accept our prayers and oblations: and graciously hearken unto us, whom thou dost cleanse by thy heavenly mysteries. Through.

Communion. Zech. 14, 5-6. Behold, the Lord shall come, and all his Saints with him: and in that day there shall be a great light.

Postcommunion.

GRANT, O Lord, that this holy Sacrament, which we have now received, may in such wise deliver us from the sins of our former nature: that we may be worthy to enter into the fellowship of thy saving mysteries. Through.

Ember Saturday in Advent

Station at St. Peter.

Introit. Ps. 80, 4 and 2. Veni et ostende.

COME and shew us the light of thy countenance, O Lord, thou that sittest upon the Cherubim: and we shall be whole. Ps. ibid., 1. Hear, O thou Shepherd of Israel: thou that leadest Joseph like a sheep. ℣. Glory.

After Kýrie, eléison is said: Let us pray. Let us bow the knee. ℟. Arise.

Collect.

O GOD, who seest us to be sore afflicted by reason of our iniquity: mercifully grant; that we may be comforted by thy visitation: Who livest and reignest.

The Lesson from the Prophet Isaiah.

Is. 19, 20-22.

IN those days: They shall cry unto the Lord because of the oppressors, and he shall send them a saviour, and a great one, and he shall deliver them. And the Lord shall be known to Egypt, and the Egyptians shall know the Lord in that day: and shall do sacrifice and oblation: yea, they shall vow a vow unto the Lord, and perform it. And the Lord shall smite Egypt, he shall smite and heal it: and they shall return even to the Lord, and he shall be intreated of them, and shall heal them, even he the Lord our God.

Gradual. Ps. 19, 7 and 2. He goeth forth from the uttermost part of the heaven: and runneth about unto the end of it again. ℣. The heavens declare the glory of God: and the firmament sheweth his handywork.

Let us pray.   Let us bow the knee.
℟. Arise.

Collect.

GRANT, we beseech thee, almighty God: that we, who by reason of our ancient bondage are bowed beneath the yoke of sin; may by the new birth of thine only-begotten Son which we await obtain deliverance: Who liveth.

The Lesson from the Prophet Isaiah.

Is. 35, 1-7.

THUS saith the Lord: The wilderness and the solitary place shall be glad for them, and the desert shall rejoice, and blossom as the rose. It shall blossom abundantly, and rejoice even with joy and singing: the glory of Lebanon shall be given unto it: the excellency of Carmel and Sharon, they shall see the glory of the Lord, and the excellency of our God. Strengthen ye the weak hands, and confirm the feeble knees. Say to them that are of a fearful heart: Be strong, fear not: behold, your God will come with vengeance, even God with a recompence: he will come and save you. Then the eyes of the blind shall be opened, and the ears of the deaf shall be unstopped. Then shall the lame man leap as an hart, and the tongue of the dumb sing: for in the wilderness shall waters break out, and streams in the desert. And the parched ground shall become a pool, and the thirsty land springs of water: saith the Lord almighty.

Gradual. Ps. 19, 6 and 7. He hath set his tabernacle in the sun: and he cometh forth as a bridegroom out of his chamber. ℣. He goeth forth from the uttermost part of the heaven: and runneth about unto the end of it again.

Let us pray.   Let us bow the knee.
℟. Arise.

Collect.

WE beseech thee, O Lord, that we thine unworthy servants, who now bewail the guilt of our misdeeds, may be gladdened by the advent of thy only-begotten Son: Who liveth and reigneth.

The Lesson from the Prophet Isaiah.

Is. 40, 9-11.

THUS saith the Lord: O Sion, that bringest good tidings, get thee up into the high mountain: O Jerusalem, that bringest good tidings, lift up thy voice with strength: lift it up, be not afraid. Say unto the cities of Judah: Behold your God: behold, the Lord God will come with strong hand, and his arm shall rule for him: behold his reward is with him, and his work before him. He shall feed his flock like a shepherd: he shall gather the lambs with his arm, and carry them in his bosom, even he the Lord our God.

Gradual. Ps. 80, 20 and 3. Turn us again, O Lord God of hosts: shew the light of thy countenance, and we shall be whole. ℣. Stir up thy strength, O Lord, and come, and save us.

Let us pray.   Let us bow the knee.
℟. Arise.

Collect.

GRANT, we beseech thee, almighty God: that the coming festival of thy Son may bring healing to our souls in this present life, and obtain for us the rewards of everlasting felicity. Through the same.

Ember Saturday in Advent

The Lesson from the Prophet Isaiah.
Is. 45, 1-8.

THUS saith the Lord to his anointed, to Cyrus, whose right hand I have holden, to subdue nations before him, and I will loose the loins of kings, to open before him the two leaved gates, and the gates shall not be shut. I will go before thee: and make the crooked places straight: I will break in pieces the gates of brass, and cut in sunder the bars of iron. And I will give thee the treasures of darkness, and hidden riches of secret places: that thou mayest know that I, the Lord, which call thee by thy name, am the God of Israel. For Jacob my servant's sake, and Israel mine elect, I have even called thee by thy name: I have surnamed thee, though thou hast not known me. I am the Lord, and there is none else: there is no God beside me: I girded thee, though thou hast not known me: that they may know from the rising of the sun, and from the west, that there is none beside me. I am the Lord, and there is none else, I form the light, and create darkness, I make peace, and create evil: I the Lord do all these things. Drop down, ye heavens, from above, and let the skies pour down righteousness: let the earth open, and let them bring forth salvation: and let righteousness spring up together: I the Lord have created it.

Gradual. Ps. 80, 3, 2 and 3. Stir up, O Lord, thy strength, and come, and save us. ℣. Hear, O thou Shepherd of Israel: thou that leadest Joseph like a sheep: shew thyself, thou that sittest upon the Cherubim, before Ephraim, Benjamin, and Manasses.

Let us pray.   Let us bow the knee.
   ℟. Arise.

Collect.

O LORD, we beseech thee favourably to hear the prayers of thy people: that we, who are justly punished for our offences, may be comforted by the visitation of thy mercy: Who livest and reignest.

The Lesson from the Prophet Daniel.

Song of the Three Children 26-30.

IN those days: The Angel of the Lord came down into the oven together with Azarias and his fellows: and smote the flame of the fire out of the oven, and made the midst of the furnace as it had been a moist whistling wind. Now the flame streamed forth above the furnace forty and nine cubits: and it passed through, and burned of the Chaldeans it found about the furnace the king's servants that made it hot. And the fire touched them not at all, neither hurt nor troubled them. Then the three, as out of one mouth, praised, glorified, and blessed God in the furnace, saying:

Here is not said, Thanks be to God.

Hymn. Song, ibid., 31-35.

BLESSED art thou, O Lord God of our fathers. And to be praised and glorified for ever.

And blessed is the name of thy glory, which is holy. And to be praised and glorified for ever.

Blessed art thou in the holy temple of thy glory. And to be praised and glorified for ever.

Blessed art thou on the holy throne of thy kingdom. And to be praised and glorified for ever.

Blessed art thou in the sceptre of thy Godhead. And to be praised and glorified for ever.

Blessed art thou that sittest upon the Cherubim, and beholdest the depths. And to be praised and glorified for ever.

Ember Saturday in Advent

Blessed art thou that walkest on the wings of the winds and on the waves of the sea. And to be praised and glorified for ever.

Let all thine Angels and Saints bless thee. And let them praise thee and glorify thee for ever.

Let the heavens, the earth, the sea, and all that in them is, bless thee. And let them praise thee and glorify thee for ever.

Glory be to the Father, and to the Son, and to the Holy Ghost. And to be praised and glorified for ever.

As it was in the beginning, is now, and ever shall be: world without end. Amen. And to be praised and glorified for ever.

Blessed art thou, O Lord God of our fathers. And to be praised and glorified for ever.

Here is said ℣. The Lord be with you without Let us bow the knee.

Let us pray. *Collect.*

O GOD, who for the deliverance of the three children didst assuage the flames of fire: mercifully grant; that the flames of sin may have no power upon us thy servants. Through.

The Lesson from the Epistle of blessed Paul the Apostle to the Thessalonians.

II Thess. 2, 1-8.

BRETHREN: We beseech you, by the coming of our Lord Jesus Christ, and by our gathering together unto him: that ye be not soon shaken in mind, or be troubled, neither by spirit, nor by word, nor by letter as from us, as that the day of Christ is at hand. Let no man deceive you by any means: for that day shall not come, except there come a falling away first, and that man of sin be revealed, the son of perdition, who opposeth and exalteth himself above all that is called God, or that is worshipped, so that he as God sitteth in the temple of God, shewing himself that he is God. Remember ye not, that, when I was yet with you, I told you these things? And now ye know what withholdeth, that he might be revealed in his time. For the mystery of iniquity doth already work: only he who now letteth will let, until he be taken out of the way. And then shall that wicked be revealed, whom the Lord shall consume with the spirit of his mouth, and shall destroy with the brightness of his coming.

Tract. Ps. 80, 2-3. Hear, O thou Shepherd of Israel: thou that leadest Joseph like a sheep. ℣. Thou that sittest upon the Cherubim, shew thyself before Ephraim, Benjamin, and Manasses. ℣. Stir up thy strength, O Lord, and come, and save us.

✠ The Continuation of the holy Gospel according to Luke.

Luke 3, 1-6.

IN the fifteenth year of the reign of Tiberius Cæsar, Pontius Pilate being governor of Judæa, and Herod being tetrarch of Galilee, and his brother Philip tetrarch of Ituræa and of the region of Trachonitis, and Lysanias the tetrarch of Abilene, Annas and Caiaphas being the high priests: the word of God came unto John the son of Zacharias in the wilderness. And he came into all the country about Jordan, preaching the baptism of repentance for the remission of sins, as it is written in the book of the words of Esaias the prophet, saying: The voice of one crying in the wilderness: Prepare ye the way of the Lord: make his paths straight: every valley shall be filled: and every mountain and hill shall be brought low: and the crooked shall be made straight, and the rough ways shall be made smooth: and all flesh shall see the salvation of God.

Offertory. Zech. 9, 9. Rejoice greatly, O daughter of Sion, shout aloud, O daughter of Jerusalem: behold, thy King cometh to thee, the holy one and the Saviour.

Secret.

WE beseech thee, O Lord, mercifully to have respect unto these our sacrifices: that they may increase our devotion and set forward our salvation. Through.

Communion. Ps. 19, 6-7. He rejoiceth as a giant to run his course: he goeth forth from the uttermost part of the heaven, and runneth about unto the end of it again.

Postcommunion.

WE beseech, O Lord our God: that these holy mysteries which thou hast given unto us for the assurance of our redemption; may both in this life and in that which is to come be profitable unto us for the healing of our souls. Through.

The Fourth Sunday in Advent

1st class.   Double of 1st class.

Station at the twelve Holy Apostles.

Introit. Is. 45. 8. Rorate.

DROP down, ye heavens, from above, and let the skies pour down righteousness: let the earth open, and bring forth the Saviour. Ps. 19, 1. The heavens declare the glory of God: and the firmament sheweth his handywork. ℣. Glory.

Collect.

O LORD, raise up, we pray thee, thy power, and come among us: and with great might succour us; that whereas, through our sins and wickedness, we are sore let and hindered in running the race that is set before us, thy bountiful grace and mercy may speedily help and deliver us. Through the satisfaction of thy Son our Lord, to whom with thee and the Holy Ghost be honour and glory, world without end. ℟. Amen.

Or, Collect.

O LORD, raise up, we pray thee, thy power, and come among us: and with great might succour us; that whereas through our sins we are sore let and hindered, thy bountiful grace and mercy may speedily help and deliver us: Who livest and reignest with God the Father.

The Lesson from the Epistle of blessed Paul the Apostle to the Philippians.

Phil. 4, 4-7.

BRETHREN: Rejoice in the Lord alway: and again I say, Rejoice. Let your moderation be known unto all men: the Lord is at hand. Be careful for nothing: but in every thing, by prayer and supplication with thanksgiving, let your requests be made known unto God. And the peace of God, which passeth all understanding, shall keep your hearts and minds in Christ Jesu our Lord.

Or

The Lesson from the Epistle of blessed Paul the Apostle to the Corinthians.

I Cor. 4, 1-5.

BRETHREN: Let a man so account of us, as the ministers of Christ, and stewards of the mysteries of God. Moreover, it is required in stewards, that a man be found faithful. But with me it is a very small thing that I should be judged of you, or of man's judgment: yea, I judge not mine own self. For I know nothing by myself: yet am I not hereby justified: but he that judgeth me is the Lord. Therefore judge nothing before the time, until the Lord come: who both will bring to light the hidden things of darkness, and will make manifest the counsels of the hearts: and then shall every man have praise of God.

Gradual. Ps. 145, 18 and 21. The Lord is nigh unto all them that call upon him: yea, all such as call upon him faithfully. ℣.My mouth shall speak the praise of the Lord: and let all flesh give thanks unto his holy name.

¶ The following Alleluia with the Verse is said on Sunday only, on Ferias it is omitted.

Alleluia, alleluia. ℣.Come, O Lord, and tarry not: forgive the misdeeds of thy people Israel. Alleluia.

☦ The Continuation of the holy Gospel according to John.

John 1, 19-28.

AT that time: The Jews sent priests and levites from Jerusalem to John to ask him: Who art thou? And he confessed, and denied not: but confessed: I am not the Christ. And they asked him: What then? Art thou Elias? And he saith: I am not. Art thou that Prophet? And he answered: No. Then said they unto him: Who art thou, that we may give an answer to them that sent us? What sayest thou of thyself? He said: I am the voice of one crying in the wilderness: Make straight the way of the Lord, as said the prophet Esaias. And they which were sent were of the Pharisees. And they asked him, and said unto him: Why baptizest thou then, if thou be not that Christ, nor Elias, neither that Prophet? John answered them, saying: I baptize with water: but there standeth one among you, whom ye know not. He it is, who coming after me is preferred before me: whose shoe's latchet I am not worthy to unloose. These things were done in Bethabara beyond Jordan, where John was baptizing. Creed.

Or Gospel, In the fifteenth year, p. 12.

Offertory. Luke 1, 28. Hail, Mary, full of grace; the Lord is with thee: blessed art thou among women, and blessed is the fruit of thy womb.

Secret.

WE beseech thee, O Lord, mercifully to have respect unto these our sacrifices: that they may increase our devotion and set forward our salvation. Through.

Preface of the Most Holy Trinity.

Communion. Is. 7, 14. Behold, a Virgin shall conceive, and bear a son: and his name shall be called Emmanuel.

Postcommunion.

O LORD, who hast made us to be partakers of thy bounty: we beseech thee; that we, continually drawing near to this holy mystery, may thereby grow in grace to the attainment of everlasting salvation. Through.

¶ If the Vigil of the Nativity fall on Sunday, the whole Office of the Mass is of the Vigil, with Commemoration of the Sunday.

December 24th.

The Vigil of the Nativity of the Lord

1st class.   Double.

Station at St. Mary Major.

Introit. Exod. 16, 6-7. Hodie scietis.

TO-DAY shall ye know that the Lord will come and deliver us: and in the morning shall ye behold his glory. Ps. 24, 1. The earth is the Lord's, and all that therein is: the compass of the world, and they that dwell therein. ℣. Glory.

Collect.

O GOD, who makest us glad with the yearly expectation of our redemption: vouchsafe; that as we joyfully receive thine Only-begotten Son for our Redeemer, so we may with sure confidence behold him when he shall come to be our Judge, even Jesus Christ thy Son our Lord: Who liveth and reigneth with thee.

The Vigil of the Nativity of the Lord

The Lesson from the Epistle of blessed Paul the Apostle to the Romans.

Rom. 1, 1-6.

PAUL, a servant of Jesus Christ, called to be an Apostle, separated unto the Gospel of God, which he had promised afore by his Prophets in the holy Scriptures concerning his Son Jesus Christ our Lord, which was made of the seed of David according to the flesh: and declared to be the Son of God with power, according to the spirit of holiness, by the resurrection from the dead: by whom we have received grace and apostleship, for obedience to the faith among all nations, for his name, among whom are ye also the called of Jesus Christ our Lord.

Gradual. Exod. 16, 6-7. To-day shall ye know that the Lord will come and deliver us: and in the morning shall ye behold his glory. ℣. Ps. 80, 2-3. Hear, O thou Shepherd of Israel: thou that leadest Joseph like a sheep: thou that sittest upon the Cherubim, shew thyself before Ephraim, Benjamin, and Manasses.

Alleluia with the following Verse is not said, unless this Vigil fall on Sunday.

Alleluia, alleluia. ℣. On the morrow the iniquity of the earth shall be blotted out: and the Saviour of the world shall reign over us. Alleluia.

✠ The Continuation of the holy Gospel according to Matthew.

Matt. 1, 18-21.

WHEN as Mary the Mother of Jesus was espoused to Joseph, before they came together, she was found with child of the Holy Ghost. Then Joseph her husband, being a just man, and not willing to make her a publick example, was minded to put her away privily. But while he thought on these things, behold, the Angel of the Lord appeared unto him in a dream, saying: Joseph, thou son of David, fear not to take unto thee Mary thy wife: for that which is conceived in her is of the Holy Ghost. And she shall bring forth a son, and thou shalt call his name Jesus: for he shall save his people from their sins.

If it fall on Sunday, the Creed is said.

Offertory. Ps. 24, 7. Lift up your heads, O ye gates: and be ye lift up, ye everlasting doors, and the King of glory shall come in.

Secret.

GRANT to us, we beseech thee, almighty God: that like as we now prevent the feast of the wondrous Birth of thy Son, so we may joyfully receive his everlasting gifts: Who with thee liveth.

Common Preface, even if it fall on Sunday.

Communion. Is. 40, 5. The glory of the Lord shall be revealed: and all flesh shall see the salvation of our God.

Postcommunion.

GRANT to us, we beseech thee, O Lord: that like as thine only-begotten Son in this heavenly mystery doth give himself to be our meat and drink; so we may be renewed by the remembrance of his birth. Through the same.

December 25.

THE NATIVITY OF OUR LORD, OR THE BIRTHDAY OF CHRIST, COMMONLY CALLED

CHRISTMAS DAY

DOUBLE OF THE 1ST CLASS WITH OCTAVE.

AT THE FIRST MASS

IN THE NIGHT

Station at St. Mary Major at the Crib.

Introit. Ps. 2, 7. Dominus dixit.

THE Lord said unto me: Thou art my Son, this day have I begotten thee. Ps. ibid., 1. Why do the heathen so furiously rage together: and why do the people imagine a vain thing? ℣. Glory.

Collect.

O GOD, who hast made this most holy night to shine with the brightness of the true light: grant, we beseech thee; that we, who have known the mystery of his light on earth, may also attain to the fruition of his joys in heaven: Who liveth and reigneth with thee in the unity of the Holy Ghost.

The Lesson from the Epistle of blessed Paul the Apostle to Titus.

Tit. 2, 11-15.

DEARLY beloved: The grace of God that bringeth salvation hath appeared to all men, teaching us that, denying ungodliness and worldly lusts, we should live soberly, righteously, and godly, in this present world, looking for that blessed hope, and the glorious appearing of the great God and our Saviour Jesus Christ: who gave himself for us: that he might redeem us from all iniquity, and purify unto himself a peculiar people, zealous of good works. These things speak, and exhort: in Christ Jesu our Lord.

Gradual. Ps. 110, 3 and 1. In the day of thy power shall the people offer thee freewill offerings with an holy worship: the dew of thy birth is of the womb of the morning. ℣. The Lord said unto my Lord: Sit thou on my right hand: until I make thine enemies thy footstool.

Alleluia, alleluia. ℣. Ps. 2, 7. The Lord said unto me: Thou art my Son, this day have I begotten thee. Alleluia.

✠ The Continuation of the holy Gospel according to Luke.

Luke 2, 1-14.

AT that time: There went out a decree from Cæsar Augustus, that all the world should be taxed. And this taxing was first made when Cyrenius was governor of Syria: and all went to be taxed, every one into his own city. And Joseph also went up from Galilee, out of the city of Nazareth, into Judæa, unto the city of David, which is called Bethlehem: because he was of the house and lineage of David: to be taxed with Mary his espoused wife, being great with child. And so it was, that, while they were there, the days were accomplished that she should be delivered. And she brought forth her firstborn son, and wrapped him in swaddling clothes, and laid him in a manger:

because there was no room for them in the inn. And there were in the same country shepherds abiding in the field, keeping watch over their flock by night. And, lo, the Angel of the Lord came upon them, and the glory of the Lord shone round about them, and they were sore afraid. And the Angel said unto them: Fear not: for behold, I bring you good tidings of great joy, which shall be to all people: for unto you is born this day in the city of David a Saviour, which is Christ the Lord. And this shall be a sign unto you: Ye shall find the babe wrapped in swaddling clothes, lying in a manger. And suddenly there was with the Angel a multitude of the heavenly host praising God, and saying: Glory to God in the highest, and on earth peace, good will toward men [or peace toward men of good will.] Creed.

Offertory. Ps. 96, 11 and 13. Let the heavens rejoice, and let the earth be glad before the Lord: for he is come.

Secret.

WE beseech thee, O Lord, that the oblation of this day's festival may be acceptable unto thee: that by thy bountiful grace we may, through this holy Communion, be found in the likeness of him in whom our substance is united unto thee: Who liveth and reigneth with thee.

¶ Preface of the Nativity, which is said throughout the Octave in all Masses, even in those which would otherwise have a proper Preface, provided that there be a Commemoration in them of the Octave, or of the Sunday within the Octave, and that the Mass itself or the Commemoration do not demand another Preface of the Divine Mysteries or Persons. It is also said, according to the Rubrics, until January 5th inclusive.

¶ Infra Actionem: Communicating, and celebrating the most sacred night, (Communicántes et noctem sacratíssimam) which is said daily until the Octave of the Nativity, inclusive; but in this Mass only is said night (noctem), afterwards day (diem).

¶ In the first and second Mass, if the Priest is to celebrate another Mass, immediately, having consumed the divine Blood, he does not purify nor wipe the Chalice, but places it upon the Corporal and covers it with a Pall; then with hands joined he says in the middle of the Altar: Quod ore súmpsimus, etc., and then washes his fingers in a vessel made ready with water, saying Corpus tuum, Dómine, etc., and wipes them. This done, he removes the Pall and again arranges the Chalice still remaining on the Corporal, and covers it in the accustomed manner, namely, first with the linen Purificator, then the Paten with the Host to be consecrated and the Pall, and finally with the Veil.

Communion. Ps. 110, 3. With an holy worship, the dew of thy birth is of the womb of the morning.

Postcommunion.

GRANT to us, we beseech thee, O Lord our God: that we who in these mysteries draw near with gladness unto the Birth of Jesus Christ our Lord; may so walk in godliness of life, that we may be found worthy to attain unto his fellowship in heaven; Who liveth and reigneth with thee.

¶ The Priest must say the Confession before the following Masses also, and bless the people at the end of each. But at the end of this and the following Mass he reads, as usual, the Gospel of St. John, In the beginning.

AT THE SECOND MASS
AT DAWN

Station at St. Anastasia.

Introit. Is. 9, 2 and 6. Lux fulgebit.

LIGHT shall shine upon us to-day: for unto us the Lord is born; and he shall be called Wonderful, God, the Prince of Peace, Father of the world to come: of whose kingdom there shall be no end. Ps. 93, 1. The Lord is King, and hath put on glorious apparel: the Lord hath put on his apparel, and girded himself with strength. ℣. Glory.

Collect.

GRANT to us, we beseech thee, almighty God: that as thou dost pour forth on us the new light of thine incarnate Word; so he who doth illuminate our minds by faith may likewise in our works shew forth his brightness. Through the same.

And Commemoration is made of St. Anastasia, Martyr:

Collect.

GRANT we beseech thee, almighty God: that we who devoutly keep the festival of thy blessed Martyr Anastasia; may by her effectual intercession be holpen in thy sight. Through.

The Lesson from the Epistle of blessed Paul the Apostle to Titus.

Tit. 2, 4-7.

DEARLY beloved: The kindness and love of God our Saviour toward man hath appeared: not by works of righteousness which we have done, but according to his mercy he saved us, by the washing of regeneration, and renewing of the Holy Ghost, which he shed on us abundantly through Jesus Christ our Saviour: that being justified by his grace, we should be made heirs according to the hope of eternal life: in Christ Jesu our Lord.

Gradual. Ps. 118, 26, 27 and 23. Blessed is he that cometh in the name of the Lord: God is the Lord who hath shewed us light. ℣. This is the Lord's doing: and it is marvellous in our eyes.

Alleluia, alleluia. ℣. Ps. 93, 1. The Lord is King, and hath put on glorious apparel: the Lord hath put on his apparel, and girded himself with strength. Alleluia.

✠ The Continuation of the holy Gospel according to Luke.

Luke 2, 15-20.

AT that time: The shepherds said one to another: Let us now go even unto Bethlehem, and see this thing which is come to pass, which the Lord hath made known unto us. And they came with haste: and found Mary and Joseph, and the Babe lying in a manger. And when they had seen it, they made known abroad the saying which was told them concerning this Child. And all they that heard it wondered: at those things which were told them by the shepherds. But Mary kept all these things, and pondered them in her heart. And the shepherds returned, glorifying and praising God for all the things that they had heard and seen, as it was told unto them. Creed.

Offertory. Ps. 93, 1-2. God hath made the round world so sure, that it cannot be moved: ever since the world began, hath thy seat, O God, been prepared, thou art from everlasting.

¶ In the second and third Mass, if they follow the first immediately, the Priest, on coming to the Offertory, removes the Veil from the Chalice, which he places a little towards the Epistle corner, but not outside the Corporal; and having offered the Host he does not wipe the Chalice with the Purificator, but leaving it within the Corporal, slightly raises it, and carefully pours wine and water into it, and offers the Chalice in the accustomed manner, without wiping the inside.

But if he celebrates the three Masses at intervals, all is done as usual, save that in the first and second he takes the ablutions in water only.

Secret.

WE beseech thee, O Lord, that these our gifts may be worthy of the mysteries of this day's Nativity, and may evermore shed forth thy peace upon us: that even as he who was born in our manhood did shew forth therein the glory of the Godhead, so we in these thy earthly creatures may be made partakers of that which is heavenly. Through the same.

For St. Anastasia. Secret.

ACCEPT, we beseech thee, O Lord, the gifts which we duly offer: that, by the merits and intercession of blessed Anastasia thy Martyr, they may be profitable to the advancement of our salvation. Through.

Preface and Communicántes, as above in the first Mass, p. 18.

Communion. Zech. 9, 9. Rejoice greatly, O daughter of Sion, shout, O daughter of Jerusalem: behold, thy King cometh, the holy one and the Saviour of the world.

Postcommunion.

O LORD, who by the wondrous Nativity of thy Son hast put off from us the old nature of our manhood: grant that by this Sacrament of his new Birth we may ever be inwardly restored in our souls. Through the same.

For St. Anastasia. Postcommunion.

O LORD, who hast satisfied this thy family with sacred gifts: we beseech thee, that we may at all times be comforted by the intercession of her whose festival we celebrate. Through.

AT THE THIRD MASS
ON THE DAY OF THE NATIVITY OF THE LORD

Station at St. Mary Major.

Introit. Is. 9, 6. Puer natus est.

UNTO us a child is born, unto us a son is given: and the government shall be upon his shoulder: and his name shall be called Angel of mighty counsel. Ps. 98, 1. O sing unto the Lord a new song, for he hath done marvellous things. ℣. Glory.

Collect.

ALMIGHTY God, who hast given us thy only-begotten Son to take our nature upon him, and as at this time to be born of a pure Virgin: grant that we being regenerate, and made thy children by adoption and grace; may daily be renewed by thy Holy Spirit. Through the same our Lord Jesus Christ, who liveth and reigneth with thee and the same Spirit, ever one God, world without end. ℟. Amen.

Or, Collect.

GRANT, we beseech thee, almighty God: that we who through our ancient bondage are held beneath the yoke of sin; may by the new Birth of thy only-begotten Son in the flesh obtain deliverance. Through the same.

The Lesson from the Epistle of blessed Paul the Apostle to the Hebrews.

Heb. 1, 1-12.

GOD, who at sundry times and in divers manners spake in time past unto the fathers by the Prophets: hath in these last days spoken unto us by his Son, whom he hath appointed heir of all things, by whom also he made the worlds: who being the brightness of his glory, and the express image of his person, and upholding all things by the word of his power, when he had by himself purged our sins, sat down on the right hand of the Majesty on high: being made so much better than the Angels, as he hath by inheritance obtained a more excellent name than they. For unto which of the Angels said he at any time: Thou art my Son, this day have I begotten thee? And again: I will be to him a Father, and he shall be to me a Son? And again, when he bringeth in the First-begotten into the world, he saith: And let all the Angels of God worship him. And of the Angels he saith: Who maketh his Angels spirits, and his ministers a flame of fire. But unto the Son he saith: Thy throne, O God, is for ever and ever: a sceptre of righteousness is the sceptre of thy kingdom. Thou hast loved righteousness, and hated iniquity: therefore God, even thy God, hath anointed thee with the oil of gladness above thy fellows. And: Thou, Lord, in the beginning hast laid the foundation of the earth: and the heavens are the works of thine hands. They shall perish, but thou remainest; and they all shall wax old as doth a garment: and as a vesture shalt thou fold them up, and they shall be changed: but thou art the same, and thy years shall not fail.

Gradual. Ps. 98, 3-4 and 2. All the ends of the earth have seen the salvation of our God: O be joyful in God, all ye lands. ℣. The Lord hath declared his salvation: in the sight of the heathen hath he openly shewed his righteousness.

Alleluia, alleluia. ℣. A hallowed day hath dawned upon us: come, ye nations, and worship the Lord: for on this day a great light hath descended upon the earth. Alleluia.

Christmas Day

✠ The Beginning of the holy Gospel, according to John.

John 1, 1-14.

IN the beginning was the Word, and the Word was with God, and the Word was God. The same was in the beginning with God. All things were made by him: and without him was not anything made that was made: in him was life, and the life was the light of men: and the light shineth in darkness, and the darkness comprehended it not. There was a man sent from God, whose name was John. The same came for a witness, to bear witness of the light, that all men through him might believe. He was not that light, but was sent to bear witness of that light. That was the true light, which lighteth every man that cometh into the world. He was in the world, and the world was made by him, and the world knew him not. He came unto his own, and his own received him not. But as many as received him, to them gave he power to become the sons of God, even to them that believe on his name: which were born, not of blood, nor of the will of the flesh, nor of the will of man, but of God. (Here genuflect) And the Word was made flesh, and dwelt among us: and we beheld his glory, the glory as of the only-begotten of the Father, full of grace and truth. Creed.

Offertory. Ps. 89, 12 and 15. The heavens are thine, the earth also is thine: thou hast laid the foundation of the round world, and all that therein is: righteousness and equity are the habitation of thy seat.

Secret.

SANCTIFY, O Lord, by the new Birth of thine only-begotten Son, the gifts which we offer: and cleanse us from the defilements of our iniquities. Through the same.

Preface and Communicántes, as above in the first Mass, p. 18.

Communion. Ps. 98, 3. All the ends of the world have seen the salvation of our God.

Postcommunion.

GRANT, we beseech thee, almighty God: that like as thy Son, born this day the Saviour of the world, is the author of our heavenly birth; so he may likewise bestow on us the gift of everlasting life: Who liveth and reigneth with thee.

At the end of this Mass the following Gospel is read:

✠ The Continuation of the holy Gospel according to Matthew.

Matt. 2, 1-12.

WHEN Jesus was born in Bethlehem of Judæa, in the days of Herod the king, behold, there came wise men from the East to Jerusalem, saying: Where is he that is born king of the Jews? For we have seen his star in the East, and are come to worship him. When Herod the king had heard these things, he was troubled, and all Jerusalem with him. And when he had gathered all the chief priests and scribes of the people together, he demanded of them, where Christ should be born. And they said unto him: In Bethlehem of Judæa; for thus it is written by the prophet: And thou, Bethlehem, in the land of Juda, art not the least among the princes of Juda; for out of thee shall come a governor that shall rule my people Israel. Then Herod, when he had privily called the wise men, inquired of them diligently what time the star appeared: and he sent them to Bethlehem, and said:

Christmas Day

Go, and search diligently for the young child: and when ye have found him, bring me word again, that I may come and worship him also. When they had heard the king, they departed. And lo, the star which they saw in the East went before them, till it came and stood over where the young Child was. When they saw the star, they rejoiced with exceeding great joy. And when they were come into the house, they saw the young Child with Mary his mother, (Here genuflect) and fell down and worshipped him. And when they had opened their treasures, they presented unto him gifts, gold, and frankincense, and myrrh. And being warned of God in a dream that they should not return to Herod, they departed into their own country another way.

¶ If within the Octave of the Nativity and thereafter from the 2nd to the 5th of January inclusive, any solemn Votive Mass of our Lord which is of the Nativity or of a Mystery for which no Votive Mass is provided is to be said, the Mass Puer natus est, which is given below, p. 35 for the 30th December is to be used.

December 26.
ST. STEPHEN THE FIRST MARTYR
Double of 2nd class.

Station at St. Stephen on the Cælian Hill.

Introit. Ps. 119, 23, 86 and 23. Sederunt.

PRINCES did sit, and speak against me, and the wicked persecuted me: help me, O Lord my God, for thy servant is occupied in thy commandments. Ps. ibid., 1. Blessed are those that are undefiled in the way, and walk in the law of the Lord. ℣. Glory.

Collect.

GRANT, O Lord, that, in all our sufferings here upon earth for the testimony of thy truth, we may stedfastly look up to heaven, and by faith behold the glory that shall be revealed; and, being filled with the Holy Ghost, may learn to love and bless our persecutors by the example of thy first Martyr Saint Stephen; who prayed for his murderers to thee, O blessed Jesus: Who standest at the right hand of God to succour all those that suffer for thee, our only Mediator and Advocate. ℟. Amen.

Or, Collect.

GRANT us, we beseech thee, O Lord, so to imitate that which we honour: that we may learn to love also our enemies; forasmuch as we celebrate the birthday of him who prayed even for his persecutors to our Lord Jesus Christ thy Son: Who liveth.

And Commemoration is made of the Octave of the Nativity.

Collect.

ALMIGHTY God, who hast given us thy only-begotten Son to take our nature upon him, and as at this time to be born of a pure Virgin: grant that we being regenerate, and made thy children by adoption and grace; may daily be renewed by thy Holy Spirit. Through the same our Lord Jesus Christ, who liveth and reigneth with thee and the same Spirit, ever one God, world without end. Amen.

Or, Collect.

GRANT, we beseech thee, almighty God: that we who through our ancient bondage are held beneath the yoke of sin: may by the new birth of thine only-begotten Son obtain deliverance. Through the same.

In B.C.P. the Lesson begins †Stephen, being full, p. 25.

The Lesson from the Acts of the Apostles.
Acts. 6, 8-10; 7, 54-60.

IN those days: Stephen, full of faith and power, did great wonders and miracles among the people. Then there arose certain of the synagogue, which is called the synagogue of the Libertines and Cyrenians, and Alexandrians, and of them of Cilicia and of Asia, disputing with Stephen: and they were not able to resist the wisdom and the spirit by which he spake. When they heard these things, they were cut to the heart, and they gnashed on him with their teeth.

St. Stephen the First Martyr

But †Stephen, being full of the Holy Ghost, looked up stedfastly into heaven, and saw the glory of God, and Jesus standing on the right hand of God. And said: Behold, I see the heavens opened, and the Son of man standing on the right hand of God. Then they cried out with a loud voice, and stopped their ears, and ran upon him with one accord. And cast him out of the city, and stoned him: and the witnesses laid down their clothes at a young man's feet, whose name was Saul. And they stoned Stephen, calling upon God and saying: Lord Jesus, receive my spirit. And he kneeled down, and cried with a loud voice: Lord, lay not this sin to their charge. And when he had said this, he fell asleep† in the Lord.

Gradual. Ps. 119, 23 and 86. Princes did sit, and speak against me; and the wicked persecuted me. ℣. Ps. 6, 5. Help me, O Lord my God: save me for thy mercy's sake.

Alleluia, alleluia. ℣. Acts 7, 56. I see the heavens opened, and Jesus standing on the right hand of the power of God. Alleluia.

¶ In Votive Masses after Septuagesima, the Alleluia and ℣. following being omitted, the Tract Thou hast given him from the Common of One Martyr, p. [4] is said.

¶ In Eastertide the Gradual is omitted, and in its place is said:

Alleluia, alleluia. ℣. Acts 7, 56. I see the heavens opened, and Jesus standing on the right hand of the power of God. Alleluia. ℣. Ps. 21, 4. Thou hast set, O Lord, a crown of pure gold upon his head. Alleluia.

✠ The Continuation of the holy Gospel according to Matthew.

Matt. 23, 34-39.

AT that time: Jesus said unto the scribes and Pharisees: Behold, I send unto you prophets, and wise men, and scribes, and some of them ye shall kill and crucify, and some of them shall ye scourge in your synagogues, and persecute them from city to city: that upon you may come all the righteous blood shed upon the earth, from the blood of righteous Abel unto the blood of Zacharias, son of Barachias, whom ye slew between the temple and the altar. Verily I say unto you, All these things shall come upon this generation. O Jerusalem, Jerusalem, thou that killest the prophets, and stonest them which are sent unto thee, how often would I have gathered thy children together, even as a hen gathered her chickens under her wings, and ye would not? Behold, your house is left unto you desolate. For I say unto you, Ye shall not see me henceforth, till ye shall say: Blessed is he that cometh in the name of the Lord. Creed, because of the Octave.

Offertory. Acts 6, 5 and 7, 59. The Apostles chose Stephen the Levite, a man full of faith and of the Holy Ghost: whom the Jews stoned as he prayed, saying: Lord Jesus, receive my spirit, alleluia.

Secret.

ACCEPT, O Lord, these gifts for the commemoration of thy Saints: that like as their passion hath raised them to glory; so our devotion may lead us to innocency of life. Through.

For the Octave of the Nativity. Secret.

SANCTIFY, O Lord, by the new birth of thine only-begotten Son the gifts which we offer: and cleanse us from the defilements of our iniquities. Through the same.

Preface and Communicántes of the Nativity, because of the Octave.

Communion. Acts 7, 56, 59 and 60. I see the heavens opened, and Jesus standing on the right hand of the power of God: Lord Jesus, receive my spirit, and lay not this sin to their charge.

Postcommunion.

ASSIST us mercifully, O Lord: that we, who have received these holy mysteries, may at the intercession of thy blessed Martyr Stephen be defended by thy everlasting protection. Through.

For the Octave of the Nativity.
Postcommunion.

GRANT, we beseech thee, almighty God, that like as thy Son, born this day the Saviour of the world, is the author of our heavenly birth: so he may likewise bestow on us the gift of everlasting life: Who liveth and reigneth with thee.

December 27.

ST. JOHN APOSTLE AND EVANGELIST

Double of 2nd class.

Station at St. Mary Major

Introit. Ecclus. 15, 5. In medio Ecclesiæ.

IN the midst of the Church he opened his mouth: and the Lord filled him with the spirit of wisdom and understanding: he clothed him with a robe of glory. Ps. 92, 2. It is a good thing to give thanks unto the Lord: and to sing praises unto thy name, O Most Highest. ℣. Glory.

Collect.

MERCIFUL Lord, we beseech thee to cast thy bright beams of light upon thy Church: that it, being enlightened by the doctrine of thy blessed Apostle and Evangelist Saint John, may so walk in the light of thy truth, that it may at length attain to the light of everlasting life. Through.

Or, Collect.

MERCIFUL Lord, cast thy bright beams of light upon thy Church: that it, being lightened by the doctrine of thy blessed Apostle and Evangelist John, may attain to thy everlasting gifts. Through.

And Commemoration is made of the Octave of the Nativity:

Collect.

ALMIGHTY God, who hast given us thy only-begotten Son to take our nature upon him, and as at this time to be born of a pure Virgin: grant that we being regenerate, and made thy children by adoption and grace; may daily be renewed by thy Holy Spirit. Through the same our Lord Jesus Christ, who liveth and reigneth with thee and the same Spirit, ever one God, world without end. ℟. Amen.

Or, Collect.

GRANT, we beseech thee, almighty God: that we who through our ancient bondage are held beneath the yoke of sin: may by the new Birth of thine only-begotten Son obtain deliverance. Through the same.

The Lesson from the Epistle of blessed John the Apostle.

I John 1, 1-10.

THAT which was from the beginning, which we have heard, which we have seen with our eyes, which we have looked upon, and our hands have handled of the word of life; (for the life was manifested, and we have seen it, and bear witness, and shew unto you that eternal life, which was with the Father, and was manifested unto us); That which we have seen and heard declare we unto you, that we also may have fellowship with us; and truly our fellowship is with the Father, and with his Son Jesus Christ. And these things write we unto you, that your joy may be full. This then is the message which we have heard of him, and declare unto you, That God is light, and in him is no darkness at all. If we say that we have fellowship with him, and walk in darkness, we lie, and do not the truth: but if we walk in the light, as he is in the light, we have fellowship one with another, and the blood of

Jesus Christ his Son cleanseth us from all sin. If we say that we have no sin, we deceive ourselves, and the truth is not in us. If we confess our sins, he is faithful and just to forgive us our sins, and to cleanse us from all unrighteousness. If we say that we have not sinned, we make him a liar, and his word is not in us.

Or,

The Lesson from the book of Wisdom.

Ecclus. 15, 1-6.

HE that feareth the Lord will do good: and he that possesseth justice shall lay hold on her, and as a mother shall she meet him, and receive him as a wife married of a virgin. With the bread of understanding shall she feed him, and give him the water of wisdom to drink; he shall be stayed upon her, and shall not be confounded: she shall exalt him above his neighbours, and in the midst of the church shall she open his mouth, and she shall fill him with the spirit of wisdom and understanding, and clothe him with a robe of glory. He shall find joy and a crown of gladness, and the Lord our God shall cause him to inherit an everlasting name.

Gradual. John 21, 23 and 19. Then went this saying abroad among the brethren: That that disciple should not die: yet Jesus said not: He shall not die. ℣. But, If I will that he tarry till I come: follow thou me.

Alleluia, alleluia. ℣. Ibid., 24. This is the disciple which testifieth of these things: and we know that his testimony is true. Alleluia.

¶ In Votive Masses after Septuagesima, the Alleluia and Verse following being omitted, the Tract Blessed is the man, as in the Common of Doctors, p. [23], is said.

¶ But in Eastertide the Gradual is omitted, and in its place is said:

Alleluia, alleluia. ℣. John 21, 24. This is the disciple which testifieth of these things, and we know that his testimony is true. Alleluia.

℣. Ps. 92, 13. The righteous shall flourish like a palm-tree: and shall spread abroad like a cedar in Libanus. Alleluia.

✠ The Continuation of the holy Gospel according to John.

John 21, 19-24.

AT that time: Jesus, said unto Peter: Follow me. Then Peter, turning about, seeth the disciple whom Jesus loved following, which also leaned on his breast at supper, and said: Lord, which is he that betrayeth thee? Peter seeing him saith to Jesus: Lord, and what shall this man do? Jesus saith unto him: If I will that he tarry till I come, what is that to thee? Follow thou me. Then went this saying abroad among the brethren, that that disciple should not die. Yet Jesus said not unto him: He shall not die; but: If I will that he tarry till I come: what is that to thee? This is the disciple which testifieth of these things, and wrote these things: and we know that his testimony is true.*

And there are also many other things which Jesus did, the which if they should be written every one, I suppose, that even the world itself could not contain the books that should be written. Creed.

Offertory. Ps. 92, 13. The righteous shall flourish like a palm-tree: and shall spread abroad like a cedar in Libanus.

Secret.

RECEIVE, O Lord, these our gifts, which we offer unto thee on the festival of him, in whose advocacy we trust for deliverance. Through.

For the Octave of the Nativity.   Secret.

SANCTIFY, O Lord, by the new Birth of thine only-begotten Son the gifts which we offer: and cleanse us from the defilements of our iniquities. Through the same.

Preface and Communicántes of the Nativity, because of the Octave; but if the Commemoration of the Octave is to be omitted, the Preface of the Apostles is said, without Communicántes of the Nativity.

Communion. John 21, 23. Then went abroad this saying among the brethren, that that disciple should not die: yet Jesus said not: He shall not die; but: If I will that he tarry till I come.

Postcommunion.

O GOD, who hast refreshed us with heavenly meat and drink, we humbly beseech thee: that we may be defended by the prayers of him, in whose memory we have received the same. Through.

For the Octave of the Nativity.

Postcommunion.

GRANT, we beseech thee, almighty God: that like as thy Son, born this day the Saviour of the world, is the author of our heavenly birth; so he may likewise bestow on us the gift of everlasting life: Who liveth and reigneth with thee.

December 28.

THE HOLY INNOCENTS, MARTYRS

Double of 2nd class with simple octave.

Station at St. Paul.

Introit. Ps. 8, 2. Ex ore infantium.

OUT of the mouth of very babes, O God, and sucklings, hast thou ordained strength because of thine enemies. Ps. ibid., 1. O Lord our Governor: how excellent is thy name in all the world. ℣. Glory.

¶ Glória in excélsis is not said, nor Allelúia, nor Ite, Missa est, unless this Feast fall on Sunday, or enjoy the rite of a double of the First Class.

Collect.

O ALMIGHTY God, who out of the mouths of babes and sucklings hast ordained strength, and madest infants to glorify thee by their deaths: mortify and kill all vices in us; and so strengthen us by thy grace, that by the innocency of our lives, and constancy of our faith even unto death, we may glorify thy holy name. Through.

Or, Collect.

O GOD, whose praise this day the Innocents thy Martyrs confessed not in speaking but in dying: mortify and kill all vices in us; that in our conversation our life may express thy faith, which with our tongues we do shew forth. Through.

And Commemoration is made of the Octave of the Nativity.

Collect.

ALMIGHTY God, who hast given us thy only-begotten Son to take our nature upon him, and as at this time to be born of a pure Virgin: grant that we being regenerate, and made thy children by adoption and grace; may daily be renewed by thy Holy Spirit. Through the same our Lord Jesus Christ, who liveth and reigneth with thee and the same Spirit, ever one God, world without end. ℟. Amen.

Or, Collect.

GRANT, we beseech thee, almighty God: that we who through our ancient bondage are held beneath the yoke of sin: may by the new Birth of thine only-begotten Son obtain deliverance. Through the same.

The Lesson from the book of the Revelation of blessed John the Apostle.

Rev. 14, 1-5.

IN those days: I beheld a Lamb standing on the mount Sion, and with him an hundred forty and four thousand, having his Father's name written in their foreheads. And I heard a voice from heaven, as the voice of many waters, and as the voice of a great thunder: and I heard the voice of harpers harping with their harps. And they sung as it were a new song before the throne, and before the four beasts, and the elders: and no man could learn that song, but the hundred and forty and four thousand, which were redeemed from the earth. These are they which were not defiled with women: for they are virgins. These are they which follow the Lamb whithersoever he goeth. These were redeemed from among men, being the first-fruits unto God, and to the Lamb: and in their mouth was found no guile: for they are without fault before the throne of God.

Gradual. Ps. 124, 7-8. Our soul is escaped, even as a bird, out of the snare of the fowler. ℣. The snare is broken, and we are delivered: our help standeth in the name of the Lord, who hath made heaven and earth.

¶ The following Alleluia with its Verse is said when this Feast falls on Sunday or enjoys the rite of a double of the First Class: and it is always said in Votive Masses before Septuagesima or after Pentecost.

Alleluia, alleluia. ℣. Ps. 113, 1. Praise the Lord, ye children: O praise the name of the Lord. Alleluia.

The Tract is not said when the Alleluia has been said as above.

Tract. Ps. 79, 3 and 10. The blood of thy Saints have they shed like water on every side of Jerusalem. ℣. And there was no man to bury them. ℣. Avenge, O Lord, the blood of thy Saints, that is shed upon the earth.

In Votive Masses in Eastertide, the Gradual and Tract being omitted, is said:

Alleluia, alleluia. ℣. Ps. 113, 1. Praise ye the Lord, ye children: O praise the name of the Lord. Alleluia. ℣. Ecclus. 39, 19. Thy Saints, O Lord, shall grow as the lily, and as the odour of balsam shall they be before thee. Alleluia.

✠ The Continuation of the holy Gospel according to Matthew.

Matt. 2, 3-18.

AT that time: The Angel of the Lord appeared to Joseph in a dream, saying: Arise, and take the young Child, and his Mother, and flee into Egypt, and be thou there until I bring thee word. For Herod will seek the young Child to destroy him. When he arose, he took the young Child and his Mother by night, and departed into Egypt: and was there until the death of Herod: that it might be fulfilled which was spoken of the Lord by the Prophet, saying: Out of Egypt have I called my Son. Then Herod, when he saw that he was mocked of the wise men, was exceeding wroth, and sent forth, and slew all the children that were in Bethlehem, and in all the coasts thereof, from two years old and under, according to the time which he had diligently enquired of the wise men. Then was fulfilled that which was spoken by Jeremy the Prophet, saying: In Rama was there a voice heard, lamentation, and weeping, and great mourning: Rachel weeping for her children, and would not be comforted, because they are not. Creed, because of the Octave.

Offertory. Ps. 124, 7. Our soul is escaped, even as a bird out of the snare of the fowler: the snare is broken, and we are delivered.

Secret.

O LORD, let the devout prayers of thy Saints continually assist us; that they may render our gifts acceptable unto thee, and ever obtain for us thy pardon. Through.

For the Octave of the Nativity. Secret.

SANCTIFY, O Lord, by the new Birth of thine only-begotten Son, the gifts which we offer: and cleanse us from the defilement of our iniquities. Through the same.

Preface and Communicántes of the Nativity, because of the Octave.

Communion. Matt. 2, 18. In Rama a voice was heard, lamentation and mourning: Rachel weeping for her children, and would not be comforted, because they are not.

Postcommunion.

WE beseech thee, O Lord: that the gifts which we have received in these holy mysteries may through the prayers of thy Saints effectually avail for our succour both in this life and in that which is to come. Through.

For the Octave of the Nativity.

Postcommunion.

GRANT, we beseech thee, almighty God: that like as thy Son, born this day the Saviour of the world, is the author of our heavenly birth; so he may likewise bestow on us the gift of everlasting life: Who liveth and reigneth with thee.

The Sunday in the Octave of the Nativity

Double.

Introit. Wisd. 18, 14-15. Dum medium.

WHILE all things were in quiet silence, and that night was in the midst of her swift course, thine almighty Word, O Lord, leaped down from heaven out of thy royal throne. Ps. 93, 1. The Lord is King, and hath put on glorious apparel: the Lord hath put on his apparel, and girded himself with strength. ℣. Glory.

Collect.

ALMIGHTY and everlasting God, direct us in all our doings according to thy good pleasure: that we, serving thee in the name of thy well-beloved Son, may worthily abound in good works: Who liveth and reigneth with thee.

Or, Collect.

ALMIGHTY God, who hast given us thy only-begotten Son to take our nature upon him, and as at this time to be born of a pure Virgin: grant that we being regenerate, and made thy children by adoption and grace; may daily be renewed by thy Holy Spirit. Through the same our Lord Jesus Christ, who liveth and reigneth with thee and the same Spirit, ever one God, world without end. ℞. Amen.

And Commemoration is made of the Octave of the Nativity.

Collect.

GRANT, we beseech thee, almighty God: that we, who through our ancient bondage are held beneath the yoke of sin; may by the new Birth of thy only-begotten Son in the flesh obtain deliverance. Through the same.

The Lesson from the Epistle of blessed Paul the Apostle to the Galatians.

Gal. 4, 1-7.

BRETHREN: So long as the heir is a child, he differeth nothing from a servant, though he be lord of all: but is under tutors and governors, until the time appointed of the father: even so we, when we were children, were in bondage under the elements of the world. But when the fulness of the time was come, God sent forth his Son, made of a woman, made under the law, to redeem them that were under the law, that we might receive the adoption of sons. And because ye are sons, God hath sent forth the Spirit of his Son into your hearts, crying: Abba, Father. Wherefore thou art no more a servant, but a son: and if a son, then an heir through God.

Gradual. Ps. 45, 3 and 2. Thou art fairer than the children of men: full of grace are thy lips. ℣. My heart is inditing of a good matter, I speak of the things which I have made unto the King: my tongue is the pen of a ready writer.

Sunday in the Octave of the Nativity

Alleluia, alleluia. ℣. Ps. 93, 1. The Lord is King, and hath put on glorious apparel: the Lord hath put on his apparel, and girded himself with strength. Alleluia.

✠ The Continuation of the holy Gospel according to Matthew.

Matt. 1, 18-23.

THE birth of Jesus Christ was on this wise: When as his Mother Mary was espoused to Joseph, before they came together, she was found with child of the Holy Ghost. Then Joseph her husband, being a just man, and not willing to make her a publick example, was minded to put her away privily. But while he thought on these things, behold, the Angel of the Lord appeared unto him in a dream, saying: Joseph thou son of David, fear not to take unto thee Mary thy wife: for that which is conceived in her is of the Holy Ghost. And she shall bring forth a son, and thou shalt call his name Jesus: for he shall save his people from their sins. Now all this was done, that it might be fulfilled which was spoken of the Lord by the prophet, saying: Behold, a Virgin shall be with child, and shall bring forth a Son: and they shall call his name Emmanuel, which being interpreted is: God with us. Then Joseph, being raised from sleep, did as the Angel of the Lord had bidden him, and took unto him his wife: and knew her not till she had brought forth her first-born Son: and he called his name Jesus. Creed.

Or,

✠ The Continuation of the holy Gospel according to Luke.

Luke 2, 33-40.

AT that time: Joseph and Mary, the Mother of Jesus, marvelled at those things which were spoken of him. And Simeon blessed them, and said unto Mary his Mother: Behold this child is set for the fall and rising again of many in Israel: and for a sign which shall be spoken against: yea, a sword shall pierce through thy own soul also, that the thoughts of many hearts may be revealed. And there was one Anna, a prophetess, the daughter of Phanuel, of the tribe of Aser: she was of a great age, and had lived with an husband seven years from her virginity. And she was a widow of about fourscore and four years: which departed not from the temple, but served God with fastings and prayers night and day. And she, coming in that instant, gave thanks likewise unto the Lord, and spake of him to all them that looked for redemption in Jerusalem. And when they had performed all things according to the law of the Lord, they returned into Galilee to their own city Nazareth. And the child grew, and waxed strong in spirit, filled with wisdom: and the grace of God was upon him. Creed.

Offertory. Ps. 93, 1-2. God hath made the round world so sure, that it cannot be moved: ever since the world began, hath thy seat, O God, been prepared, thou art from everlasting.

Secret.

GRANT, we beseech thee, almighty God: that the gifts which we here offer in the sight of thy majesty, may obtain for us grace to serve thee with all godliness, and bring us in the end to everlasting felicity. Through.

For the Octave of the Nativity.   Secret.

SANCTIFY, O Lord, by the new Birth of thine only-begotten Son, the gifts which we offer; and cleanse us from the defilements of our iniquities. Through the same.

Preface and Communicántes of the Nativity.

Communion. Matt. 2, 20. Take the young Child and his Mother, and go into the land of Israel: for they are dead which sought the young Child's life.

Postcommunion.

GRANT, O Lord, that by the operation of these thy mysteries we may be cleansed from all our sins, and obtain that which we have asked according to thy will. Through.

For the Octave of the Nativity.

Postcommunion.

GRANT, we beseech thee, almighty God: that like as thy Son, born this day the Saviour of the world, is the author of our heavenly birth; so he may likewise bestow on us the gift of everlasting life: Who liveth and reigneth with thee.

December 29.

St. Thomas of Canterbury

Bishop and Martyr.

Double.

(England and Wales: Double of 2nd class.)

Introit. Gaudeamus.

REJOICE we all in the Lord, keeping feast day in honour of blessed Thomas the Martyr: in whose passion the Angels rejoice, and glorify the Son of God. Ps. 33, 1. Rejoice in the Lord, O ye righteous: for it becometh well the just to be thankful. ℣. Glory.

Collect.

O GOD, who for the defence of thy Church didst suffer thy glorious Bishop Thomas to fall by the swords of wicked men: grant, we beseech thee; that all who call upon him for succour may rejoice in the fulfilment of their petitions. Through.

And Commemoration is made of the Octave of the Nativity.

Collect.

ALMIGHTY God, who hast given us thy only-begotten Son to take our nature upon him, and as at this time to be born of a pure Virgin: grant that we being regenerate, and made thy children by adoption and grace; may daily be renewed by thy Holy Spirit. Through the same our Lord Jesus Christ, who liveth and reigneth with thee and the same Spirit, ever one God, world without end. ℟. Amen.

Or, Collect.

GRANT, we beseech thee, almighty God: that we who through our ancient bondage are held beneath the yoke of sin: may by the new Birth of thine only-begotten Son obtain deliverance. Through the same.

The Lesson from the Epistle of blessed Paul the Apostle to the Hebrews.

Heb. 5, 1-6.

BRETHREN: Every high priest taken from among men is ordained for men in things pertaining to God: that he may offer both gifts and sacrifices for sins: who can have compassion on the ignorant, and on them that are out of the way: for that he himself also is compassed with infirmity: and by reason hereof he ought, as for the people, so also for himself to offer for sins. And no man taketh this honour unto himself, but he that is called of God, as was Aaron. So also Christ glorified not himself to be made an high priest: but he that said unto him: Thou art my Son, to-day have I begotten thee. As he saith also in another place: Thou art a priest for ever after the order of Melchisedec.

Gradual. Ecclus. 44, 16. Behold a great priest, who in his days pleased God. ℣. Ibid., 20. There was none found like unto him, to keep the law of the Most High.

Alleluia, alleluia. ℣. John 10, 14. I am the good shepherd: and know my sheep, and am known of mine. Alleluia.

✠ The Continuation of the holy Gospel according to John.

John 10, 11-16.

AT that time: Jesus said unto the Pharisees: I am the good shepherd. The good shepherd giveth his life for the sheep. But he that is an hireling, and not the shepherd, whose own the sheep are not, seeth the wolf coming, and leaveth the sheep, and fleeth: and the wolf catcheth them, and scattereth the sheep; the hireling fleeth, because he is an hireling, and careth not for the sheep. I am the good shepherd: and know my sheep, and am known of mine. As the Father knoweth me, even so know I the Father, and I lay down my life for the sheep. And other sheep I have, which are not of this fold: them also must I bring, and they shall hear my voice, and there shall be one fold, and one shepherd.

Creed, because of the Octave.

Offertory. Ps. 21, 4-5. Thou hast set, O Lord, a crown of pure gold upon his head: he asked life of thee, and thou gavest it him, alleluia.

Secret.

SANCTIFY, O Lord, the gifts which we dedicate unto thee: that through the intercession of blessed Thomas thy Martyr and Bishop, they may obtain for us thy gracious favour. Through.

For the Octave of the Nativity. Secret.

SANCTIFY, O Lord, by the new Birth of thine only-begotten Son the gifts which we offer: and cleanse us from the defilements of our iniquities. Through the same.

Preface and Communicántes of the Nativity, because of the Octave.

Communion. John 10, 14. I am the good shepherd: and know my sheep, and am known of mine.

Postcommunion.

O LORD, let this holy Communion cleanse us from every guilty stain: that at the intercession of blessed Thomas thy Martyr and Bishop, we may be made partakers thereby of thy healing unto life eternal. Through.

For the Octave of the Nativity.

Postcommunion.

GRANT, we beseech thee, almighty God: that like as thy Son, born this day the Saviour of the world, is the author of our heavenly birth; so he may likewise bestow on us the gift of everlasting life: Who liveth and reigneth with thee.

¶ For a Votive, Mass is said as above, but the Introit and after Septuagesima the Tract also are taken from the Mass Statuit p. [4].

December 30.

The Sixth Day within the Octave of the Nativity

Double.

Introit. Is. 9, 6. Puer natus est.

UNTO us a Child is born, unto us a son is given: and the government shall be upon his shoulder: and his name shall be called, Angel of mighty counsel. Ps. 98, 1. O sing unto the Lord a new song: for he hath done marvellous things. ℣. Glory.

Collect.

GRANT, we beseech thee, almighty God: that we who through our ancient bondage are held beneath the yoke of sin; may by the new Birth of thy only-begotten Son in the flesh obtain deliverance. Through the same.

The Lesson from the Epistle of blessed Paul the Apostle to Titus.

Tit. 3, 4-7.

DEARLY beloved: The kindness and love of God our Saviour toward man hath appeared: not by works of righteousness which we have done, but according to his mercy he saved us, by the washing of regeneration, and renewing of the Holy Ghost, which he shed on us abundantly through Jesus Christ our Saviour: that being justified by his grace, we should be made heirs according to the hope of eternal life: in Christ Jesu our Lord.

Gradual. Ps. 98, 3-4 and 2. All the ends of the earth have seen the salvation of our God: O be joyful in God, all ye lands. ℣. The Lord declared his salvation: his righteousness hath he openly shewed in the sight of the heathen.

Alleluia, alleluia. ℣. A hallowed day hath dawned upon us: come, ye nations, and worship the Lord: for on this day a great light hath descended upon the earth. Alleluia.

✠ The Continuation of the holy Gospel according to Luke.

Luke 2, 15-20.

AT that time: The shepherds said one to another: Let us now go even unto Bethlehem, and see this thing which is come to pass, which the Lord hath made known unto us. And they came with haste: and found Mary and Joseph, and the Babe lying in a manger. And when they had seen it, they made known abroad the saying which was told them concerning this Child. And all they that heard it wondered: at those things which were told them by the shepherds. But Mary kept all these things, and pondered them in her heart. And the shepherds returned, glorifying and praising God for all the things that they had heard and seen, as it was told unto them. Creed.

Offertory. Ps. 89, 12 and 15. The heavens are thine, the earth also is thine: thou hast laid the foundation of the round world, and all that therein is: righteousness and equity are the habitation of thy seat.

Secret.

SANCTIFY, O Lord, by the new Birth of thine only-begotten Son, the gifts which we offer: and cleanse us from the defilements of our iniquities. Through the same.

Preface and Communicántes of the Nativity.

Communion. Ps. 98, 3. All the ends of the world have seen the salvation of our God.

Postcommunion.

GRANT, we beseech thee, almighty God: that like as thy Son, born this day the Saviour of the world, is the author of our heavenly birth; so he may likewise bestow on us the gift of everlasting life: Who liveth and reigneth with thee.

December 31.

St. Silvester I

Pope and Confessor.

Double.

Introit. John 21, 15-17. Si diligis me.

IF thou lovest me, Simon Peter, feed my lambs, feed my sheep. Ps. 30, 1. I will magnify thee, O Lord, for thou hast set me up, and not made my foes to triumph over me. ℣. Glory.

St. Silvester I, Pope and Confessor

Collect.

O EVERLASTING Shepherd, look down in mercy on thy flock: and as thou didst choose blessed Silvester thy Chief Bishop to be pastor and ruler of thy Church; so at his intercession defend it with thy continual protection. Through.

And Commemoration is made of the Octave of the Nativity.

Collect.

ALMIGHTY God, who didst give thy only-begotten Son to take our nature upon him, and as at this time to be born of a pure Virgin: grant that we being regenerate, and made thy children by adoption and grace; may daily be renewed by thy Holy Spirit. Through the same our Lord Jesus Christ, who liveth and reigneth with thee and the same Spirit, ever one God, world without end. R̝. Amen.

Or, Collect.

GRANT, we beseech thee, almighty God: that we who through our ancient bondage are held beneath the yoke of sin: may by the new Birth of thine only-begotten Son obtain deliverance. Through the same.

The Lesson from the Epistle of blessed Peter the Apostle.

I Peter 5, 1-4 and 10-11.

DEARLY beloved: The elders which are among you I exhort, who am also an elder, and a witness of the sufferings of Christ, and also a partaker of the glory that shall be revealed: feed the flock of God which is among you, taking the oversight thereof, not by constraint, but willingly, not for filthy lucre, but of a ready mind; neither as being lords over God's heritage, but being ensamples to the flock. And when the chief Shepherd shall appear, ye shall receive a crown of glory that fadeth not away. Now the God of all grace, who hath called us unto his eternal glory by Christ Jesus, after that ye have suffered a while, make you perfect, stablish, strengthen, settle you. To him be glory and dominion for ever and ever. Amen.

Gradual. Ps. 107, 32 and 31. Let them exalt him in the congregation of the people: and praise him in the seat of the elders. V̝. O that men would praise the Lord for his goodness; and declare the wonders that he doeth for the children of men.

Alleluia, alleluia. Matt. 16, 18. Thou art Peter, and upon this rock I will build my Church. Alleluia.

✠ The Continuation of the holy Gospel according to Matthew.

Matt. 16, 13-19.

AT that time: Jesus came into the coasts of Cæsarea Philippi, and asked his disciples, saying: Whom do men say that I, the Son of man, am? And they said: Some say that thou art John the Baptist, some Elias, and others Jeremias, or one of the prophets. He saith unto them: But whom say ye that I am? And Simon Peter answered and said: Thou art the Christ, the Son of the living God. And Jesus answered and said unto him: Blessed art thou, Simon Bar-jona: for flesh and blood hath not revealed it unto thee, but my Father which is in heaven. And I say also unto thee, That thou art Peter, and upon this rock I will build my Church, and the gates of hell shall not prevail against it. And I will give unto thee the keys of the kingdom of heaven. And whatsoever thou shalt bind on earth shall be bound in heaven: and whatsoever thou shalt loose on earth shall be loosed in heaven. Creed, because of the Octave.

Offertory. Jer. 1, 9-10. Behold, I have put my words in thy mouth: see, I have set thee over the nations and over the kingdoms, to pull down and to destroy, to build and to plant.

Secret.

WE beseech thee, O Lord, graciously enlighten thy Church by the gifts which we here offer: that in every place thy flock may increase and prosper, and the shepherds by thy governance may be made pleasing to thy name. Through.

For the Octave of the Nativity, Secret.

SANCTIFY, O Lord, by the new Birth of thine only-begotten Son the gifts which we offer: and cleanse us from the defilements of our iniquities. Through the same.

Preface and Communicántes of the Nativity, because of the Octave.

Communion. Matt. 16, 18. Thou art Peter, and upon this rock I will build my Church.

Postcommunion.

MERCIFUL Lord, we beseech thee to govern and preserve thy Church, which thou hast here refreshed with heavenly food: that by the guiding of thy mighty power it may serve thee in more abundant freedom, and ever keep thy true religion whole and undefiled. Through.

For the Octave of the Nativity.

Postcommunion.

GRANT, we beseech thee, almighty God: that like as thy Son, born this day the Saviour of the world, is the author of our heavenly birth; so he may likewise bestow on us the gift of everlasting life: Who liveth and reigneth with thee.

January 1.

THE CIRCUMCISION OF THE LORD

AND OCTAVE OF THE NATIVITY

Double of 2nd class.

Station at St. Mary beyond the Tiber.

Introit. Is. 9, 6. Puer natus est.

UNTO us a Child is born, unto us a son is given; and the government shall be upon his shoulder: and his name shall be called, Angel of mighty counsel. Ps. 98, 1. O sing unto the Lord a new song: for he hath done marvellous things. ℣. Glory.

Collect.

ALMIGHTY God, who madest thy blessed Son to be circumcised, and obedient to the law for man: grant us the true circumcision of the Spirit; that, our hearts, and all our members, being mortified from all worldly and carnal lusts, we may in all things obey thy blessed will. Through the same... in the unity of the same Holy Spirit.

Or, Collect.

O GOD, who by the child-bearing of the blessed Virgin Mary hast bestowed upon mankind the rewards of eternal salvation: grant, we beseech thee; that we may know the succour of her intercession for us, through whom we have been found worthy to receive the author of life, even Jesus Christ thy Son our Lord: Who liveth.

The Lesson from the Epistle of blessed Paul the Apostle to the Romans.

Rom. 4, 8-14.

BRETHREN: Blessed is the man to whom the Lord will not impute sin. Cometh this blessedness then upon the circumcision only, or upon the uncircumcision also? For we say, that faith was reckoned to Abraham for righteousness. How was it then reckoned? When he was in circumcision, or in uncircumcision? Not in circumcision, but in uncircumcision. And he received the sign of circumcision, a seal of the righteousness of the faith which he had yet being uncircumcised: that he might be the father of all them that believe, though they be not circumcised: that righteousness might be imputed unto them also: and the father of circumcision to them who are not of the circumcision only, but also walk in the steps of that faith of our father Abraham, which he had being yet uncircumcised. For the promise, that he should be the heir of the world, was not to Abraham, or to his seed, through the law, but through the righteousness of faith. For if they which are of the law be heirs, faith is made void, and the promise made of none effect.

The Circumcision of the Lord

Or,

The Lesson from the Epistle of blessed Paul the Apostle to Titus.

Tit. 2, 11-16.

DEARLY beloved: The grace of God that bringeth salvation hath appeared to all men, teaching us that, denying ungodliness and worldly lusts, we should live soberly, righteously, and godly, in this present world, looking for that blessed hope, and the glorious appearing of the great God and our Saviour Jesus Christ: who gave himself for us: that he might redeem us from all iniquity, and purify unto himself a peculiar people, zealous of good works. These things speak, and exhort: in Christ Jesu our Lord.

Gradual. Ps. 98, 3-4 and 2. All the ends of the earth have seen the salvation of our God: O be joyful in God, all ye lands. ℣. The Lord declared his salvation: his righteousness hath he openly shewed in the sight of the heathen.

Alleluia, alleluia. ℣. Hebr. 1, 1-2. God, who at sundry times spake in time past unto the fathers by the Prophets, hath in these last days spoken unto us by his Son. Alleluia.

✠ The Continuation of the holy Gospel according to Luke.

Luke 2, 15-21.

AT that time: It came to pass, as the Angels were gone away from them into heaven, the shepherds said one to another: Let us now go even unto Bethlehem, and see this thing which is come to pass, which the Lord hath made known unto us. And they came with haste: and found Mary and Joseph, and the Babe lying in a manger. And when they had seen it, they made known abroad the saying which was told them concerning this Child. And all they that heard it wondered: at those things which were told them by the shepherds. But Mary kept all these things, and pondered them in her heart. And the shepherds returned, glorifying and praising God for all the things that they had heard and seen, as it was told unto them. And when eight days were accomplished for the circumcising of the Child: his name was called Jesus, which was so named of the Angel before he was conceived in the womb. Creed.

Or,

✠ The Continuation of the holy Gospel according to Luke.

Luke 2, 21.

AT that time: When eight days were accomplished for the circumcising of the Child: his name was called Jesus, which was so named of the Angel before he was conceived in the womb. Creed.

Offertory. Ps. 89, 12 and 15. The heavens are thine, the earth also is thine: thou hast laid the foundation of the round world, and all that therein is: righteousness and equity are the habitation of thy seat.

Secret.

WE beseech thee, O Lord, to accept our prayers and oblations: and graciously hearken unto us, whom thou dost cleanse by thy heavenly mysteries. Through.

Preface and Communicántes of the Nativity.

Communion. Ps. 98, 3. All the ends of the world have seen the salvation of our God.

Postcommunion.

O LORD, let this holy Communion cleanse us from every guilty stain: that, at the intercession of the blessed Virgin Mary, Mother of God, we may be made partakers thereby of thy healing unto life eternal. Through the same.

¶ On Ferias from January 2nd to 5th inclusive Mass is said as above, but the Creed and Communicántes of the Nativity are omitted.

The Sunday between the Circumcision and the Epiphany, or, if it does not occur, on the 2nd day of January.

THE MOST HOLY NAME OF JESUS
Double of 2nd class.

Introit. Phil. 2, 10-11. In nomine Jesu.

AT the name of Jesus every knee shall bow, of things in heaven, and things in earth, and things under the earth: and every tongue shall confess that Jesus Christ is Lord, to the glory of God the Father. Ps. 8, 1. O Lord our Governor, how excellent is thy name in all the world. ℣. Glory.

Collect.

O GOD, who didst appoint thine only-begotten Son to be the Saviour of mankind, and didst command that he should be called Jesus: mercifully grant; that we, who venerate his holy name on earth, may rejoice to behold him for ever in heaven. Through the same.

The Lesson from the Acts of the Apostles.

Acts 4, 8-12.

IN those days: Peter, filled with the Holy Ghost, said: Ye rulers of the people, and elders of Israel: If we this day be examined of the good deed done to the impotent man, by what means he is made whole, be it known unto you all, and to all the people of Israel: that by the name of Jesus Christ of Nazareth, whom ye crucified, whom God raised from the dead, even by him doth this man stand here before you whole. This is the stone which was set at nought of you builders: which is become the head of the corner: neither is there salvation in any other. For there is none other name under heaven given among men, whereby we must be saved.

Gradual. Ps. 106, 47. Deliver us, O Lord our God, and gather us from among the heathen: that we may give thanks unto thy holy name, and make our boast of thy praise. ℣. Is. 63, 16. Thou, O Lord, art our Father, our Redeemer: thy name is from everlasting.

Alleluia, alleluia. ℣. Ps. 145, 21. My mouth shall speak the praise of the Lord: and let all flesh give thanks unto his holy name. Alleluia.

In Votive Masses after Septuagesima, omitting Alleluia and the Verse following, is said:

Tract. Ps. 80, 20, and Cant. 2, 14. Turn us again, O Lord God of hosts: shew the light of thy countenance, and we shall be whole: let me hear thy voice. For sweet is thy voice, and thy countenance is exceeding comely. ℣. Cant. 1, 2. Thy name, O Jesu, is as ointment poured forth: therefore do the virgins love thee.

In Eastertide the Gradual is omitted, and in its place is said:

Alleluia, alleluia. ℣. Ps. 145, 21. My mouth shall speak the praise of the Lord, and let all flesh give thanks unto his holy name. Alleluia. Ibid., 1. I will magnify thee, O God, my King: and I will praise thy holy name, O Jesu, for ever and ever. Alleluia.

✠ The Continuation of the holy Gospel according to Luke.

Luke 2, 21.

AT that time: When eight days were accomplished for the circumcising of the Child: his name was called Jesus, which was so named of the Angel before he was conceived in the womb. Creed.

Offertory. Ps. 86, 12 and 5. I will thank thee, O Lord my God, with all my heart, and will praise thy name for evermore: for thou, Lord, art good and gracious: and of great mercy unto all them that call upon thee, alleluia.

Secret.

WE beseech thee, most merciful God, let thy benediction, whereby all created things are sustained, hallow this our sacrifice, which we offer unto thee to the glory of the name of thy Son, Jesus Christ our Lord: that it may be acceptable for the praise of thy majesty, and profitable for our salvation. Through the same.

Preface of the Nativity.

Communion. Ps. 86, 9-10. All nations whom thou hast made shall come and worship thee, O Lord, and shall glorify thy name: for thou art great, and doest wondrous things: thou art God alone, alleluia.

Postcommunion.

ALMIGHTY and everlasting God, who art our Creator and Redeemer, mercifully have respect unto these our prayers: and vouchsafe to receive with favourable and gracious countenance this sacrifice of our salvation, which we have offered to thy majesty, to the honour of the name of thy Son Jesus Christ our Lord; that by the merits of his glorious name of Jesus, thy grace may in such wise be shed forth upon us, that, being predestined thereby to eternal life, we may rejoice that our names are written in heaven. Through the same.

January 5.

For St. Telesphorus

Pope and Martyr.

The Mass Si diligis me, p. [2].

Collect. C

O EVERLASTING Shepherd, look down in mercy on thy flock: and as thou didst choose blessed Telesphorus, thy Martyr and Chief Bishop, to be pastor and ruler of thy Church; so at his intercession defend it with thy continual protection. Through.

Secret. C

WE beseech thee, O Lord, graciously enlighten thy Church by the gifts which we here offer: that in every place thy flock may increase and prosper, and the shepherds by thy governance may be made pleasing to thy name. Through.

Postcommunion. C

MERCIFUL Lord, we beseech thee to govern and preserve thy Church, which thou hast here refreshed with heavenly food: that by the guiding of thy mighty power it may serve thee in more abundant freedom, and ever keep thy true religion whole and undefiled. Through.

January 6.

THE EPIPHANY OF THE LORD

Double of 1st class.

Station at St. Peter

Introit. Mal. 3, 1; 29, 12. Ecce, advénit.

BEHOLD, he is come, the Lord and Ruler: and in his hand the kingdom, and power, and dominion. Ps. 72, 1. Give the King thy judgments, O God: and thy righteousness unto the King's Son. ℣. Glory.

Collect.

O GOD, who by the leading of a star didst manifest thy only-begotten Son to the Gentiles: mercifully grant; that we, which know thee now by faith, may after this life have the fruition of thy glorious Godhead. Through the same.

Or, Collect.

O GOD, who on this day didst by the leading of a star manifest thy only-begotten Son to the Gentiles: mercifully grant that we, which know thee now by faith, may finally attain unto the contemplation of the beauty of thy majesty. Through the same.

The Lesson from the Epistle of blessed Paul the Apostle to the Ephesians.

Ephes. 3, 1.

BRETHREN: For this cause, I Paul, the prisoner of Jesus Christ for you Gentiles: if ye have heard of the dispensation of the grace of God, which is given me to youward. How that by revelation he made known unto me the mystery (as I wrote afore in few words, whereby, when ye read, ye may understand my knowledge in the mystery of Christ) which in other ages was not made known unto the sons of men, as it is now revealed unto his holy Apostles and Prophets by the Spirit: that the Gentiles should be fellow-heirs, and of the same body, and partakers of his promise in Christ, by the Gospel: whereof I was made a minister, according to the gift of the grace of God given unto me by the effectual working of his power. Unto me, who am less than the least of all saints, is this grace given, that I should preach among the Gentiles the unsearchable riches of Christ; and to make all men see what is the fellowship of the mystery, which from the beginning of the world hath been hid in God, who created all things by Jesus Christ. To the intent, that now unto the principalities and powers in heavenly places might be known by the Church the manifold wisdom of God, according to the eternal purpose which he purposed in Christ Jesus our Lord: in whom we have boldness and access with confidence by the faith of him.

Or,

The Lesson from the Prophet Isaiah.

Is. 60, 1-6.

ARISE, shine, O Jerusalem: for thy light is come, and the glory of the Lord is risen upon thee. For, behold, the darkness shall cover the earth, and gross darkness the people: but the Lord shall arise upon thee, and his glory shall be seen upon thee. And the Gentiles shall come to thy light, and kings to the brightness of thy rising. Lift up thine eyes round about, and see: all they gather themselves together, they come to thee: thy sons shall come from far, and thy daughters shall be

The Epiphany of the Lord

nursed at thy side. Then thou shalt see, and flow together, and thine heart shall fear, and be enlarged, because the abundance of the sea shall be converted unto thee, the forces of the Gentiles shall come unto thee. The multitude of camels shall cover thee, the dromedaries of Midian and Ephah: all they from Saba shall come, bringing gold and incense, and shall shew forth the praise of the Lord.

Gradual. Is. 60, 6 and 1. All they from Saba shall come, bringing gold and incense, and shall shew forth the praise of the Lord. ℣. Arise and shine, O Jerusalem: for the glory of the Lord is risen upon thee.

Alleluia, alleluia. ℣. Matt. 2, 2. We have seen his star in the East: and are come with gifts to worship the Lord. Alleluia.

✠ The Continuation of the holy Gospel according to Matthew.

Matt. 2, 1-12.

WHEN Jesus was born in Bethlehem of Judæa, in the days of Herod the king, behold, there came wise men from the East to Jerusalem, saying: Where is he that is born King of the Jews? for we have seen his star in the East, and are come to worship him. When Herod the king had heard these things, he was troubled, and all Jerusalem with him. And when he had gathered all the chief priests and scribes of the people together, he demanded of them, where Christ should be born. And they said unto him: In Bethlehem of Judæa: for thus it is written by the Prophet: And thou, Bethlehem, in the land of Juda, art not the least among the princes of Juda; for out of thee shall come a governor that shall rule my people Israel. Then Herod, when he had privily called the wise men, inquired of them diligently what time the star appeared: and he sent them to Bethlehem, and said: Go, and search diligently for the young child: and when ye have found him, bring me word again, that I may come and worship him also. When they had heard the king, they departed. And lo, the star which they saw in the East went before them, till it came and stood over where the young Child was. When they saw the star, they rejoiced with exceeding great joy. And when they were come into the house, they saw the young Child with Mary his Mother, (Here genuflect) and fell down and worshipped him. And when they had opened their treasures, they presented unto him gifts, gold, and frankincense, and myrrh. And being warned of God in a dream that they should not return to Herod, they departed into their own country another way. Creed.

Offertory. Ps. 72, 10-11. The kings of Tharsis and of the isles shall give presents: the kings of Arabia and Saba shall bring gifts: all kings shall fall down before him, all nations shall do him service.

Secret.

WE beseech thee, O Lord, mercifully to look upon the oblations of thy Church: wherein no longer offering gold and frankincense and myrrh; we sacrifice and receive him who by those gifts was signified, even Jesus Christ thy Son our Lord: Who liveth and reigneth with thee.

Preface and Communicántes proper.

Communion. Matt. 1, 2. We have seen his star in the East, and are come with gifts to worship the Lord.

Postcommunion.

GRANT, we beseech thee, almighty God: that we, who here celebrate thy holy mysteries, may in purity of heart and mind receive the benefits of the same. Through.

¶ On Ferias from January 7th to 12th inclusive Mass is said as above, but the Creed and Communicántes of the Epiphany are omitted.

The Holy Family, Jesus, Mary and Joseph

THE FIRST SUNDAY AFTER THE EPIPHANY

The Holy Family, Jesus, Mary and Joseph

Greater double.

Introit. Prov. 23, 24-25. Exsultat.

THE father of the Righteous greatly rejoiceth: let thy Father and thy Mother be glad, and let her that bare thee rejoice. Ps. 84, 1-2. O, how amiable are thy dwellings, thou Lord of hosts! my soul hath a desire and longing to enter into the courts of the Lord. ℣. Glory.

Collect.

O LORD Jesu Christ, who being made subject unto Mary and Joseph, didst by thy wondrous holiness consecrate the life of home: grant us, through the assistance of them both, so to be taught by the example of thy holy Family; that we may attain unto their everlasting fellowship: Who livest and reignest.

And Commemoration is made of the First Sunday after the Epiphany.

Collect.

O LORD, we beseech thee mercifully to receive the prayers of thy people which call upon thee: and grant that they may both perceive and know what things they ought to do, and also may have grace and power faithfully to fulfil the same. Through.

The Lesson from the Epistle of blessed Paul the Apostle to the Colossians.

Col. 3, 12-17.

BRETHREN: Put on, as the elect of God, holy and beloved, bowels of mercies, kindness, humbleness of mind, meekness, longsuffering: forbearing one another and forgiving one another, if any man have a quarrel against any: even as Christ forgave you, so also do ye. And above all these things put on charity, which is the bond of perfectness: and let the peace of God rule in your hearts, to the which also ye are called in one body: and be ye thankful. Let the word of Christ dwell in you richly in all wisdom, teaching and admonishing one another in psalms and hymns and spiritual songs, singing with grace in your hearts to the Lord. And whatsoever ye do in word or deed, do all in the name of the Lord Jesus, giving thanks to God and the Father through him.

Gradual. Ps. 27, 4. One thing have I desired of the Lord, which I will require: even that I may dwell in the house of the Lord all the days of my life. ℣. Ps. 84, 5. Blessed are they that dwell in thy house, O Lord: they will be alway praising thee.

. Alleluia, alleluia. ℣. Is. 45, 15. Verily thou art a King that hidest thyself, O God of Israel, the Saviour. Alleluia.

In votive Masses after Septuagesima, omitting Alleluia and the Verse following, is said:

Tract. Heb. 10, 5. Sacrifice and offering, thou wouldest not, but a body hast thou prepared me. ℣. Ps. 40, 7-8. Burnt-offerings, and sacrifice for sin, hast thou not required: then said I: Lo, I come. ℣ Heb. 10, 7. In the volume of the book it is written of me: To do thy will, O God.

In Eastertide the Gradual is omitted, and in its place is said:

Alleluia, alleluia. ℣. Prov. 8, 34. Blessed is the man that heareth me, watching daily at my gates, waiting at the posts of my doors. Alleluia. ℣. Col. 3, 3. Our life is hid with Christ in God. Alleluia.

✠ The Continuation of the holy Gospel according to Luke.

Luke 2, 42-52.

WHEN Jesus was twelve years old, they went up to Jerusalem after the custom of the feast, and when they had fulfilled the days, as they returned, the child Jesus tarried behind in Jerusalem, and Joseph and his Mother knew not of it. But they, supposing him to have been in the company, went a day's journey, and they sought him among their kinsfolk and acquaintance. And when they found him not, they turned back again to Jerusalem, seeking him. And it came to pass, that after three days they found him in the temple, sitting in the midst of the doctors, both hearing them, and asking them questions. And all that heard him were astonished at his understanding and answers. And when they saw him, they were amazed. And his Mother said unto him: Son, why hast thou thus dealt with us? Behold, thy father and I have sought thee sorrowing. And he said unto them: How is it that ye sought me? Wist ye not that I must be about my Father's business? And they understood not the saying which he spake unto them. And he went down with them, and came to Nazareth: and was subject unto them. But his Mother kept all these sayings in her heart. And Jesus increased in wisdom, and stature, and in favour with God and man. Creed.

Offertory. Luke 2, 22. His parents brought Jesus to Jerusalem, to present him to the Lord.

Secret.

WE offer unto thee, O Lord, this sacrifice of propitiation, humbly beseeching thee: that, at the intercession of the Virgin Mother of God with blessed Joseph, thou wouldest surely stablish our families in thy peace and favour. Through the same.

For the Sunday.

Secret.

MAY the sacrifice which we offer unto thee, O Lord, evermore quicken and defend us. Through.

Preface of the Epiphany.

Communion. Luke 2, 51. Jesus went down with them, and came to Nazareth, and was subject unto them.

Postcommunion.

O LORD Jesu, who dost refresh us with these heavenly sacraments, make us continually to follow the example of thy holy Family: that in the hour of our death, by the assistance of thy glorious Virgin Mother with blessed Joseph; we may be found worthy to be received by thee into everlasting habitations: Who livest and reignest with God the Father.

For the Sunday.

Postcommunion.

WE humbly beseech thee, almighty God: that as thou dost refresh us with thy sacraments: so thou wouldest grant unto us to do thee worthy and acceptable service. Through.

For the First Sunday after the Epiphany

Introit. In excelso throno.

ON a throne exalted I beheld a man sitting, whom a legion of Angels worship, singing together: behold, his rule and governance endure to all ages. Ps. 100, 1. O be joyful in the Lord, all ye lands: serve the Lord with gladness. ℣. Glory.

The First Sunday after the Epiphany

Collect.

O LORD, we beseech thee mercifully to receive the prayers of thy people which call upon thee: and grant that they may both perceive and know what things they ought to do, and also may have grace and power faithfully to fulfil the same. Through.

The Lesson from the Epistle of blessed Paul the Apostle to the Romans.

Rom. 12, 1-5.

BRETHREN: I beseech you by the mercies of God, that ye present your bodies a living sacrifice, holy, acceptable unto God, which is your reasonable service. And be not conformed to this world, but be ye transformed by the renewing of your mind: that ye may prove what is that good, and acceptable, and perfect will of God. For I say, through the grace given unto me, to every man that is among you: Not to think of himself more highly than he ought to think, but to think soberly: according as God hath dealt to every man the measure of faith. For as we have many members in one body, and all members have not the same office: so we, being many, are one body in Christ, and every one members one of another: in Christ Jesu our Lord.

Gradual. Ps. 72, 18 and 3. Blessed be the Lord, even the God of Israel, which only doeth wondrous things from the beginning. ℣. The mountains shall bring peace, and the little hills righteousness unto the people.

Alleluia, alleluia. ℣. Ps. 100, 1. O be joyful in the Lord, all ye lands: serve the Lord with gladness. Alleluia.

✠ The Continuation of the holy Gospel according to Luke.

Luke 2, 42-52.

NOW his parents went to Jerusalem every year at the feast of the Passover. And when Jesus was twelve years old, they went up to Jerusalem after the custom of the feast. And when they had fulfilled the days, as they returned, the child Jesus tarried behind in Jerusalem, and Joseph and his Mother knew not of it. But they, supposing him to have been in the company, went a day's journey, and they sought him among their kinsfolk and acquaintance. And when they found him not, they turned back again to Jerusalem, seeking him. And it came to pass, that after three days they found him in the temple, sitting in the midst of the doctors, both hearing them, and asking them questions. And all that heard him were astonished at his understanding and answers. And when they saw him, they were amazed. And his Mother said unto him: Son, why hast thou thus dealt with us? Behold, thy father and I have sought thee sorrowing. And he said unto them: How is it that ye sought me? Wist ye not that I must be about my Father's business? And they understood not the saying which he spake unto them. And he went down with them, and came to Nazareth: and was subject unto them. But his Mother kept all these sayings in her heart. And Jesus increased in wisdom, and stature, and in favour with God and man. Creed.

Offertory. Ps. 100, 1-2. O be joyful in the Lord, all ye lands, serve the Lord with gladness: and come before his presence with a song: for the Lord he is God.

Secret.

MAY the sacrifice which we offer unto thee, O Lord, evermore quicken and defend us. Through.

Preface of the Epiphany.

Communion. Luke 2, 48-49. Son, why hast thou thus dealt with us? behold, thy father and I have sought thee sorrowing. And how is it that ye sought me? wist ye not that I must be about my Father's business?

Postcommunion.

WE humbly beseech thee, almighty God: that as thou dost refresh us with thy sacraments, so thou wouldest vouchsafe unto us to do thee worthy and acceptable service. Through.

January 8.

For St. Lucian and his Companions
Martyrs.

The Mass Sapientiam, p. [11].

January 11.

For St. Hyginus
Pope and Martyr.

The Mass Si diligis me, p. [2].

Collect.   C

O EVERLASTING Shepherd, look down in mercy on thy flock: and as thou didst choose blessed Hyginus, thy Martyr and Chief Bishop, to be pastor and ruler of thy Church; so at his intercession defend it with thy continual protection. Through.

Secret.   C

WE beseech thee, O Lord, graciously enlighten thy Church by the gifts which we here offer: that in every place thy flock may increase and prosper, and the shepherds by thy governance may be made pleasing to thy name. Through.

Postcommunion.   C

MERCIFUL Lord, we beseech thee, to govern and preserve thy Church, which thou hast here refreshed with heavenly food: that by the guiding of thy mighty power it may serve thee in more abundant freedom, and ever keep thy true religion whole and undefiled. Through.

January 13.

Commemoration of the Baptism of Our Lord Jesus Christ
Greater double.

Introit. Mal. 3, 1; Chron. 29, 12. Ecce, advénit.

BEHOLD, he is come, the Lord and Ruler: and in his hand the kingdom, and power, and dominion. Ps. 72, 1. Give the King thy judgments, O God: and thy righteousness unto the King's Son. ℣. Glory.

Collect.

O GOD, whose only-begotten Son hath been made manifest in substance of our flesh: grant, we beseech thee; that, as we have known him after the fashion of our outward likeness, so we may inwardly be made regenerate in him: Who liveth and reigneth with thee.

The Lesson from the Prophet Isaiah.
Is. 60, 1-6.

ARISE, shine, O Jerusalem: for thy light is come, and the glory of the Lord is risen upon thee. For, behold, the darkness shall cover the earth, and gross darkness the people: but the Lord shall arise upon thee, and his glory shall be seen upon thee. And the Gentiles shall come to thy light, and kings to the brightness of thy rising. Lift up thine eyes round about, and see: all they gather themselves together, they come to thee: thy sons shall come from far, and thy daughters shall be nursed at thy side. Then thou shalt see, and flow together, and thine heart shall fear, and be enlarged, because the abundance of the sea shall be converted unto thee, the forces of the Gentiles shall come unto thee. The multitude of camels shall cover thee, the dromedaries of Midian and Ephah: all they from Saba shall come, bringing gold and incense, and they shall shew forth the praise of the Lord.

Gradual. Ibid., 6 and 11. All they from Saba shall come, bringing gold and incense, and they shall shew forth the praise of the Lord. ℣. Arise and shine, O Jerusalem: for the glory of the Lord is risen upon thee.

Alleluia, alleluia. ℣. Matt. 2, 2. We have seen his star in the East, and are come with gifts to worship the Lord. Alleluia.

✠ The Continuation of the holy Gospel according to John.

John 1, 29-34.

AT that time: John seeth Jesus coming unto him, and saith: Behold the Lamb of God, which taketh away the sin of the world. This is he of whom I said: After me cometh a man which is preferred before me: for he was before me. And I knew him not: but that he should be made manifest to Israel, therefore am I come baptizing with water. And John bare record, saying: I saw the Spirit descending from heaven like a dove, and it abode upon him. And I knew him not: but he that sent me to baptize with water, the same said unto me: Upon whom thou shalt see the Spirit descending, and remaining on him, the same is he which baptizeth with the Holy Ghost. And I saw: and bare record that this is the Son of God. Creed.

Offertory. Ps. 72, 10-11. The kings of Tharsis and of the isles shall give presents: the kings of Arabia and Saba shall bring gifts: all kings shall fall down before him, all nations shall do him service.

Secret.

WE offer this our sacrifice unto thee, O Lord, in remembrance of the manifestation of thy new-born Son, humbly beseeching thee: that like as he is himself the author of our gifts, so he may also in his mercy receive the same, even Jesus Christ our Lord: Who liveth.

Preface of the Epiphany.

Communion. Matt. 2, 2. We have seen his star in the East, and are come with gifts to worship the Lord.

Postcommunion.

PREVENT us, O Lord, we beseech thee, at all times and in all places with thy heavenly light: that as thou hast vouchsafed to make us partakers of this mystery, so we may understand it aright in purity of heart, and worthily receive it with devout affection. Through.

¶ If January 13th fall on Sunday, Mass is said of the Holy Family, p. 45, with Commemoration of the Sunday only.

The Second Sunday after the Epiphany

Double.

Introit. Ps. 66, 4. Omnis terra.

ALL the earth shall worship thee, O God, and sing of thee: they shall sing praise unto thy name, O thou Most Highest. Ps. ibid., 1-2. O be joyful in God, all ye lands: sing praises unto the honour of his name: make his praise to be glorious. ℣. Glory.

Glória in excélsis is said on all Sundays before Septuagesima. But on ferial days, when the Mass of the preceding Sunday is resumed, it is not said.

Collect.

ALMIGHTY and everlasting God, who dost govern all things in heaven and earth: mercifully hear the supplications of thy people; and grant us thy peace all the days of our life. Through.

The Second Sunday after the Epiphany

The Lesson from the Epistle of blessed Paul the Apostle to the Romans.

Rom. 12, 6-16.

BRETHREN: Having gifts differing according to the grace that is given to us: whether prophecy, let us prophesy according to the proportion of faith, or ministry, let us wait on our ministering, or he that teacheth, on teaching, or he that exhorteth, on exhortation, he that giveth, let him do it with simplicity, he that ruleth, with diligence, he that sheweth mercy, with cheerfulness. Let love be without dissimulation. Abhor that which is evil, cleave to that which is good: Be kindly affectioned one to another with brotherly love: In honour preferring one another: Not slothful in business: Fervent in spirit: Serving the Lord: Rejoicing in hope: Patient in tribulation: Continuing instant in prayer: Distributing to the necessity of saints: Given to hospitality. Bless them which persecute you: bless, and curse not. Rejoice with them that do rejoice, and weep with them that weep: Be of the same mind one towards another: Mind not high things, but condescend to men of low estate.

Gradual. Ps. 107, 20-21. The Lord sent his word, and healed them: and they were saved from their destruction. ℣. O that men would therefore praise the Lord for his goodness: and declare the wonders that he doeth for the children of men.

Alleluia, alleluia. ℣. Ps. 148, 2. Praise the Lord, all ye Angels of his: praise him, all his hosts. Alleluia.

¶ Alleluia is said thus, with its Verse after the Gradual on all lesser Sundays after the Epiphany, even if the Mass of Sunday be resumed on Ferias.

✠ The Continuation of the holy Gospel according to John.

John 2, 1-11.

AT that time: There was a marriage in Cana of Galilee: and the Mother of Jesus was there. And both Jesus was called, and his disciples, to the marriage. And when they wanted wine, the Mother of Jesus saith unto him: They have no wine. Jesus saith unto her: Woman, what have I to do with thee? Mine hour is not yet come. His Mother saith unto the servants: Whatsoever he saith unto you, do it. And there were set there six water-pots of stone, after the manner of the purifying of the Jews, containing two or three firkins apiece. Jesus saith unto them: Fill the water-pots with water. And they filled them up to the brim. And he saith unto them: Draw out now, and bear unto the governor of the feast. And they bare it. When the ruler of the feast had tasted the water that was made wine, and knew not whence it was, but the servants which drew the water knew: the governor of the feast called the bridegroom, and saith unto him: Every man at the beginning doth set forth good wine, and when men have well drunk, then that which is worse. But thou hast kept the good wine until now. This beginning of miracles did Jesus in Cana of Galilee: and manifested forth his glory, and his disciples believed on him. Creed.

Offertory. Ps. 66, 1-2 and 16. O be joyful in God, all ye lands: sing praises unto the honour of his name: O come hither, and hearken, all ye that fear God, and I will tell you what the Lord hath done for my soul, alleluia.

Secret.

SANCTIFY, O Lord, these our oblations: and cleanse us from the defilement of our iniquities. Through.

Preface of the Most Holy Trinity.

Communion. John 2, 7-9 and 10-11. The Lord saith: Fill the water-pots with water, and bear unto the ruler of the feast. When the ruler of the feast had tasted the water that was made wine, he saith unto the bridegroom: Thou hast kept the good wine until now. This miracle did Jesus first before his disciples.

Postcommunion.

INCREASE, O Lord, we beseech thee, and multiply upon us the operation of thy power: that we, whom thou hast quickened with these heavenly sacraments, may by thy bounty be made ready to receive the benefits which thou dost promise. Through.

The Third Sunday after the Epiphany
Double.
Introit. Ps. 97 7-8. Adorate.

WORSHIP God, all ye Angels of his: Sion heard, and rejoiced: and the daughters of Judah were glad. Ps. ibid., 1. The Lord is King, the earth may be glad thereof: yea, the multitude of the isles may be glad thereof. ℣. Glory.

Collect.

ALMIGHTY and everlasting God, mercifully look upon our infirmities: and in all our dangers and necessities stretch forth thy right hand to help and defend us. Through.

Or, Collect.

ALMIGHTY and everlasting God, mercifully look upon our infirmity: and stretch forth the right hand of thy majesty to defend us. Through.

The Lesson from the Epistle of blessed Paul the Apostle to the Romans.
Rom. 12, 16-21.

BRETHREN: Be not wise in your own conceits: recompense to no man evil for evil: provide things honest in the sight of all men. If it be possible, as much as lieth in you, live peaceably with all men: Dearly beloved, avenge not yourselves, but rather give place unto wrath. For it is written: Vengeance is mine: I will repay, saith the Lord. Therefore, if thine enemy hunger, feed him: if he thirst, give him drink: for in so doing thou shalt heap coals of fire on his head. Be not overcome of evil, but overcome evil with good.

Gradual. Ps. 102, 16-17. The heathen shall fear thy name, O Lord, and all the kings of the earth thy majesty. ℣. When the Lord shall build up Sion, and when his glory shall appear.

Alleluia, alleluia. ℣. Ps. 97, 1. The Lord is King, the earth may be glad thereof: yea, the multitude of the isles may be glad thereof. Alleluia.

✠ The Continuation of the holy Gospel according to Matthew.
Matt. 8, 1-13.

AT that time: When Jesus was come down from the mountain, great multitudes followed him: and behold, there came a leper and worshipped him, saying: Lord, if thou wilt, thou canst make me clean. And Jesus put forth his hand, and touched him, saying: I will. Be thou clean. And immediately his leprosy was cleansed. And Jesus saith unto him: See thou tell no man: but go thy way, shew thyself to the priest, and offer the gift that Moses commanded, for a testimony unto them. And when Jesus was entered into Capernaum, there came unto him a centurion beseeching him, and saying: Lord, my servant lieth at home sick of the palsy, grievously tormented. And Jesus saith unto him: I will come and heal him. The centurion answered and said: Lord, I am not worthy that thou shouldest come under my roof: but speak the word only, and my servant shall be healed. For I am a man under authority, having soldiers under me, and I say unto this man: Go, and he goeth; and to another: Come, and he cometh; and to my servant: Do this, and he doeth it. When Jesus heard it, he marvelled, and said to them that followed: Verily I say unto you, I have not found so great faith, no, not in Israel. And I say unto you, That many shall come from the East and West, and shall sit down with Abraham, and Isaac, and Jacob, in the kingdom of heaven: but the children of the kingdom shall be cast out into the outer darkness: there shall be weeping and gnashing of teeth. And Jesus said unto the centurion: Go thy way, and as thou hast believed, so be it done unto thee. And his servant was healed in the self-same hour. Creed.

Offertory. Ps. 118, 1 and 17. The right hand of the Lord bringeth mighty things to pass, the right hand of the Lord hath exalted me: I shall not die, but live, and declare the works of the Lord.

Secret.

WE beseech thee, O Lord, that this oblation may cleanse us from our sins: and sanctify thy servants both in body and soul for the celebration of this sacrifice. Through.

Preface of the Most Holy Trinity.

Communion. Luke 4, 22. All wondered at these things which proceeded out of the mouth of God.

Postcommunion.

O LORD, who dost vouchsafe unto us to be made partakers of so great a mystery: we beseech thee; that thou wouldest vouchsafe to render us worthy thereby to enjoy the benefits of the same. Through.

The Fourth Sunday after the Epiphany
Double.

Introit. Ps. 97, 7-8. Adorate.

WORSHIP God, all ye Angels of his: Sion heard and rejoiced: and the daughters of Judah were glad. Ps. ibid., 1. The Lord is King, the earth may be glad thereof: yea the multitude of the isles may be glad thereof. ℣. Glory.

Collect.

O GOD, who knowest us to be set in the midst of so many and great dangers, that by reason of the frailty of our nature we cannot always stand upright: grant to us such strength and protection; as may support us in all dangers, and carry us through all temptations. Through.

Or, Collect.

O GOD, who knowest us to be set in the midst of so many and great dangers, that for man's frailness we cannot always stand uprightly: grant to us health of body and soul; that all those things which we suffer for sin, by thy help we may overcome. Through.

The Lesson from the Epistle of blessed Paul the Apostle to the Romans.
Rom. 13, 1-7.

BRETHREN: Let every soul be subject unto the higher powers: for there is no power but of God: the powers that be are ordained of God. Whosoever therefore resisteth the power resisteth the ordinance of God: and they that resist shall receive to themselves damnation. For rulers are not a terror to good works, but to the evil. Wilt thou then not be afraid of the power? do that which is good, and thou shalt have praise of the same: for he is the minister of God to thee for good. But if thou do that which is evil, be afraid: for he beareth not the sword in vain: for he is the minister of God, a revenger to execute wrath upon him that doeth evil. Wherefore ye must needs be subject, not only for wrath, but also for conscience sake. For this cause pay ye tribute also: for they are God's ministers, attending continually upon this very thing. Render therefore to all their dues: tribute to whom tribute is due, custom to whom custom, fear to whom fear, honour to whom honour.

Or,

The Lesson from the Epistle of blessed Paul the Apostle to the Romans.

Rom. 13, 8-10.

BRETHREN: Owe no man any thing, but to love one another: for he that loveth another hath fulfilled the law. For this: Thou shalt not commit adultery, Thou shalt not kill, Thou shalt not steal, Thou shalt not bear false witness, Thou shalt not covet: and if there be any other commandment, it is briefly comprehended in this saying namely: Thou shalt love thy neighbour as thyself. Love worketh no ill to his neighbour. Therefore love is the fulfilling of the law.

Gradual. Ps. 102, 16-17. The heathen shall fear thy name, O Lord, and all the kings of the earth thy majesty. ℣. When the Lord shall build up Sion, and when his glory shall appear.

Alleluia, alleluia. ℣. Ps. 97, 1. The Lord is King, the earth may be glad thereof: yea, the multitude of the isles may be glad thereof. Alleluia.

✠ The Continuation of the holy Gospel according to Matthew.

Matt. 8, 23-27.

AT that time: When Jesus was entered into a ship, his disciples followed him: and behold, there arose a great tempest in the sea, insomuch that the ship was covered with the waves, but he was asleep. And his disciples came to him, and awoke him, saying: Lord, save us, we perish. And he saith unto them: Why are ye fearful, O ye of little faith? Then he arose, and rebuked the winds and the sea, and there was a great calm. But the men marvelled, saying: What manner of man is this, that even the winds and the sea obey him? *

And when he was come to the other side into the country of the Gergesenes, there met him two possessed with devils, coming out of the tombs, exceeding fierce, so that no man might pass by that way. And behold, they cried out, saying: What have we to do with thee, Jesus, thou Son of God? art thou come hither to torment us before the time? And there was a good way off from them an herd of many swine, feeding. So the devils besought him, saying: If thou cast us out, suffer us to go away into the herd of swine. And he said unto them: Go. And when they were come out, they went into the herd of swine: and behold, the whole herd of swine ran violently down a steep place into the sea, and perished in the waters. And they that kept them fled, and went their ways into the city, and told everything, and what was befallen to the possessed of the devils. And behold, the whole city came out to meet Jesus: and when they saw him, they besought him, that he would depart out of their coasts. Creed.

Offertory. Ps. 118, 16-17. The right hand of the Lord bringeth mighty things to pass, the right hand of the Lord hath exalted me: I shall not die, but live, and declare the works of the Lord.

Secret.

GRANT, we beseech thee, almighty God: that this oblation of our sacrifice may cleanse our frailty from all evil and evermore defend us. Through.

Preface of the Most Holy Trinity.

Communion. Luke 4. 22. All wondered at these things which proceeded out of the mouth of God.

Postcommunion.

LET these thy gifts, O God, deliver us from earthly desires: and evermore strengthen us with heavenly refreshment. Through.

The Fifth Sunday after the Epiphany
Double.

Introit. Ps. 97, 7-8. Adorate.

WORSHIP God, all ye Angels of his: Sion heard, and rejoiced: and the daughters of Judah were glad. Ps. ibid., 1. The Lord is King, the earth may be glad thereof: yea, the multitude of the isles may be glad thereof. ℣. Glory.

Collect.

O LORD, we beseech thee to keep thy Church and household continually in thy true religion: that they who do lean only upon the hope of thy heavenly grace may evermore be defended by thy mighty power. Through.

Or, Collect.

O LORD, we beseech thee to keep this thy family in continual godliness: that they who do lean only upon the hope of thy heavenly grace, may evermore be defended by thy protection. Through.

The Lesson from the Epistle of blessed Paul the Apostle to the Colossians.

Col. 3, 12-17.

BRETHREN: Put on as the elect of God, holy and beloved, bowels of mercies, kindness, humbleness of mind, meekness, long-suffering: forbearing one another, and forgiving one another, if any man have a quarrel against any: even as Christ forgave you, so also do ye. And above all these things put on charity, which is the bond of perfectness: and let the peace of God rule in your hearts, to the which also ye are called in one body: and be ye thankful. Let the word of Christ dwell in you richly in all wisdom, teaching and admonishing one another in psalms, and hymns, and spiritual songs, singing with grace in your hearts to the Lord. And whatsoever ye do, in word or deed, do all in the name of the Lord Jesus, giving thanks to God and the Father through Jesus Christ our Lord.

Gradual. Ps. 102, 16-17. The heathen shall fear thy name, O Lord, and all the kings of the earth thy majesty. ℣. When the Lord shall build up Sion, and when his glory shall appear.

Alleluia, alleluia. ℣. Ps. 97, 1. The Lord is King, the earth may be glad thereof: yea, the multitude of the isles may be glad thereof. Alleluia.

✠ The Continuation of the holy Gospel according to Matthew.

Matt. 13, 24-30.

AT that time: Jesus spake this parable unto the multitudes: The kingdom of heaven is likened unto a man which sowed good seed in his field. But while men slept, his enemy came and sowed tares among the wheat, and went his way. But when the blade was sprung up, and brought forth fruit, then appeared the tares also. So the servants of the householder came, and said unto him: Sir, didst not thou sow good seed in thy field? From whence then hath it tares? He said unto them: An enemy hath done this. The servants said unto him: Wilt thou then that we go and gather them up? But he said: Nay: lest while ye gather up the tares, ye root up also the wheat with them. Let both grow together until the harvest, and in the time of harvest, I will say to the reapers: Gather ye together first the tares, and bind them in bundles to burn them, but gather the wheat into my barn. Creed.

Offertory. Ps. 118, 16-17. The right hand of the Lord bringeth mighty things to pass, the right hand of the Lord hath exalted me: I shall not die, but live, and declare the works of the Lord.

Secret.

WE offer unto thee, O Lord, this sacrifice of atonement: beseeching thee of thy great goodness to absolve our offences, and to guide the hearts of them that go astray. Through.

Preface of the Most Holy Trinity.

Communion. Luke 4, 22. All wondered at these things which proceeded out of the mouth of God.

Postcommunion.

WE beseech thee, almighty God: that as through these holy mysteries we have received the pledge of our salvation, so we may effectually be brought unto the fulfilment of the same. Through.

The Sixth Sunday after the Epiphany

Double.

Introit. Ps. 97, 7-8. Adorate.

WORSHIP God, all ye Angels of his: Sion heard, and rejoiced: and the daughters of Judah were glad. Ps. ibid., 1. The Lord is King, the earth may be glad thereof: yea, the multitude of the isles may be glad. ℣. Glory.

Collect.

O GOD, whose blessed Son was manifested that he might destroy the works of the devil, and make us the sons of God, and heirs of eternal life: grant us, we beseech thee, that, having this hope, we may purify ourselves, even as he is pure; that, when he shall appear again with power and great glory, we may be made like unto him in his eternal and glorious kingdom: Where with thee, O Father, and thee, O Holy Ghost, he liveth and reigneth, ever one God, world without end. ℟. Amen.

Or, Collect.

GRANT, we beseech thee, almighty God: that we, ever thinking on such things as be reasonable and pleasing unto thee, may both in word and deed fulfil the same. Through.

The Lesson from the Epistle of blessed John the Apostle.

I John 3, 1-8.

DEARLY beloved: Behold, what manner of love the Father hath bestowed upon us, that we should be called the sons of God: therefore the world knoweth us not, because it knew him not. Beloved, now are we the sons of God, and it doth not yet appear what we shall be: but we know, that, when he shall appear, we shall be like him, for we shall see him as he is. And every man that hath this hope in him purifieth himself, even as he is pure. Whosoever committeth sin transgresseth also the law: for sin is the transgression of the law. And ye know that he was manifested to take away our sins: and in him is no sin. Whosoever abideth in him sinneth not: whosoever sinneth hath not seen him, neither known him. Little children, let no man deceive you: he that doeth righteousness is righteous, even as he is righteous. He that committeth sin is of the devil: for the devil sinneth from the beginning. For this purpose the Son of God was manifested, that he might destroy the works of the devil.

Or,

The Lesson from the Epistle of blessed Paul the Apostle to the Thessalonians.

I Thess. 1, 2-10.

BRETHREN: We give thanks to God always for you all, making mention of you in our prayers, remembering without ceasing your work of faith, and labour of love, and patience of hope in our Lord Jesus Christ, in the sight of God

The Sixth Sunday after the Epiphany

and our Father: knowing, brethren beloved, your election of God: for our Gospel came not unto you in word only, but also in power and in the Holy Ghost, and in much assurance, as ye know what manner of men we were among you for your sake. And ye became followers of us, and of the Lord, having received the word in much affliction, with joy of the Holy Ghost: so that ye were ensamples to all that believe in Macedonia and Achaia. For from you sounded out the word of the Lord not only in Macedonia and Achaia, but also in every place your faith to Godward is spread abroad, so that we need not to speak any thing. For they themselves shew of us what manner of entering in we had unto you: and how ye turned to God from idols to serve the living and true God, and to wait for his Son from heaven (whom he raised from the dead), even Jesus, which delivereth us from the wrath to come.

Gradual. Ps. 102, 16-17. The heathen shall fear thy name, O Lord, and all the kings of the earth thy majesty. ℣. When the Lord shall build up Sion, and when his glory shall appear.

Alleluia, alleluia. ℣. Ps. 97, 1. The Lord is King, the earth may be glad thereof: yea, the multitude of the isles may be glad thereof. Alleluia.

✠ The Continuation of the holy Gospel according to Matthew.

Matt. 24, 23-31.

AT that time: Jesus said unto his disciples: If any man shall say unto you: Lo, here is Christ, or there, believe it not. For there shall arise false Christs, and false prophets, and shall shew great signs and wonders: insomuch that (if it were possible) they shall deceive the very elect. Behold, I have told you before. Wherefore, if they shall say unto you: Behold, he is in the desert: go not forth. Behold, he is in the secret chambers: believe it not. For as the lightning cometh out of the East, and shineth even unto the West, so shall also the coming of the Son of man be. For wheresoever the carcase is, there will the eagles be gathered together. Immediately after the tribulation of those days shall the sun be darkened, and the moon shall not give her light: and the stars shall fall from heaven, and the powers of the heaven shall be shaken. And then shall appear the sign of the Son of man in heaven, and then shall all the tribes of the earth mourn, and they shall see the Son of man coming in the clouds of heaven, with power and great glory. And he shall send his Angels with a great sound of a trumpet: and they shall gather together his elect from the four winds, from one end of heaven to the other. Creed.

Or,

✠ The Continuation of the holy Gospel according to Matthew.

Matt. 13, 31-35.

AT that time: Jesus spake this parable unto the multitudes: The kingdom of heaven is like to a grain of mustard seed, which a man took, and sowed in his field: which indeed is the least of all seeds: but when it is grown, it is the greatest among herbs, and becometh a tree, so that the birds of the air come and lodge in the branches thereof. Another parable spake he unto them: The kingdom of heaven is like unto leaven, which a woman took, and hid in three measures of meal, till the whole was leavened. All these things spake Jesus unto the multitude in parables: and without a parable spake he not unto them: that it might be fulfilled which was spoken by the Prophet, saying: I will open my mouth in parables, I will utter things which have been kept secret from the foundation of the world. Creed.

Offertory. Ps. 118, 16-17. The right hand of the Lord bringeth mighty things to pass, the right hand of the Lord hath exalted me: I shall not die, but live, and declare the works of the Lord.

Secret.

WE beseech thee, O God, that this oblation may cleanse and regenerate, govern and defend us. Through.

Preface of the Most Holy Trinity.

Communion. Luke 4, 22. All wondered at these things which proceeded out of the mouth of God.

Postcommunion.

O LORD, who hast fulfilled us with thy heavenly delights: we beseech thee; that we may ever earnestly seek after those things whereby we truly live. Through.

Septuagesima Sunday

2nd class.   Double.

Station at St. Lawrence without the walls

Introit. Ps. 18, 5-7. Circumdederunt.

THE sorrows of death compassed me, the pains of hell came about me: and in my tribulation I called upon the Lord, and he heard my voice out of his holy temple. Ps. ibid., 1-2. I will love thee, O Lord, my strength: the Lord is my stony rock, my fortress, and my saviour. ℣. Glory.

¶ Glória in excélsis is not said in Masses of the Season from this Sunday until Wednesday in Holy Week, inclusive, either on Sundays or Ferias.

Collect.

O LORD, we beseech thee favourably to hear the prayers of thy people: that we, who are justly punished for our offences, may be mercifully delivered by thy goodness, for the glory of thy name. Through.

The Lesson from the Epistle of blessed Paul the Apostle to the Corinthians.

I Cor. 9, 24-27; 10, 1-5.

BRETHREN: Know ye not, that they which run in a race run all, but one receiveth the prize? So run that ye may obtain. And every man that striveth for the mastery is temperate in all things: now they do it to obtain a corruptible crown; but we an incorruptible. I therefore so run, not as uncertainly: so fight I, not as one that beateth the air: but I keep under my body, and bring it into subjection: lest that by any means, when I have preached to others, I myself should be a castaway.†

For I would not that ye should be ignorant, brethren, how that all our fathers were under the cloud, and all passed through the sea, and were all baptized unto Moses in the cloud and in the sea: and did all eat the same spiritual meat, and did all drink the same spiritual drink, (for they drank of that spiritual rock that followed them: and that rock was Christ): but with many of them God was not well pleased.

Gradual. Ps. 9, 10-11 and 19-20. A refuge in due time of trouble: they that know thee will put their trust in thee: for thou, Lord, never failest them that seek thee. ℣. For the poor shall not alway be forgotten: the patient abiding of the meek shall not perish for ever: up, Lord, and let not man have the upper hand.

The following Tract is said on Sunday only.

Tract. Ps. 130, 1-4. Out of the deep have I called unto thee, O Lord: Lord, hear my voice. ℣. O let thine ears consider well the prayer of thy servant. ℣. If thou, Lord, wilt be extreme to mark what is done amiss: O Lord, who may abide it? ℣. For there is mercy with thee, therefore shalt thou be feared.

¶ From Septuagesima until the Tuesday after Quinquagesima Sunday inclusive, when on Ferias the Mass of Sunday is resumed, the Tract is not said, but only the Gradual.

✠ The Continuation of the holy Gospel according to Matthew.

Matt. 20, 1-16.

AT that time: Jesus spake this parable unto his disciples: The kingdom of heaven is like unto a man that is an householder, which went out early in the morning to hire labourers into his vineyard. And when he had agreed with the labourers for a penny a day, he sent them into his vineyard. And he went out about the third hour, and saw others standing idle in the market-place, and said unto them: Go ye also into the vineyard, and whatsoever is right I will give you. And they went their way. Again he went out about the sixth and ninth hour: and did likewise. And about the eleventh hour he went out, and found others standing idle, and saith unto them: why stand ye here all the day idle? They say unto him: Because no man hath hired us. He saith unto them: Go ye also into the vineyard, and whatsoever is right, that shall ye receive. So when even was come, the lord of the vineyard saith unto his steward: Call the labourers, and give them their hire, beginning from the last unto the first. And when they came that were hired about the eleventh hour, they received every man a penny. But when the first came, they supposed that they should have received more: and they likewise received every man a penny. And when they had received it, they murmured against the goodman of the house, saying: These last have wrought but one hour, and thou hast made them equal unto us, which have borne the burden and heat of the day. But he answered one of them, and said: Friend, I do thee no wrong: didst not thou agree with me for a penny? Take that thine is, and go thy way: I will give unto this last even as unto thee. Is it not lawful for me to do what I will with mine own? Is thine eye evil, because I am good? So the last shall be first, and the first last. For many be called, but few chosen. Creed.

Offertory. Ps. 92, 1. It is a good thing to give thanks unto the Lord, and to sing praises unto thy name, O Most Highest.

Secret.

WE beseech thee, O Lord, to accept our prayers and oblations: and graciously hearken unto us, whom thou dost cleanse by thy heavenly mysteries. Through.

Preface of the Most Holy Trinity.

Communion. Ps. 31, 17-18. Shew thy servant the light of thy countenance, and save me for thy mercy's sake: let me not be confounded, O Lord, for I have called upon thee.

Postcommunion.

STRENGTHEN, O God, with these thy gifts the wills of thy faithful people: that they receiving the same may seek them the more, and seeking them may obtain them everlastingly. Through.

℣. Let us bless the Lord.
℟. Thanks be to God.

Sexagesima Sunday

2nd class. Double.

Station at St. Paul

Introit. Ps. 44, 23-26. Exsurge.

ARISE, O Lord, wherefore sleepest thou? Awake, and cast us not away for ever: wherefore hidest thou thy countenance, and forgettest our trouble? Our belly cleaveth unto the ground: arise, O Lord, help us, and deliver us. Ps. ibid., 1. O God, we have heard with our ears: our fathers have told us. ℣. Glory.

Sexagesima Sunday

Collect.

O LORD God, who seest that we put not our trust in any thing that we do: mercifully grant; that by thy power we may be defended against all adversity. Through.

Or, Collect.

O GOD, who seest that we put not our trust in any thing that we do: mercifully grant; that by the protection of the Doctor of the Gentiles we may be defended against all adversity. Through.

The Lesson from the Epistle of blessed Paul the Apostle to the Corinthians.
II Cor. 11, 19-23; 12, 1-9.

BRETHREN: Ye suffer fools gladly, seeing ye yourselves are wise. For ye suffer if a man bring you into bondage, if a man devour you, if a man take of you, if a man exalt himself, if a man smite you on the face. I speak as concerning reproach, as though we had been weak. Howbeit, wheresoever any is bold, (I speak foolishly,) I am bold also: Are they Hebrews? so am I: Are they Israelites? so am I: Are they the seed of Abraham? so am I: Are they ministers of Christ? (I speak as a fool), I am more: in labours more abundant, in stripes above measure, in prisons more frequent, in deaths oft. Of the Jews five times received I forty stripes save one. Thrice was I beaten with rods, once was I stoned, thrice I suffered ship-wreck, a night and a day I have been in the deep: in journeyings often, in perils of waters, in perils of robbers, in perils by mine own countrymen, in perils by the heathen, in perils in the city, in perils in the wilderness, in perils in the sea, in perils among false brethren: in weariness and painfulness, in watchings often, in hunger and thirst, in fastings often, in cold and nakedness: besides those things that are without, that which cometh upon me daily, the care of all the Churches. Who is weak, and I am not weak? who is offended, and I burn not? If I must needs glory: I will glory of the things which concern mine infirmities. The God and Father of our Lord Jesus Christ, which is blessed for evermore, knoweth that I lie not.†

In Damascus the governor under Aretas the king kept the city of the Damascenes with a garrison desirous to apprehend me: and through a window in a basket was I let down by the wall, and escaped his hands. It is not expedient for me doubtless to glory, I will come to visions and revelations of the Lord. I knew a man in Christ above fourteen years ago, (whether in the body, I cannot tell, or whether out of the body, I cannot tell, God knoweth:) such an one caught up to the third heaven. And I knew such a man, (whether in the body, or out of the body, I cannot tell, God knoweth:) how that he was caught up into paradise: and heard unspeakable words, which it is not lawful for a man to utter. Of such an one will I glory: yet of myself I will not glory, but in mine infirmities. For though I would desire to glory, I shall not be a fool: for I will say the truth: but now I forbear, lest any man should think of me above that which he seeth me to be, or that he heareth of me. And lest I should be exalted above measure through the abundance of the revelations, there was given to me a thorn in the flesh, the messenger of Satan to buffet me. For this thing I besought the Lord thrice, that it might depart from me: and he said unto me: My grace is sufficient for thee: for my strength is made perfect in weakness. Most gladly therefore will I rather glory in my infirmities, that the power of Christ may rest upon me.

Gradual. Ps. 83, 10-14. Let the nations know that thou, whose name is Jehovah: art only the Most Highest over all the earth. ℣. O my God, make them like unto a wheel, and as the stubble before the wind.

¶ The following Tract is said on Sunday only, on Ferias it is omitted.

Tract. Ps. 60, 4 and 6. Thou hast moved the land, O Lord, and divided it. ℣. Heal the sores thereof, for it shaketh. ℣. That they may triumph because of the truth: that thy beloved may be delivered.

✠ The Continuation of the holy Gospel according to Luke.

Luke 8, 4-15.

AT that time: When much people were gathered together, and were come to Jesus out of every city, he spake by a parable: A sower went out to sow his seed: and as he sowed, some fell by the way-side, and it was trodden down, and the fowls of the air devoured it. And some fell upon a rock: and as soon as it was sprung up it withered away, because it lacked moisture. And some fell among thorns, and the thorns sprang up with it, and choked it. And other fell on good ground: and sprang up, and bare fruit an hundred-fold. And when he had said these things, he cried: He that hath ears to hear, let him hear. And his disciples asked him, saying: What might this parable be? And he said: Unto you it is given to know the mysteries of the kingdom of God: but to others in parables: that seeing they might not see, and hearing they might not understand. Now the parable is this: The seed is the word of God. Those by the way-side are they that hear: then cometh the devil, and taketh away the word out of their hearts, lest they should believe, and be saved. They on the rock: are they which, when they hear, receive the word with joy: and these have no root, which for a while believe, and in time of temptation fall away. And that which fell among thorns: are they, which, when they have heard, go forth, and are choked with cares, and riches, and pleasures of this life, and bring no fruit to perfection. But that on the good ground: are they, which in an honest and good heart having heard the word, keep it, and bring forth fruit with patience. Creed.

Offertory. Ps. 17, 5-7. O hold thou up my goings in thy paths, that my footsteps slip not: incline thine ear to me, and hearken unto my words: shew thy marvellous loving-kindness, O Lord, thou that art the Saviour of them which put their trust in thee.

Secret.

MAY the sacrifice which we offer unto thee, O Lord, evermore quicken and defend us. Through.

Preface of the Most Holy Trinity.

Communion. Ps. 43, 4. I will go unto the altar of God, even unto the God of my joy and gladness.

Postcommunion.

WE humbly beseech thee, almighty God: that as thou dost refresh us with thy sacraments, so thou wouldest vouchsafe unto us to do thee worthy and acceptable service. Through.

℣. Let us bless the Lord.

℟. Thanks be to God.

Quinquagesima Sunday

2nd class.   Double.

Station at St. Peter

Introit. Ps. 31, 3-4. *Esto mihi.*

BE thou my strong rock, and house of defence, that thou mayest save me: for thou art my strong rock, and my castle: be thou also my guide, and lead me for thy name's sake. Ps. ibid., 1. In thee, O Lord, have I put my trust, let me never be put to confusion: deliver me in thy righteousness and save me. ℣. Glory.

Quinquagesima Sunday

Collect.

O LORD, who hast taught us that all our doings without charity are nothing worth: send thy Holy Ghost, and pour into our hearts that most excellent gift of charity, the very bond of peace and of all virtues; without which whosoever liveth is counted dead before thee. Grant this for thine only Son Jesus Christ's sake: Who liveth and reigneth with thee in the unity of the same Holy Ghost.

Or, Collect.

WE beseech thee, O Lord, graciously hear our prayers: that we, being loosed from the bonds of our sins, may by thee be defended against all adversity. Through.

The Lesson from the Epistle of blessed Paul the Apostle to the Corinthians.

I Cor. 13, 1-13.

BRETHREN: Though I speak with the tongues of men and of Angels, and have not charity, I am become as sounding brass, or a tinkling cymbal. And though I have the gift of prophecy, and understand all mysteries, and all knowledge: and though I have all faith, so that I could remove mountains, and have not charity, I am nothing. And though I bestow all my goods to feed the poor, and though I give my body to be burned, and have not charity, it profiteth me nothing. Charity suffereth long, and is kind: charity envieth not, charity vaunteth not itself, is not puffed up, doth not behave itself unseemly, seeketh not her own, is not easily provoked, thinketh no evil, rejoiceth not in iniquity, but rejoiceth in the truth: beareth all things, believeth all things, hopeth all things, endureth all things. Charity never faileth: but whether there be prophecies, they shall fail, whether there be tongues, they shall cease, whether there be knowledge, it shall vanish away. For we know in part, and we prophesy in part. But when that which is perfect is come, then that which is in part shall be done away. When I was a child, I spake as a child, I understood as a child, I thought as a child. But when I became a man, I put away childish things. For now we see through a glass darkly: but then face to face. Now I know in part: but then shall I know even as also I am known. And now abideth faith, hope, charity, these three: but the greatest of these is charity.

Gradual. Ps. 77, 15-16. Thou art the God that only doeth wonders: and hast declared thy power among the people. ℣. Thou hast mightily delivered thy people, even the sons of Jacob and Joseph.

¶ The following Tract is said on Sunday only, on Ferias it is omitted.

Tract. Ps. 100, 1-2. O be joyful in the Lord, all ye lands: serve the Lord with gladness. ℣. Come before his presence with a song: be ye sure that the Lord he is God. ℣. It is he that hath made us, and not we ourselves: we are his people, and the sheep of his pasture.

✠ The Continuation of the holy Gospel according to Luke.

Luke 18, 31-43.

AT that time: Jesus took unto him the twelve, and said unto them: Behold, we go up to Jerusalem, and all things that are written by the Prophets concerning the Son of man shall be accomplished. For he shall be delivered unto the Gentiles, and shall be mocked, and spitefully entreated, and spitted on: and they shall scourge him, and put him to death, and the third day he shall rise again. And they understood none of these things, and this saying was hid from them, neither knew they the things which were spoken. And it came to pass, that as he was come nigh unto Jericho, a certain blind man sat by the way-side begging. And hearing the multitude pass by, he asked what it meant.

And they told him, that Jesus of Nazareth passeth by. And he cried, saying: Jesus, thou Son of David, have mercy on me. And they which went before rebuked him, that he should hold his peace: but he cried so much the more: Thou Son of David, have mercy on me. And Jesus stood, and commanded him to be brought unto him. And when he was come near, he asked him, saying: What wilt thou that I should do unto thee? And he said: Lord, that I may receive my sight. And Jesus said unto him: Receive thy sight, thy faith hath saved thee. And immediately he received his sight, and followed him, glorifying God. And all the people, when they saw it, gave praise unto God. Creed.

Offertory. Ps. 119, 12-13. Blessed art thou, O Lord, O teach me thy statutes: with my lips have I been telling of all the judgments of thy mouth.

Secret.

WE beseech thee, O Lord, that this oblation may cleanse us from our sins: and sanctify thy servants both in body and soul for the celebration of this sacrifice. Through.

Preface of the Most Holy Trinity.

Communion. Ps. 78, 29-30. They did eat, and were well filled, for the Lord gave them their own desire: they were not disappointed of their lust.

Postcommunion.

WE beseech thee, almighty God: that we who have received this heavenly food may be defended thereby against all adversities. Through.

℣. Let us bless the Lord.

℟. Thanks be to God.

ASH WEDNESDAY

Privileged feria.

1st class.

¶ Before Mass ashes, made from the branches of olive or other trees blessed the year before, are blessed in this manner:

None being said, the Priest vested in a violet Cope, or without a Chasuble, accompanied by the ministers similarly vested, proceeds to bless ashes placed in some vessel on the Altar. And first the following Antiphon is sung by the choir:

Ps. 69, 17. Exaudi nos.

HEAR us, O Lord, for thy loving-kindness is comfortable: turn thee unto us, O Lord, according to the multitude of thy mercies. Ps. ibid., 1. Save me, O God: for the waters are come in even unto my soul.

℣. Glory.

Hear us is repeated.

¶ Then the Priest at the Epistle corner, not turning to the people, with hands joined (which is observed in the Prayers of all benedictions as regards hands joined), says:

℣. The Lord be with you.

℟. And with thy spirit.

Let us pray. Collect.

ALMIGHTY and everlasting God, spare them that are penitent, be favourable to them that call upon thee; and vouchsafe to send thy holy Angel from heaven, to bl ✠ ess, and sanc ✠ tify these ashes, that they may be a wholesome medicine to all who humbly call upon thy holy name, who in their consciences by sin are accused, who in the sight of thy divine compassion bewail their faults, and earnestly and meekly implore thy most gracious loving-kindness: and grant to all them that call upon thy most holy name; that they, being sprinkled therewith for the redemption of their transgressions, may be preserved evermore both in body and soul. Through Christ our Lord. ℟. Amen.

Let us pray. Collect.

O GOD, who wouldest not the death of a sinner, but rather that he should repent: mercifully look upon the frailty of our mortal nature; and of thy goodness vouchsafe to bl ✠ ess these ashes which we purpose to have set upon our heads for the increase of humility, and the meriting of pardon; that we, acknowledging that we are but ashes, and that by reason of our vileness unto dust we shall return; may through thy mercy be found meet to receive forgiveness of all our sins, and the rewards which thou hast promised to them that are penitent. Through Christ our Lord. ℟. Amen.

Let us pray.   Collect.

O GOD, who dost turn unto them that abase themselves, and art favourable unto them that make satisfaction: incline thy gracious ear to our prayers; and mercifully pour forth upon the heads of thy servants now to be sprinkled with these ashes the grace of thy benediction: that they being filled with the spirit of true penitence may effectually obtain those things that they have asked according to thy will. And we beseech thee to ordain that we, being stablished in these thy blessings, may cleave to the same unto life everlasting. Through Christ our Lord. ℟. Amen.

Let us pray.   Collect.

ALMIGHTY and everlasting God, who upon the people of Nineveh, repenting in sackcloth and ashes, didst bestow the healing of thy loving-kindness: mercifully grant; that we may so imitate them in outward fashion that we may be made like unto them in the obtaining of thy pardon. Through.

¶ Then the Celebrant, having put incense in the thurible, thrice sprinkles the ashes with blessed water, saying the Antiphon, Thou shalt purge me, without chant and without the Psalm, and thrice censes them.

¶ Then the senior Priest from the Clergy approaches the Altar, and sets ashes on the Celebrant, who does not kneel. But if there be no other Priest present, the Celebrant himself, turning to the Altar, sets ashes upon his own head, saying nothing, and forthwith the choir sing the Antiphon.

Joel 2, 13. Immutemur.

LET us change our raiment for sackcloth and ashes: let us fast and mourn before the Lord; for our God is exceeding merciful to forgive us our sins.

Another Antiphon, Ibid., 17. Let the priests, the ministers of the Lord, weep between the porch and the altar, and let them say: Spare, O Lord, spare thy people: and shut not up, O Lord, the mouths of them that praise thee.

The Responsory follows:

Esther 13; Joel 2. Let us amend the sins that in our ignorance we have committed: lest the day of death come suddenly upon us, and we find no place for repentance, though we seek it.* Hear, O Lord, and have mercy: for we have sinned against thee. ℣. Ps. 79, 9. Help us, O God of our salvation: and for the glory of thy name deliver us, O Lord. Hear, O Lord. ℣. Glory be to the Father, and to the Son, and to the Holy Ghost. Hear, O Lord.

¶ While the Antiphons and Responsory are in singing, the Priest with uncovered head first sets ashes on the senior Priest from whom he himself has received them, and then on the Ministers, vested and kneeling before the Altar, saying:

Gen. 3, 19. Remember, O man, that dust thou art, and unto dust shalt thou return.

¶ Then come the others, first the Clergy in order, then the people: and kneeling before the Altar receive the ashes severally from the Priest, as has been said of the Ministers.

The imposition of ashes being finished, the Priest says:

℣. The Lord be with you.

℟. And with thy spirit.

Let us pray.   Collect.

GRANT to us, O Lord, to put on the armour of our Christian warfare with prayer and fasting: that we, who are to fight against all spiritual wickedness, may be defended by the power of abstinence. Through Christ our Lord. ℟. Amen.

¶ Then Mass is said.

Ash Wednesday

Station at St. Sabina

Introit. Wisd. 11, 24, 25 and 27.

Misereris omnium.

THOU hast mercy upon all, O Lord, and hatest nothing that thou hast created: and winkest at the sins of men, because they should amend, and sparest them: for thou art the Lord our God. Ps. 57, 1. Be merciful unto me, O God, be merciful unto me: for my soul trusteth in thee. ℣. Glory.

Collect.

ALMIGHTY and everlasting God, who hatest nothing that thou hast made, and dost forgive the sins of all them that are penitent: create and make in us new and contrite hearts; that we worthily lamenting our sins, and acknowledging our wretchedness, may obtain of thee, the God of all mercy, perfect remission and forgiveness. Through.

Or, Collect.

GRANT, O Lord, to thy faithful people: that they may enter upon the solemn observance of this fast with reverence and godly fear, and in peace and quietness may fulfil the same. Through.

The Lesson from the Prophet Joel.

Joel 2, 12-19.

THUS saith the Lord: Turn ye even to me with all your heart, and with fasting, and with weeping, and with mourning. And rend your heart, and not your garments, and turn unto the Lord your God: for he is gracious and merciful, slow to anger, and of great kindness, and repenteth him of the evil. Who knoweth if he will return, and repent, and leave a blessing behind him, even a meat-offering and a drink-offering unto the Lord your God? Blow the trumpet in Sion, sanctify a fast, call a solemn assembly, gather the people, sanctify the congregation, assemble the elders, gather the children, and those that suck the breasts: let the bridegroom go forth of his chamber, and the bride out of her closet. Let the priests, the ministers of the Lord, weep between the porch and the altar, and let them say: Spare thy people, O Lord, and give not thine heritage to reproach, that the heathen should rule over them. Wherefore should they say among the people: Where is their God?†

Then will the Lord be jealous for his land, and pity his people. Yea, the Lord will answer and say unto his people: Behold I will send you corn, and wine, and oil, and ye shall be satisfied therewith: and I will no more make you a reproach among the heathen: saith the Lord almighty.

Gradual. Ps. 57, 2 and 4. Be merciful unto me, O God, be merciful unto me: for my soul trusteth in thee. ℣. He shall send from heaven, and save me from the reproof of him that would eat me up.

The following Tract is said in the Masses of Monday, Wednesday, and Friday, until Monday in Holy Week inclusive, except on Ember Wednesday.

Tract. Ps. 103, 10. O Lord, deal not with us after our sins: nor reward us according to our wickedness. ℣. Ps. 79, 8-9. O Lord, remember not our old sins: but have mercy upon us, and that soon, for we are come to great misery. (Here genuflect) ℣. Help us, O God of our salvation: and for the glory of thy name, O Lord, deliver us: and be merciful unto our sins, for thy name's sake.

✠ The Continuation of the holy Gospel according to Matthew.

Matt. 6, 16-21.

AT that time: Jesus said unto his disciples: When ye fast, be not as the hypocrites, of a sad countenance. For they disfigure their faces, that they may appear unto men to fast. Verily I say unto you: They have their reward. But thou, when thou fastest, anoint thine head, and wash thy face, that thou appear not unto men to fast, but unto thy Father which is in secret: and thy Father, which seeth in secret, shall reward thee openly. Lay not up for yourselves treasures upon earth: where moth and rust doth corrupt: and where thieves break through and steal. But lay up for yourselves treasures in heaven: where neither moth nor rust doth corrupt; and where thieves do not break through nor steal. For where your treasure is, there will your heart be also.

Offertory. Ps. 30, 2-3. I will magnify thee, O Lord, for thou hast set me up, and not made my foes to triumph over me: O Lord, I cried unto thee, and thou hast healed me.

Secret.

GRANT, we beseech thee, O Lord, that like as we by these our gifts do celebrate the institution of this holy Sacrament: so we may by thee be enabled worthily to offer the same. Through.

¶ Preface of Lent; which is said until Saturday before Passion Sunday, inclusive, according to the Rubrics.

Communion. Ps. 1, 2-3. He who doth meditate on the law of the Lord day and night will bring forth his fruit in due season.

Postcommunion.

PROTECT us, O Lord, by thy holy Sacrament which we have here received: that this our fast may be acceptable unto thee, and profitable for the healing of our souls. Through.

¶ Then the Priest says at once: Let us pray, and the Deacon (if any be serving in the office of Deacon), turning to the people, with joined hands, says: Humble your heads before God. Otherwise the Priest himself says it, standing in the same place before the book, without turning to the people.

Prayer.

LOOK down in mercy, O Lord, upon those who bow before thy majesty: that they, who have been refreshed by thy sacred gifts, may evermore be strengthened by thy heavenly succour. Through.

¶ And this manner of saying the Prayer over the people is observed only in Masses of the Feria, until Wednesday in Holy Week inclusive.

℣. Let us bless the Lord.

℞. Thanks be to God.

Thursday

Station at St. George

Introit. Ps. 55, 17, 19, 20 and 23.

Dum clamarem.

WHEN I called upon the Lord, he heard my voice from the battle that was against me, yea, even God, that endureth for ever, shall bring them down: O cast thy burden upon the Lord, and he shall nourish thee. Ps. ibid, 1-2. Hear my prayer, O God, and hide not thyself from my petition: take heed unto me, and hear me. ℣. Glory.

Collect.

O GOD, who art wroth with them that sin against thee, and sparest them that are penitent: mercifully have respect to the prayers of thy people which call upon thee; and turn away the scourges of thy wrath which for our sins we most justly deserve. Through.

The Thursday after Ash Wednesday

The Lesson from the Prophet Isaiah.
Is. 38, 1-6.

IN those days: Was Hezekiah sick unto death: and Isaiah the Prophet the son of Amoz came unto him, and said unto him: Thus saith the Lord: Set thine house in order, for thou shalt die, and not live. Then Hezekiah turned his face toward the wall, and prayed unto the Lord, and said: Remember now, O Lord, I beseech thee, how I have walked before thee in truth and with a perfect heart, and have done that which is good in thy sight. And Hezekiah wept sore. Then came the word of the Lord to Isaiah, saying: Go, and say to Hezekiah: Thus saith the Lord, the God of David thy father: I have heard thy prayer, I have seen thy tears: behold, I will add unto thy days fifteen years: and I will deliver thee and this city out of the hand of the king of Assyria, and I will defend this city, saith the Lord almighty.

Gradual. Ps. 55, 23, 17-19. O cast thy burden upon the Lord, and he shall nourish thee. ℣. When I called upon the Lord, he heard my voice from the battle that was against me.

✠ The Continuation of the holy Gospel according to Matthew.

Matt. 8, 5-13.

AT that time: When Jesus was entered into Capernaum, there came unto him a centurion, beseeching him, and saying: Lord, my servant lieth at home sick of the palsy, grievously tormented. And Jesus saith unto him: I will come and heal him. The centurion answered and said: Lord, I am not worthy that thou shouldest come under my roof: but speak the word only, and my servant shall be healed. For I am a man under authority, having soldiers under me, and I say to this man: Go, and he goeth; and to another: Come, and he cometh; and to my servant: Do this, and he doeth it. When Jesus heard it, he marvelled, and said to them that followed: Verily I say unto you, I have not found so great faith, no, not in Israel. And I say unto you, That many shall come from the East and West, and shall sit down with Abraham, and Isaac, and Jacob, in the kingdom of heaven: but the children of the kingdom shall be cast out into outer darkness: there shall be weeping and gnashing of teeth. And Jesus said unto the centurion: Go thy way, and as thou hast believed, so be it done unto thee. And his servant was healed in the selfsame hour.

Offertory. Ps. 25, 1-3. Unto thee, O Lord, will I lift up my soul: my God, I have put my trust in thee, O let me not be confounded: neither let mine enemies triumph over me: for all they that hope in thee shall not be ashamed.

Secret.

WE beseech thee, O Lord, mercifully to have respect unto this our sacrifice; that the same may be profitable for our increase in all godliness, and for the attainment of everlasting salvation. Through.

Preface of Lent.

Communion. Ps. 51, 21. Thou shalt be pleased with the sacrifice of righteousness, with the burnt-offerings and oblations upon thine altar, O Lord.

Postcommunion.

WE humbly beseech thee, almighty God: that as thou hast made us partakers of thy heavenly benediction; so likewise the pledge which thou hast given us in this holy Sacrament may be fulfilled in us unto everlasting salvation. Through.

Over the people:

Let us pray. Humble your heads before God.

Collect.

SPARE, O Lord, spare thy people: that they who are justly chastised by thy scourges, may by the pardon of thy mercy be relieved. Through.

Friday

Station at SS. John and Paul

Introit. Ps. 30, 11. Audivit Dominus.

THE Lord heard, and had mercy upon me: the Lord became my helper. Ps. ibid., 1. I will magnify thee, O Lord, for thou hast set me up: and not made my foes to triumph over me. ℣. Glory.

Collect.

WE beseech thee, O Lord, to prosper with thy gracious favour the fast which we have here begun: that as with our bodies we therein do thee outward worship, so we may have strength also to perform the same in singleness of heart. Through.

The Lesson from the Prophet Isaiah.

Is. 58, 1-9.

THUS saith the Lord God: Cry aloud, spare not, lift up thy voice like a trumpet: and shew my people their transgression, and the house of Jacob their sins. Yet they seek me daily, and delight to know my ways: as a nation that did righteousness, and forsook not the ordinance of their God: they ask of me the ordinances of justice: they take delight in approaching to God. Wherefore have we fasted, say they, and thou seest not: wherefore have we afflicted our soul, and thou takest no knowledge? Behold, in the day of your fast ye find pleasure, and exact all your labours. Behold, ye fast for strife and debate, and to smite with the fist of wickedness. Ye shall not fast as ye do this day, to make your voice to be heard on high. Is it such a fast that I have chosen, a day for a man to afflict his soul? is it to bow down his head as a bulrush, and to spread sackcloth and ashes under him? wilt thou call this a fast, and an acceptable day to the Lord? Is not this the fast that I have chosen? to loose the bands of wickedness, to undo the heavy burdens: and to let the oppressed go free, and that ye break every yoke. Is it not to deal thy bread to the hungry, and that thou bring the poor that are cast out to thy house? when thou seest the naked, that thou cover him; and that thou hide not thyself from thine own flesh? Then shall thy light break forth as the morning, and thine health shall spring forth speedily, and thy righteousness shall go before thee, the glory of the Lord shall be thy rereward. Then shalt thou call, and the Lord shall answer; thou shalt cry, and he shall say: Here I am. For I the Lord thy God am merciful.

Gradual. Ps. 27, 4. One thing have I desired of the Lord, which I will require, even that I may dwell in the house of the Lord. ℣. To behold the fair beauty of the Lord, and to hide me in his holy temple.

Tract. Ps. 103, 10. O Lord, deal not with us after our sins: nor reward us according to our wickednesses. ℣. Ps. 79, 8-9. O Lord, remember not our old sins: but have mercy upon us, and that soon, for we are come to great misery. (Here genuflect) ℣. Help us, O God of our salvation: and for the glory of thy name, O Lord, deliver us: and be merciful unto our sins, for thy name's sake.

✠ The Continuation of the holy Gospel according to Matthew.

Matt. 5, 43-48; 6, 1-4.

AT that time: Jesus said unto his disciples: Ye have heard that it hath been said: Thou shalt love thy neighbour, and hate thine enemy. But I say unto you: Love your enemies, bless them that curse you: do good to them that hate you, and pray for them which despitefully use you, and persecute you, that ye may be the children of your Father which is in heaven: for he maketh his sun to rise on the evil and on the good, and sendeth rain on the just and on the unjust. For if ye love them which love you, what reward have ye? do not even the publicans the same? And if ye salute your brethren only, what do ye more than others? do not even the publicans so? Be ye therefore perfect, even as your Father which is in heaven is perfect. Take heed that ye do not your alms before men, to be seen of them: otherwise ye have no reward of your Father which is in heaven. Therefore when thou doest thine alms, do not sound a trumpet before thee, as the hypocrites do in the synagogues and in the streets, that they may have glory of men. Verily I say unto you, They have their reward. But when thou doest alms, let not thy left hand know what thy right hand doeth, that thine alms may be in secret, and thy Father which seeth in secret himself shall reward thee openly.

Offertory. Ps. 119, 154 and 125. Quicken me, O Lord, according to thy word: that I may know thy testimonies.

Secret.

GRANT, we beseech thee, O Lord, that this sacrifice of Lenten observance which we offer: may both render our souls acceptable unto thee, and make us more readily to serve thee in continence. Through.

Preface of Lent.

Communion. Ps. 2, 11-12. Serve the Lord in fear, and rejoice unto him with reverence: lay hold on discipline, lest ye perish from the right way.

Postcommunion.

POUR forth upon us, O Lord, the Spirit of thy charity: that as thou hast now fulfilled us with one heavenly bread, so of thy goodness thou wouldest make us to be of one heart and mind. Through ... in the unity of the same Holy Spirit.

Over the people:

Let us pray. Humble your heads before God.

Collect.

DEFEND, O Lord, thy people, and of thy mercy cleanse them from all their sins: that they, being delivered from the dominion of iniquity, may be preserved from all the assaults of adversity. Through.

Saturday

Station at St. Tryphon

Introit. Ps. 30, 11. Audivit Dominus.

THE Lord heard, and had mercy upon me: the Lord became my helper. Ps. ibid., 1. I will magnify thee, O Lord, for thou hast set me up: and not made my foes to triumph over me. ℣. Glory.

Collect.

ASSIST us, mercifully, O Lord, in these our supplications: and grant; that like as this solemn fast hath been ordained for the safety and healing of our bodies and our souls, so we may in all godliness and lowliness observe the same. Through.

The Lesson from the Prophet Isaiah.

Is. 58, 9-14.

THUS saith the Lord God: If thou take away from the midst of thee the yoke, the putting forth of the finger, and speaking vanity. And if thou draw out thy soul to the hungry, and satisfy the afflicted soul, then shall thy light rise in obscurity, and thy darkness be as the noonday. And the Lord shall guide thee continually, and satisfy thy soul in drought, and make fat thy bones, and thou shalt be like a watered garden, and like a spring of water, whose waters fail not. And they that shall be of thee shall build the old waste places: thou shalt raise up the foundations of many generations; and thou shalt be called, The repairer of the breach, The restorer of paths to dwell in.

If thou turn away thy foot from the sabbath, from doing thy pleasure on my holy day, and call the sabbath a delight, the holy of the Lord, honourable, and shalt honour him, not doing thine own ways, nor finding thine own pleasure, nor speaking thine own words: then shalt thou delight thyself in the Lord: and I will cause thee to ride upon the high places of the earth, and feed thee with the heritage of Jacob thy father. For the mouth of the Lord hath spoken it.

Gradual. Ps. 27, 4. One thing have I desired of the Lord, which I will require, even that I may dwell in the house of the Lord. ℣. To behold the fair beauty of the Lord, and to visit his temple.

☨ The Continuation of the holy Gospel according to Mark.

Mark 6, 47-56.

AT that time: When even was come, the ship was in the midst of the sea, and Jesus alone on the land. And he saw his disciples toiling in rowing (for the wind was contrary unto them), and about the fourth watch of the night he cometh unto them, walking upon the sea: and would have passed by them. But when they saw him walking upon the sea, they supposed it had been a spirit, and cried out. For they all saw him, and were troubled. And immediately he talked with them, and saith unto them: Be of good cheer, it is I, be not afraid. And he went up unto them into the ship, and the wind ceased. And they were sore amazed in themselves beyond measure, and wondered: for they considered not the miracle of the loaves: for their heart was hardened. And when they had passed over, they came into the land of Gennesaret, and drew to the shore. And when they were come out of the ship, straightway they knew him: and ran through that whole region round about, and began to carry about in beds those that were sick, where they heard he was. And whithersoever he entered, into villages, or cities, or country, they laid the sick in the streets, and besought him that they might touch if it were but the border of his garment: and as many as touched him were made whole.

Offertory. Ps. 119, 154 and 125. Quicken me, O Lord, according to thy word: that I may know thy testimonies.

Secret.

ACCEPT, O Lord, the sacrifice which thou hast ordained to be a worthy propitiation unto thee: and grant, we beseech thee, that we being cleansed by the operation of the same may offer unto thee the acceptable devotion of our hearts. Through.

Preface of Lent.

Communion. Ps. 2, 11-12. Serve the Lord in fear, and rejoice unto him with reverence: lay hold on discipline, lest ye perish from the right way.

Postcommunion.

O LORD, who here hast quickened us with thy gift of heavenly life: we beseech thee, that those things which in this present life we do receive in a mystery, may be our succour unto life eternal. Through.

Over the people:

Let us pray. Humble your heads before God.

Collect.

STRENGTHEN, O God, by these thy gifts the wills of thy faithful people: that they receiving the same may seek them the more, and seeking them may obtain them everlastingly. Through.

The First Sunday in Lent

1st class.   Double of 1st class.

Station at St. John Lateran

Introit. Ps. 91, 15-16. Invocabit me.

HE shall call upon me, and I will hear him: I will deliver him, and bring him to honour: with long life will I satisfy him. Ps. ibid., 1. Whoso dwelleth under the defence of the Most High, shall abide under the shadow of the Almighty. ℣. Glory.

Collect.

O LORD, who for our sake didst fast forty days and forty nights: give us grace to use such abstinence; that, our flesh being subdued to the Spirit, we may ever obey thy godly motions in righteousness, and true holiness, to thy honour and glory: Who livest and reignest with the Father and the Holy Ghost, one God, world without end. ℟. Amen.

Or, Collect.

O GOD, who year by year through this Lenten observance dost cleanse and renew thy Church: grant unto us thy servants; that as by abstinence we strive to win thy pardon, so by good works we may effectually obtain the same. Through.

The Lesson from the Epistle of blessed Paul the Apostle to the Corinthians.

II Cor. 6, 1-10.

BRETHREN: We beseech you, that ye receive not the grace of God in vain. For he saith: I have heard thee in a time accepted, and in the day of salvation have I succoured thee. Behold, now is the accepted time, behold, now is the day of salvation. Giving no offence in any thing, that the ministry be not blamed: but in all things approving ourselves as the ministers of God, in much patience, in afflictions, in necessities, in distresses, in stripes, in imprisonments, in tumults, in labours, in watchings, in fastings, by pureness, by knowledge, by long-suffering, by kindness, by the Holy Ghost, by love unfeigned, by the word of truth, by the power of God, by the armour of righteousness on the right hand and on the left: by honour and dishonour: by evil report and good report: as deceivers, and yet true: as unknown, and yet well known: as dying, and behold, we live: as chastened, and not killed: as sorrowful, yet alway rejoicing: as poor, yet making many rich: as having nothing, and yet possessing all things.

Gradual. Ps. 91, 11-12. God shall give his Angels charge over thee, to keep thee in all thy ways. ℣. They shall bear thee in their hands, that thou hurt not thy foot against a stone.

Tract. Ibid., 1-7 and 11-16. Whoso dwelleth under the defence of the Most High, shall abide under the shadow of the Almighty. ℣. I will say unto the Lord: Thou art my hope and my stronghold: my God, in him will I trust. ℣. For he shall deliver thee from the snare of the hunter, and from the noisome pestilence. ℣. He shall defend thee under his wings, and thou shalt be safe under his feathers. ℣. His faithfulness and truth shall be thy shield and buckler: thou shalt not be afraid for any terror by night. ℣. Nor for the arrow that flieth by day, for the pestilence that walketh in darkness, nor for the sickness that destroyeth in the noonday. ℣. A thousand shall fall beside thee, and ten thousand at thy right hand: but it shall not come nigh thee. ℣. For he shall give his Angels charge over thee, to keep thee in all thy ways. ℣. They shall bear thee in their hands: that thou hurt not thy foot against a stone. ℣. Thou shalt go upon the lion and adder, the young lion and the dragon shalt thou tread under thy feet. ℣. Because he hath set his love upon me, therefore will I deliver him: I will set him up, because he hath known my name. ℣. He shall call upon me, and I will hear him: yea, I am with him in trouble. ℣. I will deliver him and bring him to honour: with long life will I satisfy him, and shew him my salvation.

✠ The Continuation of the holy Gospel according to Matthew.

Matt. 4, 1-11.

AT that time: Jesus was led up of the Spirit into the wilderness, to be tempted of the devil. And when he had fasted forty days and forty nights, he was afterward an hungred. And when the tempter came to him, he said: If thou be the Son of God, command that these stones be made bread. But he answered and said: It is written: Man shall not live by bread alone, but by every word that proceedeth out of the mouth of God. Then the devil taketh him up into the holy city, and setteth him on a pinnacle of the temple, and saith unto him: If thou be the Son of God, cast thyself down. For it is written: He shall give his Angels charge concerning thee, and in their hands they shall bear thee up, lest at any time thou dash thy foot against a stone. Jesus said unto him: It is written again: Thou shalt not tempt the Lord thy God. Again, the devil taketh him up into an exceeding high mountain: and sheweth him all the kingdoms of the world, and the glory of them; and saith unto him: All these things will I give thee, if thou wilt fall down and worship me. Then saith Jesus unto him: Get thee hence, Satan; for it is written: Thou shalt worship the Lord thy God, and him only shalt thou serve. Then the devil leaveth him: and behold, Angels came and ministered unto him. Creed.

Offertory. Ps. 91, 4-5. The Lord shall defend thee under his wings, and thou shalt be safe under his feathers: his faithfulness and truth shall be thy shield and buckler.

Secret.

WE solemnly offer unto thee, O Lord, this sacrifice in the beginning of Lent, beseeching thee: that, while we abstain from carnal feastings, we may likewise refrain from hurtful pleasures. Through.

Preface of Lent.

Communion. Ps. 91, 4-5. The Lord shall defend thee under his wings, and thou shalt be safe under his feathers: his faithfulness and truth shall be thy shield and buckler.

Postcommunion.

GRANT, O Lord, that this holy Sacrament, which we have now received, may in such wise deliver us from the sins of our former nature: that we may be worthy to enter into the fellowship of thy saving mysteries. Through.

Monday

Station at St. Peter ad Vincula

Introit. Ps. 123, 2. Sicut oculi.

AS the eyes of servants look unto the hand of their masters: even so our eyes wait upon the Lord our God, until he have mercy upon us: have mercy upon us, O Lord, have mercy upon us. Ps. ibid., 1. Unto thee lift I up mine eyes: O thou that dwellest in the heavens. ℣. Glory.

Collect.

TURN thou us, O God our Saviour: and that this Lenten fast may be profitable unto us, instruct our minds in all heavenly learning. Through.

The Lesson from the Prophet Ezekiel.

Ezek. 34, 11-16.

THUS saith the Lord God: Behold, I, even I, will both search my sheep, and seek them out. As a shepherd seeketh out

The Monday after the First Sunday in Lent

his flock in the day that he is among his sheep that are scattered: so will I seek out my sheep, and will deliver them out of all places where they have been scattered in the cloudy and dark day. And I will bring them out from the people, and gather them from the countries, and will bring them to their own land: and feed them upon the mountains of Israel by the rivers, and in all the inhabited places of the country. I will feed them in a good pasture, and upon the high mountains of Israel shall their fold be: there shall they lie in a good fold, and in a fat pasture shall they feed upon the mountains of Israel. I will feed my flock, and I will cause them to lie down, saith the Lord God. I will seek that which was lost; and bring again that which was driven away; and will bind up that which was broken; and will strengthen that which was sick; but I will destroy the fat and the strong: I will feed them with judgment, saith the Lord almighty.

Gradual. Ps. 84, 10 and 9. Behold, O God our defender, and look upon thy servants. ℣. O Lord God of hosts, hear the prayers of thy servants.

Tract. Ps. 103, 10. O Lord, deal not with us after our sins: nor reward us according to our wickednesses. ℣. Ps. 79. O Lord, remember not our old sins: but have mercy upon us, and that soon, for we are come to great misery. (Here genuflect) ℣. Help us, O God of our salvation: and for the glory of thy name, O Lord, deliver us: and be merciful unto our sins, for thy name's sake.

✠ The Continuation of the holy Gospel according to Matthew.

Matt. 25, 31-46.

AT that time: Jesus said unto his disciples: When the Son of man shall come in his glory, and all the holy Angels with him, then shall he sit upon the throne of his glory: and before him shall be gathered all nations, and he shall separate them one from another, as a shepherd divideth his sheep from the goats: and he shall set the sheep on his right hand, but the goats on the left. Then shall the King say unto them on his right hand: Come, ye blessed of my Father, inherit the kingdom prepared for you from the foundation of the world. For I was an hungred, and ye gave me meat; I was thirsty, and ye gave me drink; I was a stranger, and ye took me in; naked, and ye clothed me; I was sick, and ye visited me; I was in prison, and ye came unto me. Then shall the righteous answer him, saying: Lord, when saw we thee an hungred, and fed thee; or thirsty, and gave thee drink? When saw we thee a stranger, and took thee in? or naked, and clothed thee? Or when saw we thee sick, or in prison, and came unto thee? And the King shall answer and say unto them: Verily I say unto you: Inasmuch as ye have done it unto one of the least of these my brethren, ye have done it unto me. Then shall he say also unto them on the left hand: Depart from me, ye cursed, into everlasting fire, prepared for the devil and his angels. For I was an hungred, and ye gave me no meat; I was thirsty, and ye gave me no drink; I was a stranger, and ye took me not in; naked, and ye clothed me not; sick, and in prison, and ye visited me not. Then shall they also answer him, saying: Lord, when saw we thee an hungred, or athirst, or a stranger, or naked, or sick, or in prison, and did not minister unto thee? Then shall he answer them, saying: Verily I say unto you: Inasmuch as ye did it not to one of the least of these, ye did it not to me. And these shall go away into everlasting punishment: but the righteous into life eternal.

Offertory. Ps. 119, 18, 26 and 73. I will lift up mine eyes and see thy wondrous things, O Lord, that thou mayest teach me thy judgments: O give me understanding, and I shall learn thy commandments.

Secret.

SANCTIFY, O Lord, the gifts which we offer unto thee: and cleanse us from the stains of our sins. Through.

Preface of Lent.

Communion. Matt. 25, 40 and 34. Verily I say unto you, whatsoever ye have done unto one of the least of mine, ye have done unto me: come, ye blessed of my Father, inherit the kingdom prepared for you from the foundation of the world.

Postcommunion.

O LORD, who hast fulfilled us with the gift of thy salvation, we humbly beseech thee: that as we do rejoice in the partaking of the same, so thereby our souls may be effectually renewed. Through.

Over the people:

Let us pray. Humble your heads before God.

Collect.

WE beseech thee, O Lord, loose the chains of our sins: and of thy great mercy turn aside the punishment which for the same we most righteously deserve. Through.

Tuesday

Station at St. Anastasia

Introit. Ps. 90, 1-2. Domine, refugium.

LORD, thou hast been our refuge from one generation to another: thou art from everlasting, and world without end. Ps. ibid., 2. Before the mountains were brought forth, or ever the earth and the world were made: thou art God from everlasting, and world without end. ℣. Glory.

Collect.

O LORD, graciously behold this thy family: and vouchsafe; that whereas we now chasten our bodies by the mortifying of the flesh, our souls may shine in thy sight with longing after thee. Through.

The Lesson from the Prophet Isaiah.

Is. 55, 6-11.

IN those days: Spake Isaiah the Prophet, saying: Seek ye the Lord while he may be found: call ye upon him while he is near. Let the wicked forsake his way, and the unrighteous man his thoughts, and let him return unto the Lord: and he will have mercy upon him, and to our God, for he will abundantly pardon. For my thoughts are not your thoughts, neither are your ways my ways, saith the Lord. For as the heavens are higher than the earth, so are my ways higher than your ways, and my thoughts than your thoughts. For as the rain cometh down, and the snow from heaven, and returneth not thither, but watereth the earth, and maketh it bring forth and bud, that it may give seed to the sower, and bread to the eater: so shall my word be that goeth forth out of my mouth: it shall not return unto me void, but it shall accomplish that which I please, and it shall prosper in the thing whereto I sent it: saith the Lord almighty.

Gradual. Ps. 141, 2. Let my prayer be set forth in thy sight, O Lord, as the incense. ℣. Let the lifting up of my hands be an evening sacrifice.

✠ The Continuation of the holy Gospel according to Matthew.

Matt. 21, 10-17.

AT that time: When Jesus was come into Jerusalem, all the city was moved, saying: Who is this? And the multitude said: This is Jesus the Prophet of Nazareth of Galilee. And Jesus went into the temple of God, and cast out all them that sold and bought in the temple;

and overthrew the tables of the money-changers, and the seats of them that sold doves: and said unto them: It is written: My house shall be called the house of prayer: but ye have made it a den of thieves. And the blind and the lame came to him in the temple: and he healed them. And when the chief priests and scribes saw the wonderful things that he did, and the children crying in the temple, and saying: Hosanna to the Son of David: they were sore displeased, and said unto him: Hearest thou what these say? And Jesus saith unto them: Yea. Have ye never read: Out of the mouths of babes and sucklings thou hast perfected praise? And he left them, and went out of the city into Bethany: and he lodged there.

Offertory. Ps. 31, 15-16. My hope hath been in thee, O Lord; I have said: Thou art my God, my time is in thy hand.

Secret.

WE beseech thee, O Lord, have respect unto the gifts which we offer: and defend us against all dangers. Through.

Preface of Lent.

Communion. Ps. 4, 2. Thou hast heard me when I called upon thee, O God of my righteousness: thou hast set me at liberty when I was in trouble; have mercy upon me, O Lord, and hearken unto my prayer.

Postcommunion.

WE beseech thee, almighty God: that as through these holy mysteries we have received the pledge of our salvation, so we may effectually be brought unto the fulfilment of the same. Through.

Over the people:

Let us pray. Humble your heads before God.

Collect.

O LORD, let our prayers ascend unto thee: and drive far from thy Church all wickedness. Through.

Ember Wednesday in Lent

Station at St. Mary Major

Introit. Ps. 25, 6, 3 and 22. Reminiscere.

CALL to remembrance thy tender mercies, O Lord, and thy loving-kindnesses, which have been ever of old: neither let our enemies triumph over us: deliver us, O God of Israel, out of all our troubles. Ps. ibid., 1. Unto thee, O Lord, will I lift up my soul: my God, I have put my trust in thee, O let me not be confounded. ℣. Glory.

After Kýrie, eléison is said: Let us pray. Let us bow the knee. ℟. Arise.

Collect.

WE beseech thee, O Lord, graciously hear our prayers; and stretch forth the right hand of thy majesty to be our defence against all adversities. Through.

The Lesson from the book Exodus.

Exod. 24, 12-18.

IN those days: The Lord said unto Moses: Come up to me into the mount, and be there: and I will give thee tables of stone, and a law, and commandments which I have written: that thou mayest teach them unto the children of Israel. And Moses rose up, and his minister Joshua: and Moses went up into the mount of God, and he said unto the elders: Tarry ye here for us, until we come again unto you: and, behold, Aaron and Hur are with you: if any man have any matters to do, let him come unto them. And Moses went up into the mount, and a cloud covered the mount, and the glory of the Lord abode upon mount Sinai, and the cloud covered it six days: and the seventh day he called unto Moses out of the midst of the cloud. And the sight of the glory of the Lord was like devouring fire on the top of the mount in the eyes of the children of Israel. And Moses went into the midst of the cloud, and gat him up into the mount: and Moses was in the mount forty days and forty nights.

Gradual. Ps. 25, 17-18. The sorrows of my heart are enlarged: O Lord, bring thou me out of my troubles. ℣. Look upon my adversity and misery: and forgive me all my sin.

Here is said ℣. The Lord be with you, without Let us bow the knee.

Let us pray. Collect.

WE beseech thee, O Lord, graciously to regard the devout prayers of thy people: that they, who by abstinence do mortify the body, may by the fruit of good works be renewed in the spirit of their minds. Through.

The Lesson from the book of the Kings.

I Kings 19, 3-8.

IN those days: Elijah came to Beersheba, which belongeth to Judah, and left his servant there, but he himself went a day's journey into the wilderness. And he came and sat down under a juniper tree: and he requested for himself that he might die, and said: It is enough, now, O Lord, take away my life: for I am not better than my fathers. And as he lay and slept under a juniper tree: behold, then an Angel touched him, and said unto him: Arise and eat. And he looked, and, behold, there was a cake baken on the coals, and a cruse of water at his head: and he did eat and drink, and laid him down again. And the Angel of the Lord came again the second time, and touched him, and said: Arise and eat: because the journey is too great for thee. And he arose, and did eat and drink, and went in the strength of that meat forty days and forty nights unto Horeb the mount of God.

Tract. Ps. 25, 17-18 and 1-4. O Lord, bring thou me out of my troubles: look upon my adversity and misery: and forgive me all my sin. ℣. Unto thee, O Lord, will I lift up my soul: my God, I have put my trust in thee: O let me not be confounded: neither let mine enemies triumph over me. ℣. For all they that hope in thee shall not be ashamed: but such as transgress without a cause shall be put to confusion.

✠ The Continuation of the holy Gospel according to Matthew.

Matt. 12, 38-50.

AT that time: Certain of the scribes and of the Pharisees answered Jesus, saying: Master, we would see a sign from thee. But he answered and said unto them: An evil and adulterous generation seeketh after a sign: and there shall no sign be given to it, but the sign of the prophet Jonas. For as Jonas was three days and three nights in the whale's belly: so shall the Son of man be three days and three nights in the heart of the earth. The men of Nineveh shall rise in judgment with this generation, and shall condemn it: because they repented at the preaching of Jonas. And, behold, a greater than Jonas is here. The queen of the south shall rise up in the judgment with this generation, and shall condemn it: for she came from the uttermost parts of the earth to hear the wisdom of Solomon. And, behold, a greater than Solomon is here. When the unclean spirit is gone out of a man, he walketh through dry places, seeking rest, and findeth none. Then he saith: I will return into my house from whence I came out. And when he is come, he findeth it empty, swept, and garnished. Then goeth he, and taketh with himself seven other spirits more wicked than himself, and they enter in and dwell there: and the last state of that man is worse than the first. Even so shall it be also unto this wicked generation. While he yet talked to the people, behold, his Mother and his brethren stood without, desiring to speak with him. Then one said unto him: Behold, thy mother and thy brethren stand without, desiring to speak with thee. But he answered and said unto him that told him: Who is my mother, and who are my brethren? And he stretched forth his hand toward his disciples, and said: Behold my mother and my brethren! For whosoever shall do the will of my Father which is in heaven: the same is my brother, and sister, and mother.

Offertory. Ps. 119, 47-48. My delight shall be in thy commandments, which I have loved exceedingly: my hands also will I lift up to thy commandments which I have loved.

Secret.

WE offer unto thee, O Lord, this sacrifice of propitiation: beseeching thee, that thou wouldest mercifully absolve our offences, and direct the hearts of them that go astray. Through.

Preface of Lent.

Communion. Ps. 5, 2-4. Consider my meditation: O hearken thou unto the voice of my calling, my King, and my God: for unto thee, O Lord, will I make my prayer.

Postcommunion.

O LORD, let this holy Sacrament, which we have here received, both cleanse us from our secret faults, and deliver us from all the snares of our enemies. Through.

Over the people:

Let us pray. Humble your heads before God.

Collect.

O LORD, we beseech thee, illumine our minds with the bright beams of thy light: that we may be able to perceive those things which we ought to do; and have strength to do those things which be right. Through.

Thursday

Station at St. Laurence in Paneperna

Introit. Ps. 96, 6. Confessio.

GLORY and worship are before him: power and honour are in his sanctuary. Ps. ibid., 1. O sing unto the Lord a new song: sing unto the Lord, all the whole earth. ℣. Glory.

Collect.

WE beseech thee, O Lord, graciously to regard the devout prayers of thy people: that they who by abstinence do mortify the body, may by the fruit of good works be renewed in the spirit of their minds. Through.

The Lesson from the Prophet Ezekiel.
Ezek. 18, 1-9.

IN those days: The word of the Lord came unto me, saying: What mean ye, that ye use this proverb concerning the land of Israel, saying: The fathers have eaten sour grapes, and the children's teeth are set on edge? As I live, saith the Lord God, ye shall not have occasion any more to use this proverb in Israel. Behold, all souls are mine: as the soul of the father, so also the soul of the son is mine, the soul that sinneth, it shall die. But if a man be just, and do that which is lawful and right, and hath not eaten upon the mountains, neither hath lifted up his eyes to the idols of the house of Israel: neither hath defiled his neighbour's wife, neither hath come near to a menstruous woman: and hath not oppressed any, but hath restored to the debtor his pledge, hath spoiled none by violence, hath given his bread to the hungry, and hath covered the naked with a garment: he that hath not given forth upon usury, neither hath taken any increase: that hath withdrawn his hand from iniquity, hath executed true judgment between man and man: hath walked in my statutes, and hath kept my judgments, to deal truly: he is just, he shall surely live, saith the Lord almighty.

Gradual. Ps. 17, 8 and 2. Keep me, O Lord, as the apple of an eye: hide me under the shadow of thy wings. ℣. Let my sentence come forth from thy presence: and let thine eyes look upon the thing that is equal.

✠ The Continuation of the holy Gospel according to Matthew.

Matt. 15, 21-28.

AT that time: Jesus went thence, and departed into the coasts of Tyre and Sidon. And, behold, a woman of Canaan came out of the same coasts, and cried unto him, saying: Have mercy on me, O Lord, thou Son of David: my daughter is grievously vexed with a devil. But he answered her not a word. And his disciples came and besought him, saying: Send her away; for she crieth after us. But he answered and said: I am not sent but unto the lost sheep of the house of Israel. Then came she and worshipped him, saying: Lord, help me. But he answered and said: It is not meet to take the children's bread, and to cast it to dogs. And she said: Truth, Lord: yet the dogs eat of the crumbs which fall from their masters' table. Then Jesus answered and said unto her: O woman, great is thy faith: be it unto thee even as thou wilt. And her daughter was made whole from that very hour.

Offertory. Ps. 34, 8-9. The Angel of the Lord tarrieth round about them that fear him, and delivereth them: O taste, and see, how gracious the Lord is.

Secret.

WE beseech thee, O Lord: that this sacrifice, which we offer in this time of fasting appointed for our healing, may effectually avail for the salvation of our souls. Through.

Preface of Lent.

Communion. John 6, 52. The bread that I will give is my flesh, which I will give for the life of the world.

Postcommunion.

O LORD, support us in this life with the abundance of thy gifts, and by the same renew us unto life everlasting. Through.

Over the people:

Let us pray. Humble your heads before God.

Collect.

GRANT, O Lord, we beseech thee, unto all Christian peoples: that they may both acknowledge the faith which they profess, and likewise love the heavenly gift to which they continually draw near. Through.

Ember Friday in Lent

Station at the twelve Holy Apostles

Introit. Ps. 25, 17-18. De necessitatibus.

O LORD, bring thou me out of my troubles: look upon my adversity and misery, and forgive me all my sin. Ps. ibid., 1. Unto thee, O Lord, will I lift up my soul; my God, I have put my trust in thee, O let me not be confounded. ℣. Glory.

Collect.

BE merciful, O Lord, unto thy people: that they who by thee are enabled to serve thee in all godliness, may ever be comforted by thy gracious and ready help. Through.

The Lesson from the Prophet Ezekiel.
Ezek. 18, 20-28.

THUS saith the Lord God: The soul that sinneth, it shall die: the son shall not bear the iniquity of the father, neither shall the father bear the iniquity of the son: the righteousness of the righteous shall be upon him, and the wickedness of the wicked shall be upon him. But if the wicked will turn from all his sins that he hath committed, and keep all my statutes, and do that which is lawful and right: he shall surely live, he shall not die. All his transgressions that he hath committed, they shall not be mentioned unto him: in his righteousness that he hath done he shall live. Have I any pleasure at all that the wicked should die, saith the Lord God: and not that he should return from his ways, and live? But when the righteous turneth away from his righteousness, and committeth iniquity, and doeth according to all the abominations that the wicked man doeth, shall he live? All his righteousness that he hath done shall not be mentioned: in his trespass that he hath trespassed, and in his sin that he hath sinned, in them shall he die. Yet ye say: The way of the Lord is not equal. Hear now, O house of Israel: Is not my way equal, are not your ways unequal? When a righteous man turneth away from his righteousness, and committeth iniquity, and dieth in them: for his iniquity that he hath done shall he die. Again, when the wicked man turneth away from his wickedness that he hath committed, and doeth that which is lawful and right: he shall save his soul alive. Because he considereth, and turneth away from all his transgressions that he hath committed, he shall surely live, he shall not die, saith the Lord almighty.

Gradual. Ps. 86, 2 and 6. My God, save thy servant that putteth his trust in thee. ℣. Give ear, Lord, unto my prayer.

Tract. Ps. 103, 10. O Lord, deal not with us after our sins: nor reward us according to our wickednesses. ℣. Ps. 79, 10. O Lord, remember not our old sins: but have mercy upon us, and that soon, for we are come to great misery. (Here genuflect) ℣. Help us, O God of our salvation: and for the glory of thy name, O Lord, deliver us; and be merciful unto our sins, for thy name's sake.

✠ The Continuation of the holy Gospel according to John.
John 5, 1-15.

AT that time: There was a feast of the Jews, and Jesus went up to Jerusalem. Now there is at Jerusalem by the sheep market a pool, which is called in the Hebrew tongue Bethesda, having five porches. In these lay a great multitude of impotent folk, of blind, halt, withered, waiting for the moving of the water. For an Angel went down at a certain season into the pool, and troubled the water. Whosoever then first after the troubling of the water stepped in was made whole of whatsoever disease he had. And a certain man was there, which had an infirmity thirty and eight years. When Jesus saw him lie, and knew that he had been now a long time in that case, he saith unto him: Wilt thou be made whole? The impotent man answered him: Sir, I have no man, when the water is troubled, to put me into the pool: but while I am coming, another steppeth down before me. Jesus saith unto him: Rise, take up thy bed, and walk. And immediately the man was made whole: and took up his bed, and walked. And on the same day was the sabbath. The Jews therefore said unto him that was cured: It is the sabbath day, it is not lawful for thee to carry thy bed. He answered them: He that made me whole, the same said unto me: Take up thy bed, and walk. Then asked they him: What man is that which said unto thee:

Take up thy bed, and walk? And he that was healed wist not who it was. For Jesus had conveyed himself away, a multitude being in that place. Afterward Jesus findeth him in the temple, and said unto him: Behold, thou art made whole: sin no more, lest a worse thing come unto thee. The man departed, and told the Jews that it was Jesus, which had made him whole.

Offertory. Ps. 103, 2 and 5. Praise the Lord, O my soul, and forget not all his benefits: who maketh thee young and lusty as an eagle.

Secret.

ACCEPT, O Lord, we pray thee, this oblation of our bounden service: and graciously sanctify these thy gifts. Through.

Preface of Lent.

Communion. Ps. 6, 11. All mine enemies shall be confounded, and sore vexed: they shall be turned back, and put to shame suddenly.

Postcommunion.

GRANT, O Lord, that by the operation of these thy mysteries we may be cleansed from all our sins, and obtain that which we have asked according to thy will. Through.

Over the people:

Let us pray. Humble your heads before God.

Collect.

GRACIOUSLY hear us, O merciful God: and shew forth in our hearts the light of thy grace. Through.

Ember Saturday in Lent

Station at St. Peter

Introit. Ps. 88, 3. Intret.

O LET my prayer enter into thy presence: incline thine ear, O Lord, unto my calling. Ps. ibid., 1. O Lord God of my salvation: I have cried day and night before thee. ℣. Glory.

After Kýrie, eléison is said: Let us pray. Let us bow the knee. ℟. Arise.

Collect.

WE beseech thee, O Lord, graciously to look upon thy people: and of thy great goodness turn aside from them the scourges of thine anger. Through.

The Lesson from the book Deuteronomy.

Deut. 26, 12-19.

IN those days: Spake Moses unto the people, saying: When thou hast made an end of tithing all the tithes of thine increase, then thou shalt say before the Lord thy God: I have brought away the hallowed things out of mine house, and also have given them unto the Levite, and unto the stranger, to the fatherless, and to the widow, according to all thy commandments which thou hast commanded me: I have not transgressed thy commandments, neither have I forgotten them. I have hearkened to the voice of the Lord my God, and have done according to all that thou hast commanded me. Look down from thy holy habitation, from heaven, and bless thy people Israel, and the land which thou hast given us, as thou swarest unto our fathers, a land that floweth with milk and honey. This day the Lord thy God hath commanded thee to do these statutes and judgments: thou shalt therefore keep and do them with all thine heart, and with all thy soul. Thou hast avouched the Lord this day to be thy God, and to walk in his ways, and to keep his statutes, and his commandments, and his judgments, and to hearken unto his voice. And the Lord hath avouched thee this day to be his peculiar people, as he hath promised thee, and that thou shouldest keep all his commandments: and to make thee high above all nations which he hath made, in praise, and in name, and in honour: and that thou mayest be an holy people unto the Lord thy God, as he hath spoken.

Gradual. Ps. 79, 9-10. Be merciful, O Lord, unto our sins: wherefore do the heathen say: Where is now their God? ℣. Help us, O God of our salvation: and for the glory of thy name, O Lord, deliver us.

Let us pray. Let us bow the knee. ℟. Arise.

Collect.

BEHOLD, O God our defender: that we who are sore oppressed by the burden of our sins may by thy mercy be relieved from the same to serve thee in perfect freedom. Through.

The Lesson from the book Deuteronomy.

Deut. 11, 22-25.

IN those days: Moses said unto the children of Israel: If ye shall diligently keep all these commandments which I command you, to do them, to love the Lord your God, to walk in all his ways, and to cleave unto him, then will the Lord drive out all these nations from before you, and ye shall possess greater nations and mightier than yourselves. Every place whereon the soles of your feet shall tread shall be yours. From the wilderness and Lebanon, from the river, the river Euphrates, even unto the uttermost sea shall your coast be. There shall no man be able to stand before you: for the Lord your God shall lay the fear of you and the dread of you upon all the land that ye shall tread upon, as he hath said unto you, the Lord your God.

Gradual. Ps. 84, 10 and 9. Behold, O God our defender, and look upon thy servants. ℣. O Lord God of hosts, hear the prayers of thy servants.

Let us pray. Let us bow the knee. ℟. Arise.

Collect.

ASSIST us mercifully, O Lord, we beseech thee, in these our supplications: that by thy bountiful grace we may walk humbly in all time of our wealth, and in all time of tribulation may serve thee without fear. Through.

The Lesson from the book of the Maccabees.

II Macc. 1, 23-27.

IN those days: The priests made a prayer whilst the sacrifice was consuming, Jonathan beginning, and the rest answering thereunto, as Neemias did. And the prayer was after this manner: O Lord, Lord God, Creator of all things, who art fearful and strong, and righteous, and merciful, and the only and gracious King, the only giver of all things, the only just, almighty, and everlasting, thou that deliverest Israel from all trouble, and didst choose the fathers, and sanctify them: receive the sacrifice for thy whole people Israel, and preserve thine own portion, and sanctify it: and let the heathen know that thou art our God.

Gradual. Ps. 90, 13 and 1. Turn thee again, O Lord, at the last, and be gracious unto thy servants. ℣. Lord, thou hast been our refuge, from one generation to another.

Let us pray. Let us bow the knee. ℟. Arise.

Collect.

O LORD, we beseech thee favourably to hear the prayers of thy people: that we, who are justly punished for our offences, may be mercifully delivered by thy goodness for the glory of thy name. Through.

The Lesson from the book of Wisdom.

Ecclus. 36, 1-10.

HAVE mercy upon us, O Lord God of all, and behold us, and send thy fear upon all the nations that seek not after thee. Lift up thy hand against the strange nations, and let them see thy power. As thou wast sanctified in us before them, so be thou magnified among them before us, and let them know thee, as we have known thee, that there is no God but only thou, O God. Shew new signs, and make other strange wonders. Glorify thy hand and thy right arm, that they may set forth thy wondrous works. Raise up indignation, and pour out wrath. Take away the adversary, and destroy the enemy. Make the time short, remember the covenant, and let them declare thy wonderful works, O Lord our God.

Gradual. Ps. 141, 2. Let my prayer be set forth in thy sight, O Lord, as the incense. ℣. Let the lifting up of my hands be an evening sacrifice.

Let us pray. Let us bow the knee. ℟. Arise.

Collect.

PREVENT us, O Lord, we beseech thee, in all our doings with thy most gracious favour, and further us with thy continual help: that all our prayer and work may be begun, continued and ended in thee. Through.

The Lesson from the Prophet Daniel.

Song of the Three Children, 24-28.

IN those days: The Angel of the Lord came down into the oven together with Azarias and his fellows: and smote the flame of the fire out of the oven, and made the midst of the furnace as it had been a moist whistling wind. Now the flame streamed forth above the furnace forty and nine cubits: and it passed through, and burned of the Chaldeans it found about the furnace, the king's servants, that made it hot. And the fire touched them not at all, neither hurt nor troubled them. Then the three, as out of one mouth, praised, glorified, and blessed God in the furnace, saying:

Here the response Thanks be to God is not made.

Hymn. Song, ibid., 29-39.

BLESSED art thou, O Lord God of our fathers. And to be praised and glorified for ever.

And blessed is the name of thy glory, which is holy. And to be praised and glorified for ever.

Blessed art thou in the holy temple of thy glory. And to be praised and glorified for ever.

Blessed art thou on the holy throne of thy kingdom. And to be praised and glorified for ever.

Blessed art thou in the sceptre of thy Godhead. And to be praised and glorified for ever.

Blessed art thou that sittest upon the Cherubim, and beholdest the depths. And to be praised and glorified for ever.

Blessed art thou that walkest on the wings of the winds and on the waves of the sea. And to be praised and glorified for ever.

Let all thine Angels and Saints bless thee. And let them praise thee and glorify thee for ever.

Let the heavens, the earth, the sea, and all that in them is bless thee. And let them praise thee and glorify thee for ever.

Glory be to the Father, and to the Son, and to the Holy Ghost. And to be praised and glorified for ever.

As it was in the beginning, is now, and ever shall be: world without end. Amen. And to be praised and glorified for ever.

Blessed art thou, O Lord God of our fathers. And to be praised and glorified for ever.

Here is said ℣. The Lord be with you, without Let us bow the knee.

Ember Saturday in Lent

Let us pray.   Collect.

O GOD, who for the deliverance of the three children didst assuage the flames of fire: mercifully grant; that the flames of sin may have no power upon us thy servants. Through.

The Lesson from the Epistle of blessed Paul the Apostle to the Thessalonians.

I Thess. 5, 14-23.

BRETHREN: We exhort you, warn them that are unruly, comfort the feebleminded, support the weak, be patient toward all men. See that none render evil for evil unto any man: but ever follow that which is good, both among yourselves, and to all men. Rejoice evermore. Pray without ceasing. In everything give thanks: for this is the will of God in Christ Jesus concerning you. Quench not the Spirit. Despise not prophesyings. Prove all things: hold fast that which is good. Abstain from all appearance of evil. And the very God of peace sanctify you wholly: and I pray God your whole spirit and soul and body be preserved blameless unto the coming of our Lord Jesus Christ.

Tract. Ps. 117, 1-2. O praise the Lord, all ye heathen: praise him, all ye nations. ℣. For his merciful kindness is ever more and more towards us: and the truth of the Lord endureth for ever.

☩ The Continuation of the holy Gospel according to Matthew.

Matt 17, 1-9.

AT that time: Jesus taketh Peter, James, and John his brother, and bringeth them up into an high mountain apart: and was transfigured before them. And his face did shine as the sun, and his raiment was white at the light. And, behold, there appeared unto them Moses and Elias talking with him. Then answered Peter, and said unto Jesus: Lord, it is good for us to be here: if thou wilt, let us make here three tabernacles, one for thee, and one for Moses, and one for Elias. While he yet spake, behold, a bright cloud overshadowed them. And behold a voice out of the cloud, which said: This is my beloved Son, in whom I am well pleased: hear ye him. And when the disciples heard it, they fell on their face, and were sore afraid. And Jesus came and touched them, and said: Arise, and be not afraid. And when they had lifted up their eyes, they saw no man, save Jesus only. And as they came down from the mountain, Jesus charged them, saying: Tell the vision to no man, until the Son of man be risen again from the dead.

Offertory. Ps. 88, 2-3. O Lord God of my salvation, I have cried day and night before thee: let my prayer enter into thy presence, O Lord.

Secret.

SANCTIFY, we beseech thee, O Lord, our fast by this our sacrifice: that those things, which our observance outwardly shews forth, it may inwardly effect. Through.

Preface of Lent.

Communion. Ps. 7, 2. O Lord my God, in thee have I put my trust: save me from all them that persecute me, and deliver me.

Postcommunion.

O ALMIGHTY God, let thy sanctifying power effectually cleanse us from all our sins, and be profitable for our healing unto life everlasting. Through.

Over the people:

Let us pray.   Humble your heads before God.

Collect.

GRANT, O God, that thy faithful people which here do seek thy blessing: may in such wise be strengthened by the same, that they may never turn aside from the following of thy will, and may alway rejoice in thy bountiful goodness. Through.

The Second Sunday in Lent

1st class.   Double of 1st class.

Station at St. Mary in Dominica

Introit. Ps. 25, 6, 3 and 22. Reminiscere.

CALL to remembrance thy tender mercies, O Lord, and thy lovingkindnesses, which have been ever of old: neither let our enemies triumph over us: deliver us, O God of Israel, out of all our troubles. Ps. ibid., 1. Unto thee, O Lord, do I lift up my soul: my God, in thee have I trusted, let me not be confounded. ℣. Glory.

Collect.

ALMIGHTY God, who seest that we have no power of ourselves to help ourselves: keep us both outwardly in our bodies, and inwardly in our souls; that we may be defended from all adversities which may happen to the body, and from all evil thoughts which may assault and hurt the soul. Through.

The Lesson from the Epistle of blessed Paul the Apostle to the Thessalonians.

I Thess. 4, 1-7.

BRETHREN: We beseech you, and exhort you by the Lord Jesus: that as ye have received of us how ye ought to walk, and to please God, so ye would abound more and more. For ye know what commandments we gave you by the Lord Jesus. For this is the will of God, even your sanctification: that ye should abstain from fornication, that every one of you should know how to possess his vessel in sanctification and honour; not in the lust of concupiscence, even as the Gentiles which know not God: that no man go beyond and defraud his brother in any matter: because that the Lord is the avenger of all such, as we also have forewarned you, and testified. For God hath not called us unto uncleanness, but unto holiness: [in Christ Jesu our Lord.*]

He therefore that despiseth, despiseth not man, but God, who hath also given unto us his Holy Spirit.

Gradual. Ps. 25, 17-18. The sorrows of my heart are enlarged: O bring thou me out of my troubles, O Lord. ℣. Look upon my adversity and misery: and forgive me all my sin.

Tract. Ps. 106, 1-4. O give thanks unto the Lord, for he is gracious: and his mercy endureth for ever. ℣. Who can express the noble acts of the Lord: or shew forth all his praise? ℣. Blessed are they that alway keep judgment, and do righteousness. ℣. Remember us, O Lord, according to the favour that thou bearest unto thy people: O visit us with thy salvation.

✠ The Continuation of the holy Gospel according to Matthew.

Matt. 15, 21-28.

AT that time: Jesus went thence, and departed into the coasts of Tyre and Sidon. And behold, a woman of Canaan came out of the same coasts, and cried unto him, saying: Have mercy on me, O Lord, thou Son of David; my daughter is grievously vexed with a devil. But he answered her not a word. And his disciples came and besought him, saying: Send her away, for she crieth after us. But he answered and said: I am not sent, but unto the lost sheep of the house of Israel. Then came she and worshipped him, saying: Lord, help me. But he answered and said: It is not meet to take the children's bread, and to cast it to dogs. And she said: Truth, Lord; yet the dogs eat of the crumbs which fall from their masters' table. Then Jesus answered and said unto her: O woman, great is thy faith: be it unto thee even as thou wilt. And her daughter was made whole from that very hour. Creed.

Or Gospel Jesus taketh Peter p. 83.

The Monday after the Second Sunday in Lent

Offertory. Ps. 119, 47-48. My delight shall be in thy commandments, which I have loved exceedingly: my hands also will I lift up unto thy commandments, which I have loved.

Secret.

WE beseech thee, O Lord, mercifully to have respect unto these our sacrifices: that they may increase our devotion and set forward our salvation. Through.

Preface of Lent.

Communion. Ps. 5, 2-4. Consider my meditation: O hearken thou unto the voice of my calling, my King and my God: for unto thee will I make my prayer, O Lord.

Postcommunion.

WE humbly beseech thee, almighty God: that as thou dost refresh us with thy sacraments, so thou wouldest vouchsafe unto us to do thee worthy and acceptable service. Through.

Monday

Station at St. Clement

Introit. Ps. 26, 11-12. Redime me.

DELIVER me, O Lord, and be merciful unto me: my foot standeth right: I will praise the Lord in the congregations. Ps. ibid., 1. Be thou my judge, O Lord, for I have walked innocently: my trust hath been also in the Lord, therefore shall I not fall. ℣. Glory.

Collect.

GRANT, we beseech thee, almighty God: that like as we thy family do abstain from food to the mortifying of the flesh; so we may likewise fast from sin to the following after righteousness. Through.

The Lesson from the Prophet Daniel.

Dan. 9, 15-19.

IN those days: Daniel prayed unto the Lord, and said: O Lord our God, that hast brought thy people forth out of the land of Egypt with a mighty hand, and hast gotten thee renown, as at this day: we have sinned, we have done wickedly: O Lord, according to all thy righteousness, I beseech thee, let thine anger and thy fury be turned away from thy city Jerusalem, thy holy mountain. Because for our sins, and for the iniquities of our fathers, Jerusalem and thy people are become a reproach to all that are about us. Now therefore, O our God, hear the prayer of thy servant, and his supplications: and cause thy face to shine upon thy sanctuary that is desolate, for the Lord's sake. O my God, incline thine ear, and hear: open thine eyes, and behold our desolations, and the city which is called by thy name: for we do not present our supplications before thee for our righteousnesses, but for thy great mercies. O Lord, hear, O Lord, forgive: O Lord, hearken and do: defer not, for thine own sake, O my God: for thy city and thy people are called by thy name, O Lord our God.

Gradual. Ps. 70, 6 and 3. Thou art my helper, and my redeemer: O Lord, make no long tarrying. ℣. Let mine enemies be ashamed and confounded that seek after my soul.

Tract. Ps. 103, 10. O Lord, deal not with us after our sins: nor reward us according to our wickednesses. ℣. Ps. 79. O Lord, remember not our old sins: but have mercy upon us, and that soon, for we are come to great misery. (Here genuflect) ℣. Help us, O God of our salvation: and for the glory of thy name, O Lord, deliver us: and be merciful unto our sins, for thy name's sake.

✠ The Continuation of the holy Gospel according to John.

John 8, 21-29.

AT that time: Jesus said unto the multitudes of the Jews: I go my way, and ye shall seek me, and shall die in your sins. Whither I go, ye cannot come. Then said the Jews: Will he kill himself, because he saith: Whither I go, ye cannot come? And he said unto them: Ye are from beneath, I am from above. Ye are of this world, I am not of this world. I said therefore unto you, that ye shall die in your sins: for if ye believe not that I am he, ye shall die in your sins. Then said they unto him: Who art thou? And Jesus saith unto them: Even the same that I said unto you from the beginning. I have many things to say and to judge of you. But he that sent me is true: and I speak to the world those things which I have heard of him. They understood not that he spake to them of the Father. Then said Jesus unto them: When ye have lifted up the Son of man, then shall ye know that I am he, and that I do nothing of myself: but as my Father hath taught me, I speak these things: and he that sent me is with me, the Father hath not left me alone: for I do always those things that please him.

Offertory. Ps. 16, 7-8. I will thank the Lord for giving me warning: I have set God always before me: for he is on my right hand, therefore I shall not fall.

Secret.

MAY this sacrifice, O Lord, of atonement and praise make us worthy of thy protection. Through.

Preface of Lent.

Communion. Ps. 8, 2. O Lord our Governor, how excellent is thy name in all the world!

Postcommunion.

O LORD, let this holy Communion cleanse us from every guilty stain; that we may thereby be made partakers of thy healing unto life eternal. Through.

Over the people:

Let us pray. Humble your heads before God.

Collect.

ASSIST us mercifully, almighty God, in these our supplications: that we whom thou dost suffer to put our trust and confidence in thy mercy; may of thy goodness obtain the wonted effects of thy compassion. Through.

Tuesday

Station at St. Balbina

Introit. Ps. 27, 8-9. Tibi dixit.

MY heart hath talked of thee, seek ye my face, thy face, Lord, will I seek: O hide not thou thy face from me. Ps. ibid., 1. The Lord is my light, and my salvation; whom then shall I fear? ℣. Glory.

Collect.

WE beseech thee, O Lord, of thy mercy so to perfect in us the work of this holy observance: that we, who by thine inspiration, know those things which we ought to do, may by thee be enabled to fulfil the same. Through.

The Lesson from the book of the Kings.

I Kings 17, 8-16.

IN those days: The word of the Lord came unto Elijah the Tishbite, saying: Arise, get thee to Zarephath, which belongeth to Zidon, and dwell there: behold, I have commanded a widow woman there to sustain thee. So he arose and went to Zarephath. And when he came to the gate of the city, behold the widow woman was there gathering of sticks, and he called to her, and said: Fetch me, I pray thee, a little water in a vessel, that I may drink. And as she was going to fetch it, he called to her, and said: Bring me, I pray thee, a morsel of bread in thine hand. And she said: As the Lord thy God liveth, I have not a cake, but an handful of meal in a barrel, and a little oil in a cruse: and, behold, I am gathering two sticks, that I may go in and dress it for me and my son, that we may eat it, and die. And Elijah said unto her: Fear not, go and do as thou hast said: but make me thereof a little cake first, and bring it unto me: and after make for thee and for thy son. For thus saith the Lord God of Israel: The barrel of meal shall not waste, neither shall the cruse of oil fail, until the day that the Lord sendeth rain upon the earth. And she went and did according to the saying of Elijah: and she, and he, and her house, did eat many days: and the barrel of meal wasted not, neither did the cruse of oil fail, according to the word of the Lord, which he spake by Elijah.

Gradual. Ps. 55, 23, 17-18. O cast thy burden upon the Lord, and he shall nourish thee. ℣. When I called upon the Lord, he heard my voice from the battle that was against me.

☩ The Continuation of the holy Gospel according to Matthew.

Matt. 23, 1-12.

AT that time: Spake Jesus to the multitude, and to his disciples, saying: The scribes and the Pharisees sit in Moses' seat. All therefore whatsoever they bid you observe, that observe and do: but do not ye after their works: for they say, and do not. For they bind heavy burdens and grievous to be borne, and lay them on men's shoulders: but they themselves will not move them with one of their fingers. But all their works they do for to be seen of men: they make broad their phylacteries, and enlarge the borders of their garments. And love the uppermost rooms at feasts, and the chief seats in the synagogues, and greetings in the markets, and to be called of men, Rabbi, Rabbi. But be not ye called Rabbi: for one is your Master, even Christ, and all ye are brethren. And call no man your father upon the earth, for one is your Father, which is in heaven. Neither be ye called masters: for one is your Master, even Christ. But he that is greatest among you shall be your servant. And whosoever shall exalt himself shall be abased; and he that shall humble himself shall be exalted.

Offertory. Ps. 51, 3. Have mercy upon me, O Lord, after thy great goodness: O Lord, do away mine offences.

Secret.

VOUCHSAFE, O Lord, that these mysteries may accomplish thy sanctification within us: that we, being cleansed from all earthly vices, may attain unto thy gift of everlasting life. Through.

Preface of Lent.

Communion. Ps. 9, 2-3. I will speak of all thy marvellous works: I will be glad and rejoice in thee: yea, my songs will I make of thy name, O thou most Highest.

Postcommunion.

WE beseech thee, O Lord, make us ever to obey thy commandments: that we may be rendered worthy to partake of thy holy gifts. Through.

Over the people:

Let us pray. Humble your heads before God.

Collect.

BE merciful, O Lord, unto these our supplications, and heal the infirmities of our souls: that we, obtaining the remission of our sins, may evermore rejoice in thy heavenly benediction. Through.

Wednesday

Station at St. Cecilia

Introit. Ps. 38, 22-23. Ne derelinquas.

FORSAKE me not, O Lord my God: be not thou far from me: haste thee to help me, O Lord, thou strength of my salvation. Ps. ibid., 2. Put me not to rebuke, O Lord, in thine anger: neither chasten me in thy heavy displeasure. ℣. Glory.

Collect.

WE beseech thee, O Lord, look down in mercy on thy people: that we, whom thou dost command to abstain from carnal food, may likewise be delivered from all sins that hurt the soul. Through.

The Lesson from the book of Esther.

Esther 13, 8-11 and 15-17.

IN those days: Mardocheus made his prayer unto the Lord, saying: O Lord, Lord, the King almighty, for the whole world is in thy power, and if thou hast appointed to save Israel, there is no man that can gainsay thee. For thou hast made heaven and earth, and all the wondrous things under the heaven. Thou art Lord of all things, and there is no man that can resist thee, which art the Lord. And now, O Lord God and King, spare thy people, for their eyes are upon us to bring us to nought, yea, they desire to destroy the inheritance, that hath been thine from the beginning. Despise not the portion, which thou hast delivered out of Egypt for thine own self. Hear my prayer, and be merciful unto thine inheritance, turn our sorrow into joy, that we may live, O Lord, and praise thy name, and destroy not the mouths of them that praise thee, O Lord our God.

Gradual. Ps. 28, 19 and 1. Save thy people, O Lord, and give thy blessing unto thine inheritance. ℣. Unto thee have I cried, O Lord my strength: think no scorn of me, lest I become like them that go down into the pit.

Tract. Ps. 103, 10. O Lord, deal not with us after our sins: nor reward us according to our wickednesses. ℣. Ps. 79, 8-9. O Lord, remember not our old sins: but have mercy upon us, and that soon, for we are come to great misery. (Here genuflect) ℣. Help us, O God of our salvation: and for the glory of thy name, O Lord, deliver us: and be merciful unto our sins, for thy name's sake.

✠ The Continuation of the holy Gospel according to Matthew.

Matt. 20, 17-28.

AT that time: Jesus going up to Jerusalem took the twelve disciples apart in the way, and said unto them: Behold, we go up to Jerusalem, and the Son of man shall be betrayed unto the chief priests and unto the scribes, and they shall condemn him to death, and shall deliver him to the Gentiles to mock, and to scourge, and to crucify him, and the third day he shall rise again. Then came to him the mother of Zebedee's children with her sons, worshipping him, and desiring a certain thing of him. And he said unto her: What wilt thou? She saith unto him: Grant that these my two sons may sit, the one on thy right hand, and the other on the left, in thy kingdom. But Jesus answered and said: Ye know not what ye ask. Are ye able to drink of the cup that I shall drink of, and to be baptized with the baptism that I am baptized with? They say unto him: We are able. And he saith unto them: Ye shall drink indeed of my cup: and be baptized with the baptism that I am baptized with: but to sit on my right hand, and on my left, is not mine to give, but it shall be given to them for whom it is prepared of my Father. And when the ten heard it, they were moved with indignation against the two brethren.

But Jesus called them unto him, and said: Ye know that the princes of the Gentiles exercise dominion over them: and they that are great exercise authority upon them. But it shall not be so among you: but whosoever will be great among you, let him be your minister; and whosoever will be chief among you, let him be your servant. Even as the Son of man came not to be ministered unto, but to minister, and to give his life a ransom for many.

Offertory. Ps. 25, 1-3. Unto thee, O Lord, will I lift up my soul: my God, I have put my trust in thee, O let me not be confounded: neither let mine enemies triumph over me: for all they that hope in thee shall not be ashamed.

Secret.

O LORD, mercifully regard the sacrifices which we offer unto thee: and by this holy Communion absolve us from the bonds of our sins. Through.

Preface of Lent.

Communion. Ps. 11, 8. The righteous Lord loveth righteousness: his countenance will behold the thing that is just.

Postcommunion.

WE beseech thee, O Lord: that we who have here received thy holy sacraments; may thereby grow and increase toward the attainment of eternal redemption. Through.

Over the people:

Let us pray. Humble your heads before God.

Collect.

O GOD, the restorer and lover of innocency, direct unto thyself the hearts of us thy servants: that being kindled with the fire of thy spirit, we may be found steadfast in faith, and effectually given to all good works. Through.

Thursday

Station at St. Mary beyond the Tiber

Introit. Ps. 70, 2-3. Deus in adjutorium.

HASTE thee, O God, to deliver me: make haste to help me, O Lord: let mine enemies be ashamed and confounded that seek after my soul. Ps. ibid., 4. Let them be turned backward and put to confusion: that wish me evil. ℣. Glory.

Collect.

GRANT to us, Lord, we beseech thee, the help of thy grace; that we, being devoutly given to fasting and prayer, may be delivered from all enemies of body and soul. Through.

The Lesson from the Prophet Jeremiah.
Jer. 17, 5-10.

THUS saith the Lord God: Cursed be the man that trusteth in man, and maketh flesh his arm, and whose heart departeth from the Lord. For he shall be like the heath in the desert, and shall not see when good cometh: but shall inhabit the parched places in the wilderness, in a salt land and not inhabited. Blessed is the man that trusteth in the Lord, and whose hope the Lord is. For he shall be as a tree planted by the waters, and that spreadeth out her roots by the river: and shall not see when heat cometh. But her leaf shall be green, and shall not be careful in the year of drought, neither shall cease from yielding fruit. The heart is deceitful above all things, and desperately wicked: who can know it? I the Lord search the heart, I try the reins: even to give every man according to his ways, and according to the fruit of his doings: saith the Lord almighty.

Gradual. Ps. 79, 9-10. Be merciful unto our sins, O Lord: wherefore do the heathen say: Where is now their God? ℣. Help us, O God of our salvation: and for the glory of thy name, O Lord, deliver us.

The Friday after the Second Sunday in Lent

✠ The Continuation of the holy Gospel according to Luke.

Luke 16, 19-31.

AT that time: Jesus said unto the Pharisees: There was a certain rich man, which was clothed in purple and fine linen: and fared sumptuously every day. And there was a certain beggar named Lazarus, which was laid at his gate, full of sores, and desiring to be fed with the crumbs which fell from the rich man's table: moreover the dogs came and licked his sores. And it came to pass, that the beggar died, and was carried by the Angels into Abraham's bosom. The rich man also died, and was buried. And in hell he lift up his eyes, being in torments, and seeth Abraham afar off, and Lazarus in his bosom: and he cried and said: Father Abraham, have mercy on me, and send Lazarus, that he may dip the tip of his finger in water, and cool my tongue, for I am tormented in this flame. But Abraham said: Son, remember that thou in thy lifetime receivedst thy good things, and likewise Lazarus evil things: but now he is comforted, and thou art tormented. And beside all this, between us and you there is a great gulf fixed: so that they which would pass from hence to you cannot, neither can they pass to us, that would come from thence. Then he said: I pray thee therefore, father, that thou wouldest send him to my father's house. For I have five brethren, that he may testify unto them, lest they also come into this place of torment. Abraham saith unto him: They have Moses and the Prophets: let them hear them. And he said: Nay, father Abraham: but if one went unto them from the dead, they will repent. And he said unto him: If they hear not Moses and the Prophets, neither will they be persuaded, though one rose from the dead.

Offertory. Exod. 11, 13-14. Moses besought the Lord his God, and said: Lord, why doth thy wrath wax hot against thy people? turn from thy fierce wrath: remember Abraham, Isaac, and Jacob, to whom thou swarest to give a land flowing with milk and honey. And the Lord repented of the evil which he thought to do unto his people.

Secret.

LET the fast which we have dedicated to the honour of thy name, O Lord, by this present sacrifice sanctify us in thy sight: that this profession of our outward observance may inwardly work in us to good effect. Through.

Preface of Lent.

Communion. John 6, 57. He that eateth my flesh, and drinketh my blood, dwelleth in me, and I in him, saith the Lord.

Postcommunion.

WE beseech thee, O Lord, that we thy servants, never failing of the succour of thy grace, may be devoutly given to thy holy service and stablished by thy continual help. Through.

Over the people:

Let us pray.   Humble your heads before God.

Collect.

ASSIST, O Lord, thy servants, and grant the perpetual bounty of thy lovingkindness to them that call upon thee: that forasmuch as we do glory in thee our author and our governor, we may be united and restored by thee, and evermore preserved in that state to which thou dost restore us. Through.

Friday

Station at St. Vitalis

Introit. Ps. 17, 15. Ego autem.

AS for me, I will behold thy presence in righteousness: and when I awake up after thy likeness, I shall be satisfied with it. Ps. ibid., 1. Hear the right, O Lord: consider my complaint. ℣. Glory.

The Friday after the Second Sunday in Lent

Collect.

GRANT, we beseech thee, almighty God: that we may in such wise be cleansed by this holy time of fasting, that we may with pure hearts and minds approach the coming feast. Through.

The Lesson from the book Genesis.
Gen. 37, 6-22.

IN those days: Joseph said unto his brethren: Hear, I pray you, this dream which I have dreamed: For, behold, we were binding sheaves in the field: and, lo, my sheaf arose, and also stood upright, and, behold, your sheaves stood round about, and made obeisance to my sheaf. And his brethren said to him: Shalt thou indeed reign over us? or shalt thou indeed have dominion over us? And they hated him the more for his dreams, and for his words. And he dreamed yet another dream, and told it to his brethren, and said: Behold, I have dreamed a dream more, and, behold, the sun and the moon and the eleven stars made obeisance to me. And he told it to his father, and to his brethren: and his father rebuked him, and said unto him: What is this dream that thou hast dreamed? Shall I and thy mother and thy brethren indeed come to bow down ourselves to thee to the earth? And his brethren envied him: but his father observed the saying. And his brethren went to feed their father's flock in Shechem, and Israel said unto Joseph: Do not thy brethren feed the flock in Shechem? come, and I will send thee unto them. And he said to him: Here am I, and he said to him: Go, I pray thee, see whether it be well with thy brethren, and well with the flocks: and bring me word again. So he sent him out of the vale of Hebron, and he came to Shechem: and a certain man found him, and, behold, he was wandering in the field, and the man asked him, saying: What seekest thou? And he said, I seek my brethren: tell me, I pray thee, where they feed their flocks. And the man said: They are departed hence; for I heard them say: Let us go to Dothan. And Joseph went after his brethren, and found them in Dothan. And when they saw him afar off, even before he came near unto them, they conspired against him to slay him, and they said one to another: Behold, this dreamer cometh: come now therefore, and let us slay him, and cast him into some pit, and we will say: Some evil beast hath devoured him: and we shall see what will become of his dreams. And Reuben heard it, and he delivered him out of their hands, and said: Let us not kill him. And Reuben said unto them: Shed no blood: but cast him into this pit that is in the wilderness, and lay no hand upon him: that he might rid him out of their hands, to deliver him to his father again.

Gradual. Ps. 120, 1-2. When I was in trouble I called upon the Lord, and he heard me. ℣. Deliver my soul, O Lord, from lying lips: and from a deceitful tongue.

Tract. Ps. 103, 10. O Lord, deal not with us after our sins: nor reward us according to our wickednesses. ℣. Ps. 79, 8-9. O Lord, remember not our old sins: but have mercy upon us, and that soon, for we are come to great misery. (Here genuflect) ℣. Help us, O God of our salvation: and for the glory of thy name, O Lord, deliver us: and be merciful unto our sins, for thy name's sake.

✠ The Continuation of the holy Gospel according to Matthew.
Matt. 21, 33-46.

AT that time: Jesus spake this parable unto the multitudes of the Jews and the chief priests: There was a certain householder, which planted a vineyard, and hedged it round about, and digged a winepress in it, and built a tower, and let it out to husbandmen, and went into a far country. And when the time of the fruit drew near, he sent his servants to the husbandmen, that they might receive the fruits of it. And the husbandmen took his servants, and beat one, and killed another, and stoned another. Again, he sent other servants more than the first, and they did unto them likewise. But last of all he sent unto them his son, saying: They will reverence my son. But when the husbandmen saw the son, they said among themselves: This is the heir, come, let us kill him, and let us seize on his inheritance. And they caught him, and cast him out of the vineyard, and slew him. When the lord therefore of the vineyard cometh, what will he do unto those husbandmen? They say unto him: He will miserably destroy those wicked men, and will let out his vineyard unto other husbandmen, which shall render him the fruits in their seasons. Jesus said unto them: Did ye never read in the Scriptures: The stone which the builders rejected, the same is become the head of the corner? this is the Lord's doing, and it is marvellous in our eyes. Therefore say I unto you, The kingdom of God shall be taken from you, and given to a nation bringing forth the fruits thereof. And whosoever shall fall on this stone shall be broken: but on whomsoever it shall fall, it will grind him to powder. And when the chief priests and Pharisees had heard his parables, they perceived that he spake of them. But when they sought to lay hands on him, they feared the multitude: because they took him for a Prophet.

Offertory. Ps. 40, 14-15. Make haste, O Lord, to help me: let them be ashamed, and confounded, that seek after my soul to destroy it: make haste, O Lord, to help me.

Secret.

MAY this sacrifice, O God, continually work in us to good effect, and be strengthened in the power of its operation. Through.

Preface of Lent.

Communion. Ps. 12, 8. Thou shalt keep us, O Lord: thou shalt preserve us from this generation for ever.

Postcommunion.

O LORD, who hast bestowed on us this pledge of salvation: grant us, we beseech thee, so to walk worthily of the same, that we may attain unto the fulfilment thereof in everlasting life. Through.

Over the people:

Let us pray. Humble your heads before God.

Collect.

KEEP, we beseech thee, O Lord, thy people, both outwardly in their bodies and inwardly in their souls: that they cleaving steadfastly to all good works, may ever be defended by thy mighty power. Through.

Saturday

Station at SS. Marcellinus and Peter

Introit. Ps. 19, 8. Lex Domini.

THE law of the Lord is an undefiled law, converting the soul: the testimony of the Lord is sure, and giveth wisdom unto the simple. Ps. ibid., 2. The heavens declare the glory of God: and the firmament sheweth his handy-work. ℣. Glory.

Collect.

GRANT, we beseech thee, O Lord, that this our fast may so work in us to good effect: that we, who now do submit ourselves to the chastening of the flesh, may be profited thereby to the quickening of our souls. Through.

The Lesson from the book Genesis.

Gen. 27, 6-40.

IN those days: Rebekah spake unto Jacob her son, saying: Behold, I heard thy father speak unto Esau thy brother, saying: Bring me venison, and make me savoury meat, that I may eat, and bless thee before the Lord before my death. Now therefore, my son, obey my voice according to that which I command thee: go now to the flock, and fetch me from thence two good kids of the goats, and I will make them savoury meat for thy father, such as he loveth: and thou shalt bring it to thy father, that he may eat, and that he may bless thee before his death. And Jacob said to Rebekah his mother: Behold, Esau my brother is a hairy man, and I am a smooth man: my father peradventure will feel me, and I shall seem to him as a deceiver, and I shall bring a curse upon me, and not a blessing. And his mother said unto him: Upon me be thy curse, my son: only obey my voice, and go fetch me them. And he went, and fetched, and brought them to his mother. And his mother made savoury meat, such as his father loved. And Rebekah took goodly raiment of her eldest son Esau, which were with her in the house, and put them upon Jacob her younger son: and she put the skins of the kids of the goats upon his hands, and upon the smooth of his neck. And she gave the savoury meat and the bread, which she had prepared, into the hand of her son Jacob. And he came unto his father, and said: My father. And he said: Here am I. Who art thou, my son? And Jacob said unto his father: I am Esau thy firstborn: I have done according as thou badest me: arise, I pray thee, sit and eat of my venison, that thy soul may bless me. And Isaac said unto his son: How is it that thou hast found it so quickly, my son? and he said: Because the Lord thy God brought it to me. And Isaac said unto Jacob: Come near, I pray thee, that I may feel thee, my son, whether thou be my very son Esau or not. And Jacob went near unto Isaac his father, and he felt him, and said: The voice is Jacob's voice, but the hands are the hands of Esau. And he discerned him not, because his hands were hairy, as his brother Esau's hand. So he blessed him, and he said: Art thou my very son Esau? And he said: I am. And he said: Bring it near to me, and I will eat of my son's venison, that my soul may bless thee. And he brought it near to him, and he did eat, and he brought him wine, and he drank. And his father Isaac said unto him: Come near now, and kiss me, my son. And he came near, and kissed him. And he smelled the smell of his raiment, and blessed him, and said: See, the smell of my son is as the smell of a field which the Lord hath blessed. Therefore God give thee of the dew of heaven, and the fatness of the earth, and plenty of corn and wine. Let people serve thee, and nations bow down to thee: be lord over thy brethren, and let thy mother's sons bow down to thee. Cursed be every one that curseth thee: and blessed be he that blesseth thee. And it came to pass, as soon as Isaac had made an end of blessing Jacob, and Jacob was yet scarce gone out from the presence of Isaac his father, that Esau his brother came in from his hunting, and he also had made savoury meat, and brought it unto his father, and said unto his father: Let my father arise, and eat of his son's venison, that thy soul may bless me. And Isaac his father said unto him: Who art thou? And he said: I am thy son, thy firstborn Esau. And Isaac trembled very exceedingly, and said: Who? where is he that hath taken venison, and brought it me, and I have eaten of all before thou camest? And I have blessed him, yea, and he shall be blessed. And when Esau heard the words of his father, he cried with a great and exceeding bitter cry, and said unto his father: Bless me, even me also, O my father. And he said: Thy brother came with subtilty, and hath taken away thy blessing. And he said: Is not he rightly named Jacob? for he hath supplanted me these two times: he took away my birthright, and, behold, now he hath taken away my blessing. And he said: Hast thou not reserved a blessing for me? And Isaac answered and said unto Esau: Behold, I have made him thy lord, and all his brethren have I given to him for servants: and with corn and wine have I sustained him, and what shall I do now unto thee, my son? And Esau said unto his father: Hast thou but one blessing, my father? bless me, even me also, O my father. And Esau lifted up his voice, and wept, and Isaac his father answered and said unto him: Behold, thy dwelling shall be the fatness of the earth, and of the dew of heaven from above.

Gradual. Ps. 92, 2-3. It is a good thing to give thanks unto the Lord: and to sing praises unto thy name, O most Highest. ℣. To tell of thy loving-kindness early in the morning: and of thy truth in the night-season.

✠ The Continuation of the holy Gospel according to Luke.

Luke 15, 11-32.

AT that time: Jesus spake this parable unto the scribes and Pharisees: A certain man had two sons: and the younger of them said to his father: Father, give me the portion of goods that falleth to me. And he divided unto them his living. And not many days after the younger son gathered all together, and took his journey into a far country, and there wasted his substance with riotous living. And when he had spent all, there arose a mighty famine in that land, and he began to be in want. And he went and joined himself to a citizen of that country. And he sent him into his fields to feed swine. And he would fain have filled his belly with the husks that the swine did eat: and no man gave unto him. And when he came to himself, he said: How many hired servants of my father's have bread enough and to spare, and I perish with hunger? I will arise and go to my father, and will say unto him: Father, I have sinned against heaven, and before thee: and am no more worthy to be called thy son: make me as one of thy hired servants. And he arose, and came to his father. But when he was yet a great way off, his father saw him, and had compassion and ran, and fell on his neck, and kissed him. And the son said unto him: Father, I have sinned against heaven, and in thy sight, and am no more worthy to be called thy son. But the father said to his servants: Bring forth the best robe, and put it on him, and put a ring on his hand, and shoes on his feet: and bring hither the fatted calf, and kill it, and let us eat, and be merry, for this my son was dead, and is alive again: he was lost, and is found. And they began to be merry. Now his elder son was in the field: and as he came and drew nigh to the house, he heard musick and dancing: and he called one of the servants, and asked what these things meant. And he said unto him: Thy brother is come, and thy father hath killed the fatted calf, because he hath received him safe and sound. And he was angry, and would not go in. Therefore came his father out, and intreated him. And he answering said to his father: Lo, these many years do I serve thee, neither transgressed I at any time thy commandment: and yet thou never gavest me a kid, that I might make merry with my friends: but as soon as this thy son was come, which hath devoured thy living with harlots, thou hast killed for him the fatted calf. And he said unto him: Son, thou art ever with me, and all that I have is thine: it was meet that we should make merry, and be glad, for this thy brother was dead, and is alive again: and was lost, and is found.

Offertory. Ps. 13, 4-5. Lighten mine eyes, that I sleep not in death: lest mine enemy say: I have prevailed against him.

The Third Sunday in Lent

Secret.

WE beseech thee, O Lord, mercifully to accept these sacrifices: and grant that we who pray to be absolved from our own offences may not be burdened with the sins of other men. Through.

Preface of Lent.

Communion. Luke 15, 32. Son, it is meet that thou shouldest be glad, for this thy brother was dead, and is alive again: and was lost, and is found.

Postcommunion.

LET this heavenly Sacrament, O Lord, which we have here received: in such wise possess our inmost hearts; that we may be partakers of the grace and power of the same. Through.

Over the people:

Let us pray. Humble your heads before God.

Collect.

O LORD, we beseech thee to keep thy household continually in thy true religion: that they who do lean only upon the hope of thy heavenly grace may evermore be defended by thy heavenly protection. Through Jesus Christ thy Son our Lord: Who liveth and reigneth with thee.

The Third Sunday in Lent

1st class.   Double of 1st class.

Station at St. Lawrence without the Walls

Introit. Ps. 25, 15-16. Oculi mei.

MINE eyes are ever looking unto the Lord: for he shall pluck my feet out of the net: look thou upon me and have mercy upon me, for I am desolate, and in misery. Ps. ibid., 1-2. Unto thee, O Lord, do I lift up my soul; my God, in thee have I trusted: let me not be confounded. ℣. Glory.

Collect.

WE beseech thee, almighty God, look upon the hearty desires of thy humble servants: and stretch forth the right hand of thy majesty, to be our defence against all our enemies. Through. Amen.

The Lesson from the Epistle of blessed Paul the Apostle to the Ephesians.

Ephes. 5, 1-9.

BRETHREN: Be ye followers of God, as dear children: and walk in love, as Christ also hath loved us, and hath given himself for us, an offering and a sacrifice to God for a sweet-smelling savour. But fornication, and all uncleanness, or covetousness, let it not be once named amongst you, as becometh saints: neither filthiness, nor foolish-talking, nor jesting, which are not convenient: but rather giving of thanks. For this ye know, that no whoremonger, nor unclean person, nor covetous man, who is an idolater, hath any inheritance in the kingdom of Christ, and of God. Let no man deceive you with vain words: for because of these things cometh the wrath of God upon the children of disobedience. Be not ye therefore partakers with them. For ye were sometimes darkness: but now are ye light in the Lord. Walk as children of light: for the fruit of the Spirit is in all goodness, and righteousness, and truth:*

Proving what is acceptable unto the Lord. And have no fellowship with the unfruitful works of darkness, but rather reprove them: for it is a shame even to speak of those things which are done of them in secret. But all things that are reproved are made manifest by the light: for whatsoever doth make manifest is light. Wherefore he saith, Awake, thou that sleepest, and arise from the dead, and Christ shall give thee light.

The Third Sunday in Lent

Gradual. Ps. 9, 20 and 4. Up, Lord, and let not man have the upper hand: let the heathen be judged in thy sight. ℣. While mine enemies are driven back: they shall fall and perish at thy presence.

Tract. Ps. 123, 1-3. Unto thee lift I up mine eyes: O thou that dwellest in the heavens. ℣. Behold, even as the eyes of servants: look unto the hand of their masters. ℣. And as the eyes of a maiden unto the hand of her mistress: even so our eyes wait upon the Lord our God, until he have mercy upon us. ℣. Have mercy upon us, O Lord: have mercy upon us.

☩ The Continuation of the holy Gospel according to Luke.

Luke 11, 14-28.

AT that time: Jesus was casting out a devil, and it was dumb. And it came to pass, when the devil was gone out, the dumb spake, and the people wondered. But some of them said: He casteth out devils through Beelzebub, the chief of the devils. And others, tempting him, sought of him a sign from heaven. But he, knowing their thoughts, said unto them: Every kingdom divided against itself is brought to desolation, and a house divided against a house falleth. If Satan also be divided against himself, how shall his kingdom stand? because ye say, that I cast out devils through Beelzebub. And if I by Beelzebub cast out devils: by whom do your sons cast them out? Therefore shall they be your judges. But if I with the finger of God cast out devils: no doubt the kingdom of God is come upon you. When a strong man armed keepeth his palace, his goods are in peace. But when a stronger than he shall come upon him, and overcome him, he taketh from him all his armour wherein he trusted, and divideth his spoils. He that is not with me is against me: and he that gathereth not with me scattereth. When the unclean spirt is gone out of a man, he walketh through dry places, seeking rest: and finding none, he saith: I will return unto my house whence I came out. And when he cometh, he findeth it swept and garnished. Then goeth he and taketh to him seven other spirits more wicked than himself, and they enter in, and dwell there. And the last state of that man is worse than the first. And it came to pass, as he spake these things: a certain woman of the company lift up her voice, and said unto him: Blessed is the womb that bare thee, and the paps which thou hast sucked. But he said: Yea rather, blessed are they that hear the word of God and keep it. Creed.

Offertory. Ps. 19, 9-12. The statutes of the Lord are right, and rejoice the heart; his judgments also are sweeter than honey and the honey-comb: moreover, thy servant keepeth them.

Secret.

WE beseech thee, O Lord, that this oblation may cleanse us from our sins: and sanctify thy servants both in body and soul for the celebration of this sacrifice. Through.

Preface of Lent.

Communion. Ps. 84, 4-5. The sparrow hath found her an house, and the swallow a nest, where she may lay her young: even thy altars, O Lord of hosts, my King and my God; blessed are they that dwell in thy house: they will be alway praising thee.

Postcommunion.

O LORD, who sufferest us to be partakers of thy wondrous mysteries: we beseech thee, that by thy mercy we may be absolved from all our iniquities, and defended against all dangers. Through.

Monday

Station at St. Mark

Introit. Ps. 56, 11. In Deo.

IN God's word will I rejoice; in the Lord's word will I comfort me; yea, in God will I put my trust: I will not be afraid what man can do unto me. Ps. ibid., 1. Be merciful unto me, O God, for man goeth about to devour me: he is daily fighting, and troubling me. ℣. Glory.

Collect.

WE beseech thee, O Lord, mercifully to pour thy grace into our hearts: that as we do abstain from carnal feastings; so we may inwardly refrain ourselves from all wantonness that may hurt the soul. Through.

The Lesson from the book of the Kings.

II Kings 5, 1-15.

IN those days: Naaman, captain of the host of the king of Syria, was a great man with his master, and honourable: because by him the Lord had given deliverance unto Syria: he was also a mighty man in valour, but he was a leper. And the Syrians had gone out by companies, and had brought away captive out of the land of Israel a little maid, and she waited on Naaman's wife, and she said unto her mistress: Would God my lord were with the Prophet that is in Samaria: for he would recover him of his leprosy. And one went in, and told his lord, saying: Thus and thus said the maid that is of the land of Israel. And the king of Syria said: Go to, go, and I will send a letter unto the king of Israel. And he departed, and took with him ten talents of silver, and six thousand pieces of gold, and ten changes of raiment, and he brought the letter to the king of Israel, saying: Now when this letter is come unto thee, behold, I have therewith sent Naaman my servant to thee, that thou mayest recover him of his leprosy. And it came to pass, when the king of Israel had read the letter, that he rent his clothes, and said: Am I God, to kill and to make alive, that this man doth send unto me to recover a man of his leprosy? wherefore consider, I pray you, and see how he seeketh a quarrel against me. And it was so, when Elisha the man of God had heard that the king of Israel had rent his clothes, that he sent to the king, saying: Wherefore hast thou rent thy clothes? let him come now to me, and he shall know that there is a prophet in Israel. So Naaman came with his horses and with his chariot, and stood at the door of the house of Elisha: and Elisha sent a messenger unto him, saying: Go and wash in Jordan seven times, and thy flesh shall come again to thee, and thou shalt be clean. But Naaman was wroth, and went away, and said: Behold, I thought, He will surely come out to me, and stand, and call on the name of the Lord his God, and strike his hand over the place, and recover the leper. Are not Abana and Pharpar, rivers of Damascus, better than all the waters of Israel, may I not wash in them, and be clean? So he turned and went away in a rage, and his servants came near, and spake unto him, and said: My father, if the Prophet had bid thee do some great thing, wouldest thou not have done it: how much rather then, when he saith to thee: Wash, and be clean? Then went he down, and dipped himself seven times in Jordan, according to the saying of the man of God, and his flesh came again like unto the flesh of a little child, and he was clean. And he returned to the man of God, he and all his company, and came, and stood before him, and he said: Behold, now I know that there is no God in all the earth, but in Israel.

Gradual. Ps. 56, 9 and 2. Thou, O God, tellest my flittings: put my tears into thy bottle. ℣. Be merciful unto me, O God, for man goeth about to devour me: he is daily fighting, and troubling me.

Tract. Ps. 103, 10. O Lord, deal not with us after our sins: nor reward us according to our wickednesses. ℣. Ps. 79, 8-9. O Lord, remember not our old sins: but have mercy upon us, and that soon, for we are come to great misery. (Here genuflect) ℣. Help us, O God of our salvation: and for the glory of thy name, O Lord, deliver us: and be merciful unto our sins, for thy name's sake.

✠ The Continuation of the holy Gospel according to Luke.

Luke 4, 23-30.

AT that time: Jesus said unto the Pharisees: Ye will surely say unto me this proverb: Physician, heal thyself: whatsoever we have heard done in Capernaum, do also here in thy country. And he said: Verily I say unto you, No prophet is accepted in his own country. But I tell you of a truth, many widows were in Israel in the days of Elias, when the heaven was shut up three years and six months, when great famine was throughout all the land: but unto none of them was Elias sent, save unto Sarepta, a city of Sidon, unto a woman that was a widow. And many lepers were in Israel in the time of Eliseus the Prophet: and none of them was cleansed, saving Naaman the Syrian. And all they in the synagogue, when they heard these things, were filled with wrath, and rose up, and thrust him out of the city: and led him unto the brow of the hill whereon their city was built, that they might cast him down headlong. But he passing through the midst of them went his way.

Offertory. Ps. 55, 2-3. Hear my prayer, O God: and hide not thyself from my petition: take heed unto me, and hear me.

Secret.

MAY this oblation, which we thy servants offer unto thee, O Lord, be made by thee a Sacrament effectual unto our salvation. Through.

Preface of Lent.

Communion. Ps. 14, 7. Who shall give salvation unto Israel out of Sion? When the Lord turneth the captivity of his people, then shall Jacob rejoice, and Israel shall be glad.

Postcommunion.

GRANT, we beseech thee, almighty and merciful God: that those things which we have taken with our outward lips; we may inwardly receive in purity of heart. Through.

Over the people:

Let us pray. Humble your heads before God.

Collect.

LET thy merciful kindness, O Lord, be upon us: that whereas through our sins and wickedness we are sore beset by many and great dangers, we may be found worthy to be defended from the same by thy protection and preserved by thy deliverance. Through.

Tuesday

Station at St. Pudentiana

Introit. Ps. 17, 6 and 8. Ego clamavi.

I HAVE called upon thee, O God, for thou hast heard me: incline thine ear to me, and hearken unto my words: keep me, O Lord, as the apple of an eye: hide me under the shadow of thy wings. Ps. ibid., 1. Hear the right, O Lord: consider my complaint. ℣. Glory.

Collect.

GRACIOUSLY hear us, almighty and merciful God: and of thy great goodness grant us the gift of continence unto our salvation. Through.

The Lesson from the book of the Kings.

II Kings 4, 1-7.

IN those days: There cried a certain woman unto the Prophet Elisha, saying: Thy servant my husband is dead, and thou knowest that thy servant did fear the Lord: and the creditor is come to take unto him my two sons to be bondmen. And Elisha said unto her: What shall I do for thee? Tell me, what hast thou in the house? And she said: Thine handmaid hath not any thing in the house, save a pot of oil. Then he said: Go, borrow thee vessels abroad of all thy neighbours, even empty vessels, borrow not a few. And when thou art come in, thou shalt shut the door upon thee and upon thy sons: and shalt pour out into all those vessels: and thou shalt set aside that which is full. So she went from him, and shut the door upon her and upon her sons: who brought the vessels to her, and she poured out. And it came to pass, when the vessels were full, that she said unto her son: Bring me yet a vessel. And he said unto her: There is not a vessel more. And the oil stayed. Then she came and told the man of God. And he said: Go, sell the oil, and pay thy debt: and live thou and thy children of the rest.

Gradual. Ps. 19, 13-14. Cleanse thou me, O Lord, from my secret faults: keep thy servant also from presumptuous sins. V. Lest they get the dominion over me, so shall I be undefiled: and innocent from the great offence.

☩ The Continuation of the holy Gospel according to Matthew.

Matt. 18, 15-22.

AT that time: Jesus said unto his disciples: If thy brother shall trespass against thee, go and tell him his fault between thee and him alone. If he shall hear thee, thou hast gained thy brother. But if he will not hear thee, then take with thee one or two more, that in the mouth of two or three witnesses every word may be established. And if he shall neglect to hear them: tell it unto the church. But if he neglect to hear the church: let him be unto thee as an heathen man and a publican. Verily I say unto you, Whatsoever ye shall bind on earth shall be bound in heaven: and whatsoever ye shall loose on earth shall be loosed in heaven. Again I say unto you, That if two of you shall agree on earth as touching any thing that they shall ask, it shall be done for them of my Father which is in heaven. For where two or three are gathered together in my name, there am I in the midst of them. Then came Peter to him, and said: Lord, how oft shall my brother sin against me, and I forgive him? till seven times? Jesus saith unto him: I say not unto thee, Until seven times, but, Until seventy times seven.

Offertory. Ps. 118, 16-17. The right hand of the Lord bringeth mighty things to pass: the right hand of the Lord hath exalted me. I shall not die, but live: and declare the works of the Lord.

Secret.

WE beseech thee, O Lord, that this Sacrament may effectually accomplish in us the work of our redemption: that we, being delivered from the lusts of the flesh, may attain to thy gift of everlasting salvation. Through.

Preface of Lent.

Communion. Ps. 15, 1-2. Lord, who shall dwell in thy tabernacle? or who shall rest upon thy holy hill? Even he, that leadeth an uncorrupt life, and doeth the thing which is right.

Postcommunion.

O LORD, who hast cleansed us by these sacred mysteries: we beseech thee, that we may obtain of thy mercy pardon and grace. Through.

The Wednesday after the Third Sunday in Lent

Over the people:
Let us pray. Humble your heads before God.

Collect.

DEFEND us, O Lord, with thy protection: and evermore keep us from all iniquity. Through.

Wednesday
Station at St. Xystus

Introit. Ps. 31, 7-8. Ego autem.

MY trust hath been in the Lord: I will be glad, and rejoice in thy mercy: for thou hast considered my trouble. Ps. ibid., 2. In thee, O Lord, have I put my trust: let me never be put to confusion, deliver me in thy righteousness and save me. ℣. Glory.

Collect.

GRANT to us, we beseech thee, O Lord: that we, being taught by fasting in the way of salvation, and likewise abstaining from all vices that may hurt the soul, may more readily obtain the pardon of thy loving-kindness. Through.

The Lesson from the book Exodus.
Exod. 20, 12-24.

THUS saith the Lord God: Honour thy father and thy mother: that thy days may be long upon the land which the Lord thy God giveth thee. Thou shalt not kill. Thou shalt not commit adultery. Thou shalt not steal. Thou shalt not bear false witness against thy neighbour. Thou shalt not covet thy neighbour's house: thou shalt not covet thy neighbour's wife, nor his manservant, nor his maidservant, nor his ox, nor his ass, nor any thing that is thy neighbour's. And all the people saw the thunderings, and the lightnings, and the noise of the trumpet, and the mountain smoking: and when the people saw it, they removed, and stood afar off, and they said unto Moses: Speak thou with us, and we will hear: but let not God speak with us, lest we die. And Moses said unto the people: Fear not: for God is come to prove you, and that his fear may be before your faces, that ye sin not. And the people stood afar off. And Moses drew near unto the thick darkness where God was. And the Lord said unto Moses: Thus thou shalt say unto the children of Israel: Ye have seen that I have talked with you from heaven. Ye shall not make with me gods of silver, neither shall ye make unto you gods of gold. An altar of earth thou shalt make unto me, and shalt sacrifice thereon thy burnt offerings, and thy peace offerings, thy sheep, and thine oxen, in all places where I record my name.

Gradual. Ps. 6, 3-4. Have mercy upon me, O Lord, for I am weak: O Lord, heal me. ℣. For my bones are vexed: my soul also is sore troubled.

Tract. Ps. 103, 10. O Lord, deal not with us after our sins: nor reward us according to our wickednesses. ℣. Ps. 79, 8-9. O Lord, remember not our old sins: but have mercy upon us, and that soon, for we are come to great misery. (Here genuflect) ℣. Help us, O God of our salvation: and for the glory of thy name, O Lord, deliver us: and be merciful unto our sins, for thy name's sake.

✠ The Continuation of the holy Gospel according to Matthew.
Matt. 15, 1-20.

AT that time: There came to Jesus scribes and Pharisees, which were of Jerusalem, saying: Why do thy disciples transgress the tradition of the elders? For they wash not their hands when they eat bread. But he answered and said unto them: Why do ye also transgress the commandment of God by your tradition? For God commanded, saying: Honour thy father and mother. And: He that curseth father or mother, let him die the death. But ye say: Whosoever shall say to his father or his mother: It is a gift, by whatsoever thou mightest be profited by me: and honour not his father or his mother, he shall be free: thus have ye made the commandment of God of none effect by your tradition. Ye hypocrites, well did Esaias prophesy of you, saying: This people draweth nigh unto me with their mouth, and honoureth me with their lips: but their heart is far from me. But in vain they do worship me, teaching for doctrines the commandments of men. And he called the multitude, and said unto them: Hear, and understand. Not that which goeth into the mouth defileth a man: but that which cometh out of the mouth, this defileth a man. Then came his disciples, and said unto him: Knowest thou that the Pharisees were offended, after they heard this saying? But he answered and said: Every plant, which my heavenly Father hath not planted, shall be rooted up. Let them alone: they be blind leaders of the blind. And if the blind lead the blind, both shall fall into the ditch. Then answered Peter and said unto him: Declare unto us this parable. And Jesus said: Are ye also yet without understanding? Do not ye yet understand, that whatsoever entereth in at the mouth goeth into the belly, and is cast out into the draught? But those things which proceed out of the mouth come forth from the heart, and they defile the man: for out of the heart proceed evil thoughts, murders, adulteries, fornications, thefts, false witness, blasphemies. These are the things which defile a man. But to eat with unwashen hands defileth not a man.

Offertory. Ps. 109, 21. Deal thou with me, O Lord, according unto thy name: for sweet is thy mercy.

Secret.

ACCEPT, we beseech thee, O Lord, the prayers of thy people, and the oblation of their sacrifice; and as we celebrate thy mysteries defend us from all perils. Through.

Preface of Lent.

Communion. Ps. 16, 10. Thou hast shewn me the path of life; in thy presence, O Lord, shall be the fulness of joy.

Postcommunion.

SANCTIFY us, O Lord, who have now partaken of thy holy table: that, we being cleansed thereby from all perversities, may be made worthy to obtain thy heavenly promises. Through.

Over the people:

Let us pray. Humble your heads before God.

Collect.

GRANT, we beseech thee, almighty God: that we who seek the grace of thy protection, may by thee be delivered from all evils, and serve thee with a quiet mind. Through.

Thursday

Station at SS. Cosmas and Damian

Introit. Salus populi.

I AM the salvation of the people, saith the Lord: out of whatsoever tribulation they shall cry unto me, I will hear them: and I will be their Lord for ever. Ps. 78, 1. Hear my law, O my people: incline your ears unto the words of my mouth. ℣. Glory.

Collect.

O LORD, who in this solemn festival hast bestowed upon thy blessed Saints Cosmas and Damian everlasting glory, and upon us the assistance of thy unspeakable providence; grant that we may observe the same to the honour of thy name. Through.

The Thursday after the Third Sunday in Lent

The Lesson from the Prophet Jeremiah.

Jer. 7, 1-7.

IN those days: The word of the Lord came unto me, saying: Stand in the gate of the Lord's house: and proclaim there this word, and say: Hear the word of the Lord, all ye of Judah, that enter in at these gates to worship the Lord. Thus saith the Lord of hosts, the God of Israel: Amend your ways and your doings: and I will cause you to dwell in this place. Trust ye not in lying words, saying: The temple of the Lord, The temple of the Lord, The temple of the Lord, are these. For if ye throughly amend your ways and your doings: if ye throughly execute judgment between a man and his neighbour, if ye oppress not the stranger, the fatherless, and the widow, and shed not innocent blood in this place, neither walk after other gods to your hurt: then will I cause you to dwell in this place, in the land that I gave to your fathers, for ever and ever: saith the Lord almighty.

Gradual. Ps. 145, 15-16. The eyes of all wait upon thee, O Lord: and thou givest them their meat in due season. ℣. Thou openest thine hand: and fillest all things living with plenteousness.

✠ The Continuation of the holy Gospel according to Luke.

Luke 4, 38-44.

AT that time: Jesus arose out of the synagogue, and entered into Simon's house. And Simon's wife's mother was taken with a great fever: and they besought him for her. And he stood over her, and rebuked the fever: and it left her. And immediately she arose and ministered unto them. Now when the sun was setting, all they that had any sick with divers diseases brought them unto him. And he laid his hands on every one of them, and healed them. And devils also came out of many, crying out, and saying: Thou art Christ the Son of God; and he rebuking them suffered them not to speak, for they knew that he was Christ. And when it was day, he departed and went into a desert place, and the people sought him, and came unto him, and stayed him, that he should not depart from them. And he said unto them: I must preach the kingdom of God to other cities also: for therefore am I sent. And he preached in the synagogues of Galilee.

Offertory. Ps. 138, 7. Though I walk in the midst of trouble, yet shalt thou refresh me, O Lord: thou shalt stretch forth thy hand upon the furiousness of mine enemies, and thy right hand shall save me.

Secret.

O LORD, who in this sacrifice hast given unto us the beginning of all martyrdom; we offer unto thee the same in honour of the precious death of thy Saints. Through.

Preface of Lent.

Communion. Ps. 119, 4-5. Thou hast charged that we shall diligently keep thy commandments: O that my ways were made so direct, that I might keep thy statutes!

Postcommunion.

GRANT, O Lord, that we who have here received this holy Sacrament, pleading the merits of thy blessed Martyrs, Cosmas and Damian: may obtain thereby the assurance of our everlasting salvation. Through.

Over the people:

Let us pray. Humble your heads before God.

Collect.

WE beseech thee, O Lord, that the abundance of thy heavenly favour may strengthen and increase thy people: and make them ever to walk obediently after thy commandments. Through.

Friday

Station at St. Lawrence in Lucina

Introit. Ps. 86, 17. *Fac mecum.*

SHEW some token upon me, O Lord, for good: that they who hate me may see it, and be ashamed: because thou, Lord, hast holpen me, and comforted me. Ps. ibid., 1. Bow down thine ear, O Lord, and hear me: for I am poor, and in misery. ℣. Glory.

Collect.

ASSIST, O Lord, we beseech thee, this our fasting with thy gracious favour: that like as we do abstain from food in our bodies; so we may fast from sin in our souls. Through.

The Lesson from the book Numbers.

Num. 20, 1-3 and 6-13.

IN those days: The children of Israel gathered themselves together against Moses and against Aaron: and the people chode with Moses, and spake, saying: Give us water to drink. And Moses and Aaron went from the presence of the assembly unto the door of the tabernacle of the congregation, and they fell upon their faces: and the glory of the Lord appeared unto them. And the Lord spake unto Moses, saying: Take the rod, and gather thou the assembly together, thou, and Aaron thy brother, and speak ye unto the rock before their eyes, and it shall give forth his water. And thou shalt bring forth to them water out of the rock, so thou shalt give the congregation and their beasts drink. And Moses took the rod from before the Lord, as he commanded him, and Moses and Aaron gathered the congregation together before the rock, and he said unto them: Hear now, ye rebels: must we fetch you water out of this rock? And Moses lifted up his hand, and with his rod he smote the rock twice, and the water came out abundantly, and the congregation drank, and their beasts also. And the Lord spake unto Moses and Aaron: Because ye believed me not, to sanctify me in the eyes of the children of Israel, therefore ye shall not bring this congregation into the land which I have given them. This is the water of Meribah, because the children of Israel strove with the Lord, and he was sanctified in them.

Gradual. Ps. 28, 7 and 1. My heart hath trusted in God, and I am helped: therefore my heart danceth for joy, and in my song will I praise him. ℣. Unto thee have I cried, O Lord: O my God, keep not still silence, depart not from me.

Tract. Ps. 103, 10. O Lord, deal not with us after our sins: nor reward us according to our wickednesses. ℣. Ps. 79, 8-9. O Lord, remember not our old sins: but have mercy upon us, and that soon, for we are come to great misery. (Here genuflect) ℣. Help us, O God of our salvation: and for the glory of thy name, O Lord, deliver us: and be merciful unto our sins, for thy name's sake.

☩ The Continuation of the holy Gospel according to John.

John 4, 5-42.

AT that time: Jesus cometh to a city of Samaria, which is called Sychar: near to the parcel of ground that Jacob gave to his son Joseph. Now Jacob's well was there. Jesus therefore, being wearied with his journey, sat thus on the well. And it was about the sixth hour. There cometh a woman of Samaria to draw water. Jesus saith unto her: Give me to drink. (For his disciples were gone away unto the city to buy meat.) Then saith the woman of Samaria unto him: How is it that thou, being a Jew, askest drink of me, which am a woman of Samaria? for the Jews have no dealings with the Samaritans. Jesus answered and said unto her: If thou knewest the gift of God, and who it is that saith to thee: Give me to drink: thou wouldest have asked of him, and he would have given thee living water. The woman saith unto him: Sir, thou hast nothing to draw with, and the well is deep: from whence then hast thou that living water? Art thou greater than our father Jacob, which gave us the well, and drank thereof himself, and his children, and his cattle? Jesus answered and said unto her: Whosoever drinketh of this water shall thirst again: but whosoever drinketh of the water that I shall give him shall never thirst: but the water that I shall give him shall be in him a well of water springing up into everlasting life. The woman saith unto him: Sir, give me this water, that I thirst not, neither come hither to draw. Jesus saith unto her: Go, call thy husband, and come hither. The woman answered and said: I have no husband. Jesus said unto her: Thou hast well said, I have no husband: for thou hast had five husbands, and he whom thou now hast is not thy husband: in that saidst thou truly. The woman saith unto him: Sir, I perceive that thou art a Prophet. Our fathers worshipped in this mountain; and ye say, that in Jerusalem is the place where men ought to worship. Jesus saith unto her: Woman, believe me, the hour cometh, when ye shall neither in this mountain, nor yet at Jerusalem, worship the Father. Ye worship ye know not what: we know what we worship: for salvation is of the Jews. But the hour cometh, and now is, when the true worshippers shall worship the Father in spirit and in truth. For the Father seeketh such to worship him. God is a spirit: and they that worship him must worship him in spirit and in truth. The woman saith unto him: I know that Messias cometh, which is called Christ. When he is come, he will tell us all things. Jesus saith unto her: I that speak unto thee am he. And upon this came his disciples: and marvelled that he talked with the woman. Yet no man said: What seekest thou, or, Why talkest thou with her? The woman then left her waterpot, and went her way into the city, and saith to the men: Come, see a man, which told me all things that ever I did: is not this the Christ? Then they went out of the city, and came unto him. In the mean while his disciples prayed him, saying: Master, eat. But he said unto them: I have meat to eat that ye know not of. Therefore said the disciples one to another: Hath any man brought him ought to eat? Jesus saith unto them: My meat is to do the will of him that sent me, and to finish his work. Say not ye, There are yet four months, and then cometh harvest? Behold, I say unto you: Lift up your eyes, and look on the fields, for they are white already to harvest. And he that reapeth receiveth wages, and gathereth fruit unto life eternal: that both he that soweth and he that reapeth may rejoice together. And herein is that saying true: One soweth, and another reapeth. I sent you to reap that whereon ye bestowed no labour: other men laboured, and ye are entered into their labours. And many of the Samaritans of that city believed on him for the saying of the woman, which testified: He told me all that ever I did. So when the Samaritans were come unto him, they besought him that he would tarry with them. And he abode there two days. And many more believed because of his own word. And said unto the woman: Now we believe, not because of thy saying: for we have heard him ourselves, and know that this is indeed the Christ, the Saviour of the world.

Offertory. Ps. 5, 3-4. O hearken thou unto the voice of my calling, my King, and my God: for unto thee, O Lord, will I make my prayer.

Secret.

LOOK favourably, we beseech thee, O Lord, upon the gifts which we consecrate; that they may be pleasing unto thee, and ever be profitable unto us for our salvation. Through.

The Saturday after the Third Sunday in Lent

Preface of Lent.

Communion. John 4, 13-14. Whosoever drinketh of the water that I shall give him, saith the Lord, it shall be in him a well of water springing up into everlasting life.

Postcommunion.

LET this holy Sacrament, O Lord, whereof we have been made partakers, cleanse us from all our sins: and bring us at the last unto thy heavenly kingdom. Through.

Over the people:

Let us pray. Humble your heads before God.

Collect.

GRANT, we beseech thee, almighty God: that we who put our confidence in thy protection may by thy help overcome all things that may hurt us. Through.

Saturday

Station at St. Susanna

Introit. Ps. 5, 1-2. Verba mea.

PONDER my words, O Lord: consider my meditation: O hearken thou unto the voice of my calling, my King, and my God. Ps. ibid., 3. For unto thee will I make my prayer: my voice shalt thou hear betimes, O Lord. ℣. Glory.

Collect.

GRANT, we beseech thee, almighty God: that they who do abstain from food to the mortifying of the flesh; may likewise fast from sin, to the following after righteousness. Through.

The Lesson from the Prophet Daniel.

Dan. 13, 1-9, 15-17, 19-30 and 33-62.

IN those days: There dwelt a man in Babylon, called Joacim: and he took a wife, whose name was Susanna, the daughter of Chelcias, a very fair woman, and one that feared the Lord: her parents also were righteous, and taught their daughter according to the law of Moses. Now Joacim was a great rich man, and had a fair garden joining unto his house: and to him resorted the Jews, because he was more honourable than all others. The same year were appointed two of the ancients of the people to be judges: such as the Lord spake of: That wickedness came from Babylon from ancient judges, who seemed to govern the people. These kept much at Joacim's house, and all that had any suits in law came unto them. Now when the people departed away at noon, Susanna went into her husband's garden to walk. And the two elders saw her going in every day, and walking: so that their lust was inflamed toward her. And they perverted their own mind, and turned away their eyes, that they might not look unto heaven, nor remember just judgments. And it fell out, as they watched a fit time, she went in as before with two maids only, and she was desirous to wash herself in the garden: for it was hot, and there was no body there save the two elders, that had hid themselves, and watched her. Then she said to her maids: Bring me oil and washing balls, and shut the garden doors, that I may wash me. Now when the maids were gone forth, the two elders rose up, and ran unto her, saying: Behold, the garden doors are shut, that no man can see us, and we are in love with thee: therefore consent unto us, and lie with us. If thou wilt not, we will bear witness against thee, that a young man was with thee, and therefore thou didst send away thy maids from thee. Then Susanna sighed, and said: I am straitened on every side: for if I do this thing, it is death unto me: and if I do not, I cannot escape your hands. It is better for me to fall into your hands, and not do it, than to sin in the sight of the Lord. With that Susanna cried with a loud voice: and the two elders cried out against her. Then ran the one, and opened the garden door. So when the servants of the house heard the cry in the garden, they rushed in at a privy door, to see what was done unto her. But when the elders had declared their matter, the servants were greatly ashamed: for there was never such a report made of Susanna. And it came to pass the next day, when the people were assembled to her husband Joacim, the two elders came also full of mischievous imagination against Susanna to put her to death. And said before the people: Send for Susanna, the daughter of Chelcias, Joacim's wife. And so they sent. So she came with her father and mother, her children, and all her kindred. Therefore her friends and all that saw her wept. Then the two elders stood up in the midst of the people, and laid their hands upon her head. And she weeping looked up toward heaven: for her heart trusted in the Lord. And the elders said: As we walked in the garden alone, this woman came in with two maids: and shut the garden doors, and sent the maids away. Then a young man, who there was hid, came unto her, and lay with her. Then we that stood in a corner of the garden, seeing this wickedness, ran unto them. And when we saw them together, the man we could not hold, for he was stronger than we, and opened the door, and leaped out: but having taken this woman, we asked who the young man was, but she would not tell us: these things do we testify. Then the assembly believed them, as those that were the elders and judges of the people, so they condemned her to death. Then Susanna cried out with a loud voice, and said: O everlasting God, that knowest the secrets, and knowest all things before they be, thou knowest that they have borne false witness against me: and, behold, I must die, whereas I never did such things as these men have maliciously invented against me. And the Lord heard her voice. Therefore when she was led to be put to death, the Lord raised up the holy spirit of a young youth, whose name was Daniel. Who cried with a loud voice: I am clear from the blood of this woman. Then all the people turned them toward him, and said: What mean these words that thou hast spoken? So he standing in the midst of them said: Are ye such fools, ye sons of Israel, that without examination or knowledge of the truth ye have condemned a daughter of Israel? Return again to the place of judgment, for they have borne false witness against her. Wherefore all the people turned again in haste. Then said Daniel unto them: Put these two aside one far from another, and I will examine them. So when they were put asunder one from another, he called one of them, and said unto him: O thou that art waxen old in wickedness, now thy sins which thou hast committed aforetime are come to light: for thou hast pronounced false judgment, and hast condemned the innocent, and hast let the guilty go free, albeit the Lord saith: The innocent and righteous shalt thou not slay. Now then, if thou hast seen her, tell me, Under what tree sawest thou them companying together? Who answered: Under a mastick tree. And Daniel said: Very well, thou hast lied against thine own head. For even now the Angel of God hath received the sentence of God to cut thee in two. So he put him aside, and commanded to bring the other, and said unto him: O thou seed of Chanaan, and not of Juda, beauty hath deceived thee, and lust hath perverted thine heart: thus have ye dealt with the daughters of Israel, and they for fear companied with you: but the daughter of Juda would not abide your wickedness. Now therefore tell me, Under what tree didst thou take them companying together? Who answered:

Under an holm tree. Then said Daniel unto him: Well, thou hast also lied against thine own head: for the Angel of God waiteth with the sword to cut thee in two, that he may destroy you. With that all the assembly cried out with a loud voice, and praised God, who saveth them that trust in him. And they arose against the two elders, for Daniel had convicted them of false witness by their own mouth, and they did unto them in such sort as they maliciously intended to do to their neighbour: and they put them to death, thus the innocent blood was saved the same day.

Gradual. Ps. 23, 4. Though I walk through the valley of the shadow of death, I will fear no evil: for thou art with me, O Lord. ℣. Thy rod and thy staff comfort me.

✠ The Continuation of the holy Gospel according to John.

John 8, 1-11.

AT that time: Jesus went unto the mount of Olives: and early in the morning he came again into the temple, and all the people came unto him, and he sat down, and taught them. And the scribes and Pharisees brought unto him a woman taken in adultery: and when they had set her in the midst, they say unto him: Master, this woman was taken in adultery, in the very act. Now Moses in the law commanded us, that such should be stoned. But what sayest thou? This they said, tempting him, that they might have to accuse him. But Jesus stooped down, and with his finger wrote on the ground, as though he heard them not. So when they continued asking him, he lifted up himself, and said unto them: He that is without sin among you, let him first cast a stone at her. And again he stooped down, and wrote on the ground. And they which heard it, being convicted by their own conscience, went out one by one, beginning at the eldest, even unto the last: and Jesus was left alone, and the woman standing in the midst. When Jesus had lifted up himself, and saw none but the woman, he said unto her: Woman, where are those thine accusers? hath no man condemned thee? She said: No man, Lord. And Jesus said unto her: Neither do I condemn thee: Go, and sin no more.

Offertory. Ps. 119, 133. Order my steps in thy word: and so shall no wickedness have dominion over me, O Lord.

Secret.

GRANT, we beseech thee, almighty God: that this oblation of our sacrifice may cleanse our frailty from all evil and evermore defend us. Through.

Preface of Lent.

Communion. John 8, 10-11. Woman, hath no man condemned thee? No man, Lord. Neither do I condemn thee: sin no more.

Postcommunion.

WE beseech thee, almighty God: that we may be made very members incorporate in him, of whose body and blood we are here partakers: Who liveth and reigneth with thee.

Over the people:

Let us pray. Humble your heads before God.

Collect.

STRETCH forth, O Lord, upon thy faithful people the right hand of thy heavenly succour: that they, seeking thee with their whole heart; may be found worthy to obtain those things which they have asked according to thy will. Through.

The Fourth Sunday in Lent

1st class. Double of 1st class.

Station at St. Cross in Jerusalem

Introit. Is. 66, 10-11. Laetare.

REJOICE, O Jerusalem, and come together, all ye that love her; rejoice for joy, all ye that have mourned: that ye may be glad, and be satisfied with the breasts of your consolation. Ps. 122, 1. I was glad when they said unto me: We will go into the house of the Lord. ℣. Glory.

Collect.

GRANT, we beseech thee, almighty God: that we, who for our evil deeds do worthily deserve to be punished, by the comfort of thy grace may mercifully be relieved. Through.

The Lesson from the Epistle of blessed Paul the Apostle to the Galatians.

Gal. 4, 22-31.

BRETHREN: It is written: That Abraham had two sons, the one by a bond maid, the other by a free-woman. But he who was of the bondwoman was born after the flesh: but he of the free-woman was by promise: which things are an allegory. For these are the two covenants. The one from the mount Sinai, which gendereth to bondage: which is Agar: for this Agar is mount Sinai in Arabia, and answereth to Jerusalem which now is, and is in bondage with her children. But Jerusalem which is above is free, which is the mother of us all. For it is written: Rejoice, thou barren that barest not: break forth and cry, thou that travailest not: for the desolate hath many more children than she which hath an husband. Now we, brethren, as Isaac was, are the children of promise. But as then he that was born after the flesh persecuted him that was born after the Spirit: even so it is now. Nevertheless, what saith the Scripture? Cast out the bond-woman and her son: for the son of the bond-woman shall not be heir with the son of the free-woman. So then, brethren, we are not children of the bond-woman, but of the free: by the liberty wherewith Christ hath made us free.

Gradual. Ps. 122, 1 and 7. I was glad when they said unto me: We will go into the house of the Lord. ℣. Peace be within thy walls: and plenteousness within thy palaces.

Tract. Ps. 125, 1-2. They that put their trust in the Lord shall be even as the mount Sion: which may not be removed, but standeth fast for ever. ℣. The hills stand about Jerusalem: even so standeth the Lord round about his people, from this time forth for evermore.

✠ The Continuation of the holy Gospel according to John.

John 6, 1-15.

AT that time: Jesus went over the sea of Galilee, which is the sea of Tiberias: and a great multitude followed him, because they saw his miracles which he did on them that were diseased. And Jesus went up into a mountain, and there he sat with his disciples. And the Passover, a feast of the Jews, was nigh. When Jesus then lift up his eyes, and saw a great company come unto him, he saith unto Philip: Whence shall we buy bread, that these may eat? And this he said to prove him, for he himself knew what he would do. Philip answered him: Two hundred pennyworth of bread is not sufficient for them, that every one of them may take a little. One of his disciples, Andrew, Simon Peter's brother, saith unto him: There is a lad here, which hath five barley-loaves, and two small fishes: but what are they among so many? And Jesus said: Make the men sit down. And there was much grass in the place. So the men sat down, in number about five thousand. And Jesus took the loaves, and when he had given thanks he distributed to the disciples, and the disciples to them that were set down: and likewise of the fishes as much as they would. When they were filled, he said unto his disciples: Gather up the fragments that remain, that nothing be lost. Therefore they gathered them together, and filled twelve baskets with the fragments of the five barley-loaves, which remained over and above unto them that had eaten. Then those men, when they had seen the miracle that Jesus did, said: This is of a truth that Prophet that should come into the world.†

When Jesus therefore perceived that they would come and take him by force, to make him a king, he departed again into a mountain himself alone. Creed.

Offertory. Ps. 135, 3 and 6. O praise the Lord, for he is gracious: O sing praises unto his name, for he is lovely: whatsoever he pleased, that did he in heaven, and in earth.

Secret.

WE beseech thee, O Lord, mercifully to have respect unto these our sacrifices: that they may increase our devotion and set forward our salvation. Through.

Preface of Lent.

Communion. Ps. 122, 3-4. Jerusalem is built as a city, that is at unity in itself: for thither the tribes go up, even the tribes of the Lord, to give thanks unto thy name, O Lord.

Postcommunion.

O MERCIFUL God, who never failest to fulfil us with thy holy mysteries: grant to us, we beseech thee, that we may ever perform them in lowliness and sincerity, and receive them in faithfulness of heart. Through.

Monday

Station at the Four Crowned Saints

Introit. Ps. 54, 1-2. Deus in nomine.

SAVE me, O God, for thy name's sake: and avenge me in thy strength: hear my prayer, O God: and hearken unto the words of my mouth. Ps. ibid., 3. For strangers are risen up against me: and tyrants seek after my soul. ℣. Glory.

Collect.

GRANT, we beseech thee, almighty God: that we, who year by year devoutly keep this holy observance, may be acceptable unto thee both in body and in soul. Through.

The Lesson from the book of the Kings.

I Kings 3, 16-28.

IN those days: Came there two women, that were harlots, unto king Solomon, and stood before him, and the one woman said: O my lord, I and this woman dwell in one house, and I was delivered of a child with her in the house. And it came to pass the third day after that I was delivered, that this woman was delivered also: and we were together, there was no stranger with us in the house, save we two in the house. And this woman's child died in the night: because she overlaid it. And she arose at midnight, and took my son from beside me, while thine handmaid slept, and laid it in her bosom: and laid her dead child in my bosom. And when I rose in the morning to give my child suck, behold, it was dead: but when I had considered it in the morning, behold, it was not my son, which I did bear. And the other woman said: Nay, but the living is my son, and the dead is thy son. And this said: No: but the dead is thy son, and the living is my son. Thus they spake before the king. Then said the king: The one saith: This is my son that liveth, and thy son is dead. And the other saith: Nay, but thy son is the dead, and my son is the living. And the king said: Bring me a sword. And they brought a sword before the king: and the king said: Divide the living child in two, and give half to the one, and half to the other. Then spake the woman whose the living child was unto the king, for her bowels yearned upon her son, and she said: O my lord, give her the living child, and in no wise slay it. But the other said: Let it be neither mine nor thine, but divide it. Then the king answered and said: Give her the living child, and in no wise slay it: she is the mother thereof. And all Israel heard of the judgment which the king had judged, and they feared the king, for they saw that the wisdom of God was in him, to do judgment.

Gradual. Ps. 31, 3. Be thou my strong rock, and house of defence, that thou mayest save me. ℣. Ps. 71, 1. In thee, O God, have I put my trust: let me never be put to confusion, O Lord.

Tract. Ps. 103, 10. O Lord, deal not with us after our sins: nor reward us according to our wickednesses. ℣. Ps. 79, 8-9. O Lord, remember not our old sins: but have mercy upon us, and that soon, for we are come to great misery. (Here genuflect) ℣. Help us, O God of our salvation: and for the glory of thy name, O Lord, deliver us: and be merciful unto our sins, for thy name's sake.

✠ The Continuation of the holy Gospel according to John.

John 2, 13-25.

AT that time: The Jews' passover was at hand, and Jesus went up to Jerusalem: and found in the temple those that sold oxen and sheep and doves, and the changers of money sitting. And when he had made a scourge of small cords, he drove them all out of the temple, and the sheep, and the oxen, and poured out the changers' money, and overthrew the tables. And said unto them that sold doves: Take these things hence, make not my Father's house an house of merchandise. And his disciples remembered that it was written: The zeal of thine house hath eaten me up. Then answered the Jews and said unto him: What sign shewest thou unto us, seeing that thou doest these things? Jesus answered and said unto them: Destroy this temple, and in three days I will raise it up. Then said the Jews: Forty and six years was this temple in building, and wilt thou rear it up in three days? But he spake of the temple of his body. When therefore he was risen from the dead, his disciples remembered that he had said this unto them, and they believed the Scripture, and the word which Jesus had said. Now when he was in Jerusalem at the passover, in the feast day, many believed in his name, when they saw the miracles which he did. But Jesus did not commit himself unto them, because he knew all men, and needed not that any should testify of man: for he knew what was in man.

Offertory. Ps. 100, 1-2. O be joyful in God, all ye lands: serve the Lord with gladness, and come before his presence with a song: for the Lord he is God.

Secret.

MAY this sacrifice which we offer unto thee, O Lord, evermore quicken and defend us. Through.

Preface of Lent.

Communion. Ps. 19, 13-14. Cleanse thou me, O Lord, from my secret faults: keep thy servant also from presumptuous sins.

Postcommunion.

WE beseech thee, O Lord: that we who have here received this Sacrament of our salvation: may thereby grow and increase toward the attainment of eternal redemption. Through.

The Tuesday after the Fourth Sunday in Lent

Over the people:

Let us pray. Humble your heads before God.

Collect.

O LORD, we beseech thee graciously to hear our prayers: and grant that we, to whom thou dost give an hearty desire to pray, may be defended by thy succour. Through.

Tuesday

Station at St. Lawrence in Damaso

Introit. Ps. 55, 2-3. Exaudi.

HEAR my prayer, O God: and hide not thyself from my petition: take heed unto me, and hear me. Ps. ibid., 3-4. I mourn in my prayer, and am vexed: the enemy crieth so, and the ungodly cometh on so fast. ℣. Glory.

Collect.

WE beseech thee, O Lord, that we, devoutly observing this solemn ordinance of fasting; may thereby increase in godliness of conversation, and effectually obtain the continual succour of thy mercy. Through.

The Lesson from the book Exodus.

Exod. 32, 7-14.

IN those days: The Lord spake unto Moses, saying: Go, get thee down from the mount: for thy people, which thou broughtest out of the land of Egypt, have corrupted themselves. They have turned aside quickly out of the way which I commanded them: they have made them a molten calf, and have worshipped it, and have sacrificed thereunto, and said: These be thy gods, O Israel, which have brought thee up out of the land of Egypt. And the Lord said unto Moses: I have seen this people, and, behold, it is a stiffnecked people: now therefore let me alone, that my wrath may wax hot against them, and that I may consume them, and I will make of thee a great nation. And Moses besought the Lord his God, and said: Lord, why doth thy wrath wax hot against thy people, which thou hast brought forth out of the land of Egypt with great power, and with a mighty hand? Wherefore should the Egyptians speak, and say: For mischief did he bring them out, to slay them in the mountains, and to consume them from the face of the earth: turn from thy fierce wrath, and repent of this evil against thy people. Remember Abraham, Isaac, and Israel, thy servants, to whom thou swarest by thine own self, and saidst unto them: I will multiply your seed as the stars of heaven, and all this land that I have spoken of will I give unto your seed, and they shall inherit it for ever. And the Lord repented of the evil which he thought to do unto his people.

Gradual. Ps. 44, 26 and 2. Arise, O Lord, and help us: and deliver us for thy name's sake. ℣. We have heard with our ears, O God: our fathers have told us, what thou hast done in their days and in the days of old.

✠ The Continuation of the holy Gospel according to John.

John 7, 14-31.

AT that time: About the midst of the feast Jesus went up into the temple, and taught. And the Jews marvelled, saying: How knoweth this man letters, having never learned? Jesus answered them, and said: My doctrine is not mine, but his that sent me. If any man will do his will, he shall know of the doctrine, whether it be of God, or whether I speak of myself. He that speaketh of himself seeketh his own glory. But he that seeketh his glory that sent him, the same is true, and no unrighteousness is in him. Did not Moses give you the law: and yet none of you keepeth the law? Why go ye about to kill me? The people answered and said: Thou hast a devil: who goeth about to kill thee? Jesus answered and said unto them: I have done one work, and ye all marvel. Moses therefore gave unto you circumcision (not because it is of Moses, but of the fathers): and ye on the sabbath day circumcise a man. If a man on the sabbath day receive circumcision, that the law of Moses should not be broken: are ye angry at me, because I have made a man every whit whole on the sabbath day? Judge not according to the appearance but judge righteous judgment. Then said some of them of Jerusalem: Is not this he, whom they seek to kill? But, lo, he speaketh boldly, and they say nothing unto him. Do the rulers know indeed that this is the very Christ? Howbeit we know this man whence he is: but when Christ cometh, no man knoweth whence he is. Then cried Jesus in the temple as he taught, saying: Ye both know me, and ye know whence I am, and I am not come of myself, but he that sent me is true, whom ye know not. But I know him, for I am from him, and he hath sent me. Then they sought to take him: but no man laid hands on him, because his hour was not yet come. And many of the people believed on him.

Offertory. Ps. 40, 2-4. I waited patiently for the Lord, and he inclined unto me: and heard my calling: and he hath put a new song in my mouth, even a thanksgiving unto our God.

Secret.

WE beseech thee, O Lord, that this oblation may cleanse us from our sins: and sanctify thy servants both in body and soul, for the celebration of this sacrifice. Through.

Preface of Lent.

Communion. Ps. 20, 6. We will rejoice in thy salvation: and triumph in the name of the Lord our God.

Postcommunion.

LET this holy Sacrament, O Lord, whereof we have been made partakers, cleanse us from all our sins: and bring us in the end to thy heavenly kingdom. Through.

Over the people:

Let us pray.   Humble your heads before God.

Collect.

HAVE mercy, O Lord, upon thy people: and grant that they who are sore vexed by continual tribulations may by the comfort of thy grace be relieved. Through.

Wednesday

Station at St. Paul

Introit. Ezek. 36, 23-26. Cum sanctificatus.

WHEN I shall be sanctified in you, I will gather you out of all countries: then will I sprinkle clean water upon you, and ye shall be clean from all your filthiness: and a new spirit will I put within you. Ps. 34, 1. I will alway give thanks unto the Lord: his praise shall ever be in my mouth. ℣. Glory.

After Kýrie eléison is said Let us pray. Let us bow the knee. ℟. Arise.

Collect.

O GOD, who through fasting dost grant unto the righteous the reward of their godliness, and to sinners the pardon of their offences: have mercy upon us thy humble servants; that we, confessing the sins which we have committed, may obtain of thee the forgiveness of our iniquities. Through.

The Wednesday after the Fourth Sunday in Lent

The Lesson from the Prophet Ezekiel.

Ezek. 36, 23-28.

THUS saith the Lord God: I will sanctify my great name, which was profaned among the heathen, which ye have profaned in the midst of them: and the heathen shall know that I am the Lord, when I shall be sanctified in you before their eyes. For I will take you from among the heathen, and gather you out of all countries, and will bring you into your own land. Then will I sprinkle clean water upon you, and ye shall be clean from all your filthiness, and from all your idols will I cleanse you. A new heart also will I give you, and a new spirit will I put within you: and I will take away the stony heart out of your flesh, and I will give you an heart of flesh. And I will put my spirit within you: and cause you to walk in my statutes, and ye shall keep my judgments, and do them. And ye shall dwell in the land that I gave to your fathers: and ye shall be my people, and I will be your God: saith the Lord almighty.

Gradual. Ps. 34, 12 and 6. Come, ye children, and hearken unto me: I will teach you the fear of the Lord. ℣. Come ye to him, and be enlightened: and your faces shall not be ashamed.

Here is said: ℣. The Lord be with you without Let us bow the knee.

Let us pray. Collect.

GRANT, we beseech thee, almighty God: that we, duly chastening the flesh by this our fast, may inwardly rejoice in holiness of spirit; that, our earthly affections being subdued, we may more readily obtain thy heavenly promises. Through.

The Lesson from the Prophet Isaiah.

Is. 1, 16-19.

THUS saith the Lord God: Wash you, make you clean, put away the evil of your doings from before mine eyes: cease to do evil, learn to do well: seek judgment, relieve the oppressed, judge the fatherless, plead for the widow. Come now, and let us reason together, saith the Lord: though your sins be as scarlet, they shall be as white as snow: though they be red like crimson, they shall be as wool. If ye be willing and obedient, ye shall eat the good of the land: saith the Lord almighty.

Gradual. Ps. 33. 12 and 6. Blessed are the people, whose God is the Lord: and blessed are the folk, that the Lord hath chosen to him to be his inheritance. ℣. By the word of the Lord were the heavens made: and all the hosts of them by the breath of his mouth.

Tract. Ps. 103, 10. O Lord, deal not with us after our sins: nor reward us according to our wickednesses. ℣. Ps. 79, 8-9. O Lord, remember not our old sins: but have mercy upon us, and that soon, for we are come to great misery. (Here genuflect) ℣. Help us, O God of our salvation: and for the glory of thy name, O Lord, deliver us: and be merciful unto our sins, for thy name's sake.

✠ The Continuation of the holy Gospel according to John.

John 9, 1-38.

AT that time: As Jesus passed by, he saw a man which was blind from his birth: and his disciples asked him, saying: Master, who did sin, this man, or his parents, that he was born blind? Jesus answered: Neither hath this man sinned, nor his parents: but that the works of God should be made manifest in him. I must work the works of him that sent me, while it is day: the night cometh, when no man can work. As long as I am in the world, I am the light of the world. When he had thus spoken, he spat on the ground, and made clay of the spittle, and he anointed the eyes of the blind man with the clay, and said unto him: Go, wash in the pool of Siloam, (which is by interpretation, Sent.) He went his way therefore, and washed, and came seeing. The neighbours therefore, and they which before had seen him that he was blind, said: Is not this he that sat and begged? Some said: This is he. Others said: He is like him. But he said: I am he. Therefore said they unto him: How were thine eyes opened? He answered and said: A man that is called Jesus made clay, and anointed mine eyes, and said unto me: Go to the pool of Siloam, and wash. And I went and washed, and I received sight. Then said they unto him: Where is he? He said: I know not. They brought to the Pharisees him that aforetime was blind. And it was the sabbath day when Jesus made the clay, and opened his eyes. Then again the Pharisees also asked him how he had received his sight. He said unto them: He put clay upon mine eyes, and I washed, and do see. Therefore said some of the Pharisees: This man is not of God, because he keepeth not the sabbath day. Others said: How can a man that is a sinner do such miracles? And there was a division among them. They say unto the blind man again: What sayest thou of him, that he hath opened thine eyes? He said: He is a Prophet. But the Jews did not believe concerning him, that he had been blind, and received his sight, until they called the parents of him that had received his sight: and they asked them, saying: Is this your son, who ye say was born blind? How then doth he now see? His parents answered them and said: We know that this is our son, and that he was born blind: but by what means he now seeth, we know not: or who hath opened his eyes, we know not: he is of age, ask him, he shall speak for himself. These words spake his parents, because they feared the Jews: for the Jews had agreed already, that if any man did confess that he was Christ, he should be put out of the synagogue. Therefore said his parents: He is of age, ask him. Then again called they the man that was blind, and said unto him: Give God the praise. We know that this man is a sinner. He answered and said: Whether he be a sinner or no, I know not: one thing I know, that, whereas I was blind, now I see. Then said they to him again: What did he to thee? how opened he thine eyes? He answered them: I have told you already, and ye did not hear: wherefore would ye hear it again? Will ye also be his disciples? Then they reviled him, and said: Thou art his disciple: but we are Moses' disciples. We know that God spake unto Moses: as for this fellow, we know not from whence he is. The man answered and said unto them: Why herein is a marvellous thing, that ye know not from whence he is, and yet he hath opened mine eyes: now we know that God heareth not sinners: but if any man be a worshipper of God, and doeth his will, him he heareth. Since the world began was it not heard that any man opened the eyes of one that was born blind. If this man were not of God, he could do nothing. They answered and said unto him: Thou wast altogether born in sins, and dost thou teach us? And they cast him out. Jesus heard that they had cast him out, and when he had found him, he said unto him: Dost thou believe on the Son of God? He answered, and said: Who is he, Lord, that I might believe on him? And Jesus said unto him: Thou hast both seen him, and it is he that talketh with thee. And he said: Lord, I believe. (Here genuflect). And he worshipped him.

Offertory. Ps. 66, 8-9 and 20. O praise the Lord our God, ye people, and make the voice of his praise to be heard: who holdeth our soul in life, and suffereth not our feet to slip: praised be the Lord who hath not cast out my prayer, nor turned his mercy from me.

The Thursday after the Fourth Sunday in Lent

Secret.

WE humbly beseech thee, almighty God: that by these sacrifices our sins may be cleansed; for therein thou dost grant us true healing both of body and soul. Through.

Preface of Lent.

Communion. John 9, 11. The Lord made clay of spittle, and anointed mine eyes: and I went and washed, and received sight, and believed in God.

Postcommunion.

O LORD our God, who hast made us partakers of this holy Sacrament: grant that we may thereby inwardly be satisfied with heavenly food, and outwardly be defended against all adversities. Through.

Over the people:

Let us pray. Humble your heads before God.

Collect.

LET thy merciful ears, O Lord, be open to the prayers of thy humble servants: and that they may obtain their petitions: make them to ask such things as shall please thee. Through.

Thursday

Station at SS. Silvester and Martin

Introit. Ps. 105, 3-4. Laetetur cor.

LET the heart of them rejoice that seek the Lord: seek the Lord and his strength: seek his face evermore. Ps. ibid., 1. O give thanks unto the Lord, and call upon his name: tell the people what things he hath done. ℣. Glory.

Collect.

GRANT, we beseech thee, almighty God: that we, duly chastening the flesh by this our fast, may inwardly rejoice in holiness of spirit; that, our earthly affections being subdued, we may more readily obtain thy heavenly promises. Through.

The Lesson from the book of the Kings.

II Kings 4, 25-38.

IN those days: There came a woman of Shunem unto Elisha to mount Carmel: and it came to pass, when the man of God saw her afar off, that he said to Gehazi his servant: Behold, yonder is that Shunammite. Run now, I pray thee, to meet her, and say unto her: Is it well with thee, is it well with thy husband, is it well with the child? And she answered: It is well. And when she came to the man of God to the hill, she caught him by the feet: but Gehazi came near to thrust her away. And the man of God said: Let her alone: for her soul is vexed within her, and the Lord hath hid it from me, and hath not told me. Then she said: Did I desire a son of my lord? Did I not say: Do not deceive me? Then he said to Gehazi: Gird up thy loins, and take my staff in thine hand, and go thy way. If thou meet any man, salute him not: and if any salute thee, answer him not again: and lay my staff upon the face of the child. And the mother of the child said: As the Lord liveth, and as thy soul liveth, I will not leave thee. And he arose, and followed her. And Gehazi passed on before them, and laid the staff upon the face of the child, but there was neither voice, nor hearing: wherefore he went again to meet him, and told him, saying: The child is not awaked. And when Elisha was come into the house, behold, the child was dead, and laid upon his bed: he went in therefore, and shut the door upon them twain: and prayed unto the Lord. And he went up, and lay upon the child: and put his mouth upon his mouth, and his eyes upon his eyes, and his hands upon his hands: and he stretched himself upon the child: and the flesh of the child waxed warm. Then he returned, and walked in the house to and fro: and went up, and stretched himself upon him: and the child sneezed seven times, and the child opened his eyes. And he called Gehazi, and said: Call this Shunammite. So he called her. And when she was come in unto him, he said: Take up thy son. Then she went in, and fell at his feet, and bowed herself to the ground: and took up her son, and went out, and Elisha came again to Gilgal.

Gradual. Ps. 74, 20, 19 and 22. Look, O Lord, upon the covenant: and forget not the congregation of the poor for ever. ℣. Arise, O Lord, maintain thine own cause: remember the rebuke that thy servants have.

✠ The Continuation of the holy Gospel according to Luke.

Luke 7, 11-16.

AT that time: Jesus went into a city called Nain: and many of his disciples went with him, and much people. Now when he came nigh to the gate of the city, behold, there was a dead man carried out, the only son of his mother: and she was a widow, and much people of the city was with her. And when the Lord saw her, he had compassion on her, and said unto her: Weep not. And he came and touched the bier. And they that bare him stood still. And he said: Young man, I say unto thee, Arise. And he that was dead sat up, and began to speak. And he delivered him to his mother. And there came a fear on all: and they glorified God, saying: That a great Prophet is risen up among us: and, That God hath visited his people.

Offertory. Ps. 70, 2-4. Make haste, O Lord, to help me: let them be ashamed that think evil against thy servants.

Secret.

CLEANSE us, O merciful God: that, like as the prayers and devout oblations of thy Church are acceptable in thy sight, so they may be rendered yet more acceptable by reason of the cleansing of our hearts. Through.

Preface of Lent.

Communion. Ps. 71, 16-18. O Lord, I will make mention of thy righteousness only: thou, O God, hast taught me from my youth up until now: forsake me not, O God, in mine old age, when I am greyheaded.

Postcommunion.

O LORD, who hast bestowed upon us thy heavenly gifts: we pray thee, that those things which thou hast ordained for the healing of thy faithful people, may not be turned unto their judgment. Through.

Over the people:

Let us pray. Humble your heads before God.

Collect.

O GOD, the creator and ruler of thy people, drive far from us all the assaults of temptation: that we, being ever found acceptable in thy sight, may by thee be defended from the fear of our enemies. Through.

Friday

Station at St. Eusebius

Introit. Ps. 19, 15. Meditatio.

LET the meditation of my heart be alway acceptable in thy sight: O Lord, my strength, and my redeemer. Ps. ibid., 1. The heavens declare the glory of God: and the firmament sheweth his handy-work. ℣. Glory.

Collect.

O GOD, who by thy ineffable sacraments dost regenerate the world: grant, we beseech thee; that thy Church, being profited by thine eternal ordinances, may likewise fail not of thy succour in all things temporal. Through.

The Friday after the Fourth Sunday in Lent

The Lesson from the book of the Kings.

I Kings 17, 17-24.

IN those days: The son of the woman, the mistress of the house, fell sick, and his sickness was so sore, that there was no breath left in him. And she said unto Elijah: What have I to do with thee, O thou man of God? Art thou come unto me to call my sin to remembrance, and to slay my son? And he said unto her: Give me thy son. And he took him out of her bosom, and carried him up into a loft, where he abode, and laid him upon his own bed, and he cried unto the Lord, and said: O Lord my God, hast thou also brought evil upon the widow with whom I sojourn, by slaying her son? And he stretched himself upon the child three times, and cried unto the Lord, and said: O Lord my God, I pray thee, let this child's soul come into him again. And the Lord heard the voice of Elijah: and the soul of the child came into him again, and he revived. And Elijah took the child, and brought him down out of the chamber into the house, and delivered him unto his mother, and Elijah said: See, thy son liveth. And the woman said to Elijah: Now by this I know that thou art a man of God, and that the word of the Lord in thy mouth is truth.

Gradual. Ps. 118, 8-9. It is better to trust in the Lord, than to put any confidence in man. ℣. It is better to trust in the Lord, than to put any confidence in princes.

Tract. Ps. 103, 10. O Lord, deal not with us after our sins: nor reward us according to our wickednesses. ℣. Ps. 79, 8-9. O Lord, remember not our old sins: but have mercy upon us, and that soon, for we are come to great misery. (Here genuflect) ℣. Help us, O God of our salvation: and for the glory of thy name, O Lord, deliver us: and be merciful unto our sins, for thy name's sake.

✠ The Continuation of the holy Gospel according to John.

John 11, 1-45.

AT that time: A certain man was sick, named Lazarus, of Bethany, the town of Mary and her sister Martha. (It was that Mary which anointed the Lord with ointment, and wiped his feet with her hair: whose brother Lazarus was sick.) Therefore his sisters sent unto him, saying: Lord, behold, he whom thou lovest is sick. When Jesus heard that, he said: This sickness is not unto death, but for the glory of God, that the Son of God might be glorified thereby. Now Jesus loved Martha, and her sister, and Lazarus. When he had heard therefore that he was sick, he abode two days still in the same place where he was. Then after that saith he to his disciples: Let us go into Judæa again. His disciples say unto him: Master, the Jews of late sought to stone thee, and goest thou thither again? Jesus answered: Are there not twelve hours in the day? If any man walk in the day, he stumbleth not, because he seeth the light of this world: but if a man walk in the night, he stumbleth, because there is no light in him. These things said he, and after that he saith unto them: Our friend Lazarus sleepeth: but I go, that I may awake him out of sleep. Then said his disciples: Lord, if he sleep, he shall do well. Howbeit Jesus spake of his death: but they thought that he had spoken of taking of rest in sleep. Then said Jesus unto them plainly: Lazarus is dead: and I am glad for your sakes that I was not there, to the intent ye may believe: nevertheless let us go unto him. Then said Thomas, which is called Didymus, unto his fellow-disciples: Let us also go, that we may die with him. Then when Jesus came, he found that he had lain in the grave four days already. Now Bethany was nigh unto Jerusalem, about fifteen furlongs off. And many of the Jews came to Martha and Mary, to comfort them concerning their brother. Then Martha, as soon as she heard that Jesus was coming, went and met him: but Mary sat still in the house. Then said Martha unto Jesus: Lord, if thou hadst been here, my brother had not died: but I know, that even now, whatsoever thou wilt ask of God, God will give it thee. Jesus saith unto her: Thy brother shall rise again. Martha saith unto him: I know that he shall rise again in the resurrection at the last day. Jesus said unto her: I am the resurrection, and the life: he that believeth in me, though he were dead, yet shall he live: and whosoever liveth and believeth in me shall never die. Believest thou this? She saith unto him: Yea, Lord, I believe that thou art the Christ, the Son of God, which should come into the world. And when she had so said, she went her way, and called Mary her sister secretly, saying: The Master is come, and calleth for thee. As soon as she heard that, she arose quickly, and came unto him: now Jesus was not yet come into the town; but was in that place where Martha met him. The Jews then which were with her in the house, and comforted her, when they saw Mary, that she rose up hastily and went out, followed her, saying: She goeth unto the grave to weep there. Then when Mary was come where Jesus was, and saw him, she fell down at his feet, saying unto him: Lord, if thou hadst been here, my brother had not died. When Jesus therefore saw her weeping, and the Jews also weeping which came with her, he groaned in the spirit, and was troubled, and said: Where have ye laid him? They said unto him: Lord, come and see. Jesus wept. Then said the Jews: Behold how he loved him. And some of them said: Could not this man, which opened the eyes of the blind, have caused that even this man should not have died? Jesus therefore again groaning in himself cometh to the grave. It was a cave, and a stone lay upon it. Jesus said: Take ye away the stone. Martha, the sister of him that was dead, saith unto him: Lord, by this time he stinketh, for he hath been dead four days. Jesus saith unto her: Said I not unto thee, that, if thou wouldest believe, thou shouldest see the glory of God? Then they took away the stone from the place where the dead was laid: and Jesus lifted up his eyes, and said: Father, I thank thee that thou hast heard me. And I knew that thou hearest me always, but because of the people which stand by I said it: that they may believe that thou hast sent me. And when he thus had spoken, he cried with a loud voice: Lazarus, come forth. And he that was dead came forth, bound hand and foot with graveclothes, and his face was bound about with a napkin. Jesus saith unto them: Loose him, and let him go. Then many of the Jews which came to Mary, and had seen the things which Jesus did, believed on him.

Offertory. Ps. 18, 28 and 32. Thou, O Lord, shalt save the people that are in adversity, and shalt bring down the high looks of the proud: for who is God, but thou, O Lord?

Secret.

WE beseech thee, O Lord, that the gifts which we have offered may purify us: and evermore cause thee to be favourable unto us. Through.

Preface of Lent.

Communion. John 11, 33, 35, 43, 44 and 39. When the Lord saw the sisters of Lazarus weeping at the grave, he wept before the Jews, and cried out: Lazarus, come forth: and he that had been dead four days came forth, bound hand and foot.

Postcommunion.

WE beseech thee, O Lord, that we, who have here received this holy Sacrament; may thereby be delivered evermore from the bonds of our sins, and defended against all adversities. Through.

Over the people:

Let us pray. Humble your heads before God.

Collect.

GRANT to us, we beseech thee, almighty God: that we who, knowing our own infirmity, do put our confidence in thy power; may evermore rejoice in the abundance of thy loving-kindness. Through.

Saturday

Station at St. Nicholas in prison

Introit. Is. 55, 1. Sitientes.

HO, every one that thirsteth, come ye to the waters, saith the Lord: and he that hath no money, come ye and drink with gladness. Ps. 78, 1. Hear my law, O my people: incline your ears unto the words of my mouth. ℣. Glory.

Collect.

O LORD, forasmuch as this our fast will be unprofitable unto us, unless it be acceptable unto thy lovingkindness: we beseech thee that the devout affection of our hearts may by thy grace be made fruitful in all good works. Through.

The Lesson from the Prophet Isaiah.

Is. 49, 8-15.

THUS saith the Lord: In an acceptable time have I heard thee, and in a day of salvation have I helped thee: and I will preserve thee, and give thee for a covenant of the people, to establish the earth, to cause to inherit the desolate heritages: that thou mayest say to the prisoners: Go forth: to them that are in darkness: Shew yourselves. They shall feed in the ways, and their pastures shall be in all high places. They shall not hunger nor thirst, neither shall the heat nor sun smite them: for he that hath mercy on them shall lead them, even by the springs of water shall he guide them. And I will make all my mountains a way, and my highways shall be exalted. Behold, these shall come from far, and, lo, these from the north and from the west, and these from the land of Sinim. Sing, O heavens, and be joyful, O earth, and break forth into singing, O mountains: for the Lord hath comforted his people, and will have mercy upon his afflicted. But Sion said: The Lord hath forsaken me, and my Lord hath forgotten me. Can a woman forget her sucking child, that she should not have compassion on the son of her womb? yea, they may forget, yet will I not forget thee, saith the Lord almighty.

Gradual. Ps. 10, 14 and 1-2. The poor, O Lord, committeth himself unto thee: for thou art the helper of the friendless. ℣. Why standest thou so far off, O Lord, and hidest thy face in the needful time of trouble? The ungodly for his own lust doth persecute the poor.

✠ The Continuation of the holy Gospel according to John.

John 8, 12-20.

AT that time: Spake Jesus unto the multitudes of the Jews, saying: I am the light of the world: he that followeth me shall not walk in darkness, but shall have the light of life. The Pharisees therefore said unto him: Thou bearest record of thyself: thy record is not true. Jesus answered and said unto them: Though I bear record of myself, yet my record is true: for I know whence I came, and whither I go: but ye cannot tell whence I come, and whither I go. Ye judge after the flesh: I judge no man: and yet if I judge, my judgment is true, for I am not alone: but I and the Father that sent me. It is also written in your law, that the testimony of two men is true. I am one that bear witness of myself: and the Father that sent me beareth witness of me. Then said they unto him: Where is thy Father? Jesus answered: Ye neither know me, nor my Father: if ye had known me, ye should have known my Father also. These words spake Jesus in the treasury, as he taught in the temple: and no man laid hands on him; for his hour was not yet come.

Offertory. Ps. 18, 3. The Lord is my stony rock, and my defence; and my saviour, in whom I will trust.

Secret.

WE beseech thee, O Lord, mercifully to receive our oblations: and in thy mercy make even our rebel wills to turn to thee. Through.

Preface of Lent.

Communion. Ps. 23, 1-2. The Lord is my shepherd, therefore can I lack nothing: he shall feed me in a green pasture: and lead me forth beside the waters of comfort.

Postcommunion.

WE beseech thee, O Lord, that thy holy mysteries may cleanse us from our sins: and by their operation render us an acceptable people in thy sight. Through.

Over the people:

Let us pray.   Humble your heads before God.

Collect.

O GOD, who choosest to shew mercy rather than wrath to them that put their trust in thee: grant to us so worthily to bewail the sins which we have committed; that we may be found worthy to obtain the comfort of thy grace. Through.

¶ Mass being ended, before Vespers, Crosses and Images are covered throughout the church; and they remain covered, the Crosses until after the adoration of the Cross by the Celebrant on Good Friday, but the Images till the intonation of the Angelic Hymn on Holy Saturday.

PASSION SUNDAY

1st class.   Double of 1st class.

¶ From this Sunday until Maundy Thursday inclusive, in Masses of the Season the Psalm Júdica me is not said before the Confession, nor Glória Patri at the Introit and after the Psalm Lavábo.

Station at St. Peter

Introit. Ps. 43, 1-2. Judica me.

GIVE sentence with me, O God, and defend my cause against the ungodly people: O deliver me from the deceitful and wicked man: for thou art the God of my strength. Ps. ibid., 3. O send out thy light and thy truth: that they may lead me and bring me unto thy holy hill, and to thy dwelling. Give sentence.

Collect.

WE beseech thee, almighty God, mercifully to look upon thy people: that by thy great goodness they may be governed and preserved evermore, both in body and soul. Through.

The Lesson from the Epistle of blessed Paul the Apostle to the Hebrews.

Heb. 9, 11-15.

BRETHREN: Christ being come an High Priest of good things to come, by a greater and more perfect tabernacle, not made with hands, that is to say, not of this building: neither by the blood of goats and calves; but by his own blood he entered in once into the Holy Place, having obtained eternal redemption for us. For if the blood of bulls and of goats, and the ashes of an heifer sprinkling the unclean, sanctifieth to the purifying of the flesh: how much more shall the blood of Christ, who, through the eternal Spirit, offered himself without spot to God, purge your conscience from dead works to serve the living God? And for this cause he is the Mediator of the new Testament: that by means of death, for the redemption of the transgressions that were under the first Testament, they which are called might receive the promise of eternal inheritance, in Christ Jesus our Lord.

Gradual. Ps. 143, 9-10. **Deliver me, O Lord, from mine enemies: teach me to do the thing that pleaseth thee.** ℣. Ps. 18, 48-49. It is thou, Lord, that deliverest me from my cruel enemies: and settest me up above mine adversaries: thou shalt rid me from the wicked man.

Tract. Ps. 129, 1-4. **Many a time have they fought against me from my youth up.** ℣. May Israel now say: yea, many a time have they vexed me from my youth up. ℣. But they have not prevailed against me: the plowers plowed upon my back. ℣. And made long furrows: but the righteous Lord hath hewn the snares of the ungodly in pieces.

✠ The Continuation of the holy Gospel according to John.

John 8, 46-59.

AT that time: Jesus said unto the multitudes of the Jews: which of you convinceth me of sin? And if I say the truth, why do ye not believe me? He that is of God heareth God's words. Ye therefore hear them not, because ye are not of God. Then answered the Jews, and said unto him: Say we not well, that thou art a Samaritan, and hast a devil? Jesus answered: I have not a devil, but I honour my Father, and ye do dishonour me. And I seek not mine own glory: there is one that seeketh and judgeth. Verily, verily, I say unto you: If a man keep my saying, he shall never see death. Then said the Jews unto him: Now we know that thou hast a devil. Abraham is dead, and the Prophets; and thou sayest: If a man keep my saying, he shall never taste of death. Art thou greater than our father Abraham, which is dead? and the Prophets are dead. Whom makest thou thyself? Jesus answered: If I honour myself, my honour is nothing: it is my Father that honoureth me, of whom ye say, that he is your God, yet ye have not known him: but I know him: and if I should say, I know him not, I shall be a liar like unto you. But I know him, and keep his saying. Your father Abraham rejoiced to see my day, and he saw it, and was glad. Then said the Jews unto him: Thou art not yet fifty years old, and hast thou seen Abraham? Jesus said unto them: Verily, verily I say unto you, before Abraham was, I am. Then took they up stones to cast at him: but Jesus hid himself, and went out of the temple. Creed.

Offertory. Ps. 119, 17 and 107. I will give thanks unto thee, O Lord, with my whole heart: O do well unto thy servant, that I may live, and keep thy word: quicken thou me, O Lord, according to thy word.

Secret.

WE beseech thee, O Lord, that these our oblations may both loose the bonds of our iniquity, and obtain for us the gifts of thy lovingkindness. Through.

¶ Preface of the Cross; which is said until Maundy Thursday inclusive, according to the Rubrics.

Communion. I Cor. 11, 24-25. This is my body, which is given for you: this cup is the new Testament in my blood, saith the Lord: this do ye, as oft as ye drink it, in remembrance of me.

Postcommunion.

ASSIST us mercifully, O Lord our God: that we, whom thou hast here refreshed with thy holy mysteries, may be defended by thy perpetual succour. Through.

Monday

Station at St. Chrysogonus

Introit. Ps. 56, 2. Miserere mihi.

BE merciful unto me, O Lord, for man goeth about to devour me: he is daily fighting, and troubling me. Ps. ibid., 3. Mine enemies are daily in hand to swallow me up: for they be many that fight against me. Be merciful.

Collect.

SANCTIFY, we beseech thee, O Lord, this our fast: and mercifully bestow upon us the remission of all our offences. Through.

The Lesson from the Prophet Jonah.

Jonah 3, 1-10.

IN those days: The word of the Lord came unto Jonah the second time, saying: Arise, go unto Nineveh, that great city, and preach unto it the preaching that I bid thee. So Jonah arose, and went unto Nineveh, according to the word of the Lord. Now Nineveh was an exceeding great city of three days' journey. And Jonah began to enter into the city a day's

The Monday after Passion Sunday

journey: and he cried, and said: Yet forty days, and Nineveh shall be overthrown. So the people of Nineveh believed God: and proclaimed a fast, and put on sackcloth, from the greatest of them even to the least of them. For word came unto the king of Nineveh: and he arose from his throne, and he laid his robe from him, and covered him with sackcloth, and sat in ashes. And he caused it to be proclaimed and published through Nineveh by the decree of the king and his nobles, saying: Let neither man nor beast, herd nor flock, taste any thing: let them not feed, nor drink water. But let man and beast be covered with sackcloth, and cry mightily unto God, yea, let them turn every one from his evil way, and from the violence that is in their hands. Who can tell if God will turn and repent: and turn away from his fierce anger, that we perish not? And God saw their works, that they turned from their evil way: and the Lord our God had mercy on his people.

Gradual. Ps. 54, 4 and 3. Hear my prayer, O God: and hearken unto the words of my mouth. ℣. Save me, O God, for thy name's sake, and avenge me in thy strength.

Tract. Ps. 103, 10. O Lord, deal not with us after our sins: nor reward us according to our wickednesses. ℣. Ps. 79, 8-9. O Lord, remember not our old sins: but have mercy upon us, and that soon, for we are come to great misery. (Here genuflect) ℣. Help us, O God of our salvation: and for the glory of thy name, O Lord, deliver us: and be merciful unto our sins, for thy name's sake.

✠ The Continuation of the holy Gospel according to John.

John 7, 32-39.

AT that time: The Pharisees and the chief priests sent officers to take Jesus. Then said Jesus unto them: Yet a little while am I with you: and then I go unto him that sent me. Ye shall seek me, and shall not find me: and where I am, thither ye cannot come. Then said the Jews among themselves: Whither will he go, that we shall not find him? will he go unto the dispersed among the Gentiles, and teach the Gentiles? What manner of saying is this that he said: Ye shall seek me, and shall not find me: and where I am, thither ye cannot come? In the last day, that great day of the feast, Jesus stood and cried, saying: If any man thirst, let him come unto me, and drink. He that believeth on me, as the Scripture hath said, out of his belly shall flow rivers of living water. But this spake he of the Spirit, which they that believe on him should receive.

Offertory. Ps. 6, 5. Turn thee, O Lord, and deliver my soul: O save me for thy mercy's sake.

Secret.

GRANT unto us, O Lord our God: that this saving victim may avail both for the purging of our offences, and for the obtaining of the favour of thy divine majesty. Through.

Preface of the Cross.

Communion. Ps. 24, 10. The Lord of hosts, he is the King of Glory.

Postcommunion.

O LORD, who hast made us partakers of thy Sacrament of salvation, we beseech thee: that it may be profitable unto us both for the cleansing and the healing of our souls. Through.

Over the people:

Let us pray. Humble your heads before God.

Collect.

KEEP, we beseech thee, O Lord, thy faithful people both outwardly in their bodies and inwardly in their souls: that they, cleaving steadfastly to all good works, may ever be defended by thy mighty power. Through.

Tuesday

Station at St. Cyriacus

Introit. Ps. 27, 14. Exspecta.

O TARRY thou the Lord's leisure, be strong: and he shall comfort thine heart, and put thou thy trust in the Lord. Ps. ibid., 1. The Lord is my light, and my salvation: whom then shall I fear? O tarry thou.

Collect.

WE beseech thee, O Lord, let this our fasting be acceptable in thy sight: that we, being cleansed thereby and made worthy of thy grace, may finally attain unto everlasting life. Through.

The Lesson from the Prophet Daniel.

Bel and the Dragon, 29-42.

IN those days: The Babylonians came to the king, and said: Deliver us Daniel, who hath destroyed Bel, and slain the dragon, or else we will destroy thee and thine house. Now when the king saw that they pressed him sore: being constrained, he delivered Daniel unto them. Who cast him into the lions' den, where he was six days. And in the den there were seven lions, and they had given them every day two carcases, and two sheep: which then were not given to them, to the intent they might devour Daniel. Now there was in Jewry a prophet, called Habbacuc, who had made pottage, and had broken bread in a bowl: and was going into the field, for to bring it to the reapers. But the Angel of the Lord said unto Habbacuc: Go, carry the dinner that thou hast into Babylon unto Daniel, who is in the lions' den. And Habbacuc said: Lord, I never saw Babylon, neither do I know where the den is. Then the Angel of the Lord took him by the crown, and bare him by the hair of his head, and through the vehemency of his spirit set him in Babylon over the den. And Habbacuc cried, saying: O Daniel, Daniel, take the dinner which God hath sent thee. And Daniel said: Thou hast remembered me, O God, neither hast thou forsaken them that seek thee and love thee. So Daniel arose, and did eat. And the Angel of the Lord set Habbacuc in his own place again immediately. Upon the seventh day the king went to bewail Daniel: and when he came to the den, he looked in, and, behold, Daniel was sitting. Then cried the king with a loud voice, saying: Great art thou, O Lord God of Daniel. And he drew him out. And cast those that were the cause of his destruction into the den, and they were devoured in a moment before his face. Then said the king: Let all the inhabitants of the whole earth fear the God of Daniel: for he is the saviour, working signs, and wonders in the earth: who hath delivered Daniel out of the lions' den.

Gradual. Ps. 43, 1 and 3. O Lord, defend my cause: O deliver me from the deceitful and wicked man. ℣. O send out thy light and thy truth: that they may lead me, and bring me unto thy holy hill.

✠ The Continuation of the holy Gospel according to John.

John 7, 1-13.

AT that time: Jesus walked in Galilee, for he would not walk in Jewry, because the Jews sought to kill him. Now the Jews' feast of tabernacles was at hand. His brethren therefore said unto him: Depart hence, and go into Judæa, that thy disciples also may see the works that thou doest. For there is no man that doeth any thing in secret, and he himself seeketh to be known openly: if thou do these things, shew thyself to the world. For neither did his brethren believe in him. Then Jesus said unto them: My time is not yet come: but your time is alway ready. The world cannot hate you: but me it hateth, because I testify of it, that the works thereof are evil. Go ye up unto this feast, I go not up yet unto this feast: for my time is not yet full come. When he had said these words unto them, he abode still in Galilee. But when his brethren were gone up, then went he also up unto the feast, not openly, but as it were in secret. Then the Jews sought him at the feast, and said: Where is he? And there was much murmuring among the people concerning him. For some said: He is a good man. Others said: Nay, but he deceiveth the people. Howbeit no man spake openly of him for fear of the Jews.

Offertory. Ps. 9, 11-13. All they that know thy name will put their trust in thee, O Lord: for thou never failest them that seek thee: O praise the Lord which dwelleth in Sion: who forgetteth not the complaint of the poor.

Secret.

WE offer and present unto thee, O Lord, these sacrifices: that they may in such wise be a token of comfort to us in this life; that we fail not to hope in thy everlasting promises. Through.

Preface of the Cross.

Communion. Ps. 25, 22. Deliver me, O God of Israel, out of all my troubles.

Postcommunion.

GRANT, we beseech thee, almighty God: that we, ever following diligently after things eternal, may be found worthy to attain unto the gifts of thy heavenly bounty. Through.

Over the people:

Let us pray.   Humble your heads before God.

Collect.

GRANT to us, Lord, we beseech thee, grace so to continue steadfastly in obedience to thy will: that in our time the number of thy faithful people may be multiplied, and the worthiness of their service increased. Through.

Wednesday

Station at St. Marcellus

Introit. Ps. 18, 48-49. Liberator.

IT is thou that deliverest me from my cruel enemies: and settest me up above mine adversaries: thou shalt rid me from the wicked man, O Lord. Ps. ibid., 1-2. I will love thee, O Lord, my strength: the Lord is my stony rock, my defence, and my Saviour. It is thou that.

Collect.

O MERCIFUL God, sanctify this our fasting to the enlightenment of the hearts of thy faithful people: that we, to whom thou dost give an hearty desire to pray, may obtain of thy lovingkindness the fulfilment of all our petitions. Through.

The Lesson from the book Leviticus.

Lev. 19, 1-2, 11-19 and 25.

IN those days: The Lord spake unto Moses, saying: Speak unto all the congregation of the children of Israel, and say unto them: I am the Lord your God. Ye shall not steal, neither deal falsely, neither lie one to another. And ye shall not swear by my name falsely, neither shalt thou profane the name of thy God. I am the Lord. Thou shalt not defraud thy neighbour; neither rob him. The wages of him that is hired shall not abide with thee all night until the morning. Thou shalt not curse the deaf, nor put a stumbling-block before the blind: but shalt fear thy God. I am the Lord. Ye shall do no unrighteousness in judgment. Thou shalt not respect the person of the poor, nor honour the person of the mighty. But in righteousness shalt thou judge thy neighbour. Thou shalt not go

The Wednesday after Passion Sunday

up and down as a talebearer among thy people. Neither shalt thou stand against the blood of thy neighbour. I am the Lord. Thou shalt not hate thy brother in thine heart, thou shalt in any wise rebuke thy neighbour, and not suffer sin upon him. Thou shalt not avenge, nor bear any grudge against the children of thy people. But thou shalt love thy neighbour as thyself. I am the Lord. Ye shall keep my statutes. For I am the Lord your God.

Gradual. Ps. 30, 1-3. I will magnify thee, O Lord, for thou hast set me up: and not made my foes to triumph over me. ℣. O Lord my God, I cried unto thee, and thou hast healed me: thou, Lord, hast brought my soul out of hell, thou hast kept my life from them that go down to the pit.

Tract. Ps. 103, 10. O Lord, deal not with us after our sins: nor reward us according to our wickednesses. ℣. Ps. 79, 8-9. O Lord, remember not our old sins: but have mercy upon us, and that soon, for we are come to great misery. (Here genuflect) ℣. Help us, O God of our salvation: and for the glory of thy name, O Lord, deliver us: and be merciful unto our sins, for thy name's sake.

✠ The Continuation of the holy Gospel according to John.

John 10, 22-38.

AT that time: It was at Jerusalem the feast of the Dedication: and it was winter. And Jesus walked in the temple in Solomon's porch. Then came the Jews round about him, and said unto him: How long dost thou make us to doubt? If thou be the Christ, tell us plainly. Jesus answered them: I told you, and ye believed not: The works that I do in my Father's name, they bear witness of me: but ye believe not, because ye are not of my sheep, as I said unto you. My sheep hear my voice: and I know them, and they follow me: and I give unto them eternal life: and they shall never perish, neither shall any man pluck them out of my hand. My Father, which gave them me, is greater than all: and no man is able to pluck them out of my Father's hand. I and my Father are one. Then the Jews took up stones again to stone him. Jesus answered them: Many good works have I shewed you from my Father, for which of those works do ye stone me? The Jews answered him, saying: For a good work we stone thee not, but for blasphemy: and because that thou, being a man, makest thyself God. Jesus answered them: Is it not written in your law: I said, Ye are gods? If he called them gods, unto whom the word of God came, and the Scripture cannot be broken: say ye of him, whom the Father hath sanctified, and sent into the world: Thou blasphemest: because I said, I am the Son of God? If I do not the works of my Father, believe me not. But if I do, though ye believe not me, believe the works: that ye may know, and believe, that the Father is in me, and I in him.

Offertory. Ps. 59, 2. Deliver me from mine enemies, O God: defend me from them that rise up against me, O Lord.

Secret.

GRANT, O merciful God, that we may bring unto thee with sincere worship this our sacrifice of propitiation and praise. Through.

Preface of the Cross.

Communion. Ps. 26, 6-7. I will wash my hands in innocency, O Lord, and so will I go to thine altar: that I may shew the voice of thanksgiving, and tell of all thy wondrous works.

Postcommunion.

WE humbly beseech thee, almighty God: that as thou hast made us partakers of thy heavenly benediction; so likewise the pledge which thou hast given us in this holy Sacrament may be fulfilled in us unto everlasting salvation. *Through.*

Over the people:

Let us pray. Humble your heads before God.

Collect.

ASSIST us mercifully, almighty God, in these our supplications: that we, whom thou dost suffer to put our trust and confidence in thy mercy; may of thy goodness obtain the wonted effects of thy compassion. *Through.*

Thursday

Station at St. Apollinaris

Introit. Song of the Three Children, 8, 19. *Omnia quae.*

EVERYTHING that thou hast done to us, O Lord, thou hast done in true judgment: for we have sinned, and not obeyed thy commandments: but give glory to thy name, and deal with us according to the multitude of thy mercies. Ps. 119, 1. Blessed are those that are undefiled in the way: and walk in the law of the Lord. *Everything that thou hast done.*

Collect.

GRANT, we beseech thee, almighty God: that we, who by our incontinence have corrupted the dignity of man's condition, may by devout abstinence heal and restore the same. *Through.*

The Lesson from the Prophet Daniel.

Song of the Three Children 11-22.

IN those days: Azarias prayed unto the Lord, saying: O Lord our God: deliver us not up wholly, for thy name's sake, neither disannul thou thy covenant: and cause not thy mercy to depart from us, for thy beloved Abraham's sake, for thy servant Isaac's sake, and for thy holy Israel's sake: to whom thou hast spoken and promised, that thou wouldest multiply their seed as the stars of heaven, and as the sand that lieth upon the seashore: for we, O Lord, are become less than any nation, and be kept under this day in all the world because of our sins. Neither is there at this time prince, or prophet, or leader, or burnt offering, or sacrifice, or oblation, or incense, or place to sacrifice before thee, and to find mercy: nevertheless in a contrite heart and an humble spirit let us be accepted. Like as in the burnt offerings of rams and bullocks, and like as in ten thousands of fat lambs: so let our sacrifice be in thy sight this day, that it may please thee: for they shall not be confounded that put their trust in thee. And now we follow thee with all our heart, we fear thee, and seek thy face. Put us not to shame: but deal with us after thy lovingkindness, and according to the multitude of thy mercies. Deliver us also according to thy marvellous works, and give glory to thy name, O Lord: and let all them that do thy servants hurt be ashamed, and let them be confounded in all their power and might: and let their strength be broken: and let them know that thou art Lord, the only God, and glorious over the whole world, O Lord our God.

Gradual. Ps. 96, 8-9. Bring presents, and come into his courts: O worship the Lord in the beauty of holiness. ℣. Ps. 29, 9. The Lord discovereth the thick bushes: in his temple doth every man speak of his honour.

The Thursday after Passion Sunday

✠ The Continuation of the holy Gospel according to Luke.

Luke 7, 36-50.

AT that time: One of the Pharisees desired Jesus that he would eat with him. And he went into the Pharisee's house, and sat down to meat. And, behold, a woman in the city, which was a sinner, when she knew that Jesus sat at meat in the Pharisee's house, brought an alabaster box of ointment: and stood at his feet behind him weeping, and began to wash his feet with tears, and did wipe them with the hairs of her head, and kissed his feet, and anointed them with the ointment. Now when the Pharisee which had bidden him saw it, he spake within himself, saying: This man, if he were a Prophet, would have known who and what manner of woman this is that toucheth him: for she is a sinner. And Jesus answering said unto him: Simon, I have somewhat to say unto thee. And he saith: Master, say on. There was a certain creditor which had two debtors: the one owed five hundred pence, and the other fifty. And when they had nothing to pay, he frankly forgave them both. Tell me therefore, which of them will love him most? Simon answered and said: I suppose that he, to whom he forgave most. And he said unto him: Thou hast rightly judged. And he turned to the woman, and said unto Simon: Seest thou this woman? I entered into thine house, thou gavest me no water for my feet: but she hath washed my feet with tears, and wiped them with the hairs of her head. Thou gavest me no kiss: but this woman since the time I came in hath not ceased to kiss my feet. My head with oil thou didst not anoint: but this woman hath anointed my feet with ointment. Wherefore I say unto thee: Her sins, which are many, are forgiven, for she loved much. But to whom little is forgiven, the same loveth little. And he said unto her: Thy sins are forgiven. And they that sat at meat with him began to say within themselves: Who is this that forgiveth sins also? And he said to the woman: Thy faith hath saved thee: go in peace.

Offertory. Ps. 137, 1. By the waters of Babylon we sat down and wept: when we remembered thee, O Sion.

Secret.

O LORD our God, who of the creatures, which thou hast ordained for the succour of our frailty, hast commanded that an oblation should be appointed to be offered to thy name: grant, we beseech thee; that the same may become unto us a help in this present life, and a Sacrament availing unto life eternal. Through.

Preface of the Cross.

Communion. Ps. 119, 49-50. Think upon thy servant, O Lord, as concerning thy word, wherein thou hast caused me to put my trust: the same is my comfort in my trouble.

Postcommunion.

GRANT, O Lord, that those things which we have taken with our outward lips we may inwardly receive in purity of heart: that, being in this life partakers of thy gifts, we may thereby be healed unto life eternal. Through.

Over the people:

Let us pray.   Humble your heads before God.

Collect.

BE merciful, we beseech thee, O Lord, unto us thy people: that we, eschewing those things that are contrary to thy good pleasure, may in keeping of thy commandments be fulfilled with heavenly joy. Through.

Friday

Station at St. Stephen on the Caelian Hill

Introit. Ps. 31, 10, 16 and 18. *Miserere mihi.*

HAVE mercy upon me, O Lord, for I am in trouble: save me and deliver me from the hand of mine enemies and from them that persecute me: let me not be confounded, O Lord, for I have called upon thee. Ps. ibid., 1. In thee, O Lord, have I put my trust, let me never be put to confusion: deliver me in thy righteousness. Have mercy.

Collect.

WE beseech thee, O Lord, mercifully to pour thy grace into our hearts: that we, who willingly by the chastisement of the flesh do restrain our sins; may in such wise mortify ourselves in this life, that we be not delivered unto everlasting punishments. Through.

The Lesson from the Prophet Jeremiah.

Jer. 17, 13-18.

IN those days: Jeremiah said: O Lord, all that forsake thee shall be ashamed: and they that depart from me shall be written in the earth: because they have forsaken the Lord, the fountain of living waters. Heal me, O Lord, and I shall be healed: save me, and I shall be saved: for thou art my praise. Behold, they say unto me: Where is the word of the Lord? Let it come now. As for me, I have not hastened from being a pastor to follow thee: neither have I desired the woeful day, thou knowest. That which came out of my lips was right before thee. Be not a terror unto me, thou art my hope in the day of evil. Let them be confounded that persecute me, but let not me be confounded: let them be dismayed, but let not me be dismayed. Bring upon them the day of evil, and destroy them with double destruction, O Lord our God.

Gradual. Ps. 35, 20 and 22. The communing of mine enemies is not for peace: and maliciously are they set against me. ℣. This thou hast seen, O Lord, hold not thy tongue: go not far from me.

Tract. Ps. 103, 10. O Lord, deal not with us after our sins: nor reward us according to our wickednesses. ℣. Ps. 79, 8-9. O Lord, remember not our old sins: but have mercy upon us, and that soon, for we are come to great misery. (Here genuflect) ℣. Help us, O God of our salvation: and for the glory of thy name, O Lord, deliver us: and be merciful unto our sins, for thy name's sake.

✠ The Continuation of the holy Gospel according to John.

John 11, 47-54.

AT that time: The chief priests and the Pharisees gathered a council against Jesus, and said: What do we, for this man doeth many miracles? If we let him thus alone, all men will believe on him: and the Romans shall come and take away both our place and nation. And one of them, named Caiaphas, being the high priest that same year, said unto them: Ye know nothing at all, nor consider that it is expedient for us, that one man should die for the people, and that the whole nation perish not. And this spake he not of himself: but being high priest that year, he prophesied that Jesus should die for that nation, and not for that nation only, but that also he should gather together in one the children of God that were scattered abroad. Then from that day forth they took counsel together for to put him to death. Jesus therefore walked no more openly among the Jews: but went thence unto a country near to the wilderness, into a city called Ephraim, and there continued with his disciples.

Offertory. Ps. 119, 12, 121 and 42. Blessed art thou, O Lord, O teach me thy statutes: and give me not over unto mine oppressors: so shall I make answer unto my blasphemers.

Secret.

GRANT unto us, merciful God: that we, being ever found meet to do thee worthy service at thine altars, may continually be made partakers of the same to our salvation. Through.

Preface of the Cross.

Communion. Ps. 27, 12. Deliver me not over, O Lord, into the will of mine adversaries: for there are false witnesses risen up against me, and such as speak wrong.

Postcommunion.

LET this holy sacrifice, O Lord, which we have here received, be our continual defence: and evermore drive far from us all things that may hurt us. Through.

Over the people:

Let us pray.　　Humble your heads before God.

Collect.

GRANT, we beseech thee, almighty God: that we, who seek the grace of thy protection, may be delivered from all evils and serve thee with a quiet mind. Through.

Saturday

Station at St. John before the Latin Gate

Introit. Ps. 31, 10, 16 and 18. Miserere mihi.

HAVE mercy upon me, O Lord, for I am in trouble: save me and deliver me from the hand of mine enemies: and from them that persecute me: let me not be confounded, O Lord, for I have called upon thee. Ps. ibid., 1. In thee, O Lord, have I put my trust, let me never be put to confusion: deliver me in thy righteousness. Have mercy.

Collect.

WE beseech thee, O Lord, that thy people who are consecrated to thy service may increase in godly and devout affection: that, being instructed in all holy learning, they may both be made the more acceptable unto thy majesty, and prospered more abundantly with thy gifts. Through.

The Lesson from the Prophet Jeremiah.

Jer. 18, 18-23.

IN those days: The wicked Jews said one to another: Come, and let us devise devices against the righteous: for the law shall not perish from the priest, nor counsel from the wise, nor the word from the prophet: come, and let us smite him with the tongue, and let us not give heed to any of his words. Give heed to me, O Lord, and hearken to the voice of them that contend with me. Shall evil be recompensed for good, for they have digged a pit for my soul? Remember that I stood before thee to speak good for them, and to turn away thy wrath from them. Therefore deliver up their children to the famine, and pour out their blood by the force of the sword: and let their wives be bereaved of their children, and be widows: and let their men be put to death: let their young men be slain by the sword in battle. Let a cry be heard from their houses, when thou shalt bring a troop suddenly upon them: for they have digged a pit to take me, and hid snares for my feet. Yet, Lord, thou knowest all their counsel against me to slay me: forgive not their iniquity, neither blot out their sin from thy sight. But let them be overthrown before thee, deal thus with them in the time of thine anger, O Lord our God.

Gradual. Ps. 35, 20 and 22. The communing of mine enemies is not for peace: and maliciously are they set against me. ℣. This thou hast seen, O Lord, hold not thy tongue: go not far from me.

✠ The Continuation of the holy Gospel according to John.

John 12, 10-30.

AT that time: The chief priests consulted that they might put Lazarus also to death: because that by reason of him many of the Jews went away, and believed on Jesus. On the next day much people that were come to the feast, when they heard that Jesus was coming to Jerusalem, took branches of palm trees, and went forth to meet him, and cried: Hosanna, blessed is the King of Israel that cometh in the name of the Lord. And Jesus, when he had found a young ass, sat thereon, as it is written: Fear not, daughter of Sion: behold, thy King cometh, sitting on an ass's colt. These things understood not his disciples at the first: but when Jesus was glorified, then remembered they that these things were written of him: and that they had done these things unto him. The people therefore that was with him when he called Lazarus out of his grave, and raised him from the dead, bare record. For this cause the people also met him: for that they heard that he had done this miracle. The Pharisees therefore said among themselves: Perceive ye how ye prevail nothing? Behold, the world is gone after him. And there were certain Greeks among them that came up to worship at the feast. The same came therefore to Philip, which was of Bethsaida of Galilee: and desired him, saying: Sir, we would see Jesus. Philip cometh and telleth Andrew: and again Andrew and Philip tell Jesus. And Jesus answered them, saying: The hour is come, that the Son of man should be glorified. Verily, verily, I say unto you, Except a corn of wheat fall into the ground and die, it abideth alone: but if it die, it bringeth forth much fruit. He that loveth his life shall lose it: and he that hateth his life in this world shall keep it unto life eternal. If any man serve me, let him follow me: and where I am, there shall also my servant be. If any man serve me, him will my Father honour. Now is my soul troubled. And what shall I say? Father, save me from this hour. But for this cause came I unto this hour. Father, glorify thy name. Then came there a voice from heaven, saying: I have both glorified it, and will glorify it again. The people therefore, that stood by, and heard it, said that it thundered. Others said: An Angel spake to him. Jesus answered and said: This voice came not because of me, but for your sakes. Now is the judgment of this world, now shall the prince of this world be cast out. And I, if I be lifted up from the earth, will draw all men unto me. This he said, signifying what death he should die. The people answered him: We have heard out of the law that Christ abideth for ever, and how sayest thou: The Son of man must be lifted up? Who is this Son of man? Then Jesus said unto them: Yet a little while is the light with you. Walk while ye have the light, lest darkness come upon you: for he that walketh in darkness knoweth not whither he goeth. While ye have light, believe in the light: that ye may be the children of light. These things spake Jesus: and departed, and did hide himself from them.

Offertory. Ps. 119, 12, 121 and 42. Blessed art thou, O Lord, O teach me thy statutes: and give me not over unto mine oppressors: so shall I make answer unto my blasphemers.

Secret.

O LORD, who sufferest us to be made partakers of this wondrous mystery: we beseech thee, that by thy mercy we may be delivered from all perils and iniquities. Through.

Preface of the Cross.

Communion. Ps. 27, 12. Deliver me not over, O Lord, into the will of mine adversaries: for there are false witnesses risen up against me, and such as speak wrong.

Postcommunion.

O LORD our God, who hast fulfilled us with the bounty of thy heavenly gifts: we beseech thee, that we may ever live by the partaking of the same. Through.

Over the people:

Let us pray. Humble your heads before God.

Collect.

WE beseech thee, O Lord, that thy right hand may defend thy people who call upon thee: and vouchsafe so to cleanse and instruct them; that they may obtain thy comfort in this present life, and grow in grace unto the attainment of everlasting felicity. Through.

THE COLLECTS, EPISTLES AND GOSPELS

for

HOLY WEEK

according to

THE BOOK OF COMMON PRAYER

Sunday before Easter

Collect and Epistle Let this mind, as on p. 148.

Gospel, †When the morning was come, p. 151, ending at this was the Son of God.†

Monday before Easter

For the Epistle. Is. 63, 1.

WHO is this that cometh from Edom, with dyed garments from Bozrah? this that is glorious in his apparel, travelling in the greatness of his strength? I that speak in righteousness, mighty to save. Wherefore art thou red in thine apparel, and thy garments like him that treadeth in the wine-fat? I have trodden the wine-press alone, and of the people there was none with me: for I will tread them in mine anger, and trample them in my fury, and their blood shall be sprinkled upon my garments, and I will stain all my raiment. For the day of vengeance is in mine heart, and the year of my redeemed is come. And I looked, and there was none to help; and I wondered that there was none to uphold: therefore mine own arm brought salvation unto me, and my fury it upheld me. And I will tread down the people in mine anger, and make them drunk in my fury, and I will bring down their strength to the earth. I will mention the loving-kindnesses of the Lord, and the praises of the Lord, according to all that the Lord hath bestowed on us, and the great goodness towards the house of Israel, which he hath bestowed on them, according to his mercies, and according to the multitude of his loving-kindnesses. For he said, Surely they are my people, children that will not lie: so he was their Saviour. In all their affliction he was afflicted, and the Angel of his presence saved them: in his love, and in his pity, he redeemed them, and he bare them, and carried them all the days of old. But they rebelled, and vexed his Holy Spirit; therefore he was turned to be their enemy, and he fought against them. Then he remembered the days of old, Moses and his people, saying, Where is he that brought them up out of the sea with the shepherd of his flock? where is he that put his Holy Spirit within him? that led them by the right hand of Moses, with his glorious arm, dividing the water before them, to make himself an everlasting Name? that led them through the deep as an horse in the wilderness, that they should not stumble? As a beast goeth down into the valley, the Spirit of the Lord caused him to rest: so didst thou lead thy people, to make thyself a glorious Name. Look down from heaven, and behold from the habitation of thy holiness, and of thy glory: where is thy zeal, and thy strength, the sounding of thy bowels, and of thy mercies towards me? Are they restrained? Doubtless thou art our Father, though Abraham be ignorant of us, and Israel acknowledge us not: Thou, O Lord, art our Father, our Redeemer, thy Name is from everlasting. O Lord, why hast thou made us to err from thy ways? and hardened our hearts from thy fear? Return for thy servants sake, the tribes of thine inheritance. The people of thy holiness have possessed it but a little while: our adversaries have trodden down thy sanctuary. We are thine: thou never barest rule over them; they were not called by thy Name.

The Gospel. Mark 14, 1.

AFTER two days was the feast of the Passover, and of unleavened bread: and the chief priests and the scribes sought how they might take him by craft, and put him to death. But they said, Not on the feast-day, lest there be an uproar of the people. And being in Bethany, in the house of Simon the leper, as he sat at meat, there came a woman having an alabaster box of ointment of spikenard, very precious; and she brake the box, and poured it on his head. And there were some that had indignation within themselves, and said, Why was this waste of the ointment made? for it might have been sold for more than three hundred pence, and have been given to the poor: and they murmured against her. And Jesus said, Let her alone; why trouble ye her? she hath wrought a good work on me: for ye have the poor with you always, and whensoever ye will ye may do them good; but me ye have not always. She hath done what she could; she is come aforehand to anoint my body to the burying. Verily I say unto you, Wheresoever this Gospel shall be preached throughout the whole world, this also that she hath done shall be spoken of for a memorial of her. And Judas Iscariot, one of the twelve, went unto the chief priests to betray him unto them. And when they heard it they were glad, and promised to give him money. And he sought how he might conveniently betray him. And the first day of unleavened bread, when they killed the passover, his disciples said unto him, Where wilt thou that we go and prepare, that thou mayest eat the passover? And he sendeth forth two of his disciples, and saith unto them, Go ye into the city, and there shall meet you a man bearing a pitcher of water; follow him: And wheresoever he shall go in, say ye to the good-man of the house, The Master saith, Where is the guest-chamber, where I shall eat the passover with my disciples? And he will shew you a large upper-room furnished, and prepared: there make ready for us. And his disciples went forth, and came into the city, and found as he had said unto them: and they made ready the passover. And in the evening he cometh with the twelve. And as they sat, and did eat, Jesus said, Verily I say unto you, One of you which eateth with me shall betray me. And they began to be sorrowful, and to say unto him one by one, Is it I? and another said, Is it I? And he answered and said unto them, It is one of the twelve that dippeth with me in the dish. The Son of Man indeed goeth, as it is written of him: but woe to that man by whom the Son of Man is betrayed: good were it for that man if he had never been born. And as they did eat, Jesus took bread, and blessed, and brake it, and gave to them, and said, Take, eat: this is my body. And he took the cup, and when he had given thanks he gave it to them: and they all drank of it. And he said unto them, This is my blood of the new testament, which is shed for many. Verily I say unto you, I will drink no more of the fruit of the vine, until that day that I drink it new in the Kingdom of God. And when they had sung an hymn they went out into the mount of Olives. And Jesus saith unto them, All ye shall be offended because of me this night: for it is written, I will smite the shepherd, and the sheep shall be scattered. But, after that I am risen, I will go before you into Galilee. But Peter said unto him, Although all shall be offended, yet will not I. And Jesus saith unto him, Verily I say unto thee, That this day, even in this night, before the cock crow twice, thou shalt deny me thrice. But he spake the more vehemently, If I should die with thee, I will not deny thee in any wise. Likewise also said they all. And they came to a place which was named Gethsemane: and he saith to his disciples, Sit ye here, while I shall pray. And he taketh with him Peter, and James, and John, and began to be sore amazed, and to be very heavy, and saith unto them, My soul is exceeding sorrowful unto death; tarry ye here, and watch. And he went forward a little, and fell on the ground, and prayed, that, if it were possible, the hour might pass from him. And he said, Abba, Father, all things are possible unto thee; take away this cup from me; nevertheless, not what I will, but what thou wilt. And he cometh and findeth them sleeping, and saith unto Peter, Simon, sleepest thou? couldest not thou watch one hour? Watch ye and pray, lest ye enter into temptation: the spirit truly is ready, but the flesh is weak. And again he went away, and prayed, and spake the same words. And when he returned he found them asleep again, (for their eyes were heavy,) neither wist they what to answer him. And he cometh the third time, and saith unto them, Sleep on now, and take your rest: it is enough, the hour is come; behold, the Son of Man is betrayed into the hands of sinners. Rise up, let us go; lo, he that betrayeth me is at hand. And immediately, while he yet spake, cometh Judas, one of the twelve, and with him a great multitude with swords and staves, from the chief priests, and the scribes, and the elders. And he that betrayed him had given them a token, saying, Whomsoever I shall kiss, that same is he; take him, and lead him away safely. And as soon as he was come he goeth straightway to him, and saith, Master, master; and kissed him. And they laid their hands on him, and took him. And one of them that stood by drew a sword, and smote a servant of the high priest, and cut off his ear. And Jesus answered, and said unto them, Are ye come out as against a thief, with swords and with staves, to take me? I was daily with you in the temple teaching, and ye took me not: but the Scriptures must be fulfilled. And they all forsook him, and fled. And there followed him a certain young man, having a linen cloth cast about his naked body; and the young men laid hold on him: and he left the linen cloth, and fled from them naked. And they led Jesus away to the high priest: and with him were assembled all the chief priests, and the elders, and the scribes. And Peter followed him afar off, even into the palace of the high priest: and he sat with the servants, and warmed himself at the fire. And the chief priests and all the council sought for witness against Jesus to put him to death; and found none. For many bare false witness against him, but their witness agreed not together. And there arose certain, and bare false witness against him, saying, We heard him say, I will destroy this temple that is made with hands, and within three days I will build another made without hands. But neither so did their witness agree together. And the high priest stood up in the midst, and asked Jesus, saying, Answerest thou nothing? what is it which these witness against thee? But he held his peace, and answered nothing. Again the high priest asked him, and said unto him, Art thou the Christ, the Son of the Blessed? And Jesus said, I am; and ye shall see the Son of Man sitting on the right hand of power, and coming in the clouds of heaven. Then the high priest rent his clothes, and saith, What need we any further witnesses? ye have heard the blasphemy: what think ye? And they all condemned him to be guilty of death.

And some began to spit on him, and to cover his face, and to buffet him, and to say unto him, Prophesy: and the servants did strike him with the palms of their hands. And as Peter was beneath in the palace there cometh one of the maids of the high priest; and when she saw Peter warming himself she looked upon him, and said, And thou also wast with Jesus of Nazareth. But he denied, saying, I know not, neither understand I what thou sayest. And he went out into the porch; and the cock crew. And a maid saw him again, and began to say to them that stood by, This is one of them. And he denied it again. And a little after, they that stood by said again to Peter, Surely thou art one of them; for thou art a Galilean, and thy speech agreeth thereto. But he began to curse and to swear, saying, I know not this man of whom ye speak. And the second time the cock crew. And Peter called to mind the word that Jesus said unto him, Before the cock crow twice, thou shalt deny me thrice. And when he thought thereon, he wept.

Tuesday before Easter

For the Epistle. Is. 50, 5.

THE Lord God hath opened mine ear, and I was not rebellious, neither turned away back. I gave my back to the smiters, and my cheeks to them that plucked off the hair: I hid not my face from shame and spitting. For the Lord God will help me, therefore shall I not be confounded: therefore have I set my face like a flint, and I know that I shall not be ashamed. He is near that justifieth me; who will contend with me? Let us stand together; who is mine adversary? let him come near to me. Behold, the Lord God will help me; who is he that shall condemn me? Lo, they all shall wax old as a garment: the moth shall eat them up. Who is among you that feareth the Lord, that obeyeth the voice of his servant, that walketh in darkness, and hath no light? let him trust in the Name of the Lord, and stay upon his God. Behold, all ye that kindle a fire, that compass yourselves about with sparks; walk in the light of your fire, and in the sparks that ye have kindled. This shall ye have of mine hand, ye shall lie down in sorrow.

The Gospel †And straightway in the morning, p.159, ending at this man was the Son of God.†

Wednesday before Easter

The Epistle. Heb. 9, 16.

WHERE a testament is, there must also of necessity be the death of the testator: for a testament is of force after men are dead; otherwise it is of no strength at all whilst the testator liveth. Whereupon, neither the first testament was dedicated without blood: for when Moses had spoken every precept to all the people, according to the law, he took the blood of calves and of goats, with water, and scarlet wool, and hyssop, and sprinkled both the book, and all the people, saying, This is the blood of the testament, which God hath enjoined unto you. Moreover, he sprinkled with blood both the tabernacle, and all the vessels of the ministry. And almost all things are by the law purged with blood: and without shedding of blood is no remission. It was therefore necessary that the patterns of things in the heavens should be purified with these; but the heavenly things themselves with better sacrifices than these. For Christ is not entered into the holy places made with hands, which are the figures of the true, but into heaven itself, now to appear in the presence of God for us; nor yet that he should offer himself often, as the high priest entereth into the holy place every year with blood of others: for then must he often have suffered since the foundation of the world; but now once in the end of the world hath he appeared to put away sin by the sacrifice of himself. And as it is appointed unto men once to die, but after this the judgment: so Christ was once offered to bear the sins of many; and unto them that look for him shall he appear the second time without sin unto salvation.

The Gospel. Luke 22, 1.

NOW the feast of unleavened bread drew nigh, which is called the Passover. And the chief priests and scribes sought how they might kill him; for they feared the people. Then entered Satan into Judas surnamed Iscariot, being of the number of the twelve. And he went his way, and communed with the chief priests and captains, how he might betray him unto them. And they were glad, and covenanted to give him money. And he promised, and sought opportunity to betray him unto them in the absence of the multitude. Then came the day of unleavened bread, when the passover must be killed. And he sent Peter and John, saying, Go and prepare us the passover, that we may eat. And they said unto him, Where wilt thou that we prepare? And he said unto them, Behold, when ye are entered into the city, there shall a man meet you, bearing a pitcher of water; follow him into the house where he entereth in. And ye shall say unto the goodman of the house, The Master saith unto thee, Where is the guest-chamber, where I shall eat the passover with my disciples? And he shall shew you a large upper room furnished; there make ready. And they went, and found as he had said unto them: and they made ready the passover. And when the hour was come he sat down, and the twelve Apostles with him. And he said unto them, With desire I have desired to eat this passover with you before I suffer: for I say unto you, I will not any more eat thereof, until it be fulfilled in the Kingdom of God. And he took the cup, and gave thanks, and said, Take this, and divide it among yourselves. For I say unto you, I will not drink of the fruit of the vine, until the Kingdom of God shall come. And he took bread, and gave thanks, and brake it, and gave unto them, saying, This is my body, which is given for you: this do in remembrance of me. Likewise also the cup after supper, saying, This cup is the new testament in my blood, which is shed for you. But behold, the hand of him that betrayeth me is with me on the table. And truly the Son of Man goeth as it was determined; but woe unto that man by whom he is betrayed. And they began to enquire among themselves, which of them it was that should do this thing. And there was also a strife among them, which of them should be accounted the greatest. And he said unto them, The kings of the Gentiles exercise lordship over them, and they that exercise authority upon them are called benefactors. But ye shall not be so: but he that is greatest among you, let him be as the younger; and he that is chief, as he that doth serve. For whether is greater, he that sitteth at meat, or he that serveth? is not he that sitteth at meat? but I am among you as he that serveth. Ye are they which have continued with me in my temptations. And I appoint unto you a kingdom, as my Father hath appointed unto me; that ye may eat and drink at my table in my kingdom, and sit on thrones, judging the twelve tribes of Israel. And the Lord said, Simon, Simon, behold, Satan hath desired to have you, that he may sift you as wheat: but I have prayed for thee, that thy faith fail not; and when thou art converted, strengthen thy brethren. And he said unto him, Lord, I am ready to go with thee both into prison and to death. And he said, I tell thee, Peter, the cock shall not crow this day, before that thou shalt thrice deny that thou knowest me. And he said unto them, When I sent you without purse, and scrip, and shoes, lacked ye anything? And they said, Nothing. Then said he unto them, But now, he that hath a purse, let him take it, and likewise his scrip: and he that hath no sword, let him sell his garment, and buy one. For I say unto you, that this that is written must yet be accomplished in me, And he was reckoned among the transgressors: for the things concerning me have an end. And they said, Lord, behold, here are two swords. And he said unto them, It is enough. And he came out, and went, as he was wont, to the mount of Olives, and his disciples also followed him. And when he was at the place, he said unto them, Pray, that ye enter not into temptation. And he was withdrawn from them about a stone's cast, and kneeled down and prayed, saying, Father, if thou be willing, remove this cup from me: nevertheless, not my will, but thine be done. And there appeared an Angel unto him from heaven, strengthening him. And being in an agony, he prayed more earnestly; and his sweat was as it were great drops of blood falling down to the ground. And when he rose from prayer, and was come to his disciples, he found them sleeping for sorrow, and said unto them, Why sleep ye? rise and pray, lest ye enter into temptation. And while he yet spake, behold, a multitude, and he that was called Judas, one of the twelve, went before them, and drew near unto Jesus to kiss him. But Jesus said unto him, Judas, betrayest thou the Son of Man with a kiss? When they who were about him saw what would follow, they said unto him, Lord, shall we smite with the sword? And one of them smote the servant of the high priest, and cut off his right ear. And Jesus answered and said, Suffer ye thus far. And he touched his ear, and healed him. Then Jesus said unto the chief priests, and captains of the temple, and the elders who were come to him, Be ye come out as against a thief, with swords and staves? When I was daily with you in the temple, ye stretched forth no hands against me: but this is your hour, and the power of darkness. Then took they him, and led him, and brought him into the high priest's house: and Peter followed afar off. And when they had kindled a fire in the midst of the hall, and were set down together, Peter sat down among them. But a certain maid beheld him, as he sat by the fire, and earnestly looked upon him, and said, This man was also with him. And he denied him, saying, Woman, I know him not. And after a little while another saw him, and said, Thou art also of them. And Peter said, Man, I am not. And about the space of one hour after, another confidently affirmed, saying, Of a truth this fellow also was with him; for he is a Galilean. And Peter said, Man, I know not what thou sayest. And immediately, while he yet spake, the cock crew. And the Lord turned, and looked upon Peter; and Peter remembered the word of the Lord, how he had said unto him, Before the cock crow, thou shalt deny me thrice. And Peter went out, and wept bitterly. And the men that held Jesus mocked him, and smote him. And when they had blindfolded him, they struck him on the face, and asked him, saying, Prophesy, who is it that smote thee? And many other things blasphemously spake they against him. And as soon as it was day, the elders of the people, and the chief priests, and the scribes, came together, and led him into their council, saying, Art thou the Christ? tell us. And he said unto them, If I tell you, ye will not believe: and if I also ask you, ye will not answer me, nor let me go. Hereafter shall the Son of Man sit on the right hand of the power of God. Then said they all, Art thou then the Son of God? And he said unto them, Ye say that I am. And they said, What need we any further witness? for we ourselves have heard of his own mouth.

Thursday before Easter
The Epistle. I Cor. 11, 17.

IN this that I declare unto you, I praise you not; that ye come together not for the better, but for the worse. For first of all, when ye come together in the church, I hear that there be divisions among you, and I partly believe it. For there must be also heresies among you, that they who are approved may be made manifest among you. When ye come together therefore into one place, this is not to eat the Lord's supper: for in eating every one taketh before other his own supper; and one is hungry, and another is drunken. What, have ye not houses to eat and to drink in? or despise ye the church of God, and shame them that have not? What shall I say to you? shall I praise you in this? I praise you not. For I have received of the Lord that which also I delivered unto you, That the Lord Jesus, the same night in which he was betrayed, took bread; and when he had given thanks, he brake it, and said, Take, eat; this is my body, which is broken for you: this do in remembrance of me. After the same manner also he took the cup, when he had supped, saying, This cup is the new testament in my blood: this do ye, as oft as ye drink it, in remembrance of me. For as often as ye eat this bread, and drink this cup, ye do shew the Lord's death till he come. Wherefore, whosoever shall eat this bread, or drink this cup of the Lord, unworthily, shall be guilty of the body and blood of the Lord. But let a man examine himself, and so let him eat of that bread, and drink of that cup. For he that eateth and drinketh unworthily eateth and drinketh judgment to himself, not discerning the Lord's body. For this cause many are weak and sickly among you, and many sleep. For if we would judge ourselves, we should not be judged. But when we are judged, we are chastened of the Lord, that we should not be condemned with the world. Wherefore, my brethren, when ye come together to eat, tarry one for another. And if any man hunger, let him eat at home; that ye come not together unto condemnation. And the rest will I set in order when I come.

The Gospel †The whole multitude of them arose, as on p. 163, ending at beholding these things.†

Good Friday

The Collects.

ALMIGHTY God, we beseech thee graciously to behold this thy family, for which our Lord Jesus Christ was contented to be betrayed, and given up into the hands of wicked men, and to suffer death upon the cross, who now liveth and reigneth with thee and the Holy Ghost, ever one God, world without end. ℟. Amen.

ALMIGHTY and everlasting God, by whose Spirit the whole body of the Church is governed and sanctified; Receive our supplications and prayers, which we offer before thee for all estates of men in thy holy Church, that every member of the same, in his vocation and ministry, may truly and godly serve thee; through our Lord and Saviour Jesus Christ. ℟. Amen.

O MERCIFUL God, who hast made all men, and hatest nothing that thou hast made, nor wouldest the death of a sinner, but rather that he should be converted and live; Have mercy upon all Jews, Turks, Infidels, and Hereticks, and take from them all ignorance, hardness of heart, and contempt of thy Word; and so fetch them home, blessed Lord, to thy flock, that they may be saved among the remnant of the true Israelites, and be made one fold under one shepherd, Jesus Christ our Lord, who liveth and reigneth with thee and the Holy Spirit, one God, world without end. ℟. Amen.

The Epistle. Heb. 10, 1.

THE law having a shadow of good things to come, and not the very image of the things, can never with those sacrifices, which they offered year by year continually, make the comers thereunto perfect: for then would they not have ceased to be offered? because that the worshippers once purged should have had no more conscience of sins. But in those sacrifices there is a remembrance again made of sins every year. For it is not possible that the blood of bulls and of goats should take away sins. Wherefore, when he cometh into the world, he saith, Sacrifice and offering thou wouldest not, but a body hast thou prepared me: In burnt-offerings and sacrifices for sin thou hast had no pleasure: Then said I, Lo, I come (in the volume of the book it is written of me) to do thy will, O God. Above, when he said, Sacrifice and offering, and burnt-offerings, and offering for sin thou wouldest not, neither hadst pleasure therein, which are offered by the Law: then said he, Lo, I come to do thy will, O God. He taketh away the first, that he may establish the second. By the which will we are sanctified, through the offering of the body of Jesus Christ once for all. And every priest standeth daily ministering, and offering oftentimes the same sacrifices, which can never take away sins. But this man, after he had offered one sacrifice for sins, for ever sat down on the right hand of God; from henceforth expecting till his enemies be made his foot-stool. For by one offering he hath perfected for ever them that are sanctified: Whereof the Holy Ghost also is a witness to us: for after that he had said before, This is the covenant that I will make with them after those days, saith the Lord, I will put my laws into their hearts, and in their minds will I write them; and their sins and iniquities will I remember no more. Now where remission of these is, there is no more offering for sin. Having therefore, brethren, boldness to enter into the holiest by the blood of Jesus, by a new and living way, which he hath consecrated for us, through the vail, that is to say, his flesh; and having an High Priest over the house of God; let us draw near with a true heart, in full assurance of faith, having our hearts sprinkled from an evil conscience, and our bodies washed with pure water. Let us hold fast the profession of our faith without wavering; (for he is faithful that promised;) and let us consider one another to provoke unto love, and to good works: not forsaking the assembling of ourselves together, as the manner of some is; but exhorting one another: and so much the more, as ye see the day approaching.

The Gospel †Pilate therefore took Jesus, p. 179, ending at whom they pierced.†

Easter Even

Collect.

GRANT, O Lord, that as we are baptized into the death of thy blessed Son our Saviour Jesus Christ, so by continual mortifying our corrupt affections we may be buried with him; and that through the grave, and gate of death, we may pass to our joyful resurrection; for his merits, who died, and was buried, and rose again for us, thy Son Jesus Christ our Lord. ℟. Amen.

The Epistle. I Peter 3, 17.

IT is better, if the will of God be so, that ye suffer for well-doing, than for evil-doing. For Christ also hath once suffered for sins, the just for the unjust, that he might bring us to God, being put to death in the flesh, but quickened by the Spirit. By which also he went and preached unto the spirits in prison; which sometime were disobedient, when once the long-suffering of God waited in the days of Noah, while the ark was a preparing; wherein few, that is, eight souls, were saved by water. The like figure whereunto, even baptism, doth also now save us, (not the putting away the filth of the flesh, but the answer of a good conscience towards God,) by the resurrection of Jesus Christ: who is gone into heaven, and is on the right hand of God, Angels and authorities and powers being made subject unto him.

The Gospel. Matt. 27, 57.

WHEN the even was come, there came a rich man of Arimathæa, named Joseph, who also himself was Jesus' disciple. He went to Pilate, and begged the body of Jesus. Then Pilate commanded the body to be delivered. And when Joseph had taken the body, he wrapped it in a clean linen cloth, and laid it in his own new tomb, which he had hewn out in the rock; and he rolled a great stone to the door of the sepulchre, and departed. And there was Mary Magdalene, and the other Mary, sitting over against the sepulchre. Now the next day that followed the day of the preparation, the chief priests and Pharisees came together unto Pilate, saying, Sir, we remember that that deceiver said, while he was yet alive, After three days I will rise again. Command therefore that the sepulchre be made sure until the third day, lest his disciples come by night and steal him away, and say unto the people, He is risen from the dead: so the last error shall be worse than the first. Pilate said unto them, Ye have a watch; go your way, make it as sure as you can. So they went and made the sepulchre sure, sealing the stone, and setting a watch.

THE SECOND SUNDAY IN PASSION TIDE

COMMONLY CALLED

PALM SUNDAY

Double of 1st class.

THE SOLEMN PROCESSION OF PALMS
IN HONOUR OF CHRIST THE KING

All which is printed in italics in the following rubrics refers to the simple celebration, when the sacred ceremonies are performed by the priest, without sacred ministers.

THE BLESSING OF PALMS

1. At the appointed hour, in choir after Terce, the sprinkling of water being omitted, the blessing of branches of palms or olives or other trees takes place.

2. The colour of the vestments is red.

3. The celebrant is vested in amice, alb, girdle, stole and cope, or remains without the chasuble; the sacred ministers wear dalmatic and tunicle.

3a. *The celebrant is vested in amice, alb, girdle, stole, and cope, or remains without the chasuble.*

4. The palms, unless they are already held in their hands by the faithful, are made ready on a table, covered with a white cloth, and placed in a position in the sanctuary, where they may best be seen by the people.

5. All things being duly disposed, the celebrant, with the sacred ministers, *or servers,* having made due reverence to the Altar, stands behind the table, turned towards the people.

Meanwhile the following antiphon is sung.

Antiphon.   Matt. 21, 9.

Hosanna to the Son of David: blessed is he that cometh in the name of the Lord. O King of Israel: Hosanna in the highest.

6. Then the celebrant, with joined hands, blesses the palms, saying in the tone of the ferial Collect:

℣. The Lord be with you.

       To which all respond:

℟. And with thy spirit.

7. In the following Collect the celebrant shall say, as is suitable to the kind of branches, these branches of palm, or these branches of olive, or these branches of trees, or these branches of palm and olive, or these branches of palm (olive) and other trees.

Let us pray.   Collect.

BL✠ESS, O Lord, we beseech thee, these branches of palm (or olive or trees or palm and olive or palm (olive) and other trees): and grant; that as thy people on this day perform this outward observance to thine honour, so they, inwardly fulfilling the same with reverence and purity of heart, may win the victory over the enemy, and continually abound in all good works. Through.

8. Then the celebrant first sprinkles the palms, set upon the table, thrice, then, at the rails, the palms of the faithful, where they themselves, as has been said, already hold them in their hands, unless it is desired to perform the sprinkling of them, passing through the body of the church.

9. Then the celebrant puts incense into the thurible, in the usual manner, and first thrice censes the blessed palms, set upon the table, then, at the rails, or passing through the body of the church, those of the faithful.

The sacred ministers, *or the servers,* accompany the celebrant, both at the sprinkling and the censing of the palms, holding the edge of the cope.

THE DISTRIBUTION OF THE PALMS

10. The blessing being completed, the distribution of the palms is made, according to the custom of the place.

11. The celebrant, standing on the predella of the Altar, turning to the people, the sacred ministers, *or servers,* assisting him, gives the blessed palms first to all the clergy in order, then to the servers, finally, at the rails, to the faithful.

12. And when he begins to distribute, the following antiphons and psalms are sung, in this manner:

Antiphon 1.

The children of the Hebrews, bearing branches of olive, went out to meet the Lord, crying out and saying: Hosanna in the highest.

Ps. 24, 1-2 and 7-10. *Domini est terra.*

THE earth is the Lord's, and all that therein is, * the compass of the world, and they that dwell therein.

For he hath founded it upon the seas, * and prepared it upon the floods.

And the antiphon is repeated:

The children of the Hebrews, bearing branches of olive, went out to meet the Lord, crying out and saying: Hosanna in the highest.

Lift up your heads, O ye gates, and be ye lift up, ye everlasting doors, * and the King of glory shall come in!

Who is the King of glory? * it is the Lord strong and mighty, even the Lord mighty in battle.

Ant. The children of the Hebrews, bearing.

Lift up your heads, O ye gates, and be ye lift up, ye everlasting doors, * and the King of glory shall come in.

Who is the King of glory? * even the Lord of hosts, he is the King of glory.

Ant. The children of the Hebrews, bearing.

Glory be to the Father, and to the Son, * and to the Holy Ghost,

As it was in the beginning, is now, and ever shall be, * world with end. Amen.

Ant. The children of the Hebrews, bearing.

Antiphon 2.

The children of the Hebrews spread their garments in the way, and cried out, saying: Hosanna to the Son of David: blessed is he that cometh in the name of the Lord.

Ps. 47. *Plaudite manibus.*

O CLAP your hands together, all ye people, * sing unto God with the voice of melody.

For the Lord is high, and to be feared, * he is the great King upon all the earth.

And the antiphon is repeated:

The children of the Hebrews spread their garments in the way, and cried out, saying: Hosanna to the Son of David: blessed is he that cometh in the name of the Lord.

He shall subdue the people unto us * and the nations under our feet.

He shall choose out an heritage for us, * even the worship of Jacob, whom he loved.

And the antiphon is repeated:

The children of the Hebrews spread their garments in the way, and cried out, saying: Hosanna to the Son of David: blessed is he that cometh in the name of the Lord.

God is gone up with a merry noise, * and the Lord with the sound of the trump.

O sing praises, sing praises unto our God, * O sing praises, sing praises unto our King.

And the antiphon is repeated:

The children of the Hebrews spread their garments in the way, and cried out, saying: Hosanna to the Son of David: blessed is he that cometh in the name of the Lord.

For God is the King of all the earth, * sing ye praises with understanding.

God reigneth over the heathen, * God sitteth upon his holy seat.

And the antiphon is repeated:

The children of the Hebrews spread their garments in the way, and cried out, saying: Hosanna to the Son of David: blessed is he that cometh in the name of the Lord.

The princes of the people * are joined unto the people of the God of Abraham.

For God, which is very high exalted, * doth defend the earth as it were with a shield.

And the antiphon is repeated:

The children of the Hebrews spread their garments in the way, and cried out, saying: Hosanna to the Son of David: blessed is he that cometh in the name of the Lord.

Glory be to the Father and to the Son, * and to the Holy Ghost.

As it was in the beginning, is now, and ever shall be, * world without end. Amen.

And the antiphon is repeated:

The children of the Hebrews spread their garments in the way, and cried out, saying: Hosanna to the Son of David: blessed is he that cometh in the name of the Lord.

If the above do not suffice, they shall be repeated until the distribution be ended; but if it be ended earlier, then the singing ends with Glória Patri, and the antiphon is repeated.

THE READING OF THE GOSPEL

13. The distribution of palms being ended and the table removed, the celebrant washes his hands, saying nothing: then, ascending the Altar, he kisses it in the midst, and puts incense into the thurible, in the usual manner. The deacon carries the book of the gospels to the Altar and sets it down thereon, and all things are done as in Mass, when the gospel is to be sung.

13a. The celebrant shall do all things as is usual at other times, when the priest alone celebrates Mass with chant.

14.

☩ The Continuation of the holy Gospel according to Matthew.

Matt. 21, 1-9.

AT that time: When Jesus drew nigh unto Jerusalem, and was come to Bethphage unto the Mount of Olives; then sent he two disciples, saying unto them: Go into the village over against you, and straightway ye shall find an ass tied, and a colt with her: loose them and bring them unto me: and if any man say ought unto you, ye shall say, The Lord hath need of them, and straightway he will send them. All this was done, that it might be fulfilled which was spoken by the Prophet, saying: Tell ye the daughter of Sion: Behold thy King cometh unto thee, meek and sitting upon an ass, and a colt the foal of an ass. And the disciples went, and did as Jesus commanded them. And brought the ass, and the colt, and put on them their clothes, and they set him thereon. And a very great multitude spread their garments in the way: others cut down branches from the trees, and strawed them in the way: and the multitudes that went before, and that followed, cried, saying: Hosanna to the Son of David: blessed is he that cometh in the name of the Lord.

15. The Gospel ended, the subdeacon carries the book to be kissed by the celebrant, who is not censed by the deacon.

THE PROCESSION WITH BLESSED PALMS

16. These things being done, the celebrant puts incense into the thurible, in the usual manner. And the deacon, turning to the people, says:

℣. Let us proceed in peace.

All respond:

℟. In the name of Christ. Amen.

The Procession begins. The thurifer goes first with smoking censer: then another subdeacon vested, or an acolyte, *or one of the servers,* carrying the cross not veiled, between two acolytes, *or servers,* with lighted candles: the clergy follow in order, last of all the celebrant with deacon and subdeacon, after them the faithful, carrying blessed branches in their hands.

17. The Procession shall go, if possible, outside the church, by some longer route. If in any place there be a second church, in which the blessing of palms can be conveniently performed, nothing need prevent the blessing of palms being done there, and then the Procession going to the principal church.

18. As the Procession begins, the following antiphons may be sung, all, or some, according to opportunity:

Antiphon 1.

The multitudes with flowers and palms go forth to meet the Redeemer: and render worthy homage to the triumphant conqueror: the Gentiles with their lips proclaim the Son of God: and in the praise of Christ their voices thunder through the skies: Hosanna!

Antiphon 2.

With the Angels and the children may we be found faithful, crying unto the vanquisher of death: Hosanna in the highest!

Antiphon 3.

A great multitude, that were come together to the feast, cried unto the Lord: Blessed is he that cometh in the name of the Lord: Hosanna in the highest!

Palm Sunday

Antiphon 4. Luke 19, 37-38.

The whole multitude of them that went down began to rejoice and praise God with a loud voice, for all the mighty works which they had seen, saying: Blessed is the King that cometh in the name of the Lord; peace on earth, and glory in the highest.

19. As the Procession goes forward, the following hymn is sung, the people, if possible, continually repeating the first verse, as noted below.

Hymn to Christ the King.

Choir: Gloria, laus et honor.

GLORY and honour and praise be to thee, our King and Redeemer,
Christ, to whom children of old loved their Hosannas to raise.

All:

Glory and honour and praise be to thee, our King and Redeemer,
Christ, to whom children of old loved their Hosannas to raise.

Choir:

Israel's Monarch art thou, and the glorious Offspring of David,
Thou that approachest, a King blest in the Name of the Lord.

All:

Glory and honour and praise be to thee, our King and Redeemer,
Christ, to whom children of old loved their Hosannas to raise.

Choir:

Glory to thee in the highest, the heavenly armies are singing;
Glory to thee upon earth, man and creation reply.

All:

Glory and honour and praise be to thee, our King and Redeemer,
Christ, to whom children of old loved their Hosannas to raise.

Choir:

Met thee with palms in their hands that day the folk of the Hebrews,
We with our prayers and our hymns now to thy presence approach.

All:

Glory and honour and praise be to thee, our King and Redeemer,
Christ, to whom children of old loved their Hosannas to raise.

Choir:

They to thee offered their praise for to herald thy sorrowful Passion;
We to the King on his throne utter the jubilant hymn.

All:

Glory and honour and praise be to thee, our King and Redeemer,
Christ, to whom children of old loved their Hosannas to raise.

Choir:

They were then pleasing to thee, unto thee our devotion be pleasing;
Merciful King, kind King, who in all goodness art pleased.

All:

Glory and honour and praise be to thee, our King and Redeemer,
Christ, to whom children of old loved their Hosannas to raise.

Antiphon 5.

All men praise thy name, and say: Blessed is he that cometh in the name of the Lord: Hosanna in the highest.

Ps. 147. Lauda, Jerusalem.

PRAISE the Lord, O Jerusalem: * praise thy God, O Sion.

For he hath made fast the bars of thy gates: * and hath blessed thy children within thee.

He maketh peace in thy borders: * and filleth thee with the flour of wheat.

Palm Sunday

He sendeth forth his commandment upon earth: * and his word runneth very swiftly.

He giveth snow like wool: * and scattereth the hoar-frost like ashes.

He casteth forth his ice like morsels: * who is able to abide his frost?

He sendeth out his word, and melteth them: * he bloweth with his wind, and the waters flow.

He sheweth his word unto Jacob: * his statutes and ordinances unto Israel.

He hath not dealt so with any nation: * neither have the heathen knowledge of his laws.

Glory be to the Father and to the Son, * and to the Holy Ghost.

As it was in the beginning, is now, and ever shall be, * world without end. Amen.

And the antiphon is repeated:

All men praise thy name, and say: Blessed is he that cometh in the name of the Lord: Hosanna in the highest.

Antiphon 6.

With palms bright shining we fall low before the Lord: let us all go forth to meet him with hymns and songs, glorifying him and saying: Blessed be the Lord.

Antiphon 7.

Hail, our King, Son of David, Redeemer of the world, whom the Prophets foretold should come to be the Saviour of the house of Israel. For the Father hath sent thee into the world to be the saving victim, whom all the Saints awaited from the foundation of the world, and now: Hosanna to the Son of David. Blessed is he that cometh in the name of the Lord.

20. The hymn Christus vincit or some other hymn in honour of Christ the King may be sung by the faithful.

21. As the Procession enters the church, while the celebrant passes through the doors of the church, the last antiphon is begun.

Antiphon 8.

When the Lord entered the holy city, the children of the Hebrews, foretelling the resurrection of Life,

With branches of palm: Hosanna, they cried, in the highest.

When the people heard that Jesus was coming to Jerusalem, they went forth to meet him

With branches of palm: Hosanna, they cried, in the highest.

22. The celebrant, having arrived and reverenced the Altar, goes up with the sacred ministers, and standing between them, facing the people, a clerk, *or server,* holding the book, sings, in the ferial tone, the Collect to end the procession, with joined hands.

℣. The Lord be with you.

All: ℟. And with thy spirit.

Let us pray.   Collect.

O LORD Jesu Christ, our King and Redeemer, to whose honour we, bearing these branches, have sung our solemn praises: mercifully grant; that whithersoever these branches may be carried, there the grace of thy benediction may descend, and, all the wickedness and craft of the devil being put to nought, thy right hand may protect those whom thou hast redeemed: Who livest and reignest.

23. The Collect ended, the celebrant and ministers, having reverenced the Altar, lay aside the red vestments, putting on violet for the Mass.

24. Branches are not held in the hands, while the story of the Passion of the Lord is sung or read.

THE MASS

Station at St. John Lateran

1. The colour of the vestments is violet. The sacred ministers wear dalmatic and tunicle; as is observed also on Monday, Tuesday and Wednesday.

2. When the blessing and procession of palms has taken place before Mass, the celebrant with the sacred ministers, *or servers,* approaches the Altar, and, omitting the Psalm Júdica me, and the Confession, straightway goes up, kisses it in the midst, and incenses it in the usual manner.

3. Antiphon at the Entrance. (Introit.)

Ps. 22, 20 and 22. Domine, ne longe.

BE not thou far from me, O Lord, thou art my succour, haste thee to help me: save me from the lion's mouth, thou hast heard me also from among the horns of the unicorns. Ps. ibid., 1. My God, my God, look upon me, why hast thou forsaken me: and art so far from my health, and from the words of my complaint? Be not.

4. Let us pray.   Collect.

ALMIGHTY and everlasting God, who, *of thy tender love towards mankind, hast sent thy Son, our Saviour Jesus Christ,* to take upon him our flesh, and to suffer death upon the cross, that all mankind should follow the example of his great humility: mercifully grant; that we may both follow the example of his patience, and also be made partakers of his resurrection. Through the same.

or:* didst cause our Saviour* to take....

And this Collect only is said.

The Lesson from the Epistle of blessed Paul the Apostle to the Philippians.

Phil. 2, 5-11.

BRETHREN: Let this mind be in you, which was also in Christ Jesus: who, being in the form of God, thought it not robbery to be equal with God: but made himself of no reputation, and took upon him the form of a servant, and was made in the likeness of men. And being found in fashion as a man, he humbled himself, and became obedient unto death, even the death of the cross. Wherefore God also hath highly exalted him, and given him a name which is above every name: (Here genuflect) that at the name of Jesus every knee should bow, of things in heaven, and things in earth, and things under the earth: and that every tongue should confess that Jesus Christ is Lord, to the glory of God the Father.

6. Gradual. Ps. 73, 24 and 1-3. Thou has holden me by my right hand; thou shalt guide me with thy counsel: and after that receive me with glory. ℣. Truly God is loving unto Israel, even unto such as are of a clean heart; nevertheless, my feet were almost gone; my treadings had well nigh slipt: and why? I was grieved at the wicked, I do also see the ungodly in such prosperity.

7. Tract. Ps. 22, 2-9, 18-19, 22, 24 and 32. My God, my God, look upon me: why hast thou forsaken me? ℣. And art so far from my health, and from the words of my complaint? ℣. O my God, I cry in the daytime, but thou hearest not: and in the night season also I take no rest. ℣. And

The Second Sunday of the Passion

thou continuest holy, O thou worship of Israel. ℣. Our fathers hoped in thee: they trusted in thee, and thou didst deliver them. ℣. They called upon thee, and were holpen: they put their trust in thee, and were not confounded. ℣. But as for me, I am a worm, and no man: a very scorn of men, and the outcast of the people. ℣. All they that see me laugh me to scorn: they shoot out their lips, and shake their heads, saying: ℣. He trusted in God, that he would deliver him: let him deliver him, if he will have him. ℣. They stand staring and looking upon me: they part my garments among them, and cast lots upon my vesture. ℣. Save me from the lion's mouth: thou hast heard me also from among the horns of the unicorns. ℣. O praise the Lord, ye that fear him: magnify him, all ye of the seed of Jacob. ℣. They shall be counted unto the Lord for a generation: they shall come, and the heavens shall declare his righteousness: ℣. Unto a people that shall be born, whom the Lord hath made.

8. The reading of the Epistle being ended, bare lecterns are set on the Gospel side, on the floor of the sanctuary, and the singing or reading of the story of the Passion of the Lord is done in this manner:

It is sung or read by ministers at least in the order of Deacons, who come before the Altar, accompanied by two acolytes, *or servers,* without lights and without incense, and there kneeling on the lowest step, bowing low, they recite in a low voice, as usual, Cleanse my heart, and ask a blessing of the celebrant, saying **Bid, sir,** a blessing. The celebrant, turned towards them, answers in an audible voice:

The Lord be in your hearts, and on your lips, that ye may worthily and fitly proclaim his Gospel: in the name of the Father, and of the Son, ✠ and of the Holy Ghost. And they say: Amen.

Then together with the acolytes, *or servers,* they make a reverence, and go to the lecterns; they do not sign the book, nor themselves, as they begin to sing or read.

8a. The priest, having read the Gradual and Tract, says in the usual manner in the midst of the Altar, Cleanse my heart, Bid, Lord, *and* The Lord be in my heart.

Then on the Gospel side, at the Altar, he reads or sings in a clear voice the story of the Passion of the Lord, and he does not sign the book, nor himself, as he begins to read or sing.

9. This manner of singing or reading is observed also on Tuesday and Wednesday, when the story of the Passion of the Lord is sung or read.

10. The Gospel of the Passion and Death of the Lord according to Matthew: 26, 36-75; 27, 1-54.

The Passion of our Lord Jesus Christ according to Matthew.

AT that time: Cometh Jesus with his disciples unto a place called Gethsemane, and saith unto the disciples: ✠ Sit ye here, while I go and pray yonder. C. And he took with him Peter and the two sons of Zebedee, and began to be sorrowful and very heavy. Then saith he unto them: ✠ My soul is exceeding sorrowful, even unto death: tarry ye here, and watch with me. C. And he went a little farther, and fell on his face, and prayed, saying: ✠ O my Father, if it be possible, let this cup pass from me. Nevertheless not as I will, but as thou wilt. C. And he cometh unto the disciples, and findeth them asleep: and saith unto Peter: ✠ What, could ye not watch with me one hour? Watch and pray, that ye enter not into temptation. The spirit indeed is willing, but the flesh is weak. C. He went away again the second time, and prayed, saying: ✠ O my Father, if this cup may not pass away from me, except I drink it, thy will be done. C. And he came and found them asleep again: for their eyes were heavy. And he left them, and went away again, and prayed the third time, saying the same words. Then cometh he to his disciples, and saith unto them: ✠ Sleep on now, and take your rest: behold, the hour is at hand, and the Son of man is betrayed into the hands of sinners. Rise, let us be going: behold, he is at hand that doth betray me.

C. And while he yet spake, lo, Judas, one of the twelve, came, and with him a great multitude with swords and staves, from the chief priests and elders of the people. Now he that betrayed him gave them a sign, saying: S. Whomsoever I shall kiss, that same is he, hold him fast. C. And forthwith he came to Jesus, and said: S. Hail, Master. C. And kissed him. And Jesus said unto him: ✠ Friend, wherefore art thou come? C. Then came they, and laid hands on Jesus, and took him. And, behold, one of them which were with Jesus stretched out his hand, and drew his sword, and struck a servant of the high priest's, and smote off his ear. Then said Jesus unto him: ✠ Put up again thy sword into his place. For all they that take the sword shall perish with the sword. Thinkest thou that I cannot now pray to my Father, and he shall presently give me more than twelve legions of Angels? But how then shall the Scriptures be fulfilled, that thus it must be?

C. In that same hour said Jesus to the multitudes: ✠ Are ye come out as against a thief with swords and staves for to take me? I sat daily with you teaching in the temple, and ye laid no hold on me. C. But all this was done, that the Scriptures of the Prophets might be fulfilled. Then all the disciples forsook him, and fled.

And they that had laid hold on Jesus led him away to Caiaphas the high priest, where the scribes and the elders were assembled. But Peter followed him afar off unto the high priest's palace. And went in, and sat with the servants, to see the end. Now the chief priests, and elders, and all the council, sought false witness against Jesus, to put him to death: but found none, yea, though many false witnesses came, yet found they none. At the last came two false witnesses, and said: S. This fellow said: I am able to destroy the temple of God, and to build it in three days. C. And the high priest arose, and said unto him: S. Answerest thou nothing? what is it which these witness against thee? C. But Jesus held his peace. And the high priest answered and said unto him: S. I adjure thee by the living God, that thou tell us whether thou be the Christ, the Son of God. C. Jesus saith unto him: ✠ Thou hast said. Nevertheless I say unto you: Hereafter shall ye see the Son of man sitting on the right hand of power, and coming in the clouds of heaven. C. Then the high priest rent his clothes, saying: S. He hath spoken blasphemy: what further need have we of witnesses? Behold, now ye have heard his blasphemy: what think ye? C. They answered and said: S. He is guilty of death.

C. Then did they spit in his face, and buffeted him, and others smote him with the palms of the hands, saying: S. Prophesy unto us, thou Christ, who is he that smote thee? C. Now Peter sat without in the palace: and a damsel came unto him, saying: S. Thou also wast with Jesus of Galilee. C. But he denied before them all, saying: S. I know not what thou sayest. C. And when he was gone out into the porch, another maid saw him, and said unto them that were there: S. This fellow was also with Jesus of Nazareth. C. And again he denied with an oath: I do not know the man. And after a while came unto him they that stood by, and said to Peter: S. Surely thou also art one of them:

for thy speech bewrayeth thee. C. Then began he to curse and to swear, saying: S. I know not the man. C. And immediately the cock crew. And Peter remembered the word of Jesus, which said unto him: Before the cock crow, thou shalt deny me thrice. And he went out, and wept bitterly.

(† Matt. 27, 1.)

When the morning was come, all the chief priests and elders of the people took counsel against Jesus, to put him to death. And when they had bound him, they led him away, and delivered him to Pontius Pilate the governor. Then Judas who had betrayed him, when he saw that he was condemned, repented himself, and brought again the thirty pieces of silver to the chief priests and elders, saying: S. I have sinned, in that I have betrayed the innocent blood. C. And they said: S. What is that to us? See thou to that. C. And he cast down the pieces of silver in the temple, and departed: and went and hanged himself. And the chief priests took the silver pieces, and said: S. It is not lawful for to put them into the treasury: because it is the price of blood. C. And they took counsel, and bought with them the potter's field, to bury strangers in. Wherefore that field was called: The field of blood, unto this day. Then was fulfilled that which was spoken by Jeremy the Prophet, saying: And they took the thirty pieces of silver, the price of him that was valued, whom they of the children of Israel did value: and gave them for the potter's field, as the Lord appointed me.

And Jesus stood before the governor, and the governor asked him, saying: S. Art thou the King of the Jews? C. And Jesus said unto him: ✠ Thou sayest. C. And when he was accused of the chief priests and elders, he answered nothing. Then saith Pilate unto him: S. Hearest thou not how many things they witness against thee? C. And he answered him to never a word, insomuch that the governor marvelled greatly. Now at that feast the governor was wont to release unto the people a prisoner, whom they would. And they had then a notable prisoner, called Barabbas. Therefore when they were gathered together, Pilate said unto them: S. Whom will ye that I release unto you: Barabbas, or Jesus which is called Christ? C. For he knew that for envy they had delivered him. When he was set down on the judgment-seat, his wife sent unto him, saying: S. Have thou nothing to do with that just man: for I have suffered many things this day in a dream because of him. C. But the chief priests and elders persuaded the multitude that they should ask Barabbas, and destroy Jesus. The governor answered and said unto them: S. Whether of the twain will ye that I release unto you? C. They said: S. Barabbas. C. Pilate saith unto them: S. What shall I do then with Jesus, which is called Christ? C. They all say unto him: S. Let him be crucified. C. And the governor said: S. Why, what evil hath he done? C. But they cried out the more, saying: S. Let him be crucified. C. When Pilate saw that he could prevail nothing, but that rather a tumult was made: he took water, and washed his hands before the multitude, saying: S. I am innocent of the blood of this just person: see ye to it. C. Then answered all the people, and said: S. His blood be on us, and on our children. C. Then released he Barabbas unto them: and when he had scourged Jesus he delivered him to be crucified.

Then the soldiers of the governor took Jesus into the common hall, and gathered unto him the whole band of soldiers: and they stripped him, and put on him a scarlet robe: and when they had platted a crown of thorns they put it upon his head, and a reed in his right hand. And they bowed the knee before him, and mocked him, saying: S. Hail, King of the

Jews. C. And they spit upon him, and took the reed, and smote him on the head. And after that they had mocked him they took the robe off from him, and put his own raiment on him, and led him away to crucify him.

And as they came out they found a man of Cyrene, Simon by name: him they compelled to bear his cross. And when they were come unto a place called Golgotha, that is to say, a place of a skull, they gave him vinegar to drink mingled with gall. And when he had tasted thereof, he would not drink. And they crucified him, and parted his garments, casting lots: that it might be fulfilled, which was spoken by the Prophet: They parted my garments among them, and upon my vesture did they cast lots. And sitting down they watched him there. And set up over his head his accusation written: This is Jesus the King of the Jews.

Then were there two thieves crucified with him: one on the right hand, and another on the left. And they that passed by reviled him, wagging their heads, and saying: S. Thou that destroyest the temple, and buildest it in three days: save thyself. If thou be the Son of God, come down from the cross. C. Likewise also the chief priests mocking him, with the scribes and elders, said: S. He saved others, himself he cannot save: if he be the King of Israel, let him now come down from the cross, and we will believe him: he trusted in God: let him deliver him now, if he will have him; for he said: I am the Son of God. C. The thieves also, which were crucified with him, cast the same in his teeth.

Now from the sixth hour there was darkness over all the land unto the ninth hour. And about the ninth hour Jesus cried with a loud voice, saying: ✠ Eli, Eli, lama sabachtháni? C. That is to say: ✠ My God, my God, why hast thou forsaken me? C. Some of them that stood there, when they heard that, said: S. This man calleth for Elias. C. And straightway one of them ran, and took a spunge, and filled it with vinegar, and put it on a reed, and gave him to drink. The rest said: S. Let be, let us see whether Elias will come to save him. C. Jesus, when he had cried again with a loud voice, yielded up the ghost.

Here genuflect, and pause awhile.

And behold, the vail of the temple was rent in twain from the top to the bottom: and the earth did quake, and the rocks rent, and the graves were opened: and many bodies of saints which slept arose, and came out of the graves after his resurrection, and went into the holy city, and appeared unto many. Now when the centurion, and they that were with him, watching Jesus, saw the earthquake, and those things that were done, they feared greatly, saying: S. Truly this was the Son of God.†

C. And many women were there beholding afar off, which followed Jesus from Galilee, ministering unto him: among which was Mary Magdalene, and Mary the mother of James and Joses, and the mother of Zebedee's children.

When the even was come, there came a rich man of Arimathea, named Joseph, who also himself was Jesus' disciple. He went to Pilate, and begged the body of Jesus. Then Pilate commanded the body to be delivered. And when Joseph had taken the body, he wrapped it in a clean linen cloth, and laid it in his own new tomb, which he had hewn out in the rock. And he rolled a great stone to the door of the sepulchre, and departed.

After the singing or reading of the story of the Passion of the Lord, the celebrant does not kiss the book, nor is he incensed;

The Second Sunday of the Passion

which is observed also on Tuesday, Wednesday and Friday, when the story of the Passion of the Lord is sung or read.

11. He, who today celebrates a second or a third read Mass, is not bound to repeat the reading of the Passion of the Lord, but in place thereof reads the following Gospel, in the usual manner:

✠ The Continuation of the holy Gospel according to Matthew.

Matt. 27, 45-52.

AFTER they had crucified Jesus, from the sixth hour there was darkness over all the land unto the ninth hour. And about the ninth hour Jesus cried with a loud voice, saying: Eli, Eli, lama sabachtháni? That is to say: My God, my God, why hast thou forsaken me? Some of them that stood there, when they heard that, said: This man calleth for Elias. And straightway one of them ran, and took a spunge, and filled it with vinegar, and put it on a reed, and gave him to drink. The rest said: Let be, let us see whether Elias will come to save him. Jesus, when he had cried again with a loud voice, yielded up the ghost.

Here genuflect, and pause awhile.

And behold, the vail of the temple was rent in twain from the top to the bottom: and the earth did quake, and the rocks rent, and the graves were opened: and many bodies of saints which slept arose.

12. The Creed is said.

13. Antiphon at the Offertory. Ps. 69, 21-22. Thy rebuke hath broken my heart; I am full of heaviness: I looked for some to have pity on me, but there was no man, neither found I any to comfort me. They gave me gall to eat: and when I was thirsty they gave me vinegar to drink.

14. Secret.

GRANT, we beseech thee, O Lord: that the gift which we offer in the sight of thy majesty may obtain for us grace to serve thee with all godliness, and bring us in the end to everlasting felicity. Through.

15. Preface of the holy Cross.

16. Antiphon at the Communion.
Matt. 26, 42. Father, if this cup may not pass away from me, except I drink it: thy will be done.

17. Let us pray. Postcommunion.

O LORD, let the operation of this mystery avail for the cleansing of our sins: that we may thereby obtain those things which we ask, according to thy will. Through.

18. The celebrant, at the end of Mass, having given the blessing in the usual manner, omits the last Gospel, and all return to the sacristy.

In other Masses, without the blessing of palms, the following Gospel is read at the end:

✠ The Continuation of the holy Gospel according to Matthew.

Matt. 21, 1-9.

AT that time: When Jesus drew nigh unto Jerusalem, and was come to Bethphage unto the Mount of Olives; then sent he two disciples, saying unto them: Go into the village over against you, and straightway ye shall find an ass tied, and a colt with her: loose them and bring them unto me: and if any man say ought unto you, ye shall say, The Lord hath need of them, and straightway he will send them. All this was done, that it might be fulfilled which was spoken by the Prophet, saying: Tell ye the daughter of Sion: Behold thy King cometh unto thee, meek and sitting upon an ass, and a colt the foal of an ass. And the disciples went, and did as Jesus commanded them. And brought the ass, and the colt, and put on them their clothes, and they set him thereon. And a very great multitude spread their garments in the way: others cut down branches from the trees, and strawed them in the way: and the multitudes that went before, and that followed, cried, saying: Hosanna to the Son of David: blessed is he that cometh in the name of the Lord.

MONDAY IN HOLY WEEK

Simple.

Station at St. Praxedes

1. Antiphon at the Entrance. (Introit.)

Ps. 35, 1-2. Judica.

PLEAD thou my cause, O Lord, with them that strive with me, and fight thou against them that fight against me: lay hand upon the shield and buckler, and stand up to help me, O Lord, thou strength of my salvation. Ps. ibid., 3. Bring forth the spear, and stop the way against them that persecute me: say unto my soul: I am thy salvation. Plead thou.

2. Let us pray. Collect.

GRANT, we beseech thee, almighty God: that we who amidst so many and great adversities do fail by reason of our weakness; may be renewed through the merits of the Passion of thy only-begotten Son: Who liveth and reigneth with thee.

And this Collect only is said.

3. †Epistle, p. 133, or:

The Lesson from the Prophet Isaiah.

Is. 50, 5-10.

IN those days: Said Isaiah: The Lord God hath opened mine ear, and I was not rebellious: neither turned away back. I gave my back to the smiters, and my cheeks to them that plucked off the hair: I hid not my face from shame and spitting. For the Lord God will help me, therefore shall I not be confounded: therefore have I set my face like a flint, and I know that I shall not be ashamed. He is near that justifieth me, who will contend with me? Let us stand together, who is mine adversary? Let him come near to me. Behold, the Lord God will help me: who is he that shall condemn me? lo, they all shall wax old as a garment; the moth shall eat them up. Who is among you that feareth the Lord, that obeyeth the voice of his servant, that walketh in darkness, and hath no light? Let him trust in the name of the Lord, and stay upon his God.

4. Gradual. Ps. 35, 23 and 3.

Awake, O Lord, and stand up to judge my quarrel, avenge thou my cause, my God, and my Lord. ℣. Bring forth the spear, and stop the way against them that persecute me.

5. Tract. Ps. 103, 10.

O Lord, deal not with us after our sins which we have committed: nor reward us according to our wickednesses. ℣. Ps. 79, 8-9. Lord, remember not our old sins, but have mercy upon us, and that soon: for we are come to great misery.

(Here genuflect). ℣. Help us, O God of our salvation: and for the glory of thy name, O Lord, deliver us: and be merciful unto our sins, for thy name's sake.

6. Gospel, p. 134, or:

✠ The Continuation of the holy Gospel according to John.

John 12, 1-9.

SIX days before the passover Jesus came to Bethany, where Lazarus was which had been dead, whom he raised from the dead. There they made him a supper: and Martha served, but Lazarus was one of them that sat at the table with him. Then took Mary a pound of ointment of spikenard, very costly, and anointed the feet of Jesus, and wiped his feet with her hair: and the house was filled with the odour of the ointment. Then saith one of his disciples, Judas Iscariot, Simon's son, which should betray him: Why was not this ointment sold for three hundred pence, and given to the poor? This he said, not that he cared for the poor, but because he was a thief, and had the bag, and bare what was put therein. Then said Jesus: Let her alone, against the day of my burying hath she kept this. For the poor always ye have with you: but me ye have not always. Much people of the Jews therefore knew that he was there: and they came not for Jesus' sake only, but that they might see Lazarus also, whom he had raised from the dead.

7. Antiphon at the Offertory.

Ps. 143, 9-10. Deliver me, O Lord, from mine enemies: for I flee unto thee to hide me, teach me to do the thing that pleaseth thee: for thou art my God.

8. Secret.

ALMIGHTY God, let the effectual power of this sacrifice in such wise cleanse us from our iniquities, that we may thereby attain in purity unto the origin of the same. Through.

9. Preface of the holy Cross.

10. Antiphon at the Communion. Ps. 35, 26. Let them be put to confusion and shame together, that rejoice at my trouble: let them be clothed with rebuke and dishonour, that boast themselves against me.

11. Let us pray. Postcommunion.

O LORD, let thy holy mysteries kindle our hearts with heavenly fire: that we may delight in the performance of the same, and likewise in bringing forth the fruits thereof. Through.

12. Then the celebrant says at once: Let us pray. And the deacon, turning to the people, with joined hands, says: Humble your heads before God.

12a. *The celebrant, standing in the same place before the book, and not turning to the people, says: Let us pray. Humble your heads before God.*

Over the people:

Let us pray. Humble your heads before God.

Collect.

HELP us, O God of our salvation: and grant, that we, whom thou hast vouchsafed to redeem by thy inestimable benefits, may come with gladness to commemorate the same. Through.

TUESDAY IN HOLY WEEK

Simple.

Station at St. Prisca

1. Antiphon at the Entrance. (Introit.)

Gal. 6, 14. Nos autem.

BUT as for us, it behoveth us to glory in the Cross of our Lord Jesus Christ: in whom is our salvation, life, and resurrection: by whom we are saved and set free. Ps. 67, 1. God be merciful unto us, and bless us: and shew us the light of his countenance, and be merciful unto us. But it behoveth.

2. Let us pray.   Collect.

ALMIGHTY and everlasting God: grant unto us so to celebrate the mysteries of the passion of the Lord; that we may be worthy to obtain thy pardon. Through the same.

And this Collect only is said.

3. †Epistle, p. 136, or:

The Lesson from the Prophet Jeremiah.

Jer. 11, 18-20.

IN those days: Said Jeremiah: The Lord hath given me knowledge, and I know: then thou shewedst me their doings. But I was like a lamb or an ox that is brought to the slaughter: and I knew not that they had devised devices against me, saying: Let us destroy the tree with the fruit thereof, and let us cut him off from the land of the living, that his name may be no more remembered. But, O Lord of Hosts, that judgest righteously, that triest the reins and the heart, let me see thy vengeance on them: for unto thee have I revealed my cause, O Lord my God.

4. Gradual. Ps. 35, 13 and 1-2.

Nevertheless, when they were sick, I put on sackcloth, and humbled my soul with fasting: and my prayer shall turn into mine own bosom. ℣. Plead thou my cause, O Lord, with them that strive with me, and fight thou against them that fight against me: lay hand upon the shield and buckler, and stand up to help me.

5. The Gospel of the Passion and Death of the Lord according to Mark.

14, 32-72; 15, 1-46.

Cleanse my heart is said, and the rest is done as noted on Sunday, p. 149.

The Passion of our Lord Jesus Christ according to Mark.

AT that time: Jesus and his disciples came to a place which was named Gethsemane. And he saith to his disciples: ✠ Sit ye here, while I shall pray. C. And he taketh with him Peter, and James, and John: and began to be sore amazed, and to be very heavy. And saith unto them: ✠ My soul is exceeding sorrowful unto death: tarry ye here, and watch. C. And he went forward a little and fell on the ground: and prayed, that, if it were possible, the hour might pass from him: and he said: ✠ Abba, Father, all things are possible unto thee, take away this cup from me: nevertheless, not what I will, but what thou wilt. C. And he cometh and findeth them sleeping. And saith unto Peter: ✠ Simon, sleepest thou? couldest not thou watch one hour? Watch ye and pray, lest ye enter into temptation. The spirit truly is ready, but the flesh is weak. C. And again he went away, and prayed, and spake the same words. And when he returned he found them asleep again, (for their eyes were heavy), neither wist they what to answer him. And he cometh the third time, and saith unto them: ✠ Sleep on now, and take your rest. It is enough: the hour is come: behold, the Son of man is betrayed into the hands of sinners. Rise up, let us go: lo, he that betrayeth me is at hand. C. And immediately, while he yet spake, cometh Judas, one of the twelve, and with him a great multitude with swords and staves, from the chief priests, and the scribes, and the elders. And he that betrayed him had given them a token, saying: S. Whomsoever I shall kiss, that same is he, take him, and lead him away safely. C. And as soon as he was come he goeth straightway to him, and saith: S. Master, master. C. And kissed him. And they laid their hands on him, and took him. And one of them that stood by drew a sword, and smote a servant of the high priest: and cut off his ear. And Jesus answered, and said unto them: ✠ Are ye come out as against a thief, with swords and with staves, to take me? I was daily with you in the temple teaching, and ye took me not. But the Scriptures must be fulfilled. C. And they all forsook him, and fled. And there followed him a certain young man, having a linen cloth cast about his naked body: and the young men laid hold on him. And he left the linen cloth, and fled from them naked.

And they led Jesus away to the high priest: and with him were assembled all the chief priests, and the elders, and the scribes. And Peter followed him afar off, even into the palace of the high priest: and he sat with the servants, and warmed himself at the fire. And the chief priests and all the council sought for witness against Jesus to put him to death, and found none. For many bare false witness against him: but their witness agreed not together. And there arose certain, and bare false witness against him, saying: S. We heard him say: I will destroy this temple that is made with hands, and within three days I will build another made without hands. C. But neither so did their witness agree together. And the high priest stood up in the midst, and asked Jesus, saying: S. Answerest thou nothing, what is it which these witness against thee? C. But he held his peace, and answered nothing. Again the high priest asked him, and said unto him: S. Art thou the Christ, the Son of the Blessed? C. And Jesus said: ✠ I am: and ye shall see the Son of man sitting on the right hand of power, and coming in the clouds of heaven. C. Then the high priest rent his clothes, and saith: S. What need we any further witnesses? Ye have heard the blasphemy: what think ye? C. And they all condemned him to be guilty of death.

And some began to spit on him, and to cover his face, and to buffet him, and to say unto him: S. Prophesy. C. And the servants did strike him with the palms of their hands.

And as Peter was beneath in the palace there cometh one of the maids of the high priest: and when she saw Peter warming himself she looked upon him, and said: S. And thou also wast with Jesus of Nazareth. C. But he denied, saying: S. I know not, neither understand I what thou sayest. C. And he went out into the porch, and the cock crew. And a maid saw him again, and began to say to them that stood by: S. This is one of them. C. And he denied it again. And a little after, they that stood by said again to Peter: S. Surely thou art one of them: for thou art a Galilean, and thy speech agreeth thereto. C. But he began to curse and to swear, saying: S. I know not this man of whom ye speak. C. And the second time the cock crew. And Peter called to mind the word that Jesus said unto him: Before the cock crow twice, thou shalt deny me thrice. And when he thought thereon he wept.

(†Mark 15, 1.)

And straightway in the morning the chief priests held a consultation with the elders, and scribes, and the whole council, and bound Jesus, and carried him away, and delivered him to Pilate. And Pilate asked him: S. Art thou the King of the Jews? C. And he answering said unto him: ✠ Thou sayest it. C. And the chief priests accused him of many things: but he answered nothing. And Pilate asked him again, saying: S. Answerest thou nothing? behold how many things they witness against thee. C. But Jesus yet answered nothing, so that Pilate marvelled.

Now at that feast he released unto them one prisoner, whomsoever they desired. And there was one named Barabbas, which lay bound with them that had made insurrection with him, who had committed murder in the insurrection. And the multitude, crying aloud, began to desire him to do as he had ever done unto them. But Pilate answered them, saying: S. Will ye that I release unto you the King of the Jews? C. For he knew that the chief priests had delivered him for envy. But the chief priests moved the people, that he should rather release Barabbas unto them. And Pilate answered, and said again unto them: S. What will ye then that I shall do unto him whom ye call the King of the Jews? C. And they cried out again: S. Crucify him. C. Then Pilate said unto them: S. Why, what evil hath he done? C. And they cried out the more exceedingly: S. Crucify him. C. And so Pilate, willing to content the people, released Barabbas unto them, and delivered Jesus, when he had scourged him, to be crucified.

And the soldiers led him away into the hall, called Prætorium, and they call together the whole band, and they clothed him with purple, and platted a crown of thorns, and put it about his head. And began to salute him: Hail King of the Jews. And they smote him on the head with a reed, and did spit upon him, and bowing their knees worshipped him. And when they had mocked him they took off the purple from him, and put his own clothes on him, and led him out to crucify him. And they compel one Simon a Cyrenian, who passed by, coming out of the country, the father of Alexander and Rufus, to bear his cross.

And they bring him unto the place Golgotha, which is, being interpreted, The place of a skull. And they gave him to drink wine mingled with myrrh: but he received it not. And when they had crucified him they parted his garments, casting lots upon them, what every man should take. And it was the third hour, and they crucified him. And the superscription of his accusation was written over: The King of the Jews. And with him they crucify two thieves: the one on his right hand, and the other on his left. And the Scripture was fulfilled, which saith: And he was numbered with the transgressors. And they that passed by railed on him, wagging their heads, and saying: S. Ah, thou that destroyest the temple, and buildest it in three days: save thyself, and come down from the cross. C. Likewise also the chief priests mocking said among themselves, with the scribes: S. He saved others, himself he cannot save. Let Christ the King of Israel descend now from the cross, that we may see and believe. C. And they that were crucified with him reviled him. And when the sixth hour was come, there was darkness over the whole land until the ninth hour. And at the ninth hour Jesus cried with a loud voice, saying: ✠ Eloi, Eloi, lama sabachtháni? C. Which is, being interpreted: ✠ My God, my God, why hast thou forsaken me? C. And some of them that stood by, when they heard it, said: S. Behold, he calleth Elias. C. And one ran and filled a spunge full of vinegar, and put it on a reed, and gave him to drink, saying: S. Let alone, let us see whether Elias will come to take him down. C. And Jesus cried with a loud voice, and gave up the ghost.

Here genuflect, and pause awhile.

And the vail of the temple was rent in twain from the top to the bottom. And when the centurion, which stood over against him, saw that he so cried out, and gave up the ghost, he said: S. Truly this man was the Son of God.†

C. There were also women looking on afar off: among whom was Mary Magdalene, and Mary the mother of James the less and of Joses, and Salome: who also, when he was in Galilee, followed him, and ministered unto him, and many other women which came up with him unto Jerusalem.

And now when the even was come, (because it was the Preparation, that is, the day before the sabbath), Joseph of Arimathæa, an honourable counsellor, which also waited for the kingdom of God, came, and went in boldly unto Pilate, and craved the body of Jesus. And Pilate marvelled if he were already dead. And calling unto him the centurion, he asked whether he had been any while dead. And when he knew it of the centurion, he gave the body to Joseph. And he bought fine linen, and took him down, and wrapped him in the linen, and laid him in a sepulchre which was hewn out of a rock, and rolled a stone unto the door of the sepulchre.

6. Antiphon at the Offertory. Ps. 140, 5.

Keep me, O Lord, from the hands of the ungodly: preserve me from the wicked men.

7. Secret.

WE beseech thee, O Lord: that this sacrifice which we offer unto thee in the time of fasting, ordained for the healing of our souls, may effectually avail for our salvation. Through.

8. Preface of the Holy Cross.

9. Antiphon at the Communion.

Ps. 69, 13-14. They that sit in the gate speak against me: and the drunkards make songs upon me: but, Lord, I make my prayer unto thee: in an acceptable time, O God, in the multitude of thy mercy.

10. Let us pray. Postcommunion.

ALMIGHTY God, let thy holy mysteries both cleanse us from all our sins, and avail for our healing unto life eternal. Through.

11. Over the people:

Let us pray. Humble your heads before God.

Collect.

LET thy merciful kindness, O God, cleanse us throughly from the corruption of our former nature, and effectually renew us unto holiness of life. Through.

WEDNESDAY IN HOLY WEEK

Simple.

Station at St. Mary Major

1. Antiphon at the Entrance. (Introit.)

Phil. 2, 10, 8 and 11. In nomine.

AT the name of Jesus every knee shall bow, of things in heaven, and things in earth, and things under the earth: for the Lord became obedient unto death, even the death of the cross: wherefore Jesus Christ is Lord, to the glory of God the Father. Ps. 102, 1. Hear my prayer, O Lord: and let my crying come unto thee. At the name.

2. After Kýrie, eléison, the celebrant, standing at the Epistle side, says Let us pray, the Deacon Let us bow the knee, and all kneel and pray for a space in silence; the Deacon having said Arise, all rise, and the celebrant says the prayer.

2a. *After Kýrie, eléison, the celebrant, standing at the Epistle side, says: Let us pray, Let us bow the knee, and, having made a short prayer, kneeling and in silence, he says: Arise, then he rises and says the prayer.*

Which is also observed in read Masses.

3. Let us pray. Collect.

GRANT, we beseech thee, almighty God: that we, who are continually afflicted by reason of our transgressions, may be delivered by the passion of thine only-begotten Son: Who liveth and reigneth with thee.

4. The Lesson from the Prophet Isaiah.

Is. 62, 11; 63, 1-7.

THUS saith the Lord God: Say ye to the daughter of Sion: Behold, thy Salvation cometh: behold, his reward is with him. Who is this that cometh from Edom, with dyed garments from Bozrah? This that is glorious in his apparel, travelling in the greatness of his strength? I that speak in righteousness, mighty to save. Wherefore art thou red in thine apparel, and thy garments like him that treadeth in the winefat? I have trodden the winepress alone, and of the people there was none with me: for I will tread them in mine anger, and trample them in my fury: and their blood shall be sprinkled upon my garments, and I will stain all my raiment. For the day of vengeance is in mine heart, and the year of my redeemed is come. And I looked, and there was none to help: and I wondered that there was none to uphold: therefore mine own arm brought salvation unto me, and my fury, it upheld me. And I will tread down the people in mine anger, and make them drunk in my fury, and I will bring down their strength to the earth. I will mention the lovingkindnesses of the Lord, and the praises of the Lord, according to all that the Lord our God hath bestowed on us.

5. Gradual. Ps. 69, 18 and 2-3.

Hide not thy face from thy servant, for I am in trouble: O haste thee, and hear me. ℣. Save me, O God: for the waters are come in, even unto my soul: I stick fast in the deep mire, where no ground is.

Wednesday in Holy Week

6. Here is said ℣. The Lord be with you, without Let us bow the knee.

Let us pray.   Collect.

O GOD, who for our sakes didst will that thy Son should suffer death upon the Cross, that thou mightest drive far from us the power of the enemy: grant to us thy servants; that we may attain unto the grace of his resurrection: Through the same.

And this Collect only is said.

7. †Epistle, p. 136, or:

The Lesson from the Prophet Isaiah.

Is. 53, 1-12.

IN those days: Said Isaiah: Lord, who hath believed our report? and to whom is the arm of the Lord revealed? For he shall grow up before him as a tender plant, and as a root out of a dry ground: he hath no form nor comeliness: and when we shall see him, there is no beauty that we should desire him: he is despised and rejected of men, a man of sorrows, and acquainted with grief: and we hid as it were our faces from him, he was despised, and we esteemed him not. Surely he hath borne our griefs, and carried our sorrows: yet we did esteem him stricken, smitten of God, and afflicted. But he was wounded for our transgressions, he was bruised for our iniquities: the chastisement of our peace was upon him, and with his stripes we are healed. All we like sheep have gone astray, we have turned every one to his own way: and the Lord hath laid on him the iniquity of us all. He was oppressed, and he was afflicted, yet he opened not his mouth: he is brought as a lamb to the slaughter, and as a sheep before her shearers is dumb, so he openeth not his mouth. He was taken from prison and from judgment: and who shall declare his generation? for he was cut off out of the land of the living: for the transgression of my people was he stricken. And he made his grave with the wicked, and with the rich in his death: because he had done no violence, neither was any deceit in his mouth. Yet it pleased the Lord to bruise him, he hath put him to grief: when thou shalt make his soul an offering for sin, he shall see his seed, he shall prolong his days, and the pleasure of the Lord shall prosper in his hand. He shall see of the travail of his soul, and shall be satisfied: by his knowledge shall my righteous servant justify many, for he shall bear their iniquities. Therefore will I divide him a portion with the great: and he shall divide the spoil with the strong, because he hath poured out his soul unto death, and he was numbered with the transgressors: and he bare the sin of many, and made intercession for the transgressors.

8.   Tract. Ps. 102, 1-4 and 14.

Hear my prayer, O Lord, and let my crying come unto thee. ℣. Hide not thy face from me in the time of my trouble. ℣. Incline thine ear unto me when I call, O hear me, and that right soon. ℣. For my days are consumed away like smoke: and my bones are burnt up as it were a fire-brand. ℣. My heart is smitten down, and withered like grass: so that I forget to eat my bread. ℣. Thou shalt arise, O Lord, and have mercy upon Sion: for it is time that thou have mercy upon her.

9. The Gospel of the Passion and Death of the Lord according to Luke.
22, 39-71; 23, 1-53.

Cleanse my heart is said, and the rest is done as noted on Sunday, p. 149.

The Passion of our Lord Jesus Christ according to Luke.

AT that time: Jesus came out, and went, as he was wont, to the mount of Olives. And his disciples also followed

Wednesday in Holy Week

him. And when he was at the place, he said unto them: ✠ Pray, that ye enter not into temptation. C. And he was withdrawn from them about a stone's cast, and kneeled down and prayed, saying: ✠ Father, if thou be willing, remove this cup from me: nevertheless, not my will, but thine be done. C. And there appeared an Angel unto him from heaven, strengthening him. And being in an agony, he prayed more earnestly. And his sweat was as it were great drops of blood falling down to the ground. And when he rose up from prayer, and was come to his disciples, he found them sleeping for sorrow. And said unto them: ✠ Why sleep ye? rise and pray, lest ye enter into temptation.

C. And while he yet spake, behold, a multitude: and he that was called Judas, one of the twelve, went before them, and drew near unto Jesus to kiss him. But Jesus said unto him: ✠ Judas, betrayest thou the Son of man with a kiss? C. When they who were about him saw what would follow, they said unto him: S. Lord, shall we smite with the sword? C. And one of them smote the servant of the high priest, and cut off his right ear. And Jesus answered and said: ✠ Suffer ye thus far. C. And he touched his ear, and healed him. Then Jesus said unto the chief priests, and captains of the temple, and the elders who were come to him: ✠ Be ye come out as against a thief, with swords and staves? When I was daily with you in the temple, ye stretched forth no hands against me: but this is your hour, and the power of darkness.

C. Then took they him, and led him, and brought him into the high priest's house: and Peter followed afar off. And when they had kindled a fire in the midst of the hall, and were set down together, Peter sat down among them. But a certain maid beheld him, as he sat by the fire, and earnestly looked upon him, and said: S. This man was also with him. C. And he denied him, saying: S. Woman, I know him not. C. And after a little while another saw him, and said: S. Thou art also of them. C. And Peter said: S. Man, I am not. C. And about the space of one hour after, another confidently affirmed, saying: S. Of a truth this fellow also was with him: for he is a Galilean. C. And Peter said: S. Man, I know not what thou sayest. C. And immediately, while he yet spake, the cock crew. And the Lord turned, and looked upon Peter. And Peter remembered the word of the Lord, how he had said unto him: Before the cock crow, thou shalt deny me thrice. And Peter went out, and wept bitterly.

And the men that held Jesus mocked him, and smote him. And when they had blindfolded him, they struck him on the face, and asked him, saying: S. Prophesy, who is it that smote thee? C. And many other things blasphemously spake they against him.

And as soon as it was day, the elders of the people, and the chief priests, and the scribes, came together, and led him into their council, saying: S. Art thou the Christ? tell us. C. And he said unto them: ✠ If I tell you, ye will not believe: and if I also ask you, ye will not answer me, nor let me go. Hereafter shall the Son of man sit on the right hand of the power of God. C. Then said they all: S. Art thou then the Son of God? C. And he said unto them: ✠ Ye say that I am. C. And they said: S. What need we any further witness? For we ourselves have heard of his own mouth.

(†Luke 23, 1.)

And the whole multitude of them arose, and led him unto Pilate. And they began to accuse him, saying: S. We found this fellow perverting the nation, and forbidding to give tribute to Cæsar, saying, That he himself is Christ a king. C. And Pilate asked him, saying: S. Art thou the

King of the Jews? C. And he answered him, and said: ✠ Thou sayest it. C. Then said Pilate to the chief priests, and to the people: S. I find no fault in this man. C. And they were the more fierce, saying: S. He stirreth up the people, teaching throughout all Jewry, beginning from Galilee to this place.

C. When Pilate heard of Galilee, he asked whether the man were a Galilean. And as soon as he knew that he belonged unto Herod's jurisdiction, he sent him to Herod, who himself was also at Jerusalem at that time. And when Herod saw Jesus he was exceeding glad. For he was desirous to see him of a long season, because he had heard many things of him, and he hoped to have seen some miracle done by him. Then he questioned with him in many words. But he answered him nothing. And the chief priests and scribes stood and vehemently accused him. And Herod with his men of war set him at nought: and mocked him, and arrayed him in a gorgeous robe, and sent him again to Pilate. And the same day Pilate and Herod were made friends together: for before they were at enmity between themselves. And Pilate, when he had called together the chief priests, and the rulers, and the people, said unto them: S. Ye have brought this man unto me, as one that perverteth the people, and behold, I, having examined him before you, have found no fault in this man touching those things whereof ye accuse him. No, nor yet Herod: for I sent you to him, and lo, nothing worthy of death is done unto him. I will therefore chastise him, and release him.

C. For of necessity he must release one unto them at the feast. And they cried out all at once, saying: S. Away with this man, and release unto us Barabbas. C. Who for a certain sedition made in the city, and for murder, was cast into prison. Pilate, therefore, willing to release Jesus, spake again to them. But they cried, saying: S. Crucify him, crucify him. C. And he said unto them the third time: S. Why, what evil hath he done? I have found no cause of death in him: I will therefore chastise him, and let him go. C. And they were instant with loud voices, requiring that he might be crucified. And the voices of them and of the chief priests prevailed. And Pilate gave sentence that it should be as they required. And he released unto them him that for sedition and murder was cast into prison, whom they had desired: but he delivered Jesus to their will.

And as they led him away, they laid hold upon one Simon a Cyrenian, coming out of the country: and on him they laid the cross, that he might bear it after Jesus. And there followed him a great company of people, and of women, which also bewailed and lamented him. But Jesus, turning unto them, said: ✠ Daughters of Jerusalem, weep not for me, but weep for yourselves, and for your children. For behold, the days are coming, in the which they shall say: Blessed are the barren, and the wombs that never bare, and the paps which never gave suck. Then shall they begin to say to the mountains: Fall on us; and to the hills: Cover us. For if they do these things in a green tree, what shall be done in the dry?

C. And there were also two other, malefactors, led with him to be put to death. And when they were come to the place which is called Calvary, there they crucified him: and the malefactors, one on the right hand, and the other on the left. Then said Jesus: ✠ Father, forgive them: for they know not what they do. C. And they parted his raiment, and cast lots. And the people stood beholding, and the rulers also with them derided him, saying: S. He saved others: let him save himself, if he be Christ, the chosen of God. C. And the soldiers also mocked him, coming to him, and offering him vinegar, and saying: S. If thou be the King of the Jews, save thyself. C. And a superscription also was written over him in letters of Greek, and Latin, and Hebrew: This is the King of the Jews. And one of the malefactors, which were hanged, railed on him, saying: S. If thou be Christ, save thyself, and us. C. But the other answering rebuked him, saying: S. Dost not thou fear God, seeing thou art in the same condemnation? And we indeed justly, for we receive the due reward of our deeds: but this man hath done nothing amiss. C. And he said unto Jesus: S. Lord, remember me when thou comest into thy kingdom. C. And Jesus said unto him: ✠ Verily I say unto thee: To-day shalt thou be with me in paradise.

C. And it was about the sixth hour, and there was a darkness over all the earth until the ninth hour. And the sun was darkened: and the vail of the temple was rent in the midst. And when Jesus had cried with a loud voice, he said: ✠ Father, into thy hands I commend my spirit. C. And having said thus, he gave up the ghost.

Here genuflect, and pause awhile.

Now when the centurion saw what was done, he glorified God, saying: S. Certainly this was a righteous man. C. And all the people that came together to that sight, beholding the things that were done, smote their breasts, and returned. And all his acquaintance, and the women that followed him from Galilee, stood afar off, beholding these things.†

And, behold, there was a man named Joseph, a counseller, and he was a good man, and a just: the same had not consented to the counsel and deed of them, he was of Arimathæa, a city of the Jews, who also himself waited for the kingdom of God. This man went unto Pilate, and begged the body of Jesus: and he took it down, and wrapped it in linen, and laid it in a sepulchre that was hewn in stone, wherein never man before was laid.

10. Antiphon at the Offertory. Ps. 102, 1-2. Hear my prayer, O Lord, and let my crying come unto thee: hide not thy face from me.

11. Secret.

ACCEPT, we beseech thee, O Lord, these our oblations, and vouchsafe so to work in us: that as we shew forth in a mystery the passion of thy Son our Lord, so by devout affection we may receive the benefit of the same. Through the same.

12. Preface of the Holy Cross.

13. Antiphon at the Communion. Ps. 102, 10, 13-14. I have mingled my drink with weeping: for thou hast taken me up, and cast me down: and I am withered like grass: but thou, O Lord, shalt endure for ever: thou shalt arise, and have mercy upon Sion, for it is time that thou have mercy upon her.

14. Let us pray.   Postcommunion.

ALMIGHTY God, enlighten our understanding: that, as these wondrous mysteries do testify to the temporal death of thy Son, so thereby we may have assurance that thou hast bestowed upon us life eternal. Through the same.

15. Over the people:

Let us pray.   Humble your heads before God.

Collect.

O LORD, we beseech thee graciously to behold this thy family, for which our Lord Jesus Christ was contented to be betrayed, and given up into the hands of wicked men, and to suffer death upon the Cross: Who liveth and reigneth with thee.

THE THURSDAY OF THE SUPPER OF THE LORD

COMMONLY CALLED

MAUNDY THURSDAY

Double of 1st class.

1. The tabernacle, if there be one on the High Altar, is to be entirely empty; but for communicating the clergy and people today and tomorrow, there shall be set on the Altar a ciborium (or ciboria) with particles to be consecrated in this Mass.

2. In sung Mass the incensing of the Altar, as in solemn Mass, is permitted.

3. Each of the clergy present wears his choir habit; priests also wear a white stole; the celebrant and ministers wear white vestments.

4. All being thus vested, the procession is made through the church to the Altar.

5. Meanwhile is sung by the choir the antiphon ad introitum.

Antiphon at the Entrance. (Introit.)

Gal. 6, 14. Nos autem.

BUT as for us, it behoveth us to glory in the Cross of our Lord Jesus Christ: in whom is our salvation, life, and resurrection: by whom we are saved, and set free. Ps. 67, 1. God be merciful unto us, and bless us: and shew us the light of his countenance, and be merciful unto us. But as for us.

6. The celebrant, after he has come to the Altar with the ministers, *or servers,* having made the confession, goes up and kisses it in the midst, and incenses it in the usual manner, even when he celebrates alone with chant.

7. The incensing of the Altar being done, the celebrant, having recited the Introit and Kýrie, eléison, solemnly intones Glory be to God on high, and the bells and organ are sounded, and, the hymn being finished, are silent until the paschal vigil.

8. Let us pray. Collect.

O GOD, from whom Judas received the punishment of his guilt, and the thief the reward of his confession, grant unto us the effectual fruits of thy redemption: that as in his passion Jesus Christ, our Lord, gave unto each the due recompense of his deeds; so he may deliver us from the transgressions of our old nature, and bestow upon us the grace of his resurrection: Who liveth and reigneth with thee.

9. †The Epistle, p. 138, or:

The Lesson from the Epistle of blessed Paul the Apostle to the Corinthians.

I Cor. 11, 20-32.

BRETHREN: When ye come together into one place, this is not to eat the Lord's supper. For in eating every one taketh before other his own supper. And one is hungry, and another is drunken. What, have ye not houses to eat and to drink in? or despise ye the Church of God, and shame them that have not? What shall I say to you? Shall I praise you in this? I praise you not. For I have received of the Lord that which also I delivered unto you, That the Lord Jesus, the same night in which he was betrayed, took bread; and when he had given thanks, he brake it, and said: Take, eat: this is my body, which is broken for you: this do in remembrance of me. After the same manner also he took the cup, when he had supped, saying: This cup is the new Testament in my blood: this do ye, as oft as ye drink it, in remembrance of me. For as often as ye eat this bread, and drink this cup: ye do shew the Lord's death till he come. Wherefore, whosoever shall eat this bread, or drink this cup of the Lord, unworthily, shall be guilty of the body and blood of the Lord. But let a man examine himself: and so let him eat of that bread, and drink of that cup. For he that eateth and drinketh unworthily eateth and drinketh judgment to himself: not discerning the Lord's body. For this cause many are weak and sickly among you, and many sleep. For if we would judge ourselves, we should not be judged. But when we are judged, we are chastened of the Lord, that we should not be condemned with the world.

10. Gradual. Phil. 2, 8-9. Christ for us became obedient unto death, even the death of the cross. ℣. Wherefore God also hath highly exalted him: and given him a name which is above every name.

11. Cleanse my heart, etc., and The Lord be in my heart, are said as usual.

12. †Gospel, p. 163, or:

✠ The Continuation of the holy Gospel according to John.

John 13, 1-15.

BEFORE the feast of the passover, when Jesus knew that his hour was come that he should depart out of this world unto the Father: having loved his own which were in the world, he loved them unto the end. And supper being ended, the devil having now put into the heart of Judas Iscariot, Simon's son, to betray him: Jesus knowing that the Father had given all things into his hands, and that he was come from God, and went to God: he riseth from supper, and laid aside his garments: and took a towel, and girded himself. After that he poureth water into a bason, and began to wash the disciples' feet, and to wipe them with the towel wherewith he was girded. Then cometh he to Simon Peter. And Peter saith unto him: Lord, dost thou wash my feet? Jesus answered and said unto him: What I do thou knowest not now; but thou shalt know hereafter. Peter saith unto him: Thou shalt never wash my feet. Jesus answered him: If I wash thee not, thou hast no part with me. Simon Peter saith unto him: Lord, not my feet only, but also my hands and my head. Jesus saith to him: He that is washed needeth not save to wash his feet, but is clean every whit. And ye are clean, but not all. For he knew who should betray him: therefore said he: Ye are not all clean. So after he had washed their feet, and had taken his garments: and was set down again, he said unto them: Know ye what I have done to you? Ye call me Master and Lord: and ye say well: for so I am. If I then, your Lord and Master, have washed your feet: ye also ought to wash one another's feet. For I have given you an example, that ye should do as I have done to you.

13. It is very fitting that after the Gospel, there should be a brief homily to illustrate the wondrous mysteries, which are recalled in this Mass, namely the institution of the Holy Eucharist and the order of priesthood, as also the commandment of the Lord concerning brotherly love.

14. The Creed is not said today.

(The Mass continues, No. 23, p. 170.)

THE WASHING OF THE FEET

15. After the homily in the Mass, there follows, if for pastoral reasons it be considered desirable, the washing of the feet.

16. In the midst of the sanctuary, or in the body of the church, seats shall be prepared on either side for twelve men, whose feet are to be washed: other things needful shall be prepared on a small table.

17. Meanwhile the deacon and subdeacon, *or the two senior servers,* lead the twelve men chosen, two and two, to the place prepared, while the choir or the clergy present begin to sing or recite the antiphons and psalms following.

The twelve chosen men, having made a reverence to the Altar and the celebrant, who sits in the sanctuary, are arranged on the seats; then the sacred ministers, *or the servers,* shall approach the celebrant. All put off the maniple, the celebrant also the chasuble.

As the washing of the feet draws to an end, the 8th antiphon, with its verses, is begun, the others if need be, being omitted.

18. The antiphons, psalms and verses to be sung or recited, are:

Antiphon 1.

John 13, 34. Mandatum novum. A new commandment I give unto you: that ye love one another, as I have loved you, saith the Lord. Ps. 119, 1. Blessed are those that are undefiled in the way: and walk in the law of the Lord.

And immediately is repeated the Antiphon, A new commandment. And so with the other Antiphons, which have Psalms or Verses. And of any Psalm only the first verse is said.

Antiphon 2.

John 13, 4-5 and 15. After the Lord had risen from supper, he poured water into a bason, and began to wash his disciples' feet: this example left he unto them. Ps. 48. Great is the Lord, and highly to be praised: in the city of our God, even upon his holy hill. After the Lord had risen.

Antiphon 3.

John 13, 12-13 and 15. The Lord Jesus, after he had supped with his disciples, washed their feet, and said to them: Know ye what I, your Lord and Master, have done to you? I have given you an example, that ye also should so do. Ps. 85, 1. Lord, thou art become gracious unto thy land: thou hast turned away the captivity of Jacob. The Lord Jesus.

Antiphon 4.

John 13, 6-8. Lord, dost thou wash my feet? Jesus answered, and said unto him: If I wash not thy feet, thou hast no part with me. ℣. Then cometh he to Simon Peter, and Peter saith unto him.

And the Antiphon is repeated, Lord, dost thou.

℣. What I do, thou knowest not now: but thou shalt know hereafter.

The Antiphon is repeated for the third time, Lord, dost thou.

Antiphon 5.

If I, your Lord and Master, have washed your feet: how much more ought ye to wash one another's feet? Ps. 49, 1. O hear ye this, all ye people: ponder it with your ears, all ye that dwell in the world. If I, your Lord.

Antiphon 6.

John 13, 35. By this shall all men know that ye are my disciples, if ye have love one to another. ℣. Jesus said to his disciples. By this shall all men.

Antiphon 7.

I Cor. 13, 13. Let there abide in you faith, hope, charity, these three: but the greatest of these is charity. ℣. And now abideth faith, hope, charity, these three, but the greatest of these is charity. Let there abide in you.

8.

The following Antiphon with its verses is never omitted: and it is begun, the preceding ones being omitted, if need be, as the washing of the feet draws to an end.

Antiphon.

Where charity and love are, there is God. ℣. The love of Christ hath gathered us together in one. ℣. Let us rejoice and be glad in him. ℣. Let us fear and love the living God. ℣. And love one another in sincerity of heart.

The Antiphon is repeated, Where charity and love are, there is God.

℣. When therefore we are gathered together in one: ℣. Take we heed that we be not divided in mind. ℣. Let malicious quarrels, let contentions cease. ℣. And let Christ our God be in the midst of us.

And the Antiphon is repeated, Where charity and love are, there is God.

℣. So may we also with the Blessed see. ℣. In glory thy countenance, O Christ our God: ℣. Joy, that is infinite and undefiled. ℣. For ever and for evermore. Amen.

19. Meanwhile the celebrant proceeds to the washing of the feet in this manner: he girds himself with a towel, and those who are to be washed being arranged in order, the acolytes ministering a bason and water, the subdeacon holding the right foot of each, he kneels before each, washes and wipes the foot, the deacon providing the linen cloth for wiping.

19a. *The offices, which in the solemn rite are fulfilled by the deacon and subdeacon, are performed by the servers.*

20. After the washing, the celebrant washes his hands, and wipes them, saying nothing.

Then all resume the maniple, and the celebrant also the chasuble, and they return and stand before the midst of the Altar, where the celebrant says:

Our Father, secretly.

℣. And lead us not into temptation.

℟. But deliver us from evil.

℣. Thou hast charged, O Lord.

℟. That we shall diligently keep thy commandments.

℣. Thou didst wash the feet of thy disciples.

℟. Despise not thou the works of thine own hands.

℣. O Lord, hear my prayer.

℟. And let my cry come unto thee.

℣. The Lord be with you.

℟. And with thy spirit.

Let us pray.   Collect.

ASSIST us, we beseech thee, O Lord, in this our bounden service: and whereas thou wast pleased to wash the feet of thy disciples, despise not thou the works of thine own hands, which thou hast bidden us to follow: that as here outward defilements by us and from us are washed away; so also the secret sins of us all may be cleansed by thee. And this we ask of thee, who livest and reignest God: throughout all ages, world without end. ℟. Amen.

21. The Collect being ended the twelve men, having made a reverence to the Altar and the celebrant, are led back to their places.

22. After the washing of the feet, or, where this does not take place, after the sermon the celebration of Mass proceeds in the usual manner.

23. Antiphon at the Offertory. Ps. 118, 16-17. The right hand of the Lord bringeth mighty things to pass, the right hand of the Lord hath exalted me: I shall not die, but live, and declare the works of the Lord.

24. Secret.

WE beseech thee, O Lord holy, Father almighty, everlasting God: that he may render our sacrifice acceptable unto thee, who on this day commanded and taught his disciples to do this in remembrance of him, even Jesus Christ thy Son our Lord: Who liveth and reigneth with thee.

25. Preface, Sanctus and Benedictus, are said in the accustomed manner. And the Preface of the Holy Cross is said.

Infra Actionem.

COMMUNICANTES, et diem sacratíssimum celebrántes, quo Dóminus noster Jesus Christus pro nobis est tráditus: sed et memóriam venerántes, in primis gloriósæ semper Vírginis Maríæ, Genitrícis ejúsdem Dei et Dómini nostri Jesu Christi: sed et beatórum Apostolórum ac Mártyrum tuórum, Petri et Pauli, Andréæ, Jacóbi, Joánnis, Thomæ, Jacóbi, Philíppi, Bartholomæi, Matthæi, Simónis et Thaddæi: Lini, Cleti, Cleméntis, Xysti, Cornélii, Cypriáni, Lauréntii, Chrysógoni, Joánnis et Pauli, Cosmæ et Damiáni: et ómnium Sanctórum tuórum; quorum méritis precibúsque concédas, ut in ómnibus protectiónis tuæ muniámur auxílio. Jungit manus. Per eúndem Christum Dóminum nostrum. Amen.

UNITED in one communion, we celebrate the most sacred day whereon our Lord Jesus Christ was betrayed for us: we venerate moreover the memory, first, of the glorious ever Virgin Mary, Mother of the same our God and Lord Jesus Christ: as also of thy blessed Apostles and Martyrs, Peter and Paul, Andrew, James, John, Thomas, James, Philip, Bartholomew, Matthew, Simon and Thaddeus: Linus, Cletus, Clement, Xystus, Cornelius, Cyprian, Lawrence, Chrysogonus, John and Paul, Cosmas and Damian: and of all thy Saints; grant that by their merits and prayers we may in all things be defended with the help of thy protection. He joins his hands. Through the same Christ our Lord. Amen.

Tenens manus expansas super Oblata, dicit:

Holding his hands spread out over the Oblations, he says:

HANC ígitur oblatiónem servitútis nostræ, sed et cunctæ famíliæ tuæ, quam tibi offérimus ob diem, in qua Dóminus noster Jesus Christus trádidit discípulis suis Córporis et Sánguinis sui mystéria celebránda: quæsumus, Dómine, ut placátus accípias: diésque nostros in tua pace dispónas, atque ab ætérna damnatióne nos éripi et in electórum tuórum

WE beseech thee then, O Lord, graciously to accept this oblation from us thy servants, and from thy whole family, which we present unto thee in remembrance of the day whereon our Lord Jesus Christ commanded his disciples to celebrate the mysteries of his Body and Blood: and do thou order our days in thy peace, and bid us to be delivered from

Maundy Thursday

júbeas grege numerári. Jungit manus. Per eúndem Christum Dóminum nostrum. Amen.

QUAM oblatiónem tu, Deus, in ómnibus, quæsumus, Signat ter super Oblata, bene ✠ díctam, adscríp ✠ tam, ra ✠ tam, rationábilem acceptabilémque fácere dignéris: Signat semel super Hostiam, ut nobis Cor ✠ pus, Et semel super Calicem, et San ✠ guis fiat dilectíssimi Fílii tui, Jungit manus, Dómini nostri Jesu Christi.

27. Incensatio Sacramenti, ut in Missa solemni moris est, hodie fit etiam si Missa absque ministris sacris celebratur: tunc autem ab acolytis, *seu ministrantibus,* peragitur.

QUI prídie, quam pro nostra omniúmque salúte paterétur, hoc est hódie, Accípit Hostiam, accépit panem in sanctas ac venerábiles manus suas, Elevat oculos ad cælum, et elevátis óculis in cælum ad te Deum, Patrem suum omnipoténtem, Caput inclinat, tibi grátias agens, Signat super Hostiam, bene ✠ díxit, fregit, dedítque discípulis suis, dicens: Accípite, et manducáte ex hoc omnes.

Hoc est enim Corpus meum

Et reliqua ut in Canone Missae, praeter sequentia.

eternal damnation, and to be numbered in the fold of thine elect. He joins his hands. Through the same Christ our Lord. Amen.

VOUCHSAFE, O God, we beseech thee, in all things, He signs thrice over the Oblations, to make this oblation bles ✠ sed, ap ✠ proved, and ac ✠ cepted, a perfect and worthy offering: He signs once over the Host, that it may become for us the Bo ✠ dy, And once over the Chalice, and Blo ✠ od of thy dearly beloved Son, He joins his hands, our Lord Jesus Christ.

The incensing of the Sacrament, which is usual in solemn Mass, is done today even if Mass is celebrated without sacred Ministers: for then it is performed by the acolytes, *or servers.*

WHO the day before he suffered for our salvation and that of all mankind, that is, on this day, He takes the Host, took bread into his holy and venerable hands, He lifts his eyes to heaven, and with eyes lifted up to heaven unto thee, God, his almighty Father, He bows his head, giving thanks to thee, He signs over the Host, he ble ✠ ssed, brake, and gave it to his disciples: saying: Take, and eat ye all of this.

For this is my Body

And the rest as in the Canon of the Mass, except the following.

28. To the three-fold O Lamb of God is answered thrice: have mercy upon us, as below:

O LAMB of God, that takest away the sins of the world: have mercy upon us,

O Lamb of God, that takest away the sins of the world: have mercy upon us,

O Lamb of God, that takest away the sins of the world: have mercy upon us.

The kiss of peace is not given today, and the Prayer Dómine Jesu Christe, qui dixísti is omitted.

29. Having received the most sacred Blood, the celebrant, omitting the confession and absolution, proceeds to the distribution of Communion, in the usual manner. The sacred ministers come first; after them the rest of the clergy in order, then the servers.

These all come before the Altar, two and two, or four and four, and, having genuflected, ascend the steps, and kneeling reverently receive the Body of the Lord; then in the same order they withdraw. The faithful receive the Sacrament at the rails.

If however the number of the faithful approaching the Holy Table be great, other priests also, either with the celebrant at the rails, or in some other fitting place, may distribute Communion, provided that care be taken to secure good order and reverence among the faithful.

If the Bishop distribute Holy Communion, the faithful do not kiss his ring before Communion.

30. The antiphon at the Communion may be sung by the choir, while the celebrant distributes the sacred particles.

31. Antiphon at the Communion. John 13, 12-13 and 15. The Lord Jesus after he had supped with his disciples, washed their feet, and said to them: Know ye what I, your Lord and Master, have done to you? I have given you an example, that ye also should so do.

According to the number of communicants, the following Psalms may be added: Psalm 23 The Lord is my shepherd. And the Antiphon The Lord Jesus is repeated. Psalm 72 Give the King thy judgments, O God, Psalm 104 Praise the Lord, O my soul, Psalm 150 O praise God in his holiness. And after each Psalm the Antiphon The Lord Jesus is repeated.

32. The Communion of the faithful ended, the ciborium or ciboria are placed on the corporal. The celebrant proceeds to the ablution of the chalice and his fingers, reciting the accustomed prayers.

33. All things being thus completed, the Mass proceeds in the accustomed manner; but the celebrant genuflects, whenever he approaches, or departs from the midst of the Altar, or passes before the Sacrament: and when he says The Lord be with you, he does not turn to the people in the midst of the Altar, lest he turn his back toward the Sacrament, but at the Gospel side.

34. Let us pray.   Postcommunion.

O LORD our God, who hast refreshed us with life-giving sustenance, we beseech thee: that we who observe this institution in the time of our mortal life, may obtain the benefit thereof in thy gift of immortality. Through.

35. In place of Ite, Missa est, today is sung Let us bless the Lord, and Pláceat tibi is said as usual.

36. The blessing and last Gospel of St. John are omitted today; the celebrant and ministers put off the maniple, and the celebrant also the chasuble, and he takes a cope of white colour.

37. In read Masses, which are allowed to be celebrated by the Ordinary, Mass is ended in the usual manner.

THE SOLEMN TRANSLATION AND REPOSITION OF THE SACRAMENT AND THE STRIPPING OF THE ALTARS

1. Mass being ended, there follows at once the solemn translation and reservation of the Sacrament, which is kept in the ciborium for the Communion to be made on the following day.

2. A suitable place is to be made ready in some chapel or on some Altar of the church, adorned with lights and hangings. A simplicity and severity, suitable to the liturgy of these days, is to be observed.

3. In the translation and reservation of the Sacrament, the following method is to be observed:

Torches are lighted, and the procession is made in the usual manner.

Another subdeacon, if one can be had, duly vested, carries the Cross: otherwise one of the clerks, *or servers*.

The celebrant, standing before the Altar, puts incense in two thuribles, without a blessing. Then, kneeling in the middle, he thrice incenses the Sacrament.

Then he takes a humeral veil of white colour, and going up to the Altar in the midst, having genuflected, he stands, and takes the ciborium, which the deacon hands to him, and covers it with the ends of the veil.

Then, descending from the Altar, he proceeds beneath the canopy, two acolytes, *or servers*, continually incensing the Sacrament, to the place prepared.

The sacred ministers, *or servers*, accompany the celebrant, proceeding on his right and left.

During the procession, the hymn **Pange, lingua, gloriósi Córporis mystérium**, is sung as far as the words **Tantum ergo**; if need be, the same hymn is repeated.

4. When they are come to the place prepared, the celebrant, aided, if need be, by the deacon, sets down the ciborium on the Altar, genuflects, puts in incense again, and incenses it; meanwhile Tantum ergo is sung.

Then the deacon, *or the celebrant himself*, puts back the ciborium in the tabernacle or urn.

5. Then all kneeling for some time adore the Sacrament in silence. At a signal, the celebrant and sacred ministers, *and the servers*, rise, again kneel and adore, and return to the sacristy, where the celebrant and sacred ministers put off the vestments of white colour; then the celebrant and deacon put on a violet stole.

6. If there be more ciboria to be transferred, the celebrant, (or, if they be available, another priest or deacon wearing surplice, stole and humeral veil of the same colour), shall transfer them to the appointed place, before he begins the stripping of the Altars, in simple form, namely, with two acolytes, *or servers*, with lighted torches, and another carrying the small canopy.

7. Then the celebrant, with the ministers, *or servers*, go before the High Altar; and, having reverenced it, begin, standing, the stripping of the Altars, in this manner:

The celebrant says in a clear voice the following antiphon:

Ps. 22, 19. They part my garments among them, and upon my vesture they cast lots, adding the beginning of the same Psalm:

My God, my God, why hast thou forsaken me?

The clergy, if they be present, continue the recitation of this Psalm, until the stripping of the Altars has been completed; otherwise the celebrant himself continues the Psalm.

The celebrant with the sacred ministers, *or with the servers,* strips all the Altars of the church, excepting that at which the Sacrament is solemnly adored.

The Altars having been stripped, they return to the High Altar, and the celebrant having repeated the antiphon They part, they return to the sacristy.

8. Then Compline is said in choir, with the candles extinguished, and without chant.

9. Public adoration is made at the place of reservation of the most Holy Eucharist at least, if possible, until midnight.

FRIDAY OF THE PASSION AND DEATH OF THE LORD
COMMONLY CALLED

GOOD FRIDAY

Double of 1st class.

THE SOLEMN LITURGY ON THE AFTERNOON OF THE PASSION AND DEATH OF THE LORD

Station at St. Cross in Jerusalem

1. The Altar shall be completely bare: without cross, candlesticks or linen cloths.

2. The solemn afternoon liturgy of this feria, where there is a lack of clergy and priests, is performed by the celebrant with the assistance of servers, as noted below; but where there are clerics, it is most fitting that they should assist in choir at the liturgical function.

3. Each one then vests in his choir habit; the celebrant and deacon wear amice, alb, girdle and black stole; the subdeacon amice, alb and girdle.

THE FIRST PART OF THE LITURGY
OR
THE LESSONS

4. All being thus vested, the procession moves through the church to the Altar in silence.

5. The clergy, ministers, *or servers,* and the celebrant, when they are come to the Altar, make reverence thereto; then the celebrant and sacred ministers, *but not the servers,* lie prostrate on their faces, but the others go to the stalls in choir, and there remain, kneeling and bowing low; and all pray awhile in silence.

6. The signal being given, all raise themselves, but remain kneeling: the celebrant alone, standing before the steps of the Altar, says with joined hands and in the ferial tone the following Collect:

Collect.

O GOD, who hast destroyed the death of our old sin, whereto all flesh fell heir, by the Passion of thy Christ, our Lord: grant that, being conformed unto the same; we, who by nature have borne the image of the earthy, may by thy sanctifying grace bear also the image of the heavenly. Through the same Christ our Lord.

All answer: Amen.

7. The Collect ended, the celebrant and ministers, *or the servers,* go to the seats. Meanwhile a bare lectern is set in the midst of the sanctuary, and a reader

begins the first lesson, all sitting and listening. It is begun without title, and ended without Thanks be to God.

7a. If a lector be not available, the celebrant himself reads the lesson, standing in his place.

The first Lesson. Hosea 6, 1-6.

THUS saith the Lord: In their affliction they will seek me early: Come, and let us return unto the Lord: for he hath torn, and he will heal us: he hath smitten, and he will bind us up. After two days will he revive us: in the third day he will raise us up, and we shall live in his sight. Then shall we know, if we follow on to know the Lord: his going forth is prepared as the morning, and he shall come unto us as the rain, as the latter and former rain unto the earth. O Ephraim, what shall I do unto thee? O Judah, what shall I do unto thee? for your goodness is as a morning cloud: and as the early dew it goeth away. Therefore have I hewed them by the prophet, I have slain them by the words of my mouth: and thy judgments are as the light that goeth forth. For I desired mercy, and not sacrifice, and the knowledge of God more than burnt offerings.

The responsory follows, to be sung by the choir, or recited by the clergy present.

Responsory. Habak. 3.

O Lord, I have heard thy speech, and was afraid: I have considered thy works, and was confounded. ℣. O Lord, revive thy work in the midst of the years: in the midst of the years make it known. ℣. In the time of confusion of my soul: in wrath, remember mercy. ℣. God came from Teman, and his Holy One from the thick woods of the mountains. ℣. His glory covered the heavens: and the earth was full of his praise.

8. The Responsory ended, all rise; the celebrant, standing at the seat, says Let us pray, the deacon Let us bow the knee, and all, kneeling, pray for a space in silence; the deacon having said Arise, all rise, and the celebrant, with hands joined and in the ferial tone, says the Collect.

8a. The celebrant, remaining in his place, says Let us pray, Let us bow the knee, and having prayed for a short time, kneeling and in silence, says Arise; then he rises, and, with hands joined and in the ferial tone, says the following Collect.

Let us pray.

℣. Let us bow the knee.   ℟. Arise.

[†Three Collects and Epistle, p. 139.]

Collect.

O GOD, from whom Judas received the punishment of his guilt, and the thief the reward of his confession: grant unto us the effectual fruits of thy redemption; that, like as in his passion Jesus Christ, our Lord, gave unto each the due recompense of his deeds; so he may deliver us from the transgressions of our old nature, and bestow on us the grace of his resurrection: Who liveth and reigneth with thee.

9. The Collect ended, the second lesson follows, to be said by the subdeacon at the lectern, likewise without title, and without Thanks be to God at the end.

9a. A lector shall read the lesson at the lectern; otherwise the celebrant himself, standing in his place.

The second Lesson. Exod. 12, 1-11.

IN those days: The Lord spake unto Moses and Aaron in the land of Egypt, saying: This month shall be unto you the beginning of months: it shall be the first month of the year to you. Speak ye unto all the congregation of Israel, saying: In the tenth day of this month they shall take to them every man a lamb, according to the house of their fathers, a lamb for an house. And if the household be too little for the lamb, let him and his neighbour next unto his house take it according to the number of the souls, every man according to his eating shall make your count for the lamb. Your lamb shall be without blemish, a male of the first year: ye shall take it out from the sheep, or from the goats. And ye shall keep it up until the fourteenth day of the same month: and the whole assembly of the congregation of Israel shall kill it in the evening. And they shall take of the blood, and strike it on the two side posts and on the upper door post of the houses, wherein they shall eat it. And they shall eat the flesh in that night, roast with fire, and unleavened bread, and with bitter herbs they shall eat it. Eat not of it raw, nor sodden at all with water, but roast with fire: his head with his legs, and with the purtenance thereof. And ye shall let nothing of it remain until the morning. And that which remaineth of it until the morning ye shall burn with fire. And thus shall ye eat it: With your loins girded, your shoes on your feet, and your staff in your hand, and ye shall eat it in haste: it is the Lord's Passover.

Responsory. Ps. 140, 1-9 and 14.

Deliver me, O Lord, from the evil man: and preserve me from the wicked man. ℣. Who imagine mischief in their hearts: and stir up strife all the day long. ℣. They have sharpened their tongues like a serpent: adders' poison is under their lips. ℣. Keep me, O Lord, from the hands of the ungodly: and preserve me from the wicked men. ℣. Who are purposed to overthrow my goings: the proud have laid a snare for me. ℣. And spread a net abroad with cords: yea, and set traps in my way. ℣. I said unto the Lord: Thou art my God: hear the voice of my prayers, O Lord. ℣. O Lord God, thou strength of my health: thou hast covered my head in the day of battle. ℣. Let not the ungodly have his desire, O Lord: let not his mischievous imagination prosper, lest they be too proud. ℣. Let the mischief of their own lips fall upon the head of them: that compass me about. ℣. The righteous also shall give thanks unto thy name: and the just shall continue in thy sight.

10. The second lesson with its responsory being ended, there are set on the Gospel side, on the level space of the sanctuary, bare lecterns with books, and they proceed to the singing or reading of the story of the Passion according to John in this manner: it is sung or read by ministers, being at least in the Order of Deacon, who, accompanied by two acolytes, *or servers,* without lights, and without incense, having made a reverence to the Altar, stand before the celebrant; while they bow low, the celebrant says over them in a clear voice:

The Lord be in your hearts,
and on your lips.

They stand erect, and answer: Amen.

Then, having again made a reverence to the Altar, they go to the Gospel side, and there, on a bare lectern, they begin to sing or to read the story of the Passion of the Lord, all listening.

10a, The celebrant reads or sings the story of the Passion of the Lord, in a clear and distinct voice. Before he begins, he says, in the midst of the sanctuary, bowing low, in a clear voice:

The Lord be in my heart,
and on my lips. Amen.

Then, having made a reverence to the Altar, he goes to the Gospel side, and there, on a bare lectern, he begins to read or to sing the story of the Passion of the Lord.

11. The Gospel of the Passion and Death of the Lord according to John. 18, 1-40; 19, 1-42.

The Passion of our Lord Jesus Christ according to John.

AT that time: Jesus went forth with his disciples over the brook Cedron, where was a garden, into the which he entered, and his disciples. And Judas also, which betrayed him, knew the place: for Jesus oft times resorted thither with his disciples. Judas then, having received a band of men and officers from the chief priests and Pharisees, cometh thither with lanterns and torches and weapons. Jesus therefore, knowing all things that should come upon him, went forth, and said unto them: ✠Whom seek ye? C. They answered him: S. Jesus of Nazareth. C. Jesus saith unto them: ✠I am he. C. And Judas also, which betrayed him, stood with them. As soon then as he had said unto them: I am he: they went backward, and fell to the ground. Then asked he them again: ✠Whom seek ye? C. And they said: S. Jesus of Nazareth. C. Jesus answered: ✠I have told you that I am he: if therefore ye seek me, let these go their way. C. That the saying might be fulfilled, which he spake: Of them which thou gavest me have I lost none.

Then Simon Peter having a sword drew it: and smote the high priest's servant: and cut off his right ear. The servant's name was Malchus. Then said Jesus unto Peter: ✠Put up thy sword into the sheath. The cup which my Father hath given me, shall I not drink it? C. Then the band and the captain and officers of the Jews took Jesus, and bound him.

And led him away to Annas first, for he was father in law to Caiaphas, which was the high priest that same year. Now Caiaphas was he, which gave counsel to the Jews: That it was expedient that one man should die for the people. And Simon Peter followed Jesus, and so did another disciple. That disciple was known unto the high priest, and went in with Jesus into the palace of the high priest.

But Peter stood at the door without. Then went out that other disciple, which was known unto the high priest, and spake unto her that kept the door: and brought in Peter. Then saith the damsel that kept the door unto Peter: S. Art not thou also one of this man's disciples? C. He saith: S. I am not. C. And the servants and officers stood there, who had made a fire of coals, for it was cold, and they warmed themselves: and Peter stood with them, and warmed himself.

The high priest then asked Jesus of his disciples, and of his doctrine. Jesus answered him: ✠I spake openly to the world: I ever taught in the synagogue, and in the temple, whither the Jews always resort: and in secret have I said nothing. Why askest thou me? ask them which heard me, what I have said unto them: behold, they know what I said. C. And when he had thus spoken, one of the officers which stood by struck Jesus with the palm of his hand, saying: S. Answerest thou the high priest so? C. Jesus answered him: ✠If I have spoken evil, bear witness of the evil: but if well, why smitest thou me?

C. Now Annas had sent him bound unto Caiaphas the high priest. And Simon Peter stood and warmed himself. They said therefore unto him: S. Art not thou also one of his disciples? C. He denied it, and said: S. I am not. C. One of the servants of the high priest, being his kinsman whose ear Peter cut off, saith: S. Did not I see thee in the garden with him? C. Peter then denied again: and immediately the cock crew.

Then led they Jesus from Caiaphas unto the hall of judgment. And it was early: and they themselves went not into the judgment-hall, lest they should be defiled, but that they might eat the Passover. Pilate then went out unto them, and said: S. What accusation bring ye against this man? C. They answered and said unto him: S. If he were not a malefactor, we would not have delivered him up unto thee. C. Then said Pilate unto them: S. Take ye him, and judge him according to your law. C. The Jews therefore said unto him: S. It is not lawful for us to put any man to death. C. That the saying of Jesus might be fulfilled, which he spake, signifying what death he should die.

Then Pilate entered into the judgment-hall again, and called Jesus, and said unto him: S. Art thou the King of the Jews? C. Jesus answered him: ✠ Sayest thou this thing of thyself, or did others tell it thee of me? C. Pilate answered: S. Am I a Jew? Thine own nation and the chief priests have delivered thee unto me: what hast thou done? C. Jesus answered: ✠ My kingdom is not of this world. If my kingdom were of this world, then would my servants fight, that I should not be delivered to the Jews: but now is my kingdom not from hence. C. Pilate therefore said unto him: S. Art thou a King then? C. Jesus answered: ✠ Thou sayest that I am a King. To this end was I born, and for this cause came I into the world, that I should bear witness unto the truth: every one that is of the truth heareth my voice. C. Pilate saith unto him: S. What is truth? C. And when he had said this, he went out again unto the Jews, and saith unto them: S. I find in him no fault at all. But ye have a custom, that I should release unto you one at the Passover: will ye therefore that I release unto you the King of the Jews? C. Then cried they all again, saying: S. Not this man, but Barabbas. C. Now Barabbas was a robber.

(†John 19, 1.)

Pilate therefore took Jesus, and scourged him. And the soldiers platted a crown of thorns, and put it on his head: and they put on him a purple robe. And said: S. Hail, King of the Jews. C. And they smote him with their hands.

Pilate therefore went forth again, and saith unto them: S. Behold, I bring him forth to you, that ye may know that I find no fault in him. C. Then came Jesus forth, wearing the crown of thorns, and the purple robe. And Pilate saith unto them: S. Behold the man. C. When the chief priests therefore and officers saw him, they cried out, saying: S. Crucify him, crucify him. C. Pilate saith unto them: S. Take ye him, and crucify him: for I find no fault in him. C. The Jews answered him: S. We have a law, and by our law he ought to die, because he made himself the Son of God. C. When Pilate therefore heard that saying, he was the more afraid.

And went again into the judgment-hall: and saith unto Jesus: S. Whence art thou? C. But Jesus gave him no answer. Then saith Pilate unto him: S. Speakest thou not unto me? knowest thou not that I have power to crucify thee, and have power to release thee? C. Jesus answered: ✠ Thou couldest have no power at all against me, except it were given thee from above. Therefore he that delivered me unto thee hath the greater sin. C. And from thenceforth Pilate sought to release him. But the Jews cried out, saying: S. If thou let this man go, thou art not Cæsar's friend. Whosoever maketh himself a king speaketh against Cæsar. C. When Pilate therefore heard that saying, he brought Jesus forth, and sat down in the judgment-seat, in a place that is called the Pavement, but in the Hebrew, Gabbatha. And it was the Preparation of the Passover, and about the sixth hour, and he saith unto the Jews: S. Behold your King. C. But they cried out: S. Away with him, away with him, crucify him. C. Pilate saith unto them: S. Shall I crucify your King? C. The chief priests answered: S. We have no king but Cæsar. C. Then delivered he him therefore unto them to be crucified.

And they took Jesus, and led him away. And he bearing his Cross, went forth into a place called the place of a skull, which is called in the Hebrew, Golgotha: where they crucified him, and two other with him, on either side one, and Jesus in the midst.

And Pilate wrote a title: and put it on the cross. And the writing was: Jesus of Nazareth the King of the Jews. This title then read many of the Jews, for the place where Jesus was crucified was nigh to the city. And it was written in Hebrew, and Greek, and Latin. Then said the chief priests of the Jews to Pilate: S. Write not, The King of the Jews, but that he said: I am the King of the Jews. C. Pilate answered: S. What I have written, I have written.

C. Then the soldiers, when they had crucified Jesus, took his garments, and made four parts: to every soldier a part, and also his coat. Now the coat was without seam, woven from the top throughout. They said therefore among themselves: S. Let us not rend it, but cast lots for it, whose it shall be. C. That the Scripture might be fulfilled which saith: They parted my raiment among them: and for my vesture they did cast lots. These things therefore the soldiers did.

Now there stood by the cross of Jesus, his Mother, and his Mother's sister, Mary the wife of Cleophas, and Mary Magdalene. When Jesus therefore saw his Mother, and the disciple standing by, whom he loved, he saith unto his Mother: ✠ Woman, behold thy son. C. Then saith he to the disciple: ✠ Behold thy mother. C. And from that hour that disciple took her unto his own home.

After this, Jesus, knowing that all things were now accomplished, that the Scripture might be fulfilled, saith ✠ I thirst. C. Now there was set a vessel full of vinegar. And they filled a spunge with vinegar, and put it upon hyssop, and put it to his mouth. When Jesus therefore had received the vinegar, he said: ✠ It is finished. C. And he bowed his head and gave up the ghost.

Here genuflect, and pause awhile.

The Jews therefore, because it was the Preparation, that the bodies should not remain upon the cross on the sabbath-day, for that sabbath-day was an high-day, besought Pilate that their legs might be broken, and that they might be taken away. Then came the soldiers: and brake the legs of the first, and of the other which was crucified with him. But when they came to Jesus, and saw that he was dead already, they brake not his legs, but one of the soldiers with a spear pierced his side, and forthwith came there out blood and water. And he that saw it bare record: and his record is true. And he knoweth that he saith true: that ye might believe. For these things were done that the Scripture should be fulfilled: A bone of him shall not be broken. And again, another Scripture saith: They shall look on him whom they pierced.†

And after this Joseph of Arimathæa, being a disciple of Jesus, but secretly for fear of the Jews, besought Pilate that he might take away the body of Jesus. And Pilate gave him leave. He came therefore and took the body of Jesus. And there came also Nicodemus, which at the first came to Jesus by night, and brought a mixture of myrrh and aloes, about an hundred pound weight. Then took they the body of Jesus, and wound it in linen clothes with the spices, as the manner of the Jews is to bury. Now in the place where he was crucified there was a garden: and in the garden a new sepulchre, wherein was never man yet laid. There laid they Jesus therefore because of the Jews' Preparation day, for the sepulchre was nigh at hand.

THE SECOND PART OF THE LITURGY
OR
THE SOLEMN PRAYERS
ALSO CALLED
THE PRAYER OF THE FAITHFUL

12. The singing or reading of the story of the Passion of the Lord being ended, the celebrant puts on a cope of black colour; and the deacon and subdeacon dalmatic and tunicle of the same.

Meanwhile two acolytes, *or servers,* spread one linen cloth only upon the Altar, placing the book in the middle. Then the celebrant, accompanied by the ministers, *or the servers,* approaches the Altar; and, going up, he kisses it in the midst, and standing in the same place, having the book before him, he begins the solemn Prayers, the sacred ministers standing on either side.

13. They are said in this manner: The preface of the celebrant, whereby the particular intention is indicated, comes first, and is sung in the special tone noted below, with joined hands; then the celebrant says Let us pray, the deacon Let us bow the knee, and all kneel, and pray in silence for a space; the deacon having said Arise, all rise, and the celebrant, with hands extended and in the ferial tone, says the Prayer.

13*a*. *The celebrant says Let us pray, Let us bow the knee, and after a short prayer, kneeling and in silence, he says Arise, then he rises and with hands extended, and in the ferial tone, says the Prayer.*

1. For the Holy Church

LET us práy, déar-ly be-lóv-ed, for the hó-ly Church of Gód: that our Gód and Lórd would vouch-sáfe to gíve her péace and ú-ni-ty, and pre-sérve her through-óut all the wórld: má-king súb-ject ún-to hér prin-ci-pá- li- ties and pów-ers: and gránt that, léad-ing a quí- et and péace-ful lífe, we may gló-ri-fy Gód the Fá-ther Al-migh-ty. Let us pray.

℣ Let us bów the knee. ℟. A-ríse.

ALMIGHTY and everlasting God, who in Christ hast revealed thy glory to all nations: preserve the works of thy mercy; that thy Church, spread abroad over the whole world, may with steadfast faith persevere in the confession of thy name. Through the same.
All: ℟. Amen.

2. For the Chief Bishop

LET us práy ál-so for óur most blés-sed Fá-ther N. : that our Gód and Lórd, who hath chó-sen him un-to the ór-der of Bísh-ops, may pre-sérve him in héalth and sáfe-ty to his hó-ly Chúrch, for the góv-ern-ance of the hó-ly péo-ple of Gód. Let us práy.

℣. Let us bów the knee. ℟. A-ríse.

ALMIGHTY and everlasting God, by whose judgment all things are established: mercifully regard our prayers, and in thy goodness preserve him whom thou hast chosen to be our Bishop; that the Christian people who are governed by thine authority may under so great a Pontiff increase in the merits of their faith. Through.
All: ℟. Amen.

Good Friday

3. For all Orders and Estates of the Faithful

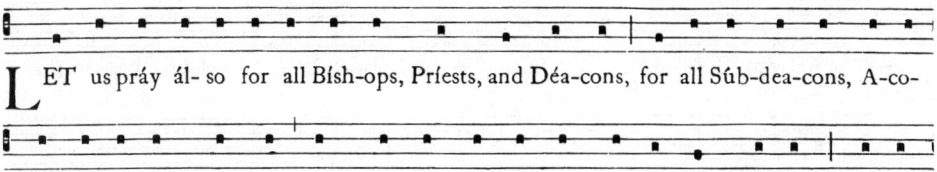

LET us práy ál- so for all Bísh-ops, Príests, and Déa-cons, for all Súb-dea-cons, A-co-lytes, Ex-or-cists, Réad-ers, Dóor-keep-ers, Con-féss-ors, Vír-gins, and Wí-dows: and for áll the hó-ly péo-ple of Gód. Let us práy.   ℣. Let us bów the knee.   ℟. A- ríse.

ALMIGHTY and everlasting God, by whose spirit the whole body of the Church is governed and sanctified: receive our supplications, which we offer before thee for all orders of the same; that by the bounty of thy grace they may faithfully serve thee in their several estates. Through.

All: ℟. Amen.

4. For Rulers and Governors

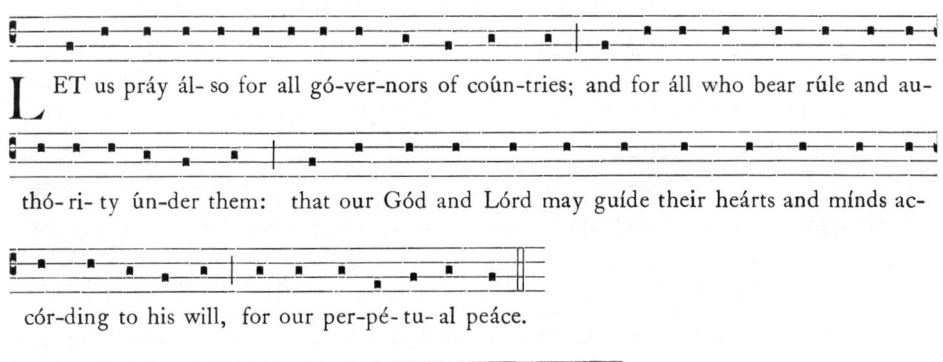

LET us práy ál- so for all gó-ver-nors of coún-tries; and for áll who bear rúle and au- thó- ri- ty ún-der them: that our Gód and Lórd may guíde their heárts and mínds ac- córd-ing to his will, for our per-pé- tu- al peáce.

Let us práy.   ℣. Let us bów the knee.   ℟. A- ríse.

ALMIGHTY and everlasting God, in whose hand are the dominion and government of all peoples: look graciously on those who bear rule and authority over us; that all nations, by the protection of thy right hand, may continue in true religion, and abide in continual safety. Through. All: ℟. Amen.

Good Friday

5. For Catechumens

LET us pray al-so for our ca-te-chu-mens: that our God and Lord would o-pen the ears of their hearts, and the gate of mer-cy; that, re-ceiv-ing in the wa-ters of re-ge-ne-ra-tion the re-mis-sion of all their sins, they al-so may be found in Christ Je-sus our Lord.

Let us pray. ℣. Let us bow the knee. ℟. A-rise.

ALMIGHTY and everlasting God, who dost continually enrich thy Church with a new offspring: increase the faith and understanding of our catechumens: that they, being born again in the water of baptism, may be numbered among the sons of thine adoption. Through.
All: ℟. Amen.

6. For the needs of the Faithful

LET us pray, dear-ly be-lov-ed, un-to God the Fa-ther Al-migh-ty, that he would purge the world from all er-rors: would take a-way dis-eas-es: drive a-way fa-mine: o-pen the pri-sons: loos-en the chains: grant un-to pil-grims a safe re-turn: to the sick heal-ing: and to them that tra-vel by sea a ha-ven of safe-ty. Let us pray. ℣. Let us bow the knee.

℟. A-rise.

Good Friday

ALMIGHTY and everlasting God, the comfort of them that mourn, the strength of them that travail: let the prayers of them that cry out of any tribulation ascend unto thee; that in their necessities all may rejoice in the succour of thy loving kindness. Through.

All: ℟. Amen.

7. For the Unity of the Church

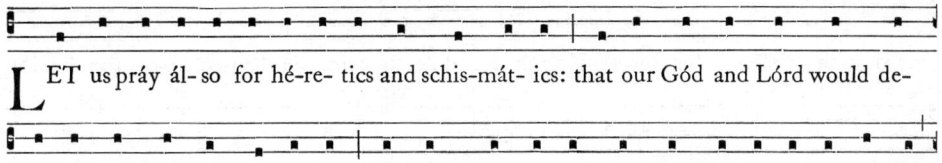

LET us pray ál-so for hé-re-tics and schis-mát-ics: that our Gód and Lórd would de-li-ver them from áll their ér-rors; and vouch-sáfe to cáll them báck to their ho-ly mó-ther, the Cá-tho lic and A-pos-to- lic Chúrch. Let us práy. ℣.Let us bów the knee. ℟. A-ríse.

ALMIGHTY and everlasting God, who savest all men, and wouldest not that any should perish: look upon the souls that are deceived by the craft of the devil; that the hearts of them that are gone astray, being delivered from all perversity of heresy, may turn to wisdom and come again to the unity of thy truth. Through.

All: ℟. Amen.

8. For the Conversion of the Jews

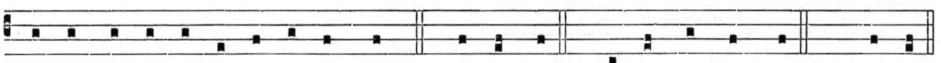

LET us práy ál-so for the fáith-less Jéws: that our Gód and Lórd would táke a-wáy the véil

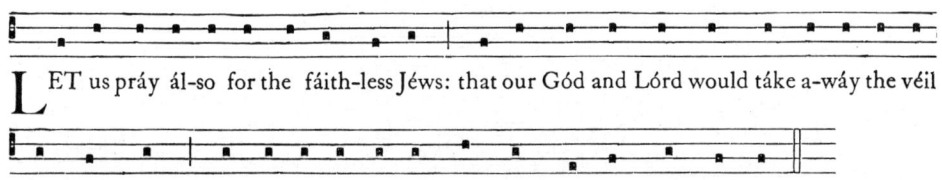

from their héarts; that they ál- so may ac-knów-ledge Jé- sus Chríst, our Lórd.

Let us práv. ℟. Let us bów the knee. ℣. A- ríse.

ALMIGHTY and everlasting God, who deniest not thy mercy even to the faithless Jews: graciously hear our prayers, which we offer for the blindness of this people: that they, acknowledging the light of thy truth, which is Christ, may be delivered from their darkness. Through the same.

All: ℟. Amen.

9. For the Conversion of the Heathen

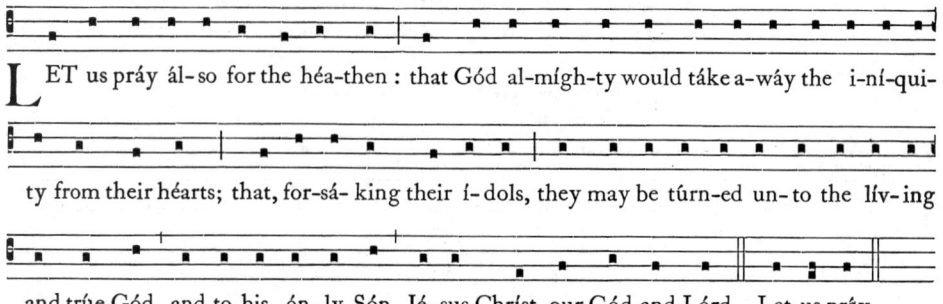

LET us pray ál-so for the héa-then : that Gód al-mígh-ty would táke a-wáy the i-ní-qui-ty from their héarts; that, for-sá- king their í-dols, they may be túrn-ed un-to the lív-ing and trúe Gód, and to his ón- ly Són, Jé-sus Chríst, our Gód and Lórd. Let us práy.

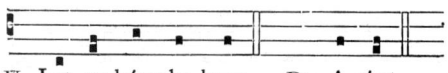

℣. Let us bów the knee. ℟. A-ríse.

ALMIGHTY and everlasting God, who desirest not the death of sinners but rather that they should live: mercifully receive our prayer, and deliver them from the worship of idols; and gather them unto thy holy Church, to the praise and glory of thy name. Through.

All: ℟. Amen.

THE THIRD PART OF THE LITURGY
OR
THE SOLEMN ADORATION OF THE HOLY CROSS

14. The solemn Prayers ended, the celebrant and ministers return to the seats, where the celebrant puts off the cope, the ministers the dalmatic or tunicle; and they begin the solemn adoration of the Cross.

A sufficiently large Cross must be provided, with the figure of the Crucified, covered with a violet veil which can be easily removed.

15. First the holy Cross is carried from the sacristy to the midst of the sanctuary, all standing. And it is carried in this manner:

The celebrant and subdeacon remain standing at the seats: the deacon with the acolytes *or servers* goes to the sacristy, from which he brings the Cross in procession to the church: the acolytes *or servers* go first, the deacon follows with the Cross, in the midst between two other acolytes, *or servers,* carrying lighted candles.

When they have entered the sanctuary, the celebrant and subdeacon come to meet them, and in the midst, before the Altar, the celebrant receives the Cross from the hands of the deacon.

15a. *The celebrant with the servers goes to the sacristy, and brings the Cross thence, as above.*

16. Then the unveiling of the holy Cross proceeds in this manner:

The celebrant, going to the Epistle side, and there standing on the floor, with face turned toward the people, unveils the Cross a little, from the top. Then he alone begins the antiphon **Behold the wood of the Cross**, and thereafter is assisted in the chant by the sacred ministers, as far as **O come, let us worship**, which is sung by the choir, all present singing with them.

The singing ended, all kneel, the celebrant excepted, and worship for a moment in silence.

Then the celebrant ascends the Altar from the Epistle side, and unveils the right arm of the Crucifix; then raising the Cross a little, the sacred ministers, if need be, helping him, he sings again, higher than before, **Behold the wood of the Cross**, the others continuing, and, after the singing, kneeling, as before.

Finally the celebrant proceeds to the middle of the Altar, and completely unveils the Cross, and raising it, begins a third time in a higher key Behold the wood of the Cross, the others, as above, continuing, and after the chant worshipping.

Two acolytes, *or servers,* with lighted candles accompany the Cross, on the right and left of the celebrant.

16a. *The celebrant, in unveiling the holy Cross, is assisted by the servers: but he sings alone the antiphon Behold the wood of the Cross, as far as O come, let us worship.*

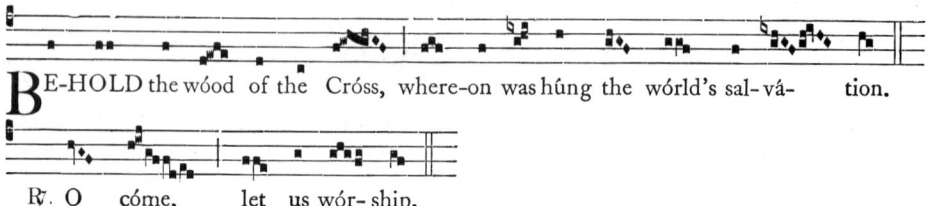

BE-HOLD the wóod of the Cróss, where-on was húng the wórld's sal-vá-tion.

℟. O cóme, let us wór-ship.

17. After the unveiling of the Cross there follows the solemn adoration thereof, in this manner: the Cross, after it has been unveiled, is given by the celebrant to two acolytes, *or servers,* who, standing on the foot-pace, before the midst of the Altar, and with faces turned toward the people, sustain it on either side by the arms, so that the foot of the Cross stands upon the foot-pace. The two other acolytes, *or servers,* who were carrying lighted candles, having set down the candles to the right and left of the Cross on the foot-pace, remain kneeling at the sides of the foot-pace, on the highest step, facing the Cross.

Then the adoration of the holy Cross begins in the following order: first the celebrant approaches alone: then the ministers, after that the clergy, finally the servers. All of these, if it can conveniently be done, first put off their shoes, and, one after another, approach the Cross, having thrice made a simple genuflexion, and kiss the feet of the Crucified.

18. The holy Cross, the adoration on the part of the celebrant, ministers, clergy and servers being performed, is carried to the rails by the two acolytes, *or servers,* accompanied by the two other acolytes, *or servers,* with lighted candles, and there sustained, as above, so that the faithful, passing as in procession before the Cross, first the men, then the women, can devoutly kiss the feet of the Crucifix, having first made one simple genuflexion.

19. While the adoration of the holy Cross is being performed, the singers, divided into two choirs, sing the Reproaches, and other things that follow; the celebrant, sacred ministers and servers and all others who have performed the adoration of the holy Cross, sit and listen.

REPROACHES
I

1 and 2. O my people, what have I done unto thee? or wherein have I wearied thee? Answer me!

℣. Because I brought thee forth from the land of Egypt: thou hast prepared a Cross for thy Saviour.

    1. Hágios o Theós.

    2. Holy God.

    1. Hágios Ischyrós.

    2. Holy, mighty.

    1. Hágios Athánatos, eléison hymás.

    2. Holy and Immortal, have mercy upon us.

1 and 2. Because I led thee through the desert forty years, and fed thee with manna, and brought thee into a land exceeding good: thou hast prepared a Cross for thy Saviour.

    1. Hágios o Theós.

    2. Holy God.

    1. Hágios Ischyrós.

    2. Holy, mighty.

    1. Hágios Athánatos, eléison hymás.

    2. Holy and Immortal, have mercy upon us.

1 and 2. What more could I have done for thee that I have not done? I indeed did plant thee, my vineyard, exceeding fair: and thou art become very bitter unto me: for vinegar thou gavest to quench my thirst: and hast pierced with a spear the side of thy Saviour.

    1. Hágios o Theós.

    2. Holy God.

    1. Hágios Ischyrós.

    2. Holy, mighty.

    1. Hágios Athánatos, eléison hymás.

    2. Holy and Immortal, have mercy upon us.

II

1. I did scourge Egypt with her first-born for thy sake: and thou hast scourged me and delivered me up.
2. O my people, what have I done unto thee? or wherein have I wearied thee? Answer me!

1. I led thee out of Egypt, drowning Pharaoh in the Red Sea: and thou hast delivered me unto the chief priests.
2. O my people, what have I done unto thee? or wherein have I wearied thee? Answer me!

1. I opened the sea before thee: and thou hast opened my side with a spear.
2. O my people, what have I done unto thee? or wherein have I wearied thee? Answer me!

1. I went before thee in a pillar of cloud: and thou hast led me unto the judgment hall of Pilate.
2. O my people, what have I done unto thee? or wherein have I wearied thee? Answer me!

1. I fed thee with manna in the desert: and thou hast stricken me with blows and scourges.
2. O my people, what have I done unto thee? or wherein have I wearied thee? Answer me!

1. I gave thee to drink of the water of salvation from the rock: and thou hast given me gall and vinegar to drink.
2. O my people, what have I done unto thee? or wherein have I wearied thee? Answer me!

1. For thee I smote the kings of the Canaanites: and thou hast smitten my head with a reed.
2. O my people, what have I done unto thee? or wherein have I wearied thee? Answer me!

1. I gave thee a royal sceptre: and thou hast given unto my head a crown of thorns.
2. O my people, what have I done unto thee? or wherein have I wearied thee? Answer me!

1. I exalted thee with great power: and thou hast hanged me upon the gibbet of the Cross.
2. O my people, what have I done unto thee? or wherein have I wearied thee? Answer me!

III

1 and 2. Antiphon. **We worship thy Cross, O Lord: and praise and glorify thy holy resurrection: for behold, by virtue of the tree joy hath come to the whole world.**

1. Ps. 67, 1. **God be merciful unto us and bless us:**

2. **And shew us the light of his countenance, and be merciful unto us.**

1 and 2. Antiphon. **We worship thy Cross, O Lord: and praise and glorify thy holy resurrection: for behold, by virtue of the tree joy hath come to the whole world.**

IV

1 and 2. Antiphon. **Faithful Cross, above all other, one and only noble tree: none in foliage, none in blossom, none in fruit thy peer may be.
Sweetest wood and sweetest iron, sweetest weight is hung on thee.**

1. Hymn. **Sing, my tongue, the glorious battle, sing the ending of the fray, now above the Cross, the trophy, sound the loud triumphant lay: tell how Christ, the world's Redeemer, as a victim won the day.**

2. **Faithful Cross, above all other, one and only noble tree: none in foliage, none in blossom, none in fruit thy peer may be.**

1. **God in pity saw man fallen, shamed and sunk in misery, when he fell on death by tasting fruit of the forbidden tree: then another tree was chosen which the world from death should free.**

2. **Sweetest wood and sweetest iron, sweetest weight is hung on thee.**

1. **Thus the scheme of our salvation, was of old in order laid: that the manifold deceiver's art by art might be outweighed: and the lure the foe put forward into means of healing made.**

2. **Faithful Cross, above all other, one and only noble tree: none in foliage, none in blossom, none in fruit thy peer may be.**

1. **Therefore when the appointed fulness of the holy time was come, he was sent who maketh all things forth from God's eternal home; thus he came to earth, incarnate, offspring of a virgin's womb.**

2. **Sweetest wood and sweetest iron, sweetest weight is hung on thee.**

1. **Lo! he lies, an Infant weeping, where the narrow manger stands, while the Mother-Maid his members wraps in mean and lowly bands, and the swaddling clothes is winding round God's helpless feet and hands.**

2. Faithful Cross, above all other, one and only noble tree: none in foliage, none in blossom, none in fruit thy peer may be.

1. Thirty years among us dwelling, his appointed time fulfilled, born for this, he meets his Passion, for that this he freely willed, on the Cross the Lamb is lifted where his life-blood shall be spilled.

2. Sweetest wood and sweetest iron, sweetest weight is hung on thee.

1. He endured the nails, the spitting, vinegar, and spear, and reed; from that holy Body broken blood and water forth proceed: earth, and stars, and sky, and ocean by that flood from stain are freed.

2. Faithful Cross, above all other, one and only noble tree: none in foliage, none in blossom, none in fruit thy peer may be.

1. Bend thy boughs, O tree of glory! thy relaxing sinews bend; for awhile the ancient rigour that thy birth bestowed, suspend; and the King of heavenly beauty on thy bosom gently tend!

2. Sweetest wood and sweetest iron, sweetest weight is hung on thee.

1. Thou alone wast counted worthy this world's ransom to uphold; for a shipwreck'd race preparing harbour, like the ark of old; with the sacred Blood anointed from the smitten Lamb that rolled.

2. Faithful Cross, above all other, one and only noble tree: none in foliage, none in blossom, none in fruit thy peer may be.

The conclusion, never to be omitted:

1. To the Trinity be glory everlasting as it meet; equal to the Father, equal to the Son, and Paraclete; Trinal Unity, whose praises all created things repeat.
Amen.

2. Sweetest wood and sweetest iron, sweetest weight is hung on thee.

THE FOURTH PART OF THE LITURGY
OR
THE COMMUNION

20. The worship of the Cross being ended, the Cross itself is carried back to the Altar by the acolytes, *or servers,* who had sustained it, accompanied by the other two acolytes, *or servers,* with lighted candles, and there placed in the midst, and, if the arrangement of the Altar permit, so high that it may be conveniently seen by the faithful, without incommoding the celebrant in the following ceremonies, which are to be performed at the Altar. And the lighted candles are set down on the Altar.

21. Then the celebrant and deacon, having put off the stole of black colour, put on violet vestments, namely, the celebrant the stole and chasuble, the deacon the stole and dalmatic, the subdeacon the tunicle.

22. Next the deacon, having placed the burse on the Altar, spreads the corporal, in the usual manner; an acolyte, *or server,* sets on the Altar a vessel of water with purificator, for washing and drying the fingers after the Communion, and arranges the book on the Gospel side.

22a. *Before the procession begins, the priest brings and spreads the corporal on the Altar, in the usual manner.*

23. All things being thus ordered, the Sacrament is brought back from the place of reservation to the High Altar for the Communion. And it is carried in this manner:

The celebrant and subdeacon, the clergy and people, remain in their places, in silence.

The deacon with two acolytes, and another clerk to carry the small canopy, go to the Altar of reposition, on which two candlesticks are ready with lighted candles, afterwards to be taken by the acolytes.

At the Altar of reposition they kneel: then the deacon withdraws the sacred pyx from the tabernacle or urn, and having put on a humeral veil of white colour, he covers the pyx with the ends of the veil and brings it to the High Altar.

23a. *All these things are done by the celebrant himself with his servers.*

24. They proceed in the order in which they came: a small canopy is carried over the Sacrament: the acolytes, walking on either side carry lighted candles, and all kneel.

Meanwhile the choir sings the following antiphons:

1. We adore thee, O Christ, and we bless thee, because by thy Cross thou hast redeemed the world.

2. Through the tree we were made slaves, and through the holy Cross we are set free: the fruit of the tree betrayed us, the Son of God redeemed us.

3. O Saviour of the world, who by thy Cross and precious Blood hast redeemed us, save us and help us, we humbly beseech thee, O Lord.

25. When they are come to the High Altar, they go up, the deacon sets down the sacred pyx upon the corporal, the acolytes their candlesticks upon the Altar. The deacon, having genuflected, withdraws to the Epistle side; the acolytes descend, one on each side, and kneel on the lowest step of the Altar.

26. Then the celebrant and subdeacon go to the Altar, adore on both knees, ascend it, and having made, together with the deacon, a genuflexion, the celebrant recites in a clear voice, but does not sing, the preface of the Lord's Prayer: Let us pray. Commanded by saving precepts.

The whole Our Father, since it is the Prayer for Communion, is recited by all present, clergy and faithful, together with the celebrant, solemnly, gravely and distinctly, all adding: Amen.

The celebrant, with joined hands, says alone:

Let us pray. Commanded by saving precepts, and taught by divine institution, we are bold to say:

The celebrant, with hands still joined, and all present continue:

OUR Father, which art in heaven;*

Hallowed be thy name.*

Thy Kingdom come.*

Thy will be done, in earth as it is in heaven.*

Give us this day our daily bread:*

And forgive us our trespasses,*

As we forgive them that trespass against us.*

And lead us not into temptation;*

But deliver us from evil.*   Amen.

Good Friday

27. The celebrant alone, in a clear and distinct voice with hands joined, continues:

DELIVER us, O Lord, we beseech thee, from all evils, past, present and to come: and at the intercession of the blessed and glorious ever Virgin Mary, Mother of God, with thy blessed Apostles Peter and Paul, and with Andrew, and all thy Saints, he does not sign himself, graciously grant us peace in our days; that by the help of thine availing mercy we may ever both be free from sin, and safe from all distress. Through the same Jesus Christ thy Son our Lord: Who liveth and reigneth with thee in the unity of the Holy Ghost God, world without end.

And all answer: Amen.

28. And straightway the celebrant recites, in a low voice, the following Prayer, bowing as usual, with joined hands placed upon the Altar:

PERCEPTIO Córporis tui, Dómine Jesu Christe, quod ego indígnus súmere præsúmo, non mihi provéniat in judícium et condemnatiónem: sed pro tua pietáte prosit mihi ad tutaméntum mentis et córporis, et ad medélam percipiéndam; Qui vivis et regnas cum Deo Patre in unitáte Spíritus Sancti Deus, per ómnia sæcula sæculorum. Amen.

LET not the partaking of thy Body, O Lord Jesu Christ, which I, unworthy, presume to receive, turn to my judgment and condemnation; but of thy goodness let it avail unto me for protection of body and soul, that I may receive thy healing; Who livest and reignest with God the Father in the unity of the Holy Ghost God, world without end. Amen.

29. Then he uncovers the ciborium, and, having genuflected, he takes a sacred particle in his right hand, and bowing low and striking his breast, he says thrice, in the usual manner:

Dómine, non sum dignus, ut intres sub tectum meum: sed tantum dic verbo, et sanábitur anima mea.

Lord, I am not worthy that thou shouldest enter under my roof: but speak the word only, and my soul shall be healed.

30. Then, signing himself with the Sacrament, he adds in a low voice:

Corpus Dómini nostri Jesu Christi custódiat ánimam meam in vitam ætérnam. Amen.

The Body of our Lord Jesus Christ preserve my soul unto everlasting life. Amen.

And he reverently receives the Body, and rests a while in meditation on the Sacrament.

31. And straightway the deacon makes the confession, in the usual manner. Then the celebrant, having made a genuflexion, turning to the people, with hands joined before his breast, says in a clear voice:

Almighty God have mercy upon you, forgive you your sins, and bring you to everlasting life. All answer: Amen.

The celebrant continues:

The almighty and merciful Lord grant unto you pardon, absolution, ✠ and remission of your sins. All answer: Amen.

32. Then he turns to the Altar, genuflects, takes the ciborium, and turning to the people in the usual manner, in the midst of the Altar, he says in a clear voice:

Behold the Lamb of God, behold him that taketh away the sins of the world.

Then he adds: Lord, I am not worthy that thou shouldest enter under my roof: but speak the word only, and my soul shall be healed: which he repeats a second and a third time.

And he proceeds to the distribution of Communion, as has been said above on Maundy Thursday, p. 172. Priests communicating wear a violet stole.

33. While the Holy Communion is being distributed, Psalm 22 **My God, my God,** may be sung; or one or other responsory from Mattins of this Friday.

34. The Communion being done, the celebrant washes his fingers in a vessel, and wipes them with a purificator, saying nothing; and he places the ciborium in the tabernacle.

35. These things being done, the celebrant standing at the middle of the Altar, having the book before him, and the sacred ministers on his right and left, says for thanksgiving in the ferial tone and with hands joined, the three following Collects, all standing and answering: Amen.

Let us pray. First Collect.

WE beseech thee, O Lord, that as thy people have now with devout heart and mind recalled the passion and death of thy Son: so likewise thy plenteous benediction may descend upon them, thy pardon and consolation be granted unto them, their holy faith increased, their eternal redemption made sure. Through the same Christ our Lord. ℟. Amen.

Let us pray. Second Collect.

ALMIGHTY and merciful God, who hast redeemed us by the blessed passion and death of thine Anointed: preserve in us this work of thy mercy; that through our partaking of this mystery, we may evermore continue steadfast in thy service. Through the same Christ our Lord. ℟. Amen.

Let us pray. Third Collect.

CALL to remembrance, O Lord, thy tender mercies, and sanctify thy servants by thine eternal protection: for whose sake Christ thy Son through his blood did institute this paschal mystery. Through the same Christ our Lord. ℟. Amen.

36. The celebrant and sacred minsters descend from the Altar, and, having made a genuflexion, together with the acolytes, *or servers,* return to the sacristy.

37. Compline is said in choir, (in monotone), the candles being extinguished.

38. At a convenient time, the Most Holy Eucharist is carried back privately to the place of reservation, and there kept, a lamp being kindled, as usual. And the Altar is stripped.

HOLY SATURDAY

Double of 1st class.

THE PASCHAL VIGIL

Station at St. John Lateran

THE BLESSING OF THE NEW FIRE

1. At a suitable hour the altars are covered with linen cloths, but the candles remain extinguished till the beginning of Mass. Meanwhile fire is struck from flint outside the church, and from it coals are kindled.

2. The celebrant is vested in amice, alb, girdle, stole and violet cope: the sacred ministers in amice, alb and girdle, the deacon in stole and dalmatic, the sub-deacon in tunicle of the same colour.

2a. *The priest is vested in amice, alb, girdle, stole and violet cope, or remains without the chasuble.*

3. The ministers, *or servers*, standing by with the cross, blessed water and incense, either before the door, or in the entry of the church, or within it, namely where the people can better follow the sacred rite, the celebrant blesses the new fire, saying:

℣. The Lord be with you.

℟. And with thy spirit.

Let us pray.   Collect.

O GOD, who through thy Son, the true cornerstone, hast bestowed upon the faithful the fire of thy brightness: sanct ✠ ify this new fire, now struck from the flint-stone, to be profitable to our service: and grant unto us that by this paschal feast we may be so inflamed with heavenly desires; that we may with pure hearts attain unto the feast of thy eternal brightness. Through the same Christ our Lord. ℟. Amen.

Then he sprinkles the fire thrice, saying nothing.

4. An acolyte takes some of the blessed coals, and sets them in the thurible; and the celebrant puts incense from the boat into the thurible, blessing it in the usual manner, and thrice censes the fire.

THE BLESSING OF THE PASCHAL CANDLE

5. The new fire having been blessed, an acolyte, *or one of the servers,* bears the paschal candle into the midst, before the priest, who with a knife, between the outermost points prepared for the inserting of the grains of incense, cuts a cross. Then he makes above it the greek letter Alpha, and beneath it the letter Omega, and between the arms of the cross four numbers expressing the current year, saying meanwhile:

(1) Christ yesterday and today (he cuts the vertical line)

(2) The Beginning and the End (he cuts the transverse line)

(3) Alpha (he cuts above the vertical line the letter A)

(4) and Oméga (he cuts beneath the vertical line the letter Ω)

(5) His are the times (he cuts the first number of the current year in the left upper angle of the cross)

(6) and ages (he cuts the second number of the current year in the right upper angle of the cross)

(7) To him be glory and dominion (he cuts the third number of the current year in the left lower angle of the cross)

(8) through all the ages of eternity. Amen. (He cuts the fourth number of the current year in the right lower angle of the cross).

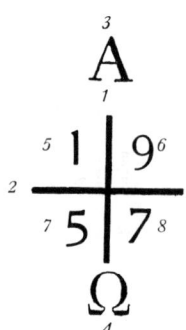

6. The cutting of the cross and other signs being done, the deacon, *or one of the servers,* presents to the celebrant the grains of incense, which, if they are not blessed, the celebrant sprinkles thrice and censes thrice, saying nothing. Then he fixes the five grains of incense in the places prepared for the purpose, meanwhile saying:

(1) Through his holy and glorious

(2) wounds

(3) may Christ the Lord

(4) guard

(5) and preserve us. Amen.

```
        1
    4   2   5
        3
```

7. Then the deacon, *or a server,* hands to the celebrant a small candle, kindled from the new fire, with which he lights the candle saying:

May the light of Christ gloriously rising Scatter the darkness of heart and mind.

Holy Saturday

8. Then the celebrant blesses the lighted candle saying:

℣. The Lord be with you.

℟. And with thy spirit.

Let us pray.   Collect.

WE beseech thee, almighty God, that the abundance of thy bles✠sing may come down upon this lighted candle: and as thou, thyself unseen, art the regenerator of all things, so kindle a light to lighten our darkness; that not only may our sacrifice, which is offered on this night, be illumined by the inward presence of thy light; but that in all places wheresoever the same shall be carried from this mystery here sanctified, the wickedness of the crafts of the devil may be driven forth, and the power of thy majesty ever be present. Through Christ our Lord. ℟. Amen.

9. Meanwhile all the lights of the church are extinguished.

THE SOLEMN PROCESSION AND THE PASCHAL PRAECONIUM

10. Then the celebrant again puts incense into the thurible; then the deacon, vested in a stole and dalmatic of white colour, takes the lighted paschal candle, and the procession is arranged: the thurifer goes first, the subdeacon follows with the cross, the deacon with the lighted candle, immediately after him the celebrant, then the clergy in order and the people.

10a. *If there be no deacon, the celebrant himself vests in like manner. A server carries the cross.*

11. When the deacon has entered the church, he raises the blessed candle, and standing erect, sings alone:

℣. The Líght of Chríst.

to which all the others, genuflecting towards the blessed candle, answer:

℟. Thánks be to Gód.

Then the celebrant lights his own candle from the blessed candle, *or a server does so for him.*

The deacon, *or the celebrant himself,* proceeding to the middle of the church, sings there in a higher tone:

The Light of Christ,

to which all, as above genuflecting, answer:

Thanks be to God.

And the candles of the clergy are lighted from the blessed candle.

The third time, proceeding before the altar, in the midst of the choir, he sings in a still higher tone:

The Light of Christ,

to which for the third time all, as above genuflecting, answer:

Thanks be to God.

And the candles of the people, and the lights of the church are kindled from the blessed candle.

12. Then the celebrant goes to his place in choir, on the epistle side; the

Holy Saturday

subdeacon, *or servers*, with the cross stands on the gospel side; the clergy occupy their places in the stalls.

The deacon sets down the paschal candle in the midst of the choir, on a small stand, and, taking the book, asks a blessing from the celebrant, as is done at the gospel, the celebrant saying:

THE Lord be in thy heart, and on thy lips: that thou mayest worthily and fitly proclaim his paschal praise: In the name of the Father, and of the Son, ✠ and of the Holy Ghost. Amen.

12a. The celebrant himself does so, and goes to the credence: then taking the book from the credence, he says at the foot of the altar:

Bid, Lord, a blessing.—The Lord be in my heart, and on my lips: that I may worthily and fitly proclaim his paschal praise. Amen.

13. He then goes to the lectern, which is covered with a white hanging, and sets the book upon it, and censes it; then going around the paschal candle, he censes it also.

Then, all rising, and standing, as at the gospel, and holding their candles lighted, the deacon, *or the priest himself*, sings the paschal praeconium, having the paschal candle before him, the altar on his right, the nave of the church on his left.

PRAECONIUM PASCHALE

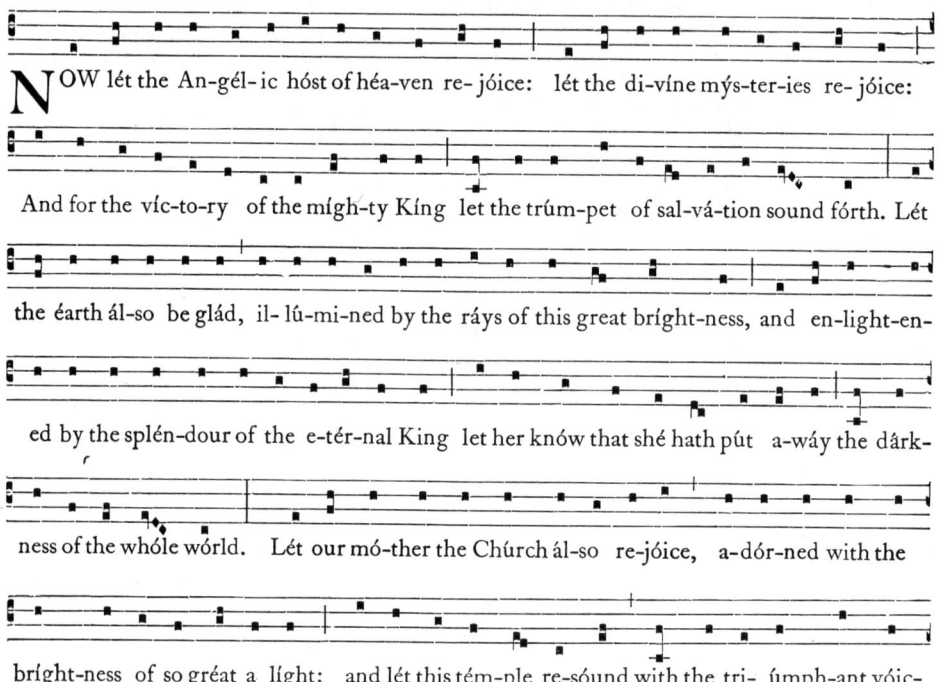

NOW lét the An-gél-ic hóst of héa-ven re-jóice: lét the di-víne mýs-ter-ies re-jóice: And for the víc-to-ry of the mígh-ty Kíng let the trúm-pet of sal-vá-tion sound fórth. Lét the éarth ál-so be glád, il-lú-mi-ned by the ráys of this great bríght-ness, and en-light-en-ed by the splén-dour of the e-tér-nal King let her knów that shé hath pút a-wáy the dárk-ness of the whóle wórld. Lét our mó-ther the Chúrch ál-so re-jóice, a-dór-ned with the bríght-ness of so gréat a líght: and lét this tém-ple re-sóund with the tri-úmph-ant vóic-

Holy Saturday

es of the péo-ples: Whére-fore, déar-ly be-lóv-ed bréth-ren, who are hére pré-sent in the wón-drous cléar-ness of this hó-ly líght, jóin with mé, I be-séech you, in cáll-ing up-ón the mér-cy of al-míght-y Gód. That hé who hath been pléa-sed, for no mé-rit of míne, to ad-mít me ín-to the núm-ber of his Lé-vites: may póur on mé the bríght-ness of his líght, and máke me méet to pro-cláim the práis-es of this Cán-dle. Through Jé-sus Chríst his Són our Lórd : Who lív-eth and reígn-eth with hím in the ú-ni-ty of the Hó-ly Ghóst, Gód. Through-óut all á-ges, wórld with-óut énd. ℟. A-men. ℣. The Lórd be with you. ℟. And with thy spí-rit. ℣. Líft up your héarts. ℟. We líft them úp ún-to the Lórd. ℣. Lét us give thánks ún-to our Lórd Gód. ℟. It is méet and ríght só to dó.

IT is vé-ry méet and ríght that wé should, with the whóle af-féct-ion of our héart and mínd, and with the sér-vice of our líps, give práise un-to the in-ví-si-ble Gód, the Fá-ther

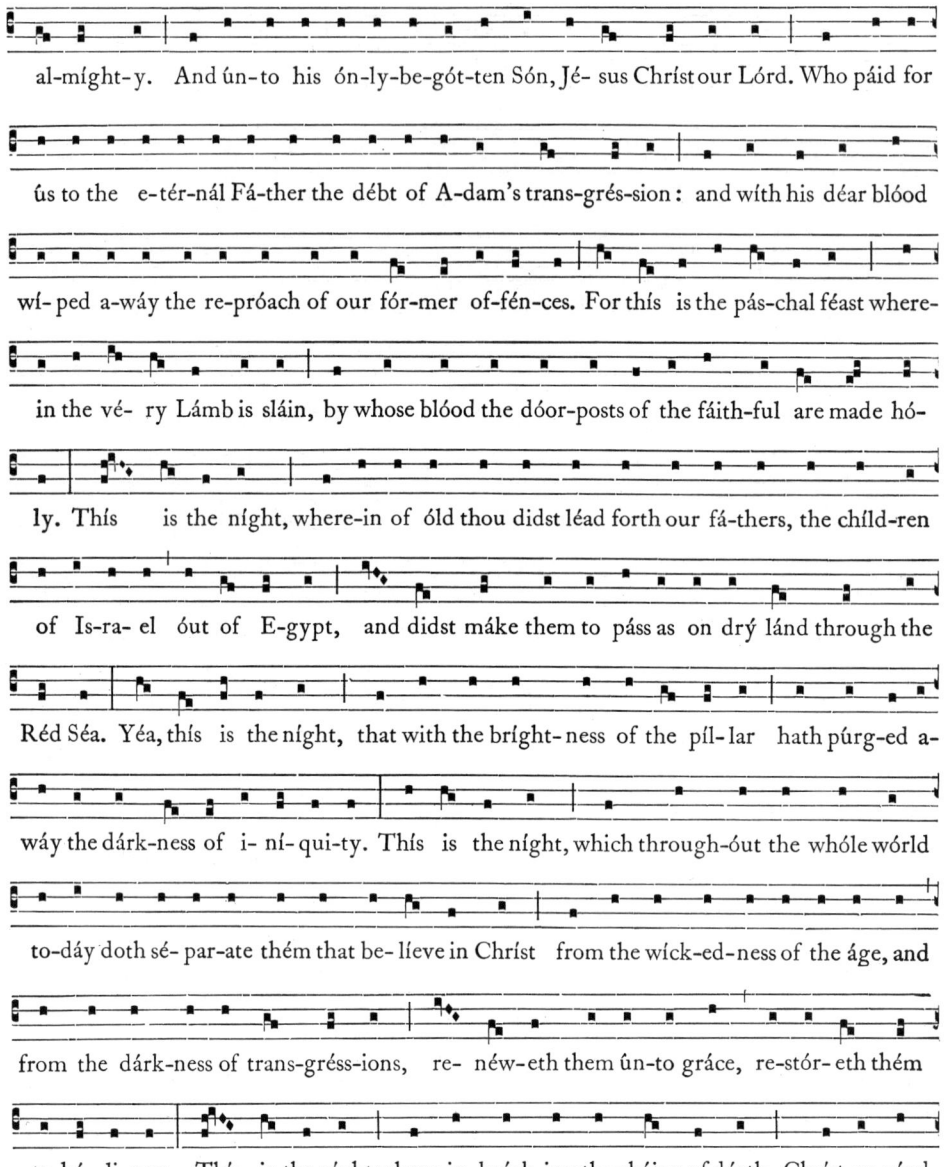

Holy Saturday

eth from hell in triumph. For nought indeed had it profited us to be born, if it had not profited us to be redeemed. O how wonderful the condescension of thy loving kindness! O how inestimable the goodness of thy love: who to redeem a slave didst deliver up thy Son! O truly necessary sin of Adam, which by the death of Christ was done away! O happy fault, which was counted worthy to have such and so great a Redeemer! O night truly blessed, which alone was worthy to know the time and the hour wherein Christ rose again from hell! This is the night whereof it is written: And the night is as clear as the day: and, Then shall my night be turned into day. The sanctifying power therefore of this night putteth to flight the deeds of wickedness, washeth away sins: restoreth innocence to the fallen, and joy to them that mourn: casteth out enmities, prepareth concord, and

Holy Saturday

bów-eth down prín-ci-pá -li- ties.

Thére-fore in this níght of gráce ac-cépt, O hó - ly Fá-ther, the éve-ning sá-cri-fice of this ín-cense: which, bý the hánds of thy mín-is-ters, hó - ly Chúrch doth láy be - fóre thee, in the só-lemn óf - fer-ing of this Cán-dle, máde from the wórk of bées. But we al-réad -y knów the éx - cel-len -cy óf thís píl-lar, which for the hón-our of Gód the spárk-ling fíre doth kín-dle.

Which, thóugh it be di - víded in - to párts, súf-fer-eth not lóss by the bór-row-ing of its líght. For it is féd by mélt-ing wáx, which the bée the mó-ther hath wróught in - to the súb-stance of this pré-cious Cán-dle.

O níght trú-ly bléss-ed, which did spóil the E-gýpt-ians, and made rích the Héb-rews!

O níght where-in héa-ven-ly thíngs are jóin-ed un - to éarth-ly, thíngs hú-man un-to

Holy Saturday

things di-vine. We thére-fore práy thée, O Lórd: that this Cán-dle, cón-se-crá-ted to the hón-our of thy náme, may con-tin-ue with-out céas-íng to ván-quish the dárk-ness of this night.

That, bé-ing ac-cept-ed for a sá-vour of swéet-ness, it may be mín-gled with the líghts of héa-ven. May the mórn-ing stár find it búrn-ing: that mórn-ing stár, I sáy, which knów-eth nót his gó-ing down. That stár, which, rís-ing a-gáin from héll, steád-fast-ly gív-eth líght to áll man-kínd. We thére-fore práy thée, O Lórd: that thou wóuld-est vouch-sáfe to rúle, góv-ern and pre-sérve with thy con-tín-u-al pro-téct-ion ús thy sér-vants, the whóle clér-gy and thý most faíth-ful péo-ple: to-géth-er with our most bléss-ed Fá-ther N. and our Bísh-op N., gránt-ing us péace-ful times in this our pásch-al jóy.

Look ál-so on those who rule us in pów-er, and by the in-éf-fa-ble gift of thy góod-ness and mér-cy, di-rect their thoughts to jús-tice and peace, that from the bú-sy toil

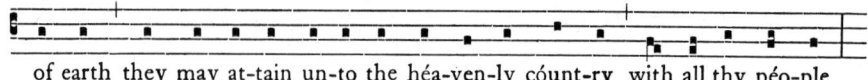
of earth they may at-tain un-to the héa-ven-ly cóunt-ry with all thy péo-ple.

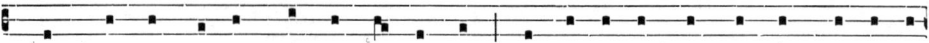
Through the sáme Jé-sus Christ thy Son our Lórd: Who lív-eth and réign-eth with thée in the

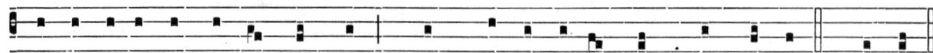
ú - ni - ty of the Hó - ly Ghóst Gód: through-óut all á-ges, wórld with-óut énd. ℟.A-men.

The clergy, servers and people extinguish their candles.

THE LESSONS

14. After the paschal praeconium, the deacon, laying aside his white vestments, puts on violet, and goes to the celebrant.

14a. The celebrant lays aside the white dalmatic and stole, puts on violet stole and cope, and returns to the lectern.

15. Then the lessons are read, without title, and at the end the response **Thanks be to God** is not made. They are read by a lector, in the midst of the choir, before the blessed candle, so standing as to have the Altar on his right and the nave of the church on his left. The celebrant and ministers, clergy and people sit and listen.

15a. If there be no lectors, the celebrant himself in violet stole and cope reads the Lessons and Collects at the Lectern, so standing as noted above. The servers and people sit and listen.

16. At the end of the lesson, or after the canticle, the collects are said, in this manner: all rise, the celebrant says **Let us pray,** the deacon, *or the priest himself,* **Let us bow the knee,** and all, kneeling, the priest included, pray for some time in silence; the deacon, *or the priest,* having said **Arise,** all rise, and the priest says the collect.

17. The four lessons following are read with their canticles and collects.

THE FIRST LESSON.

Gen. 1, 1-31, and 2, 1-2.

IN the beginning God created the heaven and the earth. And the earth was without form and void, and darkness was upon the face of the deep: and the Spirit of God moved upon the face of the waters. And God said: Let there be light. And there was light. And God saw the light, that it was good: and God divided the light from the darkness. And God called the light Day, and the darkness he called Night: and the evening and the morning were the first day. And God said: Let there be a firmament in the midst of the waters: and let it divide the waters from the waters. And God made the firmament, and divided the waters which were under the firmament from the waters which were above the firmament. And it was so. And God called the firmament Heaven: and the evening and the morning were the second day. And God

Holy Saturday

said: Let the waters under the heaven be gathered together unto one place: and let the dry land appear. And it was so. And God called the dry land Earth: and the gathering together of the waters called he Seas. And God saw that it was good. And God said: Let the earth bring forth grass, the herb yielding seed, and the fruit tree yielding fruit after his kind, whose seed is in itself, upon the earth. And it was so. And the earth brought forth grass, and herb yielding seed after his kind, and the tree yielding fruit, whose seed was in itself, after his kind. And God saw that it was good. And the evening and the morning were the third day. And God said: Let there be lights in the firmament of the heaven to divide the day from the night, and let them be for signs, and for seasons, and for days, and years: and let them be for lights in the firmament of the heaven to give light upon the earth. And it was so. And God made two great lights: the greater light to rule the day: and the lesser light to rule the night: he made the stars also. And God set them in the firmament of the heaven to give light upon the earth, and to rule over the day and over the night, and to divide the light from the darkness. And God saw that it was good. And the evening and the morning were the fourth day. And God said: Let the waters bring forth abundantly the moving creature that hath life, and fowl that may fly above the earth in the open firmament of heaven. And God created great whales, and every living creature that moveth, which the waters brought forth abundantly, after their kind, and every winged fowl after his kind. And God saw that it was good. And God blessed them, saying: Be fruitful, and multiply, and fill the waters in the seas: and let fowl multiply in the earth. And the evening and the morning were the fifth day. And God said: Let the earth bring forth the living creature after his kind: cattle, and creeping thing, and beast of the earth after his kind. And it was so. And God made the beast of the earth after his kind, and cattle after their kind, and every thing that creepeth upon the earth after his kind. And God saw that it was good, and God said: Let us make man in our image, after our likeness: and let them have dominion over the fish of the sea, and over the fowl of the air, and over the cattle, and over all the earth, and over every creeping thing that creepeth upon the earth. So God created man in his own image: in the image of God created he him, male and female created he them. And God blessed them, and God said unto them: Be fruitful, and multiply, and replenish the earth, and subdue it, and have dominion over the fish of the sea, and over the fowl of the air, and over every living thing that moveth upon the earth. And God said: Behold, I have given you every herb bearing seed, which is upon the face of all the earth, and every tree, in the which is the fruit of a tree yielding seed; to you it shall be for meat: and to every beast of the earth, and to every fowl of the air, and to every thing that creepeth upon the earth, wherein there is life, I have given every green herb for meat. And it was so. And God saw everything that he had made: and, behold, it was very good. And the evening and the morning were the sixth day. Thus the heavens and the earth were finished, and all the host of them. And on the seventh day God ended his work which he had made: and he rested on the seventh day from all his work which he had made.

Let us pray.

℣. Let us bow the knee. ℟. Arise.

Collect.

O GOD, who didst wonderfully create man, and hast more wonderfully redeemed him: grant us, we beseech thee, such strength of mind to withstand the enticements of sin; that we may be found worthy to attain to everlasting joys. Through.

THE SECOND LESSON.

Exod. 14, 24-31; and 15, 1.

IN those days: It came to pass, that in the morning watch the Lord looked unto the host of the Egyptians through the pillar of fire and of the cloud, and troubled the host of the Egyptians: and took off their chariot wheels, that they drave them heavily. So that the Egyptians said: Let us flee from the face of Israel: for the Lord fighteth for them against the Egyptians. And the Lord said unto Moses: Stretch out thine hand over the sea, that the waters may come again upon the Egyptians, upon their chariots, and upon their horsemen. And Moses stretched forth his hand over the sea, and the sea returned to his strength when the morning appeared: and the Egyptians fled against it, and the Lord overthrew the Egyptians in the midst of the sea. And the waters returned, and covered the chariots, and the horsemen, and all the host of Pharaoh that came into the sea after them: there remained not so much as one of them. But the children of Israel walked upon dry land in the midst of the sea, and the waters were a wall unto them on their right hand, and on their left: thus the Lord saved Israel that day out of the hand of the Egyptians. And Israel saw the Egyptians dead upon the sea shore, and Israel saw that great work which the Lord did upon the Egyptians: and the people feared the Lord, and believed the Lord, and his servant Moses. Then sang Moses and the children of Israel this song unto the Lord, and spake saying:

Canticle. Exod. 15, 1-2.

WE will sing unto the Lord: for he hath triumphed gloriously: the horse and his rider hath he thrown into the sea: the Lord is my strength and song, and he is become my salvation. ℣. He is my God, and I will praise him: my father's God, and I will exalt him. ℣. The Lord is a man of war: the Lord is his name.

Let us pray.

℣. Let us bow the knee.   ℞. Arise.

Collect.

O GOD, whose miracles of old we perceive to shine forth even in our times: who didst deliver one people from the pursuit of the Eyptians by the power of thy right hand, and dost now through the water of regeneration bestow thy saving health upon all nations: vouchsafe; that the fulness of the whole world may be numbered among the sons of Abraham and made partakers of the dignity of Israel. Through.

THE THIRD LESSON.

Is. 4, 2-6.

IN that day shall the branch of the Lord be beautiful and glorious, and the fruit of the earth shall be excellent and comely for them that are escaped of Israel. And it shall come to pass: That he that is left in Sion, and he that remaineth in Jerusalem, shall be called holy, even every one that is written among the living in Jerusalem. When the Lord shall have washed away the filth of the daughters of Sion, and shall have purged the blood of Jerusalem from the midst thereof by the spirit of judgment, and by the spirit of burning. And the Lord will create upon every dwelling place of mount Sion, and upon her assemblies, a cloud of smoke by day, and the shining of a flaming fire by night: for upon all the glory shall be a defence. And there shall be a tabernacle for a shadow in the daytime from the heat, and for a place of refuge, and for a covert from storm and from rain.

Canticle. Is. 5, 1-2.

MY well-beloved hath a vineyard in a very fruitful hill. ℣. And he fenced it, and gathered out the stones thereof: and planted it with the choicest vine, and built a tower in the midst of it. ℣. And also made a wine-press therein: for the vineyard of the Lord of hosts is the house of Israel.

Let us pray.

℣. Let us bow the knee. ℟. Arise.

Collect.

O GOD, who by the mouth of thy holy prophets hast manifested thyself in all the children of thy Church, to be in all places of thy dominion the sower of good seed and the husbandman of thine elect branches: grant unto thy peoples, who are named thy vineyard and thy harvest field; that being purged from all thorns and briars, they may be made to bring forth worthy fruit in abundance. Through.

THE FOURTH LESSON.
Deut. 31, 22-30.

IN those days: Moses wrote this song, and taught it to the children of Israel. And he gave Joshua the son of Nun a charge, and said: Be strong and of a good courage: for thou shalt bring the children of Israel into the land which I sware unto them, and I will be with thee. And it came to pass, when Moses had made an end of writing the words of this law in a book, until they were finished: that Moses commanded the Levites, which bare the ark of the covenant of the Lord, saying: Take this book of the law, and put it in the side of the ark of the covenant of the Lord your God: that it may be there for a witness against thee. For I know thy rebellion, and thy stiff neck. Behold, while I am yet alive with you this day, ye have been rebellious against the Lord: and how much more after my death? Gather unto me all the elders of your tribes, and your officers, that I may speak these words in their ears, and call heaven and earth to record against them. For I know that after my death ye will utterly corrupt yourselves, and turn aside from the way which I have commanded you: and evil will befall you in the latter days, because ye will do evil in the sight of the Lord, to provoke him to anger through the work of your hands. And Moses spake in the ears of all the congregation of Israel the words of this song, until they were ended.

Canticle. Deut. 32, 1-4.

GIVE ear, O ye heavens, and I will speak: and hear, O earth, the words of my mouth. ℣. My doctrine shall drop as the rain: my speech shall distil as the dew. ℣. As the small rain upon the tender herb, and as the showers upon the grass: because I will publish the name of the Lord. ℣. Ascribe ye greatness unto our God: he is the rock, his work is perfect, for all his ways are judgment. ℣. A God of truth and without iniquity: just and right is the Lord.

Let us pray.

℣. Let us bow the knee. ℟. Arise.

Collect.

O GOD, the exaltation of the humble and the strength of them that do stand, who by thy holy servant Moses didst vouchsafe so to instruct thy people in the chanting of thy sacred song, that the repeating of the law by them might be profitable for our learning: stir up thy power among all the fulness of the nations whom thou hast justified, and grant us gladness, assuaging fear; that the sins of all may be blotted out by thy forgiveness, and that which was denounced of old in vengeance may turn to our salvation. Through.

THE FIRST PART OF THE LITANIES

18. The lessons being ended, the litanies of the saints are sung by two cantors as far as the invocation **Be thou merciful**, all kneeling and responding; but they are not doubled.

18a. *In the absence of cantors, the litanies are sung (or said) by the priest himself, kneeling on the lowest step of the altar, at the Epistle side.*

19. If the church has a baptismal font, the rite proceeds as below, No. 20; otherwise as below, No. 24.

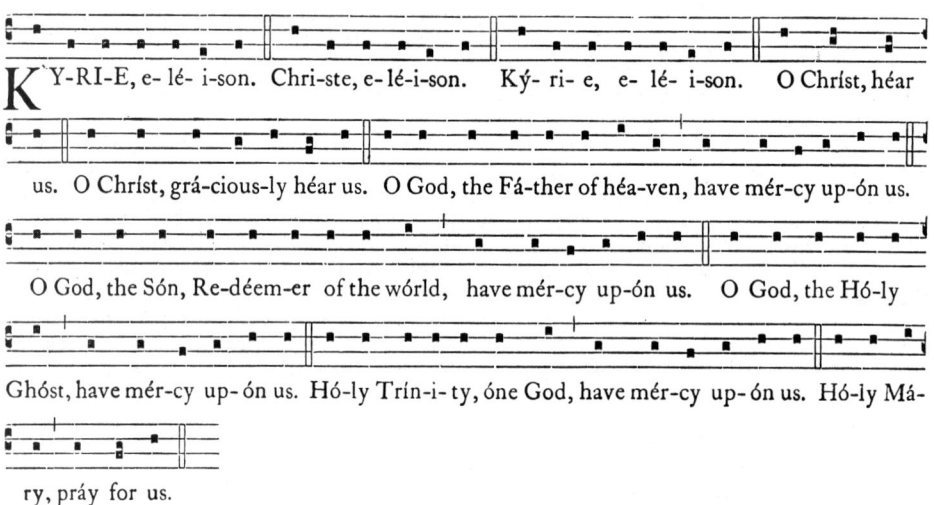

KY-RI-E, e- lé- i-son. Chri-ste, e-lé-i-son. Ký- ri- e, e- lé- i-son. O Christ, héar us. O Christ, grá-cious-ly héar us. O God, the Fá-ther of héa-ven, have mér-cy up-ón us. O God, the Són, Re-déem-er of the wórld, have mér-cy up-ón us. O God, the Hó-ly Ghóst, have mér-cy up- ón us. Hó-ly Trín-i- ty, óne God, have mér-cy up- ón us. Hó-ly Má-ry, práy for us.

Holy Mother of God, pray.
Holy Virgin of virgins, pray.
Holy Michael, pray.
Holy Gabriel, pray.
Holy Raphael, pray.
All ye holy Angels and Archangels, pray.
All ye holy orders of blessed Spirits, pray.
Holy John Baptist, pray.
Holy Joseph, pray.
All ye holy Patriarchs and Prophets, pray.
Holy Peter, pray.
Holy Paul, pray.
Holy Andrew, pray.
Holy John, pray.
All ye holy Apostles and Evangelists, pray.
All ye holy Disciples of the Lord, pray.

Holy Stephen, pray.
Holy Lawrence, pray.
Holy Vincent, pray.
All ye holy Martyrs, pray.
Holy Silvester, pray.
Holy Gregory, pray.
Holy Augustine, pray.
All ye holy Bishops and Confessors, pray.
All ye holy Doctors, pray.
Holy Antony, pray.
Holy Benedict, pray.
Holy Dominic, pray.
Holy Francis, pray.
All ye holy Priests and Levites, pray.
All ye holy Monks and Hermits, pray.
Holy Mary Magdalen, pray.

Holy Saturday

Holy Agnes, pray.
Holy Cecilia, pray.
Holy Agatha, pray.
Holy Anastasia, pray.

All ye holy Virgins and Widows, pray for us.
All ye holy men and women, Saints of God, intercede for us.

THE BLESSING OF THE BAPTISMAL WATER

20. While the litanies of the saints are being sung, a vessel of baptismal water to be blessed, and all else which is needed for the blessing, is prepared in the midst of the choir before the blessed candle, in the sight of the faithful.

21. In blessing the baptismal water, the celebrant, standing before the people, shall have the vessel of water to be blessed before him, the blessed candle on his right, the subdeacon, *or servers,* on his left, standing with the cross.

The celebrant, with hands joined, says in the ferial tone:

℣. The Lord be with you.

℟. And with thy spirit.

Let us pray. *Collect.*

ALMIGHTY and everlasting God, be present at the mysteries, be present at the sacraments of thy great goodness: and send forth the spirit of adoption for the regeneration of the new peoples, whom the font of baptism doth bring forth unto thee; that this office and ministry of thy unworthy servants may be effectually fulfilled by thy power. Through Jesus Christ, thy Son, our Lord: Who liveth and reigneth with thee in the unity of the Holy Ghost, God.

Then raising his voice to the tone of the Preface, he proceeds with joined hands:

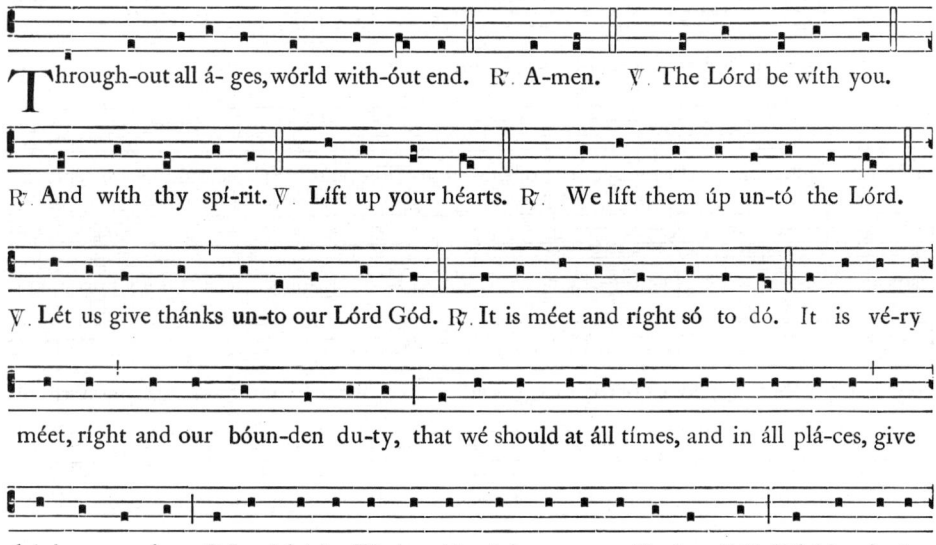

Through-out all á-ges, wórld with-óut end. ℟. A-men. ℣. The Lórd be wíth you. ℟. And with thy spí-rit. ℣. Líft up your héarts. ℟. We líft them úp un-tó the Lórd. ℣. Lét us give thánks un-to our Lórd Gód. ℟. It is méet and ríght só to dó. It is vé-ry méet, ríght and our bóun-den du-ty, that wé should at áll tímes, and in áll plá-ces, give thánks un-to thee: O Lord hó-ly Fá-ther Al-mígh-ty ev-er-lást-ing Gód: Whó by thy in-vís-i-ble pówer dost wónd-rous-ly give ef-féct to the wórk of thy sá-cra-ments: And thóugh we be un-wór-thy to per-fórm mýs-ter-ies so gréat: yét thou dóst not léave us dés-ti-tute of the gífts of thy gráce, but mér-ci-ful-ly in-clín-est thíne éars ev-en ún-to thése our súp-pli-cá-tions. O Gód, whose Spí-rit in the fírst be-gín-nings of the wórld mó-ved ó-ver the wá-ters: that é-ven thén the ná-ture of wá-ter might con-céive the vír-tue of sánc-ti-fi-cá-tion. O Gód, who didst wásh a-wáy in the wá-ters the in-í-qui-ties of a sín-ful wórld, and didst, é-ven in the out-póur-ing of the flóod, shew fórth in a fí-gure our re-gé-ne-rá-tion: that by the mýs-te-ry of thís same é-le-ment thére should bé an énd to sín and líke-wise a be-gín-ning of vír-tue. Lóok, O Lórd, up-ón the fáce of thy Chúrch, and múl-ti-ply in hér the pów-er of thy re-gén-er-á-tion, for thóu dost by the stréams of thine ab-únd-ant gráce make glád thy cí-ty: and ó-pen-est the fóunt of báp-tism through-óut the

Holy Saturday

whóle wórld for the re-néw-ing of the nâ-tions: that by the com-mánd of thy má-jes- ty she may re-céive from the Hó- ly Ghóst the gráce of thine ón-ly-be-gót-ten Són.

Here the celebrant divides the water in the form of a cross with his extended hand, which he wipes at once with a linen cloth, saying:

May hé, by the sé-cret míng-ling of his div- íne pów-er, make frúit-ful this wá-ter pre- párt- ed for the re-gen-er- á-tion of man-kínd: that, háv-ing re-ceív-ed sánc-ti- fi- cá- tion, and bé- ing bórn a-gáin a new créat-ure, thére may come fórth an óff-spring of héa-ven from the spót-less wómb of this di- víne fóun-tain: that áll, whe-ther séx di-víde them in bó-dy, or áge in tíme, may a- líke be bróught fórth in- to one chíld-hood by gráce, their mó-ther. Far hénce, O Lórd, at thý com-mánd let év- ery ûn-clean spí- rit de-párt: Far hénce be áll the wíck-ed-ness of the cráft of the dé- vil: let no pów-er of the én- e-my hére have pláce or pórt-ion: let it nót en-snáre and cóm-pass us a-róund: let it nót way-láy us in séc-ret: lét it not táint us with cor-rúp-tion.

Holy Saturday

He touches the water with his hand.

Máy this hó-ly and ún-de-fíl-ed créat-ure be frée from év-ery as-sáult of the é-ne-my, and pú-ri-fi-ed by the de-párt-ure of áll in-iqu-i-ty. Máy it be a lív-ing fóun-tain, wa-ter that dóth re-gé-ne-rate, a pú-ri-fy-ing stréam: that áll who shall be wásh-ed in this láv-er of sal-vá-tion máy, by the óp-er-át-ion of the Hó-ly Ghóst with-ín them, ob-tain the gráce of pér-fect pú-ri-fi-cá-tion.

He makes three crosses over the water, saying:

Whére-fore I bléss thee, O créa-ture of wá-ter, by the lív-ing ✠ Gód, by the trúe ✠ Gód, by the hó-ly ✠ Gód: by Gód who ín the be-gín-ning through his wórd di-ví-ded thee fróm the dry lánd: whose spí-rit móv-ed up-ón thee.

Here he divides the water with his hand, and scatters it towards the four quarters of the world, saying:

Who máde thee to flów from the fóun-tain of pá-ra-dise, and com-mánd-ed thee to wá-ter the whóle eárth with thý four rí-vers. Whó in the dés-ert be-stów-ed up-ón thee swéet-ness

Holy Saturday

when thóu wast bít-ter, that mén might drink, and bróught thee fórth from the róck for the thírst-ing péo-ple. I ble✠ss thee ál-so by Jé-sus Chríst his ón-ly Són, our Lórd: whó in Cá-na of Gá-li-lee by a wónd-rous mí-ra-cle did chánge thee thróugh his pów-er ín-to wíne. Who wálk-ed up-ón thee with his féet: and was bap-tí-sed in thee by Jóhn in Jór-dan. Who bróught thee fórth to-géth-er with blóod from his síde: and com-mánd-ed his dís-ci-ples that be-líev-ing they should bé bap-tís-ed in thee, sáy-ing: Gó yé, téach all ná-tions, bap-tíz-ing them in the name of the Fa-ther, and of the Són, and óf the Hó-ly Ghóst.

He changes his voice, and proceeds in the tone of the Lesson:	He breathes thrice upon the water in the form of a cross, saying:
ALMIGHTY God, mercifully assist our prayers, who keep these thy commandments: graciously breathe thou upon us.	Bless with thy word and power this element of water: that as by nature it hath power to cleanse and wash the body, so also it may be effectual for the purifying of the soul.

Here the celebrant lowers the candle into the water a little way: and resuming the tone of the Preface, says:

May the pów-er of the Hó-ly Ghóst des-cénd up-ón the fúl-ness of thís fónt.

Then withdrawing the candle from the water, he again dips it more deeply, and repeats in a somewhat higher voice, May the power. Then he again withdraws the candle from the water, and the third time dips it to the bottom, repeating in a still higher voice: May the power, as above.

Holy Saturday

Then breathing three times on the water in this form ℣, he proceeds:

And máke the whole súb-stance of this wá-ter to be fruít-ful ún-to re-gén-er-á-tion.

Here the candle is taken out of the water, and he proceeds:

Hére may the stáins of ev-ery sín be blót-ted out: hére may nát-ure, cre-á-ted in thine ím-age, be re-stór-ed to the hón-our of its fírst e-státe, and cléan-sed from áll the de-fíle-ment of its óld con-díť-ion: that év-ery mán who cóm-eth to this sá-cra-ment of ré-gen-er-á-tion may be bórn a-gáin ún-to the new chíld-hood of true ín-no-cence.

He says that which follows in the reading voice:

Through Jesus Christ thy Son, our Lord: Who shall come to judge the quick and the dead, and the world by fire. ℟. Amen.

Then some clerk, *or server,* takes some of the water in a vessel, for sprinkling the people at the end of the renewal of promises of baptism as below (no. 25), and for sprinkling in houses and other places.

Which done, the celebrant who is blessing the Font, pours some of the Oil of Catechumens into the water in the form of a cross, saying in an audible voice:

May this font be sanctified and made fruitful by the Oil of salvation, for such as shall be born again therefrom, unto life everlasting. ℟. Amen.

Then in the same manner, he pours in some of the Chrism, saying:

May this inpouring of the Chrism of our Lord Jesus Christ, and of the Holy Ghost the Paraclete, be wrought in the name of the holy Trinity. ℟. Amen.

Lastly he takes both phials of the said holy Oil and the Chrism, and pouring in some of both together in the form of a cross, says:

May this commingling of the Chrism of sanctification, and of the Oil of unction, and of the Water of baptism, likewise be wrought in the name of the Fa ☩ ther, and of the S ☩ on, and of the Holy ☩ Ghost. ℟. Amen.

Then he mingles the Oil itself with the water. If there be any to be baptized, he baptizes them in the usual manner.

Holy Saturday

22. The blessing having been performed, the baptismal water is carried processionally to the Font, in this manner: the thurifer goes before, there follow another subdeacon, *or server,* with the cross, the clergy, the deacon, *or one or more servers,* carrying the vessel of baptismal water, unless it be convenient for it to be carried by the acolytes, and the celebrant; but the paschal candle remains in its place; and meanwhile is sung the following:

Canticle. Ps. 42, 1-3.

LIKE as the hart desireth the water-brooks: so longeth my soul after thee, O God. ℣. My soul is athirst for God, yea, even for the living God: when shall I come to appear before the presence of God? ℣. My tears have been my meat day and night, while they daily say unto me: Where is now thy God?

The blessed water having been put into the Font, the celebrant, with hands joined and in the ferial tone, says:

℣. The Lord be with you.

℟. And with thy spirit.

Let us pray.   Collect.

ALMIGHTY and everlasting God, mercifully look upon the devout prayers of this people now called to a new birth, who, like the hart, seek the fountain of thy waters: and mercifully grant; that the thirst of their faith may, by the mystery of Baptism, sanctify them in body and soul. Through. ℟. Amen.

And he censes the Font.

Then all return in silence to the choir, and the renewal of the promises of baptism is begun.

23. But if in any place a baptistery exists separate from the church, and it be preferred that the blessing of baptismal water be done in the baptistery itself, after the invocation Holy Trinity, one God, have mercy upon us, they go down to the Font in this manner: a clerk goes first with the blessed Candle, another subdeacon follows with the cross, in the midst between two acolytes with lighted candles, then the clergy in order, finally the celebrant with the sacred ministers. But the cantors and people remain in their places, and continue the singing of the litanies, repeating, if need be, the invocations from Holy Mary, pray for us.

The blessing of baptismal water is done as above, with these changes only; as they go to the Font, the canticle Like as the hart is sung, and the celebrant, before he goes in to bless the Font, says the prayer Almighty and everlasting God, as above, no. 22, then he proceeds to the benediction of the Font, no. 21, p. 211.

THE RENEWAL OF THE PROMISES OF BAPTISM

All stand, holding their candles lighted.

24. The blessing of the baptismal water and the carrying thereof to the Font being completed, or, where this does not take place, at the conclusion of the first part of the litanies, there follows the renewal of the promises of baptism.

25. The celebrant, having put off the violet vestments, takes a white stole and cope. Then, after putting in incense and censing the candle, standing before it in the midst of the choir, or from the ambo or pulpit, he begins, as follows:

On this most holy night, dearly beloved brethren, holy Mother Church keeps vigil. Calling to mind the death and burial of our Lord Jesus Christ, she renders him love for love; and celebrating his glorious resurrection she rejoices with great gladness.

Now since, as the Apostle teaches, we have by baptism been buried with Christ into death, so, just as Christ rose from the dead, we too must walk in newness of life; knowing that our former nature has been crucified with Christ, so that we are the slaves of guilt no longer. Let us, therefore, reckon ourselves dead to sin, but alive unto God through Christ Jesus our Lord.

Wherefore, dearly beloved brethren, now that our lenten exercises are done, let us renew the promises of our holy baptism, by which we once renounced Satan and his works, together with the world which is at enmity with God, and promised to serve God faithfully in the holy Catholic Church.

Now, therefore:

Celebrant: Do you renounce Satan?

All: We do renounce him.

Celebrant: And all his works?

All: We do renounce them.

Celebrant: And all his pomps?

All: We do renounce them.

Celebrant: Do you believe in God, the Father almighty, Creator of heaven and earth?

All: We do believe.

Celebrant: Do you believe in Jesus Christ, his only Son, our Lord, who was born into this world and who suffered for us?

All: We do believe.

Celebrant: Do you also believe in the Holy Ghost, the holy Catholic Church, the communion of saints, the forgiveness of sins, the resurrection of the body, and life everlasting?

All: We do believe.

Celebrant: Now let us pray to God all together, as our Lord Jesus Christ himself taught us to pray:

All: Our Father ...

Celebrant: And may almighty God, the Father of our Lord Jesus Christ, who made us to be born again of water and the Holy Ghost, and granted us forgiveness of sins, keep us by his grace in the same Jesus Christ our Lord unto everlasting life.

All: Amen.

And he sprinkles the people with the blessed water, taken out, as has been said above (no. 21), at the blessing of baptismal water; or, where the blessing of baptismal water does not take place, with "ordinary" blessed water.

The candles of the clergy and people are extinguished.

THE SECOND PART OF THE LITANIES

26. The renewal of the promises of baptism being accomplished, the cantors, *or the priest himself*, begin the second part of the litanies, from the invocation Be thou merciful to the end, all kneeling and responding.

If on this sacred paschal vigil Holy Orders be conferred, the usual prostration and blessing of the ordinands shall be performed, while this second part of the litanies is being chanted.

27. The celebrant and the ministers, *or servers*, go to the sacristy, and put on vestments of white colour for the Mass to be solemnly celebrated.

27a. If there be no cantors, the celebrant himself must sing the litanies, and when they are ended, he goes with the servers to the sacristy.

28. Meanwhile the paschal candle is placed in its candlestick, on the Gospel side, and the altar is made ready for solemn Mass, with kindled lights and flowers.

Bé thou mér-ci-ful, Spáre us, O Lórd.

Be thou merciful, graciously hear us, O Lord.

From all evil, deliver us, O Lord.

From all sin, deliver.

From everlasting death, deliver.

By the mystery of thy holy Incarnation, deliver.

By thine Advent, deliver.

By thy Nativity, deliver.

By thy Baptism and holy Fasting, deliver.

By thy Cross and Passion, deliver.

By thy Death and Burial, deliver.

By thy holy Resurrection, deliver.

By thy wonderful Ascension, deliver.

By the coming of the Holy Ghost the Paraclete, deliver.

In the day of judgment, deliver.

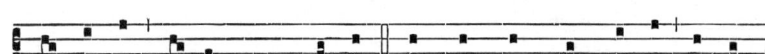
We sín-ners be-séech thee, héar us. That thou wóuld-est spáre us, we be-séech thee, hear us.

That it may please thee to govern and preserve thy holy Church, we beseech thee.

That it may please thee to preserve our apostolic lord and all orders of the Church in thy true religion, we beseech thee.

That it may please thee to humble the enemies of holy Church, we beseech thee.

That it may please thee to give to Christian kings and rulers peace and true concord, we beseech thee, hear us.

That it may please thee to strengthen and preserve us in thy holy service, we beseech thee.

That thou wouldest reward all our benefactors with everlasting blessings, we beseech thee, hear us.

That it may please thee to give and preserve the fruits of the earth, we beseech thee.

That it may please thee to grant to all the faithful departed rest eternal, we beseech thee.

That it may please thee graciously to hear us, we beseech thee, hear us.

O Lamb of Gód, that tá-kest a-wáy the síns of the wórld, spáre us, O Lórd. O Lámb of God,

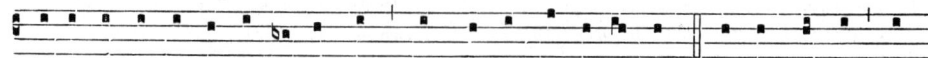

that tá-kest a-wáy the síns of the wórld, grá-cióus-ly héar us, O Lórd. O Lámb of God, that

tá-kest a-way the síns of the wórld, have mér-cy up-on us. O Christ, héar us. O Christ, grá-

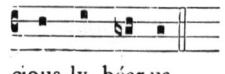

cious-ly héar us.

THE SOLEMN MASS
OF THE PASCHAL VIGIL

1. At the end of the Litanies, the cantors solemnly begin Kýrie, eléison, as usual at Mass. Meanwhile the priest with the ministers, in white vestments, *or with the servers*, approaches the altar, and omitting the psalm Give sentence, and the confession, goes up and kisses it in the midst, and censes it in the accustomed manner.

2. Kýrie, eléison being ended by the choir, the celebrant solemnly begins Glory be to God on high, and the bells are rung, and the images uncovered.

Then the celebrant says:

℣. The Lord be with you.

℟. And with thy spirit.

Let us pray.   Collect.

O GOD, who dost illumine this most holy night with the glory of the Resurrection of the Lord: preserve in these persons, now made incorporate in thy family, the spirit of adoption, which thou hast given them; that they, being regenerate both in body and soul, may continually serve thee in purity of heart. Through the same.

3.

The Lesson from the Epistle of blessed Paul the Apostle to the Colossians.

Col. 3, 1-4.

BRETHREN: If ye be risen with Christ, seek those things which are above, where Christ sitteth on the right hand of God: set your affection on things above, not on things on the earth. For ye are dead, and your life is hid with Christ in God. When Christ, who is our life, shall appear: then shall ye also appear with him in glory.

4. The Epistle ended, the celebrant begins:

Al- le-   lú- ia.

And he sings it through thrice, raising his voice gradually: and all repeat it each time in the same tone.

Afterwards the cantors continue:

℣. Ps. 118, 1. O give thanks unto the Lord, for he is gracious: because his mercy endureth for ever.

Then is said: ℣. Ps. 117. O praise the Lord, all ye heathen: praise him, all ye nations. ℣. For his merciful kindness is ever more and more towards us: and the truth of the Lord endureth for ever.

5. At the Gospel lights are not carried, but only incense. A blessing is asked, and other things are done as usual.

Holy Saturday

✠ The Continuation of the holy Gospel according to Matthew.

Matt. 28, 1-7.

IN the end of the sabbath, as it began to dawn toward the first day of the week, came Mary Magdalen and the other Mary to see the sepulchre. And, behold, there was a great earthquake. For the Angel of the Lord descended from heaven: and came and rolled back the stone from the door, and sat upon it: his countenance was like lightning: and his raiment white as snow. And for fear of him the keepers did shake, and became as dead men. And the Angel answered and said unto the women: Fear not ye: for I know that ye seek Jesus, who was crucified: he is not here: for he is risen, as he said. Come, see the place where the Lord lay. And go quickly, and tell his disciples that he is risen from the dead: and behold, he goeth before you into Galilee: there shall ye see him. Lo, I have told you.

The Creed is not said, but, the Gospel ended, the celebrant says: The Lord be with you, then: Let us pray. The antiphon at the Offertory is not said. At the Lavabo Glória Patri is said.

6. Secret.

ACCEPT, we beseech thee, O Lord, the prayers and oblations of thy people; that this beginning of thy paschal mysteries may by the operation of thy grace be unto us a wholesome medicine unto everlasting life. Through.

Preface. Thee, O Lord, at all times, but chiefly on this night.

7. Infra Actionem, Communicántes and Hanc ígitur, proper, as in the Canon.

The peace of the Lord be alway with you is said, but the kiss of peace is not given.

Agnus Dei is not said: but, the prayer O Lord Jesu Christ, who saidst, being omitted, the other accustomed prayers before Communion are said.

8. After the receiving of the Sacrament, the distribution of Communion, the purification and ablution are done in the usual manner: then for Lauds of the Sunday of the Resurrection there is sung in choir the antiphon:

Al- le- lú- ia, * al- le- lú- ia, al- le- lú- ia.

Psalm 150. Laudate Dominum.

O PRAISE God in his hó- li-ness,* praise him in the fír-ma-ment of his pów- er.

Praise him in his noble acts,* praise him according to his excellent greatness.

Praise him in the sound of the trumpet,* praise him upon the lute and harp.

Praise him in the cymbals and dances,* praise him upon the strings and pipe.

Praise him upon the well-tuned cymbals,* praise him upon the loud cymbals.

Let everything that hath breath,* praise the Lord.

Holy Saturday

Glory be to the Father and to the Son,* and to the Holy Ghost,

As it was in the beginning, is now, and ever shall be,* world without end. Amen.

The antiphon is repeated: Allelúia, allelúia, allelúia.

The Chapter, hymn and verse are not said, but immediately the celebrant intones the antiphon to the Benedictus:

And the cantors continue:

And vé-ry eár-ly * the first day of the week, they came un-to the sé-pul-chre, at

the rí-sing of the sun, al- le- lú- ia.

Then the Benedictus is sung with Glória Patri at the end, and the censing is done, as at other times at Lauds.

Song of Zacharias. Luke 1, 68-79.   Benedictus.

BLES-SED be the Lord God of Is-ra-el,* for he hath ví-si-ted and re-dée-med his peó-ple.

And hath raised up a mighty salvation for us:* in the house of his servant David.

As he spake by the mouth of his holy Prophets,* which have been since the world began:

That we should be saved from our enemies,* and from the hands of all that hate us:

To perform the mercy promised to our forefathers:* and to remember his holy covenant.

To perform the oath which he sware to our forefather Abraham,* that he would give us:

That we being delivered out of the hand of our enemies,* might serve him without fear.

In holiness and righteousness before him,* all the days of our life.

And thou, child, shalt be called the Prophet of the Highest:* for thou shalt go before the face of the Lord to prepare his ways:

To give knowledge of salvation unto his people:* for the remission of their sins:

Through the tender mercy of our God:* whereby the day-spring from on high hath visited us:

To give light to them that sit in darkness, and in the shadow of death:* and to guide our feet into the way of peace.

Glory be to the Father, and to the Son,* and to the Holy Ghost.

As it was in the beginning, is now, and ever shall be,* world without end. Amen.

Antiphon. And very early the first day of the week, they came unto the sepulchre at the rising of the sun, alleluia.

Holy Saturday

9. The antiphon having been repeated, the celebrant says in the usual manner:

℣. The Lord be with you.

℟. And with thy spirit.

Let us pray. *Postcommunion or Collect.*

POUR forth upon us, O Lord, the Spirit of thy charity: that as thou hast now fulfilled us with this paschal Sacrament, so we may by thy mercy be enabled to dwell together in unity and concord. Through Jesus Christ thy Son our Lord: Who liveth and reigneth with thee in the unity of the same Holy Spirit.

10. Then the celebrant says:

℣. The Lord be with you.

℟. And with thy spirit.

And the deacon, turning himself to the people, *or the priest himself,* sings:

I -te, mis-sa est, al-le-lú-ia, al-le- lú -ia.

℟. Thanks be to God, alleluia, alleluia.

And the celebrant, having said **Pláceat tibi, sancta Trínitas**, gives the blessing in the usual manner and, the last gospel being omitted, all return to the sacristy.

THE ORDER OF THE ADMINISTRATION OF THE LORD'S SUPPER

or

HOLY COMMUNION

¶ The Table, at the Communion-time having a fair white linen cloth upon it, shall stand in the Body of the Church, or in the Chancel, where Morning and Evening Prayer are appointed to be said. And the Priest standing at the North-side of the Table shall say the Lord's Prayer, with the Collect following, the people kneeling.

OUR Father which art in heaven, Hallowed be thy Name. Thy kingdom come. Thy will be done in earth, As it is in heaven. Give us this day our daily bread. And forgive us our trespasses, As we forgive them that trespass against us. And lead us not into temptation; But deliver us from evil. Amen.

Collect.

ALMIGHTY God, unto whom all hearts be open, all desires known, and from whom no secrets are hid; Cleanse the thoughts of our hearts by the inspiration of thy Holy Spirit, that we may perfectly love thee, and worthily magnify thy holy Name; through Christ our Lord. Amen.

¶ Then shall the Priest, turning to the people, rehearse distinctly all the Ten Commandments; and the people still kneeling shall, after every Commandment, ask God mercy for their transgression thereof for the time past, and grace to keep the same for the time to come, as followeth.

Minister.

GOD spake these words, and said; I am the Lord thy God: Thou shalt have none other gods but me.

People. Lord, have mercy upon us, and incline our hearts to keep this law.

Minister. Thou shalt not make to thyself any graven image, nor the likeness of any thing that is in heaven above, or in the earth beneath, or in the water under the earth. Thou shalt not bow down to them, nor worship them: for I the Lord thy God am a jealous God, and visit the sins of the fathers upon the children, unto the third and fourth generation of them that hate me, and shew mercy unto thousands in them that love me, and keep my commandments.

People. Lord, have mercy upon us, and incline our hearts to keep this law.

Minister. Thou shalt not take the Name of the Lord thy God in vain: for the Lord will not hold him guiltless, that taketh his Name in vain.

People. Lord, have mercy upon us, and incline our hearts to keep this law.

Minister. Remember that thou keep holy the Sabbath-day. Six days shalt thou labour, and do all that thou hast to do; but the seventh day is the Sabbath of the Lord thy God. In it thou shalt do no manner of work, thou, and thy son, and thy daughter, thy man-servant, and thy maid-servant, thy cattle, and the stranger that is within thy gates. For in six days the Lord made heaven and earth, the sea, and all that in them is, and rested the seventh day: wherefore the Lord blessed the seventh day, and hallowed it.

People. Lord, have mercy upon us, and incline our hearts to keep this law.

Minister. Honour thy father and thy mother; that thy days may be long in the land, which the Lord thy God giveth thee.

People. Lord, have mercy upon us, and incline our hearts to keep this law.

Minister. Thou shalt do no murder.

People. Lord, have mercy upon us, and incline our hearts to keep this law.

Minister. Thou shalt not commit adultery.

People. Lord, have mercy upon us, and incline our hearts to keep this law.

Minister. Thou shalt not steal.

People. Lord, have mercy upon us, and incline our hearts to keep this law.

Minister. Thou shalt not bear false witness against thy neighbour.

People. Lord, have mercy upon us, and incline our hearts to keep this law.

Minister. Thou shalt not covet thy neighbour's house, thou shalt not covet thy neighbour's wife, nor his servant, nor his maid, nor his ox, nor his ass, nor any thing that is his.

People. Lord, have mercy upon us, and write all these thy laws in our hearts, we beseech thee.

¶ Then shall follow one of these two Collects for the Queen, the Priest standing as before, and saying,

Let us pray.

ALMIGHTY God, whose kingdom is everlasting, and power infinite; Have mercy upon the whole Church; and so rule the heart of thy chosen Servant Elizabeth, our Queen and Governour, that she (knowing whose minister she is) may above all things seek thy honour and glory: and that we, and all her subjects (duly considering whose authority she hath) may faithfully serve, honour, and humbly obey her, in thee, and for thee, according to thy blessed Word and ordinance; through Jesus Christ our Lord, who with thee and the Holy Ghost liveth and reigneth, ever one God, world without end. *Amen.*

Or

ALMIGHTY and everlasting God, we are taught by thy holy Word, that the hearts of Kings are in thy rule and governance, and that thou dost dispose and turn them as it seemeth best to thy godly wisdom: We humbly beseech thee so to dispose and govern the heart of Elizabeth thy Servant, our Queen and Governour, that, in all her thoughts, words, and works, she may ever seek thy honour and glory, and study to preserve thy people committed to her charge, in wealth, peace, and godliness: Grant this, O merciful Father, for thy dear Son's sake, Jesus Christ our Lord. *Amen.*

¶ Then shall be said the Collect of the Day. And immediately after the Collect the Priest shall read the Epistle, saying, **The Epistle** [or, **The portion of Scripture appointed for the Epistle**] **is written in the—Chapter of—beginning at the—Verse.** And the Epistle ended, he shall say, **Here endeth the Epistle.** Then shall he read the Gospel (the people all standing up) saying, **The holy Gospel is written in the—Chapter of—beginning at the—Verse.** And the Gospel ended, shall be sung or said the Creed following, the people still standing, as before.

I BELIEVE in one God the Father Almighty, Maker of heaven and earth, And of all things visible and invisible:

And in one Lord Jesus Christ, the only-begotten Son of God, Begotten of his Father before all worlds, God of God, Light of Light, Very God of very God, Begotten, not made, Being of one substance with the Father; By whom all things were made, Who for us men, and for our salvation came down from heaven, And was incarnate by the Holy Ghost of the Virgin Mary, And was made man, And was crucified also for us under Pontius Pilate. He suffered and was buried, And the third day he rose again according to the Scriptures, And ascended into heaven, And sitteth on the right hand of the Father. And he shall come again with glory to judge both the quick and the dead: Whose kingdom shall have no end.

And I believe in the Holy Ghost, The Lord and Giver of life, Who proceedeth from the Father and the Son, Who with the Father and the Son together is worshipped and glorified, Who spake by the Prophets. And I believe one Catholick and Apostolick Church. I acknowledge one Baptism for the remission of sins, And I look for the Resurrection of the dead, And the life of the world to come. Amen.

¶ Then the Curate shall declare unto the people what Holy-days, or Fasting-days, are in the Week following to be observed. And then also (if occasion be) shall notice be given of the Communion; and Briefs, Citations, and Excommunications read, and the Banns of Matrimony published. And nothing shall be proclaimed or published in the Church, during the time of Divine Service, but by the Minister: nor by him any thing, but what is prescribed in the Rules of this Book, or enjoined by the Queen, or by the Ordinary of the place.

¶ Then shall follow the Sermon, or one of the Homilies already set forth, or hereafter to be set forth, by authority.

¶ Then shall the Priest return to the Lord's Table, and begin the Offertory, saying one or more of these Sentences following, as he thinketh most convenient in his discretion.

LET your light so shine before men, that they may see your good works, and glorify your Father which is in heaven. Matt. 5.

Lay not up for yourselves treasure upon the earth; where the rust and moth doth corrupt, and where thieves break through and steal: but lay up for yourselves treasures in heaven; where neither rust nor moth doth corrupt, and where thieves do not break through and steal. Matt. 6.

Whatsoever ye would that men should do unto you, even so do unto them; for this is the Law and the Prophets. Matt. 7.

Not every one that saith unto me, Lord, Lord, shall enter into the Kingdom of heaven; but he that doeth the will of my Father which is in heaven. Matt. 7.

Zacchæus stood forth, and said unto the Lord, Behold, Lord, the half of my goods I give to the poor; and if I have done any wrong to any man, I restore four-fold. Luke 19.

Who goeth a warfare at any time of his own cost? Who planteth a vineyard, and eateth not of the fruit thereof? Or who feedeth a flock, and eateth not of the milk of the flock? I Cor. 9.

If we have sown unto you spiritual things, is it a great matter if we shall reap your worldly things? I Cor. 9.

Do ye not know, that they who minister about holy things live of the sacrifice; and they who wait at the altar are partakers with the altar? Even so hath the Lord also ordained, that they who preach the Gospel should live of the Gospel. I Cor. 9.

He that soweth little shall reap little; and he that soweth plenteously shall reap plenteously. Let every man do according as he is disposed in his heart, not grudgingly, or of necessity; for God loveth a cheerful giver. II Cor. 9.

Let him that is taught in the Word minister unto him that teacheth, in all good things. Be not deceived, God is not mocked: for whatsoever a man soweth that shall he reap. Gal. 6.

While we have time, let us do good unto all men; and specially unto them that are of the household of faith. Gal. 6.

Godliness is great riches, if a man be content with that he hath: for we brought nothing into the world, neither may we carry any thing out. I Tim. 6.

Charge them who are rich in this world, that they may be ready to give, and glad to distribute; laying up in store for themselves a good foundation against the time to come, that they may attain eternal life. I Tim. 6.

God is not unrighteous, that he will forget your works, and labour that proceedeth of love; which love ye have shewed for his Name's sake, who have ministered unto the saints, and yet do minister. Heb. 6.

To do good, and to distribute, forget not; for with such sacrifices God is well pleased. Heb. 13.

Whoso hath this world's good, and seeth his brother have need, and shutteth up his compassion from him, how dwelleth the love of God in him? I John 3.

Give alms of thy goods, and never turn thy face from any poor man; and then the face of the Lord shall not be turned away from thee. Tobit 4.

Be merciful after thy power. If thou hast much, give plenteously: if thou hast little, do thy diligence gladly to give of that little: for so gatherest thou thyself a good reward in the day of necessity. Tobit 4.

He that hath pity upon the poor lendeth unto the Lord: and look, what he layeth out, it shall be paid him again. Prov. 19.

Blessed be the man that provideth for the sick and needy: the Lord shall deliver him in the time of trouble. Ps. 41.

¶ Whilst these Sentences are in reading, the Deacons, Churchwardens, or other fit person appointed for that purpose, shall receive the Alms for the Poor, and other devotions of the people, in a decent bason to be provided by the Parish for that purpose; and reverently bring it to the Priest, who shall humbly present and place it upon the holy Table.

¶ And when there is a Communion, the Priest shall then place upon the Table so much Bread and Wine, as he shall think sufficient.

The Communion

After which done, the Priest shall say,

Let us pray for the whole state of Christ's Church militant here in earth.

ALMIGHTY and everliving God, who by thy holy Apostle hast taught us to make prayers, and supplications, and to give thanks, for all men; We humbly beseech thee most mercifully [to accept our alms and oblations, and] to receive these our prayers, which we offer unto thy Divine Majesty; beseeching thee to inspire continually the universal Church with the spirit of truth, unity, and concord: And grant, that all they that do confess thy holy Name may agree in the truth of thy holy Word, and live in unity, and godly love. We beseech thee also to save and defend all Christian Kings, Princes, and Governours; and specially thy Servant ELIZABETH our Queen; that under her we may be godly and quietly governed: And grant unto her whole Council, and to all that are put in authority under her, that they may truly and indifferently minister justice, to the punishment of wickedness and vice, and to the maintenance of thy true religion, and virtue. Give grace, O heavenly Father, to all Bishops and Curates, that they may both by their life and doctrine set forth thy true and lively Word, and rightly and duly administer thy holy Sacraments: And to all thy people give thy heavenly grace; and especially to this congregation here present; that, with meek heart and due reverence, they may hear, and receive thy holy Word; truly serving thee in holiness and righteousness all the days of their life. And we most humbly beseech thee of thy goodness, O Lord, to comfort and succour all them, who in this transitory life are in trouble, sorrow, need, sickness, or any other adversity. And we also bless thy holy Name for all thy servants departed this life in thy faith and fear; beseeching thee to give us grace so to follow their good examples, that with them we may be partakers of thy heavenly kingdom: Grant this, O Father, for Jesus Christ's sake, our only Mediator and Advocate. *Amen.*

If there be no alms or oblations, then shall the words [of accepting our alms and oblations] be left out unsaid.

¶ At the time of the celebration of the Communion, the Communicants being conveniently placed for the receiving of the holy Sacrament, the Priest shall say this Exhortation.

DEARLY beloved in the Lord, ye that mind to come to the holy Communion of the Body and Blood of our Saviour Christ, must consider how Saint Paul exhorteth all persons diligently to try and examine themselves, before they presume to eat of that Bread, and drink of that Cup. For as the benefit is great, if with a true penitent heart and lively faith we receive that holy Sacrament; (for then we spiritually eat the flesh of Christ, and drink his blood; then we dwell in Christ, and Christ in us; we are one with Christ, and Christ with us;) so is the danger great, if we receive the same unworthily. For then we are guilty of the Body and Blood of Christ our Saviour; we eat and drink our own damnation, not considering the Lord's Body; we kindle God's wrath against us; we provoke him to plague us with divers diseases, and sundry kinds of death. Judge therefore yourselves, brethren, that ye be not judged of the Lord; repent you truly for your sins past; have a lively and stedfast faith in Christ our Saviour; amend your lives, and be in perfect charity with all men; so shall ye be meet partakers of those holy mysteries. And above all things ye must give most humble and hearty thanks to God, the Father, the Son, and the Holy Ghost, for the redemption of the world by the death and passion of our Saviour Christ, both God and man; who did humble himself, even to the death upon the Cross, for us, miserable sinners, who lay in darkness and the shadow of death; that he might make us the children of God, and exalt us to everlasting life. And to the end that we should alway remember the exceeding great love of our Master, and only Saviour, Jesus Christ, thus dying for us, and the innumerable benefits which by his precious blood-shedding he hath obtained to us; he hath instituted and ordained holy mysteries, as pledges of his love, and for a continual remembrance of his death, to our great and endless comfort. To him therefore, with the Father and the Holy Ghost, let us give (as we are most bounden) continual thanks; submitting ourselves wholly to his holy will and pleasure, and studying to serve him in true holiness and righteousness all the days of our life. *Amen.*

¶ Then shall the Priest say to them that come to receive the holy Communion.

YE that do truly and earnestly repent you of your sins, and are in love and charity with your neighbours, and intend to lead a new life, following the commandments of God, and walking from henceforth in his holy ways; Draw near with faith, and take this holy Sacrament to your comfort; and make your humble confession to Almighty God, meekly kneeling upon your knees.

¶ Then shall this general Confession be made, in the name of all those that are minded to receive the holy Communion, by one of the Ministers; both he and all the people kneeling humbly upon their knees, and saying,

ALMIGHTY God, Father of our Lord Jesus Christ, Maker of all things, Judge of all men; We acknowledge and bewail our manifold sins and wickedness, Which we, from time to time, most grievously have committed, By thought, word, and deed, Against thy Divine Majesty, Provoking most justly thy wrath and indignation against us. We do earnestly repent, And are heartily sorry for these our misdoings; The remembrance of them is grievous unto us; The burden of them is intolerable. Have mercy upon us, Have mercy upon us, most merciful Father; For thy Son our Lord Jesus Christ's sake, Forgive us all that is past; And grant that we may ever hereafter Serve and please thee In newness of life, To the honour and glory of thy Name; Through Jesus Christ our Lord. Amen.

¶ Then shall the Priest (or the Bishop, being present,) stand up, and turning himself to the people, pronounce this Absolution.

ALMIGHTY God, our heavenly Father, who of his great mercy hath promised forgiveness of sins to all them that with hearty repentance and true faith turn unto him; Have mercy upon you; pardon and deliver you from all your sins; confirm and strengthen you in all goodness; and bring you to everlasting life; through Jesus Christ our Lord. *Amen.*

¶ Then shall the Priest say.

Hear what comfortable words our Saviour Christ saith unto all that truly turn to him.

COME unto me all that travail and are heavy laden, and I will refresh you. Matt. 11, 28.

So God loved the world, that he gave his only-begotten Son, to the end that all that believe in him should not perish, but have everlasting life. John 3, 16.

Hear also what Saint Paul saith.

This is a true saying, and worthy of all men to be received, That Christ Jesus came into the world to save sinners. I Tim. 1, 15.

Hear also what Saint John saith.

If any man sin, we have an Advocate with the Father, Jesus Christ the righteous; and he is the propitiation for our sins. I John 2, 1.

¶ After which the Priest shall proceed, saying,

Lift up your hearts.

Answer. We lift them up unto the Lord.

Priest. Let us give thanks unto our Lord God.

Answer. It is meet and right so to do.

¶ Then shall the Priest turn to the Lord's Table, and say,

IT is very meet, right, and our bounden duty, that we should at all times, and *These words [Holy Father] must be omitted on Trinity Sunday.* in all places, give thanks unto thee, O Lord, Holy Father, Almighty, Everlasting God.

¶ Here shall follow the Proper Preface, according to the time, if there be any specially appointed: or else immediately shall follow,

THEREFORE with Angels and Archangels, and with all the company of heaven, we laud and magnify thy glorious Name; evermore praising thee, and saying, Holy, holy, holy, Lord God of Hosts, heaven and earth are full of thy glory: Glory be to thee, O Lord most High. *Amen.*

PROPER PREFACES

Upon Christmas-day, and seven days after.

BECAUSE thou didst give Jesus Christ thine only Son to be born as at this time for us; who, by the operation of the Holy Ghost, was made very man of the substance of the Virgin Mary his mother; and that without spot of sin, to make us clean from all sin. Therefore with Angels, etc.

Upon Easter-day, and seven days after.

BUT chiefly are we bound to praise thee for the glorious Resurrection of thy Son Jesus Christ our Lord: for he is the very Paschal Lamb, which was offered for us, and hath taken away the sin of the world; who by his death hath destroyed death, and by his rising to life again hath restored to us everlasting life. Therefore with Angels, etc.

Upon Ascension-day, and seven days after.

THROUGH thy most dearly beloved Son Jesus Christ our Lord; who after his most glorious Resurrection manifestly appeared to all his Apostles, and in their sight ascended up into heaven to prepare a place for us; that where he is, thither we might also ascend, and reign with him in glory. Therefore with Angels, etc.

Upon Whit-Sunday, and six days after.

THROUGH Jesus Christ our Lord; according to whose most true promise, the Holy Ghost came down as at this time from heaven with a sudden great sound, as it had been a mighty wind, in the likeness of fiery tongues, lighting upon the Apostles, to teach them, and to lead them to all truth; giving them both the gift of divers languages, and also boldness with fervent zeal constantly to preach the Gospel unto all nations; whereby we have been brought out of darkness and error into the clear light and true knowledge of thee, and of thy Son Jesus Christ. Therefore with Angels, etc.

Upon the Feast of Trinity only.

WHO art one God, one Lord; not one only Person, but three Persons in one Substance. For that which we believe of the glory of the Father, the same we believe of the Son, and of the Holy Ghost, without any difference or inequality. Therefore with Angels, etc.

¶ After each of which Prefaces shall immediately be sung or said,

THEREFORE with Angels and Archangels, and with all the company of heaven, we laud and magnify thy glorious Name; evermore praising thee, and saying, Holy, holy, holy, etc., as above.

¶ *Then shall the Priest, kneeling down at the Lord's Table, say in the name of all them that shall receive the Communion this Prayer following.*

WE do not presume to come to this thy Table, O merciful Lord, trusting in our own righteousness, but in thy manifold and great mercies. We are not worthy so much as to gather up the crumbs under thy Table. But thou art the same Lord, whose property is always to have mercy: Grant us therefore, gracious Lord, so to eat the flesh of thy dear Son Jesus Christ, and to drink his blood, that our sinful bodies may be made clean by his body, and our souls washed through his most precious blood, and that we may evermore dwell in him, and he in us. *Amen.*

¶ *When the Priest, standing before the Table, hath so ordered the Bread and Wine, that he may with the more readiness and decency break the Bread before the people, and take the Cup into his hands, he shall say the Prayer of Consecration, as followeth.*

ALMIGHTY God, our heavenly Father, who of thy tender mercy didst give thine only Son Jesus Christ to suffer death upon the cross for our redemption; who made there (by his one oblation of himself once offered) a full, perfect, and sufficient sacrifice, oblation, and satisfaction, for the sins of the whole world; and did institute, and in his holy Gospel command us to continue, a perpetual memory of that his precious death, until his coming again; Hear us, O merciful Father, we most humbly beseech thee; and grant that we receiving these thy creatures of bread and wine, according to thy Son our Saviour Jesus Christ's holy institution, in remembrance of his death and passion, may be partakers of his most blessed Body and Blood:

The Communion

* *Here the Priest is to take the Paten into his hand:*

† *And here to break the Bread:*

‡ *And here to lay his hand upon all the Bread.*

Who, in the same night that he was betrayed, *took Bread; and, when he had given thanks, †he brake it, and gave it to his disciples, saying: Take, eat, ‡ This is my Body which is given for you: Do this in remembrance of me.

* *Here he is to take the Cup into his hand:*

Likewise after supper he *took the Cup; and, when he had given thanks, he gave it to them saying, Drink ye all of this:

† *And here to lay his hand upon every vessel (be it Chalice or flagon) in which there is any Wine to be consecrated.*

For this †is my Blood of the New Testament, which is shed for you and for many, for the remission of sins:

Do this, as oft as ye shall drink it in remembrance of me. *Amen.*

¶ Then shall the Minister first receive the Communion in both kinds himself, and then proceed to deliver the same to the Bishops, Priests, and Deacons, in like manner, (if any be present,) and after that to the people also in order, into their hands, all meekly kneeling. And, when he delivereth the Bread to any one, he shall say,

THE Body of our Lord Jesus Christ, which was given for thee, preserve thy body and soul unto everlasting life. Take and eat this in remembrance that Christ died for thee, and feed on him in thy heart by faith with thanksgiving.

¶ And the Minister that delivereth the Cup to any one shall say,

THE Blood of our Lord Jesus Christ, which was shed for thee, preserve thy body and soul unto everlasting life. Drink this in remembrance that Christ's Blood was shed for thee, and be thankful.

¶ When all have communicated, the Minister shall return to the Lord's Table, and reverently place upon it what remaineth of the consecrated Elements, covering the same with a fair linen cloth.

¶ Then shall the Priest say the Lord's Prayer, the people repeating after him every Petition.

OUR Father, which art in heaven, Hallowed be thy Name. Thy Kingdom come. Thy will be done in earth, As it is in heaven. Give us this day our daily bread. And forgive us our trespasses, As we forgive them that trespass against us. And lead us not into temptation; But deliver us from evil: For thine is the kingdom, The power, and the glory, For ever and ever. Amen.

¶ After shall be said as followeth.

O LORD and heavenly Father, we thy humble servants entirely desire thy fatherly goodness mercifully to accept this our sacrifice of praise and thanksgiving; most humbly beseeching thee to grant, that by the merits and death of thy Son Jesus Christ, and through faith in his blood, we and all thy whole Church may obtain remission of our sins, and all other benefits of his passion. And here we offer and present unto thee, O Lord, ourselves, our souls and bodies, to be a reasonable, holy, and lively sacrifice unto thee; humbly beseeching thee, that all we, who are partakers of this holy Communion, may be fulfilled with thy grace and heavenly benediction. And although we be unworthy, through our manifold sins, to offer unto thee any sacrifice, yet we beseech thee to accept this our bounden duty and service; not weighing our merits, but pardoning our offences, through Jesus Christ our Lord; by whom, and with whom, in the unity of the Holy Ghost, all honour and glory be unto thee, O Father Almighty, world without end. *Amen.*

Or this.

ALMIGHTY and everliving God, we most heartily thank thee, for that thou dost vouchsafe to feed us, who have duly received these holy mysteries, with the spiritual food of the most precious Body and Blood of thy Son our Saviour Jesus Christ; and dost assure us thereby of thy favour and goodness towards us; and that we are very members incorporate in the mystical body of thy Son, which is the blessed company of all faithful people; and are also heirs through hope of thy everlasting kingdom, by the merits of the most precious death and passion of thy dear Son. And we most humbly beseech thee, O heavenly Father, so to assist us with thy grace, that we may continue in that holy fellowship, and do all such good works as thou hast prepared for us to walk in; through Jesus Christ our Lord, to whom, with thee and the Holy Ghost, be all honour and glory, world without end. *Amen.*

¶ Then shall be said or sung,

GLORY be to God on high, and in earth peace, good will towards men. We praise thee, we bless thee, we worship thee, we glorify thee, we give thanks to thee for thy great glory, O Lord God, heavenly King, God the Father Almighty.

O Lord, the only-begotten Son Jesu Christ; O Lord God, Lamb of God, Son of the Father, that takest away the sins of the world, have mercy upon us. Thou that takest away the sins of the world, have mercy upon us. Thou that takest away the sins of the world, receive our prayer. Thou that sittest at the right hand of God the Father, have mercy upon us.

For thou only art holy; thou only art the Lord; thou only, O Christ, with the Holy Ghost, art most high in the glory of God the Father. *Amen.*

The Communion

¶ Then the Priest (or Bishop if he be present) shall let them depart with this Blessing.

THE peace of God, which passeth all understanding, keep your hearts and minds in the knowledge and love of God, and of his Son Jesus Christ our Lord: and the blessing of God Almighty, the Father, the Son, and the Holy Ghost, be amongst you and remain with you always. *Amen.*

¶ Collects which may be said as often as occasion shall serve, after the Collects of the Communion, by the discretion of the Minister.

ASSIST us mercifully, O Lord, in these our supplications and prayers, and dispose the way of thy servants towards the attainment of everlasting salvation; that, among all the changes and chances of this mortal life, they may ever be defended by thy most gracious and ready help: through Jesus Christ our Lord. *Amen.*

O ALMIGHTY Lord, and everlasting God, vouchsafe, we beseech thee, to direct, sanctify, and govern, both our hearts and bodies, in the ways of thy laws, and in the works of thy commandments; that through thy most mighty protection, both here and ever, we may be preserved in body and soul; through our Lord and Saviour Jesus Christ. *Amen.*

GRANT, we beseech thee, Almighty God, that the words, which we have heard this day with our outward ears, may through thy grace be so grafted inwardly in our hearts, that they may bring forth in us the fruit of good living, to the honour and praise of thy Name; through Jesus Christ our Lord. *Amen.*

PREVENT us, O Lord, in all our doings with thy most gracious favour, and further us with thy continual help; that in all our works begun, continued, and ended in thee, we may glorify thy holy Name, and finally by thy mercy obtain everlasting life; through Jesus Christ our Lord. *Amen.*

ALMIGHTY God, the fountain of all wisdom, who knowest our necessities before we ask, and our ignorance in asking; We beseech thee to have compassion upon our infirmities; and those things, which for our unworthiness we dare not, and for our blindness we cannot ask, vouchsafe to give us, for the worthiness of thy Son Jesus Christ our Lord. *Amen.*

ALMIGHTY God, who hast promised to hear the petitions of them that ask in thy Son's Name; We beseech thee mercifully to incline thine ears to us that have made now our prayers and supplications unto thee; and grant, that those things, which we have faithfully asked according to thy will, may effectually be obtained, to the relief of our necessity, and to the setting forth of thy glory; through Jesus Christ our Lord. *Amen.*

¶ Upon the Sundays and other Holy-days (if there be no Communion) shall be said all that is appointed at the Communion, until the end of the general Prayer For the whole state of Christ's Church militant here in earth together with one or more of these Collects last before rehearsed, concluding with the Blessing.

¶ And there shall be no celebration of the Lord's Supper, except there be a convenient number to communicate with the Priest, according to his discretion.

¶ And if there be not above twenty persons in the Parish of discretion to receive the Communion; yet there shall be no Communion, except four (or three at the least) communicate with the Priest.

¶ And in Cathedral and Collegiate Churches, and Colleges, where there are many Priests and Deacons, they shall all receive the Communion with the Priest every Sunday at the least, except they have a reasonable cause to the contrary.

¶ And to take away all occasions of dissention, and superstition, which any person hath or might have concerning the Bread and Wine, it shall suffice that the Bread be such as is usual to be eaten; but the best and purest Wheat Bread that conveniently may be gotten.

¶ And if any of the Bread and Wine remain unconsecrated, the Curate shall have it to his own use: but if any remain of that which was consecrated, it shall not be carried out of the Church, but the Priest and such other of the Communicants as he shall then call unto him, shall, immediately after the Blessing, reverently eat and drink the same.

The Bread and Wine for the Communion shall be provided by the Curate and the Churchwardens at the charges of the Parish.

¶ And note, that every Parishioner shall communicate at the least three times in the year, of which Easter to be one. And yearly at Easter every Parishioner shall reckon with the Parson, Vicar, or Curate, or his or their Deputy or Deputies; and pay to them or him all Ecclesiastical Duties, accustomably due, then and at that time to be paid.

¶ After the Divine Service ended, the money given at the Offertory shall be disposed of to such pious and charitable uses, as the Minister and Churchwardens shall think fit. Wherein if they disagree, it shall be disposed of as the Ordinary shall appoint.

ORDER OF THE MASS

When the Priest, having vested, approaches the Altar, he makes the due reverence, and signs himself with the sign of the cross from forehead to breast, and says in a clear voice:

IN the name of the Father, and of the Son, and of the Holy Ghost. Amen.

Then with hands joined before his breast he begins the Antiphon:

I will go unto the altar of God.

The Ministers respond:

Even unto the God of my joy and gladness.

Then alternately with the Ministers he says the following:

Ps. 43, 1-6.

GIVE sentence with me, O God, and defend my cause against the ungodly people: O deliver me from the deceitful and wicked man.

M. For thou art the God of my strength, why hast thou put me from thee: and why go I so heavily, while the enemy oppresseth me?

P. O send out thy light and thy truth, that they may lead me: and bring me unto thy holy hill, and to thy dwelling.

M. And that I may go unto the altar of God, even unto the God of my joy and gladness: and upon the harp will I give thanks unto thee, O God, my God.

P. Why art thou so heavy, O my soul: and why art thou so disquieted within me?

M. O put thy trust in God: for I will yet give him thanks, which is the help of my countenance, and my God.

P. Glory be to the Father, and to the Son, and to the Holy Ghost.

M. As it was in the beginning, is now, and ever shall be: world without end. Amen.

P. repeats the Antiphon:

I will go unto the altar of God.

℟. Even unto the God of my joy and gladness.

He signs himself, saying:

℣. Our help is in the name of the Lord.

℟. Who hath made heaven and earth.

Then with hands joined, bowing profoundly, he makes the Confession.

¶ In Masses of the Dead, and in Masses of the Season from Passion Sunday to Holy Saturday exclusive, the Psalm Give sentence is omitted, with Glory be to the Father, and the repetition of the Antiphon; but In the name of the Father, I will go, and Our help having been said, the Confession is made as follows:

I CONFESS to almighty God, to blessed Mary ever Virgin, to blessed Michael the Archangel, to blessed John Baptist, to the holy Apostles Peter and Paul, to all the Saints, and to you, brethren: that I have sinned exceedingly in thought, word and deed: (He strikes his breast thrice, saying:) through my fault, through my fault, through my most grievous fault. Therefore I beg blessed Mary ever Virgin, blessed Michael the Archangel, blessed John Baptist, the holy Apostles Peter and Paul, all the Saints, and you, brethren, to pray for me to the Lord our God.

The Ministers respond:

Almighty God have mercy upon thee, forgive thee thy sins, and bring thee to everlasting life.

P. Amen.

He stands erect, and the Ministers repeat the Confession; and where you, brethren was said by the Priest, there is said by the Ministers thee, father.

Then the Priest, with joined hands, makes the absolution, saying:

Almighty God have mercy upon you, forgive you your sins, and bring you to everlasting life. R̷. Amen.

He signs himself with the sign of the cross, saying:

The almighty and merciful Lord grant unto us pardon, absolution and remission of our sins. R̷. Amen.

And bowing he proceeds:

V̷. Wilt thou not turn again, and quicken us, O God?

R̷. That thy people may rejoice in thee.

V̷. O Lord, shew thy mercy upon us.

R̷. And grant us thy salvation.

V̷. O Lord, hear my prayer.

R̷. And let my cry come unto thee.

V̷. The Lord be with you.

R̷. And with thy spirit.

And extending and joining his hands, he says in a clear voice:

Let us pray, and ascending to the Altar, says secretly:

TAKE away from us, we beseech thee, O Lord, our iniquities: that we may be worthy to enter with pure minds into the Holy of holies. Through Christ our Lord. Amen.

Then, with hands joined upon the Altar, he says, bowing:

WE pray thee, O Lord, through the merits of thy Saints, (He kisses the Altar in the midst) whose relics are here, and of all the Saints: that thou wouldest vouchsafe to pardon all my sins. Amen.

¶ At solemn Mass the Celebrant, before he reads the Introit, blesses incense, saying: Be thou bles✠sed by him in whose honour thou shalt be burned. Amen. And receiving the thurible from the deacon, he censes the Altar, saying nothing. Then the deacon takes the thurible from the Celebrant, and censes him only. Then the Celebrant, signing himself with the sign of the cross, begins the Introit: which ended, with joined hands he says alternately with the Ministers:

Kyrie, eléison.   Kyrie, eléison.   Kyrie, eléison.

Christe eléison.   Christe, eléison.   Christe, eléison.

Kyrie, eléison.   Kyrie, eléison.   Kyrie, eléison.

or:

Lord, have mercy. Lord, have mercy. Lord, have mercy.

Christ, have mercy. Christ, have mercy. Christ, have mercy.

Lord, have mercy. Lord, have mercy. Lord, have mercy.

Then in the midst of the Altar he extends and joins his hands, and bowing his head a little, says, if it is to be said, Glory be to God on high, and continues with joined hands. When he says **We worship thee, We give thanks unto thee, Jesu Christ,** and **Receive our prayer,** he bows his head; and at the end, saying **With the Holy Ghost,** he signs himself from forehead to breast.

Order of the Mass

I. On Doubles, and solemn days

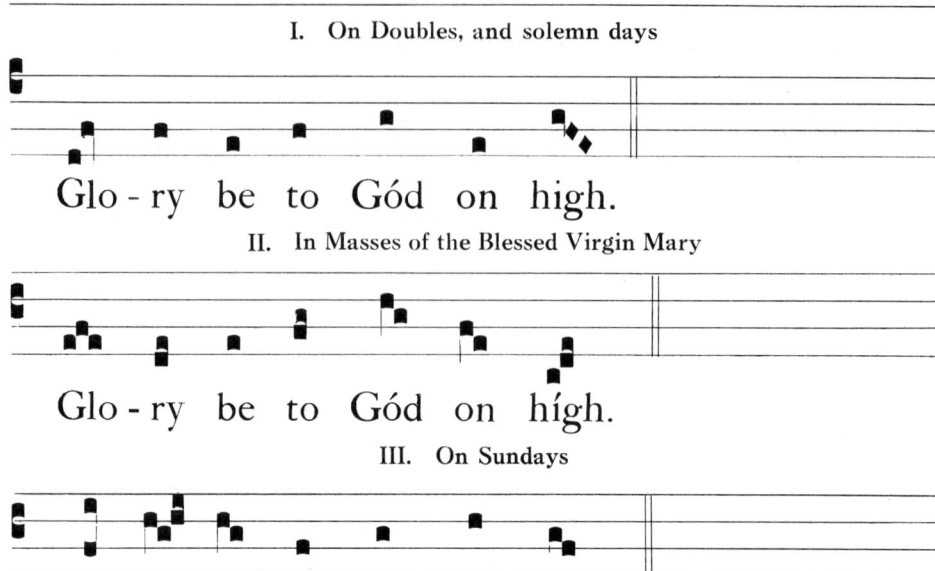

Glo-ry be to God on high.

II. In Masses of the Blessed Virgin Mary

Glo-ry be to God on high.

III. On Sundays

Glo-ry be to God on high.

And in earth peace towards men of good will. We praise thee. We bless thee. We worship thee. We glorify thee. We give thanks to thee for thy great glory. O Lord God, heavenly King, God the Father almighty. O Lord, the only-begotten Son Jesu Christ. O Lord God, Lamb of God, Son of the Father. That takest away the sins of the world, have mercy upon us. Thou that takest away the sins of the world, receive our prayer. Thou that sittest at the right hand of the Father, have mercy upon us.

For thou only art Holy. Thou only art the Lord. Thou only, O Jesu Christ, with the Holy Ghost, art Most High in the glory of God the Father. Amen.

Then he kisses the Altar in the midst, and turning to the people, says: ℣. The Lord be with you. ℟. And with thy spirit. Then he says: Let us pray, and the Collects, one or more, as the order of the Office demands. Then follow the Epistle, Gradual, and Tract, or Alleluia, with the Verse, or Sequence, as the Season or quality of the Mass requires.

These being ended, if it be a solemn Mass, the deacon places the book of the Gospels on the middle of the Altar, and the celebrant blesses incense as above: then the Deacon, kneeling before the Altar, says with joined hands:

CLEANSE my heart and my lips, almighty God, who didst cleanse the lips of Isaiah the prophet with a live coal: so of thy gracious mercy vouchsafe to cleanse me, that I may worthily proclaim thy holy Gospel. Through Christ our Lord. Amen.

Then he takes the book from the Altar, and again kneeling asks a blessing from the Priest, saying: Bid, Sir, a blessing.

The Priest answers:

The Lord be in thy heart and on thy lips: that thou mayst worthily and fitly proclaim his Gospel: In the name of the Father, and of the Son, ✠ and of the Holy Ghost. Amen.

And having received the blessing, he kisses the hand of the celebrant: and going with the other ministers, the incense and the lights, to the place of the Gospel, he stands with joined hands and says: ℣. The Lord be with you. ℟. And with thy spirit. And announcing: The Continuation of the holy Gospel according to N., or The Beginning, he signs the book with the thumb of his right hand at the beginning of the Gospel which he is to read, then himself on the forehead, the mouth, and the breast: and while the ministers respond, Glory be to thee, O Lord, he censes the book thrice, then reads the Gospel with joined hands. Which ended, the Subdeacon carries the book to the Priest, who kisses the Gospel, saying: Through the words of the Gospel may our sins be blotted out.

Then the Priest is censed by the Deacon.

If, however, the Priest celebrates without Deacon and Subdeacon, when the book has been carried to the other corner of the Altar, he bows in the midst, and with joined hands says:

Cleanse my heart, as above, and **Bid**, Lord, a blessing. The Lord be in my heart and on my lips: that I may worthily and fitly proclaim his Gospel. Amen.

Then turning to the book, he says, with joined hands: ℣. The Lord be with you. ℟. And with thy spirit.

And announcing: The Beginning, or The Continuation of the holy Gospel. he signs the book, and himself on forehead, mouth, and breast, and reads the Gospel, as said before. At the end of which the minister responds: Praise be to thee, O Christ, and the Priest kisses the Gospel, saying: Through the words of the Gospel, as above.

¶ In Masses of the Dead Cleanse my heart is said, but a blessing is not asked, lights are not carried, and the celebrant does not kiss the book.

Then at the midst of the Altar, extending, raising and joining his hands, he says, if it is to be said, I believe in one God, and proceeds with joined hands. When he says God, he bows his head to the Cross: which he does likewise when he says Jesus Christ, and together is worshipped. But at the words And was incarnate he genuflects until And was made man is said. At the end at the words And the life of the world to come he signs himself with the sign of the cross from forehead to breast.

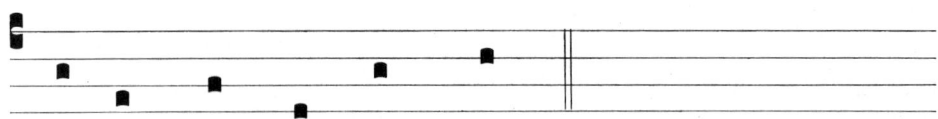

I be-lieve in óne Gód.

The Father almighty, maker of heaven and earth, and of all things visible and invisible.

And in one Lord Jesus Christ, the only-begotten Son of God. Begotten of his Father before all worlds, God of God, light of light, very God of very God. Begotten not made, being of one substance with the Father: by whom all things were made. Who for us men, and for our salvation came down from heaven. (Here genuflect) And was incarnate by the Holy Ghost of the Virgin Mary: And was made man. And was crucified also for us: under Pontius Pilate he suffered, and was buried. And the third day he rose again according to the Scriptures. And ascended into heaven: and sitteth on the right hand of the Father. And he shall come again with glory to judge both the quick and the dead: Whose kingdom shall have no end.

And I believe in the Holy Ghost, the Lord, and giver of life: who proceedeth from the Father and the Son. Who with the Father and the Son together is worshipped and glorified: who spake by the Prophets. And I believe one holy, catholick and apostolick Church. I acknowledge one baptism for the remission of sins. And I look for the resurrection of the dead. And the life of the world to come.   Amen.

Then he kisses the Altar, and turning to the people says: ℣. The Lord be with you. ℟. And with thy spirit. Then he says. Let us pray. and the Offertory.

Quo dicto, si est Missa solemnis, Diaconus porrigit celebranti Patenam cum Hostia: si privata, Sacerdos ipse accipit Patenam cum Hostia, quam offerens, dicit:	Which having been said, if the Mass be solemn, the Deacon presents the Paten with the Host to the celebrant: if it be private, the Priest himself takes the Paten with the Host, which he offers, saying:
SUSCIPE, sancte Pater, omnípotens ætérne Deus, hanc immaculátam hóstiam, quam ego indígnus fámulus tuus óffero tibi Deo meo vivo et vero, pro innumerabílibus peccátis et offensiónibus et neglegéntiis meis, et pro ómnibus circumstántibus, sed et pro ómnibus fidélibus christiánis vivis atque defúnctis: ut, mihi et illis profíciat ad salútem in vitam ætérnam. Amen.	RECEIVE, O holy Father, almighty everlasting God, this spotless host, which I, thine unworthy servant, offer unto thee, my living and true God, for my numberless sins, offences, and negligences, and for all who stand here around, as also for all faithful christians, both living and departed: that to me and to them it may avail for salvation unto life eternal. Amen.
Deinde faciens crucem cum eadem Patena, deponit Hostiam super Corporale. Diaconus ministrat vinum, Subdiaconus aquam in Calice: vel, si privata est Missa, utrumque infundit Sacerdos, et aquam miscendam in Calice benedicit signo crucis, dicens:	Then making a cross with the same Paten, he places the Host upon the Corporal. The Deacon ministers the wine, the Subdeacon the water in the Chalice: or if it be a private Mass, the Priest pours in both, and blesses with the sign of the Cross the water to be mixed in the Chalice, saying:
DEUS qui humánæ substántiæ dignitátem mirabíliter condidísti, et mirabílius reformásti: da nobis per hujus aquæ et vini mystérium, ejus divinitátis esse consórtes, qui humanitátis nostræ fíeri dignátus est párticeps, Jesus Christus, Filius tuus, Dominus noster: Qui tecum vivit et regnat in unitáte Spíritus Sancti Deus: per ómnia sæcula sæculorum. Amen.	O GOD, who didst wondrously create, and yet more wondrously renew the dignity of human nature: grant that by the mystery of this water and wine we may be made co-heirs of his divinity, who vouchsafed to be made partaker of our humanity, even Jesus Christ thy Son our Lord: Who liveth and reigneth with thee in the unity of the Holy Ghost, one God: world without end. Amen.

Order of the Mass

¶ In Missis Defunctorum dicitur prædicta Oratio: sed aqua non benedicitur.

Postea accipit Calicem, et offert dicens:

OFFERIMUS tibi, Dómine, cálicem salutáris, tuam deprecántes cleméntiam: ut in conspéctu divínæ majestátis tuæ, pro nostra et totíus mundi salúte, cum odóre suavitátis ascéndat. Amen.

Deinde facit signum crucis cum Calice, et illum ponit super Corporale, et Palla cooperit: tum junctis manibus super Altare, aliquantulum inclinatus, dicit:

IN spíritu humilitátis, et in ánimo contríto suscipiámur a te, Dómine: et sic fiat sacrifícium nostrum in conspéctu tuo hódie, ut pláceat tibi, Dómine Deus.

Erectus expandit manus, easque in altum porrectas jungens, elevatis ad cœlum oculis, et statim demissis, dicit:

VENI, sanctificátor omnípotens ætérne Deus: Benedicit Oblata, prosequendo: et béne✠dic hoc sacrifícium tuo sancto nómini præparátum.

Postea, si solemniter celebrat, benedicit incensum, dicens:

PER intercessiónem beáti Michaélis Archángeli stantis a dextris altáris incénsi, et ómnium electórum suórum, incénsum istud dignétur Dóminus bene✠dícere, et in odórem suavitátis accípere. Per Christum Dóminum nostrum. Amen.

¶ In Masses of the Dead the foregoing Prayer is said: but the water is not blessed.

Then he receives the Chalice, and offers it, saying:

WE offer unto thee, O Lord, the cup of salvation, humbly beseeching thy mercy: that in the sight of thy divine majesty it may ascend as a sweet-smelling savour for our salvation, and for that of the whole world. Amen.

Then he makes the sign of the cross with the Chalice, and places it upon the Corporal, and covers it with the Pall: then with hands joined upon the Altar, he says, bowing slightly:

IN a humble spirit, and with a contrite heart, may we be accepted of thee, O Lord: and so let our sacrifice be offered in thy sight this day, that it may be pleasing unto thee, O Lord God.

Standing erect, he extends his hands, raises them and joins them, and lifting his eyes to heaven and straight way lowering them, he says:

COME, O thou Fount of holiness, almighty, eternal God: He blesses the Oblations, proceeding: and bl✠ess this sacrifice, made ready for thy holy name.

Then, if he is celebrating solemnly, he blesses incense, saying:

THROUGH the intercession of blessed Michael the Archangel standing at the right hand of the altar of incense, and of all his elect, may the Lord vouchsafe to bl✠ess this incense, and to receive it for a sweet smelling savour. Through Christ our Lord. Amen.

Et accepto thuribulo a Diacono, incensat Oblata, modo in Rubricis generalibus præscripto, dicens:

INCENSUM istud a te benedíctum ascéndat ad te, Dómine: et descéndat super nos misericórdia tua.

Deinde incensat Altare, dicens:

Ps. 140, 1-3.

DIRIGATUR, Dómine, orátio mea sicut incénsum in conspéctu túo: elevátio mánuum meárum sacrifícium vespertínum. Pone, Dómine, custódiam ori meo, et óstium circumstántiæ lábiis meis: ut non declínet cor meum in verba malítiæ, ad excusándas excusatiónes in peccátis.

Dum reddit thuribulum Diacono, dicit:

ACCENDAT in nobis Dóminus ignem sui amóris, et flammam ætérnæ caritátis. Amen.

Postea incensatur Sacerdos a Diacono, deinde alii per ordinem. Interim Sacerdos lavat manus, dicens:

Ps. 25, 6-12.

LAVABO inter innocéntes manus meas: et circúmdabo altáre tuum, Dómine:

Ut áudiam vocem laudis, et enárrem univérsa mirabília tua.

Dómine, diléxi decórem domus tuæ et locum habitatiónis glóriæ tuæ.

Ne perdas cum ímpiis, Deus, ánimam meam, et cum viris sánguinum vitam meam:

In quorum mánibus iniquitátes sunt: déxtera eórum repléta est munéribus.

Ego autem in innocéntia mea ingréssus sum: rédime me, et miserére mei.

And receiving the thurible from the Deacon, he censes the Oblations, in the manner prescribed in the general Rubrics, saying:

MAY this incense, which thou hast blessed, ascend unto thee, O Lord: and may thy mercy descend upon us.

Then he censes the Altar, saying:

Ps. 141, 1-3.

LET my prayer, O Lord, be set forth in thy sight as the incense: and let the lifting up of my hands be an evening sacrifice. Set a watch, O Lord, before my mouth, and keep the door of my lips: O let not mine heart be inclined to any evil thing, let me not be occupied in ungodly works.

While he returns the thurible to the Deacon, he says:

THE Lord kindle in us the fire of his love, and the flame of eternal charity. Amen.

Then the Priest is censed by the Deacon, and afterwards the others in order. Meanwhile the Priest washes his hands, saying:

Ps. 26, 6-12.

I WILL wash my hands in innocency, O Lord: and so will I go to thine altar:

That I may shew the voice of thanksgiving, and tell of all thy wondrous works.

Lord, I have loved the habitation of thy house and the place where thine honour dwelleth.

O shut not up my soul with the sinners, nor my life with the blood-thirsty:

In whose hands is wickedness: and their right hand is full of gifts.

But as for me, I will walk innocently: O deliver me, and be merciful unto me.

Pes meus stetit in dirécto: in ecclésiis benedícam te, Dómine.	My foot standeth right: I will praise the Lord in the congregations.
Glória Patri, et Fílio, et Spirítui Sancto.	Glory be to the Father, and to the Son, and to the Holy Ghost.
Sicut erat in princípio, et nunc, et semper: et in saécula sæculórum. Amen.	As it was in the beginning, is now, and ever shall be: world without end. Amen.
¶ In Missis Defunctorum, et tempore Passionis in Missis de Tempore omittitur Glória Patri.	¶ In Masses of the Dead, and during Passion Tide in Masses of the Season, Glory be is omitted.
Deinde aliquantulum inclinatus in medio Altaris, junctis manibus super eo, dicit:	Then bowing slightly in the middle of the Altar, with hands joined upon it, he says:
SUSCIPE, sancta Trínitas, hanc oblatiónem, quam tibi offérimus ob memóriam passiónis, resurrectiónis, et ascensiónis Jesu Christi Dómini nostri: et in honórem beátæ Maríæ semper Vírginis, et beáti Joánnis Baptístæ, et sanctórum Apostolórum Petri et Pauli, et istórum et ómnium Sanctórum: ut illis profíciat ad honórem, nobis autem ad salútem: et illi pro nobis intercédere dignéntur in cælis, quorum memóriam ágimus in terris. Per eúndem Christum Dóminum nostrum. Amen.	RECEIVE, O holy Trinity, this oblation which we offer unto thee in memory of the passion, resurrection, and ascension of our Lord Jesus Christ: and to the honour of blessed Mary ever Virgin, of blessed John Baptist, of the holy Apostles Peter and Paul, of these and of all the Saints: that it may avail for their honour, and for our salvation: and may they vouchsafe to intercede for us in heaven, whose memory we keep on earth. Through the same Christ our Lord. Amen.
Postea osculatur Altare, et versus ad populum extendens, et jungens manus, voce paululum elevata, dicit:	Then he kisses the Altar, and turning to the people, he extends and joins his hands, and says, raising his voice a little:
ORATE, fratres: ut meum ac vestrum sacrifícium acceptábile fiat apud Deum Patrem omnipoténtem.	PRAY, brethren: that my sacrifice and yours may be acceptable to God the Father almighty.
Minister, seu circumstantes respondent: alioquin ipsemet Sacerdos:	The minister, or those standing around, respond: otherwise the Priest himself:
SUSCIPIAT Dóminus sacrifícium de mánibus tuis (vel meis) ad laudem et glóriam nóminis sui, ad utilitátem quoque nostram, totiúsque Ecclésiæ suæ sanctæ.	THE Lord receive the sacrifice at thy (or my) hands, to the praise and glory of his name, to our benefit also, and that of all his holy Church.
Sacerdos submissa voce dicit: **Amen.**	The Priest in a low voice says: **Amen.**

Deinde, manibus extensis, absolute sine Orémus subjungit Orationes secretas. Quibus finitis, cum pervenerit ad conclusionem, clara voce dicit **Per ómnia sæcula sæculórum**, cum Præfatione, ut in sequentibus.

Præfationem incipit ambabus manibus positis hinc inde super Altare: quas aliquantulum elevat, cum dicit: **Sursum corda**. Jungit eas ante pectus, et caput inclinat, cum dicit: **Grátias agámus Dómino Deo nostro**.

Deinde disjungit manus, et disjunctas tenet usque ad finem Præfationis: qua finita, iterum jungit eas, et inclinatus dicit: **Sanctus**. Et cum dicit: **Benedíctus qui venit**, signum crucis sibi producit a fronte ad pectus.

Then with hands extended, immediately without **Let us pray** he adds the secret Prayers, which ended, when he has come to the conclusion, he says in a clear voice: **Throughout all ages, world without end**, with the Preface, as below.

He begins the Preface with both hands placed apart on the Altar: and raises them a little when he says: **Lift up your hearts**. He joins them before his breast, and bows his head, when he says: **Let us give thanks unto our Lord God**.

Then he separates his hands, and holds them separated till the end of the Preface: which ended, he again joins them, and says, bowing: **Holy**. And when he says: **Blessed is he that cometh**, he makes the sign of the cross on himself from forehead to breast.

The Priest shall say:

Let us pray for the whole state of Christ's Church militant here in earth.

ALMIGHTY and everliving God, who by thy holy Apostle hast taught us to make prayers, and supplications, and to give thanks, for all men: We humbly beseech thee most mercifully [*to accept our alms and oblations, and] to receive these our prayers which we offer unto thy divine Majesty, beseeching thee to inspire continually the universal Church with the spirit of truth, unity, and concord. *If there be no alms or oblations, then shall the words [of accepting our alms and oblations] be left out unsaid.

And grant, that all they that do confess thy holy Name may agree in the truth of thy holy word, and live in unity, and godly love.

We beseech thee also to save and defend all christian Kings, Princes and Governors, and specially thy servant Elizabeth, our Queen, that under her we may be godly and quietly governed: and grant unto her whole Council, and to all that are put in authority under her, that they may truly and indifferently minister justice, to the punishment of wickedness and vice, and to the maintenance of thy true religion, and virtue.

Give grace, O heavenly Father, to all Bishops, and Curates, that they may both by their life and doctrine set forth thy true and lively word, and rightly and duly administer thy holy Sacraments.

And to all thy people give thy heavenly grace, and specially to this congregation here present; that, with meek heart and due reverence, they may hear and receive thy holy word, truly serving thee in holiness and righteousness all the days of their life.

And we most humbly beseech thee of thy goodness, O Lord, to comfort and succour all them who in this transitory life are in trouble, sorrow, need, sickness, or any other adversity.

And we also bless thy holy name for all thy servants departed this life in thy faith and fear, beseeching thee to give us grace so to follow their good examples, that with them we may be partakers of thy heavenly kingdom.

Grant this, O Father, for Jesus Christ's sake:
Our only Mediator and Advocate.
℟. Amen.

Or he sings:

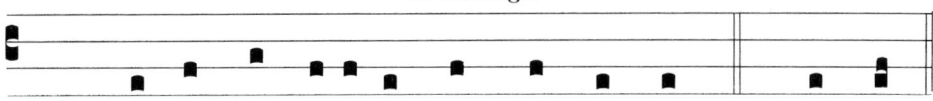

Our ón-ly Med-i-á-tor and Ad-voc-ate.   ℟. A-men.

PREFACES

PREFACES IN SOLEMN CHANT

are to be used in all Masses of any double office, and in Votive Masses for a grave and at the same time public cause. They are never used in Masses of simple rite, or in Votive Masses which are not for a grave and at the same time public cause.

PREFACES IN FERIAL CHANT

are to be used in all Masses of simple rite, and in Votive Masses, which are not for a grave and at the same time public cause. The ferial chant is to be used in the Mass of the Greater Rogation within the Octave of Easter, and the prayers Communicántes and Hanc oblatiónem (as below in the Canon) are said, unless Commemoration of the Octave be omitted.

NOTE.—Where two Prefaces are given for the same day, the former, marked †, is that appointed in the Book of Common Prayer: the latter, marked *, is that appointed in the Missal.

PREFACES IN SOLEMN CHANT

PREFACE OF THE NATIVITY OF THE LORD ✟

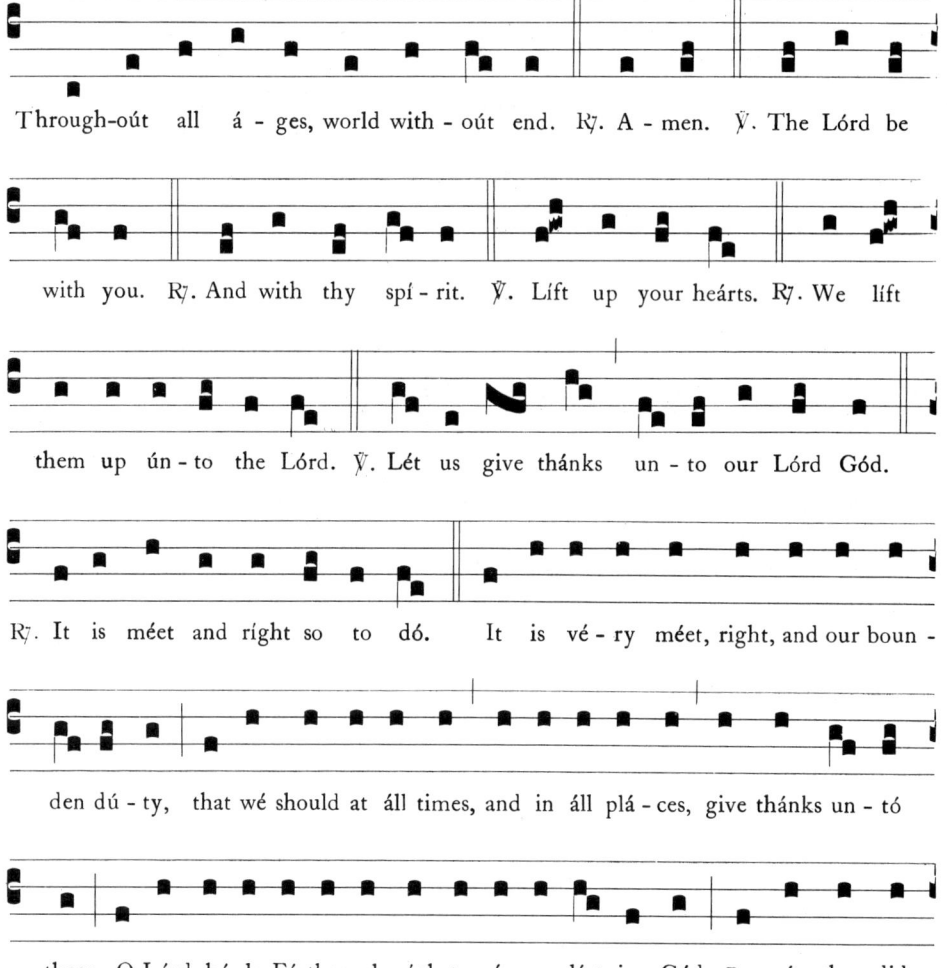

Solemn Preface of the Nativity of the Lord †

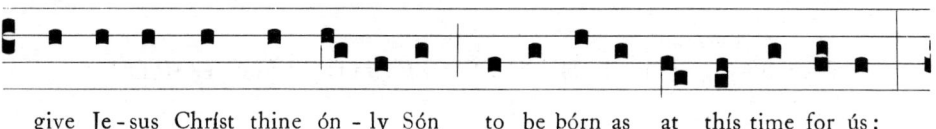
give Je-sus Chríst thine ón-ly Són to be bórn as at thís time for ús:

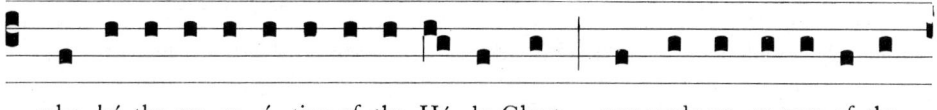
who, bý the op-er-á-tion of the Hó-ly Ghost, was made ve-ry man of the

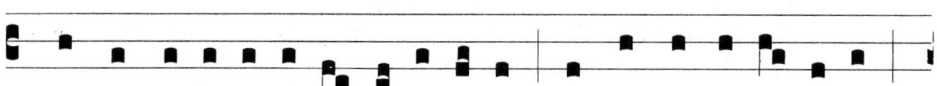
súb-stance of the Vir-gin Ma-ry his mo-ther: and thát with-out spót of sin

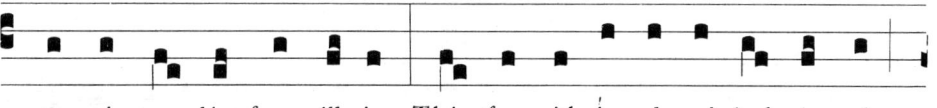
to make us cléan from áll sin. Thére-fore with Án-gels and Arch-án-gels,

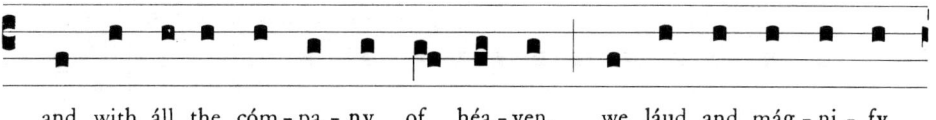
and with áll the cóm-pa-ny of héa-ven, we láud and mág-ni-fy

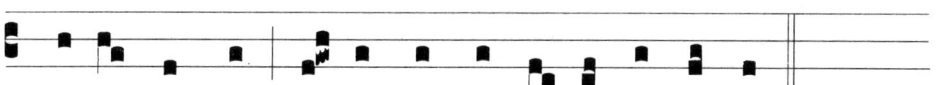
thy gló-rious Náme, év-er-more praís-ing thée, and sáy-ing: Holy, etc.

PREFACE OF THE NATIVITY OF THE LORD*

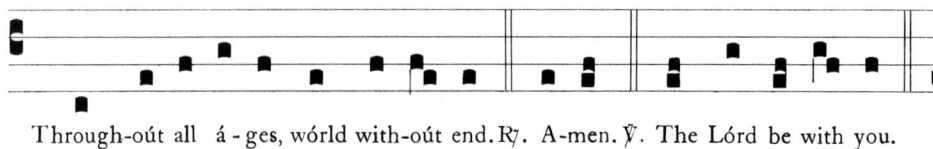

Through-oút all á-ges, wórld with-oút end. R̂. A-men. V̂. The Lórd be with you.

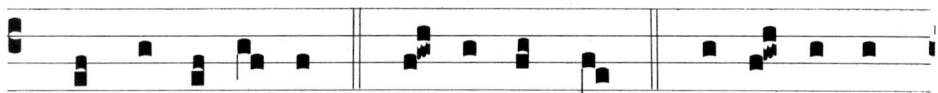

R̂. And with thy spí-rit. V̂. Líft up your heárts. R̂. We líft them up

ún-to the Lórd. V̂. Lét us give thánks un-to our Lórd Gód. R̂. It is

méet and ríght so to dó. It is vé-ry méet, right, and our boun-den dú-ty,

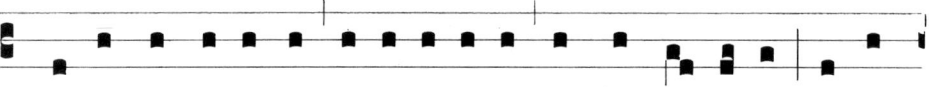

that wé should at áll times and in áll plá-ces give thánks un-tó thee: O Lórd,

hó-ly Fá-ther, al-míght-y, év-er-lást-ing Gód: Be-cáuse through the mýs-te-ry

Solemn Preface of the Nativity of the Lord

of the Wórd made flesh the líght of thy gló-ry. hath shone a-new up-ón the éyes of our mínd : that as we ac-knów-ledge God, made ví-si-ble to man, we may through hím be cáught up to lóve of thíngs in-vís-i-ble. And thére-fore with Án-gels and Arch-án-gels, with Thrónes and Do-mi-ná-tions, and with áll the cóm-pa-ny of the héa-ven-ly host, we síng the má-jes-ty of thy gló-ry, év-er-more práis-ing thee, and sáy-ing : Holy, holy, holy, etc.

Infra Actionem **Communicántes** proper, as below in the Canon.

But in the first Mass of the Nativity of the Lord is said: **We celebrate the most sacred night, wherein,** etc.; thereafter is always said: **We celebrate the most sacred day, whereon,** etc.; until the Octave of the Nativity of the Lord inclusive, in all Masses which are celebrated of the Octave or of the Sunday within the Octave, or which have a Commemoration of either or both.

PREFACE OF THE EPIPHANY OF THE LORD

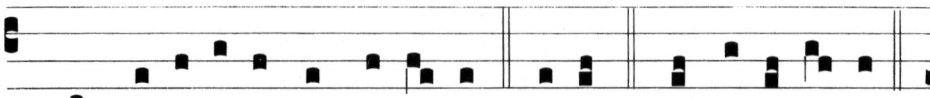
Through-oút all á-ges, wórld with-oút end. R̷. A-men. V̷. The Lórd be with you.

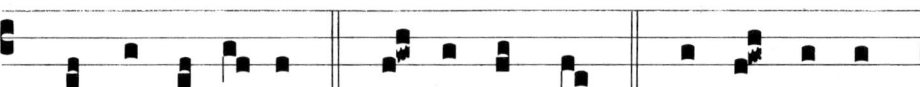
R̷. And with thy spí-rit. V̷. Líft up your heárts. R̷. We líft them up

ún-to the Lórd. V̷. Lét us give thánks un-to our Lórd Gód. R̷. It is

méet and ríght so to dó. It is vé-ry méet, right, and our boun-den dú-ty,

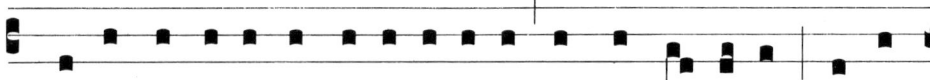
that wé should at áll times and in áll plá-ces give thánks un-tó thee: O Lórd,

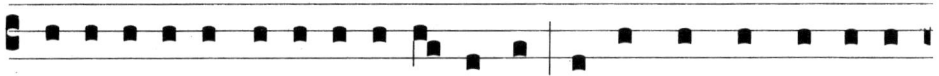
hó-ly Fá-ther, al-míght-y, év-er-lást-ing Gód: Be-cáuse that, whén thine ón-ly-

Solemn Preface of the Epiphany of the Lord

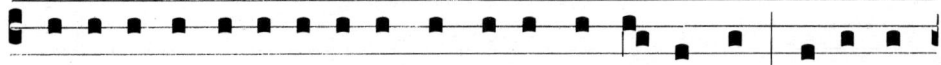
be-gót-ten Són man- i- fest- ly ap-péared in súb-stance óf our flésh, he re-stóred

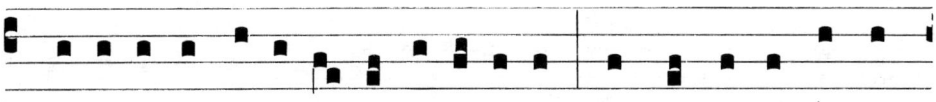
us by the new líght of his ím-mor-tál - i - ty. † And thére-fore with Án - gels

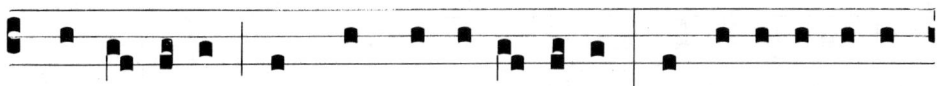
and Arch-án-gels, with Thrónes and Do- mi - ná-tions, and with all the cóm-pa-

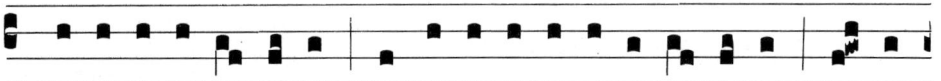
ny of the héa-ven- ly host, we síng the má-jes- ty of thy gló-ry, év- er-

more praís-ing thée, and sáy - ing : Holy, holy, holy, Lord God of hosts, etc.

Infra Actionem, Communicántes proper, as below in the Canon.
This Preface is said until January 13th inclusive in all Masses of double rite.

258   Solemn Preface of the Epiphany of the Lord

† B.C.P. conclusion.

Thére-fore with Án - gels and Arch- án - gels, and with all the cóm - pa - ny

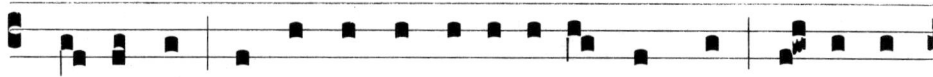
of héa - ven, we láud and mág - ni - fy thy gló - rious Náme : év - er - more

práis - ing thée, and sáy - ing : Holy, holy, holy, Lord God of hosts, etc.

PREFACE OF LENT

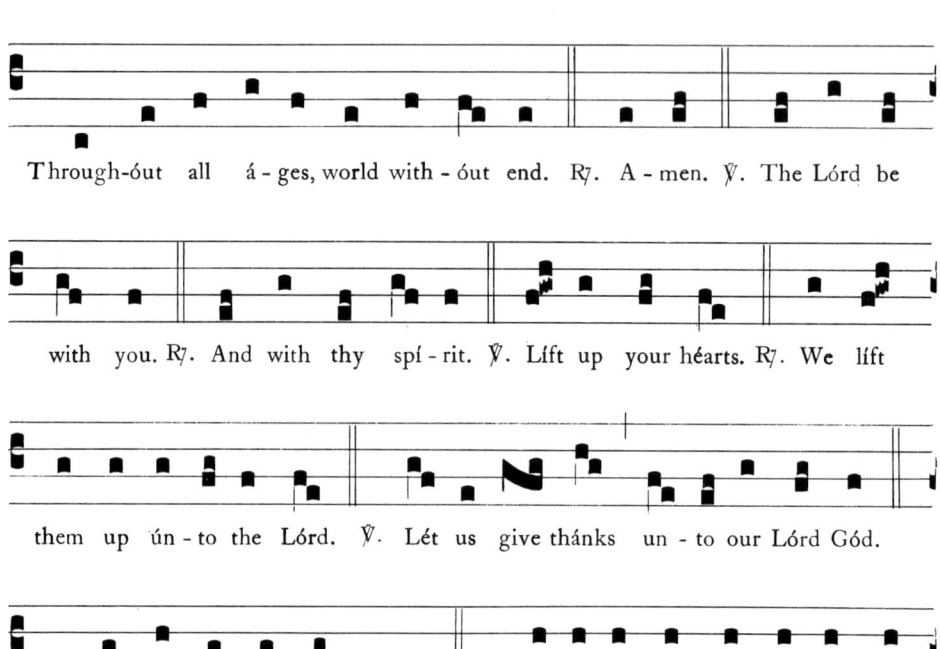

Through-out all a-ges, world with-out end. R/. A-men. V/. The Lord be with you. R/. And with thy spi-rit. V/. Lift up your hearts. R/. We lift them up un-to the Lord. V/. Let us give thanks un-to our Lord God.

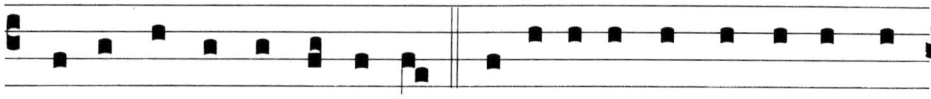

R/. It is meet and right so to do. It is ve-ry meet, right, and our boun-

den du-ty, that we should at all times, and in all pla-ces, give thanks un-to

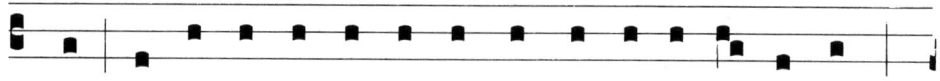

thee, O Lord, ho-ly Fa-ther, al-might-y, ev-er-last-ing God:

Solemn Preface of Lent

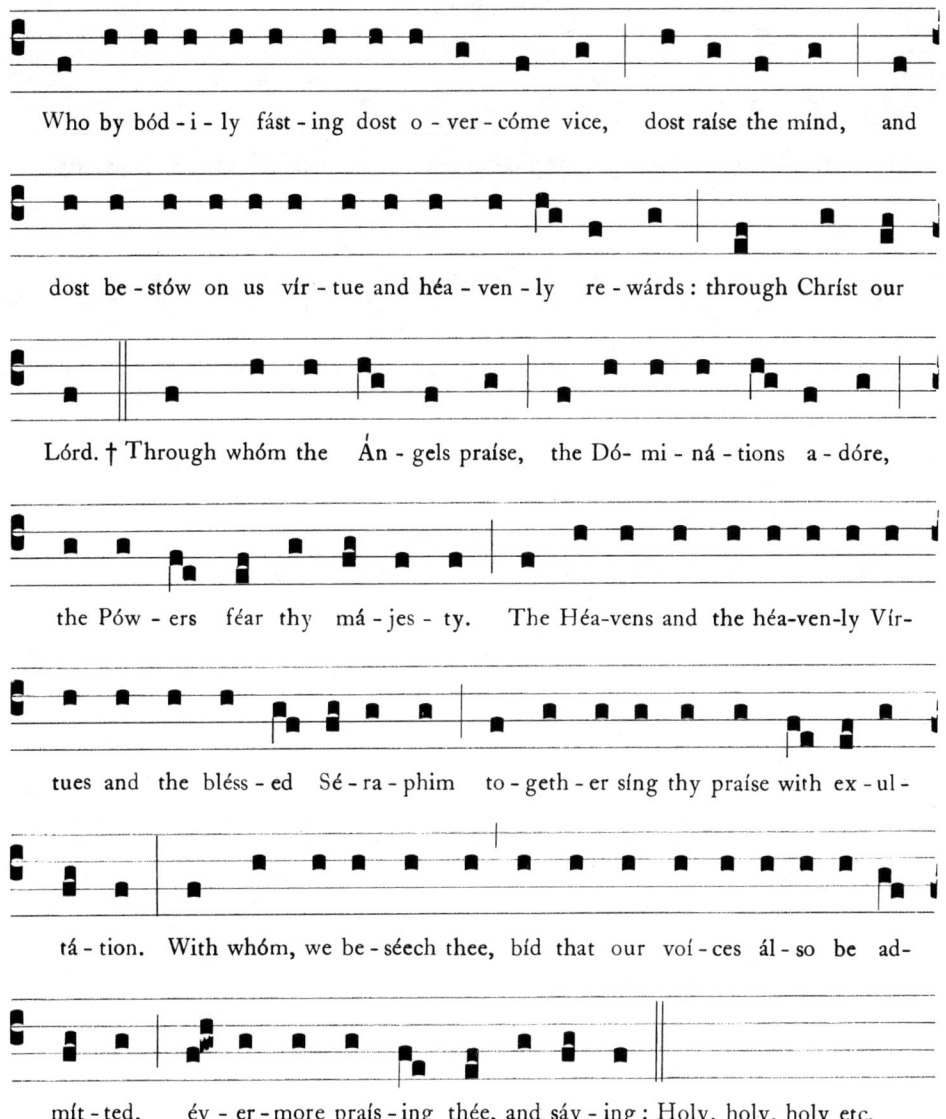

Who by bód-i-ly fást-ing dost o-ver-cóme vice, dost raíse the mínd, and dost be-stów on us vír-tue and héa-ven-ly re-wárds: through Chríst our Lórd. † Through whóm the Án-gels praíse, the Dó-mi-ná-tions a-dóre, the Pów-ers féar thy má-jes-ty. The Héa-vens and the héa-ven-ly Vír-tues and the bléss-ed Sé-ra-phim to-geth-er síng thy praíse with ex-ul-tá-tion. With whóm, we be-séech thee, bíd that our voí-ces ál-so be ad-mít-ted, év-er-more praís-ing thée, and sáy-ing: Holy, holy, holy etc.

[or Therefore, etc., p. 262.]

Solemn Preface of Lent

†B.C.P. conclusion.

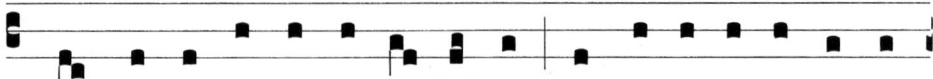

There-fore with An-gels and Arch-án-gels, and with all the cóm-pa-ny

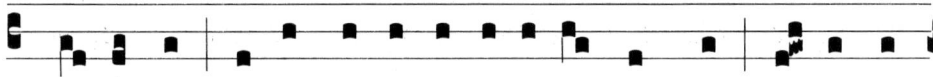

of héa-ven, we láud and mág-ni-fy thy gló-rious Náme, év-er-more

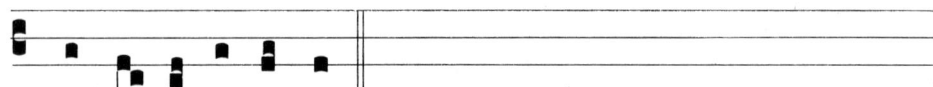

práis-ing thée, and sáy-ing : Holy, holy, holy, Lord God of hosts, etc.

PREFACE OF THE HOLY CROSS

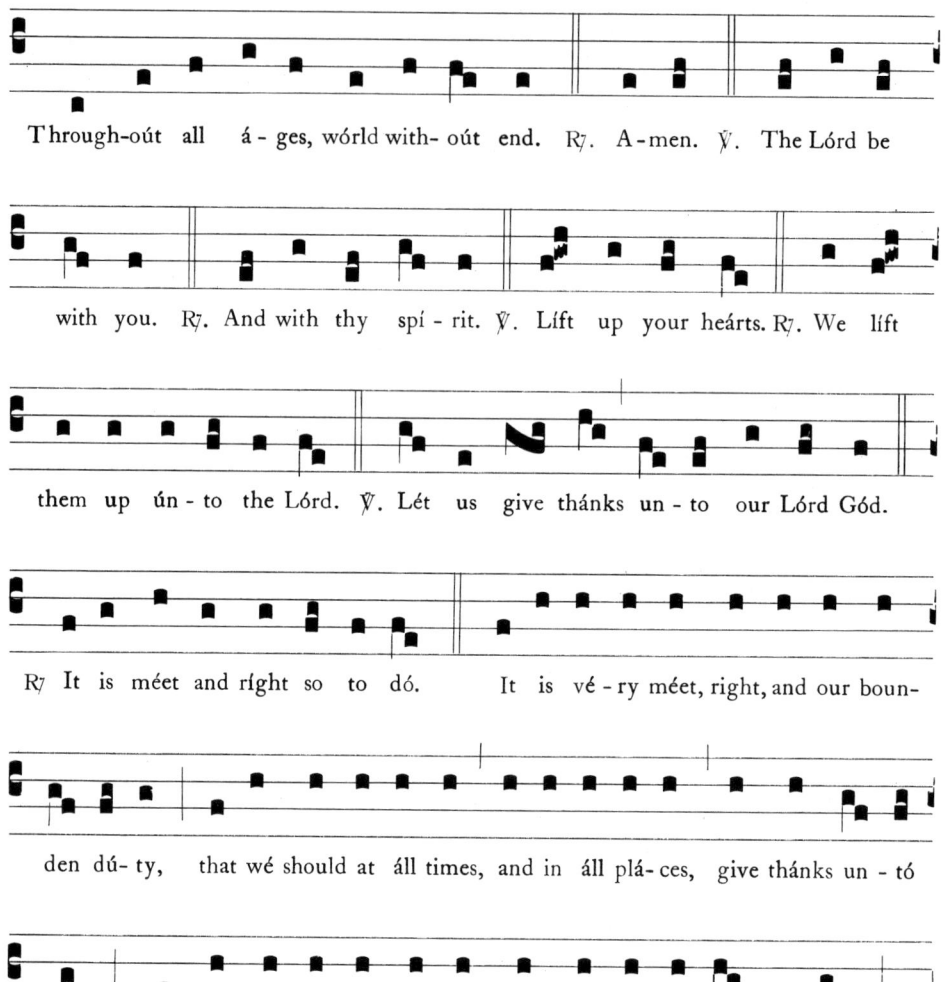

Through-oút all á-ges, wórld with-oút end. R̷. A-men. V̷. The Lórd be with you. R̷. And with thy spí-rit. V̷. Líft up your heárts. R̷. We líft them up ún-to the Lórd. V̷. Lét us give thánks un-to our Lórd Gód. R̷ It is méet and ríght so to dó. It is vé-ry méet, right, and our boun-den dú-ty, that wé should at áll times, and in áll plá-ces, give thánks un-tó thee, O Lórd, hó-ly Fá-ther, al-míght-y, év-er-lást-ing Gód:

Solemn Preface of the Holy Cross

Whó by the trée of the Cróss didst give sal-vá-tion un-to man-kind: that whence deáth a-róse, thence lífe might ríse a-gain: and that hé who by a trée ó-ver-cáme, might al-so by a trée be ó-ver-cóme: through Christ our Lórd. †Through whóm the An-gels praíse, the Dó-mi-ná-tions a-dóre, the Pów-ers féar thy má-jes-ty. The Héa-vens and the héa-ven-ly Vír-tues, and the bléss-ed Sé-ra-phim to-ge-ther síng thy praíse with ex-ul-tá-tion. With whom, we be-séech thee, bíd that our voi-ces ál-so

Solemn Preface of the Holy Cross

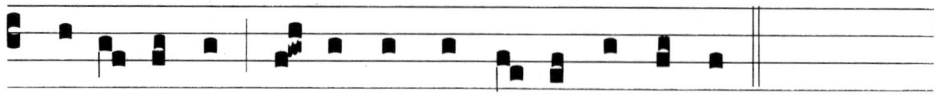
be ad-mitt-ed, év-er-more práis-ing thée and sáy-ing : Holy, holy, etc.

† B.C.P. conclusion.

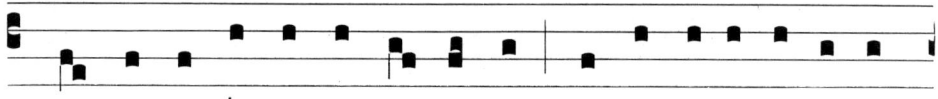
Thére-fore with Án-gels and Arch-án-gels, and with áll the cóm-pa-ny

of héa-ven, we láud and mág-ni-fy thy gló-rious Náme, év-er-

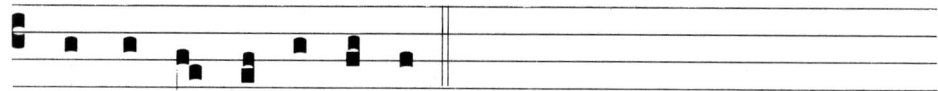
more praís-ing thée and sáy-ing : Holy, holy, holy, Lord God of hosts, etc

PREFACE OF EASTER †

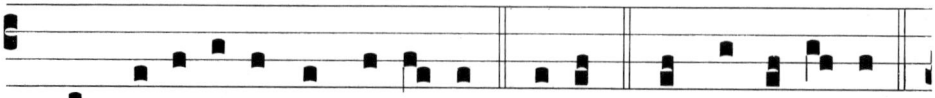
Through-oút all á-ges, wórld with-oút end. ℟. A-men. ℣. The Lórd be with you.

℟. And with thy spí-rit. ℣. Líft up your heárts. ℟. We líft them up

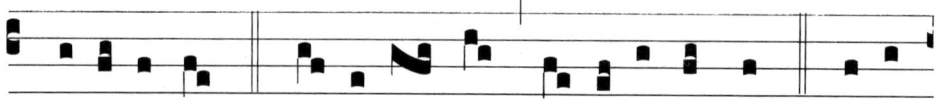
ún-to the Lórd. ℣. Lét us give thánks un-to our Lórd Gód. ℟. It is

méet and ríght so to dó. It is vé-ry méet, right, and our boun-den dú-ty,

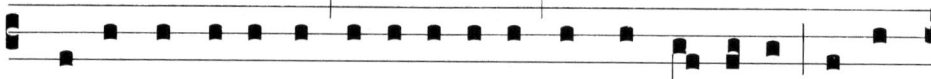
that wé should at áll times and in áll plá-ces give thánks un-tó thee: O Lórd,

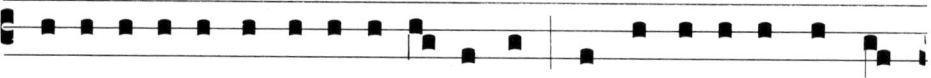
hó-ly Fá-ther, al-míght-y, év-er-lást-ing Gód: But chíef-ly are we bóund to

Solemn Preface of Easter ☩

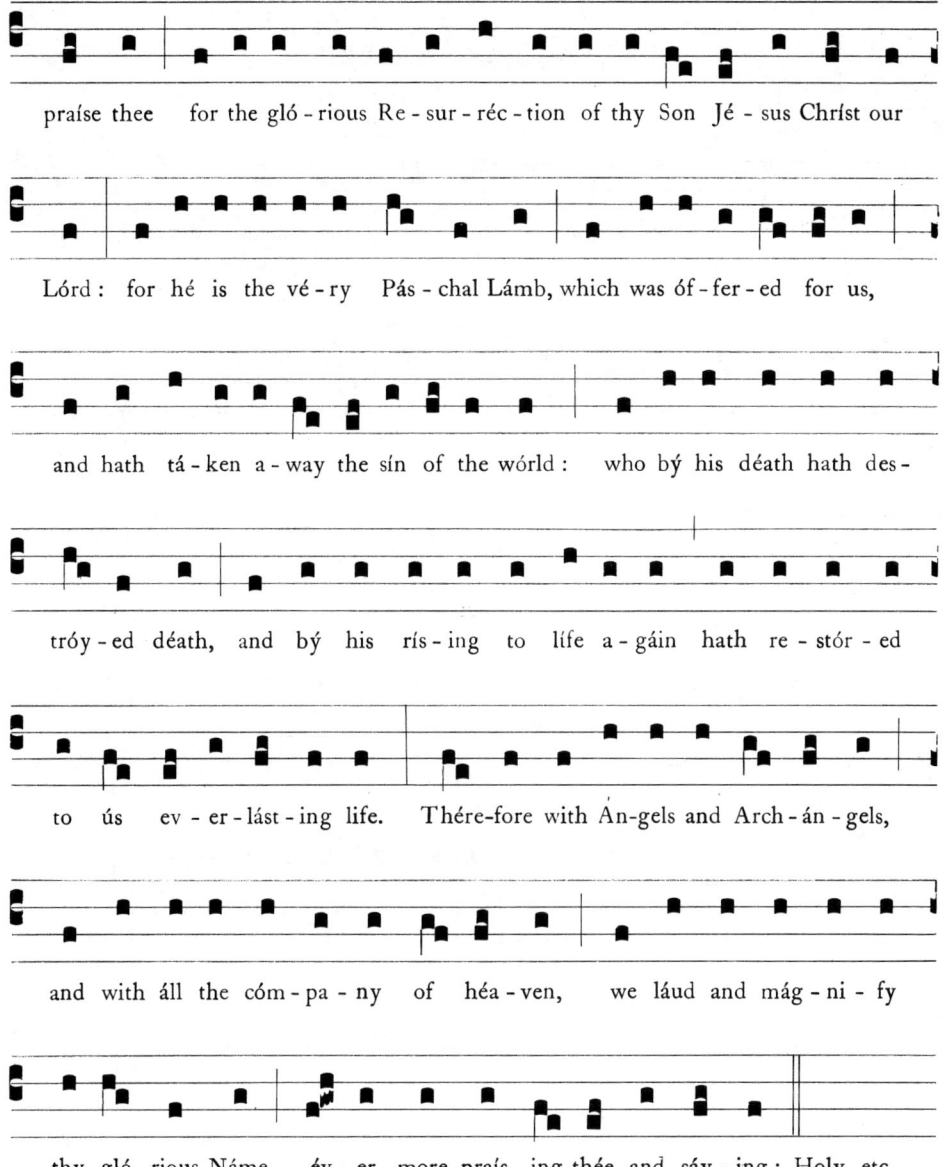

praise thee for the gló-rious Re-sur-réc-tion of thy Son Jé-sus Chríst our Lórd: for hé is the vé-ry Pás-chal Lámb, which was óf-fer-ed for us, and hath tá-ken a-way the sín of the wórld: who bý his déath hath des-tróy-ed déath, and bý his rís-ing to lífe a-gáin hath re-stór-ed to ús ev-er-lást-ing life. Thére-fore with Án-gels and Arch-án-gels, and with áll the cóm-pa-ny of héa-ven, we láud and mág-ni-fy thy gló-rious Náme, év-er-more praís-ing thée, and sáy-ing: Holy, etc.

PREFACE OF EASTER *

Through-oút all á - ges, world with - oút end. R⁷. A - men. V̌. The Lórd be

with you. R⁷. And with thy spí - rit. V̌. Líft up your heárts. R⁷. We líft

them up ún - to the Lórd. V̌. Lét us give thánks un - to our Lórd Gód.

R⁷. It is méet and ríght so to dó. It is vé - ry méet, right, and our boun -

den dú - ty, that wé should at áll times in - deed gló - ri - fy thée, O Lórd,

chíef - ly on this night,
but chíef - ly on this day, when Chríst our Páss - o - ver is sác -
chíef - ly at this time,

Solemn Preface of Easter *

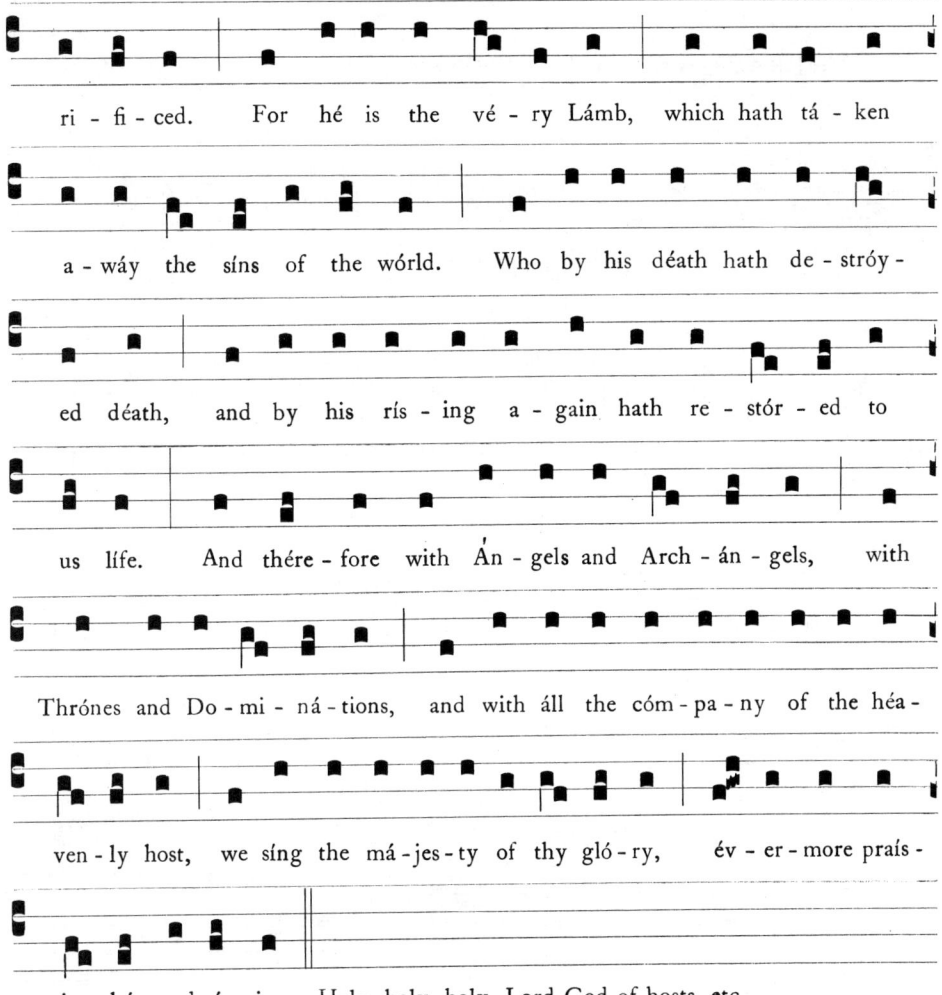

ri - fi - ced. For hé is the vé - ry Lámb, which hath tá - ken a - wáy the síns of the wórld. Who by his déath hath de - stróy - ed déath, and by his rís - ing a - gain hath re - stór - ed to us life. And thére - fore with An - gels and Arch - án - gels, with Thrónes and Do - mi - ná - tions, and with áll the cóm - pa - ny of the héa - ven - ly host, we síng the má - jes - ty of thy gló - ry, év - er - more praís - ing thée, and sáy - ing : Holy, holy, holy, Lord God of hosts, etc.

¶ In the Mass of Holy Saturday is said: **chiefly on this night**: on Easter Day and up to the Saturday following: **chiefly on this day**: thereafter: **chiefly at this time**.

Infra Actionem Communicántes and Hanc ígitur proper, as below in the Canon. So it is said from Holy Saturday up to Saturday after Easter inclusive. But in the Mass of Holy Saturday Infra Actionem is said **we celebrate the most sacred night** (et noctem sacratíssimam celebrántes.)

19

PREFACE OF THE ASCENSION OF THE LORD †

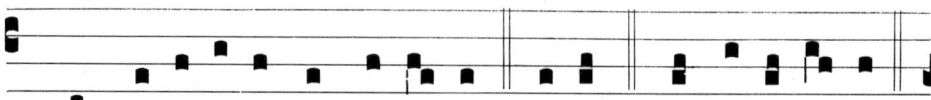
Through-oút all á-ges, wórld with-oút end. ℟. A-men. ℣. The Lórd be with you.

℟. And with thy spí-rit. ℣. Líft up your heárts. ℟. We líft them up

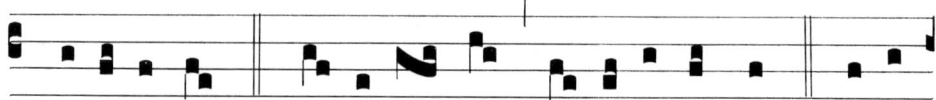
ún-to the Lórd. ℣. Lét us give thánks un-to our Lórd Gód. ℟. It is

méet and ríght so to dó. It is vé-ry méet, right, and our boun-den dú-ty,

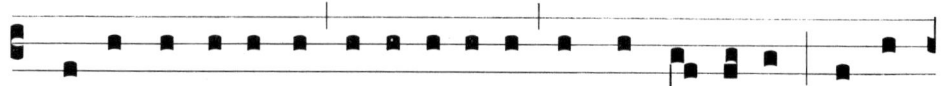
that wé should at áll times, and in áll plá-ces give thánks un-tó thee, O Lórd,

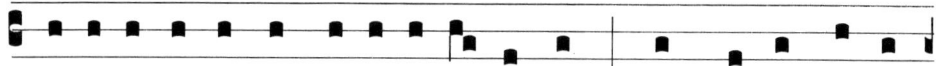
hó-ly Fá-ther, al-míght-y, év-er-lást-ing Gód: Through thy most dear-ly

Solemn Preface of the Ascension of the Lord †

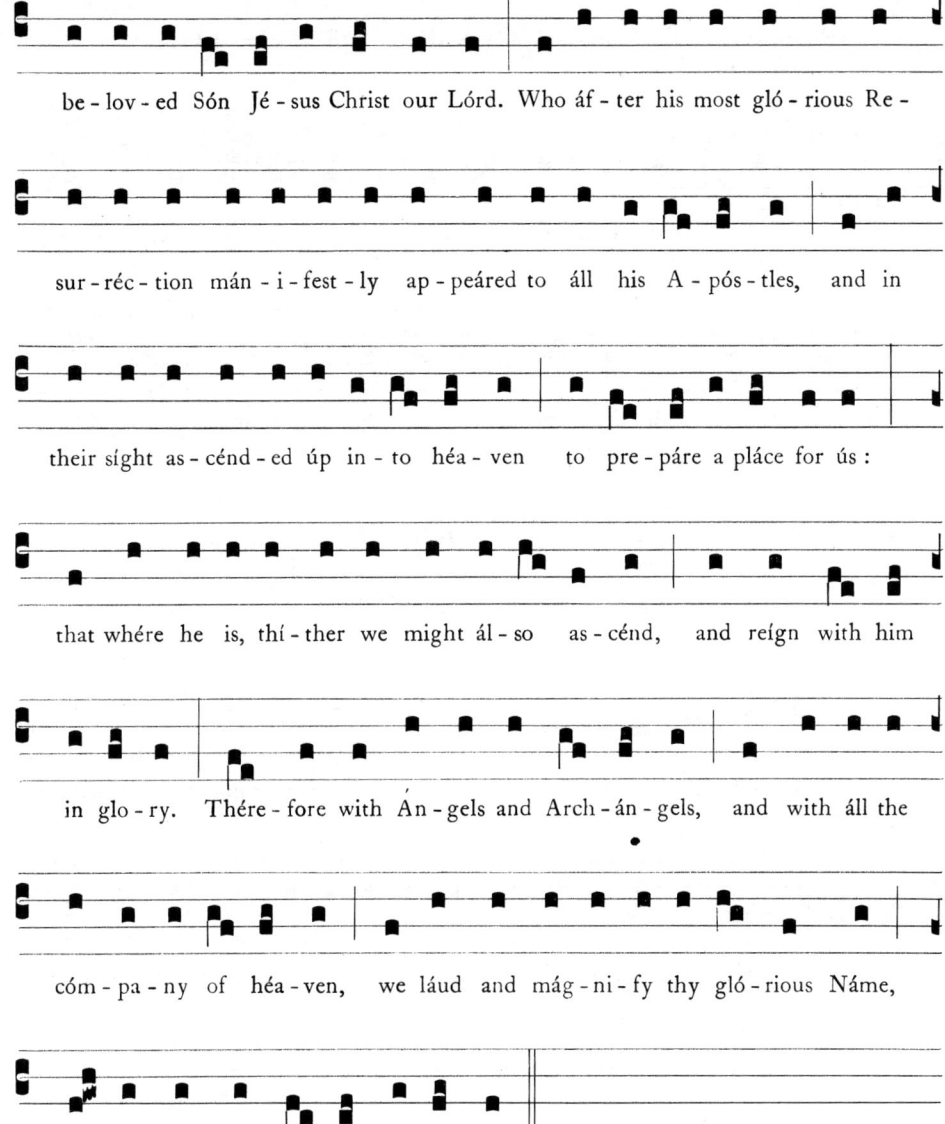

be-lov-ed Són Jé-sus Christ our Lórd. Who áf-ter his most gló-rious Re-sur-réc-tion mán-i-fest-ly ap-peáred to áll his A-pós-tles, and in their síght as-cénd-ed úp in-to héa-ven to pre-páre a pláce for ús: that whére he is, thí-ther we might ál-so as-cénd, and reígn with him in glo-ry. Thére-fore with Án-gels and Arch-án-gels, and with áll the cóm-pa-ny of héa-ven, we láud and mág-ni-fy thy gló-rious Náme, év-er-more praís-ing thée, and sáy-ing: Holy, holy, holy, etc.

PREFACE OF THE ASCENSION OF THE LORD*

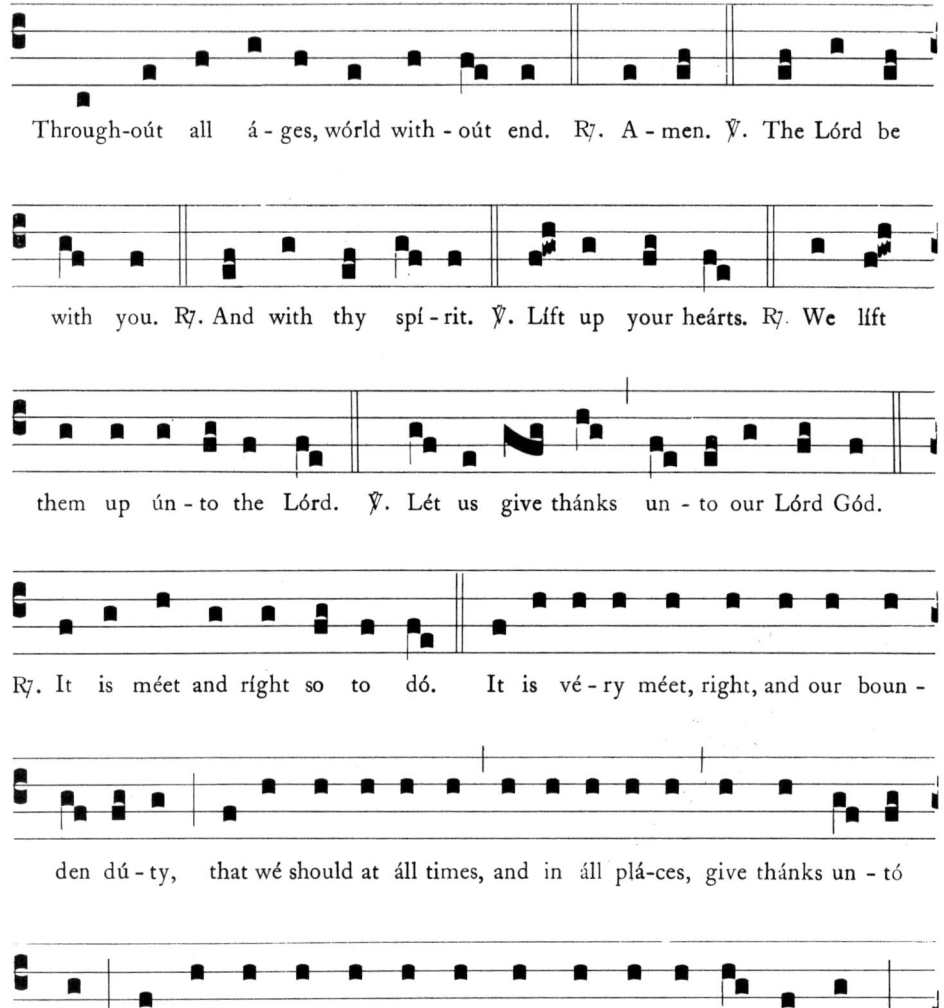

Through-oút all á-ges, wórld with-oút end. ℟. A-men. ℣. The Lórd be with you. ℟. And with thy spí-rit. ℣. Líft up your heárts. ℟. We líft them up ún-to the Lórd. ℣. Lét us give thánks un-to our Lórd Gód. ℟. It is méet and ríght so to dó. It is vé-ry méet, right, and our bounden dú-ty, that wé should at áll times, and in áll plá-ces, give thánks un-tó thee, O Lórd, hó-ly Fá-ther, al-míght-y, év-er-lást-ing Gód:

Solemn Preface of the Ascension of the Lord *

Through Chríst our Lórd. Who áf-ter his Re-sur-réc-tion mán-i-fest-ly ap-péared to áll his dis-cí-ples, and in their síght as-cénd-ed úp in-to héa-ven, that hé might máke us par-tá-kers of his Gód-head. And thére-fore with Án-gels and Arch-án-gels, with Thrónes and Do-mi-ná-tions, and with áll the cóm-pa-ny of the héa-ven-ly host, we síng the má-jes-ty of thy gló-ry, év-er-more praís-ing thée, and sáy-ing : Holy, etc.

Infra Actionem, Communicántes proper, as below in the Canon. And it is thus said on the Feast only.

PREFACE OF THE MOST SACRED HEART OF JESUS

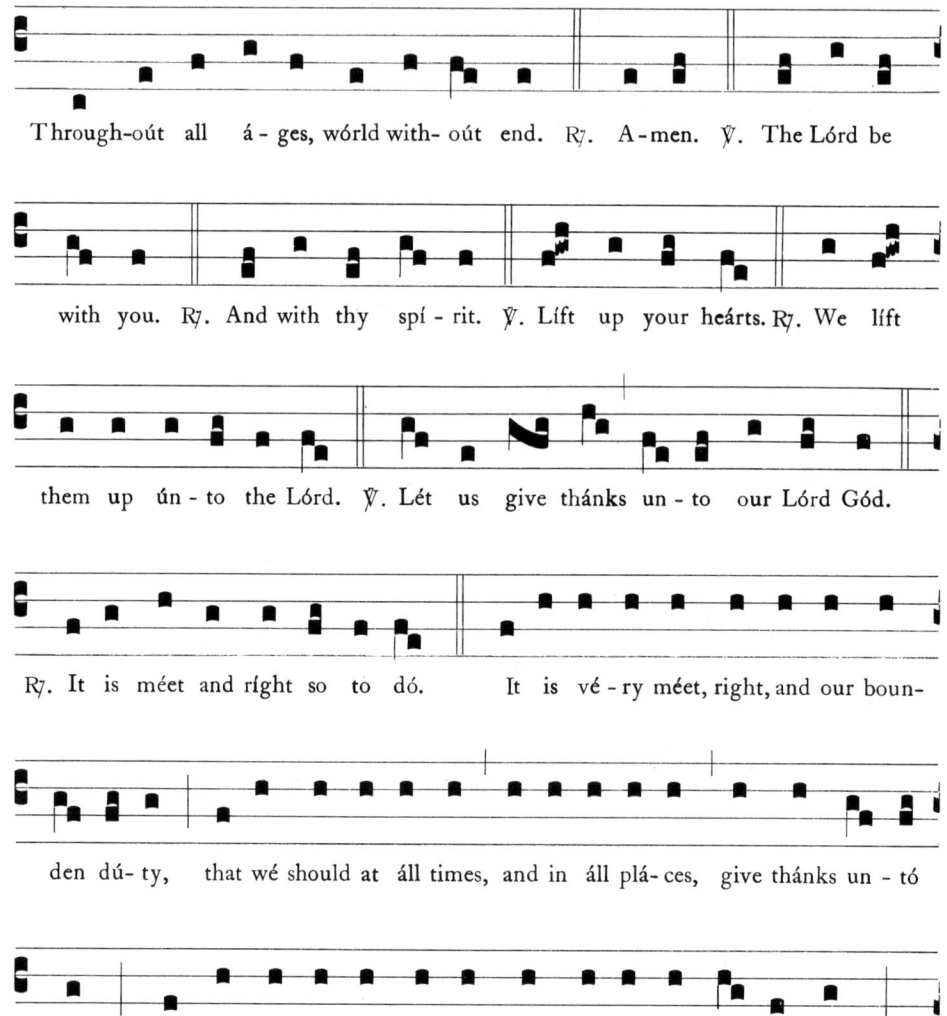

Through-oút all á-ges, wórld with-oút end. R⁊. A-men. V̊. The Lórd be with you. R⁊. And with thy spí-rit. V̊. Líft up your heárts. R⁊. We líft them up ún-to the Lórd. V̊. Lét us give thánks un-to our Lórd Gód. R⁊. It is méet and ríght so to dó. It is vé-ry méet, right, and our bounden dú-ty, that wé should at áll times, and in áll plá-ces, give thánks un-tó thee, O Lórd, hó-ly Fá-ther, al-míght-y, év-er-lást-ing Gód:

Solemn Preface of the most Sacred Heart of Jesus

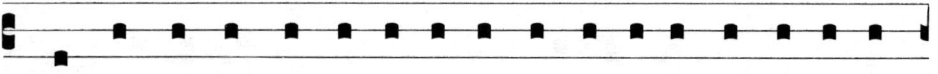

Who didst will that thine ón-ly-be-gót-ten Són, as he húng up-on the

Cróss, should be píerc-ed by the sól-dier's spéar: that his Heárt thus o-pen-

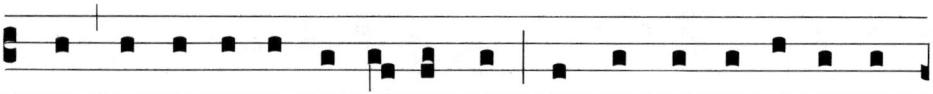

ed, the shríne of héav-en-ly bóun-ty, might pour fórth up-ón us stréams

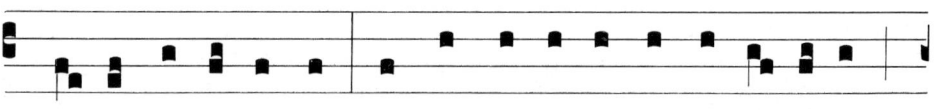

of mér-cy and of gráce; and, búrn-ing with un-céas-ing lóve for us,

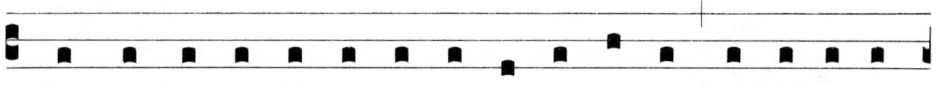

might líke-wise be a pláce of rést for the gód-ly, and an a-bíd-

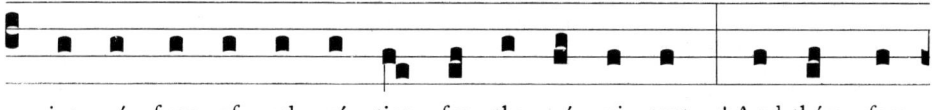

ing ré-fuge of sal-vá-tion for the pé-ni-tent. †And thére-fore

Solemn Preface of the most Sacred Heart of Jesus

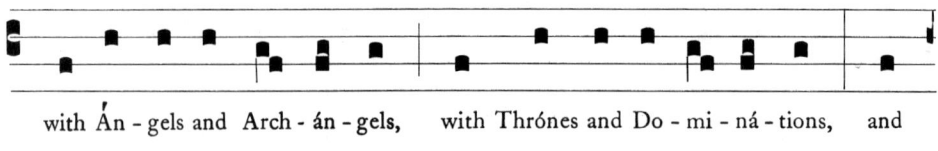
with Án - gels and Arch - án - gels, with Thrónes and Do - mi - ná - tions, and

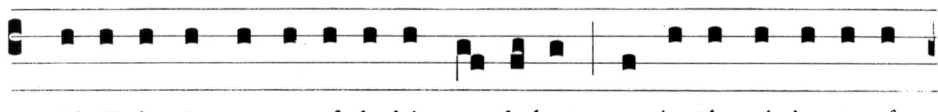
with áll the cóm - pa - ny of the héa - ven - ly host, we síng the má - jes - ty of

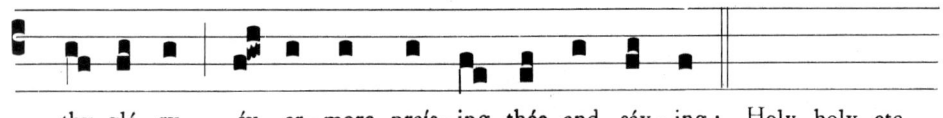
thy gló - ry, év - er - more praís - ing thée, and sáy - ing : Holy, holy, etc

† B.C.P. conclusion.

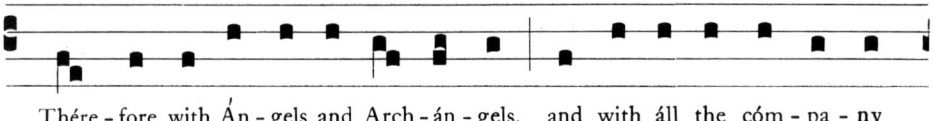
Thére - fore with Án - gels and Arch - án - gels, and with áll the cóm - pa - ny

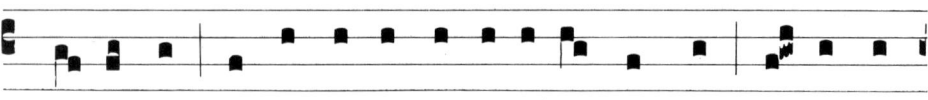
of héa - ven, we láud and mág - ni - fy thy gló - rious Náme, év - er - more

praís - ing thée, and sáy - ing : Holy, holy, holy, Lord God of hosts, etc.

PREFACE OF JESUS CHRIST THE KING

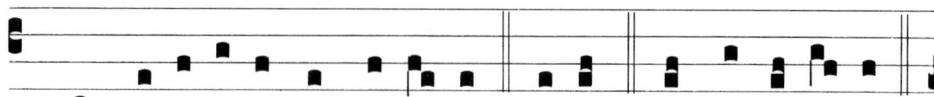
Through-out all a-ges, world with-out end. R⁊. A-men. ℣. The Lord be with you.

R⁊. And with thy spi-rit. ℣. Lift up your hearts. R⁊. We lift them up

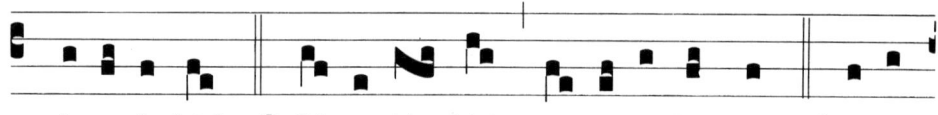
un-to the Lord. ℣. Let us give thanks un-to our Lord God. R⁊. It is

meet and right so to do. It is ve-ry meet, right, and our boun-den du-ty,

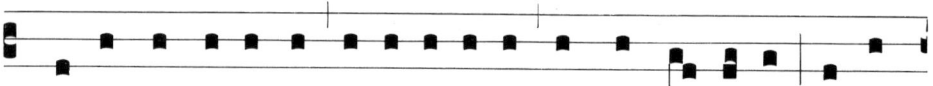
that we should at all times and in all pla-ces give thanks un-to thee: O Lord,

ho-ly Fa-ther, al-might-y, ev-er-last-ing God: Who didst a-noint thine on-ly-

Solemn Preface of Jesus Christ the King

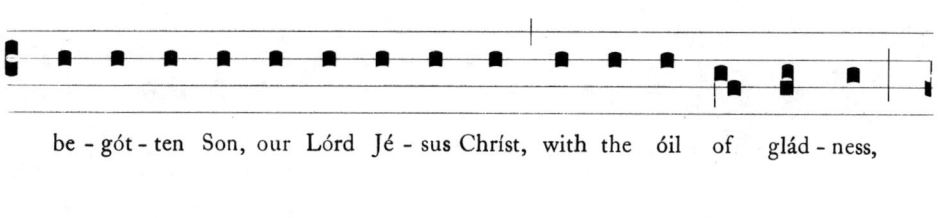
be-gót-ten Son, our Lórd Jé-sus Chríst, with the óil of glád-ness,

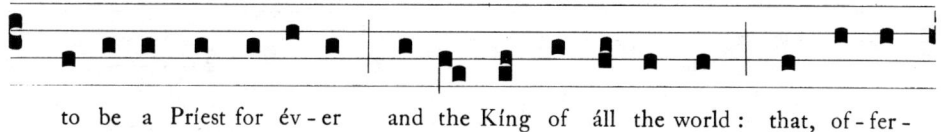
to be a Príest for év-er and the Kíng of áll the world: that, of-fer-

ing him-sélf an un-spót-ted sác-ri-fice of péace up-ón the ál-tar of

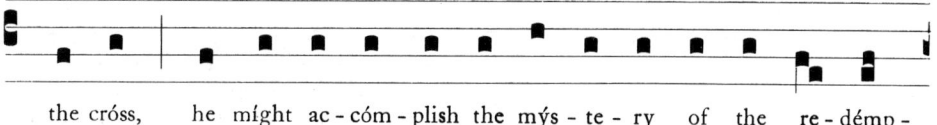
the cróss, he míght ac-cóm-plish the mýs-te-ry of the re-démp-

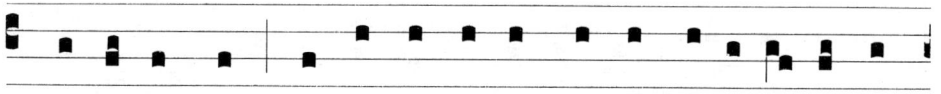
tion of man-kínd: and má-king all créa-tures súb-ject to his góv-ern-

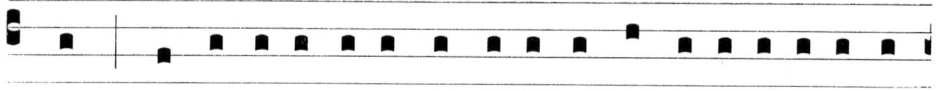
ance, might de-lív-er up to thine ín-fi-nite Má-jes-ty an e-tér-nal

Solemn Preface of Jesus Christ the King

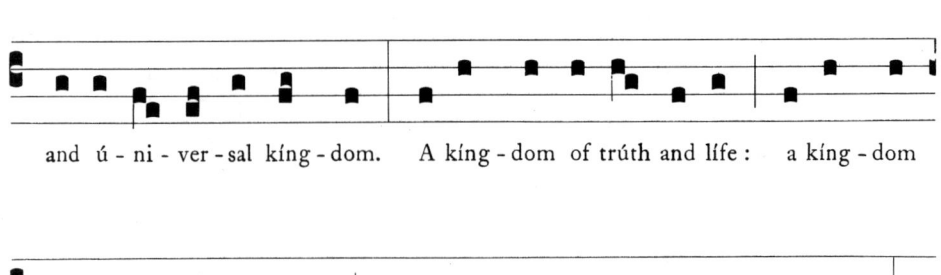
and ú - ni - ver - sal kíng - dom. A kíng - dom of trúth and lífe : a kíng - dom

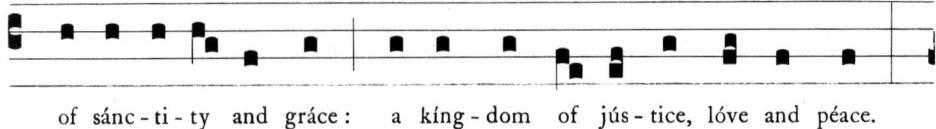
of sánc - ti - ty and gráce : a kíng - dom of jús - tice, lóve and péace.

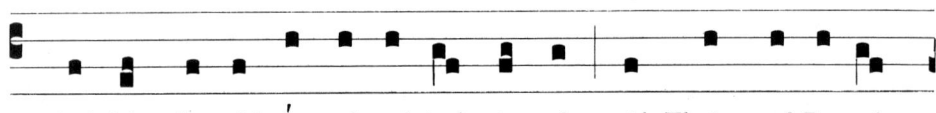
† And thére - fore with Án - gels and Arch - án - gels, with Thrónes and Do - mi -

ná - tions, and with áll the cóm - pa - ny of the héa - ven - ly host, we síng

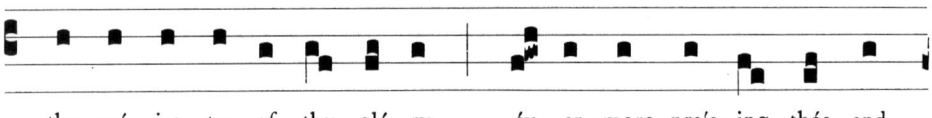
the má - jes - ty of thy gló - ry, év - er - more praís - ing thée, and

sáy - ing : Holy, holy, holy, Lord God of hosts, etc.

Solemn Preface of Jesus Christ the King

†B.C.P. conclusion.

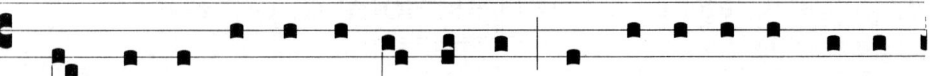

Thére-fore with An-gels and Arch-án-gels, and with all the cóm-pa-ny

of héa-ven, we láud and mág-ni-fy thy gló-rious Náme: év-er-more

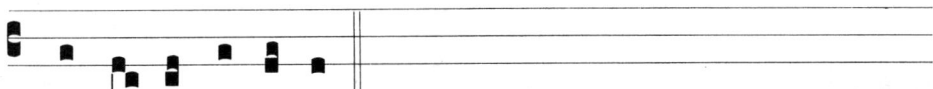

praís-ing thée, and sáy-ing: Holy, holy, holy, Lord God of hosts, etc.

PREFACE OF THE HOLY GHOST ✝

Through-out all á - ges, world with - out end. ℟. A - men. ℣. The Lórd be with you. ℟. And with thy spí - rit. ℣. Líft up your heárts. ℟. We líft them up ún - to the Lórd. ℣. Lét us give thánks un - to our Lórd Gód. ℟. It is méet and ríght so to dó. It is vé - ry méet, right, and our boun - den dú - ty, that wé should at áll times, and in áll plá - ces, give thánks un - to thée, O Lórd, hó - ly Fá - ther, al - mígh - ty, év - er - lást - ing God:

Solemn Preface of the Holy Ghost ✝

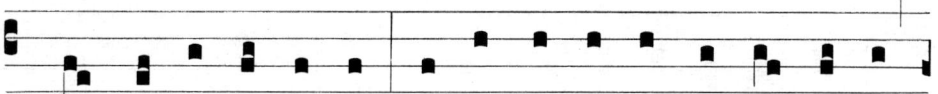
Through Jésus Christ our Lórd, Ac-córd-ing to whóse most trúe pró-mise,

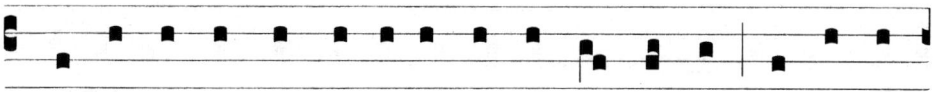
the Hó-ly Ghóst came dówn as at this tíme from héa-ven with a súd-

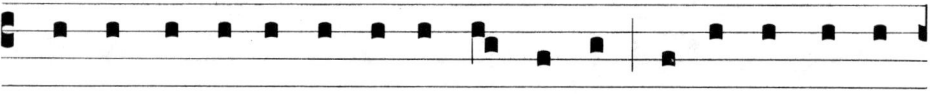
den great sóund, as it had been a míght-y wínd, in the líke-ness of

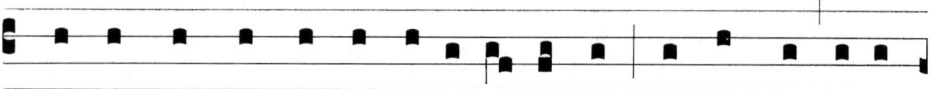
fí-ery tóngues, líght-ing up-ón the A-pós-tles, to teách them, and to

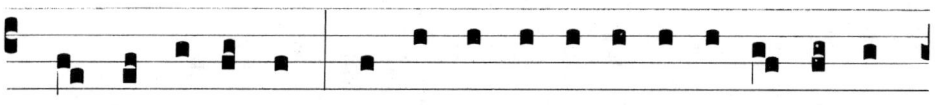
léad them to áll trúth: gív-ing them bóth the gíft of dí-vers lan-gua-

ges, and ál-so bóld-ness with fér-vent zéal cón-stant-ly to préach the

286 Solemn Preface of the Holy Ghost ✝

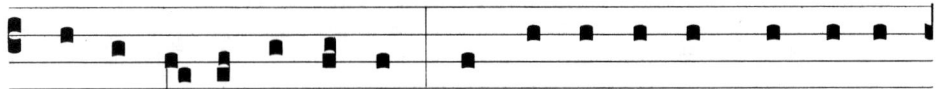
Gós-pel un-tó all ná-tions: whére-by we have been bróught out of

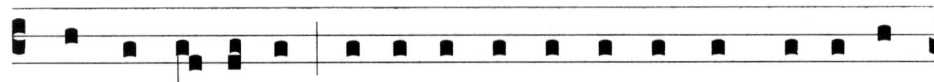
dárk-ness and ér-ror in-to the clear líght and true knów-ledge of thée,

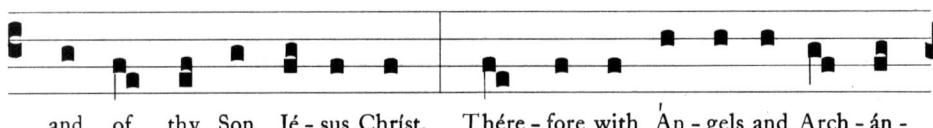
and of thy Son Jé-sus Chríst. Thére-fore with An-gels and Arch-án-

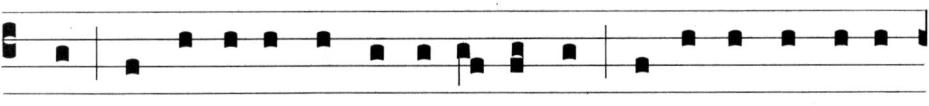
gels, and with áll the cóm-pa-ny of héa-ven, we láud and mág-ni-fy

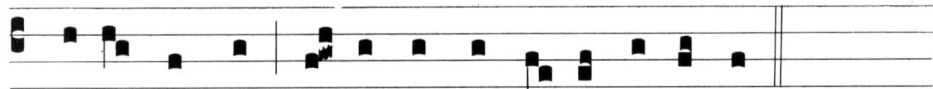
thy gló-rious Náme, év-er-more praís-ing thée, and say-ing: Holy, etc.

PREFACE OF THE HOLY GHOST *

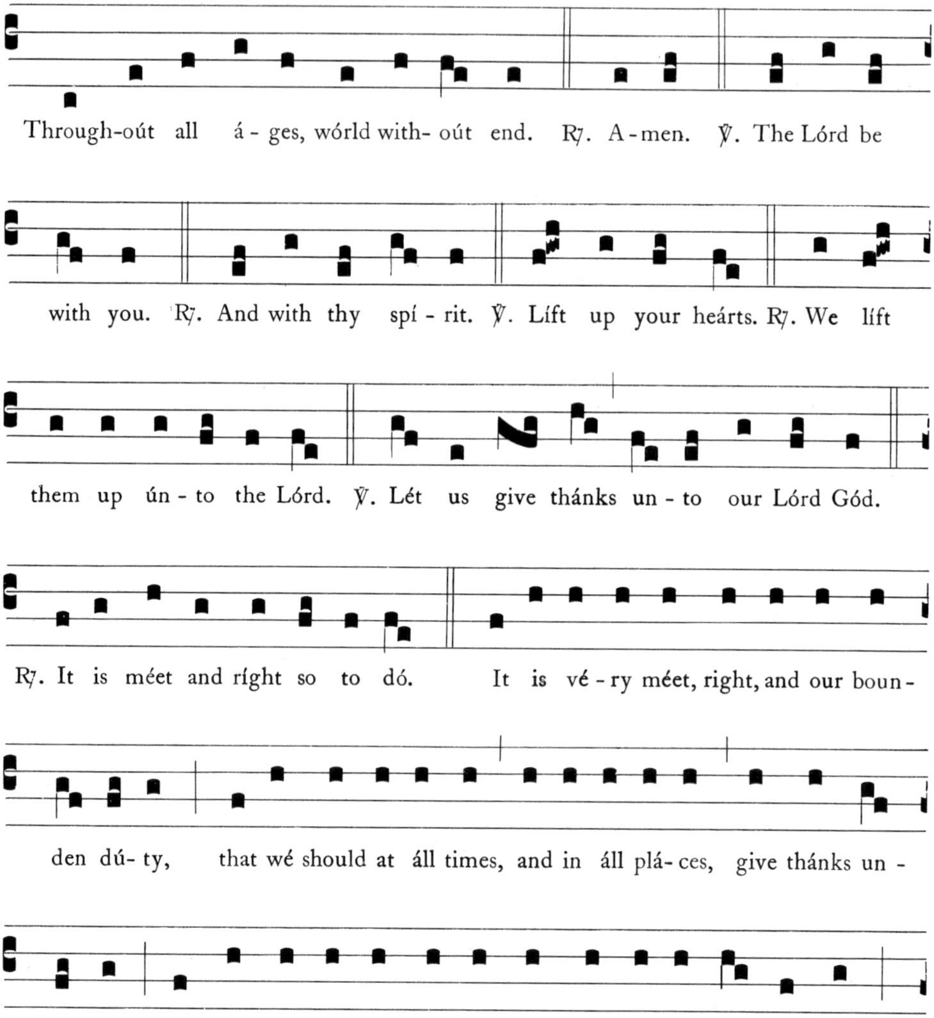

Through-out all a-ges, world with-out end. R7. A-men. V. The Lord be

with you. R7. And with thy spi-rit. V. Lift up your hearts. R7. We lift

them up un-to the Lord. V. Let us give thanks un-to our Lord God.

R7. It is meet and right so to do. It is ve-ry meet, right, and our boun-

den du-ty, that we should at all times, and in all pla-ces, give thanks un-

to thee, O Lord, ho-ly Fa-ther, al-migh-ty, ev-er-last-ing God:

Solemn Preface of the Holy Ghost *

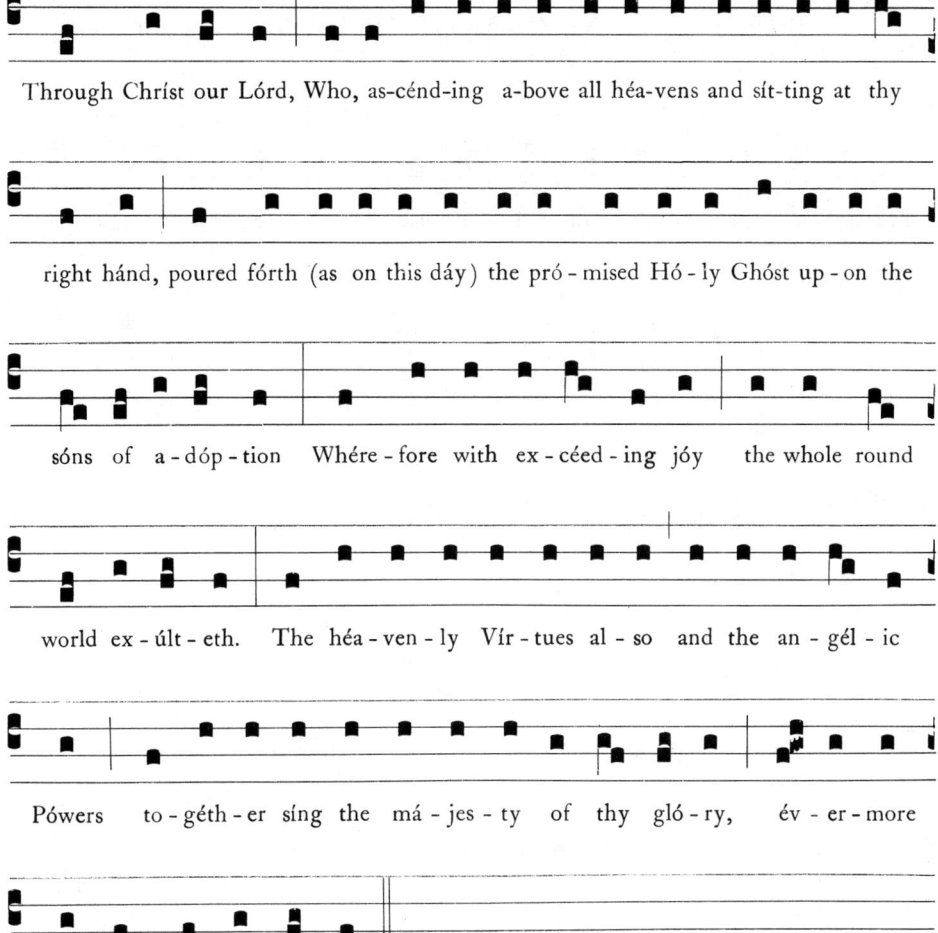

Through Christ our Lórd, Who, as-cénd-ing a-bove all héa-vens and sít-ting at thy right hánd, poured fórth (as on this dáy) the pró-mised Hó-ly Ghóst up-on the sóns of a-dóp-tion Whére-fore with ex-céed-ing jóy the whole round world ex-últ-eth. The héa-ven-ly Vír-tues al-so and the an-gél-ic Pówers to-géth-er síng the má-jes-ty of thy gló-ry, év-er-more praís-ing thée, and sáy-ing: Holy, holy, holy, Lord God of hosts, etc.

Infra Actionem Communicántes and **Hanc oblatiónem** proper, as below in the Canon.

And it is said only from the Vigil of Pentecost until the following Saturday inclusive, in all Masses which are celebrated of the Vigil or the Octave, or which have a Commemoration of either.

PREFACE OF THE MOST HOLY TRINITY †

Through-out all á-ges, world with-out end. ℟. A-men. ℣. The Lord be with you. ℟. And with thy spí-rit. ℣. Líft up your heárts. ℟. We lift them up ún-to the Lórd. ℣. Lét us give thánks un-to our Lórd Gód. ℟. It is méet and ríght so to dó. It is vé-ry méet, right, and our boun-den dú-ty, that wé should at áll times, and in áll plá-ces, give thánks un-tó thee, O Lórd, [hó-ly Fá-ther], al-mígh-ty, év-er-lást-ing Gód :

† On Trinity Sunday only the words in brackets may be omitted.

Solemn Preface of the Most Holy Trinity †

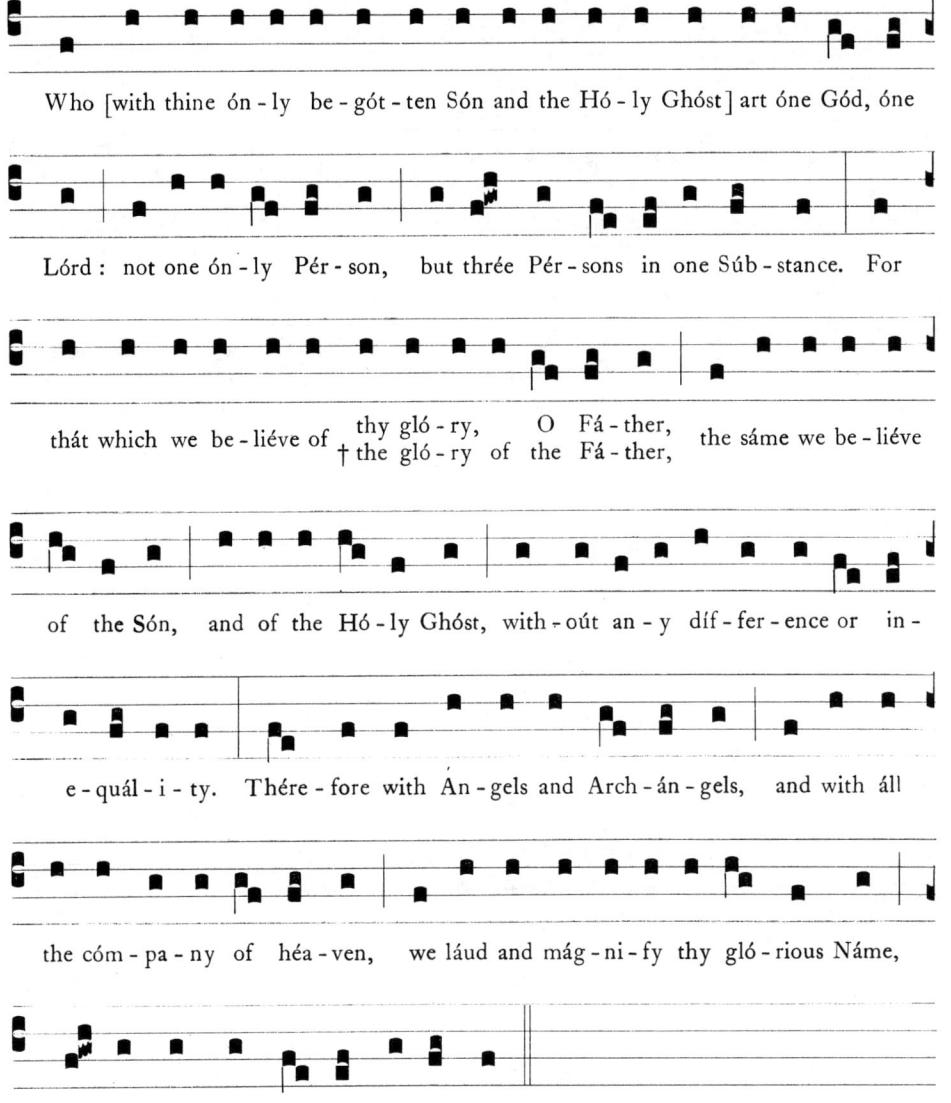

Who [with thine ón-ly be-gót-ten Són and the Hó-ly Ghóst] art óne Gód, óne Lórd: not one ón-ly Pér-son, but thrée Pér-sons in one Súb-stance. For thát which we be-liéve of thy gló-ry, O Fá-ther, the sáme we be-liéve
† the gló-ry of the Fá-ther,
of the Són, and of the Hó-ly Ghóst, with-oút an-y díf-fer-ence or in-e-quál-i-ty. Thére-fore with Án-gels and Arch-án-gels, and with áll the cóm-pa-ny of héa-ven, we láud and mág-ni-fy thy gló-rious Náme, év-er-more praís-ing thée, and sáy-ing: Holy, holy, holy, etc.

† On Trinity Sunday only these words are sung.

PREFACE OF THE MOST HOLY TRINITY *

Solemn Preface of the Most Holy Trinity

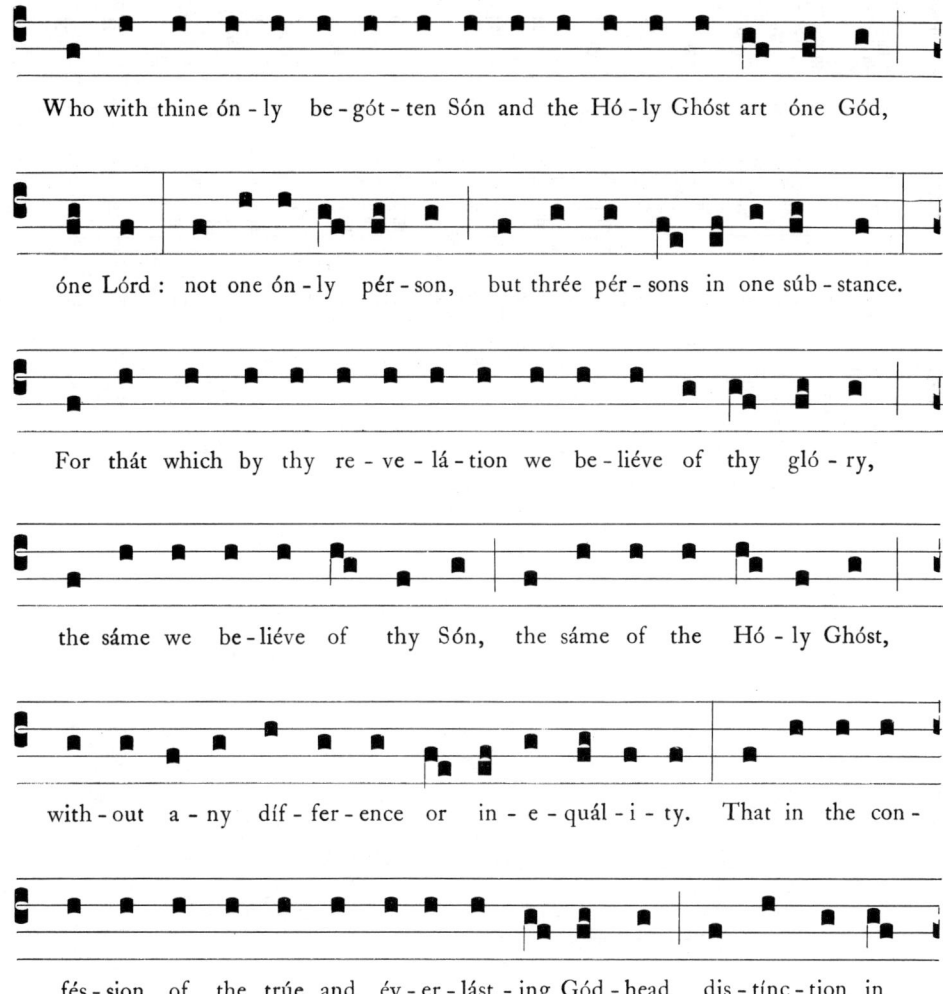

Who with thine ón-ly be-gót-ten Són and the Hó-ly Ghóst art óne Gód, óne Lórd : not one ón-ly pér-son, but thrée pér-sons in one súb-stance. For thát which by thy re-ve-lá-tion we be-liéve of thy gló-ry, the sáme we be-liéve of thy Són, the sáme of the Hó-ly Ghóst, with-out a-ny díf-fer-ence or in-e-quál-i-ty. That in the con-fés-sion of the trúe and év-er-lást-ing Gód-head dis-tínc-tion in Pér-sons, ú-ni-ty in és-sence, and e-quál-i-ty ín má-jes-ty

Solemn Preface of the Most Holy Trinity *

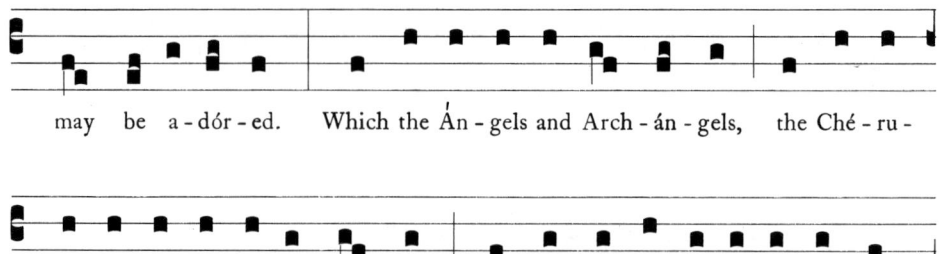
may be a-dór-ed. Which the Án-gels and Arch-án-gels, the Ché-ru-

bim al-so and Sé-ra-phim práise: who céase not dái-ly to cry out, with

one voíce, sáy-ing: Holy, holy, holy, Lord God of hosts, etc.

PREFACE OF THE BLESSED VIRGIN MARY

Either And that on the Annunciation, or Visitation, or Assumption, or Nativity, or Presentation, is said, according to the name of the Feast.

In Masses of the immaculate Conception is said: And that in the immaculate Conception.

In Masses of the Seven Sorrows is said: And that in the Transfixion.

On the Feast of Mount Carmel is said: And that in the Commemoration.

On all other Feasts is said: And that on the Festival.

In Votive Masses, in which a special Mystery has not to be expressed: And that in the Veneration.

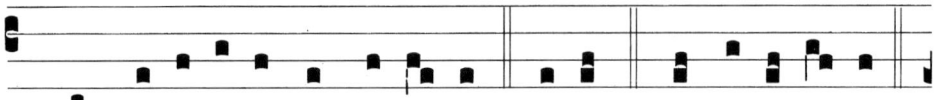

Through-oút all á-ges, wórld with-oút end. R7. A-men. V. The Lórd be with you.

R7. And with thy spí-rit. V. Líft up your heárts. R7. We líft them up

ún-to the Lórd. V. Lét us give thánks un-to our Lórd Gód. R7. It is

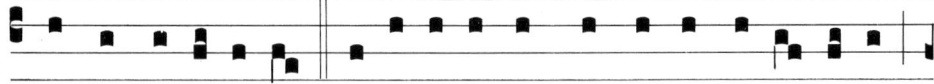

méet and right so to dó. It is vé-ry méet, right, and our boun-den dú-ty,

Solemn Preface of the Blessed Virgin Mary 297

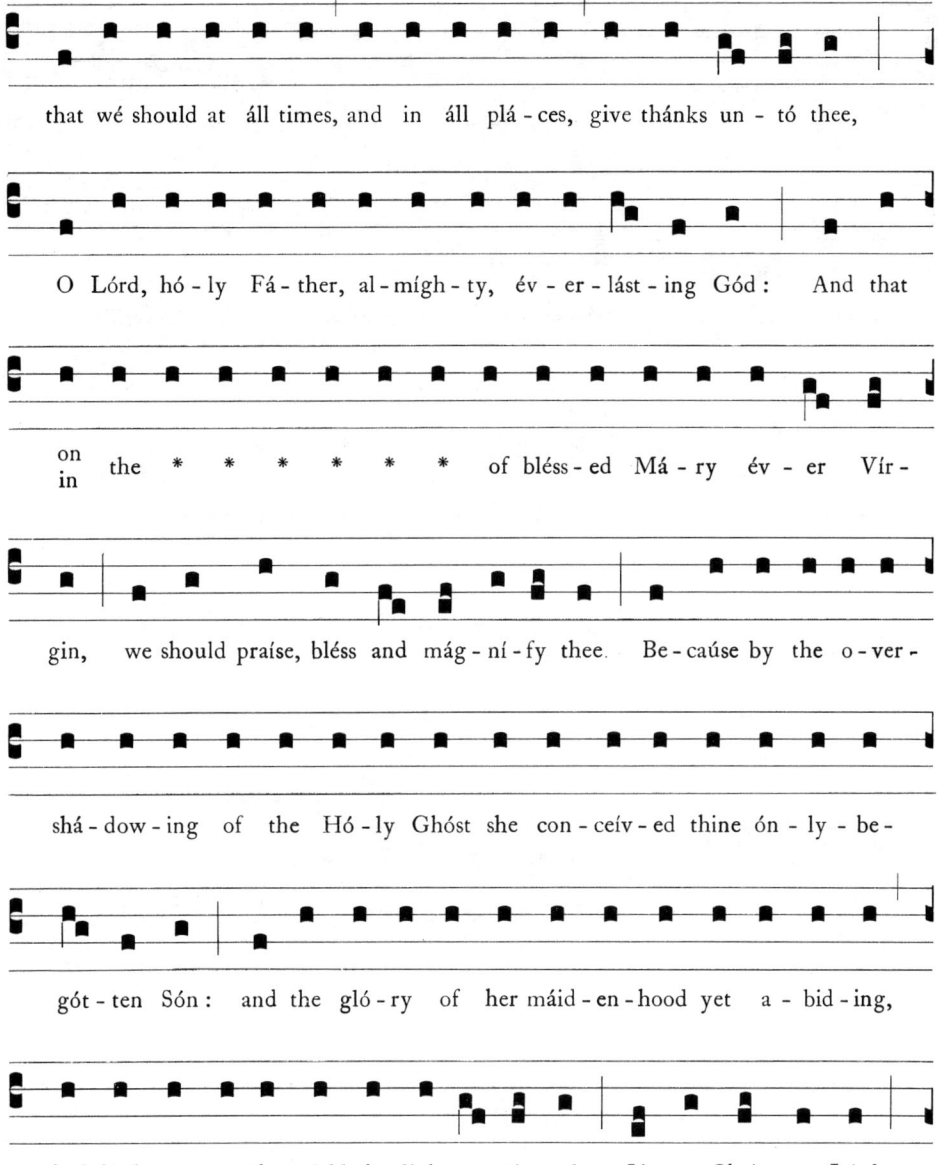

that wé should at áll times, and in áll plá - ces, give thánks un - tó thee,

O Lórd, hó - ly Fá - ther, al - mígh - ty, év - er - lást - ing Gód: And that

on the * * * * * * of bléss - ed Má - ry év - er Vír -
in

gin, we should praíse, bléss and mág - ní - fy thee. Be - caúse by the o - ver -

shá - dow - ing of the Hó - ly Ghóst she con - ceív - ed thine ón - ly - be -

gót - ten Són: and the gló - ry of her máid - en - hood yet a - bíd - ing,

shed fórth up - on the wórld the líght e - tér - nal, Jé - sus Chríst, our Lórd.

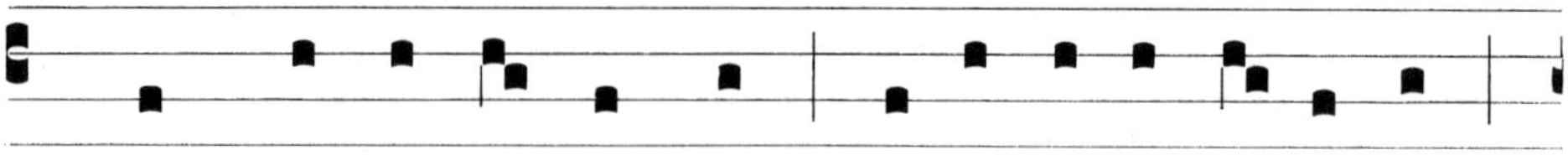

298   **Solemn Preface of the Blessed Virgin Mary**

♪ Through whóm the Án - gels praíse, the Dó - mi - ná - tions a - dóre,

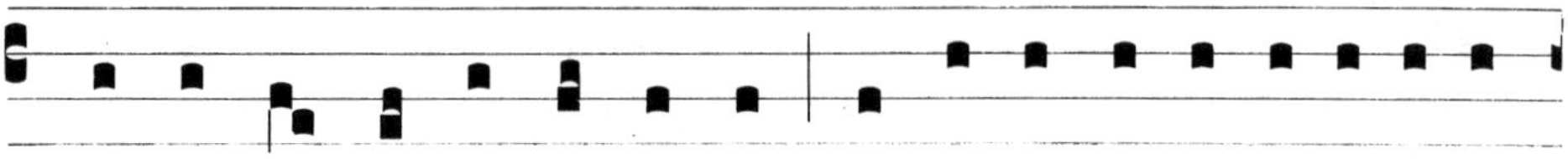

the Pów - ers féar thy má - jes - ty. The Héa-vens and the héa-ven-ly Vír-

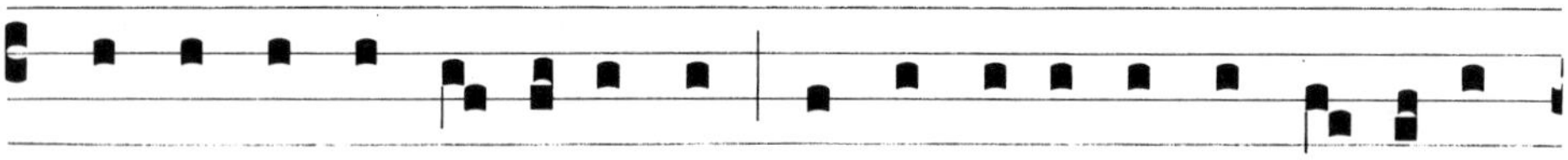

tues and the bléss - ed Sé - ra - phim to - géth - er síng thy praíse with ex - ul -

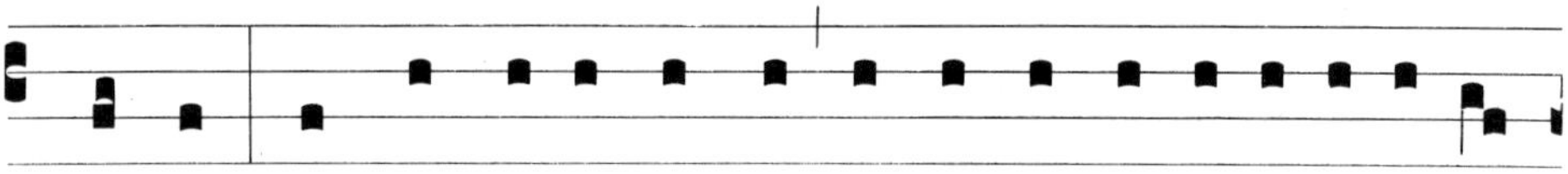

tá - tion. With whóm, we be - séech thee, bíd that our voí - ces ál - so be ad -

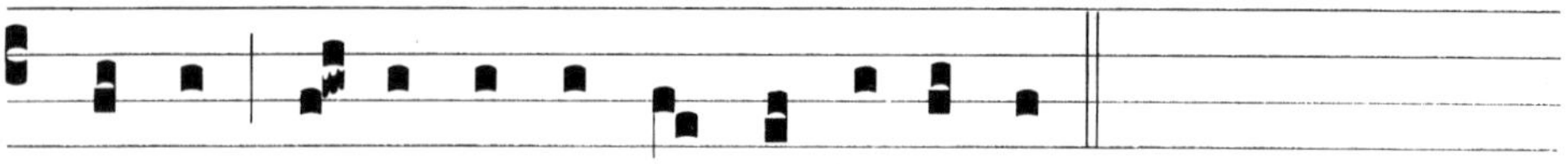

mít - ted, év - er - more praís - ing thée, and sáy - ing : Hóly, holy, holy etc.

B.C.P. Conclusion.

Thére - fore with Án - gels and Arch - án - gels, and with áll the cóm - pa - ny

Solemn Preface of the Blessed Virgin Mary

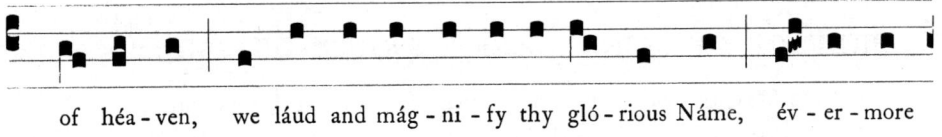

of héa-ven, we láud and mág-ni-fy thy gló-rious Náme, év-er-more

praís-ing thée, and sáy-ing : Holy, holy, holy, Lord God of hosts, etc.

PREFACE OF SAINT JOSEPH, SPOUSE OF THE B.V.M.

On May 1st (St. Joseph the Worker) is said: In the Solemnity.

In Votive Masses of St. Joseph is said: In the Veneration.

Through-oút all á-ges, wórd with-oút end. R̷. A-men. V̷. The Lórd be with you.

R̷. And with thy spí-rit. V̷. Líft up your heárts. R̷. We líft them up

ún-to the Lórd. V̷. Lét us give thánks un-to our Lórd Gód. R̷. It is

méet and ríght so to dó. It is vé-ry méet, right, and our boun-den

dú-ty, that wé should at áll times, and in áll plá-ces, give thánks un-tó

thee, O Lórd, hó-ly Fá-ther, al-mígh-ty, év-er-lást-ing Gód: And that

Solemn Preface of Saint Joseph, Spouse of the B.V.M.

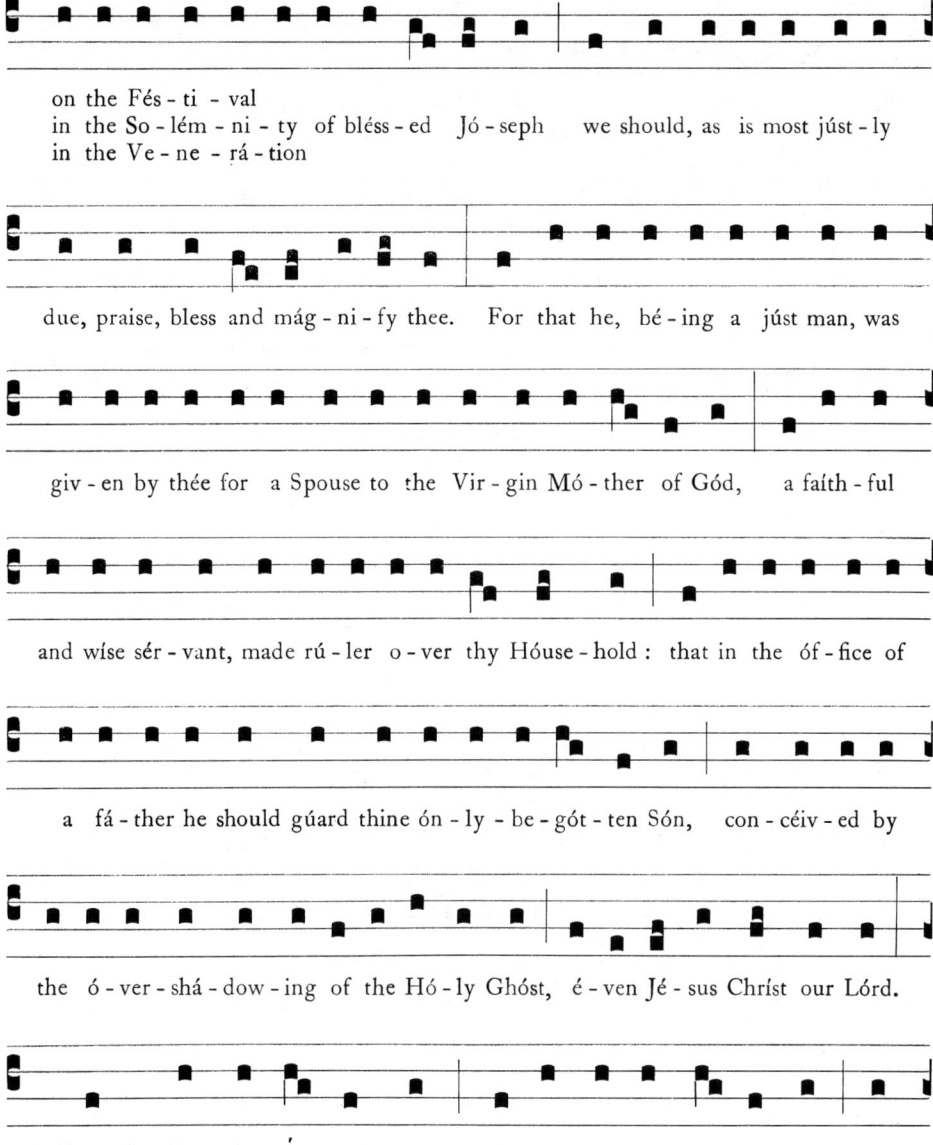

on the Fés-ti-val
in the So-lém-ni-ty of bléss-ed Jó-seph we should, as is most júst-ly
in the Ve-ne-rá-tion

due, praise, bless and mág-ni-fy thee. For that he, bé-ing a júst man, was

giv-en by thée for a Spouse to the Vir-gin Mó-ther of Gód, a faith-ful

and wíse sér-vant, made rú-ler o-ver thy Hóuse-hold: that in the óf-fice of

a fá-ther he should gúard thine ón-ly-be-gót-ten Són, con-céiv-ed by

the ó-ver-shá-dow-ing of the Hó-ly Ghóst, é-ven Jé-sus Chríst our Lórd.

†Through whóm the Án-gels praise, the Dó-mi-ná-tions a-dóre, the

Solemn Preface of Saint Joseph, Spouse of the B.V.M.

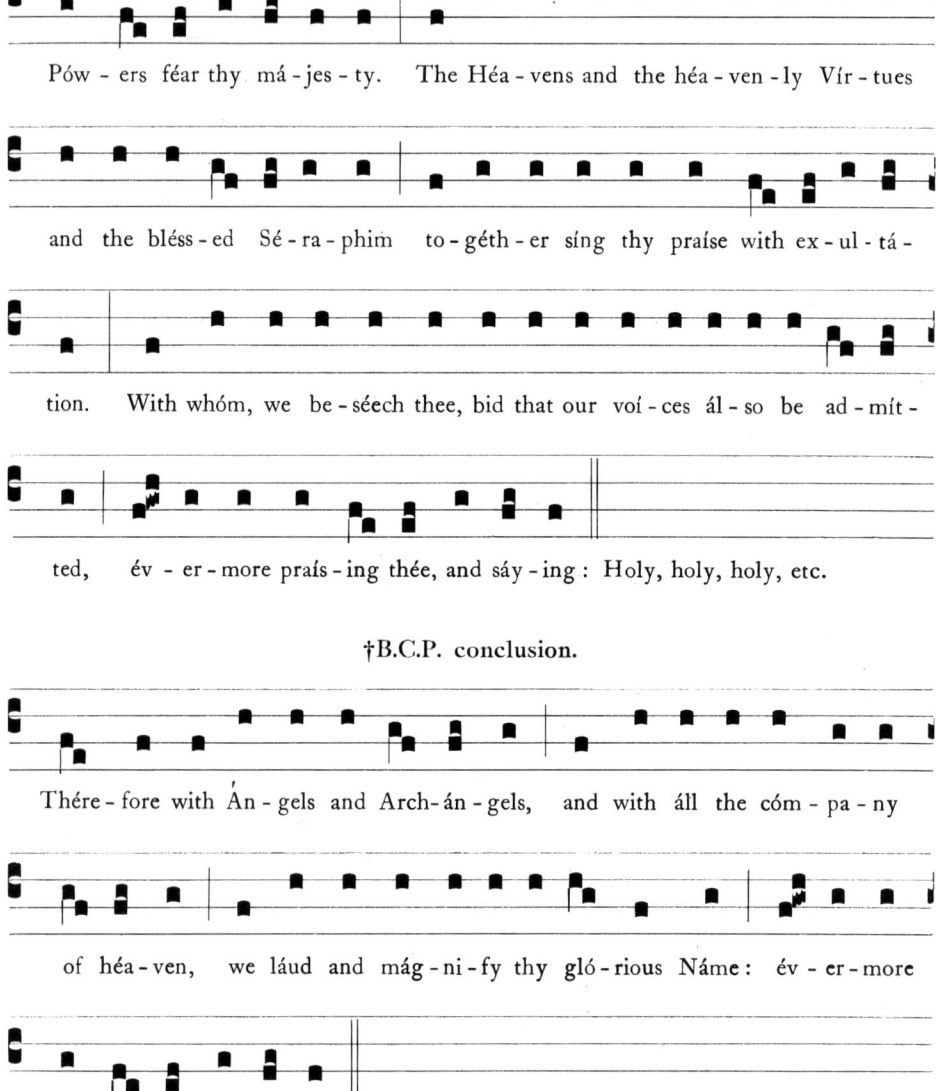

Pów-ers féar thy má-jes-ty. The Héa-vens and the héa-ven-ly Vír-tues and the bléss-ed Sé-ra-phim to-géth-er síng thy praíse with ex-ul-tá-tion. With whóm, we be-séech thee, bid that our voí-ces ál-so be ad-mít-ted, év-er-more praís-ing thée, and sáy-ing : Holy, holy, holy, etc.

†B.C.P. conclusion.

Thére-fore with Án-gels and Arch-án-gels, and with áll the cóm-pa-ny of héa-ven, we láud and mág-ni-fy thy gló-rious Náme: év-er-more praís-ing thée, and sáy-ing : Holy, holy, holy, Lord God of hosts, etc.

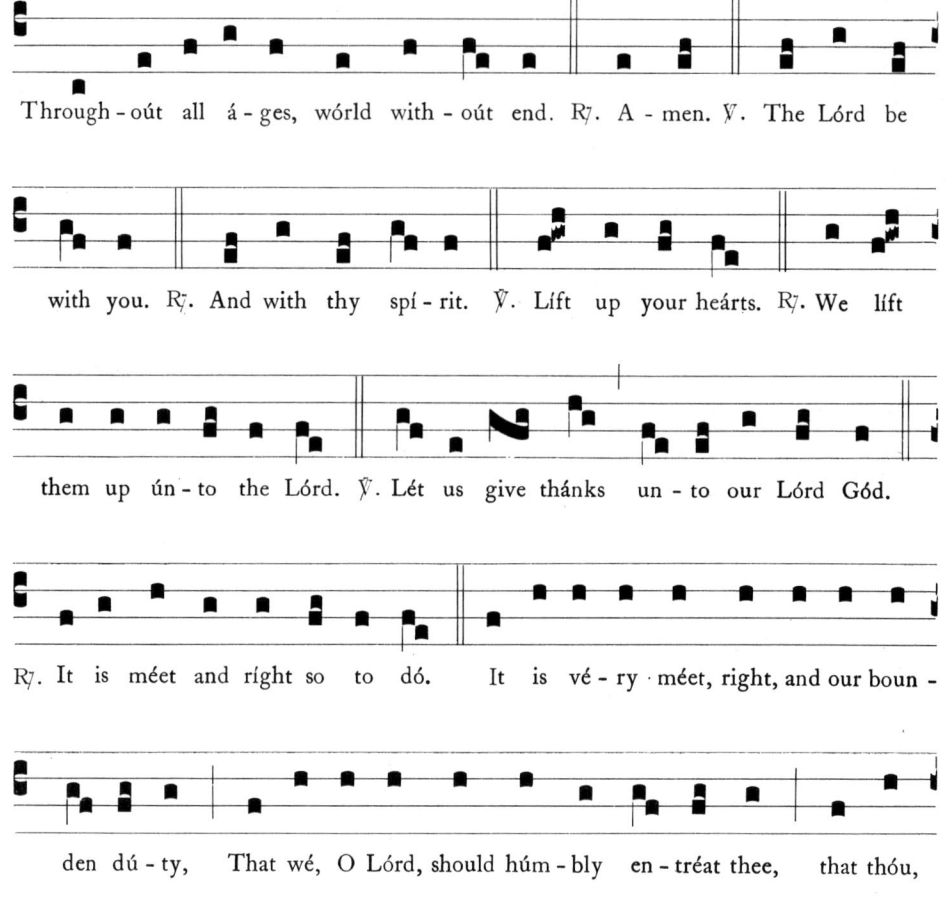

Solemn Preface of the Apostles

Solemn Preface of the Apostles

† B.C.P. conclusion.

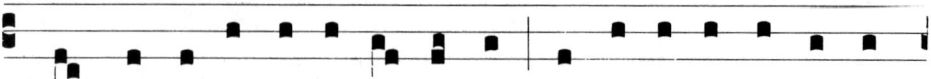
Thére-fore with Án-gels and Arch-án-gels, and with áll the cóm-pa-ny

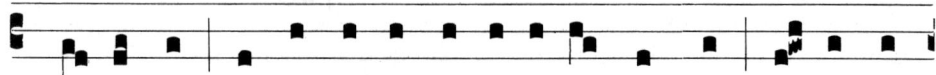
of héa-ven, we láud and mág-ni-fy thy gló-rious Náme, év-er-more

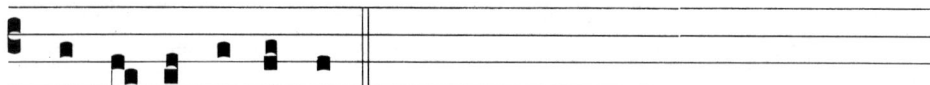
práis-ing thée, and sáy-ing : Holy, holy, holy, Lord God of hosts, etc.

COMMON PREFACE ✝

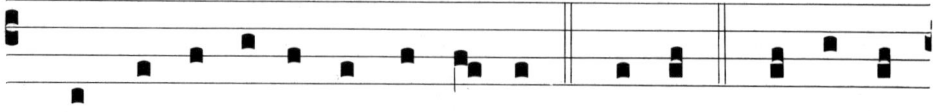
Through-out all á-ges, wórld with-oút end. ℟. A-men. ℣. The Lórd be

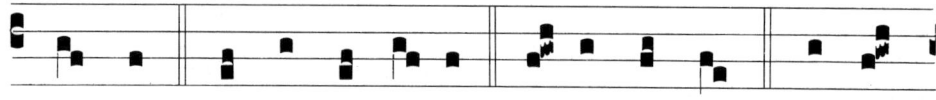
with you. ℟. And with thy spí-rit. ℣. Líft up your heárts. ℟. We lift

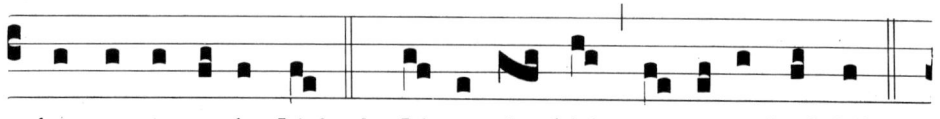
them up ún-to the Lórd. ℣. Lét us give thánks un-to our Lórd Gód.

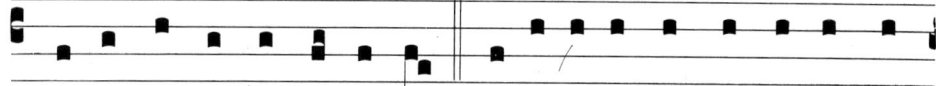
℟. It is méet and ríght so to dó. It is vé-ry méet, right, and our boun

den dú-ty, that wé should at áll times, and in áll plá-ces, give thánks un-

tó thee, O Lórd, hó-ly Fá-ther, al-mígh-ty, év-er-lást-ing Gód:

Solemn Common Preface ✝

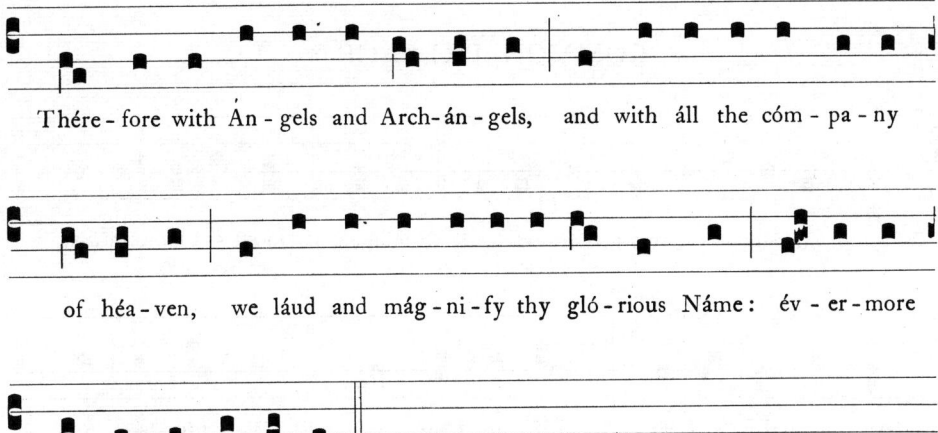

Thére-fore with Án-gels and Arch-án-gels, and with áll the cóm-pa-ny of héa-ven, we láud and mág-ni-fy thy gló-rious Náme: év-er-more práis-ing thée, and sáy-ing: Holy, holy, holy, Lord God of hosts, etc.

COMMON PREFACE *

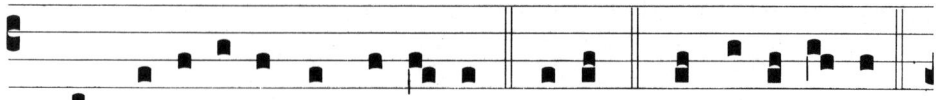

Through-oút all á-ges, wórld with-oút end. ℟. A-men. ℣. The Lórd be with you.

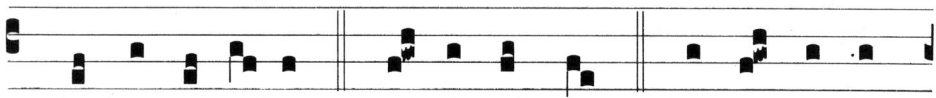

℟. And with thy spí-rit. ℣. Líft up your heárts. ℟. We líft them up

ún-to the Lórd. ℣. Lét us give thánks un-to our Lórd Gód. ℟. It is

méet and ríght so to dó. It is vé-ry méet, right, and our boun-den dú-ty,

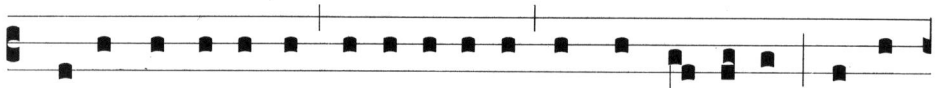

that wé should at áll times, and in áll plá-ces, give thánks un-tó thee, O Lórd,

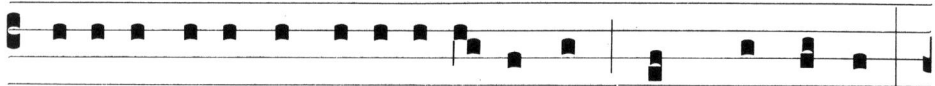

hó-ly Fá-ther, al-mígh-ty, év-er-lást-ing Gód : Through Chríst, our Lórd.

Solemn Common Preface

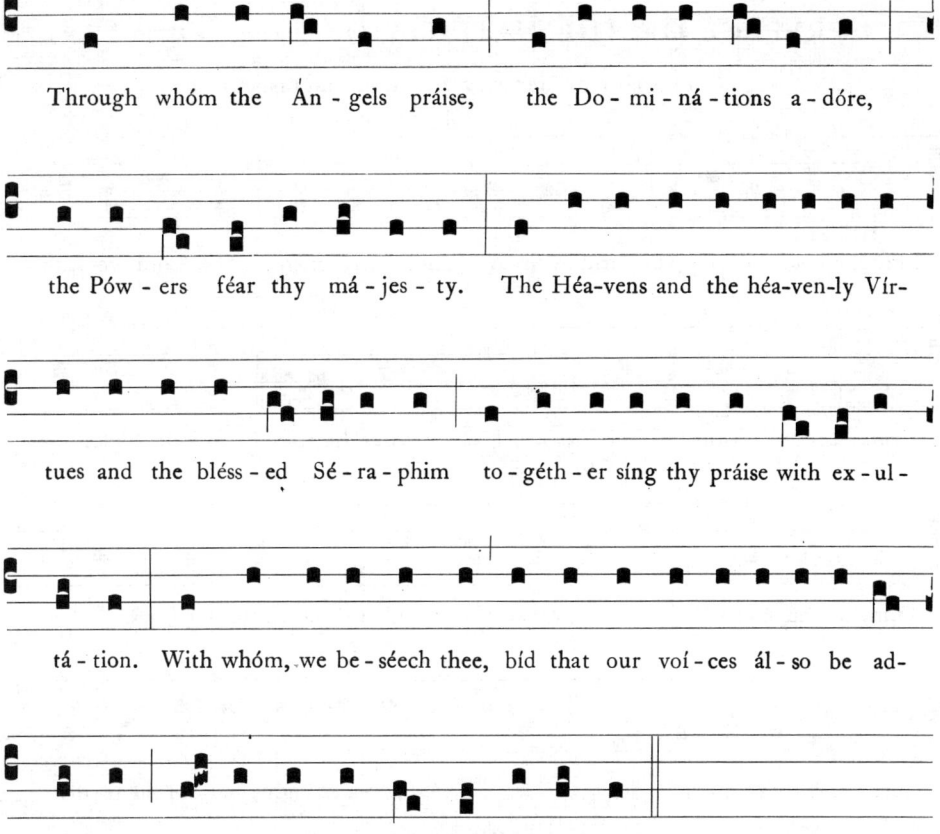

Through whóm the Án - gels práise, the Do - mi - ná - tions a - dóre, the Pów - ers féar thy má - jes - ty. The Héa-vens and the héa-ven-ly Vír-tues and the bléss - ed Sé - ra - phim to - géth - er síng thy práise with ex - ul - tá - tion. With whóm, we be - séech thee, bíd that our voí - ces ál - so be ad - mít - ted, év - er - more práis - ing thée, and sáy - ing : Holy, holy, holy etc.

Ferial Preface of the Nativity of the Lord *

PREFACE OF THE NATIVITY OF THE LORD *
(on Ferias from January 2nd to 5th inclusive.)

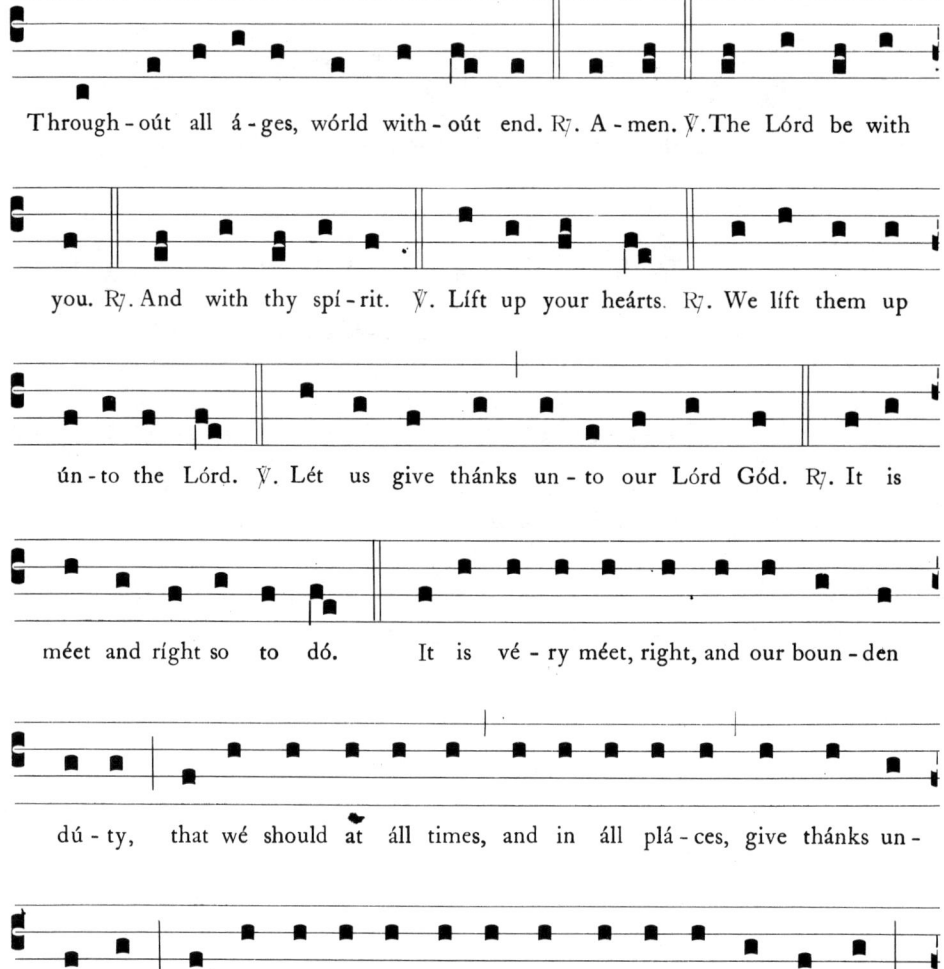

Ferial Preface of the Nativity of the Lord

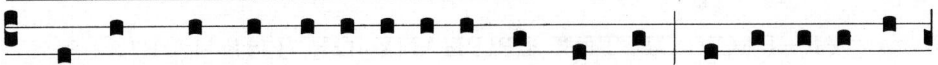
Be-cáuse through the mýs-te-ry of the Wórd made flésh the líght of thy gló-

ry hath shóne a-néw up-ón the éyes of our mínd: that as we ac-knów-ledge God

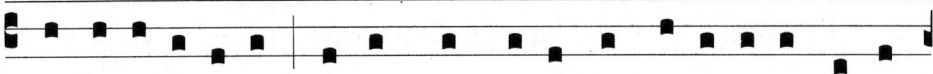
made vís-i-ble to mán. we may through hím be cáught up to lóve of thíngs in-

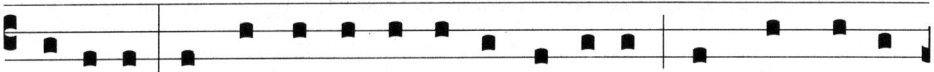
vís-i-ble. And thére-fore with An-gels and Arch-án-gels, with Thrónes and Do-

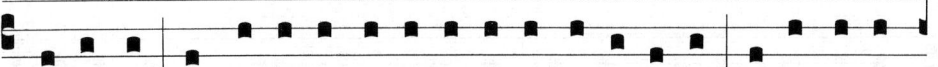
mi-ná-tions, and with áll the cóm-pa-ny of the héa-ven-ly hóst, we síng the má-

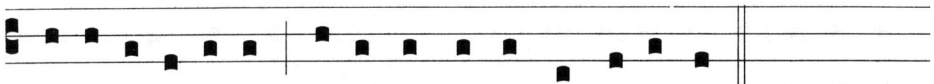
jes-ty of thy gló-ry, év-er-more práis-ing thée, and sáy-ing : Holy, holy, etc.

PREFACE OF THE EPIPHANY OF THE LORD

(on Ferias from January 7th to 12th inclusive.)

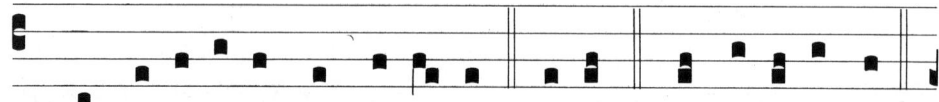

Through-oút all á-ges, wórld with-oút end. R̷. A-men. V̷. The Lórd be with you

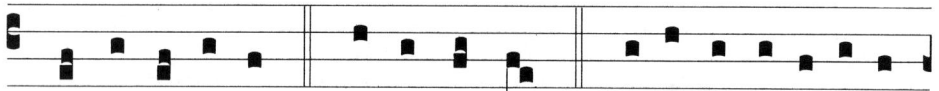

R̷. And with thy spí-rit. V̷. Líft up your heárts. R̷. We líft them up ún-to the

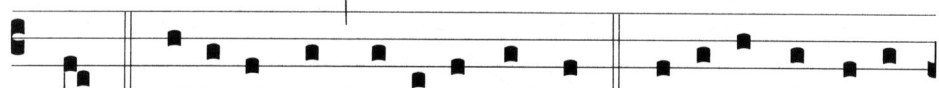

Lórd. V̷. Lét us give thánks un-to our Lórd Gód. R̷. It is méet and ríght so

to dó. It is vé-ry méet, right, and our boun-den dú-ty, that wé should

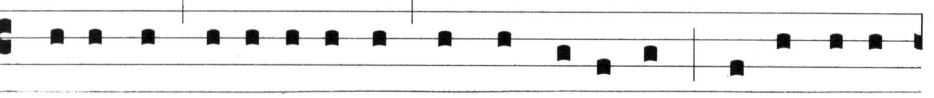

at áll times, and in áll pla-ces, give thánks un-tó thee: O Lórd, hó-ly

Fá-ther, al-mígh-ty, év-er-lást-ing Gód: Be-cáuse that, whén thine ón-ly-

Ferial Preface of the Epiphany of the Lord 315

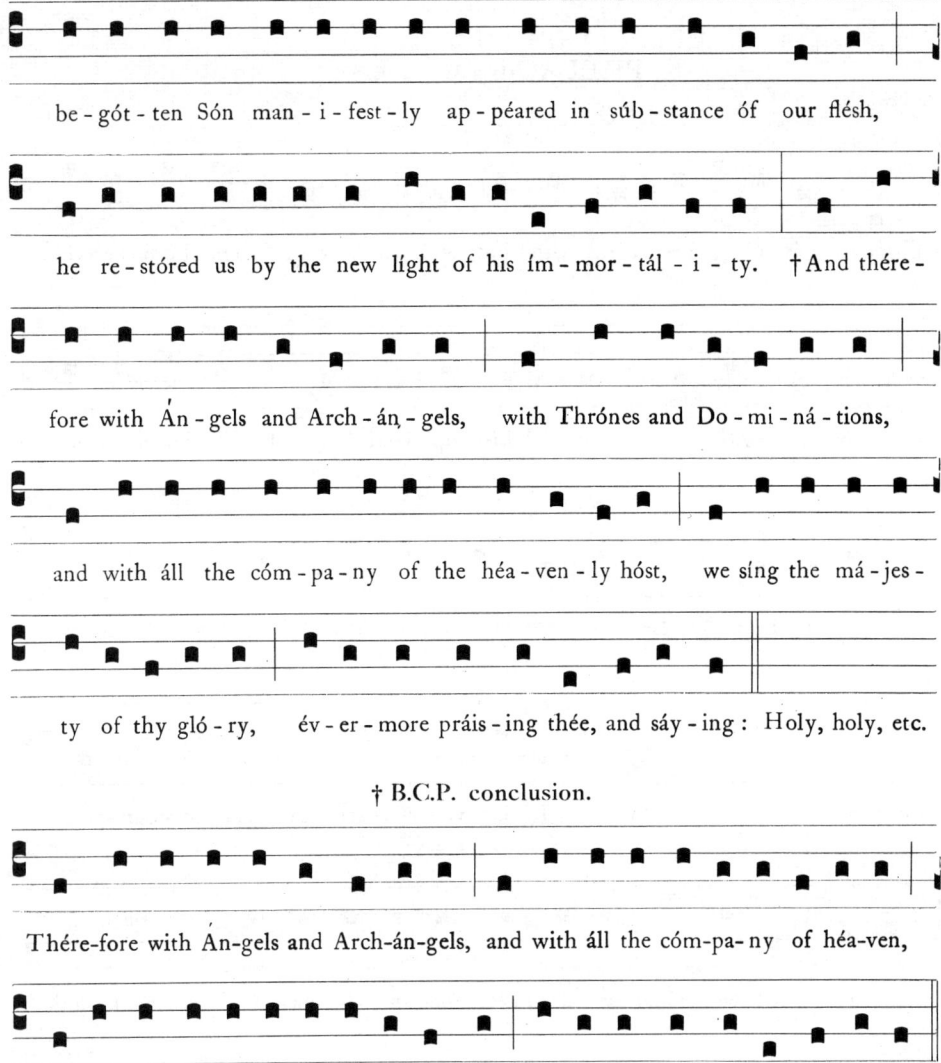

be-gót-ten Són man-i-fest-ly ap-péared in súb-stance óf our flésh, he re-stóred us by the new líght of his ím-mor-tál-i-ty. †And thére-fore with Án-gels and Arch-án-gels, with Thrónes and Do-mi-ná-tions, and with áll the cóm-pa-ny of the héa-ven-ly hóst, we síng the má-jes-ty of thy gló-ry, év-er-more práis-ing thée, and sáy-ing: Holy, holy, etc.

† B.C.P. conclusion.

Thére-fore with Án-gels and Arch-án-gels, and with áll the cóm-pa-ny of héa-ven, we láud and mág-ni-fy thy gló-ri-ous Náme, év-er-more práis-ing thée, and sáy-ing: Holy, holy, holy, Lord God of hosts, etc.

This Preface is said on Ferias from January 7th to 12th inclusive in Masses of the Epiphany.

PREFACE OF LENT

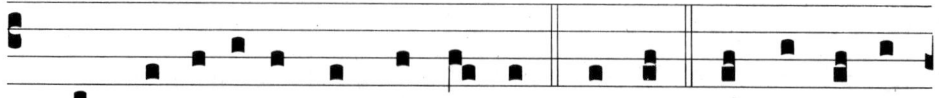
Through-oút all á-ges, wórld with-oút end. ℟. A-men. ℣.The Lórd be with

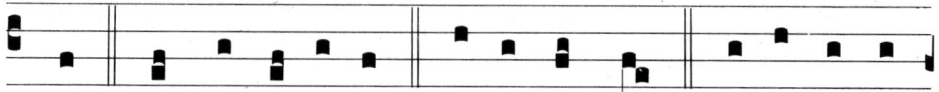
you ℟. And with thy spí-rit. ℣. Líft up your heárts. ℟. We líft them up

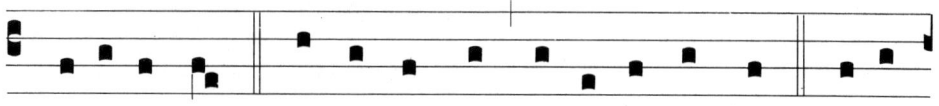
ún-to the Lórd. ℣. Lét us give thánks un-tó our Lórd Gód. ℟. It is

méet and ríght so to dó. It is vé-ry méet, ríght, and our boun-den

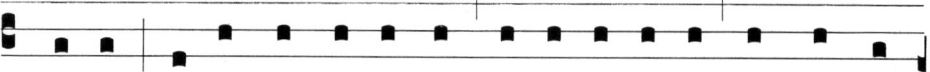
dú-ty, that wé should at áll times, and in áll plá-ces, give thánks un-

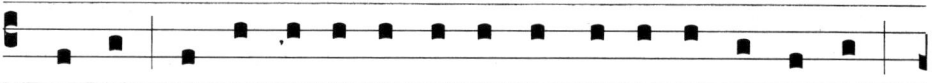
tó thee, O Lórd, hó-ly Fá-ther, al-mígh-ty, év-er-lást-ing Gód:

Ferial Preface of Lent

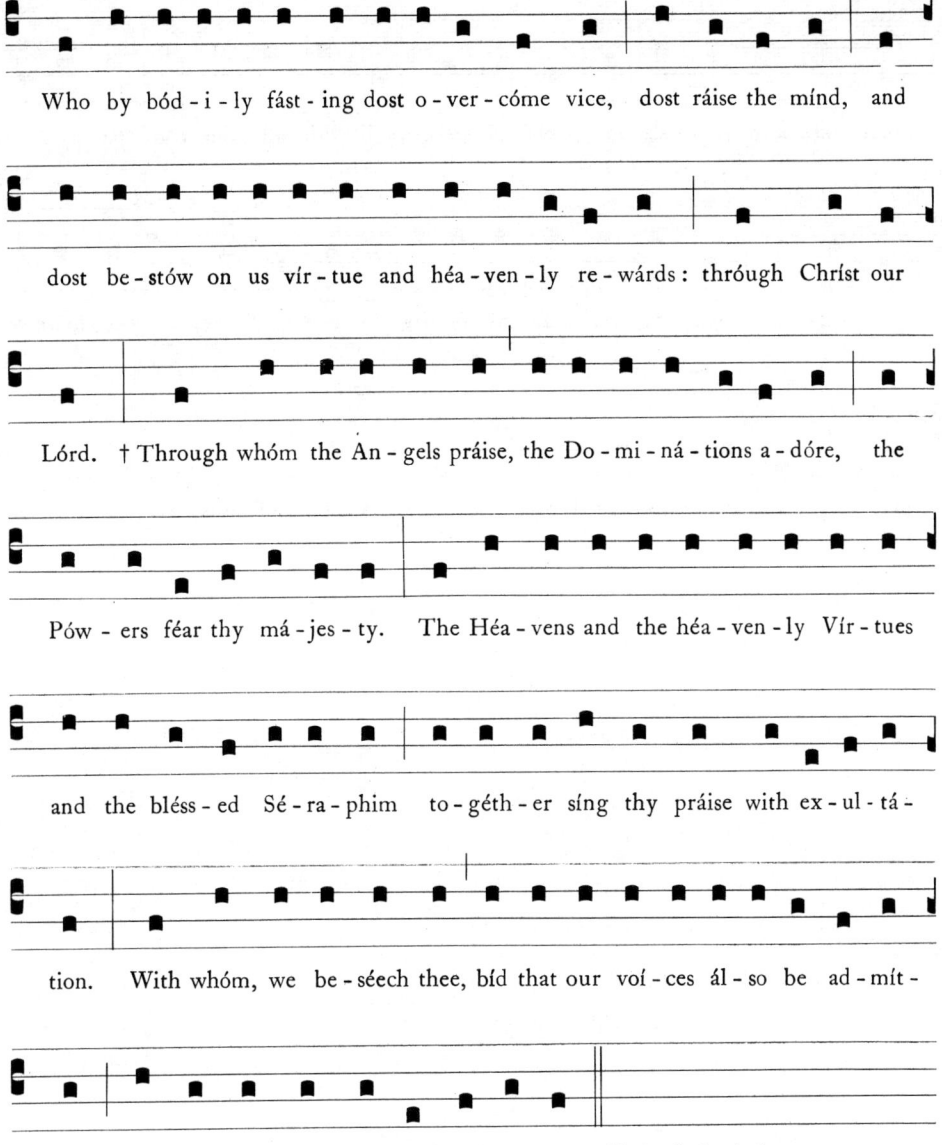

Who by bód-i-ly fást-ing dost o-ver-cóme vice, dost ráise the mínd, and dost be-stów on us vír-tue and héa-ven-ly re-wárds: thróugh Chríst our Lórd. † Through whóm the Án-gels práise, the Do-mi-ná-tions a-dóre, the Pów-ers féar thy má-jes-ty. The Héa-vens and the héa-ven-ly Vír-tues and the bléss-ed Sé-ra-phim to-géth-er síng thy práise with ex-ul-tá-tion. With whóm, we be-séech thee, bíd that our voí-ces ál-so be ad-mít-ted, év-er-more práis-ing thée, and sáy-ing: Holy, holy, holy, etc.

Ferial Preface of Lent 318

† B.C.P. conclusion.

Thére-fore with Án-gels and Arch-án-gels, and with áll the cóm-pa-ny

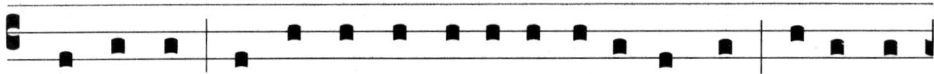

of héa-ven, we láud and mág-ni-fy thy gló-ri-ous Náme, év-er-more

práis-ing thée, and sáy-ing : Holy, holy, holy, Lord God of hosts, etc.

PREFACE OF THE HOLY CROSS

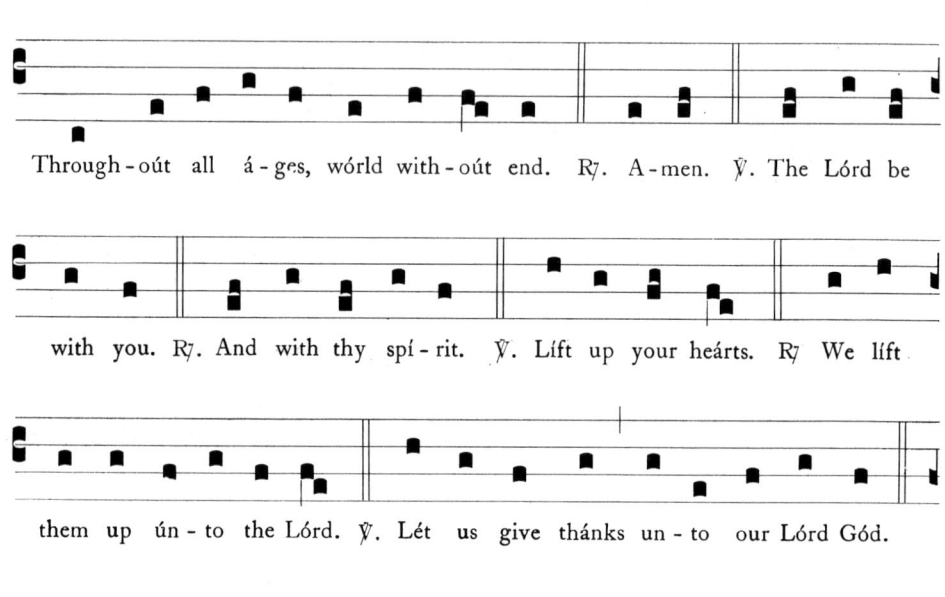

Through-out all á-ges, wórld with-oút end. ℟. A-men. ℣. The Lórd be with you. ℟. And with thy spí-rit. ℣. Líft up your heárts. ℟ We líft them up ún-to the Lórd. ℣. Lét us give thánks un-to our Lórd Gód.

℟. It is méet and ríght so to dó. It is vé-ry méet, right, and our boun-

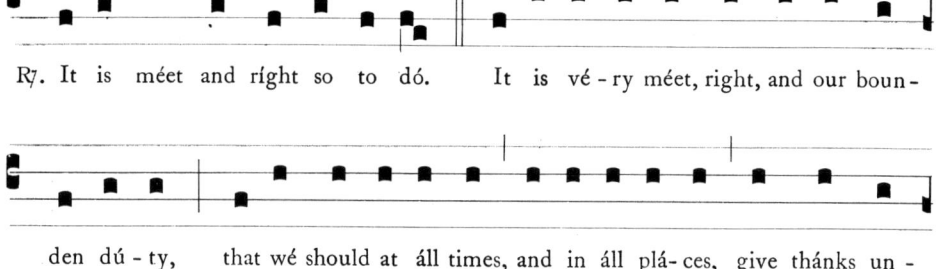

den dú-ty, that wé should at áll times, and in áll plá-ces, give thánks un-

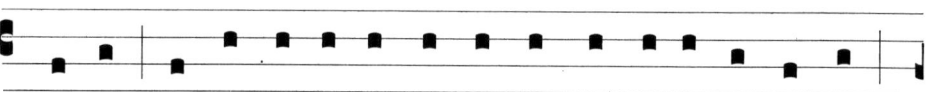

tó thee, O Lórd, hó-ly Fá-ther, al-mígh-ty, év-er-lást-ing Gód:

Ferial Preface of the Holy Cross

Who by the trée of the Cróss didst gíve sal-vá-tion un-to man-kínd: that whénce

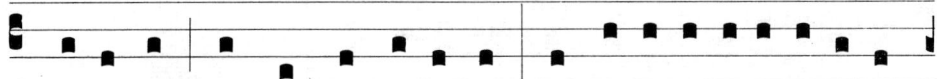
death a-róse, thence lífe might ríse a-gáin: and that hé who by a trée o-ver-

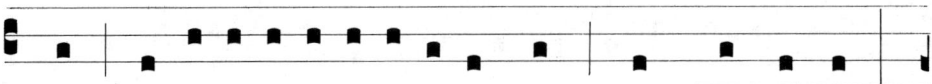
cáme might ál-so by a trée be ó-ver-cóme: through Chríst, our Lórd.

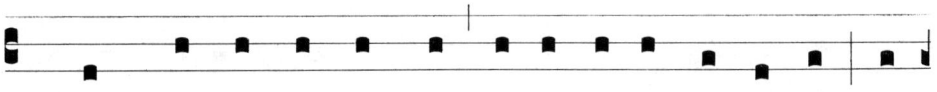
† Through whóm the Án-gels práise, the Do-mi-ná-tions a-dóre, the

Pów-ers féar thy má-jes-ty. The Héa-vens and the héa-ven-ly Vír-

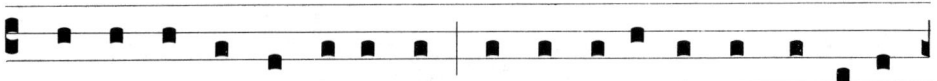
tues and the bléss-ed Sé-ra-phim to-géth-er síng thy práise with ex-ul-

Ferial Preface of the Holy Cross

tá - tion. With whóm, we be - séech thee, bíd that our voí - ces ál - so be ad-

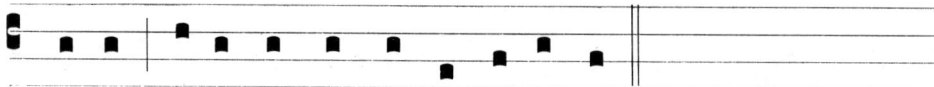
mít - ted, év - er - more práis - ing thée, and sáy - ing : Holy, holy, holy etc.

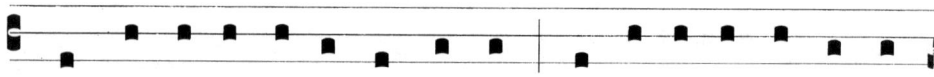
Thére - fore with Án - gels and Arch - án - gels, and with áll the cóm - pa - ny

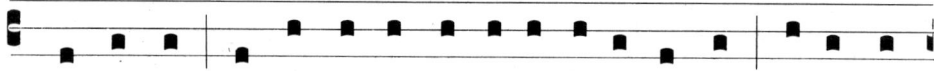
of héa - ven, we láud and mág - ni - fy thy gló - ri - ous Náme, év - er - more

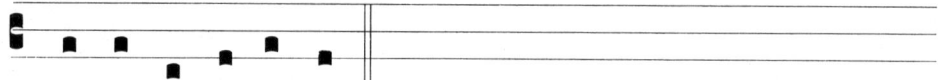
práis - ing thée, and sáy - ing : Holy, holy, holy, Lord God of hosts, etc.

PREFACE OF EASTER ✝

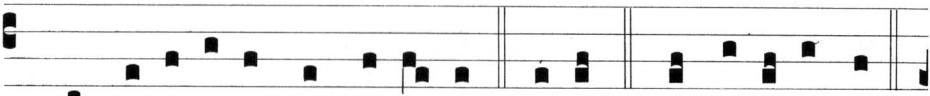
Through-out all á-ges, wórld with-oút end. ℟. A-men. ℣. The Lórd be with you.

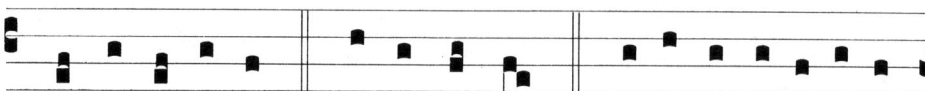
℟. And with thy spí-rit. ℣. Líft up your heárts. ℟. We líft them up ún-to the

Lórd. ℣. Lét us give thánks un-to our Lórd Gód. ℟. It is méet and ríght so

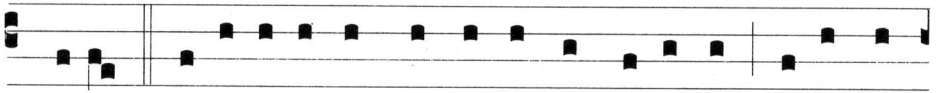
to dó. It is vé-ry méet, right, and our boun-den dú-ty, that wé should

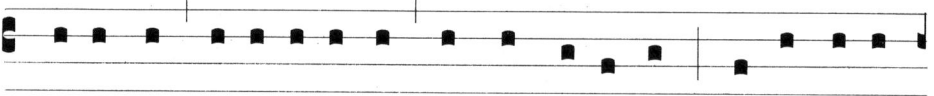
at áll times, and in áll plá-ces, give thánks un-tó thee: O Lórd, hó-ly

Fá-ther, al-mígh-ty, év-er-lást-ing Gód: But chíef-ly are we boúnd to

Ferial Preface of Easter †

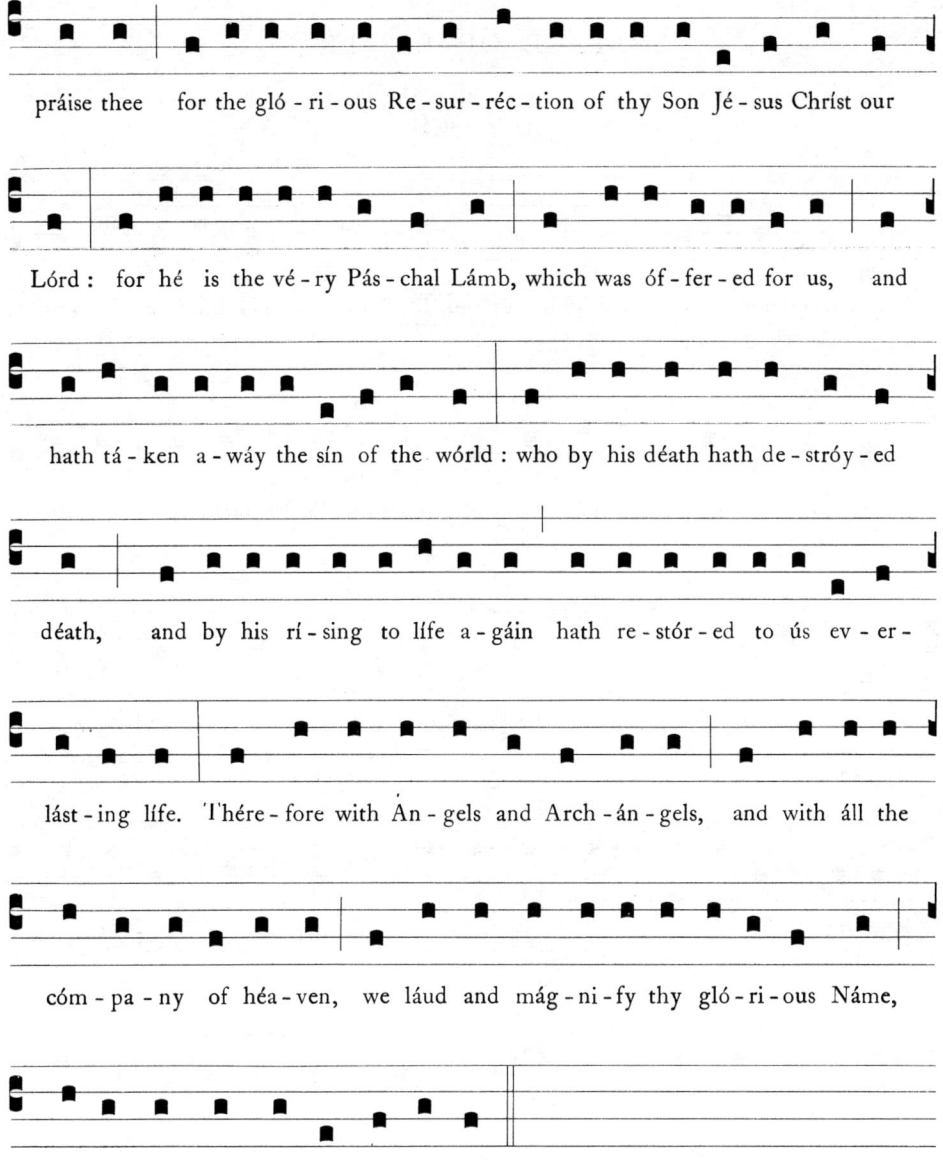

praise thee for the glo-ri-ous Re-sur-rec-tion of thy Son Je-sus Christ our Lord: for he is the ve-ry Pas-chal Lamb, which was of-fer-ed for us, and hath ta-ken a-way the sin of the world: who by his death hath de-stroy-ed death, and by his ri-sing to life a-gain hath re-stor-ed to us ev-er-last-ing life. There-fore with An-gels and Arch-an-gels, and with all the com-pa-ny of hea-ven, we laud and mag-ni-fy thy glo-ri-ous Name, ev-er-more prais-ing thee, and say-ing: Holy, holy, holy, etc.

PREFACE OF EASTER *

In the Mass of the Rogation, if it occur within the Octave of Easter is said: chiefly on this day.

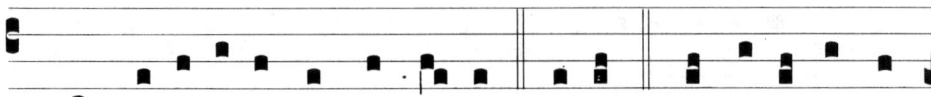
Through-oút all á-ges, wórld with-oút end. ℟. A-men. ℣. The Lórd be with you.

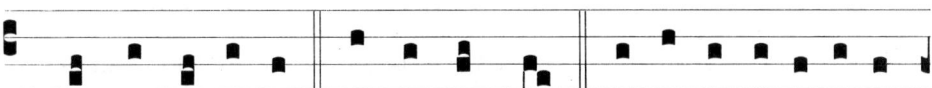
℟. And with thy spí-rit. ℣. Líft up your heárts. ℟. We líft them up ún-to the

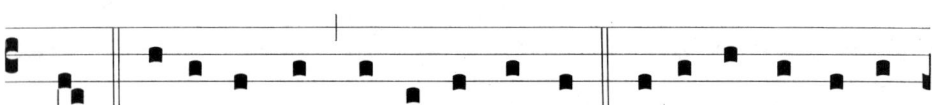
Lórd. ℣. Lét us give thánks un-to our Lórd Gód. ℟. It is méet and ríght so

to dó. It is vé-ry méet, right, and our boun-den dú-ty, that wé should

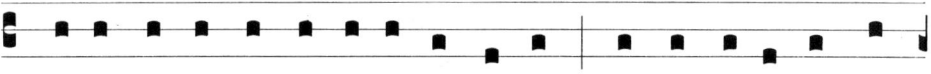
at áll times in-déed gló-ri-fy thée, O Lórd, but chíef-ly at this tíme,
                                                                      chíef-ly on this dáy,

Ferial Preface of Easter *

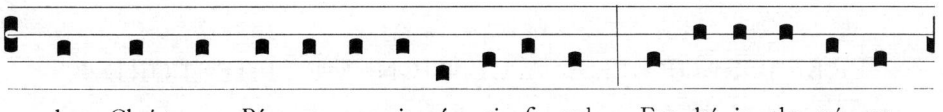
when Christ our Páss-o-ver is sác-ri-fi-ced. For hé is the vé-ry

Lámb, which hath tá-ken a-wáy the síns of the wórld. Who by his déath

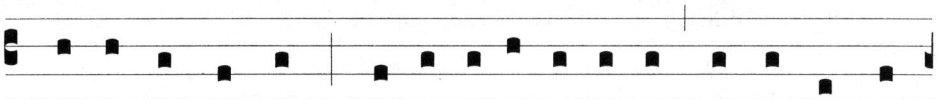
hath de-stróy-ed déath, and by his rí-sing a-gáin hath re-stóred to

us lífe. And thére-fore with Án-gels and Arch-án-gels, with Thrónes and Do-

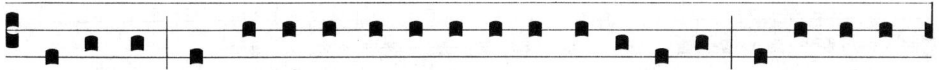
mi-ná-tions, and with áll the cóm-pa-ny of the héa-ven-ly hóst, we síng the má-

jes-ty of thy gló-ry, év-er-more práis-ing thée, and sáy-ing : Holy, holy, etc.

PREFACE OF THE ASCENSION OF THE LORD †

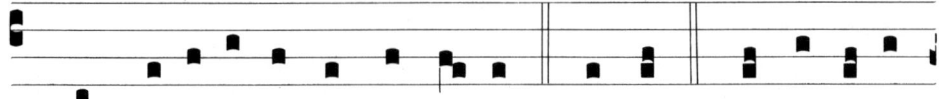
Through-oút all á-ges, wórld with-oút end. R̃. A-men. V̄. The Lórd be with

you. R̃. And with thy spí-rit. V̄. Líft up your heárts. R̃. We líft them up ún-

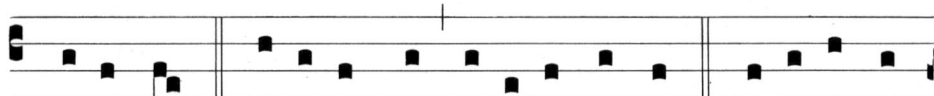
to the Lórd. V̄. Lét us give thánks un-to our Lórd Gód. R̃. It is méet and

ríght so to dó. It is vé-ry méet, right, and our boun-den dú-ty,

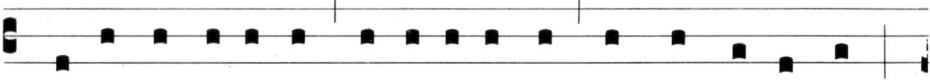
that wé should at áll times, and in áll plá-ces, give thánks un-tó thee,

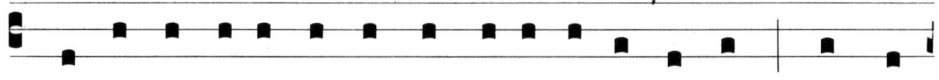
O Lórd, hó-ly Fá-ther, al-mígh-ty, év-er-lást-ing Gód: Through thy

Ferial Preface of the Ascension of the Lord †

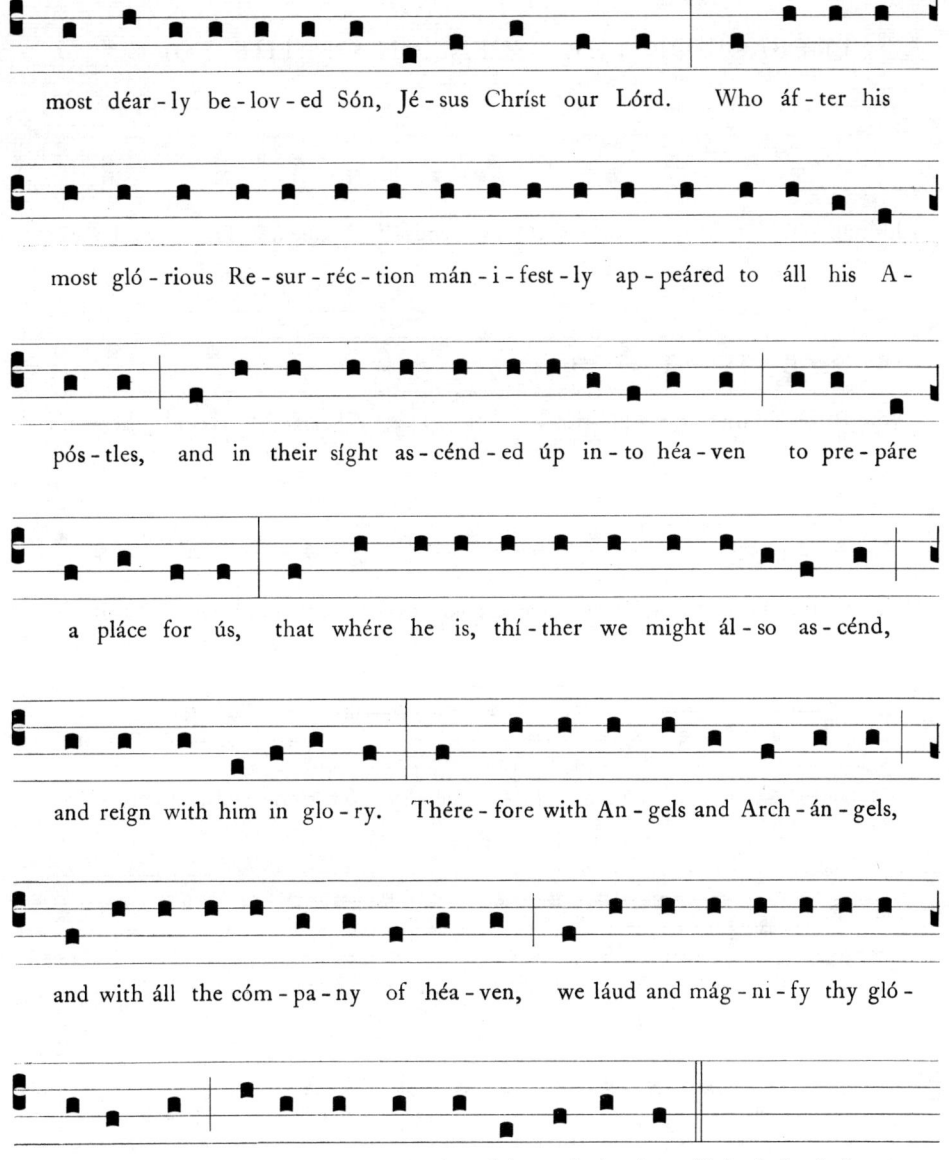

most dear-ly be-lov-ed Són, Jé-sus Christ our Lórd. Who áf-ter his most gló-rious Re-sur-réc-tion mán-i-fest-ly ap-peáred to áll his A-pós-tles, and in their síght as-cénd-ed úp in-to héa-ven to pre-páre a pláce for ús, that whére he is, thí-ther we might ál-so as-cénd, and reígn with him in glo-ry. Thére-fore with An-gels and Arch-án-gels, and with áll the cóm-pa-ny of héa-ven, we láud and mág-ni-fy thy gló-ri-ous Náme, év-er-more práis-ing thée, and sáy-ing: Holy, holy, holy, etc.

Ferial Preface of the Ascension of the Lord *

PREFACE OF THE ASCENSION OF THE LORD *

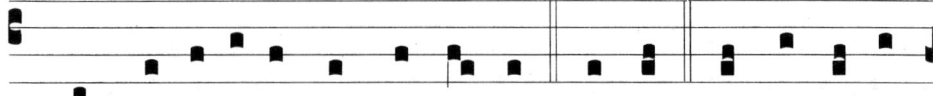
Through-oút all á-ges, wórld with-oút end. R̷. A-men. V̷. The Lórd be with

you. R̷. And with thy spí-rit. V̷. Líft up your heárts. R̷. We líft them up

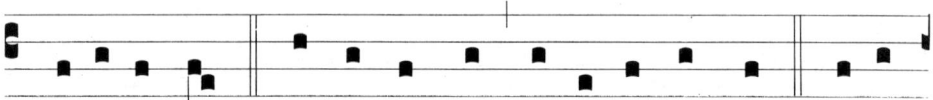
ún-to the Lórd. V̷. Lét us give thánks un-to our Lórd Gód. R̷. It is

méet and ríght so to dó. It is vé-ry méet, ríght, and our boun-den

dú-ty, that wé should at áll times, and in áll plá-ces, give thánks un-

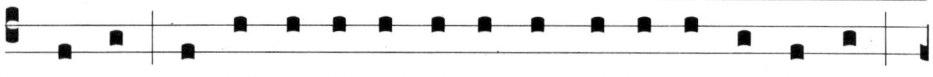
tó thee, O Lórd, hó-ly Fá-ther, al-mígh-ty, év-er-lást-ing Gód:

Ferial Preface of the Ascension of the Lord *

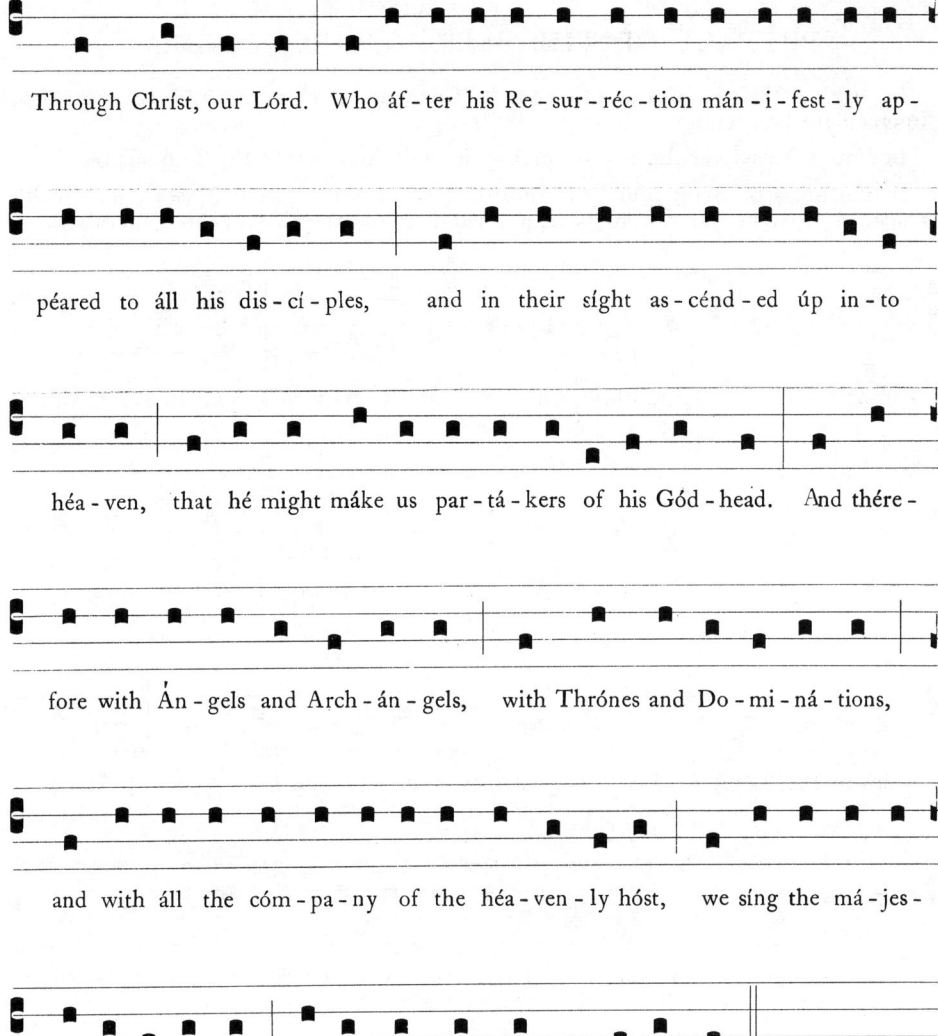

Through Christ, our Lórd. Who áf-ter his Re-sur-réc-tion mán-i-fest-ly ap-peared to áll his dis-cí-ples, and in their síght as-cénd-ed úp in-to héa-ven, that hé might máke us par-tá-kers of his Gód-head. And thére-fore with Án-gels and Arch-án-gels, with Thrónes and Do-mi-ná-tions, and with áll the cóm-pa-ny of the héa-ven-ly hóst, we síng the má-jes-ty of thy gló-ry, év-er-more práis-ing thée, and sáy-ing: Holy, holy, etc.

And it is said until the Vigil of Pentecost exclusive in all Masses of simple and ferial rite.

PREFACE OF THE BLESSED VIRGIN MARY

In Votive Masses of the Immaculate Conception is said: And that in the Immaculate Conception.

In Votive Masses of the Seven Sorrows is said: And that in the Transfixion.

In the Mass of Saint Mary on Saturday, as also in Votive Masses, in which a special Mystery has not to be expressed, is said: And that in the Veneration.

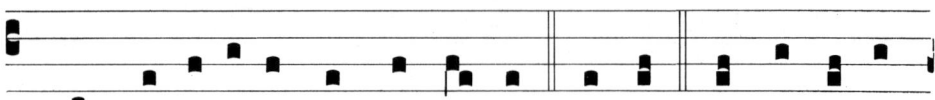
Through-oút all á-ges, wórld with-oút end. ℟. A-men. ℣. The Lórd be with

you. ℟. And with thy spí-rit. ℣. Líft up your heárts. ℟. We líft them up

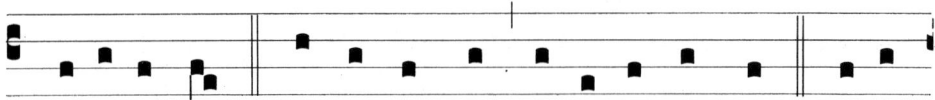
ún-to the Lórd. ℣. Lét us give thánks un-to our Lórd Gód. ℟. It is

méet and ríght so to dó. It is vé-ry méet, right, and our boun-den

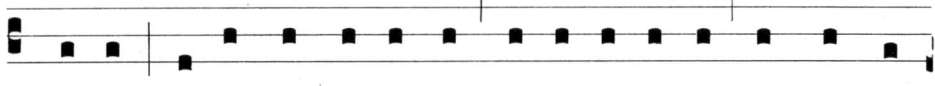
dú-ty, that wé should at áll times, and in áli plá-ces, give thánks un-

Ferial Preface of the Blessed Virgin Mary 333

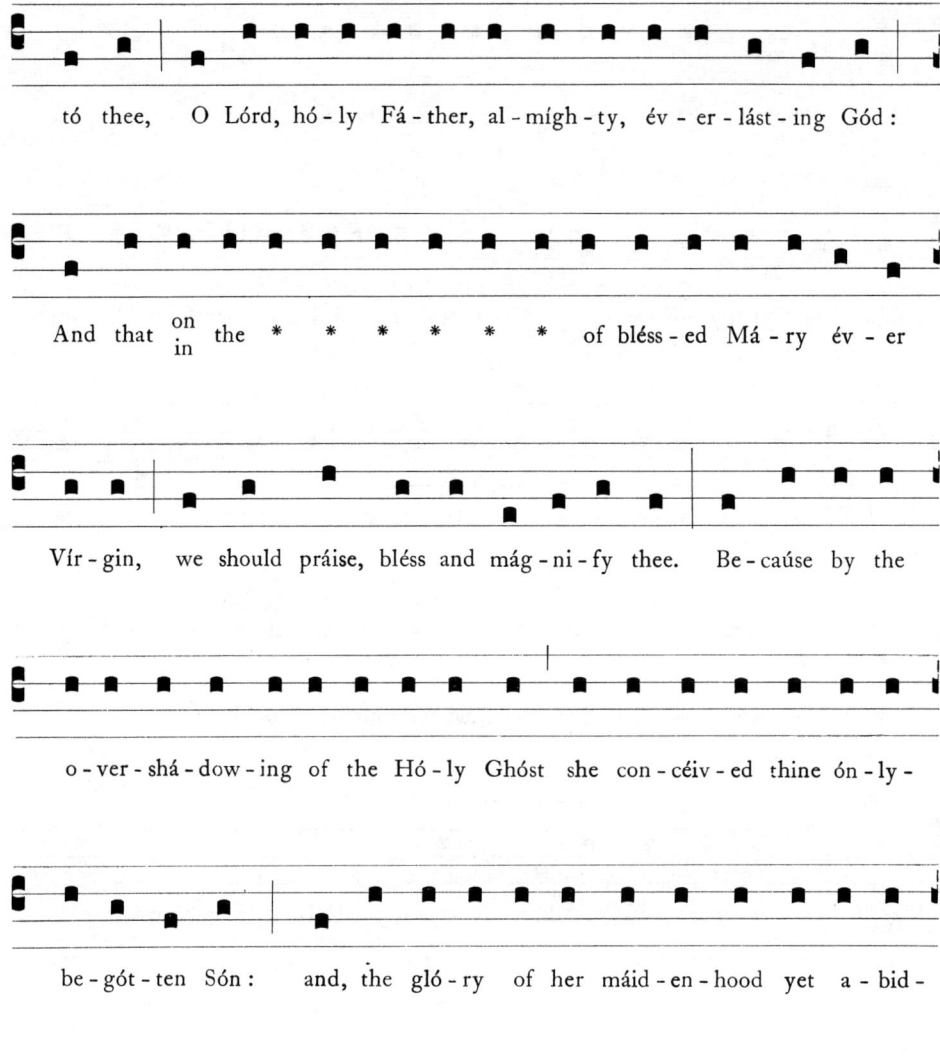

tó thee, O Lórd, hó-ly Fá-ther, al-mígh-ty, év-er-lást-ing Gód:

And that on/in the * * * * * * of bléss-ed Má-ry év-er

Vír-gin, we should práise, bléss and mág-ni-fy thee. Be-caúse by the

o-ver-shá-dow-ing of the Hó-ly Ghóst she con-céiv-ed thine ón-ly-

be-gót-ten Són: and, the gló-ry of her máid-en-hood yet a-bid-

ing, shed fórth up-on the wórld the líght e-tér-nal, Jé-sus Chríst our

Ferial Preface of the Blessed Virgin Mary

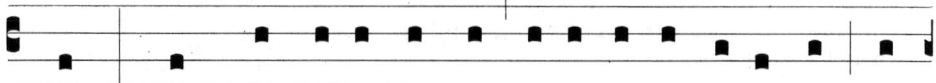
Lórd. † Through whóm the Án - gels práise, the Do - mi - ná - tions a - dóre, the

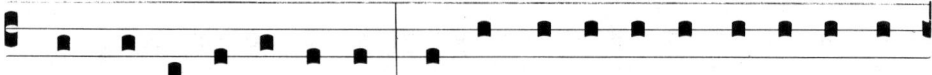
Pów - ers féar thy má - jes - ty. The Héa - vens and the héa - ven - ly Vír - tues

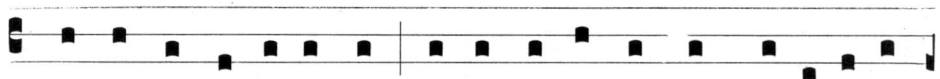
and the bléss - ed Sé - ra - phim to - géth - er síng thy práise with ex - ul - tá -

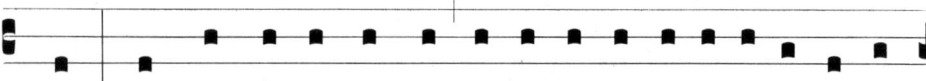
tion. With whóm, we be - séech thee, bíd that our voí - ces ál - so be ad - mít -

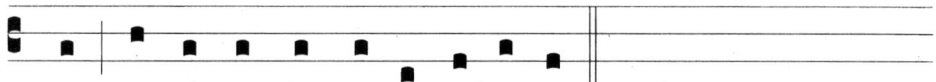
ted, év - er - more práis - ing thée, and sáy - ing : Holy, holy, holy, etc.

Ferial Preface of the Blessed Virgin Mary

†B.C.P. conclusion.

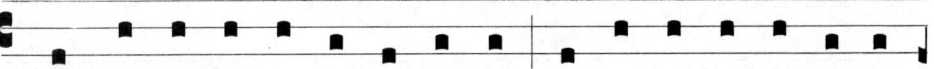

Thére-fore with Án-gels and Arch-án-gels, and with áll the cóm-pa-ny

of héa-ven, we láud and mág-ni-fy thy gló-ri-ous Náme, év-er-more

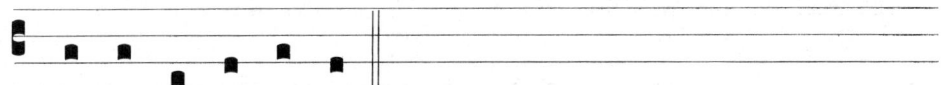

práis-ing thée, and sáy-ing : Holy, holy, holy, Lord God of hosts, etc.

COMMON PREFACE ✝

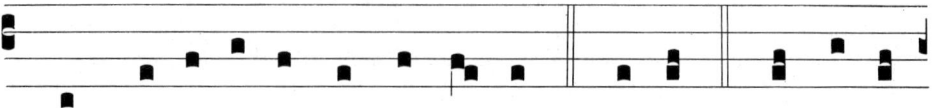
Through-oút all á-ges, wórld with-oút end. ℟. A-men. ℣. The Lórd be

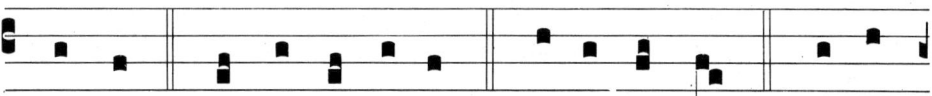
with you. ℟. And with thy spí-rit. ℣. Líft up your heárts. ℟ We líft

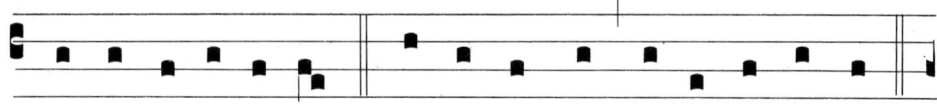
them up ún-to the Lórd. ℣. Lét us give thánks un-to our Lórd Gód.

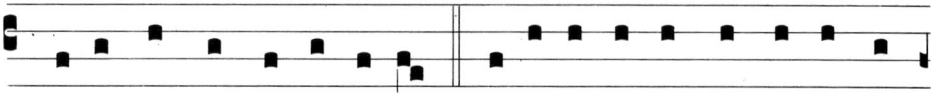
℟. It is méet and ríght so to dó. It is vé-ry méet, right, and our boun-

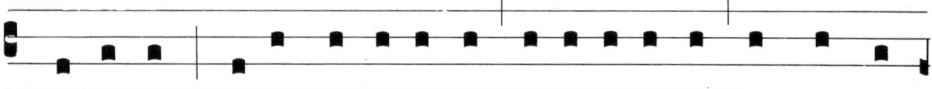
den dú-ty, that wé should at áll times, and in áll plá-ces, give thánks un-

tó thee, O Lórd, hó-ly Fá-ther, al-mígh-ty, év-er-lást-ing Gód:

Common Ferial Preface †   337

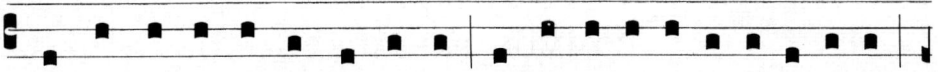

Thére-fore with Án-gels and Arch- án-gels, and with áll the cóm-pa-ny of héa-ven,

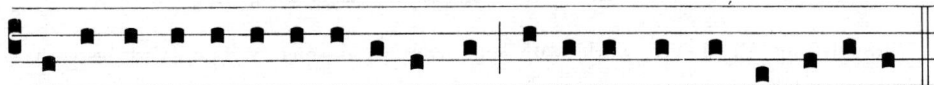

we láud and mág-ni- fy thy gló- ri- ous Náme, év- er-more práis-ing thée, and sáy-ing :

>Holy, holy, holy, Lord God of hosts.
>Heaven and earth are full of thy glory.
>Glory be to thee, O Lord most high. Amen.

COMMON PREFACE *

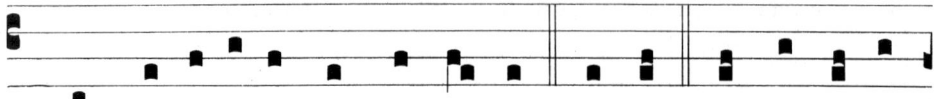
Through-oút all á-ges, wórld with-oút end. R︦. A-men. V︦. The Lórd be with

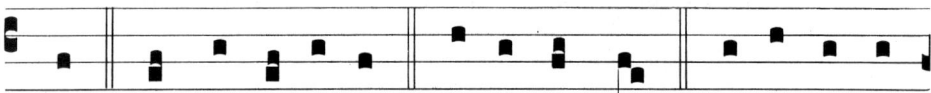
you. R︦. And with thy spí-rit. V︦. Líft up your heárts. R︦. We líft them up

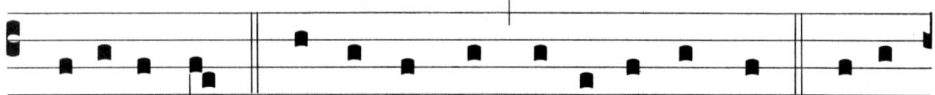
ún-to the Lórd. V︦. Lét us give thánks un-to our Lórd Gód. R︦. It is

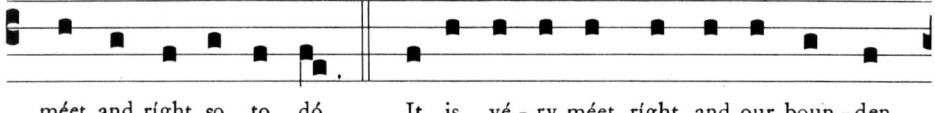
méet and ríght so to dó. It is vé-ry méet, ríght, and our boun-den

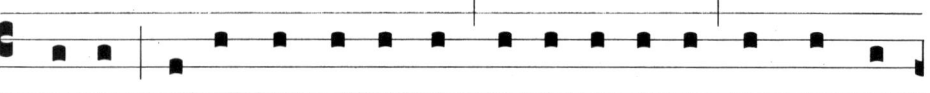
dú-ty, that wé should at áll times, and in áll plá-ces, give thánks un-

tó thee, O Lórd, hó-ly Fá-ther, al-mígh-ty, év-er-lást-ing Gód:

Common Ferial Preface

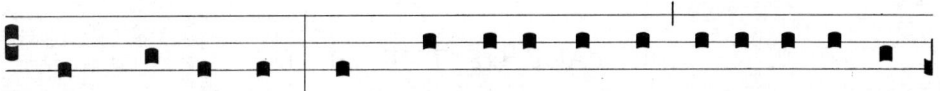
through Christ, our Lórd. Through whóm the An-gels práise, the Do-mi-ná-tions

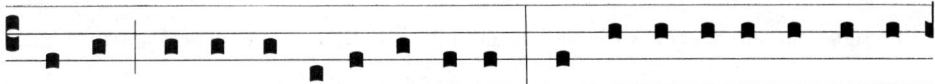
a-dóre, the Pów-ers féar thy má-jes-ty. The Héa-vens and the héa-ven-ly

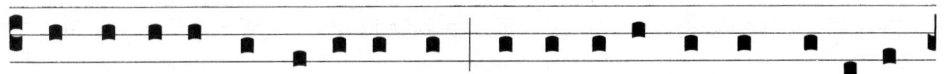
Vír-tues and the bléss-ed Sé-ra-phim to-géth-er síng thy práise with ex-ul-

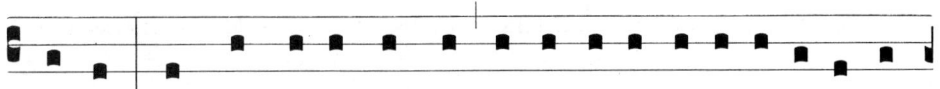
tá-tion. With whóm, we be-séech thee, bíd that our voí-ces ál-so be ad-mít-

ted, év-er-more práis-ing thée, and sáy-ing:

Holy, holy, holy, Lord God of hosts.
Heaven and earth are full of thy glory.
Hosanna in the highest.
Blessed is he that cometh in the name of the Lord.
Hosanna in the highest.

PREFACE OF THE DEAD

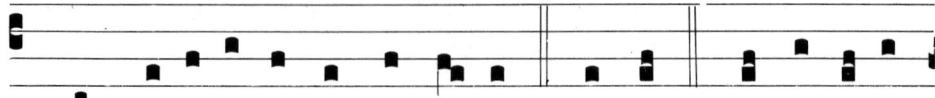
Through-oút all á-ges, wórld with-oút end. R͗. A-men. V͗. The Lórd be with

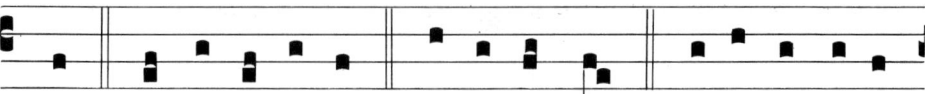
you. R͗. And with thy spí-rit. V͗. Líft up your heárts. R͗. We líft them up ún-

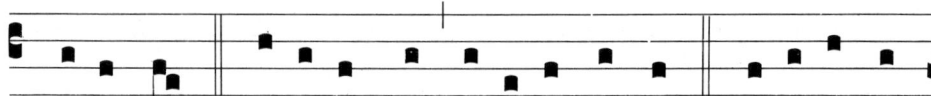
to the Lórd. V͗. Lét us give thánks un-to our Lórd Gód. R͗. It is méet and

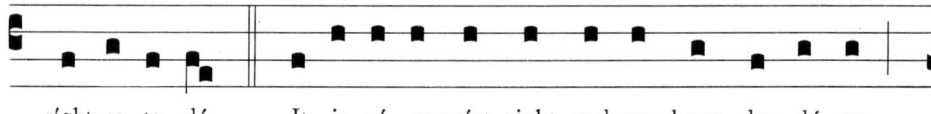
ríght so to dó.   It is vé-ry méet, right, and our boun-den dú-ty,

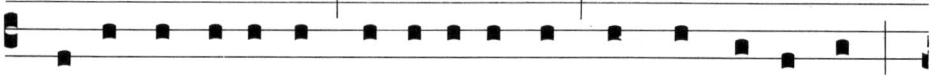
that wé should at áll times, and in áll plá-ces, give thánks un-tó thee,

O Lórd, hó-ly Fá-ther, al-mígh-ty, év-er-lást-ing Gód: through Chríst

Preface of the Dead

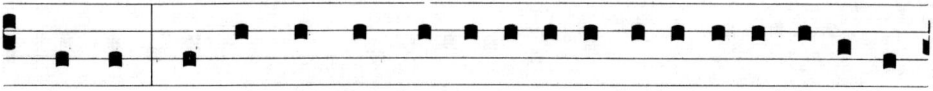
our Lórd. In whóm hath shone fórth un-to us the hópe of a bléss-ed ré-sur-

réc-tion, that théy who be-wáil the cér-tain con-di-tion of their mor-tá-li-

ty may be con-sól-ed by the pró-mise of im-mor-tá-li-ty to cóme.

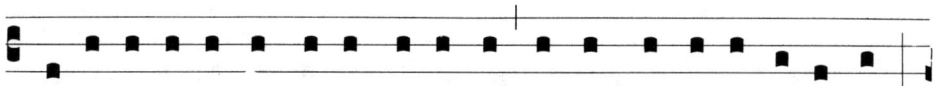
For the life of thy fáith-ful péo-ple, O Lórd, is cháng-ed, not tá-ken a-wáy,

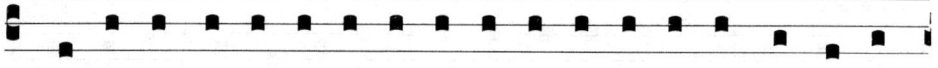
and at the dis-so-lú-tion of the ta-ber-ná-cle of this éarth-ly só-

journ-ing, a dwéll-ing-place e-tér-nal is made réa-dy in the héa-vens.

Preface of the Dead

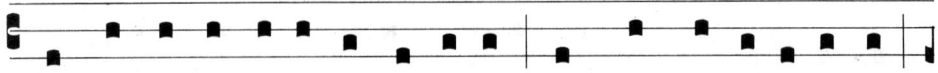
† And thére-fore with Án-gels and Arch-án-gels, with Thrónes and Do- mi- ná-tions,

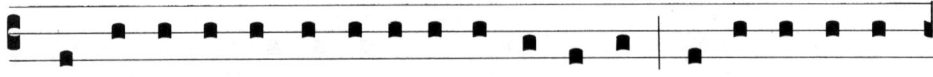
and with áll the cóm - pa - ny of the héa - ven - ly hóst, we síng the má - jes -

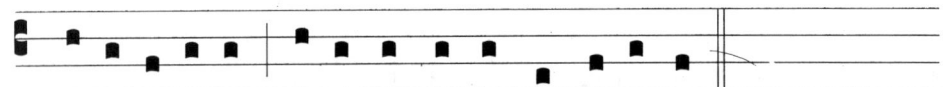
ty of thy gló-ry, év - er-more práis-ing thée, and sáy-ing : Holy, holy, etc.

†B.C.P. conclusion.

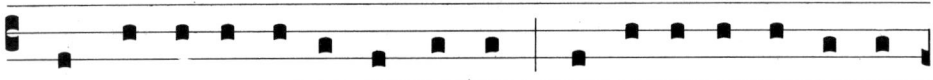
Thére - fore with Án - gels and Arch - án - gels, and with áll the cóm - pa - ny

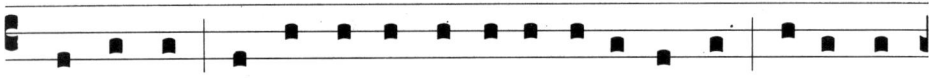
of héa - ven, we láud and mág - ni - fy thy gló - ri - ous Náme, év - er - more

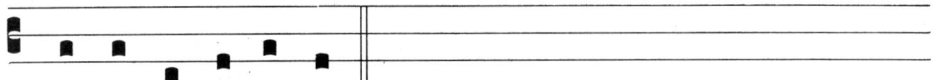
práis - ing thée, and sáy - ing : Holy, holy, holy, Lord God of hosts, etc.

PREFACES

Preface of the Nativity of the Lord

This Preface is said: (1) in Masses of the Nativity of the Lord, and of the Sunday or other day within the Octave, as also in Masses of the Circumcision of the Lord, of the Most Holy Name of Jesus, and of the Purification of the Blessed Virgin Mary. (2) It is also said in all Masses which are celebrated from January 2nd to January 5th inclusive, unless the Mass itself has a Proper Preface.

Preface of the Epiphany of the Lord

This Preface is said in Masses of the Epiphany of the Lord, and in all Masses celebrated from January 7th to 13th (inclusive), unless the Mass itself has a Proper Preface.

Preface of Lent

This Preface is said: (1) in Masses of the Season from Ash Wednesday to the Saturday within the fourth week of Lent inclusive. (2) It is also said in all Masses celebrated during the Season, provided that the Mass itself has not a Proper Preface.

Preface of the Holy Cross

This Preface is said: (1) in Masses of the Season from Passion Sunday to Maundy Thursday inclusive; and in all Masses of the Holy Cross, of the Passion of the Lord, and of the most precious Blood of Our Lord Jesus Christ; but not in Masses of Our Lord Jesus Christ the Eternal High Priest. (2) It is also said in all Masses celebrated during the Season, provided that the Mass itself has not a Proper Preface.

Preface of Easter

This Preface is said: (1) in Masses of the Season from Holy Saturday to the Vigil of the Ascension of the Lord inclusive, and in the Masses of the greater and lesser Litanies. (2) It is also said in all Masses celebrated during the Season, provided that the Mass itself has not a Proper Preface.

Preface of the Ascension

This Preface is said: (1) in Masses of the Ascension of the Lord, and of the Sunday after the Ascension (2) It is also said in all Masses celebrated from the Ascension to the Vigil of Pentecost exclusive, provided that the Mass itself has not a Proper Preface.

Preface of the Most Sacred Heart of Jesus

This Preface is said in Masses of the Most Sacred Heart of Jesus.

Preface of Jesus Christ the King

This Preface is said in Masses of Our Lord Jesus Christ the King.

Preface of the Holy Ghost

This Preface is said in Masses of the Season from the Vigil of Pentecost to the following Saturday inclusive; and in votive Masses of the Holy Ghost. Outside the Vigil and Octave the words *on this day* are omitted.

Preface of the Most Holy Trinity

This Preface is said in Masses of the Most Holy Trinity, of the greater Sundays of Advent, Septuagesima, Sexagesima and Quinquagesima, and of the lesser Sundays after Epiphany (from January 14th), and after Trinity (or Pentecost). It is not said on Sundays, if the Mass of the Sunday itself is not said.

Preface of the B.V. Mary

This Preface is said in all Masses of the Blessed Virgin Mary, but not on the Feast of the Purification of the Blessed Virgin Mary.

Preface of St. Joseph, Spouse of the B.V.M.

This Preface is said in all Masses of St. Joseph.

Preface of the Apostles

This Preface is said in Masses of Apostles outside the Octave of the Nativity. It is also said in Masses of Evangelists (not being Apostles), but not of Supreme Pontiffs.

Common Preface

This Preface is said: (1) in all Masses which have no Proper Preface. (2) In Masses of the Dedication of the Church. (3) On Sundays when the Mass of the Feast celebrated has no Proper Preface; unless, in each case, the Preface of the occurring Season be appointed to be said.

Preface of the Dead

This Preface is said in all Masses of the Dead.

PREFACES WITHOUT CHANT

Note:—† = Preface according to the Book of Common Prayer.

* = Preface according to the Missal.

PREFACE OF THE NATIVITY OF THE LORD †

THROUGHOUT all ages, world without end. ℟. Amen.

℣. The Lord be with you.　℟. And with thy spirit.

℣. Lift up your hearts.　℟. We lift them up unto the Lord.

℣. Let us give thanks unto our Lord God.　℟. It is meet and right so to do.

It is very meet, right, and our bounden duty, that we should at all times, and in all places, give thanks unto thee, O Lord, Holy Father, Almighty, Everlasting God: Because thou didst give Jesus Christ thine only Son to be born as at this time for us: who, by the operation of the Holy Ghost, was made very man of the substance of the Virgin Mary his mother: and that without spot of sin, to make us clean from all sin. Therefore with Angels and Archangels, and with all the company of heaven, we laud and magnify thy glorious name; evermore praising thee and saying:

Holy, Holy, Holy, Lord God of hosts, heaven and earth are full of thy glory: Glory be to thee, O Lord most High. Amen.

PREFACE OF THE NATIVITY OF THE LORD *

THROUGHOUT all ages, world without end. ℟. Amen.
℣. The Lord be with you. ℟. And with thy spirit.
℣. Lift up your hearts. ℟. We lift them up unto the Lord.
℣. Let us give thanks unto our Lord God. ℟. It is meet and right so to do.

It is very meet, right, and our bounden duty, that we should at all times, and in all places, give thanks unto thee: O Lord, Holy Father, Almighty, Everlasting God: Because through the mystery of the Word made flesh the light of thy glory hath shone anew upon the eyes of our mind: that as we acknowledge God, made visible to man, we may through him be caught up to love of things invisible. And therefore with Angels and Archangels, with Thrones and Dominations, and with all the company of the heavenly host, we sing the majesty of thy glory, evermore praising thee, and saying:

Holy, Holy, Holy, Lord God of hosts, heaven and earth are full of thy glory. Hosanna in the highest.

Blessed is he that cometh in the name of the Lord. Hosanna in the highest.

Infra Actionem, Communicántes proper, as below in the Canon.

But in the first Mass of the Nativity of the Lord is said: we celebrate the most sacred night, wherein, etc., (noctem sacratíssimam celebrántes, qua, etc.;) thereafter is always said: celebrate the most holy day whereon, etc., (diem sacratíssimum celebrántes, quo etc.;) until the Octave of the Nativity of the Lord inclusive.

PREFACE OF THE EPIPHANY OF THE LORD*

℣. THROUGHOUT all ages, world without end. ℟. Amen.

℣. The Lord be with you. ℟. And with thy spirit.

℣. Lift up your hearts. ℟. We lift them up unto the Lord.

℣. Let us give thanks unto our Lord God. ℟. It is meet and right so to do.

It is very meet, right, and our bounden duty, that we should at all times, and in all places, give thanks unto thee, O Lord, Holy Father, Almighty, Everlasting God: Because that when thine only-begotten Son manifestly appeared in substance of our flesh, he restored us by the new light of his immortality.

†And therefore with Angels and Archangels, with Thrones and Dominations, and with all the company of the heavenly host, we sing the majesty of thy glory, evermore praising thee, and saying:

Holy, Holy, Holy, Lord God of hosts, heaven and earth are full of thy glory.   Hosanna in the highest.

Blessed is he that cometh in the name of the Lord. Hosanna in the highest.

B.C.P. conclusion.

☦ Therefore with Angels and Archangels, and with all the company of heaven, we laud and magnify thy glorious name; evermore praising thee and saying:

Holy, Holy, Holy, Lord God of hosts, heaven and earth are full of thy glory: Glory be to thee, O Lord most High.   Amen.

Infra Actionem, Communicántes proper, as below in the Canon, on the Feast only.

PREFACE OF LENT

THROUGHOUT all ages, world without end. ℟. Amen.
℣. The Lord be with you. ℟. And with thy spirit.
℣. Lift up your hearts. ℟. We lift them up unto the Lord.
℣. Let us give thanks unto our Lord God. ℟. It is meet and right so to do.

It is very meet, right, and our bounden duty, that we should at all times, and in all places, give thanks unto thee, O Lord, Holy Father, Almighty, Everlasting God: Who by bodily fasting dost overcome vice, dost raise the mind, and dost bestow on us virtue and heavenly rewards: through Christ our Lord.

*Through whom the Angels praise, the Dominations adore, the Powers fear thy Majesty. The Heavens and the heavenly Virtues, and the blessed Seraphim together sing thy praise with exultation. With whom, we beseech thee, bid that our voices also be admitted, evermore praising thee, and saying:

Holy, Holy, Holy, Lord God of hosts, heaven and earth are full of thy glory: Hosanna in the highest.

Blessed is he that cometh in the name of the Lord. Hosanna in the highest.

B.C.P. conclusion.

✝Therefore with Angels and Archangels, and with all the company of heaven, we laud and magnify thy glorious name, evermore praising thee and saying:

Holy, Holy, Holy, Lord God of hosts, heaven and earth are full of thy glory: Glory be to thee, O Lord most High. Amen.

PREFACE OF THE HOLY CROSS

Note. This Preface is not said in Masses of Our Lord Jesus Christ, the Eternal Priest.

THROUGHOUT all ages, world without end. ℞. Amen.

℣. The Lord be with you. ℞. And with thy spirit.

℣. Lift up your hearts. ℞. We lift them up unto the Lord.

℣. Let us give thanks unto our Lord God. ℞. It is meet and right so to do.

It is very meet, right, and our bounden duty, that we should at all times, and in all places, give thanks unto thee, O Lord, Holy Father, Almighty, Everlasting God: Who by the tree of the Cross didst give salvation unto mankind: that whence death arose, thence life might rise again: and that he who by a tree overcame might also by a tree be overcome: ✝through Christ our Lord. Through whom the Angels praise, the Dominations adore, the Powers fear thy Majesty. The heavens and the heavenly Virtues, and the blessed Seraphim together sing thy praise with exultation. With whom, we beseech thee, bid that our voices also be admitted, evermore praising thee and saying:

Holy, Holy, Holy, Lord God of hosts, heaven and earth are full of thy glory.   Hosanna in the highest.

Blessed is he that cometh in the name of the Lord. Hosanna in the highest.

†B.C.P. conclusion.

†Therefore with Angels and Archangels, and with all the company of heaven, we laud and magnify thy glorious name: evermore praising thee and saying:

Holy, Holy Holy, Lord God of hosts, heaven and earth are full of thy glory: Glory be to thee, O Lord most high.

PREFACE OF EASTER ☦

THROUGHOUT all ages, world without end. ℟. Amen.

℣. The Lord be with you. ℟. And with thy spirit.

℣. Lift up your hearts. ℟. We lift them up unto the Lord.

℣. Let us give thanks unto our Lord God. ℟. It is meet and right so to do.

It is very meet, right, and our bounden duty, that we should at all times, and in all places, give thanks unto thee, O Lord, Holy Father, Almighty, Everlasting God: But chiefly are we bound to praise thee for the glorious Resurrection of thy Son Jesus Christ our Lord: for he is the very Paschal Lamb, which was offered for us, and hath taken away the sin of the world; who by his death hath destroyed death, and by his rising to life again hath restored to us everlasting life. Therefore with Angels and Archangels, and with all the company of heaven, we laud and magnify thy glorious name, evermore praising thee, and saying:

Holy, Holy, Holy, Lord God of hosts, heaven and earth are full of thy glory: Glory be to thee, O Lord most high. Amen.

PREFACE OF EASTER *

In the Mass of Holy Saturday is said: **chiefly on this night;** on Easter Day and up to the Saturday following inclusive, **chiefly on this day;** otherwise, and also in the Mass of the greater Litanies, if it be celebrated within the Octave of Easter without a Commemoration thereof, **chiefly at this time.**

℣. THROUGHOUT all ages, world without end. ℟. Amen.

℣. The Lord be with you. ℟. And with thy spirit.

℣. Lift up your hearts. ℟. We lift them up unto the Lord.

℣. Let us give thanks unto our Lord God. ℟. It is meet and right so to do.

It is very meet, right, and our bounden duty, that we should at all times indeed glorify thee, O Lord, but chiefly on this day (or chiefly at this time) when Christ our Passover is sacrificed. For he is the very Lamb which hath taken away the sins of the world. Who by his death hath destroyed death, and by his rising again hath restored to us life. And therefore with Angels and Archangels, with Thrones and Dominations, and with all the company of the heavenly host, we sing the majesty of thy glory, evermore praising thee and saying:

Holy, Holy, Holy, etc.

Infra Actionem, **Communicántes** and **Hanc oblatiónem** proper, as below in the Canon.

So it is said from Holy Saturday up to Saturday after Easter inclusive. But in the Mass of Holy Saturday Infra Actionem is said **we celebrate the most sacred night (et noctem sacratíssimam celebrántes).**

PREFACE OF THE ASCENSION OF THE LORD ✝

℣. THROUGHOUT all ages, world without end. ℟. Amen.
℣. The Lord be with you. ℟. And with thy spirit.
℣. Lift up your hearts. ℟. We lift them up unto the Lord.
℣. Let us give thanks unto our Lord God. ℟. It is meet and right so to do.

It is very meet, right, and our bounden duty, that we should at all times, and in all places, give thanks unto thee, O Lord, Holy Father, Almighty, Everlasting God: Through thy most dearly beloved Son Jesus Christ our Lord. Who after his most glorious Resurrection manifestly appeared to all his Apostles, and in their sight ascended up into heaven to prepare a place for us: that where he is, thither we might also ascend, and reign with him in glory. Therefore with Angels and Archangels, and with all the company of heaven, we laud and magnify thy glorious name, evermore praising thee, and saying:

Holy, Holy, Holy, etc.

PREFACE OF THE ASCENSION OF THE LORD*

THROUGHOUT all ages, world without end. ℞. Amen.

℣. The Lord be with you. ℞. And with thy spirit.

℣. Lift up your hearts. ℞. We lift them up unto the Lord.

℣. Let us give thanks unto our Lord God. ℞. It is meet and right so to do.

It is very meet, right, and our bounden duty, that we should at all times, and in all places, give thanks unto thee, O Lord, Holy Father, Almighty, Everlasting God: Through Christ our Lord. Who after his Resurrection manifestly appeared to all his disciples, and in their sight ascended up into heaven, that he might make us partakers of his Godhead. And therefore with Angels and Archangels, with Thrones and Dominations, and with all the company of the heavenly host, we sing the majesty of thy glory, evermore praising thee, and saying:

Holy, Holy, Holy, etc.

Infra Actionem, Communicántes proper, as below in the Canon, on the Feast only.

PREFACE OF THE MOST SACRED HEART OF JESUS

℣. THROUGHOUT all ages, world without end. ℟. Amen.

℣. The Lord be with you. ℟. And with thy spirit.

℣. Lift up your hearts. ℟. We lift them up unto the Lord.

℣. Let us give thanks unto our Lord God. ℟. It is meet and right so to do.

It is very meet, right, and our bounden duty, that we should at all times, and in all places, give thanks unto thee, O Lord, Holy Father, Almighty, Everlasting God: Who didst will that thine only-begotten Son, as he hung upon the Cross, should be pierced by the soldier's spear: that his Heart thus opened, the shrine of heavenly bounty, might pour forth upon us streams of mercy and of grace; and, burning with unceasing love for us, might likewise be a place of rest for the godly, and an abiding refuge of salvation for the penitent. *And therefore with Angels and Archangels, with Thrones and Dominations, and with all the company of the heavenly host, we sing the majesty of thy glory, evermore praising thee, and saying:

Holy, Holy, Holy, etc.

†B.C.P. conclusion.

Therefore with Angels and Archangels, etc.

Holy, Holy, Holy, etc.

PREFACE OF OUR LORD JESUS CHRIST THE KING

THROUGHOUT all ages, world without end. ℟. Amen.

℣. The Lord be with you. ℟. And with thy spirit.

℣. Lift up your hearts. ℟. We lift them up unto the Lord.

℣. Let us give thanks unto our Lord God. ℟. It is meet and right so to do.

It is very meet, right, and our bounden duty, that we should at all times, and in all places, give thanks unto thee, O Lord, Holy Father, Almighty, Everlasting God: Who didst anoint thine only-begotten Son, our Lord Jesus Christ, with the oil of gladness, to be a Priest for ever and the King of all the world: that, offering himself an unspotted sacrifice of peace upon the altar of the cross, he might accomplish the mystery of the redemption of mankind: and making all creatures subject to his governance, might deliver up to thine infinite Majesty an eternal and universal kingdom. A kingdom of truth and life: a kingdom of sanctity and grace: a kingdom of justice, love and peace.

*And therefore with Angels and Archangels, with Thrones and Dominations, and with all the company of the heavenly host, we sing the majesty of thy glory, evermore praising thee, and saying: Holy, Holy, Holy, etc., †or Therefore, etc.

PREFACE OF THE HOLY GHOST †

THROUGHOUT all ages, world without end. ℟. Amen.

℣. The Lord be with you. ℟. And with thy spirit.

℣. Lift up your hearts. ℟. We lift them up unto the Lord.

℣. Let us give thanks unto our Lord God. ℟. It is meet and right so to do.

It is very meet, right, and our bounden duty, that we should at all times, and in all places, give thanks unto thee, O Lord, Holy Father, Almighty, Everlasting God: through Jesus Christ our Lord: according to whose most true promise, the Holy Ghost came down as at this time from heaven with a sudden great sound, as it had been a mighty wind, in the likeness of fiery tongues, lighting upon the Apostles, to teach them, and to lead them to all truth: giving them both the gift of divers languages, and also boldness with fervent zeal constantly to preach the Gospel unto all nations: whereby we have been brought out of darkness and error into the clear light and true knowledge of thee, and of thy Son Jesus Christ. Therefore with Angels and Archangels, and with all the company of heaven, we laud and magnify thy glorious name, evermore praising thee, and saying:

Holy, Holy, Holy, etc.

PREFACE OF THE HOLY GHOST *

Outside the Vigil and Octave of Pentecost the words *as on this day* are omitted.

℣. THROUGHOUT all ages, world without end. ℟. Amen.

℣. The Lord be with you. ℟. And with thy spirit.

℣. Lift up your hearts. ℟. We lift them up unto the Lord.

℣. Let us give thanks unto our Lord God. ℟. It is meet and right so to do.

It is very meet, right, and our bounden duty, that we should at all times, and in all places, give thanks unto thee, O Lord, Holy Father, Almighty, Everlasting God: Through Christ our Lord. Who, ascending above all heavens and sitting at thy right hand, poured forth (as on this day) the promised Holy Ghost upon the sons of adoption. Wherefore with exceeding joy the whole round world exulteth. The heavenly Virtues also and the Angelic Powers together sing the majesty of thy glory, evermore praising thee, and saying:

Holy, Holy, Holy, etc.

Infra Actionem, Communicántes, and Hanc oblatiónem, proper, as below in the Canon.

And it is said only from the Vigil of Pentecost until the following Saturday inclusive, in all Masses of the Vigil or Octave.

PREFACE OF THE MOST HOLY TRINITY †

℣. THROUGHOUT all ages, world without end.　℟. Amen.
℣. The Lord be with you.　℟. And with thy spirit.
℣. Lift up your hearts.　℟. We lift them up unto the Lord.
℣. Let us give thanks unto our Lord God.　℟. It is meet and right so to do.

It is very meet, right, and our bounden duty, that we should at all times, and in all places, give thanks unto thee, O Lord, Holy Father, Almighty, Everlasting God: Who with thine only-begotten Son and the Holy Ghost art one God, one Lord: not one only person, but three persons in one substance. For that which we believe of thy glory, O Father, the same we believe of the Son, and of the Holy Ghost, without any difference or inequality.

Therefore with Angels and Archangels, and with all the company of heaven, we laud and magnify thy glorious name: evermore praising thee, and saying:

Holy, Holy, Holy, etc.

On Trinity Sunday only the Preface may be said as on p. 231.
On other occasions it is said as above.

PREFACE OF THE MOST HOLY TRINITY*

℣. THROUGHOUT all ages, world without end.   ℟. Amen.
℣. The Lord be with you.   ℟. And with thy spirit.
℣. Lift up your hearts.   ℟. We lift them up unto the Lord.
℣. Let us give thanks unto our Lord God.   ℟. It is meet and right so to do.

It is very meet, right, and our bounden duty, that we should at all times, and in all places, give thanks unto thee, O Lord, Holy Father, Almighty, Everlasting God: Who with thine only begotten Son and the Holy Ghost art one God, one Lord: not one only person, but three persons in one substance. For that which by thy revelation we believe of thy glory, the same we believe of thy Son, the same of the Holy Ghost, without any difference or inequality. That in the confession of the true and everlasting Godhead, distinction in Persons, unity in essence, and equality in majesty, may be adored. Which the Angels and Archangels, the Cherubim also and Seraphim praise: who cease not daily to cry out, with one voice saying:

Holy, Holy, Holy, etc.

PREFACE OF THE BLESSED VIRGIN MARY

Either the Annunciation, or the Visitation, or the Assumption, or the Nativity, or the Presentation is said, according to the title of the Feast. In Masses of the immaculate Conception is said: the immaculate Conception. On the Feast of the Seven Sorrows: the Transfixion. On the Feast of Mt. Carmel: the Commemoration. In all other Feasts: the Festival. In Votives in which a special Mystery is not to be expressed, and in the Mass of St. Mary on Saturday: in the Veneration.

THROUGHOUT all ages, world without end. ℟. Amen.

℣. The Lord be with you. ℟. And with thy spirit.

℣. Lift up your hearts. ℟. We lift them up unto the Lord.

℣. Let us give thanks unto our Lord God. ℟. It is meet and right so to do.

It is very meet, right, and our bounden duty, that we should at all times, and in all places, give thanks unto thee, O Lord, Holy Father, Almighty, Everlasting God: And that on (in) *** of Blessed Mary ever Virgin, we should praise, bless and magnify thee. Because by the overshadowing of the Holy Ghost she conceived thine only begotten Son: and, the glory of her maidenhood yet abiding, shed forth upon the world the light eternal, Jesus Christ our Lord.* Through whom the Angels praise, the Dominations adore, the Powers fear thy majesty. The Heavens and the heavenly Virtues and the blessed Seraphim together sing thy praise with exultation. With whom, we beseech thee, bid that our voices also be admitted, evermore praising thee, and saying:

Holy, Holy, Holy, Lord God of hosts, Heaven and earth are full of thy glory. Hosanna in the highest.

Blessed is he that cometh in the name of the Lord. Hosanna in the highest.

† B.C.P. conclusion.

†Therefore with Angels and Archangels, and with all the company of heaven, we laud and magnify thy glorious name: evermore praising thee and saying:

Holy, Holy, Holy, Lord God of hosts, heaven and earth are full of thy glory. Glory be to thee, O Lord most high.

PREFACE OF ST. JOSEPH, SPOUSE OF THE B.V.M.

On May 1st (St. Joseph the Worker) is said: And that in the Solemnity.
In Votive Masses is said: And that in the Veneration.

THROUGHOUT all ages, world without end. ℟. Amen.
℣. The Lord be with you. ℟. And with thy spirit.
℣. Lift up your hearts. ℟. We lift them up unto the Lord.
℣. Let us give thanks unto our Lord God. ℟. It is meet and right so to do.

It is very meet, right, and our bounden duty, that we should at all times, and in all places, give thanks unto thee, O Lord, Holy Father, Almighty, Everlasting God: And that on the Festival (in the Solemnity or Veneration) of blessed Joseph, we should, as is most justly due, praise, bless and magnify thee. For that he, being a just man, was given by thee for a Spouse to the Virgin Mother of God, a faithful and wise servant, made ruler over thy Household: that in the office of a father he should guard thine only begotten Son, conceived by the overshadowing of the Holy Ghost, even Jesus Christ our Lord.

*Through whom the Angels praise, the Dominations adore, the Powers fear thy majesty. The Heavens and the heavenly Virtues and the blessed Seraphim together sing thy praise with exultation. With whom, we beseech thee, bid that our voices also be admitted, evermore praising thee, and saying:

Holy, Holy, Holy, etc.

† B.C.P. conclusion.

Therefore with Angels and Archangels, etc.

PREFACE OF THE APOSTLES

THROUGHOUT all ages, world without end.   ℟. Amen.

℣. The Lord be with you.   ℟. And with thy spirit.

℣. Lift up your hearts.   ℟. We lift them up unto the Lord.

℣. Let us give thanks unto our Lord God.   ℟. It is meet and right so to do.

It is very meet, right, and our bounden duty: That we, O Lord, should humbly entreat thee, that thou, the everlasting Shepherd, do not forsake thy flock: but through thy blessed Apostles keep it by thy continual protection. That it may be governed by those same rulers whom, in thy stead, thou hast appointed for thy work as shepherds of thy people.

*And therefore with Angels and Archangels, with Thrones and Dominations, and with all the company of the heavenly host, we sing the majesty of thy glory, evermore praising thee, and saying:

Holy, Holy, Holy, etc.

† B.C.P. conclusion.

Therefore with Angels and Archangels, etc.

Holy, Holy, Holy, etc.

THE COMMON PREFACE ✝

Throughout all ages, world without end. ℟. Amen.
℣. The Lord be with you. ℟. And with thy Spirit.
℣. Lift up your hearts.
℟. We lift them up unto the Lord.
℣. Let us give thanks unto our Lord God.
℟. It is meet and right so to do.

It is very meet, right, and our bounden duty, that we should at all times, and in all places, give thanks unto thee, O Lord, Holy Father, Almighty, Everlasting God: Therefore with Angels and Archangels, and with all the company of heaven, we laud and magnify thy glorious name, evermore praising thee, and saying:

Holy, Holy, Holy, Lord God of hosts, heaven and earth are full of thy glory. Glory be to thee, O Lord most high. Amen.

[Blessed is he that cometh in the name of the Lord. Hosanna in the highest.]

THE COMMON PREFACE*

Throughout all ages, world without end. ℟. Amen.
℣. The Lord be with you. ℟. And with thy spirit.
℣. Lift up your hearts.
℟. We lift them up unto the Lord.
℣. Let us give thanks unto our Lord God.
℟. It is meet and right so to do.

It is very meet, right, and our bounden duty, that we should at all times, and in all places, give thanks unto thee, O Lord, Holy Father, Almighty, Everlasting God: through Christ, our Lord. Through whom the Angels praise, the Dominations adore, the Powers fear thy majesty. The Heavens and the heavenly Virtues and the blessed Seraphim together sing thy praise with exultation. With whom, we beseech thee, bid that our voices also be admitted, evermore praising thee, and saying:

Holy, Holy, Holy, Lord God of hosts. Heaven and earth are full of thy glory. Hosanna in the highest.

Blessed is he that cometh in the name of the Lord. Hosanna in the highest.

PREFACE OF THE DEAD

THROUGHOUT all ages, world without end. ℟. Amen.

℣. The Lord be with you. ℟. And with thy spirit.

℣. Lift up your hearts. ℟. We lift them up unto the Lord.

℣. Let us give thanks unto our Lord God. ℟. It is meet and right so to do.

It is very meet, right, and our bounden duty, that we should at all times, and in all places, give thanks unto thee, O Lord, Holy Father, Almighty, Everlasting God: through Christ our Lord. In whom hath shone forth unto us the hope of a blessed resurrection: that they who bewail the certain condition of their mortality may be consoled by thy promise of immortality to come. For the life of thy faithful people, O Lord, is changed, not taken away: and at the dissolution of the tabernacle of this earthly sojourning, a dwelling-place eternal is made ready in the heavens.

*And therefore with Angels and Archangels, with Thrones and Dominations, and with all the company of the heavenly host, we sing the majesty of thy glory, evermore praising thee, and saying:

Holy, Holy, Holy, Lord God of hosts, Heaven and earth are full of thy glory.   Hosanna in the highest.

Blessed is he that cometh in the name of the Lord.   Hosanna in the highest.

† B.C.P. conclusion.

Therefore with Angels and Archangels, and with all the company of heaven, we laud and magnify thy glorious name, evermore praising thee, and saying:

Holy, Holy, Holy, Lord God of hosts, Heaven and earth are full of thy glory.   Glory be to thee, O Lord most high.   Amen.

PRAYER OF ADDRESS

OR

HUMBLE ACCESS

(When it is to be said here).

WE do not presume to come to this thy Table, O merciful Lord, trusting in our own righteousness, but in thy manifold and great mercies. We are not worthy so much as to gather up the crumbs under thy Table. But thou art the same Lord, whose property is always to have mercy:

Grant us therefore, gracious Lord, so to eat the flesh of thy dear Son Jesus Christ, and to drink his blood, that our sinful bodies may be made clean by his body, and our souls washed through his most precious blood, and that we may evermore dwell in him, and he in us. ℟. Amen.

The Preface (or the foregoing Prayer) being ended, the Priest, extending, raising somewhat and joining his hands, raising his eyes towards heaven, and immediately lowering them, bowed profoundly before the Altar with his hands placed thereon kisses it, and then says with hands extended: (p. 371, or 395).

CANON OF THE MASS

Most merciful Father, we humbly pray thee, through Jesus Christ thy Son our Lord, and we ask, *He kisses the Altar,* and, *with hands joined before his breast, says:* that thou accept and bless *He signs thrice over the Host and Chalice together, saying:* these ✙ gifts, these ✙ presents, these ✙ holy and unspoiled sacrifices. *With extended hands he proceeds:* We offer them unto thee, first, for thy holy catholic Church: that thou vouchsafe to keep it in peace, to guard, unite, and govern it throughout the whole world: together with thy servant N. our Pontiff and N. our Bishop and all the faithful guardians of the catholic and apostolic faith.

Commemoration for the Living

Remember, O Lord, thy servants and handmaids N. and N. *He joins his hands and prays awhile for those for whom he intends to pray: then with extended hands proceeds:* and all who here around us stand, whose faith is known unto thee and their steadfastness manifest, on whose behalf we offer unto thee: or who themselves offer unto thee this sacrifice of praise, for themselves, and for all who are theirs: for the redemption of their souls, for the hope of their salvation and safety: and who offer their prayers unto thee, the eternal God, the living and the true.

Canon of the Mass

* Infra Actionem

United in one communion, we venerate the memory, first, of the glorious ever Virgin Mary, Mother of our God and Lord Jesus Christ: ✝ as also of thy blessed Apostles and Martyrs, Peter and Paul, Andrew, James, John, Thomas, James, Philip, Bartholomew, Matthew, Simon and Thaddæus: Linus, Cletus, Clement, Xystus, Cornelius, Cyprian, Lawrence, Chrysogonus, John and Paul, Cosmas and Damian: and of all thy Saints; grant that by their merits and prayers we may in all things be defended with the help of thy protection. *He joins his hands.* Through the same Christ our Lord. Amen.

¶ *Holding his hands spread out over the Oblations, he says:*

We beseech thee then, O Lord, graciously to accept this oblation from us thy servants, and from thy whole family: order thou our days in thy peace, and bid us to be delivered from eternal damnation, and to be numbered in the fold of thine elect. *He joins his hands.* Through Christ our Lord. Amen.

Vouchsafe, O God, we beseech thee, in all things *He signs thrice over the Oblations,* to make this oblation bles✠sed, appro✠ved and ac✠cepted, a perfect and worthy offering: *He signs once over the Host,* that it may become for us the Bo✠dy and *once over the Chalice* and Blo✠od of thy dearly beloved Son, *He joins his hands,* our Lord Jesus Christ.

The Canon continues, p. 378.

Canon of the Mass

* On the Nativity of the Lord and through the Octave is said:

United in one communion, we celebrate the most sacred day, (most sacred night,) whereon the undefiled virginity of blessed Mary brought forth the Saviour to this world: we venerate moreover the memory, first, of the same glorious ever Virgin Mary, Mother of the same our God and Lord Jesus Christ:†

On the Epiphany of the Lord is said:

United in one communion, we celebrate the most sacred day, whereon thine only begotten Son, co-eternal with thee in thy glory, visibly appeared in the body, in the true substance of our flesh: we venerate moreover the memory, first, of the glorious ever Virgin Mary, Mother of the same our God and Lord Jesus Christ:†

From Holy Saturday to the following Saturday is said:

United in one communion, we celebrate the most sacred day (most sacred night) of the Resurrection of our Lord Jesus Christ according to the flesh: we venerate moreover the memory, first, of the glorious ever Virgin Mary, Mother of the same our God and Lord Jesus Christ:†

On the Ascension of the Lord is said:

United in one communion, we celebrate the most sacred day, whereon our Lord, thine only-begotten Son, set at the right hand of thy glory the substance of our frailty united to himself: we venerate moreover the memory, first, of the glorious ever Virgin Mary, Mother of the same our God and Lord Jesus Christ:†

From the Vigil of Pentecost to the following Saturday inclusive is said:

United in one communion, we celebrate the most sacred day of Pentecost, whereon the Holy Ghost appeared to the Apostles in tongues innumerable: we venerate moreover the memory, first, of the glorious ever Virgin Mary, Mother of our God and Lord Jesus Christ:†

¶ From Holy Saturday until Saturday in Easter Week inclusive and from the Vigil of Pentecost until the following Saturday inclusive is said:

We beseech thee then, O Lord, graciously to accept this oblation from us thy servants, and from thy whole family: we present it unto thee on behalf also of those whom thou hast vouchsafed to regenerate by water and the Holy Ghost, granting unto them remission of all their sins: order thou our days in thy peace, and bid us to be delivered from eternal damnation, and to be numbered in the fold of thine elect. He joins his hands. Through Christ our Lord. Amen.

Vouchsafe, etc.

PRAYER OF CONSECRATION

The Priest shall say the Prayer of Consecration as follows:

Almighty God, our heavenly Father, who of thy tender mercy didst give thine only Son Jesus Christ to suffer death upon the Cross for our redemption; who made there (by his one oblation of himself once offered) a full, perfect, and sufficient sacrifice, oblation, and satisfaction, for the sins of the whole world; and did institute, and in his holy Gospel command us to continue, a perpetual memory of that his precious death, *He joins his hands,* until his coming again:

Holding his hands extended over the Oblations, he says:

Hear us, O merciful Father, we most humbly beseech thee; and grant that we receiving *He signs thrice over the Oblations,* these thy crea✠tures of br✠ead and wi✠ne, according to thy Son our Saviour Jesus Christ's holy institution, in remembrance of his death and passion, *He signs once over the Host,* may be partakers of his most blessed Bo✠dy and once over the Chalice and Blo✠od.

Who, in the same night that he was betrayed, *He takes the Host,* took bread, *He raises his eyes to heaven, bows his head, and signs once over the Host, and, when he had given* ✠ *thanks, he brake it, and gave it to his disciples, saying:* Take, eat.

Holding the Host with both hands between the thumbs and forefingers, he utters the words of consecration secretly, distinctly, and with great care over the Host, and at the same time over all, if more are to be consecrated.

This is my Body which is given for you.

Do this in remembrance of me.

Having pronounced these words, he straightway genuflects and adores the consecrated Host: he rises, shews it to the people, replaces it upon the Corporal, and genuflecting again adores: and he does not any more separate his forefingers and thumbs, except when the Host is to be handled, until the ablution of his fingers. Then, having uncovered the Chalice, he says.

Likewise after supper, *He takes the Chalice with both hands,* he took the Cup: *He bows his head, and with his left hand holding the Chalice, he signs over it with his right, and when* he had given ✠ *thanks, he gave it to them, saying:* Drink ye all of this.

He pronounces the words of consecration carefully, continuously and secretly, over the Chalice, holding it slightly raised.

For this is my Blood of the New Testament: which is shed for you and for many for the remission of sins.

Having pronounced these words, he sets down the Chalice upon the Corporal, and saying secretly:

Do this, as oft as ye shall drink it, in remembrance of me.

The Canon continues, p. 379.
[or The Prayer of Oblation, p. 376.]

Genuflecting he adores: he rises, shows it to the people, sets it down, covers it, and again genuflecting adores. Afterward, with hands separated, he says:

Wherefore, O Lord and heavenly Father, we thy humble servants entirely desire thy fatherly goodness mercifully to accept, *He joins his hands and signs thrice over the Host and Chalice together, saying:* this✢our ✢Sacri✢fice, *He signs once over the Host saying:* of pra✢ise, *and once over the Chalice, saying:* and thanks✢giving.

With hands extended, he proceeds:

Most humbly beseeching thee to grant, that by the merits and death of thy Son Jesus Christ, and through faith in his blood, we and all thy whole Church may obtain remission of our sins, and all other benefits of his passion.

Bowing profoundly, and with hands joined and placed upon the Altar, he says:

And here we offer and present unto thee, O Lord, ourselves, our souls and bodies, to be a reasonable, holy, and lively sacrifice unto thee; humbly beseeching thee, that all we, *He kisses the Altar,* who are partakers, *He joins his hands and signs once over the Host, and once over the Chalice,* of this ho✢ly Com✢munion, *He signs himself, saying:* may be fulfilled with thy grace and heavenly benediction.

Prayer of Oblation

Commemoration for the Departed

He joins his hands and prays awhile for those departed for whom he intends to pray, then separating his hands, he strikes his breast with his right hand, and slightly raising his voice, says:

And although we be unworthy, *With hands extended as before, he proceeds secretly:* through our manifold sins, to offer unto thee any sacrifice; yet we beseech thee to accept this our bounden duty and service; not weighing our merits, but pardoning our offences. *He joins his hands and signs thrice over the Host and Chalice together, saying:* Through ✠ Jesus ✠ Christ ✠ our Lord.

He uncovers the Chalice, genuflects, and takes the Host between the thumb and forefinger of his right hand: and holding the Chalice with his left, he signs with the Host three times from lip to lip of the Chalice, saying:

By wh✠om, and with wh✠om, in the un✠ity of the Holy Ghost, *With the Host itself he signs twice between himself and the Chalice, saying:* all hon✠our and glo✠ry be unto thee, *Elevating a little the Chalice and Host, he says:* O Father almighty.

He replaces the Host, covers the Chalice with the Pall, genuflects, rises and says in an audible voice or sings:

World without end. ℟. Amen.

He joins his hands.

Let us pray: As our Saviour Christ hath commanded and taught us, we are bold to say:

Our Father (p. 382 or 383)

Canon of the Mass

Who the day before he suffered, He takes the Host, took bread into his holy and venerable hands, He lifts up his eyes to heaven, and with eyes lifted up to heaven unto thee, God, his almighty Father, He bows his head, giving thanks to thee, He signs over the Host, he bles✠sed, brake and gave it to his disciples, saying: Take, and eat ye all of this.

Holding the Host with both hands between the thumbs and forefingers, he utters the words of consecration secretly, distinctly, and attentively over the Host, and at the same time over all, if more are to be consecrated.

For this is my Body

Having uttered these words, he immediately genuflects and adores the consecrated Host: rises, shews it to the people, replaces it upon the Corporal, and again genuflects and adores: and does not disjoin his forefingers and thumbs henceforth, except when the Host is to be handled, till after ablution of his fingers. Then, having uncovered the Chalice, he says:

Likewise after supper, He takes the Chalice in both hands, taking also this goodly Chalice into his holy and venerable hands: again He bows his head, giving thanks to thee, Holding the Chalice in his left hand, he signs over it with his right, he bles✠sed, and gave it to his disciples, saying: Take, and drink ye all of it.

He utters the words of consecration over the Chalice, attentively, continuously and secretly, holding it slightly raised.

For this is the Chalice of my Blood, of the new and eternal testament: the mystery of faith: which shall be shed for you and for many for the remission of sins

Canon of the Mass

<small>Having uttered these words, he sets down the Chalice upon the Corporal, and saying secretly:</small>

As oft as ye shall do these things, ye shall do them in remembrance of me.

<small>He genuflects and adores: rises, shews it to the people, sets it down, covers it, and again adores. Then with hands extended he says:</small>

Wherefore, O Lord, we thy servants, and thy holy people also, remembering the blessed passion of the same Christ thy Son our Lord, as also his resurrection from the dead, and his glorious ascension into heaven: do offer unto thine excellent majesty of thine own gifts and bounty, <small>He joins his hands and signs thrice over the Host and Chalice together, saying:</small> the pure ✠ victim, the holy ✠ victim, the immaculate ✠ victim, <small>He signs once over the Host,</small> saying: the holy ✠ Bread of eternal life, and once over the Chalice, saying: and the Chalice ✠ of everlasting salvation.

<small>With extended hands he proceeds:</small>

Vouchsafe to look upon them with a merciful and pleasant countenance: and to accept them, even as thou didst vouchsafe to accept the gifts of thy servant Abel the Righteous, and the sacrifice of our Patriarch Abraham: and the holy sacrifice, the immaculate victim, which thy high priest Melchisedech offered unto thee.

<small>Bowing profoundly, he says with hands joined and placed upon the Altar:</small>

We humbly beseech thee, almighty God: command these offerings to be brought by the hands of thy holy Angel to thine altar on high, in sight of thy divine majesty: that all we *He kisses the Altar,* who at this partaking of the altar shall receive the most sacred *He joins his hands, and signs once over the Host, and once over the Chalice,* Bo✠dy and Blo✠od of thy Son, *He signs himself, saying:* may be fulfilled with all heavenly benediction and grace. *He joins his hands.* Through the same Christ our Lord. Amen.

Commemoration for the Departed

Remember also, O Lord, thy servants and handmaids N. and N., who have gone before us sealed with the seal of faith, and who sleep the sleep of peace.

He joins his hands and prays awhile for those departed for whom he intends to pray, then with extended hands proceeds:

To them, O Lord, and to all that rest in Christ, we beseech thee to grant the abode of refreshing, of light, and of peace. *He joins his hands, and bows his head, saying:* Through the same Christ our Lord. Amen.

He strikes his breast with his right hand, saying in a slightly louder voice:

To us sinners also, *With hands extended as before, he proceeds secretly:* thy servants, who hope in the multitude of thy mercies, vouchsafe to grant some part and fellowship with thy holy Apostles and Martyrs: with John, Stephen, Matthias, Barnabas, Ignatius, Alexander, Marcellinus, Peter, Felicitas, Perpetua, Agatha, Lucy, Agnes, Cecilia, Anastasia, and with all thy Saints: within whose

Canon of the Mass

fellowship, we beseech thee, admit us, not weighing our merit, but granting us forgiveness. *He joins his hands.* Through Christ our Lord.

Through whom, O Lord, thou dost ever create all these good things, *He signs thrice over the Host and Chalice together, saying:* dost sanc ✠ tify, quick ✠ en, ble ✠ ss, and bestow them upon us. *He uncovers the Chalice, genuflects, and takes the Host between the thumb and first finger of his right hand: and holding the Chalice with his left, he signs with the Host thrice from lip to lip of the Chalice, saying:*

Through ✠ him, and with ✠ him, and in ✠ him, *He signs twice with the Host itself between himself and the Chalice, saying:* O God the Father ✠ almighty, in the unity of the Holy ✠ Ghost, *Elevating the Chalice a little with the Host, he says:* all honour and glory are thine. *He replaces the Host, covers the Chalice with the Pall, genuflects, rises and says in an audible voice or sings:*

Through-out all á-ges, wórld with-oút end. ℟. A-men.

He joins his hands:

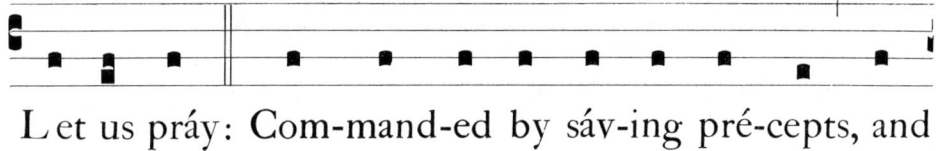

Let us práy: Com-mand-ed by sáv-ing pré-cepts, and

táught by di-víne in-sti-tú-tion, we are bóld to say:

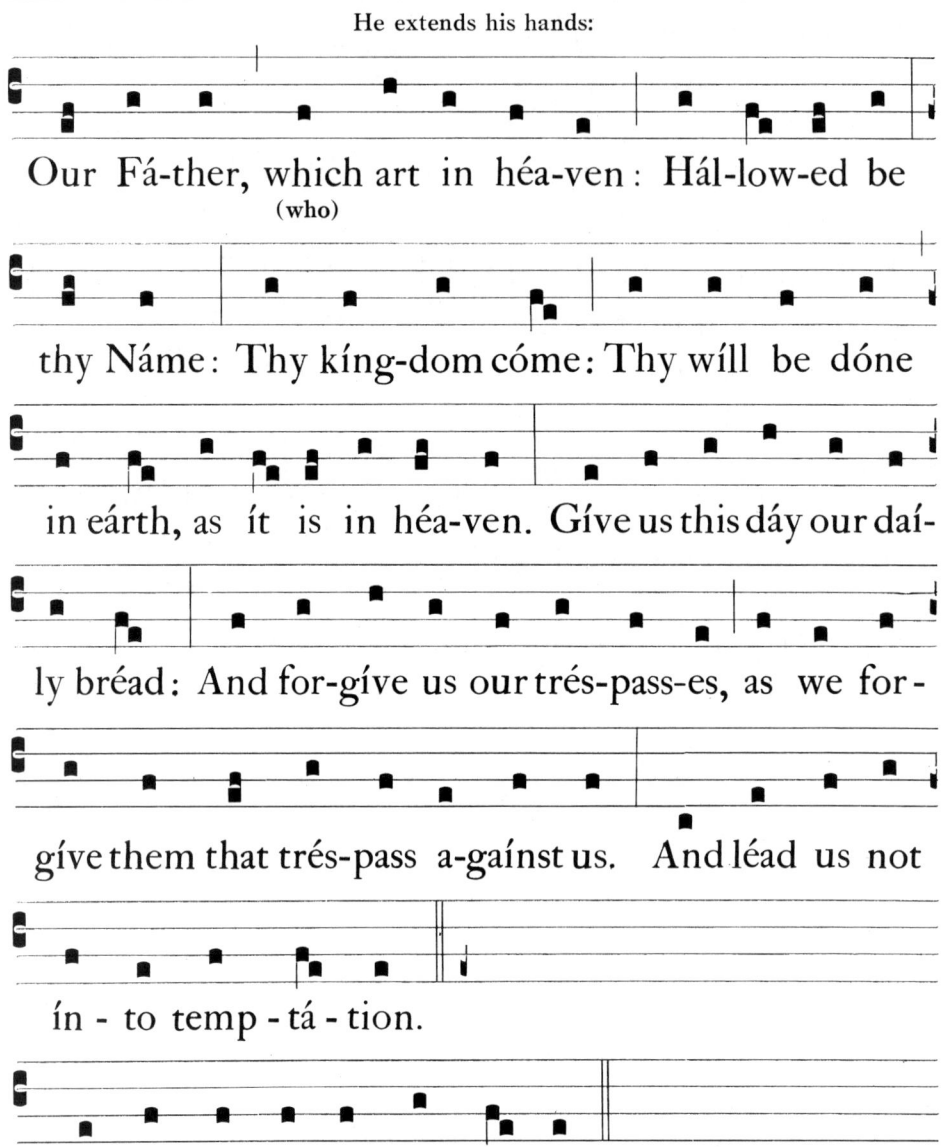

Canon of the Mass

¶ The following chant is used on simple Feasts, on Ferial days, in Votive Masses which are not for a grave and at the same time public cause, and in Masses of the Dead.

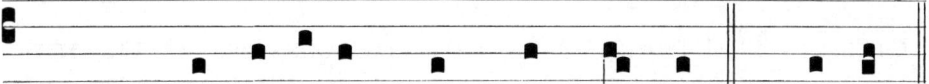
Through-oút all á-ges, wórld with-óut end.   ℟. A-men.

He joins his hands:
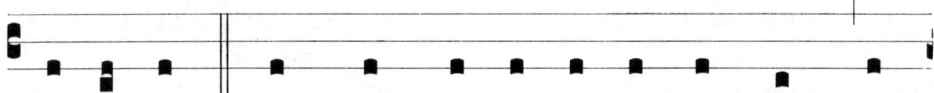
Lét us práy : Com-mand-ed by sav-ing pré-cepts, and

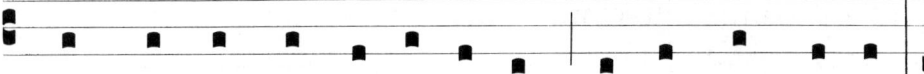
táught by di - víne in-sti-tú-tion, we are bóld to say :

He extends his hands:

Our Fá-ther, which árt in héa-ven : Hál-low-ed be
(who)

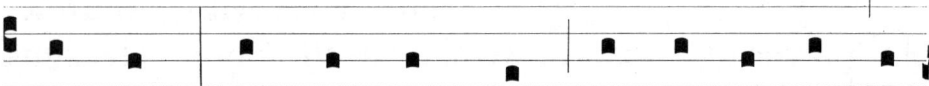
thy Náme : Thy king-dom cóme. Thy will be dóne, in

éarth as it ís in héa-ven. Gíve us this dáy our dái-ly

Canon of the Mass

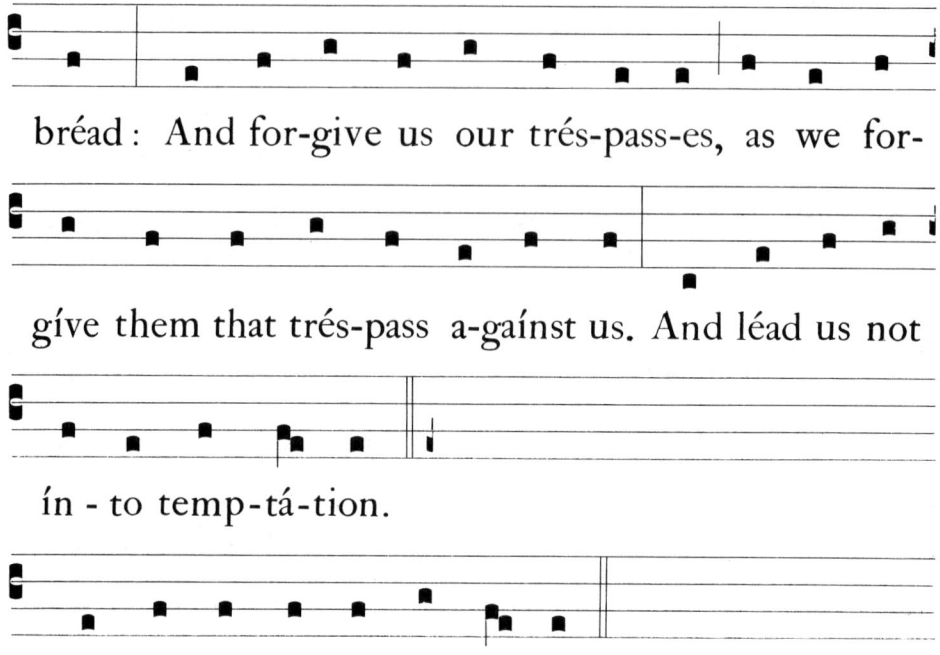

bréad: And for-give us our trés-pass-es, as we for-gíve them that trés-pass a-gaínst us. And léad us not ín - to temp-tá-tion.

℟. But de - lív - er us from é - vil.

The Priest says secretly: Amen.

Then he takes the Paten between the fore and middle fingers of his right hand, and holding it upright upon the Altar, says secretly:

Deliver us, O Lord, we beseech thee, from all evils, past, present, and to come: and at the intercession of the blessed and glorious ever Virgin Mary, Mother of God, with thy blessed Apostles Peter and Paul, and with Andrew, and all the Saints, *He signs himself with the Paten from forehead to breast,* favourably grant peace in our days: *He kisses the Paten,* that by the help of

Canon of the Mass

thine availing mercy we may ever both be free from sin and safe from all distress.

He puts the Paten under the Host, uncovers the Chalice, genuflects, rises, takes the Host, and holding it with both hands over the Chalice, breaks it in the middle, saying:

Through the same Jesus Christ thy Son our Lord.

He places the half which he holds in his right hand on the Paten. Then from the part which remains in his left hand, he breaks a particle, saying:

Who liveth and reigneth with thee in the unity of the Holy Ghost, God.

He joins the other half, which he holds in his left hand, to the half laid upon the Paten, and retaining the small particle in his right hand over the Chalice, which he holds with his left by the knop below the cup, he says in an audible voice, or sings:

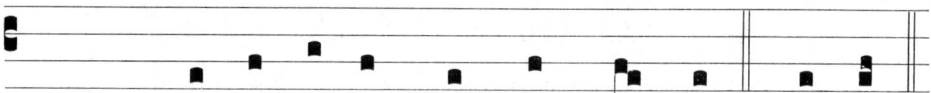

Through-oút all á-ges, wórld withoút end. ℟. A-men.

With the particle itself he signs thrice over the Chalice, saying:

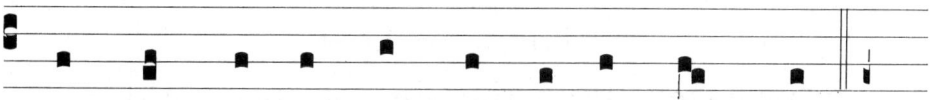

The peáce ✠ of the Lórd be ✠ al-way wíth ✠ you.

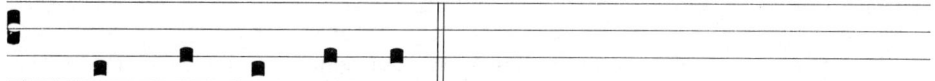

℟. And wíth thy spí-rit.

He puts the particle into the Chalice, saying secretly:

May this mingling and hallowing of the Body and Blood of our Lord Jesus Christ avail us who receive it unto everlasting life. Amen.

He covers the Chalice, genuflects, rises, and bowing to the Sacrament, joins his hands, and beating his breast thrice, says in an audible voice:

O Lamb of God,
that takest away the sins of the world:
have mercy upon us.

O Lamb of God,
that takest away the sins of the world:
have mercy upon us.

O Lamb of God,
that takest away the sins of the world:
grant us peace.

In Masses of the Dead **have mercy upon us** is not said, but in its place **grant them rest**, and the third time is added **everlasting**.

Then bowing, with hands joined upon the Altar, he says secretly the following Prayers:

O Lord Jesu Christ, who saidst to thine Apostles, Peace I leave with you, my peace I give unto you: regard not my sins, but the faith of thy Church: and vouchsafe to grant her peace and unity according to thy will: Who livest and reignest God, throughout all ages; world without end. Amen.

If the pax is to be given, he kisses the Altar, and giving the pax, says:

Peace be with you.

℟. And with thy spirit.

In Masses of the Dead the pax is not given, nor is the preceding Prayer said:

O Lord Jesu Christ, Son of the living God, who by the will of the Father, and the co-operation of the Holy Ghost, hast through thy death given life unto the world: deliver me by this thy most sacred Body and Blood from all mine iniquities, and from every evil: and make me ever to cleave unto thy commandments, and suffer me never to be separated from thee: Who with the same God the Father and the Holy Ghost livest and reignest God, world without end. Amen.

Let the partaking of thy Body, O Lord Jesu Christ, which I, unworthy, presume to receive, turn not to my judgment and condemnation: but of thy goodness let it avail unto me for protection of soul and of body, that I may receive thy healing: Who livest and reignest with God the Father in the unity of the Holy Ghost God, throughout all ages, world without end. Amen.

He genuflects, rises, and says:

I will receive the bread of heaven, and call upon the name of the Lord.

Then bowing slightly, he takes both parts of the Host between the thumb and forefinger of his left hand, and places the Paten between the same forefinger and the middle finger, and beating his breast three times with his right hand, he says thrice, devoutly and humbly, raising his voice a little:

Lord, I am not worthy, *And he proceeds secretly:* that thou shouldest enter under my roof: but speak the word only, and my soul shall be healed.

Afterwards signing himself with his right hand with the Host over the Paten, he says:

The Body of our Lord Jesus Christ preserve my soul unto everlasting life. Amen.

And bowing himself, he reverently takes both parts of the Host: which having been consumed, he puts the Paten down upon the Corporal, and raising himself, joins his hands, and is still for a little space in meditation on the Most Holy Sacrament. Then he uncovers the Chalice, genuflects, collects the fragments, if there be any, and cleanses the Paten over the Chalice, saying meanwhile:

What reward shall I give unto the Lord for all the benefits that he hath done unto me? I will receive the cup of salvation, and call upon the name of the Lord. I will call upon the Lord which is worthy to be praised, so shall I be safe from mine enemies.

He takes the Chalice in his right hand and signing himself with it, says:

The Blood of our Lord Jesus Christ preserve my soul unto everlasting life. Amen.

Holding the Paten under the Chalice with his left hand, he reverently receives the Blood with the particle. Having received it, if there be any to be communicated, let him communicate them, before he purify himself. (See p. 393.)

Afterwards he says:

Grant, O Lord, that what we have taken with our mouths we may receive in purity of heart: and let this temporal gift avail for our healing unto life eternal.

Meanwhile he presents the Chalice to the minister, who pours into it a little wine, wherewith he purifies himself: then he continues:

Let thy Body, O Lord, which I have taken, and thy Blood which I have drunk, cleave unto my members: and grant; that no stain of sin may remain in me, whom thou hast refreshed with these pure and holy sacraments: Who livest and reignest world without end. Amen.

He washes and wipes his fingers, and takes the ablution: he wipes his mouth and the Chalice, which, having folded the Corporal, he covers and places on the Altar as before: then he proceeds with the Mass.

¶ After shall be said as follows:

Almighty and everliving God, we most heartily thank thee, for that thou dost vouchsafe to feed us, who have duly received these holy mysteries, with the spiritual food of the most precious Body and Blood of thy Son our Saviour Jesus Christ.

And dost assure us thereby of thy favour and goodness towards us; and that we are very members incorporate in the mystical body of thy Son, which is the blessed company of all faithful people; and are also heirs through hope of thy everlasting kingdom, by the merits of the most precious death and passion of thy dear Son.

And we most humbly beseech thee, O heavenly Father, so to assist us with thy grace, that we may continue in that holy fellowship, and do all such good works as thou hast prepared for us to walk in. Through Jesus Christ our Lord, to whom with thee and the Holy Ghost be all honour and glory, world without end. ℟. Amen.

Canon of the Mass

Having said after the last Prayer: ℣. The Lord be with you. ℟. And with thy spirit, He says, according to the quality of the Mass, either Ite, Missa est, or Let us bless the Lord. ℟. Thanks be to God.

In Masses of the Dead he says: ℣. May they rest in peace. ℟. Amen.

[For Chant, see pp. 409-411.]

Having said Ite, Missa est, or Let us bless the Lord, the Priest bows himself before the midst of the Altar, and with hands joined thereon, says secretly:

LET this my bounden duty and service be pleasing to thee, O holy Trinity: and grant; that the sacrifice, which I, unworthy, have offered before the eyes of thy majesty, may be acceptable to thee, and may through thy mercy obtain thy gracious favour for me and all for whom I have offered it. Through Christ our Lord. Amen.

Then he kisses the Altar: and raising his eyes, extending, raising, and joining his hands, and bowing his head to the Cross, he says: May God almighty, and turning to the people, blessing them once only, even in solemn Masses, he proceeds: the Father, the ✠ Son and the Holy Ghost, bless you. ℟. Amen.

In Pontifical Mass the blessing is threefold, as is ordered in the Pontifical.

Then the Priest at the Gospel corner says with hands joined: ℣. The Lord be with you. ℟. And with thy spirit.

And signing with the sign of the Cross first the Altar or book, then himself on forehead, mouth and breast, he says:

✠ The Beginning of the holy Gospel according to John.

Or if another Gospel is to be read: The Continuation of the holy Gospel etc.

℟. Glory be to thee, O Lord.

He proceeds with joined hands:

John 1, 1-14.

IN the beginning was the Word, and the Word was with God, and the Word was God. The same was in the beginning with God. All things were made by him: and without him was not anything made that was made: in him was life, and the life was the light of men: and the light shineth in darkness, and the darkness comprehended it not. There was a man sent from God whose name was John. The same came for a witness, to bear witness of the light, that all men through him might believe. He was not that light, but was sent to bear witness of that light. That was the true light, which lighteth every man that cometh into the world. He was in the world, and the world was made by him, and the world knew him not. He came unto his own, and his own received him not. But as many as received him, to them gave he power to become the sons of God, even to them that believe on his name: which were born, not of blood, nor of the will of the flesh, nor of the will of man, but of God. He genuflects, saying: And the Word was made flesh, And rising proceeds: and dwelt among us: and we beheld his glory, the glory as of the Only-begotten of the Father, full of grace and truth.

℟. Thanks be to God.

In Masses of the Dead the Blessing is not given, but having said **May they rest in peace** and **Let this my bounden duty,** he kisses the Altar, and reads the Gospel of Saint John.

The Gospel of Saint John being ended, he says for thanksgiving as he goes from the Altar the Antiphon **Let us sing,** with the rest.

ORDER

FOR THE ADMINISTRATION

OF

HOLY COMMUNION

If there are some to be communicated within the Mass, the Priest, having received the most sacred Blood, before he purifies himself, having made a genuflexion, shall place the consecrated particles in a ciborium, or, if there are few to be communicated, on the paten, unless from the beginning they had been placed in a ciborium or another chalice. Meanwhile the minister, kneeling at the Epistle side, and facing the Gospel side, makes the confession for them, saying: **I confess to God almighty, etc.** Then the Priest again genuflects, and with joined hands, turning to the people at the Gospel side, says:

Almighty God have mercy upon you, forgive you your sins, and bring you to everlasting life.

℞. **Amen.**

And he adds: **The almighty and merciful Lord grant unto you pardon, absolution,** ✠ **and remission of your sins.**

℞. **Amen.**

As he says: **pardon, etc.**, he signs those who are to be communicated with his right hand in the form of a cross.

Then he turns to the Altar, genuflects, and with his left hand takes the ciborium; and with his right takes one particle, which he holds between his thumb and forefinger somewhat raised above the ciborium: and turning to the people in the midst of the Altar, he says in a clear voice:

Behold the Lamb of God, behold him who taketh away the sins of the world. Then he continues: **Lord, I am not worthy that thou shouldest enter under my roof, but speak the word only, and my soul shall be healed;** which he repeats a second and third time: and the same form is to be used, when Communion is ministered to a woman.

Then he proceeds to communicate them, beginning from those who are on the Epistle side; but first, if Communion is to be given to Priests, or others of the Clergy, it shall be ministered to them, kneeling at the steps of the Altar. Priests or Deacons, when communicating, shall wear a stole either of white colour, or of the same colour as the administering Priest wears.

The Priest, when giving the Sacrament to each one, and making with it the sign of the cross over the ciborium, says at the same time:

The Body of our Lord Jesus Christ preserve thy soul unto everlasting life. Amen.

The Communion ended, he returns to the Altar, saying nothing, nor does he give the blessing, as he will give it at the end of Mass. Then he says secretly: **Quod ore súmpsimus,** etc., as in the Missal, purifies himself, and completes the Mass.

N.B. The Communion of the people should always take place within the Mass immediately after the Communion of the celebrating Priest (unless for some reasonable cause it is to be done immediately before or after a Low Mass), since the Prayers which are said in the Mass after the Communion refer not only to the Priest but to the other communicants.

CANON MISSAE

Finita Præfatione, Sacerdos extendens, elevans aliquantulum et jungens manus, elevansque ad cælum oculos, et statim demittens, profunde inclinatus ante Altare, manibus super eo positis, dicit:

Te ígitur, clementíssime Pater, per Jesum Christum, Fílium tuum, Dóminum nostrum, súpplices rogámus, ac pétimus, Osculatur Altare et, junctis manibus ante pectus, dicit: uti accépta hábeas et benedícas, Signat ter super Hostiam et Calicem simul, dicens: hæc ✠ dona, hæc ✠ múnera, hæc ✠ sancta sacrifícia illibáta, Extensis manibus prosequitur: in primis, quæ tibi offérimus pro Ecclésia tua sancta cathólica: quam pacificáre, custodíre, adunáre et régere dignéris toto orbe terrárum: una cum fámulo tuo Papa nostro N. et Antístite nostro N. et ómnibus orthodóxis, atque cathólicæ et apostólicæ fídei cultóribus.

Commemoratio pro vivis

Meménto, Dómine, famulórum famularúmque tuárum N. et N. Jungit manus, orat aliquantulum pro quibus orare intendit: deinde manibus extensis prosequitur: et ómnium circumstántium, quorum tibi fides cógnita est et nota devótio, pro quibus tibi offérimus: vel qui tibi ófferunt hoc sacrifícium laudis, pro se, suísque ómnibus: pro redemptióne animárum suárum, pro spe salútis et incolumitátis suæ: tibíque reddunt vota sua ætérno Deo, vivo et vero.

* Infra Actionem

Communicántes, et memóriam venerántes, in primis gloriósæ semper Vírginis Maríæ, Genitrícis Dei et Dómini nostri Jesu Christi: †sed et beatórum Apostolórum ac Mártyrum tuórum, Petri et Pauli, Andréæ, Jacóbi, Joánnis, Thomæ, Jacóbi, Philíppi, Bartholomæi, Matthæi, Simónis et Thaddæi: Lini, Cleti, Cleméntis, Xysti, Cornélii, Cypriáni, Lauréntii, Chrysógoni, Joánnis et Pauli, Cosmæ et Damiáni: et ómnium Sanctórum tuórum; quorum méritis precibúsque concédas, ut in ómnibus protectiónis tuæ muniámur auxílio. Jungit manus. Per eúndem Christum Dóminum nostrum. Amen.

¶ Tenens manus expansas super Oblata, dicit:

Hanc ígitur oblatiónem servitútis nostræ, sed et cunctæ famíliæ tuæ, quæsumus, Dómine, ut placátus accípias: diésque nostros in túa pace dispónas, atque ab ætérna damnatióne nos éripi, et in electórum tuórum júbeas grege numerári. Jungit manus. Per Christum Dóminum nostrum. Amen.

Quam oblatiónem tu, Deus, in ómnibus, quæsumus, Signat ter super Oblata, bene✠díctam, adscríp✠tam, ra✠tam, rationábilem, acceptabilémque fácere dignéris: Signat semel super Hostiam, ut nobis Cor✠pus, et semel super Calicem, et San✠guis fiat dilectíssimi Fílii tui, Jungit manus, Dómini nostri Jesu Christi.

*In Nativitate Domini et per Octavam dicitur:

Communicántes, et diem sacratíssimum celebrántes, quo (vel noctem sacratíssimam celebrántes, qua) beátæ Maríæ intemeráta virgínitas huic mundo édidit Salvatórem: sed et memóriam venerántes, in primis ejúsdem gloriósæ semper Vírginis Maríæ, Genitrícis ejúsdem Dei et Dómini nostri Jesu Christi: †

In Epiphania Domini dicitur:

Communicántes, et diem sacratíssimum celebrántes, quo Unigénitus tuus, in tua tecum glória coætérnus, in veritáte carnis nostræ visibíliter corporális appáruit: sed et memóriam venerántes, in primis gloriósæ semper Vírginis Maríæ, Genitrícis ejúsdem Dei et Dómini nostri Jesu Christi: †

A Sabbato sancto usque ad Sabbatum in Albis dicitur:

Communicántes, et diem sacratíssimum (vel noctem sacratíssimam) celebrántes Resurrectiónis Dómini nostri Jesu Christi secúndum carnem: sed et memóriam venerántes, in primis gloriósæ semper Vírginis Maríæ, Genitrícis ejúsdem Dei et Dómini nostri Jesu Christi: †

In Ascensione Domini dicitur:

Communicántes, et diem sacratíssimum celebrántes, quo Dóminus noster, unigénitus Fílius tuus, unítam sibi fragilitátis nostræ substántiam in glóriæ tuæ déxtera collocávit: sed et memóriam venerántes, in primis gloriósæ semper Vírginis Maríæ, Genitrícis ejúsdem Dei et Dómini nostri Jesu Christi: †

A Vigilia Pentecostes usque ad sequens Sabbatum inclusive dicitur:

Communicántes, et diem sacratíssimum Pentecóstes celebrántes, quo Spíritus Sanctus Apóstolis innúmeris linguis appáruit: sed et memóriam venerántes, in primis gloriósæ semper Vírginis Maríæ, Genitrícis Dei et Dómini nostri Jesu Christi: †

¶ A Sabbato sancto usque ad Sabbatum in Albis inclusive et a Vigilia Pentecostes usque ad sequens Sabbatum inclusive dicitur:

Hanc igitur oblatiónem servitútis nostræ, sed et cunctæ famíliæ tuæ, quam tibi offérimus pro his quoque, quos regeneráre dignátus es ex aqua et Spíritu Sancto, tríbuens eis remissiónem ómnium peccatórum, quæsumus, Dómine, ut placátus accípias: diésque nostros in tua pace dispónas, atque ab ætérna damnatióne nos éripi, et in electórum tuórum júbeas grege numerári. Jungit manus. Per Christum Dóminum nostrum. Amen.

Quam oblatiónem, etc.

Qui prídie quam paterétur, Accipit Hostiam, accépit panem in sanctas ac venerábiles manus suas, Elevat oculos ad caelum, et elevátis óculis in cælum ad te Deum, Patrem suum omnipoténtem, Caput inclinat, tibi grátias agens, Signat super Hostiam, bene ✠ díxit, fregit, dedítque discípulis suis, dicens: Accípite, et manducáte ex hoc omnes.

Tenens ambabus manibus Hostiam inter indices et pollices, profert verba consecrationis secrete, distincte, et attente super Hostiam, et simul super omnes, si plures sint consecrandæ.

Hoc est enim Corpus meum

Quibus verbis prolatis, statim Hostiam consecratam genuflexus adorat: surgit, ostendit populo, reponit super Corporale, et genuflexus iterum adorat: nec amplius pollices et indices disjungit, nisi quando Hostia tractanda est, usque ad ablutionem digitorum. Tunc, detecto Calice, dicit:

Símili modo postquam cœnátum est, Ambabus manibus accipit Calicem, accípiens et hunc præclárum Cálicem in sanctas ac venerábiles manus suas: item Caput inclinat, tibi grátias agens, Sinistra tenens Calicem, dextera signat super eum bene ✠ díxit, dedítque discípulis suis, dicens: Accípite, et bíbite ex eo omnes.

Profert verba consecrationis super Calicem, attente, continuate, et secrete, tenens illum parum elevatum.

Hic est enim Calix Sánguinis mei, novi et ætérni testaménti: mystérium fídei: qui pro vobis et pro multis effundétur in remissiónem peccatórum

Canon Missae 399

Quibus verbis prolatis, deponit Calicem super Corporale, et dicens secrete:

Hæc quotiescúmque fecéritis, in mei memóriam faciétis.

Genuflexus adorat: surgit, ostendit populo, deponit, cooperit, et genuflexus iterum adorat. Deinde disjunctis manibus dicit:

Unde et mémores, Dómine, nos servi tui, sed et plebs tua sancta, ejúsdem Christi Fílii tui, Domini nostri, tam beátæ passiónis, nec non et ab ínferis resurrectiónis, sed et in cælos gloriósæ ascensiónis: offérimus præcláræ majestáti tuæ de tuis donis ac datis, Jungit manus, et signat ter super Hostiam, et Calicem simul, dicens: hóstiam ✠ puram, hóstiam ✠ sanctam, hóstiam ✠ immaculátam, Signat semel super Hostiam, dicens: Panem ✠ sanctum vitæ ætérnæ, et semel super Cálicem, dicens: et Cálicem ✠ salútis perpétuæ.

Extensis manibus prosequitur:

Supra quæ propítio ac seréno vultu respícere dignéris: et accépta habére, sícuti accépta habére dignátus es múnera púeri tui justi Abel, et sacrifícium Patriárchæ nostri Abrahæ: et quod tibi óbtulit summus sacérdos tuus Melchísedech, sanctum sacrifícium, immaculátam hóstiam.

Profunde inclinatus, junctis manibus et super Altare positis, dicit:

Súpplices te rogámus, omnípotens Deus: jube hæc perférri per manus sancti Angeli tui in sublíme altáre tuum, in conspéctu divínæ majestátis tuæ: ut, quotquot Osculatur Altare, ex hac altáris participatióne sacrosánctum Fílii tui *Jungit manus, et signat semel super Hostiam, et semel super Calicem,* Cor ✠ pus, et Sán ✠ guinem sumpsérimus, *Seipsum signat, dicens:* omni benedictióne cælésti et grátia repleámur. *Jungit manus.* Per eúndem Christum Dóminum nostrum. Amen.

Commemoratio pro defunctis

Meménto étiam, Dómine, famulórum famularúmque tuárum N. et N., qui nos præcessérunt cum signo fídei, et dórmiunt in somno pacis.

Jungit manus, orat aliquantulum pro iis defunctis, pro quibus orare intendit, deinde extensis manibus prosequitur:

Ipsis, Dómine, et ómnibus in Christo quiescéntibus, locum refrigérii, lucis et pacis ut indúlgeas, deprecámur. *Jungit manus, et caput inclinat, dicens:* Per eúndem Christum Dóminum nostrum. Amen.

Manu dextera percutit sibi pectus, elata aliquantulum voce dicens:

Nobis quoque peccatóribus *Extensis manibus ut prius, secrete prosequitur:* fámulis tuis, de multitúdine miseratiónum tuárum sperántibus, partem áliquam et societátem donáre dignéris, cum tuis sanctis Apóstolis et Martyribus: cum Joánne, Stéphano, Matthía, Bárnaba, Ignátio, Alexándro, Marcellíno, Petro, Felicitáte, Perpétua, Agatha, Lúcia, Agnéte, Cæcília, Anastásia, et ómnibus Sanctis tuis: intra quorum nos consórtium, non æstimator mériti, sed véniæ, quæsumus, largítor admítte. Jungit manus. Per Christum Dóminum nostrum.

Per quem hæc ómnia, Dómine, semper bona creas, Signat ter super Hostiam, et Calicem simul, dicens: sanctí✠ficas, viví✠ficas, bene✠dícis et præstas nobis.

Discooperit Calicem, genuflectit, accipit Hostiam inter pollicem et indicem manus dexteræ: et tenens sinistra Calicem, cum Hostia signat ter a labio ad labium Calicis, dicens:

Per ip✠sum, et cum ip✠so, et in ip✠so, Cum ipsa Hostia signat bis inter se et Calicem, dicens: est tibi Deo Patri✠omnipoténti, in unitáte Spíritus ✠Sancti, Elevans parum Calicem cum Hostia, dicit: omnis honor, et glória.

Reponit Hostiam, Calicem Palla cooperit, genuflectit, surgit, et dicit intelligibili voce vel cantat:

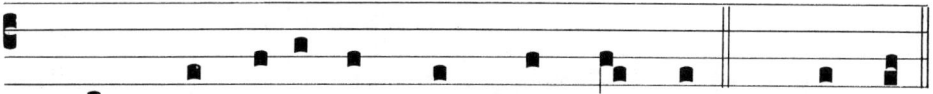

Through-out all á-ges, wórld with-oút end. ℟. A-men.

Jungit manus

Let us práy: Com-mand-ed by sáv-ing pré-cepts, and

táught by di-víne in-sti-tú-tion, we are bóld to say:

Canon Missae

402

Extendit manus

Our Fá-ther, which art in héa-ven : Hál-low-ed be
(who)
thy Náme : Thy kíng-dom cóme : Thy will be dóne
in eárth, as it is in héa-ven, Gíve us this dáy our daí-
ly bréad : And for-gíve us our trés-pass-es, as we for-
gíve them that trés-pass a-gaínst us. And léad us not
ín - to temp - tá - tion.

℟. But de - lív - er us from é - vil.

Sacerdos dicit secrete: Amen.

Canon Missae 403

¶ Sequens cantus dicitur in Festis simplicibus, in diebus Ferialibus, in Missis votivis quae non sint pro re gravi et publica simul causa, et in Missis Defunctorum.

Through-oút all á-ges, wórld with-óut end. ℟. A-men.

Jungit manus

Lét us práy : Com-mand-ed by sav-ing pré-cepts, and táught by di - víne in-sti-tú-tion, we are bóld to say :

Extendit manus

Our Fá-ther, which árt in héa-ven : Hál-low-ed be
(who)
thy Náme : Thy king-dom cóme. Thy will be dóne, in éarth as it ís in héa-ven. Gíve us this dáy our dái-ly

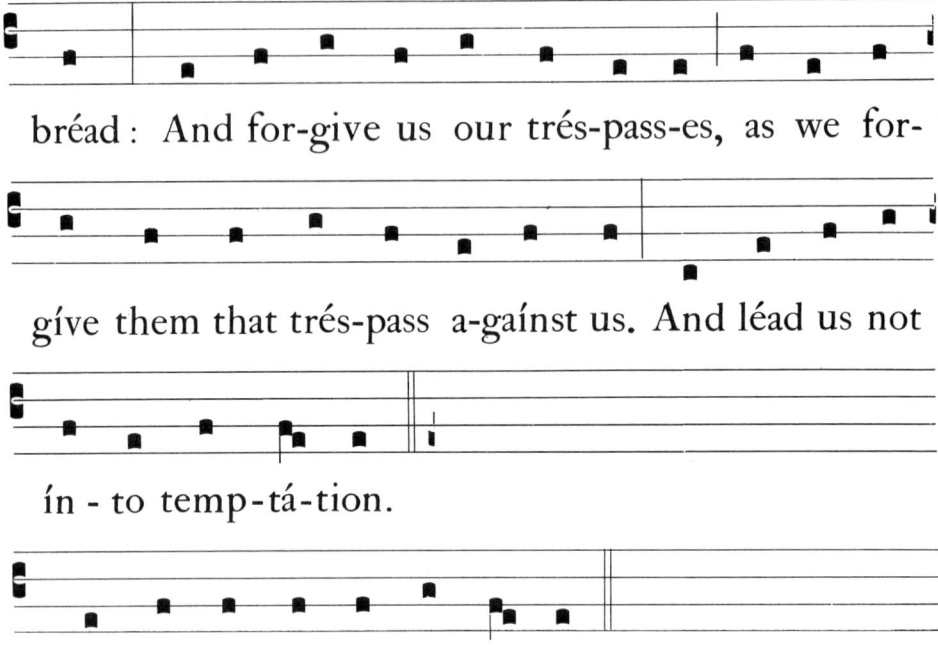

bréad: And forgive us our tréspasses, as we forgíve them that tréspass against us. And léad us not into temptátion.

℟. But delíver us from évil.

Sacerdos dicit secrete: Amen.

Deinde manu dextera accipit inter indicem et medium digitos Patenam, quam tenens super Altare erectam, dicit secrete:

Líbera nos, quæsumus, Dómine, ab ómnibus malis, prætéritis, præséntibus et futúris: et intercedénte beáta et gloriósa semper Vírgine Dei Genitríce María, cum beátis Apóstolis tuis Petro et Paulo, atque Andréa, et ómnibus Sanctis, *Signat se cum Patena a fronte ad pectus,* da propítius pacem in diébus nostris: *Patenam osculatur,* ut ope misericórdiæ tuæ adjúti, et a peccáto simus semper líberi et ab omni perturbatióne secúri.

Submittit Patenam Hostiæ, discooperit Calicem, genuflectit, surgit, accipit Hostiam, et eam super Calicem tenens utraque manu, frangit per medium, dicens:

Per eúndem Dóminum nostrum Jesum Christum Fílium tuum.

Et mediam partem, quam in dextera manu tenet, ponit super Patenam. Deinde ex parte, quæ in sinistra remanserat, frangit particulam, dicens:

Qui tecum vivit et regnat in unitáte Spíritus Sancti Deus.

Aliam mediam partem, quam in sinistra manu habet, adjungit mediæ super Patenam positæ, et particulam parvam dextera retinens super Calicem, quem sinistra per nodum infra cuppam tenet, dicit intelligibili voce vel cantat:

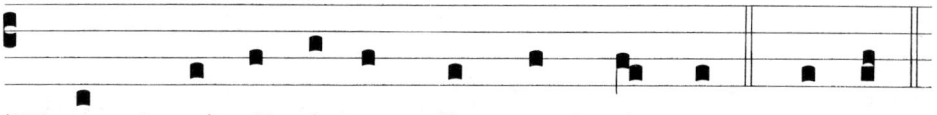

Through-oút all á-ges, wórld withoút end. ℟. A-men.

Cum ipsa particula signat ter super Calicem, dicens:

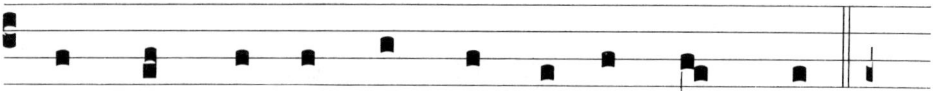

The peáce ✠ of the Lórd be ✠ al-way wíth ✠ you.

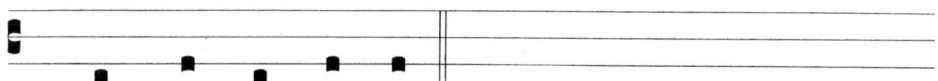

℟. And wíth thy spí-rit.

Particulam ipsam mittit in Calicem, dicens secrete:

Hæc commíxtio, et consecrátio Córporis et Sánguinis Dómini nostri Jesu Christi, fiat accipiéntibus nobis in vitam ætérnam. Amen.

Cooperit Calicem, genuflectit, surgit, et inclinatus Sacramento, junctis manibus, et ter pectus percutiens, intelligibili voce dicit:

Agnus Dei, qui tollis peccáta mundi: miserére nobis.

Agnus Dei, qui tollis peccáta mundi: miserére nobis.

Agnus Dei, qui tollis peccáta mundi: dona nobis pacem.

In Missis Defunctorum non dicitur miserére nobis, sed ejus loco dona eis réquiem, et in tertio additur sempiternam.

Canon Missae

Deinde, junctis manibus super Altare, inclinatus dicit secrete sequentes Orationes:

Dómine Jesu Christe, qui dixísti Apóstolis tuis: Pacem relínquo vobis, pacem meam do vobis: ne respícias peccáta mea, sed fidem Ecclésiæ tuæ; eámque secúndum voluntátem tuam pacificáre et coadunáre dignéris: Qui vivis et regnas Deus per ómnia sæcula sæculórum. Amen.

Si danda est pax, osculatur Altare, et dans pacem, dicit:

Pax tecum.

R℈. Et cum spíritu tuo.

In Missis Defunctorum non datur pax, neque dicitur præcedens Oratio.

Dómine Jesu Christe, Fili Dei vivi, qui ex voluntáte Patris, cooperánte Spíritu Sancto, per mortem tuam mundum vivificásti: líbera me per hoc sacrosánctum Corpus et Sánguinem tuum ab ómnibus iniquitátibus meis, et univérsis malis: et fac me tuis semper inhærére mandátis, et a te numquam separári permíttas: Qui cum eódem Deo Patre et Spíritu Sancto vivis et regnas Deus in sæcula sæculórum. Amen.

Percéptio Córporis tui, Dómine Jesu Christe, quod ego indígnus súmere præsúmo, non mihi provéniat in judícium et condemnatiónem: sed pro tua pietáte prosit mihi ad tutaméntum mentis et córporis, et ad medélam percipiéndam: Qui vivis et regnas cum Deo Patre in unitáte Spíritus Sancti Deus, per ómnia sæcula sæculórum. Amen.

Genuflectit, surgit, et dicit:

Panem cæléstem accípiam, et nomen Dómini invocábo.

Deinde parum inclinatus, accipit ambas partes Hostiæ inter pollicem et indicem sinistræ manus, et Patenam inter eundem indicem et medium supponit, et dextera tribus vicibus percutiens pectus, elata aliquantulum voce, ter dicit devote et humiliter:

Dómine, non sum dignus, Et secrete prosequitur: ut intres sub tectum meum: sed tantum dic verbo, et sanábitur ánima mea.

Postea dextera se signans cum Hostia super Patenam, dicit:

Corpus Dómini nostri Jesu Christi custódiat ánimam meam in vitam ætérnam. Amen.

Et se inclinans, reverenter sumit ambas partes Hostiæ: quibus sumptis, deponit Patenam super Corporale, et erigens se jungit manus, et quiescit aliquantulum in meditatione Sanctissimi Sacramenti. Deinde discooperit Calicem, genuflectit, colligit fragmenta, si quæ sint, extergit Patenam super Calicem, interim dicens:

Quid retríbuam Dómino pro ómnibus, quæ retríbuit mihi? Cálicem salutáris accípiam, et nomen Dómini invocábo. Laudans invocábo Dóminum, et ab inimícis meis salvus ero.

Accipit Calicem manu dextera, et eo se signans, dicit:

Sanguis Dómini nostri Jesu Christi custódiat ánimam meam in vitam ætérnam. Amen.

Et sinistra supponens Patenam Calici, reverenter sumit totum Sanguinem cum particula. Quo sumpto, si qui sunt communicandi, eos communicet, antequam se purificet. Postea dicit:

Quod ore súmpsimus, Dómine, pura mente capiámus: et de múnere temporáli fiat nobis remédium sempitérnum.

Canon Missae

Interim porrigit Calicem ministro, qui infundit in eo parum vini, quo se purificat: deinde prosequitur:

Corpus tuum, Dómine, quod sumpsi, et Sanguis, quem potávi, adhǽreat viscéribus meis: et prǽsta; ut in me non remáneat scélerum mácula, quem pura et sancta refecérunt sacraménta: Qui vivis et regnas in sǽcula sæculórum. Amen.

Ábluit et extergit digitos, ac sumit ablutiónem: extergit os et Cálicem, quem, plicato Corporali, operit et collocat in Altari ut prius: deinde prosequitur Missam.

Dicto, post ultimam Orationem, ℣. Dóminus vobíscum. ℟. Et cum spíritu tuo, dicit pro Missæ qualitate, vel Ite, Missa est, vel Benedicámus Dómino. ℟. Deo gratias.

In Missis Defunctorum dicit: ℣. Requiéscant in pace. ℟. Amen.

I. Tempore Paschali
hoc est a Missa Sabbati sancti usque ad Sabbatum in Albis inclusive in Missis de Tempore

I - te, Mis-sa est, al-le-lú-ja, al-le - lú-ja.

II. In Festis solemnibus

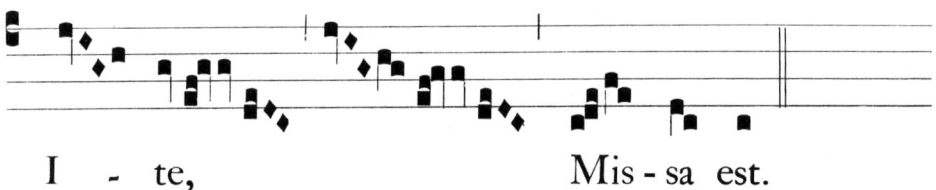

I - te, Mis - sa est.

III. In Festis duplicibus

I - te, Mis-sa est.

IV. In Missis B. Mariæ Virg.

I - te, Mis-sa est.

V. In Dominicis infra annum, et infra Octavas

I - te, Mis - sa est.

VI. In Festis simplicibus

I - te, Mis-sa est.

VII. In Dominicis Tempore Adventus, Quadragesimae et Passionis

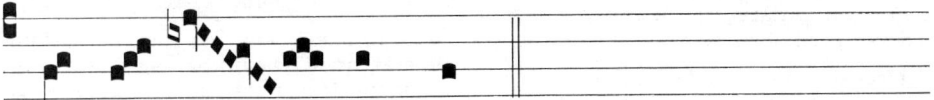

Let us bléss   the Lórd.

VIII. In omnibus Feriis extra Tempus Paschale, in Litaniis majoribus et minoribus, in Vigiliis communibus item extra Tempus Paschale, atque, si omissum fuerit Glória in excélsis, in Missis Votivis, quae pro re gravi et publica simul causa non sint

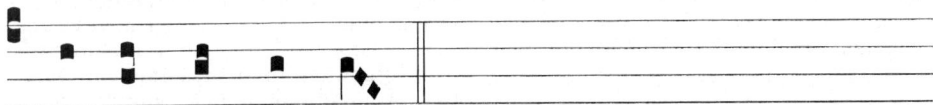

Let us bléss the Lórd.

IX. In Dominicis Septuagesimae, Sexagesimae et Quinquagesimae

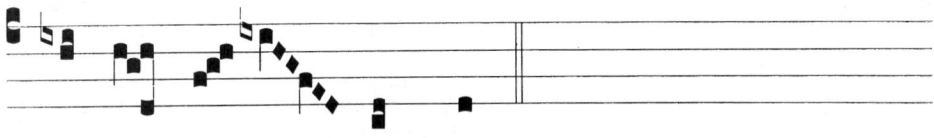

Let us   bléss   the Lórd.

X. In Vigilia Nativitatis Domini, etiamsi in Dominica occurrat, in Festo SS. Innocentium, et in Missis votivis pro re gravi et publica simul causa, quando non dicitur Glória in excélsis

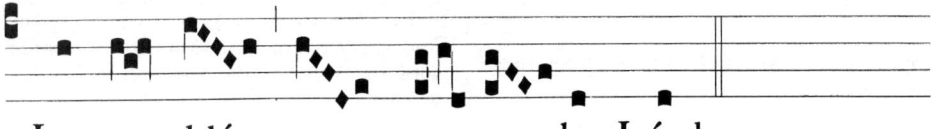

Let us bléss   the Lórd.

XI. In Missis Defunctorum

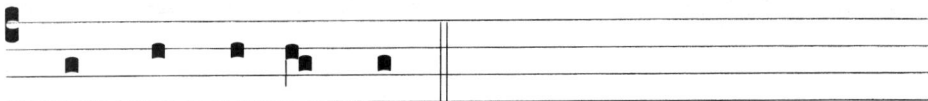

May they rést in peáce.

Dicto Ite, Missa est, vel Benedicámus Dómino, Sacerdos inclinat se ante medium Altaris, et manibus junctis super illud, dicit secrete:

Pláceat tibi, sancta Trínitas, obséquium servitútis meæ: et præsta; ut sacrifícium, quod óculis tuæ majestátis indígnus óbtuli, tibi sit acceptábile, mihíque et ómnibus, pro quibus illud óbtuli, sit, te miseránte, propitiábile. Per Christum, Dóminum nostrum. Amen.

Deinde osculatur Altare: et elevatis oculis, extendens, elevans et jungens manus, caputque Cruci inclinans, dicit:

Benedícat vos omnípotens Deus, et versus ad populum, semel tantum benedicens, etiam in Missis solemnibus, prosequitur: Pater, et Fílius, ✠ et Spíritus Sanctus. ℟. Amen.

In Missa Pontificali ter benedicitur, ut in Pontificali habetur.

Deinde Sacerdos in cornu Evangelii, junctis manibus dicit:

℣. Dóminus vobíscum.

℟. Et cum spíritu tuo.

Et signans signo crucis primum Altare vel librum, deinde se in fronte, ore et pectore, dicit:

✠ Inítium sancti Evangélii secúndum Joánnem.

Vel si aliud Evangelium legendum sit:

Sequéntia sancti Evangélii etc.

℟. Glória tibi, Dómine.

Junctis manibus prosequitur:

Joann. 1, 1-14.

IN princípio erat Verbum, et Verbum erat apud Deum, et Deus erat Verbum. Hoc erat in princípio apud Deum. Omnia per ipsum facta sunt: et sine ipso factum est nihil, quod factum est: in ipso vita erat, et vita erat lux hóminum: et lux in ténebris lucet, et ténebræ eam non comprehendérunt. Fuit homo missus a Deo, cui nomen erat Joánnes. Hic venit in testimónium, ut testimónium perhibéret de lúmine, ut omnes créderent per illum. Non erat ille lux, sed ut testimónium perhibéret de lúmine. Erat lux vera, quæ illúminat omnem hóminem veniétem in hunc mundum. In mundo erat, et mundus per ipsum factus est, et mundus eum non cognóvit. In própria venit, et sui eum non recepérunt. Quotquot autem recepérunt eum, dedit eis potestátem fílios Dei fíeri, his, qui credunt in nómine ejus: qui non ex sanguínibus, neque ex voluntáte carnis, neque ex voluntáte viri, sed ex Deo nati sunt. Genuflectit dicens: Et Verbum caro factum est, Et surgens prosequitur: et habitávit in nobis: et vídimus glóriam ejus, glóriam quasi Unigéniti a Patre, plenum grátiæ et veritátis.

℟. Deo grátias.

In Missis Defunctorum non datur benedictio, sed dicto Requiéscant in pace, dicit: Pláceat tibi, sancta Trínitas; deinde, osculato Altari, legit Evangelium sancti Joannis.

Finito Evangelio sancti Joannis, discedens ab Altari, pro gratiarum actione dicit Antiphonam Trium puerórum, cum reliquis, ut habetur in principio Missalis.

EASTER DAY

THE SUNDAY OF THE RESURRECTION

Double of 1st class with Octave.

Station at St. Mary Major

Introit. Ps. 139, 18 and 5-6. Resurrexi.

I AM risen, and am still with thee, alleluia: thou hast laid thine hand upon me, alleluia: thy knowledge is too wonderful, alleluia, alleluia. Ps. ibid., 1-2. O Lord, thou hast searched me out, and known me: thou knowest my downsitting, and mine uprising. ℣. Glory.

Collect.

ALMIGHTY God, who through thine only-begotten Son Jesus Christ hast overcome death, and opened unto us the gate of everlasting life: we humbly beseech thee, that, as by thy special grace preventing us thou dost put into our minds good desires; so by thy continual help we may bring the same to good effect. Through the same Jesus Christ our Lord: Who liveth and reigneth with thee and the Holy Ghost, ever one God, world without end. ℟. Amen.

Or, Collect.

O GOD, who on this day hast through thine only-begotten Son overcome death, and opened unto us the gate of everlasting life: we beseech thee; that as by thy preventing grace thou dost breathe into our minds these our desires, so by thy continual help thou wouldest bring the same to good effect. Through the same.

The Lesson from the Epistle of blessed Paul the Apostle to the Colossians.

Col. 3, 1-7.

BRETHREN: If ye be risen with Christ, seek those things which are above, where Christ sitteth on the right hand of God: set your affection on things above, not on things on the earth. For ye are dead, and your life is hid with Christ in God. When Christ, who is our life, shall appear: then shall ye also appear with him in glory. Mortify therefore your members which are upon the earth: fornication, uncleanness, inordinate affection, evil concupiscence, and covetousness, which is idolatry: for which things' sake the wrath of God cometh on the children of disobedience. In the which ye also walked some time, when ye lived in them.

or:

The Lesson from the Epistle of blessed Paul the Apostle to the Corinthians.

I Cor. 5, 7-8.

BRETHREN: Purge out the old leaven, that ye may be a new lump, as ye are unleavened. For even Christ our passover is sacrificed for us. Therefore let us keep the feast: not with old leaven, neither with the leaven of malice and wickedness: but with the unleavened bread of sincerity and truth.

Easter Day

Gradual. Ps. 118, 24 and 1. This is the day which the Lord hath made: we will rejoice and be glad in it. ℣. O give thanks unto the Lord, for he is gracious: and his mercy endureth for ever.

Alleluia, alleluia. ℣. I Cor. 5, 7. Christ our Passover is sacrificed for us.

Sequence.   Victimae paschali.

CHRISTIANS, to the paschal victim offer your thankful praises.

A Lamb the sheep redeemeth: Christ, who only is sinless, reconcileth sinners to the Father.

Death and life have contended in that combat stupendous: the prince of life, who died, reigns immortal.

Speak, Mary, declaring what thou sawest wayfaring.

The tomb of Christ, who is living: the glory of Jesu's resurrection.

Bright Angels attesting, the shroud and napkin resting.

Yea, Christ my hope is arisen: to Galilee he goes before you.

Christ indeed from death is risen, our new life obtaining: have mercy, victor King, ever reigning. Amen. Alleluia.

¶ The Sequence is said until Saturday before Low Sunday, inclusive.

✠ The Continuation of the holy Gospel according to John.

John 20, 1-10.

AT that time: On the first day of the week cometh Mary Magdalene early, when it was yet dark, unto the sepulchre: and seeth the stone taken away from the sepulchre. Then she runneth and cometh to Simon Peter, and to the other disciple whom Jesus loved, and saith unto them: They have taken away the Lord out of the sepulchre, and we know not where they have laid him. Peter therefore went forth, and that other disciple, and came to the sepulchre. So they ran both together, and the other disciple did outrun Peter, and came first to the sepulchre. And he, stooping down and looking in, saw the linen clothes lying, yet went he not in. Then cometh Simon Peter following him, and went into the sepulchre, and seeth the linen clothes lie, and the napkin that was about his head, not lying with the linen clothes, but wrapped together in a place by itself. Then went in also that other disciple which came first to the sepulchre: and he saw, and believed: for as yet they knew not the Scripture, that he must rise again from the dead. Then the disciples went away again unto their own home.   Creed.

or:

✠ The Continuation of the holy Gospel according to Mark.

Mark 16, 1-7.

AT that time: Mary Magdalene, and Mary the mother of James, and Salome, bought sweet spices, that they might come and anoint Jesus. And very early in the morning the first day of the week, they came unto the sepulchre at the rising of the sun. And they said among themselves: Who shall roll us away the stone from the door of the sepulchre? And when they looked, they saw that the stone was rolled away. For it was very great. And entering into the sepulchre, they saw a young man sitting on the right side, clothed in a long white garment, and they were affrighted. And he said unto them: Be not affrighted: ye seek Jesus of Nazareth, which was crucified: he is risen, he is not here, behold the place where they laid him. But go your way, tell his disciples and Peter that he goeth before you into Galilee: there shall ye see him as he said unto you.   Creed.

Offertory. Ps. 76, 9-10. The earth trembled and was still, when God arose to judgment, alleluia.

Secret.

RECEIVE, we beseech thee, O Lord, the prayers and oblations of thy people: that this beginning of thy paschal mysteries may, by thine operation, be unto us a wholesome medicine unto everlasting life. Through.

¶ Easter Preface, Thee, O Lord, but chiefly on this day.

Infra Actionem, Communícantes and Hanc oblatiónem proper.

And so it is said until the Saturday before Low Sunday, inclusive.

Communion. I Cor. 5, 7-8. Christ our Passover is sacrificed for us, alleluia: therefore let us keep the feast with the unleavened bread of sincerity and truth, alleluia, alleluia, alleluia.

Postcommunion.

POUR forth upon us, O Lord, the Spirit of thy charity: that as thou hast now fulfilled us with this paschal Sacrament, so we may by thy mercy be enabled to dwell together in unity and concord. Through ... in the unity of the same Holy Spirit.

¶ After The Lord be with you is said: Ite, Missa est, alleluia, alleluia.

℟. Thanks be to God, alleluia, alleluia.

And so it is said until Saturday inclusive.

MONDAY

IN THE OCTAVE OF EASTER

Double of 1st class.

Station at St. Peter

Introit. Exod. 13. 5 and 9. Introduxit.

THE Lord hath brought you into a land flowing with milk and honey, alleluia: that the law of the Lord may alway be in your mouth, alleluia, alleluia. Ps. 105, 1. O give thanks unto the Lord, and call upon his name: tell the people what things he hath done. ℣. Glory.

Collect Almighty God, p. 415.

Or, Collect.

O GOD, who by this paschal festival hast bestowed thy saving health upon all nations: prosper, we beseech thee, thy people with the gift of thy heavenly grace; that they may worthily serve thee in perfect freedom, and finally attain unto everlasting life. Through.

The Lesson from the Acts of the Apostles.

Acts 10, 34-43.

IN those days: Peter opened his mouth, and said: Of a truth I perceive that God is no respecter of persons: but in every nation he that feareth him, and worketh righteousness, is accepted with him. The word which God sent unto the children of Israel, preaching peace by Jesus Christ, (He is Lord of all:) that word (I say) ye know, which was published throughout all Judæa: and began from Galilee, after the baptism which John preached: how God anointed Jesus of Nazareth with the Holy Ghost, and with power, who went about doing good, and healing all that were oppressed of the devil, for God was with him. And we are witnesses of all things, which he did both in the land of the Jews and in Jerusalem, whom they slew and hanged on a tree. Him God raised up the third day, and shewed him openly, not to all the people, but unto witnesses chosen before of God: even to us, who did eat and drink with him, after he rose from the dead. And he commanded us to preach unto the people, and to testify, that it is he who was ordained of God to be the judge of quick and dead. To him give all the Prophets witness, that through his name whosoever believeth in him shall receive remission of sins.

Or:

The Lesson from the Acts of the Apostles.

Acts 10, 37-43.

IN those days: Peter standing in the midst of the people, said: Men and brethren, ye know the word which was published throughout all Judæa: and began from Galilee, after the baptism which John preached: how God anointed Jesus of Nazareth with the Holy Ghost, and with power, who went about doing good, and healing all that were oppressed of the devil, for God was with him. And we are witnesses of all things, which he did both in the land of the Jews and in Jerusalem, whom they slew and hanged on a tree. Him God raised up the third day, and shewed him openly, not to all the people, but unto witnesses chosen before of God: even to us, who did eat and drink with him, after he rose from the dead.

Monday in the Octave of Easter

And he commanded us to preach unto the people, and to testify, that it is he who was ordained of God to be the judge of quick and dead. To him give all the Prophets witness, that through his name whosoever believeth in him shall receive remission of sins.

Gradual. Ps. 118, 24 and 2. This is the day which the Lord hath made: we will rejoice and be glad in it. ℣. Let Israel now confess, that he is gracious: and that his mercy endureth for ever.

Alleluia, alleluia. ℣. Matt. 28, 2. The Angel of the Lord descended from heaven: and came and rolled back the stone and sat upon it.

Sequence.   Victimae paschali.

CHRISTIANS, to the paschal victim offer your thankful praises.

A Lamb the sheep redeemeth: Christ, who only is sinless, reconcileth sinners to the Father.

Death and life have contended in that combat stupendous: the prince of life, who died, reigns immortal.

Speak, Mary, declaring what thou sawest wayfaring.

The tomb of Christ, who is living: the glory of Jesu's resurrection.

Bright Angels attesting, the shroud and napkin resting.

Yea, Christ my hope is arisen: to Galilee he goes before you.

Christ indeed from death is risen, our new life obtaining: have mercy, victor King, ever reigning. Amen. Alleluia.

✠ The Continuation of the holy Gospel according to Luke.

Luke 24, 13-35.

AT that time: Behold two of Jesus' disciples went that same day to a village called Emmaus, which was from Jerusalem about threescore furlongs. And they talked together of all these things which had happened. And it came to pass, that while they communed together, and reasoned: Jesus himself drew near, and went with them: but their eyes were holden, that they should not know him. And he said unto them: What manner of communications are these that ye have one to another, as ye walk, and are sad? And the one of them, whose name was Cleopas, answering, said unto him: Art thou only a stranger in Jerusalem, and hast not known the things which are come to pass there in these days? And he said unto them: What things? And they said unto him: Concerning Jesus of Nazareth, who was a Prophet mighty in deed and word, before God and all the people: and how the chief priests and our rulers delivered him to be condemned to death, and have crucified him. But we trusted that it had been he which should have redeemed Israel: and besides all this, to-day is the third day since these things were done. Yea, and certain women also of our company made us astonished, which were early at the sepulchre, and when they found not his body, they came, saying, that they had also seen a vision of Angels, which said that he was alive. And certain of them which were with us went to the sepulchre: and found it even so as the women had said, but him they saw not. Then he said unto them: O fools, and slow of heart to believe all that the Prophets have spoken. Ought not Christ to have suffered these things, and to enter into his glory? And beginning at Moses, and all the Prophets, he expounded unto them in all the Scriptures the things concerning himself. And they drew nigh unto the village whither they went: and he made as though he would have gone further. But they constrained him, saying: Abide with us, for it is towards evening, and the day is far spent. And he went in to tarry with them. And it came to pass, as he sat at meat with them, he took bread, and blessed it, and brake, and gave to them. And their eyes were opened, and they knew him: and he vanished out of their sight. And they said one to another: Did not our heart burn within us, while he talked with us by the way, and while he opened to us the Scriptures? And they rose up the same hour, and returned to Jerusalem: and found the eleven gathered together, and them that were with them, saying: The Lord is risen indeed, and hath appeared to Simon. And they told what things were done in the way: and how he was known of them in breaking of bread. Creed.

Offertory. Matt. 28, 2, 5-6. The Angel of the Lord descended from heaven, and said unto the women: He whom ye seek is risen as he said, alleluia.

Secret.

RECEIVE, O Lord, the prayers and oblations of thy people: that this beginning of thy paschal mysteries may, by thine operation, be unto us a wholesome medicine unto everlasting life. Through.

Preface, Communicántes and Hanc oblatiónem as on Easter Day.

Communion. Luke 24, 34. The Lord is risen, and hath appeared to Peter, alleluia.

Postcommunion.

POUR forth upon us, O Lord, the Spirit of thy charity: that as thou hast now fulfilled us with this paschal Sacrament, so we may by thy mercy be enabled to dwell together in unity and concord. Through ... in the unity of the same Holy Spirit.

TUESDAY

IN THE OCTAVE OF EASTER

Double of 1st class.

Station at St. Paul

Introit. Ecclus. 15, 3-4. Aqua sapientiæ.

THE water of wisdom hath he given them to drink, alleluia: he shall be stayed upon them, and shall not be moved, alleluia: and he shall exalt them for ever, alleluia, alleluia. Ps. 105, 1. O give thanks unto the Lord, and call upon his name: tell the people what things he hath done. ℣. Glory.

Collect Almighty God, p. 415.

Or, Collect.

O GOD, who dost ever multiply thy Church with new offspring: grant unto thy servants; that as by faith they have received the Sacrament of their regeneration, so in their life and conversation they may ever cleave unto the same. Through.

The Lesson from the Acts of the Apostles.

Acts 13, 16 and 26-33.

IN those days: Paul stood up, and beckoning with his hand to keep silence, said: Men and brethren, children of the stock of Abraham, and whosoever among you feareth God, to you is the word of this salvation sent. For they that dwell at Jerusalem, and their rulers, because they knew not Jesus, nor yet the voices of the Prophets which are read every sabbath-day, they have fulfilled them in condemning him: and though they found no cause of death in him, yet desired they Pilate that he should be slain. And when they had fulfilled all that was written of him, they took him down from the tree, and laid him in a sepulchre. But God raised him from the dead: and he was seen many days of them which came up with him from Galilee to Jerusalem, who are his witnesses unto the people. And we declare unto you glad tidings, how that the promise which was made unto the fathers, God hath fulfilled the same unto us their children, in that he hath raised up Jesus [Christ our Lord*] again.

As it is also written in the second Psalm: Thou art my Son, this day have I begotten thee. And as concerning that he raised him up from the dead, now no more to return to corruption, he said on this wise: I will give you the sure mercies of David. Wherefore he saith also in another Psalm: Thou shalt not suffer thine Holy One to see corruption. For David, after he had served his own generation by the will of God, fell on sleep, and was laid unto his fathers, and saw corruption: but he whom God raised again saw no corruption. Be it known unto you therefore, men and brethren, that through this man is preached unto you the forgiveness of sins: and by him all that believe are justified from all things, from which ye could not be justified by the law of Moses. Beware therefore, lest that come upon you which is spoken of in the Prophets: Behold ye despisers, and wonder, and perish: for I work a work in your days, a work which ye shall in no wise believe, though a man declare it unto you.

Gradual. Ps. 118, 24 and 16. This is the day which the Lord hath made: we will rejoice and be glad in it. ℣. Ps. 107, 2. Let them now give thanks whom the Lord hath redeemed: and delivered from the hand of the enemy, and gathered them out of the lands.

Alleluia, alleluia. ℣. The Lord is risen from the tomb, who for us hung upon the tree.

Sequence.   Victimae paschali.

CHRISTIANS, to the paschal victim offer your thankful praises.

A Lamb the sheep redeemeth: Christ, who only is sinless, reconcileth sinners to the Father.

Death and life have contended in that combat stupendous: the prince of life, who died, reigns immortal.

Speak, Mary, declaring what thou sawest wayfaring.

The tomb of Christ, who is living: the glory of Jesu's resurrection.

Bright Angels attesting, the shroud and napkin resting.

Yea, Christ my hope is arisen: to Galilee he goes before you.

Christ indeed from death is risen, our new life obtaining: have mercy, victor King, ever reigning. Amen. Alleluia.

✠ The Continuation of the holy Gospel according to Luke.

Luke 24, 36-47.

AT that time: Jesus stood in the midst of his disciples, and saith unto them: Peace be unto you: [it is I, fear not.] But they were terrified and affrighted, and supposed that they had seen a spirit. And he said unto them: Why are ye troubled, and why do thoughts arise in your hearts? Behold my hands and my feet, that it is I myself: handle me, and see: for a spirit hath not flesh and bones, as ye see me have. And when he had thus spoken, he shewed them his hands and his feet. And while they yet believed not for joy, and wondered, he said unto them: Have ye here any meat? And they gave him a piece of a broiled fish, and of an honeycomb. And he took it, and did eat before them. And he said unto them: These are the words which I spake unto you, while I was yet with you, that all things must be fulfilled which were written in the law of Moses, and in the Prophets, and in the Psalms concerning me. Then opened he their understanding, that they might understand the Scriptures. And said unto them: Thus it is written, and thus it behoved Christ to suffer, and to rise from the dead the third day: and that repentance and remission of sins should be preached in his name among all nations,* beginning at Jerusalem. And ye are witnesses of these things. Creed.

Offertory. Ps. 18, 14 and 16. The Lord thundered out of heaven: and the Highest gave his thunder: and the springs of waters were seen, alleluia.

Secret.

RECEIVE, O Lord, the prayers and oblations of thy people: that through this observance of our bounden devotion we may attain unto heavenly glory. Through.

Preface, Communicántes and Hanc oblatiónem as on Easter Day.

Communion. Col. 3, 1-2. If ye be risen with Christ, seek those things which are above, where Christ sitteth on the right hand of God, alleluia: set your affection on things above, alleluia.

Postcommunion.

GRANT, we beseech thee, almighty God: that this paschal Sacrament, which we have here received, may continually bring forth fruit in our souls. Through.

Wednesday in the Octave of Easter

Double.

Station of St. Lawrence without the Walls

Introit. Matt. 25, 34. Venite.

COME, ye blessed of my Father, inherit the kingdom, alleluia: which hath been prepared for you from the foundation of the world, alleluia, alleluia, alleluia. Ps. 96, 1. O sing unto the Lord a new song: sing unto the Lord, all the whole earth. ℣. Glory.

Collect.

O GOD, who dost gladden us with the yearly festival of the Resurrection of the Lord: mercifully grant; that through this temporal feast which we now observe, we may be found worthy to attain unto everlasting felicity. Through the same.

The Lesson from the Acts of the Apostles.

Acts 3, 12-15 and 17-19.

IN those days: Peter opened his mouth and said: Ye men of Israel, and ye that fear God, hearken. The God of Abraham, and of Isaac, and of Jacob, the God of our fathers, hath glorified his Son Jesus, whom ye delivered up, and denied him in the presence of Pilate, when he was determined to let him go. But ye denied the holy one and the just, and desired a murderer to be granted unto you: and killed the prince of life, whom God hath raised from the dead, whereof we are witnesses. And now, brethren, I wot that through ignorance ye did it, as did also your rulers. But those things, which God before had shewed by the mouth of all his Prophets, that Christ should suffer, he hath so fulfilled. Repent ye therefore, and be converted, that your sins may be blotted out.

Gradual. Ps. 118, 24 and 16. This is the day which the Lord hath made: we will rejoice and be glad in it. ℣. The right hand of the Lord bringeth mighty things to pass, the right hand of the Lord hath exalted me.

Alleluia, alleluia. ℣. Luke 24, 34. The Lord is risen indeed: and hath appeared to Peter.

Sequence.   Victimae paschali.

CHRISTIANS, to the paschal victim offer your thankful praises.

A Lamb the sheep redeemeth: Christ, who only is sinless, reconcileth sinners to the Father.

Death and life have contended in that combat stupendous: the prince of life, who died, reigns immortal.

Speak, Mary, declaring what thou sawest wayfaring.

The tomb of Christ, who is living: the glory of Jesu's resurrection.

Bright Angels attesting, the shroud and napkin resting.

Yea, Christ my hope is arisen: to Galilee he goes before you.

Christ indeed from death is risen, our new life obtaining: have mercy, victor King, ever reigning. Amen. Alleluia.

✠ The Continuation of the holy Gospel according to John.

John 21, 1-14.

AT that time: Jesus shewed himself again to the disciples at the sea of Tiberias. And on this wise shewed he himself. There were together Simon Peter, and Thomas called Didymus, and Nathanael of Cana in Galilee, and the sons of Zebedee, and two other of his disciples. Simon Peter saith unto them: I go a fishing. They say unto him: We also go with thee. They went forth, and entered into a ship immediately: and that night they caught nothing. But when the morning was now come, Jesus stood on the shore: but the disciples knew not that it was Jesus. Then Jesus saith unto them: Children, have ye any meat? They answered him: No. And he said unto them: Cast the net on the right side of the ship, and ye shall find. They cast therefore: and now they were not able to draw it for the multitude of fishes. Therefore that disciple whom Jesus loved saith unto Peter: It is the Lord. Now when Simon Peter heard that it was the Lord, he girt his fisher's coat unto him, (for he was naked,) and did cast himself into the sea. And the other disciples came in a little ship, (for they were not far from land, but as it were two hundred cubits,) dragging the net with fishes. As soon then as they were come to land, they saw a fire of coals there, and fish laid thereon and bread. Jesus saith unto them: Bring of the fish which ye have now caught. Simon Peter went up, and drew the net to land full of great fishes, an hundred and fifty and three. And for all there were so many, yet was not the net broken. Jesus saith unto them: Come and dine. And none of the disciples durst ask him: Who art thou? knowing that it was the Lord. Jesus then cometh, and taketh bread, and giveth them, and fish likewise. This is now the third time that Jesus shewed himself to his disciples, after that he was risen from the dead. Creed.

Offertory. Ps. 78, 23-25. The Lord opened the doors of heaven: and rained down manna upon them for to eat: he gave them food from heaven: so man did eat Angels' food, alleluia.

Secret.

WE offer unto thee, O Lord, this sacrifice of our paschal gladness: whereby thou dost wondrously bestow upon thy Church both food and sustenance. Through.

Preface, Communicántes and Hanc oblatiónem as on Easter Day.

Communion. Rom. 6, 9. Christ, being raised from the dead, dieth no more, alleluia: death hath no more dominion over him, alleluia, alleluia.

Postcommunion.

WE beseech thee, O Lord, that we, being cleansed from the corruption of our former nature: may by the devout receiving of thy Sacrament be transformed into a new creature: Who livest and reignest with God the Father.

Thursday in the Octave of Easter
Double.

Station at the Twelve Holy Apostles

Introit. Wisd. 10, 20-21. Victricem.

THY victorious hand, O Lord, have they magnified, with one accord, alleluia: for wisdom hath opened the mouth of the dumb, and made eloquent the tongues of babes, alleluia, alleluia. Ps. 98, 1. O sing unto the Lord a new song: for he hath done marvellous things. V. Glory.

Collect.

O GOD, who hast united the diversity of nations in the confession of thy name: grant that they who are born again in the font of Baptism may agree in steadfastness of faith and godliness of life. Through.

The Lesson from the Acts of the Apostles.

Acts 8, 26-40.

IN those days: The Angel of the Lord spake unto Philip, saying: Arise, and go toward the south unto the way that goeth down from Jerusalem unto Gaza: which is desert. And he arose, and went. And, behold, a man of Ethiopia, an eunuch of great authority under Candace queen of the Ethiopians, who had the charge of all her treasure, and had come to Jerusalem for to worship: was returning, and sitting in his chariot read Esaias the Prophet. Then the Spirit said unto Philip: Go near, and join thyself to this chariot. And Philip ran thither to him, and heard him read the Prophet Esaias, and said: Understandest thou what thou readest? And he said: How can I, except some man should guide me? And he desired Philip that he would come up and sit with him. The place of the Scripture which he read was this: He was led as a sheep to the slaughter: and like a lamb dumb before his shearer, so opened he not his mouth. In his humiliation his judgment was taken away. And who shall declare his generation, for his life is taken from the earth? And the eunuch answered Philip, and said: I pray thee, of whom speaketh the Prophet this? of himself, or of some other man? Then Philip opened his mouth, and began at the same Scripture, and preached unto him Jesus. And as they went on their way, they came unto a certain water: and the eunuch said: See, here is water, what doth hinder me to be baptized? And Philip said: If thou believest with all thine heart, thou mayest. And he answered and said: I believe that Jesus Christ is the Son of God. And he commanded the chariot to stand still: and they went down both into the water, both Philip and the eunuch, and he baptized him. And when they were come up out of the water, the Spirit of the Lord caught away Philip, that the eunuch saw him no more. And he went on his way rejoicing. But Philip was found at Azotus, and passing through he preached in all the cities (till he came to Caesarea) the name of the Lord Jesus Christ.

Gradual. Ps. 118, 24 and 22-23. This is the day which the Lord hath made: we will rejoice and be glad in it. ℣. The same stone, which the builders refused, is become the head stone in the corner: this is the Lord's doing, and it is marvellous in our eyes.

Alleluia, alleluia. ℣. Christ, who created all things, is risen: and he hath had compassion on mankind.

Sequence. Victimae paschali.

CHRISTIANS, to the paschal victim offer your thankful praises.

A Lamb the sheep redeemeth: Christ, who only is sinless, reconcileth sinners to the Father.

Death and life have contended in that combat stupendous: the prince of life, who died, reigns immortal.

Speak, Mary, declaring what thou sawest wayfaring.

The tomb of Christ, who is living: the glory of Jesu's resurrection.

Bright Angels attesting, the shroud and napkin resting.

Yea, Christ my hope is arisen: to Galilee he goes before you.

Christ indeed from death is risen, our new life obtaining: have mercy, victor King, ever reigning. Amen. Alleluia.

✠ The Continuation of the holy Gospel according to John.

John 20, 11-18.

AT that time: Mary stood without at the sepulchre weeping. And as she wept, she stooped down, and looked into the sepulchre: and seeth two Angels in white sitting, the one at the head, and the other at the feet, where the body of Jesus had lain. And they say unto her: Woman, why weepest thou? She saith unto them: Because they have taken away my Lord: and I know not where they have laid him. And when she had thus said, she turned herself back, and saw Jesus standing: and knew not that it was Jesus. Jesus saith unto her: Woman, why weepest thou? whom seekest thou? She, supposing him to be the gardener, said unto him: Sir, if thou have borne him hence, tell me where thou hast laid him: and I will take him away. Jesus saith unto her: Mary. She turned herself, and saith unto him: Rabboni (which is to say, Master). Jesus said unto her: Touch me not, for I am not yet ascended to my Father: but go to my brethren, and say unto them: I ascend unto my Father, and your Father, and to my God, and your God. Mary Magdalene came and told the disciples that she had seen the Lord, and that he had spoken these things unto her. Creed.

Offertory. Exod. 13. 5. In the day of your solemnity, saith the Lord, I will bring you into a land flowing with milk and honey, alleluia.

Secret.

WE beseech thee, O Lord, mercifully to accept the oblations of thy people: that they, being made regenerate by the confession of thy name and by baptism, may attain unto everlasting felicity. Through.

Preface, Communicántes and Hanc oblatiónem as on Easter Day.

Communion. I Pet. 2, 9. Ye are a peculiar people, shew ye forth the praises of him, alleluia: who hath called you out of darkness into his marvellous light, alleluia.

Postcommunion.

GRACIOUSLY hear our prayers, O Lord: that this holy Communion of our redemption may obtain for us thy succour in this present life, and bring us to the gladness of life everlasting. Through.

Friday in the Octave of Easter

Double.

Station at St. Mary of the Martyrs

Introit. Ps. 78, 53. Eduxit eos.

THE Lord hath brought them out safely, alleluia: and overwhelmed their enemies with the sea, alleluia, alleluia, alleluia. Ps. ibid., 1. Hear my law, O my people: incline your ears unto the words of my mouth. ℣. Glory.

Collect.

ALMIGHTY and everlasting God, who hast bestowed on us this paschal Sacrament for a pledge of the reconciliation of mankind: vouchsafe; that those things which we celebrate in outward profession we may effectually imitate within our souls. Through.

The Lesson from the Epistle of blessed Peter the Apostle.

I Peter 3, 18-32.

DEARLY beloved: Christ hath once suffered for sins, the just for the unjust, that he might bring us to God, being put to death in the flesh, but quickened by the Spirit. By which also he went and preached unto the spirits in prison: which sometime were disobedient, when once the longsuffering of God waited in the days of Noah, while the ark was a preparing, wherein few, that is, eight souls, were saved by water. The like figure whereunto even baptism doth also now save us: not the putting away of the filth of the flesh, but the answer of a good conscience toward God, by the resurrection of Jesus Christ our Lord, who is gone into heaven, and is on the right hand of God.

Gradual. Ps. 118, 24 and 26-27. This is the day which the Lord hath made: we will rejoice and be glad in it. ℣. Blessed is he that cometh in the name of the Lord: God is the Lord who hath shewed us light.

Alleluia, alleluia. ℣. Ps. 96, 10. Tell it out among the heathen: that the Lord hath reigned from the tree.

Sequence.   Victimae paschali.

CHRISTIANS, to the paschal victim offer your thankful praises.

A Lamb the sheep redeemeth: Christ, who only is sinless, reconcileth sinners to the Father.

Death and life have contended in that combat stupendous: the prince of life, who died, reigns immortal.

Speak, Mary, declaring what thou sawest wayfaring.

The tomb of Christ, who is living: the glory of Jesu's resurrection.

Bright Angels attesting, the shroud and napkin resting.

Yea, Christ my hope is arisen: to Galilee he goes before you.

Christ indeed from death is risen, our new life obtaining: have mercy, victor King, ever reigning. Amen. Alleluia.

✠ The Continuation of the holy Gospel according to Matthew.

Matt. 28, 16-20.

AT that time: The eleven disciples went away into Galilee, into a mountain where Jesus had appointed them. And when they saw him, they worshipped him: but some doubted. And Jesus came and spake unto them, saying: All power is given unto me in heaven and in earth. Go ye therefore, and teach all nations, baptizing them in the name of the Father, and of the Son, and of the Holy Ghost: teaching them to observe all things whatsoever I have commanded you. And, lo, I am with you alway, even unto the end of the world. Creed.

Offertory. Exod. 12, 14. This day shall be unto you for a memorial, alleluia: and ye shall keep it a feast to the Lord throughout your generations: ye shall keep it a feast by an ordinance for ever, alleluia, alleluia, alleluia.

Secret.

WE beseech thee, O Lord, mercifully to accept our oblations: which we offer unto thee for the expiation of the sins of them that are born again, and for the speedy attaining of thy heavenly succour. Through.

Preface, Communicántes and Hanc oblatiónem as on Easter Day.

Communion. Matt. 28, 18-19. All power is given to me in heaven and in earth, alleluia: go ye, and teach all nations, baptizing them in the name of the Father, and of the Son, and of the Holy Ghost, alleluia, alleluia.

Postcommunion.

WE beseech thee, O Lord, mercifully to look upon thy people: and as thou hast vouchsafed to renew them with thine eternal mysteries, so of thy goodness deliver them from guilt in all things temporal. Through.

Low Saturday
Sabbato in Albis
Double.

Station at St. John Lateran

Introit. Ps. 105, 43. Eduxit Dominus.

THE Lord hath brought forth his people with joy, alleluia: and his chosen with gladness, alleluia, alleluia. Ps. ibid., 1. O give thanks unto the Lord, and call upon his name: tell the people what things he hath done. ℣. Glory.

Collect.

GRANT, we beseech thee, almighty God: that we who have devoutly kept this paschal festival may thereby be found worthy to attain unto everlasting felicity. Through.

The Lesson from the Epistle of blessed Peter the Apostle.

I Peter 2, 1-10.

DEARLY beloved: Laying aside therefore all malice, and all guile, and hypocrisies, and envies, and all evil speakings, as newborn babes, desire the sincere milk of the word: that ye may grow thereby: if so be ye have tasted that the Lord is gracious. To whom coming, as unto a living stone, disallowed indeed of men, but chosen of God, and precious: ye also, as lively stones, are built up a spiritual house, an holy priesthood, to offer up spiritual sacrifices, acceptable to God by Jesus Christ. Wherefore also it is contained in the Scripture: Behold, I lay in Sion a chief corner stone, elect, precious: and he that believeth on him shall not be confounded. Unto you therefore which believe he is precious: but unto them which be disobedient, the stone which the builders disallowed, the same is made the head of the corner, and a stone of stumbling, and a rock of offence, even to them which stumble at the word, being disobedient, whereunto also they were appointed. But ye are a chosen generation, a royal priesthood, an holy nation, a peculiar people: that ye should shew forth the praises of him who hath called you out of darkness into his marvellous light. Which in time past were not a people, but are now the people of God: which had not obtained mercy, but now have obtained mercy.

¶ From this day until Ember Saturday in Whitsun Week inclusive, in all Masses, the Gradual is not said, but four Alleluias with two Verses are said in the order given below; but in the Mass of the Rogations, on the Vigil of Pentecost, and after each Lesson on Ember Saturday, one Alleluia is said with one Verse only.

Alleluia, alleluia. ℣. Ps. 118, 24. This is the day which the Lord hath made: we will rejoice and be glad in it. Alleluia. ℣. Ps. 113, 1. Praise the Lord, ye servants, O praise the name of the Lord.

Sequence. *Victimae paschali.*

CHRISTIANS, to the paschal victim offer your thankful praises.

A Lamb the sheep redeemeth: Christ, who only is sinless, reconcileth sinners to the Father.

Death and life have contended in that combat stupendous: the prince of life, who died, reigns immortal.

Speak, Mary, declaring what thou sawest wayfaring.

The tomb of Christ, who is living: the glory of Jesu's resurrection.

Bright Angels attesting, the shroud and napkin resting.

Yea, Christ my hope is arisen: to Galilee he goes before you.

Christ indeed from death is risen, our new life obtaining: have mercy, victor King, ever reigning. Amen. Alleluia.

✠ The Continuation of the holy Gospel according to John.

John 20, 1-9.

AT that time: On the first day of the week cometh Mary Magdalene early, when it was yet dark, unto the sepulchre, and seeth the stone taken away from the sepulchre. Then she runneth, and cometh to Simon Peter, and to the other disciple, whom Jesus loved, and saith unto them: They have taken away the Lord out of the sepulchre, and we know not where they have laid him. Peter therefore went forth, and that other disciple, and came to the sepulchre. So they ran both together, and the other disciple did outrun Peter, and came first to the sepulchre. And he stooping down, and looking in, saw the linen clothes lying, yet went he not in. Then cometh Simon Peter following him, and went into the sepulchre, and seeth the linen clothes lie, and the napkin, that was about his head, not lying with the linen clothes, but wrapped together in a place by itself. Then went in also that other disciple, which came first to the sepulchre: and he saw, and believed: for as yet they knew not the Scripture, that he must rise again from the dead. Creed.

Offertory. Ps. 118, 26-27. Blessed is he that cometh in the name of the Lord: we have wished you good luck, ye that are of the house of the Lord: God is the Lord who hath shewed us light, alleluia, alleluia.

Secret.

GRANT us, we beseech thee, O Lord, alway to rejoice in these paschal mysteries: that the continual working of our redemption may effectually lead us to everlasting gladness. Through.

Preface, Communicántes and Hanc oblatiónem as on Easter Day.

Communion. Gal. 3, 27. As many of you as have been baptized into Christ have put on Christ, alleluia.

Postcommunion.

O LORD, who hast quickened us with the gift of our redemption, we beseech thee: that this means of everlasting salvation may avail for our advancement in thy true religion. Through.

LOW SUNDAY

Dominica in Albis

THE OCTAVE OF EASTER

Double of 1st class.

Station at St. Pancras

Introit. I Pet. 2, 2. Quasimodo.

AS new-born babes, alleluia: desire ye the sincere milk of the word, alleluia, alleluia, alleluia. Ps. 81, 2. Sing we merrily unto God our helper: make a cheerful noise unto the God of Jacob. ℣. Glory.

¶ Glória in excélsis is said on this and the following Sundays after Easter, even when during the week the Mass of the preceding Sunday is resumed.

Collect.

ALMIGHTY Father, who hast given thine only Son to die for our sins, and to rise again for our justification: grant us so to put away the leaven of malice and wickedness; that we may alway serve thee in pureness of living and truth. Through the merits of the same thy Son Jesus Christ our Lord: Who liveth and reigneth with thee.

Or, Collect.

GRANT, we beseech thee, almighty God: that as we have now fulfilled this paschal festival, so in our life and conversation we may by thy grace continually shew forth the same. Through.

The Lesson from the Epistle of blessed John the Apostle.

I John 5, 4-10.

DEARLY beloved: Whatsoever is born of God overcometh the world: and this is the victory that overcometh the world, even our faith. Who is he that overcometh the world, but he that believeth that Jesus is the Son of God? This is he that came by water and blood, even Jesus Christ: not by water only, but by water and blood. And it is the Spirit that beareth witness, because the Spirit is truth. For there are three that bear record in heaven: the Father, the Word and the Holy Ghost: and these three are one. And there are three that bear witness in earth: The spirit, and the water, and the blood: and these three agree in one. If we receive the witness of men, the witness of God is greater: for this is the witness of God which he hath testified of his Son. He that believeth on the Son of God hath the witness in himself.*

He that believeth not God hath made him a liar, because he believeth not the record that God gave of his Son. And this is the record, that God hath given to us eternal life: and this life is in his Son. He that hath the Son hath life: and he that hath not the Son hath not life.

Alleluia, alleluia. ℣. Matt. 28, 7. In the day of my resurrection, saith the Lord, I will go before you into Galilee. Alleluia. ℣. John 20, 26. After eight days, when the doors were shut, Jesus stood in the midst of his disciples, and said: Peace be unto you. Alleluia.

✠ The Continuation of the holy Gospel according to John.

John 20, 19-31.

AT that time: The same day at evening, being the first day of the week, when the doors were shut, where the disciples were assembled for fear of the Jews: came Jesus and stood in the midst, and saith unto them: Peace be unto you. And when he had so said, he shewed unto them his hands and his side. Then were the disciples glad when they saw the Lord. Then said Jesus to them again: Peace be unto you. As my Father hath sent me, even so send I you. And when he had said this, he breathed on them, and saith unto them: Receive ye the Holy Ghost: whosesoever sins ye remit, they are remitted unto them; and whosesoever sins ye retain, they are retained.†

Now, Thomas, one of the twelve, called Didymus, was not with them when Jesus came. The other disciples therefore said unto him: We have seen the Lord. But he said unto them: Except I shall see in his hands the print of the nails and put my finger into the print of the nails, and thrust my hand into his side, I will not believe. And after eight days again his disciples were within, and Thomas with them. Then came Jesus, the doors being shut, and stood in the midst, and said: Peace be unto you. Then saith he to Thomas: Reach hither thy finger, and behold my hands, and reach hither thy hand, and thrust it into my side: and be not faithless, but believing. And Thomas answered and said unto him: My Lord, and my God. Jesus saith unto him: Thomas, because thou hast seen me, thou hast believed: blessed are they that have not seen, and yet have believed. And many other signs truly did Jesus in the presence of his disciples, which are not written in this book. But these are written, that ye might believe that Jesus is the Christ, the Son of God: and that believing ye might have life through his name. Creed.

Offertory. Matt. 28, 2, 5-6. The Angel of the Lord descended from heaven, and saith unto the women: He whom ye seek is risen, as he said, alleluia.

Secret.

ACCEPT, O Lord, we beseech thee, the offerings of thy Church exultant: and grant unto her, on whom thou hast bestowed cause for so great joy, the fruit of perpetual gladness. Through.

Preface of Easter, in which is said: but chiefly at this time.

Communion. John 20, 27. Reach hither thy hand, and behold the print of the nails, alleluia: and be not faithless, but believing, alleluia, alleluia.

Postcommunion.

WE beseech thee, O Lord our God: that these holy mysteries which thou hast given us for the assurance of our redemption; may both in this life and in that which is to come be profitable for the healing of our souls. Through.

The Second Sunday after Easter

Double.

Introit. Ps. 33, 5-6. Misericordia.

THE loving-kindness of the Lord filleth the whole world, alleluia: by the word of the Lord the heavens were stablished, alleluia, alleluia. Ps. ibid., 1. Rejoice in the Lord, O ye righteous: for it becometh well the just to be thankful. ℣.Glory.

Collect.

ALMIGHTY God, who hast given thine only Son to be unto us both a sacrifice for sin, and also an ensample of godly life: give us grace that we may always most thankfully receive that his inestimable benefit; and also daily endeavour ourselves to follow the blessed steps of his most holy life. Through the same.

The Second Sunday after Easter

Or, Collect.

O GOD, who hast given thy Son to take our low estate upon him, and hast thereby raised up this fallen world: grant unto thy faithful people perpetual gladness; that they, whom thou hast delivered from the peril of eternal death, may by thee be brought to the fruition of everlasting joy. Through the same.

The Lesson from the Epistle of blessed Peter the Apostle.

I Peter 2, 19-25.

DEARLY beloved: This is thankworthy, if a man for conscience toward God endure grief, suffering wrongfully. For what glory is it, if when ye be buffeted for your faults, ye shall take it patiently? But if, when ye do well, and suffer for it, ye take it patiently; this is acceptable with God. For even hereunto were ye called. Because Christ also suffered for us, leaving us an example, that ye should follow his steps. Who did no sin, neither was guile found in his mouth: who, when he was reviled, reviled not again: when he suffered, he threatened not: but committed himself to him that judgeth righteously: who his own self bare our sins in his own body on the tree: that we, being dead to sins, should live unto righteousness: by whose stripes ye were healed. For ye were as sheep going astray: but are now returned unto the shepherd and bishop of your souls.

or:

The Lesson from the Epistle of blessed Peter the Apostle.

I Peter 2, 21-25.

DEARLY beloved: Christ suffered for us, leaving us an example, that ye should follow his steps. Who did no sin, neither was guile found in his mouth: who, when he was reviled, reviled not again: when he suffered, he threatened not: but committed himself to him that judgeth righteously: who his own self bare our sins in his own body on the tree: that we, being dead to sins, should live unto righteousness: by whose stripes ye were healed. For ye were as sheep going astray: but are now returned unto the shepherd and bishop of your souls.

Alleluia, alleluia. V. Luke 24, 35. The disciples knew the Lord Jesus in the breaking of bread. Alleluia. V. John 10, 14. I am the good shepherd: and know my sheep, and am known of mine. Alleluia.

✠ The Continuation of the holy Gospel according to John.

John 10, 11-16.

AT that time: Jesus said unto the Pharisees: I am the good shepherd. The good shepherd giveth his life for the sheep. But he that is an hireling, and not the shepherd, whose own the sheep are not, seeth the wolf coming, and leaveth the sheep, and fleeth: and the wolf catcheth them, and scattereth the sheep: the hireling fleeth because he is an hireling, and careth not for the sheep. I am the good shepherd: and know my sheep and am known of mine. As the Father knoweth me, even so know I the Father, and I lay down my life for the sheep. And other sheep I have, which are not of this fold: them also I must bring, and they shall hear my voice, and there shall be one fold, and one shepherd. Creed.

Offertory. Ps. 63, 2 and 5. O God, thou art my God, early will I seek thee: and lift up my hands in thy name, alleluia.

Secret.

MAY this sacred oblation, O Lord, ever bestow upon us thy saving benediction: that those things which we shew forth in an outward mystery may effectually be accomplished in our inward souls. Through.

Preface of Easter, But chiefly at this time.

Communion. John 10, 14. I am the good shepherd, alleluia: and know my sheep, and am known of mine, alleluia, alleluia.

Postcommunion.

GRANT to us, we beseech thee, almighty God: that we, receiving the quickening of thy grace, may ever glory in the gift which thou bestowest. Through.

The Third Sunday after Easter

Double.

Introit. Ps. 66 1-2. Jubilate Deo.

O BE joyful in God, all ye lands, alleluia: sing ye praises unto the honour of his name, alleluia: make his praise to be exceeding glorious, alleluia, alleluia, alleluia. Ps. ibid., 2. Say unto God, O how wonderful art thou in thy works, O Lord! through the greatness of thy power shall thine enemies be found liars unto thee. ℣. Glory.

Collect.

ALMIGHTY God, who shewest to them that be in error the light of thy truth, to the intent that they may return into the way of righteousness: grant unto all them that are admitted into the fellowship of Christ's religion, that they may eschew those things that are contrary to their profession; and follow all such things as are agreeable to the same. Through the same.

The Lesson from the Epistle of blessed Peter the Apostle.

I Peter 2, 11-19.

DEARLY beloved: I beseech you as strangers and pilgrims, abstain from fleshly lusts, which war against the soul, having your conversation honest among the Gentiles: that, whereas they speak against you as evil doers, they may, by your good works which they shall behold, glorify God in the day of visitation. Submit yourselves to every ordinance of man for the Lord's sake: whether it be to the King, as supreme: or unto governors, as unto them that are sent by him, for the punishment of evil doers, and for the praise of them that do well: for so is the will of God, that with well-doing ye may put to silence the ignorance of foolish men: as free, and not using your liberty for a cloke of maliciousness, but as the servants of God. Honour all men: love the brotherhood: fear God: honour the King.†

Servants, be subject to your masters with all fear, not only to the good and gentle, but also to the froward. For this is thankworthy: in Christ Jesu our Lord.

Alleluia, alleluia. ℣. Ps. 111, 9. The Lord hath sent redemption unto his people. Alleluia. ℣. Luke 24, 46. It behoved Christ to suffer, and to rise from the dead: and so to enter into his glory. Alleluia.

✠ The Continuation of the holy Gospel according to John.

John 16, 16-22.

AT that time: Jesus said to his disciples: A little while and ye shall not see me: and again, a little while and ye shall see me: because I go to the Father. Then said some of his disciples among themselves: What is this that he saith unto us: A little while and ye shall not see me: and again, a little while and ye shall see me, and, Because I go to the Father? They said therefore: What is this that he saith: A little while? we cannot tell what he saith. Now Jesus knew that they were desirous to ask him, and said unto them: Do ye enquire among yourselves of that I said: A little while and ye shall not see me: and again, a little while and ye shall see me?

Verily, verily I say unto you: That ye shall weep and lament, but the world shall rejoice: and ye shall be sorrowful, but your sorrow shall be turned into joy. A woman, when she is in travail, hath sorrow, because her hour is come: but as soon as she is delivered of the child, she remembereth no more the anguish, for joy that a man is born into the world. And ye now therefore have sorrow, but I will see you again, and your heart shall rejoice: and your joy no man taketh from you. Creed.

Offertory. Ps. 146, 1. Praise the Lord, O my soul: while I live will I praise the Lord: yea, as long as I have any being, I will sing praises unto my God, alleluia.

Secret.

GRANT to us, O Lord, that through these mysteries we may so assuage our earthly desires, that we may learn to love things heavenly. Through.

Preface of Easter, but chiefly at this time.

Communion. John 16, 16. A little while, and ye shall not see me, alleluia; and again, a little while and ye shall see me, because I go to the Father, alleluia, alleluia.

Postcommunion.

O LORD our God, who hast made us partakers of this holy Sacrament: grant that we may thereby inwardly be satisfied with heavenly food, and outwardly be defended against all adversities. Through.

The Fourth Sunday after Easter

Double.

Introit. Ps. 98, 1-2. Cantate Domino.

O SING unto the Lord a new song, alleluia: for the Lord hath done marvellous things, alleluia: in the sight of the nations hath he shewed his righteousness, alleluia, alleluia, alleluia. Ps. ibid., 2. With his own right hand, and with his holy arm: hath he gotten himself the victory. ℣. Glory.

Collect.

O ALMIGHTY God, who alone canst order the unruly wills and affections of sinful men: grant unto thy people, that they may love the thing which thou commandest, and desire that which thou dost promise; that so, among the sundry and manifold changes of the world, our hearts may surely there be fixed where true joys are to be found. Through.

Or, Collect.

O GOD, who makest the faithful to be of one mind and will: grant unto thy people, that they may love the thing which thou commandest, and desire that which thou dost promise; that so amid the sundry and manifold changes of the world our hearts may surely there be fixed, where true joys are to be found. Through.

The Lesson from the Epistle of blessed James the Apostle.

James 1, 17-21.

DEARLY beloved: Every good gift, and every perfect gift is from above, and cometh down from the Father of lights, with whom is no variableness, neither shadow of turning. Of his own will begat he us with the Word of truth, that we should be a kind of first-fruits of his creatures. Wherefore, my beloved brethren, let every man be swift to hear: slow to speak, slow to wrath. For the wrath of man worketh not the righteousness of God. Wherefore lay apart all filthiness and superfluity of naughtiness, and receive with meekness the engrafted word which is able to save your souls.

Alleluia, alleluia. ℣. Ps. 118, 16. The right hand of the Lord bringeth mighty things to pass: the right hand of the Lord hath exalted me. Alleluia. ℣. Rom. 6, 9. Christ being raised from the dead dieth no more: death hath no more dominion over him. Alleluia.

✠ The Continuation of the holy Gospel according to John.

John 16, 5-14.

AT that time: Jesus said unto his disciples: I go my way to him that sent me: and none of you asketh me: Whither goest thou? But, because I have said these things unto you, sorrow hath filled your heart. Nevertheless, I tell you the truth: it is expedient for you that I go away: for if I go not away, the Comforter will not come unto you: but if I depart, I will send him unto you. And when he is come, he will reprove the world of sin, and of righteousness, and of judgment. Of sin, because they believe not on me: of righteousness, because I go to my Father, and ye see me no more: of judgment, because the prince of this world is judged. I have yet many things to say unto you: but ye cannot bear them now. Howbeit when he, the Spirit of truth, is come, he will guide you into all truth. For he shall not speak of himself: but whatsoever he shall hear, that shall he speak, and he will shew you things to come. He shall glorify me: for he shall receive of mine, and shall shew it unto you.*

All things that the Father hath are mine. Therefore said I, that he shall take of mine, and shall shew it unto you. Creed.

Offertory. Ps. 66, 1-2 and 16. O be joyful in God, all ye lands, sing praises unto the honour of his name: O come hither and hearken, all ye that fear God, and I will tell you what the Lord hath done for my soul, alleluia.

Secret.

O GOD, who by communion in this venerable sacrifice hast made us partakers of the one supreme Godhead: grant, we beseech thee; that as we have the knowledge of thy truth, so by worthy conversation we may attain unto the fulness of the same. Through.

Preface of Easter, but chiefly at this time.

Communion. John 16, 8. When the Comforter, the Spirit of truth, is come, he will reprove the world of sin, and of righteousness, and of judgment, alleluia, alleluia.

Postcommunion.

ASSIST us, mercifully, O Lord our God; that we, who have faithfully received this holy Sacrament, may thereby be cleansed from our iniquities, and delivered from all dangers that beset us. Through.

The Fifth Sunday after Easter

Double.

Introit. Is. 48, 20. Vocem jucunditatis.

WITH a voice of singing declare ye this, and let it be heard, alleluia: utter it even unto the end of the earth: the Lord hath delivered his people, alleluia, alleluia. Ps. 66, 1. O be joyful in God, all ye lands, sing praises unto the honour of his name: make his praise to be glorious. ℣. Glory.

Collect.

O LORD, from whom all good things do come, grant to us thy humble servants: that by thy holy inspiration we may think those things that be good; and by thy merciful guiding may perform the same. Through.

Or, Collect.

O GOD, from whom all good things do come, grant to us thy humble servants; that by thy inspiration we may think those things that be right; and by thy guiding may perform the same. Through.

The Fifth Sunday after Easter

The Lesson from the Epistle of blessed James the Apostle.

James 1, 22-27.

DEARLY beloved: Be ye doers of the Word, and not hearers only: deceiving your own selves. For if any be a hearer of the Word, and not a doer: he is like unto a man beholding his natural face in a glass: for he beholdeth himself, and goeth his way, and straightway forgetteth what manner of man he was. But whoso looketh into the perfect law of liberty, and continueth therein, he being not a forgetful hearer, but a doer of the work: this man shall be blessed in his deed. If any man among you seem to be religious, and bridleth not his tongue, but deceiveth his own heart, this man's religion is vain. Pure religion, and undefiled before God and the Father, is this: To visit the fatherless and widows in their affliction, and to keep himself unspotted from the world.

Alleluia, alleluia. ℣. Christ is risen, and hath shewed light unto us, whom he hath redeemed with his blood. Alleluia. ℣. John 16, 28. I came forth from the Father, and am come into the world: again I leave the world, and go to the Father. Alleluia.

✠ The Continuation of the holy Gospel according to John.

John 16, 23-30.

AT that time: Jesus said unto his disciples: Verily, verily I say unto you: Whatsoever ye shall ask the Father in my name, he will give it you. Hitherto have ye asked nothing in my name: Ask, and ye shall receive, that your joy may be full. These things have I spoken unto you in proverbs. The time cometh when I shall no more speak unto you in proverbs, but I shall shew you plainly of the Father. At that day ye shall ask in my name: and I say not unto you, that I will pray the Father for you: for the Father himself loveth you, because ye have loved me, and have believed that I came out from God. I came forth from the Father, and am come into the world: again, I leave the world, and go to the Father. His disciples said unto him: Lo, now speakest thou plainly, and speakest no proverb. Now are we sure that thou knowest all things, and needest not that any man should ask thee: by this we believe that thou camest forth from God.*

Jesus answered them: Do ye now believe? Behold, the hour cometh, yea, is now come, that ye shall be scattered every man to his own, and shall leave me alone: and yet I am not alone, because the Father is with me. These things I have spoken unto you, that in me ye might have peace. In the world, ye shall have tribulation: but be of good cheer, I have overcome the world. Creed.

Offertory. Ps. 66, 8-9 and 20. O praise the Lord our God, ye people, and make the voice of his praise to be heard: who holdeth our soul in life, and suffereth not our feet to slip: praised be the Lord who hath not cast out my prayer, nor turned his mercy from me, alleluia.

Secret.

RECEIVE, O Lord, the prayers and oblations of thy faithful people: that through this observance of our bounden duty we may attain unto heavenly glory. Through.

Preface of Easter, but chiefly at this time.

Communion. Ps. 96, 1. O sing unto the Lord, alleluia: sing unto the Lord, and praise his name: be telling of his salvation from day to day, alleluia, alleluia.

Postcommunion.

GRANT unto us, O Lord, that we, who have been fulfilled with the grace and power of this heavenly table: may both desire those things which be right, and effectually obtain all things that we desire. Through.

THE GREATER AND LESSER LITANIES

On the greater Litanies on the Feast of St. Mark the Evangelist, or, if this Feast fall on Easter Day, on the Tuesday following, the Station is at St. Peter. And on the lesser Litanies before Ascension: on Rogation Monday, Station at St. Mary major: on Tuesday, Station at St. John Lateran: on Wednesday, Station at St. Peter.

¶ The following Mass is sung on the Greater and Lesser Rogation-days at the Procession, without Commemoration of an occurring Feast and without the Creed, even on a Sunday. The Commemoration is not to be omitted, however, if a conventual Mass is said in Choir of a Double of the First or Second Class, which is celebrated on that day, or of the occurring Octave of Easter. But if only one Mass is said in the church, at the Procession the Mass of the Rogations is said, but if the Office be a double of first class, in such a case Mass is said of the day.

¶ On Rogation Monday, if the Office is of the Feria, even if there be no Procession, the following conventual Mass is similarly said; otherwise if the office shall be of a Double Feast, two conventual Masses are said. Low Masses, however, may be said ad libitum, of the Office of the Day or of the Feria, according to the Rubrics.

¶ On Tuesday, if the office be of the Feria, the following Mass is similarly said without Glória in excélsis, although Te Deum has been said at Matins.

On a Feast, however, even a Simple, Mass is said of it with Commemoration of the Rogations; but, if there be a Procession, the Rubrics are to be observed.

¶ The same rule is observed as regards the Commemoration of the Rogations on the Vigil of the Ascension, but on it Mass is not said of the Rogations, except at the Procession, as above.

¶ On all days of the Litanies, Commemoration is always made of the Rogations in all Low Masses, which are not of the Dead. In sung Masses Commemoration is made only of the Greater Rogation (April 25).

Introit. Ps. 18, 7. Exaudivit.

HE hath heard my voice out of his holy temple, alleluia: and my complaint hath come before him, it hath entered even into his ears, alleluia, alleluia. Ps. ibid., 1. I will love thee, O Lord, my strength: the Lord is my stony rock, my fortress and my saviour. ℣. Glory.

¶ In this Mass Glória in excélsis is not said, nor the Creed.

Collect.

GRANT, we beseech thee, almighty God: that we, who in all our troubles do put our whole trust and confidence in thy mercy; may ever be defended by thy protection against all adversities. Through.

The Lesson from the Epistle of blessed James the Apostle.

James 5, 16-20.

DEARLY beloved: Confess your faults one to another, and pray one for another, that ye may be healed: the effectual fervent prayer of a righteous man availeth much. Elias was a man subject to like passions as we are: and he prayed earnestly that it might not rain, and it rained not on the earth by the space of three years and six months. And he prayed again, and the heaven gave rain, and the earth brought forth her fruit. Brethren, if any of you do err from the truth, and one convert him: let him know that he which converteth the sinner from the error of his way shall save a soul from death, and shall hide a multitude of sins.

Alleluia. ℣. Ps. 118, 1. O give thanks unto the Lord, for he is gracious: and his mercy endureth for ever.

☩ The Continuation of the holy Gospel according to Luke.

Luke 11, 5-13.

AT that time: Jesus said unto his disciples: Which of you shall have a friend, and shall go unto him at midnight, and say unto him: Friend, lend me three loaves, for a friend of mine in his journey is come to me, and I have nothing to set before him: and he from within shall answer and say: Trouble me not, the door is now shut, and my children are with me in bed, I cannot rise and give thee. I say unto you: Though he will not rise and give him because he is his friend, yet because of his importunity he will rise and give him as many as he needeth. And I say unto you: Ask, and it shall be given you: seek, and ye shall find: knock, and it shall be opened unto you. For every one that asketh receiveth: and he that seeketh findeth: and to him that knocketh it shall be opened. If a son shall ask bread of any of you that is a father, will he give him a stone? Or if he ask a fish: will he for a fish give him a serpent? Or if he shall ask an egg: will he offer him a scorpion? If ye then, being evil, know how to give good gifts unto your children: how much more shall your heavenly Father give the Holy Spirit to them that ask him?

Offertory. Ps. 109, 30-31. I will give great thanks unto the Lord with my mouth: and praise him among the multitude, for he shall stand at the right hand of the poor: to save his soul from unrighteous judges, alleluia.

Secret.

WE beseech thee, O Lord, that these our oblations may deliver us from the bonds of our iniquity, and obtain for us the gifts of thy mercy. Through.

Preface of Easter.

Communion. Luke 11, 9-10. Ask, and ye shall receive: seek, and ye shall find: knock, and it shall be opened unto you: for every one that asketh receiveth: and he that seeketh findeth: and to him that knocketh it shall be opened, alleluia.

Postcommunion.

WE beseech thee, O Lord, to prosper with thy gracious favour these our supplications: that we, receiving thy gifts in this time of our tribulation, may increase in thy love by the consolation of the same. Through.

The Vigil of the Ascension

¶ To-day, if a Double Feast (but not of the First Class) occur, three conventual Masses are said, the first after Terce of the Office of the Day, the second after Sext of the Vigil, the third after None of the Rogations at the Procession. But if there be no Procession, a Commemoration is

The Vigil of the Ascension

made of the Rogations in a read Mass of the Vigil. But on a Double of the First Class nothing is said of the Vigil or the Rogations. If, however, the Office be of the Vigil, the conventual Mass is said of it; but if there be a Procession, the Rogation Mass is not omitted.

Introit. Is. 48, 20. Vocem jucunditatis.

WITH a voice of singing declare ye this, and let it be heard, alleluia: utter it even unto the end of the earth: the Lord hath delivered his people, alleluia, alleluia. Ps. 66, 1. O be joyful in God, all ye lands: sing praises unto his name, make his praise to be glorious. ℣. Glory.

Glória in excélsis is said.

Collect.

O LORD, from whom all good things do come, grant to us thy humble servants: that by thy holy inspiration we may think those things that be good; and by thy merciful guiding may perform the same. Through.

Or, Collect.

O GOD, from whom all good things do come, grant to us thy humble servants: that by thy inspiration we may think those things that be right; and by thy guiding may perform the same. Through.

2nd of the Rogations (in private Masses).

Collect.

GRANT, we beseech thee, almighty God: that we, who in all our troubles do put our whole trust and confidence in thy mercy; may ever be defended by thy protection against all adversities. Through.

The Lesson from the Epistle of blessed Paul the Apostle to the Ephesians.

Ephes. 4, 7-13.

BRETHREN: Unto every one of us is given grace according to the measure of the gift of Christ. Wherefore he saith: When he ascended up on high, he led captivity captive: and gave gifts unto men. Now that he ascended, what is it but that he also descended first into the lower parts of the earth? He that descended is the same also that ascended up far above all heavens, that he might fill all things. And he gave some, apostles, and some, prophets, and some, evangelists, and some, pastors and teachers, for the perfecting of the saints, for the work of the ministry, for the edifying of the body of Christ: till we all come in the unity of the faith, and of the knowledge of the Son of God, unto a perfect man, unto the measure of the stature of the fulness of Christ.

Alleluia, alleluia. ℣. Christ is risen, and hath shewed light unto us, whom he hath redeemed with his blood. Alleluia. ℣. John 16, 28. I came forth from the Father, and am come into the world: again I leave the world, and go to the Father. Alleluia.

✠ The Continuation of the holy Gospel according to John.

John 17, 1-11.

AT that time: Jesus lifted up his eyes to heaven, and said: Father, the hour is come, glorify thy Son, that thy Son also may glorify thee: as thou hast given him power over all flesh, that he should give eternal life to as many as thou hast given him. And this is life eternal: that they might know thee the only true God, and Jesus Christ, whom thou hast sent. I have glorified thee on the earth: I have finished the work which thou gavest me to do: and now, O Father, glorify thou me with thine own self with the glory which I had with thee before the world was. I have manifested thy name unto the men which thou gavest me out of the world. Thine they were, and thou gavest them me: and they have kept thy word. Now they have known that all things whatsoever thou hast given me are of thee: for I have given unto them the words which thou gavest me: and they have received them, and have known surely that I came out from thee, and they have believed that thou didst send me. I pray for them, I pray not for the world, but for them which thou hast given me: for they are thine: and all mine are thine, and thine are mine: and I am glorified in them. And now I am no more in the world, but these are in the world, and I come to thee.

Offertory. Ps. 66, 8-9 and 20. O praise the Lord our God, ye people, and make the voice of his praise to be heard: who holdeth our soul in life, and suffereth not our feet to slip: praised be the Lord, who hath not cast out my prayer, nor turned his mercy from me, alleluia.

Secret.

RECEIVE, O Lord, the prayers and oblations of thy faithful people: that through this observance of our bounden duty and service, we may attain unto heavenly glory. Through.

For the Rogations.   Secret.

WE beseech thee, O Lord, that these our oblations may deliver us from the bonds of our iniquity, and obtain for us the gifts of thy mercy. Through.

Preface of Easter.

Communion. Ps. 96, 1. O sing unto the Lord, alleluia: sing unto the Lord, and praise his name: be telling of his salvation from day to day, alleluia, alleluia.

Postcommunion.

GRANT unto us, O Lord, that we who have been fulfilled with the grace and power of this heavenly table: may both desire those things which be right, and obtain all things that we desire. Through.

For the Rogations.   Postcommunion.

WE beseech thee, O Lord, to prosper with thy gracious favour these our supplications: that we, receiving thy gifts in this time of our tribulation, may increase in thy love by the consolation of the same. Through.

THE ASCENSION OF THE LORD

Double of 1st class.

Station at St. Peter

Introit. Acts 1, 11. Viri Galilæi.

YE men of Galilee, why marvel ye gazing up into heaven? alleluia: in like manner as ye have seen him going up into heaven, so shall he come again, alleluia, alleluia, alleluia. Ps. 47, 1. O clap your hands together, all ye people: O sing unto God with the voice of melody. V. Glory.

Collect.

GRANT, we beseech thee, almighty God: that like as we do believe thy only-begotten Son our Lord Jesus Christ to have ascended into the heavens; so we may also in heart and mind thither ascend, and with him continually dwell: Who liveth and reigneth with thee.

Or, Collect.

GRANT, we beseech thee, almighty God: that like as we do believe thy only-begotten Son our Redeemer this day to have ascended into the heavens; so we also in heart and mind may there continually dwell. Through the same.

The Lesson from the Acts of the Apostles.

Acts 1, 1-11.

THE former treatise have I made, O Theophilus, of all that Jesus began both to do and teach, until the day in which he was taken up, after that he through the Holy Ghost had given commandments unto the Apostles whom he had chosen: to whom also he shewed himself alive after his passion, by many infallible proofs, being seen of them forty days, and speaking of the things pertaining to the kingdom of God. And, being assembled together with them, commanded them that they should not depart from Jerusalem, but wait for the promise of the Father, which, saith he, ye have heard of me: for John truly baptized with water, but ye shall be baptized with the Holy Ghost not many days hence. When they therefore were come together, they asked of him, saying: Lord, wilt thou at this time restore again the kingdom to Israel? And he said unto them: It is not for you to know the times or the seasons, which the Father hath put in his own power: but ye shall receive power after that the Holy Ghost is come upon you, and ye shall be witnesses unto me, both in Jerusalem, and in all Judæa, and in Samaria, and unto the uttermost part of the earth. And when he had spoken these things, while they beheld, he was taken up, and a cloud received him out of their sight. And while they looked stedfastly toward heaven, as he went up, behold, two men stood by them in white apparel, which also said: Ye men of Galilee, why stand ye gazing up into heaven? This same Jesus, which is taken up from you into heaven, shall so come in like manner as ye have seen him go into heaven.

Alleluia, alleluia. V. Ps. 47, 6. God is gone up with a merry noise, and the Lord with the sound of the trump. Alleluia. V. Ps. 68, 18-19. The Lord in the holy place of Sinai, ascending up on high, hath led captivity captive. Alleluia.

Sunday after the Ascension

☩ The Continuation of the holy Gospel according to Mark.

Mark 16, 14-20.

AT that time: Jesus appeared unto the eleven as they sat at meat: and upbraided them with their unbelief and hardness of heart: because they believed not them which had seen him after he was risen. And he said unto them: Go ye into all the world, and preach the Gospel to every creature. He that believeth and is baptized shall be saved: but he that believeth not shall be damned. And these signs shall follow them that believe: In my name shall they cast out devils: they shall speak with new tongues: they shall take up serpents: and if they drink any deadly thing, it shall not hurt them: they shall lay hands on the sick, and they shall recover. So then after the Lord had spoken unto them, he was received up into heaven, and sat on the right hand of God. And they went forth and preached everywhere, the Lord working with them, and confirming the word with signs following.

¶ The Gospel having been read, the paschal Candle is extinguished, nor is it lighted again.

The Creed is said.

Offertory. Ps. 47, 6. God is gone up with a merry noise: and the Lord with the sound of the trump, alleluia.

Secret.

ACCEPT, O Lord, the gifts which, in remembrance of the glorious Ascension of thy Son, we offer unto thee: and mercifully grant; that we may be delivered from present dangers, and attain unto everlasting life. Through the same.

Preface and Communicántes proper.

Communion. Ps. 68, 33-34. Sing ye to the Lord, who ascended above the heaven of heavens, to the Sunrising, alleluia.

Postcommunion.

GRANT to us, we beseech thee, almighty and merciful God: that we, who have outwardly received these holy mysteries, may inwardly be partakers of the benefits of the same. Through.

¶ On ferias, until the Friday following the Sunday after Ascension inclusive, Mass is said as above, but the Creed and Communicántes of the Ascension are omitted.

Sunday after the Ascension

Double.

Introit. Ps. 27, 7-9. Exaudi.

HEARKEN unto my voice, O Lord, when I cry unto thee, alleluia: unto thee my heart hath said, Thy face have I sought, thy face, Lord, will I seek: O hide not thou thy face from me, alleluia, alleluia. Ps. ibid., 1. The Lord is my light, and my salvation: whom then shall I fear. ℣. Glory.

Collect.

O GOD, the King of glory, who hast exalted thine only Son Jesus Christ with great triumph unto thy kingdom in heaven: we beseech thee, leave us not comfortless; but send to us thine Holy Ghost to comfort us, and exalt us unto the same place whither our Saviour Christ is gone before: Who liveth and reigneth with thee and the Holy Ghost, one God, world without end. ℟. Amen.

Or, Collect.

ALMIGHTY and everlasting God: vouchsafe that we, being devoutly given in all things to do thy holy will; may ever serve thy divine majesty in sincerity of heart. Through.

Sunday after the Ascension

The Lesson from the Epistle of blessed Peter the Apostle.

I Peter 4, 7-11.

DEARLY beloved: The end of all things is at hand. Be ye therefore sober, and watch unto prayer. And above all things have fervent charity among yourselves: for charity shall cover the multitude of sins. Use hospitality one to another without grudging: as every man hath received the gift, even so minister the same one to another, as good stewards of the manifold grace of God. If any man speak, let him speak as the oracles of God: if any man minister, let him do it as of the ability which God giveth: that God in all things may be glorified through Jesus Christ, to whom be praise and dominion for ever and ever. Amen.

or:

The Lesson from the Epistle of blessed Peter the Apostle.

I Peter 4, 7-11.

DEARLY beloved: Be sober, and watch unto prayer. And above all things have fervent charity among yourselves: for charity shall cover the multitude of sins. Use hospitality one to another without grudging: as every man hath received the gift, even so minister the same one to another, as good stewards of the manifold grace of God. If any man speak, let him speak as the oracles of God: if any man minister, let him do it as of the ability which God giveth: that God in all things may be glorified through Jesus Christ our Lord.

Alleluia, alleluia. ℣. Ps. 47, 9. The Lord reigneth over all the heathen: God sitteth upon his holy seat. Alleluia. ℣. John 14, 18. I will not leave you comfortless: I go away and come again unto you, and your heart shall rejoice. Alleluia.

✠ The Continuation of the holy Gospel according to John.

John 15, 26-27; 16, 1-4.

AT that time: Jesus said unto his disciples: When the Comforter is come, whom I will send unto you from the Father, even the Spirit of truth, which proceedeth from the Father, he shall testify of me: and ye shall also bear witness, because ye have been with me from the beginning. These things have I spoken unto you that ye should not be offended. They shall put you out of the synagogues: yea, the time cometh, that whosoever killeth you will think that he doeth God service. And these things will they do unto you, because they have not known the Father, nor me. But these things have I told you: that, when the time shall come, ye may remember that I told you of them. Creed.

Offertory. Ps. 47, 6. God is gone up with a merry noise: and the Lord with the sound of the trump, alleluia.

Secret.

MAY these spotless sacrifices purify us, O Lord: and give unto our souls the strength of thy heavenly grace. Through.

Preface only of the Ascension.

Communion. John 17, 12-13 and 15. Father, while I was with them, I kept those that thou gavest me, alleluia: and now I come to thee: I pray not that thou shouldest take them out of the world; but that thou shouldest keep them from the evil, alleluia, alleluia.

Postcommunion.

GRANT, we beseech thee, O Lord: that we, whom thou hast fulfilled with thy sacred gifts; may continually render thanks unto thee for the same. Through.

SATURDAY THE VIGIL OF PENTECOST

Double.

Station at St. John Lateran

Introit. Ezek. 36, 23-26.

Cum sanctificatus fuero.

WHEN I shall be sanctified in you, I will gather you out of all countries: then will I sprinkle clean water upon you, and ye shall be clean from all your filthiness: and a new spirit will I put within you, alleluia, alleluia. Ps. 34, 1. I will alway give thanks unto the Lord: his praise shall ever be in my mouth. ℣. Glory.

Glória in excélsis is said.

Collect.

GRANT, we beseech thee, almighty God: that the splendour of thy glory may shine forth upon us; and that the light of thy light may, by the illumination of the Holy Spirit, strengthen the hearts of them who through thy grace are born again. Through... in the unity of the same Holy Spirit.

¶ This Collect only is is said.

The Lesson from the Acts of the Apostles.

Acts 19, 1-8.

IN those days: It came to pass, that, while Apollos was at Corinth, Paul having passed through the upper coasts came to Ephesus: and finding certain disciples, he said unto them: Have ye received the Holy Ghost since ye believed? And they said unto him: We have not so much as heard whether there be any Holy Ghost. And he said unto them: Unto what then were ye baptized? And they said: Unto John's baptism. Then said Paul: John verily baptized with the baptism of repentance, saying unto the people, that they should believe on him which should come after him, that is, on Christ Jesus. When they heard this, they were baptized in the name of the Lord Jesus. And when Paul had laid his hands upon them, the Holy Ghost came on them, and they spake with tongues, and prophesied. And all the men were about twelve. And he went into the synagogue, and spake boldly for the space of three months, disputing and persuading the things concerning the kingdom of God.

Alleluia. ℣. Ps. 107, 1. O give thanks unto the Lord, for he is gracious: and his mercy endureth for ever.

Alleluia is not repeated, but there immediately follows:

Tract. Ps. 117, 1-2. O praise the Lord, all ye heathen: praise him, all ye nations. ℣. For his merciful kindness is ever more and more towards us: and the truth of the Lord endureth for ever.

Saturday the Vigil of Pentecost

✠ The Continuation of the holy Gospel according to John.

John 14, 15-21.

AT that time: Jesus said unto his disciples: If ye love me, keep my commandments. And I will pray the Father, and he shall give you another Comforter, that he may abide with you for ever, even the Spirit of truth, whom the world cannot receive, because it seeth him not, neither knoweth him. But ye know him: for he dwelleth with you, and shall be in you. I will not leave you comfortless: I will come to you. Yet a little while, and the world seeth me no more. But ye see me, because I live, ye shall live also. At that day ye shall know that I am in my Father, and ye in me, and I in you. He that hath my commandments and keepeth them: he it is that loveth me. And he that loveth me shall be loved of my Father: and I will love him, and will manifest myself to him.

The Creed is not said.

Offertory. Ps. 104, 30-31. O send forth thy Spirit, and they shall be made, and thou shalt renew the face of the earth: the glorious majesty of the Lord shall endure for ever, alleluia.

Secret.

SANCTIFY, we beseech thee, O Lord, these our oblations: and cleanse our hearts by the enlightening of thy Holy Spirit. Through... in the unity of the same Holy Spirit.

¶ Preface, Communicántes, and Hanc oblatiónem proper of Pentecost; which are said until the following Saturday, inclusive.

Communion. John 7, 37-39. In the last day of the feast, Jesus said: He that believeth on me, out of his belly shall flow rivers of living water: but this spake he of the Spirit, which they that believe on him should receive, alleluia, alleluia.

Postcommunion.

POUR thy Holy Spirit upon us, O Lord, and cleanse our hearts: that by the inward sprinkling of his dew they may bring forth fruit unto thee. Through... in the unity of the same Holy Spirit.

WHITSUNDAY or PENTECOST

Double of 1st class with Octave.

Station at St. Peter

Introit. Wisd. 1, 7. Spiritus Domini.

THE Spirit of the Lord hath filled the whole world, alleluia: and that which containeth all things hath knowledge of the voice, alleluia, alleluia, alleluia. Ps. 68, 1. Let God arise, and let his enemies be scattered: let them also that hate him flee before him. ℣. Glory.

Collect.

GOD, who as* at this time* didst teach the hearts of thy faithful people, by the sending to them the light of thy Holy Spirit: grant us by the same Spirit to have a right judgment in all things; and evermore to rejoice in his holy comfort. Through ... in the unity of the same Holy Spirit.

*or: on this day.

The Lesson from the Acts of the Apostles.

Acts 2, 1-11.

WHEN the day of Pentecost was fully come, they were all with one accord in one place: And suddenly there came a sound from heaven, as of a rushing mighty wind: and it filled all the house where they were sitting. And there appeared unto them cloven tongues, like as of fire, and it sat upon each of them: and they were all filled with the Holy Ghost, and began to speak with other tongues, as the Spirit gave them utterance. And there were dwelling at Jerusalem Jews, devout men, out of every nation under heaven. Now when this was noised abroad, the multitude came together, and were confounded, because that every man heard them speak in his own language. And they were all amazed, and marvelled, saying one to another: Behold, are not all these which speak Galileans? And how hear we every man in our own tongue wherein we were born? Parthians, and Medes, and Elamites, and the dwellers in Mesopotamia, and in Judæa, and Cappadocia, in Pontus, and Asia, Phrygia, and Pamphylia, in Egypt, and in the parts of Libya about Cyrene, and strangers of Rome, Jews, and Proselytes, Cretes, and Arabians: we do hear them speak in our tongues the wonderful works of God.

Alleluia, alleluia. ℣. Ps. 104, 30. O send forth thy Spirit and they shall be made, and thou shalt renew the face of the earth. Alleluia. (Here genuflect.) ℣. Come, Holy Ghost, fill the hearts of thy faithful: and kindle in them the fire of thy love.

Sequence.   Veni, Sancte Spiritus.

COME, thou Holy Spirit, come, and from thy celestial home send thy light and brilliancy.

Come, thou Father of the poor; come thou source of all our store; come, the soul's true radiancy.

Thou of comforters the best, of the soul the sweetest guest, come in toil refreshingly.

In our labour rest most sweet, grateful shadow from the heat, comfort in adversity.

O thou light most pure and blest, shine within the inmost breast of thy faithful company.

Where thou art not, man hath nought, every holy deed and thought comes from thy divinity.

What is soiléd, make thou pure, what is wounded, work its cure, water what is parched and dry.

What is rigid, gently bend, what is frozen, warmly tend, strengthen what goes erringly.

Fill thy faithful, who confide in thy power to guard and guide, with thy sevenfold mystery.

Here thy grace and virtue send, grant salvation in the end, and in heaven felicity. Amen. Alleluia.

¶ And it is said daily until the following Saturday, inclusive.

✠ The Continuation of the holy Gospel according to John.

John 14, 15-31.

AT that time: Jesus said unto his disciples: If ye love me, keep my commandments. And I will pray the Father, and he shall give you another Comforter, that he may abide with you for ever, even the Spirit of truth, whom the world cannot receive, because it seeth him not, neither knoweth him. But ye know him: for he dwelleth with you, and shall be in you. I will not leave you comfortless: I will come to you. Yet a little while: and the world seeth me no more. But ye see me, because I live, ye shall live also. At that day ye shall know, that I am in my Father, and ye in me, and I in you. He that hath my commandments, and keepeth them: he it is that loveth me. And he that loveth me shall be loved of my Father: and I will love him, and will manifest myself to him. Judas saith unto him, (not Iscariot,): Lord, how is it that thou wilt manifest thyself unto us, and not unto the world? Jesus answered and said unto him: If a man love me, he will keep my words, and my Father will love him, and we will come unto him, and make our abode with him: he that loveth me not keepeth not my sayings. And the word which ye hear is not mine: but the Father's which sent me. These things have I spoken unto you, being yet present with you. But the Comforter, which is the Holy Ghost, whom the Father will send in my name, he shall teach you all things, and bring all things to your remembrance, whatsoever I have said unto you. Peace I leave with you, my peace I give unto you: not as the world giveth, give I unto you. Let not your heart be troubled, neither let it be afraid. Ye have heard how I said unto you: I go away and come again unto you. If ye loved me, ye would rejoice, because I said, I go unto the Father: for my Father is greater than I. And now I have told you before it come to pass: that, when it is come to pass, ye might believe. Hereafter I will not talk much with you. For the prince of this world cometh, and hath nothing in me. But that the world may know that I love the Father, and as the Father gave me commandment, even so I do. Creed.

or:

✠ The Continuation of the holy Gospel according to John.

John 14, 23-31.

AT that time: Jesus said unto his disciples: If a man love me, he will keep my words, and my Father will love him, and we will come unto him, and make our abode with him: he that loveth me not keepeth not my sayings. And the word which ye hear is not mine: but the Father's which sent me. These things have I spoken unto you, being yet present with you. But the Comforter, which is the Holy Ghost, whom the Father will send in my name, he shall teach you all things, and bring all things to your remembrance, whatsoever I have said unto you. Peace I leave with you, my peace I give unto you: not as the world giveth, give I unto you. Let not your heart be troubled, neither let it be afraid. Ye have heard how I said unto you: I go away and come again unto you. If ye loved me, ye would rejoice, because I said, I go unto the Father: for my Father is greater than I. And now I have told you before it come to pass: that, when it is come to pass, ye might believe. Hereafter I will not talk much with you. For the prince of this world cometh, and hath nothing in me. But that the world may know that I love the Father, and as the Father gave me commandment, even so I do. Creed.

Offertory. Ps. 68, 29-30. Stablish the thing, O God, that thou hast wrought in us: for thy temple's sake at Jerusalem shall kings bring presents unto thee, alleluia.

Secret.

SANCTIFY, we beseech thee, O Lord, the gifts which we offer: and cleanse our hearts by the enlightening of the Holy Spirit. Through.... in the unity of the same Holy Spirit.

Preface, Communicántes and Hanc oblatiónem proper.

Communion. Acts 2, 2 and 4. Suddenly there came a sound from heaven as of a rushing mighty wind, where they were sitting, alleluia: and they were all filled with the Holy Ghost, speaking the wonderful works of God, alleluia, alleluia.

Postcommunion.

POUR thy Holy Spirit upon us, O Lord, and cleanse our hearts: that by the inward sprinkling of his dew they may bring forth fruit unto thee. Through... in the unity of the same Holy Spirit.

MONDAY

IN THE OCTAVE OF PENTECOST

Double of 1st class.

Station at St. Peter ad Vincula

Introit. Ps. 81, 17. Cibavit eos.

HE fed them with the finest wheat-flour, alleluia: and with honey out of the stony rock hath he satisfied them, alleluia, alleluia. Ps. ibid., 1. Sing we merrily unto God our strength: make a cheerful noise unto the God of Jacob. ℣. Glory.

Collect God, who as, p. 446.

Or, Collect.

O GOD, who didst bestow the Holy Spirit on thine Apostles: grant unto thy people who devoutly call upon thee the fulfilment of all their petitions; that they who have received thy gift of faith, may likewise obtain of thy bountiful goodness the blessing of peace. Through ... in the unity of the same Holy Spirit.

The Lesson from the Acts of the Apostles.

Acts 10, 34 and 42-48.

IN those days: Peter opened his mouth, and said: Of a truth I perceive that God is no respecter of persons: but in every nation he that feareth him, and worketh righteousness, is accepted with him. The word which God sent unto the children of Israel, preaching peace by Jesus Christ, (he is Lord of all;) that word, I say, ye know, which was published throughout all Judæa: and began from Galilee, after the baptism which John preached: how God anointed Jesus of Nazareth with the Holy Ghost, and with power, who went about doing good, and healing all that were oppressed of the devil, for God was with him. And we are witnesses of all things which he did, both in the land of the Jews, and in Jerusalem, whom they slew, and hanged on a tree. Him God raised up the third day, and shewed him openly, not to all the people, but unto witnesses chosen before of God: even to us who did eat and drink with him after he rose from the dead. And he commanded us to preach unto the people, and to testify that it is he which was ordained of God to be the judge of quick and dead. To him give all the Prophets witness, that through his name whosoever believeth in him shall receive remission of sins. While Peter yet spake these words, the Holy Ghost fell on all them which heard the word. And they of the circumcision, which believed, were astonished, as many as came with Peter, because that on the Gentiles also was poured out the gift of the Holy Ghost. For they heard them speak with tongues, and magnify God. Then answered Peter: Can any man forbid water, that these should not be baptized, which have received the Holy Ghost as well as we? And he commanded them to be baptized in the name of the Lord. Then prayed they him to tarry certain days.

or:

The Lesson from the Acts of the Apostles.

Acts 10, 34 and 42-48.

IN those days: Peter opened his mouth and said: Men and brethren, the Lord commanded us to preach unto the people, and to testify that it is he which was ordained of God to be the judge of quick and dead. To him give all the Prophets witness, that through his name whosoever believeth in him shall receive remission of sins. While Peter yet spake these words, the Holy Ghost fell on all them which heard the word. And they of the circumcision, which believed, were astonished, as many as came with Peter: because that on the Gentiles also was poured out the gift of the Holy Ghost. For they heard them speak with tongues, and magnify God. Then answered Peter: Can any man forbid water, that these should not be baptized, which have received the Holy Ghost as well as we? And he commanded them to be baptized in the name of the Lord Jesus Christ.

Alleluia, alleluia. ℣. Acts 2, 4. The Apostles spake with other tongues the wonderful works of God. Alleluia. (Here genuflect). ℣. Come, Holy Ghost, fill the hearts of thy faithful: and kindle in them the fire of thy love.

Sequence.   Veni, Sancte Spiritus.

COME, thou Holy Spirit, come, and from thy celestial home send thy light and brilliancy.

Come, thou Father of the poor; come thou source of all our store; come, the soul's true radiancy.

Thou of comforters the best, of the soul the sweetest guest, come in toil refreshingly.

In our labour rest most sweet, grateful shadow from the heat, comfort in adversity.

O thou light most pure and blest, shine within the inmost breast of thy faithful company.

Where thou art not, man hath nought, every holy deed and thought comes from thy divinity.

What is soiléd, make thou pure, what is wounded, work its cure, water what is parched and dry.

What is rigid, gently bend, what is frozen, warmly tend, strengthen what goes erringly.

Fill thy faithful, who confide in thy power to guard and guide, with thy sevenfold mystery.

Here thy grace and virtue send, grant salvation in the end, and in heaven felicity. Amen. Alleluia.

✠ The Continuation of the holy Gospel according to John.

John 3, 16-21.

AT that time: Jesus said unto Nicodemus: God so loved the world, that he gave his only-begotten Son: that whosoever believeth in him should not perish, but have everlasting life. For God sent not his Son into the world to condemn the world, but that the world through him might be saved. He that believeth on him is not condemned; but he that believeth not is condemned already: because he hath not believed in the name of the only-begotten Son of God. And this is the condemnation: that light is come into the world, and men loved darkness rather than light: because their deeds were evil. For every one that doeth evil hateth the light, neither cometh to the light, lest his deeds should be reproved: but he that doeth truth cometh to the light, that his deeds may be made manifest, that they are wrought in God. Creed.

Offertory. Ps. 18, 14 and 16. The Lord thundered out of heaven, and the Highest gave forth his voice: and the springs of waters were seen, alleluia.

Secret.

WE beseech thee, O Lord, graciously to sanctify these our gifts: and by the acceptable offering of our spiritual sacrifice, render us ourselves an everlasting oblation unto thee. Through.

Preface, Communicántes and Hanc oblatiónem, as on the day of Pentecost.

Communion. John 14, 26. The Holy Ghost shall teach you, alleluia: whatsoever I have said unto you, alleluia, alleluia.

Postcommunion.

WE beseech thee, O Lord, mercifully to assist thy people: that they whom thou hast fulfilled with these heavenly mysteries may by thee be defended from the fierceness of their enemies. Through.

TUESDAY

IN THE OCTAVE OF PENTECOST

Double of 1st class.

Station at St. Anastasia

Introit. II Esd. 2, 36-37. Accipite.

RECEIVE the joyfulness of your glory, alleluia: giving thanks unto God, alleluia: who hath called you to the heavenly kingdom, alleluia, alleluia, alleluia. Ps. 78, 1. Hear my law, O my people: incline your ears unto the words of my mouth. ℣. Glory.

Collect God, who as, p. 446.

Or, Collect.

WE beseech thee, O Lord, let the power of the Holy Ghost effectually work within us: that by his merciful goodness he may cleanse our hearts and ever defend us against all adversities. Through . . . in the unity of the same Holy Ghost.

The Lesson from the Acts of the Apostles.

Acts 8, 14-17.

IN those days: When the Apostles, which were at Jerusalem, heard that Samaria had received the word of God, they sent unto them Peter and John. Who, when they were come down, prayed for them, that they might receive the Holy Ghost: for as yet he was fallen upon none of them, only they were baptized in the name of the Lord Jesus. Then laid they their hands on them, and they received the Holy Ghost.

Alleluia, alleluia. ℣. John 14, 26. The Holy Ghost shall teach you whatsoever I have said unto you. Alleluia. (Here genuflect). ℣. Come, Holy Ghost, fill the hearts of thy faithful: and kindle in them the fire of thy love.

Sequence. Veni, Sancte Spiritus.

COME, thou Holy Spirit, come, and from thy celestial home send thy light and brilliancy.

Come, thou Father of the poor; come thou source of all our store; come, the soul's true radiancy.

Thou of comforters the best, of the soul the sweetest guest, come in toil refreshingly.

In our labour rest most sweet, grateful shadow from the heat, comfort in adversity.

O thou light most pure and blest, shine within the inmost breast of thy faithful company.

Where thou art not, man hath nought, every holy deed and thought comes from thy divinity.

What is soiléd, make thou pure, what is wounded, work its cure, water what is parched and dry.

What is rigid, gently bend, what is frozen, warmly tend, strengthen what goes erringly.

Fill thy faithful, who confide in thy power to guard and guide, with thy sevenfold mystery.

Here thy grace and virtue send, grant salvation in the end, and in heaven felicity. Amen. Alleluia.

✠ The Continuation of the holy Gospel according to John.

John 10, 1-10.

AT that time: Jesus said unto the Pharisees: Verily, verily, I say unto you: He that entereth not by the door into the sheepfold, but climbeth up some other way, the same is a thief and a robber. But he that entereth in by the door is the shepherd of the sheep. To him the porter openeth, and the sheep hear his voice, and he calleth his own sheep by name, and leadeth them out. And when he putteth forth his own sheep, he goeth before them: and the sheep follow him, for they know his voice. And a stranger will they not follow, but will flee from him; for they know not the voice of strangers. This parable spake Jesus unto them. But they understood not what things they were which he spake unto them. Then said Jesus unto them again: Verily, verily, I say unto you: I am the door of the sheep. All that ever came before me are thieves and robbers, but the sheep did not hear them. I am the door. By me if any man enter in, he shall be saved: and shall go in and out, and find pasture. The thief cometh not but for to steal and to kill, and to destroy. I am come that they might have life, and that they might have it more abundantly. Creed.

Offertory. Ps. 78, 23-25. The Lord opened the doors of heaven: and rained down manna upon them for to eat: he gave them food from heaven, so man did eat Angels' food, alleluia.

Secret.

CLEANSE us, O Lord, we beseech thee, by the oblation of these our gifts: and make us worthy thereby to be partakers of this holy Sacrament. Through.

Preface, Communicántes and Hanc oblatiónem as on the day of Pentecost.

Communion. John 15, 26; 16, 14; 17, 1 and 5. The Spirit which proceedeth from the Father, alleluia: he shall glorify me, alleluia, alleluia.

Postcommunion.

WE beseech thee, O Lord, that thy Holy Spirit, who is himself the remission of all our iniquities, may in this heavenly Sacrament regenerate our souls. Through ... in the unity of the same Holy Spirit.

Ember Wednesday of Pentecost
Double.
Station at St. Mary Major

Introit. Ps. 68, 8-9.

Deus, dum egredereris.

O GOD, when thou wentest forth before the people, journeying and dwelling with them, alleluia: the earth shook, and the heavens dropped, alleluia, alleluia. Ps. ibid., 1. Let God arise, and let his enemies be scattered: let them also that hate him flee before him. ℣. Glory.

After Kýrie eléison is said Let us pray, without Let us bow the knee.

Collect.

WE beseech thee, O Lord, that the Paraclete, who proceedeth from thee, may enlighten our minds: and lead us, as thy Son hath promised, into all truth: Who liveth and reigneth with thee in the unity of the same Holy Ghost.

The Lesson from the Acts of the Apostles.

Acts 2, 14-21.

IN those days: Peter, standing up with the eleven, lifted up his voice, and said unto them: Ye men of Judæa, and all ye that dwell at Jerusalem, be this known unto you, and hearken to my words. For these are not drunken, as ye suppose, seeing it is but the third hour of the day: this is that which was spoken by the Prophet Joel: And it shall come to pass in the last days, saith God, I will pour out of my Spirit upon all flesh, and your sons and your daughters shall prophesy, and your young men shall see visions, and your old men shall dream dreams. And on my servants and on my handmaidens I will pour out in those days of my Spirit, and they shall prophesy: and I will shew wonders in heaven above, and signs in the earth beneath, blood, and fire, and vapour of smoke. The sun shall be turned into darkness, and the moon into blood, before that great and notable day of the Lord come. And it shall come to pass: that whosoever shall call on the name of the Lord shall be saved.

Alleluia. ℣. Ps. 33, 6. By the word of the Lord were the heavens made, and all the hosts of them by the breath of his mouth.

Here is said Glória in excélsis, and then The Lord be with you.

Collect.

GRANT, we beseech thee, almighty and merciful God: that the Holy Ghost descending on us may by his gracious indwelling render us a temple of his glory. Through... in the unity of the same Holy Ghost.

The Lesson from the Acts of the Apostles.

Acts 5, 12-16.

IN those days: By the hands of the Apostles were many signs and wonders wrought among the people. And they were all with one accord in Solomon's porch. And of the rest durst no man join himself to them: but the people magnified them. And believers were the more added to the Lord, multitudes both of men and women, insomuch that they brought forth the sick into the streets, and laid them on beds and couches, that at the least the shadow of Peter passing by might overshadow some of them. There came also a multitude out of the cities round about unto Jerusalem, bringing sick folks, and them which were vexed with unclean spirits: and they were healed every one.

Alleluia, alleluia. (Here genuflect). ℣. Come, Holy Ghost, fill the hearts of thy faithful: and kindle in them the fire of thy love.

Sequence.　　　　　Veni, Sancte Spiritus.

COME, thou Holy Spirit, come, and from thy celestial home send thy light and brilliancy.

Come, thou Father of the poor; come thou source of all our store; come, the soul's true radiancy.

Thou of comforters the best, of the soul the sweetest guest, come in toil refreshingly.

In our labour rest most sweet, grateful shadow from the heat, comfort in adversity.

O thou light most pure and blest, shine within the inmost breast of thy faithful company.

Where thou art not, man hath nought, every holy deed and thought comes from thy divinity.

What is soiléd, make thou pure, what is wounded, work its cure, water what is parched and dry.

What is rigid, gently bend, what is frozen, warmly tend, strengthen what goes erringly.

Fill thy faithful, who confide in thy power to guard and guide, with thy sevenfold mystery.

Here thy grace and virtue send, grant salvation in the end, and in heaven felicity. Amen. Alleluia.

✠ The Continuation of the holy Gospel according to John.

John 6, 44-52.

AT that time: Jesus said to the multitudes of the Jews: No man can come to me, except the Father which hath sent me draw him: and I will raise him up at the last day. It is written in the Prophets: And they shall be all taught of God. Every man therefore that hath heard, and hath learned of the Father, cometh unto me. Not that any man hath seen the Father, save he which is of God, he hath seen the Father. Verily, verily, I say unto you: He that believeth on me hath everlasting life. I am that bread of life. Your fathers did eat manna in the wilderness, and are dead. This is the bread which cometh down from heaven: that a man may eat thereof, and not die. I am the living bread which came down from heaven, if any man eat of this bread, he shall live for ever: and the bread that I will give is my flesh, which I will give for the life of the world. Creed.

Offertory. Ps. 119, 47-48. My delight shall be in thy commandments which I have loved exceedingly: my hands also will I lift up unto thy commandments which I have loved, alleluia.

Secret.

ACCEPT, we beseech thee, O Lord, these our oblations: and vouchsafe so to work in us, that we, who outwardly perform thy mysteries, may inwardly celebrate the same with all godly and devout affection. Through.

Preface, Communicántes and Hanc oblatiónem, as on the day of Pentecost.

Communion. John 14, 27. Peace I leave with you, alleluia: my peace I give unto you, alleluia, alleluia.

Postcommunion.

O LORD, who has suffered us to receive these heavenly sacraments, we humbly beseech thy mercy: that as we celebrate thy holy mysteries in this present life, so we may be brought unto the fulfilment of the same in everlasting felicity. Through.

Thursday in the Octave of Pentecost

Double.

Station at St. Lawrence without the walls

Introit. Wisd. 1, 7. Spiritus Domini.

THE Spirit of the Lord hath filled the whole world, alleluia: and that which containeth all things hath knowledge of the voice, alleluia, alleluia, alleluia. Ps. 68, 1. Let God arise, and let his enemies be scattered: let them also that hate him flee before him. ℣. Glory.

Collect.

GOD, who as on this day didst teach the hearts of thy faithful people, by the sending to them the light of thy Holy Spirit: grant us by the same Spirit to have a right judgment in all things, and evermore to rejoice in his holy comfort. Through ... in the unity of the same Holy Spirit.

The Lesson from the Acts of the Apostles.

Acts 8, 5-8.

IN those days: Philip went down to the city of Samaria, and preached Christ unto them. And the people with one accord gave heed unto those things which Philip spake, hearing and seeing the miracles which he did. For unclean spirits, crying with loud voice, came out of many that were possessed with them. And many taken with palsies, and that were lame, were healed. And there was great joy in that city.

Alleluia, alleluia. ℣. Ps. 104, 30. O send forth thy Spirit and they shall be made: and thou shalt renew the face of the earth. Alleluia. (Here genuflect). ℣. Come, Holy Ghost, fill the hearts of thy faithful, and kindle in them the fire of thy love.

Sequence.   Veni, Sancte Spiritus.

COME, thou Holy Spirit, come, and from thy celestial home send thy light and brilliancy.

Come, thou Father of the poor; come thou source of all our store; come, the soul's true radiancy.

Thou of comforters the best, of the soul the sweetest guest, come in toil refreshingly.

In our labour rest most sweet, grateful shadow from the heat, comfort in adversity.

O thou light most pure and blest, shine within the inmost breast of thy faithful company.

Where thou art not, man hath nought, every holy deed and thought comes from thy divinity.

What is soiléd, make thou pure, what is wounded, work its cure, water what is parched and dry.

What is rigid, gently bend, what is frozen, warmly tend, strengthen what goes erringly.

Fill thy faithful, who confide in thy power to guard and guide, with thy sevenfold mystery.

Here thy grace and virtue send, grant salvation in the end, and in heaven felicity. Amen. Alleluia.

✠ The Continuation of the holy Gospel according to Luke.

Luke 9, 1-6.

AT that time: Jesus called his twelve disciples together, and gave them power and authority over all devils, and to cure diseases. And he sent them to preach the kingdom of God, and to heal the sick. And he said unto them: Take nothing for your journey, neither staves, nor scrip, neither bread, nor money, neither have two coats apiece. And whatsoever house ye enter into, there abide, and thence depart. And whosoever will not receive you: when ye go out of that city, shake off the very dust from your feet for a testimony against them. And they departed, and went through the towns, preaching the gospel, and healing everywhere. Creed.

Offertory. Ps. 68, 29-30. Stablish the thing, O God, that thou hast wrought in us: for thy temple's sake at Jerusalem shall kings bring presents unto thee, alleluia.

Secret.

SANCTIFY, we beseech thee, O Lord, these our oblations: and cleanse our hearts by the enlightening of thy Holy Spirit. Through...in the unity of the same Holy Spirit.

Preface, Communicántes and Hanc oblatiónem, as on the day of Pentecost.

Communion. Acts 2, 2 and 4. Suddenly there came a sound from heaven, as of a rushing mighty wind, where they were sitting, alleluia: and they were all filled with the Holy Ghost, speaking the wonderful works of God, alleluia, alleluia.

Postcommunion.

POUR thy Holy Spirit upon us, O Lord, and cleanse our inmost hearts: that they, being sprinkled by the dew of his grace, may bring forth fruit unto thee. Through...in the unity of the same Holy Spirit.

Ember Friday of Pentecost
Double.
Station at the Twelve Holy Apostles

Introit. Ps. 71, 8 and 23. Repleatur os.

LET my mouth be filled with thy praise, alleluia: that I may sing, alleluia: my lips will be fain when I sing unto thee, alleluia, alleluia. Ps. ibid., 1-2. In thee, O Lord, have I put my trust, let me never be put to confusion: but rid me, and deliver me in thy righteousness. ℣. Glory.

Collect.

GRANT, we beseech thee, O merciful God: that thy Church, being knit together in the fellowship of the Holy Ghost, may not fear the assaults of any adversary. Through ... in the unity of the same Holy Ghost.

The Lesson from the Prophet Joel.

Joel 2, 23-24 and 26-27.

THUS saith the Lord God: Be glad, ye children of Sion, and rejoice in the Lord your God: for he hath given you the former rain moderately, and he will cause to come down for you the rain, the former rain, and the latter rain in the first month. And the floors shall be full of wheat, and the fats shall overflow with wine and oil. And ye shall eat in plenty, and be satisfied, and praise the name of the Lord your God, that hath dealt wondrously with you: and my people shall never be ashamed. And ye shall know that I am in the midst of Israel: and that I am the Lord your God, and none else: and my people shall never be ashamed: saith the Lord almighty.

Alleluia, alleluia. ℣. Wisd. 12, 1. O how good and sweet, O Lord, is thy Spirit within us! Alleluia. (Here genuflect). ℣. Come, Holy Ghost, fill the hearts of thy faithful: and kindle in them the fire of thy love.

Sequence. Veni, Sancte Spiritus.

COME, thou Holy Spirit, come, and from thy celestial home send thy light and brilliancy.

Come, thou Father of the poor; come thou source of all our store; come, the soul's true radiancy.

Thou of comforters the best, of the soul the sweetest guest, come in toil refreshingly.

In our labour rest most sweet, grateful shadow from the heat, comfort in adversity.

O thou light most pure and blest, shine within the inmost breast of thy faithful company.

Where thou art not, man hath nought, every holy deed and thought comes from thy divinity.

What is soiléd, make thou pure, what is wounded, work its cure, water what is parched and dry.

What is rigid, gently bend, what is frozen, warmly tend, strengthen what goes erringly.

Fill thy faithful, who confide in thy power to guard and guide, with thy sevenfold mystery.

Here thy grace and virtue send, grant salvation in the end, and in heaven felicity. Amen. Alleluia.

✠ The Continuation of the holy Gospel according to Luke.

Luke 5, 17-26.

AT that time: It came to pass on a certain day, as Jesus was teaching, that there were Pharisees and doctors of the law sitting by, which were come out of every town of Galilee, and Judæa, and Jerusalem: and the power of the Lord was present to heal them. And, behold, men brought in a bed a man which was taken with a palsy: and they sought means to bring him in, and to lay him before him. And when they could not find by what way they might bring him in because of the multitude, they went upon the housetop, and let him down through the tiling with his couch into the midst before Jesus. And when he saw their faith, he said unto him: Man, thy sins are forgiven thee. And the scribes and the Pharisees began to reason, saying: Who is this which speaketh blasphemies? Who can forgive sins, but God alone? But when Jesus perceived their thoughts, he answering said unto them: What reason ye in your hearts? Whether is easier, to say: Thy sins be forgiven thee, or to say: Rise up and walk? But that ye may know that the Son of man hath power upon earth to forgive sins (he said unto the sick of the palsy): I say unto thee, Arise, and take up thy couch, and go into thine house. And immediately he rose up before them, and took up that whereon he lay: and departed to his own house, glorifying God. And they were all amazed, and they glorified God. And were filled with fear, saying: We have seen strange things to-day. Creed.

Offertory. Ps. 146, 1. Praise the Lord, O my soul: while I live will I praise the Lord: yea, as long as I have any being, I will sing praises unto my God, alleluia.

Secret.

GRANT, O Lord, that the same heavenly fire, which through the Holy Spirit enkindled the hearts of the disciples of Christ thy Son: may likewise consume this our sacrifice which we offer in thy sight. Through the same... in the unity of the same Holy Spirit.

Preface, Communicántes and Hanc oblatiónem, as on the day of Pentecost.

Communion. John 14, 18. I will not leave you comfortless: I will come to you again, alleluia: and your heart shall rejoice, alleluia.

Postcommunion.

O LORD, who hast made us partakers of the gifts of these sacred mysteries: we humbly beseech thee; that those things, which thou hast commanded us to do in remembrance of thee, may be profitable to the succour of all our infirmities: Who livest and reignest.

Ember Saturday of Pentecost
Double.
Station at St. Peter

Introit. Rom. 5, 5. Caritas Dei.

THE love of God is shed abroad in our hearts, alleluia: by the Holy Ghost which dwelleth in us, alleluia, alleluia. Ps. 103, 1. Praise the Lord, O my soul: and all that is within me praise his holy name. ℣. Glory.

After Kýrie, eléison is said Let us pray only, without Let us bow the knee, and likewise before the following Prayers.

Collect

WE beseech thee, O Lord, that thy Holy Spirit, by whose wisdom we were created, and by whose providence we are governed, may of thy mercy be poured into our hearts. Through... in the unity of the same Holy Spirit.

The Lesson from the Prophet Joel.
Joel 2, 28-32.

THUS saith the Lord God: I will pour out my Spirit upon all flesh: and your sons and your daughters shall prophesy: your old men shall dream dreams, your young men shall see visions. And also upon the servants and upon the hand-

Ember Saturday of Pentecost

maids in those days will I pour out my Spirit. And I will shew wonders in the heavens and in the earth, blood, and fire, and pillars of smoke. The sun shall be turned into darkness, and the moon into blood: before the great and the terrible day of the Lord come. And it shall come to pass: that whosoever shall call on the name of the Lord shall be delivered.

Alleluia. ℣. John 6, 64. It is the Spirit that quickeneth: the flesh profiteth nothing.

Let us pray. Collect.

WE beseech thee, O Lord, that thy Holy Spirit may inflame our hearts with that same fire, which our Lord Jesus Christ sent upon earth, and willed that it should be kindled exceedingly: Who liveth and reigneth with thee in the unity of the same Holy Spirit.

The Lesson from the book Leviticus.

Lev. 23, 9-11, 15-17 and 21.

IN those days: The Lord spake to Moses, saying: Speak unto the children of Israel, and say unto them: When ye be come into the land which I give unto you, and shall reap the harvest thereof, then ye shall bring a sheaf of the firstfruits of your harvest unto the priest: and he shall wave the sheaf before the Lord, to be accepted for you, on the morrow after the sabbath the priest shall wave it. And ye shall count unto you from the morrow after the sabbath, from the day that ye brought the sheaf of the wave offering, seven sabbaths shall be complete, even unto the morrow after the seventh sabbath shall ye number fifty days: and ye shall offer a new meat offering unto the Lord, ye shall bring out of your habitations two wave loaves of two tenth deals, they shall be of fine flour, they shall be baken with leaven, they are the firstfruits unto the Lord. And ye shall proclaim on the selfsame day, that it may be an holy convocation unto you: ye shall do no servile work therein. It shall be a statute for ever in all your dwellings throughout your generations: saith the Lord almighty.

Alleluia. ℣. Job. 26, 13. By his Spirit he hath garnished the heavens.

Let us pray. Collect.

O GOD, who for the healing of our souls hast commanded us to chasten our bodies with godly fasting: mercifully grant unto us; that both in body and soul we may ever be devoutly given to thy service. Through.

The Lesson from the book Deuteronomy.

Deut. 26, 1-11.

IN those days: Moses said to the children of Israel: Hear, O Israel, that which I command thee this day. When thou art come in unto the land which the Lord thy God giveth thee for an inheritance, and possessest it, and dwellest therein: thou shalt take of the first of all the fruit of the earth, and shalt put it in a basket, and shalt go unto the place which the Lord thy God shall choose to place his name there: and thou shalt go unto the priest that shall be in those days, and say unto him: I profess this day unto the Lord thy God, which hath heard our voice, and looked on our affliction, and our labour, and our oppression: and hath brought us forth out of Egypt with a mighty hand, and with an outstretched arm, and with great terribleness, and with signs, and with wonders: and hath brought us into this place, and hath given us this land, that floweth with milk and honey. And now, behold, I have brought the firstfruits of the land, which thou, O Lord, hast given me. And thou shalt set it before the Lord thy God, and worship before the Lord thy God. And thou shalt rejoice in every good thing which the Lord thy God hath given unto thee.

Alleluia. ℣. Acts 2, 1. When the day of Pentecost was fully come, they were all sitting with one accord.

Let us pray. Collect.

GRANT to us, we beseech thee, O Lord: that we, being taught by fasting in the way of salvation, and likewise abstaining from all vices that may hurt the soul, may more readily obtain the pardon of thy loving-kindness. Through.

The Lesson from the book Leviticus.

Lev. 26, 3-12.

IN those days: The Lord said unto Moses: Speak unto the children of Israel, and say unto them: If ye walk in my statutes, and keep my commandments, and do them, then I will give you rain in due season, and the land shall yield her increase and the trees of the field shall yield their fruit. And your threshing shall reach unto the vintage, and the vintage shall reach unto the sowing time: and ye shall eat your bread to the full, and dwell in your land safely. And I will give peace in the land: and ye shall lie down, and none shall make you afraid. And I will rid evil beasts out of the land, neither shall the sword go through your land. And ye shall chase your enemies, and they shall fall before you by the sword. And five of you shall chase an hundred, and an hundred of you shall put ten thousand to flight: and your enemies shall fall before you by the sword. For I will have respect unto you, and make you fruitful: and multiply you, and establish my covenant with you. And ye shall eat old store, and bring forth the old because of the new. And I will set my tabernacle among you, and my soul shall not abhor you. And I will walk among you, and will be your God, and ye shall be my people: saith the Lord almighty.

Alleluia. (Here genuflect). ℣. Come, Holy Ghost; fill the hearts of thy faithful: and kindle in them the fire of thy love.

Let us pray. Collect.

GRANT, we beseech thee, almighty God: that we may in suchwise abstain from carnal feasting; that we may likewise fast from all sins that beset us. Through.

The Lesson from the Prophet Daniel.

Dan. 3, 47-51.

IN those days: The Angel of the Lord came down into the oven together with Azarias and his fellows: and smote the flame of the fire out of the oven, and made the midst of the furnace as it had been a moist whistling wind. Now the flame streamed forth above the furnace forty and nine cubits: and it passed through and burnt of the Chaldeans it found about the furnace, the king's servants that made it hot. And the fire touched them not at all, neither hurt nor troubled them. Then the three, as out of one mouth, praised, glorified, and blessed God in the furnace, saying:

Here the response Thanks be to God is not made.

Alleluia. ℣. ibid., 52. Blessed art thou, O Lord God of our fathers, and worthy to be praised for ever.

The Verse being ended, Glória in excélsis is said. Then ℣. The Lord be with you. ℞. And with thy spirit.

Let us pray. Collect.

O GOD, who for the deliverance of the three children didst assuage the flames of fire: mercifully grant; that the flames of sin may have no power upon us thy servants. Through.

The Lesson from the Epistle of blessed Paul the Apostle to the Romans.

Rom. 5, 1-5.

BRETHREN: Being justified by faith, we have peace with God through our Lord Jesus Christ: by whom also we have access by faith into this grace wherein we stand, and rejoice in hope of the glory of God. And not only so, but we glory in tribulations also: knowing that tribulation worketh patience, and patience, experience, and experience, hope, and hope maketh not ashamed: because the love of God is shed abroad in our hearts by the Holy Ghost which is given unto us.

Tract. Ps. 117, 1-2. O praise the Lord, all ye heathen: praise him, all ye nations. ℣. For his merciful kindness is ever more and more towards us: and the truth of the Lord endureth for ever.

Sequence. Veni, Sancte Spiritus.

COME, thou Holy Spirit, come, and from thy celestial home send thy light and brilliancy.

Come, thou Father of the poor; come thou source of all our store; come, the soul's true radiancy.

Thou of comforters the best, of the soul the sweetest guest, come in toil refreshingly.

In our labour rest most sweet, grateful shadow from the heat, comfort in adversity.

O thou light most pure and blest, shine within the inmost breast of thy faithful company.

Where thou art not, man hath nought, every holy deed and thought comes from thy divinity.

What is soiléd, make thou pure, what is wounded, work its cure, water what is parched and dry.

What is rigid, gently bend, what is frozen warmly tend, strengthen what goes erringly.

Fill thy faithful, who confide in thy power to guard and guide, with thy sevenfold mystery.

Here thy grace and virtue send, grant salvation in the end, and in heaven felicity. Amen.

At the end Alleluia is not said.

✠ The Continuation of the holy Gospel according to Luke.

Luke 4, 38-44.

AT that time: Jesus arose out of the synagogue, and entered into Simon's house. And Simon's wife's mother was taken with a great fever: and they besought him for her. And he stood over her, and rebuked the fever: and it left her. And immediately she arose and ministered unto them. Now when the sun was setting, all they that had any sick with divers diseases brought them unto him. And he laid his hands on everyone of them, and healed them. And devils also came out of many, crying out, and saying: Thou art Christ the Son of God: and he rebuking them suffered them not to speak, for they knew that he was Christ. And when it was day, he departed and went into a desert place, and the people sought him, and came unto him: and stayed him, that he should not depart from them. And he said unto them: I must preach the kingdom of God to other cities also: for therefore am I sent. And he preached in the synagogues of Galilee. Creed.

Offertory. Ps. 88, 1. O Lord God of my salvation, I have cried day and night before thee: let my prayer enter into thy presence, O Lord, alleluia.

Secret.

GRANT us, O Lord, we beseech thee, by the power of this Sacrament to offer unto thee a pure and clean heart: to the end that this our fasting may be acceptable in thy sight. Through.

Preface, Communicántes and Hanc oblatiónem as on the day of Pentecost.

Communion. John 3, 8. The Spirit bloweth where it listeth: and thou hearest the sound thereof, alleluia, alleluia: but canst not tell whence it cometh and whither it goeth, alleluia, alleluia, alleluia.

Postcommunion.

O LORD, let thy holy mysteries kindle us with heavenly fire: that we may evermore delight in the performance of the same, and likewise in bringing forth the fruits thereof. Through.

¶ After Mass Eastertide ends.

* (For another Mass of the Feast of the Most Holy Trinity, and for Masses of the Sundays after Pentecost, see p. 511.)

TRINITY SUNDAY

Double of 1st class.

Introit. Tob. 12, 6. Benedicta sit.

BLESSED be the holy Trinity, and the undivided Unity: we will praise and glorify him, because he hath showed his mercy upon us. Ps. 8, 1. O Lord our governor: how excellent is thy name in all the world! ℣. Glory.

Collect.

ALMIGHTY and everlasting God, who hast given unto us thy servants grace by the confession of a true faith to acknowledge the glory of the eternal Trinity, and in the power of the Divine Majesty to worship the Unity: we beseech thee; that thou wouldest keep us stedfast in this faith, and evermore defend us from all adversities: Who livest and reignest, one God, world without end. ℟. Amen.

The Lesson from the book of the Revelation of blessed John the Apostle.

Rev. 4, 1-11.

IN those days: I looked, and behold, a door was opened in heaven: and the first voice which I heard was as it were of a trumpet talking with me; which said: Come up hither, and I will shew thee things which must be hereafter. And immediately I was in the Spirit: and behold, a throne was set in heaven, and one sat on the throne: and he that sat was to look upon like a jasper and a sardine stone: and there was a rainbow round about the throne, in sight like unto an emerald. And round about the throne were four and twenty seats; and upon the seats I saw four and twenty elders sitting, clothed in white raiment; and they had on their heads crowns of gold: and out of the throne proceeded lightnings, and thunderings, and voices. And there were seven lamps of fire burning before the throne, which are the seven spirits of God. And before the throne there was a sea of glass like unto crystal: and in the midst of the throne, and round about the throne, were four beasts full of eyes before and behind. And the first beast was like a lion, and the second beast like a calf, and the third beast had a face as a man, and the fourth beast was like a flying eagle. And the four beasts had each of them six wings about him; and they were full of eyes within: and they rest not day and night, saying: Holy, holy, holy, Lord God Almighty, which was, and is, and is to come. And when those beasts give glory, and honour, and thanks to him that sat on the throne, who liveth for ever and ever, the four and twenty elders fall down before him that sat on the throne, and worship him that liveth for ever and ever, and cast their crowns before the throne, saying: Thou art worthy, O Lord, to receive glory, and honour, and power: for thou hast created all things, and for thy pleasure they are and were created.

Gradual. Dan. 3, 55-56. Blessed art thou, O Lord, that beholdest the depths, and sittest upon the Cherubim. ℣. Blessed art thou, O Lord, in the firmament of heaven, and worthy to be praised for ever.

Alleluia, alleluia. ℣. Ibid., 52. Blessed art thou, O Lord God of our fathers, and worthy to be praised for evermore. Alleluia.

✠ The Continuation of the holy Gospel according to John.

John 3, 1-15.

AT that time: There was a man of the Pharisees, named Nicodemus, a ruler of the Jews. The same came to Jesus by night, and said unto him: Rabbi, we know that thou art a teacher come from God; for no man can do these miracles that thou doest, except God be with him. Jesus answered and said unto him: Verily, verily, I say unto thee, Except a man be born again, he cannot see the kingdom of God. Nicodemus saith unto him: How can a man be born when he is old? can he enter the second time into his mother's womb, and be born? Jesus answered: Verily, verily, I say unto thee, Except a man be born of water and of the Spirit, he cannot enter into the Kingdom of God. That which is born of the flesh is flesh: and that which is born of the spirit is spirit. Marvel not that I said unto thee: Ye must be born again. The wind bloweth where it listeth, and thou hearest the sound thereof, but canst not tell whence it cometh, and whither it goeth: so is every one that is born of the Spirit. Nicodemus answered and said unto him: How can these things be? Jesus answered and said unto him: Art thou a master of Israel, and knowest not these things? Verily, verily, I say unto thee, We speak that we do know, and testify that we have seen, and ye receive not our witness. If I have told you earthly things, and ye believe not: how shall ye believe, if I tell you of heavenly things? And no man hath ascended up to heaven, but he that came down from heaven, even the Son of man, who is in heaven. And as Moses lifted up the serpent in the wilderness: even so must the Son of man be lifted up, that whosoever believeth in him should not perish, but have eternal life. Creed.

Offertory. Tob. 12, 6. Blessed be God the Father, and the only-begotten Son of God, and the Holy Spirit: because he hath shewed his mercy upon us.

Secret.

SANCTIFY, we beseech thee, O Lord our God, through the invocation of thy holy name, this oblation of our sacrifice: and make us thereby an oblation unto thee for evermore. Through.

Preface of the Most Holy Trinity.

Communion. Tob. 12, 6. We bless the God of heaven, and will praise him in the sight of all that live: because he hath shewed his mercy upon us.

Postcommunion.

O LORD our God, who hast given unto us to acknowledge the holy and everlasting Trinity, and likewise the undivided Unity: grant that we, who have now received this holy Sacrament, may be thereby preserved from all evil both in body and soul. Through.

FEAST OF THE MOST HOLY BODY OF CHRIST

CORPUS CHRISTI

Double of 1st class.

Introit. Ps. 81, 17. Cibavit.

HE fed them with the finest wheat-flour, alleluia: and with honey out of the stony rock hath he satisfied them, alleluia, alleluia, alleluia. Ps. ibid., 1. Sing we merrily unto God, our strength: make a cheerful noise unto the God of Jacob. ℣. Glory.

Collect

O GOD, who in a wonderful Sacrament hast left us a memorial of thy Passion: grant that we may so reverence the sacred mysteries of thy Body and Blood; that we may ever enjoy within ourselves the fruit of thy redemption: Who livest and reignest with God the Father.

(Another version.)
Collect

O GOD, who under a wonderful Sacrament hast left unto us a memorial of thy Passion: grant us, we beseech thee, so to venerate the sacred mysteries of thy Body and Blood; that we may ever perceive within ourselves the fruit of thy redemption: Who livest and reignest with God the Father.

The Lesson from the Epistle of blessed Paul the Apostle to the Corinthians.
I Cor. 11, 23-29.

BRETHREN: I have received of the Lord that which also I delivered unto you. That the Lord Jesus the same night in which he was betrayed took bread, and when he had given thanks, he brake it, and said: Take, eat: this is my body, which is broken for you: this do in remembrance of me. After the same manner also he took the cup, when he had supped, saying: This cup is the new Testament in my blood. This do ye, as oft as ye drink it, in remembrance of me. For as often as ye eat this bread, and drink this cup, ye do shew the Lord's death till he come. Wherefore whosoever shall eat this bread, or drink this cup of the Lord, unworthily, shall be guilty of the body and blood of the Lord. But let a man examine himself: and so let him eat of that bread, and drink of that cup. For he that eateth and drinketh unworthily, eateth and drinketh judgment to himself, not discerning the Lord's body.

Gradual. Ps. 145, 15-16. The eyes of all wait upon thee, O Lord: and thou givest them their meat in due season. ℣. Thou openest thine hand: and fillest all things living with plenteousness.

Alleluia, alleluia. ℣. John 6, 56-57. My flesh is meat indeed, and my blood is drink indeed: he that eateth my flesh and drinketh my blood, dwelleth in me, and I in him.

Sequence.   Lauda, Sion, Salvatorem.

LAUD, O Sion, thy salvation, laud with hymns of exultation Christ, thy king and shepherd true.

Spend thyself, his honour raising: who surpasseth all thy praising, never canst thou reach his due.

Sing to-day, the mystery shewing of the living, life-bestowing bread from heaven before thee set.

E'en the same of old provided, where the twelve, divinely guided, at the holy table met.

Full and clear ring out thy chanting, joy nor sweetest grace be wanting to thy heart and soul today.

When we gather up the measure of that supper and its treasure, keeping feast in glad array.

Lo, the new King's table gracing, this new Passover of blessing hath fulfilled the elder rite.

Now the new the old effaceth, truth revealed the shadow chaseth, day is breaking on the night.

What he did at supper seated, Christ ordained to be repeated, his memorial ne'er to cease.

And, his word for guidance taking, bread and wine we hallow, making thus our sacrifice of peace.

This the truth to Christians given—bread becomes his flesh from heaven, wine becomes his holy blood.

Doth it pass thy comprehending? yet by faith, thy sight transcending, wondrous things are understood.

Under diverse forms are hidden glorious things to sight forbidden, signs alone, not things, we see.

Wine is poured and bread is broken: but in either sacred token Christ entire we know to be.

Whoso of this food partaketh rendeth not the Lord nor breaketh: Christ is whole to all that taste.

Thousands are, as one, receivers: one, as thousands of believers, takes the food that cannot waste.

Good and evil men are sharing one repast: a doom preparing varied as the heart of man.

Doom of life or death awarded: as their days shall be recorded which from one beginning ran.

When the Sacrament is broken, doubt not in each severed token, hallowed by the word once spoken, resteth all the true content.

Nought the precious gift divideth: breaking but the sign betideth: he himself the same abideth, nothing of his fulness spent.

Lo! the Angels' food is given to the pilgrim who hath striven: see the children's bread from heaven, which to dogs may not be cast.

Truth the ancient types fulfilling, Isaac bound, a victim willing: paschal lamb, its life-blood spilling: manna sent in ages past.

Very bread, good shepherd, tend us: Jesu, of thy love befriend us: thou refresh us, thou defend us: thine eternal goodness send us in the land of life to see.

Thou who all things canst and knowest: who on earth such food bestowest: grant us with thy saints, though lowest, where the heavenly feast thou shewest, fellow-heirs and guests to be. Amen. Alleluia.

✠ The Continuation of the holy Gospel according to John.

John 6, 56-59.

AT that time: Jesus said unto the multitudes of the Jews: My flesh is meat indeed, and my blood is drink indeed. He that eateth my flesh and drinketh my blood, dwelleth in me, and I in him. As the living Father hath sent me, and I live by the Father: so he that eateth me, even he shall live by me. This is that bread which came down from heaven. Not as your fathers did eat manna, and are dead. He that eateth this bread shall live for ever. Creed.

Offertory. Lev. 21, 6. The priests of the Lord do offer the offerings of the Lord made by fire and the bread of their God: and therefore they shall be holy unto their God, and shall not profane the name of their God, alleluia.

Secret.

GRACIOUSLY grant, we beseech thee, O Lord, unto thy Church the gifts of unity and peace: which are shewn forth in a mystery in the gifts we offer. Through.

Common Preface.

Communion. I Cor. 11, 26-27. As often as ye eat this bread, and drink this cup, ye do shew the Lord's death till he come: wherefore whosoever shall eat this bread or drink this cup of the Lord, unworthily, shall be guilty of the body and blood of the Lord, alleluia.

Postcommunion.

WE beseech thee, O Lord: that like as the receiving of thy precious Body and Blood in this life doth foreshadow the everlasting fruition of thy Godhead, so thou wouldest vouchsafe unto us to be fulfilled with the same: Who livest and reignest with God the Father.

The First Sunday after Trinity

Double.

Introit. Ps. 13, 5-6.

Domine, in tua misericordia.

O LORD, my trust is in thy mercy: and my heart is joyful in thy salvation: I will sing of the Lord, because he hath dealt so lovingly with me. Ps. ibid., 1. How long wilt thou forget me, O Lord, for ever? how long wilt thou hide thy face from me? ℣. Glory.

¶ Glória in excélsis is said on all Sundays after Trinity. But it is not said on ferial days, when the Mass of the preceding Sunday is resumed.

Collect.

O GOD, the strength of all them that put their trust in thee, mercifully accept our prayers: and because through the weakness of our mortal nature we can do no good thing without thee, grant us the help of thy grace; that in keeping of thy commandments we may please thee, both in will and deed. Through.

The Lesson from the Epistle of blessed John the Apostle.

I John 4, 8-21.

DEARLY beloved: Let us love one another: for love is of God, and every one that loveth is born of God, and knoweth God. He that loveth not knoweth not God: for God is love. In this was manifested the love of God towards us, because that God sent his only-begotten Son into the world, that we might live through him. Herein is love: not that we loved God, but that he loved us, and sent his Son to be the propitiation for our sins. Beloved, if God so loved us: we ought also to love one another. No man hath seen God at any time. If we love one another, God dwelleth in us, and his love is perfected in us. Hereby know we that we dwell in him, and he in us: because he hath given us of his Spirit. And we have seen, and do testify, that the Father sent the Son to be the Saviour of the world. Whosoever shall confess that Jesus is the Son of God, God dwelleth in him, and he in God. And we have known and believed the love that God hath to us. God is love: and he that dwelleth in love dwelleth in God, and God in him. Herein is our love made perfect, that we may have boldness in the day of judgment: because as he is, so are we in this world. There is no fear in love: but perfect love casteth out fear, because fear hath torment. He that feareth is not made perfect in love. We love him, because he first loved us. If a man say, I love God, and hateth his brother, he is a liar. For he that loveth not his brother, whom he hath seen, how can he love God, whom he hath not seen? And this commandment have we from him: That he who loveth God love his brother also.

Gradual. Ps. 41, 5 and 2. I said, Lord, be merciful unto me: heal my soul, for I have sinned against thee. ℣. Blessed is he that considereth the poor and needy: the Lord shall deliver him in the time of trouble.

Alleluia, alleluia. ℣. Ps. 5, 1. Ponder my words, O Lord: consider my meditation. Alleluia.

¶ Alleluia is thus said with its Verse after the Gradual on all Sundays after Trinity, even if the Mass of Sunday be resumed on ferial days.

✠ The Continuation of the holy Gospel according to Luke.

Luke 16, 19-31.

AT that time: Jesus said unto the Pharisees: There was a certain rich man, which was clothed in purple, and fine linen, and fared sumptuously every day. And there was a certain beggar named Lazarus, which was laid at his gate full of sores, and desiring to be fed with the crumbs, which fell from the rich man's table: moreover, the dogs came and licked his sores. And it came to pass, that the beggar died, and was carried by the angels into Abraham's bosom. The rich man also died, and was buried: and in hell he lift up his eyes, being in torments, and seeth Abraham afar off, and Lazarus in his bosom. And he cried and said: Father Abraham, have mercy on me, and send Lazarus, that he may dip the tip of his finger in water, and cool my tongue: for I am tormented in this flame. But Abraham said: Son, remember that thou in thy life-time receivedst thy good things, and likewise Lazarus evil things: but now he is comforted, and thou art tormented. And besides all this, between us and you there is a great gulf fixed: so that they who would pass from hence to you cannot; neither can they pass to us, that would come from thence. Then he said: I pray thee therefore, father, that thou wouldest send him to my father's house: for I have five brethren; that he may testify unto them, lest they also come into this place of torment. Abraham saith unto him: They have Moses and the Prophets: let them hear them. And he said: Nay, father Abraham, but if one went unto them from the dead, they will repent. And he said unto him: If they hear not Moses and the Prophets, neither will they be persuaded, though one rose from the dead.

Creed, which is said on all Sundays after Trinity, but it is not said on ferial days, when the Mass of the preceding Sunday is resumed.

Offertory. Ps. 5, 3-4. O hearken thou unto the voice of my calling, my King and my God: for unto thee will I make my prayer.

Secret.

WE beseech thee, O Lord, graciously to accept this our sacrifice which we offer unto thee: and grant that it may avail for our perpetual succour. Through.

Preface of the Most Holy Trinity.

Communion. Ps. 9, 2-3. I will speak of all thy marvellous works: I will be glad, and rejoice in thee: yea, my songs will I make of thy name, O most Highest.

Postcommunion.

O LORD, who hast fulfilled us with thy wondrous bounty: grant, we beseech thee, that we, receiving these gifts of our salvation, may never cease to shew forth thy praise. Through.

FRIDAY IN THE WEEK AFTER CORPUS CHRISTI

FEAST OF

THE MOST SACRED HEART
OF JESUS

Double of 1st class.

Introit. Ps. 33, 11 and 19. Cogitationes.

THE thoughts of his Heart shall endure from generation to generation: to deliver their soul from death, and to feed them in the time of dearth. (E.T. Alleluia, alleluia.) Ps. ibid., 1. Rejoice in the Lord, O ye righteous: for it becometh well the just to be thankful. ℣. Glory.

Collect.

O GOD, who in the Heart of thy Son wounded by our sins, dost vouchsafe in thy mercy to bestow on us the abundant riches of thy love: grant, we beseech thee; that the devout homage of our worship, which we render unto him, may be deemed an oblation and satisfaction acceptable in thy sight. Through the same.

The Lesson from the Epistle of blessed Paul the Apostle to the Ephesians.

Ephes. 3, 8-19.

BRETHREN: Unto me who am less than the least of all saints is this grace given, that I should preach among the Gentiles the unsearchable riches of Christ, and to make all men see what is the fellowship of the mystery, which from the beginning of the world hath been hid in God, who created all things by Jesus Christ: to the intent that now unto the principalities and powers in heavenly places might be known by the Church the manifold wisdom of God, according to the eternal purpose which he purposed in Christ Jesus our Lord, in whom we have boldness and access with confidence by the faith of him. For this cause I bow my knees unto the Father of our Lord Jesus Christ, of whom the whole family in heaven and earth is named, that he would grant you according to the riches of his glory, to be strengthened with might by his Spirit in the inner man, that Christ may dwell in your hearts by faith: that ye, being rooted and grounded in love, may be able to comprehend with all saints what is the breadth and length and depth and height: and to know the love of Christ, which passeth knowledge, that ye might be filled with all the fulness of God.

Gradual. Ps. 25, 8-9. Gracious and righteous is the Lord: therefore will he teach sinners in the way. ℣. Them that are meek shall he guide in judgment, and such as are gentle, them shall he learn his way.

Alleluia, alleluia. ℣. Matt. 11, 29. Take my yoke upon you and learn of me, for I am meek and lowly in heart, and ye shall find rest unto your souls. Alleluia.

In votive Masses after Septuagesima, omitting Alleluia and the Verse following, is said:

Tract. Ps. 103, 8-10. The Lord is full of compassion and mercy, long suffering and of great goodness. ℣. He will not always be chiding, neither keepeth he his anger for ever. ℣. He hath not dealt with us after our sins, nor rewarded us according to our wickednesses.

In Eastertide, the Gradual and Tract being omitted, is said:

Alleluia, alleluia. ℣. Matt. 11, 29 and 28. Take my yoke upon you and learn of me, for I am meek and lowly in heart: and ye shall find rest unto your souls. Alleluia. ℣. Come unto me all ye that labour and are heavy laden, and I will refresh you. Alleluia.

✠ The Continuation of the holy Gospel according to John.

John 19, 31-37.

AT that time: The Jews, because it was the Preparation, that the bodies should not remain upon the cross on the sabbath day (for that sabbath day was an high day), besought Pilate that their legs might be broken, and that they might be taken away. Then came the soldiers: and brake the legs of the first and of the other which was crucified with him. But when they came to Jesus and saw that he was dead already, they brake not his legs, but one of the soldiers with a spear pierced his side, and forthwith came there out blood and water. And he that saw it bare record: and his record is true. And he knoweth that he saith true, that ye might believe. For these things were done that the Scripture should be fulfilled: A bone of him shall not be broken. And again another Scripture saith: They shall look on him whom they pierced. Creed.

Offertory. Ps. 69, 21. Thy rebuke hath broken my heart, I am full of heaviness: I looked for some to have pity upon me, but there was no man: neither found I any to comfort me.

But in Eastertide in votive Masses the Offertory is varied as follows:

Offertory. Ps. 40, 7-9. Burnt offerings and sacrifice for sin hast thou not required; then said I: Lo I come. In the volume of the book it is written of me that I should fulfil thy will, O my God: I am content to do it, yea thy law is within my heart, alleluia.

Secret.

REGARD, we beseech thee, O Lord, the ineffable charity of the Heart of thy beloved Son: that the gift which we offer may be acceptable unto thee, and avail for the expiation of our offences. Through the same.

Preface of the Most Sacred Heart of Jesus.

Communion. John 19, 34. One of the soldiers with a spear pierced his side, and forthwith came there out blood and water.

In Eastertide in votive Masses the Communion is varied as follows:

Communion. John 7, 37. If any man thirst, let him come unto me and drink, alleluia, alleluia.

Postcommunion.

O LORD Jesu, who hast given us to taste of the sweetness of thy most gracious Heart: kindle in us by these holy mysteries the fire of thy heavenly love; that we may learn to despise the things of earth, and to set our affection on things above: Who livest and reignest with God the Father.

The Second Sunday after Trinity
Double.

Introit. Ps. 18, 19-20. Factus est.

THE Lord was my upholder, he brought me forth also into a place of liberty: he delivered me, even because he had a favour unto me. Ps. ibid., 1. I will love thee, O Lord my strength: the Lord is my stony rock, my defence, and my Saviour. ℣. Glory.

The Second Sunday after Trinity

Collect.

O LORD, who never failest to help and govern them whom thou dost bring up in thy stedfast fear and love: keep us, we beseech thee, under the protection of thy good providence; and make us to have a perpetual fear and love of thy holy name. Through.

The Lesson from the Epistle of blessed John the Apostle.

I John 3, 13-18.

DEARLY beloved: Marvel not, if the world hate you. We know that we have passed from death unto life, because we love the brethren. He that loveth not his brother abideth in death: whosoever hateth his brother is a murderer. And ye know that no murderer hath eternal life abiding in him. Hereby perceive we the the love of God, because he laid down his life for us: and we ought to lay down our lives for the brethren. But whoso hath this world's good, and seeth his brother have need, and shutteth up his bowels of compassion from him: how dwelleth the love of God in him? My little children, let us not love in word, neither in tongue: but in deed, and in truth. And hereby we know that we are of the truth, and shall assure our hearts before him. For if our heart condemn us, God is greater than our heart, and knoweth all things. Beloved, if our heart condemn us not, then have we confidence towards God. And whatsoever we ask, we receive of him, because we keep his commandments, and do those things that are pleasing in his sight. And this is his commandment: That we should believe on the name of his Son Jesus Christ, and love one another, as he gave us commandment. And he that keepeth his commandments dwelleth in him, and he in him: and hereby we know that he abideth in us, by the Spirit which he hath given us.

Gradual. Ps. 120, 1-2. When I was in trouble I called upon the Lord, and he heard me. ℣. Deliver my soul, O Lord, from lying lips, and from a deceitful tongue.

Alleluia, alleluia. ℣. Ps. 7, 1. O Lord my God, in thee have I put my trust: save me from all them that persecute me, and deliver me. Alleluia.

✠ The Continuation of the holy Gospel according to Luke.

Luke 14, 16-24.

AT that time: Jesus spake this parable unto the Pharisees: A certain man made a great supper, and bade many. And sent his servant at supper-time to say to them that were bidden, Come, for all things are now ready. And they all with one consent began to make excuse. The first said unto him: I have bought a piece of ground, and I must needs go and see it: I pray thee have me excused. And another said: I have bought five yoke of oxen, and I go to prove them: I pray thee have me excused. And another said: I have married a wife: and therefore I cannot come. So that servant came, and shewed his lord these things. Then the master of the house being angry said to his servant: Go out quickly into the streets and lanes of the city: and bring in hither the poor, and the maimed, and the halt, and the blind. And the servant said: Lord, it is done as thou hast commanded, and yet there is room. And the lord said unto the servant: Go out into the highways and hedges: and compel them to come in, that my house may be filled. For I say unto you, That none of those men which were bidden shall taste of my supper. Creed.

Offertory. Ps. 6, 5. Turn thee, O Lord, and deliver my soul: O save me for thy mercy's sake.

Secret.

CLEANSE us, O Lord, by this oblation now to be hallowed to the honour of thy name: and daily renew us thereby to the attainment of heavenly life. Through.

Preface of the Most Holy Trinity.

Communion. Ps. 13, 6. I will sing of the Lord, because he hath dealt so lovingly with me: yea, I will praise the name of the Lord most Highest.

Postcommunion.

O LORD, who hast made us to be partakers of thy bounty: we beseech thee; that we, continually drawing near to this holy mystery, may thereby grow in grace to the attainment of everlasting salvation. Through.

The Third Sunday after Trinity

Double.

Introit. Ps. 25, 15 and 17. Respice in me.

TURN thee unto me, and have mercy upon me, O Lord: for I am desolate and in misery: look upon my adversity and misery: and forgive me all my sin, O my God. Ps. ibid., 1-2. Unto thee, O Lord, will I lift up my soul: my God, I have put my trust in thee, let me not be confounded. ℣. Glory.

Collect.

O LORD, we beseech thee mercifully to hear us: and grant that we, to whom thou hast given an hearty desire to pray; may by thy mighty aid be defended and comforted in all dangers and adversities. Through.

The Lesson from the Epistle of blessed Peter the Apostle.

I Peter 5, 6-11.

DEARLY beloved: All of you be subject one to another, and be clothed with humility: for God resisteth the proud, and giveth grace to the humble. Humble yourselves therefore under the mighty hand of God, that he may exalt you in due time: casting all your care upon him, for he careth for you. Be sober, be vigilant: because your adversary the devil, as a roaring lion, walketh about seeking whom he may devour: whom resist stedfast in the faith: knowing that the same afflictions are accomplished in your brethren that are in the world. But the God of all grace, who hath called us into his eternal glory by Christ Jesus, after that ye have suffered a while, make you perfect, stablish, strengthen, settle you. To him be glory and dominion for ever and ever. Amen.

Gradual. Ps. 55, 23, 17 and 19. O cast thy burden upon the Lord: and he shall nourish thee. ℣. When I called upon the Lord, he heard my voice from the battle that was against me.

Alleluia, alleluia. ℣. Ps. 7, 12. God is a righteous judge, strong and patient, and God is provoked every day. Alleluia.

✠ The Continuation of the holy Gospel according to Luke.

Luke 15, 1-10.

AT that time: There drew near unto Jesus all the publicans and sinners for to hear him. And the Pharisees and Scribes murmured, saying: This man receiveth sinners, and eateth with them. And he spake this parable unto them, saying: What man of you having an hundred sheep: if he lose one of them, doth not leave the ninety and nine in the wilderness, and go after that which is lost, until he find it? And when he hath found it, he layeth it on his shoulders, rejoicing: and when he cometh home, he calleth together his friends and neighbours, saying unto them: Rejoice with me, for I have found my sheep which was lost? I say unto you, that likewise joy shall be in heaven over one sinner that repenteth, more than over ninety and nine just persons, which need no repentance. Either what woman having ten pieces of silver, if she lose one piece, doth not light a candle, and sweep the house, and seek diligently till she find it? And when she hath found it, she calleth her friends and her neighbours together, saying: Rejoice with me, for I have found the piece which I had lost. Likewise, I say unto you: There is joy in the presence of the Angels of God over one sinner that repenteth. Creed.

Offertory. Ps. 9, 10-12. They that know thy name will put their trust in thee: for thou, Lord, hast never failed them that seek thee: O praise the Lord which dwelleth in Sion: for he forgetteth not the complaint of the poor.

Secret.

SANCTIFY, O Lord, we beseech thee, the gifts which we offer unto thee: that they may be made unto us the Body and Blood of thine only-begotten Son: Who liveth.

Preface of the Most Holy Trinity.

Communion. Luke 15, 10. I say unto you: There is joy in the presence of the Angels of God over one sinner that repenteth.

Postcommunion.

WE beseech thee, O Lord, that we who have received these holy mysteries may by their power be cleansed from all our iniquities, and evermore be filled with the bounteous gifts of thy grace. Through.

The Fourth Sunday after Trinity

Double.

Introit. Ps. 27, 1-2.

Dominus illuminatio mea.

THE Lord is my light, and my salvation, whom then shall I fear? the Lord is the strength of my life, of whom then shall I be afraid? When mine enemies came upon me, they stumbled and fell. Ps. ibid., 3. Though an host of men were laid against me: yet shall not my heart be afraid. ℣. Glory.

Collect.

O GOD, the protector of all that trust in thee, without whom nothing is strong, nothing is holy: increase and multiply upon us thy mercy; that, thou being our ruler and guide, we may so pass through things temporal, that we finally lose not the things eternal. Grant this, O heavenly Father, for Jesus Christ's sake our Lord: Who liveth.

The Lesson from the Epistle of blessed Paul the Apostle to the Romans.

Rom. 8, 18-23.

BRETHREN: I reckon that the sufferings of this present time are not worthy to be compared with the glory which shall be revealed in us. For the earnest expectation of the creature waiteth for the manifestation of the sons of God. For the creature was made subject to vanity, not willingly, but by reason of him who hath subjected the same in hope: because the creature itself also shall be delivered from the bondage of corruption, into the glorious liberty of the children of God. For we know that the whole creation groaneth, and travaileth in pain together until now. And not only they, but ourselves also, which have the firstfruits of the Spirit, even we ourselves groan within ourselves, waiting for the adoption, to wit, the redemption of our body: in Christ Jesu our Lord.

Gradual. Ps. 79, 9-10. Be merciful, O Lord, unto our sins: wherefore do the heathen say: Where is now their God? ℣. Help us, O God of our salvation: and for the glory of thy name, O Lord, deliver us.

Alleluia, alleluia ℣. Ps. 9, 5 and 10. O God, who art set in the throne and judgest right: be thou the refuge of the oppressed in time of trouble. Alleluia.

☩ The Continuation of the holy Gospel according to Luke.

Luke 6, 36-42.

AT that time: Jesus said unto his disciples: Be ye therefore merciful, as your Father also is merciful. Judge not, and ye shall not be judged: condemn not, and ye shall not be condemned: forgive, and ye shall be forgiven: give, and it shall be given unto you: good measure, pressed down, and shaken together, and running over, shall men give into your bosom. For with the same measure that ye mete withal, it shall be measured to you again. And he spake a parable unto them, Can the blind lead the blind? shall they not both fall into the ditch? The disciple is not above his master: but every one that is perfect shall be as his master. And why beholdest thou the mote that is in thy brother's eye, but perceivest not the beam that is in thine own eye? Either how canst thou say to thy brother: Brother, let me pull out the mote that is in thine eye, when thou thyself beholdest not the beam that is in thine own eye? Thou hypocrite, cast out first the beam out of thine own eye, and then shalt thou see clearly to pull out the mote that is in thy brother's eye. Creed.

Offertory. Ps. 13, 4-5. Lighten mine eyes, that I sleep not in death: lest mine enemy say: I have prevailed against him.

Secret.

REGARD, O Lord, the prayers and oblations of thy Church: and grant that the partaking thereof may avail for the salvation and continual sanctification of thy faithful people. Through.

Preface of the Most Holy Trinity.

Communion. Ps. 18, 1. The Lord is my stony rock, and my defence, my Saviour, my God, and my might.

Postcommunion.

WE beseech thee, O Lord: that we, being quickened by thy holy mysteries which we have now received; may be cleansed from our offences, and made ready for the obtaining of thy everlasting mercy. Through.

The Fifth Sunday after Trinity

Double.

Introit. Ps. 27, 8 and 11. Exaudi, Domine.

HEARKEN unto my voice, O Lord, when I cry unto thee: thou hast been my succour, leave me not, neither forsake me, O God of my salvation. Ps. ibid., 1. The Lord is my light, and my salvation: whom then shall I fear? ℣. Glory.

Collect.

GRANT, O Lord, we beseech thee: that the course of this world may be so peaceably ordered by thy governance; that thy Church may joyfully serve thee in all godly quietness. Through.

The Lesson from the Epistle of blessed Peter the Apostle.

I Peter 3, 8-15.

DEARLY beloved: Be ye all of one mind, having compassion one of another, love as brethren, be pitiful, be courteous: not rendering evil for evil, or railing for railing, but contrariwise blessing: knowing that ye are thereunto called, that ye should inherit a blessing. For he that will love life, and see good days, let him refrain his tongue from evil, and his lips that they speak no guile. Let him eschew evil, and do good: let him seek peace and ensue it. For the eyes of the

Lord are over the righteous, and his ears are open unto their prayers: but the face of the Lord is against them that do evil. And who is he that will harm you, if ye be followers of that which is good? But and if ye suffer for righteousness' sake, happy are ye. And be not afraid of their terror: neither be troubled. But sanctify the Lord God in your hearts.

Gradual. Ps. 84, 10 and 9. Behold, O God, our defender: and look upon thy servants. ℣. O Lord God of hosts, hear the prayer of thy servants.

Alleluia, alleluia. ℣. Ps. 21, 1. The king shall rejoice in thy strength, O Lord: exceeding glad shall he be of thy salvation. Alleluia.

✠ The Continuation of the holy Gospel according to Luke.

Luke 5, 1-11.

AT that time: It came to pass, that as the people pressed upon Jesus to hear the word of God, he stood by the lake of Gennesaret. And saw two ships standing by the lake: but the fishermen were gone out of them, and were washing their nets. And he entered into one of the ships, which was Simon's, and prayed him that he would thrust out a little from the land. And he sat down, and taught the people out of the ship. Now when he had left speaking, he said unto Simon: Launch out into the deep, and let down your nets for a draught. And Simon answering said unto him: Master, we have toiled all the night, and have taken nothing: nevertheless, at thy word I will let down the net. And when they had this done, they inclosed a great multitude of fishes: and their net brake. And they beckoned unto their partners which were in the other ship, that they should come and help them. And they came, and filled both the ships, so that they began to sink. When Simon Peter saw it, he fell down at Jesus' knees, saying: Depart from me, for I am a sinful man, O Lord. For he was astonished, and all that were with him, at the draught of the fishes which they had taken: and so was also James, and John, the sons of Zebedee, which were partners with Simon. And Jesus said unto Simon: Fear not: from henceforth thou shalt catch men. And when they had brought their ships to land, they forsook all, and followed him. Creed.

Offertory. Ps. 16, 7-8. I will bless the Lord who hath given me counsel: I have set God always before me: for he is on my right hand, therefore I shall not fall.

Secret.

O LORD, we beseech thee mercifully to receive our oblations: and graciously turn our rebel wills to thee. Through.

Preface of the Most Holy Trinity.

Communion. Ps. 27, 4. One thing have I desired of the Lord, which I will require: even that I may dwell in the house of the Lord all the days of my life.

Postcommunion.

WE beseech thee, O Lord, that the mysteries which we have received may cleanse us from all our sins: and by the gifts therein bestowed defend us from all adversities. Through.

The Sixth Sunday after Trinity

Double.

Introit. Ps. 28, 8-9. Dominus fortitudo.

THE Lord is the strength of his people, and he is the wholesome defence of his Anointed: O Lord, save thy people, and give thy blessing unto thine inheritance: feed them, and set them up for ever. Ps. ibid., 1. Unto thee will I cry, O Lord my strength, think no scorn of me: lest, if thou make as though thou hearest not, I become like them that go down into the pit. ℣. Glory.

The Sixth Sunday after Trinity

Collect.

O GOD, who hast prepared for them that love thee such good things as pass man's understanding: pour into our hearts such love toward thee: that we, loving thee above all things, may obtain thy promises, which exceed all that we can desire. Through.

The Lesson from the Epistle of blessed Paul the Apostle to the Romans.

Rom. 6, 3-11.

BRETHREN: So many of us as were baptized into Jesus Christ were baptized into his death. Therefore we are buried with him by baptism into death: that like as Christ was raised up from the dead by the glory of the Father, even so we also should walk in newness of life. For if we have been planted together in the likeness of his death: we shall be also in the likeness of his resurrection. Knowing this, that our old man is crucified with him: that the body of sin might be destroyed, that henceforth we should not serve sin. For he that is dead is freed from sin. Now if we be dead with Christ: we believe that we shall also live with him: knowing that Christ being raised from the dead dieth no more, death hath no more dominion over him. For in that he died, he died unto sin once: but in that he liveth, he liveth unto God. Likewise reckon ye also yourselves to be dead indeed unto sin, but alive unto God through Jesus Christ our Lord.

Gradual. Ps. 90, 13 and 1. Turn thee again, O Lord, at the last, and be gracious unto thy servants. ℣. Lord, thou hast been our refuge, from one generation to another.

Alleluia, alleluia. ℣. Ps. 31, 1-2. In thee, O Lord, have I put my trust, let me never be put to confusion: rid me and deliver me in thy righteousness: bow down thine ear to me, make haste to deliver me. Alleluia.

✠ The Continuation of the holy Gospel according to Matthew.

Matt. 5, 20-24.

AT that time: Jesus said unto his disciples, Except your righteousness shall exceed the righteousness of the Scribes and Pharisees, ye shall in no case enter into the kingdom of heaven. Ye have heard that it was said by them of old time: Thou shalt not kill: and whosoever shall kill, shall be in danger of the judgment. But I say unto you: that whosoever is angry with his brother without a cause shall be in danger of the judgment. And whosoever shall say to his brother, Raca: shall be in danger of the judgment. And whosoever shall say, Thou fool: shall be in danger of hell-fire. Therefore if thou bring thy gift to the altar, and there rememberest that thy brother hath ought against thee: leave there thy gift before the altar, and go thy way, first be reconciled to thy brother: and then come and offer thy gift. Agree with thine adversary quickly, whiles thou art in the way with him: lest at any time the adversary deliver thee to the judge, and the judge deliver thee to the officer, and thou be cast into prison. Verily I say unto thee: Thou shalt by no means come out thence, till thou hast paid the uttermost farthing. Creed.

Offertory. Ps. 17, 5-7. O hold thou up my goings in thy paths, that my footsteps slip not: incline thine ear unto me, and hearken unto my words: shew thy marvellous lovingkindness, thou that art the Saviour of them which put their trust in thee, O Lord.

Secret.

ASSIST us mercifully, O Lord, in these our supplications: and graciously accept the oblations of thy servants and handmaids; that those things which each hath offered to the honour of thy name may be profitable unto all for their salvation. Through.

Preface of the Most Holy Trinity.

Communion. Ps. 27, 6. I will offer in his dwelling an oblation with great gladness: I will sing, and speak praises unto the Lord.

Postcommunion.

O LORD, who hast satisfied us with thy heavenly gift: grant, we beseech thee; that we may be cleansed from our secret faults, and delivered from the snares of our enemies. Through.

The Seventh Sunday after Trinity
Double.

Introit. Ps. 47, 1. Omnes gentes.

O CLAP your hands together, all ye people: O sing unto God with the voice of melody. Ps. ibid., 2. For the Lord is high, and to be feared: he is the great King upon all the earth. ℣. Glory.

Collect.

LORD of all power and might, who art the author and giver of all good things: graft in our hearts the love of thy name, increase in us true religion; nourish us with all goodness, and of thy great mercy keep us in the same. Through.

The Lesson from the Epistle of blessed Paul the Apostle to the Romans.

Rom. 6, 19-23.

BRETHREN: I speak after the manner of men, because of the infirmity of your flesh: for as ye have yielded your members servants to uncleanness, and to iniquity unto iniquity, even so now yield your members servants to righteousness, unto holiness. For when ye were the servants of sin, ye were free from righteousness. What fruit had ye then in those things whereof ye are now ashamed? For the end of those things is death. But now being made free from sin, and become servants to God, ye have your fruit unto holiness, and the end everlasting life. For the wages of sin is death. But the gift of God is eternal life, through Jesus Christ our Lord.

Gradual. Ps. 34, 12 and 6. Come, ye children, and hearken unto me: I will teach you the fear of the Lord. ℣. They had an eye unto him and were enlightened: and their faces were not ashamed.

Alleluia, alleluia. ℣. Ps. 47, 1. O clap your hands together, all ye people: O sing unto God with the voice of melody. Alleluia.

✠ The Continuation of the holy Gospel according to Mark.

Mark 8, 1-9.

AT that time: The multitude being very great, and having nothing to eat, Jesus called his disciples unto him, and saith unto them: I have compassion on the multitude: because they have now been with me three days, and have nothing to eat: and if I send them away fasting to their own houses, they will faint by the way: for divers of them came from far. And his disciples answered him: From whence can a man satisfy these men with bread here in the wilderness? And he asked them: How many loaves have ye? And they said: Seven. And he commanded the people to sit down on the ground. And he took the seven loaves, and gave thanks, and brake, and gave to his disciples to set before them, and they did set them before the people. And they had a few small fishes: and he blessed and commanded to set them also before them. So they did eat, and were filled, and they took up of the broken meat that was left seven baskets. And they that had eaten were about four thousand: and he sent them away. Creed.

Offertory. Dan. 3, 40. Like as in the burnt offerings of rams and bullocks, and like as in ten thousands of fat lambs: so let our sacrifice be in thy sight this day that it may please thee: for they shall not be confounded that put their trust in thee, O Lord.

Secret.

ASSIST us mercifully, O Lord, in these our supplications, and graciously accept the oblations of thy people: and that none may ask amiss or fail in his petition, grant; that those things which we ask faithfully, we may obtain effectually. Through.

Preface of the Most Holy Trinity.

Communion. Ps. 31, 3. Bow down thine ear, make haste to deliver me.

Postcommunion.

O LORD, who hast fulfilled us with these gifts: we beseech thee; that we may both be cleansed by their operation, and defended by their succour. Through.

The Eighth Sunday after Trinity

Double.

Introit. Ps. 48, 8-9. Suscepimus.

WE wait for thy loving kindness, O God, in the midst of thy temple: O God, according to thy name, so is thy praise unto the world's end: thy right hand is full of righteousness. Ps. ibid., 1. Great is the Lord, and highly to be praised: in the city of our God, even upon his holy hill. ℣. Glory.

Collect.

O GOD, whose never-failing providence ordereth all things both in heaven and earth: we humbly beseech thee; to put away from us all hurtful things, and to give us those things which be profitable for us. Through.

The Lesson from the Epistle of blessed Paul the Apostle to the Romans.

Rom. 8, 12-17.

BRETHREN: We are debtors, not to the flesh, to live after the flesh. For if ye live after the flesh, ye shall die: but if ye through the Spirit do mortify the deeds of the body, ye shall live. For as many as are led by the Spirit of God, they are the sons of God. For ye have not received the spirit of bondage again to fear, but ye have received the spirit of adoption, whereby we cry: Abba, Father. The Spirit itself beareth witness with our spirit, that we are the children of God. And if children, then heirs: heirs of God, and joint-heirs with Christ: if so be that we suffer with him, that we may be also glorified together.

Gradual. Ps. 31, 3. Be thou my strong rock and house of defence, that thou mayest save me. ℣. Ps. 71, 1. In thee, O God, have I put my trust: let me never be put to confusion, O Lord.

Alleluia, alleluia. ℣. Ps. 48, 1. Great is the Lord, and highly to be praised, in the city of our God, even upon his holy hill. Alleluia.

✠ The Continuation of the holy Gospel according to Matthew.

Matt. 7, 15-21.

AT that time: Jesus said unto his disciples: Beware of false prophets, which come to you in sheep's clothing, but inwardly they are ravening wolves: ye shall know them by their fruits. Do men gather grapes of thorns, or figs of thistles? Even so every good tree bringeth forth good fruit: but a corrupt tree bringeth forth evil fruit. A good tree cannot bring forth evil fruit: neither can a corrupt tree bring forth good fruit. Every tree that bringeth not forth good fruit is hewn down, and cast into the fire. Wherefore by their fruits ye shall know them. Not every one that saith unto me, Lord, Lord, shall enter into the kingdom of heaven: but he that doeth the will of my Father which is in heaven. Creed.

Offertory. Ps. 18, 28 and 32. Thou shalt save the people that are in adversity, O Lord, and shalt bring down the high looks of the proud: for who is God, but thou, O Lord?

Secret.

O GOD, who by the one perfect sacrifice didst ratify the manifold offerings of the law: accept this sacrifice from thy bounden servants, and sanctify it with that benediction wherewith thou didst bless the gifts of Abel: that what each hath offered to the honour of thy majesty may be profitable unto all for their salvation. Through.

Preface of the Most Holy Trinity.

Communion. Ps. 34, 8. O taste, and see, how gracious the Lord is: blessed is the man that trusteth in him.

Postcommunion.

GRANT, O Lord, that the power of thy healing may by thy mercy cleanse us from our perversities, and lead us to those things that be right. Through.

The Ninth Sunday after Trinity
Double.

Introit. Ps. 54, 4-5. Ecce Deus.

BEHOLD, God is my helper: the Lord is with them that uphold my soul: he shall reward evil unto mine enemies: destroy thou them in thy truth, O Lord, my defender. Ps. ibid., 1. Save me, O God, for thy name's sake: and avenge me in thy strength. ℣. Glory.

Collect.

GRANT to us, Lord, we beseech thee, the spirit to think and do always such things as be rightful: that we who cannot do any thing that is good without thee, may by thee be enabled to live according to thy will. Through.

The Lesson from the Epistle of blessed Paul the Apostle to the Corinthians.
I Cor. 10, 6-13.

BRETHREN: I would not that ye should be ignorant, how that all our fathers were under the cloud, and all passed through the sea; and were all baptized unto Moses in the cloud, and in the sea; and did all eat the same spiritual meat, and did all drink the same spiritual drink: for they drank of that spiritual rock that followed them; and that rock was Christ. But with many of them God was not well pleased: for they were overthrown in the wilderness. Now these things were our examples to the intent we should not lust after evil things, as they also lusted. Neither be ye idolaters, as were some of them: as it is written: The people sat down to eat and drink and rose up to play. Neither let us commit fornication, as some of them committed, and fell in one day three and twenty thousand. Neither let us tempt Christ, as some of them also tempted, and were destroyed of serpents. Neither murmur ye, as some of them also murmured, and were destroyed of the destroyer. Now all these things happened unto them for ensamples: and they are written for our admonition, upon whom the ends of the world are come. Wherefore let him that thinketh he standeth take heed lest he fall. There hath no temptation taken you, but such as is common to man: but God is faithful, who will not suffer you to be tempted above that ye are able: but will with the temptation also make a way of escape, that ye may be able to bear it.

Gradual. Ps. 8, 1. O Lord our governor: how excellent is thy name in all the world! ℣. Thou that hast set thy glory above the heavens.

Alleluia, alleluia. ℣. Ps. 59, 1. Deliver me from mine enemies, O God: defend me from them that rise up against me. Alleluia.

☩ The Continuation of the holy Gospel according to Luke.

Luke 16, 1-9.

AT that time: Jesus spake this parable unto his disciples: There was a certain rich man which had a steward: and the same was accused unto him that he had wasted his goods. And he called him, and said unto him: How is it that I hear this of thee? Give an account of thy stewardship: for thou mayest be no longer steward. Then the steward said within himself: What shall I do, for my lord taketh away from me the stewardship? I cannot dig, to beg I am ashamed. I am resolved what to do, that, when I am put out of the stewardship, they may receive me into their houses. So he called every one of his lord's debtors unto him, and said unto the first: How much owest thou unto my lord? And he said: An hundred measures of oil. And he said unto him: Take thy bill: and sit down quickly, and write fifty. Then said he to another: And how much owest thou? And he said: An hundred measures of wheat. And he said unto him: Take thy bill, and write four score. And the lord commended the unjust steward, because he had done wisely: for the children of this world are in their generation wiser than the children of light. And I say unto you: Make to yourselves friends of the mammon of unrighteousness: that when ye fail, they may receive you into everlasting habitations. Creed.

Offertory. Ps. 19, 8-11. The statutes of the Lord are right, and rejoice the heart, his judgments are sweeter also than honey, and the honey-comb: moreover by them is thy servant taught.

Secret.

ACCEPT, O Lord, we beseech thee, the gifts which of thine own bounty we do offer unto thee: that, by the mighty working of thy grace, these most holy mysteries may sanctify our conversation in this life present, and bring us to everlasting felicity. Through.

Preface of the Most Holy Trinity.

Communion. John 6, 57. He that eateth my flesh and drinketh my blood, dwelleth in me, and I in him, saith the Lord.

Postcommunion.

LET these heavenly mysteries, O Lord, renew us both in body and soul: that we, who therein offer unto thee our outward worship, may inwardly feel the effectual benefit of the same. Through.

The Tenth Sunday after Trinity

Double.

Introit. Ps. 55, 18-19, 20 and 23.

Cum clamarem.

WHEN I called upon the Lord, he heard my voice from the battle that was against me: and he hath brought them down, even he that is of old, and endureth for ever: O cast thy burden upon the Lord, and he shall nourish thee. Ps. ibid., 1. Hear my prayer, O Lord, and hide not thy self from my petition: take heed unto me, and hear me. ℣. Glory.

Collect.

LET thy merciful ears, O Lord, be open to the prayers of thy humble servants: and that they may obtain their petitions; make them to ask such things as shall please thee. Through.

The Tenth Sunday after Trinity

The Lesson from the Epistle of blessed Paul the Apostle to the Corinthians.

I Cor. 12, 1-11.

BRETHREN: Concerning spiritual gifts, I would not have you ignorant. Ye know that ye were Gentiles, carried away unto these dumb idols, even as ye were led. Wherefore I give you to understand, that no man speaking by the Spirit of God calleth Jesus accursed. And that no man can say that Jesus is the Lord, but by the Holy Ghost. Now there are diversities of gifts, but the same Spirit. And there are differences of administrations, but the same Lord. And there are diversities of operations, but it is the same God, who worketh all in all. But the manifestation of the Spirit is given to every man to profit withal. For to one is given by the Spirit the word of wisdom: to another the word of knowledge by the same Spirit: to another faith by the same Spirit: to another the gifts of healing by the same Spirit: to another the working of miracles, to another prophecy, to another discerning of spirits, to another divers kinds of tongues, to another the interpretation of tongues. But all these worketh that one and the self-same Spirit, dividing to every man severally as he will.

Gradual. Ps. 17, 8 and 2. Keep me, O Lord, as the apple of an eye: hide me under the shadow of thy wings. ℣. Let my sentence come forth from thy presence: and let thine eyes look upon the thing that is equal.

Alleluia, alleluia. ℣. Ps. 65, 1. Thou, O God, art praised in Sion: and unto thee shall the vow be performed in Jerusalem. Alleluia.

✠ The Continuation of the holy Gospel according to Luke.

Luke 19, 41-47.

AT that time: When Jesus was come near Jerusalem, he beheld the city, and wept over it, saying: If thou hadst known, even thou, at least in this thy day, the things which belong unto thy peace, but now they are hid from thine eyes. For the days shall come upon thee: that thine enemies shall cast a trench about thee; and compass thee round: and keep thee in on every side: and shall lay thee even with the ground, and thy children within thee, and they shall not leave in thee one stone upon another: because thou knewest not the time of thy visitation. And he went into the temple, and began to cast out them that sold therein, and them that bought, saying unto them: It is written: My house is the house of prayer. But ye have made it a den of thieves. And he taught daily in the temple. Creed.

Offertory. Ps. 25, 1-2. Unto thee, O Lord, will I lift up my soul: my God, I have put my trust in thee, O let me not be confounded: neither let mine enemies triumph over me: for all they that hope in thee shall not be ashamed.

Secret.

GRANT to us, we beseech thee, O Lord, to draw near in worthiness to these thy mysteries: for as oft as the commemoration of this victim is celebrated, the work of our redemption is performed. Through.

Preface of the Most Holy Trinity.

Communion. Ps. 51, 19. Thou shalt be pleased with the sacrifice of righteousness, with the burnt-offerings and oblations, upon thine altar, O Lord.

Postcommunion.

WE beseech thee, O Lord, that this Sacrament, whereof we have been partakers, may cleanse us from all our sins, and may bestow upon us unity and concord. Through.

The Eleventh Sunday after Trinity
Double.

Introit. Ps. 68, 5-6 and 35. Deus in loco sancto.

GOD in his holy habitation: he is the God that maketh men to be of one mind in an house: he will give strength and power unto his people. Ps. ibid., 1. Let God arise, and let his enemies be scattered: let them also that hate him flee before him. ℣. Glory.

Collect.

O GOD, who declarest thy almighty power most chiefly in shewing mercy and pity: mercifully grant unto us such a measure of thy grace; that we, running the way of thy commandments, may obtain thy gracious promises, and be made partakers of thy heavenly treasure. Through.

The Lesson from the Epistle of blessed Paul the Apostle to the Corinthians.

I Cor. 15, 1-10.

BRETHREN: I declare unto you the Gospel which I preached unto you, which also ye have received, and wherein ye stand, by which also ye are saved: if ye keep in memory what I preached unto you, unless ye have believed in vain. For I delivered unto you first of all, that which I also received: how that Christ died for our sins, according to the Scriptures: and that he was buried, and that he rose again the third day, according to the Scriptures: and that he was seen of Cephas, then of the twelve. After that, he was seen of about five hundred brethren at once, of whom the greater part remain unto this present, but some are fallen asleep. After that, he was seen of James, then of all the Apostles: and last of all, he was seen of me also, as of one born out of due time. For I am the least of the Apostles, that am not meet to be called an Apostle, because I persecuted the Church of God. But by the grace of God I am what I am, and his grace which was bestowed upon me was not in vain. But I laboured more abundantly than they all: yet not I, but the grace of God which was with me. Therefore whether it were I or they, so we preach, and so ye believed.

Gradual. Ps. 28, 8 and 1. My heart hath trusted in God, and I am helped: therefore my heart danceth for joy and in my song will I praise him. ℣. Unto thee will I cry, O Lord: be not silent, O my God, nor depart from me.

Alleluia, alleluia. ℣. Ps. 81, 1-2. Sing we merrily unto God our strength, make a cheerful noise unto the God of Jacob: take the merry harp, with the lute. Alleluia.

✠ The Continuation of the holy Gospel according to Luke.

Luke 19, 9-14.

AT that time: Jesus spake this parable unto certain which trusted in themselves that they were righteous, and despised others: Two men went up into the temple to pray: the one a Pharisee, and the other a Publican. The Pharisee stood and prayed thus with himself: God, I thank thee, that I am not as other men are: extortioners, unjust, adulterers: or even as this Publican. I fast twice in the week: I give tithes of all that I possess. And the Publican, standing afar off, would not lift up so much as his eyes unto heaven: but smote upon his breast, saying: God be merciful to me a sinner. I tell you: this man went down to his house justified rather than the other: for every one that exalteth himself shall be abased: and he that humbleth himself shall be exalted. Creed.

Offertory. Ps. 30, 1-2. I will magnify thee O Lord, for thou hast set me up, and not made my foes to triumph over me: O Lord, I cried unto thee, and thou hast healed me.

Secret.

O LORD, who hast granted unto us to present this sacrifice to the honour of thy name, to the end that it may avail for the healing of our souls; grant that the same may be acceptable in thy sight. Through.

Preface of the Most Holy Trinity.

Communion. Prov. 3, 9-10. Honour the Lord with thy substance, and with the first-fruits of all thine increase: so shall thy barns be filled with plenty, and thy presses shall burst out with new wine.

Postcommunion.

WE beseech thee, O Lord our God: that as thou ceasest not to renew us with thy heavenly sacraments; so thou wouldest ever bestow on us thy gracious and ready help. Through.

The Twelfth Sunday after Trinity

Double.

Introit. Ps. 70, 1-2. Deus in adjutorium.

HASTE thee, O God, to deliver me: make haste to help me, O Lord: let mine enemies be ashamed and confounded, that seek after my soul. Ps. ibid., 4. Let them be turned backward and put to confusion: that wish me evil. ℣. Glory.

Collect.

ALMIGHTY and everlasting God, who art always more ready to hear than we to pray, and art wont to give more than either we desire or deserve: pour down upon us the abundance of thy mercy; forgiving us those things whereof our conscience is afraid, and giving us those good things which we are not worthy to ask, but through the merits and mediation of Jesus Christ, thy Son our Lord: Who liveth.

The Lesson from the Epistle of blessed Paul the Apostle to the Corinthians.

II Cor. 3, 4-9.

BRETHREN: Such trust have we through Christ to Godward: not that we are sufficient of ourselves to think any thing as of ourselves: but our sufficiency is of God: who also hath made us able ministers of the New Testament: not of the letter, but of the Spirit: for the letter killeth, but the Spirit giveth life. But if the ministration of death written and engraven in stones was glorious; so that the children of Israel could not stedfastly behold the face of Moses for the glory of his countenance, which glory was to be done away: how shall not the ministration of the Spirit be rather glorious? For if the ministration of condemnation be glory: much more doth the ministration of righteousness exceed in glory.

Gradual. Ps. 34, 1-2. I will alway give thanks unto the Lord: his praise shall ever be in my mouth. ℣. My soul shall make her boast in the Lord: the humble shall hear thereof, and be glad.

Alleluia, alleluia. Ps. 88, 1. O Lord God of my salvation, I have cried day and night before thee. Alleluia.

☩ The Continuation of the holy Gospel according to Mark.

Mark 7, 31-37.

AT that time: Jesus, departing from the coasts of Tyre and Sidon, came unto the sea of Galilee, through the midst of the coast of Decapolis. And they bring unto him one that was deaf, and had an impediment in his speech, and they beseech him to put his hand upon him. And he took him aside from the multitude, and put his fingers into his ears, and he spit, and touched his tongue: and looking up to heaven, he sighed, and said unto him: Ephphatha, that is, Be opened. And straightway his ears were opened, and the string of his tongue was loosed, and he spake plain. And he charged them that they should tell no man. But the more he charged them, so much the more a great deal they published it: and were beyond measure astonished, saying: He hath done all things well: he maketh both the deaf to hear, and the dumb to speak. Creed.

Offertory. Exod. 32, 11, 13-14. Moses besought the Lord his God, and said: Why, O Lord, doth thy wrath wax hot against thy people? Turn from thy fierce wrath: remember Abraham, Isaac, and Jacob, to whom thou swarest to give a land flowing with milk and honey. And the Lord repented of the evil which he thought to do unto his people.

Secret.

LOOK favourably, O Lord, we beseech thee, on this our bounden duty and service: that this sacrifice which we offer may be an oblation acceptable to thee, and effectually avail for the succour of our frailty. Through.

Preface of the Most Holy Trinity.

Communion. Ps. 104, 13-15. The earth, O Lord, is filled with the fruit of thy works: that thou mayest bring food out of the earth, and wine that maketh glad the heart of man, and oil to make him a cheerful countenance, and bread to strengthen man's heart.

Postcommunion.

WE beseech thee, O Lord, that we, who have received this holy Sacrament, may in such wise feel the effectual succour of the same: that, being preserved both in body and soul, we may glory in the fulness of thy heavenly healing. Through.

The Thirteenth Sunday after Trinity

Double.

Introit. Ps. 74, 21, 20 and 23. Respice, Domine.

LOOK, O Lord, upon thy covenant, and forsake not the congregation of the poor for ever: arise, O God, maintain thine own cause, and forget not the voices of them that seek thee. Ps. ibid., 1. O God, wherefore art thou absent from us so long: why is thy wrath so hot against the sheep of thy pasture? ℣. Glory.

Collect.

ALMIGHTY and merciful God, of whose only gift it cometh that thy faithful people do unto thee true and laudable service: grant, we beseech thee; that we may so faithfully serve thee in this life, that we fail not finally to attain thy heavenly promises. Through.

The Lesson from the Epistle of blessed Paul the Apostle to the Galatians.

Gal. 3, 16-22.

BRETHREN: To Abraham and his seed were the promises made. He saith not: And to seeds, as of many; but as of one: And to thy seed, which is Christ. And this I say: That the covenant that was confirmed before of God in Christ, the Law, which was four hundred and thirty years after, cannot disannul, that it should make the promise of none effect. For if the inheritance be of the Law, it is no more of promise. But God gave it to Abraham by promise. Wherefore then serveth the Law? It was added because of transgressions, till the seed should come, to whom the promise was made, and it was ordained by Angels in the hand of a mediator. Now a mediator is not a mediator of one: but God is one. Is the Law then against the promises of God? God forbid. For if there had been a law given which could have given life, verily righteousness should have been by the Law. But the Scripture hath concluded all under sin, that the promise by faith of Jesus Christ might be given to them that believe.

Gradual. Ps. 74, 20, 19 and 22. Look upon thy covenant, O Lord, and forget not the congregation of the poor for ever. ℣. Arise, O God, maintain thine own cause: remember the rebuke that thy servants have.

Alleluia, alleluia. ℣. Ps. 90, 1. Lord, thou hast been our refuge: from one generation to another. Alleluia.

✠ The Continuation of the holy Gospel according to Luke.

Luke 19, 23-37.

AT that time: Jesus said unto his disciples: Blessed are the eyes which see the things that ye see. For I tell you, That many prophets and kings have desired to see those things which ye see, and have not seen them: and to hear those things which ye hear, and have not heard them. And behold, a certain lawyer stood up, and tempted him, saying: Master, what shall I do to inherit eternal life? He said unto him: What is written in the Law? how readest thou? And he answering said: Thou shalt love the Lord thy God with all thy heart, and with all thy soul, and with all thy strength, and with all thy mind: and thy neighbour as thyself. And he said unto him: Thou hast answered right: this do, and thou shalt live. But he, willing to justify himself, said unto Jesus: And who is my neighbour? And Jesus answering said: A certain man went down from Jerusalem to Jericho, and fell among thieves, which stripped him of his raiment: and wounded him, and departed leaving him half dead. And by chance there came down a certain Priest that way: and, when he saw him, he passed by on the other side. And likewise a Levite, when he was at the place, came and looked on him, and passed by on the other side. But a certain Samaritan, as he journeyed, came where he was: and, when he saw him, he had compassion on him. And went to him, and bound up his wounds, pouring in oil and wine, and set him on his own beast, and brought him to an inn, and took care of him. And on the morrow, when he departed, he took out two pence, and gave them to the host, and said unto him: Take care of him: and whatsoever thou spendest more, when I come again, I will repay thee. Which now of these three, thinkest thou, was neighbour unto him that fell among thieves? And he said: He that shewed mercy on him. Then said Jesus unto him: Go, and do thou likewise. Creed.

Offertory. Ps. 31, 16-17. My hope hath been in thee, O Lord; I have said: Thou art my God, my time is in thy hand.

Secret.

WE beseech thee, O Lord, mercifully look upon these sacrifices which we present on thy holy altars: that they may bestow on us thy pardon to the honour and glory of thy name. Through.

Preface of the Most Holy Trinity.

Communion. Wisd. 16, 20. Thou hast given us bread from heaven, O Lord, having every delight, and every taste of sweetness.

Postcommunion.

QUICKEN us, O Lord, we pray thee, who have duly received these holy mysteries: that we may be cleansed thereby from all our sins, and defended against all adversities. Through.

The Fourteenth Sunday after Trinity

Double.

Introit. Ps. 84, 9-10. Protector noster.

BEHOLD, O God, our defender, and look upon the face of thine Anointed: for one day in thy courts is better than a thousand. Ps. ibid., 1-2. O how amiable are thy dwellings, thou Lord of hosts! my soul hath a desire and longing to enter into the courts of the Lord. ℣. Glory.

Collect.

ALMIGHTY and everlasting God, give unto us the increase of faith, hope, and charity: and, that we may obtain that which thou dost promise, make us to love that which thou dost command. Through.

The Lesson from the Epistle of blessed Paul the Apostle to the Galatians.

Gal. 5, 16-24.

BRETHREN: Walk in the Spirit, and ye shall not fulfil the lust of the flesh. For the flesh lusteth against the spirit and the spirit against the flesh: and these are contrary the one to the other, so that ye cannot do the things that ye would. But if ye be led by the spirit, ye are not under the law. Now the works of the flesh are manifest, which are these: adultery, fornication, uncleanness, lasciviousness, idolatry, witchcraft, hatred, variance, emulations, wrath, strife, seditions, heresies, envyings, murders, drunkenness, revellings, and such like: of the which I tell you before, as I have also told you in time past: that they who do such things shall not inherit the kingdom of God. But the fruit of the Spirit is: love, joy, peace, long-suffering, gentleness, goodness, faith, meekness, temperance. Against such there is no law. And they that are Christ's have crucified the flesh, with the affections and lusts.

Gradual. Ps. 118, 8-9. It is better to trust in the Lord, than to put any confidence in man. ℣. It is better to trust in the Lord, than to put any confidence in princes.

Alleluia, alleluia. ℣. Ps. 95, 1. O come let us sing unto the Lord: let us heartily rejoice in the strength of our salvation. Alleluia.

✠ The Continuation of the holy Gospel according to Luke.

Luke 17, 11-19.

AT that time: As Jesus went to Jerusalem, he passed through the midst of Samaria, and Galilee. And as he entered into a certain village, there met him ten men that were lepers, which stood afar off; and they lifted up their voices, and said: Jesus, Master, have mercy on us. And when he saw them, he said unto them: Go, shew yourselves unto the priests. And it came to pass, that, as they went, they were cleansed. And one of them, when he saw that he was healed, turned back, and with a loud voice glorified God, and fell down on his face at his feet, giving him thanks: and he was a Samaritan. And Jesus answering said: Were there not ten cleansed? but where are the nine? There are not found that returned to give glory to God, save this stranger. And he said unto him: Arise, go thy way: thy faith hath made thee whole. Creed.

Offertory. Ps. 34, 8-9. The Angel of the Lord tarrieth round about them that fear him, and delivereth them: O taste, and see, how gracious the Lord is.

Secret.

LOOK mercifully, O Lord, upon thy people, look mercifully upon our oblations: that we, being rendered thereby acceptable in thy sight, may obtain of thee remission of all our sins, and the effectual fulfilment of our desires. Through.

Preface of the Most Holy Trinity.

Communion. Matt. 6, 33. Seek ye first the kingdom of God, and all things shall be added unto you, saith the Lord.

Postcommunion.

WE beseech thee, O Lord: that we, who have here received thy heavenly sacraments, may thereby grow in grace toward the attainment of eternal redemption. Through.

The Fifteenth Sunday after Trinity

Double.

Introit. Ps. 86, 1-3. Inclina, Domine.

BOW down thine ear, O Lord, and hear me: my God, save thy servant that putteth his trust in thee: be merciful unto me, O Lord, for I will call daily upon thee. Ps. ibid., 4. Comfort the soul of thy servant: for unto thee, O Lord, do I lift up my soul. ℣. Glory.

Collect.

KEEP, we beseech thee, O Lord, thy Church with thy perpetual mercy: and, because the frailty of man without thee cannot but fall; keep us ever by thy help from all things hurtful, and lead us to all things profitable to our salvation. Through.

The Lesson from the Epistle of blessed Paul the Apostle to the Galatians.

Gal. 6, 11-18.

BRETHREN: Ye see how large a letter I have written unto you with mine own hand. As many as desire to make a fair shew in the flesh, they constrain you to be circumcised: only lest they should suffer persecution for the cross of Christ. For neither they themselves who are circumcised keep the law: but desire to have you circumcised, that they may glory in your flesh. But God forbid that I should glory, save in the cross of our Lord Jesus Christ, by whom the world is crucified unto me, and I unto the world. For in Christ Jesus neither circumcision availeth any thing, nor uncircumcision, but a new creature. And as many as walk according to this rule, peace be on them, and mercy, and upon the Israel of God. From henceforth let no man trouble me: for I bear in my body the marks of the Lord Jesus. Brethren, the grace of our Lord Jesus Christ be with your spirit. Amen.

Gradual. Ps. 92, 1-2. It is a good thing to give thanks unto the Lord: and to sing praises unto thy name, O most Highest. ℣. To tell of thy loving-kindness early in the morning, and of thy truth in the night-season.

Alleluia, alleluia. ℣. Ps. 95, 3. For the Lord is a great God, and a great King above all the earth. Alleluia.

✠ The Continuation of the holy Gospel according to Matthew.

Matt. 6, 24-33.

AT that time: Jesus said unto his disciples: No man can serve two masters: for either he will hate the one, and love the other: or else he will hold to the one, and despise the other. Ye cannot serve God and mammon. Therefore I say unto you, Take no thought for your life, what ye shall eat, or what ye shall drink, nor yet for your body, what ye shall put on. Is not the life more than meat: and the body than raiment? Behold the fowls of the air, for they sow not, neither do they reap, nor gather into barns: yet your heavenly Father feedeth them. Are ye not much better than they? Which of you by taking thought can add one cubit unto his stature? And why take ye thought for raiment? Consider the lilies of the field how they grow: they toil not, neither do they spin. And yet I say unto you, That even Solomon in all his glory was not arrayed like one of these. Wherefore, if God so clothe the grass of the field, which to-day is, and to-morrow is cast into the oven: shall he not much more clothe you, O ye of little faith? Therefore take no thought, saying: What shall we eat, or what shall we drink, or wherewithal shall we be clothed? For after all these things do the Gentiles seek. For your heavenly Father knoweth that ye have need of all these things. But seek ye first the kingdom of God, and his righteousness: and all these things shall be added unto you. Take therefore no thought for the morrow: for the morrow shall take thought for the things of itself: sufficient unto the day is the evil thereof. Creed.

Offertory. Ps. 40, 1-3. I waited patiently for the Lord, and he inclined unto me: and heard my calling: and he hath put a new song in my mouth, even a thanksgiving unto our God.

Secret.

GRANT to us, Lord, we beseech thee, that this saving victim may avail, both for the cleansing of our offences, and for the obtaining of the favour of thy almighty power. Through.

Preface of the Most Holy Trinity.

Communion. John 6, 52. The bread that I will give is my flesh, which I will give for the life of the world.

Postcommunion.

LET thy holy Sacrament, O God, evermore cleanse and defend us: that we may be brought thereby to the attainment of everlasting salvation. Through.

The Sixteenth Sunday after Trinity
Double.

Introit. Ps. 86, 3 and 5. Miserere mihi.

BE merciful unto me, O Lord: for I will call daily upon thee: for thou, Lord, art good and gracious, and of great mercy unto all them that call upon thee. Ps. ibid., 1. Bow down thine ear, O Lord, and hear me: for I am poor and in misery. ℣. Glory.

Collect.

O LORD, we beseech thee, let thy continual pity cleanse and defend thy Church: and, because it cannot continue in safety without thy succour; preserve it evermore by thy help and goodness. Through.

The Lesson from the Epistle of blessed Paul the Apostle to the Ephesians.

Eph. 3, 13-21.

BRETHREN: I desire that ye faint not at my tribulations for you: which is your glory. For this cause I bow my knees unto the Father of our Lord Jesus Christ, of whom the whole family in heaven and earth is named, that he would grant you, according to the riches of his glory, to be strengthened with might by his Spirit in the inner man, that Christ may dwell in your hearts by faith: that ye, being rooted and grounded in love, may be able to comprehend with all saints, what is the breadth, and length, and depth, and height: and to know the love of Christ, which passeth knowledge, that ye might be filled with all the fulness of God. Now unto him that is able to do exceeding abundantly above all that we ask or think, according to the power that worketh in us: unto him be glory in the Church by Christ Jesus, throughout all ages, world without end. Amen.

Gradual. Ps. 102, 15-16. The heathen shall fear thy name, O Lord, and all the kings of the earth thy majesty. ℣. When the Lord shall build up Sion, and when his glory shall appear.

Alleluia, alleluia. ℣. Ps. 98, 1. O sing unto the Lord a new song: for the Lord hath done marvellous things. Alleluia.

✠ The Continuation of the holy Gospel according to Luke.

Luke 7, 11-16.

AT that time: Jesus went into a city called Nain: and many of his disciples went with him, and much people. Now when he came nigh to the gate of the city, behold, there was a dead man carried out, the only son of his mother: and she was a widow: and much people of the city was with her. And when the Lord saw her, he had compassion on her, and said unto her: Weep not. And he came and touched the bier. And they that bare him stood still. And he said: Young man, I say unto thee, Arise. And he that was dead sat up, and began to speak. And he delivered him to his mother. And there came a fear on all: and they glorified God, saying: That a great Prophet is risen up among us: and that God hath visited his people. And this rumour of him went forth throughout all Judæa, and throughout all the region round about. Creed.

Offertory. Ps. 40, 16-17. Look down, O Lord, to help me: let them be ashamed and confounded that seek after my soul to destroy it: look down, O Lord, to help me.

Secret.

GRANT, O Lord, that by the protection of these thy sacraments we may ever be defended against the assaults of the devil. Through.

Preface of the Most Holy Trinity.

Communion. Ps. 71, 15-17. O Lord, I will make mention of thy righteousness only: thou, O God, hast taught me from my youth up until now: forsake me not, O God, in mine old age, when I am gray-headed.

Postcommunion.

O LORD, we beseech thee, let the operation of thy heavenly bounty in such wise possess our souls and bodies: that not our own desires, but the effectual working of thy grace may ever prevail within us. Through.

Ember Wednesday in September

Station at St. Mary Major

Introit. Ps. 81, 1-3 and 5. Exsultate Deo.

SING we merrily unto God our strength: make a cheerful noise unto the God of Jacob: take the merry harp with the lute: blow up the trumpet in the new-moon, for this was made a statute for Israel, and a law of the God of Jacob. Ps. ibid., 6. This he ordained in Joseph for a testimony, when he came out of the land of Egypt: and had heard a strange language. ℣. Glory.

After Kýrie eléison is said Let us pray. Let us bow the knee. ℟. Arise.

Collect.

WE beseech thee, O Lord, to succour our infirmity with the healing of thy loving kindness: that we, who by the frailty of our nature are ready to fall, may by thy merciful goodness be renewed. Through.

The Lesson from the Prophet Amos.

Amos 9, 13-15.

THUS saith the Lord God: Behold, the days come: that the plowman shall overtake the reaper, and the treader of grapes him that soweth seed: and the mountains shall drop sweet wine, and all the hills shall melt. And I will bring again the captivity of my people of Israel: and they shall build the waste cities, and inhabit them: and they shall plant vineyards, and drink the wine thereof: they shall also make gardens, and eat the fruit of them. And I will plant them upon their land: and they shall no more be pulled up out of their land which I have given them: saith the Lord thy God.

Gradual. Ps. 113, 5-7. Who is like unto the Lord our God, that hath his dwelling so high, and yet humbleth himself to behold the things that are in heaven and earth? ℣. He taketh up the simple out of the dust, and lifteth the poor out of the mire.

Here is said: ℣. The Lord be with you, without Let us bow the knee.

Let us pray. Collect.

GRANT, we beseech thee, O Lord, unto thy humble servants: that, as they do abstain from bodily food, so they may also fast from sin within their souls. Through.

The Lesson from the book of Esdras.

Nehem, or II Esdr. 8, 1-10.

IN those days: All the people gathered themselves together as one man into the street that was before the water gate: and they spake unto Ezra the scribe to bring the book of the law of Moses, which the Lord had commanded to Israel. And Ezra the priest brought the law before the congregation both of men and women, and all that could hear with understanding, upon the first day of the seventh month. And he read therein before the street that was before the water gate from the morning until midday, before the men and the women, and those that could understand: and the ears of all the people were attentive unto the book of the law. And Ezra the scribe stood upon a pulpit of wood, which they had made for the purpose. And Ezra opened the book in the sight of all the people: for he was above all the people: and when he opened it, all the people stood up. And Ezra blessed the Lord, the great God: and all the people answered: Amen, Amen: with lifting up their hands: and they bowed their heads, and worshipped the Lord with their faces to the ground. And the Levites caused the people to understand the law: and the people stood in their place. So they read in the book in the law of God distinctly, and gave the sense: and caused them to understand the reading. And Nehemiah, and Ezra the priest the scribe, and the Levites that taught the people, said unto all the people: This day is holy unto the Lord your God, mourn not, nor weep. Then he said unto them: Go your way, eat the fat, and drink the sweet, and send portions unto them for whom nothing is prepared: for this day is holy unto our Lord, neither be ye sorry: for the joy of the Lord is your strength.

Gradual. Ps. 33, 12 and 6. Blessed are the people, whose God is the Lord, and blessed are the folk, that he hath chosen to him to be his inheritance. ℣. By the word of the Lord were the heavens made: and all the host of them by the breath of his mouth.

✠ The Continuation of the holy Gospel according to Mark.

Mark 9, 17-28.

AT that time: One of the multitude answered and said unto Jesus: Master, I have brought unto thee my son, which hath a dumb spirit: and wheresoever he taketh him, he teareth him, and he foameth, and gnasheth with his teeth, and pineth away: and I spake to thy disciples that they should cast him out, and they could not. He answereth him, and saith: O faithless generation, how long shall I be with you? how long shall I suffer you? Bring him unto me. And they brought him unto him. And when he saw him, straightway the spirit tare him: and he fell on the ground, and wallowed foaming. And he asked his father: How long is it ago since this came unto him? And he said: Of a child. And ofttimes it hath cast him into the fire, and into the waters, to destroy him. But if thou canst do any thing, have compassion on us, and help us. Jesus said unto him: If thou canst believe, all things are possible to him that believeth. And straightway the father of the child cried out, and said with tears: Lord, I believe: help thou mine unbelief. When Jesus saw that the people came together, he rebuked the foul spirit, saying unto him: Thou dumb and deaf spirit, I charge thee, come out of him: and enter no more into him. And the spirit cried, and rent him sore, and came out of him, and he was as one dead, insomuch that many said: He is dead. But Jesus took him by the hand, and lifted him up, and he arose. And when he was come into the house, his disciples asked him privately: Why could not we cast him out? And he said unto them: This kind can come forth by nothing, but by prayer and fasting.

Offertory. Ps. 119, 47-48. My delight shall be in thy commandments, which I have loved exceedingly: my hands also will I lift up unto thy commandments, which I have loved.

Secret.

WE beseech thee, O Lord, that this oblation may cleanse us from our sins: and sanctify thy servants both in body and soul for the celebration of this sacrifice. Through.

Communion. Nehem. 8, 10. Eat the fat, and drink the sweet, and send portions unto them for whom nothing is prepared: for this day is holy unto our Lord, neither be ye sorry: for the joy of the Lord is your strength.

Postcommunion.

O LORD, who hast made us partakers of thy heavenly gifts, we humbly beseech thee: that like as of thy bounty we devoutly offer the same unto thee, so by thy goodness we may worthily receive them in our souls. Through.

Ember Friday in September

Station at the Twelve Holy Apostles

Introit. Ps. 105, 3-4. Laetetur cor.

LET the heart of them rejoice that seek the Lord: seek the Lord and his strength: seek his face evermore. Ps. ibid., 1. O give thanks unto the Lord, and call upon his name: tell the people what things he hath done. ℣. Glory.

Collect.

GRANT, we beseech thee, almighty God: that we, who year by year devoutly keep this holy ordinance, may serve thee acceptably both in body and soul. Through.

The Lesson from the Prophet Hosea.

Hosea 14, 2-10.

THUS saith the Lord God: O Israel, return unto the Lord thy God: for thou hast fallen by thine iniquity. Take with you words, and turn to the Lord, say unto him: Take away all iniquity, and receive us graciously: so will we render the calves of our lips. Asshur shall not save us, we will not ride upon horses, neither will we say any more to the work of our hands: Ye are our Gods: for in thee the fatherless findeth mercy. I will heal their backsliding, I will love them freely: for mine anger is turned away from him. I will be as the dew unto Israel, he shall grow as the lily, and cast forth his roots as Lebanon. His branches shall spread, and his beauty shall be as the olive tree: and his smell as Lebanon. They that dwell under his shadow shall return: they shall revive as the corn, and grow as the vine: the scent thereof shall be as the wine of Lebanon. Ephraim shall say: What have I to do any more with idols? I have heard him, and observed him, I am like a green fir tree: from me is thy fruit found. Who is wise, and he shall understand these things? prudent, and he shall know them? for the ways of the Lord are right, and the just shall walk in them: but the transgressors shall fall therein.

Gradual. Ps. 90, 13 and 1. Turn thee again, O Lord, at the last, and be gracious unto thy servants. ℣. Lord thou hast been our refuge, from one generation to another.

☩ The Continuation of the holy Gospel according to Luke.

Luke 7, 36-50.

AT that time: One of the Pharisees desired Jesus that he would eat with him. And he went into the Pharisee's house, and sat down to meat. And, behold, a woman in the city, which was a sinner, when she knew that Jesus sat at meat in the Pharisee's house, brought an alabaster box of ointment: and stood at his feet behind him weeping, and began to wash his feet with tears, and did wipe them with the hairs of her head, and kissed his feet, and anointed them with the ointment. Now when the Pharisee which had bidden him saw it, he spake within himself, saying: This man, if he were a Prophet, would have known who and what manner of woman this is that toucheth him: for she is a sinner. And Jesus answering said unto him: Simon, I have somewhat to say unto thee. And he saith: Master, say on. There was a certain creditor which had two debtors: the one owed five hundred pence, and the other fifty. And when they had nothing to pay, he frankly forgave them both. Tell me, therefore, which of them will love him most? Simon answered and said: I suppose that he, to whom he forgave most. And he said unto him: Thou hast rightly judged. And he turned to the woman, and said unto Simon: Seest thou this woman? I entered into thine house, thou gavest me no water for my feet: but she hath washed my feet with tears, and wiped them with the hairs of her head. Thou gavest me no kiss: but this woman since the time I came in hath not ceased to kiss my feet. My head with oil thou didst not anoint: but this woman hath anointed my feet with ointment. Wherefore I say unto thee: Her sins, which are many, are forgiven, for she loved much. But to whom little is forgiven, the same loveth little. And he said unto her: Thy sins are forgiven. And they that sat at meat with him began to say within themselves: Who is this that forgiveth sins also? And he said to the woman: Thy faith hath saved thee: go in peace.

Offertory. Ps. 103, 2 and 5. Praise the Lord, O my soul, and forget not all his benefits: who maketh thee young and lusty as an eagle.

Secret.

O LORD, we beseech thee, let this our fast be acceptable in thy sight: that we, being cleansed thereby and made worthy of thy grace, may be brought unto thine everlasting promises. Through.

Communion. Ps. 119, 22 and 24. O turn from me shame and rebuke, for I have kept thy commandments, O Lord: for thy testimonies are my delight.

Postcommunion.

WE beseech thee, almighty God: that we, shewing forth our thankfulness for the gifts which we have received, may obtain yet more abundant mercies. Through.

Ember Saturday in September

Station at St. Peter

Introit. Ps. 95. 6-7. Venite.

O COME, let us worship and fall down, and kneel before the Lord our maker: for he is the Lord our God. Ps. ibid., 1. O come, let us sing unto the Lord: let us heartily rejoice in the strength of our salvation. ℣. Glory.

After Kýrie, eléison is said: Let us pray. Let us bow the knee. ℟. Arise.

Collect.

ALMIGHTY and everlasting God, who through godly continence bestowest healing both of body and soul: we humbly beseech thy majesty; that thou wouldest mercifully look upon the devout prayers and fasting of thy people, granting us in this world the succour of thy grace, and in the world to come life everlasting. Through.

The Lesson from the book Leviticus.

Lev. 23, 26-32.

IN those days: The Lord spake unto Moses, saying: On the tenth day of this seventh month there shall be a day of atonement, it shall be an holy convocation unto you: and ye shall afflict your souls, and offer an offering made by fire unto the Lord. And ye shall do no work in that same day: for it is a day of atonement, to make an atonement for you before the Lord your God. For whatsoever soul it be that shall not be afflicted in that same day, he shall be cut off from among his people: and whatsoever soul it be that doeth any work in that same day, the same soul will I destroy from among his people. Ye shall do no manner of work: it shall be a statute for ever throughout your generations in all your dwellings. It shall be unto you a sabbath of rest, and ye shall afflict your souls in the ninth day of the month: at even, from even unto even, shall ye celebrate your sabbath: saith the Lord almighty.

Gradual. Ps. 79, 9-10. Be merciful unto our sins, O Lord: wherefore do the heathen say: Where is now their God? ℣. Help us, O God of our salvation: and for the glory of thy name, O Lord, deliver us.

Let us pray.   Let us bow the knee.
℟. Arise.

Collect.

GRANT to us, we beseech thee, almighty God: that we may through fasting be fulfilled with thy grace; and through abstinence strengthened to overcome all our enemies. Through.

The Lesson from the book Leviticus.

Lev. 22, 39-43.

IN those days: The Lord spake unto Moses, saying: In the fifteenth day of the seventh month, when ye have gathered in the fruit of the land, ye shall keep a feast unto the Lord seven days: on the first day shall be a sabbath, and on the eighth day shall be a sabbath. And ye shall take you on the first day the boughs of goodly trees, branches of palm trees, and the boughs of thick trees, and willows of the brook, and ye shall rejoice before the Lord your God seven days. And ye shall keep it a feast unto the Lord seven days in the year: it shall be a statute for ever in your generations. Ye shall celebrate it in the seventh month, ye shall dwell in booths seven days. All that are Israelites born shall dwell in booths: that your generations may know that I made the children of Israel to dwell in booths, when I brought them out of the land of Egypt. I am the Lord your God.

Gradual. Ps. 84, 10 and 19. Behold, O God our defender: and look upon thy servants. ℣. O Lord God of hosts, hear the prayers of thy servants.

Let us pray. Let us bow the knee.
℞. Arise.

Collect.

WE beseech thee, O Lord, graciously to behold this thy family: that as by thine inspiration we do seek thy healing unto everlasting salvation, so by thy bounteous goodness we may effectually obtain the same. Through.

The Lesson from the Prophet Micah.

Micah. 7, 14, 16 and 18-20.

O LORD our God, feed thy people with thy rod, the flock of thine heritage, which dwell solitarily in the wood, as in the days of old. The nations shall see and be confounded at all their might. Who is a God like unto thee, that pardoneth iniquity, and passeth by the transgression of the remnant of his heritage? He retaineth not his anger for ever, because he delighteth in mercy. He will turn again, he will have compassion upon us: he will subdue our iniquities, and thou wilt cast all their sins into the depths of the sea. Thou wilt perform the truth to Jacob, and the mercy to Abraham: which thou hast sworn unto our fathers from the days of old: O Lord our God.

Gradual. Ps. 90, 13 and 1. Turn thee again, O Lord, at the last, and be gracious unto thy servants. ℣. Lord, thou hast been our refuge, from one generation to another.

Let us pray. Let us bow the knee.
℞. Arise.

Collect.

GRANT, we beseech thee, almighty God: that we may in such wise abstain from carnal feasting; that we may likewise fast from all vices that beset us. Through.

The Lesson from the Prophet Zechariah.

Zec. 8, 14-19.

IN those days: The word of the Lord came unto me, saying: Thus saith the Lord of hosts: As I thought to punish you, when your fathers provoked me to wrath, saith the Lord of hosts, and I repented not, so again have I thought in these days to do well unto Jerusalem and to the house of Judah: fear ye not. These are the things that ye shall do: Speak ye every man the truth to his neighbour: execute the judgment of truth and peace in your gates. And let none of you imagine evil in your hearts against his neighbour: and love no false oath: for all these are things that I hate, saith the Lord. And the word of the Lord of hosts came unto me, saying: Thus saith the Lord of hosts: The fast of the fourth month, and the fast of the fifth, and the fast of the seventh, and the fast of the tenth, shall be to the house of Judah joy and gladness, and cheerful feasts: therefore love the truth and peace: saith the Lord of hosts.

Gradual. Ps. 141, 2. Let my prayer be set forth in thy sight, O Lord, as the incense. ℣. Let the lifting up of my hands be an evening sacrifice.

Let us pray. Let us bow the knee.
℞. Arise.

Collect.

O LORD, who sufferest us to offer unto thee the observance of our solemn fast: we beseech thee, that thou wouldest likewise bestow upon us the succour of thy pardon. Through.

The Lesson from the Prophet Daniel.

Song of the Three Children 24-28.

IN those days: The Angel of the Lord came down into the oven together with Azarias and his fellows: and smote the flame of the fire out of the oven, and made the midst of the furnace as it had been a moist whistling wind. Now the flame streamed forth above the furnace forty and nine cubits: and it passed through and burned of the Chaldeans it found about the furnace, the king's servants that made it hot. And the fire touched them not at all, neither hurt nor troubled them. Then the three, as out of one mouth, praised, glorified, and blessed God in the furnace, saying:

Here the response Thanks be to God is not made.

Hymn. Song, ibid., 29-39.

BLESSED art thou, O Lord God of our fathers. And to be praised and glorified for ever.

And blessed is the name of thy glory, which is holy. And to be praised and glorified for ever.

Blessed art thou in the holy temple of thy glory. And to be praised and glorified for ever.

Blessed art thou on the holy throne of thy kingdom. And to be praised and glorified for ever.

Blessed art thou in the sceptre of thy Godhead. And to be praised and glorified for ever.

Blessed art thou that sittest upon the Cherubim, and beholdest the depths. And to be praised and glorified for ever.

Blessed art thou that walkest on the wings of the winds and on the waves of the sea. And to be praised and glorified for ever.

Let all thine Angels and Saints bless thee. And let them praise thee and glorify thee for ever.

Let the heavens, the earth, the sea, and all that in them is bless thee. And let them praise thee and glorify thee for ever.

Glory be to the Father, and to the Son, and to the Holy Ghost. And to be praised and glorified for ever.

As it was in the beginning, is now, and ever shall be: world without end. Amen. And to be praised and glorified for ever.

Blessed art thou, O Lord God of our fathers. And to be praised and glorified for ever.

Here is said ℣. The Lord be with you, without Let us bow the knee.

Let us pray.   Collect.

O GOD, who for the deliverance of the three children didst assuage the flames of fire: mercifully grant; that the flames of sin may have no power upon us thy servants. Through.

The Lesson from the Epistle of blessed Paul the Apostle to the Hebrews.

Heb. 9, 2-12.

BRETHREN: There was a tabernacle made, the first, wherein was the candlestick, and the table, and the shewbread, which is called the Sanctuary. And after the second veil, the tabernacle which is called the Holiest of all: which had the golden censer, and the ark of the covenant overlaid round about with gold, wherein was the golden pot that had manna, and Aaron's rod that budded, and the tables of the covenant, and over it the Cherubims of glory shadowing the mercy-seat: of which we cannot now speak particularly. Now when these things were thus ordained; the priests went always into the first tabernacle, accomplishing the service of God: but into the second went the high priest alone once every year, not without blood, which he offered for himself, and for the errors of the people: the Holy Ghost this signifying, that the way into the holiest of all was not yet made manifest, while as the first tabernacle was yet standing. Which was a figure for the time then present: in which were offered both gifts and sacrifices, that could not make him that did the service perfect, as pertaining to the conscience, which stood only in meats and drinks, and divers washings, and carnal ordinances, imposed on them until the time of reformation. But Christ being come an high priest of good things to come, by a greater and more perfect tabernacle, not made with hands, that is to say, not of this building; neither by the blood of goats and calves, but by his own blood he entered in once into the Holy place, having obtained eternal redemption.

Tract. Ps. 117, 1-2. O praise the Lord, all ye heathen: praise him, all ye nations. ℣. For his merciful kindness is ever more and more towards us: and the truth of the Lord endureth for ever.

✠ The Continuation of the holy Gospel according to Luke.

Luke 13, 6-17.

AT that time: Jesus spake this parable unto the multitudes: A certain man had a fig tree planted in his vineyard, and he came and sought fruit thereon, and found none. Then said he unto the dresser of his vineyard: Behold, these three years I come seeking fruit on this fig tree, and find none: cut it down: why cumbereth it the ground? And he answering said unto him: Lord, let it alone this year also, till I shall dig about it, and dung it: and if it bear fruit, well: and if not, then after that thou shalt cut it down. And he was teaching in one of the synagogues on the sabbath. And, behold, there was a woman which had a spirit of infirmity eighteen years: and was bowed together, and could in no wise lift up herself. And when Jesus saw her, he called her to him, and said unto her: Woman, thou art loosed from thine infirmity. And he laid his hands on her, and immediately she was made straight, and glorified God. And the ruler of the synagogue answered with indignation, because that Jesus had healed on the sabbath-day, and said unto the people: There are six days in which men ought to work: in them therefore come and be healed, and not on the sabbath-day. The Lord then answered him, and said: Thou hypocrite, doth not each one of you on the sabbath loose his ox or his ass from the stall, and lead him away to watering? And ought not this woman, being a daughter of Abraham, whom Satan hath bound, lo, these eighteen years, be loosed from this bond on the sabbath-day? And when he had said these things, all his adversaries were ashamed: and all the people rejoiced for all the glorious things that were done by him.

Offertory. Ps. 88, 1-2. O Lord God of my salvation, I have cried day and night before thee: let my prayer enter into thy presence, O Lord.

Secret.

GRANT, we beseech thee, almighty God: that these gifts which we offer in the sight of thy majesty may both win for us grace to do thee faithful service, and bring us in the end to everlasting felicity. Through.

Communion. Lev. 23, 41 and 43. In the seventh month ye shall celebrate a feast, when I made the children of Israel to dwell in booths, when I brought them out of the land of Egypt: I am the Lord your God.

Postcommunion.

WE beseech thee, O Lord, that thy holy mysteries may in such wise accomplish in us their perfect work: that we, who now offer them in outward fashion, may inwardly receive them in verity and truth. Through.

The Seventeenth Sunday after Trinity
Double.

Introit. Ps. 119, 137 and 124.

Justus es, Domine.

RIGHTEOUS art thou, O Lord, and true is thy judgment: O deal with thy servant according unto thy loving mercy. Ps. ibid., 1. Blessed are those that are undefiled in the way: and walk in the law of the Lord. ℣. Glory.

Collect.

LORD, we pray thee that thy grace may always prevent and follow us: and make us continually to be given to all good works. Through.

The Lesson from the Epistle of blessed Paul the Apostle to the Ephesians.

Ephes. 4, 1-6.

BRETHREN: I, the prisoner of the Lord, beseech you, that ye walk worthy of the vocation wherewith ye are called, with all lowliness and meekness, with long-suffering, forbearing one another in love, endeavouring to keep the unity of the spirit in the bond of peace. There is one body, and one Spirit, even as ye are called in one hope of your calling. One Lord, one faith, one baptism. One God and Father of all, who is above all, and through all, and in you all:†
[Who is blessed for ever and ever. Amen.]

Gradual. Ps. 33, 12 and 6. Blessed are the people whose God is the Lord: and blessed are the folk, that he hath chosen to him to be his inheritance. ℣. By the word of the Lord were the heavens made: and all the hosts of them by the breath of his mouth.

Alleluia, alleluia. ℣. Ps. 102, 1. Hear my prayer, O Lord, and let my cry come unto thee. Alleluia.

✠ The Continuation of the holy Gospel according to Luke.

Luke 14, 1-11.

AT that time: As Jesus went into the house of one of the chief Pharisees to eat bread on the sabbath-day, they watched him. And behold, there was a certain man before him which had the dropsy. And Jesus answering spake unto the lawyers and Pharisees, saying: Is it lawful to heal on the sabbath-day? And they held their peace. And he took him, and healed him, and let him go. And answered them, saying: Which of you shall have an ass, or an ox, fallen into a pit, and will not straightway pull him out on the sabbath-day? And they could not answer him again to these things. And he put forth a parable to those which were bidden, when he marked how they chose out the chief rooms, saying unto them: When thou art bidden of any man to a wedding, sit not down in the highest room, lest a more honourable man than thou be bidden of him, and he that bade thee and him come and say to thee: Give this man place: and thou begin with shame to take the lowest room. But when thou art bidden, go and sit down in the lowest room: that, when he that bade thee cometh, he may say unto thee: Friend, go up higher. Then shalt thou have worship in the presence of them that sit at meat with thee: for whosoever exalteth himself shall be abased: and he that humbleth himself shall be exalted. Creed.

Offertory. Dan. 9, 17-19. I, Daniel, prayed unto my God, and said: Hear, O Lord, the prayers of thy servant: cause thy face to shine upon thy sanctuary: and behold, O God, this thy people, who are called by thy name.

Secret.

CLEANSE us, O Lord, we pray thee, by the effectual working of this our sacrifice: and so accomplish in us the work of thy mercy; that we may be found worthy to be made partakers of the same. Through.

Preface of the Most Holy Trinity.

Communion. Ps. 76, 11-12. Promise unto the Lord your God, and keep it, all ye that are round about him, bring presents unto him that ought to be feared: he shall refrain the spirit of princes: and is wonderful among the kings of the earth.

Postcommunion.

WE beseech thee, O Lord, mercifully to cleanse and renew our souls with thy heavenly mysteries: that we may thereby both now and ever be defended from all bodily temptations. Through.

The Eighteenth Sunday after Trinity
Double.

Introit. Eccli. 36, 18. Da pacem.

GIVE peace, O Lord, to them that wait for thee, and let thy prophets be found faithful: hear the prayers of thy servant, and of thy people Israel. Ps. 122, 1. I was glad when they said unto me: We will go into the house of the Lord. ℣. Glory.

Collect.

LORD, we beseech thee, grant thy people grace to withstand the temptations of the world, the flesh and the devil: and with pure hearts and minds to follow thee the only God. Through.

The Lesson from the Epistle of blessed Paul the Apostle to the Corinthians.
I Cor. 1, 4-8.

BRETHREN: I thank my God always on your behalf, for the grace of God which is given you by Jesus Christ: that in every thing ye are enriched by him, in all utterance, and in all knowledge: even as the testimony of Christ was confirmed in you: so that ye come behind in no gift, waiting for the coming of our Lord Jesus Christ, who shall also confirm you unto the end, that ye may be blameless in the day of our Lord Jesus Christ.

Gradual. Ps. 122, 1 and 7. I was glad when they said unto me: We will go into the house of the Lord. ℣. Peace be within thy walls: and plenteousness within thy palaces.

Alleluia, alleluia. ℣. Ps. 102, 16. The heathen shall fear thy name, O Lord, and all the kings of the earth thy majesty. Alleluia.

✠ The Continuation of the holy Gospel according to Matthew.
Matt. 22, 34-46.

AT that time: When the Pharisees had heard that Jesus had put the Sadducees to silence, they were gathered together. Then one of them, who was a lawyer, asked him a question, tempting him, and saying: Master, which is the great commandment in the Law? Jesus said unto him: Thou shalt love the Lord thy God with all thy heart, and with all thy soul, and with all thy mind. This is the first and great commandment. And the second is like unto it: Thou shalt love thy neighbour as thyself. On these two commandments hang all the law and the prophets. While the Pharisees were gathered together, Jesus asked them, saying: What think ye of Christ? whose son is he? They say unto him: The son of David. He saith unto them: How then doth David in spirit call him Lord, saying: The Lord said unto my Lord, sit thou on my right hand, till I make thine enemies thy footstool? If David then call him Lord, how is he his son? And no man was able to answer him a word: neither durst any man from that day forth ask him any more questions. Creed.

Offertory. Exod. 24, 4-5. Moses consecrated an altar unto the Lord, offering burnt offerings upon it, and sacrificing peace offerings: and he made an evening sacrifice for a sweet-smelling savour unto the Lord God, in the sight of the children of Israel.

Secret.

WE humbly beseech thy majesty, O Lord: that these holy mysteries which we here perform may cleanse us from our former sins, and defend us against all temptations. Through.

Preface of the Most Holy Trinity.

Communion. Ps. 96, 8-9. Bring offerings and come into his courts: O worship the Lord in the beauty of holiness.

Postcommunion.

ALMIGHTY God, let thy sanctifying power cleanse us from all our sins, and avail for the healing of our souls unto life eternal. Through.

The Nineteenth Sunday after Trinity

Double.

Introit. Salus populi.

I AM the saving health of the people, saith the Lord: out of whatsoever tribulation they shall cry to me, I will hear them: and I will be their Lord for ever. Ps. 78, 1. Hear my law, O my people: incline your ears unto the words of my mouth. ℣. Glory.

Collect.

O GOD, forasmuch as without thee we are not able to please thee: mercifully grant; that thy Holy Spirit may in all things direct and rule our hearts. Through... in the unity of the same Holy Spirit.

The Lesson from the Epistle of blessed Paul the Apostle to the Ephesians.

Ephes. 4, 17-28.

BRETHREN: This I say therefore, and testify in the Lord: that ye henceforth walk not as other Gentiles walk, in the vanity of their mind: having the understanding darkened, being alienated from the life of God through the ignorance that is in them, because of the blindness of their heart: who, being past feeling, have given themselves over unto lasciviousness, to work all uncleanness with greediness. But ye have not so learned Christ: if so be that ye have heard him, and have been taught by him, as the truth is in Jesus: that ye put off, concerning the former conversation, the old man, which is corrupt according to the deceitful lusts: and* be renewed in the spirit of your mind, and that ye put on the new man, which after God is created in righteousness and true holiness. Wherefore, putting away lying, speak every man truth with his neighbour: for we are members one of another. Be ye angry and sin not: let not the sun go down upon your wrath. Neither give place to the devil: let him that stole steal no more; but rather let him labour, working with his hands the thing which is good, that he may have to give to him that needeth. Let no corrupt communication proceed out of your mouth, but that which is good to the use of edifying, that it may minister grace unto the hearers. And grieve not the Holy Spirit of God, whereby ye are sealed unto the day of redemption. Let all bitterness, and wrath, and anger, and clamour, and evil-speaking, be put away from you, with all malice. And be ye kind one to another, tender-hearted, forgiving one another, even as God for Christ's sake hath forgiven you.

Gradual. Ps. 41, 1. Let my prayer be set forth in thy sight, O Lord, as the incense. ℣. Let the lifting up of my hands be an evening sacrifice.

Alleluia, alleluia. ℣. Ps. 105, 1. O give thanks unto the Lord, and call upon his name: tell the people what things he hath done. Alleluia.

☩ The Continuation of the holy Gospel according to Matthew.

Matt. 9, 1-8.

AT that time: Jesus entered into a ship, and passed over, and came into his own city. And behold, they brought to him a man sick of the palsy, lying on a bed. And Jesus, seeing their faith, said unto the sick of the palsy: Son, be of good cheer, thy sins be forgiven thee. And behold, certain of the scribes said within themselves: This man blasphemeth. And Jesus, knowing their thoughts, said: Wherefore think ye evil in your hearts? For whether is easier to say: Thy sins be forgiven thee; or to say: Arise, and walk? But that ye may know that the Son of man hath power on earth to forgive sins, then saith he to the sick of the palsy: Arise, take up thy bed, and go unto thine house. And he arose, and departed to his house. But when the multitude saw it, they marvelled, and glorified God, who had given such power unto men. Creed.

Offertory. Ps. 138, 7. Though I walk in the midst of trouble, yet shalt thou refresh me, O Lord: thou shalt stretch forth thy hand upon the furiousness of mine enemies, and thy right hand shall save me.

Secret.

O GOD, who through communion in this wondrous sacrifice dost make us partakers of thy glorious Godhead: grant, we beseech thee; that as we have the knowledge of thy truth, so in all our conversation we may walk worthy of the same. Through.

Preface of the Most Holy Trinity.

Communion. Ps. 119, 4-5. Thou hast charged that we shall diligently keep thy commandments: O that my ways were made so direct, that I might keep thy statutes.

Postcommunion.

WE render thanks unto thee, O Lord, for that thou hast quickened us with thy heavenly gifts: humbly beseeching thy mercy; that thou wouldest make us worthy partakers of the same. Through.

The Twentieth Sunday after Trinity

Double.

Introit. Dan. 3, 31, 29 and 35.

Omnia quae fecisti.

ALL things that thou hast done to us, O Lord, thou hast done in true judgment, for we have sinned and have not obeyed thy commandments: but give glory to thy name, and deal with us according to the multitude of thy mercies. Ps. 119, 1. Blessed are those that are undefiled in the way: and walk in the law of the Lord. ℣. Glory.

Collect.

O ALMIGHTY and most merciful God, of thy bountiful goodness keep us, we beseech thee, from all things that may hurt us: that we, being ready both in body and soul; may cheerfully accomplish those things that thou wouldest have done. Through.

The Lesson from the Epistle of blessed Paul the Apostle to the Ephesians.

Ephes. 5, 15-21.

BRETHREN: See that ye walk circumspectly: not as fools, but as wise, redeeming the time, because the days are evil. Wherefore be ye not unwise, but understanding what the will of the Lord

The Twenty-first Sunday after Trinity

is. And be not drunk with wine, wherein is excess: but be filled with the Spirit, speaking to yourselves in psalms, and hymns, and spiritual songs, singing and making melody in your heart to the Lord: giving thanks always for all things unto God and the Father, in the name of our Lord Jesus Christ. Submitting yourselves one to another in the fear of God.

Gradual. Ps. 145, 15-16. The eyes of all wait upon thee, O Lord: and thou givest them their meat in due season. ℣. Thou openest thine hand: and fillest all things living with plenteousness.

Alleluia, alleluia. Ps. 108, 1. O God, my heart is ready, my heart is ready: I will sing and give praise unto thee. Alleluia.

✠ The Continuation of the holy Gospel according to Matthew.

Matt. 22, 1-14.

AT that time: Jesus spake unto the chief priests and Pharisees in parables, saying: The kingdom of heaven is like unto a certain king, who made a marriage for his son. And sent forth his servants to call them that were bidden to the wedding, and they would not come. Again, he sent forth other servants, saying: Tell them which are bidden: Behold, I have prepared my dinner, my oxen and my fatlings are killed, and all things are ready: come unto the marriage. But they made light of it, and went their ways, one to his farm, another to his merchandise: and the remnant took his servants, and entreated them spitefully, and slew them. But when the king heard thereof, he was wroth: and he sent forth his armies and destroyed those murderers, and burnt up their city. Then saith he to his servants: The wedding is ready, but they who were bidden were not worthy. Go ye therefore into the highways, and as many as ye shall find bid to the marriage. So those servants went out into the highways, and gathered together all, as many as they found, both bad and good: and the wedding was furnished with guests. And when the king came in to see the guests, he saw there a man which had not on a wedding-garment. And he saith unto him: Friend, how camest thou in hither, not having a wedding garment? And he was speechless. Then said the king to the servants: Bind him hand and foot, and take him away, and cast him into outer darkness: there shall be weeping and gnashing of teeth. For many are called, but few are chosen. Creed.

Offertory. Ps. 137, 1. By the waters of Babylon we sat down and wept: when we remembered thee, O Sion.

Secret.

GRANT, we beseech thee, O Lord, that these gifts, which we offer in the sight of thy majesty, may avail for our salvation. Through.

Preface of the Most Holy Trinity.

Communion. Ps. 119, 49-50. O think upon thy servant, O Lord, as concerning thy word, wherein thou hast caused me to put my trust: the same is my comfort in my trouble.

Postcommunion.

GRANT, O Lord, that the power of thy healing may in thy mercy cleanse us from our perversities, and make us ever to cleave stedfastly unto thy commandments. Through.

The Twenty-first Sunday after Trinity
Double.

Introit. Esther 13, 9-11. In voluntate tua.

O LORD, everything is in subjection to thy will, and there is no man that is able to resist thy power: for thou hast created everything, heaven and earth, and all the wonders which under heaven's vault are contained: thou art Lord of all things. Ps. 119, 1. Blessed are those that are undefiled in the way: and walk in the law of the Lord. ℣. Glory.

The Twenty-first Sunday after Trinity

Collect.

GRANT, we beseech thee, merciful Lord, to thy faithful people pardon and peace: that they may be cleansed from all their sins, and serve thee with a quiet mind. Through.

The Lesson from the Epistle of blessed Paul the Apostle to the Ephesians.

Ephes. 6, 10-17.

BRETHREN: Be strong in the Lord, and in the power of his might. Put on the whole armour of God, that ye may be able to stand against the wiles of the devil. For we wrestle not against flesh and blood: but against principalities, against powers, against the rulers of the darkness of this world, against spiritual wickedness in high places. Wherefore take unto you the whole armour of God, that ye may be able to withstand in the evil day, and having done all, to stand. Stand therefore, having your loins girt about with truth, and having on the breast-plate of righteousness, and your feet shod with the preparation of the Gospel of peace: above all, taking the shield of faith, wherewith ye shall be able to quench all the fiery darts of the wicked: and take the helmet of salvation: and the sword of the Spirit, which is the word of God:* praying always with all prayer and supplication in the Spirit, and watching thereunto with all perseverance, and supplication for all saints: and for me, that utterance may be given unto me, that I may open my mouth boldly, to make known the mystery of the Gospel, for which I am an ambassador in bonds: that therein I may speak boldly, as I ought to speak.

Gradual. Ps. 90, 1-2. Lord, thou hast been our refuge, from one generation to another. ℣. Before the mountains were brought forth, or ever the earth and the world were made: thou art God from everlasting, and world without end.

Alleluia, alleluia. ℣. Ps. 114, 1. When Israel came out of Egypt, and the house of Jacob from among the strange people. Alleluia.

✠ The Continuation of the holy Gospel according to John.

John 4, 46-53.

AT that time: There was a certain nobleman, whose son was sick at Capernaum. When he heard that Jesus was come out of Judæa into Galilee, he went unto him, and besought him that he would come down and heal his son: for he was at the point of death. Then said Jesus unto him: Except ye see signs and wonders, ye will not believe. The nobleman saith unto him: Sir, come down ere my child die. Jesus saith unto him: Go thy way, thy son liveth. And the man believed the word that Jesus had spoken unto him, and he went his way. And, as he was now going down, his servants met him, and told him, saying: Thy son liveth. Then enquired he of them the hour when he began to amend. And they said unto him: Yesterday at the seventh hour the fever left him. So the father knew that it was at the same hour, in the which Jesus said unto him: Thy son liveth: and himself believed, and his whole house. This is again the second miracle that Jesus did, when he was come out of Judæa into Galilee. Creed.

Offertory. Job. 1. There was a man in the land of Uz, whose name was Job: perfect and upright, and one that feared God: and Satan sought to tempt him: and power was given him by the Lord over his possessions and over his flesh: and he destroyed all his substance and his sons: and he smote his flesh with sore boils.

Secret.

WE beseech thee, O Lord, that these mysteries may bestow upon us thy heavenly healing: and purge away the iniquities of our hearts. Through.

Preface of the Most Holy Trinity.

Communion. Ps. 119, 81, 84 and 86. My soul hath longed for thy salvation, and I have a good hope because of thy word: when wilt thou be avenged of them that persecute me? they persecute me falsely, be thou my help, O Lord my God.

Postcommunion.

WE beseech thee, O Lord, make us ever to obey thy commandments: that we may be rendered worthy of thy holy gifts. Through.

The Twenty-second Sunday after Trinity

Double.

Introit. Ps. 130, 3-4. Si iniquitates.

IF thou, Lord, wilt be extreme to mark what is done amiss: O Lord, who may abide it? for there is mercy with thee, O God of Israel. Ps. ibid., 1. Out of the deep have I called unto thee, O Lord: Lord, hear my voice. ℣. Glory.

Collect.

LORD, we beseech thee to keep thy household the Church in continual godliness: that through thy protection it may be free from all adversities, and devoutly given to serve thee in good works, to the glory of thy name. Through.

The Lesson from the Epistle of blessed Paul the Apostle to the Philippians.

Phil. 1, 3-11.

BRETHREN: I thank my God upon every remembrance of you, always in every prayer of mine for you all making request with joy, for your fellowship in the Gospel from the first day until now: being confident of this very thing, that he who hath begun a good work in you will perform it until the day of Jesus Christ. Even as it is meet for me to think this of you all: because I have you in my heart, inasmuch as both in my bonds, and in the defence and confirmation of the Gospel, ye all are partakers of my grace. For God is my record, how greatly I long after you all in the bowels of Jesus Christ. And this I pray, that your love may abound yet more and more in knowledge and in all judgment: that ye may approve things that are excellent, that ye may be sincere and without offence till the day of Christ, being filled with the fruits of righteousness, which are by Jesus Christ, unto the glory and praise of God.

Gradual. Ps. 133, 1-2. Behold how good and joyful a thing it is, brethren, to dwell together in unity! ℣. It is like the precious ointment upon the head, that ran down unto Aaron's beard.

Alleluia, alleluia. ℣. Ps. 115, 11. Ye that fear the Lord, put your trust in him: he is their helper and defender. Alleluia.

✠ The Continuation of the holy Gospel according to Matthew.

Matt. 18, 21-35.

AT that time: Peter said unto Jesus: Lord, how oft shall my brother sin against me, and I forgive him? till seven times? Jesus saith unto him: I say not unto thee, until seven times: but until seventy times seven. Therefore is* the kingdom of heaven likened unto a certain king, which would take account of his servants. And when he had begun to reckon, one was brought unto him, which owed him ten thousand talents. But forasmuch as he had not to pay, his lord commanded him to be sold, and his wife and children, and all that he had, and payment to be made.

The servant therefore fell down and worshipped him, saying: Lord, have patience with me, and I will pay thee all. Then the lord of that servant was moved with compassion, and loosed him, and forgave him the debt. But the same servant went out, and found one of his fellow-servants, which owed him an hundred pence: and he laid hands on him, and took him by the throat, saying: Pay me that thou owest. And his fellow-servant fell down at his feet, and besought him, saying: Have patience with me, and I will pay thee all. And he would not: but went and cast him into prison, till he should pay the debt. So when his fellow-servants saw what was done, they were very sorry: and came and told unto their lord all that was done. Then his lord, after that he had called him, said unto him: O thou wicked servant, I forgave thee all that debt, because thou desiredst me: shouldest not thou also have had compassion on thy fellow-servant, even as I had pity on thee? And his lord was wroth, and delivered him to the tormentors, till he should pay all that was due unto him. So likewise shall my heavenly Father do also unto you, if ye from your hearts forgive not every one his brother their trespasses. Creed.

Offertory. Esther 14, 12-13. Remember me, O Lord, King of all power: and put a well-ordered speech in my mouth, that my words may be pleasing in the sight of the prince.

Secret.

MERCIFULLY receive, O Lord, this our sacrifice: whereby thou hast willed that atonement should be made unto thee, and that salvation should be restored to us by the power of thy loving kindness. Through.

Preface of the Most Holy Trinity.

Communion. Ps. 17, 6. I have called upon thee, O God, for thou shalt hear me: incline thine ear to me, and hearken unto my words.

Postcommunion.

O LORD, who hast bestowed on us the food of everlasting life, we beseech thee: that those things which we have received with our outward lips we may ever inwardly seek in purity of heart. Through.

The Twenty-third Sunday after Trinity

Double.

Introit. Jer. 29, 11, 12 and 14.

Dicit Dominus.

THUS saith the Lord: I think thoughts of peace, and not of affliction: ye shall call upon me, and I will hearken unto you: and will bring again your captivity from all places. Ps. 85, 1. Lord, thou art become gracious unto thy land: thou hast turned away the captivity of Jacob. ℣. Glory.

Collect.

O GOD, our refuge and strength, who art the author of all godliness: be ready, we beseech thee, to hear the devout prayers of thy Church, and grant; that those things which we ask faithfully we may obtain effectually. Through.

The Lesson from the Epistle of blessed Paul the Apostle to the Philippians.

Phil. 3, 17-21; 4, 1-3.

BRETHREN: Be followers together of me, and mark them which walk so as ye have us for an ensample. For many walk, of whom I have told you often, (and now tell you even weeping), that they are the enemies of the Cross of Christ: whose end is destruction: whose god is their belly: and whose glory is in their shame, who mind earthly things. For our conversation is in heaven: from whence also we look for the Saviour, the Lord Jesus Christ, who shall change our vile body, that it may be fashioned like unto his glorious body, according to the working whereby he is able even to subdue all things unto himself.

Gradual. Ps. 44, 8-9. It is thou, Lord, that savest us from our enemies: and puttest them to confusion that hate us. ℣. We make our boast of God all day long, and will praise thy name for ever.

Alleluia, alleluia. ℣. Ps. 130, 1-2. Out of the deep have I called unto thee, O Lord: Lord, hear my voice. Alleluia.

✠ The Continuation of the holy Gospel according to Matthew.

Matt. 22, 15-21.

AT that time: The Pharisees went and took counsel how they might entangle Jesus in his talk. And they sent out unto him their disciples with the Herodians, saying: Master, we know that thou art true, and teachest the way of God in truth, neither carest thou for any man: for thou regardest not the person of men: tell us therefore, what thinkest thou, is it lawful to give tribute unto Cæsar, or not? But Jesus perceived their wickedness, and said: Why tempt ye me, ye hypocrites? Shew me the tribute-money. And they brought unto him a penny. And he saith unto them: Whose is this image and superscription? They say unto him: Cæsar's. Then saith he unto them: Render therefore unto Cæsar the things which are Cæsar's; and unto God the things that are God's.* When they had heard these words, they marvelled, and left him, and went their way. Creed.

Offertory. Ps. 130, 1-2. Out of the deep have I called unto thee, O Lord: Lord, hear my voice: out of the deep have I called unto thee, O Lord.

Secret.

GRANT, O merciful God: that this saving oblation may evermore deliver us from our sins, and defend us against all adversities. Through.

Preface of the Most Holy Trinity.

Communion. Mark 11, 24. Verily, I say unto you. What things soever ye desire, when ye pray, believe that ye receive them, and it shall be done unto you.

Postcommunion.

O LORD, who hast made us partakers of the gifts of these sacred mysteries, we humbly beseech thee: that those things, which thou hast commanded us to do in remembrance of thee, may be profitable to the succour of our infirmities: Who livest and reignest with God the Father.

The Twenty-fourth Sunday after Trinity

Double.

Introit. Jer. 29, 11, 12 and 14.

Dicit Dominus.

THUS saith the Lord: I think thoughts of peace, and not of affliction: ye shall call upon me, and I will hearken unto you: and will bring again your captivity from all places. Ps. 85, 1. Lord, thou art become gracious unto thy land: thou hast turned away the captivity of Jacob. ℣. Glory.

Collect.

O LORD, we beseech thee, absolve thy people from their offences: that through thy bountiful goodness we may all be delivered from the bands of those sins, which by our frailty we have committed. Grant this, O heavenly Father, for Jesus Christ's sake, our blessed Lord and Saviour: Who liveth.

The Twenty-fourth Sunday after Trinity

The Lesson from the Epistle of blessed Paul the Apostle to the Colossians.

Col. 1, 3-12.

BRETHREN: We give thanks to God and the Father of our Lord Jesus Christ, praying always for you: since we heard of your faith in Christ Jesus, and of the love which ye have to all the saints, for the hope which is laid up for you in heaven, whereof ye heard before in the word of the truth of the Gospel: which is come unto you, as it is in all the world, and bringeth forth fruit, as it doth also in you, since the day ye heard of it, and knew the grace of God in truth, as ye also learned of Epaphras, our dear fellow-servant, who is for you a faithful minister of Christ, who also declared unto us your love in the Spirit. For this cause we also, since the day we heard it, do not cease to pray for you, and to desire that ye might be filled with the knowledge of his will in all wisdom and spiritual understanding: that ye might walk worthy of the Lord unto all pleasing: being fruitful in every good work, and increasing in the knowledge of God: strengthened with all might, according to his glorious power, unto all patience and long-suffering with joyfulness, giving thanks unto the Father, which hath made us meet to be partakers of the inheritance of the saints in light.

Gradual. Ps. 44, 8-9. It is thou, Lord, that savest us from our enemies: and puttest them to confusion that hate us. ℣. We make our boast of God all day long, and will praise thy name for ever.

Alleluia, alleluia. ℣. Ps. 130, 1-2. Out of the deep have I called unto thee, O Lord: Lord, hear my voice. Alleluia.

✠ The Continuation of the holy Gospel according to Matthew.

Matt. 9, 18-26.

AT that time: While Jesus spake unto the multitudes, behold, there came a certain ruler and worshipped him, saying: My daughter is even now dead: but come and lay thy hand upon her, and she shall live. And Jesus arose, and followed him, and so did his disciples. And behold, a woman, which was diseased with an issue of blood twelve years, came behind him, and touched the hem of his garment. For she said within herself: If I may but touch his garment, I shall be whole. But Jesus turned him about, and, when he saw her, he said: Daughter, be of good comfort, thy faith hath made thee whole. And the woman was made whole from that hour. And when Jesus came into the ruler's house, and saw the minstrels and the people making a noise, he said unto them: Give place: for the maid is not dead but sleepeth. And they laughed him to scorn. But when the people were put forth, he went in, and took her by the hand. And the maid arose. And the fame hereof went abroad into all that land. Creed.

Offertory. Ps. 130, 1-2. Out of the deep have I called unto thee, O Lord: Lord, hear my voice: out of the deep have I called unto thee, O Lord.

Secret.

WE offer unto thee, O Lord, this sacrifice of praise to the increasing of our faithful service: beseeching thee, that although we be unworthy of thy bounty, yet thou wouldest accomplish in us the effectual working of the same. Through.

Preface of the Most Holy Trinity.

Communion. Mark 11, 24. Verily I say unto you, What things soever ye desire, when ye pray, believe that ye receive them, and it shall be done unto you.

Postcommunion.

WE beseech thee, almighty God: that we, whom thou makest to rejoice in the partaking of heavenly things, may by thee be defended against all earthly perils. Through.

¶ If there be more than 25 Sundays after Trinity, then after the 25th the Masses of the Sundays which were left over after the Epiphany are resumed as below, according to the order given in the Rubrics. And in the last place is always said the Mass of the 25th Sunday, as below, p. 509.

The Fifth Sunday

which remained over after the Epiphany.

Double.

Introit. Jer. 29, 11, 12 and 14.

Dicit Dominus.

THUS saith the Lord: I think thoughts of peace, and not of affliction: ye shall call upon me, and I will hearken unto you: and will bring again your captivity from all places. Ps. 85, 1. Lord, thou art become gracious unto thy land: thou hast turned away the captivity of Jacob. ℣. Glory.

Collect.

O LORD, we beseech thee to keep thy [Church and] household continually in thy true religion: that they who do lean only upon the hope of thy heavenly grace may evermore be defended by thy mighty power. Through.

The Lesson from the Epistle of blessed Paul the Apostle to the Colossians.

Col. 3, 12-17.

BRETHREN: Put on as the elect of God, holy and beloved, bowels of mercies, kindness, humbleness of mind, meekness, long-suffering: forbearing one another, and forgiving one another, if any man have a quarrel against any: even as Christ forgave you, so also do ye. And above all these things put on charity, which is the bond of perfectness: and let the peace of God rule in your hearts, to the which also ye are called in one body: and be ye thankful. Let the word of Christ dwell in you richly in all wisdom, teaching and admonishing one another in psalms and hymns, and spiritual songs, singing with grace in your hearts to the Lord. And whatsoever ye do, in word or deed, do all in the name of the Lord Jesus, giving thanks to God and the Father through Jesus Christ our Lord.

Gradual. Ps. 44, 8-9. It is thou, Lord, that savest us from our enemies: and puttest them to confusion that hate us. ℣. We make our boast of God all day long, and will praise thy name for ever.

Alleluia, alleluia. ℣. Ps. 130, 1-2. Out of the deep have I called unto thee, O Lord: Lord, hear my voice. Alleluia.

☩ The Continuation of the holy Gospel according to Matthew.

Matt. 13, 24-30.

AT that time: Jesus spake unto the multitudes this parable: The kingdom of heaven is likened unto a man which sowed good seed in his field. But while men slept, his enemy came and sowed tares among the wheat, and went his way. But, when the blade was sprung up and brought forth fruit, then appeared the tares also. So the servants of the householder came, and said unto him: Sir, didst not thou sow good seed in thy field? From whence then hath it tares? He said unto them: An enemy hath done this. The servants said unto him: Wilt thou then that we go and gather them up? But he said: Nay: lest while ye gather up the tares, ye root up also the wheat with them. Let both grow together until the harvest, and in the time of harvest I will say to the reapers: Gather ye together first the tares, and bind them in bundles to burn them, but gather the wheat into my barn. Creed.

Offertory. Ps. 130, 1-2. Out of the deep have I called unto thee, O Lord: Lord, hear my voice: out of the deep have I called unto thee, O Lord.

Secret.

WE offer unto thee, O Lord, this sacrifice of propitiation for our sins: beseeching thee of thy merciful goodness to absolve our offences, and to guide the hearts of them that go astray. Through.

Preface of the Most Holy Trinity.

Communion. Mark 11, 24. Verily I say unto you, what things soever ye desire when ye pray, believe that ye receive them, and it shall be done unto you.

Postcommunion.

WE beseech thee, almighty God: that as through these holy mysteries we have received the pledge of our salvation, so we may effectually be brought unto the fulfilment of the same. Through.

The Sixth Sunday
which remained over after the Epiphany.
Double.
Introit. Jer. 29, 11, 12 and 14.
Dicit Dominus.

THUS saith the Lord: I think thoughts of peace, and not of affliction: ye shall call upon me, and I will hearken unto you: and will bring again your captivity from all places. Ps. 85, 1. Lord, thou art become gracious unto thy land: thou hast turned away the captivity of Jacob. ℣. Glory.

Collect.

O GOD, whose blessed Son was manifested that he might destroy the works of the devil, and make us the sons of God, and heirs of eternal life: grant us, we beseech thee, that, having this hope, we may purify ourselves, even as he is pure; that, when he shall appear again with power and great glory, we may be made like unto him in his eternal and glorious kingdom: Where with thee, O Father, and thee, O Holy Ghost, he liveth and reigneth, ever one God, world without end. ℟. Amen.

The Lesson from the Epistle of blessed John the Apostle.
I John 3, 1-8.

DEARLY beloved: Behold what manner of love the Father hath bestowed upon us, that we should be called the sons of God: therefore the world knoweth us not, because it knew him not. Beloved, now are we the sons of God: and it doth not yet appear what we shall be. But we know that, when he shall appear, we shall be like him: for we shall see him as he is. And every man that hath this hope in him purifieth himself, even as he is pure. Whosoever committeth sin transgresseth also the law: for sin is the transgression of the law. And we know that he was manifested to take away our sins: and in him is no sin. Whosoever abideth in him sinneth not: whosoever sinneth hath not seen him, neither known him. Little children, let no man deceive you. He that doeth righteousness is righteous, even as he is righteous. He that committeth sin is of the devil: for the devil sinneth from the beginning. For this purpose the Son of God was manifested, that he might destroy the works of the devil.

Gradual. Ps. 44, 8-9. It is thou, Lord, that savest us from our enemies: and puttest them to confusion that hate us. ℣. We make our boast of God all day long, and will praise thy name for ever.

Alleluia, alleluia. Ps. 130, 1-2. Out of the deep have I called unto thee, O Lord: Lord, hear my voice. Alleluia.

✠ The Continuation of the holy Gospel according to Matthew.

Matt. 24, 23-31.

AT that time: Jesus said unto his disciples: If any man shall say unto you: Lo, here is Christ, or there, believe it not. For there shall arise false Christs, and false prophets, and shall shew great signs and wonders, insomuch that (if it were possible) they shall deceive the very elect. Behold, I have told you before. Wherefore, if they shall say unto you: Behold, he is in the desert, go not forth: behold, he is in the secret chambers, believe it not. For as the lightning cometh out of the East, and shineth even unto the West: so shall also the coming of the Son of man be. For wheresoever the carcase is, there will the eagles be gathered together. Immediately after the tribulation of those days shall the sun be darkened, and the moon shall not give her light, and the stars shall fall from heaven, and the powers of the heavens shall be shaken: and then shall appear the sign of the Son of man in heaven: and then shall all the tribes of the earth mourn: and they shall see the Son of man coming in the clouds of heaven with power and great glory. And he shall send his Angels with a great sound of a trumpet: and they shall gather together his elect from the four winds, from one end of heaven to the other. Creed.

Offertory. Ps. 130, 1-2. Out of the deep have I called unto thee, O Lord: Lord, hear my voice: out of the deep have I called unto thee, O Lord.

Secret.

WE beseech thee, O God, that this oblation may cleanse and regenerate, govern and defend us. Through.

Preface of the Most Holy Trinity.

Communion. Mark 11, 24. Verily I say unto you, what things soever ye desire when ye pray, believe that ye receive them, and it shall be done unto you.

Postcommunion.

O LORD, who hast fulfilled us with thy heavenly delights: we beseech thee; that we may ever earnestly seek after those things whereby we truly live. Through.

The Twenty-fifth and last Sunday after Trinity

Double.

Introit. Jer. 29, 11, 12 and 14.

Dicit Dominus.

THUS saith the Lord: I think thoughts of peace, and not of affliction: ye shall call upon me, and I will hearken unto you: and will bring again your captivity from all places. Ps. 85, 1. Lord, thou art become gracious unto thy land: thou hast turned away the captivity of Jacob. ℣. Glory.

Collect.

STIR up, we beseech thee, O Lord, the wills of thy faithful people: that they, plenteously bringing forth the fruit of good works; may of thee be plenteously rewarded. Through.

The Lesson from the Prophet Jeremiah.

Jer. 23, 5-8.

IN those days: Jeremiah the Prophet spake, saying: Behold, the days come, saith the Lord: that I will raise unto David a righteous branch, and a king shall reign, and prosper: and shall execute judgment and justice in the earth. In his days Judah shall be saved, and Israel shall dwell safely: and this is his name whereby he shall be called, The Lord our Righteousness. Therefore behold, the days come, saith the Lord, that they shall no more say: The Lord liveth, which brought up the children of Israel out of the land of Egypt: but:

The Lord liveth, which brought up and which led the seed of the house of Israel out of the north-country, and from all countries whither I had driven them: and they shall dwell in their own land.

Gradual. Ps. 44, 8-9. It is thou, Lord, that savest us from our enemies: and puttest them to confusion that hate us. ℣. We make our boast of God all day long, and will praise thy name for ever.

Alleluia, alleluia. ℣. Ps. 130, 1-2. Out of the deep have I called unto thee, O Lord: Lord, hear my voice. Alleluia.

✠ The Continuation of the holy Gospel according to John.

John 6, 5-14.

AT that time: Jesus saw a great company come unto him, and he saith unto Philip: Whence shall we buy bread that these may eat? And this he said to prove him: for he himself knew what he would do. Philip answered him: Two hundred pennyworth of bread is not sufficient for them, that every one of them may take a little. One of his disciples, Andrew, Simon Peter's brother, saith unto him: There is a lad here, which hath five barley-loaves, and two small fishes: but what are they among so many? And Jesus said: Make the men sit down. Now there was much grass in the place. So the men sat down, in number about five thousand. And Jesus took the loaves: and when he had given thanks, he distributed to the disciples: and the disciples to them that were set down: and likewise of the fishes, as much as they would. When they were filled, he said unto his disciples: Gather up the fragments that remain, that nothing be lost. Therefore they gathered them together, and filled twelve baskets with the fragments of the five barley-loaves which remained over and above unto them that had eaten. Then those men, when they had seen the miracle that Jesus did, said: This is of a truth that Prophet that should come into the world. Creed.

Offertory. Ps. 130, 1. Out of the deep have I called unto thee, O Lord: Lord, hear my voice: out of the deep have I called unto thee, O Lord.

Secret.

WE beseech thee, O Lord, to have compassion on our supplications, and to accept the prayers and oblations of thy people: that the hearts of all men being turned unto thee, we may be delivered from the desire of things temporal, and follow stedfastly after things eternal. Through.

Communion. Mark 11, 24. Verily I say unto you, what things soever ye desire when ye pray, believe that ye receive them, and it shall be done unto you.

Postcommunion.

GRANT, O Lord, that the effectual healing of this Sacrament which we have received may deliver us from all the diseases of our souls. Through.

MASSES
OF THE SUNDAYS AFTER PENTECOST

THE FEAST OF
THE MOST HOLY TRINITY

Double of 1st class.

Introit. Tob. 12, 6. Benedicta sit.

BLESSED be the holy Trinity, and the undivided Unity: we will praise and glorify him, because he hath showed his mercy upon us. Ps. 8, 1. O Lord our governor: how excellent is thy name in all the world! ℣. Glory.

Collect.

ALMIGHTY and everlasting God, who hast given unto us thy servants grace by the confession of a true faith to acknowledge the glory of the eternal Trinity, and in the power of the Majesty to worship the Unity: we beseech thee; that through the steadfastness of this faith we may evermore be defended from all adversities. Through.

And Commemoration is made of the first Sunday after Pentecost:

Collect.

O GOD, the strength of all them that put their trust in thee, mercifully accept our prayers: and because through the weakness of our mortal nature we can do no good thing without thee, grant us the help of thy grace; that in keeping of thy commandments we may please thee, both in will and deed. Through.

The Lesson from the Epistle of blessed Paul the Apostle to the Romans.

Rom. 11, 33-36.

O THE depth of the riches both of the wisdom and knowledge of God: how unsearchable are his judgments and his ways past finding out! For who hath known the mind of the Lord? Or who hath been his counsellor? Or who hath first given to him, and it shall be recompensed unto him again? For of him, and through him, and to him, are all things: to whom be glory for ever. Amen.

Gradual. Dan. 3, 55-56. Blessed art thou, O Lord, that beholdest the depths, and sittest upon the Cherubim. ℣. Blessed art thou, O Lord, in the firmament of heaven, and worthy to be praised for ever.

Alleluia, alleluia. ℣. ibid., 52. Blessed art thou, O Lord God of our fathers, and worthy to be praised for evermore. Alleluia.

✠ The Continuation of the holy Gospel according to Matthew.

Matt. 28, 18-20.

AT that time: Jesus said unto his disciples: All power is given unto me in heaven and in earth. Go ye therefore, and teach all nations, baptizing them in the name of the Father, and of the Son, and of the Holy Ghost: teaching them to observe all things whatsoever I have commanded you. And lo, I am with you alway, even unto the end of the world. Creed.

Offertory. Tob. 12, 6. Blessed be God the Father, and the only-begotten Son of God, and the Holy Spirit: because he hath shewed his mercy upon us.

Secret.

SANCTIFY, we beseech thee, O Lord our God, this oblation of our sacrifice through the invocation of thy holy name: and make us thereby an offering acceptable unto thee for evermore. Through.

For the Sunday:
Secret.

WE beseech thee, O Lord, graciously to accept this our sacrifice which we offer unto thee: and grant that it may avail for our perpetual succour. Through.

Preface of the Most Holy Trinity.

Communion. Tob. 12, 6. We bless the God of heaven, and will praise him in the sight of all that live: because he hath shewed his mercy upon us.

Postcommunion.

O LORD our God, who hast given unto us to acknowledge the holy and everlasting Trinity, and likewise the undivided Unity; grant that we may be thereby preserved from all evil both in body and soul. Through.

For the Sunday:
Postcommunion.

O LORD, who hast fulfilled us with thy wondrous bounty: grant, we beseech thee; that we, receiving these gifts of our salvation, may never cease to shew forth thy praise. Through.

The First Sunday after Pentecost

Double.

Introit. Ps. 13, 6. Domine in tua.

O LORD, my trust is in thy mercy: and my heart is joyful in thy salvation: I will sing of the Lord, because he hath dealt so lovingly with me. Ps. ibid., 1. How long wilt thou forget me, O Lord, for ever? how long wilt thou hide thy face from me? Glory.

¶ Glória in excélsis is said on all Sundays after Pentecost. But it is not said on ferial days, when the Mass of the preceding Sunday is resumed.

Collect.

O GOD, the strength of all them that put their trust in thee, mercifully accept our prayers: and because through the weakness of our mortal nature we can do no good thing without thee, grant us the help of thy grace; that in keeping of thy commandments we may please thee, both in will and deed. Through.

The Lesson from the Epistle of blessed John the Apostle.

I John 4, 8.

DEARLY beloved: God is love. In this was manifested the love of God towards us, because that God sent his only-begotten Son into the world, that we might live through him. Herein is love: not that we loved God, but that he loved us, and sent his Son to be the propitiation for our sins. Beloved, if God so loved us: we ought also to love one another. No man hath seen God at any time. If we love one another, God dwelleth in us, and his love is perfected in us. Hereby know we that we dwell in him, and he in us: because he hath given us of his Spirit. And we have seen, and do testify, that the Father sent the Son to be the Saviour of

The First Sunday after Pentecost

the world. Whosoever shall confess that Jesus is the Son of God, God dwelleth in him, and he in God. And we have known and believed the love that God hath to us. God is love: and he that dwelleth in love dwelleth in God, and God in him. Herein is our love made perfect, that we may have boldness in the day of judgment: because as he is, so are we in this world. There is no fear in love: but perfect love casteth out fear, because fear hath torment. He that feareth is not made perfect in love. We love him, because he first loved us. If a man say, I love God, and hateth his brother, he is a liar. For he that loveth not his brother, whom he hath seen, how can he love God whom he hath not seen? And this commandment have we from him: That he who loveth God love his brother also.

Gradual. Ps. 41, 5 and 2. I said, Lord, be merciful unto me: heal my soul, for I have sinned against thee. ℣. Blessed is he that considereth the poor and needy: the Lord shall deliver him in the time of trouble.

Alleluia, alleluia. ℣. Ps. 5, 1. Ponder my words, O Lord: consider my meditation. Alleluia.

¶ Alleluia with its Verse is said thus after the Gradual on all Sundays after Pentecost, and also if the Mass of the Sunday be resumed on ferias.

✠ The Continuation of the holy Gospel according to Luke.

Luke 6, 36-42.

AT that time: Jesus said unto his disciples: Be ye merciful, as your Father also is merciful. Judge not, and ye shall not be judged: condemn not, and ye shall not be condemned. Forgive, and ye shall be forgiven. Give, and it shall be given unto you: good measure, pressed down, and shaken together, and running over, shall men give into your bosom. For with the same measure that ye mete withal it shall be measured to you again. And he spake a parable unto them: Can the blind lead the blind? shall they not both fall into the ditch? The disciple is not above his master: but every one that is perfect shall be as his master. And why beholdest thou the mote that is in thy brother's eye, but perceivest not the beam that is in thine own eye? Either how canst thou say to thy brother: Brother, let me pull out the mote that is in thine eye: when thou thyself beholdest not the beam that is in thine own eye? Thou hypocrite, cast out first the beam out of thine own eye: and then shalt thou see clearly to pull out the mote that is in thy brother's eye.

Creed, which is said on all Sundays after Pentecost, but it is not said on ferial days, when the Mass of the preceding Sunday is resumed.

Offertory. Ps. 5. 3-4. O hearken thou unto the voice of my calling, my King and my God: for unto thee, O Lord, will I make my prayer.

Secret.

WE beseech thee, O Lord, graciously to accept this our sacrifice which we offer unto thee: and grant that it may avail for our perpetual succour. Through.

¶ Preface of the Most Holy Trinity, which is said on all Sundays after Pentecost if the Mass be of the Sunday. But whenever within the week the Mass of the preceding Sunday is resumed, the Common Preface is said, according to the Rubrics.

Communion. Ps. 9, 2-3. I will speak of all thy marvellous works: I will be glad and rejoice in thee: yea, my songs will I make of thy name, O Most Highest.

Postcommunion.

O LORD, who hast fulfilled us with thy wondrous bounty: grant we beseech thee; that we, receiving these gifts of our salvation, may never cease to shew forth thy praise. Through.

The Second Sunday after Pentecost
Double.

Introit. Ps. 18, 19-20. Factus est.

THE Lord was my upholder, he brought me forth also into a place of liberty: he brought me forth, even because he had a favour unto me. Ps. ibid., 1. I will love thee, O Lord my strength: the Lord is my stony rock, my defence and my saviour. ℣. Glory.

Collect.

LORD, make us to have a perpetual fear and love of thy holy name: for thou never failest to govern them whom thou dost bring up in thy stedfast love. Through.

The Lesson from the Epistle of blessed John the Apostle.

I John 3, 13-18.

DEARLY beloved: Marvel not, if the world hate you. We know that we have passed from death unto life, because we love the brethren. He that loveth not his brother abideth in death: whosoever hateth his brother is a murderer. And ye know that no murderer hath eternal life abiding in him. Hereby perceive we the love of God, because he laid down his life for us: and we ought to lay down our lives for the brethren. But whoso hath this world's goods and seeth his brother have need, and shutteth up his bowels of compassion from him: how dwelleth the love of God in him? My little children, let us not love in word, neither in tongue, but in deed, and in truth.

Gradual. Ps. 120, 1-2. When I was in trouble I called upon the Lord, and he heard me. ℣. Deliver my soul, O Lord, from lying lips, and from a deceitful tongue.

Alleluia, alleluia. ℣. Ps. 7, 1. O Lord my God, in thee have I put my trust: save me from all them that persecute me, and deliver me. Alleluia.

✠ The Continuation of the holy Gospel according to Luke.

Luke 14, 16-24.

AT that time: Jesus spake this parable unto the Pharisees: A certain man made a great supper, and bade many. And sent his servant at supper-time to say to them that were bidden, Come, for all things are now ready. And they all with one consent began to make excuse. The first said unto him: I have bought a piece of ground, and I must needs go and see it: I pray thee have me excused. And another said: I have bought five yoke of oxen, and I go to prove them: I pray thee have me excused. And another said: I have married a wife: and therefore I cannot come. So that servant came, and shewed his lord these things. Then the master of the house being angry said to his servant: Go out quickly into the streets and lanes of the city: and bring in hither the poor, and the maimed, and the halt, and the blind. And the servant said: Lord it is done as thou hast commanded, and yet there is room. And the lord said unto the servant: Go out into the highways and hedges: and compel them to come in, that my house may be filled. For I say unto you, That none of those men which were bidden shall taste of my supper. Creed.

Offertory. Ps. 6, 5. Turn thee, O Lord, and deliver my soul: O save me for thy mercy's sake.

Secret.

CLEANSE us, O Lord, by this oblation now to be hallowed to the honour of thy name: and daily renew us thereby to the attainment of heavenly life. Through.

Communion. Ps. 13, 6. I will sing of the Lord, because he hath dealt so lovingly with me: yea, I will praise the name of the Lord Most Highest.

Postcommunion.

O LORD, who hast made us to be partakers of thy bounty: we beseech thee; that we, continually drawing near to this holy mystery, may thereby grow in grace to the attainment of everlasting salvation. Through.

The Third Sunday after Pentecost

Double.

Introit. Ps. 25, 16 and 18. Respice in me. TURN thee unto me, and have mercy upon me, O Lord: for I am desolate and in misery: look upon my adversity and misery: and forgive me all my sin, O my God. Ps. ibid., 1. Unto thee, O Lord, will I lift up my soul: my God, I have put my trust in thee, O let me not be confounded. ℣. Glory.

Collect.

O GOD, the protector of them that trust in thee, without whom nothing is strong, nothing is holy: increase and multiply upon us thy mercy; that, thou being our ruler and guide, we may so pass through good things temporal, that we lose not the things eternal. Through.

The Lesson from the Epistle of blessed Peter the Apostle.

I Peter 5, 6-11.

DEARLY beloved: Humble yourselves under the mighty hand of God, that he may exalt you in due time: casting all your care upon him for he careth for you. Be sober, be vigilant: because your adversary the devil, as a roaring lion, walketh about, seeking whom he may devour: whom resist steadfast in the faith: knowing that the same afflictions are accomplished in your brethren that are in the world. But the God of all grace, who hath called us into his eternal glory by Christ Jesus, after that ye have suffered a while, make you perfect, stablish, strengthen, settle you. To him be glory and dominion for ever and ever. Amen.

Gradual. Ps. 55, 23, 17 and 19. O cast thy burden upon the Lord: and he shall nourish thee. ℣. When I called upon the Lord, he heard my voice from the battle that was against me.

Alleluia, alleluia. ℣. Ps. 7, 12. God is a righteous judge, strong and patient, and God is provoked every day. Alleluia.

✠ *The Continuation of the holy Gospel according to Luke.*

Luke 15, 1-10.

AT that time: There drew near unto Jesus all the publicans and sinners for to hear him. And the Pharisees and scribes murmured, saying: This man receiveth sinners, and eateth with them. And he spake this parable unto them, saying: What man of you having an hundred sheep: if he lose one of them, doth not leave the ninety and nine in the wilderness, and go after that which is lost, until he find it? And when he hath found it, he layeth it on his shoulders, rejoicing: and when he cometh home, he calleth together his friends and neighbours, saying unto them: Rejoice with me, for I have found my sheep, which was lost? I say unto you, That likewise joy shall be in heaven over one sinner that repenteth more than over ninety and nine just persons, which need no repentance. Either what woman having ten pieces of silver, if she lose one piece, doth not light a candle, and sweep the house, and seek diligently till she find it? And when she hath found it she calleth her friends and her neighbours together, saying: Rejoice with me, for I have found the piece which I had lost? Likewise, I say unto you: There is joy in the presence of the Angels of God over one sinner that repenteth. Creed.

Offertory. Ps. 9, 11-13. They that know thy name will put their trust in thee: for thou, Lord, hast never failed them that seek thee: O praise the Lord which dwelleth in Sion: for he forgetteth not the complaint of the poor.

Secret.

REGARD, O Lord, the gifts of thy suppliant Church: and grant that the partaking thereof may avail for the salvation and continual sanctification of them that believe. Through.

Communion. Luke 15, 10 I say unto you: There is joy in the presence of the Angels of God over one sinner that repenteth.

Postcommunion.

O LORD, through whom we have received these sacred gifts: we beseech thee; that by the power of the same, thou wouldest both cleanse us from all vices, and evermore fulfil us with the gifts of thy grace. Through.

The Fourth Sunday after Pentecost

Introit. Ps. 27, 1-2.

Dominus illuminatio mea.

THE Lord is my light, and my salvation, whom then shall I fear? the Lord is the strength of my life, of whom then shall I be afraid? When mine enemies came upon me, they stumbled and fell. Ps. ibid., 4. Though an host of men were laid against me, yet shall not my heart be afraid. ℣. Glory.

Collect.

GRANT to us, Lord, we beseech thee: that the course of this world may be so peaceably ordered by thy governance; that thy Church may joyfully serve thee in godly quietness. Through.

The Lesson from the Epistle of blessed Paul the Apostle to the Romans.

Rom. 8, 18-23.

BRETHREN: I reckon that the sufferings of this present time are not worthy to be compared with the glory which shall be revealed in us. For the earnest expectation of the creature waiteth for the manifestation of the sons of God. For the creature was made subject to vanity, not willingly, but by reason of him who hath subjected the same in hope: because the creature itself also shall be delivered from the bondage of corruption, into the glorious liberty of the children of God. For we know that the whole creation groaneth, and travaileth in pain together until now. And not only they, but ourselves also which have the firstfruits of the Spirit, even we ourselves groan within ourselves, waiting for the adoption, to wit, the redemption of our body: in Christ Jesu our Lord.

Gradual. Ps. 79, 9-10. Be merciful, O Lord, unto our sins: wherefore do the heathen say: Where is now their God? ℣. Help us, O God of our salvation: and for the glory of thy name, O Lord, deliver us.

Alleluia, alleluia. ℣. Ps. 9, 5 and 10. O God, who art set in the throne and judgest right: be thou the refuge of the oppressed in time of trouble. Alleluia.

✠ The Continuation of the holy Gospel according to Luke.

Luke 5, 1-11.

AT that time: When the people pressed upon Jesus to hear the word of God, he stood by the lake of Gennesareth. And saw two ships, standing by the lake: but the fishermen were gone out of them, and were washing their nets. And he entered one of the ships, which was Simon's, and prayed him that he would thrust out a little from the land. And he sat down, and taught the people out of the ship. Now when he had left speaking, he said unto Simon: Launch out into the deep, and let down your nets for a draught. And Simon answering said unto him: Master, we have toiled all the night, and have taken nothing: nevertheless, at thy word I will let down the net. And when they had this done, they inclosed a great multitude of fishes: and their net brake. And they beckoned unto their partners which were in the other ship, that they should come and help them. And they came, and filled both the ships, so that they began to sink. When Simon Peter saw it, he fell down at Jesus' knees, saying: Depart from me, for I am a sinful man, O Lord. For he was astonished, and all that were with him, at the draught of the fishes which they had taken: and so was also James and John, the sons of Zebedee, which were partners with Simon. And Jesus said unto Simon: Fear not: from henceforth thou shalt catch men. And when they had brought their ships to land, they forsook all, and followed him. Creed.

Offertory. Ps. 13, 4-5. Lighten mine eyes, that I sleep not in death: lest mine enemy say: I have prevailed against him.

Secret.

O LORD, we beseech thee mercifully to receive our oblations: and graciously turn our rebel wills to thee. Through.

Preface of the Most Holy Trinity.

Communion. Ps. 18, 1. The Lord is my stony rock and my defence, my saviour, my God, and my might.

Postcommunion.

WE beseech thee, O Lord, that the mysteries which we have here received may cleanse us from all our sins: and by the gifts therein bestowed defend us from all adversities. Through.

The Fifth Sunday after Pentecost

Double.

Introit. Ps. 27, 7 and 9. Exaudi, Domine.

HEARKEN unto my voice, O Lord, when I cry unto thee: be thou my succour, O cast me not away, neither forsake me, O God of my salvation. Ps. ibid., 1. The Lord is my light, and my salvation: whom then shall I fear? ℣. Glory.

Collect.

O GOD, who hast prepared for them that love thee such good things as pass man's understanding: pour into our hearts such love toward thee; that we, loving thee in all things and above all things, may obtain thy promises, which exceed all that we can desire. Through.

The Lesson from the Epistle of blessed Peter the Apostle.

I Peter 3, 8-15.

DEARLY beloved: Be ye all of one mind, having compassion one of another, love as brethren, be pitiful, be courteous: not rendering evil for evil, or railing for railing, but contrariwise blessing: knowing that ye are thereunto called, that ye should inherit a blessing. For he that will love life, and see good days, let him refrain his tongue from evil, and his lips that they speak no guile. Let him eschew evil, and do good: let him seek peace and ensue it. For the eyes of the Lord are over the righteous, and his ears are open unto their prayers: but the face of the Lord is against them that do evil. And who is he that will harm you, if ye be followers of that which is good? But and if ye suffer for righteousness' sake, happy are ye. And be not afraid of their terror: neither be troubled. But sanctify the Lord Christ in your hearts.

Gradual. Ps. 84, 10 and 9. Behold, O God, our defender: and look upon thy servants. ℣. O Lord God of hosts, hear the prayer of thy servants.

Alleluia, alleluia. ℣. Ps. 21, 1. The king shall rejoice in thy strength, O Lord: exceeding glad shall he be of thy salvation. Alleluia.

✠ The Continuation of the holy Gospel according to Matthew.

Matt. 5, 20.

AT that time: Jesus said unto his disciples: Except your righteousness shall exceed the righteousness of the Scribes and Pharisees, ye shall in no case enter into the kingdom of heaven. Ye have heard that it was said by them of old time: Thou shalt not kill: and whosoever shall kill, shall be in danger of the judgment. But I say unto you: that whosoever is angry with his brother without a cause shall be in danger of the judgment. And whosoever shall say to his brother, Raca: shall be in danger of the council. But whosoever shall say, Thou fool: shall be in danger of hell-fire. Therefore if thou bring thy gift to the altar, and there rememberest that thy brother hath ought against thee: leave there thy gift before the altar, and go thy way, first be reconciled to thy brother: and then come and offer thy gift. Creed.

Offertory. Ps. 16, 7-8. I will bless the Lord who hath given me counsel: I have set God always before me: for he is on my right hand, therefore I shall not fall.

Secret.

ASSIST us, O Lord, in these our supplications: and graciously accept the oblations of thy servants and handmaids; that those things which each hath offered to the honour of thy name, may be profitable unto all for their salvation. Through.

Preface of the Most Holy Trinity.

Communion. Ps. 27, 4. One thing have I desired of the Lord, which I will require: even that I may dwell in the house of the Lord all the days of my life.

Postcommunion.

O LORD, who hast satisfied us with thy heavenly gift: grant, we beseech thee; that we may be cleansed from our secret faults, and delivered from the snares of our enemies. Through.

The Sixth Sunday after Pentecost

Double.

Introit. Ps. 28, 8-9. Dominus fortitudo.

THE Lord is the strength of his people, and he is the wholesome defence of his Anointed: O Lord, save thy people, and give thy blessing unto thine inheritance: feed them, and set them up for ever. Ps. ibid., 1. Unto thee will I cry, O Lord my strength, think no scorn of me: lest, if thou make as though thou hearest not, I become like them that go down into the pit. ℣. Glory.

Collect.

GOD of all power and might, who art the author of all good things: graft in our hearts the love of thy name, increase in us true religion; nourish us with all goodness, and of thy great mercy keep us in the same. Through.

The Sixth Sunday after Pentecost

The Lesson from the Epistle of blessed Paul the Apostle to the Romans.

Rom. 6, 3-11.

BRETHREN: So many of us as were baptized into Jesus Christ were baptized into his death. Therefore we are buried with him by baptism into death: that like as Christ was raised up from the dead by the glory of the Father, even so we also should walk in newness of life. For if we have been planted together in the likeness of his death: we shall be also in the likeness of his resurrection. Knowing this, that our old man is crucified with him: that the body of sin might be destroyed, that henceforth we should not serve sin. For he that is dead is freed from sin. Now if we be dead with Christ: we believe that we shall also live with him: knowing that Christ being raised from the dead dieth no more, death hath no more dominion over him. For in that he died, he died unto sin once: but in that he liveth he liveth unto God. Likewise reckon ye also yourselves to be dead indeed unto sin, but alive unto God, in Christ Jesu our Lord.

Gradual. Ps. 90, 13 and 1. Turn thee again, O Lord, at the last, and be gracious unto thy servants. ℣.Lord, thou hast been our refuge, from one generation to another.

Alleluia, alleluia. ℣. Ps. 31, 1-2. In thee, O Lord, have I put my trust, let me never be put to confusion: rid me and deliver me in thy righteousness: bow down thine ear to me, make haste to deliver me. Alleluia.

✠ The Continuation of the holy Gospel according to Mark.

Mark 8, 1-9.

AT that time: When there was a great multitude with Jesus, and they had nothing to eat, he called his disciples and saith unto them: I have compassion on the multitude: because they have now been with me three days, and have nothing to eat: and if I send them away fasting to their own houses, they will faint by the way: for divers of them came from far. And his disciples answered him: From whence can a man satisfy these men with bread here in the wilderness? And he asked them: How many loaves have ye? And they said: Seven. And he commanded the people to sit down on the ground. And he took the seven loaves, and gave thanks, and brake, and gave to his disciples to set before them, and they did set them before the people. And they had a few small fishes: and he blessed, and commanded to set them also before them. So they did eat, and were filled, and they took up of the broken meat that was left seven baskets. And they that had eaten were about four thousand: and he sent them away. Creed.

Offertory. Ps. 1, 5-7. O hold thou up my goings in thy paths, that my footsteps slip not: incline thine ear unto me, and hearken unto my words: shew thy marvellous loving-kindness, thou that art the Saviour of them which put their trust in thee, O Lord.

Secret.

ASSIST us mercifully, O Lord, in these our supplications, and graciously receive these oblations of thy people: and to the intent that none may ask amiss, or fail in his petition, grant; that those things which we ask faithfully, we may obtain effectually. Through.

Preface of the Most Holy Trinity.

Communion. Ps. 27, 6. I will offer in his dwelling an oblation with great gladness: I will sing, and speak praises unto the Lord.

Postcommunion.

O LORD, who hast fulfilled us with these gifts: we beseech thee; that we may both be cleansed by their operation, and defended by their succour. Through.

The Seventh Sunday after Pentecost
Double.

Introit. Ps. 47, 1. Omnes gentes.

O CLAP your hands together, all ye people: O sing unto God with the voice of melody. Ps. ibid., 2. For the Lord is high, and to be feared: he is the great King upon all the earth. ℣. Glory.

Collect.

O GOD, whose never-failing providence ordereth all things: we humbly beseech thee; to put away from us all hurtful things, and to give us all things which be profitable for us. Through.

The Lesson from the Epistle of blessed Paul the Apostle to the Romans.

Rom. 6, 19-23.

BRETHREN: I speak after the manner of men, because of the infirmity of your flesh: for as ye have yielded your members servants to uncleanness, and to iniquity unto iniquity, even so now yield your members servants to righteousness, unto holiness. For when ye were the servants of sin, ye were free from righteousness. What fruit had ye then in those things whereof ye are now ashamed? For the end of those things is death. But now being made free from sin, and become servants to God, ye have your fruit unto holiness, and the end everlasting life. For the wages of sin is death. But the gift of God is eternal life, in Christ Jesu our Lord.

Gradual. Ps. 34, 12 and 6. Come ye children, and hearken unto me: I will teach you the fear of the Lord. ℣. They had an eye unto him and were enlightened: and their faces were not ashamed.

Alleluia, alleluia. ℣. Ps. 47, 1. O clap your hands together, all ye people: O sing unto God with the voice of melody. Alleluia.

✠ The Continuation of the holy Gospel according to Matthew.

Matt. 7, 15-21.

AT that time: Jesus said unto his disciples: Beware of false prophets, which come to you in sheep's clothing, but inwardly they are ravening wolves: ye shall know them by their fruits. Do men gather grapes of thorns, or figs of thistles? Even so every good tree bringeth forth good fruit: but a corrupt tree bringeth forth evil fruit. A good tree cannot bring forth evil fruit: neither can a corrupt tree bring forth good fruit. Every tree that bringeth not forth good fruit is hewn down, and cast into the fire. Wherefore by their fruits ye shall know them. Not every one that saith unto me, Lord, Lord, shall enter into the kingdom of heaven: but he that doeth the will of my Father who is in heaven, he shall enter into the kingdom of heaven. Creed.

Offertory. Dan. 3, 40. Like as in the burnt offerings of rams and bullocks, and like as in ten thousands of fat lambs: so let our sacrifice be in thy sight this day, that it may please thee: for they shall not be confounded that put their trust in thee, O Lord.

Secret.

O GOD, who by the one perfect sacrifice didst ratify the manifold offerings of the law: accept this sacrifice from thy bounden servants, and sanctify it with that benediction wherewith thou didst bless the gifts of Abel: that what each hath offered to the honour of thy majesty may be profitable unto all for their salvation. Through.

Preface of the Most Holy Trinity.

Communion. Ps. 31, 3. Bow down thine ear, make haste to deliver me.

Postcommunion.

GRANT, O Lord, that the power of thy healing may by thy mercy cleanse us from our perversities, and lead us to those things that be right. Through.

The Eighth Sunday after Pentecost
Double.

Introit. Ps. 48, 8-9. Suscepimus.

WE wait for thy loving-kindness, O God, in the midst of thy temple: O God, according to thy name, so is thy praise unto the world's end: thy right hand is full of righteousness. Ps. ibid., 1. Great is the Lord, and highly to be praised: in the city of our God, even upon his holy hill. ℣. Glory.

Collect.

GRANT to us, Lord, we beseech thee, the spirit to think and do always such things as be rightful: that we, who cannot be without thee, may be enabled to live according to thy will. Through.

The Lesson from the Epistle of blessed Paul the Apostle to the Romans.
Rom. 8, 12-17.

BRETHREN: We are debtors, not to the flesh, to live after the flesh. For if ye live after the flesh, ye shall die: but if ye through the spirit do mortify the deeds of the body, ye shall live. For as many as are led by the Spirit of God, they are the sons of God. For ye have not received the spirit of bondage again to fear, but ye have received the spirit of adoption, whereby we cry: Abba, Father. The Spirit itself beareth witness with our spirit, that we are the children of God. And if children, then heirs: heirs of God, and joint-heirs with Christ.

Gradual. Ps. 31, 3. Be thou my strong rock and house of defence, that thou mayest save me. ℣. In thee, O God, have I put my trust: let me never be put to confusion, O Lord.

Alleluia, alleluia. ℣. Ps. 48, 1. Great is the Lord, and highly to be praised, in the city of our God, even upon his holy hill. Alleluia.

✠ The Continuation of the holy Gospel according to Luke.
Luke 16, 1-9.

AT this time: Jesus spake this parable unto his disciples: There was a certain rich man which had a steward: and the same was accused unto him that he had wasted his goods. And he called him, and said unto him: How is it that I hear this of thee? Give an account of thy stewardship: for thou mayest be no longer steward. Then the steward said within himself: What shall I do, for my lord taketh away from me the stewardship? I cannot dig, to beg I am ashamed. I am resolved what to do, that, when I am put out of the stewardship, they may receive me into their houses. So he called every one of his lord's debtors unto him, and said unto the first: How much owest thou unto my lord? And he said: An hundred measures of oil. And he said unto him: Take thy bill: and sit down quickly, and write fifty. Then said he to another: And how much owest thou? And he said: An hundred measures of wheat. And he said unto him: Take thy bill, and write fourscore. And the lord commended the unjust steward, because he had done wisely: for the children of this world are in their generation wiser than the children of light. And I say unto you: Make to yourselves friends of the mammon of unrighteousness: that when ye fail, they may receive you into everlasting habitations. Creed.

Offertory. Ps. 18, 28 and 32. Thou shalt save the people that are in adversity, O Lord, and shalt bring down the high looks of the proud: for who is God, but thou, O Lord?

Secret.

ACCEPT, O Lord, we beseech thee, the gifts which of thine own bounty we offer unto thee: that, by the mighty working of thy grace, these most holy mysteries may sanctify our conversation in this life present, and bring us to everlasting felicity. Through.

Preface of the Most Holy Trinity.

Communion. Ps. 34, 9. O taste, and see, how gracious the Lord is: blessed is the man that trusteth in him.

Postcommunion.

LET these heavenly mysteries, O Lord, renew us both in body and soul: that we, who therein offer unto thee our outward worship, may inwardly feel the effectual benefit of the same. Through.

The Ninth Sunday after Pentecost
Double.

Introit. Ps. 54, 4-5. Ecce Deus.

BEHOLD, God is my helper: the Lord is with them that uphold my soul: he shall reward evil unto mine enemies: destroy thou them in thy truth. O Lord, my defender. Ps. ibid., 1. Save me O God, for thy name's sake: and avenge me in thy strength. ℣. Glory.

Collect.

LET thy merciful ears, O Lord, be open to the prayers of thy humble servants: and that they may obtain their petitions; make them to ask such things as shall please thee. Through.

The Lesson from the Epistle of blessed Paul the Apostle to the Corinthians.

I Cor. 10, 6-13.

BRETHREN: Let us not lust after evil things, as they also lusted. Neither be ye idolaters, as were some of them: as it is written: The people sat down to eat and drink, and rose up to play. Neither let us commit fornication, as some of them committed, and fell in one day three and twenty thousand. Neither let us tempt Christ, as some of them also tempted, and were destroyed of serpents. Neither murmur ye, as some of them also murmured and were destroyed of the destroyer. Now all these things happened unto them for ensamples: and they are written for our admonition, upon whom the ends of the world are come. Wherefore let him that thinketh he standeth take heed lest he fall. There hath no temptation taken you, but such as is common to man: but God is faithful, who will not suffer you to be tempted above that ye are able, but will with the temptation also make a way of escape, that ye may be able to bear it.

Gradual. Ps. 8, 1. O Lord our governor, how excellent is thy name in all the world! ℣. Thou that hast set thy glory above the heavens.

Alleluia, alleluia. ℣. Ps. 59, 1. Deliver me from mine enemies, O God: defend me from them that rise up against me. Alleluia.

✠ The Continuation of the holy Gospel according to Luke.

Luke 19, 41-47.

AT that time: When Jesus drew near to Jerusalem, he beheld the city, and wept over it, saying: If thou hadst known, even thou, at least in this thy day, the things which belong unto thy peace, but now they are hid from thine eyes. For the days shall come upon thee: that thine enemies shall cast a trench about thee, and compass thee round: and keep thee in on every side: and shall lay thee even with the ground, and thy children within thee, and they shall not leave in thee one stone upon another: because thou knewest not the time of thy visitation. And he went into the temple, and began to cast out them that sold therein, and them that bought, saying unto them: It is written: My house is the house of prayer. But ye have made it a den of thieves. And he taught daily in the temple. Creed.

Offertory. Ps. 19, 9-12. The statutes of the Lord are right, and rejoice the heart, his judgments are sweeter also than honey, and the honey-comb: moreover by them is thy servant taught.

Secret.

GRANT to us, we beseech thee, O Lord, to draw near in worthiness to these thy mysteries: for as oft as the commemoration of this victim is celebrated, the work of our redemption is performed. Through.

Preface of the Most Holy Trinity.

Communion. John 6, 57. He that eateth my flesh and drinketh my blood, dwelleth in me, and I in him, saith the Lord.

Postcommunion.

WE beseech thee, O Lord, that this Sacrament, whereof we have been partakers, may cleanse us from all our sins, and may bestow upon us unity and concord. Through.

The Tenth Sunday after Pentecost
Double.

Introit. Ps. 55, 17, 18, 20 and 23.

Cum clamarem.

WHEN I called upon the Lord, he heard my voice from the battle that was against me: and he hath brought them down, even he that is of old, and endureth for ever: O cast thy burden upon the Lord, and he shall nourish thee. Ps. ibid. Hear my prayer, O Lord, and hide not thyself from my petition: take heed unto me, and hear me. ℣. Glory.

Collect.

O GOD, who declarest thy almighty power most chiefly in shewing mercy and pity: give unto us abundantly thy grace; that we, running toward thy promises, may be made partakers of thy heavenly treasure. Through.

The Lesson from the Epistle of blessed Paul the Apostle to the Corinthians.

I Cor. 12, 2-11.

BRETHREN: Ye know that ye were Gentiles, carried away unto these dumb idols, even as ye were led. Wherefore I give you to understand, that no man speaking by the Spirit of God calleth Jesus accursed. And that no man can say that Jesus is the Lord, but by the Holy Ghost. Now there are diversities of gifts, but the same Spirit. And there are differences of administrations, but the same Lord. And there are diversities of operations, but it is the same God, who worketh all in all. But the manifestation of the Spirit is given to every man to profit withal. For to one is given by the Spirit the word of wisdom: to another the word of knowledge by the same Spirit: to another faith by the same Spirit: to another the gifts of healing by the same Spirit: to another the working of miracles, to another prophecy, to another discerning of spirits, to another divers kinds of tongues, to another the interpretation of tongues. But all these worketh that one and the self-same Spirit, dividing to every man severally as he will.

Gradual. Ps. 17. 8 and 2. Keep me O Lord, as the apple of an eye: hide me under the shadow of thy wings. ℣. Let my sentence come forth from thy presence: and let thine eyes look upon the thing that is equal.

Alleluia, alleluia. Ps. 65, 1. Thou, O God, art praised in Sion: and unto thee shall the vow be performed in Jerusalem. Alleluia.

✠ The Continuation of the holy Gospel according to Luke.

Luke 18, 9-14.

AT that time: Jesus spake this parable unto certain which trusted in themselves that they were righteous, and despised others: Two men went up into the temple to pray: the one a pharisee, and the other a publican. The pharisee stood and prayed thus with himself: God, I thank thee, that I am not as other men are: extortioners, unjust, adulterers: or even as this publican. I fast twice in the week: I give tithes of all that I possess. And the publican, standing afar off, would not lift up so much as his eyes unto heaven: but smote upon his breast, saying: God be merciful to me a sinner. I tell you: this man went down to his house justified rather than the other: for every one that exalteth himself shall be abased: and he that humbleth himself shall be exalted. Creed.

Offertory. Ps. 25, 1-3. Unto thee, O Lord, will I lift up my soul: my God, I have put my trust in thee, O let me not be confounded: neither let mine enemies triumph over me: for all they that hope in thee shall not be ashamed.

Secret.

O LORD, who hast granted unto us to present this sacrifice to the honour of thy name, to the end that it may avail for the healing of our souls: grant that the same may be acceptable in thy sight. Through.

Preface of the Most Holy Trinity.

Communion. Ps. 51, 21. Thou shalt be pleased with the sacrifice of righteousness, with the burnt offerings and oblations, upon thine altar, O Lord.

Postcommunion.

WE beseech thee, O Lord our God: that as thou ceasest not to renew us with thy heavenly Sacraments; so thou wouldest bestow on us thy gracious and ready help. Through.

The Eleventh Sunday after Pentecost

Double.

Introit. Ps. 68, 6-7 and 36.

Deus in loco sancto.

GOD in his holy habitation: he is the God that maketh men to be of one mind in an house: he will give strength and power unto his people. Ps. ibid., 1. Let God arise, and let his enemies be scattered: let them also that hate him flee before him. ℣. Glory.

Collect.

ALMIGHTY and everlasting God, who in the abundance of thy loving-kindness art wont to give more than we thy humble servants either desire or deserve: pour down upon us thy mercy; forgiving us those things whereof our conscience is afraid, and giving unto us that which our prayer dare not presume to ask. Through.

The Lesson from the Epistle of blessed Paul the Apostle to the Corinthians.

I Cor. 15, 1-10.

BRETHREN: I declare unto you the Gospel which I preached unto you, which also ye have received, and wherein ye stand, by which also ye are saved: if ye keep in memory what I preached unto

The Eleventh Sunday after Pentecost

you, unless ye have believed in vain. For I delivered unto you first of all, that which I also received: how that Christ died for our sins, according to the Scriptures: and that he was buried, and that he rose again the third day, according to the Scriptures: and that he was seen of Cephas, then of the twelve. After that, he was seen of about five hundred brethren at once, of whom the greater part remain unto this present, but some are fallen asleep. After that, he was seen of James, then of all the Apostles: and last of all, he was seen of me also, as of one born out of due time. For I am the least of the Apostles that am not meet to be called an Apostle, because I persecuted the Church of God. But by the grace of God I am what I am, and his grace which was bestowed upon me was not in vain.

Gradual. Ps. 28, 7 and 1. My heart hath trusted in God, and I am helped: therefore my heart danceth for joy and in my song will I praise him. ℣. Unto thee will I cry, O Lord: be not silent, O my God, nor depart from me.

Alleluia, alleluia. ℣. Ps. 81, 1-2. Sing we merrily unto God our strength, make a cheerful noise unto the God of Jacob: take the merry psalm with the lute. Alleluia.

✠ The Continuation of the holy Gospel according to Mark.

Mark 7, 31-37.

AT that time: Jesus, departing from the coasts of Tyre and Sidon, came unto the sea of Galilee, through the midst of the coasts of Decapolis. And they bring unto him one that was deaf, and had an impediment in his speech, and they beseech him to put his hand upon him. And he took him aside from the multitude, and put his fingers into his ears, and he spit, and touched his tongue: and looking up to heaven, he sighed, and saith unto him: Ephphatha, that is, Be opened. And straightway his ears were opened, and the string of his tongue was loosed, and he spake plain. And he charged them that they should tell no man. But the more he charged them, so much the more a great deal they published it: and were beyond measure astonished, saying: He hath done all things well: he maketh both the deaf to hear and the dumb to speak. Creed.

Offertory. Ps. 30, 1-2. I will magnify thee, O Lord, for thou hast set me up, and not made my foes to triumph over me: O Lord, I cried unto thee, and thou hast healed me.

Secret.

LOOK favourably, O Lord, we beseech thee, on this our bounden duty and service: that this sacrifice which we offer may be an oblation acceptable to thee, and avail for the succour of our frailty. Through.

Preface of the Most Holy Trinity.

Communion. Prov. 3, 9-10. Honour the Lord with thy substance, and with the firstfruits of all thine increase: so shall thy barns be filled with plenty, and thy presses shall burst out with new wine.

Postcommunion.

WE beseech thee, O Lord, that we who have received this holy Sacrament may in such wise feel the effectual succour of the same: that being preserved both in body and soul, we may glory in the fulness of thy heavenly healing. Through.

The Twelfth Sunday after Pentecost
Double.

Introit. Ps. 70, 1-2. Deus in adjutorium.

HASTE thee, O God, to deliver me, make haste to help me, O Lord, let mine enemies be ashamed and confounded that seek after my soul. Ps. ibid., 3. Let them be turned backward and put to confusion: that wish me evil. ℣. Glory.

Collect.

ALMIGHTY and merciful God, of whose gift it cometh that thy faithful people do unto thee worthy and laudable service: grant, we beseech thee; that we may run without stumbling to thy heavenly promises. Through.

The Lesson from the Epistle of blessed Paul the Apostle to the Corinthians.

II Cor. 3, 4-9.

BRETHREN: Such trust have we through Christ to Godward: not that we are sufficient of ourselves to think anything of ourselves: but our sufficiency is of God: who also hath made us able ministers of the New Testament: not of the letter, but of the Spirit: for the letter killeth, but the Spirit giveth life. But if the ministration of death written and engraven in stones was glorious; so that the children of Israel could not stedfastly behold the face of Moses for the glory of his countenance, which glory was to be done away: how shall not the ministration of the Spirit be rather glorious? For if the ministration of condemnation be glory: much more doth the ministration of righteousness exceed in glory.

Gradual. Ps. 34, 1-2. I will alway give thanks unto the Lord: his praise shall ever be in my mouth. ℣. My soul shall make her boast in the Lord: the humble shall hear thereof, and be glad.

Alleluia, alleluia. ℣. Ps. 88, 1. O Lord God of my salvation, I have cried day and night before thee. Alleluia.

✠ The Continuation of the holy Gospel according to Luke.

Luke 10, 23-37.

AT that time: Jesus said unto his disciples: Blessed are the eyes which see the things that ye see. For I tell you, That many prophets and kings have desired to see those things which ye see, and have not seen them: and to hear those things which ye hear, and have not heard them. And behold, a certain lawyer stood up, and tempted him, saying: Master, what shall I do to inherit eternal life? He said unto him: What is written in the Law? how readest thou? And he answering said: Thou shalt love the Lord thy God with all thy heart, and with all thy soul, and with all thy strength, and with all thy mind: and thy neighbour as thyself. And he said unto him: Thou hast answered right: this do, and thou shalt live. But he, willing to justify himself said unto Jesus: And who is my neighbour? And Jesus answering said: A certain man went down from Jerusalem to Jericho, and fell among thieves, which stripped him of his raiment: and wounded him, and departed leaving him half dead. And by chance there came down a certain Priest that way, and when he saw him, he passed by on the other side. And likewise a Levite, when he was at the place, came and looked on him, and passed by on the other side. But a certain Samaritan, as he journeyed, came where he was: and, when he saw him, he had compassion on him. And went to him, and bound up his wounds, pouring in oil and wine, and set him on his own beast, and brought him to an inn, and took care of him. And on the morrow, when he departed, he took out two pence, and gave them to the host, and said unto him: Take care of him: and whatsoever thou spendest more, when I come again, I will repay thee. Which now of these three, thinkest thou, was neighbour unto him that fell among the thieves? And he said: He that shewed mercy on him. Then said Jesus unto him: Go, and do thou likewise. Creed.

Offertory. Exod. 32, 11, 13-14. Moses besought the Lord his God, and said: Why, O Lord, doth thy wrath wax hot against thy people? Turn from thy fierce wrath: remember Abraham, Isaac, and Jacob, to whom thou swarest to give a land flowing with milk and honey. And the Lord repented of the evil which he thought to do unto his people.

Secret.

WE beseech thee, O Lord, mercifully look upon these sacrifices, which we present on thy holy altars: that they may bestow on us thy pardon to the honour and glory of thy name. Through.

Preface of the Most Holy Trinity.

Communion. Ps. 104, 13-15. The earth, O Lord, is filled with the fruit of thy works: that thou mayest bring food out of the earth, and wine that maketh glad the heart of man: and oil to make him a cheerful countenance, and bread to strengthen man's heart.

Postcommunion.

QUICKEN us, O Lord, we pray thee, who have duly received these holy mysteries: that we may be cleansed thereby from all our sins, and defended against all adversities. Through.

The Thirteenth Sunday after Pentecost
Double.

Introit. Ps. 74, 20, 19 and 23.

Respice, Domine.

LOOK, O Lord, upon thy covenant, and forsake not the congregation of the poor for ever: arise, O Lord, maintain thine own cause, and forget not the voices of them that seek thee. Ps. ibid., 1. O God, wherefore art thou absent from us so long: why is thy wrath so hot against the sheep of thy pasture? ℣. Glory.

Collect.

ALMIGHTY and everlasting God, give unto us the increase of faith, hope, and charity: and, that we may be worthy to obtain that which thou dost promise, make us to love that which thou dost command. Through.

The Lesson from the Epistle of blessed Paul the Apostle to the Galatians.

Gal. 3, 16-22.

BRETHREN: To Abraham and his seed were the promises made. He saith not: And to seeds, as of many; but as of one: And to thy seed, which is Christ. And this I say: That the covenant that was confirmed before of God in Christ, the Law, which was four hundred and thirty years after, cannot disannul, that it should make the promise of none effect. For if the inheritance be of the Law, it is no more of promise. But God gave it to Abraham by promise. Wherefore then serveth the Law? It was added because of transgressions, till the seed should come, to whom the promise was made, and it was ordained by Angels in the hand of a mediator. Now a mediator is not a mediator of one: but God is one. Is the Law then against the promises of God? God forbid. For if there had been a law given which could have given life, verily righteousness should have been by the Law. But the Scripture hath concluded all under sin, that the promise by faith of Jesus Christ might be given to them that believe.

Gradual. Ps. 74, 20, 19 and 22. Look upon thy covenant, O Lord, and forget not the congregation of the poor for ever. ℣. Arise, O Lord, maintain thine own cause: remember the rebuke that thy servants have.

Alleluia, alleluia. ℣. Ps. 90, 1. Lord, thou hast been our refuge: from one generation to another. Alleluia.

✠ The Continuation of the holy Gospel according to Luke.

Luke 17, 11-19.

AT that time: As Jesus went to Jerusalem, he passed through the midst of Samaria and Galilee. And as he entered into a certain village, there met him ten men who were lepers, which stood afar off; and they lifted up their voices and said: Jesus, Master, have mercy on us. And when he saw them, he said unto them: Go, shew yourselves unto the priests. And it came to pass, that, as they went, they were cleansed. And one of them, when he saw that he was healed, turned back, and with a loud voice glorified God, and fell down on his face at his feet, giving him thanks: and he was a Samaritan. And Jesus answering said: Were there not ten cleansed? but where are the nine? There are not found that returned to give glory to God, save this stranger. And he said unto him: Arise, go thy way; thy faith hath made thee whole. Creed.

Offertory. Ps. 31, 15-16. My hope hath been in thee, O Lord; I have said: Thou art my God, my time is in thy hand.

Secret.

LOOK mercifully, O Lord, upon thy people, look mercifully upon their oblations: that we, being rendered thereby acceptable in thy sight, may obtain of thee remission of all our sins, and the effectual fulfilment of our desires. Through.

Preface of the Most Holy Trinity.

Communion. Wisd. 16, 20. Thou hast given us bread from heaven, O Lord, having every delight, and every taste of sweetness.

Postcommunion.

WE beseech thee, O Lord, that we who have here received thy heavenly sacraments: may thereby grow in grace toward the attainment of eternal redemption. Through.

The Fourteenth Sunday after Pentecost
Double.

Introit. Ps. 84, 10-11. Protector noster.

BEHOLD, O God, our defender, and look upon the face of thine Anointed: for one day in thy courts is better than a thousand. Ps. ibid., 1-2. O how amiable are thy dwellings, thou Lord of hosts! my soul hath a desire and longing to enter into the courts of the Lord. ℣. Glory.

Collect.

KEEP, we beseech thee, O Lord, thy Church with thy perpetual mercy: and, because the frailty of man without thee cannot but fall; keep it ever by thy help from all things hurtful, and lead it to all things profitable to salvation. Through.

The Fourteenth Sunday after Pentecost

The Lesson from the Epistle of blessed Paul the Apostle to the Galatians.

Gal. 5, 16-24.

BRETHREN: Walk in the Spirit, and ye shall not fulfil the lust of the flesh. For the flesh lusteth against the spirit, and the spirit against the flesh: and these are contrary the one to the other, so that ye cannot do the things that ye would. But if ye be led by the spirit ye are not under the law. Now the works of the flesh are manifest, which are these, adultery, fornication, uncleanness, lasciviousness, idolatry, witchcraft, hatred, variance, emulations, wrath, strife, seditions, heresies, envyings, murders, drunkenness, revellings, and such like: of the which I tell you before, as I have also told you in time past: that they who do such things shall not inherit the kingdom of God. But the fruit of the Spirit is: love, joy, peace, longsuffering, gentleness, faith, meekness, temperance. Against such there is no law. And they that are Christ's have crucified the flesh, with the affections and lusts.

Gradual. Ps. 118, 8-9. It is better to trust in the Lord, than to put any confidence in man. ℣. It is better to trust in the Lord, than to put any confidence in princes.

Alleluia, alleluia. ℣. Ps. 95, 1. O come let us sing unto the Lord: let us heartily rejoice in the strength of our salvation. Alleluia.

✠ The Continuation of the holy Gospel according to Matthew.

Matt. 6, 24-33.

AT that time: Jesus said unto his disciples: No man can serve two masters: for either he will hate the one, and love the other: or else he will hold to the one, and despise the other. Ye cannot serve God and mammon. Therefore I say unto you, Take no thought for your life, what ye shall eat, or what ye shall drink, nor yet for your body, what ye shall put on. Is not the life more than meat: and the body than raiment? Behold the fowls of the air, for they sow not, neither do they reap, not gather into barns: yet your heavenly Father feedeth them. Are ye not much better than they? Which of you by taking thought can add one cubit unto his stature? And why take ye thought for raiment? Consider the lilies of the field how they grow: they toil neither do they spin. And yet I say unto you, That even Solomon in all his glory was not arrayed like one of these. Wherefore, if God so clothe the grass of the field, which to-day is, and tomorrow is cast into the oven: shall he not much more clothe you, O ye of little faith? Therefore take no thought, saying: What shall we eat, or what shall we drink, or wherewithal we shall be clothed? For after all these things do the Gentiles seek. For your heavenly Father knoweth that ye have need of all these things. But seek ye first the kingdom of God, and his righteousness: and all these things shall be added unto you. Creed.

Offertory. Ps. 34, 8-9. The Angel of the Lord tarrieth round about them that fear him, and delivereth them: O taste, and see, how gracious the Lord is.

Secret.

GRANT to us, Lord, we beseech thee, that this saving victim may avail both for the cleansing of our offences, and for the obtaining of the favour of thine almighty power. Through.

Preface of the Most Holy Trinity.

Communion. Matt. 6, 33. Seek ye first the kingdom of God, and all things shall be added unto you, saith the Lord.

Postcommunion.

LET thy holy Sacrament, O God, evermore cleanse and defend us: that we may be brought thereby to the attainment of everlasting salvation. Through.

The Fifteenth Sunday after Pentecost
Double.

Introit. Ps. 86, 1-3. Inclina, Domine.

BOW down thine ear, O Lord, and hear me: my God, save thy servant, that putteth his trust in thee: be merciful unto me, O Lord, for I will call daily upon thee. Ps. ibid., 4. Comfort the soul of thy servant: for unto thee, O Lord, do I lift up my soul. ℣. Glory.

Collect.

O LORD, let thy continual pity cleanse and defend thy Church: and because without thee it cannot continue in safety; preserve it evermore by thy help and goodness. Through.

The Lesson from the Epistle of blessed Paul the Apostle to the Galatians.

Gal. 5, 25-26; 6, 1-10.

BRETHREN: If we live in the Spirit, let us also walk in the Spirit. Let us not be desirous of vain glory, provoking one another, envying one another. Brethren, if a man be overtaken in a fault, ye, which are spiritual, restore such an one in the spirit of meekness, considering thyself, lest thou also be tempted. Bear ye one another's burdens, and so fulfil the law of Christ. For if a man think himself to be something, when he is nothing, he deceiveth himself. But let every man prove his own work, and then shall he have rejoicing in himself alone, and not in another. For every man shall bear his own burden. Let him that is taught in the word communicate unto him that teacheth in all good things. Be not deceived: God is not mocked. For whatsoever a man soweth, that shall he also reap. For he that soweth to his flesh shall of the flesh reap corruption: but he that soweth to the Spirit shall of the Spirit reap life everlasting. And let us not be weary in well doing: for in due season we shall reap, if we faint not. As we have therefore opportunity, let us do good unto all men, especially unto them who are of the household of faith.

Gradual. Ps. 92, 1-2. It is a good thing to give thanks unto the Lord: and to sing praises unto thy name, O Most Highest. ℣. To tell of thy loving-kindness early in the morning, and of thy truth in the night-season.

Alleluia, alleluia. ℣. Ps. 95, 2. For the Lord is a great God, and a great King above all the earth. Alleluia.

✠ The Continuation of the holy Gospel according to Luke.

Luke 7, 11-16.

AT that time: Jesus went into a city called Nain: and many of his disciples went with him, and much people. Now when he came nigh to the gate of the city, behold, there was a dead man carried out, the only son of his mother: and she was a widow: and much people of the city was with her. And when the Lord saw her, he had compassion on her, and said unto her: Weep not. And he came and touched the bier. And they that bare him stood still. And he said: Young man, I say unto thee, Arise. And he that was dead sat up, and began to speak. And he delivered him to his mother. And there came a fear on all: and they glorified God, saying: That a great Prophet is risen up among us: and that God hath visited his people. Creed.

Offertory. Ps. 40, 1-3. I waited patiently for the Lord, and he inclined unto me: he heard my calling: and hath put a new song in my mouth, even a thanksgiving unto our God.

Secret.

GRANT, O Lord, that by the protection of these thy sacraments we may ever be defended against the assaults of the devil. Through.

Preface of the Most Holy Trinity.

Communion. John 6, 52. The bread that I will give is my flesh, which I will give for the life of the world.

Postcommunion

O LORD, we beseech thee, let the operation of thy heavenly bounty in such wise possess our souls and bodies: that not our own desires, but the effectual working of thy grace may ever prevail within us. Through.

The Sixteenth Sunday after Pentecost

Double

Introit. Ps. 86, 3 and 5. Miserere mihi.

BE merciful unto me, O Lord, for I will call daily upon thee: for thou, Lord, art good and gracious, and of great mercy unto all them that call upon thee. Ps. ibid., 1. Bow down thine ear, O Lord, and hear me: for I am poor and in misery. ℣. Glory.

Collect.

LORD, we pray thee that thy grace may always prevent and follow us: and make us continually to be given to good works. Through.

The Lesson from the Epistle of blessed Paul the Apostle to the Ephesians.

Eph. 3, 13-21.

BRETHREN: I desire that ye faint not at my tribulations for you: which is your glory. For this cause I bow my knees unto the Father of our Lord Jesus Christ, of whom the whole family in heaven and earth is named, that he would grant you, according to the riches of his glory, to be strengthened with might by his Spirit in the inner man, that Christ may dwell in your hearts by faith: that ye, being rooted and grounded in love, may be able to comprehend with all saints, what is the breadth, and length, and depth, and height: and to know the love of Christ, which passeth knowledge, that ye might be filled with all the fulness of God. Now unto him that is able to do exceeding abundantly above all that we ask or think, according to the power that worketh in us: unto him be glory in the Church by Christ Jesus, throughout all ages, world without end. Amen.

Gradual. Ps. 102, 16-17. The heathen shall fear thy name, O Lord, and all the kings of the earth thy majesty. ℣. When the Lord shall build up Sion, and when his glory shall appear.

Alleluia, alleluia. ℣. Ps. 98, 1. O sing unto the Lord a new song: for the Lord hath done marvellous things. Alleluia.

✠ The Continuation of the holy Gospel according to Luke.

Luke 14, 1-11.

AT that time: When Jesus went into the house of one of the chief Pharisees to eat bread on the sabbath-day, they watched him. And behold there was a certain man before him which had the dropsy. And Jesus answering spake unto the lawyers and Pharisees, saying: Is it lawful to heal on the sabbath-day? And they held their peace. And he took him, and healed him, and let him go. And answered them, saying: Which of you shall have an ass, or an ox, fallen into a pit, and will not straightway pull him out on the sabbath-day? And they could not answer him again to those things. And he put forth a parable to those which were bidden, when he marked how they chose out the chief rooms, saying unto them:

The Seventeenth Sunday after Pentecost

Double

Introit: Ps. 119, 137 and 124.

Justus es, Domine.

RIGHTEOUS art thou O Lord, and true is thy judgment: O deal with thy servant according unto thy loving mercy. Ps. ibid., 1. Blessed are those that are undefiled in the way: and walk in the law of the Lord. ℣. Glory.

Collect.

LORD, we beseech thee, grant thy people grace to avoid the infections of the devil: and with pure heart and mind to follow thee, the only God. Through.

The Lesson from the Epistle of blessed Paul the Apostle to the Ephesians.

Eph. 4, 1-6.

BRETHREN: I, the prisoner of the Lord, beseech you, that ye walk worthy of the vocation wherewith ye are called, with all lowliness and meekness, with long-suffering, forbearing one another in love, endeavouring to keep the unity of the spirit in the bond of peace. There is one body, and one Spirit, even as ye are called in one hope of your calling. One Lord, one faith, one baptism. One God, and Father of all, who is above all, and through all, and in you all. Who is blessed for ever and ever. Amen.

Gradual. Ps. 33, 12 and 6. Blessed are the people whose God is the Lord: and blessed are the folk that he hath chosen to him to be his inheritance. ℣. By the word of the Lord were the heavens made: and all the hosts of them by the breath of his mouth.

Alleluia, alleluia. ℣. Ps. 102, 1. Hear my prayer, O Lord, and let my cry come unto thee. Alleluia.

When thou art bidden of any man to a wedding, sit not down in the highest room, lest a more honourable man than thou be bidden of him, and he that bade thee and him come and say to thee: Give this man place: and thou begin with shame to take the lowest room. But when thou art bidden, go and sit down in the lowest room: that, when he that bade thee cometh, he may say unto thee: Friend, go up higher. Then shalt thou have worship in the presence of them that sit at meat with thee: for whosoever exalteth himself shall be abased: and he that humbleth himself shall be exalted. Creed.

Offertory. Ps. 40, 14-15. Look down, O Lord, to help me: let them be ashamed, and confounded that seek after my soul to destroy it: look down, O Lord to help me.

Secret.

CLEANSE us, O Lord, we pray thee, by the effectual working of this our sacrifice: and so accomplish in us the work of thy mercy; that we may be found worthy to be made partakers of the same. Through.

Preface of the Most Holy Trinity.

Communion. Ps. 71, 16-18. O Lord, I will make mention of thy righteousness only: thou, O God, hast taught me from my youth up until now: forsake me not, O God, in mine old age, when I am grayheaded.

Postcommunion

WE beseech thee, O Lord, mercifully to cleanse and renew our souls with thy heavenly mysteries: that we may thereby both now and ever be defended from all bodily temptations. Through.

✠ The Continuation of the holy Gospel according to Matthew.

Matt. 22, 34-46.

AT that time: The Pharisees came unto Jesus: and one of them, who was a lawyer, asked him a question, tempting him, and saying: Master, which is the great commandment in the Law? Jesus said unto him: Thou shalt love the Lord thy God with all thy heart, and with all thy soul, and with all thy mind. This is the first and great commandment. And the second is like unto it: Thou shalt love thy neighbour as thyself. On these two commandments hang all the law and the prophets. While the Pharisees were gathered together, Jesus asked them, saying: What think ye of Christ? whose son is he? They say unto him: The son of David. He saith unto them: How then doth David in spirit call him Lord, saying: The Lord said unto my Lord, sit thou on my right hand, till I make thine enemies thy footstool? If David then call him Lord, how is he his son? And no man was able to answer him a word: neither durst any man from that day forth ask him any more questions. Creed.

Offertory. Dan. 9, 17-19. I, Daniel, prayed unto my God, and said: Hear, O Lord, the prayers of thy servant: cause thy face to shine upon thy sanctuary: and behold, O God, this thy people, who are called by thy name.

Secret.

WE humbly beseech thy majesty, O Lord: that these holy mysteries which we here perform may cleanse us from our former sins, and defend us against all temptation. Through.

Preface of the Most Holy Trinity.

Communion. Ps. 76, 12-13. Promise unto the Lord your God, and keep it, all ye that are round about him, bring presents unto him that ought to be feared: he shall refrain the spirit of princes: and is wonderful among all the kings of the earth.

Postcommunion

ALMIGHTY God, let thy sanctifying power cleanse us from all our sins, and avail for the healing of our souls unto life eternal. Through.

The Ember Days

Mass as on on p. 489, et seq.

The Eighteenth Sunday after Pentecost

Double

Introit. Eccli. 36, 18. Da pacem.

GIVE peace, O Lord, to them that wait for thee, and let thy prophets be found faithful: hear the prayers of thy servant, and of thy people Israel. Ps. 122, 1. I was glad when they said unto me: We will go into the house of the Lord. ℣. Glory.

Collect.

O LORD, forasmuch as without thee we are not able to please thee: let the operation of thy mercy, we pray thee, in all things direct and rule our hearts. Through.

The Lesson from the Epistle of blessed Paul the Apostle to the Corinthians.

I Cor. 1, 4-8.

BRETHREN: I thank my God always on your behalf, for the grace of God which is given you by Jesus Christ: that in every thing ye are enriched by him, in all utterance, and in all knowledge: even as the testimony of Christ was confirmed in you: so that ye come behind in no gift, waiting for the coming of our Lord Jesus Christ, who shall also confirm you unto the end, that ye may be blameless in the day of the coming of our Lord Jesus Christ.

Gradual. Ps. 122, 1 and 7. I was glad when they said unto me: We will go into the house of the Lord. ℣. Peace be within thy walls: and plenteousness within thy palaces.

Alleluia, alleluia. ℣. Ps. 102, 16. The nations shall fear thy name, O Lord, and all the kings of the earth thy majesty. Alleluia.

✠ The Continuation of the holy Gospel according to Matthew.

Matt. 9, 1-8.

AT that time: Jesus entered into a ship, and passed over, and came into his own city. And behold, they brought to him a man sick of the palsy lying on a bed. And Jesus, seeing their faith, said unto the sick of the palsy: Son, be of good cheer, thy sins be forgiven thee. And behold, certain of the scribes said within themselves: This man blasphemeth. And Jesus, knowing their thoughts, said: Wherefore think ye evil in your hearts? For whether is easier to say: Thy sins be forgiven thee, or to say: Arise, and walk? But that ye may know that the Son of man hath power on earth to forgive sins, then saith he to the sick of the palsy: Arise, take up thy bed and go unto thine house. And he arose, and departed to his house. But when the multitude saw it, they marvelled, and glorified God, who had given such power unto men. Creed.

Offertory. Exod. 24, 4-5. Moses consecrated an altar unto the Lord, offering burnt offerings upon it, and sacrificing peace offerings: and he made an evening sacrifice for a sweet-smelling savour unto the Lord God, in the sight of the children of Israel.

Secret.

O GOD, who through communion in this wondrous sacrifice hast made us partakers of thy glorious Godhead: grant, we beseech thee, that as we have the knowledge of thy truth, so in all our conversation we may walk worthy of the same. Through.

Preface of the Most Holy Trinity.

Communion. Ps. 96, 8-9. Bring offerings and come into his courts: O worship the Lord in the beauty of holiness.

Postcommunion

WE render thanks unto thee, O Lord, for that thou hast quickened us with thy heavenly gifts: humbly beseeching thy mercy; that thou wouldest make us worthy partakers of the same. Through.

The Nineteenth Sunday after Pentecost

Double

Introit. Salus populi.

I AM the salvation of the people, saith the Lord: out of whatsoever tribulation they shall cry to me, I will hear them: and I will be their Lord for ever. Ps. 78, 1. Hear my law, O my people: incline your ears unto the words of my mouth. ℣. Glory.

Collect.

ALMIGHTY and merciful God, of thy bountiful goodness keep us from all things that may hurt us: that we, being ready both in body and soul, may with free hearts accomplish those things that thou wouldest have done. Through.

The Nineteenth Sunday after Pentecost

The Lesson from the Epistle of blessed Paul the Apostle to the Ephesians.

Eph. 4, 23-28.

BRETHREN: Be ye renewed in the spirit of your mind, and put on the new man, which after God is created in righteousness and true holiness. Wherefore, putting away lying, speak every man truth with his neighbour: for we are members one of another. Be ye angry and sin not: let not the sun go down upon your wrath. Neither give place to the devil: let him that stole steal no more; but rather let him labour, working with his hands the thing which is good, that he may have to give to him that needeth.

Gradual. Ps. 141, 2. Let my prayer be set forth in thy sight, O Lord, as the incense. ℣. Let the lifting up of my hands be an evening sacrifice.

Alleluia, alleluia. ℣. Ps. 105, 1. O give thanks unto the Lord, and call upon his name: tell the people what things he hath done. Alleluia.

✠ The Continuation of the holy Gospel according to Matthew.

Matt. 22, 1-14.

AT that time: Jesus spake unto the chief priests and Pharisees in parables, saying: The kingdom of heaven is like unto a certain king, who made a marriage for his son. And sent forth his servants to call them that were bidden to the wedding, and they would not come. Again, he sent forth other servants, saying: Tell them which are bidden: Behold, I have prepared my dinner, my oxen and my fatlings are killed and all things are ready: come unto the marriage. But they made light of it, and went their ways, one to his farm, another to his merchandise: and the remnant took his servants, and entreated them spitefully, and slew them. But when the king heard thereof, he was wroth: and he sent forth his armies, and destroyed those murderers, and burnt up their city. Then saith he to his servants: The wedding is ready, but they who were bidden were not worthy. Go ye therefore into the highways, and as many as ye shall find bid to the marriage. So those servants went out into the highways, and gathered together all, as many as they found, both bad and good: and the wedding was furnished with guests. And when the king came in to see the guests, he saw there a man which had not on a wedding-garment. And he saith unto him: Friend, how camest thou in hither, not having a wedding-garment? And he was speechless. Then said the king to the servants: Bind him hand and foot, and take him away, and cast him into outer darkness: there shall be weeping and gnashing of teeth. For many are called, but few are chosen. Creed.

Offertory. Ps. 138, 7. Though I walk in the midst of trouble, yet shalt thou refresh me, O Lord: thou shalt stretch forth thy hand upon the furiousness of mine enemies, and thy right hand shall save me.

Secret.

GRANT, we beseech thee, O Lord, that these gifts, which we offer in the sight of thy majesty, may avail for our salvation. Through.

Preface of the Most Holy Trinity.

Communion. Ps. 119, 4-5. Thou hast charged that we shall diligently keep thy commandments: O that my ways were made so direct, that I might keep thy statutes.

Postcommunion.

GRANT, O Lord, that the power of thy healing may in thy mercy cleanse us from our perversities, and make us ever to cleave stedfastly to thy commandments. Through.

The Twentieth Sunday after Pentecost
Double.

Introit. Dan. 3, 31, 29 and 35.

Omnia quæ fecisti.

ALL things that thou hast done to us, O Lord, thou hast done in true judgment, for we have sinned and have not obeyed thy commandments: but give glory to thy name, and deal with us according to the multitude of thy mercies. Ps. 119. Blessed are those that are undefiled in the way: and walk in the law of the Lord. V. Glory.

Collect.

GRANT, we beseech thee, merciful Lord, to thy faithful people pardon and peace: that they may be cleansed from all their sins and serve thee with a quiet mind. Through.

The Lesson from the Epistle of blessed Paul the Apostle to the Ephesians.

Eph. 5, 15-21.

BRETHREN: See that ye walk circumspectly: not as fools, but as wise, redeeming the time, because the days are evil. Wherefore be ye not unwise, but understanding what the will of the Lord is. And be not drunk with wine, wherein is excess: but be filled with the Spirit, speaking to yourselves in psalms, and hymns, and spiritual songs, singing and making melody in your heart to the Lord: giving thanks always for all things unto God and the Father, in the name of our Lord Jesus Christ. Submitting yourselves one to another in the fear of Christ.

Gradual. Ps. 145, 15-16. The eyes of all wait upon thee, O Lord: and thou givest them their meat in due season. V. Thou openest thine hand: and fillest all things living with plenteousness.

Alleluia, alleluia. V. Ps. 108, 1. O God, my heart is ready, my heart is ready: I will sing and give praise unto thee. Alleluia.

✠ The Continuation of the holy Gospel according to John.

John 4, 46-53.

AT that time: There was a certain nobleman, whose son was sick at Capernaum. When he heard that Jesus was come out of Judæa into Galilee, he went unto him, and besought him that he would come down and heal his son: for he was at the point of death. Then said Jesus unto him: Except ye see signs and wonders, ye will not believe. The nobleman saith unto him: Sir, come down ere my child die. Jesus saith unto him: Go thy way, thy son liveth. And the man believed the word that Jesus had spoken unto him, and he went his way. And, as he was now going down, his servants met him, and told him, saying: Thy son liveth. Then enquired he of them the hour when he began to mend. And they said unto him: Yesterday at the seventh hour the fever left him. So the father knew that it was at the same hour, in the which Jesus said unto him: Thy son liveth: and himself believed and his whole house. Creed.

Offertory. Ps. 137, 1. By the waters of Babylon we sat down and wept: when we remembered thee, O Sion.

Secret.

WE beseech thee, O Lord, that these mysteries may bestow upon us thy heavenly healing: and purge away the iniquities of our hearts. Through.

Preface of the Most Holy Trinity.

Communion. Ps. 119, 49-50. O think upon thy servant, O Lord, as concerning thy word, wherein thou hast caused me to put my trust: the same is my comfort in my affliction.

Postcommunion.

WE beseech thee, O Lord, make us ever to obey thy commandments: that we may be rendered worthy of thy holy gifts. Through.

The Twenty-first Sunday after Pentecost

Double.

Introit. Es. 13, 9-11. In voluntate tua.

O LORD, everything is in subjection to thy will, and there is no man that is able to resist thy power: for thou hast created everything, heaven and earth, and all the wonders which under heaven's vault are contained: thou art Lord of all things. Ps. 119, 1. Blessed are those that are undefiled in the way: and walk in the law of the Lord. ℣. Glory.

Collect.

LORD, we beseech thee to keep this thy family in continual godliness: that through thy protection it may be free from all adversities; and devoutly given to serve thee in good works to the glory of thy name. Through.

The Lesson from the Epistle of blessed Paul the Apostle to the Ephesians.

Eph. 6, 10-17.

BRETHREN: Be strong in the Lord, and in the power of his might. Put on the whole armour of God, that ye may be able to stand against the wiles of the devil. For we wrestle not against flesh and blood: but against principalities, against powers, against the rulers of the darkness of this world, against spiritual wickedness in high places. Wherefore take unto you the whole armour of God, that ye may be able to withstand in the evil day, and having done all, to stand. Stand therefore, having your loins girt about with truth, and having on the breastplate of righteousness, and your feet shod with the preparation of the Gospel of peace: above all, taking the shield of faith, wherewith ye shall be able to quench all the fiery darts of the wicked: and take the helmet of salvation: and the sword of the Spirit, which is the word of God.

Gradual. Ps. 90, 1-2. Lord, thou hast been our refuge, from one generation to another. ℣. Before the mountains were brought forth, or ever the earth and the world were made: thou art God from everlasting, and world without end.

Alleluia, alleluia. ℣. Ps. 114, 1. When Israel came out of Egypt, and the house of Jacob from among the strange people. Alleluia.

✠ The Continuation of the holy Gospel according to Matthew.

Matt. 18, 23-35.

AT that time: Jesus spake unto his disciples this parable: The kingdom of heaven is likened unto a certain king, which would take account of his servants. And when he had begun to reckon, one was brought unto him, which owed him ten thousand talents. But forasmuch as he had not to pay, his lord commanded him to be sold, and his wife and children, and all that he had, and payment to be made. The servant therefore fell down and worshipped him, saying: Lord have patience with me, and I will pay thee all. Then the lord of that servant was moved with compassion, and loosed him, and forgave him the debt. But the same servant went out, and found one of his fellow-servants which owed him an hundred pence: and he laid hands on him, and took him by the throat, saying: Pay me that thou owest. And his fellow-servant fell down at his feet, and besought him, saying: Have patience with me, and I will pay thee all. And he would not: but went and cast him into prison, till he should pay the debt. So when his fellow-servants saw what was done, they were very sorry: and came and told unto their lord all that was done. Then his lord, after that he had called him, said unto him: O thou wicked servant, I forgave thee all that debt, because thou desirest me, shouldest not thou also have had compassion on thy fellow-servant, even as I had pity on thee? And his lord was wroth, and delivered him to the tormentors, till he should pay all that was due unto him. So likewise shall my heavenly Father do also unto you, if ye from your hearts forgive not every one his brother their trespasses.   Creed.

Offertory. Job 1. There was a man in the land of Uz, whose name was Job: perfect and upright, and one that feared God: and Satan sought to tempt him: and power was given him by the Lord over his possessions and over his flesh: and he destroyed all his substance and his sons: and he smote his flesh with sore boils.

Secret.

MERCIFULLY receive, O Lord, this our sacrifice: whereby thou hast willed that atonement should be made unto thee, and that salvation should be restored to us by the power of thy lovingkindness. Through.

Preface of the Most Holy Trinity.

Communion. Ps. 119, 81, 84 and 86. My soul hath longed for thy salvation and I have a good hope because of thy word: when wilt thou be avenged of them that persecute me? they persecuted me falsely, be thou my help, O Lord my God.

Postcommunion.

O LORD, who hast bestowed on us the food of everlasting life: we beseech thee; that those things which we have received with our outward lips, we may ever inwardly seek in purity of heart. Through.

The Twenty-second Sunday after Pentecost

Double.

Introit. Ps. 130, 3-4. Si iniquitates.

IF thou, Lord, wilt be extreme to mark what is done amiss: O Lord, who may abide it? for there is mercy with thee, O God of Israel. Ps. ibid., 1-2. Out of the deep have I called unto thee, O Lord: Lord, hear my voice. ℣. Glory.

Collect.

O GOD, our refuge and strength, who art thyself the author of all godliness: be ready to hear the godly prayers of thy Church, and grant; that those things which we ask faithfully we may obtain effectually. Through.

The Lesson from the Epistle of blessed Paul the Apostle to the Philippians.

Phil. 1, 6-11.

BRETHREN: We are confident in the Lord Jesus, that he who hath begun a good work in you will perform it until the day of Jesus Christ. Even as it is meet for me to think this of you all: because I have you in my heart, inasmuch as both in my bonds, and in the defence and confirmation of the Gospel, ye all are partakers of my grace. For God is my record, how greatly I long after you all in the bowels of Jesus Christ. And this I pray, that your love may abound yet more and more in knowledge and in all judgment: that ye may approve things that are excellent, that ye may be sincere, and without offence, till the day of Christ, being filled with the fruits of righteousness, which are by Jesus Christ, unto the glory and praise of God.

Gradual. Ps. 133, 1-2. Behold, how good and joyful a thing it is, brethren, to dwell together in unity! ℣. It is like the precious ointment upon the head, that ran down unto the beard, even unto Aaron's beard.

Alleluia, alleluia. ℣. Ps. 115, 11. Ye that fear the Lord, put your trust in him: he is their helper and defender. Alleluia.

✠ The Continuation of the holy Gospel according to Matthew.

Matt. 22, 15-21.

AT that time: The Pharisees went and took counsel how they might entangle Jesus in his talk. And they sent out unto him their disciples, with the Herodians, saying: Master, we know that thou art true, and teachest the way of God in truth, neither carest thou for any man: for thou regardest not the person of men: tell us therefore, what thinkest thou, is it lawful to give tribute unto Cæsar, or not? But Jesus perceived their wickedness, and said: Why tempt ye me, ye hypocrites? Shew me the tribute-money. And they brought unto him a penny. And he saith unto them: Whose is this image and superscription? They say unto him: Cæsar's. Then saith he unto them: Render therefore unto Cæsar the things which are Cæsar's; and unto God the things that are God's. Creed.

Offertory. Esther 14, 12-13. Remember me, O Lord, King of all power: and put a well-ordered speech in my mouth, that my words may be pleasing in the sight of the prince.

Secret.

GRANT, O merciful God: that this saving oblation may evermore deliver us from our sins, and defend us against all adversities. Through.

Preface of the Most Holy Trinity.

Communion. Ps. 17, 6. I have called upon thee, O God, for thou shalt hear me: incline thine ear unto me, and hearken unto my words.

Postcommunion.

O LORD, who hast made us partakers of the gifts of these sacred mysteries, we humbly beseech thee: that those things, which thou hast commanded us to do in remembrance of thee, may be profitable to the succour of our infirmities: Who livest and reignest with God the Father.

The Twenty-third Sunday after Pentecost

Double.

¶ If this Sunday be superseded by the last Sunday after Pentecost, the Mass following is omitted.

Introit. Jer. 29, 11, 12 and 14.

Dicit Dominus.

THUS saith the Lord: I think thoughts of peace, and not of affliction: ye shall call upon me, and I will hearken unto you, and will bring again your captivity from all places. Ps. 85, 1. Lord, thou art become gracious unto thy land: thou hast turned away the captivity of Jacob. ℣. Glory.

Collect.

O LORD, we beseech thee, absolve thy people from their offences: that through thy bountiful goodness we may be delivered from the bands of all those sins, which by our frailty we have committed. Through.

The Lesson from the Epistle of blessed Paul the Apostle to the Philippians.

Phil. 3, 17-21; 4, 1-3.

BRETHREN: Be followers together of me, and mark them which walk so as ye have us for an ensample. For many walk, of whom I have told you often (and now tell you even weeping) that they are the enemies of the Cross of Christ: whose end is destruction: whose god is their belly: and whose glory is in their shame, who mind earthly things. For our conversation is in heaven: from whence also we look for the Saviour, the Lord Jesus Christ, who shall change our vile body, that it may be fashioned like unto his glorious body, according to the working whereby he is able even to subdue all things unto himself. Therefore, my brethren dearly beloved and longed for, my joy and crown: so stand fast in the Lord, my dearly beloved. I beseech Euodias, and beseech Syntyche, that they be of the same mind in the Lord. And I intreat thee also, true yoke-fellow, help those women which laboured with me in the Gospel, with Clement also, and with other my fellow labourers, whose names are in the book of life.

Gradual. Ps. 44, 8-9. It is thou, Lord, that savest us from our enemies: and puttest them to confusion that hate us. ℣. We make our boast of God all day long, and will praise thy name for ever.

Alleluia, alleluia. ℣. Ps. 130, 1-2. Out of the deep have I called unto thee, O Lord: Lord, hear my voice. Alleluia.

✠ The Continuation of the holy Gospel according to Matthew.

Matt. 9, 18-26.

AT that time: While Jesus spake unto the multitudes, behold, there came a certain ruler, and worshipped him, saying: My daughter is even now dead: but come and lay thy hand upon her, and she shall live. And Jesus arose, and followed him, and so did his disciples. And behold, a woman, which was diseased with an issue of blood twelve years, came behind him, and touched the hem of his garment. For she said within herself: If I may but touch his garment, I shall be whole. But Jesus turned him about, and when he saw her, he said: Daughter, be of good comfort, thy faith hath made thee whole. And the woman was made whole from that hour. And when Jesus came into the ruler's house, and saw the minstrels and the people making a noise, he said unto them: Give place: for the maid is not dead, but sleepeth. And they laughed him to scorn. But when the people were put forth, he went in, and took her by the hand. And the maid arose. And the fame hereof went abroad into all that land. Creed.

Offertory. Ps. 130, 1-2. Out of the deep have I called unto thee, O Lord: Lord, hear my voice: out of the deep have I called unto thee, O Lord.

Secret.

WE offer unto thee, O Lord, this sacrifice of praise to the increasing of our faithful service: beseeching thee; that although we be unworthy of thy bounty, yet thou wouldest accomplish in us the effectual working of the same. Through.

Preface of the Most Holy Trinity.

Communion. Mark 11, 24. Verily, I say unto you, What things soever ye desire, when ye pray, believe that ye receive them, and it shall be done unto you.

Postcommunion.

WE beseech thee, almighty God: that we, whom thou makest to rejoice in the partaking of heavenly things, may by thee be defended against all earthly perils. Through.

¶ If there be more than 24 Sundays after Pentecost, then after the 23rd the Masses of the Sundays which were left over after the Epiphany are resumed, as below, according to the order given in the Rubrics. And in the last place is always said the Mass of the 24th Sunday, as below p. 544.

The Third Sunday
which remained over after the Epiphany.

Double.

Introit. Jer. 29, 11, 12 and 14.

Dicit Dominus.

THUS saith the Lord: I think thoughts of peace, and not of affliction: ye shall call upon me, and I will hearken unto you: and will bring again your captivity from all places. Ps. 85, 1. Lord, thou art become gracious unto thy land: thou hast turned away the captivity of Jacob. ℣. Glory.

Collect.

ALMIGHTY and everlasting God, mercifully look upon our infirmity: and stretch forth the right hand of thy majesty to defend us. Through.

The Lesson from the Epistle of blessed Paul the Apostle to the Romans.

Rom. 12, 16-21.

BRETHREN: Be not wise in your own conceits: recompense to no man evil for evil: provide things honest in the sight of all men. If it be possible, as much as lieth in you, live peaceably with all men: Dearly beloved, avenge not yourselves, but rather give place unto wrath. For it is written: Vengeance is mine: I will repay, saith the Lord. Therefore, if thine enemy hunger, feed him: if he thirst, give him drink: for in so doing thou shalt heap coals of fire on his head. Be not overcome of evil, but overcome evil with good.

Gradual. Ps. 44, 8-9. It is thou, Lord, that savest us from our enemies: and puttest them to confusion that hate us. ℣. We make our boast of God all day long, and will praise thy name for ever.

Alleluia, alleluia. ℣. Ps. 130, 1. Out of the deep have I called unto thee, O Lord: Lord, hear my voice. Alleluia.

✠ The Continuation of the holy Gospel according to Matthew.

Matt. 8, 1-13.

AT that time: When Jesus was come down from the mountain, great multitudes followed him: and behold, there came a leper and worshipped him, saying: Lord, if thou wilt, thou canst make me clean. And Jesus put forth his hand, and touched him, saying: I will. Be thou clean. And immediately his leprosy was cleansed. And Jesus saith unto him: See thou tell no man: but go thy way, shew thyself to the priest, and offer the gift that Moses commanded for a testimony unto them. And when Jesus was entered into Capernaum, there came unto him a centurion, beseeching him, and saying: Lord, my servant lieth at home sick of the palsy, grievously tormented. And Jesus saith unto him: I will come and heal him. The centurion answered and said: Lord, I am not worthy that thou shouldest come under my roof: but speak the word only, and my servant shall be healed. For I am a man under authority, having soldiers under me, and I say unto this man: Go, and he goeth; and to another: Come, and he cometh: and to my servant: Do this, and he doeth it. When Jesus heard it, he marvelled, and said to them that followed: Verily I say unto you, I have not found so great a faith, no not in Israel. And I say unto you, That many shall come from the East and West, and shall sit down with Abraham, and Isaac, and Jacob, in the kingdom of heaven: but the children of the kingdom shall be cast out into outer darkness: there shall be weeping and gnashing of teeth. And Jesus said unto the centurion: Go thy way, and as thou hast believed, so be it done unto thee. And his servant was healed in the selfsame hour. Creed.

Offertory. Ps. 130, 1-2. Out of the deep have I called unto thee, O Lord: Lord hear my voice: out of the deep have I called unto thee, O Lord.

Secret.

WE beseech thee, O Lord, that this oblation may cleanse us from our sins: and sanctify thy servants both in body and soul for the celebration of this sacrifice. Through.

Preface of the Most Holy Trinity.

Communion. Mark 11, 24. Verily, I say unto you, What things soever ye desire, when ye pray, believe that ye receive them, and it shall be done unto you.

Postcommunion.

O LORD, who dost vouchsafe unto us to be made partakers of so great a mystery: we beseech thee; that thou wouldest vouchsafe to render us worthy thereby to obtain the benefits of the same. Through.

The Fourth Sunday
which remained over after the Epiphany.

Double.

Introit. Jer. 29, 11, 12 and 14.

Dicit Dominus.

THUS saith the Lord: I think thoughts of peace, and not of affliction: ye shall call upon me, and I will hearken unto you: and will bring again your captivity from all places. Ps. 85, 1. Lord thou art become gracious unto thy land: thou hast turned away the captivity of Jacob. ℣. Glory.

Collect.

O GOD, who knowest us to be set in the midst of so many and great dangers, that for man's frailness we cannot always stand uprightly: grant to us health of soul and body; that all those things which we suffer for sin, by thy help we may overcome. Through.

The Lesson from the Epistle of blessed Paul the Apostle to the Romans.

Rom. 13, 8-10.

BRETHREN: Owe no man any thing, but to love one another: for he that loveth another hath fulfilled the law. For this: Thou shalt not commit adultery: Thou shalt not kill: Thou shalt not steal: Thou shalt not bear false witness: Thou shalt not covet: and if there be any other commandment, it is briefly comprehended in this saying, namely: Thou shalt love thy neighbour as thyself. Love worketh no ill to his neighbour. Therefore love is the fulfilling of the law.

Gradual. Ps. 44, 8-9. It is thou, Lord, that savest us from our enemies: and puttest them to confusion that hate us. ℣. We make our boast of God all day long, and will praise thy name for ever.

Alleluia, alleluia. Ps. 130, 1. Out of the deep have I called unto thee, O Lord: Lord, hear my voice. Alleluia.

✠ The Continuation of the holy Gospel according to Matthew.

Matt. 8, 23-27.

AT that time: When Jesus was entered into a ship, his disciples followed him: and behold there arose a great tempest in the sea, insomuch that the ship was covered with the waves, but he was asleep. And his disciples came to him, and awoke him, saying: Lord, save us, we perish. And he saith unto them: Why are ye fearful, O ye of little faith? Then he arose, and rebuked the winds and the sea, and there was a great calm. But the men marvelled, saying: What manner of man is this, that even the winds and the sea obey him? Creed.

Offertory. Ps. 130, 1. Out of the deep have I called unto thee, O Lord: Lord, hear my voice: out of the deep have I called unto thee, O Lord.

Secret.

GRANT, we beseech thee, almighty God: that this oblation of our sacrifice may cleanse our frailty from all evil and evermore defend us. Through.

Preface of the Most Holy Trinity.

Communion. Mark 11, 24. Verily I say unto you, what things soever ye desire when ye pray, believe that ye receive them, and it shall be done unto you.

Postcommunion.

LET these thy gifts, O God, deliver us from earthly desires: and evermore strengthen us with heavenly nourishment. Through.

The Fifth Sunday

which remained over after the Epiphany.
Double.
Mass as on p. 507, except the Collect.

Collect.

O LORD, we beseech thee to keep this thy family in continual godliness: that they who now lean only upon the hope of thy heavenly grace, may evermore be defended by thy protection. Through.

The Sixth Sunday

which remained over after the Epiphany.
Double.
Introit. Jer. 11, 12 and 14.
Dicit Dominus.

THUS saith the Lord: I think thoughts of peace, and not of affliction: ye shall call upon me, and I will hearken unto you: and will bring again your captivity from all places. Ps. 85, 1. Lord, thou art become gracious unto thy land: thou hast turned away the captivity of Jacob. ℣. Glory.

Collect.

GRANT, we beseech thee, almighty God: that we, ever thinking on such things as be reasonable and pleasing unto thee, may both in word and deed fulfil the same. Through.

The Lesson from the Epistle of blessed Paul the Apostle to the Thessalonians.

I Thess. 1, 2-10.

BRETHREN: We give thanks to God always for you all, making mention of you in our prayers, remembering without ceasing your work of faith, and labour of love, and patience and hope in our Lord Jesus Christ, in the sight of God and our Father: knowing, brethren beloved, your election of God: for our Gospel came not unto you in word only, but also in power, and in the Holy Ghost, and in much assurance, as ye know what manner of men we were among you for your sake. And ye became followers of us, and of the Lord, having received the word in much affliction, with joy of the Holy Ghost: so that ye were ensamples to all that believe in Macedonia and Achaia. For from you sounded out the word of the Lord not only in Macedonia and Achaia, but also in every place your faith to Godward is spread abroad, so that we need not to speak any thing. For they themselves shew of us what manner of entering in we had unto you: and how ye turned to God from idols to serve the living and true God, and to wait for his Son from heaven (whom he raised from the dead) even Jesus, which delivered us from the wrath to come.

Gradual. Ps. 44, 8-9. It is thou, Lord, that savest us from our enemies: and puttest them to confusion that hate us. ℣. We make our boast of God all day long, and will praise thy name for ever.

Alleluia, alleluia. Ps. 130, 1. Out of the deep have I called unto thee, O Lord: Lord, hear my voice. Alleluia.

The Twenty-fourth and last Sunday after Pentecost

Double.

Introit. Jer. 29, 11, 12 and 14.

Dicit Dominus.

THUS saith the Lord: I think thoughts of peace, and not of affliction: ye shall call upon me, and I will hearken unto you: and will bring again your captivity from all places. Ps. 85, 1. Lord, thou art become gracious unto thy land: thou hast turned away the captivity of Jacob. ℣. Glory.

Collect.

STIR up, we beseech thee, O Lord, the wills of thy faithful: that they, bringing forth more plenteously the fruit of good works; may of thy loving-kindness be the more abundantly rewarded. Through.

The Lesson from the Epistle of blessed Paul the Apostle to the Colossians.

Col. 1, 9-14.

BRETHREN: We do not cease to pray for you, and to desire that ye might be filled with the knowledge of the will of God in all wisdom, and spiritual understanding: that ye might walk worthy of the Lord unto all pleasing: being fruitful in every good work, and increasing in the knowledge of God: strengthened with all might according to his glorious power, unto all patience and long-suffering with joyfulness, giving thanks unto the Father, which hath made us meet to be partakers of the inheritance of the saints in light: who hath delivered us from the power of darkness and hath translated us into the kingdom of his dear Son, in whom we have redemption through his blood, even the forgiveness of sins.

✠ The Continuation of the holy Gospel according to Matthew.

Matt. 13, 31-35.

AT that time: Jesus spake this parable unto the multitudes: The kingdom of heaven is like to a grain of mustard seed, which a man took, and sowed in his field: which indeed is the least of all seeds: but when it is grown, it is the greatest among herbs, and becometh a tree, so that the birds of the air come and lodge in the branches thereof. Another parable spake he unto them. The kingdom of heaven is like unto leaven, which a woman took, and hid in three measures of meal, till the whole was leavened. All these things spake Jesus unto the multitude in parables: and without a parable spake he not unto them: that it might be fulfilled which was spoken by the Prophet, saying: I will open my mouth in parables, I will utter things which have been kept secret from the foundation of the world. Creed.

Offertory. Ps. 130, 1-2. Out of the deep have I called unto thee, O Lord: Lord, hear my voice: out of the deep have I called unto thee, O Lord.

Secret.

WE beseech thee, O God, that this oblation may cleanse and regenerate, govern and defend us. Through.

Preface of the Most Holy Trinity.

Communion. Mark 11, 24. Verily, I say unto you, What things soever ye desire, when ye pray, believe that ye receive them, and it shall be done unto you.

Postcommunion.

O LORD, who hast fulfilled us with thy heavenly delights: we beseech thee; that we may ever earnestly seek after those things whereby we truly live. Through.

The Twenty-fourth and last Sunday after Pentecost

Gradual. Ps. 44, 8-9. It is thou, Lord, that savest us from our enemies: and puttest them to confusion that hate us. ℣. We make our boast of God all day long, and will praise thy name for ever.

Alleluia, alleluia. ℣. Ps. 130, 1. Out of the deep have I called unto thee, O Lord: Lord, hear my voice. Alleluia.

✠ The Continuation of the holy Gospel according to Matthew.

Matt. 24, 15-35.

AT that time: Jesus said unto his disciples: When ye shall see the abomination of desolation, spoken of by Daniel the Prophet, stand in the holy place: whoso readeth, let him understand: then let them which be in Judæa flee into the mountains: let him which is on the housetop not come down to take any thing out of his house: neither let him which is in the field return back to take his clothes. And woe unto them that are with child, and to them that give suck in those days. But pray ye that your flight be not in the winter, neither on the sabbath day. For then shall be great tribulation, such as was not since the beginning of the world to this time, no, nor ever shall be. And except those days should be shortened, there should no flesh be saved: but for the elect's sake those days shall be shortened. Then if any man shall say unto you: Lo, here is Christ, or there: believe it not. For there shall arise false Christs, and false prophets, and shall shew great signs and wonders, insomuch that (if it were possible) they shall deceive the very elect. Behold, I have told you before. Wherefore if they shall say unto you: Behold, he is in the desert, go not forth: behold he is in the secret chambers, believe it not. For as the lightning cometh out of the East, and shineth even unto the West: so shall also the coming of the Son of man be. For wheresoever the carcase is, there will the eagles be gathered together. Immediately after the tribulation of those days shall the sun be darkened, and the moon shall not give her light, and the stars shall fall from heaven, and the powers of the heavens shall be shaken: and then shall appear the sign of the Son of man in heaven: and then shall all the tribes of the earth mourn: and they shall see the Son of man coming in the clouds of heaven with power and great glory. And he shall send his Angels with a great sound of a trumpet: and they shall gather together his elect from the four winds, from one end of heaven to the other. Now learn a parable of the fig tree: when his branch is yet tender, and putteth forth leaves, ye know that summer is nigh: so likewise ye, when ye shall see all these things, know that it is near, even at the doors. Verily I say unto you, This generation shall not pass, till all these things be fulfilled. Heaven and earth shall pass away, but my words shall not pass away. Creed.

Offertory. Ps. 130, 1. Out of the deep have I called unto thee, O Lord: Lord, hear my voice: out of the deep have I called unto thee, O Lord.

Secret.

WE beseech thee, O Lord, to have compassion on our supplications, and to accept the prayers and oblations of thy people: that the hearts of all men being turned unto thee, we may be delivered from the desire of things temporal, and follow stedfastly after things eternal. Through.

Preface of the Most Holy Trinity.

Communion. Mark 11, 24. Verily I say unto you, what things soever ye desire, when ye pray, believe that ye receive them, and it shall be done unto you.

Postcommunion.

GRANT, O Lord, that the effectual healing of this Sacrament which we have received may deliver us from all the diseases of our souls. Through.

TABLE OF PRAYERS

First Week in Advent

Collect.

O LORD, raise up, we pray thee, thy power and come among us: that whereas through our sins and wickedness we are sore beset by many and great dangers; we may be found worthy to be defended from the same by thy protection, and preserved by thy deliverance: Who livest and reignest with God the Father in the unity of the Holy Ghost: ever one God, world without end. ℟. Amen.

Secret.

LET these sacred mysteries, O Lord, so cleanse us by their mighty power, that we, growing in purity, may attain unto thee who art the author of the same. Through.

Postcommunion.

LET us wait, O Lord, for thy lovingkindness in the midst of thy temple: that with due honour we may hail the coming feast of our redemption. Through.

Second Week in Advent

Collect.

STIR up our hearts, O Lord, to prepare the way of thine only-begotten Son: that through his advent we may be cleansed from our offences, and may serve thee with a ready mind: Who liveth.

Secret.

WE beseech thee, O Lord, mercifully to accept the prayers and sacrifices of thy humble servants: that we, who cannot of our own prayers and merits help ourselves, may be defended by thy succour. Through.

Postcommunion.

O LORD, who hast fulfilled us with spiritual food and sustenance, we humbly beseech thee: that through the partaking of these holy mysteries thou wouldest teach us to despise things earthly, and to love the things that are heavenly. Through.

Third Week in Advent

Collect.

LORD, we beseech thee, give ear to our prayers: and by thy gracious visitation lighten the darkness of our heart: Who livest and reignest with God the Father.

Secret.

WE beseech thee, O Lord, that the continual offering of this sacrifice of our bounden duty: may fulfil thine institution of this sacred mystery, and may accomplish in us the wondrous work of thy salvation. Through.

Postcommunion.

HAVE mercy upon us, O Lord, we beseech thee: and grant that these means of heavenly grace may so cleanse us from our iniquities, that we may be made ready to keep thy coming festival. Through.

Fourth Week in Advent

Collect.

O LORD, raise up, we pray thee, thy power and come among us: and with great might succour us; that whereas through our sins we are sore let and hindered, thy bountiful grace and mercy may speedily help and deliver us: Who livest and reignest with God the Father.

Secret.

WE beseech thee, O Lord, mercifully to have respect unto these our sacrifices: that they may increase our devotion and set forward our salvation. Through.

Postcommunion.

O LORD, who hast made us to be partakers of thy bounty: we beseech thee; that we, continually drawing near to this holy mystery, may thereby grow in grace to the attainment of everlasting salvation. Through.

Of the Most Holy Sacrament

Collect.

O GOD, who in a wonderful Sacrament hast left us a memorial of thy Passion: grant that we may so reverence the sacred mysteries of thy Body and Blood; that we may ever enjoy within ourselves the fruit of thy redemption: Who livest and reignest with God the Father.

Secret.

GRACIOUSLY grant, we beseech thee, O Lord, unto thy Church the gifts of unity and peace: which are shewn forth in a mystery in the gifts we here offer. Through.

Postcommunion.

WE beseech thee, O Lord: that like as the receiving of thy precious Body and Blood in this life doth foreshadow the everlasting fruition of thy Godhead, so thou wouldest vouchsafe unto us to be fulfilled with the same: Who livest and reignest with God the Father.

On the Anniversary of the Election and Consecration of the Bishop

Collect.

O GOD, the pastor and ruler of all the faithful, mercifully look upon thy servant N., whom thou hast chosen to be pastor and ruler of the Church of N.: grant unto him, we beseech thee, to be in word and conversation a wholesome example to the people committed to his charge; that he with them may attain at last to the crown of everlasting life. Through.

Secret.

WE beseech thee, O Lord, mercifully to accept these our oblations: granting unto thy servant N., that like as thou hast chosen him to be pastor and ruler of the Church of N.; so he may be governed evermore by thy defence. Through.

Postcommunion.

DEFEND us, O Lord, we beseech thee, who have here received these heavenly mysteries: and grant that thy servant, N., whom thou hast chosen to be pastor and ruler of the Church of N.; together with the flock committed to his charge, may thereby be preserved and strengthened against all adversities. Through.

* On the Anniversary of the Election and Coronation of the Chief Bishop—for Church of N., substitute thy Church.

For the Propagation of the Faith

To be said in all Masses on the last Sunday but one of October, unless a Double of the 1st class occur.

Collect.

O GOD, who wouldest that all men should be saved, and come to the knowledge of the truth: send forth, we beseech thee, labourers into thy harvest, and enable them to speak thy word with all boldness; that thy word may run and be glorified, and that all nations may know thee, the one true God, and him whom thou hast sent, even Jesus Christ thy Son our Lord: Who liveth and reigneth with thee.

Secret.

BEHOLD, O God our defender, and look upon the face of thine Anointed, who gave himself a ransom for all: and grant; that, from the rising of the sun even unto the going down of the same, thy name may be great among the Gentiles, and that in every place a pure oblation may be sacrificed and offered unto thy name. Through the same.

Postcommunion.

WE beseech thee, O Lord: that as thou hast fed us with the gift of our redemption; so also this means of eternal salvation may ever avail for the furtherance of the true faith. Through.

For the Priest Himself

Which may be said (even in a Sung Mass) on the Anniversary of his Ordination, subject to the Rubrics.

Collect.

ALMIGHTY and merciful God, graciously hearken unto my humble prayers: and make me thy servant, to whom for no merits of my own but by the boundless compassion of thy bounty thou hast vouchsafed to serve thee in these heavenly mysteries, a worthy minister at thy sacred altars; that the words which I utter with my lips may by thy sanctifying power be brought to good effect. Through.

Secret.

CLEANSE me, O Lord, by the power of this Sacrament from all the stains of my sins: and grant; that with the help of thy grace I may be made worthy thereby to fulfil the ministry committed to my charge. Through.

Postcommunion.

ALMIGHTY and everlasting God, who hast vouchsafed to me, a sinner, to stand before thy sacred altars, and to praise the power of thy holy name: mercifully grant to me through the mystery of this Sacrament the pardon of my sins; that I may offer unto thy majesty true and worthy service. Through.

(B.C.P.)

¶ *Collect to be repeated every day with the other Collects in Advent, until Christmas Eve.*

Collect.

ALMIGHTY God, give us grace that we may cast away the works of darkness, and put upon us the armour of light, now in the time of this mortal life, in which thy Son Jesus Christ came to visit us in great humility: that in the last day, when he shall come again in his glorious Majesty to judge both the quick and the dead, we may rise to the life immortal. Through him who liveth and reigneth with thee and the Holy Ghost, now and ever. ℟. Amen.

¶ *Collect to be read every day in Lent after the Collect appointed for the Day.*

Collect.

ALMIGHTY and everlasting God, who hatest nothing that thou hast made, and dost forgive the sins of all them that are penitent: create and make in us new and contrite hearts; that we worthily lamenting our sins, and acknowledging our wretchedness, may obtain of thee, the God of all mercy, perfect remission and forgiveness. Through.

THE PROPER OF SAINTS

The Masses of all Feasts contained in this Proper (except those of peculiar Mysteries of our Lord, or of Feasts of the Blessed Virgin Mary, for which no special Mass is provided, as also of Masses of St. Joseph, and of the Apostles SS. Peter and Paul) are also said as Votives. But in them, unless otherwise provided in their places, after the Epistle the Gradual with its following Verse or Tract, or in Eastertide the Alleluia, with its Verses which are wanting, is taken from the respective Common. But for Martyrs, in Eastertide, is said the Mass Protexisti or Sancti tui, as the case may be, and in it are said the proper Prayers, Epistle, and Gospel, if any are provided. But in each Prayer the words this day, yearly, and the like, when they occur, are omitted and the words birthday or festival are to be changed into commemoration or memorial. In the same way, instead of the Introit Gaudeamus, the Introit of the respective Common is said, and outside Eastertide the Alleluia, which is added to the Introit, Offertory and Communion because of Eastertide, is omitted.

NOTE—Outside Advent, Lent and Easter Tide, on the first day of each month on which the Office is said of the Feria, the Conventual Mass must be a Mass of Requiem.

FEASTS OF NOVEMBER

November 29.

For St. Saturninus

Martyr.

The Mass Laetabitur, p. [7], except the Prayers as below.

Collect. P

O GOD, who vouchsafest unto us to rejoice in the heavenly birthday of thy blessed Martyr Saturninus: grant, we pray thee; that we may feel the succour of his merits. Through.

Secret. P

SANCTIFY, O Lord, we beseech thee, the offerings which we here dedicate to thee: and, at the intercession of thy blessed Martyr Saturninus, for their sake look graciously upon us. Through.

Postcommunion. P

WE beseech thee, O Lord, that we, being sanctified by this Sacrament which we have here received: may, at the intercession of thy Saints, be thereby rendered acceptable unto thee. Through.

November 30.

ST. ANDREW APOSTLE

Double of 2nd class.

(Scotland: Double of 1st class.)

Introit. Ps. 139, 17. Mihi autem.

RIGHT dear are thy friends unto me, O God, and held in highest honour: their rule and governance is exceeding steadfast. Ps. Ibid., 1. O Lord, thou hast searched me out, and known me: thou knowest my down-sitting, and mine up-rising. ℣. Glory.

Collect.

ALMIGHTY God, who didst give such grace unto thy holy Apostle Saint Andrew, that he readily obeyed the calling of thy Son Jesus Christ, and followed him without delay: grant unto us all; that we, being called by thy holy Word, may forthwith give up ourselves obediently to fulfil thy holy commandments. Through the same.

Or, Collect.

WE humbly beseech thee, O Lord: that as thou didst choose thy blessed Apostle Andrew to be a teacher and ruler of thy Church; so he may continually intercede for us in the sight of thy divine majesty. Through.

In Advent Commemoration is made of the Feria, p. 546.

The Lesson from the Epistle of blessed Paul the Apostle to the Romans.

Rom. 10, 10-18.

BRETHREN: If thou shalt confess with thy mouth the Lord Jesus, and shalt believe in thine heart that God hath raised him from the dead, thou shalt be saved. For with the heart man believeth unto righteousness: and with the mouth confession is made unto salvation. For the Scripture saith: Whosoever believeth on him shall not be ashamed. For there is no difference between the Jew and the Greek: for the same Lord over all is rich unto all that call upon him. For whosoever shall call upon the name of the Lord shall be saved. How then shall they call on him, in whom they have not believed? And how shall they believe in him, of whom they have not heard? And how shall they hear without a preacher? And how shall they preach, except they be sent? As it is written: How beautiful are the feet of them that preach the Gospel of peace, and bring glad tidings of good things! But they have not all obeyed the Gospel. For Esaias saith: Lord, who hath believed our report? So then faith cometh by hearing, and hearing by the word of God. But I say: Have they not heard? Yes verily, their sound went into all the earth, and their words unto the ends of the world. But I say: Did not Israel know? First Moses saith: I will provoke you to jealousy by them that are no people, and by a foolish nation I will anger you. But Esaias is very bold, and saith: I was found of them that sought me not: I was made manifest unto them that asked not after me. But to Israel he saith: All day long I have stretched forth my hands unto a disobedient and gainsaying people.

or

The Lesson from the Epistle of blessed Paul the Apostle to the Romans.

Rom. 10, 10-18.

BRETHREN: With the heart man believeth unto righteousness: and with the mouth confession is made unto salvation. For the Scripture saith: Whosoever believeth on him shall not be ashamed. For there is no difference between the Jew and the Greek: for the same Lord over all is rich unto all that call upon him. For whosoever shall call upon the name of the Lord shall be saved. How then shall they call on him, in whom they have not believed? And how shall they believe in him, of whom they have not heard? And how shall they hear without a preacher? And how shall they preach, except they be sent? As it is written: How beautiful are the feet of them that preach the Gospel of peace, and bring glad tidings of good things! But they have not all obeyed the Gospel. For Esaias saith: Lord, who hath believed our report? So then faith cometh by hearing, and hearing by the word of God. But I say: Have they not heard? Yes verily, their sound went into all the earth, and their words unto the ends of the world.

Gradual. Ps. 45, 17-18. Thou shalt make them princes in all lands: they shall remember thy name, O Lord. ℣. Instead of thy fathers thou shalt have children: therefore shall the people give thanks unto thee.

Alleluia, alleluia. ℣. The Lord loved Andrew as a sweet savour. Alleluia.

✠ The Continuation of the holy Gospel according to Matthew.

Matt. 4, 18-22.

AT that time: Jesus, walking by the sea of Galilee, saw two brethren, Simon called Peter, and Andrew his brother, casting a net into the sea, (for they were fishers), and he saith unto them: Follow me, and I will make you fishers of men. And they straightway left their nets, and followed him. And going on from thence he saw other two brethren, James the son of Zebedee, and John his brother, in a ship with Zebedee their father, mending their nets: and he called them. And they immediately left the ship and their father, and followed him. Creed.

Offertory. Ps. 139, 17. Right dear are thy friends unto me, O God, and held in highest honour: their rule and governance is exceeding steadfast.

Secret.

O LORD, we beseech thee, let the devout prayers of thy blessed Apostle Andrew commend our sacrifice unto thee: that this oblation, which we offer in his honour, may by his merits be rendered acceptable in thy sight. Through.

In Advent, Commemoration is made of the Feria, p. 546.

Preface of the Apostles.

Communion. Matt. 4, 19-20. Follow me: I will make you fishers of men: and they straightway left their nets, and followed the Lord.

Postcommunion.

WE beseech thee, O Lord, that thy heavenly mysteries, which we have joyfully received on this festival of blessed Andrew thine Apostle: may effectually avail for the glory of thy Saints, and likewise for the forgiveness of our sins. Through.

In Advent, Commemoration is made of the Feria, p. 546.

¶ In Votive Masses after Septuagesima, everything is said as above, but after the Gradual, Alleluia and the Verse following being omitted, the Tract from the Mass Statuit is said, p. [4]. In Eastertide the Introit and Offertory are taken from the Mass Protexisti, p. [15]. The rest is said as above, but after the Epistle the Gradual is omitted, and in its place is said:

Alleluia, alleluia. ℣. The Lord loved Andrew as a sweet savour. Alleluia. ℣. Ps. 21, 4. Thou hast set, O Lord, a crown of pure gold upon his head. Alleluia.

FEASTS OF DECEMBER

¶ In Advent on simple Feasts Mass is said of the Feria with Commemoration of the Feast.

December 2.

St. Bibiana

Virgin and Martyr

Simple.

The Mass Me exspectaverunt, in the Common of Virgin Martyrs, p. [29], except the Collect.

Collect.

O GOD, the giver of all good gifts, who in thy handmaid Bibiana didst unite the palm of martyrdom with the flower of virginity: unite by her intercession our hearts in charity unto thee; that we, being delivered from all dangers, may attain unto the rewards of everlasting salvation. Through.

Secret.

GRACIOUSLY receive, O Lord, through the merits of blessed Bibiana, thy Virgin and Martyr, the sacrifices which we offer unto thee: and grant that they may avail for our continual help. Through.

Postcommunion.

O LORD our God, who hast fulfilled us with the bounty of thy heavenly gift: we beseech thee, that, at the intercession of blessed Bibiana, thy Virgin and Martyr, we may ever live by the partaking of the same. Through.

December 3.

St. Francis Xavier

Confessor

Greater double.

Introit. Ps. 119, 46-47. Loquebar.

I WILL speak of thy testimonies even before kings, and will not be ashamed: and my delight shall be in thy commandments, which I have loved exceedingly. Ps. 117, 1-2. O praise the Lord, all ye heathen, praise him, all ye nations: for his merciful kindness is ever more and more towards us, and the truth of the Lord endureth for ever. ℣. Glory.

Collect.

O GOD, who by the preaching and miracles of blessed Francis didst vouchsafe to gather unto thy Church the peoples of India: mercifully grant; that we, who venerate his glorious merits, may likewise follow him in all virtuous and godly living. Through.

Commemoration of the Feria, p. 546.

The Lesson from the Epistle of blessed Paul the Apostle to the Romans.

Rom. 10, 10-18.

BRETHREN: With the heart man believeth unto righteousness: and with the mouth confession is made unto salvation. For the Scripture saith: Whosoever believeth on him shall not be ashamed. For there is no difference between the Jew and the Greek: for the same Lord over all is rich unto all that call upon him. For whosoever shall call upon the name of the Lord shall be saved. How then shall they call on him, in whom they have not believed? And how shall they believe in him, of whom they have not heard? And how shall they hear without a preacher? And how shall they preach, except they be sent? As it is written: How beautiful are the feet of them that preach the Gospel of peace, and bring glad tidings of good things! But they have not all obeyed the Gospel. For Esaias saith: Lord, who hath believed our report? So then faith cometh by hearing, and hearing by the word of God. But I say: Have they not heard? Yes verily, their sound went into all the earth, and their words unto the ends of the world.

Gradual. Ps. 92, 13-14. The righteous shall flourish like a palm-tree: and shall spread abroad like a cedar in Libanus in the house of the Lord. ℣. To tell of thy loving-kindness early in the morning, and of thy truth in the night-season.

Alleluia, alleluia. ℣. Jas. 1, 12. Blessed is the man that endureth temptation: for when he is tried, he shall receive the crown of life. Alleluia.

✠ The Continuation of the holy Gospel according to Mark.

Mark 16, 15-18.

AT that time: Jesus said unto his disciples: Go ye into all the world, and preach the Gospel to every creature. He that believeth and is baptized shall be saved: but he that believeth not shall be damned. And these signs shall follow them that believe: In my name shall they cast out devils: they shall speak with new tongues: they shall take up serpents: and if they drink any deadly thing, it shall not hurt them: they shall lay hands on the sick, and they shall recover.

Offertory. Ps. 89, 25. My truth and my mercy shall be with him: and in my name shall his horn be exalted.

Secret.

GRANT to us, we beseech thee, almighty God: that this oblation of our humble service may be acceptable in thy sight to the honour of thy Saints, and may cleanse us both in body and soul. Through.

Commemoration of the Feria, p 546.

Communion. Matt. 24, 46-47. Blessed is the servant, whom his lord when he cometh shall find watching: verily I say unto you, he shall make him ruler over all his goods.

Postcommunion.

WE beseech thee, almighty God: that we, who have received this heavenly food, may at the intercession of blessed Francis thy Confessor be thereby defended against all adversities. Through.

Commemoration of the Feria, p. 546.

December 4

St. Peter Chrysologus

Bishop, Confessor and Doctor of the Church

Double.

Introit. Ecclus. 15, 5. In medio.

IN the midst of the Church he opened his mouth: and the Lord filled him with the spirit of wisdom and understanding: he clothed him with a robe of glory. Ps. 92, 1. It is a good thing to give thanks unto the Lord: and to sing praises unto thy name, O most Highest. ℣. Glory.

Collect.

O GOD, who wast pleased that by a sign from heaven blessed Peter Chrysologus thy most excellent Doctor should be chosen to rule and to teach thy Church: grant, we beseech thee; that as we have learned of him the doctrine of life on earth, so we may be found worthy to have him for our advocate in heaven. Through.

And Commemoration is made of the Feria, p. 546, then Commemoration of St. Barbara, V.M.

Collect.

O GOD, who among the manifold works of thy power hast bestowed even upon the weakness of women the victory of martyrdom: mercifully grant that we, who this day celebrate the heavenly birth of blessed Barbara thy Virgin and Martyr, may by her example be drawn nearer unto thee. Through.

The Lesson from the Epistle of blessed Paul the Apostle to Timothy.

II Tim. 4, 1-8.

DEARLY beloved: I charge thee before God, and the Lord Jesus Christ, who shall judge the quick and the dead at his appearing and his kingdom: preach the word, be instant in season, out of season: reprove, rebuke, exhort with all longsuffering and doctrine. For the time will come when they will not endure sound doctrine, but after their own lusts shall they heap to themselves teachers, having itching ears, and they shall turn away their ears from the truth, and shall be turned unto fables. But watch thou in all things, endure afflictions, do the work of an Evangelist, make full proof of thy ministry. For I am now ready to be offered, and the time of my departure is at hand. I have fought a good fight, I have finished my course, I have kept the faith. Henceforth there is laid up for me a crown of righteousness, which the Lord, the righteous judge, shall give me at that day: and not to me only, but unto all them also that love his appearing.

Gradual. Ecclus. 44, 16. Behold a great priest, who in his days pleased God. ℣. There was none like unto him, to keep the law of the most High.

Alleluia, alleluia. ℣. Ps. 110, 4. Thou art a priest for ever after the order of Melchisedech. Alleluia.

✠ The Continuation of the holy Gospel according to Matthew.

Matt. 5, 13-19.

AT that time: Jesus said unto his disciples: Ye are the salt of the earth. But if the salt have lost his savour, wherewith shall it be salted? It is thenceforth good for nothing, but to be cast out, and to be trodden under foot of men. Ye are the light of the world. A city that is set on an hill cannot be hid. Neither do men light a candle, and put it under a bushel, but on a candlestick, and it giveth light unto all that are in the house. Let your light so shine before men, that they may see your good works, and glorify your Father which is in heaven. Think not that I am come to destroy the law or the prophets: I am not come to destroy, but to fulfil. For verily I say unto you, Till heaven and earth pass, one jot or one tittle shall in no wise pass from the law, till all be fulfilled. Whosoever therefore shall break one of these least commandments, and shall teach men so, he shall be called the least in the kingdom of heaven: but whosoever shall do and teach them, the same shall be called great in the kingdom of heaven. Creed.

Offertory. Ps. 92, 13. The righteous shall flourish like a palm-tree: and shall spread abroad like a cedar in Libanus.

Secret.

MAY the devout prayers of thy Bishop and Doctor, Saint Peter Chrysologus, continually succour us, O Lord: that they may render our oblations acceptable in thy sight; and ever obtain for us thy merciful pardon. Through.

Commemoration of the Feria, p. 546.

For St. Barbara.
Secret.

RECEIVE, O Lord, the gifts which we offer on the solemnity of blessed Barbara, thy Virgin and Martyr: through whose advocacy we trust to be delivered. Through.

Communion. Matt. 25, 20-21. Lord, thou deliveredst unto me five talents: behold, I have gained beside them five talents more. Well done, thou good and faithful servant, thou hast been faithful over a few things, I will make thee ruler over many things, enter thou into the joy of thy Lord.

Postcommunion.

WE beseech thee, O Lord, that blessed Peter Chrysologus, thy Bishop and most excellent Doctor, may ever stand before thee as our advocate: that this sacrifice of thine ordinance may effectually avail for our salvation. Through.

And Commemoration is made of the Feria, p. 546.

For St. Barbara.
Postcommunion.

ASSIST us mercifully, O Lord, who have here received these holy mysteries: and at the intercession of blessed Barbara, thy Virgin and Martyr, make us ever to rejoice in thy continual protection. Through.

December 5.
For St. Sabbas
Abbot

The Mass Os justi, from the Common of an Abbot, p. [26], with the Prayers as below:

Collect. C

O LORD, we beseech thee, let the intercession of thy blessed Abbot Sabbas commend us unto thee: that those things which for our own merits we cannot ask, we may through his advocacy obtain. Through.

Secret. P

O LORD, we beseech thee, let Saint Sabbas intercede for us: that this sacrifice which we offer and present upon thy holy altar may be profitable unto us for our salvation. Through.

Postcommunion. P

LET thy Sacrament, O Lord, which we have now received and the prayers of blessed Sabbas effectually defend us: that we may both imitate the example of his conversation, and receive the succour of his intercession. Through.

¶ If to-day be Saturday, private Masses are said of the preceding Sunday with 2nd Collect of St. Sabbas; the conventual Mass however is said in Choir after Sext of St. Mary on Saturday with 2nd Collect of the Feria, according to the Rubrics.

December 6.
St. Nicholas
Bishop and Confessor
Double.

Introit. Ecclus. 45, 3. Statuit ei.

THE Lord hath established a covenant of peace with him, and made him the chief of his people: that he should have the dignity of the priesthood for ever. Ps. 132, 1. Lord, remember David: and all his trouble. ℣. Glory.

Collect.

O GOD, who didst adorn thy blessed Bishop Nicholas with power to work many and great miracles: grant, we beseech thee; that by his merits and prayers we may be delivered from the fires of everlasting torment. Through.

Commemoration of the Feria, p. 546.

The Lesson from the Epistle of blessed Paul the Apostle to the Hebrews.

Heb. 13, 7-17.

BRETHREN: Remember them which have the rule over you, who have spoken unto you the word of God: whose faith follow, considering the end of their conversation. Jesus Christ the same yesterday, and to-day: and for ever. Be not carried about with divers and strange doctrines. For it is a good thing that the heart be established with grace, not with meats, which have not profited them that have been occupied therein. We have an altar, whereof they have no right to eat which serve the tabernacle. For the bodies of those beasts whose blood is brought into the Sanctuary by the high priest for sin, are burned without the camp. Wherefore Jesus also, that he might sanctify the people with his own blood, suffered without the gate. Let us go forth therefore unto him without the camp, bearing his reproach. For here have we no continuing city, but we seek one to come. By him therefore let us offer the sacrifice of praise to God continually, that is, the fruit of our lips giving thanks to his name. But to do good and to communicate forget not: for with such sacrifices God is well pleased. Obey them that have the rule over you, and submit yourselves. For they watch for your souls, as they that must give account.

Gradual. Ps. 89, 21-23. I have found David my servant, with my holy oil have I anointed him: my hand shall hold him fast, and my arm shall strengthen him. ℣. The enemy shall not be able to do him violence, the son of wickedness shall not hurt him.

Alleluia, alleluia. ℣. Ps. 92, 13. The righteous shall flourish like a palm-tree: and shall spread abroad like a cedar in Libanus. Alleluia.

✠ The Continuation of the holy Gospel according to Matthew.

Matt. 25, 14-23.

AT that time: Jesus spake this parable to his disciples: A man travelling into a far country, called his own servants, and delivered unto them his goods. And unto one he gave five talents, to another two, and to another one, to every man according to his several ability, and straightway took his journey. Then he that had received the five talents went and traded with the same, and made them other five talents. And likewise he that had received two, he also gained other two. But he that had received one went and digged in the earth, and hid his lord's money. After a long time the lord of those servants cometh, and reckoneth with them. And so he that had received five talents, came and brought other five talents, saying: Lord, thou deliveredst unto me five talents, behold, I have gained beside them five talents more. His lord said unto him: Well done, thou good and faithful servant, thou hast been faithful over a few things, I will make thee ruler over many things: enter thou into the joy of thy lord. He also that had received two talents came and said: Lord, thou deliveredst unto me two talents, behold, I have gained two other talents beside them. His lord said unto him: Well done, good and faithful servant, thou hast been faithful over a few things, I will make thee ruler over many things: enter thou into the joy of thy lord.

Offertory. Ps. 89, 25. My truth and my mercy shall be with him: and in my name shall his horn be exalted.

Secret.

SANCTIFY, we beseech thee, O Lord God, these our gifts which we offer unto thee on the festival of thy holy Bishop Nicholas: that by the same our life may ever be governed both in prosperity and in adversity. Through.

Commemoration of the Feria, p. 546.

Communion. Ps. 89, 36-38. I have sworn once by my holiness: His seed shall endure for ever, and his seat is like as the sun before me, he shall stand fast for evermore as the moon, and as the faithful witness in heaven.

Postcommunion.

GRANT, O Lord, that like as we, remembering the festival of Saint Nicholas thy Bishop, have partaken of this sacrifice; so we may thereby be defended with thine everlasting protection. Through.

Commemoration of the Feria, p. 546.

December 7.

St. Ambrose

Bishop, Confessor and Doctor of the Church

Double.

Introit. Ecclus. 15, 5. In medio.

IN the midst of the Church he opened his mouth: and the Lord filled him with the spirit of wisdom and understanding: he clothed him with a robe of glory. Ps. 92, 1. It is a good thing to give thanks unto the Lord: and to sing praises unto thy name, O most Highest. ℣. Glory.

Collect.

O GOD, who didst send blessed Ambrose thy Doctor to guide thy people in the way of everlasting salvation: grant, we beseech thee; that as we have learned of him the doctrine of life on earth, so we may be found worthy to have him for our advocate in heaven. Through.

Commemoration of the Feria, p. 546.

The Lesson from the Epistle of blessed Paul the Apostle to Timothy.

II Tim. 4, 1-8.

DEARLY beloved: I charge thee before God, and the Lord Jesus Christ, who shall judge the quick and the dead at his appearing and his kingdom: preach the word, be instant in season, out of season: reprove, rebuke, exhort with all longsuffering and doctrine. For the time will come when they will not endure sound doctrine, but after their own lusts shall they heap to themselves teachers, having itching ears, and they shall turn away their ears from the truth, and shall be turned unto fables. But watch thou in all things, endure afflictions, do the work of an Evangelist, make full proof of thy ministry. For I am now ready to be offered, and the time of my departure is at hand. I have fought a good fight, I have finished my course, I have kept the faith. Henceforth there is laid up for me a crown of righteousness, which the Lord, the righteous judge, shall give me at that day: and not to me only, but unto all them also that love his appearing.

Gradual. Ecclus. 44, 16. Behold a great priest, who in his days pleased God. ℣. There was none found like unto him, to keep the law of the Most High.

Alleluia, alleluia. ℣. Ps. 110, 4. The Lord sware, and will not repent: Thou art a priest for ever after the order of Melchisedech. Alleluia.

After Septuagesima, omitting Alleluia and the Verse following, is said:

Tract. Ps. 112, 1-3. Blessed is the man that feareth the Lord: he hath great delight in his commandments. ℣. His seed shall be mighty upon earth: the generation of the faithful shall be blessed. ℣. Riches and plenteousness shall be in his house: and his righteousness endureth for ever.

In Eastertide the Gradual is omitted, and in its place is said:

Alleluia, alleluia. ℣. Ecclus. 45. The Lord loved him, and adorned him: he clothed him with a robe of glory. Alleluia. ℣. Hos. 14. The righteous shall grow as the lily and flourish for ever before the Lord. Alleluia.

☨ The Continuation of the holy Gospel according to Matthew.

Matt. 5, 13-19.

AT that time: Jesus said unto his disciples: Ye are the salt of the earth. But if the salt have lost his savour, wherewith shall it be salted? It is thenceforth good for nothing, but to be cast out, and to be trodden under foot of men. Ye are the light of the world. A city that is set on an hill cannot be hid. Neither do men light a candle, and put it under a bushel, but on a candlestick, and it giveth light unto all that are in the house. Let your light so shine before men, that they may see your good works, and glorify your Father which is in heaven. Think not that I am come to destroy the law or the prophets: I am not come to destroy, but to fulfil. For verily I say unto you, Till heaven and earth pass, one jot or one tittle shall in no wise pass from the law, till all be fulfilled. Whosoever therefore shall break one of these least commandments, and shall teach men so, he shall be called the least in the kingdom of heaven: but whosoever shall do and teach them, the same shall be called great in the kingdom of heaven. Creed.

Offertory. Ps. 89, 25. My truth and my mercy shall be with him: and in my name shall his horn be exalted.

Secret.

ALMIGHTY and everlasting God, grant that these oblations, which we here present unto thy majesty, may through the intercession of blessed Ambrose, thy Confessor and Bishop, be profitable unto us for the attainment of everlasting salvation. Through.

Commemoration of the Feria, p. 546.

Communion. Ps. 89, 36-38. I have sworn once by my holiness: His seed shall endure for ever, and his seat is like as the sun before me, he shall stand fast for evermore as the moon, and as the faithful witness in heaven.

Postcommunion.

ALMIGHTY God, who hast made us partakers of this Sacrament of our salvation: grant, we beseech thee; that like as we have offered our gifts unto thy majesty in honour of blessed Ambrose, thy Confessor and Bishop, so we may at all times be effectually defended by his intercession. Through.

Commemoration of the Feria, p. 546.

December 8.

THE

IMMACULATE CONCEPTION

OF

THE BLESSED VIRGIN MARY

Double of 1st class.

Introit. Is. 61, 10. *Gaudens gaudebo.*

I WILL greatly rejoice in the Lord, my soul shall be joyful in my God: for he hath clothed me with the garments of salvation: he hath covered me with the robe of righteousness, as a bride adorneth herself with her jewels. Ps. 30, 1. I will magnify thee, O Lord, for thou hast set me up: and not made my foes to triumph over me. ℣. Glory.

Collect.

O GOD, who through the immaculate Conception of the Virgin didst prepare an habitation meet for thy Son: we beseech thee; that like as thou, foreseeing the merits of the death of the same thy Son, didst thereby preserve her from all defilement, so by her intercession thou wouldest suffer us to attain in purity of heart to thee. Through the same.

Commemoration is made of the Feria.

The Lesson from the book of Wisdom.

Prov. 8, 22-35.

THE Lord possessed me in the beginning of his way, before his works of old. I was set up from everlasting, from the beginning, or ever the earth was. When there were no depths, I was brought forth: when there were no fountains abounding with water: before the mountains were settled: before the hills was I brought forth: while as yet he had not made the earth, nor the fields, nor the highest part of the dust of the world. When he prepared the heavens, I was there: when he set a compass upon the face of the depth: when he established the clouds above, when he strengthened the fountains of the deep: when he gave to the sea his decree, that the waters should not pass his commandment: when he appointed the foundations of the earth. Then I was by him, as one brought up with him: and I was daily his delight, rejoicing always before him: rejoicing in the habitable part of the earth: and my delights were with the sons of men. Now therefore hearken unto me, O ye children: for blessed are they that keep my ways. Hear instruction, and be wise, and refuse it not. Blessed is the man that heareth me, watching daily at my gates, waiting at the posts of my doors. For whoso findeth me findeth life, and shall obtain favour of the Lord.

Gradual. Judith 13, 23. Blessed art thou, O Virgin Mary, of the Lord, the most High God, above all women upon the earth. ℣. Ibid., 15, 10. Thou art the glory of Jerusalem, thou art the joy of Israel, thou art the honour of our people.

Alleluia, alleluia. ℣. Cant. 4, 7. All fair art thou, O Mary: and original sin is not in thee. Alleluia.

In Votive Masses after Septuagesima, omitting Alleluia and the Verse following, is said:

Tract. Ps. 87, 1-2. Her foundations are upon the holy hills; the Lord loveth the gates of Sion more than all the dwellings of Jacob. ℣. Very excellent things are spoken of thee, thou city of God. ℣. He was born in her, and the most High shall stablish her.

In Eastertide the Gradual is omitted, and in its place is said:

Alleluia, alleluia. ℣. Judith 15, 10. Thou art the glory of Jerusalem, thou art the joy of Israel, thou art the honour of our people. Alleluia. ℣. All fair art thou, O Mary: and original sin is not in thee. Alleluia.

✠ The Continuation of the holy Gospel according to Luke.

Luke 1, 26-28.

AT that time: The Angel Gabriel was sent from God unto a city of Galilee named Nazareth, to a Virgin espoused to a man whose name was Joseph, of the house of David, and the Virgin's name was Mary. And the Angel came in unto her, and said: Hail, full of grace; the Lord is with thee: blessed art thou among women. Creed.

Offertory. Luke 1, 28. Hail, Mary, full of grace: the Lord is with thee: blessed art thou among women, alleluia.

Secret.

ACCEPT, O Lord, this saving victim which we offer unto thee on the feast of the Immaculate Conception of the blessed Virgin Mary, and grant: that like as we do confess her through thy preventing grace to be free from all defilement; so by her intercession we may be delivered from all our iniquities. Through.

Commemoration is made of the Feria.

¶ Preface of the Blessed Virgin Mary, And that on the Immaculate Conception.

Communion. Glorious things are spoken of thee, O Mary: for he that is mighty hath done great things to thee.

Postcommunion.

GRANT, O Lord our God, that this Sacrament which we have here received: may heal in us the wounds of that sin; from which by a singular grace thou didst preserve the immaculate Conception of blessed Mary. Through.

Commemoration of the Feria.

December 10.

For St. Melchiades

Pope and Martyr

The Mass, Si diligis me, p. [2].

Collect. C

O EVERLASTING Shepherd, look down in mercy on thy flock: and as thou didst choose blessed Melchiades thy Martyr and Chief Bishop to be pastor and ruler of thy Church; so at his intercession defend it with thy continual protection. Through.

Secret. C

WE beseech thee, O Lord, graciously enlighten thy Church by the gifts which we here offer; that in every place thy flock may increase and prosper, and the shepherds by thy governance may be made pleasing to thy name. Through.

Postcommunion. C

MERCIFUL Lord, we beseech thee to govern and preserve thy Church which thou hast here refreshed with heavenly food: that, by the guiding of thy mighty power, it may serve thee in more abundant freedom, and ever keep thy true religion whole and undefiled. Through.

December 11.
St. Damasus I.
Pope and Confessor
Simple.

The Mass, Si diligis me, p. [2].

Collect.

O EVERLASTING Shepherd, look down in mercy on thy flock: and as thou didst choose blessed Damasus thy Chief Bishop to be pastor and ruler of thy Church: so at his intercession defend it with thy continual protection. Through.

Secret.

WE beseech thee, O Lord, graciously enlighten thy Church by the gifts which we here offer; that in every place thy flock may increase and prosper, and the shepherds by thy governance may be made pleasing to thy name. Through.

Postcommunion.

MERCIFUL Lord, we beseech thee to govern and preserve thy Church which thou hast here refreshed with heavenly food: that, by the guiding of thy mighty power, it may serve thee in more abundant freedom, and ever keep thy true religion whole and undefiled. Through.

December 13.
St. Lucy
Virgin and Martyr
Double.

Introit. Ps. 45, 8. Dilexisti.

THOU hast loved righteousness, and hated iniquity: therefore God, even thy God, hath anointed thee with the oil of gladness above thy fellows. Ps. ibid., 1. My heart is inditing of a good matter: I speak of the things which I have made unto the King. ℣. Glory.

Collect.

GRACIOUSLY hear us, O God of our salvation: that, like as we do rejoice in the festival of blessed Lucy thy Virgin and Martyr; so we may learn to follow her example in all godliness and charity. Through.

Commemoration is made of the Feria.

The Lesson from the Epistle of blessed Paul the Apostle to the Corinthians.

II Cor. 10, 17-18; 11, 1-2.

BRETHREN: He that glorieth, let him glory in the Lord. For not he that commendeth himself is approved; but whom the Lord commendeth. Would to God ye could bear with me a little in my folly, and indeed bear with me: for I am jealous over you with godly jealousy. For I have espoused you to one husband, that I may present you as a chaste virgin to Christ.

Gradual. Ps. 45, 8. Thou hast loved righteousness, and hated iniquity. ℣. Therefore God, even thy God, hath anointed thee with the oil of gladness.

Alleluia, alleluia. ℣. Ibid., 3. Full of grace are thy lips: because God hath blessed thee for ever. Alleluia.

¶ In Votive Masses after Septuagesima, the Tract, and in Eastertide Alleluia, with its verse, from the Mass Dilexisti, p. [31].

✠ The Continuation of the holy Gospel according to Matthew.

Matt. 13, 44-52.

AT that time: Jesus spake this parable unto his disciples: The kingdom of heaven is like unto treasure hid in a field: the which when a man hath found, he hideth, and for joy thereof goeth and selleth all that he hath, and buyeth that field. Again, the kingdom of heaven is like unto a merchant man, seeking goodly pearls. Who when he had found one pearl of great price, went and sold all that he had, and bought it. Again, the kingdom of heaven is like unto a net, that was cast into the sea, and gathered of every kind. Which, when it was full, they drew to shore, and sat down, and gathered the good into vessels, but cast the bad away. So shall it be at the end of the world: the Angels shall come forth, and sever the wicked from among the just, and shall cast them into the furnace of fire: there shall be wailing and gnashing of teeth. Jesus saith unto them: Have ye understood all these things? They say unto him: Yea, Lord. Then said he unto them: Therefore every scribe which is instructed unto the kingdom of heaven is like unto a man that is an householder, which bringeth forth out of his treasure things new and old.

Offertory. Ps. 45, 15-16. The Virgins that be her fellows shall be brought unto the King: they that bear her company shall be brought unto thee with joy and gladness: and shall enter into the palace of the Lord the King.

Secret.

GRANT, O Lord, that like as thy dedicated people do acknowledge that in tribulation they have been succoured by the merits of thy Saints: so this oblation, which they offer unto thee in honour of the same, may be acceptable in thy sight. Through.

Commemoration is made of the Feria.

Communion. Ps. 119, 161-162. Princes have persecuted me without a cause, but my heart standeth in awe of thy word: I am as glad of thy word, as one that findeth great spoils.

Postcommunion.

O LORD, who hast satisfied this thy family with thy sacred gifts: we beseech thee; that we may at all times be comforted by the intercession of her whose festival we celebrate. Through.

Commemoration is made of the Feria.

December 16.

St. Eusebius

Bishop and Martyr.

Simple.

The Mass Sacerdotes, p. [5].

Collect. C

O GOD, who makest us glad with the yearly solemnity of blessed Eusebius thy Martyr and Bishop: mercifully grant; that as we now celebrate his heavenly birthday, so we may likewise rejoice in his protection. Through.

Secret. C

SANCTIFY, O Lord, the gifts which we dedicate to thee: that at the intercession of blessed Eusebius thy Martyr and Bishop they may obtain for us thy gracious favour. Through.

Postcommunion. C

O LORD, let this holy Communion cleanse us from every guilty stain: that at the intercession of blessed Eusebius thy Martyr and Bishop we may be made partakers thereby of thy healing unto life eternal. Through.

December 21.

ST. THOMAS APOSTLE

Double of 2nd class.

¶ If to-day there occur an Ember Day, in Choir after Terce the conventual Mass is said of the Feast, and out of Choir after None a Mass is read of the Feria, of which private Masses are forbidden.

Introit. Ps. 139, 17. Mihi autem.

RIGHT dear are thy friends unto me, O God, and held in highest honour: their rule and governance is exceeding steadfast. Ps. ibid., 1-2. O Lord, thou hast searched me out, and known me: thou knowest my down-sitting, and mine up-rising. ℣. Glory.

Collect.

ALMIGHTY and everliving God, who for the more confirmation of the faith didst suffer thy holy Apostle Thomas to be doubtful in thy Son's resurrection: grant us so perfectly, and without all doubt to believe in thy Son Jesus Christ; that our faith in thy sight may never be reproved. Hear us, O Lord, through the same Jesus Christ: to whom, with thee and the Holy Ghost, be all honour and glory, now and for evermore. ℞. Amen.

Or, Collect.

GRANT to us, we beseech thee, O Lord, so to rejoice in the solemn festival of thy blessed Apostle Thomas: that we, being ever succoured by his advocacy; may steadfastly follow the example of his faith. Through.

Commemoration of the Feria, except in Conventual Masses if an Ember Day occur.

The Lesson from the Epistle of blessed Paul the Apostle to the Ephesians.

Ephes. 2, 19-22.

BRETHREN: Now ye are no more strangers and foreigners: but fellow-citizens with the saints, and of the household of God: and are built upon the foundation of the Apostles and Prophets, Jesus Christ himself being the chief corner-stone: in whom all the building, fitly framed together, groweth unto an holy temple in the Lord, in whom ye also are builded together for an habitation of God, through the Spirit.

Gradual. Ps. 139, 17. Right dear are thy friends unto me, O God, and held in highest honour: their rule and governance is exceeding steadfast. ℣. If I tell them, they are more in number than the sand.

Alleluia, alleluia. ℣. Ps. 33, 1. Rejoice in the Lord, O ye righteous: for it becometh well the just to be thankful. Alleluia.

✠ The Continuation of the holy Gospel according to John.

John 20, 24-29.

AT that time: Thomas, one of the twelve, called Didymus, was not with them when Jesus came. The other disciples therefore said unto him: We have seen the

Lord. But he said unto them: Except I shall see in his hands the print of the nails, and put my finger into the print of the nails, and thrust my hand into his side, I will not believe. And after eight days again his disciples were within, and Thomas with them. Then came Jesus, the doors being shut, and stood in the midst, and said: Peace be unto you. Then saith he to Thomas: Reach hither thy finger, and behold my hands, and reach hither thy hand, and thrust it into my side: and be not faithless, but believing. And Thomas answered and said unto him: My Lord, and my God. Jesus saith unto him: Thomas, because thou hast seen me, thou hast believed: blessed are they that have not seen, and yet have believed.*

And many other signs truly did Jesus in the presence of his disciples, which are not written in this book. But these are written, that ye might believe that Jesus is the Christ, the Son of God: and that believing ye might have life through his name. Creed.

Offertory. Ps. 19, 5. Their sound is gone out into all lands: and their words into the ends of the world.

Secret.

WE render unto thee, O Lord, this duty of our bounden service, humbly beseeching thee: that like as we do offer unto thee this sacrifice of praise in honour of the confession of thy blessed Apostle Thomas; so by his prayers thou wouldest preserve in us the effectual gifts of thy grace. Through.

Commemoration is made of the Feria, as above.

Preface of the Apostles.

Communion. John 20, 27. Reach hither thy hand, and behold the print of the nails: and be not faithless, but believing.

Postcommunion.

ASSIST us, O merciful God: and, at the intercession of thy blessed Apostle Thomas, continue towards us the gifts of thy loving kindness. Through.

Commemoration is made of the Feria, as above.

FEASTS OF JANUARY

occuring after January 13th.

January 14.

St. Hilary

Bishop, Confessor and Doctor of the Church.

Double.

Introit. Ecclus. 15, 5. In medio.

IN the midst of the Church he opened his mouth: and the Lord filled him with the spirit of wisdom and understanding: he clothed him with a robe of glory. Ps. 92, 1. It is a good thing to give thanks unto the Lord: and to sing praises unto thy name, O most Highest. ℣.Glory.

Collect.

O GOD, who didst send blessed Hilary thy Doctor to guide thy people in the way of everlasting salvation: grant, we beseech thee; that as we have learned of him the doctrine of life on earth, so we may be found worthy to have him for our advocate in heaven. Through.

And Commemoration is made of Saint Felix, P.M.

Collect.

GRANT, we beseech thee, almighty God: that by the examples of thy Saints we may so learn to amend our lives; that as we celebrate their festival, we may likewise follow them in all godly and virtuous living. Through.

The Lesson from the Epistle of blessed Paul the Apostle to Timothy.

II Tim. 4, 1-8.

DEARLY beloved: I charge thee before God, and the Lord Jesus Christ, who shall judge the quick and the dead at his appearing and his kingdom: preach the word, be instant in season, out of season: reprove, rebuke, exhort with all longsuffering and doctrine. For the time will come when they will not endure sound doctrine, but after their own lusts shall they heap to themselves teachers, having itching ears, and they shall turn away their ears from the truth, and shall be turned unto fables. But watch thou in all things, endure afflictions, do the work of an Evangelist, make full proof of thy ministry. For I am now ready to be offered, and the time of my departure is at hand. I have fought a good fight, I have finished my course, I have kept the faith. Henceforth there is laid up for me a crown of righteousness, which the Lord, the righteous judge, shall give me at that day: and not to me only, but unto all them also that love his appearing.

Gradual. Ps. 37, 30-31. The mouth of the righteous is exercised in wisdom, and his tongue will be talking of judgment. ℣. The law of his God is in his heart: and his goings shall not slide.

Alleluia, alleluia. ℣. Ecclus. 45, 9. The Lord loved him, and adorned him: he clothed him with a robe of glory. Alleluia.

✠ The Continuation of the holy Gospel according to Matthew.

Matt. 5, 13-19.

AT that time: Jesus said unto his disciples: Ye are the salt of the earth. But if the salt have lost his savour, wherewith shall it be salted? It is thenceforth good for nothing, but to be cast out, and to be trodden under foot of men. Ye are the light of the world. A city that is set on an hill cannot be hid. Neither do men light a candle, and put it under a bushel, but on a candlestick, and it giveth light unto all that are in the house. Let your light so shine before men, that they may see your good works, and glorify your Father which is in heaven. Think not that I am come to destroy the law or the prophets: I am not come to destroy, but to fulfil. For verily I say unto you, Till heaven and earth pass, one jot or one tittle shall in no wise pass from the law, till all be fulfilled. Whosoever therefore shall break one of these least commandments, and shall teach men so, he shall be called the least in the kingdom of heaven: but whosoever shall do and teach them, the same shall be called great in the kingdom of heaven. Creed.

Offertory. Ps. 92, 13. The righteous shall flourish like a palm-tree: and shall spread abroad like a cedar in Libanus.

Secret.

MAY the devout prayers of thy Bishop and Doctor Saint Hilary continually succour us, O Lord: that they may render our oblations acceptable in thy sight; and ever obtain for us thy merciful pardon. Through.

For St. Felix.   Secret.

WE beseech thee, O Lord, mercifully to accept this our sacrifice, which we offer unto thee, pleading the merits of blessed Felix, thy Martyr: that the same may avail for our perpetual succour. Through.

Communion. Luke 12, 42. A faithful and wise servant, whom his lord hath made ruler over his household: to give them their portion of meat in due season.

Postcommunion.

WE beseech thee, O Lord, that blessed Hilary, thy Bishop and most excellent Doctor, may ever stand before thee as our advocate: that this sacrifice of thine ordinance may effectually avail for our salvation. Through.

For St. Felix.   Postcommunion.

O LORD, who hast fulfilled us with these saving mysteries: we beseech thee; that as we celebrate the festival of thy blessed Martyr Felix, so we may be succoured by his prayers. Through.

Scotland:

The same day, January 14.

St. Kentigern

Bishop and Confessor

See Supplement.

January 15.

St. Paul

the First Hermit, Confessor

Double.

Introit. Ps. 92, 13-14. Justus ut palma.

THE righteous shall flourish like a palm-tree: and shall spread abroad like a cedar in Libanus: such as are planted in the house of the Lord: in the courts of the house of our God. Ps. ibid., 1. It is a good thing to give thanks unto the Lord: and to sing praises unto thy name, O Most Highest. ℣. Glory.

Collect.

O GOD, who dost make us to rejoice in the yearly festival of blessed Paul, thy Confessor: mercifully grant; that, as we now observe his heavenly birthday, so we may follow the example of his life. Through.

Commemoration of St. Maurus, Abbot.

Collect.

O LORD, we beseech thee, let the intercession of thy blessed Abbot Maurus commend us unto thee: that those things which for our own merits we cannot ask, we may through his advocacy obtain. Through.

The Lesson from the Epistle of blessed Paul the Apostle to the Philippians.

Phil. 3, 7-12.

BRETHREN: What things were gain to me, those I counted loss for Christ. Yea doubtless, and I count all things but loss for the excellency of the knowledge of Christ Jesus my Lord: for whom I have suffered the loss of all things, and do count them but dung, that I may win Christ and be found in him, not having mine own righteousness which is of the law, but that which is through the faith of Christ: the righteousness which is of God by faith, that I may know him, and the power of his resurrection, and the fellowship of his sufferings: being made conformable unto his death: if by any means I might attain unto the resurrection of the dead: not as though I had already attained, either were already perfect: but I follow after, if that I may apprehend that for which also I am apprehended of Christ Jesus.

Gradual. Ps. 92, 13-14. The righteous shall flourish like a palm-tree: and shall spread abroad like a cedar in Libanus in the house of the Lord. ℣. Ibid., 3. To tell of thy loving-kindness early in the morning, and of thy truth in the night-season.

Alleluia, alleluia. ℣. Hos. 14, 6. The just shall grow as the lily: and flourish for ever before the Lord. Alleluia.

✠ The Continuation of the holy Gospel according to Matthew.

Matt. 11, 25-30.

AT that time: Jesus answered and said: I thank thee, O Father, Lord of heaven and earth, because thou hast hid these things from the wise and prudent, and hast revealed them unto babes. Even so, Father: for so it seemed good in thy sight. All things are delivered unto me of my Father. And no man knoweth the Son, but the Father: neither knoweth any man the Father, save the Son, and he to whomsoever the Son will reveal him. Come unto me, all ye that labour and are heavy laden, and I will give you rest. Take my yoke upon you, and learn of me, for I am meek and lowly of heart: and ye shall find rest unto your souls. For my yoke is easy, and my burden is light.

Offertory. Ps. 21, 1-2. The just shall rejoice in thy strength, O Lord: exceeding glad shall he be of thy salvation: thou hast given him his heart's desire.

Secret.

WE offer thee, O Lord, this our sacrifice of praise to the honour of thy Saints: whereby we trust to be delivered from all evils both in this life and in that which is to come. Through.

For St. Maurus.   Secret.

O LORD, we beseech thee, let thy holy Abbot Maurus intercede for us: that this sacrifice which we offer and present upon thy holy altar may be profitable unto us for our salvation. Through.

Communion. Ps. 64, 11. The righteous shall rejoice in the Lord, and put his trust in him: and all they that are true of heart shall be glad.

Postcommunion.

O LORD, our God, who hast refreshed us with heavenly meat and drink, we humbly beseech thee: that we may be defended by the prayers of him in whose memory we have received the same. Through.

For St. Maurus.

Postcommunion.

LET thy Sacrament, O Lord, which we have now received, and the prayers of thy blessed Abbot Maurus, effectually defend us: that we may both imitate the example of his conversation, and receive the succour of his intercession. Through.

January 16.

St. Marcellus

Pope and Martyr

Simple.

The Mass Si diligis me, p. [2], except the Collect, as below.

Collect.

O LORD, we beseech thee favourably to hear the prayers of thy people: that, as we do rejoice in the passion of blessed Marcellus, thy Martyr and Bishop, so we may be succoured by his merits. Through.

Secret.

WE beseech thee, O Lord, graciously enlighten thy Church by the gifts which we here offer: that in every place thy flock may increase and prosper, and the shepherds by thy governance may be made pleasing to thy name. Through.

Postcommunion.

MERCIFUL Lord, we beseech thee to govern and preserve thy Church, which thou hast here refreshed with heavenly food: that by the guiding of thy mighty power it may serve thee in more abundant freedom, and ever keep thy true religion whole and undefiled. Through.

January 17.

St. Anthony

Abbot

Double.

Introit. Ps. 37, 30-31. Os justi.

THE mouth of the righteous is exercised in wisdom, and his tongue will be talking of judgment: the law of his God is in his heart. Ps. ibid., 1. Fret not thyself because of the ungodly: neither be thou envious against the evil doers. ℣. Glory.

Collect.

O LORD, we beseech thee, let the intercession of thy blessed Abbot Anthony commend us unto thee: that those things which for our own merits we cannot ask, we may through his advocacy obtain. Through.

The Lesson from the book of Wisdom.

Ecclus. 45, 1-6.

BELOVED of God and men, whose memorial is blessed. He made him like to the glorious saints, and magnified him so that his enemies stood in fear of him. By his words he caused the wonders to cease, and he made him glorious in the sight of kings, and gave him a commandment for his people, and shewed him his glory. He sanctified him in his faithfulness and meekness, and chose him out of all men. He made him to hear his voice, and brought him into the dark cloud, and gave him commandments before his face, even the law of life and knowledge.

Gradual. Ps. 21, 4-5. Thou hast prevented him, O Lord, with the blessings of goodness: thou hast set a crown of pure gold upon his head. ℣. He asked life of thee, and thou gavest him a long life, even for ever and ever.

Alleluia, alleluia. ℣. Ps. 92, 13. The righteous shall flourish like a palm-tree: and shall spread abroad like a cedar in Libanus. Alleluia.

✠ The Continuation of the holy Gospel according to Luke.

Luke 12, 35-40.

AT that time: Jesus said unto his disciples: Let your loins be girded about, and your lights burning, and ye yourselves like unto men that wait for their lord, when he will return from the wedding: that when he cometh and knocketh they may open unto him immediately. Blessed are those servants, whom the lord when he cometh shall find watching: verily I say unto you, that he shall gird himself, and make them to sit down to meat, and will come forth and serve them. And if he shall come in the second watch, or come in the third watch, and find them so, blessed are those servants. And this know, that if the good man of the house had known what hour the thief would come, he would have watched, and not have suffered his house to be broken through. Be ye therefore ready also: for the Son of man cometh at an hour when ye think not.

Offertory. Ps. 21, 3-4. Thou hast given him his heart's desire, O Lord, and hast not denied him the request of his lips: thou hast set a crown of pure gold upon his head.

Secret.

O LORD, we beseech thee, let thy holy Abbot Anthony intercede for us: that this sacrifice which we offer and present upon thy holy altar may be profitable unto us for our salvation. Through.

Communion. Luke 12, 42. A faithful and wise servant, whom his lord hath made ruler over his household, to give them their portion of meat in due season.

Postcommunion.

LET thy Sacrament, O Lord, which we have now received, and the prayers of thy blessed Abbot Anthony, effectually defend us: that we may both imitate the example of his conversation, and receive the succour of his intercession. Through.

January 18.

The Chair of St. Peter the Apostle at Rome

Greater double.

Introit. Ecclus. 45, 30. Statuit ei.

THE Lord hath established a covenant of peace with him, and made him the chief of his people: that he should have the dignity of the priesthood for ever. Ps. 132, 1. Lord, remember David: and all his trouble. ℣. Glory.

Collect.

O GOD, who didst bestow upon thy blessed Apostle Peter the keys of the kingdom of heaven, and didst appoint unto him the high priesthood for binding and loosing: vouchsafe; that by the help of his intercession we may be delivered from the bonds of our iniquities: Who livest and reignest.

Commemoration of St. Paul, Ap., which is never omitted.

Collect.

O GOD, who by the preaching of the blessed Apostle Paul didst teach the multitude of the Gentiles: grant to us, we beseech thee; that we who now celebrate his commemoration may feel the effectual benefit of his intercession. (Through.)

Commemoration of St. Prisca, V.M.

Collect.

GRANT, we beseech thee, almighty God: that we who celebrate the heavenly birthday of blessed Prisca, thy Virgin and Martyr; may both rejoice in her yearly solemnity, and follow rightly the example of her faith. Through.

The Lesson from the Epistle of blessed Peter the Apostle.

I Peter 1, 1-7.

PETER, an Apostle of Jesus Christ, to the strangers scattered throughout Pontus, Galatia, Cappadocia, Asia, and Bithynia, elect according to the foreknowledge of God the Father, through sanctification of the Spirit, unto obedience and sprinkling of the blood of Jesus Christ: grace unto you, and peace, be multiplied. Blessed be the God and Father of our Lord Jesus Christ, which according to his abundant mercy hath begotten us again unto a lively hope, by the resurrection of Jesus Christ from the dead, to an inheritance incorruptible and undefiled, and that fadeth not away, reserved in heaven for you, who are kept by the power of God through faith unto salvation, ready to be revealed in the last time. Wherein ye greatly rejoice, though now for a season, if need be, ye are in heaviness through manifold temptations: that the trial of your faith, being much more precious than of gold (that perisheth, though it be tried with fire), might be found unto praise, and honour, and glory, at the appearing of Jesus Christ our Lord.

Gradual. Ps. 107, 32 and 31. Let them exalt him in the congregation of the people: and praise him in the seat of the elders. ℣. O that men would praise the Lord for his goodness, and declare the wonders that he doeth for the children of men.

Alleluia, alleluia. ℣. Matt. 16, 18. Thou art Peter, and upon this rock I will build my Church. Alleluia.

After Septuagesima, omitting Alleluia and the Verse following, is said:

Tract. Matt. 16, 18-19. Thou art Peter, and upon this rock I will build my Church. ℣. And the gates of hell shall not prevail against it: and I will give unto thee the keys of the kingdom of heaven. ℣. Whatsoever thou shalt bind on earth shall be bound in heaven. ℣. And whatsoever thou shalt loose on earth shall be loosed in heaven.

In Votive Masses in Eastertide the Gradual is omitted, and in its place is said:

Alleluia, alleluia. ℣. Ps. 107, 15. O that men would praise the Lord for his goodness, and declare the wonders that he doeth for the children of men. Alleluia ℣. Matt. 16, 18. Thou art Peter, and upon this rock I will build my Church. Alleluia.

✠ The Continuation of the holy Gospel according to Matthew.

Matt. 16, 13-19.

AT that time: When Jesus came into the coasts of Caesarea Philippi, he asked his disciples, saying: Whom do men say that I, the Son of man, am? And they said: Some say that thou art John the Baptist, some Elias, and others Jeremias, or one of the Prophets. He saith unto them: But whom say ye that I am? And Simon Peter answered and said: Thou art the Christ, the Son of the living God. And Jesus answered and said unto him: Blessed art thou, Simon Bar-jona: for flesh and blood hath not revealed it unto thee, but my Father which is in heaven. And I say also unto thee, That thou art Peter, and upon this rock I will build my Church, and the gates of hell shall not prevail against it. And I will give unto thee the keys of the kingdom of heaven. And whatsoever thou shalt bind on earth shall be bound in heaven: and whatsoever thou shalt loose on earth shall be loosed in heaven.

The Creed is not said.

Offertory. Matt. 16, 18-19. Thou art Peter, and upon this rock I will build my Church: and the gates of hell shall not prevail against it: and I will give unto thee the keys of the kingdom of heaven.

Secret.

WE beseech thee, O Lord, let the intercession of thy blessed Apostle Peter commend unto thee the prayers and oblations of thy Church: that these gifts which we offer for his glory may avail for the remission of our sins. Through.

For St. Paul.   Secret.

SANCTIFY, O Lord, through the prayers of thine Apostle Paul, the oblations of thy people: that these gifts, which by thine institution are acceptable unto thee, may by his effectual advocacy be rendered the more acceptable in thy sight. (Through.)

For St. Prisca.   Secret.

WE beseech thee, O Lord, that this sacrifice which we offer in remembrance of the birthday of thy Saints may both loose us from the bonds of our iniquity, and obtain for us the gifts of thy mercy. Through.

Preface of the Apostles.

Communion. Matt. 16, 18. Thou art Peter, and upon this rock I will build my Church.

Postcommunion.

O LORD, let this sacrifice, which we have offered, bring forth gladness in our hearts: that as we shew forth the wonders which thou hast wrought in thy Apostle Peter; so through him we may obtain the abundance of thy loving-kindness. Through.

For St. Paul.   Postcommunion.

O LORD, who hast sanctified us with this saving mystery: we beseech thee; that he whom thou hast given to be our advocate and guide may continually intercede for us. (Through.)

For St. Prisca.   Postcommunion.

O LORD, who hast fulfilled us with these mysteries: we beseech thee, that we may be aided by the prayers of her whose festival we celebrate. Through.

January 19.
For SS. Marius, Martha, Audifax and Abachum

Martyrs.

Introit. Ps. 68, 4. Justi epulentur.

LET the righteous be glad and rejoice before God: let them also be merry and joyful. Ps. ibid., 1. Let God arise, and let his enemies be scattered: let them also that hate him flee before him. ℣. Glory.

Collect.

GRACIOUSLY hear thy people, O Lord, who call upon thee with the assistance of thy Saints: and grant us both to rejoice in peace in this our temporal life; and to obtain thy succour unto life eternal. Through.

Commemoration of St. Canute, K.M.

Collect.

O GOD, who for the glory of thy Church didst adorn the blessed King Canute with the palm of martyrdom, and wondrous miracles: mercifully grant; that, like as he did imitate the passion of the Lord, so we, following in his footsteps, may be found worthy to attain to the joys of everlasting life. Through the same.

The Epistle, Call to remembrance, p. [12].

Gradual. Wisd. 3, 1-3. The souls of the righteous are in the hand of God: and there shall no torment touch them. ℣. In the sight of the unwise they seemed to die: but they are in peace.

Alleluia, alleluia. ℣. Ps. 68, 36. Our God is wonderful in his Saints. Alleluia.

After Septuagesima, omitting Alleluia and the verse following, is said the Tract Ps. 126, p. [11].

The Gospel, As Jesus sat, No. 1, p. [14].

Offertory. Ps. 124, 7. Our soul is escaped, even as a bird out of the snare of the fowler: the snare is broken, and we are delivered.

Secret.

REGARD, O Lord, the prayers and oblations of thy faithful people: that they may be acceptable unto thee for the festival of thy Saints, and obtain for us the succour of thy mercy. Through.

For St. Canute.   Secret.

GRANT, O Lord, that this our bounden service may be acceptable in thy sight: that these our oblations may, by the prayers of him on whose solemnity they are offered, be made profitable unto our salvation. Through.

Communion. Luke 12, 4. I say unto you, my friends: Be not afraid of them that persecute you.

Postcommunion.

GRANT, O Lord, we beseech thee, that the intercession of thy Saints may render us acceptable unto thee: that this our temporal celebration may avail for our eternal salvation. Through.

For St. Canute.   Postcommunion.

WE beseech thee, O Lord our God, that like as we, whom thou hast refreshed by the partaking of thy sacred gift, do offer unto thee our outward worship: so by the intercession of blessed Canute thy Martyr, we may inwardly be profited thereby to our salvation. Through.

January 20.

SS. Fabian, Pope, and Sebastian

Martyrs.

Double.

Introit. Ps. 79, 12, 12 and 10. Intret.

LET the sorrowful sighing of the prisoners, O Lord, come before thee, reward thou our neighbours seven-fold into their bosom: avenge thou the blood of thy Saints that is shed. Ps. ibid., 1. O God, the heathen are come into thine inheritance: thy holy temple have they defiled: and made Jerusalem an heap of stones. ℣. Glory.

Collect.

ALMIGHTY God, mercifully look upon our infirmities: and whereas we are sore afflicted by the burden of our sins, let the glorious intercession of thy blessed Martyrs Fabian and Sebastian be our succour and defence. Through.

The Lesson from the Epistle of blessed Paul the Apostle to the Hebrews.

Hebr. 11, 33-39.

BRETHREN: The Saints through faith subdued kingdoms, wrought righteousness, obtained promises, stopped the mouth of lions, quenched the violence of fire, escaped the edge of the sword, out of weakness were made strong, waxed valiant in fight, turned to flight the armies of the aliens: women received their dead raised to life again: and others were tortured, not accepting deliverance, that they might obtain a better resurrection: and others had trial of cruel mockings and scourgings, yea, moreover of bonds and imprisonment: they were stoned, they were sawn asunder, were tempted, were slain with the sword: they wandered about in sheepskins and goatskins, being destitute, afflicted, tormented: of whom the world was not worthy: they wandered in deserts, and in mountains, and in dens and caves of the earth. And these all, having obtained a good report through faith, were found in Christ Jesus our Lord.

Gradual. Exod. 15, 11. God is glorious in his holy ones: fearful in praises, doing wonders. ℣. Thy right hand, O Lord, is become glorious in power: thy right hand hath dashed in pieces the enemy.

Alleluia, alleluia. ℣. Ps. 145, 10-11. Thy Saints give thanks unto thee, O Lord: they shew the glory of thy kingdom. Alleluia.

After Septuagesima, omitting Alleluia and the Verse following, is said:

Tract. Ps. 126, 5-6. They that sow in tears shall reap in joy. ℣. He that now goeth on his way weeping, and beareth forth good seed. ℣. Shall doubtless come again with joy, and bring his sheaves with him.

✠ The Continuation of the holy Gospel according to Luke.

Luke 6, 17-23.

AT that time: Jesus came down from the mountain, and stood in the plain, and the company of his disciples, and a great multitude of people out of all Judæa and Jerusalem and from the sea coast of

Tyre and Sidon, which came to hear him, and to be healed of their diseases. And they that were vexed with unclean spirits, and they were healed. And the whole multitude sought to touch him: for there went virtue out of him, and healed them all. And he lifted up his eyes on his disciples, and said: Blessed be ye poor: for yours is the kingdom of God. Blessed are ye that hunger now: for ye shall be filled. Blessed are ye that weep now: for ye shall laugh. Blessed are ye, when men shall hate you, and when they shall separate you from their company, and shall reproach you, and cast out your name as evil, for the Son of man's sake. Rejoice ye in that day, and leap for joy: for, behold, your reward is great in heaven.

Offertory. Ps. 32, 11. Be glad, O ye righteous, and rejoice in the Lord: and be joyful, all ye that are true of heart.

Secret.

WE beseech thee, O Lord, mercifully to accept this our sacrifice which we offer unto thee, pleading the merits of thy blessed Martyrs Fabian and Sebastian: that the same may avail for our perpetual succour. Through.

Communion. Luke 6, 18-19. A multitude of sick folk, and they that were vexed with unclean spirits came to him: for there went virtue out of him, and healed them all.

Postcommunion.

WE beseech thee, O Lord our God, that like as we whom thou hast refreshed by the partaking of thy sacred gift do offer unto thee our outward worship: so, at the intercession of thy holy Martyrs Fabian and Sebastian, we may inwardly be profited thereby to our salvation. Through.

January 21.

St. Agnes

Virgin and Martyr

Double.

Introit. Ps. 119, 95-96.

Me exspectaverunt.

THE ungodly laid wait for me to destroy me: O Lord, I will consider thy testimonies: I see that all things come to an end: but thy commandment is exceeding broad. Ps. ibid., 1. Blessed are those that are undefiled in the way: and walk in the law of the Lord. ℣. Glory.

Collect.

ALMIGHTY and everlasting God, who dost choose the weak things of the world to confound those things that are strong: mercifully grant; that we who keep the feast of blessed Agnes, thy Virgin and Martyr, may feel the succour of her intercession in thy sight. Through.

The Lesson from the book of Wisdom.

Ecclus. 51, 1-8 and 12.

I WILL thank thee, O Lord and King, and praise thee, O God my Saviour. I do give praise unto thy name: for thou art my defender and helper, and hast preserved my body from destruction, and from the snare of the slanderous tongue, and from the lips that forge lies, and hast been mine helper against mine adversaries. And hast delivered me, according to the multitude of thy mercies and greatness of thy name, from the teeth of them that were ready to devour me, and out of the hands of such as sought after my life, and from the manifold afflictions which I had: from the choking of fire on every side, and from the midst of the fire which I kindled not: from the depth of the belly of hell, from an unclean tongue, and from lying words, from an unjust king, and from an unrighteous tongue: my soul shall praise the Lord even unto death: for thou deliverest such as wait for thee, and savest them out of the hands of the enemies, O Lord our God.

Gradual. Ps. 45, 3. Full of grace are thy lips: because God hath blessed thee for ever. ℣. Ibid., 5. Because of the word of truth, of meekness, and righteousness: and thy right hand shall teach thee terrible things.

Alleluia, alleluia. ℣. Matt. 25, 4 and 6. The five wise virgins took oil in their vessels with their lamps: and at midnight there was a cry made: Behold, the bridegroom cometh: go ye out to meet Christ the Lord. Alleluia.

After Septuagesima, omitting Alleluia and the Verse following, is said:

Tract. Come, thou Bride of Christ, receive the crown, which the Lord hath prepared for thee for ever: for whose love thou didst shed thy blood. ℣. Ps. 45, 8. Thou hast loved righteousness and hated iniquity: therefore God, even thy God, hath anointed thee with the oil of gladness above thy fellows. ℣. Ibid., 5. In thy comeliness and in thy beauty go forth, ride prosperously and reign.

✠ The Continuation of the holy Gospel according to Matthew.

Matt. 25, 1-13.

AT that time: Jesus spake this parable unto his disciples: The kingdom of heaven shall be likened unto ten virgins: which took their lamps, and went forth to meet the bridegroom. And five of them were wise, and five were foolish: they that were foolish took their lamps, and took no oil with them: but the wise took oil in their vessels with their lamps. While the bridegroom tarried, they all slumbered and slept. And at midnight there was a cry made: Behold, the bridegroom cometh, go ye out to meet him. Then all those virgins arose, and trimmed their lamps. And the foolish said unto the wise: Give us of your oil: for our lamps are gone out. But the wise answered, saying: Not so, lest there be not enough for us and you, but go ye rather to them that sell, and buy for yourselves. And while they went to buy, the bridegroom came: and they that were ready went in with him to the marriage, and the door was shut. Afterwards came also the other virgins, saying: Lord, Lord, open to us. But he answered, and said: Verily I say unto you, I know you not. Watch therefore, for ye know neither the day nor the hour.

Offertory. Ps. 45, 15-16. The Virgins that be her fellows shall be brought unto the King: they that bear her company shall be brought unto thee with joy and gladness: and shall enter into the palace of the Lord the King.

Secret.

O LORD, mercifully regard this sacrifice which we offer unto thee: and at the intercession of blessed Agnes, thy Virgin and Martyr, absolve us from the bonds of our iniquities. Through.

Communion. Matt. 25, 4 and 6. The five wise virgins took oil in their vessels with their lamps: and at midnight there was a cry made: Behold, the bridegroom cometh: go ye out to meet him, Christ the Lord.

Postcommunion.

O LORD, our God, who hast refreshed us with heavenly meat and drink, we humbly beseech thee: that we may be defended by the prayers of her in whose memory we have received the same. Through.

January 22.
SS. Vincent and Anastasius
Martyrs

Simple.

The Mass Intret, p. [9], excepting:

Collect. P

ASSIST us mercifully, O Lord, in these our supplications: that we, who acknowledge the guilt of our sins, may by the intercession of thy blessed Martyrs Vincent and Anastasius obtain deliverance. Through.

Secret. P

WE beseech thee, O Lord, that the gifts which we offer unto thee of our bounden duty and service may be acceptable unto thee for the honour of thy Saints: and by thy mercy be profitable unto us for our salvation. Through.

Postcommunion. P

WE beseech thee, almighty God: that we, who have received this heavenly food, may at the intercession of thy blessed Martyrs Vincent and Anastasius be thereby defended against all adversities. Through.

January 23.
St. Raymund of Pennafort
Confessor

Simple.

The Mass Os justi, from the Common of a Confessor not a Bishop p. [24], the Collect excepted.

Collect. P

O GOD, who didst appoint blessed Raymund excellently to minister the sacrament of penance, and didst wondrously lead him through the waves of the sea: vouchsafe; that, through his intercession, we may be enabled to bring forth worthy fruits of repentance, and to attain to the harbour of everlasting salvation. Through.

Commemoration of St. Emerentiana, V.M.

Collect.

WE beseech thee, O Lord, that like as blessed Emerentiana, thy Virgin and Martyr, by the merit of her chastity, and by her confession of thy power was ever found acceptable in thy sight: so she may effectually intercede for our forgiveness. Through.

Secret. C

WE offer thee, O Lord, this our sacrifice of praise to the honour of thy Saints: whereby we trust to be delivered from all evils both in this life and in that which is to come. Through.

For St. Emerentiana. Secret.

GRACIOUSLY receive, O Lord, through the merits of blessed Emerentiana, thy Virgin and Martyr, this sacrifice which we offer unto thee: and grant that it may avail for our continual help. Through.

Postcommunion. C

O LORD our God, who hast refreshed us with heavenly meat and drink, we humbly beseech thee: that we may be defended by the prayers of him in whose memory we have received the same. Through.

For St. Emerentiana.   Postcommunion.

O LORD our God, who hast fulfilled us with the bounty of thy heavenly gift: we beseech thee that, at the intercession of blessed Emerentiana, thy Virgin and Martyr, we may ever live by the partaking of the same. Through.

January 24.

St. Timothy

Bishop and Martyr

Double.

Introit. Ecclus. 45, 30. Statuit ei.

THE Lord hath established a covenant of peace with him, and made him the chief of his people: that he should have the dignity of the priesthood for ever. Ps. 132, 1. Lord, remember David: and all his trouble. ℣. Glory.

Collect.

ALMIGHTY God, mercifully look upon our infirmities: and whereas we are sore afflicted by the burden of our sins, let the glorious intercession of blessed Timothy thy Martyr and Bishop be our succour and defence. Through.

The Lesson from the Epistle of blessed Paul the Apostle to Timothy.

I Tim. 6, 11-16.

DEARLY beloved: Follow after righteousness, godliness, faith, love, patience, meekness. Fight the good fight of faith, lay hold on eternal life, whereunto thou art also called, and hast professed a good profession before many witnesses. I give thee charge in the sight of God, who quickeneth all things, and before Christ Jesus, who before Pontius Pilate witnessed a good confession: that thou keep this commandment without spot, unrebukeable, until the appearing of our Lord Jesus Christ, which in his times he shall shew, who is the blessed and only Potentate, the King of kings, and Lord of lords: who only hath immortality, dwelling in the light which no man can approach unto: whom no man hath seen, nor can see: to whom be honour and power everlasting. Amen.

Gradual. Ps. 89, 21-23. I have found David my servant, with my holy oil have I anointed him: my hand shall hold him fast, and my arm shall strengthen him. ℣. The enemy shall not be able to do him violence, the son of wickedness shall not hurt him.

Alleluia, alleluia. ℣. Ps. 110, 4. Thou art a priest for ever, after the order of Melchisedech. Alleluia.

After Septuagesima, omitting Alleluia and the Verse following, is said:

Tract. Ps. 21, 3-4. Thou hast given him his heart's desire: and hast not denied him the request of his lips. ℣. For thou hast prevented him with the blessings of goodness. ℣. And hast set a crown of pure gold upon his head.

✠ The Continuation of the holy Gospel according to Luke.

Luke 14, 26-33.

AT that time: Jesus said unto the multitudes: If any man come to me, and hate not his father, and mother, and wife, and children, and brethren, and sisters, yea, and his own life also, he cannot be my disciple. And whosoever doth not bear his cross, and come after me, cannot be my disciple. For which of you, intending to build a tower, sitteth not down first, and counteth the cost, whether he have sufficient to finish it: lest haply, after he hath laid the foundation, and is not able to finish it, all that behold it begin to mock him, saying: This man began to build, and was not able to finish? Or what king, going to make war against another king, sitteth not down first, and consulteth whether he be able with ten thousand to meet him that cometh against him with twenty thousand? Or else, while the other is yet a great way off, he sendeth an ambassage, and desireth conditions of peace. So likewise, whosoever he be of you that forsaketh not all that he hath, he cannot be my disciple.

Offertory. Ps. 89, 25. My truth and my mercy shall be with him: and in my name shall his horn be exalted.

Secret.

WE beseech thee, O Lord, mercifully to accept this our sacrifice which we offer unto thee, pleading the merits of blessed Timothy thy Martyr and Bishop: that the same may avail for our perpetual succour. Through.

Communion. Ps. 89, 36-38. I have sworn once by my holiness: His seed shall endure for ever: and his seat is like as the sun before me; he shall stand fast for evermore as the moon, and as the faithful witness in heaven.

Postcommunion.

WE beseech thee, O Lord our God, that like as we whom thou hast refreshed by the partaking of thy sacred gift do offer unto thee our outward worship: so, at the intercession of blessed Timothy thy Martyr and Bishop, we may inwardly be profited thereby to our salvation. Through.

January 25.

The Conversion of St. Paul the Apostle

Greater double.

Introit. II Tim. 1, 12. Scio cui credidi.

I KNOW whom I have believed, and am persuaded that he is able to keep that which I have committed unto him against that day, a just judge. Ps. 139, 1. O Lord, thou hast searched me out, and known me: thou knowest my down-sitting, and mine up-rising. ℣. Glory.

Collect.

O GOD, who, through the preaching of the blessed Apostle Saint Paul, hast caused the light of the Gospel to shine throughout the world: grant, we beseech thee; that we, having his wonderful Conversion in remembrance, may shew forth our thankfulness unto thee for the same, by following the holy doctrine which he taught. Through.

Or, Collect.

O GOD who through the preaching of the blessed Apostle Paul hast taught the whole world: grant us, we beseech thee; that we, who this day celebrate his Conversion, may by following his example be brought nearer unto thee. Through.

In low Masses Commemoration of St. Peter, Ap., which is never omitted.

Collect.

O GOD, who didst bestow upon thy blessed Apostle Peter the keys of the kingdom of heaven, and didst appoint unto him the high priesthood for binding and loosing: vouchsafe; that by the help of his intercession we may be delivered from the bonds of our iniquities: Who livest and reignest.

The Lesson from the Acts of the Apostles. Acts 9, 1-22.

IN those days: Saul, yet breathing out threatenings and slaughter against the disciples of the Lord, went unto the high priest, and desired of him letters to Damascus to the synagogues: that, if he found any of this way, whether they were men or women, he might bring them bound unto Jerusalem. And, as he journeyed, he came near Damascus: and suddenly there shined round about him a light from heaven. And he fell to the earth, and heard a voice saying unto him: Saul, Saul, why persecutest thou me? And he said: Who art thou, Lord? And the Lord said: I am Jesus, whom thou persecutest: it is hard for thee to kick against the pricks. And he, trembling and astonished, said: Lord, what wilt thou have me to do? And the Lord said unto him: Arise, and go into the city, and it shall be told thee what thou must do. And the men which journeyed with him stood speechless, hearing a voice, but seeing no man. And Saul arose from the earth, and when his eyes were opened he saw no man. But they led him by the hand, and brought him into Damascus. And he was three days without sight, and neither did eat nor drink. And there was a certain disciple at Damascus named Ananias: and to him said the Lord in a vision: Ananias. And he said: Behold, I am here, Lord. And the Lord said unto him: Arise, and go into the street which is called Straight: and enquire in the house of Judas for one called Saul, of Tarsus: for behold, he prayeth. (And hath seen in a vision a man named Ananias, coming in, and putting his hand on him, that he might receive his sight.) Then Ananias answered: Lord, I have heard by many of this man, how much evil he hath done to thy saints at Jerusalem: and here he hath authority from the chief priests to bind all that call on thy name. But the Lord said unto him: Go thy way, for he is a chosen vessel unto me, to bear my name before the Gentiles, and kings, and the children of Israel. For I will show him how great things he must suffer for my name's sake. And Ananias went his way, and entered into the house: and, putting his hands on him, said: Brother Saul, the Lord, even Jesus that appeared unto thee in the way as thou camest, hath sent me, that thou mightest receive thy sight, and be filled with the Holy Ghost. And immediately there fell from his eyes as it had been scales, and he received sight forthwith: and arose, and was baptized. And when he had received meat he was strengthened. Then was Saul certain days with the disciples which were at Damascus. And straightway he preached Christ in the synagogues, that he is the Son of God. But all that heard him were amazed, and said: Is not this he that destroyed them which called on this name in Jerusalem: and came hither for that intent, that he might bring them bound unto the chief priests? But Saul increased the more in strength, and confounded the Jews which dwelt at Damascus, proving that this is very Christ.

Gradual. Gal. 2, 8-9. He that wrought effectually in Peter to the apostleship, the same was mighty in me towards the Gentiles: and they perceived the grace that was given unto me. ℣. The grace of God which was bestowed upon me was not in vain: but his grace ever abideth in me.

Alleluia, alleluia. ℣. Great and holy is Paul, a chosen vessel, meet indeed to be glorified, who also was worthy to inherit the twelfth throne. Alleluia.

After Septuagesima, omitting Alleluia and the Verse following, is said:

Tract. Thou art a chosen vessel, holy Apostle Paul: meet indeed art thou to be glorified. ℣. Preacher of truth and doctor of the Gentiles in faith and truth. ℣. Through thee all the Gentiles have known the grace of God. ℣. Intercede for us to God, who chose thee.

✠ The Continuation of the holy Gospel according to Matthew.

Matt. 19, 27-29.

AT that time: Peter said unto Jesus: Behold, we have forsaken all, and followed thee: what shall we have therefore? And Jesus said unto them: Verily I say unto you, That ye which have followed me, in the regeneration when the Son of man shall sit in the throne of his glory, ye also shall sit upon twelve thrones, judging the twelve tribes of Israel. And every one that hath forsaken houses, or brethren, or sisters, or father, of mother, or wife, or children, or lands, for my name's sake, shall receive an hundred-fold, and shall inherit everlasting life.*

But many that are first shall be last, and the last shall be first.

The Creed is not said.

Offertory. Ps. 139, 17. Right dear are thy friends unto me, O God, and held in highest honour: their rule and governance is exceeding steadfast.

Secret.

SANCTIFY, O Lord, through the prayers of thine Apostle Paul, these oblations of thy people: that like as thou hast appointed this ordinance to be acceptable in thy sight, so by the effectual help of his advocacy it may avail yet more for the obtaining of thy favour. Through.

For St. Peter. Secret.

WE beseech thee, O Lord, let the intercession of thy blessed Apostle Peter, commend unto thee the prayers and oblations of thy Church: that these gifts which we offer for his glory may avail for the remission of our sins. Through.

Preface of the Apostles.

Communion. Matt. 19, 28-29. Verily, I say unto you: that ye which have forsaken all and followed me, shall receive an hundred-fold, and shall inherit everlasting life.

Postcommunion.

O LORD, who hast sanctified us with this saving mystery: we beseech thee; that he, whom thou hast given to be our advocate and guide, may continually intercede for us. Through.

For St. Peter. Postcommunion.

O LORD, let this sacrifice which we have offered bring forth gladness in our hearts: that as we shew forth the wonders which thou hast wrought in thine Apostle Peter; so through him we may receive the abundance of thy loving-kindness. Through.

January 26.

St. Polycarp

Bishop and Martyr

Double.

Introit. Dan. 3, 84 and 87. Sacerdotes Dei.

O YE priests of the Lord, bless ye the Lord: O ye holy and humble men of heart, praise God. Ibid., 57. O all ye works of the Lord, bless ye the Lord: praise him, and magnify him for ever. ℣. Glory.

Collect.

O GOD, who makest us glad with the yearly solemnity of blessed Polycarp, thy Martyr and Bishop: mercifully grant; that, as we now celebrate his heavenly birthday, so we may likewise rejoice in his protection. Through.

The Lesson from the Epistle of blessed John the Apostle.

I John 3, 10-16.

DEARLY beloved: Whosoever doeth not righteousness is not of God, neither he that loveth not his brother: for this is the message that ye heard from the beginning, that we should love one another. Not as Cain, who was of that wicked one, and slew his brother. And wherefore slew he him? Because his own works were evil: and his brother's righteous. Marvel not, my brethren, if the world hate you. We know that we have passed from death unto life, because we love the brethren. He that loveth not his brother abideth in death: whosoever hateth his brother is a murderer. And ye know that no murderer hath eternal life abiding in him. Hereby perceive we the love of God, because he laid down his life for us: and we ought to lay down our lives for the brethren.

Gradual. Ps. 8, 6-7. Thou hast crowned him with glory and worship. ℣. Thou hast made him to have dominion of the works of thy hands, O Lord.

Alleluia, alleluia. ℣. This is a priest whom the Lord hath crowned. Alleluia.

After Septuagesima, omitting Alleluia and the Verse following, is said:

Tract. Ps. 112, 1-3. Blessed is the man that feareth the Lord: he hath great delight in his commandments. ℣. His seed shall be mighty upon earth: the generation of the faithful shall be blessed. ℣. Riches and plenteousness shall be in his house: and his righteousness endureth for ever.

✠ The Continuation of the holy Gospel according to Matthew.

Matt. 10, 26-32.

AT that time: Jesus said to his disciples: There is nothing covered, that shall not be revealed; and hid, that shall not be known. What I tell you in darkness, that speak ye in light: and what ye hear in the ear, that preach ye upon the housetops. And fear not them which kill the body, but are not able to kill the soul: but rather fear him which is able to destroy both soul and body in hell. Are not two sparrows sold for a farthing: and one of them shall not fall on the ground without your Father? But the very hairs of your head are all numbered. Fear ye not therefore: ye are of more value than many sparrows. Whosoever therefore shall confess me before men, him will I confess also before my Father which is in heaven.

Offertory. Ps. 89, 21-22. I have found David my servant, with my holy oil have I anointed him: my hand shall hold him fast, and my arm shall strengthen him.

Secret.

SANCTIFY, O Lord, the gifts which we dedicate to thee: that at the intercession of blessed Polycarp, thy Martyr and Bishop, they may obtain for us thy gracious favour. Through.

Communion. Ps. 21, 4. Thou hast set, O Lord, a crown of pure gold upon his head.

Postcommunion.

WE beseech thee, O Lord our God, that like as we, whom thou hast refreshed by the partaking of thy sacred gift, do offer unto thee our outward worship: so, at the intercession of blessed Polycarp, thy Martyr and Bishop, we may inwardly be profited thereby to our salvation. Through.

January 27.

St. John Chrysostom

Bishop, Confessor and Doctor of the Church

Double.

Introit. Ecclus. 15, 5. In medio.

IN the midst of the Church he opened his mouth: and the Lord filled him with the spirit of wisdom and understanding: he clothed him with a robe of glory. Ps. 92, 1. It is a good thing to give thanks unto the Lord: and to sing praises unto thy name, O most Highest. ℣. Glory.

Collect.

O LORD, who didst vouchsafe to illumine thy Church with the glorious merits and doctrine of thy blessed Confessor and Bishop John Chrysostom: increase, we beseech thee, and multiply the same by the bounty of thy heavenly grace. Through.

The Lesson from the Epistle of blessed Paul the Apostle to Timothy.

II Tim. 4, 1-8.

DEARLY beloved: I charge thee before God, and the Lord Jesus Christ, who shall judge the quick and the dead at his appearing and his kingdom: preach the word, be instant in season, out of season, reprove, rebuke, exhort with all longsuffering and doctrine. For the time will come when they will not endure sound doctrine, but after their own lusts shall they heap to themselves teachers, having itching ears, and they shall turn away their ears from the truth, and shall be turned unto fables. But watch thou in all things, endure afflictions, do the work of an Evangelist, make full proof of thy ministry. For I am now ready to be offered, and the time of my departure is at hand. I have fought a good fight, I have finished my course, I have kept the faith. Henceforth there is laid up for me a crown of righteousness, which the Lord, the righteous judge, shall give me at that day: and not to me only, but unto all them also that love his appearing.

Gradual. Ecclus 44, 16. Behold a great priest, who in his days pleased God. ℣. Ibid., 20. There was none found like unto him, to keep the law of the Most High.

Alleluia, alleluia. ℣. Jas. 1, 12. Blessed is the man that endureth temptation: for when he is tried, he shall receive the crown of life, alleluia.

After Septuagesima, omitting Alleluia and the Verse following, is said:

Tract. Ps. 112. Blessed is the man that feareth the Lord: he hath great delight in his commandments. ℣. His seed shall be mighty upon earth: the generation of the faithful shall be blessed. ℣. Riches and plenteousness shall be in his house: and his righteousness remaineth for ever.

✠ The Continuation of the holy Gospel according to Matthew.

Matt. 5, 13-19.

AT that time: Jesus said unto his disciples: Ye are the salt of the earth. But if the salt have lost his savour, wherewith shall it be salted? It is thenceforth good for nothing, but to be cast out, and to be trodden under foot of men. Ye are the light of the world. A city that is set on an hill cannot be hid. Neither do men light a candle, and put it under a bushel, but on a candlestick, and it giveth light unto all that are in the house. Let your light so shine before men, that they may see your good works, and glorify your Father which is in heaven. Think not that I am come to destroy the law, or the prophets: I am not come to destroy, but to fulfil. For verily I say unto you, Till heaven and earth pass, one jot or one tittle shall in no wise pass from the law, till all be fulfilled. Whosoever therefore shall break one of these least commandments, and shall teach men so, he shall be called the least in the kingdom of heaven: but whosoever shall do and teach them, the same shall be called great in the kingdom of heaven. Creed.

Offertory. Ps. 92, 13. The righteous shall flourish like a palm-tree: and shall spread abroad like a cedar in Libanus.

Secret.

MAY the devout prayers of thy Bishop and Doctor Saint John Chrysostom, continually succour us, O Lord: that they may render our oblations acceptable in thy sight; and may ever obtain for us thy merciful pardon. Through.

Communion. Luke 12, 42. A faithful and wise servant, whom his lord hath made ruler over his household: to give them their portion of meat in due season.

Postcommunion.

WE beseech thee, O Lord, that blessed John Chrysostom, thy Bishop and and most excellent Doctor, may ever stand before thee as our advocate: that this sacrifice of thine ordinance may effectually avail for our salvation. Through.

January 28.

St. Peter Nolasco

Confessor

Double.

Introit. Ps. 92, 13-14. Justus ut palma.

THE righteous shall flourish like a palm-tree: and shall spread abroad like a cedar in Libanus: such as are planted in the house of the Lord: in the courts of the house of our God. Ps. ibid., 1. It is a good thing to give thanks unto the Lord: and to sing praises unto thy name, O most Highest. ℣. Glory.

Collect.

O GOD, who for an ensample of thy charity didst thyself teach Saint Peter to enrich thy Church with a new offspring for the redemption of the faithful: grant to us by his intercession; that we, being delivered from the bondage of our sins, may rejoice in everlasting freedom in our heavenly country: Who livest and reignest.

Commemoration of St. Agnes, V.M.

Collect.

O GOD, who makest us glad with the yearly solemnity of blessed Agnes, thy Virgin and Martyr: grant, we beseech thee; that as we venerate her in our outward service, so we may follow the example of her godly conversation. Through.

The Lesson from the Epistle of blessed Paul the Apostle to the Corinthians.

I Cor. 4, 9-14.

BRETHREN: We are made a spectacle unto the world, and to Angels, and to men. We are fools for Christ's sake, but ye are wise in Christ: we are weak, but ye are strong: ye are honourable, but we are despised. Even unto this present hour we both hunger, and thirst, and are naked and are buffeted, and have no certain dwelling-place, and labour, working with our own hands: being reviled, we bless: being persecuted, we suffer it: being defamed, we intreat: we are made as the filth of the world, and are the offscouring of all things unto this day. I write not these things to shame you, but as my beloved sons I warn you: in Christ Jesu our Lord.

Gradual. Ps. 37, 30-31. The mouth of the righteous is exercised in wisdom, and his tongue will be talking of judgment. ℣. The law of his God is in his heart: and his goings shall not slide.

Alleluia, alleluia. ℣. Ps. 112, 1. Blessed is the man that feareth the Lord: he hath great delight in his commandments. Alleluia.

After Septuagesima, omitting Alleluia and the Verse following, is said:

Tract. Ps. 112, 1-3. Blessed is the man that feareth the Lord: he hath great delight in his commandments. ℣. His seed shall be mighty upon earth: the generation of the faithful shall be blessed. ℣. Riches and plenteousness shall be in his house: and his righteousness endureth for ever.

✠ The Continuation of the holy Gospel according to Luke.

Luke 12, 32-34.

AT that time: Jesus said unto his disciples: Fear not, little flock, for it is your Father's good pleasure to give you the kingdom. Sell that ye have, and give alms. Provide yourselves bags which wax not old, a treasure in the heavens that faileth not: where no thief approacheth, neither moth corrupteth. For where your treasure is, there will your heart be also.

Offertory. Ps. 21, 1-2. The just shall rejoice in thy strength, O Lord, exceeding glad shall he be of thy salvation: thou hast given him his heart's desire.

Secret.

WE offer thee, O Lord, this sacrifice of praise to the honour of thy Saints: whereby we trust to be delivered from all evils both in this life and in that which is to come. Through.

For St. Agnes. Secret.

LET thy plenteous benediction, we beseech thee, O Lord, come down upon these sacrifices: that by thy mercy it may effectually avail for our sanctification, and make us to rejoice in the solemnity of thy Martyrs. Through.

Communion. Matt. 19, 28-29. Verily I say unto you: that ye which have forsaken all, and followed me, shall receive an hundred-fold and shall inherit everlasting life.

Postcommunion.

O LORD our God, who hast refreshed us with heavenly meat and drink, we humbly beseech thee: that we may be defended by the prayers of him in whose memory we have received the same. Through.

For St. Agnes. Postcommunion.

GRANT, we beseech thee, O Lord, that the Sacrament which we have received in our observance of this yearly festival: may bestow on us thy healing; both in this temporal life and unto life eternal. Through.

January 29.

St. Francis of Sales

Bishop, Confessor and Doctor of the Church

Double.

The Mass In medio, p. [22], except the Collect.

And the Creed is said.

Collect. P

O GOD, who for the salvation of souls didst cause blessed Francis, thy Confessor and Bishop, to become all things to all men: mercifully grant; that we, being filled with the sweetness of thy love, may, by the direction of his counsels and the succour of his merits, attain unto the joys of everlasting life. Through.

Secret. C 1

MAY the devout prayers of thy Bishop and Doctor, Saint Francis, continually succour us, O Lord: that they may render our oblations acceptable in thy sight; and may ever obtain for us thy merciful pardon. Through.

Postcommunion. C 1

WE beseech thee, O Lord, that blessed Francis, thy Bishop and most excellent Doctor, may ever stand before thee as our advocate: that this sacrifice of thine ordinance may effectually avail for our salvation. Through.

January 30.

St. Martina

Virgin and Martyr

Simple.

The Mass Loquebar, p. [28].

Collect.

O GOD, who among the manifold works of thy power hast bestowed even upon the weakness of women the victory of martyrdom: mercifully grant; that we, who this day celebrate the heavenly birth of blessed Martina thy Virgin and Martyr, may by her example be drawn nearer unto thee. Through.

Secret.

RECEIVE, O Lord, the gifts which we offer on the solemnity of blessed Martina, thy Virgin and Martyr: through whose advocacy we trust to be delivered. Through.

Postcommunion.

ASSIST us mercifully, O Lord, who have here received these holy mysteries: and at the intercession of blessed Martina, thy Virgin and Martyr, make us ever to rejoice in thy continual protection. Through.

January 31.

St. John Bosco

Confessor

Double.

Introit. I Kings 4, 29. Dedit illi.

GOD gave him wisdom and understanding exceeding much, and largeness of heart, even as the sand that is on the seashore. Ps. 113, 1. Praise the Lord, ye children: O praise the name of the Lord. ℣. Glory.

Collect.

O GOD, who didst raise up Saint John thy Confessor to be a father and teacher of thy children, and through him, with the aid of the Virgin Mary, didst will that new homes of religion should flourish in thy Church: grant, we beseech thee; that we, being kindled by the same fire of love, may have grace to seek for souls, and to serve thee alone. Through.

The Lesson from the Epistle of blessed Paul the Apostle to the Philippians.

Phil. 4, 4-9.

BRETHREN: Rejoice in the Lord alway: and again I say, Rejoice. Let your moderation be known unto all men: the Lord is at hand. Be careful for nothing: but in everything by prayer and supplication with thanksgiving let your requests be made known unto God. And the peace of God, which passeth all understanding, shall keep your hearts and minds through Christ Jesus. Finally, brethren, whatsoever things are true, whatsoever things are honest, whatsoever things are just, whatsoever things are pure, whatsoever things are lovely, whatsoever things are of good report, if there be any virtue, and if there be any praise, think on these things. Those things, which ye have both learned, and received, and heard, and seen in me, do: and the God of peace shall be with you.

Gradual. Ps. 37, 3-5. Put thou thy trust in the Lord, and be doing good, dwell in the land, and verily thou shalt be fed. ℣. Delight thou in the Lord: and he shall give thee thy heart's desire: commit thy way unto the Lord, and put thy trust in him, and he shall bring it to pass.

Alleluia, alleluia. ℣. Ps. 74, 21. The poor and needy shall give praise unto thy name. Alleluia.

After Septuagesima, omitting Alleluia and the Verse following, is said:

Tract. Ps. 61, 4-6. Thou hast been my hope, O Lord: and a strong tower for me against the enemy. ℣. I will dwell in thy tabernacle for ever: and my trust shall be under the covering of thy wings. ℣. For thou, O Lord, hast heard my desires: and hast given an heritage unto those that fear thy name.

In Votive Masses in Eastertide the Gradual is omitted, and in its place is said:

Alleluia, alleluia. ℣. Ps. 74, 22. The poor and needy shall give praise unto thy name. Alleluia. ℣. Ps. 36, 8. They shall be satisfied with the plenteousness of thy house: and thou shalt give them drink of thy pleasures, as out of the river. Alleluia.

✠ The Continuation of the holy Gospel according to Matthew.

Matt. 18, 1-5.

AT that time: Came the disciples unto Jesus, saying: Who is the greatest in the kingdom of heaven? And Jesus called a little child unto him, and set him in the midst of them, and said: Verily I say unto you, Except ye be converted, and become as little children, ye shall not enter into the kingdom of heaven. Whosoever therefore shall humble himself as this little child, the same is greatest in the kingdom of heaven. And whoso shall receive one such little child in my name receiveth me.

Offertory. Ps. 34, 11. Come, ye children, and hearken unto me: I will teach you the fear of the Lord.

Secret.

RECEIVE, O Lord, the pure oblation of this saving Victim, and vouchsafe: that we, loving thee in all and above all things, may be made worthy to live to the praise of thy glory. Through.

Communion. Rom. 4, 18. Against hope he believed in hope, that he might become the father of many nations, according to that which was spoken to him.

Postcommunion.

O LORD, who hast fulfilled us with the mystery of thy Body and Blood, we beseech thee to grant: that at the intercession of Saint John thy Confessor we may ever abide in thanksgiving: Who livest and reignest with God the Father.

FEASTS OF FEBRUARY
February 1.

St. Ignatius
Bishop and Martyr

Double.

Introit. Gal. 6, 14. Mihi autem.

BUT God forbid that I should glory, save in the Cross of our Lord Jesus Christ: by whom the world is crucifield unto me, and I unto the world. Ps. 132, 1. Lord, remember David: and all his trouble. ℣. Glory.

Collect.

ALMIGHTY God, mercifully look upon our infirmity: and whereas we are sore afflicted by the burden of our sins, let the glorious intercession of blessed Ignatius thy Martyr and Bishop be our succour and defence. Through.

The Lesson from the Epistle of blessed Paul the Apostle to the Romans.

Rom. 8, 35-39.

BRETHREN: Who shall separate us from the love of Christ: shall tribulation, or distress, or persecution, or famine, or nakedness, or peril, or sword? As it is written: For thy sake we are killed all the day long: we are accounted as sheep for the slaughter. Nay, in all these things we are more than conquerors through him that loved us. For I am persuaded, that neither death, nor life, nor angels, nor principalities, nor powers, nor things present, nor things to come, nor height, nor depth, nor any other creature, shall be able to separate us from the love of God, which is in Christ Jesus our Lord.

Gradual. Ecclus. 44, 16. Behold a great priest who in his days pleased God. ℣. Ibid., 20. There was none found like unto him, to keep the law of the Most High.

Alleluia, alleluia. ℣. Gal. 2, 19-20. I am crucified with Christ: I live, yet not I, but Christ liveth in me. Alleluia.

After Septuagesima, omitting Alleluia and the Verse following, is said:

Tract. Ps. 21, 3-4. Thou hast given him his heart's desire: and hast not denied him the request of his lips. ℣. For thou hast prevented him with the blessings of goodness. ℣. Thou hast set a crown of pure gold upon his head.

✠ The Continuation of the holy Gospel according to John.

John 12, 24-26.

AT that time: Jesus said unto his disciples: Verily, verily, I say unto you, Except a corn of wheat fall into the ground and die, it abideth alone: but if it die, it bringeth forth much fruit. He that loveth his life shall lose it: and he that hateth his life in this world shall keep it unto life eternal. If any man serve me, let him follow me: and where I am, there shall also my servant be. If any man serve me, him will my Father honour.

Offertory. Ps. 8, 6-7. Thou hast crowned him with glory and worship: and hast made him to have dominion of the works of thy hands, O Lord.

Secret.

WE beseech thee, O Lord, mercifully to accept this our sacrifice which we offer unto thee, pleading the merits of blessed Ignatius thy Martyr and Bishop: that the same may avail for our perpetual succour. Through.

Communion. I am the wheat of Christ: let me be ground by the teeth of beasts, that I may be found pure bread.

Postcommunion.

WE beseech thee, O Lord our God, that like as we whom thou hast refreshed by the partaking of thy sacred gift do offer unto thee our outward worship: so, at the intercession of blessed Ignatius thy Martyr and Bishop; we may inwardly be profited thereby to our salvation. Through.

February 2.

THE PURIFICATION
OF
THE BLESSED VIRGIN MARY

Double of 2nd class.

¶ If it happen that this Feast be transferred, only the Blessing and Distribution of the Candles and the Procession take place to-day. Mass is said of the office occurring, and in it lighted Candles are not held in the hands.

¶ Terce being ended, the Priest vested in a violet Cope, or without a Chasuble, with the Ministers vested in like manner, proceeds to bless the Candles, which are placed in the midst before the Altar or at the Epistle corner, and he himself, standing in the same place facing the Altar, says with joined hands in the tone of the Collect of the ferial Mass:

℣. The Lord be with you.

℟. And with thy spirit.

Let us pray.   Collect.

O LORD holy, Father almighty, everlasting God, who hast created all things out of nothing, and by thy command hast made this liquid through the labours of bees to come to the perfection of wax: who didst likewise on this day fulfil the petition of the just man Simeon: we humbly pray thee; that through the invocation of thy most holy name, and the intercession of blessed Mary ever Virgin, whose festival we this day devoutly celebrate, and through the prayers of all thy Saints, thou wouldest vouchsafe to bl ✠ ess and sanc ✠ tify these candles for the use of men, and for their protection in body and soul, on land or on water: and that from thy holy heaven, and from the throne of thy majesty, thou wouldest hearken to the voice of this thy people, that seeketh to bear them forth in their hands to thine honour and to sing thy praises: and we beseech thee to have mercy on all that call upon thee, whom thou hast redeemed with the precious Blood of thy Son: Who liveth and reigneth with thee in the unity of the Holy Ghost, God: throughout all ages, world without end. ℟. Amen.

Let us pray.   Collect.

ALMIGHTY and everlasting God, who on this day didst present thine only-begotten Son in thy holy temple, to be received in the arms of Saint Simeon: we humbly implore thy mercy; that thou wouldest vouchsafe to bl ✠ ess, sanc ✠ tify, and kindle with the light of thy heavenly benediction these candles, which we thy servants, receiving to the glory of thy name, desire to kindle and bear forth: to the intent that we, being made worthy by offering them unto thee, our Lord and God, and being enkindled with the holy fire of thy most gracious charity, may be found meet to be presented in the holy temple of thy glory. Through the same Jesus Christ thy Son our Lord: Who liveth and reigneth with thee in the unity of the Holy Ghost, God: throughout all ages, world without end. ℟. Amen.

Let us pray.   Collect.

O LORD Jesu Christ, the true light, that lightenest every man that cometh into this world: pour forth thy bles✠sing upon these candles, and sanc✠tify them with the light of thy grace, and mercifully grant; that even as these lights, kindled with visible fire, do scatter the darkness of night; so our hearts, illumined by invisible fire, that is, by the brightness of the Holy Spirit, may be delivered from all blindness of iniquity: that, the eyes of our understanding being enlightened, we may discern such things as are pleasing unto thee and profitable for our salvation; so that finally after the darkness and dangers of this world, we may be found meet to attain unto the light everlasting. Through thee, Christ Jesu, Saviour of the world, who in perfect Trinity livest and reignest, God, throughout all ages, world without end. ℟. Amen.

Let us pray.   Collect.

ALMIGHTY and everlasting God, who through thy servant Moses didst command the purest liquid of oil to be prepared for the lamps to burn continually before thy face: mercifully pour upon these candles the grace of thy bene✠diction: that as they shed forth their outward light, so, by thy grace, the light of thy Spirit may continually shine within our souls. Through Jesus Christ thy Son our Lord: Who liveth and reigneth with thee in the unity of the same Holy Spirit, God: throughout all ages, world without end. ℟. Amen.

Let us pray.   Collect.

O LORD Jesu Christ, who on this day, appearing among men in substance of our flesh, wast presented by thy parents in the temple: whom the old man, Simeon, the venerable, illumined by the light of thy Spirit, acknowledged, received and blessed: mercifully grant; that we, being enlightened and instructed by the grace of the same Holy Spirit, may truly know thee and faithfully love thee: Who livest and reignest with God the Father in the unity of the same Holy Spirit, God, throughout all ages, world without end. ℟. Amen.

¶ The Prayers being ended, the Celebrant sets incense in the thurible; and thrice sprinkles the Candles with holy water, saying the Antiphon, Thou shalt purge me, without chant and without the Psalm: and then thrice incenses them.

Then the senior of the Clergy approaches the Altar, and from him the Celebrant receives a Candle, neither genuflecting nor kissing his hand. Then the Celebrant, standing in the midst before the Altar and turning to the people, distributes Candles first to the senior, from whom he himself received; then to the Deacon and Subdeacon vested, and to the rest of the Clergy, one by one in order, lastly to the lay people: all kneeling and kissing the Candle and the Celebrant's hand, excepting Prelates, if any be present. And when he begins to distribute the Candles, the Choir sings:

Antiphon. Luke 2, 32. A light to lighten the Gentiles, and the glory of thy people Israel.

Cantic. ibid., 29-31. Lord, now lettest thou thy servant depart in peace, according to thy word.

Then is repeated the whole Antiphon, A light to lighten the Gentiles, which is likewise repeated after each Verse.

For mine eyes have seen thy salvation. Ant. A light.

Which thou hast prepared before the face of all people. Ant. A light.

Glory be to the Father, and to the Son, and to the Holy Ghost. Ant. A light.

As it was in the beginning, is now, and ever shall be, world without end. Amen. Ant. A light.

These being ended, shall be sung:

Antiphon. Ps. 44, 26. O Lord, arise, help us: and deliver us for thy name's sake.

Ps. ibid. O God, we have heard with our ears: our fathers have declared unto us. ℣. Glory be.

Then is repeated: O Lord, arise.

Then the Priest says: Let us pray.

¶ If it be after Septuagesima, and not a Sunday, the Deacon says:

Let us bow the knee. ℟. Arise.

Collect.

WE beseech thee, O Lord, hearken unto thy people: and vouchsafe; that this observance, wherein thou sufferest us to do thee outward honour year by year, may by the light of thy grace bring forth fruit in our souls. Through Christ our Lord. ℟. Amen.

¶ Then follows the Procession. And first the Celebrant sets incense in the censer: then the Deacon, turning himself to the people, says: Let us proceed in peace. And the Choir answers: In the name of Christ. Amen.

¶ The Thurifer goes first, with smoking thurible: then the Subdeacon vested, carrying the Cross, in the midst between two Acolytes with lighted candles: the Clergy follow in order, last of all the Celebrant with the Deacon on his left, all with lighted Candles in their hands: and the following Antiphons are sung:

Antiphon. O Sion, adorn thy bride-chamber, and receive Christ the King: greet Mary, who is the gate of heaven: for she beareth the King of the glory of the new light: she remaineth a Virgin, yet beareth in her hands a Son begotten before the morning star: whom Simeon took into his arms, declaring to the nations that he is the Lord of life and death, and Saviour of the world.

Another Antiphon. Luke 2, 26-29. It was revealed unto Simeon by the Holy Ghost, that he should not see death, before he had seen the Lord's Christ: and when they brought the Child into the temple, then took he him up in his arms, and blessed God, and said: Lord, now lettest thou thy servant depart in peace. ℣. When his parents brought in the Child Jesus, to do for him according to the custom of the law, then took he him up in his arms.

As they enter the Church, the following is sung:

℣. They offered for him unto the Lord a pair of turtle doves or two young pigeons:* As it is written in the law of the Lord.

℣. When the days of Mary's purification according to the law of Moses were accomplished, they brought Jesus to Jerusalem to present him to the Lord.— As it is written in the law of the Lord.

℣. Glory be to the Father, and to the Son, and to the Holy Ghost.—As it is written in the law of the Lord.

¶ The Procession being ended, the Celebrant and Ministers lay aside their violet vestments, and put on white for the Mass. And Candles are held in the hands lighted while the Gospel is read, and again from the beginning of the Canon to the end of the Communion.

¶ To-day any Votive Mass, even solemn, of Christ the Lord, is forbidden.

AT THE MASS

Introit. Ps. 48, 10-11. Suscepimus.

WE wait for thy loving-kindness, O God, in the midst of thy temple: O God, according to thy name, so is thy praise unto the world's end: thy right hand is full of righteousness. Ps. ibid., 1. Great is the Lord, and highly to be praised: in the city of our God, even upon his holy hill. ℣. Glory.

Collect.

ALMIGHTY and everliving God, we humbly beseech thy majesty: that, as thy only-begotten Son was this day presented in the temple in substance of our flesh; so we may be presented unto thee with pure and clean hearts, *by the same thy Son Jesus Christ our Lord: Who liveth and reigneth. [*or: Through the same.]

The Lesson from the Prophet Malachi.

Mal. 3, 1-4.

THUS saith the Lord God: Behold, I will send my Messenger, and he shall prepare the way before me. And the Lord, whom ye seek, shall suddenly come to his temple, even the Messenger of the covenant, whom ye delight in. Behold he shall come, saith the Lord of hosts: but who may abide the day of his coming, and who shall stand when he appeareth? For he is like a refiner's fire, and like fullers' soap: and he shall sit as a refiner and purifier of silver, and he shall purify the sons of Levi, and purge them as gold and silver: that they may offer unto the Lord an offering in righteousness. Then shall the offerings of Judah and Jerusalem be pleasant unto the Lord, as in the days of old, and as in former years: [saith the Lord almighty.*]

And I will come near to you to judgment, and I will be a swift witness against the sorcerer, and against the adulterers, and against false swearers, and against those that oppress the hireling in his wages, the widow, and the fatherless, and that turn aside the stranger from his right, and fear not me: saith the Lord of hosts.

Gradual. Ps. 48, 10-11 and 9. We wait for thy loving-kindness, O God, in the midst of thy temple: O God, according to thy name, so is thy praise unto the world's end. ℣. Like as we have heard, so have we seen, in the city of our God, even upon his holy hill.

Alleluia, alleluia. ℣. The old man carried the Child: but the Child was the old man's king. Alleluia.

After Septuagesima, omitting Alleluia and the Verse following, is said:

Tract. Luke 2, 29-32. Lord, now lettest thou thy servant depart in peace, according to thy word. ℣. For mine eyes have seen thy salvation. ℣. Which thou hast prepared before the face of all people. ℣. A light to lighten the Gentiles, and the glory of thy people Israel.

✠ The Continuation of the holy Gospel according to Luke.

Luke 2, 22-32.

AT that time: When the days of Mary's purification, according to the law of Moses, were accomplished, they brought Jesus to Jerusalem, to present him to the Lord, as it is written in the Law of the Lord: Every male that openeth the womb shall be called holy to the Lord. And to offer a sacrifice, according to that which is said in the law of the Lord, A pair of turtle-doves, or two young pigeons. And behold there was a man in Jerusalem, whose name was Simeon, and the same man was just and devout, waiting for the consolation of Israel, and the Holy Ghost was upon him. And it was revealed unto him by the Holy Ghost, that he should not see death, before he had seen the Lord's Christ. And he came by the Spirit into the temple. And when the parents brought in the child Jesus, to do for him after the custom of the law: then took he him up in his arms, and blessed God, and said: Lord, now lettest thou thy servant depart in peace, according to thy word: For mine eyes have seen thy salvation: Which thou hast prepared before the face of all people: A light to lighten the Gentiles, and the glory of thy people Israel. *

And Joseph and his Mother marvelled at those things which were spoken of him. And Simeon blessed them, and said unto Mary his mother: Behold, this child is set for the fall and rising again of many in Israel: and for a sign which shall be spoken against: yea, a sword shall pierce through thy own soul also; that the thoughts of many hearts may be revealed. And there was one Anna a prophetess, the daughter of Phanuel, of the tribe of Aser: she was of a great age, and had lived with an husband seven years from her virginity. And she was a widow of about fourscore and four years, which departed not from the temple but served God with fastings and prayers night and day. And she coming in that instant gave thanks likewise unto the Lord, and spake of him to all them that looked for redemption in Jerusalem. And when they had performed all things according to the law of the Lord, they returned into Galilee to their own city Nazareth. And the child grew, and waxed strong in spirit, filled with wisdom: and the grace of God was upon him. Creed.

Offertory. Ps. 45, 3. Full of grace are thy lips: because God hath blessed thee for ever, and world without end.

Secret.

GRACIOUSLY hear our prayers, O Lord: and, that these gifts which we offer unto thy majesty may be acceptable in thy sight, do thou bestow on us the succour of thy loving-kindness. Through.

Preface of the Nativity.

Communion. Luke 2, 26. It was revealed unto Simeon by the Holy Ghost, that he should not see death, before he had seen the Lord's Christ.

Postcommunion.

WE beseech thee, O Lord our God: that these holy mysteries, which thou hast given to us for the assurance of our redemption, may, by the intercession of blessed Mary ever Virgin, both in this life and that which is to come, be profitable for the healing of our souls. Through.

February 3.

For St. Blasius

Bishop and Martyr

The Mass Sacerdotes Dei, p. [5].

Collect. C

O GOD, who makest us glad with the yearly solemnity of blessed Blasius, thy Martyr and Bishop: mercifully grant; that, as we now celebrate his heavenly birthday, so we may likewise rejoice in his protection. Through.

Secret. C

SANCTIFY, O Lord, the gifts which we dedicate to thee: that at the intercession of blessed Blasius, thy Martyr and Bishop, they may obtain for us thy gracious favour. Through.

Postcommunion. C

O LORD, let this holy Communion cleanse us from every guilty stain: that at the intercession of blessed Blasius, thy Martyr and Bishop, we may be made partakers thereby of thy healing unto life eternal. Through.

February 4.
St. Andrew Corsini
Bishop and Confessor

Double.

The Mass *Statuit ei*, from the Common of a Confessor Bishop, p. [19], excepting the Collect:

Collect.

O GOD, who in thy Church dost ever raise up new examples of holiness: grant unto thy people so to follow in the footsteps of blessed Andrew, thy Confessor and Bishop; that they may likewise attain to his reward. Through.

Secret.

WE beseech thee, O Lord, that we, remembering with gladness the merits of thy Saints, may in all places feel the succour of their intercession. Through.

Postcommunion.

GRANT, we beseech thee, almighty God: that we, shewing forth our thankfulness for the gifts which we have received, may, at the intercession of blessed Andrew, thy Confessor and Bishop, obtain yet more abundant mercies. Through.

¶ Throughout Lent, on double Feasts, the Feria is commemorated. Where the office in Choir is of obligation, two Masses must be said, one of the Feast without Commemoration of the Feria, and one of the Feria without Commemoration of the Feast. But private Masses may be said, either of the Feast with Commemoration of the Feria, or of the Feria with Commemoration of the Feast. On Doubles of the First or Second Class, a Conventual Mass is said of the Feast in Choir, and outside Choir a Mass of the Feria is read, of which, nevertheless private Masses are prohibited.

February 5.
St. Agatha
Virgin and Martyr

Double.

Introit. Gaudeamus.

REJOICE we all in the Lord, keeping feast day in honour of blessed Agatha, the Virgin and Martyr: in whose passion the Angels rejoice, and glorify the Son of God. Ps. 45, 1. My heart is inditing of a good matter: I speak of the things which I have made unto the King. ℣. Glory.

Collect.

O GOD, who among the manifold works of thy power hast bestowed even upon the weakness of women the victory of martyrdom: mercifully grant; that we, who this day celebrate the heavenly birthday of blessed Agatha, thy Virgin and Martyr, may by her example be drawn nearer unto thee. Through.

In Lent, Commemoration is made of the Feria in non-conventual Masses.

The Lesson from the Epistle of blessed Paul the Apostle to the Corinthians.

I Cor. 1, 26-31.

BRETHREN: Ye see your calling: how that not many wise men after the flesh, not many mighty, not many noble, are called: but God hath chosen the foolish things of the world to confound the wise: and God hath chosen the weak things of the world to confound the things which are mighty: and base things of the world, and things which are despised, hath God chosen, yea, and things which are not, to bring to nought things that are:

that no flesh should glory in his presence. But of him are ye in Christ Jesus, who of God is made unto us wisdom, and righteousness, and sanctification, and redemption: that, according as it is written: He that glorieth, let him glory in the Lord.

Gradual. Ps. 46, 6 and 5. God shall help her with his countenance: God is in the midst of her, therefore shall she not be removed. ℣. The rivers of the flood thereof shall make glad the city of God: the holy place of the tabernacle of the Most Highest.

Alleluia, alleluia. ℣. Ps. 119, 46. I will speak of thy testimonies even before kings: and will not be ashamed. Alleluia.

After Septuagesima, omitting Alleluia and the Verse following, is said:

Tract. Ps. 126, 5-6. They that sow in tears, shall reap in joy. ℣. They that now go on their way weeping, and bear forth good seed. ℣. Shall doubtless come again with joy, and bring their sheaves with them.

✠ The Continuation of the holy Gospel according to Matthew.

Matt. 19, 3-12.

AT that time: The Pharisees came unto Jesus, tempting him, and saying unto him: Is it lawful for a man to put away his wife for every cause? And he answered and said unto them: Have ye not read, that he which made them at the beginning made them male and female? and said: For this cause shall a man leave father and mother, and shall cleave to his wife, and they twain shall be one flesh. Wherefore they are no more twain, but one flesh. What therefore God hath joined together, let not man put asunder. They say unto him: Why did Moses then command to give a writing of divorcement, and to put her away? He saith unto them: Moses because of the hardness of your hearts suffered you to put away your wives: but from the beginning it was not so. And I say unto you. Whosoever shall put away his wife, except it be for fornication, and shall marry another, committeth adultery: and whoso marrieth her which is put away doth commit adultery. His disciples say unto him: If the case of the man be so with his wife, it is not good to marry. But he said unto them: All men cannot receive this saying, save they to whom it is given. For there are some eunuchs, which were so born from their mother's womb; and there are some eunuchs, which were made eunuchs of men; and there be eunuchs, which have made themselves eunuchs for the kingdom of heaven's sake. He that is able to receive it, let him receive it.

Offertory. Ps. 45, 15. The Virgins that be her fellows shall be brought unto the King: they that bear her company shall be brought unto thee.

Secret.

RECEIVE, O Lord, the gifts which we offer on the solemnity of blessed Agatha, thy Virgin and Martyr: through whose advocacy we trust to be deliverd. Through.

In Lent, Commemoration of the Feria.

Communion. He who deigned to heal my every wound, and to restore my breast unto my body, on him do I call, the living God.

Postcommunion.

ASSIST us mercifully, O Lord, who have here received these holy mysteries: and, at the intercession of blessed Agatha, thy Virgin and Martyr, make us ever to rejoice in thy continual protection. Through.

In Lent, Commemoration of the Feria.

February 6.

St. Titus

Bishop and Confessor

Double.

Introit. Ecclus. 45, 24. Statuit ei.

THE Lord hath established a covenant of peace with him, and made him the chief of his people: that he should have the dignity of the priesthood for ever. Ps. 132, 1. Lord, remember David: and all his trouble. ℣. Glory.

Collect.

O GOD, who didst adorn blessed Titus, thy Confessor and Bishop, with apostolic virtues: grant, through his merits and intercession; that we, living righteously and godly in this present world, may be found worthy to attain unto our heavenly country. Through.

In Lent, Commemoration of the Feria.

Then in low Masses Commemoration of St. Dorothea, Virgin and Martyr:

Collect.

WE beseech thee, O Lord, that, like as blessed Dorothea, thy Virgin and Martyr, by the merit of her chastity, and by her confession of thy power: was ever found acceptable in thy sight: so she may effectually intercede for our forgiveness. Through.

The Lesson from the book of Wisdom.

Ecclus. 44, 16-45, 15.

BEHOLD, a great priest, who in his days pleased the Lord, and was found righteous: and in the time of wrath he was taken in exchange for the world. There was none like unto him, who kept the law of the Most High. Therefore by an oath the Lord assured him that he would increase him among his people. He established with him the blessing of all men and the covenant, and made it rest upon his head. He acknowledged him in his blessing: he preserved for him his mercy: so that he found favour in the sight of the Lord. He magnified him in the sight of kings: and gave unto him a crown of glory. An everlasting covenant he made with him, and gave him a great priesthood: and blessed him with glory. That he should execute the office of the priesthood, and have praise in his name, and offer unto him incense, and a sweet savour.

Gradual. Ecclus. 44, 16. Behold a great priest, who in his days pleased the Lord. ℣. Ibid., 20. There was none like unto him to keep the law of the Most High.

Alleluia, alleluia. ℣. Ps. 110, 4. Thou art a priest for ever after the order of Melchisedech. Alleluia.

After Septuagesima, omitting, Alleluia and the Verse following, is said:

Tract. Ps. 112, 1-3. Blessed is the man that feareth the Lord: he hath great delight in his commandments. ℣. His seed shall be mighty upon earth: the generation of the faithful shall be blessed. ℣. Riches and plenteousness shall be in his house: and his righteousness endureth for ever.

✠ The Continuation of the holy Gospel according to Luke.

Luke 10, 1-9.

AT that time: The Lord appointed other seventy also: and sent them two and two before his face into every city and place whither he himself would come. Therefore said he unto them: The harvest truly is great, but the labourers are few. Pray ye therefore the Lord of the harvest, that he would send forth labourers into his harvest. Go your ways: behold, I send you forth as lambs among wolves. Carry neither purse, nor scrip, nor shoes; and salute no man by the way. And into whatsoever house ye enter, first say: Peace be to this house: and if the son of peace be there, your peace shall rest upon it: if not, it shall turn to you again. And in the same house remain, eating and drinking such things as they give: for the labourer is worthy of his hire. Go not from house to house. And into whatsoever city ye enter, and they receive you, eat such things as are set before you: and heal the sick that are therein, and say unto them: The kingdom of God is come nigh unto you.

Offertory. Ps. 89, 21-22. I have found David my servant, with my holy oil have I anointed him: my hand shall hold him fast, and my arm shall strengthen him.

Secret.

WE beseech thee, O Lord, that we, remembering with gladness the merits of thy Saints, may in all places feel the succour of their intercession. Through.

In Lent, Commemoration of the Feria. Then of St. Dorothea.

Secret.

GRACIOUSLY receive, O Lord, through the merits of blessed Dorothea, thy Virgin and Martyr, the sacrifices which we offer unto thee: and grant that they may avail for our continual help. Through.

Communion. Luke 12, 42. A faithful and wise servant, whom his lord hath made ruler over his household: to give them their portion of meat in due season.

Postcommunion.

GRANT, we beseech thee, almighty God: that we, shewing forth our thankfulness for the gifts which we have received, may, at the intercession of blessed Titus, thy Confessor and Bishop, obtain yet more abundant mercies. Through.

In Lent, Commemoration of the Feria. Then of St. Dorothea.

Postcommunion.

O LORD our God, who hast fulfilled us with the bounty of thy heavenly gift: we beseech thee that, at the intercession of blessed Dorothea, thy Virgin and Martyr, we may ever live by the partaking of the same. Through.

February 7.

St. Romuald

Abbot

Double.

The Mass Os justi, from the Common of Abbots, p. [26].

In Lent, Commemoration of the Feria.

Collect. C

O LORD, we beseech thee, let the intercession of thy blessed Abbot Romuald commend us unto thee: that those things which for our own merits we cannot ask, we may through his advocacy obtain. Through.

Secret. C

O LORD, we beseech thee, let thy holy Abbot Romuald intercede for us: that this sacrifice which we offer and present upon thy holy altar may be profitable unto us for our salvation. Through.

Postcommunion. C

LET thy Sacrament, O Lord, which we have now received, and the prayers of thy blessed Abbot Romuald, effectually defend us: that we may both imitate the example of his conversation, and receive the succour of his intercession. Through.

February 8.
St. John of Matha
Confessor

Double.

The Mass Os justi, from the Common of a Confessor not a Bishop, p. [24], excepting the Collect:

Collect.

O GOD, who through Saint John didst vouchsafe by a sign from heaven to institute the order of the most holy Trinity to redeem the captives from the power of the Saracens: grant, we beseech thee; that through the pleading of his merits we may by thy help be delivered from captivity of body and soul. Through.

In Lent, Commemoration is made of the Feria.

Secret.

WE offer thee, O Lord, this sacrifice of praise to the honour of thy Saints: whereby we trust to be delivered from all evils both in this life and in that which is to come. Through.

In Lent, Commemoration of the Feria.

Postcommunion.

O LORD, our God, who hast refreshed us with heavenly meat and drink, we humbly beseech thee: that we may be defended by the prayers of him in whose memory we have received the same. Through.

In Lent, Commemoration of the Feria.

February 9.
St. Cyril, Bishop of Alexandria
Confessor and Doctor of the Church.

Double.

Introit. Ecclus. 15, 5. In medio.

IN the midst of the Church he opened his mouth: and the Lord filled him with the spirit of wisdom and understanding: he clothed him with a robe of glory. Ps. 92, 1. It is a good thing to give thanks unto the Lord: and to sing praises unto thy name, O most Highest. ℣. Glory.

Collect.

O GOD, who didst strengthen blessed Cyril, thy Confessor and Bishop, invincibly to maintain the divine Motherhood of the most blessed Virgin Mary: grant, by his intercession; that we, believing her to be indeed the Mother of God, may as her children be saved through her protection. Through the same.

In Lent, Commemoration is made of the Feria.

Commemoration of St. Apollonia, Virgin and Martyr.

Collect.

O GOD, who among the manifold works of thy power hast bestowed even upon the weakness of women the victory of martyrdom: mercifully grant; that we, who this day celebrate the heavenly birth of blessed Apollonia, thy Virgin and Martyr, may by her example be drawn nearer unto thee. Through.

The Lesson from the Epistle of blessed Paul the Apostle to Timothy.

II Tim. 4, 1-8.

DEARLY beloved: I charge thee before God, and the Lord Jesus Christ, who shall judge the quick and the dead at his appearing and his kingdom: preach the word, be instant in season, out of season: reprove, rebuke, exhort with all longsuffering and doctrine. For the time will come when they will not endure sound doctrine, but after their own lusts shall they heap to themselves teachers, having itching ears, and they shall turn away their ears from the truth, and shall be turned unto fables. But watch thou in all things, endure afflictions, do the work of an Evangelist, make full proof of thy ministry. For I am now ready to be offered, and the time of my departure is at hand. I have fought a good fight, I have finished my course, I have kept the faith. Henceforth there is laid up for me a crown of righteousness, which the Lord, the righteous judge, shall give me at that day: and not to me only, but unto all them also that love his appearing.

Gradual. Ps. 37, 30-31. The mouth of the righteous is exercised in wisdom, and his tongue will be talking of judgment. V. The law of his God is in his heart: and his goings shall not slide.

Alleluia, alleluia. V. Ecclus. 45, 9. The Lord loved him, and adorned him: he clothed him with a robe of glory. Alleluia.

After Septuagesima, omitting Alleluia and the Verse following, is said:

Tract. Ps. 112, 1-3. Blessed is the man that feareth the Lord: he hath great delight in his commandments. V. His seed shall be mighty upon earth: the generation of the faithful shall be blessed. V. Riches and plenteousness shall be in his house: and his righteousness endureth for ever.

✠ The Continuation of the holy Gospel according to Matthew.

Matt. 5, 13-19.

AT that time: Jesus said unto his disciples: Ye are the salt of the earth. But if the salt have lost his savour, wherewith shall it be salted? It is thenceforth good for nothing, but to be cast out, and to be trodden under foot of men. Ye are the light of the world. A city that is set on an hill cannot be hid. Neither do men light a candle, and put it under a bushel, but on a candlestick, and it giveth light unto all that are in the house. Let your light so shine before men, that they may see your good works, and glorify your Father which is in heaven. Think not that I am come to destroy the law, or the prophets: I am not come to destroy, but to fulfil. For verily I say unto you, Till heaven and earth pass, one jot or one tittle shall in no wise pass from the law, till all be fulfilled. Whosoever therefore shall break one of these least commandments, and shall teach men so, he shall be called the least in the kingdom of heaven: but whosoever shall do and teach them, the same shall be called great in the kingdom of heaven. Creed.

Offertory. Ps. 92, 13. The righteous shall flourish like a palm-tree: and shall spread abroad like a cedar in Libanus.

Secret.

ALMIGHTY God, graciously look upon our gifts: and at the intercession of blessed Cyril vouchsafe; that we may be found meet worthily to receive in our hearts thine only-begotten Son, Jesus Christ our Lord, co-eternal with thee in thy glory: Who liveth and reigneth with thee.

Commemoration of the Feria: then of St. Apollonia.

Secret.

RECEIVE, O Lord, the gifts which we offer on the solemnity of blessed Apollonia, thy Virgin and Martyr: through whose advocacy we trust to be delivered. Through.

Postcommunion.

O LORD, who hast refreshed us with these heavenly mysteries, we humbly beseech thee: that, being aided by the example and merits of blessed Cyril thy Bishop, we may be enabled worthily to serve the most holy Mother of thine only-begotten Son: Who liveth and reigneth with thee.

Commemoration of the Feria: then of St. Apollonia.

Postcommunion.

ASSIST us mercifully, O Lord, who have here received these holy mysteries: and at the intercession of blessed Apollonia, thy Virgin and Martyr, make us ever to rejoice in thy continual protection. Through.

February 10.

St. Scholastica

Virgin

Double.

The Mass Dilexisti, p. [31], except the Collect.

Collect.

O GOD, who, to shew forth the way of innocence, didst cause the soul of thy blessed Virgin Scholastica to enter heaven in the appearance of a dove: grant unto us through her merits and prayers to walk in such innocency of life; that we may be worthy to attain unto everlasting joys. Through.

In Lent, Commemoration of the Feria.

Secret.

GRANT, O Lord, that like as thy dedicated people do acknowledge that in tribulation they have been succoured by the merits of thy Saints: so this oblation, which they offer unto thee in honour of the same, may be acceptable in thy sight. Through.

In Lent, Commemoration of the Feria.

Postcommunion.

O LORD, who hast satisfied this thy family with thy sacred gifts: we beseech thee, that we may at all times be comforted by the intercession of her whose festival we celebrate. Through.

In Lent, Commemoration of the Feria.

February 11.

The Appearing of the Blessed Virgin Mary Immaculate

Greater double.

Introit. Rev. 21, 2. Vidi civitatem.

I SAW the holy city, new Jerusalem, coming down from God out of heaven, prepared as a bride adorned for her husband. Ps. 45, 1. My heart is inditing of a good matter: I speak of the things which I have made unto the King. ℣. Glory.

Collect.

O GOD, who through the immaculate Conception of the Virgin didst prepare an habitation meet for thy Son: we humbly beseech thee; that we, celebrating the Appearing of the same Virgin, may obtain thy healing both in body and soul. Through the same.

In Lent Commemoration is made of the Feria in non-conventual Masses.

The Lesson from the book of the Revelation of blessed John the Apostle.

Rev. 11, 19; 12, 1 and 10.

THE temple of God was opened in heaven: and there was seen in his temple the ark of his testament, and there

Feasts of February (11)

were lightnings, and voices, and thunderings, and an earthquake, and great hail. And there appeared a great wonder in heaven: A woman clothed with the sun, and the moon under her feet, and upon her head a crown of twelve stars. And I heard a loud voice saying in heaven: Now is come salvation, and strength, and the kingdom of our God, and the power of his Christ.

Gradual. Cant. 2, 12. The flowers appear on the earth, the time of the singing of birds is come, and the voice of the turtle is heard in our land. ℣. Ibid., 10 and 14. Rise up, my love, my fair one, and come away: O my dove, that art in the clefts of the rock, in the secret places of the stairs.

Alleluia, alleluia. ℣. Let me see thy countenance, let me hear thy voice: for sweet is thy voice, and thy countenance is comely. Alleluia.

After Septuagesima, omitting Alleluia and the Verse following, is said:

Tract. Judith 15, 10. Thou art the exaltation of Jerusalem, thou art the great glory of Israel, thou art the great rejoicing of our nation. ℣. Cant. 4, 7. All fair art thou, O Mary: and original sin is not in thee. ℣. Blessed art thou, O holy Virgin Mary, and most worthy of all praise, who with thy virgin foot didst crush the serpent's head.

✠ The Continuation of the holy Gospel according to Luke.

Luke 1, 26-31.

AT that time: The Angel Gabriel was sent from God unto a city of Galilee, named Nazareth, to a Virgin espoused to a man whose name was Joseph, of the house of David, and the Virgin's name was Mary. And the Angel came in unto her, and said: Hail, full of grace; the Lord is with thee: blessed art thou among women. And when she saw him, she was troubled at his saying: and cast in her mind what manner of salutation this should be. And the Angel said unto her: Fear not, Mary, for thou hast found favour with God: and, behold, thou shalt conceive in thy womb, and bring forth a Son, and shalt call his name Jesus. Creed.

Offertory. Luke 1, 28. Hail, full of grace; the Lord is with thee: blessed art thou among women.

Secret.

MAY this sacrifice of praise, which we offer unto thee, O Lord, through the merits of the glorious and immaculate Virgin, be acceptable before thee for a savour of sweetness, and bestow upon us the healing that we seek both in body and soul. Through.

In Lent, Commemoration of the Feria.

Preface of the B.V.Mary, and that in the immaculate Conception.

Communion. Ps. 65, 10. Thou visitest the earth, and blessest it: thou makest it very plenteous.

Postcommunion.

O LORD, who hast satisfied us with heavenly food: let the right hand of thine undefiled Mother so succour and defend us, that we may by her aid be found worthy to attain to our eternal country: Who livest.

In Lent, Commemoration of the Feria.

February 12.

The Seven Holy Founders of the Order of Servants of the Blessed Virgin Mary

Confessors

Double.

Introit. Wisd. 10, 20-21.

Justi decantaverunt.

THE righteous praised thy holy name, O Lord, and magnified with one accord thine hand that fought for them: for wisdom opened the mouth of the dumb, and made the tongues of them that cannot speak eloquent. Ps. 8, 1. O Lord our Governor, how excellent is thy name in all the world. ℣. Glory.

Collect.

O LORD Jesu Christ, who, for the remembrance of the sorrows of thy most holy Mother, didst through the seven blessed Fathers enrich thy Church with the new household of her Servants: mercifully grant; that we may in such wise be joined to them in weeping, that we may likewise be partakers of their joys: Who livest and reignest.

In Lent, Commemoration of the Feria in non-conventual Masses.

The Lesson from the book of Wisdom.

Ecclus. 44, 1-15.

LET us now praise famous men, and our fathers that begat us. The Lord hath wrought great glory by them through his great power from the beginning. Such as did bear rule in their kingdoms, men renowned for their power, giving counsel by their understanding, and declaring prophecies, leaders of the people by their counsels, and by their knowledge of learning meet for the people, wise and eloquent in their instructions. Such as found out musical tunes, and recited verses in writing. Rich men furnished with ability: living peaceably in their habitations. All these were honoured in their generations, and were the glory of their times. There be of them, that have left a name behind them, that their praises might be reported. And some there be, which have no memorial: who are perished, as though they had never been: and are become as though they had never been born, and their children after them. But these were merciful men, whose righteousness hath not been forgotten: with their seed shall continually remain a good inheritance, and their children are within the covenant: their seed standeth fast, and their children for their sakes: their seed shall remain for ever, and their glory shall not be blotted out. Their bodies are buried in peace, but their name liveth for evermore. Let the people tell of their wisdom, and the Church shew forth their praise.

Gradual. Is. 65, 23. Mine elect shall not labour in vain, nor bring forth for trouble: for they are the seed of the blessed of the Lord, and their offspring with them. ℣. Ecclus. 44, 14. Their bodies are buried in peace: but their name liveth for evermore.

Alleluia, alleluia. ℣. Ibid., 15. Let the people tell of their wisdom, and let the Church shew forth their praise. Alleluia.

After Septuagesima, omitting Alleluia and the Verse following, is said:

Tract. Ps. 126, 5-6. They that sow in tears, shall reap in joy. ℣. They that now go on their way weeping, and bear forth good seed. ℣. Shall doubtless come again with joy, and bring their sheaves with them.

In votive Masses in Eastertide the Gradual is omitted, and in its place is said:

Alleluia, alleluia. ℣. Ecclus. 44, 15. Let the people tell of their wisdom, and let the Church shew forth their praise. Alleluia. V. Ps. 37, 28. The Lord forsaketh not his that be godly: but they are preserved for ever. Alleluia.

✠ The Continuation of the holy Gospel according to Matthew.

Matt. 19, 27-29.

AT that time: Peter said unto Jesus: Behold, we have forsaken all, and followed thee: what shall we have therefore? And Jesus said unto them: Verily I say unto you, That ye which have followed me, in the regeneration, when the Son of man shall sit in the throne of his glory, ye also shall sit upon twelve thrones, judging the twelve tribes of Israel. And every one that hath forsaken houses, or brethren, or sisters, or father, or mother, or wife, or children, or lands, for my name's sake, shall receive an hundredfold, and shall inherit everlasting life.

Offertory. Is. 56, 7. I will bring them to my holy mountain, and make them joyful in my house of prayer: their burnt offerings and their sacrifices shall be accepted upon mine altar.

Secret.

ACCEPT, we beseech thee, O Lord, the sacrifices which we offer unto thee: and grant; that, by the intercession of thy Saints, we may serve thee in freedom of spirit, and be inflamed with the love of the sorrowing Virgin Mother of thy Son. Through the same.

In Lent, Commemoration of the Feria.

Communion. John 15, 16. I have chosen you out of the world that ye should go and bring forth fruit: and that your fruit should remain.

Postcommunion.

O LORD, who hast refreshed us with these heavenly mysteries, we beseech thee: that, following the example of those whose feast we celebrate; we may faithfully stand by the Cross of Jesus with Mary his Mother, and be found worthy to receive the fruit of his redemption. Through the same.

In Lent, Commemoration of the Feria.

February 14.

For St. Valentine

Priest and Martyr

The Mass In virtute, p. [6], except the Prayers, as follow:

Collect. P

GRANT, we beseech thee, almighty God: that we who observe the heavenly birthday of blessed Valentine, thy Martyr; may by his intercession be delivered from all evils that beset us. Through.

Secret. P

ACCEPT, O Lord, we beseech thee, this oblation of our worthy service: and by the merits and intercession of blessed Valentine, thy Martyr, grant; that they may avail to set forward our salvation. Through.

Postcommunion. P

GRANT, O Lord, that these heavenly mysteries may renew us both in body and soul: that at the intercession of blessed Valentine, thy Martyr, we who here celebrate our outward worship may inwardly feel the effectual benefit of the same. Through.

February 15.

For SS. Faustinus and Jovita

Martyrs

The Mass Salus, p. [12], with Prayers, as below:

Collect.

O GOD, who makest us glad with the yearly solemnity of thy holy Martyrs Faustinus and Jovita: mercifully grant; that as we do rejoice in their merits, so we may be enkindled by their example. Through.

Secret.

ASSIST us mercifully, O Lord, in these our supplications which we make before thee in remembrance of thy Saints: that we who trust not in our own righteousness may be succoured by the merits of those that have found favour in thy sight. Through.

Postcommunion.

O LORD, who hast fulfilled us with these saving mysteries, we beseech thee: that we may be aided by the prayers of those whose festival we celebrate. Through.

February 18.

For St. Simeon

Bishop and Martyr

The Mass Statuit ei, from the Common of a Martyr Bishop, p. [4].

Collect.

ALMIGHTY God, mercifully look upon our infirmities: and whereas we are sore afflicted by the burden of our sins, let the glorious intercession of blessed Simeon thy Martyr and Bishop be our succour and defence. Through.

Secret.

WE beseech thee, O Lord, mercifully to accept this our sacrifice which we offer unto thee, pleading the merits of blessed Simeon, thy Martyr and Bishop: that the same may avail for our perpetual succour. Through.

Postcommunion.

WE beseech thee, O Lord our God, that like as we whom thou hast refreshed by the partaking of thy sacred gift do offer unto thee our outward worship: so, at the intercession of blessed Simeon thy Martyr and Bishop, we may inwardly be profited thereby to our salvation.

February 22.

The Chair of St. Peter, Apostle, at Antioch

Greater double.

Introit. Ecclus. 45, 30. Statuit ei.

THE Lord hath established a covenant of peace with him, and made him the chief of his people: that he should have the dignity of the priesthood for ever. Ps. 132, 1. Lord, remember David: and all his trouble. ℣. Glory.

Collect.

O GOD, who didst bestow upon thy blessed Apostle Peter the keys of the kingdom of heaven, and didst appoint unto him the high priesthood for binding and loosing: vouchsafe; that by the help of his intercession we may be delivered from the bonds of our iniquities: Who livest and reignest.

Commemoration of St. Paul, Ap., which is never omitted.

Collect.

O GOD, who by the preaching of the blessed Apostle Paul didst teach the multitude of the Gentiles: grant to us, we beseech thee; that we who now celebrate his commemoration may feel the effectual benefit of his intercession. (Through.)

Then, in Lent, Commemoration of the Feria.

The Lesson from the Epistle of blessed Peter the Apostle.
I Peter 1, 1-7.

PETER, an Apostle of Jesus Christ, to the strangers scattered throughout Pontus, Galatia, Cappadocia, Asia, and Bithynia, elect according to the foreknowledge of God the Father, through sanctification of the Spirit, unto obedience and sprinkling of the blood of Jesus Christ: grace unto you, and peace, be multiplied. Blessed be the God and Father of our Lord Jesus Christ, which according to his abundant mercy hath begotten us again unto a lively hope, by the resurrection of Jesus Christ from the dead, to an inheritance incorruptible and undefiled, and that fadeth not away, reserved in heaven for you, who are kept by the power of God through faith unto salvation, ready to be revealed in the last time. Wherein ye greatly rejoice, though now for a season, if need be, ye are in heaviness through manifold temptations: that the trial of your faith, being much more precious than of gold (that perisheth, though it be tried with fire), might be found unto praise, and honour, and glory, at the appearing of Jesus Christ our Lord.

Gradual. Ps. 107, 32 and 31. Let them exalt him in the congregation of the people: and praise him in the seat of the elders. ℣. O that men would praise the Lord for his goodness, and declare the wonders that he doeth for the children of men.

Tract. Matt. 16, 18-19. Thou art Peter, and upon this rock I will build my Church. ℣. And the gates of hell shall not prevail against it: and I will give unto thee the keys of the kingdom of heaven. ℣. Whatsoever thou shalt bind on earth shall be bound in heaven. ℣. And whatsoever thou shalt loose on earth shall be loosed in heaven.

In Votive Masses in Eastertide the Gradual is omitted, and in its place is said:

Alleluia, alleuia. ℣. Ps. 107, 15. O that men would praise the Lord for his goodness, and declare the wonders that he doeth for the children of men. Alleluia. ℣. Matt. 16, 18. Thou art Peter, and upon this rock I will build my Church. Alleluia.

✠ The Continuation of the holy Gospel according to Matthew.
Matt. 16, 13-19.

AT that time: When Jesus came into the coasts of Caesarea Philippi, he asked his disciples, saying: Whom do men say that I, the Son of man, am? And they said: Some say that thou art John the Baptist, some Elias, and others Jeremias, or one of the Prophets. He saith unto them: But whom say ye that I am? And Simon Peter answered and said: Thou art the Christ, the Son of the living God. And Jesus answered and said unto him: Blessed art thou, Simon Bar-jona: for flesh and blood hath not revealed it unto thee, but my Father which is in heaven. And I say also unto thee, That thou art Peter, and upon this rock I will build my Church, and the gates of hell shall not prevail against it. And I will give unto thee the keys of the kingdom of heaven. And whatsoever thou shalt bind on earth shall be bound in heaven: and whatsoever thou shalt loose on earth shall be loosed in heaven.

The Creed is not said.

Offertory. Matt. 16, 18-19. Thou art Peter, and upon this rock I will build my Church: and the gates of hell shall not prevail against it: and I will give unto thee the keys of the kingdom of heaven.

Secret.

WE beseech thee, O Lord, let the intercession of thy blessed Apostle Peter commend unto thee the prayers and sacrifices of thy Church: that these gifts which we offer for his glory may avail for the remission of our sins. Through.

For St. Paul. Secret.

SANCTIFY, O Lord, through the prayers of thine Apostle Paul, the oblations of thy people: that these gifts, which by thine institution are acceptable unto thee, may by his effectual advocacy be rendered the more acceptable in thy sight. (Through.)

In Lent, Commemoration of the Feria.

Preface of the Apostles.

Communion. Matt. 16, 18. Thou art Peter, and upon this rock I will build my Church.

Postcommunion.

O LORD, let this sacrifice, which we have offered, bring forth gladness in our hearts: that as we shew forth the wonders which thou hast wrought in thy Apostle Peter; so through him we may obtain the abundance of thy loving-kindness. Through.

For St. Paul. Postcommunion.

O LORD, who hast sanctified us with this saving mystery: we beseech thee; that he whom thou hast given to be our advocate and guide may continually intercede for us. (Through.)

In Lent, Commemoration of the Feria.

February 23.

St. Peter Damian

Bishop, Confessor and Doctor of the Church

Double.

The Mass **In medio**, p. [22], except the Collect as below; and the Creed is said:

Collect.

GRANT, we beseech thee, almighty God: that we may so follow the teaching and example of blessed Peter, thy Confessor and Bishop; that through contempt of things earthly we may attain to everlasting joys. Through.

In Lent, Commemoration of the Feria.

Secret.

MAY the devout prayers of thy Bishop and Doctor, Saint Peter, continually succour us, O Lord: that they may render our oblations acceptable in thy sight; and may ever obtain for us thy merciful pardon. Through.

In Lent, Commemoration of the Feria.

Postcommunion.

WE beseech thee, O Lord, that blessed Peter, thy Bishop and most excellent Doctor, may ever stand before thee as our advocate: that this sacrifice of thine ordinance may effectually avail for our salvation. Through.

In Lent, Commemoration of the Feria.

February 24 or 25.

ST. MATTHIAS THE APOSTLE

Double of 2nd class.

¶ To-day, in Lent, in Choir after Terce is said a conventual Mass of the Feast, and outside Choir after None there is read a Mass of the Feria; of which, however, private Masses are forbidden.

Introit. Ps. 139, 17. *Mihi autem.*

RIGHT dear are thy friends unto me, O God, and held in highest honour: their rule and governance is exceeding steadfast. Ps. ibid., 1-2. O Lord, thou hast searched me out, and known me: thou knowest my down-sitting, and mine up-rising. ℣. Glory.

Collect.

O ALMIGHTY God, who into the place of the traitor Judas didst choose thy faithful servant Matthias to be of the number of the twelve Apostles: grant that thy Church, being alway preserved from false apostles, may be ordered and guided by faithful and true pastors. Through.

Or, Collect.

O GOD, who didst choose blessed Matthias to be of the number of thine Apostles: grant, we beseech thee; that through his intercession we may ever know thy tender mercy toward us. Through.

In Lent, Commemoration is made of the Feria in non-conventual Masses.

The Lesson from the Acts of the Apostles.

Acts 1, 15-26.

IN those days: Peter stood up in the midst of the disciples, and said, (the number of the names together were about an hundred and twenty): Men and brethren, this Scripture must needs have been fulfilled, which the Holy Ghost by the mouth of David spake before concerning Judas, which was guide to them that took Jesus: for he was numbered with us, and had obtained part of this ministry. Now this man purchased a field with the reward of iniquity, and falling headlong he burst asunder in the midst: and all his bowels gushed out. And it was known unto all the dwellers at Jerusalem, insomuch as that field is called in their proper tongue, Aceldama, that is to say, The field of blood. For it is written in the book of Psalms: Let his habitation be desolate, and let no man dwell therein: and, His bishoprick let another take. Wherefore, of these men which have companied with us all the time that the Lord Jesus went in and out among us, beginning from the baptism of John, unto that same day that he was taken up from us, must one be ordained to be a witness with us of his resurrection. And they appointed two, Joseph called Barsabas, who was surnamed Justus, and Matthias. And they prayed, and said: Thou, Lord, which knowest the hearts of all men, shew whether of these two thou hast chosen, that he may take part of this ministry and apostleship, from which Judas by transgression fell, that he might go to his own place. And they gave forth their lots, and the lot fell upon Matthias, and he was numbered with the eleven Apostles.

Gradual. Ps. 139, 17-18. Right dear are thy friends unto me, O God, and held in highest honour: their rule and governance is exceeding steadfast. ℣. If I tell them, they are more in number than the sand.

Tract. Ps. 21, 3-4. Thou hast given him his heart's desire: and hast not denied him the request of his lips. ℣. For thou hast prevented him with the blessings of goodness. ℣. Thou hast set a crown of pure gold upon his head.

☩ The Continuation of the holy Gospel according to Matthew.

Matt. 11, 25-30.

AT that time: Jesus answered and said: I thank thee, O Father, Lord of heaven and earth, because thou hast hid these things from the wise and prudent, and hast revealed them unto babes. Even so, Father: for so it seemed good in thy sight. All things are delivered unto me of my Father. And no man knoweth the Son, but the Father: neither knoweth any man the Father, save the Son, and he to whomsoever the Son will reveal him. Come unto me, all ye that labour and are heavy laden, and I will give you rest. Take my yoke upon you, and learn of me, for I am meek and lowly in heart: and ye shall find rest unto your souls. For my yoke is easy, and my burden is light. Creed.

Offertory. Ps. 45, 17-18. Thou shalt make them princes in all lands: they shall remember thy name, O Lord, from one generation to another.

Secret.

LET the prayers of thy holy Apostle Matthias, O Lord, accompany this sacrifice which we here present to be hallowed to the glory of thy name: that we may thereby be cleansed from our iniquities and defended against all adversities. Through.

In Lent, Commemoration of the Feria.

Preface of the Apostles.

Communion. Matt. 19, 28. Ye, which have followed me, shall sit upon thrones, judging the twelves tribes of Israel.

Postcommunion.

GRANT, we beseech thee, almighty God: that through these holy mysteries which we have here received, we may, at the intercession of thy blessed Apostle Matthias, obtain of thy mercy pardon and peace. Through.

In Lent, Commemoration of the Feria.

¶ In Eastertide, the Introit, Alleluia, Offertory, and Communion from the Mass Protexisti p. [15], the rest as above.

February 27 or 28.

St. Gabriel of the Sorrowful Virgin

Confessor

Double.

Introit. Ecclus. 11, 13. Oculus Dei.

THE eye of the Lord looked upon him for good, and set him up from his low estate, and lifted up his head: and many marvelled at him, and gave honour to God. Ps. 73, 1. Truly God is loving unto Israel, even unto such as are of a clean heart! ℣. Glory.

Collect.

O GOD, who didst teach blessed Gabriel constantly to call to mind the sorrows of thy most gracious Mother, and through her didst exalt him to the glory of sanctity and miracles: grant us by his intercession and example so to be joined to thy Mother in her weeping; that we may likewise be saved through her protection: Who livest.

In Lent, Commemoration of the Feria in non-conventual Masses.

The Lesson from the Epistle of blessed John the Apostle.

I John 2, 14-17.

DEARLY beloved: I write unto you, young men, because ye are strong, and the word of God abideth in you, and ye have overcome the wicked one. Love not the world, neither the things that are in the world. If any man love the world, the love of the Father is not in him: for all that is in the world, the lust of the flesh, and the lust of the eyes, and the pride of life, is not of the Father, but is of the world. And the world passeth away, and the lust thereof. But he that doeth the will of God abideth for ever.

Gradual. Ps. 31, 20. O how plenteous is thy goodness, O Lord, which thou hast laid up for them that fear thee! ℣. And that thou hast prepared for them that put their trust in thee, even before the sons of men.

Tract. Ps. 84, 6-7, 11 and 13. Blessed is the man whose strength is in thee: in whose heart are thy ways: who going through the vale of misery useth it for a well. ℣. I had rather be a doorkeeper in the house of my God: than to dwell in the tents of ungodliness. ℣. No good thing shall he withhold from them that live a godly life: O Lord God of hosts, blessed is the man that putteth his trust in thee.

✠ The Continuation of the holy Gospel according to Mark.

Mark 10, 13-21.

AT that time: They brought young children to Jesus, that he should touch them. And his disciples rebuked those that brought them. But when Jesus saw it, he was much displeased, and said unto them: Suffer the little children to come unto me, and forbid them not: for of such is the kingdom of God. Verily I say unto you: Whosoever shall not receive the kingdom of God as a little child, he shall not enter therein. And he took them up in his arms, put his hands upon them, and blessed them. And when he was gone forth into the way, there came one running, and kneeled to him, and asked him: Good Master, what shall I do that I may inherit eternal life? And Jesus said unto him: Why callest thou me good? There is none good but one, that is God. Thou knowest the commandments: Do not commit adultery, Do not kill, Do not steal, Do not bear false witness, Defraud not, Honour thy father and mother. And he answered and said unto him: Master, all these have I observed from my youth. Then Jesus beholding him loved him, and said unto him: One thing thou lackest: go thy way, sell whatsoever thou hast, and give to the poor, and thou shalt have treasure in heaven: and come, follow me.

Offertory. Ps. 116, 16-17. Behold, O Lord, how that I am thy servant, and the son of thine handmaid: thou hast broken my bonds in sunder, I will offer to thee the sacrifice of thanksgiving.

Secret.

GRANT, O Lord, that we, who offer unto thee this saving victim in memory of Saint Gabriel, may devoutly recall the sacrifice of thy death: and through the merits of the sorrowful Virgin may receive in abundance the fruit of that same sacrifice: Who livest.

In Lent, Commemoration of the Feria.

Communion. Rev. 3, 20. Behold, I stand at the door, and knock: if any man hear my voice, and open the door, I will come in to him, and will sup with him, and he with me.

Postcommunion.

O LORD, who didst take of the glorious ever Virgin Mary that flesh, whose sweetness in this saving banquet we have been found worthy to taste: graciously receive through her hands the thanks; which, on this festival of thy Confessor Saint Gabriel, we render unto thee for the gifts thou hast bestowed upon us: Who livest.

In Lent, Commemoration of the Feria.

FEASTS OF MARCH

In Wales: March 1.

St. David

Bishop and Confessor

Patron of Wales.

See Supplement.

March 4.

St. Casimir

Confessor

Simple.

The Mass Os justi, from the Common of a Confessor not a Bishop, p. [24], the Collect excepted.

Collect. P

O GOD, who amid the pleasures of a kingdom and the enticements of the world, didst endue Saint Casimir with strength and constancy: we beseech thee; that through his intercession thy faithful people may despise things earthly, and ever seek after all things heavenly. Through.

Commemoration of St. Lucius, Pope and Martyr.

Collect. C 1

O EVERLASTING Shepherd, look down in mercy on thy flock: and as thou didst choose blessed Lucius, thy Martyr and Chief Bishop, to be pastor and ruler of thy Church; so at his intercession defend it with thy continual protection. Through.

Secret. C

WE offer thee, O Lord, this our sacrifice of praise, to the honour of thy Saints: whereby we trust to be delivered from all evils both in this life and in that which is to come. Through.

For St. Lucius. Secret.

WE beseech thee, O Lord, graciously enlighten thy Church by the gifts which we here offer: that in every place thy flock may increase and prosper, and the shepherds by thy governance may be made pleasing to thy name. Through.

Postcommunion. C

O LORD, our God, who hast refreshed us with heavenly meat and drink, we beseech thee: that we may be defended by the prayers of him in whose memory we have received the same. Through.

For St. Lucius. Postcommunion.

MERCIFUL Lord, we beseech thee to govern and preserve thy Church, which thou hast here refreshed with heavenly food: that by the guiding of thy mighty power it may serve thee in more abundant freedom, and ever keep thy true religion whole and undefiled. Through.

¶ In Lent Commemoration is made of St. Casimir and St. Lucius in low Masses of the Feria.

March 6.
SS. Perpetua and Felicity
Martyrs

Double.

The Mass Me exspectaverunt, p. [34], with the Prayers as below:

Collect. C 2

GRANT, we beseech thee, O Lord our God, that we may never cease to venerate the triumph of thy holy Martyrs, Perpetua and Felicity: and, though we cannot worthily shew forth their praises, yet we beseech thee to accept the worship we render in their honour. Through.

In Lent, Commemoration of the Feria.

Secret. C 2

O LORD, we beseech thee, look down upon these gifts, which we offer on thine altars on this festival of thy holy Martyrs, Perpetua and Felicity: that as by these blessed mysteries thou hast bestowed glory upon them, so likewise of thy bounty thou wouldest vouchsafe to us thy pardon. Through.

In Lent, Commemoration of the Feria.

Postcommunion. P

O LORD, who hast fulfilled us with gladness in these wondrous mysteries: grant, we beseech thee; that by the intercession of thy holy Martyrs, Perpetua and Felicity, we, who offer unto thee our temporal worship, may in our souls receive the benefit of the same. Through.

In Lent, Commemoration of the Feria.

March 7.
St. Thomas Aquinas

Confessor and Doctor of the Church

Double.

The Mass In medio, p. [22], except the Collect and Epistle. And the Creed is said.

Collect. P

O GOD, who dost enlighten thy Church with the wondrous learning of blessed Thomas, thy Confessor, and enrichest her through his holy labours: grant to us, we beseech thee; that we may understand aright the doctrine that he taught, and, following his example, may in our lives show forth the same. Through.

In Lent, Commemoration of the Feria.

The Lesson from the book of Wisdom.

Wisd. 7, 7-14.

I PRAYED, and understanding was given me: I called upon God, and the spirit of wisdom came to me: I preferred her before sceptres and thrones, and esteemed riches nothing in comparison of her: neither compared I unto her any precious stone: because all gold in respect of her is as a little sand, and silver shall be counted as clay before her. I loved her above health and beauty, and chose to have her instead of light: for the light that cometh from her never goeth out. All good things together came to me with her, and innumerable riches in her hands, and I rejoiced in them all: because wisdom goeth before them, and I knew not that she was the mother of them. I learned diligently, and do communicate her liberally, I do not hide her riches. For she is a treasure unto me that never faileth: which they that use become the friends of God, being commended for the gifts that come from learning.

Secret. C 2

MAY the devout prayers of thy Confessor and Doctor, Saint Thomas, continually succour us, O Lord: that they may render our oblations acceptable in thy sight; and may ever obtain for us thy merciful pardon. Through.

In Lent, Commemoration of the Feria.

Postcommunion.

WE beseech thee, O Lord, that blessed Thomas, thy Confessor and most excellent Doctor, may ever stand before thee as our advocate: that this sacrifice of thine ordinance may effectually avail for our salvation. Through.

In Lent, Commemoration of the Feria.

March 8.

St. John of God

Confessor

Double.

Introit. Ps. 37, 30-31. Os justi.

THE mouth of the righteous is exercised in wisdom: and his tongue will be talking of judgment: the law of his God is in his heart. Ps. ibid., 1. Fret not thyself because of the ungodly: neither be thou envious against the evil-doers. ℣. Glory.

Collect.

O GOD, who by the fire of thy love didst enkindle blessed John to walk unhurt amid the flames, and through him didst enrich thy Church with a new offspring: grant, by the help of his merits; that our vices may be purged by the fire of thy charity, and our souls healed to the attainment of everlasting salvation. Through.

In Lent, Commemoration of the Feria.

The Lesson from the book of Wisdom.

Ecclus. 31, 8-11.

BLESSED is the man that is found without blemish: and hath not gone after gold. Who is he, and we will call him blessed? for wonderful things hath he done among his people. Who hath been tried thereby, and found perfect? then let him glory. Who might offend, and hath not offended? or done evil, and hath not done it? His goods shall be established, and the congregation shall declare his alms.

Gradual. Ps. 92, 13-14. The righteous shall flourish like a palm-tree: and shall spread abroad like a cedar in Libanus in the house of the Lord. ℣. Ibid., 3. To tell of thy loving kindness early in the morning, and of thy truth in the night-season.

Tract. Ps. 112, 1-3. Blessed is the man that feareth the Lord: he hath great delight in his commandments. ℣. His seed shall be mighty upon earth: the generation of the faithful shall be blessed. ℣. Riches and plenteousness shall be in his house: and his righteousness endureth for ever.

✠ The Continuation of the holy Gospel according to Matthew.

Matt. 22, 34-46.

AT that time: The Pharisees came to Jesus: and one of them, who was a lawyer, asked him a question, tempting him, and saying: Master, which is the great commandment in the law? Jesus said unto him: Thou shalt love the Lord thy God, with all thy heart, and with all thy soul, and with all thy mind. This is the first and great commandment. And the second is like unto it: Thou shalt love thy neighbour as thyself. On these two commandments hang all the law and the prophets. While the Pharisees were gathered together, Jesus asked them, saying: What think ye of Christ? whose Son is he? They say unto him: The Son of David. He saith unto them: How then doth David in spirit call him Lord, saying: The Lord said unto my Lord, Sit thou on my right hand, till I make thine enemies thy foot-stool? If David then call him Lord, how is he his Son? And no man was able to answer him a word: neither durst any man from that day forth ask him any more questions.

Offertory. Ps. 89, 25. My truth and my mercy shall be with him: and in my name shall his horn be exalted.

Secret.

WE offer thee, O Lord, this sacrifice of praise to the honour of thy Saints: whereby we trust to be delivered from all evils both in this life and in that which is to come. Through.

In Lent, Commemoration of the Feria.

Communion. Matt. 24, 46-47. Blessed is the servant, whom his lord when he cometh shall find watching: verily I say unto you, he shall make him ruler over all his goods.

Postcommunion.

O LORD, our God, who hast refreshed us with heavenly meat and drink, we humbly beseech thee: that we may be defended by the prayers of him in whose memory we have received the same. Through.

In Lent, Commemoration of the Feria.

March 9.

St. Frances of Rome

Widow.

Double.

The Mass Cognovi, p. [36], the Collect excepted.

Collect. P

O GOD, who amidst the manifold gifts of thy grace didst honour blessed Frances, thy handmaid, with the familiar converse of an Angel: grant, we beseech thee; that through the help of her intercession we may be found worthy to attain hereafter unto the fellowship of the Angels. Through.

In Lent, Commemoration of the Feria.

Secret. C

GRANT, O Lord, that like as thy faithful people do acknowledge that in tribulation they have been succoured by the merits of thy Saints: so this oblation, which they here do offer unto thee in honour of the same, may be acceptable in thy sight. Through.

In Lent, Commemoration of the Feria.

Postcommunion. C

O LORD, who hast satisfied this thy family with thy sacred gifts: we beseech thee that we may at all times be comforted by the intercession of her whose festival we celebrate. Through.

In Lent, Commemoration of the Feria.

March 10.

The Holy Forty Martyrs

Simple.

Collect. P

GRANT we beseech thee, almighty God: that, like as we have known thy glorious Martyrs to be constant in their confession, so we may feel the succour of their loving intercession. Through.

Secret. P

REGARD, O Lord, the prayers and oblations of thy faithful people: that they may be acceptable unto thee for the festival of thy Saints, and bestow on us the succour of thy mercy. Through.

Postcommunion. P

O LORD, we beseech thee, let the intercession of thy Saints render us acceptable to thee: and grant; that this temporal celebration may avail to us for the attainment of eternal salvation. Through.

In Scotland: The same day, March 10.

Blessed John Ogilvie, M.

See Supplement.

March 12.

St. Gregory I

Pope, Confessor and Doctor of the Church

Greater double (or Double).

Introit. John 21, 15-17. Si diligis me.

IF thou lovest me, Simon Peter, feed my lambs, feed my sheep. Ps. 30, 1. I will magnify thee, O Lord, for thou hast set me up, and not made my foes to triumph over me. ℣. Glory.

Collect.

O GOD, who on the soul of thy servant Gregory hast bestowed the rewards of everlasting felicity: mercifully grant; that we, who are sore oppressed by the burden of our sins, may by his prayers before thee be relieved. Through.

Commemoration of the Feria.

The Lesson from the Epistle of blessed Peter the Apostle.

I Peter 5, 1-4 and 10-11.

DEARLY beloved: The elders which are among you I exhort, who am also an elder, and a witness of the sufferings of Christ, and also a partaker of the glory that shall be revealed: feed the flock of God which is among you, taking the oversight thereof, not by constraint, but willingly, not for filthy lucre, but of a ready mind; neither as being lords over God's heritage, but being ensamples to the flock. And when the chief Shepherd shall appear, ye shall receive a crown of glory that fadeth not away. Now the God of all grace, who hath called us unto his eternal glory by Christ Jesus, after that ye have suffered a while, make you perfect, stablish, strengthen, settle you. To him be glory and dominion for ever and ever. Amen.

Gradual. Ps. 107, 32 and 31. Let them exalt him in the congregation of the people: and praise him in the seat of the elders. ℣. O that men would praise the Lord for his goodness; and declare the wonders that he doeth for the children of men.

Tract. Ps. 40, 10-11. I have declared thy righteousness in the great congregation, lo, I will not refrain my lips, O Lord, and that thou knowest. ℣. I have not hid thy righteousness within my heart: my talk hath been of thy truth and thy salvation. ℣. I have not kept back thy loving mercy and truth from the great congregation.

✠ The Continuation of the holy Gospel according to Matthew.

Matt. 16, 13-19.

AT that time: Jesus came into the coasts of Cæsarea Philippi, and asked his disciples, saying: Whom do men say that I, the Son of man, am? And they said: Some say that thou art John the Baptist, some Elias, and others Jeremias, or one of the Prophets. He saith unto them: But whom say ye that I am? And Simon Peter answered and said: Thou art the Christ, the son of the living God. And Jesus answered and said unto him: Blessed art thou, Simon Bar-jona: for flesh and blood hath not revealed it unto thee, but my Father which is in heaven. And I say unto thee, That thou art Peter, and upon this rock I will build my Church, and the gates of hell shall not prevail against it. And I will give unto thee the keys of the kingdom of heaven. And whatsoever thou shalt bind on earth shall be bound in heaven: and whatsoever thou shalt loose on earth shall be loosed in heaven. Creed.

Offertory. Jer. 1, 9-10. Behold, I have put my words in thy mouth: see, I have set thee over the nations and over the kingdoms, to pull down and to destroy, to build and to plant.

Secret.

GRANT to us, we beseech thee, O Lord: that at the intercession of blessed Gregory this oblation, which thou hast instituted to be a sacrifice for the remission of the sins of the whole world, may be profitable unto us. Through.

Commemoration of the Feria.

Preface of Lent.

Communion. Matt. 16, 18. Thou art Peter, and upon this rock I will build my Church.

Postcommunion.

O GOD, who by reason of his holy life didst make thy blessed Bishop Gregory to be numbered with thy Saints: mercifully grant; that we, who celebrate this festival in his remembrance, may likewise follow the pattern of his conversation. Through.

Commemoration of the Feria.

March 17.
St. Patrick
Bishop and Confessor
(Greater) Double.

In Scotland: see Supplement.

The Mass Statuit ei, from the Common of a Confessor Bishop, p. [19], the Collect excepted.

Collect. P

O GOD, who for the preaching of thy glory to the Gentiles wast pleased to send forth blessed Patrick, thy Confessor and Bishop: grant by his merits and intercession; that we may of thy mercy be enabled to accomplish such things as thou commandest us to do. Through.

Commemoration of the Feria.

Secret. C

WE beseech thee, O Lord, that we, remembering with gladness the merits of thy Saints, may in all places feel the succour of their intercession. Through.

Commemoration of the Feria.

Postcommunion. C

GRANT, we beseech thee, almighty God: that we, shewing forth our thankfulness for the gifts which we have received, may at the intercession of blessed Patrick, thy Confessor and Bishop, obtain yet more abundant mercies. Through.

Commemoration of the Feria.

March 18.
St. Cyril, Bishop of Jerusalem
Confessor and Doctor of the Church
Double.

Introit. Ecclus. 15, 5. In medio.

IN the midst of the Church he opened his mouth: and the Lord filled him with the spirit of wisdom and understanding: he clothed him with a robe of glory. Ps. 92, 1. It is a good thing to give thanks unto the Lord: and to sing praises unto thy name, O most Highest. ℣. Glory.

Collect.

GRANT to us, we beseech thee, almighty God, at the intercession of thy blessed Bishop Cyril: so to know thee, the only true God, and Jesus Christ whom thou hast sent; that we may be found worthy to be numbered for evermore among the sheep who hear his voice. Through the same.

Commemoration of the Feria.

The Lesson from the book of Wisdom.

Ecclus. 39, 5-14.

THE righteous will give his heart to resort early to the Lord that made him, and will pray before the most High, and will open his mouth in prayer, and make supplication for his sins. When the great Lord will, he shall be filled with the spirit of understanding: he shall pour out wise sentences, and give thanks unto the Lord in his prayer. He shall direct his counsel and knowledge, and in his secrets shall he meditate. He shall shew forth that which he hath learned, and shall glory in the law of the covenant of the Lord. Many shall commend his understanding: and so long as the world endureth, it shall not be blotted out: his memorial shall not depart away, and his name shall live from generation to generation. Nations shall shew forth his wisdom, and the church shall declare his praise.

Gradual. Ps. 37, 30-31. The mouth of the righteous is exercised in wisdom, and his tongue will be talking of judgment. ℣. The law of his God is in his heart: and his goings shall not slide.

Tract. Ps. 112, 1-3. Blessed is the man that feareth the Lord: he hath great delight in his commandments. ℣. His seed shall be mighty upon earth: the generation of the faithful shall be blessed. ℣. Riches and plenteousness shall be in his house: and his righteousness endureth for ever.

✠ The Continuation of the holy Gospel according to Matthew.

Matt. 10, 23-28.

AT that time: Jesus said unto his disciples: When they persecute you in this city, flee ye into another. For verily I say unto you, Ye shall not have gone over the cities of Israel, till the Son of man be come. The disciple is not above his master, nor the servant above his lord. It is enough for the disciple that he be as his master: and the servant as his lord. If they have called the master of the house Beelzebub; how much more shall they call them of his household? Fear them not therefore. For there is nothing covered, that shall not be revealed: and hid that shall not be known. What I tell you in darkness, that speak ye in light: and what ye hear in the ear, that preach ye upon the housetops. And fear not them which kill the body, but are not able to kill the soul: but rather fear him which is able to destroy both soul and body in hell. Creed.

Offertory. Ps. 92, 13. The righteous shall flourish like a palm-tree: and shall spead abroad like a cedar in Libanus.

Secret.

LOOK down, O Lord, upon this undefiled oblation, which we here present unto thee: and grant; that by the merits of thy blessed Bishop and Confessor Cyril we may seek earnestly to receive the same in purity of heart. Through.

Commemoration of the Feria.

Communion. Luke 12, 42. A faithful and wise servant, whom his lord hath made ruler over his household: to give them their portion of meat in due season.

Postcommunion.

O LORD Jesu Christ, let this Sacrament of thy Body and Blood, which we have here received: so sanctify our hearts and minds at the prayers of thy blessed Bishop Cyril; that we may be worthy to be made partakers of the nature of thy Godhead: Who livest.

Commemoration of the Feria.

March 19.

ST. JOSEPH

SPOUSE OF THE B.V.MARY, CONFESSOR

PATRON OF THE UNIVERSAL CHURCH

Double of 1st class.

To-day in Choir after Terce the Conventual Mass of the Feast is said, and outside Choir after None is read a Mass of the Feria, of which, however, private Masses are forbidden.

Introit. Ps. 92, 13-14. Justus ut palma.

THE righteous shall flourish like a palm-tree, and shall spread abroad like a cedar in Libanus: such as are planted in the house of the Lord: in the courts of the house of our God. (E.T. Alleluia, alleluia.) Ps. ibid., 1. It is a good thing to give thanks unto the Lord: and to sing praises unto thy name, O most Highest. ℣. Glory.

Collect.

ASSIST us, O Lord, we beseech thee, by the merits of the Spouse of thy most holy Mother: that those things, which of our own power we cannot obtain, may through his intercession be granted unto us: Who livest and reignest.

In Lent, Commemoration of the Feria.

The Lesson from the book of Wisdom.

Ecclus. 45, 1-6.

BELOVED of God and men, whose memorial is blessed. He made him like to the glorious saints, and magnified him, so that his enemies stood in fear of him. By his words he caused the wonders to cease, and gave him a commandment for his people, and shewed him his glory. He sanctified him in his faithfulness and meekness, and chose him out of all men. He made him to hear his voice, and brought him into the dark cloud. And gave him commandments before his face, even the law of life and knowledge.

Gradual. Ps. 21, 4-5. Thou hast prevented him, O Lord, with the blessings of goodness: thou hast set a crown of pure gold upon his head. ℣. He asked life of thee, and thou gavest him a long life, even for ever and ever.

Tract. Ps. 112, 1-3. Blessed is the man that feareth the Lord: he hath great delight in his commandments. ℣. His seed shall be mighty upon earth: the generation of the faithful shall be blessed. ℣. Riches and plenteousness shall be in his house: and his righteousness endureth for ever.

In Eastertide, instead of the Gradual and Tract, is said:

Alleluia, alleluia. ℣. Ecclus. 45, 9. The Lord loved him and adorned him: he clothed him with a robe of glory. Alleluia. ℣. Hos. 14, 6. The righteous shall grow as the lily: and flourish for ever before the Lord. Alleluia.

☩ The Continuation of the holy Gospel according to Matthew.

Matt. 1, 18-21.

WHEN Mary the Mother of Jesus was espoused to Joseph, before they came together, she was found with child of the Holy Ghost. Then Joseph her husband, being a just man, and not willing to make her a publick example, was minded to put her away privily. But while he thought on these things, behold, the Angel of the Lord appeared unto him in a dream, saying: Joseph, thou son of David, fear not to take unto thee Mary thy wife: for that which is conceived in her is of the Holy Ghost. And she shall bring forth a son, and thou shalt call his name Jesus: for he shall save his people from their sins. Creed.

Offertory. Ps. 89, 25. My truth and my mercy shall be with him: and in my name shall his horn be exalted. (E.T. Alleluia.)

Secret.

WE render unto thee, O Lord, this duty of our bounden service, humbly beseeching thee: that like as we do offer unto thee this sacrifice of praise in honour of the festival of blessed Joseph, the Spouse of the Mother of thy Son Jesus Christ our Lord; so at his intercession thou wouldest preserve within us the effectual gifts of thy grace. Through the same.

In Lent, Commemoration of the Feria.

Preface of St. Joseph, And that on the Festival.

Communion. Matt. 1, 20. Joseph, thou son of David, fear not to take unto thee Mary thy wife: for that which is conceived in her is of the Holy Ghost. (E.T. Alleluia.)

Postcommunion.

ASSIST us, we beseech thee, O merciful God: and, at the intercession of blessed Joseph thy Confessor, continue towards us the gifts of thy loving-kindness. Through.

In Lent, Commemoration of the Feria.

¶ For a Votive of St. Joseph, the Mass Adjutor is said, p. [51].

March 21.

St. Benedict

Abbot

Greater double.

The Mass Os justi, from the Common of Abbots, p. [26].

Collect. C

O LORD, we beseech thee, let the intercession of thy blessed Abbot Benedict, commend us unto thee: that those things which for our own merits we cannot ask, we may through his advocacy obtain. Through.

Commemoration of the Feria.

Secret. C

O LORD, we beseech thee, let thy holy Abbot Benedict intercede for us: that this sacrifice which we offer and present upon thy holy altar may be profitable unto us for our salvation. Through.

Postcommunion. C

LET thy Sacrament, O Lord, which we have now received, and the prayers of thy blessed Abbot Benedict, effectually defend us: that we may both imitate the example of his conversation, and receive the succour of his intercession. Through.

March 24.

St. Gabriel the Archangel

Greater double.

Introit. Ps. 103, 20. Benedicite.

O PRAISE the Lord, ye Angels of his, ye that excel in strength: ye that fulfil his commandment, and hearken unto the voice of his words. Ps. ibid., 1. Praise the Lord, O my soul: and all that is within me praise his holy name. ℣. Glory.

Collect.

O GOD, who from the company of Angels didst choose the Archangel Gabriel to proclaim the mystery of thine Incarnation: mercifully grant; that we who celebrate his festival on earth, may find in him an advocate in heaven: Who livest and reignest.

Commemoration is made of the Feria.

The Lesson from the Prophet Daniel.

Dan. 9, 21-26.

IN those days: Behold the man Gabriel, whom I had seen in the vision at the beginning, being caused to fly swiftly, touched me about the time of the evening oblation. And he informed me, and talked with me, and said: O Daniel, I am now come forth to give thee skill and understanding. At the beginning of thy supplications the commandment came forth: and I am come to shew thee, for thou art greatly beloved: therefore understand the matter, and consider the vision. Seventy weeks are determined upon thy people and upon thy holy city, to finish the transgression, and to make an end of sins, and to make reconciliation for iniquity, and to bring in everlasting righteousness, and to seal up the vision and prophecy, and to anoint the Most Holy. Know therefore and understand: That from the going forth of the commandment to restore and to build Jerusalem unto the Messiah the Prince shall be seven weeks, and threescore and two weeks: the street shall be built again, and the wall, even in troublous times. And after threescore and two weeks shall Messiah be cut off: but not for himself. And the people of the prince that shall come shall destroy the city and the sanctuary: and the end thereof shall be with a flood, and unto the end of the war desolations are determined.

Gradual. Ps. 103, 20 and 1. O praise the Lord, ye Angels of his, ye that excel in strength, ye that fulfil his commandment. ℣. Praise the Lord, O my soul, and all that is within me praise his holy name.

Tract. Luke 1, 28, 42, 31 and 35. Hail, Mary, full of grace; the Lord is with thee. ℣. Blessed art thou among women: and blessed is the fruit of thy womb. ℣. Behold, thou shalt conceive and bring forth a Son, and shalt call his name Emmanuel. ℣. •The Holy Ghost shall come upon thee, and the power of the Highest shall overshadow thee. ℣. Therefore also that Holy Thing which shall be born of thee, shall be called the Son of God.

¶ In Votive Masses before Septuagesima or after Pentecost, the Gradual as above, but in place of the Tract is said:

Alleluia, alleluia. ℣. Ps. 103, 21. O praise the Lord, all ye his hosts: ye servants of his that do his pleasure. Alleluia.

In Eastertide, the following is said instead of the Gradual and Tract:

Alleluia, alleluia. Ps. 104, 4. Who maketh his Angels spirits: and his ministers a flaming fire. Alleluia. ℣. Luke 1, 28. Hail, Mary, full of grace; the Lord is with thee: blessed art thou among women. Alleluia.

✠ The Continuation of the holy Gospel according to Luke.

Luke 1, 26-38.

AT that time: The Angel Gabriel was sent from God unto a city of Galilee named Nazareth, to a Virgin espoused to a man whose name was Joseph, of the house of David, and the Virgin's name was Mary. And the Angel came in unto her, and said: Hail, full of grace; the Lord is with thee: blessed art thou among women. And when she saw him she was troubled at his saying: and cast in her mind what manner of salutation this should be. And the Angel said unto her: Fear not, Mary, for thou hast found favour with God: and behold, thou shalt conceive in thy womb, and bring forth a Son, and shalt call his name Jesus. He shall be great, and shall be called the Son of the Highest; and the Lord God shall give unto him the throne of his father David: and he shall reign over the house of Jacob for ever, and of his kingdom there shall be no end. Then said Mary unto the Angel: How shall this be, seeing I know not a man? And the Angel answered and said unto her: The Holy Ghost shall come upon thee, and the power of the Highest shall overshadow thee. Therefore also that Holy Thing which shall be born of thee shall be called the Son of God. And behold, thy cousin Elisabeth, she hath also conceived a son in her old age: and this is the sixth month with her who was called barren: for with God nothing shall be impossible. And Mary said: Behold the handmaid of the Lord, be it unto me according to thy word.

The Creed is not said.

Offertory. Rev. 8, 3-4. An Angel stood at the altar of the temple, having a golden censer in his hand; and there was given unto him much incense: and the smoke of the incense ascended up before God.

Secret.

LET this oblation of us thy servants, together with the prayers of thy blessed Archangel Gabriel, be made acceptable in thy sight, O Lord: that he, whom we venerate here on earth, may ever be our advocate before thee in heaven. Through.

Commemoration of the Feria.

Communion. Dan. 3, 58. O all ye Angels of the Lord, bless ye the Lord, sing ye praises, and magnify him above all for ever.

Postcommunion.

O LORD our God, who hast made us partakers of the mysteries of thy Body and Blood, we beseech thee of thy mercy to grant: that, as we have known thine Incarnation by the message of Gabriel, so by his assistance we may obtain the benefits of the same: Who livest and reignest with God the Father.

Commemoration of the Feria.

March 25.

THE ANNUNCIATION

OF

THE BLESSED VIRGIN MARY

Double of 1st class.

¶ To-day in Choir after Terce is said a Conventual Mass of the Feast, and outside Choir after None is read a Mass of the Feria; of which, however, private Masses are forbidden.

Introit. Ps. 45, 13, 15 and 16.
Vultum tuum.

THE rich also among the people shall make their supplication before thee: the Virgins that be her fellows shall be brought unto the King: they that bear her company shall be brought unto thee with joy and gladness. (E.T. Alleluia, alleluia.) Ps. ibid., 1. My heart is inditing of a good matter: I speak of the things which I have made unto the King. V. Glory.

Collect.

WE beseech thee, O Lord, pour thy grace into our hearts: that, as we have known the Incarnation of thy Son Jesus Christ by the message of an Angel; so by his cross and passion we may be brought unto the glory of his resurrection. Through the same.

Or, Collect.

O GOD, who wast pleased that thy Word should take flesh of the womb of the blessed Virgin Mary at the message of an Angel: grant to us thy humble servants; that we, believing her to be indeed the Mother of God, may by her intercession be holpen in thy sight. Through the same.

In Lent, Commemoration of the Feria in non-conventual Masses.

The Lesson from the Prophet Isaiah.
Is. 7, 10-15.

IN those days: The Lord spake unto Ahaz, saying: Ask thee a sign of the Lord thy God, ask it either in the depth, or in the height above. But Ahaz said: I will not ask, neither will I tempt the Lord. And he said: Hear ye now, O house of David: Is it a small thing for you to weary men, but will ye weary my God also? Therefore the Lord himself shall give you a sign. Behold a Virgin shall conceive, and bear a son, and shall call his name Emmanuel. Butter and honey shall he eat, that he may know to refuse the evil, and choose the good.

Gradual. Ps. 45, 3 and 5. Full of grace are thy lips: because God hath blessed thee for ever. V. Because of the word of truth, of meekness, and righteousness: and thy right hand shall teach thee terrible things.

Tract. Ibid., 11-12. Hearken, O daughter, and consider, incline thine ear: so shall the King have pleasure in thy beauty. ℣. Ibid., 13 and 10. The rich also among the people shall make their supplication before thee: kings' daughters were among thy honourable women. ℣. Ibid., 15-16. The Virgins that be her fellows shall be brought unto the King: they that bear her company shall be brought unto thee. ℣. With joy and gladness shall they be brought: and shall enter into the King's palace.

In Eastertide, omitting the Gradual and the Tract, say:

Alleluia, alleluia. ℣. Luke 1, 28. Hail, Mary, full of grace; the Lord is with thee: blessed art thou among women. Alleluia. ℣. Now hath blossomed Jesse's rod: a Virgin bears both man and God: God restoreth peace to men, high and low are one again. Alleluia.

✠ The Continuation of the holy Gospel according to Luke.

Luke 1, 26-18.

AT that time: The Angel Gabriel was sent from God unto a city of Galilee named Nazareth, to a Virgin espoused to a man whose name was Joseph, of the house of David, and the Virgin's name was Mary. and the Angel came in unto her and said: †Hail, thou that art highly favoured,† [or Hail, full of grace,] the Lord is with thee: blessed art thou among women. And when she saw him she was troubled at his saying: and cast in her mind what manner of salutation this should be. And the Angel said unto her: Fear not, Mary, for thou hast found favour with God: and behold, thou shalt conceive in thy womb, and bring forth a Son, and shalt call his name Jesus. He shall be great, and shall be called the Son of the Highest, and the Lord God shall give unto him the throne of his father David: and he shall reign over the house of Jacob for ever, and of his kingdom there shall be no end. Then said Mary unto the Angel: How shall this be, seeing I know not a man? And the Angel answered and said unto her: The Holy Ghost shall come upon thee, and the power of the Highest shall overshadow thee. Therefore also that Holy Thing which shall be born of thee shall be called the Son of God. And behold, thy cousin Elisabeth, she hath also conceived a son in her old age: and this is the sixth month with her who was called barren: for with God nothing shall be impossible. And Mary said: Behold the handmaid of the Lord, be it unto me according to thy word.*

And the Angel departed from her. Creed.

Offertory. Luke 1, 28 and 42. Hail, Mary, full of grace; the Lord is with thee: blessed art thou among women, and blessed is the fruit of thy womb. (E.T. Alleluia.)

Secret.

ESTABLISH in our hearts, we beseech thee, O Lord, the mysteries of the true faith: that like as we acknowledge thy Son conceived of a Virgin to be very God and very man; so by the power of his life-giving resurrection, we may be found worthy to attain unto everlasting gladness. Through the same.

In Lent, Commemoration of the Feria.

Preface of the B.V. Mary, And that in the Annunciation.

Communion. Is. 7, 14. Behold a Virgin shall conceive, and bear a son: and his name shall be called Emmanuel. (E.T. Alleluia.)

If the following Postcommunion was said as the Collect, then for Postcommunion the Collect O God who wast pleased, may be said, otherwise:

Postcommunion.

WE beseech thee, O Lord, pour thy grace into our hearts: that as we have known the Incarnation of Christ thy Son by the message of an Angel; so through his passion and cross we may be brought unto the glory of his resurrection. Through the same.

[Or, Collect.]

O GOD, who wast pleased that thy Word should take flesh of the womb of the blessed Virgin Mary at the message of an Angel: grant to us thy humble servants; that we, believing her to be indeed the Mother of God, may by her intercession be holpen in thy sight. Through the same.

March 27.

St. John Damascene

Confessor and Doctor of the Church

Double.

Introit. Ps. 73, 24. Tenuisti.

THOU hast holden me by my right hand: thou shalt guide me with thy counsel, and after that receive me with glory. Ps. ibid., 1. Truly God is loving unto Israel, even unto such as are of a clean heart! ℣. Glory.

Collect.

ALMIGHTY and everlasting God, who, for the defence of the veneration of sacred images, didst endue blessed John with heavenly doctrine and wondrous strength of spirit: grant unto us by his intercession and example; so to venerate the images of thy Saints, that we may follow their good examples, and feel the effectual succour of their advocacy. Through.

In Lent, Commemoration is made of the Feria.

The Lesson from the book of Wisdom.

Wisd. 10, 10-17.

THE Lord guided the just man in right paths, shewed him the kingdom of God, and gave him knowledge of holy things: made him rich in his travail, and multiplied the fruit of his labours. In the covetousness of such as oppressed him he stood by him, and made him rich. He defended him from his enemies, and kept him safe from those that lay in wait, and in a sore conflict he gave him the victory, that he might know that wisdom is stronger than all. When the just was sold, she forsook him not, but delivered him from sin: she went down with him into the pit, and left him not in bonds, till she brought him the sceptre of the kingdom, and power against those that oppressed him: as for them that had accused him, she shewed them to be liars, and gave him perpetual glory. She delivered the righteous people and blameless seed from the nation that oppressed them. She entered into the soul of the servant of the Lord, and withstood dreadful kings in wonders and signs. And she rendered to the righteous a reward of their labours.

Gradual. Ps. 18, 33 and 35. It is God that girdeth me with strength of war: and maketh my way perfect. ℣. He teacheth mine hands to fight: and mine arms shall break even a bow of steel.

Tract. Ibid., 38, 39 and 50. I will follow upon mine enemies, and overtake them. ℣. I will smite them that they shall not be able to stand: but fall under my feet. ℣. For this cause will I give thanks unto thee, O Lord, among the Gentiles, and sing praises unto thy name.

¶ In Votive Masses before Septuagesima and after Pentecost is said after the Gradual:

Alleluia, alleluia. ℣. Ps. 18, 36. Thou hast given me the defence of thy salvation: Thy right hand also shall hold me up. Alleluia.

¶ In Eastertide, the Gradual and Tract being omitted, is said:

Alleluia, alleluia. ℣. I Sam. 25, 26 and 28. The Lord hath saved thine hand unto thee: because thou fightest the battles of the Lord.
Alleluia. ℣. Ps. 144, 1. Blessed be the Lord my strength, who teacheth my hands to war, and my fingers to fight. Alleluia.

✠ The Continuation of the holy Gospel according to Luke.

Luke 6, 6-11.

AT that time: It came to pass on another sabbath, that Jesus entered into the synagogue and taught. And there was a man whose right hand was withered. And the scribes and Pharisees watched him, whether he would heal on the sabbath day: that they might find an accusation against him. But he knew their thoughts. And said to the man which had the withered hand: Rise up, and stand forth in the midst. And he arose and stood forth. Then said Jesus unto them: I will ask you one thing. Is it lawful on the sabbath days to do good, or to do evil: to save life, or to destroy it? And looking round about upon them all, he said unto the man: Stretch forth thine hand. And he did so: and his hand was restored whole as the other. And they were filled with madness, and communed one with another what they might do to Jesus. Creed.

Offertory. Job. 14, 7. There is hope of a tree, if it be cut down, that it will sprout again, and that the tender branch thereof will not cease.

Secret.

O LORD, let the devout intercession of blessed John and of the Saints, who through his labours are set forth in the temples for our veneration, avail to render the gifts which we offer acceptable in thy sight. Through.

In Lent, Commemoration of the Feria.

Communion. Ps. 37, 17. The arms of the ungodly shall be broken, and the Lord upholdeth the righteous.

Postcommunion.

WE beseech thee, O Lord, that the gifts which we have here received may defend us with heavenly armour: and that the advocacy of blessed John, united with the prayers of all the Saints, the veneration of whose images in the Church he victoriously upheld, may be our succour and defence. Through.

In Lent, Commemoration of the Feria.

March 28.

St. John of Capistrano

Confessor

Simple.

Collect.　　　　P

O GOD, who through blessed John didst cause thy faithful people in the power of the most holy name of Jesus to triumph over the enemies of the Cross: grant, we beseech thee; that, by his intercession, we may overcome the crafts of our ghostly enemies, and be found worthy to obtain of thee the crown of righteousness. Through the same.

Secret. P

O LORD, look with favour upon the sacrifice which we here offer: that at the intercession of blessed John, thy Confessor, it may so stablish us with thy sure defence, that we may beat down the snares of our enemies. Through.

Postcommunion. P

ALMIGHTY God, who has satisfied us with heavenly meat, and refreshed us with spiritual drink, we beseech thee: that, at the intercession of blessed John, thy Confessor, thou wouldest defend us against the assaults of the enemy, and preserve thy Church in continual peace. Through.

Friday after Passion Sunday.

The Seven Sorrows of the Blessed Virgin Mary

Greater double.

Introit. John 19, 25. Stabant.

THERE stood by the Cross of Jesus his Mother, and his Mother's sister, Mary the wife of Cleophas, and Salome, and Mary Magdalene. Ibid., 26-27. Woman, behold thy Son: said Jesus; and to the disciple: Behold thy Mother. ℣. Glory.

Collect.

O GOD, in whose passion, according to the prophecy of Simeon, the sword of sorrow did pierce the most loving soul of the glorious Virgin Mother Mary: mercifully grant; that we, who devoutly call to mind the suffering whereby she was pierced, may, by the glorious merits and prayers of all the Saints who have faithfully stood beneath the Cross, obtain with gladness the benefits of thy passion: Who livest and reignest.

Commemoration is made of the Feria.

Collect.

WE beseech thee, O Lord, mercifully to pour thy grace into our hearts: that we, who by willing chastisement do restrain our sins, may in such wise mortify ourselves in this life, that we be not delivered unto everlasting punishments. (Through.)

¶ In Votive Masses is said the following:

Collect.

O LORD Jesu Christ, we beseech thee: that the blessed Virgin Mary, thy Mother, whose most sacred soul was in the hour of thy passion pierced by the sword of sorrow; may both now and in the hour of death stand before thee to win for us the succour of thy mercy: Who livest.

The Lesson from the book of Judith.

Judith 13, 22-25.

THE Lord hath blessed thee in his power, because through thee he hath brought our enemies to nought. O daughter, blessed art thou of the most high God, above all the women upon the earth. And blessed be the Lord God, which hath created the heavens and the earth: because he hath so magnified thy name this day, that this thy praise shall not depart from the heart of men, which remember the power of God for ever, for whom thou hast not spared thy life for the affliction of our nation, but hast revenged our ruin, walking a straight way before our God.

Gradual. Mournful and weeping art thou, O Virgin Mary, standing by the Cross of the Lord Jesus, thy Son, the Redeemer. ℣. Virgin Mother of God, he, whom the whole world containeth not, endureth this torment of the cross, the author of life made man.

Tract. There stood by the Cross of our Lord Jesus Christ holy Mary, Queen of heaven and Lady of the world, mournful and weeping. ℣. Lam. 1, 12. O all ye that pass by, behold and see if there be any sorrow like unto my sorrow.

¶ In Votive Masses throughout the year, Gradual, Mournful...made man, as above; then:

Alleluia, alleluia. ℣. There stood by the Cross of our Lord Jesus Christ holy Mary, Queen of heaven and Lady of the world, mournful and weeping. Alleluia.

¶ In Votive Masses in Eastertide: Alleluia, alleluia. ℣. There stood.. Alleluia. O all ye.... my sorrow, Alleluia, as in the Tract above.

Sequence. Stabat Mater dolorosa.

To be omitted in votive Masses.

BY the Cross her station keeping,
Stood the mournful Mother weeping,
Where he hung, her dying Son.

Through her soul, of joy bereavéd,
Torn with anguish, deeply grievéd,
Lo! the piercing sword hath run.

O, how sad and sore distresséd
Then was she, that Mother blesséd
Of the sole-begotten One!

Torn with grief and desolation,
Mother good, the bitter Passion
Saw she of her glorious Son.

Who, on Christ's dear Mother gazing,
Torn by anguish so amazing,
Born of woman, would not weep?

Who, on Christ's dear Mother thinking,
With her Son in sorrow sinking,
Would not share her sadness deep?

For his people's sin chastiséd,
She her Jesus saw despiséd,
Saw him by the scourges rent.

Saw her own sweet Offspring taken,
And in death by all forsaken
While his spirit forth he sent.

Mother, fount of love o'erflowing,
Ah, that I, thy sorrow knowing,
In thy grief may mourn with thee.

That my heart, fresh ardour gaining,
Love of Christ my God attaining,
Unto him may pleasing be.

Holy Mother, be there written
Every wound of Jesus smitten
In my heart, and there remain.

As thy Son through tribulation
Deigned to purchase my salvation,
Let me share with thee the pain.

Let me mourn with thee beside him
For the sins which crucified him,
While my life remains in me.

Take beneath the Cross my station,
Share with thee thy desolation,
Humbly this I ask of thee.

Virgin, virgins all excelling,
Spurn me not, my prayer repelling:
Make me weep and mourn with thee.

So Christ's death within me bearing,
Let me, in his Passion sharing,
Keep his wounds in memory.

Let the five wounds penetrate me:
Let the Cross inebriate me,
And thy Son's most precious blood.

Lest I burn in hell's damnation,
Virgin, be my consolation
On the judgment day of God.

Christ, when this world's troubles leave me,
Through thy Mother then receive me
To the palm of victory.

When the bonds of flesh are riven,
Glory to my soul be given
In thy Paradise with thee. Amen.

☩ The Continuation of the holy Gospel according to John.

John 19, 25-27.

AT that time: There stood by the Cross of Jesus his Mother, and his Mother's sister, Mary the wife of Cleophas, and Mary Magdalene. When Jesus therefore saw his Mother, and the disciple standing by, whom he loved, he saith unto his Mother: Woman, behold thy Son. Then saith he to the disciple: Behold thy Mother. And from that hour that disciple took her unto his own home. Creed.

Offertory. Jer. 18, 20. Remember, O Virgin, Mother of God, when thou standest in the sight of the Lord, that thou speak good things for us, and that he may turn away his indignation from us.

Secret.

WE offer unto thee our prayers and sacrifices, O Lord Jesu Christ, humbly beseeching thee: that we, who in our prayers do recall the Piercing of the most loving soul of blessed Mary, thy Mother; may by the manifold and devout intercessions both of her and of the Saints that with her have stood beneath the Cross, through the merits of thy death, be made worthy to be partakers of the inheritance of thine elect: Who livest and reignest.

For the Feria. Secret.

GRANT unto us, O merciful God: that we, being ever found meet to do thee worthy service at thine altars, may continually be made partakers of the same unto our salvation. (Through.)

Preface of the B.V. Mary, And that in the Transfixion.

Communion. Happy the heart of the blessed Virgin Mary, which without death gained the palm of martyrdom beneath the Cross of the Lord.

Postcommunion.

O LORD Jesu Christ, let this sacrifice which we have here received in devout remembrance of the Piercing of thy Virgin Mother: obtain for us of thy mercy all such blessings as may effectually avail for our salvation: Who livest and reignest.

For the Feria. Postcommunion.

LET this holy sacrifice, O Lord, which we have here received, be our continual defence: and evermore drive far from us all things that may hurt us. (Through.)

FEASTS OF APRIL

April 2.

St. Francis of Paula

Confessor

Double.

The Mass Justus ut palma, p. [25], the Prayers and Epistle excepted:

Collect.

O GOD, the exaltation of the humble, who didst raise thy blessed Confessor Francis to the glory of thy Saints: grant, we beseech thee; that, through his merits and example, we may attain with gladness unto the rewards that thou hast promised to the humble. Through.

In Lent, Commemoration is made of the Feria.

The Lesson from the Epistle of blessed Paul the Apostle to the Philippians.

Phil. 3, 7-12.

BRETHREN: What things were gain to me, those I counted loss for Christ. Yea doubtless, and I count all things but loss for the excellency of the knowledge of Christ Jesus my Lord: for whom I have suffered the loss of all things, and do count them but dung, that I may win Christ and be found in him, not having mine own righteousness which is of the law, but that which is through the faith of Christ: the righteousness which is of God by faith, that I may know him, and the power of his resurrection, and the fellowship of his sufferings: being made conformable unto his death: if by any means I might attain unto the resurrection of the dead: not as though I had already attained, either were already perfect; but I follow after, if that I may apprehend that for which also I am apprehended of Christ Jesus.

Secret. P

THROUGH the merits of blessed Francis may these gifts of thy faithful people, with which we load thine altars, be rendered pleasing unto thee, O Lord, and, by thy mercy, profitable for our salvation. Through.

In Lent, Commemoration of the Feria.

Postcommunion. P

WE pray thee, O Lord, that the heavenly sacraments, which we have received: may, at the intercession of blessed Francis, thy Confessor; effectually avail for our succour both in this life and that which is to come. Through.

In Lent, Commemoration of the Feria.

April 4.

St. Isidore

Bishop, Confessor and Doctor of the Church

Double.

The Mass In medio, p. [22].

The Creed is said.

In Lent, Commemoration of the Feria.

Collect. C 1

O GOD, who didst send blessed Isidore thy Doctor to guide thy people in the way of everlasting salvation: grant, we beseech thee; that as we have learned of him the doctrine of life on earth, so we may be found worthy to have him for our advocate in heaven. Through.

Secret. C 1

MAY the devout prayers of thy Bishop and Doctor, Saint Isidore, continually succour us, O Lord: that they may render our oblations acceptable in thy sight; and ever obtain for us thy merciful pardon. Through.

Postcommunion. C 1

WE beseech thee, O Lord, that blessed Isidore, thy Bishop and most excellent Doctor, may ever stand before thee as our advocate: that this sacrifice of thine ordinance may effectually avail for our salvation. Through.

April 5.

St. Vincent Ferrer

Confessor

Double.

The Mass Os justi, from the Common of a Confessor not a Bishop, p. [24], except the Collect.

Collect. P

O GOD, who didst vouchsafe to illumine thy Church by the merits and preaching of blessed Vincent, thy Confessor: grant to us thy servants; that we may both be instructed by his example, and by his advocacy be delivered from all adversities. Through.

In Lent, Commemoration of the Feria.

Secret. C

WE offer thee, O Lord, this our sacrifice of praise to the honour of thy Saints: whereby we trust to be delivered from all evils both in this life and in that which is to come. Through.

In Lent, Commemoration of the Feria.

Postcommunion. C

O LORD our God, who hast refreshed us with heavenly meat and drink, we humbly beseech thee: that we may be defended by the prayers of him in whose memory we have received the same. Through.

In Lent, Commemoration of the Feria.

April 11.
St. Leo I
Pope, Confessor and Doctor of the Church

Double.

Introit. John 21, 15-17. Si diligis me.

IF thou lovest me, Simon Peter, feed my lambs, feed my sheep. (E.T. Alleluia, alleluia.) Ps. 30, 1. I will magnify thee, O Lord, for thou hast set me up, and not made my foes to triumph over me. ℣. Glory.

Collect. C 1

O EVERLASTING Shepherd, look down in mercy on thy flock: and as thou didst choose blessed Leo thy Chief Bishop to be pastor and ruler of thy Church; so at his intercession defend it with thy continual protection. Through.

In Lent Commemoration is made of the Feria.

The Lesson from the Epistle of blessed Peter the Apostle.

I Peter 5, 1-4 and 10-11.

DEARLY beloved: The elders which are among you I exhort, who am also an elder, and a witness of the sufferings of Christ, and also a partaker of the glory that shall be revealed: feed the flock of God which is among you, taking the oversight thereof, not by constraint, but willingly, not for filthy lucre, but of a ready mind; neither as being lords over God's heritage, but being ensamples to the flock. And when the chief Shepherd shall appear, ye shall receive a crown of glory that fadeth not away. Now the God of all grace, who hath called us unto his eternal glory by Christ Jesus, after that ye have suffered a while, make you perfect, stablish, strengthen, settle you. To him be glory and dominion for ever and ever. Amen.

Gradual. Ps. 107, 32 and 31. Let them exalt him in the congregation of the people: and praise him in the seat of the elders. ℣. O that men would praise the Lord for his goodness: and declare the wonders that he doeth for the children of men.

Tract. Ps. 40, 10-11. I have declared thy righteousness in the great congregation, lo, I will not refrain my lips, O Lord, and that thou knowest. ℣. I have not hid thy righteousness within my heart: my talk hath been of thy truth and thy salvation. ℣. I have not kept back thy loving mercy and truth from the great congregation.

In Eastertide in place of the Gradual and Tract is said:

Alleluia, alleluia. ℣. Matt. 16, 18. Thou art Peter, and upon this rock I will build my Church. Alleluia. ℣. Ps. 45, 17-18. Thou shalt make them princes in all lands: they shall remember thy name, O Lord. Alleluia.

✠ The Continuation of the holy Gospel according to Matthew.

Matt. 16, 13-19.

AT that time: Jesus came into the coasts of Cæsarea Philippi, and asked his disciples, saying: Whom do men say that I, the Son of man, am? And they said: Some say that thou art John the Baptist, some Elias, and others Jeremias, or one of the Prophets. He saith unto them: But whom say ye that I am? And Simon Peter answered and said: Thou art the Christ, the son of the living God. And Jesus answered and said unto him: Blessed art thou, Simon Bar-jona: for flesh and blood hath not revealed it unto thee, but my Father which is in heaven. And I say also unto thee, That thou art Peter, and upon this rock I will build my Church, and the gates of hell shall not prevail against it. And I will give unto thee the keys of the kingdom of heaven. And whatsoever thou shalt bind on earth, shall be bound in heaven: and whatsoever thou shalt loose on earth, shall be loosed in heaven. Creed.

Offertory. Jer. 1, 9-10. **Behold, I have put my words in thy mouth: see, I have set thee over the nations and over the kingdoms, to pull down and to destroy, to build and to plant. (E.T. Alleluia.)**

Secret. C 1

WE beseech thee, O Lord, graciously enlighten thy Church by the gifts which we here offer: that in every place thy flock may increase and prosper, and the shepherds by thy governance may be made pleasing to thy name. Through.

In Lent, Commemoration of the Feria.

Communion. Matt. 16, 18. **Thou art Peter, and upon this rock I will build my Church. (E.T. Alleluia.)**

Postcommunion. C 1

MERCIFUL Lord, we beseech thee to govern and preserve thy Church, which thou hast here refreshed with heavenly food: that by the guiding of thy mighty power it may serve thee in more abundant freedom, and ever keep thy true religion whole and undefiled. Through.

In Lent, Commemoration of the Feria.

April 13.

St. Hermenegild

Martyr.

Simple.

In Lent, Commemoration of this Feast in Mass of the Feria.

In Eastertide, Mass as below:

Introit. Ps. 64, 3. Protexisti.

THOU hast hidden me, O God, from the gathering together of the froward, alleluia: and from the insurrection of wicked doers, alleluia, alleluia. Ps. ibid., 1. **Hear my voice, O God, in my prayer: preserve my life from fear of the enemy.** V. Glory.

Collect. P

O GOD, who didst teach thy blessed Martyr Hermenegild to lay down an earthly for a heavenly realm: grant us, we beseech thee; that after his example we may despise all things temporal, and follow steadfastly after things eternal. Through.

The Lesson from the book of Wisdom.

Wisd. 5, 1-5.

THE righteous shall stand in great boldness before the face of such as have afflicted them, and made no account of their labours. When they see it they shall be troubled with terrible fear, and shall be amazed at the strangeness of their salvation, so far beyond all that they looked for, and they repenting and groaning for anguish of spirit shall say within themselves: These were they, whom we had sometime in derision, and a proverb of reproach. We fools accounted their life madness, and their end to be without honour: how are they numbered among the children of God, and their lot is among the Saints.

Alleluia, alleluia. ℣. Ps. 89, 6. O Lord, the very heavens shall praise thy wondrous works: and thy truth in the congregation of the saints. Alleluia. ℣. Ps. 21, 4. Thou hast set, O Lord, a crown of pure gold upon his head. Alleluia.

☩ The Continuation of the holy Gospel according to Luke.

Luke 14, 26-33.

AT that time: Jesus said unto the multitudes: If any man come to me, and hate not his father, and mother, and wife, and children, and brethren, and sisters, yea, and his own life, also, he cannot be my disciple. And whosoever doth not bear his cross, and come after me, cannot be my disciple. For which of you, intending to build a tower, sitteth not down first, and counteth the cost, whether he have sufficient to finish it; lest haply, after he hath laid the foundation, and is not able to finish it, all that behold it begin to mock him, saying: This man began to build, and was not able to finish? Or what king, going to make war against another king, sitteth not down first, and consulteth whether he be able with ten thousand to meet him that cometh against him with twenty thousand? Or else, while the other is yet a great way off, he sendeth an ambassage, and desireth conditions of peace. So likewise, whosoever he be of you that forsaketh not all that he hath, he cannot be my disciple.

Offertory. Ps. 89, 6. O Lord, the very heavens shall praise thy wondrous works: and thy truth in the congregation of the saints, alleluia, alleluia.

Secret. C3

WE beseech thee, O Lord, to accept our prayers and oblations: and graciously hearken unto us, whom thou dost cleanse by thy heavenly mysteries. Through.

Communion. Ps. 64, 11. The righteous shall rejoice in the Lord, and put his trust in him: and all they that are true of heart shall be glad, alleluia, alleluia.

Postcommunion. C3

GRANT, we beseech thee, O Lord our God: that like as we in this life do gladly honour the memory of thy Saints; so we may rejoice hereafter in their everlasting fellowship. Through.

April 14.

St. Justin

Martyr

Double.

Introit. Ps. 119, 85 and 46. Narraverunt.

THE proud have digged pits for me, which are not after thy law: I will speak of thy testimonies also, even before kings, and will not be ashamed. (E.T. Alleluia, alleluia.) Ps. ibid., 1. Blessed are those that are undefiled in the way: and walk in the law of the Lord. ℣. Glory.

Collect.

O GOD, who by the foolishness of the Cross didst wondrously teach blessed Justin Martyr the excellent knowledge of Jesus Christ: grant to us through his intercession; that we, driving away the errors that beset us, may attain unto steadfastness of faith. Through the same.

In Lent, Commemoration of the Feria.

Then Commemoration of SS. Tiburtius, Valerian and Maximus, MM.

Collect.

GRANT, we beseech thee, almighty God: that we, who celebrate the festival of thy holy Martyrs, Tiburtius, Valerian and Maximus; may likewise follow the example of their virtues. Through.

The Lesson from the Epistle of blessed Paul the Apostle to the Corinthians.

I Cor. 1, 18-25 and 30.

BRETHREN: The preaching of the cross is to them that perish foolishness: but unto us which are saved it is the power of God. For it is written: I will destroy the wisdom of the wise, and will bring to nothing the understanding of the prudent. Where is the wise? where is the scribe? where is the disputer of this world? hath not God made foolish the wisdom of this world? For after that in the wisdom of God the world by wisdom knew not God: it pleased God by the foolishness of preaching to save them that believe. For the Jews require a sign, and the Greeks seek after wisdom: but we preach Christ crucified: unto the Jews a stumbling-block, and unto the Greeks foolishness, but unto them which are called, both Jews and Greeks, Christ the power of God, and the wisdom of God: because the foolishness of God is wiser than men: and the weakness of God is stronger than men. But of him are ye in Christ Jesus, who of God is made unto us wisdom, and righteousness, and sanctification, and redemption.

Gradual. I Cor. 3, 19-22. The wisdom of this world is foolishness with God, for it is written: The Lord knoweth the thoughts of the wise, that they are vain. ℣. Ibid. 1, 19. I will destroy the wisdom of the wise, and will bring to nothing the understanding of the prudent.

Tract. I Cor. 2, 2 and 7-8. I determined not to know any thing among you, save Jesus Christ, and him crucified. ℣. We speak the wisdom of God in a mystery, even the hidden wisdom, which God ordained before the world unto our glory. ℣. Which none of the princes of this world knew. For had they known it, they would not have crucified the Lord of glory.

In Eastertide the Gradual and Tract are omitted, and instead is said:

Alleluia, alleluia. ℣. I Cor. 3, 19-20. The wisdom of this world is foolishness with God: for it is written: The Lord knoweth the thoughts of the wise, that they are vain. Alleluia. ℣. Phil. 3, 8. Yea doubtless, and I count all things but loss for the excellency of the knowledge of Christ Jesus my Lord. Alleluia.

¶ In Votive Masses before Septuagesima or after Pentecost, the Gradual is said, as above, but, the Tract being omitted, there is added:

Alleluia, alleluia. ℣. Phil. 3, 8. Yea doubtless, and I count all things but loss for the excellency of the knowledge of Christ Jesus my Lord. Alleluia.

✠ The Continuation of the holy Gospel according to Luke.

Luke 12, 2-8.

AT that time: Jesus said to his disciples: There is nothing covered, that shall not be revealed, neither hid, that shall not be known. Therefore, whatsoever ye have spoken in darkness shall be heard in the light: and that which ye have spoken in the ear in closets shall be proclaimed upon the housetops. And I say unto you my friends: Be not afraid of them that kill the body, and after that have no more that they can do. But I will forewarn you whom ye shall fear: Fear him, which after he hath killed hath power to cast into hell; yea, I say unto you, Fear him. Are not five sparrows sold for two farthings, and not one of them is forgotten before God? But even the very hairs of your head are all numbered. Fear not therefore: ye are of more value than many sparrows. Also I say unto you: Whosoever shall confess me before men, him shall the Son of man also confess before the Angels of God.

Offertory. I Cor. 2, 2. I determined not to know any thing among you, save Jesus Christ, and him crucified. (E.T. Alleluia.)

Secret.

O LORD God, graciously receive our gifts: the wondrous mystery whereof the holy Martyr Justin did manfully defend against the slanders of the ungodly. Through.

Commemoration of the Feria in Lent, and of the Saints as below.

For the SS. Martyrs.　　　Secret.

WE beseech thee, O Lord, that this oblation, which we offer unto thee in commemoration of the birthday of thy holy Martyrs: may both loose the bonds of our iniquity, and obtain for us the gifts of thy mercy. Through.

Communion. II Tim. 4, 8. There is laid up for me a crown of righteousness, which the Lord, the righteous judge, shall give me at that day. (E.T. Alleluia.)

Postcommunion.

O LORD, who hast refreshed us with heavenly food, we humbly beseech thee: that, following the teaching of blessed Justin thy Martyr; we may ever continue in thanksgiving for the gifts which we have received. Through.

Commemoration of the Feria in Lent, and of the Saints as below.

For the SS. Martyrs.　　Postcommunion.

O LORD, who hast satisfied us with thy sacred gifts, we humbly beseech thee: that we, who here do offer unto thee this service of our bounden duty, may grow and increase to the attainment of everlasting salvation. Through.

April 17.
For St. Anicetus

Pope and Martyr

The Mass Si diligis me, p. [2].

Collect.　　　C1

O EVERLASTING Shepherd, look down in mercy on thy flock: and as thou didst choose blessed Anicetus, thy Martyr and Chief Bishop, to be pastor and ruler of thy Church; so at his intercession defend it with thy continual protection. Through.

Secret.　　　C1

WE beseech thee, O Lord, graciously enlighten thy Church by the gifts which we here offer: that in every place thy flock may increase and prosper, and the shepherds by thy governance may be made pleasing to thy name. Through.

Postcommunion.　　　C1

MERCIFUL Lord, we beseech thee to govern and preserve thy Church, which thou hast here refreshed with heavenly food: that by the guiding of thy mighty power it may serve thee in more abundant freedom, and ever keep thy true religion whole and undefiled. Through.

April 21.
St. Anselm

Bishop, Confessor and Doctor
of the Church

Double.

The Mass In medio, p. [22].

And the Creed is said.

Collect.　　　C

O GOD, who didst send blessed Anselm thy Doctor to guide thy people in the way of everlasting salvation: grant, we beseech thee; that as we have learned of him the doctrine of life on earth, so we may be found worthy to have him for our advocate in heaven. Through.

Secret. C 1

MAY the devout prayers of thy Bishop and Doctor, Saint Anselm, continually succour us, O Lord: that they may render our oblations acceptable in thy sight; and ever obtain for us thy merciful pardon. Through.

Postcommunion. C 1

WE beseech thee, O Lord, that blessed Anselm, thy Bishop and most excellent Doctor, may ever stand before thee as our advocate: that this sacrifice of thine ordinance may effectually avail for our salvation. Through.

April 22.

SS. Soter and Caius

Popes and Martyrs.

Simple.

The Mass Si diligis me, p. [2].

Collect. C 1

O EVERLASTING Shepherd, look down in mercy on thy flock: and as thou didst choose blessed Soter and Caius, thy Martyrs and Chief Bishops, to be pastors and rulers of thy Church; so at their intercession defend it with thy continual protection. Through.

Secret. C 1

WE beseech thee, O Lord, graciously enlighten thy Church by the gifts which we here offer: that in every place thy flock may increase and prosper, and the shepherds by thy governance may be made pleasing to thy name. Through.

Postcommunion. C 1

MERCIFUL Lord, we beseech thee to govern and preserve thy Church, which thou hast here refreshed with heavenly food: that by the guiding of thy mighty power it may serve thee in more abundant freedom, and ever keep thy true religion whole and undefiled. Through.

April 23.

ST. GEORGE THE MARTYR

PRINCIPAL PATRON OF ENGLAND

Double of 1st class.

(Outside England and Wales: Simple. Wales: Greater Double.)

Introit. Ps. 64, 3. Protexisti.

THOU hast hidden me, O God, from the gathering together of the froward, alleluia: and from the insurrection of wicked doers, alleluia, alleluia. Ps. ibid., 1. Hear my voice, O God, in my prayer: preserve my life from fear of the enemy. V. Glory.

Collect.

O GOD, who makest us glad by the merits and intercession of blessed George, thy Martyr: mercifully grant; that we, who through his aid implore thy bounty, may by the gift of thy grace receive the same. Through.

The Lesson from the Epistle of blessed Paul the Apostle to Timothy.

II Tim. 2, 8-10; 3, 10-12.

DEARLY beloved: Remember that Jesus Christ of the seed of David was raised from the dead according to my Gospel, wherein I suffer trouble, as an evil doer, even unto bonds: but the word of God is not bound. Therefore I endure all things for the elect's sakes, that they may also obtain the salvation which is in Christ Jesus with eternal glory. But thou hast fully known my doctrine, manner of life, purpose, faith, longsuffering, charity, patience, persecutions, afflictions: which came unto me at Antioch, at Iconium, at Lystra: what persecutions I endured, but out of them all the Lord delivered me. Yea, and all that will live godly in Christ Jesus shall suffer persecution.

Alleluia, alleluia. V. Ps. 89, 6. O Lord, the very heavens shall praise thy wondrous works: and thy truth in the congregation of the saints. Alleluia. V. Ps. 21, 4. Thou hast set, O Lord, a crown of pure gold upon his head. Alleluia.

✠ The Continuation of the holy Gospel according to John.

John 15, 1-7.

AT that time: Jesus said to his disciples: I am the true vine: and my Father is the husbandman. Every branch in me that beareth not fruit he taketh away: and every branch that beareth fruit, he purgeth it, that it may bring forth more fruit. Now ye are clean through the word which I have spoken unto you. Abide in me: and I in you. As the branch cannot bear fruit of itself, except it abide in the vine: no more can ye, except ye abide in me. I am the vine, ye are the branches: he that abideth in me, and I in him, the same bringeth forth much fruit: for without me ye can do nothing. If a man abide not in me, he is cast forth as a branch, and is withered, and men gather them, and cast them into the fire and they are burned. If ye abide in me, and my words abide in you: ye shall ask what ye will, and it shall be done unto you.

In England the Creed is said.

Offertory. Ps. 89, 6. O Lord, the very heavens shall praise thy wondrous works: and thy truth in the congregation of the saints, alleluia, alleluia.

Secret.

SANCTIFY, O Lord, the gifts which we offer: and at the intercession of blessed George, thy Martyr, cleanse us thereby from the defilements of our iniquities. Through.

Communion. Ps. 64, 11. The righteous shall rejoice in the Lord, and put his trust in him: and all they that are true of heart shall be glad, alleluia, alleluia.

Postcommunion.

WE humbly beseech thee, almighty God: that as thou dost refresh us with thy sacraments, so at the intercession of blessed George, thy Martyr, thou wouldest grant unto us to do thee worthy and acceptable service. Through.

For a Votive out of Eastertide, the Mass is In virtue, p. [6], with the Prayers as above.

April 24.
St. Fidelis of Sigmaringen

Martyr

Double.

The Mass Protexisti, p. [15], except the Collect.

Collect. P

O GOD, who didst enkindle blessed Fidelis with seraphic fervour of spirit in the propagation of the true faith, and didst vouchsafe to adorn him with the palm of martyrdom and with glorious miracles: we beseech thee, that, by his merits and intercession, we may through thy grace be so stablished in faith and charity; that in thy service we may be worthy to be found faithful even unto death. Through.

Secret. C 3

WE beseech thee, O Lord, to accept our prayers and oblations: and graciously hearken unto us whom thou dost cleanse by thy heavenly mysteries. Through.

Postcommunion. C 3

GRANT, we beseech thee, O Lord our God: that like as we in this life do gladly honour the memory of thy Saints, so we may rejoice hereafter in their everlasting fellowship. Through.

April 25.

ST. MARK THE EVANGELIST

THE GREATER LITANIES.

Double of 2nd class.

Station at St. Peter

¶ At the Procession the Mass of the Rogations, p. 437, is said: and if the Feast of St. Mark is to be transferred, the Procession is not transferred, except when this Feast falls on Easter Day: it is then transferred to the following Tuesday.

Introit. Ps. 64. 3. Protexisti.

THOU hast hidden me, O God, from the gathering together of the froward, alleluia: and from the insurrection of wicked doers, alleluia, alleluia. Ps. ibid., 1. Hear my voice, O God, in my prayer: preserve my life from fear of the enemy. ℣. Glory.

Collect.

O ALMIGHTY God, who hast instructed thy holy Church with the heavenly doctrine of thy Evangelist Saint Mark: give us grace, that, being not like children carried away with every blast of vain doctrine; we may be established in the truth of thy holy Gospel. Through.

Or, Collect.

O GOD, who didst endue thy blessed Evangelist Mark with singular grace for the preaching of the Gospel: grant, we beseech thee; that we thy servants may ever profit by his learning and be defended by his prayers. Through.

Commemoration of the Rogations, even in Sung Mass, unless another conventual or sung Mass is celebrated of the Rogations.

Collect.

GRANT we beseech thee, almighty God: that we, who in all our troubles do put our whole trust and confidence in thy mercy; may ever be defended by thy protection against all adversities. Through.

The Lesson from the Epistle of blessed Paul the Apostle to the Ephesians.

Eph. 4, 7-16.

BRETHREN: Unto every one of us is given grace, according to the measure of the gift of Christ. Wherefore he saith: When he ascended up on high, he led captivity captive, and gave gifts unto men. (Now that he ascended, what is it but that he also descended first into the lower parts of the earth? He that descended is the same also that ascended up far above all heavens, that he might fill all things). And he gave some Apostles, and some Prophets, and some Evangelists, and some Pastors and Teachers: for the perfecting of the saints, for the work of the ministry, for the edifying of the body of Christ, till we all come in the unity of the faith, and of the knowledge of the Son of God, unto a perfect man, unto the measure of the stature of the fulness of Christ: that we henceforth be no more children, tossed to and fro, and carried about with every wind of doctrine, by the sleight of men, and cunning craftiness, whereby they lie in wait to deceive; but speaking the truth in love, may grow up into him in all things, which is the Head, even Christ: from whom the whole body fitly joined together, and compacted by that which every joint supplieth, according to the effectual working in the measure of every part, maketh increase of the body, unto the edifying of itself in love.

or:

The Lesson from the Prophet Ezekiel.

Ezek. 1, 10-14.

THE likeness of the faces of the four animals: they four had the face of a man, and the face of a lion, on the right side: and they four had the face of an ox on the left side, they four also had the face of an eagle. Thus were their faces, and their wings were stretched upward: two wings of every one were joined one to another, and two covered their bodies: and they went every one straight forward: whither the spirit was to go, they went, and they turned not when they went. As for the likeness of the living creatures, their appearance was like burning coals of fire, and like the appearance of lamps. It went up and down among the living creatures, and the fire was bright, and out of the fire went forth lightning. And the living creatures ran and returned as the appearance of a flash of lightning.

Alleluia, alleluia. ℣. Ps. 89, 6. O Lord, the very heavens shall praise thy wondrous works: and thy truth in the congregation of the saints. Alleluia. ℣. Ps. 21, 4. Thou hast set, O Lord, a crown of pure gold upon his head. Alleluia.

✠ The Continuation of the holy Gospel according to John.

John 15, 1-11.

AT that time: Jesus said unto his disciples: I am the true vine: and my Father is the husbandman. Every branch in me that beareth not fruit he taketh away: and every branch that beareth fruit, he purgeth it that it may bring forth more fruit. Now ye are clean through the word which I have spoken unto you. Abide in me: and I in you. As the branch cannot bear fruit of itself, except it abide in the vine: no more can ye, except ye abide in me. I am the vine, ye are the branches: he that abideth in me, and I in him, the same bringeth forth much fruit: for without me ye can do nothing. If a man abide not in me, he is cast forth as a branch, and is withered, and men gather them, and cast them into the fire, and they are burned. If ye abide in me, and my words abide in you: ye shall ask what ye will, and it shall be done unto you. Herein is my Father glorified, that ye bear much fruit; so shall ye be my disciples. As the Father hath loved me, so have I loved you: continue ye in my love. If ye keep my commandments, ye shall abide in my love: even as I have kept my Father's commandments, and abide in his love. These things have I spoken unto you, that my joy might remain in you, and that your joy might be full. Creed.

or:

✠ The Continuation of the holy Gospel according to Luke.

Luke 10, 1-9.

AT that time: The Lord appointed other seventy also, and sent them two and two before his face into every city and place whither he himself would come. Therefore said he unto them: The harvest truly is great, but the labourers are few. Pray ye therefore the Lord of the harvest, that he would send forth labourers into his harvest. Go your ways: behold, I send you forth as lambs among wolves. Carry neither purse, nor scrip, nor shoes, and salute no man by the way. And into whatsoever house ye enter, first say: Peace be to this house: and if the son of peace be there, your peace shall rest upon it: if not, it shall turn to you again. And in the same house remain, eating and drinking such things as they give: for the labourer is worthy of his hire. Go not from house to house. And into whatsoever city ye enter, and they receive you, eat such things as are set before you: and heal the sick that are therein, and say unto them: The kingdom of God is come nigh unto you. Creed.

Offertory. Ps. 89, 6. O Lord, the very heavens shall praise thy wondrous works: and thy truth in the congregation of the saints, alleluia, alleluia.

Secret.

WE present unto thee, O Lord, our oblations on this festival of thy blessed Evangelist Mark, beseeching thee: that as thou didst make him glorious in the preaching of the Gospel; so at his intercession thou wouldest make us both in word and deed acceptable unto thee. Through.

For the Rogations.

Secret.

WE beseech thee, O Lord, that these our oblations may both loose the bonds of our iniquity, and obtain for us the gifts of thy loving kindness. Through.

Preface of the Apostles.

Communion. Ps. 64, 11. The righteous shall rejoice in the Lord, and put his trust in him: and all they that are true of heart shall be glad, alleluia, alleluia.

Postcommunion.

WE beseech thee, O Lord, let thy holy mysteries evermore protect us: that through the prayers of thy blessed Evangelist Mark we may thereby be defended against all adversities. Through.

For the Rogations.

Postcommunion.

WE beseech thee, O Lord, to prosper with thy gracious favour these our supplications: that we, receiving these thy gifts in time of our tribulation, may increase in thy love by the consolation of the same. Through.

¶ For a Votive out of Eastertide, Mass of the Feast of St. Luke the Evangelist, October 18, with the Prayers and Epistle as above.

April 26.

SS. Cletus and Marcellinus

Popes and Martyrs

Simple.

The Mass Si diligis me, p. [2].

Collect. C 1

O EVERLASTING Shepherd, look down in mercy on thy flock: and as thou didst choose blessed Cletus and Marcellinus, thy Martyrs and Chief Bishops, to be pastors and rulers of thy Church; so at their intercession defend it with thy continual protection. Through.

Secret. C 1

WE beseech thee, O Lord, graciously enlighten thy Church by the gifts which we here offer: that in every place thy flock may increase and prosper, and the shepherds by thy governance may be made pleasing to thy name. Through.

Postcommunion. C1

MERCIFUL Lord, we beseech thee to govern and preserve thy Church, which thou hast here refreshed with heavenly food: that by the guiding of thy mighty power it may serve thee in more abundant freedom, and ever keep thy true religion whole and undefiled. Through.

¶ If any of the following Feasts, being a Double, occur on the Rogation Days, Commemoration thereof is made in all read Masses, except in the Conventual Mass of the Feast, if there is another Conventual or sung Mass of the Rogations. Likewise on the Wednesday, before the Commemoration of the Rogation Feria, the Vigil of the Ascension is commemorated, except in the Conventual Mass of the Feast or of the Rogations. Of the same Feasts, however, when they occur on Monday or Wednesday, unless they are Doubles of the First or Second Class, a Conventual Mass is read outside Choir and a Conventual Mass of the Feria or Vigil is said in Choir.

April 27.

St. Peter Canisius

Confessor and Doctor of the Church

Double.

The Mass In medio, p. [22], except the Collect.

And the Creed is said.

Collect. P

O GOD, who for the defence of the catholic faith didst strengthen blessed Peter thy Confessor with virtue and doctrine: mercifully grant; that by his example and teaching, all such as err may be made wise unto salvation, and the faithful may persevere in the confession of the truth. Through.

Secret. C2

MAY the devout prayers of thy Confessor and Doctor, Saint Peter, continually succour us, O Lord: that they may render our oblations acceptable in thy sight; and may ever obtain for us thy merciful pardon. Through.

Postcommunion. C2

WE beseech thee, O Lord, that blessed Peter, thy Confessor and most excellent Doctor, may ever stand before thee as our advocate: that this sacrifice of thine ordinance may effectually avail for our salvation. Through.

April 28.

St. Paul of the Cross

Confessor

Double.

Introit. Gal. 2, 19-20. Christo confixus.

I AM crucified with Christ, nevertheless I live, yet not I; but Christ liveth in me: I live by the faith of the Son of God, who loved me, and gave himself for me, alleluia, alleluia. Ps. 41, 1. Blessed is he that considereth the poor and needy: the Lord shall deliver him in the time of trouble. ℣. Glory.

Collect.

O LORD Jesu Christ, who for the preaching of the mystery of the Cross didst endue Saint Paul with singular charity, and through him didst will that a new household should flourish in thy Church: grant to us through his intercession; that we, continually recalling thy Passion on earth, may be found worthy to attain unto the benefits of the same in heaven: Who livest and reignest.

Commemoration of St. Vitalis, Martyr.

Collect.

GRANT, we beseech thee, almighty God: that we, who celebrate the heavenly birthday of blessed Vitalis, thy Martyr; may by his intercession be stablished in the love of thy name. Through.

The Lesson from the Epistle of blessed Paul the Apostle to the Corinthians.

I Cor. 1, 17-25.

BRETHREN: Christ sent me not to baptize, but to preach the Gospel: not with wisdom of words, lest the Cross of Christ should be made of none effect. For the preaching of the Cross is to them that perish foolishness: but unto us which are saved it is the power of God. For it is written: I will destroy the wisdom of the wise, and will bring to nothing the understanding of the prudent. Where is the wise? Where is the scribe? Where is the disputer of this world? Hath not God made foolish the wisdom of this world? For after that in the wisdom of God the world by wisdom knew not God: it pleased God by the foolishness of preaching to save them that believe. For the Jews require a sign, and the Greeks seek after wisdom: but we preach Christ crucified, unto the Jews a stumbling-block, and unto the Greeks foolishness, but unto them which are called, both Jews and Greeks, Christ, the power of God, and the wisdom of God: because the foolishness of God is wiser than men: and the weakness of God is stronger than men.

Alleluia, alleluia. ℣. II Cor. 5, 15. Christ died for all: that they which live should not henceforth live unto themselves, but unto him which died for them, and rose again. Alleluia. ℣. Rom. 8, 17. If children, then heirs, heirs of God, and joint-heirs with Christ: if so be that we suffer with him, that we may be also glorified together. Alleluia.

✠ The Continuation of the holy Gospel according to Luke.

Luke 10, 1-9.

AT that time: The Lord appointed other seventy also: and sent them two and two before his face into every city and place whither he himself would come. Therefore said he unto them: The harvest truly is great, but the labourers are few. Pray ye therefore the Lord of the harvest, that he would send forth labourers into his harvest. Go your ways: behold, I send you forth as lambs among wolves. Carry neither purse, nor scrip, nor shoes; and salute no man by the way. And into whatsoever house ye enter, first say: Peace be to this house: and if the son of peace be there, your peace shall rest upon it: if not, it shall turn to you again. And in the same house remain, eating and drinking such things as they give, for the labourer is worthy of his hire. Go not from house to house. And into whatsoever city ye enter, and they receive you, eat such things as are set before you: and heal the sick that are therein, and say unto them: The kingdom of God is come nigh unto you.

Offertory. Eph. 5, 2. Walk in love, as Christ also hath loved us, and hath given himself for us an offering and a sacrifice to God for a sweet-smelling savour, alleluia.

Secret.

MAY these mysteries of thy Passion and death endue us, O Lord, with that heavenly fervour: wherewith Saint Paul, in the offering of the same, presented his body a living sacrifice, holy, acceptable unto thee: Who livest and reignest.

For St. Vitalis.   Secret.

WE beseech thee, O Lord, to accept our prayers and oblations: and graciously hearken unto us whom thou dost cleanse by thy heavenly mysteries. Through.

Communion. I Pet. 4, 13. Rejoice inasmuch as ye are partakers of Christ's sufferings, that when his glory shall be revealed, ye may be glad also with exceeding joy, alleluia.

Postcommunion.

O LORD, who in this heavenly Sacrament hast bestowed on us the perpetual memorial of thine infinite love: grant, we beseech thee; that, by the merits and imitation of Saint Paul, we may draw from thy fountains water springing up unto life eternal, and in our life and conversation bear thy most sacred Passion imprinted on our hearts: Who livest and reignest.

For St. Vitalis. Postcommunion.

GRANT, we beseech thee, O Lord our God: that like as we in this life do gladly honour the memory of thy Saints; so we may rejoice hereafter in their everlasting fellowship. Through.

April 29.

St. Peter

Martyr

Double.

Introit. Ps. 64, 3. Protexisti.

THOU hast hidden me, O God, from the gathering together of the froward, alleluia: and from the insurrection of wicked doers, alleluia, alleluia. Ps. ibid., 1. Hear my voice, O God, in my prayer: preserve my life from fear of the enemy. ℣. Glory.

Collect.

GRANT, we beseech thee, almighty God: that as blessed Peter, thy Martyr, in the preaching of thy faith, was found worthy to gain the palm of martyrdom; so we likewise may do thee worthy service, and steadfastly follow the example of his faith. Through.

The Lesson from the Epistle of blessed Paul the Apostle to Timothy.

II Tim. 2, 8-10; 3, 10-12.

DEARLY beloved: Remember that Jesus Christ of the seed of David was raised from the dead according to my Gospel, wherein I suffer trouble, as an evil doer, even unto bonds: but the word of God is not bound. Therefore I endure all things for the elect's sakes, that they may also obtain the salvation which is in Christ Jesus with eternal glory. But thou hast fully known my doctrine, manner of life, purpose, faith, long suffering, charity, patience, persecutions, afflictions: which came unto me at Antioch, at Iconium, at Lystra: what persecutions I endured, but out of them all the Lord delivered me. Yea, and all that will live godly in Christ Jesus shall suffer persecution.

Alleluia, alleluia. ℣. Ps. 89, 6. O Lord, the very heavens shall praise thy wondrous works: and thy truth in the congregation of the saints. Alleluia. ℣. Ps. 21, 4. Thou hast set, O Lord, a crown of pure gold upon his head. Alleluia.

✠ The Continuation of the holy Gospel according to John.

John 15, 1-7.

AT that time: Jesus said to his disciples: I am the true vine: and my Father is the husbandman. Every branch in me that beareth not fruit he taketh away: and every branch that beareth fruit, he purgeth it, that it may bring forth more fruit. Now ye are clean through the word which I have spoken unto you. Abide in me: and I in you. As the branch cannot bear fruit of itself, except it abide in the vine: no more can ye, except ye abide in me. I am the vine, ye are the branches:

he that abideth in me, and I in him, the same bringeth forth much fruit: for without me ye can do nothing. If a man abide not in me, he is cast forth as a branch, and is withered, and men gather them, and cast them into the fire and they are burned. If ye abide in me, and my words abide in you: ye shall ask what ye will, and it shall be done unto you.

Offertory. Ps. 89, 6. O Lord, the very heavens shall praise thy wondrous works: and thy truth in the congregation of the saints, alleluia, alleluia.

Secret.

MERCIFULLY hearken, O Lord, at the intercession of thy blessed Martyr Peter, to the prayers which we here offer unto thee: and keep under thy protection the defenders of the faith. Through.

Communion. Ps. 64, 11. The righteous shall rejoice in the Lord, and put his trust in him: and all they that are true of heart shall be glad, alleluia, alleluia.

Postcommunion.

O LORD, let this holy Sacrament, which we have here received, continually avail for the protection of thy faithful people: that at the intercession of thy blessed Martyr Peter, we may be defended thereby against all the assaults of our enemies. Through.

April 30.

St. Catherine of Siena

Virgin

Double.

Introit. Ps. 45, 8. Dilexisti.

THOU hast loved righteousness, and hated iniquity: therefore God, even thy God, hath anointed thee with the oil of gladness above thy fellows, alleluia, alleluia. Ps. ibid., 1. My heart is inditing of a good matter: I speak of the things which I have made unto the King. ℣. Glory.

Collect.

GRANT, we beseech thee, almighty God: that we, who celebrate the heavenly birthday of blessed Catherine thy Virgin: may both rejoice in her yearly festival, and learn to follow her in all virtuous and godly living. Through.

The Lesson from the Epistle of blessed Paul the Apostle to the Corinthians.

II Cor. 10, 17-18; 11, 1-2.

BRETHREN: He that glorieth, let him glory in the Lord. For not he that commendeth himself is approved; but whom the Lord commendeth. Would to God ye could bear with me a little in my folly, and indeed bear with me: for I am jealous over you with godly jealousy. For I have espoused you to one husband, that I may present you as a chaste virgin to Christ.

Alleluia, alleluia. ℣. Ibid., 15-16. The Virgins that be her fellows shall be brought unto the King: they that bear her company shall be brought unto thee with joy. Alleluia. ℣. Ibid., 5. In thy comeliness and in thy beauty go forth, ride prosperously and reign. Alleluia.

✠ The Continuation of the holy Gospel according to Matthew.

Matt. 25, 1-13.

AT that time: Jesus spake this parable unto his disciples: The kingdom of heaven shall be likened unto ten virgins, which took their lamps, and went forth to meet the bridegroom. And five of them were wise, and five were foolish: they that were foolish took their lamps, and took no oil with them: but the wise took oil in their vessels with their lamps. While the bridegroom tarried, they all slumbered and slept. And at midnight there was a cry made: Behold, the bridegroom cometh; go ye out to meet him. Then all those virgins arose, and trimmed their lamps. And the foolish said unto the wise: Give us of your oil: for our lamps are gone out. But the wise answered, saying: Not so, lest there be not enough for us and you, but go ye rather to them that sell, and buy for yourselves. And while they went to buy, the bridegroom came: and they that were ready went in with him to the marriage, and the door was shut. Afterward came also the other virgins, saying: Lord, Lord, open to us. But he answered and said: Verily I say unto you, I know you not. Watch therefore, for ye know neither the day nor the hour* [wherein the Son of man cometh].

Offertory. Ps. 45, 10. Kings' daughters were among thy honourable women, upon thy right hand did stand the queen in a vesture of gold, wrought about with divers colours, alleluia.

Secret.

O LORD, let these our prayers, which we offer on this feast of Saint Catherine, in such wise ascend unto thee; that this our sacrifice may by the sweet savour of her virginity be made an oblation acceptable for our salvation. Through.

Communion. Matt. 25, 4 and 6. The five wise virgins took oil in their vessels with their lamps: and at midnight there was a cry made: Behold the bridegroom cometh: go ye out to meet Christ the Lord, alleluia.

Postcommunion.

O LORD, who by this heavenly table didst support thy blessed Virgin Catherine in her temporal life on earth: vouchsafe; that we, whom thou hast here fulfilled with the same, may thereby attain unto life eternal. Through.

May 1.

THE SOLEMNITY OF

ST. JOSEPH THE WORKER

CONFESSOR, SPOUSE OF THE B.V. MARY

Double of 1st class.

Introit. Wis. 10, 17.

WISDOM rendered to the righteous a reward of their labours, guided them in a marvellous way, and was unto them for a cover by day, and a light of stars in the night season, alleluia, alleluia. Ps. 127, 1. Except the Lord build the house: their labour is but lost that build it. ℣. Glory.

Collect.

O GOD, the creator of all things, who hast appointed unto man that he should labour and do all that he hath to do: mercifully grant; that through the example and intercession of Saint Joseph we may accomplish the work that thou commandest, and attain unto the rewards that thou dost promise. Through.

The Lesson from the Epistle of blessed Paul the Apostle to the Colossians.

Col. 3, 14-15, 17, 23-24.

BRETHREN: Put on charity, which is the bond of perfectness, and let the peace of God rule in your hearts, to the which also ye are called in one body; and be ye thankful. And whatsoever ye do in word or deed, do all in the name of the Lord Jesus, giving thanks to God and the Father by him. Whatsoever ye do, do it heartily, as to the Lord, and not unto men, knowing that of the Lord ye shall receive the reward of the inheritance. For ye serve the Lord Christ.

Alleluia, alleluia. ℣. From whatsoever tribulation they shall cry unto me, I will hear them, and I will be their defender for ever. Alleluia. ℣. Make us, O Joseph, to walk in innocency: and may our life be ever safe beneath thy care. Alleluia.

¶ In Votive Masses out of Eastertide Alleluia is omitted at the Introit, Offertory and Communion, and after the Epistle is said:

Gradual. Ps. 128, 1. Blessed are all they that fear the Lord, and walk in his ways. For thou shalt eat the labours of thine hands: O well is thee, and happy shalt thou be.

Alleluia, alleluia. ℣. Make us, O Joseph, to walk in innocency: and may our life be ever safe beneath thy care. Alleluia.

After Septuagesima, omitting Alleluia and the Verse following, is said:

Tract. Ps. 112, 1. Blessed is the man that feareth the Lord: he hath great delight in his commandments. ℣. His seed shall be mighty upon earth: the generation of the faithful shall be blessed. ℣. Riches and plenteousness shall be in his house: and his righteousness endureth for ever.

✠ The Continuation of the holy Gospel according to Matthew.

Matt. 13, 54-58.

AT that time: When Jesus was come into his own country, he taught them in their synagogue, insomuch that they were astonished and said: Whence hath this man this wisdom and these mighty works? Is not this the carpenter's son? Is not his mother called Mary, and his brethren James, and Joses, and Simon, and Judas? And his sisters, are they not all with us? Whence then hath this man all these things? And they were offended in him. But Jesus said unto them: A prophet is not without honour, save in his own country, and in his own house. And he did not many mighty works there, because of their unbelief. Creed.

Offertory. Ps. 90, 17. The glorious majesty of the Lord our God be upon us: prosper thou the work of our hands upon us, O prosper thou our handy-work, alleluia.

Secret.

MAY these sacrifices, O Lord, which we offer unto thee of the works of our hands, become for us, through the prayers and mediation of Saint Joseph, a pledge of unity and peace. Through.

Preface of St. Joseph, And that in the Solemnity.

Communion. Matt. 13, 54-55. Whence hath this man this wisdom, and these mighty works? Is not this the carpenter's son? Is not his mother called Mary? Alleluia.

Postcommunion.

GRANT, O Lord, that these holy mysteries which we have now received: through the intercession of blessed Joseph, may both fulfil that which is lacking in our work, and also avail for the assurance of our heavenly reward. Through.

¶ For the Feast of SS. Philip and James, App., see May 11th, p. 655.

May 2.

St. Athanasius

Bishop, Confessor and Doctor of the Church

Double.

Introit. Ecclus. 15, 5. In medio.

IN the midst of the Church he opened his mouth: and the Lord filled him with the spirit of wisdom and understanding: he clothed him with a robe of glory, alleluia, alleluia. Ps. 92, 1. It is a good thing to give thanks unto the Lord: and to sing praises unto thy name, O most Highest. ℣. Glory.

Collect.

WE beseech thee, O Lord, graciously to hear the prayers which we offer unto thee on this festival of blessed Athanasius, thy Confessor and Bishop: that, like as he was found worthy to do thee faithful service; so by his merits and intercession we may be absolved from all our sins. Through.

The Lesson from the Epistle of blessed Paul the Apostle to the Corinthians.

II Cor. 4, 5-14.

BRETHREN: We preach not ourselves, but Christ Jesus the Lord: and ourselves your servants for Jesus' sake: for God, who commanded the light to shine out of darkness, hath shined in our hearts, to give the light of the knowledge of the glory of God in the face of Jesus Christ. But we have this treasure in earthen vessels: that the excellency of the power may be of God, and not of us. We are troubled on every side, yet not distressed: we are perplexed, but not in despair: persecuted, but not forsaken: cast down, but not destroyed: always bearing about in the body the dying of the Lord Jesus, that the life also of Jesus might be made manifest in our body. For we which live are alway delivered unto death for Jesus' sake: that the life also of Jesus might be made manifest in our mortal flesh. So then death worketh in us, but life in you. We having the same spirit of faith, according as it is written: I believed, and therefore have I spoken: we also believe, and therefore speak: knowing that he which raised up the Lord Jesus shall raise up us also by Jesus, and shall present us with you.

Alleluia, alleluia. ℣. Ps. 110, 4. Thou art a priest for ever, after the order of Melchisedech. Alleluia. ℣. James 1, 12. Blessed is the man that endureth temptation: for when he is tried, he shall receive the crown of life. Alleluia.

In Votive Masses after Eastertide is said:

Gradual. Behold a great priest, as on January 27.

✠ The Continuation of the holy Gospel according to Matthew.

Matt. 10, 23-28.

AT that time: Jesus said unto his disciples: When they persecute you in this city, flee ye into another. For verily I say unto you, Ye shall not have gone over the cities of Israel, till the Son of man be come. The disciple is not above his master, nor the servant above his lord. It is enough for the disciple that he be as his master: and the servant as his lord. If they have called the master of the house Beelzebub: how much more shall they call them of his household? Fear them not therefore. For there is nothing covered, that shall not be revealed: and hid, that shall not be known. What I tell you in darkness, that speak ye in light: and what ye hear in the ear, that preach ye upon the housetops. And fear not them which kill the body, but are not able to kill the soul: but rather fear him which is able to destroy both soul and body in hell. Creed.

Offertory. Ps. 89, 21-22. I have found David my servant, with my holy oil have I anointed him: my hand shall hold him fast, and my arm shall strengthen him, alleluia.

Secret.

WE beseech thee, O Lord, let our devout observance of this yearly festival of Saint Athanasius, thy Confessor and Bishop, render us acceptable unto thy loving kindness: that this oblation of our bounden duty and service may be profitable unto him for the reward of everlasting felicity, and obtain for us the gifts of thy grace. Through.

Communion. Matt. 10, 27. What I tell you in darkness, that speak ye in light, saith the Lord: and what ye hear in the ear, that preach ye upon the housetops, alleluia.

Postcommunion.

O GOD, who rewardest the souls of them that put their trust in thee: vouchsafe; that we, who keep the solemn feast of blessed Athanasius, thy Confessor and Bishop, may by his prayers obtain thy merciful pardon. Through.

May 3.

THE INVENTION OF THE HOLY CROSS

Double of 2nd class.

Introit. Gal. 6, 14. Nos autem.

BUT as for us, it behoveth us to glory in the Cross of our Lord Jesus Christ: in whom is our salvation, our life and resurrection: by whom we were saved and obtained our freedom, alleluia, alleluia. Ps. 67, 1. God be merciful unto us, and bless us: and shew us the light of his countenance, and be merciful unto us. ℣. Glory.

Collect.

O GOD, who in the wondrous Finding of the Cross of our salvation didst renew the miracles of thy Passion: vouchsafe; that by the ransom of this life-giving tree, we may attain thy succour unto life eternal: Who livest.

In private Masses only, Commemoration is made of SS. Alexander, Eventius and Theodulus, Martyrs, and of St. Juvenal, Bishop and Confessor:

Collect.

GRANT, we beseech thee, almighty God: that we, who observe the heavenly birthday of thy Saints Alexander, Eventius, Theodulus and Juvenal; may by their intercession be delivered from all evils that beset us. Through.

The Lesson from the Epistle of blessed Paul the Apostle to the Philippians.

Phil. 2, 5-11.

BRETHREN: Let this mind be in you, which was also in Christ Jesus: who, being in the form of God, thought it not robbery to be equal with God: but made himself of no reputation, and took upon him the form of a servant, and was made in the likeness of men. And being found in fashion as a man, he humbled himself, and became obedient unto death, even the death of the cross. Wherefore God also hath highly exalted him, and given him a name which is above every name: (Here genuflect) that at the name of Jesus every knee should bow, of things in heaven, and things in earth, and things under the earth: and that every tongue should confess that Jesus Christ is Lord, to the glory of God the Father.

Alleluia, alleluia. ℣. Ps. 96, 10. Tell it out among the heathen that the Lord hath reigned from the tree. Alleluia. ℣. Sweetest wood and sweetest iron, sweetest weight is hung on thee: thou alone wast worthy to bear the King of heaven, and the Lord. Alleluia.

✠ The Continuation of the holy Gospel according to John.

John 3, 1-15.

AT that time: There was a man of the Pharisees, named Nicodemus, a ruler of the Jews. The same came to Jesus by night, and said unto him: Rabbi, we know that thou art a teacher come from God; for no man can do these miracles that thou doest, except God be with him. Jesus answered and said unto him: Verily, verily, I say unto thee, Except a man be born again, he cannot see the kingdom of God. Nicodemus saith unto him: How can a man be born when he is old? can he enter the second time into his mother's womb, and be born? Jesus answered: Verily, verily, I say unto thee, Except a man be born of water and of the spirit, he cannot enter into the kingdom of God. That which is born of the flesh is flesh: and that which is born of the Spirit is spirit. Marvel not that I said unto thee: Ye must be born again. The wind bloweth where it listeth, and thou hearest the sound thereof, but canst not tell whence it cometh, and whither it goeth: so is every one that is born of the Spirit. Nicodemus answered and said unto him: How can these things be? Jesus answered and said unto him: Art thou a master of Israel, and knowest not these things? Verily, verily, I say unto thee, We speak that we do know, and testify that we have seen, and ye receive not our witness. If I have told you earthly things, and ye believe not: how shall ye believe, if I tell you of heavenly things? And no man hath ascended up to heaven, but he that came down from heaven, even the Son of man which is in heaven. And as Moses lifted up the serpent in the wilderness: even so must the Son of man be lifted up, that whosoever believeth in him should not perish, but have eternal life. Creed.

Offertory. Ps. 118, 16-17. The right hand of the Lord bringeth mighty things to pass, the right hand of the Lord hath exalted me: I shall not die, but live and declare the works of the Lord, alleluia.

Secret.

LOOK down, O Lord, in mercy on this our sacrifice which we offer unto thee: that we, being preserved from all the wickedness of war, and through the standard of the holy Cross of thy Son being ever stablished with the protection of thy sure defence, may tread under foot the crafts and assaults of our adversaries. Through.

For the Holy Martyrs.

Secret.

LET thy plenteous benediction, we beseech thee, O Lord, come down upon these offerings: that of thy mercy they may avail for our sanctification, and make us to rejoice in the festival of thy Saints. Through.

Preface of the Cross.

Communion. By the sign of the Cross deliver us from our enemies, O our God, alleluia.

Postcommunion.

ALMIGHTY God who hast fulfilled us with heavenly meat, and refreshed us with spiritual drink, we beseech thee: that as thou hast commanded us to triumph by the wood of the holy Cross of thy Son, the armour of righteousness appointed for the salvation of the world; so thou wouldest defend us from the crafts and assaults of the enemy. Through the same.

For the Holy Martyrs.

Postcommunion.

WE beseech thee, O Lord our God, that like as we whom thou hast refreshed by the partaking of thy sacred gift do offer unto thee our outward worship: so, at the intercession of thy Saints, Alexander, Eventius, Theodulus and Juvenal, we may inwardly be profited thereby to our salvation. Through.

¶ For Votive Masses is said the Mass Nos autem p. [62].

May 4.

St. Monica

Widow

Double.

Introit. Ps. 119, 75 and 120.

Cognovi, Domine.

I KNOW, O Lord, that thy judgments are right, and that thou of very faithfulness hast caused me to be troubled: my flesh trembleth for fear of thee, and I am afraid of thy judgments, alleluia, alleluia. Ps. ibid., 1. Blessed are those that are undefiled in the way, and walk in the law of the Lord. ℣. Glory.

Collect.

O GOD, the comforter of them that mourn, and the salvation of them that hope in thee, who didst mercifully accept the loving tears of blessed Monica for the conversion of Augustine her son: grant to us by the intercession of them both; that we may bewail our sins, and obtain the abundant pardon of thy grace. Through.

The Lesson from the Epistle of blessed Paul the Apostle to Timothy.

I Tim. 5, 3-10.

DEARLY beloved: Honour widows that are widows indeed. But if any widow have children or nephews: let them learn first to shew piety at home, and to requite their parents: for that is good and acceptable before God. Now she that is a widow indeed, and desolate, trusteth in God, and continueth in supplications and prayers night and day. But she that liveth in pleasure is dead while she liveth. And these things give in charge that they may be blameless. But if any provide not for his own, and specially for those of his own house, he hath denied the faith, and is worse than an infidel. Let not a widow be taken into the number under threescore years old, having been the wife of one man, well reported of for good works, if she have brought up children, if she have lodged strangers, if she have washed the saints' feet, if she have relieved the afflicted, if she have diligently followed every good work.

Alleluia, alleluia. ℣. Ps. 45, 5. In thy comeliness and in thy beauty go forth, ride prosperously, and reign. Alleluia. ℣. Because of the word of truth, of meekness, and righteousness: and thy right hand shall teach thee terrible things. Alleluia.

✠ The Continuation of the holy Gospel according to Luke.

Luke 8, 11-16.

AT that time: Jesus went into a city called Nain: and many of his disciples went with him, and much people. Now when he came nigh to the gate of the city, behold, there was a dead man carried out, the only son of his mother: and she was a widow, and much people of the city was with her. And when the Lord saw her, he had compassion on her, and said unto her: Weep not. And he came and touched the bier. And they that bare him stood still. And he said: Young man, I say unto thee, Arise. And he that was dead sat up, and began to speak. And he delivered him to his mother. And there came a fear on all: and they glorified God, saying: That a great Prophet is risen up among us: and that God hath visited his people.

Offertory. Ps. 45, 3. Full of grace are thy lips: therefore God hath blessed thee for ever, and world without end, alleluia.

Secret.

GRANT, O Lord, that like as thy faithful people do acknowledge that in tribulation they have been succoured by the merits of thy Saints: so this oblation, which they here do offer unto thee in honour of the same, may be acceptable in thy sight. Through.

Communion. Ps. 45, 8. Thou hast loved righteousness, and hated iniquity: therefore God, even thy God, hath anointed thee with the oil of gladness above thy fellows, alleluia.

Postcommunion.

O LORD, who hast satisfied this thy family with sacred gifts: we beseech thee; that we may at all times be comforted by the intercession of her whose festival we celebrate. Through.

In England and Wales:

The same day, May 4.

Blessed Martyrs of England and Wales

See Supplement.

May 5.

St. Pius, V

Pope and Confessor

Double.

The Mass Si diligis me, p. [2], the Collect excepted.

Collect. P

O GOD, who for the overthrow of the enemies of thy Church and for the restoring of divine worship, wast pleased to choose blessed Pius to be the Chief Bishop: grant that we, being defended by his protection, may so devoutly serve thee; that the devices of all our enemies being brought to nought, we may rejoice in perpetual peace. Through.

Secret. C 1

WE beseech thee, O Lord, graciously enlighten thy Church by the gifts which we here offer: that in every place thy flock may increase and prosper, and the shepherds by thy governance may be made pleasing to thy name. Through.

Preface of the Season.

Postcommunion. C 1

MERCIFUL Lord, we beseech thee to govern and preserve thy Church, which thou hast here refreshed with heavenly food: that by the guiding of thy mighty power it may serve thee in more abundant freedom, and ever keep thy true religion whole and undefiled. Through.

May 6.

St. John, Apostle and Evangelist before the Latin Gate

Greater double.

Introit. Ps. 64, 4. Protexisti.

THOU hast hidden me, O God, from the gathering of the froward, alleluia: and from the insurrection of wicked doers, alleluia, alleluia. Ps. ibid., 1. Hear my voice, O God, in my prayer: preserve my life from fear of the enemy. V. Glory.

Collect.

O GOD, who seest us to be sore afflicted by evils on every side: grant, we beseech thee; that the glorious intercession of blessed John, thine Apostle and Evangelist, may be our succour and defence. Through.

The Lesson from the book of Wisdom.

Wisd. 5, 1-5.

THE righteous man shall stand in great boldness before the face of such as have afflicted him, and made no account of his labours. When they see it, they shall be troubled with terrible fear, and shall be amazed at the strangeness of his salvation, so far beyond all that they looked for, and they repenting and groaning for anguish of spirit shall say within themselves: This was he, whom he had sometimes in derision, and a proverb of reproach. We fools accounted his life madness and his end to be without honour: how is he numbered among the children of God, and his lot is among the Saints.

Alleluia, alleluia. ℣. Ps. 92, 13. The righteous shall flourish like a palm tree: and shall spread abroad like a cedar in Libanus. Alleluia. ℣. Hos. 14, 6. The righteous shall grow as the lily: and shall flourish for ever before the Lord. Alleluia.

✠ The Continuation of the holy Gospel according to Matthew.

Matt. 20, 20-23.

AT that time: There came unto Jesus the mother of Zebedee's children with her sons, worshipping him, and desiring a certain thing of him. And he said unto her: What wilt thou? She saith unto him: Grant that these my two sons may sit, the one on thy right hand, and the other on the left, in thy kingdom. But Jesus answered and said: Ye know not what ye ask. Are ye able to drink of the cup that I shall drink of, and to be baptized with the baptism that I am baptized with? They say unto him: We are able. And he saith unto them: Ye shall drink indeed of my cup, and be baptized with the baptism that I am baptized with: but to sit on my right hand, and on my left, is not mine to give, but it shall be given to them for whom it is prepared of my Father.

The Creed is not said.

Offertory. Ps. 89, 6. O Lord, the very heavens shall praise thy wondrous works: and thy truth in the congregation of the saints, alleluia, alleluia.

Secret.

WE beseech thee, O Lord, to accept our prayers and oblations: and graciously hearken unto us whom thou dost cleanse by thy heavenly mysteries. Through.

Preface of the Apostles.

Communion. Ps. 64, 11. The righteous shall rejoice in the Lord, and put his trust in him: and all they that are true of heart shall be glad, alleluia, alleluia.

Postcommunion.

WE beseech thee, O Lord, that we, who have been refreshed with heavenly bread, may be nourished unto life eternal. Through.

May 7.

St. Stanislas

Bishop and Martyr

Double.

The Mass Protexisti, p. [15], with the Prayers as below:

Collect.

O GOD, who for thine honour didst suffer the glorious Bishop Stanislas to fall by the swords of wicked men: grant, we beseech thee; that all who call upon him for succour may rejoice in the fulfilment of their petitions. Through.

Secret.

SANCTIFY, O Lord, the gifts which we dedicate to thee: that at the intercession of blessed Stanislas, thy Martyr and Bishop, they may obtain for us thy gracious favour. Through.

Postcommunion. C2

O LORD, let this holy Communion cleanse us from every guilty stain: that at the intercession of blessed Stanislas, thy Martyr and Bishop, we may be made partakers thereby of thy healing unto life eternal. Through.

May 8.
The Appearing of St. Michael the Archangel
Greater double.

Introit. Ps. 103. 20. Benedicite Dominum.

O PRAISE the Lord, all ye Angels of his: ye that excel in strength, ye that fulfil his commandment and hearken unto the voice of his words, alleluia, alleluia. Ps. ibid., 1. Praise the Lord, O my soul: and all that is within me praise his holy name. ℣. Glory.

Collect.

O GOD, who dost constitute the services of Angels and men in a wonderful order: mercifully grant; that they, who ever stand before thee and serve thee in heaven, may likewise defend our life on earth. Through.

The Lesson from the book of the Revelation of blessed John the Apostle.

Rev. 1, 1.

IN those days: God shewed that which must shortly come to pass, and he sent and signified it by his Angel unto his servant John, who bare record of the word of God, and of the testimony of Jesus Christ, and of all things that he saw. Blessed is he that readeth, and they that hear the words of this prophecy: and keep those things which are written therein: for the time is at hand. John to the seven churches which are in Asia. Grace be unto you, and peace, from him which is, and which was, and which is to come: and from the seven spirits which are before his throne: and from Jesus Christ, who is the faithful witness, and the first begotten of the dead, and the prince of the kings of the earth, who loved us, and washed us from our sins in his own blood.

Alleluia, alleluia. ℣. Holy Michael Archangel, defend us in the battle, that we perish not in the dreadful judgment. Alleluia. ℣. The sea was shaken, and the earth trembled, when the Archangel Michael came down from heaven. Alleluia.

✠ The Continuation of the holy Gospel according to Matthew.

Matt. 18, 1-10.

AT that time: The disciples came unto Jesus saying: Who is the greatest in the kingdom of heaven? And Jesus called a little child unto him, and set him in the midst of them and said: Verily I say unto you, Except ye be converted, and become as little children, ye shall not enter into the kingdom of heaven. Whosoever therefore shall humble himself as this little child, the same is greatest in the kingdom of heaven. And whoso shall receive one such little child in my name, receiveth me. But whoso shall offend one of these little ones which believe in me, it were better for him that a millstone was hanged about his neck, and that he were drowned in the depth of the sea. Woe unto the world because of offences! For it must needs be that offences come: but woe to that man by whom the offence cometh! Wherefore if thy hand or thy foot offend thee, cut them off, and cast them from thee: it is better for thee to enter into life halt or maimed, rather than having two hands or two feet to be cast into everlasting fire. And if thine eye offend thee, pluck it out, and cast it from thee: it is better for thee to enter into life with one eye, rather than having two eyes to be cast into hell-fire.

Take heed that ye despise not one of these little ones: for I say unto you, That in heaven their Angels do always behold the face of my Father which is in heaven.

The Creed is not said.

Offertory. Rev. 8, 3-4. An Angel stood by the altar of the temple, having a golden censer in his hand, and there was given unto him much incense: and the smoke of the incense ascended up before God, alleluia.

Secret.

WE offer thee, O Lord, this sacrifice of praise, humbly beseeching thee: that, at the prayers of the Angels interceding for us, thou wouldest both graciously accept the same, and grant that they may avail to our salvation. Through.

Communion. Dan. 3, 37. O all ye Angels of the Lord, bless ye the Lord: sing ye praises, and magnify him above all for ever, alleluia.

Postcommunion.

O LORD, forasmuch as we put our trust in the intercession of thy blessed Archangel Michael: we humbly beseech thee; that we, who with our outward lips have been made partakers of these holy mysteries, may inwardly in our souls receive the benefit of the same. Through.

May 9.

St. Gregory Nazianzen

Bishop, Confessor and Doctor of the Church

Double.

Introit. Ecclus. 15, 5. In medio.

IN the midst of the Church he opened his mouth: and the Lord filled him with the spirit of wisdom and understanding: he clothed him with a robe of glory, alleluia, alleluia. Ps. 92, 1. It is a good thing to give thanks unto the Lord: and to sing praises unto thy name, O Most Highest. ℣. Glory.

Collect.

O GOD, who didst send blessed Gregory thy Doctor to guide thy people in the way of everlasting salvation: grant, we beseech thee; that as we have learned of him the doctrine of life on earth, so we may be found worthy to have him for our advocate in heaven. Through.

The Lesson from the book of Wisdom.

Ecclus. 39, 6-14.

THE righteous shall give his heart to resort early to the Lord that made him, and will pray before the Most High, and will open his mouth in prayer, and make supplication for his sins. When the great Lord will, he shall be filled with the spirit of understanding: he shall pour out wise sentences, and give thanks unto the Lord in his prayers: he shall direct his counsel and knowledge, and in his secrets shall he meditate. He shall shew forth that which he hath learned, and shall glory in the law of the covenant of the Lord. Many shall commend his understanding, and so long as the world endureth, it shall not be blotted out. His memorial shall not depart away, and his name shall live from generation to generation. Nations shall shew forth his wisdom, and the Church shall declare his praise.

Alleluia, alleluia. ℣. Ecclus. 45, 9. The Lord loved him, and adorned him, he clothed him with a robe of glory. Alleluia. ℣. Hos. 14, 6. The righteous shall grow as the lily: and flourish for ever before the Lord. Alleluia.

✠ The Continuation of the holy Gospel according to Matthew.

Matt. 5, 13-19.

AT that time: Jesus said unto his disciples: Ye are the salt of the earth. But if the salt have lost his savour, wherewith shall it be salted? It is thenceforth good for nothing, but to be cast out, and to be trodden under foot of men. Ye are the light of the world. A city that is set on an hill cannot be hid. Neither do men light a candle, and put it under a bushel, but on a candlestick, and it giveth light unto all that are in the house. Let your light so shine before men, that they may see your good works, and glorify your Father which is in heaven. Think not that I am come to destroy the law, or the prophets: I am not come to destroy, but to fulfil. For verily I say unto you, Till heaven and earth pass, one jot or one tittle shall in no wise pass from the law, till all be fulfilled. Whosoever therefore shall break one of these least commandments, and shall teach men so, he shall be called the least in the kingdom of heaven: but whosoever shall do and teach them, the same shall be called great in the kingdom of heaven. Creed.

Offertory. Ps. 92, 13. The righteous shall flourish like a palm-tree: and shall spread abroad like a cedar in Libanus, alleluia.

Secret.

MAY the devout prayers of thy Bishop and Doctor Saint Gregory continually succour us, O Lord: that they may render our oblations acceptable in thy sight; and ever obtain for us thy merciful pardon. Through.

Communion. Luke 12, 42. A faithful and wise servant, whom his lord hath made ruler over his household: to give them their portion of meat in due season, alleluia.

Postcommunion.

WE beseech thee, O Lord, that blessed Gregory, thy Bishop and most excellent Doctor, may ever stand before thee as our advocate: that this sacrifice of thine ordinance may effectually avail for our salvation. Through.

May 10.
St. Antoninus
Bishop and Confessor
Double.

Introit. Ecclus. 45, 24. Statuit ei.

THE Lord hath established a covenant of peace with him, and made him the chief of his people: that he should have the dignity of the priesthood for ever, alleluia, alleluia. Ps. 132, 1. Lord, remember David: and all his trouble. ℣. Glory.

Collect.

ASSIST us, O Lord, through the merits of Saint Antoninus, thy Confessor and Bishop: that as we proclaim thy marvellous works in him, so we may glory in thy mercy toward us. Through.

Commemoration of SS. Gordian and Epimachus, Martyrs.

Collect.

GRANT, we beseech thee, almighty God: that we, who celebrate the festival of thy blessed Martyrs Gordian and Epimachus, may be aided by their intercession with thee. Through.

The Lesson from the book of Wisdom.

Ecclus. 44, 16-25, 15.

BEHOLD a great priest, who in his days pleased the Lord, and was found righteous: and in the time of wrath he was taken in exchange for the world. There was none like unto him, who kept the law of the Most High. Therefore by an oath the Lord assured him that he would increase him among his people. He established with him the blessing of all men and the covenant, and made it rest upon his head. He acknowledged him in his blessing: he preserved for him his mercy: so that he found favour in the sight of the Lord. He magnified him in the sight of kings: and gave unto him a crown of glory. An everlasting covenant he made with him, and gave him a great priesthood: and blessed him with glory. That he should execute the office of the priesthood, and have praise in his name, and offer unto him incense, and a sweet savour.

Alleluia, alleluia. ℣. Ps. 110, 4. Thou art a priest for ever after the order of Melchisedech. Alleluia. ℣. This is a priest whom the Lord hath crowned. Alleluia.

✠ The Continuation of the holy Gospel according to Matthew.

Matt. 25, 14-23.

AT that time: Jesus spake this parable unto his disciples: A man travelling into a far country called his own servants, and delivered unto them his goods. And unto one he gave five talents, to another two, and to another one, to every man according to his several ability, and straightway took his journey. Then he that had received the five talents went and traded with the same, and made them other five talents. And likewise he that had received two, he also gained other two. But he that had received one went and digged in the earth, and hid his lord's money. After a long time the lord of those servants cometh, and reckoneth with them. And so he that had received five talents came and brought other five talents, saying: Lord, thou deliveredst unto me five talents, behold, I have gained beside them five talents more. His lord said unto him: Well done, thou good and faithful servant, thou hast been faithful over a few things, I will make thee ruler over many things: enter thou into the joy of thy lord. He also that had received two talents came and said: Lord, thou deliveredst unto me two talents, behold, I have gained two other talents beside them. His lord said unto him: Well done, good and faithful servant, thou hast been faithful over a few things, I will make thee ruler over many things: enter thou into the joy of thy lord.

Offertory. Ps. 89, 21-22. I have found David my servant, with my holy oil have I anointed him: my hand shall hold him fast, and my arm shall strengthen him, alleluia.

Secret.

WE beseech thee, O Lord, that we, remembering with gladness the merits of thy Saints, may in all places feel the succour of their intercession. Through.

For the Holy Martyrs.

Secret.

WE beseech thee, O Lord, mercifully to accept this our sacrifice, which we offer unto thee, pleading the merits of thy blessed Martyrs, Gordian and Epimachus: that the same may effectually avail for our perpetual succour. Through.

Communion. Luke 12, 42. A faithful and wise servant, whom his lord hath made ruler over his household: to give them their portion of meat in due season, alleluia.

Postcommunion.

GRANT, we beseech thee, almighty God: that we, shewing forth our thankfulness for the gifts which we have received, may, at the intercession of blessed Antoninus, thy Confessor and Bishop, obtain yet more abundant mercies. Through.

For the Holy Martyrs.

Postcommunion.

WE beseech thee, almighty God: that we, who have received this heavenly food, may at the intercession of thy blessed Martyrs, Gordian and Epimachus, be thereby defended against all adversities. Through.

May 11 (formerly May 1).

SS. PHILIP AND JAMES APOSTLES

Double of 2nd class.

¶ To-day, if one of the three Rogation Days occur according to the Rubrics: 1. in Choir, after Terce is always said the Conventual Mass of the Feast, and, if the Procession take place, after None, Mass of the Rogation: 2. out of Choir, on Monday, if the Procession be omitted, after None is read the Mass of the Rogation, and on Wednesday after Sext always the Mass of the Vigil. Private Masses, moreover of the Feria and of the Vigil are forbidden.

Introit. Neh. 9, 27. Clamaverunt.

THEY cried unto thee, O Lord, in the time of their trouble: and thou didst hear them from heaven, alleluia, alleluia. Ps. 33, 1. Rejoice in the Lord, O ye righteous: for it becometh well the just to be thankful. ℣. Glory.

Collect.

O ALMIGHTY God, whom truly to know is everlasting life: grant us perfectly to know thy Son Jesus Christ to be the way, the truth, and the life; that, following the steps of thy holy Apostles, Saint Philip and Saint James, we may stedfastly walk in the way that leadeth to eternal life. Through the same thy Son Jesus Christ our Lord: Who liveth.

Or, Collect.

O GOD, who makest us glad by the yearly festival of thine Apostles Philip and James: grant, we beseech thee; that as we rejoice in their meritorious intercession; so we may learn to follow them in all virtuous and godly living. Through.

The Lesson from the Epistle of blessed James the Apostle.

James 1, 1-12.

JAMES, a servant of God and of the Lord Jesus Christ, to the twelve tribes which are scattered abroad, greeting. My brethren, count it all joy when ye fall into divers temptations: knowing this, that the trying of your faith worketh patience. But let patience have her perfect work, that ye may be perfect and entire, wanting nothing. If any of you lack wisdom, let him ask of God, that giveth to all men liberally, and upbraideth not: and it shall be given him. But let him ask in faith, nothing wavering: for he that wavereth is like a wave of the sea, driven with the wind, and tossed. For let not that man think that he shall receive any thing of the Lord. A double-minded man is unstable in all his ways. Let the brother of low degree rejoice in that he is exalted: but the rich in that he is made low: because as the flower of the grass he shall pass away. For the sun is no sooner risen with a burning heat, but it withereth the grass: and the flower thereof falleth, and the grace of the fashion of it perisheth: so also shall the rich man fade away in his ways. Blessed is the man that endureth temptation: for when he is tried, he shall receive the crown of life: which the Lord hath promised to them that love him.

Or:

The Lesson from the book of Wisdom.

Wisd. 5, 1-5.

THE righteous shall stand in great boldness before the face of such as have afflicted them, and made no account of their labours. When they see it, they shall be troubled with terrible fear, and shall be amazed at the strangeness of their salvation, so far beyond all that they looked for, and they repenting and groaning for anguish of spirit shall say within themselves: These were they, whom we had sometime in derision, and a proverb of reproach. We fools accounted their life madness, and their end to be without honour: how are they numbered among the children of God, and their lot is among the Saints.

Alleluia, alleluia. ℣. Ps. 89, 6. O Lord, the very heavens shall praise thy wondrous works: and thy truth in the congregations of the saints. Alleluia. ℣. John 14, 9. Have I been so long time with you, and yet hast thou not known me, Philip? He that hath seen me hath seen my Father also. Alleluia.

✠ The Continuation of the holy Gospel according to John.

John 14, 1-14.

AT that time: Jesus said unto his disciples: Let not your heart be troubled. Ye believe in God, believe also in me. In my Father's house are many mansions. If it were not so, I would have told you: I go to prepare a place for you. And if I go and prepare a place for you: I will come again, and receive you unto myself, that where I am, there ye may be also. And whither I go ye know, and the way ye know. Thomas saith unto him: Lord, we know not whither thou goest: and how can we know the way? Jesus saith unto him: I am the way, the truth, and the life; no man cometh unto the Father but by me: If ye had known me, ye should have known my Father also: and from henceforth ye know him, and have seen him. Philip saith unto him: Lord, shew us the Father, and it sufficeth us. Jesus saith unto him: Have I been so long time with you, and yet hast thou not known me, Philip? He that hath seen me hath seen the Father. And how sayest thou then: Shew us the Father? Believest thou not that I am in the Father, and the Father in me? The words that I speak unto you I speak not of myself. But the Father that dwelleth in me, he doeth the works. Believe me, that I am in the Father, and the Father in me. Or else believe me for the very works' sake. Verily, verily I say unto you, He that believeth on me, the works that I do shall he do also, and greater works than these shall he do: because I go unto my Father. And whatsoever ye shall ask in my name, that will I do:* that the Father may be glorified in the Son. If ye shall ask any thing in my name I will do it. Creed.

Offertory. Ps. 89, 6. O Lord, the very heavens shall praise thy wondrous works: and thy truth in the congregation of the saints, alleluia, alleluia.

Secret.

ACCEPT, O Lord, of thy mercy the gifts which on the feast of thine Apostles Philip and James we offer and present to thee: and turn aside from us all those evils which we most righteously deserve. Through.

Preface of the Apostles.

Communion. John 14, 9-10. Have I been so long time with you, and yet hast thou not known me, Philip? He that hath seen me hath seen my Father also, alleluia: believest thou not that I am in the Father, and the Father in me? Alleluia, alleluia.

Postcommunion.

O LORD, who hast fulfilled us with these saving mysteries, we beseech thee: that we may be continually assisted by the prayers of those whose festival we celebrate. Through.

May 12.

SS. Nereus, Achilles and Domitilla, Virgin, and Pancras

Martyrs

Simple.

Introit. Ps. 33, 17-19.

Ecce oculi Domini.

BEHOLD, the eye of the Lord is upon them that fear him, and put their trust in his mercy, alleluia; to deliver their soul from death: for he is our help and our shield, alleluia, alleluia. Ps. ibid., 1. Rejoice in the Lord, O ye righteous: for it becometh well the just to be thankful. ℣. Glory.

Collect.

WE beseech thee, O Lord, let this holy festival of thy Martyrs, Nereus, Achilles, Domitilla and Pancras, assist us in thy service; that we may be thereby rendered worthy to walk after thy commandments. Through.

The Lesson from the book of Wisdom.

Wisd. 5, 1-6.

THE righteous shall stand in great boldness before the face of such as have afflicted them, and made no account of their labours. When they see it, they shall be troubled with terrible fear, and shall be amazed at the strangeness of their salvation, so far beyond all that they looked for, and they repenting and groaning for anguish of spirit shall say within themselves: These were they, whom we had sometime in derision, and a proverb of reproach. We fools accounted their life madness, and their end to be without honour: how are they numbered among the children of God, and their lot is among the Saints.

Alleluia, alleluia. ℣. This is the true brotherhood, which overcame the wickedness of the world: which followed Christ, gaining heaven's glorious realms. Alleluia. ℣. The noble army of Martyrs praise thee, O Lord. Alleluia.

✠ The Continuation of the holy Gospel according to John.

John 4, 46-53.

AT that time: There was a certain nobleman, whose son was sick at Capernaum. When he heard that Jesus was come out of Judæa into Galilee, he went unto him, and besought him that he would come down and heal his son: for he was at the point of death. Then said Jesus unto him: Except ye see signs and wonders: ye will not believe. The nobleman saith unto him: Sir, come down ere my child die. Jesus saith unto him: Go thy way, thy son liveth. And the man believed the word that Jesus had spoken unto him, and he went his way. And as he was now going down, his servants met him, and told him, saying: Thy son liveth. Then enquired he of them the hour when he began to amend. And they said unto him: Yesterday at the seventh hour the fever left him. So the father knew that it was at the same hour, in the which Jesus said unto him: Thy son liveth: and himself believed, and his whole house.

Offertory. Ps. 89, 6. O Lord, the very heavens shall praise thy wondrous works: and thy truth in the congregation of the saints, alleluia, alleluia.

Secret.

WE beseech thee, O Lord, let the confession of thy holy Martyrs Nereus, Achilles, Domitilla and Pancras, be pleasing unto thee: that it may both commend our gifts, and ever implore for us thy pardon. Through.

Communion. Ps. 33, 1. Rejoice in the Lord, O ye righteous, alleluia: for it becometh well the just to be thankful, alleluia.

Postcommunion.

WE beseech thee, O Lord: that by the prayers of thy blessed Martyrs Nereus, Achilles, Domitilla and Pancras, this holy Sacrament which we have received may avail for the increase of thy mercy towards us. Through.

May 13.

St. Robert Bellarmine

Bishop, Confessor and Doctor of the Church

Double.

Introit. Ecclus. 15, 5. In medio.

IN the midst of the Church he opened his mouth: and the Lord filled him with the spirit of wisdom and understanding: he clothed him with a robe of glory, alleluia, alleluia. Ps. 92, 1. It is a good thing to give thanks unto the Lord: and to sing praises unto thy name, O Most Highest. ℣. Glory.

Collect.

O GOD, who, for the banishment of the snares of false doctrine and the defence of the rights of the Apostolic see, didst adorn blessed Robert thy Bishop and Doctor with wondrous learning and goodness: grant by his merits and intercession; that we may grow in the love of truth, and that the hearts of those that go astray may return to the unity of thy Church. Through.

The Lesson from the book of Wisdom.

Wisd. 7, 7-14.

I PRAYED, and understanding was given me: I called upon God, and the spirit of wisdom came to me: I preferred her before sceptres and thrones, and esteemed riches nothing in comparison of her. Neither compared I unto her any precious stone, because all gold in respect of her is as a little sand, and silver shall be counted as clay before her. I loved her above health and beauty, and chose to have her instead of light: for the light that cometh from her never goeth out. All good things together came to me with her, and innumerable riches in her hands. And I rejoiced in them all, because wisdom goeth before them: and I knew not that she was the mother of them. I learned diligently, and do communicate her liberally: I do not hide her riches. For she is a treasure unto men that never faileth: which they that use become the friends of God, being commended for the gifts that come from learning.

Alleluia, alleluia. ℣. Dan. 12, 3. They that be wise shall shine as the brightness of the firmament. Alleluia. ℣. And they that turn many to righteousness as the stars for ever and ever. Alleluia.

✠ The Continuation of the holy Gospel according to Matthew.

Matt. 5, 13-19.

AT that time: Jesus said unto his disciples: Ye are the salt of the earth. But if the salt have lost his savour, wherewith shall it be salted? It is thenceforth good for nothing, but to be cast out, and to be trodden under foot of men. Ye are the light of the world. A city that is set on an hill cannot be hid. Neither do men light a candle, and put it under a bushel, but on a candlestick, and it giveth light unto all that are in the house. Let your light so shine before men, that they may see your good works, and glorify your Father which is in heaven. Think not that I am come to destroy the law, or the prophets: I am not come to destroy, but to fulfil. For verily I say unto you, Till heaven and earth pass, one jot or one tittle shall in no wise pass from the law, till all be fulfilled. Whosoever therefore shall break one of these least commandments, and shall teach men so, he shall be called the least in the kingdom of heaven: but whosoever shall do and teach them, the same shall be called great in the kingdom of heaven. Creed.

Offertory. Ps. 73, 27. But it is good for me to hold me fast by God, to put my trust in the Lord God: and to speak of all thy works in the gates of the daughter of Sion, alleluia.

Secret.

WE offer unto thee, O Lord, this sacrifice for a savour of sweetness: and do thou vouchsafe; that we, being taught by the doctrine and example of blessed Robert, may run the way of thy commandments, when thou hast set our heart at liberty. Through.

Communion. Matt. 5, 14 and 16. Ye are the light of the world: let your light so shine before men, that they may see your good works, and glorify your Father which is in heaven, alleluia.

Postcommunion.

O LORD our God, let this holy Sacrament, which we have here received, inflame us with the fire of thy love: even as blessed Robert, being exceedingly enkindled with the same, did ever spend himself for thy Church. Through.

May 14.

For St. Boniface

Martyr

The Mass Protexisti, p. [15], except the Prayers:

Collect. P

GRANT, we beseech thee, almighty God: that we, who celebrate the festival of blessed Boniface, thy Martyr, may by his intercession find succour in thy sight. Through.

Secret. C

WE beseech thee, O Lord, to accept our prayers and oblations: and graciously hearken unto us whom thou dost cleanse by thy heavenly mysteries. Through.

Postcommunion. P

WE beseech thee, O Lord our God, that like as we, whom thou hast refreshed by the partaking of thy sacred gift, do offer unto thee our outward worship: so by the intercession of blessed Boniface, thy Martyr, we may inwardly be purified thereby to our salvation. Through.

For a Votive out of Eastertide the Mass In virtute, p. [6] with Prayers as above.

May 15.

St. John Baptist de la Salle

Confessor

Double.

Introit. Ps. 37, 30-31. Os justi.

THE mouth of the righteous is exercised in wisdom: and his tongue will be talking of judgment: the law of his God is in his heart, alleluia, alleluia. Ps. ibid., 1. Fret not thyself because of the ungodly: neither be thou envious against the evildoers. ℣. Glory.

Collect.

O GOD, who for the teaching of the poor in Christ's religion, and for the stablishing of the young in the way of truth, didst raise up thy Confessor, Saint John Baptist, and through him didst gather a new household in thy Church: mercifully grant; that by his intercession and example we, being kindled with zeal for thy glory and for the salvation of souls, may with him be made partakers of the crown of heavenly glory. Through the same.

The Lesson from the book of Wisdom.

Ecclus. 31, 8-11.

BLESSED is the man that is found without blemish: and hath not gone after gold. Who is he, and we will call him blessed? for wonderful things hath he done among his people. Who hath been tried thereby, and found perfect? then let him glory. Who might offend, and hath not offended? or done evil, and hath not done it? His goods shall be established, and the congregation shall declare his alms.

Alleluia, alleluia. ℣. James 1, 12. Blessed is the man that endureth temptation: for when he is tried, he shall receive the crown of life. Alleluia. ℣. Ecclus. 45, 7. The Lord loved him, and adorned him: he clothed him with a robe of glory. Alleluia.

✠ The Continuation of the holy Gospel according to Matthew.

Matt. 18, 1-5.

AT that time: The disciples came unto Jesus, saying: Who is the greatest in the kingdom of heaven? And Jesus called a little child unto him, and set him in the midst of them, and said: Verily, I say unto you, Except ye be converted, and become as little children, ye shall not enter into the kingdom of heaven. Whosoever therefore shall humble himself as this little child, the same is greatest in the kingdom of heaven. And whoso shall receive one such little one in my name, receiveth me.

Offertory. Ps. 89, 25. My truth and my mercy shall be with him: and in my name shall his horn be exalted, alleluia.

Secret.

WE offer thee, O Lord, this our sacrifice of praise to the honour of thy Saints: whereby we trust to be delivered from all evils both in this life and in that which is to come. Through.

Communion. Matt. 24, 46-47. Blessed is the servant whom his lord when he cometh shall find watching: verily I say unto you, he shall make him ruler over all his goods, alleluia.

Postcommunion.

O LORD, our God, who hast refreshed us with heavenly meat and drink, we humbly beseech thee: that we may be defended by the prayers of him in whose memory we have received the same. Through.

May 16.

St. Ubald

Bishop and Confessor

Simple.

The Mass Statuit, from the Common of a Confessor Bishop, p. [19], except the Collect:

Collect.

SEND down upon us, O Lord, the assistance of thy grace: and at the intercession of blessed Ubald, thy Confessor and Bishop, stretch forth the right hand of thy mercy to be our defence against all the wickedness of the devil. Through.

Secret.   C

WE beseech thee, O Lord, that we, remembering with gladness the merits of thy Saints, may in all places feel the succour of their intercession. Through.

Postcommunion.   C

GRANT, we beseech thee, almighty God: that we, shewing forth our thankfulness for the gifts which we have received, may, at the intercession of blessed Ubald, thy Confessor and Bishop, obtain yet more abundant mercies. Through.

May 17.

St. Paschal Baylon

Confessor

Double.

The Mass Os justi, from the Common of a Confessor not a Bishop, p. [24], except the Collect:

Collect.   P

O GOD, who didst endue thy blessed Confessor Paschal with wondrous love toward the sacred mysteries of thy Body and Blood: mercifully grant; that, as he from this heavenly banquet received abundance of spiritual grace, so we may be found worthy likewise to receive the same: Who livest and reignest with God the Father.

Secret.   C

WE offer thee, O Lord, this our sacrifice of praise to the honour of thy Saints: whereby we trust to be delivered from all evils both in this life and in that which is to come. Through.

Postcommunion.   C

O LORD, our God, who hast refreshed us with heavenly meat and drink, we humbly beseech thee: that we may be defended by the prayers of him in whose memory we have received the same. Through.

May 18.

St. Venantius

Martyr

Double.

Introit. Ps. 64, 3. Protexisti.

THOU hast hidden me, O God, from the gathering together of the froward, alleluia: and from the insurrection of wicked doers, alleluia, alleluia. Ps. ibid., 1. Hear my voice, O God, in my prayer: preserve my life from fear of the enemy. V. Glory.

Collect.

O GOD who hast hallowed this day by the triumph of blessed Venantius, thy Martyr: graciously hear the prayers of thy people, and grant; that we who venerate his merits may imitate the constancy of his faith. Through.

The Lesson from the book of Wisdom.

Wisd. 5, 1-5.

THE righteous shall stand in great boldness before the face of such as have afflicted them, and made no account of their labours. When they see it they shall be troubled with terrible fear, and shall be amazed at the strangeness of their salvation, so far beyond all that they looked for, and they repenting and groaning for anguish of spirit shall say within themselves: These were they, whom we had sometime in derision, and a proverb of reproach. We fools accounted their life madness, and their end to be without honour: how are they numbered among the children of God, and their lot is among the Saints.

Alleluia, alleluia. ℣. Ps. 89, 6. O Lord, the very heavens shall praise thy wondrous works: and thy truth in the congregation of the saints. Alleluia. ℣. Ps. 21, 4. Thou hast set, O Lord, a crown of pure gold upon his head. Alleluia.

☩ The Continuation of the holy Gospel according to John.

John 15, 1-7.

AT that time: Jesus said unto his disciples: I am the true vine: and my Father is the husbandman. Every branch in me that beareth not fruit he taketh away: and every branch that beareth fruit, he purgeth it, that it may bring forth more fruit. Now ye are clean through the word which I have spoken unto you. Abide in me: and I in you. As the branch cannot bear fruit of itself, except it abide in the vine: no more can ye, except ye abide in me. I am the vine, ye are the branches: he that abideth in me, and I in him, the same bringeth forth much fruit: for without me ye can do nothing. If a man abide not in me, he is cast forth as a branch, and is withered, and men gather them, and cast them into the fire, and they are burned. If ye abide in me, and my words abide in you: ye shall ask what ye will, and it shall be done unto you.

Offertory. Ps. 89, 6. O Lord, the very heavens shall praise thy wondrous works: and thy truth in the congregation of the saints, alleluia, alleluia.

Secret.

ALMIGHTY God, let the merits of blessed Venantius render this oblation acceptable unto thee: that we, being succoured by his assistance, may be made partakers of his glory. Through.

Communion. Ps. 64, 11. The righteous shall rejoice in the Lord, and put his trust in him: and all they that are true of heart shall be glad, alleluia. alleluia.

Postcommunion.

O LORD, who hast bestowed on us this Sacrament of everlasting life, we humbly beseech thee: that through the prayers of blessed Venantius thy Martyr on our behalf, we may obtain thereby thy pardon and grace. Through.

Out of Eastertide the Mass In virtute, p. [6], the Prayers excepted.

May 19.

St. Peter Celestine

Pope and Confessor

Double.

Introit. John 21, 15-17. Si diligis me.

IF thou lovest me, Simon Peter, feed my lambs, feed my sheep, alleluia, alleluia. Ps. 30, 1. I will magnify thee, O Lord, for thou hast set me up, and not made my foes to triumph over me. ℣. Glory.

Collect.

O GOD, who didst exalt blessed Peter Celestine to the chief bishoprick of thy Church, and didst teach him to lay it down to live in humility: mercifully grant, that we, following his example, may learn to despise all things of this world, and be found worthy to attain with gladness to the rewards which thou hast promised to the humble and meek. Through.

And Commemoration is made of St. Pudentiana, V.

Collect.

GRACIOUSLY hear us, O God of our salvation: that, like as we do rejoice in the festival of blessed Pudentiana, thy Virgin; so we may learn to follow her example in godliness and charity. Through.

The Lesson from the Epistle of blessed Peter the Apostle.

I Peter 5, 1-4 and 10-11.

DEARLY beloved: The elders which are among you I exhort, who am also an elder, and a witness of the sufferings of Christ, and also a partaker of the glory that shall be revealed: feed the flock of God which is among you, taking the oversight thereof, not by constraint, but willingly, not for filthy lucre, but of a ready mind; neither as being lords over God's heritage, but being ensamples to the flock. And when the chief Shepherd shall appear, ye shall receive a crown of glory that fadeth not away. Now the God of all grace, who hath called us unto his eternal glory by Christ Jesus, after that ye have suffered a while, make you perfect, stablish, strengthen, settle you. To him be glory and dominion for ever and ever. Amen.

Alleluia, alleluia. ℣. Matt. 16, 18. Thou art Peter, and upon this rock I will build my Church. Alleluia. ℣. Ps. 45, 17-18. Thou shalt make them princes in all lands: they shall remember thy name, O Lord. Alleluia.

✠ The Continuation of the holy Gospel according to Matthew.

Matt. 16, 13-19.

AT that time: Jesus came into the coasts of Cæsarea Philippi, and asked his disciples, saying: Whom do men say that I, the Son of man, am? And they said: Some say that thou art John the Baptist, some Elias, and others Jeremias, or one of the Prophets. He saith unto them: But whom say ye that I am? And Simon Peter answered and said: Thou art the Christ, the Son of the living God. And Jesus answered and said unto him: Blessed art thou, Simon Bar-jona: for flesh and blood hath not revealed it unto thee, but my Father which is in heaven. And I say also unto thee, That thou art Peter, and upon this rock I will build my Church, and the gates of hell shall not prevail against it. And I will give unto thee the keys of the kingdom of heaven. And whatsoever thou shalt bind on earth, shall be bound in heaven: and whatsoever thou shalt loose on earth, shall be loosed in heaven.

Offertory. Jer. 1, 9-10. Behold, I have put my words in thy mouth: see, I have set thee over the nations and over the kingdoms, to pull down and to destroy, to build and to plant, alleluia.

Secret.

WE beseech thee, O Lord, graciously enlighten thy Church by the gifts which we here offer: that in every place thy flock may increase and prosper, and the shepherds by thy governance may be made pleasing to thy name. Through.

For St. Pudentiana.   Secret.

GRANT, O Lord, that like as thy dedicated people do acknowledge that in tribulation they have been succoured by the merits of thy Saints: so this oblation, which they offer unto thee in honour of the same, may be acceptable in thy sight. Through.

Preface of the Season.

Communion. Matt. 16, 18. Thou art Peter, and upon this rock I will build my Church, alleluia.

Postcommunion.

MERCIFUL Lord, we beseech thee to govern and preserve thy Church, which thou hast here refreshed with heavenly food: that by the guiding of thy mighty power it may serve thee in more abundant freedom, and ever keep thy true religion whole and undefiled. Through.

For St. Pudentiana. Postcommunion.

O LORD, who hast satisfied this thy family with thy sacred gifts: we beseech thee; that we may at all times be comforted by the intercession of her whose festival we celebrate. Through.

May 20.

St. Bernadine of Siena

Confessor

Simple.

Introit. Ps. 37, 30-31. Os justi.

THE mouth of the righteous is exercised in wisdom: and his tongue will be talking of judgment: the law of his God is in his heart, alleluia, alleluia. Ps. ibid., 1. Fret not thyself because of the ungodly: neither be thou envious against the evildoers. ℣. Glory.

Collect.

O LORD Jesu, who didst endue blessed Bernardine, thy Confessor, with singular love of thy holy name: we beseech thee, by his merits and intercession; graciously to pour forth upon us the spirit of love toward thee: Who livest and reignest with God the Father.

The Lesson from the book of Wisdom.

Ecclus. 31, 8-11.

BLESSED is the man that is found without blemish: and hath not gone after gold. Who is he, and we will call him blessed? for wonderful things hath he done among his people. Who hath been tried thereby, and found perfect? then let him glory. Who might offend, and hath not offended? or done evil, and hath not done it? His goods shall be established, and the congregation shall declare his alms.

Alleluia, alleluia. ℣. James 1, 12. Blessed is the man that endureth temptation: for when he is tried, he shall receive the crown of life. Alleluia. ℣. Ecclus. 45, 7. The Lord loved him, and adorned him: he clothed him with a robe of glory. Alleluia.

✠ The Continuation of the holy Gospel according to Matthew.

Matt. 19, 27-29.

AT that time: Peter said unto Jesus: Behold, we have forsaken all, and followed thee: what shall we have therefore? And Jesus said unto them: Verily, I say unto you, That ye which have followed me, in the regeneration when the Son of man shall sit in the throne of his glory, ye also shall sit upon twelve thrones, judging the twelve tribes of Israel. And every one that hath forsaken houses, or brethren, or sisters, or father, or mother, or wife, or children, or lands, for my name's sake, shall receive an hundred-fold, and shall inherit everlasting life.

Offertory. Ps. 89, 25. My truth and my mercy shall be with him: and in my name shall his horn be exalted, alleluia.

Secret.

GRANT, we beseech thee, O Lord, that we who, trusting in this our sacrifice of praise, do offer it before thee to the honour of thy Saints: may by the same be delivered from all evils both in this life and in that which is to come. Through.

Communion. Matt. 24, 46-47. Blessed is the servant whom his lord when he cometh shall find watching: verily I say unto you, he shall make him ruler over all his goods, alleluia.

Postcommunion.

O LORD, our God, who hast refreshed us with heavenly meat and drink, we humbly beseech thee: that we may be defended by the prayers of him in whose memory we have received the same. Through.

May 25.
St. Gregory VII
Pope and Confessor

Double.

The Mass Si diligis me, p. [2], the Collect excepted:

Collect. P

O GOD, the strength of them that trust in thee, who didst endue blessed Gregory, thy Confessor and Bishop, with strength and constancy in the defence of thy Church: grant us, by his example and intercession, manfully to overcome all adversities that may beset us. Through.

And Commemoration is made of St. Urban I, Pope and Martyr.

Collect. C1

O EVERLASTING Shepherd, look down in mercy on thy flock: and as thou didst choose blessed Urban, thy Martyr and Chief Bishop, to be pastor and ruler of thy Church; so at his intercession defend it with thy continual protection. Through.

For St. Gregory. Secret. C1

WE beseech thee, O Lord, graciously enlighten thy Church by the gifts which we here offer: that in every place thy flock may increase and prosper, and the shepherds by thy governance may be made pleasing to thy name. Through.

For St. Urban. Secret. C2

GRACIOUSLY receive, O Lord, the gifts which we with gladness offer unto thee, and grant: that at the intercession of blessed Urban thy Church, rejoicing in purity of faith, may serve thee in all godly quietness. Through.

Common Preface (or of the Season).

For St. Gregory. Postcommunion. C1

MERCIFUL Lord, we beseech thee to govern and preserve thy Church, which thou hast here refreshed with heavenly food: that by the guiding of thy mighty power it may serve thee in more abundant freedom, and ever keep thy true religion whole and undefiled. Through.

For St. Urban. Postcommunion. C2

MULTIPLY, we beseech thee, O Lord, in thy Church the spirit of grace, which thou hast given: that through the prayers of blessed Urban thy Martyr and Chief Bishop neither the obedience of the flock may be wanting to the shepherd, nor the care of the shepherd to the flock. Through.

In England and Wales:

May 26.
St. Augustine
Bishop and Confessor, Apostle of England

See Supplement.

Elsewhere: May 26.

St. Philip Neri
Confessor

Double.

Introit. Rom. 5, 5. Caritas Dei.

THE love of God is shed abroad in our hearts by the Holy Ghost which dwelleth in us. (E.T. Alleluia, alleluia.) Ps. 103, 1. Praise the Lord, O my soul: and all that is within me, praise his holy name. ℣. Glory.

Collect.

O GOD, who hast exalted blessed Philip, thy Confessor, to the glory of thy Saints: mercifully grant; that we who rejoice in his festival may follow him in all virtuous and godly living. Through.

Commemoration of St. Eleutherius, Pope, Martyr.

Collect.

O EVERLASTING Shepherd, look down in mercy on thy flock: and as thou didst choose blessed Eleutherius thy Martyr and Chief Bishop to be pastor and ruler of thy Church; so at his intercession defend it with thy continual protection. Through.

The Lesson from the book of Wisdom.

Wisd. 7, 7.

I PRAYED, and understanding was given me: I called upon God, and the spirit of wisdom came to me: I preferred her before sceptres and thrones, and esteemed riches nothing in comparison of her: neither compared I unto her any precious stone: because all gold in respect of her is as a little sand, and silver shall be counted as clay before her. I loved her above health and beauty, and chose to have her instead of light: for the light that cometh from her never goeth out. All good things together came to me with her, and innumerable riches in her hands, and I rejoiced in them all: because wisdom goeth before them: and I knew not that she was the mother of them. I learned diligently, and do communicate her liberally: I do not hide her riches. For she is a treasure unto men that never faileth: which they that use become the friends of God, being commended for the gifts that come from learning.

Gradual. Ps. 34, 12 and 6. Come, ye children, and hearken unto me: I will teach you the fear of the Lord. ℣. Come ye unto him and be enlightened: and your faces shall not be ashamed.

Alleluia, alleluia. ℣. Lam. 1, 13. From above hath he sent fire into my bones, and hath instructed me. Alleluia.

In Eastertide the Gradual is omitted, and in its place is said:

Alleluia, alleluia. ℣. Lam. 1, 13. From above hath he sent fire into my bones, and hath instructed me. Alleluia. Ps. 39, 4. My heart was hot within me: and while I was thus musing the fire kindled. Alleluia.

☩ The Continuation of the holy Gospel according to Luke.

Luke 12, 35-40.

AT that time: Jesus said unto his disciples: Let your loins be girded about, and your lights burning, and ye yourselves like unto men that wait for their lord, when he will return from the wedding: that when he cometh and knocketh, they may open unto him immediately. Blessed are those servants, whom the lord when he cometh shall find watching: verily I say unto you, that he shall gird himself, and make them to sit down to meat, and will come forth and serve them. And if he shall come in the second watch, or come in the third watch, and find them so, blessed are those servants. And this know, that if the good man of the house had known what hour the thief would come, he would have watched, and not have suffered his house to be broken through. Be ye therefore ready also: for the Son of man cometh at an hour when ye think not.

Offertory. Ps. 119, 32. I will run the way of thy commandments, when thou hast set my heart at liberty. (E.T. Alleluia.)

Secret.

WE beseech thee, O Lord, favourably to regard these present sacrifices: and grant; that the Holy Spirit may inflame us with that fire, wherewith he wondrously penetrated the heart of blessed Philip. Through.... in the unity of the same Holy Spirit.

For St. Eleutherius.   Secret.

WE beseech thee, O Lord, graciously enlighten thy Church by the gifts which we here offer: that in every place thy flock may increase and prosper, and the shepherds by thy governance may be made pleasing to thy name. Through.

Common Preface (or of the Season).

Communion. Ps. 84, 3.   My heart and my flesh rejoice in the living God. (E.T. Alleluia.)

Postcommunion.

O LORD, who hast fulfilled us with thy heavenly delights: we beseech thee; that by the merits of thy blessed Confessor Philip, and by following him, we may ever earnestly seek after those things whereby we truly live. Through.

For St. Eleutherius.   Postcommunion.

MERCIFUL Lord, we beseech thee to govern and preserve thy Church, which thou hast here refreshed with heavenly food: that by the guiding of thy mighty power it may serve thee in more abundant freedom, and ever keep thy true religion whole and undefiled. Through.

May 27.

St. Bede the Venerable

Confessor and Doctor of the Church

Double.

Introit. Ecclus. 15, 5.   In medio.

IN the midst of the Church he opened his mouth: and the Lord filled him with the spirit of wisdom and understanding: he clothed him with a robe of glory. (E.T. Alleluia, alleluia.) Ps. 92, 1. It is a good thing to give thanks unto the Lord: and to sing praises unto thy name, O most Highest. V. Glory.

Collect.

O GOD, who dost illumine thy Church with the learning of blessed Bede, thy Confessor and Doctor: mercifully grant unto thy servants; that they may ever be enlightened by his wisdom, and succoured by his merits. Through.

Commemoration of St. John I, P.M.

Collect.

O EVERLASTING Shepherd, look down in mercy on thy flock: and as thou didst choose blessed John thy Martyr and Chief Bishop to be pastor and ruler of thy Church; so at his intercession defend it with thy continual protection. Through.

The Lesson from the Epistle of blessed Paul the Apostle to Timothy.

II Tim. 4, 1-8.

DEARLY beloved: I charge thee before God, and the Lord Jesus Christ, who shall judge the quick and the dead at his appearing and his kingdom: preach the word, be instant in season, out of season: reprove, rebuke, exhort with all longsuffering and doctrine. For the time will come when they will not endure sound doctrine, but after their own lusts shall they heap to themselves teachers, having itching ears, and they shall turn away their ears from the truth, and shall be turned unto fables. But watch thou in all things, endure afflictions, do the work of an Evangelist, make full proof of thy ministry. For I am now ready to be offered, and the time of my departure is at hand. I have fought a good fight, I have finished my course, I have kept the faith. Henceforth there is laid up for me a crown of righteousness, which the Lord, the righteous judge, shall give me at that day: and not to me only, but unto all them also that love his appearing.

Gradual. Ps. 37, 30-31. The mouth of the righteous is exercised in wisdom: and his tongue will be talking of judgment. ℣. The law of his God is in his heart: and his goings shall not slide.

Alleluia, alleluia. ℣. Ecclus. 45, 9. The Lord loved him and adorned him: he clothed him with a robe of glory. Alleluia.

In Eastertide the Gradual is omitted, and in its place is said:

Alleluia, alleluia. ℣. Ecclus. 45, 9. The Lord loved him, and adorned him: he clothed him with a robe of glory. Alleluia. ℣. Hos. 14, 6. The righteous shall grow as the lily: and flourish for ever before the Lord. Alleluia.

☩ The Continuation of the holy Gospel according to Matthew.

Matt. 5, 13-19.

AT that time: Jesus said unto his disciples: Ye are the salt of the earth. But if the salt have lost his savour, wherewith shall it be salted? It is thenceforth good for nothing, but to be cast out, and to be trodden under foot of men. Ye are the light of the world. A city that is set on an hill cannot be hid. Neither do men light a candle, and put it under a bushel, but on a candlestick, and it giveth light unto all that are in the house. Let your light so shine before men, that they may see your good works, and glorify your Father which is in heaven. Think not that I am come to destroy the law or the prophets: I am not come to destroy, but to fulfil. For verily I say unto you, Till heaven and earth pass, one jot or one tittle shall in no wise pass from the law, till all be fulfilled. Whosoever therefore shall break one of these least commandments, and shall teach men so, he shall be called the least in the kingdom of heaven: but whosoever shall do and teach them, the same shall be called great in the kingdom of heaven. Creed.

Offertory. Ps. 92, 13. The righteous shall flourish like a palm-tree: and shall spread abroad like a cedar in Libanus. (E.T. Alleluia.)

Secret.

MAY the devout prayers of thy Confessor and Doctor, Saint Bede, continually succour us, O Lord: that they may render our oblations acceptable in thy sight; and may ever obtain for us thy merciful pardon. Through.

For St. John.   Secret.

WE beseech thee, O Lord, graciously enlighten thy Church by the gifts which we here offer: that in every place thy flock may increase and prosper, and the shepherds by thy governance may be made pleasing to thy name. Through.

Common Preface (or of the Season).

Communion. Luke 12, 42. A faithful and wise servant, whom his lord hath made ruler over his household: to give them their portion of meat in due season. (E.T. Alleluia.)

Postcommunion.

WE beseech thee, O Lord, that blessed Bede, thy Confessor and most excellent Doctor, may ever stand before thee as our advocate: that this sacrifice of thine ordinance may effectually avail for our salvation. Through.

For St. John.   Postcommunion.

MERCIFUL Lord, we beseech thee to govern and preserve thy Church, which thou hast here refreshed with heavenly food: that by the guiding of thy mighty power it may serve thee in more abundant freedom, and ever keep thy true religion whole and undefiled. Through.

May 28.

(outside England and Wales.)

St. Augustine

Bishop and Confessor

Double.

Introit. Ps. 132, 9-10. Sacerdotes tui.

LET thy priests, O Lord, be clothed with righteousness, and let thy saints sing with joyfulness: for thy servant David's sake, turn not away the presence of thine Anointed. (E.T. Alleluia, alleluia.) Ps. ibid., 1. Lord, remember David: and all his trouble. ℣. Glory.

Collect.

O GOD, who by the preaching and miracles of blessed Augustine, thy Confessor and Bishop, didst vouchsafe to illumine the peoples of the English with the light of the true faith: vouchsafe; that at his intercession the hearts of those who go astray may return to the unity of thy truth, and that we may be of one heart and mind according to thy will. Through.

The Lesson from the Epistle of blessed Paul the Apostle to the Thessalonians.

I Thess. 2, 2-9.

BRETHREN: We were bold in our God to speak unto you the Gospel of God with much contention. For our exhortation was not of deceit, nor of uncleanness, nor in guile, but as we were allowed of God to be put in trust with the Gospel: even so we speak, not as pleasing men but God, which trieth our hearts. For neither at any time used we flattering words, as ye know: nor a cloke of covetousness: God is witness: nor of men sought we glory, neither of you, nor yet of others: when we might have been burdensome, as the Apostles of Christ: but we were gentle among you, even as a nurse cherisheth her children. So being affectionately desirous of you, we were willing to have imparted unto you, not the Gospel of God only, but also our own souls: because ye were dear unto us. For ye remember, brethren, our labour and travail: for labouring night and day, because we would not be chargeable unto any of you, we preached unto you the Gospel of God.

Gradual. Ps. 132, 16-17. I will deck her priests with health: and her saints shall rejoice and sing. ℣. There shall I make the horn of David to flourish: I have ordained a lantern for mine Anointed.

Alleluia, alleluia. ℣. Ps. 110, 4. The Lord sware, and will not repent: Thou art a priest for ever after the order of Melchisedech. Alleluia.

In Eastertide the Gradual is omitted, and in its place is said:

Alleluia, alleluia. ℣. Ps. 110, 4. The Lord sware, and will not repent: Thou art a priest for ever after the order of Melchisedech. Alleluia. ℣. Ecclus. 45, 9. The Lord loved him, and adorned him: he clothed him with a robe of glory. Alleluia.

✠ The Continuation of the holy Gospel according to Luke.

Luke 10, 1.

AT that time: The Lord appointed other seventy also: and sent them two and two before his face into every city and place whither he himself would come. Therefore said he unto them: The harvest truly is great, but the labourers are few. Pray ye therefore the Lord of the harvest, that he would send forth labourers into his harvest. Go your ways: behold, I send you forth as lambs among wolves. Carry neither purse, nor scrip, nor shoes; and salute no man by the way. And into whatsoever house ye enter, first say: Peace be to this house: and if the son of peace be there, your peace shall rest upon it: if not, it shall turn to you again. And in the same house remain, eating and drinking such things as they give, for the labourer is worthy of his hire. Go not from house to house. And into whatsoever city ye enter, and they receive you, eat such things as are set before you: and heal the sick that are therein, and say unto them: The kingdom of God is come nigh unto you.

Offertory. Ps. 89, 25. My truth and my mercy shall be with him: and in my name shall his horn be exalted. (E.T. Alleluia.)

Secret.

WE offer this our sacrifice unto thee, O Lord, on the solemnity of blessed Augustine, thy Confessor and Bishop, humbly beseeching thee: that the sheep which are lost, returning to the one fold, may be nourished by this saving food. Through.

Communion. Matt. 24, 46-47. Blessed is the servant, whom his lord when he cometh shall find watching: verily I say unto you, he shall make him ruler over all his goods. (E.T. Alleluia.)

Postcommunion.

O LORD, who hast refreshed us with this saving victim, we humbly beseech thee: that, through the prayers and intercession of blessed Augustine, the same may in every place be continually offered unto thy name. Through.

May 29.

St. Mary Magdalen of Pazzi

Virgin

Simple.

The Mass Dilexisti, p. [31], except the Collect:

Collect.

O GOD, the lover of virginity, who didst kindle blessed Mary Magdalen, thy Virgin, with the fire of thy love, and didst adorn her with heavenly gifts: grant; that as we celebrate her festival with gladness, so we may follow the example of her purity and love. Through.

Secret.

GRANT, O Lord, that like as thy dedicated people do acknowledge that in tribulation they have been succoured by the merits of thy Saints: so this oblation, which they offer unto thee in honour of the same, may be acceptable in thy sight. Through.

Postcommunion.

O LORD, who hast satisfied this thy family with thy sacred gifts: we beseech thee, that we may at all times be comforted by the intercession of her whose festival we celebrate. Through.

May 30.

For St. Felix I

Pope and Martyr

The Mass, Si diligis me, p. [2].

Collect.

O EVERLASTING Shepherd, look down in mercy on thy flock: and as thou didst choose blessed Felix thy Martyr and Chief Bishop to be pastor and ruler of thy Church; so at his intercession defend it with thy continual protection. Through.

Feasts of May (30)

Secret. C

WE beseech thee, O Lord, graciously enlighten thy Church by the gifts which we here offer: that in every place thy flock may increase and prosper, and the shepherds by thy governance may be made pleasing to thy name. Through.

Postcommunion. C

MERCIFUL Lord, we beseech thee to govern and preserve thy Church, which thou hast here refreshed with heavenly food: that by the guiding of thy mighty power it may serve thee in more abundant freedom, and ever keep thy true religion whole and undefiled. Through.

May 31.

THE BLESSED VIRGIN MARY, QUEEN

Double of 2nd class.

Introit. Gaudeamus.

REJOICE we all in the Lord, keeping feast day in honour of the blessed Virgin Mary the Queen: in whose solemnity the Angels rejoice, and glorify the Son of God. (E.T. Alleluia, alleluia.) Ps. 45, 1. My heart is inditing of a good matter: I speak of the things which I have made unto the King. ℣. Glory.

Collect.

GRANT to us, we beseech thee, O Lord: that we, who celebrate the festival of the blessed Virgin Mary our Queen; being defended by her succour, may obtain peace in this world, and glory in that which is to come. Through.

And, in private Masses only, Commemoration is made of St. Petronilla, V.:

Collect.

GRACIOUSLY hear us, O God of our salvation: that, like as we do rejoice in the festival of blessed Petronilla thy Virgin; so we may learn to follow her example in godliness and charity. Through.

The Lesson from the book of Wisdom.

Ecclus. 24, 3, 6, 9-11, 22.

I CAME out of the mouth of the most High, the first-born before all creatures: I dwelt in high places, and my throne is in a cloudy pillar. In all the earth, and in every people and nation, I got a possession, and by my power I have trodden under foot the hearts of all both high and low. He that obeyeth me shall never be confounded, and they that work by me shall not do amiss; they that explain me shall have life everlasting.

Alleluia, alleluia. ℣. Blessed art thou, O Virgin Mary, who didst endure beneath the cross of the Lord. Alleluia. ℣. Now with him thou reignest for ever. Alleluia.

Outside Eastertide is said:

Gradual. Rev. 19, 16. He hath on his vesture and his thigh a name written: King of Kings, and Lord of lords. ℣. Ps. 45, 10. Upon his right hand doth stand the Queen in a vesture of gold of Ophir.

Alleluia, alleluia. ℣. Hail, Queen of mercy, do thou protect us from the enemy, and in the hour of death receive us. Alleluia.

✠ The Continuation of the holy Gospel according to Luke.

Luke 1, 26-33.

AT that time: The Angel Gabriel was sent from God unto a city of Galilee named Nazareth, to a Virgin espoused to a man whose name was Joseph, of the house of David, and the Virgin's name was Mary. And the Angel came in unto her, and said: Hail, full of grace; the Lord is with thee: blessed art thou among women. But she was troubled at the saying, and cast in her mind what manner of salutation this should be. And the Angel said unto her: Fear not, Mary, for thou hast found favour with God: and behold thou shalt conceive in thy womb, and bring forth a son, and shalt call his name Jesus. He shall be great, and shall be called the Son of the Highest, and the Lord God shall give unto him the throne of his father David: and he shall reign over the house of Jacob for ever, and of his kingdom there shall be no end. Creed.

Offertory. Sprung from the royal line, Mary shineth forth: through whose prayers we with heart and soul devoutly ask for succour. (E.T. Alleluia.)

Secret.

RECEIVE, we beseech thee, O Lord, the gifts of thy Church rejoicing: and, by the merits and intercession of the blessed Virgin Mary Queen, grant that they may avail to set forward our salvation. Through.

For St. Petronilla. Secret.

GRANT, O Lord, that like as thy dedicated people do acknowledge that in tribulation they have been succoured by the merits of thy Saints: so this oblation, which they offer unto thee in honour of the same, may be acceptable in thy sight. Through.

Preface of the B.V.Mary On the Festival.

Communion. Queen of the world most worthy, Mary evermore Virgin, intercede for our peace and salvation, thou who didst bring forth Christ the Lord, the Saviour of all. (E.T. Alleluia.)

Postcommunion.

O LORD, who hast given unto us to celebrate these sacred mysteries, which we have now performed, on the festival of holy Mary our Queen: we beseech thee; that as they are now fulfilled with gladness to her honour; so at her intercession they may be made profitable for the salvation of our souls. Through.

For St. Petronilla. Postcommunion.

O LORD, who hast satisfied this thy family with thy sacred gifts: we beseech thee; that we may at all times be comforted by the intercession of her whose festival we celebrate. Through.

FEASTS OF JUNE

June 1.

St. Angela Merici

Virgin

Double.

Introit. Ps. 45, 8. Dilexisti.

THOU hast loved righteousness, and hated iniquity: therefore God, even thy God, hath anointed thee with the oil of gladness above thy fellows. (E.T. Alleluia, alleluia.) Ps. ibid., 1. My heart is inditing of a good matter: I speak of the things which I have made unto the King. ℣. Glory.

Collect.

O GOD, who wast pleased that through blessed Angela a new company of holy Virgins should flourish in thy Church: grant us by her intercession so to live after the manner of Angels; that, renouncing all things earthly, we may be worthy to rejoice in everlasting felicity. Through.

The Lesson from the Epistle of blessed Paul the Apostle to the Corinthians.

II Cor. 10, 17-18; 11, 1-2.

BRETHREN: He that glorieth, let him glory in the Lord. For not he that commendeth himself is approved; but whom the Lord commendeth. Would to God ye could bear with me a little in my folly, and indeed bear with me: for I am jealous over you with godly jealousy. For I have espoused you to one husband, that I may present you as a chaste virgin to Christ.

Gradual. Ps. 45, 5. In thy comeliness and in thy beauty go forth, ride prosperously and reign. ℣. Because of the word of truth, of meekness, and righteousness: and thy right hand shall teach thee terrible things.

Alleluia, alleluia. ℣. Ibid., 15-16. The Virgins that be her fellows shall be brought unto the King: they that bear her company shall be brought unto thee with joy. Alleluia.

In Eastertide, in place of the Gradual is said:

Alleluia, alleluia. ℣. Ibid., 15-16. The Virgins that be her fellows shall be brought unto the King: they that bear her company shall be brought unto thee with joy. Alleluia. ℣. Ibid., 5. In thy comeliness and in thy beauty go forth, ride prosperously and reign. Alleluia.

✠ The Continuation of the holy Gospel according to Matthew.

Matt. 25, 1-13.

AT that time: Jesus spake this parable unto his disciples: The kingdom of heaven shall be likened unto ten virgins, which took their lamps, and went forth to meet the bridegroom. And five of them were wise, and five were foolish: they that were foolish took their lamps, and took no oil with them: but the wise took oil in their vessels with their lamps. While the bridegroom tarried, they all slumbered and slept. And at midnight there was a cry made: Behold, the bridegroom cometh; go ye out to meet him. Then all those virgins arose, and trimmed their lamps. And the foolish said unto the wise: Give us of your oil: for our lamps are gone out. But the wise answered, saying: Not so, lest there be not enough for us and you, but go ye rather to them that sell, and buy for yourselves. And while they went to buy the bridegroom came: and they that were ready went in with him to the marriage, and the door was shut. Afterward came also the other virgins, saying: Lord, Lord, open to us. But he answered and said: Verily I say unto you, I know you not. Watch therefore, for ye know neither the day nor the hour [wherein the Son of man cometh].

Offertory. Ps. 45, 10. Kings' daughters were among thy honourable women, upon thy right hand did stand the queen in a vesture of gold, wrought about with divers colours. (E.T. Alleluia.)

Secret.

LET this sacrifice, O Lord, which we offer unto thee in memory of blessed Angela, obtain for us the pardon of our iniquity and the bounteous gifts of thy grace. Through.

Communion. Matt. 25, 4 and 6. The five wise virgins took oil in their vessels with their lamps: and at midnight there was a cry made: Behold the bridegroom cometh: go ye out to meet Christ the Lord. (E.T. Alleluia.)

Postcommunion.

O LORD, who hast refreshed us with this heavenly food, we humbly beseech thee: that we, being cleansed through the prayers and example of blessed Angela from every stain of sin, may please thee both in body and soul. Through.

June 2.
For SS. Marcellinus, Peter, and Erasmus
Bishop, Martyrs

Out of Eastertide:

Introit. Ps. 34, 18. Clamaverunt.

THE righteous cry, and the Lord heareth them: and delivereth them out of all their troubles. Ps. ibid., 1. I will alway give thanks unto the Lord: his praise shall ever be in my mouth. ℣. Glory.

Collect.

O GOD, who makest us glad with the yearly solemnity of thy blessed Martyrs, Marcellinus, Peter, and Erasmus: grant, we beseech thee; that, as we do rejoice in their merits, so we may be enkindled by their example. Through.

The Epistle, I reckon that the sufferings, p. 473.

Gradual. Ps. 34, 18-19. The righteous cry, and the Lord heareth them: and delivereth them out of all their troubles. ℣. The Lord is nigh unto them that are of a contrite heart: and will save such as be of an humble spirit.

Alleluia, alleluia. ℣. John 15, 16. I have chosen you out of the world that ye should go and bring forth fruit; and that your fruit should remain. Alleluia.

The Gospel, When ye shall hear of wars, p. [10].

Offertory. Ps. 32, 11. Be glad, O ye righteous, and rejoice in the Lord: and be joyful, all ye that are true of heart.

Secret.

WE beseech thee, O Lord, that this sacrifice which we offer in remembrance of the birthday of thy holy Martyrs: may both loose the bonds of our iniquity, and obtain for us thy bounteous forgiveness. Through.

Communion. Wisd. 3, 1-3. The souls of the righteous are in the hand of God, and there shall no torment touch them: in the sight of the unwise they seemed to die, but they are in peace.

Postcommunion.

O LORD, who hast now fulfilled us with thy heavenly gifts, we humbly beseech thee: that we, who here do offer unto thee this service of our bounden duty; may thereby grow and increase to the attainment of everlasting salvation. Through.

In Eastertide the Mass Sancti tui, p. [17], with Prayers and Epistle as above, and after the Epistle is said:

Alleluia, alleluia. ℣. John 15, 16. I have chosen you out of the world, that ye should go and bring forth fruit; and that your fruit should remain. Alleluia. ℣. Ps. 116, 15. Right dear in the sight of the Lord is the death of his saints. Alleluia.

June 4.
St. Francis Caracciolo
Confessor
Double.

Introit. Ps. 22, 15; 69, 10. Factum est cor.

MY heart in the midst of my body is even like melting wax: for the zeal of thine house hath eaten me up. (E.T. Alleluia, alleluia.) Ps. 73, 1. Truly God is loving unto Israel: even unto such as are of a clean heart. ℣. Glory.

Collect.

O GOD, who didst choose blessed Francis to found a new order in thy Church, and didst adorn him with zeal for prayer and love of penance: grant that we thy servants may so profit by following his example; that praying continually and bringing our bodies into subjection, we may be found worthy to attain unto thy heavenly glory. Through.

The Lesson from the book of Wisdom.

Wisd. 4, 7-14.

THOUGH the righteous be prevented with death, yet shall he be in rest. For honourable age is not that which standeth in length of time, nor that is measured by number of years: but wisdom is the gray hair unto men, and an unspotted life is old age. He pleased God, and was beloved of him, so that living among sinners, he was translated. Yea, speedily was he taken away, lest that wickedness should alter his understanding, or deceit beguile his soul. For the bewitching of naughtiness doth obscure things that are honest, and the wandering of concupiscence doth undermine the simple mind. He, being made perfect in a short time, fulfilled a long time, for his soul pleased the Lord: therefore hasted he to take him away from among the wicked.

Gradual. Ps. 42, 1. Like as the hart desireth the waterbrooks: so longeth my soul after thee, O God. ℣. Ps. ibid., 2. My soul is athirst for God, yea, even for the living God.

Alleluia, alleluia. ℣. Ps. 73, 26. My flesh and my heart faileth: but God is the strength of my heart, and my portion for ever. Alleluia.

In Eastertide, in place of the Gradual, is said:

Alleluia, alleluia. ℣. Ps. 65, 5. Blessed is the man whom thou choosest, and receivest unto thee: he shall dwell in thy courts. Alleluia. ℣. Ps. 112, 9. He hath dispersed abroad and given to the poor: and his righteousness remaineth for ever. Alleluia.

✠ The Continuation of the holy Gospel according to Luke.

Luke 12, 35-40.

AT that time: Jesus said unto his disciples: Let your loins be girded about, and your lights burning, and ye yourselves like unto men that wait for their lord, when he will return from the wedding: that when he cometh and knocketh, they may open unto him immediately. Blessed are those servants, whom the lord when he cometh shall find watching: verily I say unto you, that he shall gird himself, and make them to sit down to meat, and will come forth and serve them. And if he shall come in the second watch, or come in the third watch, and find them so, blessed are those servants. And this know, that if the good man of the house had known what hour the thief would come, he would have watched, and not have suffered his house to be broken through. Be ye therefore ready also: for the Son of man cometh at an hour when ye think not.

Offertory. Ps. 92, 13. The righteous shall flourish like a palm-tree: and shall spread abroad like a cedar in Libanus. (E.T. Alleluia.)

Secret.

GRANT to us, most merciful Jesu: that we, recalling the glorious merits of blessed Francis, and being inflamed with that same fire of his charity, may be enabled worthily to draw near to this thy sacred table: Who livest and reignest with God the Father.

Communion. Ps. 31, 20. How plentiful is thy goodness, O Lord, which thou hast laid up for them that fear thee. (E.T. Alleluia.)

Postcommunion.

WE beseech thee, O Lord: that like as on the feast of blessed Francis we have offered this most holy sacrifice unto thy majesty; so both the thankful remembrance and the benefits of the same may evermore abide in our souls. Through.

June 5.

St. Boniface

Bishop and Martyr

Double.

Introit. Is. 65, 19 and 23. Exsultabo.

I WILL rejoice in Jerusalem, and joy in my people: and the voice of weeping shall be no more heard in her, nor the voice of crying. Mine elect shall not labour in vain, nor bring forth for trouble: for they are the seed of the blessed of the Lord, and their offspring with them. (E.T. Alleluia, alleluia.) Ps. 44, 2. We have heard with our ears, O God: our fathers have told us, what thou hast done in their time of old. V. Glory.

Collect.

O GOD, who by the labours of blessed Boniface, thy Martyr and Bishop, didst vouchsafe to call many nations to the knowledge of thy name: mercifully grant; that we who celebrate his festival may by his advocacy find favour in thy sight. Through.

The Lesson from the book of Wisdom.

Ecclus. 44, 1-15.

LET us now praise famous men, and our fathers that begat us. The Lord hath wrought great glory by them through his great power from the beginning. Such as did bear rule in their kingdoms, men renowned for their power, giving counsel by their understanding, and declaring prophecies, leaders of the people by their counsels, and by their knowledge of learning meet for the people, wise and eloquent in their instructions. Such as found out musical tunes, and recited verses in writing. Rich men furnished with ability: living peaceably in their habitations. All these were honoured in their generations, and were the glory of their times. There be of them, that have left a name behind them, that their praises might be reported. And some there be, which have no memorial: who are perished, as though they had never been: and are become as though they had never been born, and their children after them. But these were merciful men, whose righteousness hath not been forgotten: with their seed shall continually remain a good inheritance, and their children are within the covenant: their seed standeth fast, and their children for their sakes: their seed shall remain for ever, and their glory shall not be blotted out. Their bodies are buried in peace, but their name liveth for evermore. The people will tell of their wisdom, and the Church will shew forth their praise.

Gradual. I Peter 4, 13-14. Rejoice, inasmuch as ye are partakers of Christ's sufferings, that, when his glory shall be revealed, ye may be glad also with exceeding joy. V. If ye be reproached for the name of Christ, happy are ye: for the Spirit of glory and of God resteth upon you.

Alelluia, alleluia. V. Is. 66, 12. I will extend peace to her like a river, and glory like a flowing stream. Alleluia.

In Eastertide, in place of the Gradual, is said:

Alleluia, alleluia. V. Is. 66, 10 and 14. Rejoice ye with Jerusalem, and be glad with her, all ye that love the Lord. Alleluia. V. When ye see this, your heart shall rejoice: and the hand of the Lord shall be known toward his servants. Alleluia.

✠ The Continuation of the holy Gospel according to Matthew.

Matt. 5, 1-12.

AT that time: Jesus, seeing the multitudes, went up into a mountain, and when he was set, his disciples came unto him, and he opened his mouth, and taught them, saying: Blessed are the poor in spirit: for theirs is the kingdom of heaven. Blessed are they that mourn: for they shall be comforted. Blessed are the meek: for they shall inherit the earth. Blessed are they which do hunger and thirst after righteousness: for they shall be filled. Blessed are the merciful: for they shall obtain mercy. Blessed are the pure in heart: for they shall see God. Blessed are the peacemakers: for they shall be called the children of God. Blessed are they which are persecuted for righteousness' sake: for theirs is the kingdom of heaven. Blessed are ye, when men shall revile you, and persecute you, and shall say all manner of evil against you falsely for my sake: rejoice, and be exceeding glad, for great is your reward in heaven.

Offertory. Ps. 16, 7-8. I will thank the Lord for giving me warning: I have set God always before me, for he is on my right hand, therefore I shall not fall. (E.T. Alleluia.)

Secret.

LET the abundance of thy benediction, we beseech thee, O Lord, come down upon these our oblations: that by thy mercy it may work effectually to our sanctification; and make us to rejoice in the solemnity of holy Boniface, thy Martyr and Bishop. Through.

Communion. Rev. 3, 21. To him that overcometh will I grant to sit with me in my throne: even as I also overcame, and am set down with my Father in his throne. (E.T. Alleluia.)

Postcommunion.

O LORD, who hast sanctified us with these saving mysteries: we beseech thee; that as thou hast given us thy Martyr and Bishop, Saint Boniface, to be our advocate and guide, so he may continually intercede for us. Through.

June 6.

St. Norbert

Bishop and Confessor

Double.

The Mass Statuit, from the Common of a Confessor Bishop, p. [19], the Collect excepted:

Collect. P

O GOD, who didst endue thy blessed Confessor and Bishop Norbert, with singular grace to preach thy holy word, and through him didst enrich thy Church with a new family: grant, we beseech thee; that, by the intercession of his merits, we may through thine assistance be enabled to perform those things which he taught both by word and deed. Through.

Secret. C

WE beseech thee, O Lord, that we, remembering with gladness the merits of thy Saints: may in all places feel the succour of their intercession. Through.

Postcommunion. C

GRANT, we beseech thee, almighty God: that we, shewing forth our thankfulness for the gifts we have received, may, at the intercession of blessed Norbert, thy Confessor and Bishop, obtain yet more abundant mercies. Through.

June 9.

For SS. Primus and Felician

Martyrs

Out of Eastertide:

Introit. Ecclus. 44, 15 and 14. Sapientiam sanctorum.

LET the people tell of the wisdom of the Saints, and let the Church shew forth their praise: their names shall live for evermore. Ps. 33, 1. Rejoice in the Lord, O ye righteous: for it becometh well the just to be thankful. V. Glory.

Collect.

O LORD, we beseech thee, make us alway to observe the festival of thy holy Martyrs Primus and Felician: that through their prayers we may feel the effectual succour of thy protection. Through.

Epistle, But the righteous, p. [11].

Gradual. Ps. 89, 6 and 2. O Lord, the very heavens shall praise thy wondrous works: and thy truth in the congregation of the saints. V. My song shall be alway of the loving-kindness of the Lord: from one generation to another.

Alleluia, alleluia. V. This is the true brotherhood, which overcame the wickedness of the world: which followed Christ, gaining heaven's glorious realms. Alleluia.

Gospel, I thank thee, O Father, as on the Feast of St. Matthias, p. 606.

Offertory. Ps. 68, 36. God is wonderful in his holy ones: even the God of Israel, he will give strength and power unto his people: blessed be God, alleluia.

Secret.

O LORD, we beseech thee, let this oblation, now to be hallowed in celebration of the precious death of thy Martyrs, obtain for us thy favour: that we thy servants, being cleansed thereby from our iniquities, may offer prayers and supplications acceptable in thy sight. Through.

Communion. John 15, 16. I have chosen you out of the world, that ye should go and bring forth fruit, and that your fruit should remain.

Postcommunion.

WE beseech thee, almighty God: that this solemn festival of thy holy Martyrs Primus and Felician, which we have here celebrated in these heavenly mysteries, may obtain for us the abundance of thy mercy and forgiveness. Through.

¶ In Eastertide the Mass **Sancti tui**, p. [17] with Prayers and Gospel as above, and after the Epistle is said:

Alleluia, alleluia. V. This is the true brotherhood, which overcame the wickedness of the world: which followed Christ, gaining heaven's glorious realms. Alleluia. V. The noble army of Martyrs praise thee, O Lord. Alleluia.

In Scotland:

The same day, June 9.

St. Columba

Abbot

See Supplement.

June 10. (Scotland: Nov. 16.)

St. Margaret

Queen, Widow

Simple.

The Mass Cognovi, p. [36], the Collect excepted.

Collect.

O GOD, who didst render thy blessed Queen Margaret wondrous by reason of her singular charity toward the poor: grant; that, by her intercession and example, thy charity may continually increase within our hearts. Through.

Secret.

GRANT, O Lord, that like as thy faithful people do acknowledge that in tribulation they have been succoured by the merits of thy Saints: so this oblation, which they here do offer unto thee in honour of the same, may be acceptable in thy sight. Through.

Postcommunion.

O LORD, who hast satisfied this thy family with thy sacred gifts: we beseech thee that we may at all times be comforted by the intercession of her whose festival we celebrate. Through.

Scotland: The same day, June 10th: Feria.

June 11.

St. Barnabas the Apostle

Greater double.

Out of Eastertide:

Introit. Ps. 139, 17. Mihi autem.

RIGHT dear are thy friends unto me, O God, and held in highest honour: their rule and governance is exceeding steadfast. Ps. ibid., 1. O Lord, thou hast searched me out, and known me: thou knowest my down-sitting, and mine uprising. ℣. Glory.

Collect.

O LORD God almighty, who didst endue thy holy Apostle Barnabas with singular gifts of the Holy Ghost: leave us not, we beseech thee, destitute of thy manifold gifts; nor yet of grace to use them alway to thy honour and glory. Through... in the unity of the same Holy Ghost.

Or, Collect.

O GOD, who makest us to rejoice in the merits and intercession of thy blessed Apostle Barnabas: mercifully grant; that we who through him ask thy blessings, may obtain the bountiful gifts of thy grace. Through.

The Lesson from the Acts of the Apostles.

Acts 11, 22-30.

IN those days: Tidings of these things came unto the ears of the church which was in Jerusalem: and they sent forth Barnabas, that he should go as far as Antioch. Who, when he came, and had seen the grace of God, was glad: and exhorted them all, that with purpose of heart they would cleave unto the Lord: for he was a good man, and full of the Holy Ghost and of faith. And much people was added unto the Lord. Then departed Barnabas to Tarsus, for to seek Saul: and when he had found him, he brought him unto Antioch. And it came to pass, that a whole year they assembled themselves with the church: and taught much people, and the disciples were called Christians first in Antioch. And in these days came prophets from Jerusalem unto Antioch. And there stood up one of them named Agabus, and signified by the Spirit, that there should be great dearth throughout all the world: which came to pass in the days of Claudius Cæsar. Then the disciples, every man according to his ability, determined to send relief unto the brethren which dwelt in Judæa. Which also they did, and sent it to the elders by the hands of Barnabas and Saul.

Or:

The Lesson from the Acts of the Apostles.

Acts 11, 21-26; 13, 1-3.

IN those days: A great number believed at Antioch, and turned unto the Lord. Then tidings of these things came unto

Feasts of June (11)

the ears of the church which was in Jerusalem: and they sent forth Barnabas, that he should go as far as Antioch. Who, when he came, and had seen the grace of God, was glad, and exhorted them all, that with purpose of heart they would cleave unto the Lord. For he was a good man, and full of the Holy Ghost, and of faith. And much people was added unto the Lord. Then departed Barnabas to Tarsus, for to seek Saul: and when he had found him, he brought him unto Antioch. And it came to pass, that a whole year they assembled themselves with the church and taught much people, and the disciples were called Christians first in Antioch. Now there were in the church that was at Antioch certain prophets and teachers, as Barnabas, and Simeon that was called Niger, and Lucius of Cyrene, and Manaen, which had been brought up with Herod the tetrarch, and Saul. As they ministered to the Lord, and fasted, the Holy Ghost said: Separate me Barnabas and Saul for the work whereunto I have called them. And when they had fasted and prayed, and laid their hands on them, they sent them away.

Gradual. Ps. 19, 5 and 2. Their sound is gone out into all lands: and their words into the ends of the world. ℣. The heavens declare the glory of God: and the firmament sheweth his handy-work.

Alleluia, alleluia. ℣. John 15, 16. I have chosen you out of the world, that ye should go and bring forth fruit: and that your fruit should remain. Alleluia.

✠ The Continuation of the holy Gospel according to John.

John 15, 12-16.

AT that time: Jesus said unto his disciples: This is my commandment, That ye love one another, as I have loved you. Greater love hath no man than this, that a man lay down his life for his friends. Ye are my friends, if ye do whatsoever I command you. Henceforth I call you not servants; for the servant knoweth not what his lord doeth: but I have called you friends; for all things that I have heard of my Father I have made known unto you. Ye have not chosen me, but I have chosen you, and ordained you, that ye should go and bring forth fruit, and that your fruit should remain: that whatsoever ye shall ask of the Father in my name, he may give it you. Creed.

Or:

✠ The Continuation of the holy Gospel according to Matthew.

Matt. 10, 16-22.

AT that time: Jesus said unto his disciples: Behold, I send you forth as sheep in the midst of wolves. Be ye therefore wise as serpents, and harmless as doves. But beware of men. For they will deliver you up to the councils, and they will scourge you in their synagogues: and ye shall be brought before governors and kings for my sake, for a testimony against them and the Gentiles. But when they deliver you up, take no thought how or what ye shall speak: for it shall be given you in that same hour what ye shall speak. For it is not ye that speak, but the Spirit of your Father which speaketh in you. And the brother shall deliver up the brother to death, and the father the child: and the children shall rise up against their parents, and cause them to be put to death: and ye shall be hated of all men for my name's sake: but he that endureth to the end shall be saved. Creed.

Offertory. Ps. 45, 17-18. Thou shalt make them princes in all lands: they shall remember thy name, O Lord, from one generation to another.

Secret.

SANCTIFY, O Lord, the gifts which we here offer: and, at the intercession of thy blessed Apostle Barnabas, cleanse us thereby from the defilements of our iniquities. Through.

Preface of the Apostles.

Communion. Matt. 19, 28. Ye which have followed me shall sit upon thrones, judging the twelve tribes of Israel.

Postcommunion.

WE humbly beseech thee, almighty God: that, as thou dost refresh us with thy sacraments, so, at the intercession of thy blessed Apostle Barnabas, thou wouldest vouchsafe unto us to do thee worthy and acceptable service. Through.

¶ If this Feast is celebrated in Eastertide, the Mass Protexisti, p. [15], is said, with the foregoing Prayers, Epistle, and Gospel.

June 12.

St. John of San Facundo

Confessor

Double.

Introit. Ps. 37, 30-31. Os justi.

THE mouth of the righteous is exercised in wisdom: and his tongue will be talking of judgment: the law of his God is in his heart. Ps. ibid., 1. Fret not thyself because of the ungodly: neither be thou envious against the evildoers. ℣. Glory.

Collect.

O GOD, the author of peace and lover of concord, who didst endue blessed John thy Confessor with wondrous grace for the reconciling of foes: grant by his merits and intercession; that we, being stablished in thy love, may not by any temptations be separated from thee. Through.

And Commemoration is made of SS. Basilides, Cyrinus, Nabor and Nazarius, MM.

Collect.

WE beseech thee, O Lord, cast thy bright beams of light on us thy servants, who celebrate this day the heavenly birth of the holy Martyrs Basilides, Cyrinus, Nabor and Nazarius: that as their everlasting excellence hath won for them thy glory; so through our devout observance they may more abundantly be made partakers of the same. Through.

The Lesson from the book of Wisdom.

Ecclus. 31, 8-11.

BLESSED is the man that is found without blemish: and hath not gone after gold. Who is he, and we will call him blessed? for wonderful things hath he done among his people. Who hath been tried thereby, and found perfect? then let him glory. Who might offend, and hath not offended? or done evil, and hath not done it? His goods shall be established, and the congregation shall declare his alms.

Gradual. Ps. 92, 13-14. The righteous shall flourish like a palm-tree: and shall spread abroad like a cedar in Libanus in the house of the Lord. ℣. Ibid., 3. To tell of thy loving kindness early in the morning, and of thy truth in the night-season.

Alleluia, alleluia. ℣. James 1, 12. Blessed is the man that endureth temptation: for when he is tried, he shall receive the crown of life. Alleluia.

☩ The Continuation of the holy Gospel according to Luke.

Luke 12, 35-40.

AT that time: Jesus said unto his disciples: Let your loins be girded about, and your lights burning, and ye yourselves like unto men that wait for their lord, when he will return from the wedding: that when he cometh and knocketh, they may open unto him immediately. Blessed are those servants, whom the lord when he cometh shall find watching: verily I say unto you, that he shall gird himself, and make them to sit down to meat, and will come forth and serve them. And if he shall come in the second watch, or come in the third watch, and find them so, blessed are those servants. And this know, that if the good man of the house had known what hour the thief would come, he would have watched, and not have suffered his house to be broken through. Be ye therefore ready also: for the Son of man cometh at an hour when ye think not.

Offertory. Ps. 89, 25. My truth and my mercy shall be with him: and in my name shall his horn be exalted.

Secret.

WE offer thee, O Lord, this our sacrifice of praise to the honour of thy Saints: whereby we trust to be delivered from all evils both in this life and in that which is to come. Through.

For the Martyrs. Secret.

WE offer unto thee, O Lord, this our sacrifice, and tell forth thy marvellous works, as we commemorate the shedding of the blood of thy Saints Basilides, Cyrinus, Nabor and Nazarius: whereby their glorious victory was made perfect. Through.

Communion. Matt. 24, 46-47. Blessed is the servant whom his lord when he cometh shall find watching: verily I say unto you, he shall make him ruler over all his goods.

Postcommunion.

O LORD our God, who hast refreshed us with heavenly meat and drink, we humbly beseech thee: that we may be defended by the prayers of him in whose memory we have received the same. Through.

For the Martyrs. Postcommunion.

GRANT, we beseech thee, O Lord: that as we continually celebrate the festival of thy holy Martyrs Basilides, Cyrinus, Nabor and Nazarius; so we may at all times know the succour of their intercession. Through.

June 13.

St. Antony of Padua

Confessor and Doctor of the Church

Double.

Introit. Ecclus. 15, 5. In medio.

IN the midst of the Church he opened his mouth: and the Lord filled him with the spirit of wisdom and understanding: he clothed him with a robe of glory. Ps. 92. 1. It is a good thing to give thanks unto the Lord: and to sing praises unto thy name, O most Highest. ℣. Glory.

Collect.

GRANT, O God, that the solemn festival of thy blessed Confessor and Doctor Antony may bring gladness to thy Church: that, being ever defended by thy succour in all things spiritual, it may attain unto everlasting felicity. Through.

The Lesson from the Epistle of blessed Paul the Apostle to Timothy.

II Tim. 4, 1-8.

DEARLY beloved: I charge thee before God, and the Lord Jesus Christ, who shall judge the quick and the dead at his appearing and his kingdom: preach the word, be instant in season, out of season: reprove, rebuke, exhort with all longsuffering and doctrine. For the time will come when they will not endure sound doctrine, but after their own lusts shall they heap to themselves teachers, having itching ears, and they shall turn away their ears from the truth, and shall be turned unto fables. But watch thou in all things, endure afflictions, do the work of an Evangelist, make full proof of thy ministry. For I am now ready to be offered, and the time of my departure is at hand. I have fought a good fight, I have finished my course, I have kept the faith. Henceforth there is laid up for me a crown of righteousness, which the Lord, the righteous judge, shall give me at that day: and not to me only, but unto all them also that love his appearing.

Gradual. Ps. 37, 30-31. The mouth of the righteous is exercised in wisdom, and his tongue will be talking of judgment. ℣. The law of his God is in his heart: and his goings shall not slide.

Alleluia, alleluia. ℣. Ecclus. 45, 9. The Lord loved him, and adorned him: he clothed him with a robe of glory. Alleluia.

☩ The Continuation of the holy Gospel according to Matthew.

Matt. 5, 13-19.

AT that time: Jesus said unto his disciples: Ye are the salt of the earth. But if the salt have lost his savour, wherewith shall it be salted? It is thenceforth good for nothing, but to be cast out, and to be trodden under foot of men. Ye are the light of the world. A city that is set on an hill cannot be hid. Neither do men light a candle, and put it under a bushel, but on a candlestick, and it giveth light unto all that are in the house. Let your light so shine before men, that they may see your good works, and glorify your Father which is in heaven. Think not that I am come to destroy the law or the prophets: I am not come to destroy, but to fulfil. For verily I say unto you, Till heaven and earth pass, one jot or one tittle shall in no wise pass from the law, till all be fulfilled. Whosoever therefore shall break one of these least commandments, and shall teach men so, he shall be called the least in the kingdom of heaven: but whosoever shall do and teach them, the same shall be called great in the kingdom of heaven. Creed.

Offertory. Ps. 92, 13. The righteous shall flourish like a palm-tree: and shall spread abroad like a cedar in Libanus.

Secret.

LET this present oblation, O Lord, avail for the salvation of thy people: for whom thou didst vouchsafe to offer thyself a living sacrifice unto thy Father: Who livest and reignest with the same God the Father and the Holy Ghost God, throughout all ages, world without end. Amen.

Communion. Luke 12, 42. A faithful and wise servant, whom his lord hath made ruler over his household: to give them their portion of meat in due season.

Postcommunion.

O LORD, who hast satisfied us with thy heavenly gifts: we beseech thee; that by the merits and intercession of blessed Antony thy Confessor and Doctor this sacrifice may effectually work in us to our salvation. Through.

June 14.

St. Basil

Bishop, Confessor and Doctor
of the Church

Double.

Introit. Ecclus. 15, 5. In medio.

IN the midst of the Church he opened his mouth: and the Lord filled him with the spirit of wisdom and understanding: he clothed him with a robe of glory. Ps. 92, 1. It is a good thing to give thanks unto the Lord: and to sing praises unto thy name, O Most Highest. ℣. Glory.

Collect.

WE beseech thee, O Lord, graciously to hear the prayers which we offer unto thee on this feast of blessed Basil, thy Confessor and Bishop: that, like as he was found worthy to do thee faithful service, so by his merits and intercession we may be absolved from all our sins. Through.

The Lesson from the Epistle of blessed Paul the Apostle to Timothy.

II Tim. 4, 1-8.

DEARLY beloved: I charge thee before God, and the Lord Jesus Christ, who shall judge the quick and the dead at his appearing and his kingdom: preach the word, be instant in season, out of season: reprove, rebuke, exhort with all longsuffering and doctrine. For the time will come when they will not endure sound doctrine, but after their own lusts shall they heap to themselves teachers, having itching ears, and they shall turn away their ears from the truth, and shall be turned unto fables. But watch thou in all things, endure afflictions, do the work of an Evangelist, make full proof of thy ministry. For I am now ready to be offered, and the time of my departure is at hand. I have fought a good fight, I have finished my course, I have kept the faith. Henceforth there is laid up for me a crown of righteousness, which the Lord, the righteous judge, shall give me at that day: and not to me only, but unto all them also that love his appearing.

Gradual. Ps. 37, 30-31. The mouth of the righteous is exercised in wisdom, and his tongue will be talking of judgment. ℣. The law of his God is in his heart: and his goings shall not slide.

Alleluia, alleluia. ℣. Ps. 89, 21. I have found David my servant, with my holy oil have I anointed him. Alleluia.

✠ The Continuation of the holy Gospel according to Luke.

Luke 14, 26-35.

AT that time: Jesus said unto the multitudes: If any man come to me, and hate not his father, and mother, and wife and children, and brethren, and sisters, yea, and his own life also, he cannot be my disciple. And whosoever doth not bear his cross, and come after me, cannot be my disciple. For which of you, intending to build a tower, sitteth not down first, and counteth the cost, whether he have sufficient to finish it; lest haply, after he hath laid the foundation, and is not able to finish it, all that behold it begin to mock him, saying: This man began to build, and was not able to finish? Or what king, going to make war against another king, sitteth not down first, and consulteth whether he be able with ten thousand to meet him that cometh against him with twenty thousand? Or else while the other is yet a great way off, he sendeth an ambassage, and desireth conditions of peace. So likewise, whosoever he be of you that forsaketh not all that he hath, he cannot be my disciple. Salt is good. But if the salt have lost his savour, wherewith shall it be seasoned? It is neither fit for the land, nor yet for the dung-hill, but men cast it out. He that hath ears to hear, let him hear. Creed.

Offertory. Ps. 89, 25. My truth and my mercy shall be with him: and in my name shall his horn be exalted.

Secret.

WE beseech thee, O Lord, that our devout observance of this yearly festival of thy Confessor and Bishop, Saint Basil, may render us acceptable unto thy loving kindness: that through this oblation of our bounden duty and service he may win the reward of everlasting felicity, and obtain for us the gifts of thy grace. Through.

Communion. Luke 12, 42. A faithful and wise servant, whom his lord hath made ruler over his household: to give them their portion of meat in due season.

Postcommunion.

O GOD, who rewardest the souls of them that put their trust in thee: vouchsafe; that we, who keep the solemn festival of thy blessed Confessor and Bishop Basil, may by his prayers obtain thy merciful pardon. Through.

June 15.

For SS. Vitus, Modestus and Crescentia

Martyrs

Introit. Ps. 34, 20-21. Multæ tribulationes.

GREAT are the troubles of the righteous, but the Lord delivereth him out of all: he keepeth all his bones: so that not one of them is broken. Ps. ibid., 1. I will always give thanks unto the Lord: his praise shall ever be in my mouth. ℣. Glory.

Collect.

GRANT, O Lord, we beseech thee, that, at the intercession of thy holy Martyrs, Vitus, Modestus, and Crescentia, thy Church, being not highminded, may serve and please thee in lowliness of heart: and, despising all things evil, may in freedom and charity perform such things as be right. Through.

The Epistle, The souls of the righteous, p. [9].

Gradual. Ps. 149, 5 and 1. Let the Saints be joyful with glory: let them rejoice in their beds. ℣. O sing unto the Lord a new song: let the congregation of saints praise him.

Alleluia, alleluia. ℣. Ps. 145, 10-11. Thy Saints shall give thanks unto thee, O Lord: they shew the glory of thy kingdom. Alleluia.

✠ The Continuation of the holy Gospel according to Luke.

Luke 10, 16-20.

AT that time: Jesus said unto his disciples: He that heareth you heareth me: and he that despiseth you despiseth me. And he that despiseth me despiseth him that sent me. And the seventy returned again with joy, saying: Lord, even the devils are subject unto us through thy name. And he said unto them: I beheld Satan as lightning fall from heaven. Behold, I give unto you power to tread on serpents and scorpions, and over all the power of the enemy: and nothing shall by any means hurt you. Notwithstanding in this rejoice not, that the spirits are subject unto you: but rather rejoice, because your names are written in heaven.

Offertory. Ps. 68, 36. God is wonderful in his holy ones: even the God of Israel, he will give strength and power unto his people: blessed be God.

Secret.

O LORD, forasmuch as the gifts which we offer for the honour of thy Saints do shew forth the glory of thy power: so let them achieve in us the effects of thy salvation. Through.

Communion. Wisd. 3, 1-3. The souls of the righteous are in the hand of God, and there shall no torment touch them: in the sight of the unwise they seemed to die, but they are in peace.

Postcommunion.

O LORD, who hast fulfilled us with thy heavenly benediction: we beseech thee; that, through the intercession of thy holy Martyrs Vitus, Modestus and Crescentia, this Sacrament may be profitable for our healing both in body and soul. Through.

June 18.

St. Ephraem Syrus

Deacon, Confessor and Doctor of the Church.

Double.

Introit. Ecclus. 15, 5. In medio.

IN the midst of the Church he opened his mouth: and the Lord filled him with the spirit of wisdom and understanding: he clothed him with a robe of glory. Ps. 92, 1. It is a good thing to give thanks unto the Lord: and to sing praises unto thy name, O most Highest. ℣. Glory.

Collect.

O GOD, who didst vouchsafe to enlighten thy Church with the wondrous learning and glorious merits of thy blessed Confessor and Doctor Ephraem: we humbly beseech thee; that at his intercession thou wouldest defend it by thy continual power against the snares of error and wickedness. Through.

And Commemoration is made of SS. Marcus and Marcellianus, MM.

Collect.

GRANT, we beseech thee, almighty God, that we, who observe the heavenly birthday of thy holy Martyrs Marcus and Marcellianus; may by their intercession be delivered from all evils that beset us. Through.

The Lesson from the Epistle of blessed Paul the Apostle to Timothy.

II Tim. 4, 1-8.

DEARLY beloved: I charge thee before God, and the Lord Jesus Christ, who shall judge the quick and the dead at his appearing and his kingdom: preach the word, be instant in season, out of season: reprove, rebuke, exhort with all longsuffering and doctrine. For the time will come when they will not endure sound doctrine, but after their own lusts shall they heap to themselves teachers, having itching ears, and they shall turn away their ears from the truth, and shall be turned unto fables. But watch thou in all things, endure afflictions, do the work of an Evangelist, make full proof of thy ministry. For I am now ready to be offered, and the time of my departure is at hand. I have fought a good fight, I have finished my course, I have kept the faith. Henceforth there is laid up for me a crown of righteousness, which the Lord, the righteous judge, shall give me at that day: and not to me only, but unto all them also that love his appearing.

Gradual. Ps. 37, 30-31. The mouth of the righteous is exercised in wisdom, and his tongue will be talking of judgment. ℣. The law of his God is in his heart: and his goings shall not slide.

Alleluia, alleluia. ℣. Ecclus. 45, 9. The Lord loved him, and adorned him: he clothed him with a robe of glory. Alleluia.

✠ The Continuation of the holy Gospel according to Matthew.

Matt. 5, 13-19.

AT that time: Jesus said unto his disciples: Ye are the salt of the earth. But if the salt have lost his savour, wherewith shall it be salted? It is thenceforth good for nothing, but to be cast out, and to be trodden under foot of men. Ye are the light of the world. A city that is set on an hill cannot be hid. Neither do men light a candle, and put it under a bushel, but on a candlestick, and it giveth light unto all that are in the house. Let your light so shine before men, that they may see your good works, and glorify your Father which is in heaven. Think not that I am come to destroy the law or the prophets: I am not come to destroy, but to fulfil. For verily I say unto you, Till heaven and earth pass, one jot or one tittle shall in no wise pass from the law, till all be fulfilled. Whosoever therefore shall break one of these least commandments, and shall teach men so, he shall be called the least in the kingdom of heaven: but whosoever shall do and teach them, the same shall be called great in the kingdom of heaven. Creed.

Offertory. Ps. 92, 13. The righteous shall flourish like a palm-tree: and shall spread abroad like a cedar in Libanus.

Secret.

MAY the devout prayers of thy Confessor and Doctor, Saint Ephraem, continually succour us, O Lord: that they may render our oblations acceptable in thy sight; and ever obtain for us thy merciful pardon. Through.

For the Martyrs. Secret.

SANCTIFY, O Lord, these our oblations which we present unto thee: that, at the intercession of thy holy Martyrs Marcus and Marcellianus, they may obtain for us thy gracious favour. Through.

Communion. Luke 12, 42. A faithful and wise servant, whom his lord hath made ruler over his household: to give them their portion of meat in due season.

Postcommunion.

WE beseech thee, O Lord, that blessed Ephraem, thy Confessor and most excellent Doctor, may ever stand before thee as our advocate: that this sacrifice of thine ordinance may effectually avail for our salvation. Through.

For the Martyrs. Postcommunion.

O LORD, who hast satisfied us with the gifts of thy salvation, we humbly beseech thee: that as we rejoice in the partaking of the same; so, at the intercession of thy holy Martyrs, Marcus and Marcellianus, our souls may be effectually renewed. Through.

June 19.

St. Juliana de Falconeri

Virgin.

Double.

Introit. Ps. 45, 8. Dilexisti.

THOU hast loved righteousness, and hated iniquity: therefore God, even thy God, hath anointed thee with the oil of gladness above thy fellows. Ps. ibid., 1. My heart is inditing of a good matter: I speak of the things which I have made unto the King. ℣. Glory.

Collect.

O GOD, who in the extremity of her sickness didst wondrously refresh thy blessed Virgin Juliana with the precious Body of thy Son: grant, we beseech thee; that by her merits and intercession, we also in the agony of death, being refreshed and strengthened by the same, may attain in safety to our heavenly country. Through.

Feasts of June (19)

And Commemoration is made of SS. Gervasius and Protasius, MM.

Collect.

O GOD, who makest us glad with the yearly solemnity of thy holy Martyrs Gervasius and Protasius: mercifully grant; that like as we do rejoice in their merits, so we may be enkindled by their example. Through.

The Lesson from the Epistle of blessed Paul the Apostle to the Corinthians.

II Cor. 10, 17-18; 11, 1-2.

BRETHREN: He that glorieth, let him glory in the Lord. For not he that commendeth himself is approved; but whom the Lord commendeth. Would to God ye could bear with me a little in my folly, and indeed bear with me: for I am jealous over you with godly jealousy. For I have espoused you to one husband, that I may present you as a chaste virgin to Christ.

Gradual. Ps. 45, 5. In thy comeliness and in thy beauty go forth, ride prosperously and reign. ℣. Because of the word of truth, of meekness, and righteousness: and thy right hand shall teach thee terrible things.

Alleluia, alleluia. ℣. Ibid., 15-16. The Virgins that be her fellows shall be brought unto the King: they that bear her company shall be brought unto thee with joy. Alleluia.

☩ The Continuation of the holy Gospel according to Matthew.

Matt. 25, 1-13.

AT that time: Jesus spake this parable unto his disciples: The kingdom of heaven shall be likened unto ten virgins, which took their lamps, and went forth to meet the bridegroom. And five of them were wise, and five were foolish: they that were foolish took their lamps, and took no oil with them: but the wise took oil in their vessels with their lamps. While the bridegroom tarried, they all slumbered and slept. And at midnight there was a cry made: Behold, the bridegroom cometh; go ye out to meet him. Then all those virgins arose, and trimmed their lamps. And the foolish said unto the wise: Give us of your oil: for our lamps are gone out. But the wise answered, saying: Not so, lest there be not enough for us and you, but go ye rather to them that sell, and buy for yourselves. And while they went to buy, the bridegroom came: and they that were ready went in with him to the marriage, and the door was shut. Afterward came also the other virgins, saying: Lord, Lord, open to us. But he answered and said: Verily I say unto you, I know you not. Watch therefore, for ye know neither the day nor the hour* [wherein the Son of man cometh].

Offertory. Ps. 45, 10. Kings' daughters were among thy honourable women, upon thy right hand did stand the queen in a vesture of gold, wrought about with divers colours.

Secret.

GRANT, O Lord, that like as thy dedicated people do acknowledge that in tribulation they have been succoured by the merits of thy Saints: so this oblation, which they offer unto thee in honour of the same, may be acceptable in thy sight. Through.

For the Martyrs.   Secret.

WE beseech thee, O Lord, mercifully to accept these our oblations: that at the intercession of thy holy Martyrs Gervasius and Protasius we may be defended against all adversities. Through.

Communion. Matt. 25, 4 and 6. The five wise virgins took oil in their vessels with their lamps: and at midnight there was a cry made: Behold the bridegroom cometh: go ye out to meet Christ the Lord.

Postcommunion.

O LORD, who hast satisfied this thy family with thy sacred gifts: we beseech thee; that we may at all times be comforted by the intercession of her whose festival we celebrate. Through.

For the Martyrs. Postcommunion.

O LORD, let this holy Communion cleanse us from every guilty stain: that at the intercession of thy holy Martyrs Gervasius and Protasius we may thereby be made partakers of thy healing unto life eternal. Through.

June 20.

For St. Silverius

Pope and Martyr

The Mass Si diligis me, p. [2].

Collect. C 1

O EVERLASTING Shepherd, look down in mercy on thy flock: and as thou didst choose blessed Silverius, thy Martyr and Chief Bishop, to be pastor and ruler of thy Church; so at his intercession defend it with thy continual protection. Through.

Secret. C 1

WE beseech thee, O Lord, graciously enlighten thy Church by the gifts which we here offer: that in every place thy flock may increase and prosper, and the shepherds by thy governance may be made pleasing to thy name. Through.

Postcommunion. C 1

MERCIFUL Lord, we beseech thee to govern and preserve thy Church, which thou hast here refreshed with heavenly food: that by the guiding of thy mighty power it may serve thee in more abundant freedom, and ever keep thy true religion whole and undefiled. Through.

June 21.

St. Aloysius Gonzaga

Confessor

Double.

Introit. Ps. 8, 6. Minuisti.

THOU madest him a little lower than the Angels: to crown him with glory and worship. Ps. 148, 2. Praise the Lord, all ye Angels of his: praise him, all his host. ℣. Glory.

Collect.

O GOD, the giver of all heavenly gifts, who in the angelic youth of Aloysius didst unite a wondrous innocency of life unto a wondrous penitence: grant by his merits and prayers; that though we have not followed him in his innocence; yet we may imitate his penitence. Through.

The Lesson from the book of Wisdom.

Ecclus. 31, 8-11.

BLESSED is the man that is found without blemish, and hath not gone after gold. Who is he, and we will call him blessed? for wonderful things hath he done among his people. Who hath been tried thereby, and found perfect? then let him glory. Who might offend, and hath not offended? or done evil, and hath not done it? His goods shall be established in the Lord.

Gradual. Ps. 71, 5-6. Thou, O Lord, art my hope, even from my youth: through thee have I been holden up ever since I was born: thou art he that took me out of my mother's womb. V. Ps. 41, 13. And because of my innocence thou hast received me: and hast set me before thy face for ever.

Alleluia, alleluia. V. Ps. 65, 5. Blessed is the man whom thou choosest and receivest unto thee: he shall dwell in thy courts. Alleluia.

✠ The Continuation of the holy Gospel according to Matthew.

Matt. 22, 29-40.

AT that time: Jesus answered and said unto the Sadducees: Ye do err, not knowing the Scriptures, nor the power of God. For in the resurrection they neither marry, nor are given in marriage: but are as the Angels of God in heaven. But as touching the resurrection of the dead, have ye not read that which was spoken unto you by God, saying: I am the God of Abraham, and the God of Isaac, and the God of Jacob? God is not the God of the dead, but of the living. And when the multitude heard this, they were astonished at his doctrine. But when the Pharisees had heard that he had put the Sadducees to silence, they were gathered together: then one of them, which was a lawyer, asked him a question, tempting him, and saying: Master, which is the great commandment in the law? Jesus said unto him: Thou shalt love the Lord thy God with all thy heart, and with all thy soul, and with all thy mind. This is the first and great commandment. And the second is like unto it: Thou shalt love thy neighbour as thyself. On these two commandments hang all the law and the Prophets.

Offertory. Ps. 24, 3-4. Who shall ascend into the hill of the Lord, or who shall rise up in his holy place? Even he that hath clean hands, and a pure heart.

Secret.

GRANT, O Lord, that we may sit down at the heavenly banquet clothed in the wedding-garment: which the devout preparation and continual tears of blessed Aloysius did adorn with pearls of inestimable price. Through.

Communion. Ps. 78, 24-25. He gave them food from heaven: so man did eat Angels' food.

Postcommunion.

GRANT, O Lord, that we, who have been nourished with the bread of Angels, may likewise live after the likeness of thine Angels: that, by the example of him whom we this day do honour, we may stedfastly continue in thanksgiving for the same. Through.

In England and Wales:

June 22.

St. Alban

First Martyr of Britain

See Supplement.

Elsewhere:

The same day, June 22.

St. Paulinus

Bishop and Confessor

Double.

Introit. Ps. 132, 9-10. Sacerdotes tui.

LET thy priests, O Lord, be clothed with righteousness, and let thy saints sing with joyfulness: for thy servant David's sake, turn not away the presence of thine anointed. Ps. ibid., 1. Lord, remember David, and all his trouble. V Glory.

Collect.

O GOD, who unto them that leave all things in this world for thee hast promised an hundred-fold and life eternal in the world to come: mercifully grant; that, following in the footsteps of thy holy Bishop Paulinus, we may be enabled to despise things earthly and to desire only those things that are heavenly: Who livest and reigneth with God the Father.

The Lesson from the Epistle of blessed Paul the Apostle to the Corinthians.

II Cor. 8, 9-15.

BRETHREN: Ye know the grace of our Lord Jesus Christ, that, though he was rich, yet for your sake he became poor, that ye through his poverty might be rich. And herein I give my advice: for this is expedient for you, who have begun before, not only to do, but also to be forward a year ago: now therefore perform the doing of it: that as there was a readiness to will, so there may be a performance also out of that which ye have. For if there be first a willing mind, it is accepted according to that a man hath, and not according to that he hath not. For I mean not that other men be eased, and ye burdened, but by an equality. That now at this time your abundance may be a supply for their want: that their abundance also may be a supply for your want, that there may be equality, as it is written: He that had gathered much had nothing over: and he that had gathered little had no lack.

Gradual. Ecclus. 44, 16. Behold a great priest who in his days pleased God. ℣. Ibid. There was none found like unto him, to keep the law of the Most High.

Alleluia, alleluia. ℣. Ps. 110, 4. Thou art a priest for ever after the order of Melchisedech. Alleluia.

✠ The Continuation of the holy Gospel according to Luke.

Luke 12, 32-34.

AT that time: Jesus said unto his disciples: Fear not, little flock, for it is your Father's good pleasure to give you the kingdom. Sell that ye have, and give alms. Provide yourselves bags which wax not old, a treasure in the heavens that faileth not: where no thief approacheth, neither moth corrupteth. For where your treasure is, there will your heart be also.

Offertory. Ps. 89, 21-22. I have found David my servant, with my holy oil have I anointed him: my hand shall hold him fast, and my arm shall strengthen him.

Secret.

GRANT, O Lord, that, following the example of thy holy Bishop Paulinus, we may join the sacrifice of perfect charity to the oblation of the altar: and by zeal in well-doing be found worthy of thine everlasting mercy. Through.

Communion. Luke 12, 42. A faithful and wise servant whom his lord hath made ruler over his household, to give them their portion of meat in due season.

Postcommunion.

GRANT us, O Lord, through these sacred mysteries that love of godliness and humility which thy holy Bishop Paulinus drew from this fount of heavenly blessing: and at his intercession pour forth on all who call upon thee the riches of thy bounteous grace. Through.

June 23.

Vigil of the Nativity of St. John Baptist

Introit. Luke 1, 13, 15 and 14. Ne timeas.

FEAR not, Zacharias, thy prayer is heard: and thy wife Elisabeth shall bear thee a son, and thou shalt call his name John: he shall be great in the sight of the Lord: and shall be filled with the Holy Ghost, even from his mother's womb: and many shall rejoice at his birth. Ps. 21, 1. The just shall rejoice in thy strength, O Lord: exceeding glad shall he be of thy salvation. ℣. Glory.

Glória in excélsis is not said.

Collect.

GRANT, we beseech thee, almighty God: that we thy family may ever walk in the way of salvation; and, following the teachings of blessed John the Forerunner, may attain in safety unto him whom he foretold, even Jesus Christ thy Son our Lord: Who liveth.

The Lesson from the Prophet Jeremiah.

Jer. 1, 4-10.

IN those days: The word of the Lord came unto me, saying: Before I formed thee in the belly I knew thee: and before thou camest forth out of the womb, I sanctified thee, and I ordained thee a prophet unto the nations. Then said I: Ah, Lord God: behold, I cannot speak, for I am a child. But the Lord said unto me: Say not: I am a child; for thou shalt go to all that I shall send thee: and whatsoever I command thee thou shalt speak. Be not afraid of their faces: for I am with thee to deliver thee, saith the Lord. Then the Lord put forth his hand, and touched my mouth: and the Lord said unto me: Behold, I have put my words in thy mouth; see, I have this day set thee over the nations and over the kingdoms, to root out, and to pull down, and to destroy, and to throw down, to build, and to plant: saith the Lord almighty.

Gradual. John 1, 6-7. There was a man sent from God, whose name was John. ℣. The same came to bear witness of the light, to make ready a people prepared for the Lord.

✠ The Beginning of the holy Gospel according to Luke.

Luke 1, 5-17.

THERE was in the days of Herod, the king of Judæa, a certain priest named Zacharias, of the course of Abia, and his wife was of the daughters of Aaron, and her name was Elisabeth. And they were both righteous before God, walking in all the commandments and ordinances of the Lord blameless, and they had no child, because that Elisabeth was barren, and they both were now well stricken in years. And it came to pass that while he executed the priest's office before God in the order of his course according to the custom of the priest's office, his lot was to burn incense when he went into the temple of the Lord: and the whole multitude of the people were praying without at the time of incense. And there appeared unto him an Angel of the Lord standing on the right side of the altar of incense. And when Zacharias saw him, he was troubled, and fear fell upon him. But the Angel said unto him: Fear not, Zacharias, for thy prayer is heard: and thy wife Elisabeth shall bear thee a son, and thou shalt call his name John: and thou shalt have joy and gladness, and many shall rejoice at his birth: for he shall be great in the sight of the Lord: and shall drink neither wine nor strong drink, and he shall be filled with the Holy Ghost, even from his mother's womb: and many of the children of Israel shall he turn to the Lord their God: and he shall go before him in the spirit and power of Elias: to turn the hearts of the fathers to the children, and the disobedient to the wisdom of the just, to make ready a people prepared for the Lord.

Offertory. Ps. 8, 6-7. Thou hast crowned him with glory and worship: thou hast made him to have dominion of the works of thy hands, O Lord.

Secret.

SANCTIFY, O Lord, these our oblations: and at the intercession of blessed John Baptist, cleanse us thereby from the defilements of our iniquities. Through.

Communion. Ps. 21, 6. His honour is great in thy salvation: glory and great worship shalt thou lay upon him, O Lord.

Postcommunion.

O LORD, let the glorious intercession of blessed John Baptist ever prevent and follow us: that he may implore for us the mercy of him whose coming he foretold, even Jesus Christ thy Son our Lord: Who liveth.

¶ If today be Sunday, nothing is said of the Vigil.

June 24.

THE NATIVITY OF
ST. JOHN BAPTIST

Double of 1st class.

Introit. Is. 49, 1-2. De ventre.

FROM the womb of my mother the Lord hath called me by my name: and hath made my mouth as it were a sharp sword: beneath the shadow of his hand hath he hid me, and hath made me like to a polished arrow. Ps. 92, 1. It is a good thing to give thanks unto the Lord: and to sing praises unto thy name, O most Highest. ℣. Glory.

Collect.

ALMIGHTY God, by whose providence thy servant John Baptist was wonderfully born, and sent to prepare the way of thy Son our Saviour, by preaching of repentance: make us so to follow his doctrine and holy life, that we may truly repent according to his preaching; and after his example constantly speak the truth, boldly rebuke vice, and patiently suffer for the truth's sake. Through the same.

Or, Collect:

O GOD, by whose appointment we honour on this day the nativity of blessed John: grant unto thy people the grace of spiritual gladness; and guide the hearts of all the faithful into the way of everlasting salvation. Through.

¶ In Votive Masses the Collect of the Vigil is said, as also the Secret and Postcommunion.

The Lesson from the Prophet Isaiah.

Isaiah 40, 1-11.

COMFORT ye, comfort ye my people: saith your God. Speak ye comfortably to Jerusalem, and cry unto her, that her warfare is accomplished, that her iniquity is pardoned: for she hath received of the Lord's hand double for all her sins. The voice of him that crieth in the wilderness: Prepare ye the way of the Lord, make straight in the desert a highway for our God. Every valley shall be exalted, and every mountain and hill shall be made low: and the crooked shall be made straight, and the rough places plain. And the glory of the Lord shall be revealed, and all flesh shall see it together: for the mouth of the Lord hath spoken it. The voice said: Cry. And he said: What shall I cry? All flesh is grass, and all the goodliness thereof is as the flower of the field. The grass withereth, the flower fadeth, because the Spirit of the Lord bloweth upon it: surely the people is grass. The grass withereth, the flower fadeth: but the word of our God shall stand for ever. O Sion, that bringest good tidings: get thee up into the high mountain. O Jerusalem, that bringest good tidings: lift up thy voice with strength, lift it up, be not afraid. Say unto the cities of Judah: Behold your God. Behold, the Lord God will come with strong hand, and his arm shall rule for him: behold, his reward is with him, and his work before him. He shall feed his flock like a shepherd: he shall gather the lambs with his arm, and carry them in his bosom, and shall gently lead those that are with young.

Or:

The Lesson from the Prophet Isaiah.

Isaiah. 49, 1-3, 5-7.

LISTEN, O isles, unto me, and hearken, ye people, from far: the Lord hath called me from the womb, from the bowels of my mother hath he made mention of my name. And he hath made my mouth like a sharp sword: in the shadow of his hand hath he hid me, and made me a polished shaft: in his quiver hath he hid me. And said unto me: Thou art my servant, O Israel, in whom I will be glorified. And now, saith the Lord that formed me from the womb to be his servant: Behold, I will give thee for a light to the Gentiles, that thou mayest be my salvation unto the end of the earth. Kings shall see and arise, princes also shall worship, because of the Lord, and the Holy One of Israel, and he shall choose thee.

Gradual. Jer. 1, 5 and 9. Before I formed thee in the belly I knew thee: and before thou camest forth out of the womb I sanctified thee. ℣. The Lord put forth his hand, and touched my mouth, and said unto me.

Alleluia, alleluia. ℣. Luke 1, 76. Thou child, shalt be called the Prophet of the Highest: thou shalt go before the face of the Lord, to prepare his ways. Alleluia.

✠ The Continuation of the holy Gospel according to Luke.

Luke 1, 57-68.

ELISABETH'S full time came that she should be delivered, and she brought forth a son. And her neighbours and her cousins heard how the Lord had shewed great mercy upon her, and they rejoiced with her. And it came to pass, that on the eighth day they came to circumcise the child, and they called him Zacharias, after the name of his father. And his mother answered and said: Not so, but he shall be called John. And they said unto her: There is none of thy kindred that is called by this name. And they made signs to his father, how he would have him called. And he asked for a writing-table, and wrote, saying: His name is John. And they marvelled all. And his mouth was opened immediately, and his tongue loosed, and he spake, and praised God. And fear came on all that dwelt round about them: and all these sayings were noised abroad throughout all the hill-country of Judæa: and all they that heard them laid them up in their hearts, saying: What manner of child shall this be? And the hand of the Lord was with him. And his father Zacharias was filled with the Holy Ghost, and prophesied saying: Blessed be the Lord God of Israel, for he hath visited and redeemed his people.*

And hath raised up an horn of salvation for us in the house of his servant David. As he spake by the mouth of his holy Prophets: which have been since the world began. That we should be saved from our enemies: and from the hand of all that hate us. To perform the mercy promised to our fathers: and to remember his holy covenant. The oath which he sware to our father Abraham: that he would grant unto us. That we, being delivered out of the hand of our enemies: might serve him without fear, in holiness and righteousness before him all the days of our life. And thou, child, shalt be called the Prophet of the Highest: for thou shalt go before the face of the Lord to prepare his ways. To give knowledge of salvation unto his people: by the remission of their sins. Through the tender mercy of our God: whereby the day-spring from on high hath visited us. To give light to them that sit in darkness and in the shadow of death: to guide our feet into the way of peace. And the child grew, and waxed strong in spirit: and was in the deserts till the day of his shewing unto Israel. Creed.

Offertory. Ps. 92, 13. The righteous shall flourish like a palm-tree: and shall spread abroad like a cedar in Libanus.

Secret.

WE load thine altars, O Lord, with these our oblations: celebrating with due honour the nativity of him, who sang of the coming and proclaimed the presence of the Saviour of the world, even Jesus Christ thy Son our Lord: Who liveth and reigneth with thee.

Common Preface, even if this Feast fall on Sunday.

Communion. Luke 1, 76. Thou, child, shalt be called the Prophet of the Highest: for thou shalt go before the face of the Lord to prepare his ways.

Postcommunion.

LET thy Church, O God, rejoice with gladness in the birth of blessed John Baptist: even as he made known to her the author of her new birth, Jesus Christ thy Son our Lord: Who liveth and reigneth with thee.

June 25.

St. William

Abbot

Double.

The Mass Os justi, from the Common of an Abbot, p. [26], the Collect excepted.

Collect. P

O GOD, who in thy Saints hast appointed for our infirmity a pattern and protection in treading the way of salvation: grant us so to venerate the merits of thy blessed Abbot William; that we may ever receive the succour of his intercession, and follow in his footsteps. Through.

Secret. C

WE beseech thee, O Lord, that thy holy Abbot William may intercede for us: that this sacrifice which we offer and present upon thy holy altar may be profitable unto us for our salvation. Through.

Postcommunion. C

LET thy Sacrament, O Lord, which we have now received, and the prayers of the blessed Abbot William effectually defend us: that we may both imitate the example of his conversation and receive the succour of his intercession. Through.

June 26.

SS. John and Paul

Martyrs

Double.

Introit. Ps. 34, 20-21. Multae tribulationes.

GREAT are the troubles of the righteous, but the Lord delivereth them out of all: he keepeth all their bones: so that not one of them is broken. Ps. ibid., 1. I will alway give thanks unto the Lord: his praise shall ever be in my mouth. ℣. Glory.

Collect.

WE beseech thee, almighty God: that, as their faith and passion did cause blessed John and Paul to be brethren indeed; so this day's festival may bestow on us a twofold gladness in their glory. Through.

The Lesson from the book of Wisdom.

Ecclus. 44, 10-15.

THESE were merciful men, whose righteousness hath not been forgotten: with their seed shall continually remain a good inheritance, and their children are within the covenant: their seed standeth fast, and their children for their sakes: their seed shall remain for ever, and their glory shall not be blotted out. Their bodies are buried in peace, but their name liveth for evermore. The people will tell of their wisdom, and the Church will shew forth their praise.

Gradual. Ps. 133, 1-2. Behold, how good and joyful a thing it is, brethren, to dwell together in unity! ℣. It is like the precious ointment upon the head, that ran down unto the beard, even Aaron's beard.

Alleluia, alleluia. ℣. This is the true brotherhood, which overcame the wickedness of the world: which followed Christ, gaining heaven's glorious realms. Alleluia.

✠ The Continuation of the holy Gospel according to Luke.

Luke 12, 1-8.

AT that time: Jesus said unto his disciples: Beware ye of the leaven of the Pharisees, which is hypocrisy. For there is nothing covered, that shall not be revealed: neither hid, that shall not be known. Therefore whatsoever ye have spoken in darkness shall be heard in the light: and that which ye have spoken in the ear in closets shall be proclaimed upon the housetops. And I say unto you my friends: Be not afraid of them that kill the body, and after that have no more that they can do. But I will forewarn you whom ye shall fear: fear him, which after he hath killed hath power to cast into hell. Yea, I say unto you: fear him. Are not five sparrows sold for two farthings, and not one of them is forgotten before God? But even the very hairs of your head are all numbered. Fear not therefore: ye are of more value than many sparrows. Also I say unto you: Whosoever shall confess me before men, him shall the Son of man also confess before the Angels of God.

Offertory. Ps. 5, 12-13. They that love thy name shall be joyful in thee, for thou, Lord, wilt give thy blessing unto the righteous: and with thy favourable kindness, O Lord, wilt thou defend him as with a shield.

Secret.

WE beseech thee, O Lord, mercifully to accept this our sacrifice which we offer unto thee, pleading the merits of thy holy Martyrs John and Paul: that the same may avail for our perpetual succour. Through.

Communion. Wisdom 3, 4-6. Though they be punished in the sight of men, God proved them: as gold in the furnace hath he tried them, and received them as a burnt-offering.

Postcommunion.

WE have received, O Lord, this heavenly Sacrament in commemoration of the festival of thy holy Martyrs John and Paul: grant, we beseech thee; that this our temporal observance may effectually assist us toward the attainment of everlasting felicity. Through.

June 28.

St. Irenaeus

Bishop and Martyr

Double.

Introit. Malach. 2, 6. Lex veritatis.

THE law of truth was in his mouth, and iniquity was not found in his lips: he walked with me in peace and equity, and did turn many away from iniquity. Ps. 78, 1. Hear my law, O my people: incline your ears unto the words of my mouth. ℣. Glory.

Feasts of June (28)

Collect.

O GOD, who didst bestow upon blessed Irenæus, thy Martyr and Bishop, grace to overcome false doctrine and heresy by the teaching of the truth, and to stablish thy Church in peace and prosperity: give unto thy people, we beseech thee, constancy in thy holy religion; and grant us thy peace in our time. Through.

On weekdays only, Commemoration, in private Masses, of the Vigil of SS. Peter and Paul, App., p. 700.

The Lesson from the Epistle of blessed Paul the Apostle to Timothy.

II Tim. 3, 14-17; 4, 1-5.

DEARLY beloved: Continue thou in the things which thou hast learned and hast been assured of: knowing of whom thou hast learned them: and that from a child thou hast known the holy Scriptures, which are able to make thee wise unto salvation through faith which is in Christ Jesus. All Scripture is given by inspiration of God, and is profitable for doctrine, for reproof, for correction, for instruction in righteousness: that the man of God may be perfect, throughly furnished unto all good works. I charge thee therefore, before God, and the Lord Jesus Christ, who shall judge the quick and the dead at his appearing and his kingdom: preach the word, be instant in season, out of season: reprove, rebuke, exhort, with all longsuffering and doctrine. For the time will come when they will not endure sound doctrine, but after their own lusts shall they heap to themselves teachers, having itching ears, and they shall turn away their ears from the truth, and shall be turned unto fables. But watch thou in all things, endure afflictions, do the work of an Evangelist, make full proof of thy ministry.

Gradual. Ps. 122, 8. For my brethren and companions' sakes I will wish thee prosperity. ℣. Ps. 37, 37. Keep innocency, and take heed unto the thing that is right: for that shall bring a man peace at the last.

Alleluia, alleluia. ℣. Ecclus. 6, 35. Stand in the multitude of the elders, and cleave unto him that is wise, be willing to hear every godly discourse. Alleluia.

✠ The Continuation of the holy Gospel according to Matthew.

Matt. 10, 28-33.

AT that time: Jesus said unto his disciples: Fear not them which kill the body, but are not able to kill the soul; but rather fear him which is able to destroy both soul and body in hell. Are not two sparrows sold for a farthing: and one of them shall not fall on the ground without your Father? But the very hairs of your head are all numbered. Fear ye not therefore: ye are of more value than many sparrows. Whosoever therefore shall confess me before men, him will I confess also before my Father which is in heaven. But whosoever shall deny me before men, him will I also deny before my Father which is in heaven.

Offertory. Ecclus. 24, 44. I will make doctrine to shine as the morning, and will send forth her light afar off.

Secret.

O GOD, who sufferest not any terror to confound the nations that put their trust in thee: vouchsafe to accept the prayers and oblations of the people of thine inheritance; that by thy mercy all Christian lands may be stablished in peace, and preserved from the fear of every enemy. Through.

For the Vigil, Secret as in the following Mass p. 701.

Communion. Ecclus. 24, 47. Behold that I have not laboured for myself only, but for all them that seek wisdom.

Postcommunion.

O GOD, who art the author of peace and lover of concord, in knowledge of whom standeth our eternal life, whose service is perfect freedom: defend us, thy humble servants, in all assaults of our enemies; that, at the intercession of blessed Irenæus, thy Martyr and Bishop, we, surely trusting in thy defence, may not fear the power of any adversaries. Through.

For the Vigil, Postcommunion as in the following Mass, p. 702.

The same day, June 28.

The Vigil of SS. Peter and Paul

Apostles

Introit. John 21, 18-19. Dicit Dominus.

THE Lord saith unto Peter: When thou wast young, thou girdedst thyself, and walkedst whither thou wouldest: but when thou shalt be old, thou shalt stretch forth thy hands, and another shall gird thee, and carry thee whither thou wouldest not: this spake he signifying by what death he should glorify God. Ps. 19, 1. The heavens declare the glory of God: and the firmament sheweth his handy-work. ℣. Glory.

Glória in excélsis is not said.

Collect.

GRANT, we beseech thee, almighty God: that we, whom thou hast established on the rock of the apostolic confession; may in all our troubles and adversities continue stedfast and unmoved. Through.

In private Masses Commemoration is made of St. Irenæus, B.M.

Collect.

O GOD, who didst bestow upon blessed Irenæus, thy Martyr and Bishop, grace to overcome false doctrine and heresy by the teaching of the truth, and to stablish thy Church in peace and prosperity: give unto thy people, we beseech thee, constancy in thy holy religion; and grant us thy peace in our time. Through.

The Lesson from the Acts of the Apostles.
Acts 3, 1-10.

IN those days: Peter and John went up together into the temple at the hour of prayer, being the ninth hour. And a certain man lame from his mother's womb was carried: whom they laid daily at the gate of the temple which is called Beautiful, to ask alms of them that entered into the temple. Who seeing Peter and John about to go into the temple asked an alms. And Peter, fastening his eyes upon him with John, said: Look on us. And he gave heed unto them, expecting to receive something of them. Then Peter said: Silver and gold have I none: but such as I have give I thee: In the name of Jesus Christ of Nazareth rise up and walk. And he took him by the right hand, and lifted him up, and immediately his feet and ankle bones received strength. And he leaping up stood, and walked: and entered with them into the temple walking, and leaping, and praising God. And all the people saw him walking and praising God. And they knew that it was he which sat for alms at the Beautiful gate of the temple: and they were filled with wonder and amazement at that which had happened unto him.

Gradual. Ps. 19, 5 and 2. Their sound is gone out into all lands: and their words into the ends of the world. ℣. The heavens declare the glory of God: and the firmament sheweth his handy-work.

Feasts of June (28)

✠ The Continuation of the holy Gospel according to John.

John 21, 15-19.

AT that time: Jesus said unto Simon Peter: Simon, son of Jonas, lovest thou me more than these? He saith unto him: Yea, Lord, thou knowest that I love thee. He saith unto him: Feed my lambs. He saith to him again the second time: Simon, son of Jonas, lovest thou me? He saith unto him: Yea, Lord, thou knowest that I love thee. He saith unto him: Feed my sheep. He saith unto him the third time: Simon, son of Jonas, lovest thou me? Peter was grieved because he said unto him the third time, Lovest thou me? And he said unto him: Lord, thou knowest all things: thou knowest that I love thee. Jesus saith unto him: Feed my sheep. Verily, verily, I say unto thee: when thou wast young, thou girdedst thyself, and walkedst whither thou wouldest: but when thou shalt be old thou shalt stretch forth thy hands, and another shall gird thee, and carry thee whither thou wouldest not. This spake he, signifying by what death he should glorify God.

Offertory. Ps. 139, 17. Right dear are thy friends unto me, O God, and held in highest honour: their rule and governance is exceeding stedfast.

Secret.

SANCTIFY this oblation of thy people, we beseech thee, O Lord, at the intercession of thine Apostles: and cleanse us from the defilements of our iniquities. Through.

For St. Irenæus. Secret.

O GOD, who sufferest not any terror to confound the nations that put their trust in thee: vouchsafe to accept the prayers and oblations of the people of thine inheritance; that by thy mercy all Christian lands may be stablished in peace, and preserved from the fear of every enemy. Through.

Communion. John 21, 15 and 17. Simon, son of Jonas, lovest thou me more than these? Lord, thou knowest all things: thou knowest, Lord, that I love thee.

Postcommunion.

O LORD, who hast fulfilled us with this heavenly food: defend us by the intercession of thine Apostles against all adversity. Through.

For St. Irenæus. Postcommunion.

O GOD, who art the author of peace and lover of concord, in knowledge of whom standeth our eternal life, whose service is perfect freedom: defend us, thy humble servants, in all assaults of our enemies; that, at the intercession of blessed Irenæus, thy Martyr and Bishop, we, surely trusting in thy defence, may not fear the power of any adversaries. Through.

¶ If today be Sunday, Commemoration is made, in low Masses only, of St. Irenæus, and nothing is said of the Vigil.

June 29.

SS. PETER and PAUL
THE APOSTLES
Double of 1st class.

Introit. Acts 12, 11. *Nunc scio.*

NOW I know of a surety that the Lord hath sent his Angel: and hath delivered me out of the hand of Herod, and from all the expectation of the people of the Jews. Ps. 139, 1-2. O Lord, thou hast searched me out, and known me: thou knowest my down-sitting, and mine uprising. ℣. Glory.

Collect.

O ALMIGHTY God, who by thy Son Jesus Christ didst give to thy Apostle Saint Peter many excellent gifts, and commandedst him earnestly to feed thy flock: make, we beseech thee, all Bishops and Pastors diligently to preach thy holy Word, and the people obediently to follow the same; that they may receive the crown of everlasting glory. Through the same.

Or, Collect.

O GOD, who hast hallowed this day by the martyrdom of thy Apostles Peter and Paul: vouchsafe unto thy Church; that as in the beginning it learned of them thy true religion, so it may in all things obediently follow their commandments. Through.

The Lesson from the Acts of the Apostles.

Acts 12, 1-11.

IN those days: Herod the king stretched forth his hands to vex certain of the Church. And he killed James the brother of John with the sword. And, because he saw it pleased the Jews, he proceeded further to take Peter also. Then were the days of unleavened bread. And when he had apprehended him, he put him in prison, and delivered him to four quaternions of soldiers to keep him, intending after Easter to bring him forth to the people. Peter therefore was kept in prison. But prayer was made without ceasing of the Church unto God for him. And when Herod would have brought him forth, the same night Peter was sleeping between two soldiers, bound with two chains, and the keepers before the door kept the prison. And, behold, the Angel of the Lord came upon him: and a light shined in the prison: and he smote Peter on the side, and raised him up, saying: Arise up, quickly. And his chains fell off from his hands. And the Angel said unto him: Gird thyself, and bind on thy sandals. And so he did. And he saith unto him: Cast thy garment about thee, and follow me. And he went out, and followed him, and wist not that it was true which was done by the Angel: but thought he saw a vision. When they were past the first and the second ward, they came unto the iron gate that leadeth unto the city: which opened to them of his own accord. And they went out, and passed on through one street: and forthwith the Angel departed from him. And when Peter was come to himself, he said: Now I know of a surety, that the Lord hath sent his Angel, and hath delivered me out of the hand of Herod, and from all the expectation of the people of the Jews.

Gradual. Ps. 45, 17-18. Thou shalt make them princes in all lands: they shall remember thy name, O Lord. ℣. Instead of thy fathers thou shalt have children: therefore shall the people give thanks unto thee.

Alleluia, alleluia. ℣. Matt. 16, 18. Thou art Peter, and upon this rock I will build my Church. Alleluia.

☩ The Continuation of the holy Gospel according to Matthew.

Matt. 16, 13-19.

AT that time: When Jesus came into the coasts of Caesarea Philippi, he asked his disciples, saying: Whom do men say that I, the Son of man, am? And they said: Some say that thou art John the Baptist, some Elias, and others Jeremias, or one of the Prophets. He saith unto them: But whom say ye that I am? And Simon Peter answered and said: Thou art the Christ, the Son of the living God. And Jesus answered and said unto him: Blessed art thou, Simon Barjona: for flesh and blood hath not revealed it unto thee, but my Father which is in heaven. And I say also unto thee, That thou art Peter, and upon this rock I will build my Church, and the gates of hell shall not prevail against it. And I will give unto thee the keys of the kingdom of heaven. And whatsoever thou shalt bind on earth shall be bound in heaven: and whatsoever thou shalt loose on earth shall be loosed in heaven. Creed.

Offertory. Ps. 45, 17-18. Thou shalt make them princes in all lands: they shall remember thy name, O Lord, from one generation to another.

Secret.

LET the intercession of thine Apostles, O Lord, commend the oblations which we offer for consecration to the honour of thy name: and grant that we may thereby be cleansed and defended. Through.

Preface of the Apostles.

Communion. Matt. 16, 18. Thou art Peter, and upon this rock I will build my Church.

Postcommunion.

O LORD, who hast fulfilled us with this heavenly food: defend us by the intercession of thine Apostles against all adversity. Through.

For a Votive Mass see p. [55].

June 30

Commemoration of St. Paul the Apostle

Greater double.

Introit. II Tim. 1, 12. Scio cui credidi.

I KNOW whom I have believed, and am persuaded that he is able to keep that which I have committed unto him against that day, a just judge. Ps. 139, 1. O Lord, thou hast searched me out, and known me: thou knowest my down-sitting, and mine up-rising. ℣. Glory.

Collect.

O GOD, who by the preaching of the blessed Apostle Paul didst teach the multitude of the Gentiles: grant to us, we beseech thee; that we who this day celebrate his heavenly birth may feel the effectual benefit of his intercession. Through.

And Commemoration of St. Peter Ap. is always made.

Collect.

O GOD, who didst bestow upon thy blessed Apostle Peter the keys of the kingdom of heaven, and didst appoint unto him the high priesthood for binding and loosing: vouchsafe; that by the help of his intercession we may be delivered from the bonds of our iniquities: Who livest and reignest with God the Father.

The Lesson from the Epistle of blessed Paul the Apostle to the Galatians.

Gal. 1, 11-20.

BRETHREN: I certify you that the Gospel which was preached of me is not after man: for I neither received it of man, neither was I taught it, but by the revelation of Jesus Christ. For ye have heard of my conversation in time past in the Jews' religion: how that beyond measure I persecuted the Church of God, and wasted it, and profited in the Jews' religion above many my equals in mine own nation, being more exceedingly zealous of the traditions of my fathers. But when it pleased God, who separated me from my mother's womb, and called me by his grace, to reveal his Son in me, that I might preach him among the heathen: immediately I conferred not with flesh and blood, neither went I up to Jerusalem to them which were Apostles before me: but I went into Arabia: and returned again unto Damascus: then after three years I went up to Jerusalem to see Peter, and abode with him fifteen days: but other of the Apostles saw I none, save James the Lord's brother. Now the things which I write unto you, behold, before God, I lie not.

Gradual. Gal. 2, 8-9. He that wrought effectually in Peter to the apostleship, the same was mighty in me toward the Gentiles: and they perceived the grace of God that was given unto me. ℣. I Cor. 15, 10. The grace of God which was bestowed upon me was not in vain: but his grace ever abideth in me.

Alleluia, alleluia. ℣ Holy Paul Apostle, preacher of truth and teacher of the Gentiles, intercede for us. Alleluia.

✠ The Continuation of the holy Gospel according to Matthew.

Matt. 10, 16-22.

AT that time: Jesus said unto his disciples: Behold, I send you forth as sheep in the midst of wolves. Be ye therefore wise as serpents and harmless as doves. But beware of men. For they will deliver you up to the councils, and they will scourge you in their synagogues: and ye shall be brought before governors and kings for my sake, for a testimony against them and the Gentiles. But when they deliver you up, take no thought how or what ye shall speak: for it shall be given you in that same hour what ye shall speak. For it is not ye that speak, but the Spirit of your Father which speaketh in you. And the brother shall deliver up the brother to death, and the father the child: and the children shall rise up against their parents, and cause them to be put to death: and ye shall be hated of all men for my name's sake: but he that endureth to the end shall be saved.

The Creed is not said.

Offertory. Ps. 139. 17. Right dear are thy friends unto me, O God, and held in highest honour; their rule and governance is exceeding steadfast.

Secret.

SANCTIFY, O Lord, through the prayers of thine Apostle Paul the oblations of thy people: that these gifts, which by thine institution are acceptable unto thee, may by his effectual advocacy be rendered the more acceptable in thy sight. Through.

For St. Peter.   Secret.

WE beseech, O Lord, let the intercession of thy blessed Apostle Peter commend unto thee the prayers and oblations of thy Church: that these gifts which we offer for his glory may avail for the remission of our sins. Through.

Preface of the Apostles.

Communion. Matt. 19, 28-29. Verily I say unto you: That ye which have forsaken all and followed me, shall receive an hundred-fold, and shall inherit everlasting life.

Postcommunion.

O LORD, who hast made us partakers of this holy Sacrament: we beseech thee; that at the intercession of thy blessed Apostle Paul, the mysteries which we have celebrated for the increase of his glory may be profitable to us for the healing of our souls. Through.

For St. Peter.   Postcommunion.

O LORD, let this sacrifice which we have offered bring forth gladness in our hearts: that as we shew forth the wonders which thou hast wrought in thine Apostle Peter; so through him we may obtain the abundance of thy lovingkindness. Through.

FEASTS OF JULY

July 1.

THE MOST PRECIOUS BLOOD
OF OUR LORD JESUS CHRIST

Double of 1st class.

Introit. Rev. 5, 9-10. Redemisti.

THOU hast redeemed us, O Lord, by thy blood, out of every kindred, and tongue, and people, and nation: and hast made us a kingdom unto our God. Ps. 89, 1. My song shall be alway of the loving-kindness of the Lord: with my mouth will I ever be shewing thy truth from one generation to another. ℣. Glory.

¶ In Votive Masses the words in this solemnity in the following Collect are to be omitted.

Collect.

ALMIGHTY and everlasting God, who didst appoint that thine only-begotten Son should be the Redeemer of the world, and hast vouchsafed to accept his Blood as the propitiation for our sins: grant us, we beseech thee, so to venerate in this solemnity the price of our salvation, that by its power we may be defended from all evils in this present life on earth; and may rejoice in the everlasting benefit thereof in heaven. Through the same.

The Lesson from the Epistle of blessed Paul the Apostle to the Hebrews.

Heb. 9, 11-15.

BRETHREN: Christ being come an High Priest of good things to come, by a greater and more perfect tabernacle, not made with hands, that is to say, not of this building: neither by the blood of goats and calves, but by his own blood he entered in once into the Holy Place, having obtained eternal redemption for us. For if the blood of bulls and of goats, and the ashes of an heifer sprinkling the unclean, sanctifieth to the purifying of the flesh: how much more shall the blood of Christ, who, through the eternal Spirit, offered himself without spot to God, purge your conscience from dead works to serve the living God. And for this cause he is the mediator of the new Testament: that by means of death, for the redemption of the transgressions that were under the first Testament, they which are called might receive the promise of eternal inheritance, in Christ Jesu our Lord.

Gradual. I John 5, 6-8. This is he that came by water and blood, even Jesus Christ: not by water only, but by water and blood. ℣. There are three that bear record in heaven: the Father, the Word, and the Holy Ghost; and these three are one. And there are three that bear witness in earth: the Spirit, and the water, and the blood: and these three are one.

Alleluia, alleluia. ℣. Ibid., 9. If we receive the witness of men, the witness of God is greater. Alleluia.

In Votive Masses after Septuagesima, omitting Alleluia and the Verse following, is said:

Tract. Ephes. 1, 6-8. God hath made us accepted in his beloved Son, in whom we have redemption through his blood. ℣. The forgiveness of sins, according to the riches of his grace wherein he hath abounded towards us. ℣. Rom. 3, 24-25. Being justified freely by his grace through the redemption, that is in Christ Jesus. ℣. Whom God hath set forth to be a propitiation through faith in his blood.

In Eastertide in Votive Masses is said:

Alleluia, alleluia. ℣. Rev. 5, 9. Thou art worthy, O Lord, to take the book, and to open the seals thereof: for thou wast slain, and hast redeemed us to God by thy blood. Alleluia. ℣. Exod. 12, 13. The blood shall be to you for a token: and when I see the blood, I will pass over you: and the plague shall not be upon you to destroy you. Alleluia.

✠ The Continuation of the holy Gospel according to John.

John 19, 30-35.

AT that time: When Jesus had received the vinegar, he said: It is finished. And he bowed his head and gave up the ghost. The Jews therefore, because it was the Preparation, that the bodies should not remain upon the cross on the sabbath day, (for that sabbath day was an high day), besought Pilate, that their legs might be broken, and that they might be taken away. Then came the soldiers: and brake the legs of the first, and of the other which was crucified with him. But when they came to Jesus, and saw that he was dead already, they brake not his legs, but one of the soldiers with a spear pierced his side, and forthwith came there out blood and water. And he that saw it bare record: and his record is true. Creed.

Offertory. I Cor. 10, 16. The cup of blessing which we bless, is it not the communion of the blood of Christ? the bread which we break, is it not the communion of the body of the Lord?

Secret.

WE beseech thee, that through these heavenly mysteries we may draw near unto Jesus, the mediator of the new Testament: and renew upon thine altars, O Lord of Hosts, the sprinkling of the blood that speaketh better things than that of Abel. Through the same.

Preface of the Cross.

Communion. Heb. 9, 28. Christ was once offered to bear the sins of many; and unto them that look for him shall he appear the second time without sin unto salvation.

Postcommunion.

O LORD, who has suffered us to approach thy holy table, and with joy to draw water out of the wells of the Saviour: we beseech thee, that his blood may become for us a well of water springing up unto life eternal: Who liveth and reigneth with thee.

July 2.

THE VISITATION OF THE B.V. MARY

Double of 2nd class.

Introit. Sedulius. Salve, sancta.

HAIL, O Mother most holy, who didst give birth to the Monarch: reigning o'er heaven and earth world without end. Ps. 45, 1. My heart is inditing of a good matter: I speak of the things which I have made unto the King. ℣. Glory.

Collect.

WE beseech thee, O Lord, to grant unto us thy servants the gift of thy heavenly grace: that as the child-bearing of the blessed Virgin was unto us the beginning of salvation; so the devout observance of her Visitation may avail for the increasing of our peace. Through.

Commemoration is made, in private Masses only, of SS. Processus and Martinian, Martyrs.

Collect.

O GOD, who dost encompass and protect us by the glorious confession of thy holy Martyrs Processus and Martinian: grant us both to profit by their example, and to rejoice in their intercession. Through.

The Lesson from the book of Wisdom.

Song of Songs 2, 8-14.

BEHOLD, he cometh leaping upon the mountains, skipping upon the hills; my beloved is like a roe or a young hart. Behold, he standeth behind our wall, he looketh forth at the windows, shewing himself through the lattice. My beloved spake, and said unto me: Rise up, my love, my fair one, and come away. For, lo, the winter is past, the rain is over and gone. The flowers appear on the earth, the time of the singing of birds is come: and the voice of the turtle is heard in our land: the fig tree putteth forth her green figs: and the vines with the tender grape give a good smell. Arise, my love, my fair one, and come away: O my dove, that art in the clefts of the rock, in the secret places of the stairs, let me see thy countenance, let me hear thy voice: for sweet is thy voice, and thy countenance is comely.

Gradual. Blessed and venerable art thou, O Virgin Mary: who a maiden undefiled hast our Saviour for thy child. ℣. Virgin, Mother of God, the whole world cannot contain him, yet made man for our sake, hidden he lay in thy womb.

Alleluia, alleluia. ℣. Blessed art thou, O holy Virgin Mary, and most worthy of all praise: for out of thee arose the sun of righteousness, Christ our God. Alleluia.

✠ The Continuation of the holy Gospel according to Luke.

Luke 1, 39-47.

AT that time: Mary arose and went into the hill country with haste, into a city of Juda: and entered into the house of Zacharias, and saluted Elisabeth. And it came to pass, that, when Elisabeth heard the salutation of Mary, the babe leaped in her womb: and Elisabeth was filled with the Holy Ghost, and she spake out with a loud voice, and said: Blessed art thou among women, and blessed is the fruit of thy womb. And whence is this to me, that the Mother of my Lord should come to me? For, lo, as soon as the voice of thy salutation sounded in mine ears, the babe leaped in my womb for joy. And blessed is she that believed, for there shall be a performance of those things which were told her from the Lord. And Mary said: My soul doth magnify the Lord: and my spirit hath rejoiced in God my Saviour. Creed.

Offertory. Blessed art thou, O Virgin Mary, who didst bear the Creator of all things: thou broughtest forth him who made thee, and for ever remainest a Virgin.

Secret.

LET the manhood of thine only-begotten Son, O Lord, avail for our succour: that even as he, being born of a Virgin, destroyed not but hallowed the innocence of his Mother; so on this feast of her Visitation, he may deliver us from our offences, and render us an oblation acceptable unto thee, even Jesus Christ our Lord: Who liveth.

For SS. Processus and Martinian.

Secret.

RECEIVE, O Lord, our prayers and oblations: and that they may be worthy in thy sight, may we be aided by the prayers of thy Saints. Through.

Preface of the B.V. Mary, And that on the Visitation.

Communion. Blessed is the womb of the Virgin Mary that bare the Son of the everlasting Father.

Postcommunion.

GRANT, we beseech thee, O Lord, that as we have now received thy Sacrament in the observance of this yearly festival: so it may both in this life and in that to come be profitable to us for the healing of our souls. Through.

For SS. Processus and Martinian.

Postcommunion.

O LORD our God, who hast fulfilled us with the partaking of thy sacred Body and thy precious Blood, we beseech thee: that we, who have received these holy mysteries with reverence and godly fear; may in the assurance of our redemption obtain the benefits of the same. Through.

July 3.

St. Leo

Pope and Confessor

Simple.

The Mass Si diligis me, p. [2].

Collect. C1

O EVERLASTING Shepherd, look down in mercy on thy flock: and as thou didst choose blessed Leo thy Chief Bishop to be pastor and ruler of thy Church; so at his intercession defend it with thy continual protection. Through.

Secret. C1

WE beseech thee, O Lord, graciously enlighten thy Church by the gifts which we here offer: that in every place thy flock may increase and prosper, and the shepherds by thy governance may be made pleasing to thy name. Through.

Postcommunion. C 1

MERCIFUL Lord, we beseech thee to govern and preserve thy Church, which thou hast here refreshed with heavenly food: that by the guiding of thy mighty power it may serve thee in more abundant freedom, and ever keep thy true religion whole and undefiled. Through.

July 5.

St. Antony Mary Zaccaria

Confessor.

Double.

Introit. I Cor. 2, 4. Sermo meus.

MY speech and my preaching was not with enticing words of man's wisdom, but in demonstration of the Spirit and of power. Ps. 111, 1. I will give thanks unto the Lord with my whole heart, secretly among the faithful, and in the congregation. ℣. Glory.

Collect.

GRANT, O Lord God, that we, being filled with the spirit of thine Apostle Paul, may learn that pre-eminent knowledge of Jesus Christ: whereby thou didst wondrously teach blessed Antony Mary to assemble in thy Church new households of clerks and virgins. Through the same.

The Lesson from the Epistle of blessed Paul the Apostle to Timothy.

I Tim. 4, 8-16.

DEARLY beloved: Godliness is profitable unto all things: having promise of the life that now is and of that which is to come. This is a faithful saying and worthy of all acceptation. For therefore we both labour and suffer reproach, because we trust in the living God, who is the Saviour of all men, specially of those that believe. These things command and teach. Let no man despise thy youth: but be thou an example of the believers, in word, in conversation, in charity, in spirit, in faith, in purity. Till I come, give attendance to reading, to exhortation, to doctrine. Neglect not the gift that is in thee, which was given thee by prophecy, with the laying on of the hands of the presbytery. Meditate upon these things, give thyself wholly to them: that thy profiting may appear to all. Take heed unto thyself, and unto the doctrine: continue in them. For in doing this thou shalt both save thyself, and them that hear thee.

Gradual. Phil. 1, 8-9. God is my record, how greatly I long after you all in the bowels of Jesus Christ. And this I pray, that your love may abound yet more and more in knowledge and in all judgment. ℣. Ibid., 10. That we may approve things that are excellent, that ye may be sincere and without offence till the day of Christ.

Alleluia, alleluia. ℣. Ibid., 11. Being filled with the fruits of righteousness, which are by Jesus Christ, unto the glory and praise of God. Alleluia.

After Septuagesima, omitting Alleluia and the Verse following, is said:

Tract. II Cor. 10, 17-18. He that glorieth, let him glory in the Lord: for not he that commendeth himself is approved: but whom the Lord commendeth. ℣. Gal. 6, 14. God forbid that I should glory, save in the Cross of our Lord Jesus Christ: by whom the world is crucified unto me, and I unto the world. ℣. Phil. 1, 21. To me to live is Christ, and to die is gain.

In Eastertide the Gradual is omitted, and in its place is said:

Alleluia, alleluia. ℣. II Cor. 7, 4. I am filled with comfort, I am exceeding joyful in all our tribulation. Alleluia. ℣. Ibid., 6, 13. I speak as unto my children: be ye also enlarged. Alleluia.

☩ The Continuation of the holy Gospel according to Mark.

Mark 10, 15-21.

AT that time: Jesus said unto his disciples: Whosoever shall not receive the kingdom of God as a little child, he shall not enter therein. And he took little children up in his arms, put his hands upon them, and blessed them. And when he was gone forth into the way, there came one running, and kneeled to him, and asked him: Good Master, what shall I do that I may inherit eternal life? And Jesus said unto him: Why callest thou me good? there is none good but one, that is, God. Thou knowest the commandments: Do not commit adultery, Do not kill, Do not steal, Do not bear false witness, Defraud not, Honour thy father and mother. And he answered and said unto him: Master, all these have I observed from my youth. Then Jesus beholding him loved him, and said unto him: One thing thou lackest: go thy way, sell whatsoever thou hast, and give to the poor, and thou shalt have treasure in heaven: and come and follow me.

Offertory. Ps. 138, 1-2. In the sight of the Angels will I sing praise unto thee: I will worship toward thy holy temple, and praise thy name.

Secret.

O LORD, who in the offering of this most sacred victim didst adorn blessed Antony Mary with a wondrous glory of purity in body and soul: grant, that we may in that same purity draw near unto the table of thy heavenly banquet. Through.

Communion. Phil. 3, 17. Brethren, be followers together of me, and mark them which walk so as ye have us for an ensample.

Postcommunion.

O LORD Jesu Christ, who didst endue blessed Antony Mary with the fire of thy love, to bear the standard of this sacrifice of our salvation to victory against the enemies of thy Church: vouchsafe; that through this heavenly banquet, wherewith we have been fed, that same fire may be enkindled in our hearts: Who livest and reignest with God the Father.

July 7.

SS. Cyril and Methodius

Bishops and Confessors

Double.

Introit. Ps. 132, 9-10. Sacerdotes tui.

LET thy priests, O Lord, be clothed with righteousness, and let thy Saints sing with joyfulness: for thy servant David's sake turn not away the presence of thine Anointed. Ps. ibid., 1. Lord, remember David: and all his trouble. ℣. Glory.

Collect.

ALMIGHTY and everlasting God, who by thy blessed Confessors and Bishops, Cyril and Methodius, didst suffer the peoples of Slavonia to come to the knowledge of thy name: vouchsafe; that we who glory in their festival may be united to their fellowship in heaven. Through.

The Lesson from the Epistle of blessed Paul the Apostle to the Hebrews.

Heb. 7, 23-27.

BRETHREN: They were many priests, because they were not suffered to continue by reason of death: but Jesus because he continueth ever, hath an unchangeable priesthood. Wherefore he is able also to save them to the uttermost that come unto God by him: seeing he ever liveth to make intercession for them. For such an high priest became us, who is holy, harmless, undefiled, separate from sinners, and made higher than the heavens: who needeth not daily, as those high priests, to offer up sacrifice, first for his own sins, and then for the people's: for this he did once, when he offered up himself, Jesus Christ our Lord.

Gradual. Ps. 132, 16-17. I will deck her priests with health: and her saints shall rejoice and sing. ℣. There shall I make the horn of David to flourish: I have ordained a lantern for mine Anointed.

Alleluia, alleluia. ℣. Ps. 110, 4. The Lord sware, and will not repent: Thou art a priest for ever after the order of Melchisedech. Alleluia.

✠ The Continuation of the holy Gospel according to Luke.

Luke 10, 1-9.

AT that time: the Lord appointed other seventy also: and sent them two and two before his face into every city and place whither he himself would come. Therefore said he unto them: The harvest truly is great, but the labourers are few. Pray ye therefore the Lord of the harvest, that he would send forth labourers into his harvest. Go your ways: behold I send you forth as lambs among wolves. Carry neither purse, nor scrip, nor shoes; and salute no man by the way. And into whatsoever house ye enter, first say: Peace be to this house: and if the son of peace be there, your peace shall rest upon it: if not, it shall turn to you again. And in the same house remain, eating and drinking such things as they give: for the labourer is worthy of his hire. Go not from house to house. And into whatsoever city ye enter and they receive you, eat such things as are set before you: and heal the sick that are therein, and say unto them: The kingdom of God is come nigh unto you.

Offertory. Ps. 68, 36. God is wonderful in his holy ones: even the God of Israel, he will give strength and power unto his people: blessed be God.

Secret.

WE beseech thee, O Lord, to have respect unto the prayers and oblations of thy faithful people: that they may be acceptable unto thee on this festival of thy Saints, and effectually obtain for us the assistance of thy mercy. Through.

Communion. Matt. 10, 27. What I tell you in darkness, that speak ye in light, saith the Lord: and what ye hear in the ear, that preach ye upon the house-tops.

Postcommunion.

WE beseech thee, almighty God: that as thou dost vouchsafe to bestow upon us thy heavenly gifts; so, at the intercession of thy Saints Cyril and Methodius, thou wouldest grant unto us to despise things earthly. Through.

July 8.

St. Elizabeth

Queen, Widow

Simple.

The Mass Cognovi, p. [36], the Collect excepted.

Collect. P

MOST merciful God, who among many excellent gifts didst bestow on the blessed Queen Elizabeth peculiar grace to allay the fury of war: grant to us at her intercession; that after that peace in this mortal life for which we humbly pray, we may attain unto everlasting felicity. Through.

Secret.

GRANT, O Lord, that like as thy dedicated people do acknowledge that in tribulation they have been succoured by the merits of thy Saints: so this oblation, which they here offer unto thee in honour of the same, may be acceptable in thy sight. Through.

Postcommunion.

O LORD, who hast satisfied this thy family with thy sacred gifts: we beseech thee, that we may at all times be comforted by the intercession of her whose festival we celebrate. Through.

In England and Wales.

July 9.

SS. John Fisher, Bishop, and Thomas More

Martyrs

See Supplement.

July 10.

The Seven Holy Brethren

Martyrs

and SS. Rufina and Secunda

Virgins and Martyrs

Simple.

Introit. Ps. 113, 1 and 9. Laudate.

PRAISE the Lord, ye children, O praise the name of the Lord: who maketh the barren woman to keep house, and to be a joyful mother of children. Ps. ibid., 1. Blessed be the name of the Lord: from this time forth for evermore. ℣. Glory.

Collect.

GRANT, we beseech thee, almighty God: that, as we have known thy glorious Martyrs to be constant in their confession, so we may feel the succour of their loving intercession. Through.

The Lesson from the book of Wisdom.

Prov. 31, 10-31.

WHO can find a virtuous woman? For her price is far above rubies. The heart of her husband doth safely trust in her, so that he shall have no need of spoil. She will do him good and not evil all the days of her life. She seeketh wool, and flax, and worketh willingly with her hands. She is like the merchants' ships, she bringeth her food from afar. She riseth also while it is yet night, and giveth meat to her household, and a portion to her maidens. She considereth a field, and buyeth it: with the fruit of her hands she planteth a vine-yard. She girdeth her loins with strength, and strengtheneth her arms. She perceiveth that her merchandise is good: her candle goeth not out by night. She layeth her hands to the spindle, and her hands hold the distaff. She stretcheth out her hand to the poor, yea, she reacheth forth her hands to the needy. She is not afraid of the snow for her household: for all her household are clothed with scarlet. She maketh herself coverings of tapestry: her clothing is silk and purple. Her husband is known in the gates, when he sitteth among the elders of the land. She maketh fine linen, and selleth it, and delivereth girdles unto the merchant. Strength and honour are her clothing, and she shall rejoice in time to come. She openeth her mouth with wisdom, and in her tongue is the law of kindness. She looketh well to the ways of her household, and eateth not the bread of idleness. Her children arise up, and call her blessed: her husband also, and he praiseth her. Many daughters have done virtuously, but thou excellest them all. Favour is deceitful, and beauty is vain: but a woman that feareth the Lord, she shall be praised. Give her of the fruit of her hands: and let her own works praise her in the gates.

Gradual. Ps. 124, 7-8. Our soul is escaped, even as a bird out of the snare of the fowler. ℣. The snare is broken, and we are delivered: our help is in the name of the Lord, who hath made heaven and earth.

Alleluia, alleluia. ℣. This is the true brotherhood, which overcame the wickedness of the world: which followed Christ, gaining heaven's glorious realms. Alleluia.

☧ The Continuation of the holy Gospel according to Matthew.

Matt. 12, 46-50.

AT that time: While Jesus spake to the multitudes, behold his mother and his brethren stood without, desiring to speak with him. Then one said unto him: Behold, thy mother and thy brethren stand without, desiring to speak with thee. But he answered and said unto him that told him: Who is my mother and who are my brethren? And he stretched forth his hand toward his disciples, and said: Behold my mother and my brethren. For whosoever shall do the will of my Father which is in heaven: the same is my brother, and sister, and mother.

Offertory. Ps. 124, 7. Our soul is escaped, even as a bird out of the snare of the fowler: the snare is broken, and we are delivered.

Secret.

WE beseech thee, O Lord, look with favour on these our oblations: that, through the intercession of thy Saints, they may increase our devotion, and set forward our salvation. Through.

Communion. Matt. 12, 50. Whosoever shall do the will of my Father which is in heaven: the same is my brother, and sister, and mother, saith the Lord.

Postcommunion.

WE beseech thee, almighty God: that as in these holy mysteries we have received the pledge of our salvation, so at the intercession of thy Saints we may attain unto the fulfilment of the same. Through.

July 11.

For St. Pius I

Pope and Martyr

The Mass Si diligis me, p. [2].

Collect. C 1

O EVERLASTING Shepherd, look down in mercy on thy flock: and as thou didst choose blessed Pius thy Martyr and Chief Bishop to be pastor and ruler of thy Church; so at his intercession defend it with thy continual protection. Through.

Secret. C 1

WE beseech thee, O Lord, graciously enlighten thy Church by the gifts which we here offer: that in every place thy flock may increase and prosper, and the shepherds by thy governance may be made pleasing to thy name. Through.

Postcommunion. C 1

MERCIFUL Lord, we beseech thee to govern and preserve thy Church, which thou hast here refreshed with heavenly food: that by the guiding of thy mighty power it may serve thee in more abundant freedom, and ever keep thy true religion whole and undefiled. Through.

July 12.

S. John Gualbert

Abbot

Double.

Introit. Ps. 37, 30-31. Os justi.

THE mouth of the righteous is exercised in wisdom, and his tongue will be talking of judgment: the law of his God is in his heart. Ps. ibid., 1. Fret not thyself because of the ungodly: neither be thou envious against the evil doers. ℣. Glory.

Collect.

O LORD, we beseech thee, let the intercession of thy blessed Abbot John commend us unto thee: that those things which for our own merits we cannot ask, we may through his advocacy obtain. Through.

Commemoration of SS. Nabor and Felix, MM.

Collect.

GRANT, we beseech thee, O Lord: that as the heavenly birthday of thy holy Martyrs, Nabor and Felix, faileth not to return for our observance; so at their intercession thou wouldest further us with thy continual help. Through.

The Lesson from the book of Wisdom.

Ecclus. 45, 1-6.

BELOVED of God and men, whose memorial is blessed. He made him like to the glorious saints, and magnified him so that his enemies stood in fear of him. By his words he caused the wonders to cease, and he made him glorious in the sight of kings, and gave him a commandment for his people, and shewed him his glory. He sanctified him in his faithfulness and meekness, and chose him out of all men. He made him to hear his voice, and brought him into the dark cloud, and gave him commandments before his face, even the law of life and knowledge.

Gradual. Ps. 21, 4-5. Thou hast prevented him, O Lord, with the blessings of goodness: thou hast set a crown of pure gold upon his head. ℣. He asked life of thee, and thou gavest him a long life, even for ever and ever.

Alleluia, alleluia. ℣. Ps. 92, 13. The righteous shall flourish like a palm-tree: and shall spread abroad like a cedar in Libanus. Alleluia.

✠ The Continuation of the holy Gospel according to Matthew.

Matt. 5, 43-48.

AT that time: Jesus said unto his disciples: Ye have heard that it hath been said: Thou shalt love thy neighbour, and hate thine enemy. But I say unto you: Love your enemies, bless them that curse you, do good to them that hate you, and pray for them which despitefully use you, and persecute you, that ye may be the children of your Father which is in heaven: for he maketh his sun to rise on the evil and on the good, and sendeth rain on the just and on the unjust. For if ye love them which love you, what reward have ye? do not even the publicans the same? And if ye salute your brethren only, what do ye more than others? do not even the publicans so? Be ye therefore perfect, even as your Father which is in heaven is perfect.

Offertory. Ps. 21, 3-4. Thou hast given him his heart's desire, O Lord, and hast not denied him the request of his lips: thou hast set a crown of pure gold upon his head.

Secret.

O LORD, we beseech thee, let thy holy Abbot John intercede for us: that this sacrifice which we offer and present upon thy holy altar may be profitable unto us for our salvation. Through.

For the SS. Martyrs. Secret.

WE beseech thee, O Lord, that the gifts of thy people may, by the prayers of thy holy Martyrs, Nabor and Felix, be made acceptable unto thee: that, as they are offered for their triumph to thy name, so by their merits they may be rendered worthy in thy sight. Through.

Communion. Luke 12, 42. A faithful and wise servant, whom his lord hath made ruler over his household, to give them their portion of meat in due season.

Postcommunion.

LET thy Sacrament, O Lord, which we have now received, and the prayers of thy blessed Abbot John effectually defend us: that we may both imitate the example of his conversation, and receive the succour of his intercession. Through.

For the SS. Martyrs. Postcommunion.

O LORD, who on this heavenly birthday of thy Saints hast quickened us with the gift of thy Sacrament: we beseech thee; that, as by thy grace we now receive the comfort of thy blessings, so we may be brought to the everlasting fruition of the same. Through.

July 13.

St. Anacletus

Pope and Martyr

Simple.

The Mass Si diligis me, p. [2].

Collect. C 1

O EVERLASTING Shepherd, look down in mercy on thy flock: and as thou didst choose blessed Anacletus thy Martyr and Chief Bishop to be pastor and ruler of thy Church; so at his intercession defend it with thy continual protection. Through.

Secret. C 1

WE beseech thee, O Lord, graciously enlighten thy Church by the gifts which we here offer: that in every place thy flock may increase and prosper, and the shepherds by thy governance may be made pleasing to thy name. Through.

Postcommunion. C 1

MERCIFUL Lord, we beseech thee to govern and preserve thy Church, which thou hast here refreshed with heavenly food: that by the guiding of thy mighty power it may serve thee in more abundant freedom, and ever keep thy true religion whole and undefiled. Through.

July 14.

St. Bonaventura

Bishop, Confessor, and Doctor of the Church

Double.

Introit. Ecclus. 15, 5. In medio.

IN the midst of the Church he opened his mouth: and the Lord filled him with the spirit of wisdom and understanding: he clothed him with a robe of glory. Ps. 92, 1. It is a good thing to give thanks unto the Lord: and to sing praises unto thy name, O most Highest. ℣. Glory.

Collect.

O GOD, who didst send blessed Bonaventura thy Doctor to guide thy people in the way of everlasting salvation: grant, we beseech thee; that as we have learned of him the doctrine of life on earth, so we may be found worthy to have him for our advocate in heaven. Through.

The Lesson from the Epistle of blessed Paul the Apostle to Timothy.

II Tim. 4, 1-8.

DEARLY beloved: I charge thee before God, and the Lord Jesus Christ, who shall judge the quick and the dead at his appearing and his kingdom: preach the word, be instant in season, out of season: reprove, rebuke, exhort with all longsuffering and doctrine. For the time will come when they will not endure sound doctrine, but after their own lusts shall they heap to themselves teachers, having itching ears, and they shall turn away their ears from the truth, and shall be turned unto fables. But watch thou in all things, endure afflictions, do the work of an Evangelist, make full proof of thy ministry. For I am now ready to be offered, and the time of my departure is at hand. I have fought a good fight, I have finished my course, I have kept the faith. Henceforth there is laid up for me a crown of righteousness, which the Lord, the righteous judge, shall give me at that day: and not to me only, but unto all them also that love his appearing.

Gradual. Ps. 37, 30-31. The mouth of the righteous is exercised in wisdom, and his tongue will be talking of judgment. ℣. The law of his God is in his heart, and his goings shall not slide.

Alleluia, alleluia. ℣. Ps. 110, 4. The Lord sware, and will not repent: Thou art a priest for ever, after the order of Melchisedech. Alleluia.

✠ The Continuation of the holy Gospel according to Matthew.

Matt. 5, 13-19.

AT that time: Jesus said unto his disciples: Ye are the salt of the earth. But if the salt have lost his savour, wherewith shall it be salted? It is henceforth good for nothing, but to be cast out, and to be trodden under foot of men. Ye are the light of the world. A city that is set on an hill cannot be hid. Neither do men light a candle, and put it under a bushel, but on a candlestick, and it giveth light unto all that are in the house. Let your light so shine before men, that they may see your good works, and glorify your Father which is in heaven. Think not that I am come to destroy the law or the prophets: I am not come to destroy, but to fulfil. For verily I say unto you, Till heaven and earth pass, one jot or one tittle shall in no wise pass from the law, till all be fulfilled. Whosoever therefore shall break one of these least commandments, and shall teach men so, he shall be called the least in the kingdom of heaven: but whosoever shall do and teach them, the same shall be called great in the kingdom of heaven. Creed.

Offertory. Ps. 89, 25. My truth and my mercy shall be with him: and in my name shall his horn be exalted.

Secret.

WE beseech thee, O Lord, that our devout observance of the yearly festival of Saint Bonaventura, thy Confessor and Bishop, may render us acceptable unto thy loving kindness: that this oblation of our bounden duty and service may win for him the reward of everlasting felicity, and obtain for us the gifts of thy grace. Through.

Communion. Luke 12, 42. A faithful and wise servant, whom his lord hath made ruler over his household: to give them their portion of meat in due season.

Postcommunion.

O GOD, who rewardest the souls of them that put their trust in thee: vouchsafe; that we who keep the solemn feast of blessed Bonaventura, thy Confessor and Bishop, may by his prayers obtain thy merciful pardon. Through.

July 15.

St. Henry, Emperor

Confessor.

Simple.

The Mass Os justi, from the Common of a Confessor not a Bishop, p. [24], the Collect excepted.

Collect.

O GOD, who as on this day didst cause thy blessed Confessor Henry to pass from the crown of earthly empire to thy everlasting kingdom: we humbly beseech thee; that as by the abundance of thy preventing grace thou didst enable him to overcome the temptations of this life, so thou wouldest suffer us, following his pattern, to avoid the deceits of this world, and in purity of heart to attain unto thee. Through.

Secret.

WE offer thee, O Lord, this our sacrifice of praise to the honour of thy Saints: whereby we trust to be delivered from all evils both in this life, and in that which is to come. Through.

Postcommunion.

O LORD, our God, who hast refreshed us with heavenly meat and drink, we humbly beseech thee: that we may be defended by the prayers of him in whose memory we have received the same. Through.

July 16.

Commemoration of the Blessed Virgin Mary of Mount Carmel

Greater double.

Introit. Gaudeamus.

REJOICE we all in the Lord, keeping feast day in honour of the blessed Virgin Mary: in whose solemnity the Angels rejoice, and glorify the Son of God. Ps. 45, 1. My heart is inditing of a good matter: I speak of the things which I have made unto the King. V. Glory.

Collect.

O GOD, who didst adorn the Order of Carmel with the especial title of thy most blessed Mother the ever Virgin Mary: mercifully grant; that, as we celebrate her Commemoration this day in our solemn observance, so by the help of her succour we may be found worthy to attain unto everlasting felicity: Who livest.

The Lesson from the Book of Wisdom. Ecclus. 24, 17-25.

AS the vine I brought forth a pleasant savour: and my flowers are the fruit of honour and riches. I am the mother of fair love, and fear, and knowledge, and holy hope. In me is all grace of the way and the truth: in me is all hope of life and of virtue. Come unto me, all ye that be desirous of me, and fill yourselves with my fruits. For my spirit is sweeter than honey, and mine inheritance than the honeycomb. My memorial shall be unto everlasting generations. They that eat me shall yet be hungry: and they that drink me shall yet be thirsty. He that obeyeth me shall never be confounded: and they that work by me shall not do amiss. They that expound me shall have life everlasting.

Gradual. Blessed and venerable art thou, O Virgin Mary: who, a Maiden undefiled, hast our Saviour for thy Child. ℣. Virgin, Mother of God, the whole world cannot contain him, yet made man for our sake, hidden he lay in thy womb.

Alleluia, alleluia. ℣. Through thee, O Mother of God, hath our lost life been given to us: thou who didst receive thine offspring from heaven, and bring forth to the world the Saviour. Alleluia.

✠ The Continuation of the holy Gospel according to Luke.

Luke 11, 27-28.

AT that time: As Jesus spake to the multitudes, a certain woman of the company lifted up her voice, and said unto him: Blessed is the womb that bare thee, and the paps which thou hast sucked. But he said: Yea rather, blessed are they that hear the word of God, and keep it. Creed.

Offertory. Jer. 18, 20. Remember, O Virgin Mother, in the sight of God, to speak good things for us, that he may turn away his wrath from us.

Secret.

SANCTIFY, O Lord, we beseech thee, the sacrifice which we offer: and by the most salutary intercession of blessed Mary the Mother of God, vouchsafe that the same may avail for our salvation. Through the same.

Preface of the B.V.Mary, And that on the Commemoration.

Communion. Queen of the world most worthy, Mary evermore Virgin, intercede for our peace and salvation, thou who didst bring forth Christ the Lord, the Saviour of all.

Postcommunion.

O LORD, we beseech thee, let the worshipful intercession of the ever Virgin Mary, thy glorious Mother, continually assist us: that we, being loosed from every danger and enriched by her perpetual bounty; may through her loving kindness be made of one heart and mind: Who livest.

July 17.

St. Alexius

Confessor

Simple.

Introit. Ps. 37, 30-31. Os justi.

THE mouth of the righteous is exercised in wisdom: and his tongue will be talking of judgment: the law of his God is in his heart. Ps. ibid., 1. Fret not thyself because of the ungodly: neither be thou envious against the evildoers. ℣. Glory.

Collect.

O GOD, who dost make us to rejoice in the yearly solemnity of blessed Alexius thy Confessor: mercifully grant; that, as we now observe his heavenly birthday, so we may follow the example of his life. Through.

The Lesson from the Epistle of blessed Paul the Apostle to Timothy.

I Tim. 6, 6-12.

DEARLY beloved: Godliness with contentment is great gain. For we brought nothing into this world: and it is certain we can carry nothing out. And having food and raiment let us be therewith content. But they that will be rich fall into temptation and a snare, and into many foolish and hurtful lusts: which drown men in destruction and perdition. For the love of money is the root of all evil: which while some coveted after, they have erred from the faith, and pierced themselves through with many sorrows. But thou, O man of God, flee these things: and follow after righteousness, godliness, faith, love, patience, meekness. Fight the good fight of faith, lay hold on eternal life.

Gradual. Ps. 92, 13-14. The righteous shall flourish like a palm-tree: and shall spread abroad like a cedar in Libanus in the house of the Lord. ℣. Ibid., 3. To tell of thy loving kindness early in the morning, and of thy truth in the night-season.

Alleluia, alleluia. ℣. James 1, 12. Blessed is the man that endureth temptation: for when he is tried, he shall receive the crown of life. Alleluia.

✠ The Continuation of the holy Gospel according to Matthew.

Matt. 19, 27.

AT that time: Peter said unto Jesus: Behold, we have forsaken all, and followed thee: what shall we have therefor? And Jesus said unto them: Verily I say unto you, That ye which have followed me, in the regeneration when the Son of man shall sit in the throne of his glory, ye also shall sit upon twelve thrones, judging the twelve tribes of Israel. And everyone that hath forsaken houses, or brethren, or sisters, or father, or mother, or wife, or children, or lands, for my name's sake, shall receive an hundred-fold, and shall inherit everlasting life.

Offertory. Ps. 89, 25. My truth and my mercy shall be with him: and in my name shall his horn be exalted.

Secret.

WE offer thee, O Lord, this our sacrifice of praise to the honour of thy Saints: whereby we trust to be delivered from all evils both in this life and in that which is to come. Through.

Communion. Matt. 24, 46-47. Blessed is the servant whom his lord when he cometh shall find watching: verily I say unto you, he shall make him ruler over all his goods.

Postcommunion.

O LORD our God, who hast refreshed us with heavenly meat and drink, we humbly beseech thee: that we may be defended by the prayers of him in whose memory we have received the same. Through.

July 18.

St. Camillus of Lellis

Confessor

Double.

Introit. John 15, 13. Majorem hac.

GREATER love hath no man than this, that a man lay down his life for his friends. Ps. 41, 1. Blessed is he that considereth the poor and needy: the Lord will deliver him in the time of trouble. ℣. Glory.

Collect.

O GOD, who, for the succour of souls striving in their last agony, didst endue Saint Camillus with singular gifts of charity: we beseech thee by his merits, pour into our hearts the spirit of thy love; that in the hour of our departing we may be found worthy to overcome the enemy, and to attain unto the heavenly crown. Through.

Commemoration of SS. Symphorosa and her seven Sons, Martyrs.

Collect.

O GOD, who dost vouchsafe unto us to celebrate the heavenly birthday of thy holy Martyrs Symphorosa and her Sons: grant that we may rejoice in their fellowship in everlasting bliss. Through.

The Lesson from the Epistle of blessed John the Apostle.

I John 3, 13-18.

DEARLY beloved: Marvel not if the world hate you. We know that we have passed from death unto life, because we love the brethren. He that loveth not his brother abideth in death: whosoever hateth his brother is a murderer. And ye know that no murderer hath eternal life abiding in him. Hereby perceive we the love of God, because he laid down his life for us: and we ought to lay down our lives for the brethren. But whoso hath this world's good, and seeth his brother have need, and shutteth up his bowels of compassion from him: how dwelleth the love of God in him? My little children, let us not love in word, neither in tongue, but in deed and in truth.

Gradual. Ps. 37, 30-31. The mouth of the righteous is exercised in wisdom, and his tongue will be talking of judgment. ℣. The law of his God is in his heart: and his goings shall not slide.

Alleluia, alleluia. ℣. Ps. 112, 1. Blessed is the man that feareth the Lord: he hath great delight in his commandments. Alleluia.

✠ The Continuation of the holy Gospel according to John.

John 15, 12-16.

AT that time: Jesus said unto his disciples: This is my commandment, That ye love one another, as I have loved you. Greater love hath no man than this, that a man lay down his life for his friends. Ye are my friends, if ye do whatsoever I command you. Henceforth I call you not servants: for the servant knoweth not what his lord doeth. But I have called you friends: for all things that I have heard of my Father I have made known unto you. Ye have not chosen me: but I have chosen you, and ordained you, that ye should go and bring forth fruit: and that your fruit should remain: that whatsoever ye shall ask of the Father in my name, he may give it you.

Offertory. Ps. 21, 1-2. The just shall rejoice in thy strength, O Lord, exceeding glad shall he be of thy salvation: thou hast given him his heart's desire.

Secret.

LET this spotless sacrifice, wherein we renew that work of the infinite love of our Lord Jesus Christ, avail unto us, O God the Father almighty, at the intercession of Saint Camillus, for our healing and protection against infirmities of body and soul, and in our last agony for our consolation and defence. Through the same.

For SS. Symphorosa and her seven Sons:

Secret.

WE beseech thee, O Lord, that the gifts which we offer unto thee of our bounden duty and service may be acceptable unto thee for the honour of thy Saints: and by thy mercy profitable unto us for our salvation. Through.

Communion. Matt. 25, 36 and 40. I was sick, and ye visited me. Verily, verily I say unto you: Inasmuch as ye have done it unto one of the least of these my brethren, ye have done it unto me.

Postcommunion.

GRANT, we beseech thee, O Lord, through this heavenly food, which we, who celebrate the feast of Saint Camillus, thy Confessor, have now received with reverence and godly fear: that in the hour of our death we, being refreshed by thy sacraments, and cleansed from all our offences; may be found worthy to be received with gladness into the bosom of thy mercy: Who livest and reignest with God the Father.

For SS. Symphorosa and her seven Sons:

Postcommunion.

GRANT to us we beseech thee, O Lord: at the intercession of thy holy Martyrs Symphorosa and her Sons; that we, who with our outward lips are partakers of this holy Sacrament, may inwardly receive the same in purity of heart. Through.

July 19.

St. Vincent of Paul

Confessor

Double.

Introit. Ps. 92, 13-14. Justus ut palma.

THE righteous shall flourish like a palm-tree: and shall spread abroad like a cedar in Libanus: such as are planted in the house of the Lord: in the courts of the house of our God. Ps. ibid., 1. It is a good thing to give thanks unto the Lord: and to sing praises unto thy name, O most Highest. ℣. Glory.

Collect.

O GOD, who didst endue blessed Vincent with apostolic virtue, that he should preach thy gospel to the poor, and set forward the honour of the orders of thy Church: grant we beseech thee; that we may so reverence his works of righteousness, that we may learn to follow the pattern of his godly conversation. Through.

The Lesson from the Epistle of blessed Paul the Apostle to the Corinthians.

I Cor. 4, 9-14.

BRETHREN: We are made a spectacle unto the world, and to Angels, and to men. We are fools for Christ's sake, but ye are wise in Christ: we are weak, but ye are strong: ye are honourable, but we are despised. Even unto this present hour we both hunger, and thirst, and are naked, and are buffeted, and have no certain dwelling-place, and labour, working with our own hands: being reviled, we bless: being persecuted, we suffer it: being defamed, we intreat: we are made as the filth of the world, and are the offscouring of all things unto this day. I write not these things to shame you, but as my beloved sons I warn you: in Christ Jesu our Lord.

Gradual. Ps. 37, 30-31. The mouth of the righteous is exercised in wisdom, and his tongue will be talking of judgment. ℣. The law of his God is in his heart: and his goings shall not slide.

Alleluia, alleluia. ℣. Ps. 112, 1. Blessed is the man that feareth the Lord: he hath great delight in his commandments. Alleluia.

✠ The Continuation of the holy Gospel according to Luke.

Luke 10, 1-9.

AT that time: The Lord appointed other seventy also: and sent them two and two before his face into every city and place whither he himself would come. Therefore said he unto them: The harvest truly is great, but the labourers are few. Pray ye therefore the Lord of the harvest, that he would send forth labourers into his harvest. Go your ways: behold, I send you forth as lambs among wolves. Carry neither purse, nor scrip, nor shoes, and salute no man by the way. And into whatsoever house ye enter, first say: Peace be to this house: and if the son of peace be there, your peace shall rest upon it: if not, it shall turn to you again. And in the same house remain, eating and drinking such things as they give: for the labourer is worthy of his hire. Go not from house to house. And into whatsoever city ye enter, and they receive you, eat such things as are set before you: and heal the sick that are therein, and say unto them: The kingdom of God is come nigh unto you.

Offertory. Ps. 21, 2-3. The just shall rejoice in thy strength, O Lord, exceeding glad shall he be of thy salvation: thou hast given him his heart's desire.

Secret.

GRANT to us, we beseech thee, almighty God: that this oblation of our humble service may be acceptable in thy sight to the honour of thy Saints, and may cleanse us both in body and soul. Through.

Communion. Matt. 19, 28-29. Verily I say unto you: that ye which have forsaken all, and followed me, shall receive an hundred-fold, and shall inherit everlasting life.

Postcommunion.

WE beseech thee, almighty God: that we, who have received this heavenly food, may at the intercession of blessed Vincent thy Confessor be thereby defended against all adversities. Through.

July 20.

St. Jerome Emilian

Confessor

Double.

Introit. Lam. 2, 11. Effusum est.

MY liver is poured upon the earth for the destruction of the daughter of my people, because the children and the sucklings swoon in the streets of the city. Ps. 113, 1. Praise the Lord, ye children: O praise the name of the Lord. ℣. Glory.

Collect.

O GOD, the father of mercies, who didst will that blessed Jerome should be a helper and father of the fatherless: vouchsafe; that through his merits and intercession we, who by the spirit of adoption are called and are indeed thy sons, may faithfully preserve the same within us. Through.

Commemoration of S. Margaret, Virgin and Martyr.

Collect.

WE beseech thee, O Lord, that, like as blessed Margaret, thy Virgin and Martyr, by the merit of her chastity, and by her confession of thy power, was ever found acceptable in thy sight: so she may effectually intercede for our forgiveness. Through.

The Lesson from the Prophet Isaiah.

Is. 58, 7-11.

THUS saith the Lord: Deal thy bread to the hungry, and bring the poor that are cast out to thy house: when thou seest the naked, cover him, and hide not thyself from thine own flesh. Then shall thy light break forth as the morning, and thine health shall spring forth speedily, and thy righteousness shall go before thee, the glory of the Lord shall be thy rereward. Then shalt thou call, and the Lord shall answer: thou shalt cry, and he shall say: Here I am; if thou take away from the midst of thee the yoke, the putting forth of the finger, and speaking vanity. And if thou draw out thy soul to the hungry, and satisfy the afflicted soul, then shall thy light rise in obscurity, and thy darkness be as the noonday. And the Lord shall guide thee continually, and satisfy thy soul with brightness, and deliver thy bones, and thou shalt be like a watered garden, and like a spring of water whose waters fail not.

Gradual. Prov. 5, 16. Let thy fountains be dispersed abroad, and rivers of waters in the streets. ℣. Ps. 112, 5-6. A good man is merciful and lendeth: and will guide his words with discretion, for he shall never be moved.

Alleluia, alleluia. ℣. Ibid., 9. He hath dispersed abroad, and given to the poor: and his righteousness remaineth for ever. Alleluia.

✠ The Continuation of the holy Gospel according to Matthew.
Matt. 19, 13-21.

AT that time: There were brought unto Jesus little children that he should put his hands on them, and pray. And the disciples rebuked them. But Jesus said: Suffer little children, and forbid them not, to come unto me: for of such is the kingdom of heaven. And he laid his hands on them, and departed thence. And behold, one came and said unto him: Good Master, what good thing shall I do that I may have eternal life? And he said unto him: Why callest thou me good? There is none good but one, that is, God. But if thou wilt enter into life, keep the commandments. He saith unto him: Which? Jesus said: Thou shalt do no murder: Thou shalt not commit adultery: Thou shalt not steal: Thou shalt not bear false witness: Honour thy father and thy mother, and, Thou shalt love thy neighbour as thyself. The young man saith unto him: All these things have I kept from my youth up: what lack I yet? Jesus said unto him: If thou wilt be perfect, go and sell that thou hast, and give to the poor, and thou shalt have treasure in heaven: and come and follow me.

Offertory. Tob. 12, 12. When thou didst pray with tears, and didst bury the dead, and leave thy dinner, and didst hide the dead in thy house by day, and bury them by night: I offered thy prayer unto the Lord.

Secret.

MOST merciful God, who in blessed Jerome didst vouchsafe, the old man being done away, to create a new man after thine own likeness: grant, through his merits; that we, being likewise renewed, may present this sacrifice, oblation and satisfaction for a sweet savour in thy sight. Through.

For St. Margaret.   Secret.

GRACIOUSLY receive, O Lord, through the merits of blessed Margaret, thy Virgin and Martyr, the sacrifices which we offer unto thee: and grant that they may avail for our continual help. Through.

Communion. James 1, 27. Pure religion and undefiled before God and the Father is this: To visit the fatherless and widows in their affliction, and to keep himself unspotted from the world.

Postcommunion.

O LORD, who hast refreshed us with the bread of Angels, we humbly beseech thee: that we, who celebrate with gladness the yearly remembrance of blessed Jerome thy Confessor; may likewise follow after his example, and be counted worthy to receive an exceeding great reward in thy kingdom. Through.

For St. Margaret.   Postcommunion.

O LORD our God, who hast fulfilled us with the bounty of thy heavenly gift: we beseech thee that, at the intercession of blessed Margaret, thy Virgin and Martyr, we may ever live by the partaking of the same. Through.

(For St. Margaret, V.M., the Mass Exspectaverunt, p. [29])

July 21.
For St. Praxedes
Virgin

Introit. Ps. 119, 46-47. Loquebar.

I WILL speak of thy testimonies even before kings, and will not be ashamed: and my delight shall be in thy commandments, which I have loved exceedingly. Ps. ibid., 1. Blessed are those that are undefiled in the way: and walk in the law of the Lord. ℣. Glory.

Collect.

GRACIOUSLY hear us, O God of our salvation: that, like as we do rejoice in the festival of blessed Praxedes, thy Virgin, so we may learn to follow her example in godliness and charity. Through.

Epistle Concerning virgins, p. [33].

Gradual. Ps. 45, 8. Thou hast loved righteousness and hated iniquity. ℣. Wherefore God, even thy God, hath anointed thee with the oil of gladness.

Alleluia, alleluia. ℣. Ibid., 5. In thy comeliness and in thy beauty go forth, ride prosperously and reign. Alleluia.

Gospel The kingdom of heaven is like unto treasure, p. [34].

Offertory. Ps. 45. Full of grace are thy lips, because God hath blessed thee for ever, and world without end.

Secret.

GRANT, O Lord, that like as thy dedicated people do acknowledge that in tribulation they have been succoured by the merits of thy Saints: so this oblation, which they offer unto thee in honour of the same, may be acceptable in thy sight. Through.

Communion. Matt. 13. The kingdom of heaven is like unto a merchant man, seeking goodly pearls: who when he had found one pearl of great price, gave all that he had, and bought it.

Postcommunion.

O LORD, who hast satisfied this thy family with thy sacred gifts: we beseech thee; that we may at all times be comforted by the intercession of her whose festival we celebrate. Through.

July 22.

St. Mary Magdalen

Penitent

Double.

Introit. Ps. 119, 95-96.

Me exspectaverunt.

THE ungodly laid wait for me to destroy me: but I will consider thy testimonies, O Lord: I see that all things come to an end: but thy commandment is exceeding broad. Ps. ibid., 1. Blessed are those that are undefiled in the way: and walk in the law of the Lord. ℣. Glory.

Collect.

WE beseech thee, O Lord, that as thou didst hearken to the prayers of blessed Mary Magdalen, and didst raise her brother Lazarus to life when he had been dead four days; so we may know the succour of her intercession: Who livest.

The Lesson from the book of Wisdom.

Song of Songs 3, 2-5; 8, 6-7.

I WILL rise and go about the city: in the streets and in the broad ways I will seek him whom my soul loveth: I sought him, but I found him not. The watchmen that go about the city found me. To whom I said: Saw ye him whom my soul loveth? It was but a little that I passed from them, but I found him whom my soul loveth: I held him, and would not let him go, until I had brought him into my mother's house, and into the chamber of her that conceived me. I charge you, O ye daughters of Jerusalem, by the roes and by the hinds of the field, that ye stir not up, nor awake my love, till he please. Set me as a seal upon thine heart, as a seal upon thine arm: for love is strong as death, jealousy is cruel as the grave: the coals thereof are coals of fire, which hath a most vehement flame. Many waters cannot quench love, neither can the floods drown it: if a man would give all the substance of his house for love, it would utterly be contemned.

Gradual. Ps. 45, 8. Thou hast loved righteousness and hated iniquity. ℣. Wherefore God, even thy God, hath anointed thee with the oil of gladness.

Alleluia, alleluia. ℣. Ibid., 3. Full of grace are thy lips: because God hath blessed thee for ever. Alleluia.

✠ The Continuation of the holy Gospel according to Luke.

Luke 7, 36-50.

AT that time: One of the Pharisees desired Jesus that he would eat with him. And he went into the Pharisee's house, and sat down to meat. And behold, a woman in the city, which was a sinner, when she knew that Jesus sat at meat in the Pharisee's house, brought an alabaster box of ointment: and stood at his feet behind him weeping, and began to wash his feet with tears, and did wipe them with the hairs of her head, and kissed his feet, and anointed them with the ointment. Now when the Pharisee which had bidden him saw it, he spake within himself, saying: This man, if he were a Prophet, would have known who and what manner of woman this is that toucheth him: for she is a sinner. And Jesus answering said unto him: Simon, I have somewhat to say unto thee. And he saith: Master, say on. There was a certain creditor which had two debtors: the one owed five hundred pence, and the other fifty. And when they had nothing to pay, he frankly forgave them both. Tell me therefore, which of them will love him most? Simon answered and said: I suppose that he, to whom he forgave most. And he said unto him: Thou hast rightly judged. And he turned to the woman, and said unto Simon: Seest thou this woman? I entered into thine house, thou gavest me no water for my feet: but she hath washed my feet with tears, and wiped them with the hairs of her head. Thou gavest me no kiss: but this woman since the time I came in hath not ceased to kiss my feet. My head with oil thou didst not anoint: but this woman hath anointed my feet with ointment. Wherefore I say unto thee: Her sins, which are many, are forgiven, for she loved much. But to whom little is forgiven, the same loveth little. And he said unto her: Thy sins are forgiven. And they that sat at meat with him began to say within themselves: Who is this that forgiveth sins also? And he said to the woman: Thy faith hath saved thee: go in peace.

The Creed is not said.

Offertory. Ps. 45, 10. Kings' daughters were among thy honourable women, upon thy right hand did stand the queen in a vesture of gold, wrought about with divers colours.

Secret.

WE beseech thee, O Lord, that the glorious merits of blessed Mary Magdalen may render our gifts acceptable in thy sight: even as the oblation of her devout obedience was graciously accepted by thine only-begotten Son: Who liveth and reigneth with thee.

Communion. Ps. 119, 121-122 and 128. I deal with the thing that is lawful and right, O Lord, let the proud do me no wrong: I hold straight all thy commandments, and all false ways I utterly abhor.

Postcommunion.

WE beseech thee, O Lord, that we who have received thy precious Body and Blood, the only medicine for the healing of our souls: may by the protection of Saint Mary Magdalen be delivered from all adversities: Who livest and reignest with God the Father.

July 23.

St. Apollinaris

Bishop and Martyr

Double.

Introit. Dan. 3, 84 and 87.

Sacerdotes Dei.

O YE priests of the Lord, bless ye the Lord: O ye holy and humble men of heart, praise God. Cant. ibid., 57. O all ye works of the Lord, bless ye the Lord: praise him and magnify him for ever. ℣. Glory.

Collect.

O GOD, the rewarder of faithful souls, who hast hallowed this day by the martyrdom of blessed Apollinaris, thy Priest: grant, we beseech thee, unto us thy servants; that we who keep his solemn festival may by his prayers obtain thy pardon. Through.

Commemoration of St. Liborious, B.C.

Collect.

GRANT, we beseech thee, almighty God: that we, devoutly observing this festival of blessed Liborius, thy Confessor and Bishop; may thereby advance in true godliness and attain unto everlasting salvation. Through.

The Lesson from the Epistle of blessed Peter the Apostle.

I Peter 5, 1-11.

DEARLY beloved: The elders which are among you I exhort, who am also an elder, and a witness of the sufferings of Christ: and also a partaker of the glory that shall be revealed: feed the flock of God which is among you, taking the oversight thereof, not by constraint, but willingly: not for filthy lucre, but of a ready mind: neither as being lords over God's heritage, but being ensamples to the flock. And when the chief Shepherd shall appear, ye shall receive a crown of glory that fadeth not away. Likewise, ye younger, submit yourselves unto the elder. Yea, all of you be subject one to another, and be clothed with humility: for God resisteth the proud, and giveth grace to the humble. Humble yourselves therefore under the mighty hand of God, that he may exalt you in due time: casting all your care upon him, for he careth for you. Be sober, be vigilant: because your adversary the devil, as a roaring lion, walketh about, seeking whom he may devour: whom resist stedfast in the faith: knowing that the same afflictions are accomplished in your brethren that are in the world. But the God of all grace, who hath called us unto his eternal glory in Christ Jesus, after that ye have suffered a while, make you perfect, stablish, strengthen, settle you. To him be glory and dominion for ever and ever. Amen.

Gradual. Ps. 89, 21-23. I have found David my servant, with my holy oil have I anointed him: my hand shall hold him fast, and my arm shall strengthen him. ℣. The enemy shall not be able to do him violence, the son of wickedness shall not hurt him.

Alleluia, alleluia. ℣. Ps. 110, 4. The Lord sware, and will not repent: Thou art a priest for ever, after the order of Melchisedech. Alleluia.

✠ The Continuation of the holy Gospel according to Luke.

Luke 22, 24-30.

AT that time: There was a strife among the disciples, which of them should be accounted the greatest. And Jesus said unto them: The kings of the Gentiles exercise lordship over them; and they that exercise authority upon them are called benefactors. But ye shall not be so: but he that is greatest among you, let him be as the younger: and he that is chief, as he that doth serve. For whether is greater, he that sitteth at meat, or he that serveth? is not he that sitteth at meat? But I am among you as he that serveth. Ye are they which have continued with me in my temptations: and I appoint unto you a kingdom, as my Father hath appointed unto me, that ye may eat and drink at my table in my kingdom: and sit on thrones judging the twelve tribes of Israel.

Offertory. Ps. 89, 25. My truth and my mercy shall be with him: and in my name shall his horn be exalted.

Secret.

GRACIOUSLY look, O Lord, upon these our gifts: which in remembrance of blessed Apollinaris, thy Priest and Martyr, we lay before thee, and offer up for our offences. Through.

For St. Liborius. Secret.

WE beseech thee, O Lord, that we, remembering with gladness the merits of thy Saints, may in all places feel the succour of their intercession. Through.

Communion. Matt. 25, 20-21. Lord, thou deliveredst unto me five talents, behold I have gained besides them five talents more. Well done, thou good and faithful servant, thou hast been faithful over a few things, I will make thee ruler over many things, enter thou into the joy of thy Lord.

Postcommunion.

WE beseech thee, O Lord, that the protection of blessed Apollinaris may continually defend us, who have here received thy holy mysteries: forasmuch as thou failest not to look with mercy on those to whom thou dost grant the succour of his assistance. Through.

For St. Liborius. Postcommunion.

GRANT, we beseech thee, almighty God: that we, shewing forth our thankfulness for the gifts which we have received, may, at the intercession of blessed Liborius, thy Confessor and Bishop, obtain yet more abundant mercies. Through.

July 24.

For St. Christina

Virgin and Martyr

The Mass Me exspectaverunt, p. [29].

Collect.

WE beseech thee, O Lord, that, like as blessed Christina, thy Virgin and Martyr, by the merit of her chastity, and by her confession of thy power, was ever found acceptable in thy sight: so she may effectually intercede for our forgiveness. Through.

Secret.

GRACIOUSLY receive, O Lord, through the merits of blessed Christina, thy Virgin and Martyr, the sacrifices which we offer unto thee: and grant that they may avail for our continual help. Through.

Postcommunion.

O LORD our God, who hast fulfilled us with the bounty of thy heavenly gift: we beseech thee that, at the intercession of blessed Christina, thy Virgin and Martyr, we may ever live by the partaking of the same. Through.

July 25.

ST. JAMES THE APOSTLE

Double of 2nd class.

Introit. Ps. 139, 17. Mihi autem.

RIGHT dear are thy friends unto me, O God, and held in highest honour: their rule and governance is exceeding stedfast. Ps. ibid., 1. O Lord, thou hast searched me out, and known me: thou knowest my down-sitting, and mine up-rising. ℣. Glory.

Collect.

GRANT, O merciful God: that as thine holy Apostle Saint James, leaving his father and all that he had, without delay was obedient unto the calling of thy Son Jesus Christ, and followed him; so we, forsaking all worldly and carnal affections, may be evermore ready to follow thy holy commandments. Through the same.

Or, Collect.

SANCTIFY, O Lord, and defend this thy people: that we, being strengthened by the assistance of thy Apostle James, may through our godly conversation be found acceptable in thy sight, and ever serve thee with a quiet mind. Through.

In private Masses only a Commemoration of St. Christopher, M., is made.

Collect.

GRANT, we beseech thee, almighty God: that we, who celebrate the heavenly birthday of blessed Christopher, thy Martyr, may by his intercession be stablished in the love of thy name. Through.

The Lesson from the Acts of the Apostles.

Acts 11, 27-12, 3.

IN those days: Came prophets from Jerusalem unto Antioch. And there stood up one of them named Agabus, and signified by the Spirit, that there should be great dearth throughout all the world: which came to pass in the days of Claudius Cæsar. Then the disciples, every man according to his ability, determined to send relief unto the brethren which dwelt in Judæa. Which also they did, and sent it to the elders by the hands of Barnabas and Saul. Now about that time Herod the king stretched forth his hands to vex certain of the Church. And he killed James the brother of John with the sword. And, because he saw it pleased the Jews, he proceeded further to take Peter also.

Or:

The Lesson from the Epistle of blessed Paul the Apostle to the Corinthians.

I Cor. 4, 9-15.

BRETHREN: I think that God hath set forth us the Apostles last, as it were appointed to death: for we are made a spectacle unto the world, and to Angels, and to men. We are fools for Christ's sake, but ye are wise in Christ: we are weak, but ye are strong: ye are honourable, but we are despised. Even unto this present hour we both hunger and thirst and are naked, and are buffeted, and have no certain dwelling-place, and labour, working with our own hands: being reviled, we bless: being persecuted, we suffer it: being defamed, we intreat: we are made as the filth of the world, and are the off-scouring of all things unto this day. I write not these things to shame you, but as my beloved sons I warn you. For though ye have ten thousand instructors in Christ: yet have ye not many fathers. For in Christ Jesus I have begotten you through the Gospel.

Gradual. Ps. 45, 17-18. Thou shalt make them princes in all lands: they shall remember thy name, O Lord. ℣. Instead of thy fathers thou shalt have children: therefore shall the people give thanks unto thee.

Alleluia, alleluia. ℣. John 15, 16. I have chosen you out of the world, that ye should go and bring forth fruit: and that your fruit should remain. Alleluia.

✠ The Continuation of the holy Gospel according to Matthew.

Matt. 20, 20-23.

AT that time: There came unto Jesus the mother of Zebedee's children with her sons, worshipping him, and desiring a certain thing of him. And he said unto her: What wilt thou? She saith unto him: Grant that these my two sons may sit, the one on thy right hand, and the other on the left, in thy kingdom. But Jesus answered and said: Ye know not what ye ask. Are ye able to drink of the cup that I shall drink of, and to be baptized with the baptism that I am baptized with? They say unto him: We are able. And he saith unto them: Ye shall drink indeed of my cup, and be baptized with the baptism that I am baptized with: but to sit on my right hand, and on my left, is not mine to give, but it shall be given to them for whom it is prepared of my Father.*

And when the ten heard it, they were moved with indignation against the two brethren. But Jesus called them unto him, and said: Ye know that the princes of the Gentiles exercise dominion over them, and they that are great exercise authority upon them. But it shall not be so among you: but whosoever will be great among you, let him be your minister, and whosoever will be chief among you, let him be your servant: even as the Son of man came not to be ministered unto, but to minister, and to give his life a ransom for many. Creed.

Offertory. Ps. 19, 5. Their sound is gone out into all lands: and their words into the ends of the world.

Secret.

WE beseech thee, O Lord, that the blessed passion of thy blessed Apostle James may commend unto thee the oblations of thy people: that although they may be unworthy by reason of our merits, they may through his prayers be made acceptable unto thee. Through.

For St. Christopher. Secret.

WE beseech thee, O Lord, to accept our prayers and oblations: and graciously hearken unto us, whom thou dost cleanse by thy heavenly mysteries. Through.

Preface of the Apostles.

Communion. Matt. 19, 28. Ye, which have followed me, shall sit upon thrones judging the twelve tribes of Israel.

Postcommunion.

WE beseech thee, O Lord, that we who on this feast of thy blessed Apostle James have joyfully received thy holy mysteries: may by his intercession obtain thy succour. Through.

For St. Christopher. Postcommunion.

GRANT, we beseech thee, O Lord our God: that like as we in this life do gladly honour the memory of thy Saints; so we may rejoice hereafter in their everlasting fellowship. Through.

July 26.

ST. ANNE

MOTHER OF THE BLESSED VIRGIN MARY

Double of 2nd class.

Introit. Gaudeamus.

REJOICE we all in the Lord, keeping feast day in honour of blessed Anne: in whose solemnity the Angels rejoice and glorify the Son of God. Ps. 45, 1. My heart is inditing of a good matter: I speak of the things which I have made unto the King. ℣. Glory.

Collect.

O GOD, who on blessed Anne didst vouchsafe to bestow grace, to be made worthy to bear the Mother of thine only-begotten Son: mercifully grant; that we who celebrate her festival may through her intercession find favour in thy sight. Through the same.

The Lesson from the book of Wisdom.
Prov. 31, 10-31.

WHO can find a virtuous woman? For her price is far above rubies. The heart of her husband doth safely trust in her, so that he shall have no need of spoil. She will do him good and not evil all the days of her life. She seeketh wool, and flax, and worketh willingly with her hands. She is like the merchants' ships, she bringeth her food from afar. She riseth also while it is yet night, and giveth meat to her household, and a portion to her maidens. She considereth a field and buyeth it: with the fruit of her hands she planteth a vine-yard. She girdeth her loins with strength, and strengtheneth her arms. She perceiveth that her merchandise is good: her candle goeth not out by night. She layeth her hands to the spindle, and her hands hold the distaff. She stretcheth out her hand to the poor, yea, she reacheth forth her hands to the needy. She is not afraid of the snow for her household: for all her household are clothed with scarlet. She maketh herself coverings of tapestry: her clothing is silk and purple. Her husband is known in the gates, when he sitteth among the elders of the land. She maketh fine linen, and selleth it, and delivereth girdles unto the merchant. Strength and honour are her clothing, and she shall rejoice in time to come. She openeth her mouth with wisdom, and in her tongue is the law of kindness. She looketh well to the ways of her household, and eateth not the bread of idleness. Her children arise up, and call her blessed: her husband also, and he praiseth her. Many daughters have done virtuously, but thou excellest them all. Favour is deceitful, and beauty is vain: but a woman that feareth the Lord, she shall be praised. Give her of the fruit of her hands: and let her own works praise her in the gates.

Gradual. Ps. 45, 8. Thou hast loved righteousness and hated iniquity. ℣. Wherefore God, even thy God, hath anointed thee with the oil of gladness.

Alleluia, alleluia. ℣. Ibid., 3. Full of grace are thy lips: because God hath blessed thee for ever. Alleluia.

✠ The Continuation of the holy Gospel according to Matthew.

Matt. 13, 44-52.

AT that time: Jesus spake this parable unto his disciples: The kingdom of heaven is like unto treasure hid in a field: the which when a man hath found, he hideth, and for joy thereof goeth and selleth all that he hath, and buyeth that field. Again, the kingdom of heaven is like unto a merchant man, seeking goodly pearls. Who, when he had found one pearl of great price, went and sold all that he had, and bought it. Again, the kingdom of heaven is like unto a net that was cast into the sea, and gathered of every kind. Which, when it was full, they drew to shore, and sat down, and gathered the good into vessels, but cast the bad away. So shall it be at the end of the world: the Angels shall come forth, and sever the wicked from among the just, and shall cast them into the furnace of fire: there shall be wailing and gnashing of teeth. Jesus said unto them: Have ye understood all these things? They say unto him: Yea, Lord. Then said he unto them: Therefore every scribe which is instructed unto the kingdom of heaven is like unto a man that is an householder, which bringeth forth out of his treasure things new and old.

Offertory. Ps. 45, 10. Kings' daughters were among thy honourable women, upon thy right hand did stand the queen in a vesture of gold, wrought about with divers colours.

Secret.

WE beseech thee, O Lord, mercifully to have respect unto this our sacrifice: that through the intercession of blessed Anne, who bare the Mother of thy Son, our Lord Jesus Christ, the same may be profitable unto us for the increase of our godliness, and for the attainment of everlasting felicity. Through the same.

Common Preface, even if this Feast fall on Sunday.

Communion. Ps. 45, 3. Full of grace are thy lips: because God hath blessed thee for ever, and world without end.

Postcommunion.

WE beseech thee, O Lord our God: that by the intercession of blessed Anne, whom thou didst choose to bring forth the Mother of thy Son; we, whom thou hast quickened with these heavenly sacraments, may be found worthy to attain to everlasting salvation. Through the same.

Votive Masses are said as above, but with Introit (and after Septuagesima Tract also) from the Mass Cognovi, p. [36].

July 27.

For St. Pantaleon

Martyr

The Mass Laetabitur, p. [7].

Collect. C

GRANT, we beseech thee, almighty God: that, at the intercession of blessed Pantaleon thy Martyr, we may be delivered from all adversities which may happen to the body, and from all evil thoughts which may assault and hurt the soul. Through.

Secret. C

LET this our bounden duty and service be acceptable in thy sight, O Lord: and through the supplication of him for whose solemnity it is offered, let it avail for our salvation. Through.

Postcommunion. C

WE beseech thee, O Lord our God, that like as we, whom thou hast refreshed by the partaking of thy sacred gift, do offer unto thee our outward worship: so, at the intercession of blessed Pantaleon thy Martyr, we may inwardly be profited thereby to our salvation. Through.

July 28.

SS. Nazarius and Celsus, Martyrs, Victor I, Pope and Martyr and Innocent I, Pope and Confessor

Simple.

The Mass Intret, p. [9], the Prayers and Lesson excepted.

Collect. P

O LORD, let the glorious confession of thy Saints, Nazarius, Celsus, Victor and Innocent, evermore strengthen and defend us: and obtain for our frailty thy gracious and ready help. Through.

The Lesson from the book of Wisdom.

Wisd. 10, 17.

GOD rendered to the just a reward of their labours, guided them in a marvellous way: and was unto them for a cover by day, and a light of stars in the night season: brought them through the Red Sea, and led them through much water. But he drowned their enemies, and cast them up out of the bottom of the deep. Therefore the just spoiled the ungodly, and praised thy holy name, O Lord, and magnified with one accord thine hand, that fought for them, O Lord our God.

Secret. P

GRANT to us, almighty God: that we, who present these gifts unto thee to the honour of thy Saints, Nazarius, Celsus, Victor and Innocent, may be made acceptable unto thee by the offering, and be quickened by the receiving of the same. Through.

Postcommunion. P

GRANT, O Lord, we beseech thee, that the intercession of thy Saints, Nazarius, Celsus, Victor and Innocent, may so render us acceptable unto thee: that this our temporal celebration may be profitable unto us for the obtaining of eternal salvation. Through.

July 29.

St. Martha

Virgin

Simple.

Introit. Ps. 45, 8. *Dilexisti.*

THOU hast loved righteousness, and hated iniquity: therefore God, even thy God, hath anointed thee with the oil of gladness above thy fellows. Ps. ibid., 1. My heart is inditing of a good matter: I speak of the things which I have made unto the King. ℣. Glory.

Collect.

GRACIOUSLY hear us, O God of our salvation: that, like as we do rejoice in the festival of blessed Martha, thy Virgin; so we may learn to follow her example in godliness and charity. Through.

Commemoration of SS. Felix, Pope, Simplicius, Faustinus and Beatrice, MM.

Collect.

GRANT, we beseech thee, O Lord, that as thy Christian people rejoiceth in this life in the festival of thy Martyrs, Felix, Simplicius, Faustinus and Beatrice: so they may be partakers of their everlasting felicity; and attain unto the fulness of those holy mysteries, which here they celebrate on earth. Through.

The Lesson from the Epistle of blessed Paul the Apostle to the Corinthians.

II Cor. 10, 17-18; 11, 1-2.

BRETHREN: He that glorieth, let him glory in the Lord. For not he that commendeth himself is approved; but whom the Lord commendeth. Would to God ye could bear with me a little in my folly, and indeed bear with me: for I am jealous over you with godly jealousy. For I have espoused you to one husband, that I may present you as a chaste virgin to Christ.

Gradual. Ps. 45, 5. In thy comeliness and in thy beauty go forth, ride prosperously and reign. ℣. Because of the word of truth, of meekness, and righteousness: and thy right hand shall teach thee terrible things.

Alleluia, alleluia. ℣. Ibid., 15-16. The Virgins that be her fellows shall be brought unto the King: they that bear her company shall be brought unto thee with joy. Alleluia.

✠ The Continuation of the holy Gospel according to Luke.

Luke 10, 38-42.

AT that time: Jesus entered into a certain village: and a certain woman named Martha received him into her house: and she had a sister called Mary, which also sat at Jesus' feet, and heard his word. But Martha was cumbered with much serving: and came to him, and said: Lord, dost thou not care that my sister hath left me to serve alone? bid her therefore that she help me. And Jesus answered and said unto her: Martha, Martha, thou art careful and troubled about many things, but one thing is needful. And Mary hath chosen that good part, which shall not be taken away from her.

Offertory. Ps. 45, 10. Kings' daughters were among thy honourable women, upon thy right hand did stand the queen in a vesture of gold, wrought about with divers colours.

Secret.

GRANT, O Lord, that like as thy dedicated people do acknowledge that in tribulation they have been succoured by the merits of thy Saints: so this oblation, which they offer unto thee in honour of the same, may be acceptable in thy sight. Through.

For the Martyrs.   Secret.

WE offer this our sacrifice unto thee, O Lord, in commemoration of thy holy Martyrs, Felix, Simplicius, Faustinus and Beatrice: humbly beseeching thee; that we may thereby obtain forgiveness of our sins and attain unto everlasting salvation. Through.

Communion. Matt. 25, 4 and 6. The five wise virgins took oil in their vessels with their lamps: and at midnight there was a cry made: Behold the bridegroom cometh: go ye out to meet Christ the Lord.

Postcommunion.

O LORD, who hast satisfied this thy family with thy sacred gifts: we beseech thee; that we may at all times be comforted by the intercession of her whose festival we celebrate. Through.

For the Martyrs.   Postcommunion.

GRANT, we beseech thee, almighty God; that as in these heavenly mysteries we have now celebrated the festival of thy holy Martyrs Felix, Simplicius, Faustinus and Beatrice; so we may thereby obtain thy pardon and forgiveness. Through.

July 30.

For SS. Abdon and Sennen

Martyrs.

Introit. Ps. 79, 11, 12 and 10. Intret.

LET the sorrowful sighing of the prisoners, O Lord, come before thee: reward thou our neighbours seven-fold into their bosom: avenge thou the blood of thy Saints that is shed. Ps. ibid., 1. O God, the heathen are come into thine inheritance: thy holy temple have they defiled: and made Jerusalem an heap of stones. V. Glory.

Collect.

O GOD, who on thy Saints Abdon and Sennen didst bestow abundant grace to attain unto everlasting glory: grant unto thy servants the remission of their sins; that, by the intercession of the merits of thy Saints, they may be found worthy to be delivered from all adversities. Through.

The Lesson from the Epistle of blessed Paul the Apostle to the Corinthians.

II Cor. 6, 4.

BRETHREN: Let us approve ourselves as the ministers of God, in much patience, in afflictions, in necessities, in distresses, in stripes, in imprisonments, in tumults, in labours, in watchings, in fastings, by pureness, by knowledge, by longsuffering, by kindness, by the Holy Ghost, by love unfeigned, by the word of truth, by the power of God, by the armour of righteousness on the right hand and on the left: by honour and dishonour: by evil report and good report: as deceivers, and yet true: as unknown, and yet well known: as dying, and, behold, we live: as chastened, and not killed: as sorrowful, yet alway rejoicing: as poor, yet making many rich: as having nothing, and yet possessing all things.

Gradual. Exod. 15, 11. God is glorious in his holy ones, fearful in praises, doing wonders. V. Ibid., 6. Thy right hand, O Lord, is become glorious in power: thy right hand hath dashed in pieces the enemy.

Alleluia, alleluia. V. Wisd. 3, 1. The souls of the righteous are in the hand of God, and there shall no torment touch them. Alleluia.

Gospel, Jesus, seeing the multitudes, as on the Feast of All Saints (Nov. 1).

Offertory. Ps. 68, 36. God is wonderful in his holy ones: even the God of Israel, he will give strength and power unto his people: blessed be God.

Secret.

WE beseech thee, O Lord, that this sacrifice, which we offer in remembrance of the birthday of thy holy Martyrs, may both loose the bonds of our iniquity and obtain for us the gifts of thy mercy. Through.

Communion. Ps. 79, 2 and 11. The dead bodies of thy servants, O Lord, have they given to be meat unto the fowls of the air, and the flesh of thy Saints unto the beasts of the land: according to the greatness of thy power preserve thou those that are appointed to die.

Postcommunion.

GRANT, O Lord, that by the operation of these thy mysteries we may be cleansed from all our sins: and at the intercession of thy holy Martyrs Abdon and Sennen may obtain that which we have asked according to thy will. Through.

July 31.

St. Ignatius

Confessor

Greater double.

Introit. Phil. 2, 10-11. In nomine Jesu.

AT the name of Jesus every knee shall bow, of things in heaven, and things in earth, and things under the earth: and every tongue shall confess that Jesus Christ is Lord, to the glory of God the Father. Ps. 5, 12-13. All they that love thy name shall be joyful in thee: for thou wilt give thy blessing unto the righteous. ℣. Glory.

Collect.

O GOD, who for the propagation of the greater glory of thy name, didst through blessed Ignatius stablish thy Church militant with a new defence: vouchsafe; that, by his succour and example, we may so fight manfully on earth, that we may be found worthy to be crowned with him in heaven. Through.

The Lesson from the Epistle of blessed Paul the Apostle to Timothy.

II Tim. 2, 8-10; 3, 10-12.

DEARLY beloved: Remember that Jesus Christ of the seed of David was raised from the dead according to my Gospel, wherein I suffer trouble, as an evil doer, even unto bonds: but the word of God is not bound. Therefore I endure all things for the elect's sakes, that they may also obtain the salvation which is in Christ Jesus with eternal glory. But thou hast fully known my doctrine, manner of life, purpose, faith, longsuffering, charity, patience, persecutions, afflictions: which came unto me at Antioch, at Iconium, at Lystra: what persecutions I endured, but out of them all the Lord delivered me. Yea, and all that will live godly in Christ Jesus shall suffer persecution.

Gradual. Ps. 92, 13-14. The righteous shall flourish like a palm-tree: and shall spread abroad like a cedar in Libanus in the house of the Lord. ℣. To tell of thy loving-kindness early in the morning, and of thy truth in the night-season.

Alleluia, alleluia. ℣. Jas. 1, 12. Blessed is the man that endureth temptation: for when he is tried, he shall receive the crown of life. Alleluia.

✠ The Continuation of the holy Gospel according to Luke.

Luke 10, 1.

AT that time: The Lord appointed other seventy also: and sent them two and two before his face into every city and place whither he himself would come. Therefore said he unto them: The harvest truly is great, but the labourers are few. Pray ye therefore the Lord of the harvest, that he would send forth labourers into his harvest. Go your ways: behold, I send you forth as lambs among wolves. Carry neither purse, nor scrip, nor shoes, and salute no man by the way. And into whatsoever house ye enter, first say: Peace be to this house: and if the son of peace be there, your peace shall rest upon it: if not, it shall turn to you again. And in the same house remain, eating and drinking such things as they give: for the labourer is worthy of his hire. Go not from house to house. And into whatsoever city ye enter, and they receive you, eat such things as are set before you: and heal the sick that are therein, and say unto them: The kingdom of God is come nigh unto you.

Offertory. Ps. 89, 25. My truth and my mercy shall be with him: and in my name shall his horn be exalted.

Secret.

O LORD God, let the gracious intercession of Saint Ignatius commend our oblations unto thee: that these most sacred mysteries, which thou hast appointed to be the source of all holiness, may likewise sanctify us in thy truth. Through.

Communion. Luke 12, 49. I am come to send fire on the earth: and what will I, if it be already kindled?

Postcommunion.

GRANT, O Lord, that we, who have here offered unto thee this sacrifice of praise in thanksgiving for thy Saint Ignatius: may thereby be brought hereafter to give praise unto thy majesty for evermore. Through.

FEASTS OF AUGUST

August 1.

St. Peter's Chains

St. Peter ad vincula.

Greater double.

Introit. Acts 12, 11. Nunc scio.

NOW I know of a surety, that the Lord hath sent his Angel, and hath delivered me out of the hand of Herod, and from all the expectation of the people of the Jews. Ps. 139, 1. O Lord, thou hast searched me out, and known me: thou knowest my down-sitting and mine uprising. ℣. Glory.

Collect.

O GOD, who didst deliver thy blessed Apostle Peter from his chains, and didst cause him to depart unhurt: loose, we beseech thee, the chains of our sins; and of thy mercy preserve us from all evil. Through.

Commemoration of St. Paul, Apostle, which is never omitted.

Collect.

O GOD, who by the preaching of the blessed Apostle Paul didst teach the multitude of the Gentiles: grant to us, we beseech thee; that we who now celebrate his commemoration may feel the effectual benefit of his intercession. (Through.)

Then of SS. Maccabees, MM.:

Collect.

GRANT, O Lord, that we, rejoicing in the triumph of the brethren, thy Martyrs: may be strengthened and increased in our faith; and comforted by their manifold intercession. Through.

The Lesson from the Acts of the Apostles.

Acts 12, 1-11.

IN those days: Herod the king stretched forth his hands to vex certain of the Church. And he killed James the brother of John with the sword. And, because he saw it pleased the Jews, he proceeded further to take Peter also. Then were the days of unleavened bread. And when he had apprehended him, he put him in prison, and delivered him to four quaternions of soldiers to keep him, intending after Easter to bring him forth to the people. Peter therefore was kept in prison. But prayer was made without ceasing of the Church unto God for him. And when Herod would have brought him forth, the same night Peter was sleeping between two soldiers, bound with two chains, and the keepers before the door kept the prison. And, behold, the Angel of the Lord came upon him: and a light shined in the prison: and he smote Peter on the side, and raised him up, saying: Arise up quickly. And his chains fell off from his hands. And the Angel said unto him: Gird thyself, and bind on thy sandals. And so he did. And he saith unto him: Cast thy garment about thee, and follow me. And he went out, and followed him, and wist not that it was true which was done by the Angel: but thought he saw a vision. When they were past the first and second ward, they came unto the iron gate that leadeth unto the city: which opened to them of his own accord. And they went out, and passed on through one street: and forthwith the Angel departed from him. And when Peter was come to himself, he said: Now I know of a surety, that the Lord hath sent his Angel, and hath delivered me out of the hand of Herod, and from all the expectation of the people of the Jews.

Gradual. Ps. 45, 17-18. Thou shalt make them princes in all lands: they shall remember thy name, O Lord. ℣. Instead of thy fathers thou shalt have children: therefore shall the people give thanks unto thee.

Alleluia, alleluia. ℣. Loosen at God's command, O Peter, the chains of earth's bondage: thou who dost make to lie open the heavenly realms to the blessed. Alleluia.

✠ The Continuation of the holy Gospel according to Matthew.

Matt. 16, 13-19.

AT that time: When Jesus came into the coasts of Cæsarea Philippi, he asked his disciples, saying: Whom do men say that I, the Son of man, am? And they said: Some say that thou art John the Baptist, some Elias, and others Jeremias, or one of the Prophets. He saith unto them: But whom say ye that I am? And Simon Peter answered and said: Thou art the Christ, the Son of the living God. And Jesus answered and said unto him: Blessed art thou, Simon Bar-jona: for flesh and blood hath not revealed it unto thee, but my Father which is in heaven. And I say also unto thee, that thou art Peter, and upon this rock I will build my Church, and the gates of hell shall not prevail against it. And I will give unto thee the keys of the kingdom of heaven. And whatsoever thou shalt bind on earth shall be bound in heaven: and whatsoever thou shalt loose on earth shall be loosed in heaven.

The Creed is not said.

Offertory. Ps. 45, 17-18. Thou shalt make them princes in all lands: they shall remember thy name, O Lord, from one generation to another.

Secret.

GRANT, O Lord, that this sacrifice which we offer unto thee may, at the intercession of blessed Peter thine Apostle, evermore quicken and defend us. Through.

For St. Paul. Secret.

SANCTIFY, O Lord, through the prayers of thine Apostle Paul, the oblations of thy people: that these gifts, which by thine institution are acceptable unto thee, may by his effectual advocacy be rendered the more acceptable in thy sight. (Through.)

For SS. Maccabees. Secret.

GRANT, O Lord, that we may with devout hearts celebrate thy mysteries in honour of thy holy Martyrs: and thereby obtain an increase both of protection and joy. Through.

Preface of the Apostles.

Communion. Matt. 16, 18. Thou art Peter, and upon this rock I will build my Church.

Postcommunion.

O LORD our God, who hast fulfilled us with the partaking of thy sacred Body and thy precious Blood, we beseech thee: that as we perform these mysteries with outward devotion, so we may obtain thereby the fulfilment of our redemption. Through the same.

For St. Paul. Postcommunion.

O LORD, who hast made us partakers of this holy Sacrament: we beseech thee; that, at the intercession of thy holy Apostle Paul, the mysteries which we have celebrated to the increase of his glory may be profitable for the healing of our souls. (Through.)

For SS. Maccabees. Postcommunion.

GRANT, we beseech thee, almighty God: that, we, continually advancing in godliness, may follow the faith of them whose memory by the partaking of this Sacrament we here recall. Through.

August 2.

St. Alphonsus Mary de Liguori

Bishop,
Confessor and Doctor of the Church

Double.

Introit. Luke 4, 18. Spiritus Domini.

THE Spirit of the Lord is upon me: because he hath anointed me to preach the Gospel to the poor, he hath sent me to heal the broken-hearted. Ps. 78, 1. Hear my law, O my people: incline your ears unto the words of my mouth. ℣. Glory.

Collect.

O GOD, who didst inflame blessed Alphonsus Mary, thy Confessor and Bishop, with zeal for souls, and didst through him enrich thy Church with a new family: we beseech thee; that we, being taught by his wholesome counsels and strengthened by his example, may be worthy to attain in gladness unto thee. Through.

Commemoration of St. Stephen I, P.M.

Collect.

O EVERLASTING Shepherd, look down in mercy on thy flock: and, as thou didst choose blessed Stephen thy Martyr and Chief Bishop to be pastor and ruler of thy Church; so at his intercession defend it with thy continual protection. Through.

The Lesson from the Epistle of blessed Paul the Apostle to Timothy.

II Tim. 2, 1-7.

DEARLY beloved: Be strong in the grace that is in Christ Jesus: and the things that thou hast heard of me among many witnesses, the same commit thou to faithful men, who shall be able to teach others also. Thou therefore endure hardness, as a good soldier of Jesus Christ. No man that warreth entangleth himself with the affairs of this life: that he may please him who hath chosen him to be a soldier. And if a man also strive for masteries, yet is he not crowned, except he strive lawfully. The husbandman that laboureth must be first partaker of the fruits. Consider what I say: and the Lord give thee understanding in all things.

Gradual. Ps. 119, 52-53. I remembered thine everlasting judgments, O Lord, and received comfort: I am horribly afraid for the ungodly that forsake thy law. ℣. Ps. 40, 11. I have not hid thy righteousness within my heart: my talk hath been of thy truth, and of thy salvation.

Alleluia, alleluia. ℣. Ecclus. 49, 3-4. He behaved himself uprightly in the conversion of the people, and took away the abominations of iniquity: he directed his heart unto the Lord: and in the time of the ungodly he established the worship of God. Alleluia.

✠ The Continuation of the holy Gospel according to Luke.

Luke 10, 1.

AT that time: The Lord appointed other seventy also: and sent them two and two before his face into every city and place whither he himself would come. Therefore said he unto them: The harvest truly is great, but the labourers are few. Pray ye therefore the Lord of the harvest, that he would send forth labourers into his harvest. Go your ways: behold, I send you forth as lambs among wolves. Carry neither purse, nor scrip, nor shoes, and salute no man by the way. And into whatsoever house ye enter, first say: Peace be to this house: and if the son of peace be there, your peace shall rest upon it: if not, it shall turn to you again. And in the same house remain, eating and drinking such things as they give: for the labourer is worthy of his hire. Go not from house to house. And into whatsoever city ye enter, and they receive you, eat such things as are set before you: and heal the sick that are therein, and say unto them: The kingdom of God is come nigh unto you. Creed.

Offertory. Prov. 3, 9 and 27. Honour the Lord with thy substance, and with the firstfruits of all thine increase. Withhold not good from them to whom it is due: and when it is in the power of thine hand to do it.

Secret.

O LORD Jesu Christ, who didst grant unto blessed Alphonsus Mary both to celebrate these mysteries, and through them to present himself a holy oblation unto thee: inflame our hearts by the heavenly fire of this sacrifice for a savour of sweetness: Who livest.

For St. Stephen. Secret.

WE beseech thee, O Lord, graciously enlighten thy Church by the gifts which we here offer: that in every place thy flock may increase and prosper, and the shepherds by thy governance may be made pleasing to thy name. Through.

Common Preface.

Communion. Ecclus. 50, 1 and 9. A great priest, who in his life repaired the house again, and in his days fortified the temple, as fire and incense in the censer.

Postcommunion.

O GOD, who didst render blessed Alphonsus Mary, thy Confessor and Bishop, a faithful steward and preacher of thy heavenly mysteries: grant by his merits and prayers; that thy faithful people may both frequently receive the same, and receiving them, eternally shew forth thy praise. Through.

For St. Stephen. Postcommunion.

MERCIFUL Lord, we beseech thee to govern and preserve thy Church, which thou hast here refreshed with heavenly food: that by the guiding of thy mighty power it may serve thee in more abundant freedom, and ever keep thy true religion whole and undefiled. Through.

August 3.

The Finding of St. Stephen

the First Martyr

Simple.

Introit. Ps. 119, 23, 86 and 23. Sederunt.

PRINCES did sit, and speak against me, and the wicked persecuted me: help me, O Lord my God, for thy servant is occupied in thy commandments. Ps. ibid., 1. Blessed are those that are undefiled in the way, and walk in the law of the Lord. ℣. Glory.

Collect.

GRANT us, we beseech thee, O Lord, so to imitate that which we honour: that we may learn to love also our enemies; forasmuch as we celebrate the Finding of him who prayed even for his persecutors to our Lord Jesus Christ thy Son: Who liveth and reigneth with thee.

The Lesson from the Acts of the Apostles.
Acts 6, 8-10; 7, 54-60.

IN those days: Stephen, full of faith and power, did great wonders and miracles among the people. Then there arose certain of the synagogue, which is called the synagogue of the Libertines, and Cyrenians, and Alexandrians, and of them of Cilicia and of Asia, disputing with Stephen. And they were not able to resist the wisdom and the spirit by which he spake. When they heard these things, they were cut to the heart, and they gnashed on him with their teeth. But Stephen, being full of the Holy Ghost, looked up stedfastly into heaven, and saw the glory of God, and Jesus standing on the right hand of God, and said: Behold, I see the heavens opened, and the Son of man standing on the right hand of God. Then they cried out with a loud voice, and stopped their ears, and ran upon him with one accord. And cast him out of the city, and stoned him: and the witnesses laid down their clothes at a young man's feet, whose name was Saul. And they stoned Stephen, calling upon God, and saying: Lord Jesus, receive my spirit. And he kneeled down, and cried with a loud voice: Lord, lay not this sin to their charge. And when he had said this, he fell asleep in the Lord.

Gradual. Ps. 119, 23 and 86. Princes did sit, and speak against me; and the wicked persecuted me. ℣. Ps. 6, 5. Help me, O Lord my God: save me for thy mercy's sake.

Alleluia, alleluia. ℣. Acts 7, 56. I see the heavens opened, and Jesus standing on the right hand of the power of God. Alleluia.

✠ The Continuation of the holy Gospel according to Matthew.
Matt. 23, 34-39.

AT that time: Jesus said unto the scribes and Pharisees: Behold, I send unto you prophets, and wise men, and scribes, and some of them ye shall kill and crucify, and some of them shall ye scourge in your synagogues, and persecute them from city to city: that upon you may come all the righteous blood shed upon the earth, from the blood of righteous Abel unto the blood of Zacharias, son of Barachias, whom ye slew between the temple and the altar. Verily I say unto you, All these things shall come upon this generation. O Jerusalem, Jerusalem, thou that killest the prophets, and stonest them which are sent unto thee, how often would I have gathered thy children together, even as a hen gathered her chickens under her wings, and ye would not? Behold, your house is left unto you desolate. For I say unto you, Ye shall not see me henceforth, till ye shall say: Blessed is he that cometh in the name of the Lord.

Offertory. Acts 6, 5 and 7, 59. The Apostles chose Stephen the Levite, a man full of faith and of the Holy Ghost: whom the Jews stoned as he prayed, saying: Lord Jesus, receive my spirit, alleluia.

Secret.

ACCEPT, O Lord, these gifts for the commemoration of thy Saints: that like as their passion hath raised them to glory; so our devotion may lead us to innocency of life. Through.

Communion. Acts 7, 56, 59 and 60. I see the heavens opened, and Jesus standing on the right hand of the power of God: Lord Jesus, receive my spirit, and lay not this sin to their charge.

Postcommunion.

ASSIST us mercifully, O Lord: that we, who have received these holy mysteries, may at the intercession of thy blessed Martyr Stephen be defended by thy everlasting protection. Through.

August 4.

St. Dominic

Confessor

Greater double.

Introit. Ps. 37, 30-31. Os justi.

THE mouth of the righteous is exercised in wisdom, and his tongue will be talking of judgment: the law of his God is in his heart. Ps. ibid., 1. Fret not thyself because of the ungodly: neither be thou envious against the evil doers. V. Glory.

Collect.

O GOD, who hast vouchsafed to enlighten thy Church with the merits and teaching of blessed Dominic thy Confessor: vouchsafe; that by his intercession it may fail not of thy succour in things temporal, and may continually prosper in spiritual advancement. Through.

The Lesson from the Epistle of blessed Paul the Apostle to Timothy.

II Tim. 4, 1-8.

DEARLY beloved: I charge thee before God, and the Lord Jesus Christ, who shall judge the quick and the dead at his appearing and his kingdom: preach the word, be instant in season, out of season: reprove, rebuke, exhort with all longsuffering and doctrine. For the time will come when they will not endure sound doctrine, but after their own lusts shall they heap to themselves teachers, having itching ears, and they shall turn away their ears from the truth, and shall be turned unto fables. But watch thou in all things, endure afflictions, do the work of an Evangelist, make full proof of thy ministry. For I am now ready to be offered, and the time of my departure is at hand. I have fought a good fight, I have finished my course, I have kept the faith. Henceforth there is laid up for me a crown of righteousness, which the Lord, the righteous judge, shall give me at that day: and not to me only, but unto all them also that love his appearing.

Gradual. Ps. 92, 13-14. The righteous shall flourish like a palm-tree: and shall spread abroad like a cedar in Libanus in the house of the Lord. V. Ibid., 3. To tell of thy loving-kindness early in the morning: and of thy truth in the night-season.

Alleluia, alleluia. V. Hos. 14, 6. The just shall grow as the lily: and shall flourish for ever before the Lord. Alleluia.

✠ The Continuation of the holy Gospel according to Luke.

Luke 12, 35-40.

AT that time: Jesus said unto his disciples: Let your loins be girded about and your lights burning, and ye yourselves like unto men that wait for their lord, when he will return from the wedding: that when he cometh and knocketh, they may open unto him immediately. Blessed are those servants, whom the lord when he cometh shall find watching: verily I say unto you, that he shall gird himself, and make them to sit down to meat, and will come forth and serve them. And if he shall come in the second watch, or come in the third watch, and find them so, blessed are those servants. And this know, that if the good man of the house had known what hour the thief would come, he would have watched, and not have suffered his house to be broken through. Be ye therefore ready also: for the Son of man cometh at an hour when ye think not.

Offertory. Ps. 89, 25. My truth and my mercy shall be with him: and in my name shall his horn be exalted.

Secret.

SANCTIFY, O Lord, these our oblations: that by the merits of blessed Dominic thy Confessor they may be profitable unto us for the healing of our souls. Through.

Communion. Luke 12, 42. A faithful and wise servant, whom the lord hath made ruler over his household: to give them their portion of meat in due season.

Postcommunion.

GRANT, we beseech thee, almighty God: that we, who are oppressed by the burden of our sins; may through the advocacy of blessed Dominic thy Confessor be speedily delivered from the same. Through.

August 5.

Dedication of St. Mary of the Snows

Greater double.

Introit. Sedulius. Salve, sancta Parens.

HAIL, O Mother most holy, who didst give birth to the Monarch: reigning o'er heaven and earth, world without end. Ps. 45, 1. My heart is inditing of a good matter: I speak of the things which I have made unto the King. ℣. Glory.

Collect.

GRANT, we beseech thee, O Lord God, that we thy servants may enjoy perpetual health of body and soul: and, through the glorious intercession of blessed Mary ever Virgin, be delivered from our present sadness, and attain in the end unto everlasting gladness. Through.

The Lesson from the book of Wisdom.

Ecclus. 24, 9-12.

HE created me from the beginning before the world, and I shall never fail, in the holy tabernacle I served before him. And so was I established in Sion, likewise in the beloved city he gave me rest, and in Jerusalem was my power. And I took root in an honourable people, even in the portion of the Lord's inheritance, and my abode is in the assembly of the saints.

Gradual. Blessed and venerable art thou, O Virgin Mary: who a maiden undefiled hast our Saviour for thy child. ℣. Virgin, Mother of God, the whole world cannot contain him, yet, made man for our sakes, hidden he lay in thy womb.

Alleluia, alleluia. ℣. After child-bearing thou remainedst a pure Virgin; Mother of God, intercede for us. Alleluia.

✠ The Continuation of the holy Gospel according to Luke.

Luke 11, 27-28.

AT that time: As Jesus spake to the multitudes, a certain woman of the company lifted up her voice, and said unto him: Blessed is the womb that bare thee, and the paps which thou hast sucked. But he said: Yea rather, blessed are they that hear the word of God, and keep it. Creed.

Offertory. Luke 1, 28 and 42. Hail, Mary, full of grace; the Lord is with thee: blessed art thou among women, and blessed is the fruit of thy womb.

Secret.

THROUGH thy mercy, O Lord, and the intercession of blessed Mary ever Virgin, may this oblation avail for our prosperity and peace, both now and for ever. Through.

Preface of the B.V.Mary On the Festival.

Communion. Blessed is the womb of the Virgin Mary, that bare the Son of the everlasting Father.

Postcommunion.

O LORD, who hast appointed these holy mysteries, which we have here received, to be the means of our salvation: grant, we beseech thee, that we, who have offered these our gifts unto thy majesty in honour of blessed Mary ever Virgin; may by her advocacy be at all times and in all places effectually defended. Through.

August 6.

THE TRANSFIGURATION OF OUR LORD JESUS CHRIST

Double of 2nd class.

Introit. Ps. 77, 19. Illuxerunt.

THE lightnings shone upon the ground: the earth was moved, and shook withal. Ps. 84, 1-2. O how amiable are thy dwellings, thou Lord of hosts! My soul hath a desire and longing to enter into the courts of the Lord. ℣. Glory.

Collect.

O GOD, who in the glorious Transfiguration of thine only-begotten Son didst confirm the mysteries of the faith by the testimony of the fathers, and in the voice proceeding from the bright cloud didst wondrously foreshew the perfect adoption of thy sons: mercifully vouchsafe; that we, being made fellow-heirs indeed of the King of glory, may likewise attain to be partakers of that glory. Through the same.

In private Masses only, Commemoration of St. Xystus II, Pope, and SS. Felicissimus and Agapitus, Martyrs.

Collect.

O GOD, who dost vouchsafe unto us to celebrate the heavenly birthday of thy holy Martyrs Xystus, Felicissimus and Agapitus: grant that we may rejoice in their perpetual fellowship in heaven. Through.

The Lesson from the Epistle of blessed Peter the Apostle.

II Peter 1, 16-19.

DEARLY beloved: We have not followed cunningly devised fables, when we made known unto you the power and coming of our Lord Jesus Christ: but were eye-witnesses of his majesty. For he received from God the Father honour and glory, when there came such a voice to him from the excellent glory: This is my beloved Son, in whom I am well pleased. And this voice which came from heaven we heard, when we were with him in the holy mount. We have also a more sure word of prophecy: whereunto ye do well that ye take heed, as unto a light that shineth in a dark place, until the day dawn, and the day star arise in your hearts.

Gradual. Ps. 45, 3 and 2. Thou art fairer than the children of men: full of grace are thy lips. ℣. *My heart is inditing of a good matter: I speak of the things which I have made unto the King.*

Alleluia, alleluia. ℣. Wisd. 7, 26. He is the brightness of the everlasting light, the unspotted mirror, and the image of his goodness. Alleluia.

✠ The Continuation of the holy Gospel according to Matthew.

Matt. 17, 1-9.

AT that time: Jesus taketh Peter, James, and John his brother, and bringeth them up into an high mountain apart: and was transfigured before them. And his face did shine as the sun: and his raiment was white as the light. And behold, there appeared unto them Moses and Elias talking with him. Then answered Peter, and said unto Jesus: Lord it is good for us to be here: if thou wilt, let us make here three tabernacles, one for thee, and one for Moses, and one for Elias. While he yet spake, behold a bright cloud overshadowed them. And behold a voice out of the cloud, which said: This is my beloved Son, in whom I am well pleased: hear ye him. And when the disciples heard it, they fell on their face, and were sore afraid. And Jesus came and touched them, and said: Arise, and be not afraid. And when they had lifted up their eyes, they saw no man, save Jesus only. And as they came down from the mountain, Jesus charged them, saying: Tell the vision to no man, until the Son of man be risen again from the dead. Creed.

Offertory. Ps. 112, 3. Riches and plenteousness shall be in his house: and his righteousness endureth for ever, alleluia.

Secret.

SANCTIFY, we beseech thee, O Lord, by the glorious Transfiguration of thine only-begotten Son, these our oblations: and by the splendour of his brightness cleanse us from the defilement of all our iniquities. Through the same.

For the Holy Martyrs. Secret.

WE beseech thee, O Lord, that the gifts which we offer unto thee of our bounden duty and service may be acceptable unto thee for the honour of thy Saints: and by thy mercy profitable unto us for our salvation. Through.

Common Preface, even if this Feast fall on Sunday.

Communion. Matt. 17, 9. Tell the vision which ye have seen to no man, until the Son of man be risen again from the dead.

Postcommunion.

GRANT, we beseech thee, almighty God: that we, who here celebrate in solemn worship the most sacred mysteries of the Transfiguration of thy Son, may in purity of heart and mind receive the benefits of the same. Through the same.

For the Holy Martyrs. Postcommunion.

GRANT to us, we beseech thee, O Lord: at the intercession of thy holy Martyrs Xystus, Felicissimus and Agapitus; that we, who with our outward lips are partakers of this holy Sacrament, may inwardly receive the same in purity of heart. Through.

August 7.

St. Cajetan

Confessor

Double.

Introit. Ps. 37, 30-31. Os justi.

THE mouth of the righteous is exercised in wisdom: and his tongue will be talking of judgment: the law of his God is in his heart. Ps. ibid., 1. Fret not thyself because of the ungodly: neither be thou envious against the evildoers. ℣. Glory.

Collect.

O GOD, who didst give grace unto blessed Cajetan, thy Confessor, to live after the manner of thine Apostles: grant that we, by his intercession and example, may evermore have affiance in thee; and seek after things heavenly alone. Through.

Commemoration is made of S. Donatus, Bishop and Martyr:

Collect.

O GOD, who art the glory of thy priests: grant, we beseech thee; that we, who keep the festival of thy holy Martyr and Bishop Donatus, may feel the effectual succour of his intercession. Through.

The Lesson from the book of Wisdom.

Ecclus. 31, 8-11.

BLESSED is the man that is found without blemish: and hath not gone after gold. Who is he, and we will call him blessed? for wonderful things hath he done among his people. Who hath been tried thereby, and found perfect? then let him glory. Who might offend, and hath not offended? or done evil, and hath not done it? His goods shall be established, and the congregation shall declare his alms.

Gradual. Ps. 92, 13-14. The righteous shall flourish like a palm-tree: and shall spread abroad like a cedar in Libanus in the house of the Lord. V. Ibid., 3. To tell of thy loving kindness early in the morning, and of thy truth in the night-season.

Alleluia, alleluia. V. James 1, 12. Blessed is the man that endureth temptation: for when he is tried, he shall receive the crown of life. Alleluia.

☩ The Continuation of the holy Gospel according to Matthew.

Matt. 6, 24-33.

AT that time: Jesus said unto his disciples: No man can serve two masters: for either he will hate the one, and love the other: or else he will hold to the one, and despise the other. Ye cannot serve God and mammon. Therefore I say unto you, Take no thought for your life, what ye shall eat, or what ye shall drink, nor yet for your body, what ye shall put on. Is not the life more than meat: and the body than raiment? Behold the fowls of the air, for they sow not, neither do they reap, nor gather into barns: yet your heavenly Father feedeth them. Are ye not much better than they? Which of you by taking thought can add one cubit unto his stature? And why take ye thought for raiment? Consider the lilies of the field how they grow: they toil not, neither do they spin. And yet I say unto you, That even Solomon in all his glory was not arrayed like one of these. Wherefore, if God so clothe the grass of the field, which today is, and to-morrow is cast into the oven: shall he not much more clothe you, O ye of little faith? Therefore take no thought, saying: What shall we eat, or what shall we drink, or wherewithal shall we be clothed? For after all these things do the Gentiles seek. For your heavenly Father knoweth that ye have need of all these things. But seek ye first the kingdom of God, and his righteousness: and all these things shall be added unto you.

Offertory. Ps. 89, 25. My truth and my mercy shall be with him: and in my name shall his horn be exalted.

Secret.

GRANT to us, we beseech thee, almighty God: that this oblation of our humble service may be acceptable in thy sight to the honour of thy Saints, and may cleanse us both in body and soul. Through.

For St. Donatus. Secret.

GRANT, we beseech thee, O Lord: that, as by these our gifts which we offer to the praise of thy name, we render honour to thy holy Martyr and Bishop Donatus, so by his intercession we may receive the reward of this our bounden service. Through.

Communion. Matt. 24, 46-47. Blessed is the servant whom his lord when he cometh shall find watching: verily I say unto you, he shall make him ruler over all his goods.

Postcommunion.

WE beseech thee, almighty God: that we, who have received this heavenly food, may, at the intercession of blessed Cajetan thy Confessor, be thereby defended against all adversities. Through.

For St. Donatus. Postcommunion.

ALMIGHTY and merciful God, who makest us to be alike partakers and ministers of thy sacraments: grant, we beseech thee; that at the intercession of blessed Donatus, thy Martyr and Bishop, we, following the pattern of his faith and godly conversation, may be profited thereby to our salvation. Through.

August 8.

SS. Cyriacus, Largus and Smaragdus

Martyrs.

Simple.

Introit. Ps. 34, 10-11. Timete Dominum.

O FEAR the Lord, ye that are his saints, for they that fear him lack nothing: the lions do lack, and suffer hunger: but they who seek the Lord shall want no manner of thing that is good. Ps. ibid., 1. I will alway give thanks unto the Lord: his praise shall ever be in my mouth. ℣. Glory.

Collect.

O GOD, who makest us glad with the yearly solemnity of thy holy Martyrs Cyriacus, Largus and Smaragdus: mercifully grant; that as we now celebrate their heavenly birthday, so we may imitate their constancy in suffering. Through.

The Lesson from the Epistle of blessed Paul the Apostle to the Thessalonians.

I Thess. 2, 13-16.

BRETHREN: We thank God without ceasing: because, when ye received the word of God which ye heard of us, ye received it not as the word of men, but as it is in truth, the word of God, which effectually worketh also in you that believe. For ye, brethren, became followers of the churches of God which in Judæa are in Christ Jesus: for ye also have suffered like things of your own countrymen, even as they have of the Jews: who both killed the Lord Jesus, and their own Prophets: and have persecuted us, and they please not God, and are contrary to all men, forbidding us to speak to the Gentiles that they might be saved, to fill up their sins alway: for the wrath is come upon them to the uttermost.

Gradual. Ps. 34, 10-11. O fear the Lord, ye that are his saints: for they that fear him lack nothing. ℣. But they who seek the Lord, shall want no manner of thing that is good.

Alleluia, alleluia. ℣. Wisd. 3, 7. The righteous shall shine, and run to and fro like sparks among the stubble for ever. Alleluia.

✠ The Continuation of the holy Gospel according to Mark.

Mark 16, 15.

AT that time: Jesus said to his disciples: Go ye into all the world, and preach the Gospel to every creature. He that believeth and is baptized shall be saved: but he that believeth not shall be condemned. And these signs shall follow them that believe: In my name shall they cast out devils: they shall speak with new tongues: they shall take up serpents: and if they drink any deadly thing, it shall not hurt them: they shall lay hands on the sick, and they shall recover.

Offertory. Ps. 32, 11. Be glad, O ye righteous, and rejoice in the Lord: and be joyful, all ye that are true of heart.

Secret.

O LORD, let this our bounden duty and service be acceptable in thy sight: that these our oblations may, by the prayers of those on whose festival they are presented, be made profitable unto our salvation. Through.

Communion. Mark 16, 17-18. These signs shall follow them that believe in me: they shall cast out devils: they shall lay hands on the sick, and they shall recover.

Postcommunion.

WE beseech thee, O Lord our God, that like as we, whom thou hast refreshed by the partaking of thy sacred gift, do offer unto thee our outward worship: so at the intercession of thy holy Martyrs Cyriacus, Largus and Smaragdus, we may inwardly be profited thereby to our salvation. Through.

August 9.

St. John Mary Vianney

Confessor

Double.

Introit. Ps. 37, 30-31. Os justi.

THE mouth of the righteous is exercised in wisdom: and his tongue will be talking of judgment: the law of his God is in his heart. Ps. ibid., 1. Fret not thyself because of the ungodly: neither be thou envious against the evildoers. ℣. Glory.

Collect.

ALMIGHTY and merciful God, who didst endue Saint John Mary with zeal for thy flock and a continual desire for prayer and penance: grant, we beseech thee; that by his example and intercession we may win the souls of our brethren for Christ, and with them attain unto everlasting glory. Through the same.

Commemoration is made of the Vigil of St. Lawrence.

Collect.

GRANT to us, we beseech thee, almighty God, that we may quench the flames of our sins: even as thou didst give grace to blessed Lawrence to overcome the fires of his torments. (Through.)

Then of St. Romanus, Martyr.

Collect.

GRANT, we beseech thee, almighty God: that, at the intercession of blessed Romanus thy Martyr, we may be delivered from all adversities which may happen to the body, and from all evil thoughts which may assault and hurt the soul. Through.

The Lesson from the book of Wisdom.

Ecclus. 31, 8-11.

BLESSED is the man that is found without blemish: and hath not gone after gold. Who is he, and we will call him blessed? for wonderful things hath he done among his people. Who hath been tried thereby, and found perfect? then let him glory. Who might offend, and hath not offended? or done evil, and hath not done it? His goods shall be established, and the congregation shall declare his alms.

Gradual. Ps. 92, 13-14. The righteous shall flourish like a palm-tree: and shall spread abroad like a cedar in Libanus in the house of the Lord. ℣. Ibid., 3. To tell of thy loving kindness early in the morning, and of thy truth in the night-season.

Alleluia, alleluia. ℣. James 1, 12. Blessed is the man that endureth temptation: for when he is tried, he shall receive the crown of life. Alleluia.

✠ The Continuation of the holy Gospel according to Luke.

Luke 12, 35-40.

AT that time: Jesus said unto his disciples: Let your loins be girded about, and your lights burning, and ye yourselves like unto men that wait for their lord, when he will return from the wedding: that when he cometh and knocketh, they may open unto him immediately. Blessed are those servants, whom the lord when he cometh shall find watching: verily I say unto you, that he shall gird himself, and make them to sit down to meat, and will come forth and serve them. And if he shall come in the second watch, or come in the third watch, and find them so, blessed are those servants. And this know, that if the good man of the house had known what hour the thief would come, he would have watched, and not have suffered his house to be broken through. Be ye therefore ready also: for the Son of man cometh at an hour when ye think not.

Offertory. Ps. 89, 25. My truth and my mercy shall be with him: and in my name shall his horn be exalted.

Secret.

WE offer thee, O Lord, this our sacrifice of praise to the honour of thy Saints: whereby we trust to be delivered from all evils both in this life and in that which is to come. Through.

For the Vigil. Secret.

O LORD, look favourably upon this our oblation: and at the intercession of thy blessed Martyr Lawrence absolve us from our sins. (Through.)

For St. Romanus. Secret.

WE beseech thee, O Lord, to accept our prayers and oblations: and graciously hearken unto us, whom thou dost cleanse by thy heavenly mysteries. Through.

Communion. Matt. 24, 46-47. Blessed is the servant whom his lord when he cometh shall find watching: verily I say unto you, he shall make him ruler over all his goods.

Postcommunion.

O LORD our God, who hast refreshed us with heavenly meat and drink, we humbly beseech thee: that we may be defended by the prayers of him in whose memory we have received the same. Through.

For the Vigil. Postcommunion.

GRANT, we beseech thee, O Lord, our God: that like as in this life we gladly honour the memory of thy blessed Martyr Lawrence; so in heaven we may rejoice in his everlasting fellowship. (Through.)

For St. Romanus. Postcommunion.

WE beseech thee, almighty God: that we, who have received this heavenly food, may at the intercession of blessed Romanus thy Martyr be thereby defended against all adversities. Through.

¶ If today be Sunday, Commemoration is made, in low Masses, of St. John Mary only, and nothing is said of the Vigil or of St. Romanus.

The same day, August 9.

Vigil of St. Lawrence

Martyr

Introit. Ps. 112, 9. Dispersit.

HE hath dispersed abroad, and given to the poor: his righteousness remaineth for ever: his horn shall be exalted with honour. Ps. ibid., 1. Blessed is the man that feareth the Lord: he hath great delight in his commandments. ℣. Glory.

Glória in excélsis is not said.

Collect.

ASSIST us mercifully, O Lord, in these our supplications: and at the intercession of thy blessed Martyr Lawrence, whose festival we now prevent, graciously bestow upon us thy perpetual mercy. Through.

In private Masses, Commemoration of St. John Mary.

Collect.

ALMIGHTY and merciful God, who didst endue Saint John Mary with zeal for thy flock and a continual desire for prayer and penance: grant, we beseech thee; that by his example and intercession we may win the souls of our brethren for Christ, and with them attain unto everlasting glory. (Through the same.)

3rd of St. Romanus.

Collect.

GRANT, we beseech thee, almighty God: that, at the intercession of blessed Romanus thy Martyr, we may both be delivered from all adversities which may happen to the body, and from all evil thoughts which may assault and hurt the soul. Through.

The Lesson from the book of Wisdom.

Ecclus. 51, 1-8 and 12.

I WILL thank thee, O Lord and King, and praise thee, O God my Saviour. I do give praise unto thy name: for thou art my defender and helper, and hast preserved my body from destruction, and from the snare of the slanderous tongue, and from the lips that forge lies, and hast been mine helper against mine adversaries. And hast delivered me, according to the multitude of thy mercies and greatness of thy name, from the teeth of them that were ready to devour me, and out of the hands of such as sought after my life, and from the manifold afflictions which I had: from the choking of fire on every side, and from the midst of the fire which I kindled not: from the depth of the belly of hell, from an unclean tongue, and from lying words, from an unjust king, and from an unrighteous tongue: my soul shall praise the Lord even unto death: for thou deliverest such as wait for thee, and savest them out of the hands of the enemies, O Lord our God.

Gradual. Ps. 112, 9 and 2. He hath dispersed abroad, and given to the poor: and his righteousness remaineth for ever. ℣. His seed shall be mighty upon earth: the generation of the faithful shall be blessed.

✠ The Continuation of the holy Gospel according to Matthew.

Matt. 16, 24-27.

AT that time: Jesus said unto his disciples: If any man will come after me, let him deny himself, and take up his cross, and follow me. For whosoever will save his life shall lose it: and whosoever will lose his life for my sake shall find it. For what is a man profited, if he shall gain the whole world, and lose his own soul? or what shall a man give in exchange for his soul? For the Son of man shall come in the glory of his Father with his Angels: and then he shall reward every man according to his works.

Offertory. Job 16, 20. My prayer is pure: and therefore I ask that a place be given to my voice in heaven: for there is my judge, and my record is on high: let my prayer ascend to the Lord.

Secret.

O LORD, mercifully regard the sacrifices which we offer unto thee: and at the intercession of blessed Lawrence thy Martyr absolve us from the bonds of our sins. Through.

In private Masses, 2nd Secret of St. John Mary.

Secret.

WE offer thee, O Lord, this our sacrifice of praise to the honour of thy Saints: whereby we trust to be delivered from all evils both in this life and in that which is to come. (Through.)

3rd of St. Romanus.

Secret.

WE beseech thee, O Lord, to accept our prayers and oblations: and graciously hearken unto us, whom thou dost cleanse by thy heavenly mysteries. Through.

Communion. Matt. 16, 24. He that will come after me, let him deny himself, and take up his cross, and follow me.

Postcommunion.

GRANT, we beseech thee, O Lord, our God: that like as we in this life do gladly honour the memory of blessed Lawrence thy Martyr; so we may in heaven rejoice in his eternal fellowship. Through.

In private Masses, 2nd Postcommunion of St. John Mary.

Postcommunion.

O LORD our God, who hast refreshed us with heavenly meat and drink, we humbly beseech thee: that we may be defended by the prayers of him in whose memory we have received the same. (Through.)

3rd of St. Romanus.

Postcommunion.

WE beseech thee, almighty God: that we, who have received this heavenly food, may, at the intercession of blessed Romanus thy Martyr, be thereby defended against all adversaries. Through.

August 10.

ST. LAWRENCE MARTYR

Double of 2nd class.

Introit. Ps. 96, 6. Confessio et pulcritudo.

GLORY and worship are before him: power and honour are in his sanctuary. Ps. ibid., 1. O sing unto the Lord a new song: sing unto the Lord, all the whole earth. ℣. Glory.

Collect.

GRANT to us, we beseech thee, almighty God: that we may quench the flames of our sins; even as thou didst give grace to blessed Lawrence to overcome the fires of his torments. Through.

The Lesson from the Epistle of blessed Paul the Apostle to the Corinthians.

II Cor. 9, 6-10.

BRETHREN: He which soweth sparingly shall reap also sparingly: and he which soweth bountifully shall reap also bountifully. Every man according as he purposeth in his heart, so let him give, not grudgingly, or of necessity: for God loveth a cheerful giver. And God is able to make all grace abound toward you, that ye, always having all sufficiency in all things, may abound to every good work, as it is written: He hath dispersed abroad, he hath given to the poor: his righteousness remaineth for ever. Now he that ministereth seed to the sower: both minister bread for your food, and multiply your seed sown, and increase the fruits of your righteousness.

Gradual. Ps. 17, 3. Thou hast proved and visited mine heart, O Lord, in the night-season. ℣. Thou hast tried me with fire, and hast found no wickedness in me.

Alleluia, alleluia. ℣. The Levite Lawrence wrought a good work: who by the sign of the cross gave light to the blind. Alleluia.

✠ The Continuation of the holy Gospel according to John.

John 12, 24-26.

AT that time: Jesus said unto his disciples: Verily, verily, I say unto you, Except a corn of wheat fall into the ground and die, it abideth alone: but if it die, it bringeth forth much fruit. He that loveth his life shall lose it: and he that hateth his life in this world shall keep it unto life eternal. If any man serve me, let him follow me: and where I am, there shall also my servant be. If any man serve me, him will my Father honour.

Offertory. Ps. 96, 6. Glory and worship are before him: power and honour are in his sanctuary.

Secret.

ACCEPT, we beseech thee, O Lord, the gifts which we duly offer: and grant that by the merits and intercession of blessed Lawrence they may be profitable to the advancement of our salvation. Through.

Communion. John 12, 26. He that serveth me, let him follow me: and where I am, there shall also my servant be.

Postcommunion.

O LORD, who hast satisfied us with thy sacred gifts, we humbly beseech thee: that we who celebrate this service of our bounden duty may, at the intercession of blessed Lawrence thy Martyr, be made thereby to grow in grace to the attainment of everlasting salvation. Through.

August 11.
For SS. Tiburtius and Susanna
Virgin, Martyrs.

The Mass Salus autem, p. [12], with Prayers and Epistle, as below.

Collect. P

O LORD, let the protection of thy holy Martyrs Tiburtius and Susanna continually defend us: forasmuch as thou failest not to look with mercy on those to whom thou dost grant the succour of their assistance. Through.

Epistle, The Saints through faith, as on the Feast of SS. Fabian and Sebastian, January 20.

Secret. P

ASSIST, O Lord, the prayers of thy people, assist their oblations: that the gifts which we offer in these sacred mysteries may, by the intercession of thy Saints, be acceptable unto thee. Through.

Postcommunion. P

O LORD, through whom we have received this pledge of eternal redemption: we beseech thee, that at the intercession of thy holy Martyrs it may avail for our succour both in this life and in that which is to come. Through.

August 12.
St. Clare
Virgin
Double.

The Mass Dilexisti, p. [31].

Collect. C

GRACIOUSLY hear us, O God of our salvation: that, like as we do rejoice in the festival of blessed Clare thy Virgin; so we may learn to follow her example in godliness and charity. Through.

Secret. C

GRANT, O Lord, that like as thy dedicated people do acknowledge that in tribulation they have been succoured by the merits of thy Saints: so this oblation, which they offer unto thee in honour of the same, may be acceptable in thy sight. Through.

Postcommunion. C

O LORD, who hast satisfied this thy family with thy sacred gifts: we beseech thee; that we may at all times be comforted by the intercession of her whose festival we celebrate. Through.

August 13.
For SS. Hyppolytus and Cassian
Martyrs

The Mass Salus autem, p. [12], with the following Prayers:

Collect. P

GRANT, we beseech thee, almighty God: that we, devoutly observing the festival of thy blessed Martyrs Hippolytus and Cassian, may thereby increase in godliness to the attainment of our salvation. Through

Secret. P

REGARD, O Lord, the gifts of thy people, which we offer on the festival of thy Saints: and let this confession of thy truth be profitable for our salvation. Through.

Postcommunion. P

GRANT, O Lord, that this holy Sacrament which we have here received: may avail for our deliverance from evil, and our confirmation in the light of thy truth. Through.

August 14.

Vigil of the Assumption of the Blessed Virgin Mary

Introit. Ps. 45, 13, 15-16. *Vultum tuum.*

THE rich also among the people shall make their supplication before thee: the Virgins that be her fellows shall be brought unto the King: they that bear her company shall be brought unto thee with joy and gladness. Ps. *ibid.*, 1. My heart is inditing of a good matter: I speak of the things which I have made unto the King. ℣. Glory.

Glória in excélsis is not said.

Collect.

O GOD, who didst vouchsafe to choose the Virgin womb of blessed Mary wherein to make thy dwelling-place: grant, we beseech thee; that we, being defended by her protection, may of thee be enabled to attain with gladness to her coming festival: Who livest and reignest.

Commemoration of St. Eusebius, Confessor:

Collect.

O GOD, who makest us glad with the yearly solemnity of blessed Eusebius thy Confessor: mercifully grant; that as we now celebrate his heavenly birthday, so by his example we may be drawn nearer unto thee. Through.

The Lesson from the Book of Wisdom.

Ecclus. 24, 17-25.

AS the vine I brought forth a pleasant savour: and my flowers are the fruit of honour and riches. I am the mother of fair love, and fear, and knowledge, and holy hope. In me is all grace of the way and the truth: in me is all hope of life and of virtue. Come unto me, all ye that be desirous of me, and fill yourselves with my fruits. For my spirit is sweeter than honey, and mine inheritance than the honeycomb. My memorial shall be unto everlasting generations. They that eat me shall yet be hungry: and they that drink me shall yet be thirsty. He that obeyeth me shall never be confounded: and they that work by me shall not do amiss. They that expound me shall have life everlasting.

Gradual. Blessed and venerable art thou, O Virgin Mary: who a Maiden undefiled hast our Saviour for thy child. ℣. Virgin, Mother of God, the whole world cannot contain him, yet made man for our sake, hidden he lay in thy womb.

✠ The Continuation of the holy Gospel according to Luke.

Luke 11, 27-28.

AT that time: As Jesus spake to the multitude, a certain woman of the company lifted up her voice, and said unto him: Blessed is the womb that bare thee, and the paps which thou hast sucked. But he said: Yea rather, blessed are they that hear the word of God, and keep it.

Offertory. Blessed art thou, O Virgin Mary, who didst bear the Creator of all things: thou broughtest forth him who made thee, and for ever remainest a Virgin.

Secret.

O LORD, who didst translate the Mother of God from this present life, to the intent that she might faithfully intercede before thee for our sins: grant that her prayers may render these our oblations acceptable in the sight of thy mercy. Through the same.

For St. Eusebius. Secret.

WE offer thee, O Lord, this our sacrifice of praise to the honour of thy Saints: whereby we trust to be delivered from all evils both in this life and in that which is to come. Through.

Common Preface.

Communion. Blessed is the womb of the Virgin Mary, that bare the Son of the everlasting Father.

Postcommunion.

GRANT, O merciful God, thy protection to the frailty of our mortal nature: that we who here prevent the festival of the holy Mother of God; may by the help of her intercession rise again from our iniquities. Through the same.

For St. Eusebius. Postcommunion.

O LORD, our God, who hast refreshed us with heavenly meat and drink, we humbly beseech thee: that we may be defended by the prayers of him in whose memory we have received the same. Through.

¶ If today be Sunday, Commemoration is made, in low Masses only, of St. Eusebius, and nothing is said of the Vigil.

August 15.

THE ASSUMPTION
OF THE BLESSED VIRGIN MARY

Double of 1st class.

Introit. Rev. 12, 1. Signum magnum.

A GREAT wonder appeared in heaven: a woman clothed with the sun, and the moon under her feet, and upon her head a crown of twelve stars. Ps. 98, 1. O sing unto the Lord a new song: for he hath done marvellous things. ℣. Glory.

Collect.

ALMIGHTY and everlasting God, who didst assume the immaculate Virgin Mary, Mother of thy Son, in body and soul to heavenly glory: grant, we beseech thee; that we, ever setting our affections on things above, may likewise be partakers of that glory in the world to come. Through.

The Lesson from the book of Judith.

Judith 13, 22-25; 15, 10.

THE Lord hath blessed thee by his power, because through thee he hath brought our enemies to nought. O daughter, blessed art thou of the most high God, above all the women upon the earth. And blessed be the Lord, who hath created the heavens and the earth, who directed thee to the wounding of the head of the prince of our enemies; because he hath so magnified thy name this day, that thy praise shall not depart from the mouth of men which remember the power of the Lord for ever, for whom thou hast not spared thy life, by reason of the distress and tribulation of thy people, but hast averted our ruin, in the presence of our God. Thou art the glory of Jerusalem, thou art the joy of Israel, thou art the honour of our people.

Gradual. Ps. 45, 11-12 and 14. Hearken, O daughter, and consider, and incline thine ear, so shall the king have pleasure in thy beauty. ℣. All glorious the king's daughter entereth in, her clothing is of wrought gold.

Alleluia, alleluia. ℣. Mary is taken up into heaven: the host of Angels rejoiceth. Alleluia.

✠ The Continuation of the holy Gospel according to Luke.

Luke 1, 41-50.

AT that time: Elizabeth was filled with the Holy Ghost, and she spake out with a loud voice, and said: Blessed art thou among women, and blessed is the fruit of thy womb. And whence is this to me that the mother of my Lord should come to me? For, lo, as soon as the voice of thy salutation sounded in mine ears, the babe leaped in my womb for joy. And blessed is she that believed, for there shall be a performance of those things, which were told her from the Lord. And Mary said: My soul doth magnify the Lord; and my spirit hath rejoiced in God my Saviour; for he hath regarded the lowliness of his handmaiden, for behold, from henceforth all generations shall call me blessed. For he that is mighty hath done to me great things, and holy is his name, and his mercy is on them that fear him from generation to generation. Creed.

Offertory. Gen. 3, 15. I will put enmity between thee and the Woman, and between thy seed and her Seed.

Secret.

LET this oblation of our bounden duty ascend unto thee, O Lord, and, at the intercession of the most blessed Virgin Mary, whom thou hast assumed into heaven, may our hearts, enkindled with the fire of thy love, continually long after thee. Through.

Preface of the B.V.Mary, And that on the Assumption.

Communion. Luke 1, 48-49. All generations shall call me blessed, for he that is mighty hath done to me great things.

Postcommunion.

GRANT, we beseech thee, O Lord: that we, who have received this Sacrament of our salvation; may, through the merits and intercession of the blessed Virgin Mary, whom thou hast assumed into heaven, be brought unto the glory of the resurrection. Through.

August 16.

ST. JOACHIM,
FATHER OF THE BLESSED VIRGIN MARY

Confessor

Double of 2nd class.

Introit. Ps. 112, 9. Dispersit.

HE hath dispersed abroad, and given to the poor: his righteousness remaineth for ever: his horn shall be exalted with honour. Ps. ibid., 1. Blessed is the man that feareth the Lord: he hath great delight in his commandments. V. Glory.

Collect.

O GOD, who out of all thy Saints didst choose blessed Joachim to be father of the Mother of thy Son: grant, we beseech thee; that we, who celebrate his festival, may feel the perpetual succour of his intercession. Through the same.

The Lesson from the book of Wisdom.

Ecclus. 31, 8-11.

BLESSED is the man that is found without blemish, and hath not gone after gold. Who is he, and we will call him blessed? for wonderful things hath he done among his people. Who hath been tried thereby, and found perfect? then let him glory. Who might offend, and hath not offended? or done evil, and hath not done it? His goods shall be established in the Lord, and the congregation shall declare his alms.

Gradual. Ps. 112, 9 and 2. He hath dispersed abroad, and given to the poor: his righteousness remaineth for ever. V. His seed shall be mighty upon earth: the generation of the faithful shall be blessed.

Alleluia, alleluia. V. Joachim, spouse of Saint Anne, of the gracious Virgin the father, here to thy servants bring safety and aid from on high. Alleluia.

✠ The Beginning of the holy Gospel according to Matthew.

Matt. 1, 1-16.

THE book of the generation of Jesus Christ, the son of David, the son of Abraham. Abraham begat Isaac. And Isaac begat Jacob. And Jacob begat Judas and his brethren. And Judas begat Phares and Zara of Thamar. And Phares begat Esrom. And Esrom begat Aram. And Aram begat Aminadab. And Aminadab begat Naasson. And Naasson begat Salmon. And Salmon begat Booz of Rachab. And Booz begat Obed of Ruth. And Obed begat Jesse. And Jesse begat David the king. And David the king begat Solomon of her that had been the wife of Urias. And Solomon begat Roboam. And Roboam begat Abia. And Abia begat Asa. And Asa begat Josaphat. And Josaphat begat Joram. And Joram begat Ozias. And Ozias begat Joatham. And Joatham begat Achaz. And Achaz begat Ezekias. And Ezekias begat Manasses. And Manasses begat Amon. And Amon begat Josias. And Josias begat Jechonias and his brethren about the time they were carried away to Babylon. And after they were brought to Babylon: Jechonias begat Salathiel. And Salathiel begat Zorobabel. And Zorobabel begat Abiud. And Abiud begat Eliakim. And Eliakim begat Azor. And Azor begat Sadoc. And Sadoc begat Achim. And Achim begat Eliud. And Eliud begat Eleazar. And Eleazar begat Matthan. And Matthan begat Jacob. And Jacob begat Joseph, the husband of Mary, of whom was born Jesus, who is called Christ.

The Creed is not said.

Offertory. Ps. 8, 6-7. Thou hast crowned him with glory and worship: and hast made him to have dominion of the works of thy hands, O Lord.

Secret.

ACCEPT, O most merciful God, this sacrifice which we offer to thy majesty, to the honour of the holy Patriarch Joachim, father of the Virgin Mary: and grant that, as he with his wife and their most blessed offspring intercede for us, so we may be counted worthy to receive the perfect remission of our sins, and may attain unto everlasting glory. Through.

Common Preface, even if this Feast fall on Sunday.

Communion. Luke 12, 42. A faithful and wise servant, whom his lord hath made ruler over his household: to give them their portion of meat in due season.

Postcommunion.

WE beseech thee, almighty God: that through this holy Sacrament which we have received, with the succour of the merits and prayers of blessed Joachim, father of the Mother of thy beloved Son Jesus Christ our Lord, we may be made in this world partakers of thy grace and in the world to come of glory everlasting. Through the same.

August 17.

St. Hyacinth

Confessor

Double.

The Mass Os justi, from the Common of a Confessor not a Bishop, p. [24].

Collect. C

O GOD, who dost make us to rejoice in the yearly solemnity of blessed Hyacinth thy Confessor: mercifully grant; that, as we now observe his heavenly birthday, so we may follow the example of his life. Through.

Secret. C

WE offer thee, O Lord, this our sacrifice of praise to the honour of thy Saints: whereby we trust to be delivered from all evils both in this life and in that which is to come. Through.

Postcommunion. C

O LORD our God, who hast refreshed us with heavenly meat and drink, we humbly beseech thee: that we may be defended by the prayers of him in whose memory we have received the same. Through.

August 18.

For St. Agapitus

Martyr

The Mass Laetabitur, p. [7], with the following Prayers, and Gospel.

Collect. P

O LORD, let thy Church trust with gladness in the advocacy of thy blessed Martyr Agapitus: that by his glorious prayers it may continue steadfast in godly devotion and abide in safety and quietness. Through.

The Gospel, Verily, verily, as on the Feast of St. Lawrence, August 10, p. 753.

Secret. P

RECEIVE, O Lord, the gifts which we offer on the solemnity of him through whose advocacy we trust to be delivered. Through.

Postcommunion. P

O LORD, who hast satisfied thy family with sacred gifts: we beseech thee; that we may at all times be comforted by the intercession of him whose festival we celebrate. Through.

August 19.
St. John Eudes
Confessor

Double.

The Mass Os justi, p. [24], from the Common of a Confessor not a Bishop, except the Collect:

Collect. P

O GOD, who didst enkindle blessed John thy Confessor with wondrous zeal to set forward the worship of the sacred Hearts of Jesus and Mary, and through him didst will to gather together new families in thy Church: grant, we beseech thee; that we who venerate his godly merits may likewise be taught by the example of his godly conversation. Through the same.

Secret. C

WE offer thee, O Lord, this our sacrifice of praise to the honour of thy Saints: whereby we trust to be delivered from all evils both in this life and in that which is to come. Through.

Postcommunion. C

O LORD, our God, who hast refreshed us with heavenly meat and drink, we humbly beseech thee: that we may be defended by the prayers of him in whose memory we have received the same. Through.

August 20.
St. Bernard
Abbot and Doctor of the Church.

Double.

The Mass In medio, p. [22], with the Epistle as below.

And the Creed is said.

Collect. C 2

O GOD, who didst send blessed Bernard thy Doctor to guide thy people in the way of everlasting salvation: grant, we beseech thee; that as we have learned of him the doctrine of life on earth, so we may be found worthy to have him for our advocate in heaven. Through.

The Lesson from the book of Wisdom.

Ecclus. 39, 5-14.

THE righteous will give his heart to resort early to the Lord that made him, and will pray before the most High, and will open his mouth in prayer, and make supplication for his sins. When the great Lord will, he shall be filled with the spirit of understanding: he shall pour out wise sentences, and give thanks unto the Lord in his prayer. He shall direct his counsel and knowledge, and in his secrets shall he meditate. He shall shew forth that which he hath learned, and shall glory in the law of the covenant of the Lord. Many shall commend his understanding: and so long as the world endureth, it shall not be blotted out: his memorial shall not depart away, and his name shall live from generation to generation. Nations shall shew forth his wisdom, and the Church shall declare his praise.

Secret. C2

MAY the devout prayers of thy Confessor and Doctor, Saint Bernard, continually succour us, O Lord: that they may render our oblations acceptable in thy sight; and ever obtain for us thy merciful pardon. Through.

Postcommunion. C2

WE beseech thee, O Lord, that blessed Bernard, thy Confessor and most excellent Doctor, may ever stand before thee as our advocate: that this sacrifice of thine ordinance may effectually avail for our salvation. Through.

August 21.

St. Jane Frances Fremiot de Chantal

Widow

Double.

Introit. Ps. 119, 75 and 120.
Cognovi, Domine.

I KNOW, O Lord, that thy judgments are right, and that thou of very faithfulness hast caused me to be troubled: my flesh trembleth for fear of thee, and I am afraid of thy judgments. Ps. ibid., 1. Blessed are those that are undefiled in the way, and walk in the law of the Lord. ℣. Glory.

Collect.

ALMIGHTY and merciful God, who didst enkindle blessed Jane Frances with thy love, and endue her with wondrous constancy of spirit to walk in all the paths of life on the way of perfection, and who through her didst vouchsafe to glorify thy Church with a new offspring: grant by her merits and prayers; that we who, knowing our infirmity, do put our trust in thy power, may by the help of thy heavenly grace overcome all things that are contrary to us. Through.

The Lesson from the book of Wisdom.
Prov. 31, 10-31.

WHO can find a virtuous woman? For her price is far above rubies. The heart of her husband doth safely trust in her, so that he shall have no need of spoil. She will do him good and not evil all the days of her life. She seeketh wool, and flax, and worketh willingly with her hands. She is like the merchants' ships, she bringeth her food from afar. She riseth also while it is yet night, and giveth meat to her household, and a portion to her maidens. She considereth a field, and buyeth it: with the fruit of her hands she planteth a vine-yard. She girdeth her loins with strength, and strengtheneth her arms. She perceiveth that her merchandise is good: her candle goeth not out by night. She layeth her hands to the spindle, and her hands hold the distaff. She stretcheth out her hand to the poor, yea, she reacheth forth her hands to the needy. She is not afraid of the snow for her household: for all her household are clothed with scarlet. She maketh herself coverings of tapestry: her clothing is silk and purple. Her husband is known in the gates, when he sitteth among the elders of the land. She maketh fine linen, and selleth it, and delivereth girdles unto the merchant. Strength and honour are her clothing, and she shall rejoice in time to come. She openeth her mouth with wisdom, and in her tongue is the law of kindness. She looketh well to the ways of her household, and eateth not the bread of idleness. Her children arise up, and call her blessed: her husband also, and he praiseth her. Many daughters have done virtuously, but thou excellest them all. Favour is deceitful, and beauty is vain: but a woman that feareth the Lord, she shall be praised. Give her of the fruit of her hands: and let her own works praise her in the gates.

Gradual. Ps. 45, 3 and 5. Full of grace are thy lips: therefore God hath blessed thee for ever. ℣.Because of the word of truth, of meekness, and righteousness: and thy right hand shall teach thee terrible things.

Alleluia, alleluia. ℣. Ibid., 3. In thy comeliness and in thy beauty go forth, ride prosperously, and reign. Alleluia.

☩ The Continuation of the holy Gospel according to Matthew.

Matt. 13, 44-52.

AT that time: Jesus spake this parable unto his disciples: The kingdom of heaven is like unto treasure hid in a field: the which when a man hath found, he hideth, and for joy thereof goeth and selleth all that he hath, and buyeth that field. Again, the kingdom of heaven is like unto a merchant man, seeking goodly pearls. Who, when he had found one pearl of great price, went and sold all that he had, and bought it. Again, the kingdom of heaven is like unto a net, that was cast into the sea, and gathered of every kind. Which, when it was full, they drew to shore, and sat down, and gathered the good into vessels, but cast the bad away. So shall it be at the end of the world: the Angels shall come forth, and sever the wicked from among the just, and shall cast them into the furnace of fire: there shall be wailing and gnashing of teeth. Jesus saith unto them: Have ye understood all these things? They say unto him: Yea, Lord. Then said he unto them: Therefore every scribe which is instructed unto the kingdom of heaven is like unto a man that is an householder, which bringeth forth out of his treasure things new and old.

Offertory. Ps. 45, 3. Full of grace are thy lips: therefore God hath blessed thee for ever, and world without end.

Secret.

WE beseech thee, O Lord, that this saving victim may inflame us with that fire of love: wherewith the heart of blessed Jane Frances was wondrously enkindled, and consumed by the flames of eternal charity. Through.

Communion. Ps. 45, 8. Thou hast loved righteousness, and hated iniquity: therefore God, even thy God, hath anointed thee with the oil of gladness above thy fellows.

Postcommunion.

POUR forth upon us, O Lord, the Spirit of thy charity: that by the intercession of blessed Jane Frances, we whom thou hast here satisfied with the power of this heavenly bread may by thee be enabled to despise things earthly; and with pure hearts to follow thee the only God. Through ... in the unity of the same Holy Spirit.

August 22.

THE IMMACULATE HEART OF THE BLESSED VIRGIN MARY

Double of 2nd class.

Introit. Hebr. 4, 10. Adeamus.

LET us come boldly unto the throne of grace, that we may obtain mercy, and find grace to help in time of need. Ps. 45, 1. My heart is inditing of a good matter: I speak of the things which I have made unto the King. ℣. Glory.

Collect.

ALMIGHTY and everlasting God, who in the Heart of the blessed Virgin Mary didst prepare an habitation meet for the Holy Ghost: mercifully grant; that we, celebrating with inward devotion the festival of the same immaculate Heart, may be enabled to live after thine own heart. Through.... in the unity of the same Holy Ghost.

And in private Masses only, Commemoration is made of SS. Timothy, Hippolytus and Symphorian, MM.:

Collect.

WE beseech thee, O Lord, graciously bestow on us thy help: and, at the intercession of thy blessed Martyrs Timothy, Hippolytus and Symphorian, stretch forth the right hand of thy mercy to be our defence. Through.

The Lesson from the book of Wisdom.

Ecclus. 24, 17-22.

AS the vine I brought forth a pleasant savour: and my flowers are the fruit of honour and riches. I am the mother of fair love, and fear, and knowledge, and holy hope. In me is all grace of the way and the truth: in me is all hope of life and of virtue. Come unto me, all ye that be desirous of me, and fill yourselves with my fruits. For my spirit is sweeter than honey, and mine inheritance than honey and the honey-comb. My memorial shall be unto everlasting generations. They that eat me shall yet be hungry: and they that drink me shall yet be thirsty. He that obeyeth me shall never be confounded: and they that work by me shall not do amiss. They that expound me shall have life everlasting.

Gradual. Ps. 13, 6. My heart shall be joyful in thy salvation: I will sing of the Lord, because he hath dealt so lovingly with me: yea, I will praise the name of the Lord most highest. ℣. Ps. 45, 18. They shall remember thy name from one generation to another: therefore shall the people give thanks unto thee, world without end.

Alleluia, alleluia. ℣. Luke 1, 46-47. My soul doth magnify the Lord: and my spirit hath rejoiced in God my Saviour. Alleluia.

In Votive Masses after Septuagesima, omitting Alleluia and the Verse following, is said:

Tract. Prov. 8, 32, 35. Now therefore hearken unto me, O ye children: Blessed are they that keep my ways. Hear instruction, and be wise, and refuse it not.

℣. Blessed is the man that heareth me, watching daily at my gates, waiting at the post of my doors. ℣. Whoso findeth me findeth life, and shall obtain salvation of the Lord.

In Eastertide the Gradual is omitted, and in its place is said:

Alleluia, alleluia. ℣. Luke 1, 46-47. My soul doth magnify the Lord: and my spirit hath rejoiced in God my Saviour. Alleluia. ℣. All generations shall call me blessed, for God hath regarded his lowly handmaiden. Alleluia.

✠ The Continuation of the holy Gospel according to John.

John 19, 25-27.

AT that time: There stood by the Cross of Jesus his mother, and his mother's sister, Mary the wife of Cleophas, and Mary Magdalene. When Jesus therefore saw his mother, and the disciple standing by, whom he loved, he saith unto his mother: Woman, behold thy son. Then saith he to the disciple: Behold thy mother. And from that hour that disciple took her unto his own home. Creed.

Offertory. Luke 1, 46, 49. My spirit hath rejoiced in God my Saviour; for he that is mighty hath done great things to me, and holy is his name.

Secret.

WE offer unto thy majesty, O Lord, the immaculate Lamb, beseeching thee: that our hearts may be kindled with that celestial fire, which wondrously inflamed the Heart of the blessed Virgin Mary. Through the same.

For the SS. Martyrs.   Secret.

GRANT, O Lord, that like as thy dedicated people do acknowledge that in tribulation they have been succoured by the merits of thy Saints: so this oblation, which they here offer unto thee in honour of the same, may be acceptable in thy sight. Through.

Preface of the B.V.Mary, And that on the Festival.

Communion. John 19, 27. Jesus said unto his Mother: Woman, behold thy son: then said he to the disciple: Behold thy Mother. And from that hour the disciple took her unto his own home.

Postcommunion.

O LORD, who hast refreshed us with thy heavenly gifts, we humbly beseech thee: that at the intercession of the blessed Virgin Mary, we who have devoutly celebrated the solemnity of her immaculate Heart, may be delivered from present dangers and obtain the joys of everlasting life. Through.

For the SS. Martyrs.   Postcommunion.

O LORD our God, who hast fulfilled us with the bounty of thy heavenly gift: we beseech thee, that at the intercession of thy holy Martyrs Timothy, Hippolytus and Symphorian, we may ever live by the partaking of the same. Through.

August 23.

St. Philip Benizi

Confessor

Double.

The Mass Justus ut palma, p. [25], the Collect excepted.

Collect.   P

O GOD, who in blessed Philip thy Confessor hast bestowed upon us a wondrous pattern of humility: grant unto thy servants after his example to despise the prosperity of this world, and to seek ever after things celestial. Through.

Secret. C

GRANT to us, we beseech thee, almighty God: that this oblation of our humble service may be acceptable in thy sight to the honour of thy Saints, and may cleanse us both in body and soul. Through.

Postcommunion. C

WE beseech thee, almighty God: that we, who have received this heavenly food, may, at the intercession of blessed Philip thy Confessor, be thereby defended against all adversities. Through.

August 24.

ST. BARTHOLOMEW THE APOSTLE

Double of 2nd class.

Introit. Ps. 139, 17. Mihi autem.

RIGHT dear are thy friends unto me, O God, and held in highest honour: their rule and governance is exceeding stedfast. Ps. ibid., 1. O Lord, thou hast searched me out, and known me: thou knowest my down-sitting and mine up-rising. ℣. Glory.

Collect.

O ALMIGHTY and everlasting God, who didst give to thine Apostle Bartholomew grace truly to believe and to preach thy Word: grant, we beseech thee, unto thy Church; to love that Word which he believed, and both to preach and receive the same. Through.

or, Collect.

ALMIGHTY and everlasting God, who hast vouchsafed unto us to celebrate this day the festival of thy blessed Apostle Bartholomew with holy joy and gladness: grant, we beseech thee, unto thy Church; to love that Word which he believed, and to preach that faith which he taught. Through.

The Lesson from the Acts of the Apostles.

Acts 5, 12-16.

IN those days: By the hands of the Apostles were many signs and wonders wrought among the people: and they were all with one accord in Solomon's porch. And of the rest durst no man join himself to them: but the people magnified them. And believers were the more added to the Lord, multitudes both of men and women. Insomuch that they brought forth the sick into the streets: and laid them on beds and couches; that at the least the shadow of Peter passing by might overshadow some of them. There came also a multitude out of the cities round about unto Jerusalem, bringing sick folks, and them which were vexed with unclean spirits: and they were healed every one.

Or:

The Lesson from the Epistle of blessed Paul the Apostle to the Corinthians.

I Cor. 12, 27-31.

BRETHREN: Ye are the body of Christ, and members in particular. And God hath set some in the Church, first apostles, secondarily prophets, thirdly teachers, after that miracles, then gifts of healings, helps, governments, diversities of tongues. Are all apostles? are all prophets? are all teachers? are all workers of miracles? have all the gifts of healing? do all speak with tongues? do all interpret? But covet earnestly the best gifts.

Gradual. Ps. 45, 17-18. Thou shalt make them princes in all lands: they shall remember thy name, O Lord. ℣. Instead of thy fathers thou shalt have children: therefore shall the people give thanks unto thee.

Alleluia, alleluia. ℣. The glorious company of the Apostles praise thee, O Lord. Alleluia.

☩ The Continuation of the holy Gospel according to Luke.

Luke 22, 24-30.

AT that time: There was a strife among the disciples which of them should be accounted the greatest. And Jesus said unto them: The kings of the Gentiles exercise lordship over them, and they that exercise authority upon them are called benefactors. But ye shall not be so. But he that is greatest among you, let him be as the younger. And he that is chief, as he that doth serve. For whether is greater, he that sitteth at meat, or he that serveth: is not he that sitteth at meat? But I am among you as he that serveth. Ye are they which have continued with me in my temptations. And I appoint unto you a kingdom, as my Father hath appointed me, that ye may eat and drink at my table in my kingdom, and sit on thrones judging the twelve tribes of Israel. Creed.

Or:

☩ The Continuation of the holy Gospel according to Luke.

Luke 6, 12-19.

AT that time: Jesus went out into a mountain to pray, and continued all night in prayer to God. And when it was day, he called unto him his disciples, and of them he chose twelve, (whom also he named Apostles): Simon, whom he also named Peter, and Andrew his brother, James and John, Philip and Bartholomew, Matthew and Thomas, James the son of Alphæus, and Simon called Zelotes, and Judas the brother of James, and Judas Iscariot, which also was the traitor. And he came down with them and stood in the plain, and the company of his disciples, and a great multitude of people out of all Judæa and Jerusalem, and from the sea coast of Tyre and Sidon, which came to hear him, and to be healed of their diseases; and they that were vexed with unclean spirits, and they were healed. And the whole multitude sought to touch him, for there went virtue out of him and healed them all. Creed.

Offertory. Ps. 139, 17. Right dear are thy friends unto me, O God, and held in highest honour: their rule and governance is exceeding stedfast.

Secret.

WE beseech thee, O Lord, that we, who here observe the festival of thy blessed Apostle Bartholomew: may, by the succour of him for whom we offer unto thee this our sacrifice of praise, be made partakers of thy bountiful goodness. Through.

Preface of the Apostles.

Communion. Matt. 19, 28. Ye which have followed me shall sit upon thrones, judging the twelve tribes of Israel, saith the Lord.

Postcommunion.

O LORD, who hast bestowed on us this pledge of eternal redemption: we beseech thee; that at the intercession of thy blessed Apostle Bartholomew, it may avail for our succour both in this life and that which is to come. Through.

August 25.

St. Louis

King, Confessor

Simple.

Introit. Ps. 37, 30-31. Os justi.

THE mouth of the righteous is exercised in wisdom, and his tongue will be talking of judgment: the law of his God is in his heart. Ps. ibid., 1. Fret not thyself because of the ungodly: neither be thou envious against the evildoers. ℣. Glory.

Collect.

O GOD, who didst exalt blessed Louis, thy Confessor, from an earthly realm to the glory of thy heavenly kingdom: we beseech thee, through his merits and intercession; that thou wouldest make us to be fellow-heirs of the King of kings, Jesus Christ thy Son: Who liveth and reigneth with thee.

The Lesson from the book of Wisdom.
Wisd. 10, 10-14.

THE Lord guided the just man in right paths, shewed him the kingdom of God, and gave him knowledge of holy things: made him rich in his travels, and multiplied the fruit of his labours. In the covetousness of such as oppressed him he stood by him, and made him rich. He defended him from his enemies, and kept him safe from those that lay in wait, and in a sore conflict he gave him the victory, that he might know that wisdom is stronger than all. When the righteous was sold, she forsook him not, but delivered him from sin: she went down with him in bonds, till she brought him the sceptre of the kingdom and power against those that oppressed him: as for them that had accused him, she shewed them to be liars, and the Lord our God gave him perpetual glory.

Gradual. Ps. 92, 13-14. The righteous shall flourish like a palm-tree: and shall spread abroad like a cedar in Libanus in the house of the Lord. ℣. To tell of thy loving-kindnes in the morning, and of thy truth in the night-season.

Alleluia, alleluia. James 1, 12. Blessed is the man that endureth temptation: for when he is tried, he shall receive the crown of life. Alleluia.

✠ The Continuation of the holy Gospel according to Luke.
Luke 19, 12.

AT that time: Jesus spake this parable unto his disciples: A certain nobleman went into a far country to receive for himself a kingdom, and to return. And he called his ten servants, and delivered them ten pounds, and said unto them: Occupy till I come. But his citizens hated him: and sent a message after him, saying: We will not have this man to reign over us. And it came to pass, that when he was returned, having received the kingdom: then he commanded these servants to be called unto him, to whom he had given the money, that he might know how much every man had gained by trading. Then came the first, saying: Lord, thy pound hath gained ten pounds. And he said unto him: Well, thou good servant, because thou hast been faithful in a very little, have thou authority over ten cities. And the second came, saying: Lord, thy pound hath gained five pounds. And he said likewise to him: Be thou also over five cities. And another came, saying: Lord, behold, here is thy pound, which I have kept laid up in a napkin: for I feared thee, because thou art an austere man: thou takest up that thou layedst not down, and reapest that thou didst not sow. And he saith unto him: Out of thine own mouth will I judge thee, thou wicked servant. Thou knewest that I was an austere man, taking up that I laid not down, and reaping that I did not sow: wherefore then gavest not thou my money into the bank, that at my coming I might have required mine own with usury? And he said unto them that stood by: Take from him the pound, and give it to him that hath ten pounds. And they said unto him: Lord, he hath ten pounds. For I say unto you: That unto every one which hath shall be given: and from him that hath not, even that he hath shall be taken away from him.

Offertory. Ps. 89, 25. My truth and my mercy shall be with him: and in my name shall his horn be exalted.

Secret.

GRANT, we beseech thee, almighty God: that, like as blessed Louis thy Confessor, despising the enticements of this world, sought only to be pleasing unto Christ the King; so his intercession may render us acceptable unto thee. Through the same.

Communion. Matt. 24, 46-47. Blessed is the servant, whom his lord when he cometh shall find watching: verily I say unto you, he shall make him ruler over all his goods.

Postcommunion.

O GOD, who didst make blessed Louis thy Confessor to be wondrous upon earth and glorious in heaven: we beseech thee, that by thine appointment he may ever succour and defend thy Church. Through.

August 26.

For St. Zephyrinus

Pope and Martyr

The Mass Si diligis me, p. [2].

Collect. C 1

O EVERLASTING Shepherd, look down in mercy on thy flock: and as thou didst choose blessed Zephyrinus thy Martyr and Chief Bishop to be pastor and ruler of thy Church; so at his intercession defend it with thy continual protection. Through.

Secret. C 1

WE beseech thee, O Lord, graciously enlighten thy Church by the gifts which we here offer: that in every place thy flock may increase and prosper, and the shepherds by thy governance may be made pleasing to thy name. Through.

Postcommunion. C 1

MERCIFUL Lord, we beseech thee to govern and preserve thy Church, which thou hast here refreshed with heavenly food: that by the guiding of thy mighty power it may serve thee in more abundant freedom, and ever keep thy true religion whole and undefiled. Through.

August 27.

St. Joseph of Calasanza

Confessor

Double.

Introit. Ps. 34, 12. Venite, filii.

COME, ye children, and hearken unto me: I will teach you the fear of the Lord. Ps. ibid., 1. I will alway give thanks unto the Lord: his praise shall ever be in my mouth. V. Glory.

Collect.

O GOD, who, for the teaching of youth in the spirit of understanding and godliness, didst through thy Confessor, Saint Joseph, vouchsafe to provide thy Church with a new succour: grant, we beseech thee; that by his example and intercession we may so do and teach, that we may attain unto the rewards of everlasting life. Through.

The Lesson from the book of Wisdom.

Wisd. 10, 10-14.

THE Lord guided the just man in right paths, shewed him the kingdom of God, and gave him knowledge of holy things: made him rich in his travels, and multiplied the fruit of his labours. In the covetousness of such as oppressed him he stood by him, and made him rich. He defended him from his enemies, and kept him safe from those that lay in wait, and in a sore conflict he gave him the victory, that he might know that wisdom is stronger than all. When the righteous was sold, she forsook him not, but delivered him from sin: she went down with him in bonds, till she brought him the sceptre of the kingdom and power against those that oppressed him: as for them that had accused him, she shewed them to be liars, and the Lord our God gave him perpetual glory.

Gradual. Ps. 37, 30-31. The mouth of the righteous is exercised in wisdom, and his tongue will be talking of judgment. ℣. The law of his God is in his heart: and his goings shall not slide.

Alleluia, alleluia. ℣. James 1, 12. Blessed is the man that endureth temptation: for when he is tried, he shall receive the crown of life. Alleluia.

✠ The Continuation of the holy Gospel according to Matthew.

Matt. 18, 1-5.

AT that time: The disciples came unto Jesus, saying: Who is the greatest in the kingdom of heaven? And Jesus called a little child unto him, and set him in the midst of them, and said: Verily I say unto you: Except ye be converted, and become as little children, ye shall not enter into the kingdom of heaven. Whosoever therefore shall humble himself as this little child, the same is greatest in the kingdom of heaven. And whoso shall receive one such little child in my name, receiveth me.

Offertory. Ps. 10, 17. Lord, thou hast heard the desire of the poor: thou preparest their heart, and thine ear hearkeneth thereto.

Secret.

WE set upon thine altar, O Lord, the gifts which we offer: that through the supplication of him, whose advocacy thou hast vouchsafed for our assistance, they may obtain for us thy mercy. Through.

Communion. Mark 10, 14. Suffer the little children to come unto me, and forbid them not: for of such is the kingdom of God.

Postcommunion.

O LORD, who hast here sanctified us with thy saving mystery: we beseech thee; that at the intercession of thy Confessor, Saint Joseph, we may ever increase and prosper in all godliness. Through.

August 28.

St. Augustine

Bishop, Confessor and Doctor of the Church

Double.

Introit. Ecclus. 15, 5. In medio.

IN the midst of the Church he opened his mouth: and the Lord filled him with the spirit of wisdom and understanding: he clothed him with a robe of glory. Ps. 92, 1. It is a good thing to give thanks unto the Lord: and to sing praises unto thy name, O most Highest. ℣. Glory.

Collect.

ASSIST us, almighty God, in these our supplications: that we, whom thou dost suffer to put our trust and confidence in thy mercy, may at the intercession of blessed Augustine thy Confessor and Bishop obtain of thy goodness the wonted effects of thy compassion. Through.

Commemoration of St. Hermes, Martyr.

Collect.

O GOD, who didst endue blessed Hermes thy Martyr with strength and constancy in his passion: grant unto us by his example; to despise for love of thee the prosperity of the world, and to fear none of its adversities. Through.

The Lesson from the Epistle of blessed Paul the Apostle to Timothy.

II Tim. 4, 1-8.

DEARLY beloved: I charge thee before God, and the Lord Jesus Christ, who shall judge the quick and the dead at his appearing and his kingdom: preach the word, be instant in season, out of season: reprove, rebuke, exhort with all longsuffering and doctrine. For the time will come when they will not endure sound doctrine, but after their own lusts shall they heap to themselves teachers, having itching ears, and they shall turn away their ears from the truth, and shall be turned unto fables. But watch thou in all things, endure afflictions, do the work of an Evangelist, make full proof of thy ministry. For I am now ready to be offered, and the time of my departure is at hand. I have fought a good fight, I have finished my course, I have kept the faith. Henceforth there is laid up for me a crown of righteousness, which the Lord, the righteous judge, shall give me at that day: and not to me only, but unto all them also that love his appearing.

Gradual. Ps. 37, 30-31. The mouth of the righteous is exercised in wisdom, and his tongue will be talking of judgment. ℣. The law of his God is in his heart: and his goings shall not slide.

Alleluia, alleluia. ℣. Ps. 89, 21. I have found David my servant, with my holy oil have I anointed him. Alleluia.

☩ The Continuation of the holy Gospel according to Matthew.

Matt. 5, 13-19.

AT that time: Jesus said unto his disciples: Ye are the salt of the earth. But if the salt have lost his savour, wherewith shall it be salted? It is thenceforth good for nothing, but to be cast out, and to be trodden under foot of men. Ye are the light of the world. A city that is set on an hill cannot be hid. Neither do men light a candle, and put it under a bushel, but on a candlestick, and it giveth light unto all that are in the house. Let your light so shine before men, that they may see your good works, and glorify your Father which is in heaven. Think not that I am come to destroy the law or the prophets: I am not come to destroy, but to fulfil. For verily I say unto you, Till heaven and earth pass, one jot or one tittle shall in no wise pass from the law, till all be fulfilled. Whosoever therefore shall break one of these least commandments, and shall teach men so, he shall be called the least in the kingdom of heaven: but whosoever shall do and teach them, the same shall be called great in the kingdom of heaven. Creed.

Offertory. Ps. 92, 13. The righteous shall flourish like a palm-tree: and shall spread abroad like a cedar in Libanus.

Secret.

MAY the devout prayers of thy Bishop and Doctor, Saint Augustine, continually succour us, O Lord: that they may render our oblations acceptable in thy sight; and ever obtain for us thy merciful pardon. Through.

For St. Hermes. Secret.

WE offer unto thee, O Lord, this sacrifice of praise in commemoration of thy Saints: grant, we beseech thee; that as it hath bestowed glory on them, so it may avail for our salvation. Through.

Communion. Luke 12, 42. A faithful and wise servant, whom his lord hath made ruler over his household: to give them their portion of meat in due season.

Postcommunion.

WE beseech thee, O Lord, that blessed Augustine, thy Bishop and most excellent Doctor, may ever stand before thee as our advocate: that this sacrifice of thine ordinance may effectually avail for our salvation. Through.

For St. Hermes. Postcommunion

O LORD, who hast fulfilled us with thy heavenly benediction, we beseech thy mercy: that, at the intercession of thy blessed Martyr Hermes, this offering of thy humble servants may avail for the comfort of our souls. Through.

August 29.

The Beheading of St. John Baptist

Greater Double.

Introit. Ps. 119, 46-47. Loquebar.

I WILL speak of thy testimonies, even before kings, and will not be ashamed: and my delight shall be in thy commandments, which I have loved exceedingly. Ps. 92, 1. It is a good thing to give thanks unto the Lord: and to sing praises unto thy name, O most Highest. ℣. Glory.

Collect.

WE beseech thee, O Lord: that this solemn festival of thy Forerunner and Martyr, Saint John Baptist, may effectually bestow upon us thy succour to the attainment of our salvation: Who livest and reignest with God the Father.

Commemoration of St. Sabina, Martyr.

Collect.

O GOD, who among the manifold works of thy power hast bestowed even upon the weakness of women the victory of martyrdom: mercifully grant; that we, who celebrate the birthday of blessed Sabina, thy Martyr, may by her example draw nearer unto thee. Through.

The Lesson from the Prophet Jeremiah.

Jer. 1, 17-19.

IN those days: The word of the Lord came unto me, saying: Gird up thy loins, and arise, and speak unto Judah all that I command thee. Be not dismayed at their faces: lest I confound thee before them. For, behold, I have made thee this day a defenced city, and an iron pillar, and brasen walls against the whole land, against the kings of Judah, against the princes thereof, against the priests thereof, and against the people of the land. And they shall fight against thee, but they shall not prevail against thee: for I am with thee, saith the Lord, to deliver thee.

Gradual. Ps. 92, 13-14. The righteous shall flourish like a palm-tree: and shall spread abroad like a cedar in Libanus in the house of the Lord. ℣. Ibid., 3. To tell of thy loving-kindness early in the morning, and of thy truth in the night-season.

Alleluia, alleluia. ℣. Hos. 14, 5. The righteous shall grow as the lily: and shall flourish for ever before the Lord. Alleluia.

☩ The Continuation of the holy Gospel according to Mark.

Mark 6, 17-29.

AT that time: Herod sent forth and laid hold upon John, and bound him in prison for Herodias' sake, his brother Philip's wife, for he had married her. For John had said unto Herod: It is not lawful for thee to have thy brother's wife. Therefore Herodias had a quarrel against him, and would have killed him, but she could not. For Herod feared John, knowing that he was a just man and an holy: and observed him, and when he heard him, he did many things, and heard him gladly. And when a convenient day was come, Herod on his birthday made a supper to his lords, high captains, and chief estates of Galilee. And when the daughter of the said Herodias came in, and danced, and pleased Herod and them that sat with him, the king said unto the damsel: Ask of me whatsoever thou wilt, and I will give it thee. And he sware unto her: Whatsoever thou shalt ask of me, I will give it thee, unto the half of my kingdom. And she went forth, and said unto her mother: What shall I ask? And she said: The head of John the Baptist. And she came in straightway with haste unto the king, and asked, saying: I will that thou give me by and by in a charger the head of John the Baptist. And the king was exceeding sorry: yet for his oath's sake, and for their sakes which sat with him, he would not reject her: and immediately the king sent an executioner, and commanded his head to be brought. And he went and beheaded him in the prison. And brought his head in a charger: and gave it to the damsel, and the damsel gave it to her mother. And when his disciples heard of it, they came and took up his corpse: and laid it in a tomb.

Offertory. Ps. 21, 2-3. The just shall rejoice in thy strength, O Lord, exceeding glad shall he be of thy salvation: thou hast given him his heart's desire.

Secret.

WE beseech thee, O Lord, that the gifts which we offer unto thee in remembrance of the passion of thy holy Martyr John Baptist: may through his intercession be profitable for our salvation. Through.

For St. Sabina.   Secret.

GRACIOUSLY receive, O Lord, through the merits of blessed Sabina, thy Martyr, this sacrifice which we offer unto thee: and grant that it may avail for our continual help. Through.

Communion. Ps. 21, 4. Thou hast set, O Lord, a crown of pure gold upon his head.

Postcommunion.

GRANT, O Lord, that we who observe this festival of Saint John Baptist: may learn thereby to venerate aright the meaning of the wondrous mysteries which we have here received; and to rejoice abundantly in the fruits that they bring forth in us. Through.

For St. Sabina.   Postcommunion.

O LORD our God, who hast fulfilled us with the bounty of thy heavenly gifts: we beseech thee, that, at the intercession of blessed Sabina, thy Martyr, we may ever live by the partaking of the same. Through.

August 30.

St. Rose of St. Mary

Virgin, of Lima

Double.

Introit. Ps. 45, 8. Dilexisti.

THOU hast loved righteousness, and hated iniquity: therefore God, even thy God, hath anointed thee with the oil of gladness above thy fellows. Ps. ibid., 1. My heart is inditing of a good matter: I speak of the things which I have made unto the King. ℣. Glory.

Collect.

ALMIGHTY God, the giver of all good gifts, who, by the outpouring of the dew of thy heavenly grace, didst enable blessed Rose to shew forth among the peoples of the Indies the glory of virginity and suffering: grant to us thy servants; that we, following after her in the fragrance of her beauty, may be worthy to be made the sweet fragrance of Christ: Who liveth and reigneth with thee.

Commemoration is made of SS. Felix and Adauctus, Martyrs.

Collect.

O LORD, we humbly entreat thy majesty: that like as thou dost continually gladden us with the commemoration of thy Saints; so thou wouldest evermore defend us with their supplication. Through.

The Lesson from the Epistle of blessed Paul the Apostle to the Corinthians.

II Cor. 10, 17-18; 11, 1-2.

BRETHREN: He that glorieth, let him glory in the Lord. For not he that commendeth himself is approved: but whom the Lord commendeth. Would to God ye could bear with me a little in my folly, and indeed bear with me: for I am jealous over you with godly jealousy. For I have espoused you to one husband, that I may present you as a chaste virgin to Christ.

Gradual. Ps. 45, 5. In thy comeliness and in thy beauty go forth, ride prosperously and reign. ℣. Because of the word of truth, of meekness, and righteousness: and thy right hand shall teach thee terrible things.

Alleluia. alleluia. ℣. Ibid., 15-16. The Virgins that be her fellows shall be brought unto the King: they that bear her company shall be brought unto thee with joy. Alleluia.

✠ The Continuation of the holy Gospel according to Matthew.

Matt. 25, 1-13.

AT that time: Jesus spake this parable unto his disciples: The kingdom of heaven shall be likened unto ten virgins, which took their lamps, and went forth to meet the bridegroom. And five of them were wise, and five were foolish: they that were foolish took their lamps, and took no oil with them: but the wise took oil in their vessels with their lamps. While the bridegroom tarried, they all slumbered and slept. And at midnight there was a cry made: Behold, the bridegroom cometh, go ye out to meet him. Then all those virgins arose, and trimmed their lamps. And the foolish said unto the wise: Give us of your oil: for our lamps are gone out. But the wise answered, saying: Not so, lest there be not enough for us and you, but go ye rather to them that sell, and buy for yourselves. And while they went to buy, the bridegroom came: and they that were ready went in with him to the marriage, and the door was shut. Afterward came also the other virgins, saying: Lord, Lord, open to us. But he answered and said: Verily I say unto you, I know you not. Watch therefore, for ye know neither the day nor the hour* [wherein the Son of man cometh].

Offertory. Ps. 45, 10. Kings' daughters were among thy honourable women, upon thy right hand did stand the queen in a vesture of gold, wrought about with divers colours.

Secret.

GRANT, O Lord, that like as thy dedicated people do acknowledge that in tribulation they have been succoured by the merits of thy Saints: so this oblation, which they do offer unto thee in honour of the same, may be acceptable in thy sight. Through.

For the Holy Martyrs.   Secret.

LOOK down O Lord, upon the sacrifices of thy people: that, as with devout hearts they celebrate them to the honour of thy Saints, so they may perceive them to be profitable to their salvation. Through.

Communion. Matt. 25, 4 and 6. The five wise virgins took oil in their vessels with their lamps: and at midnight there was a cry made: Behold, the bridegroom cometh: go ye out to meet Christ the Lord.

Postcommunion.   C

O LORD, who hast satisfied this thy family with thy sacred gifts: we beseech thee; that we may at all times be comforted by the intercession of her whose festival we celebrate. Through.

For the Holy Martyrs.   Postcommunion.

WE beseech thee, O Lord: that we, being filled with thy sacred gifts; may at the intercession of thy Saints ever continue in thanksgiving for the same. Through.

August 31.

St. Raymund Nonnatus

Confessor

Double.

The Mass Os justi, from the Common of a Confessor not a Bishop, p. [24], the Collect excepted.

Collect.   P

O GOD, who didst endue blessed Raymund thy Confessor with wondrous power for the deliverance of thy faithful from the captivity of the ungodly: grant to us by his intercession; that we, being delivered from the bonds of our sins, may in freedom of spirit perform those things that are acceptable unto thee. Through.

Secret.   C

WE offer thee, O Lord, this our sacrifice of praise to the honour of thy Saints: whereby we trust to be delivered from all evils both in this life and in that which is to come. Through.

Postcommunion.   C

O LORD our God, who hast refreshed us with heavenly meat and drink, we humbly beseech thee: that we may be defended by the prayers of him in whose memory we have received the same. Through.

FEASTS OF SEPTEMBER

September 1

For St. Giles

Abbot

The Mass Os justi, from the Common of Abbots, p. [26].

Collect.   C

O LORD, we beseech thee, let the intercession of thy blessed Abbot Giles commend us unto thee: that those things which for our own merits we cannot ask, we may through his advocacy obtain. Through.

Commemoration of the SS. Twelve Brethren, MM.

Collect.

GRANT, O Lord, that we, rejoicing in the truimph of the brethren thy Martyrs: may be strengthened and increased in our faith; and comforted by their manifold intercession. Through.

Feasts of September (2)

Secret. C

WE beseech thee, O Lord, that thy holy Abbot Giles may intercede for us: that this sacrifice which we offer and present upon thy holy altar may be profitable unto us for our salvation. Through.

For the SS. Martyrs. Secret.

GRANT, O Lord, that we may with devout hearts celebrate thy mysteries in honour of thy holy Martyrs: and thereby obtain an increase both of protection and joy. Through.

Postcómmunion. C

LET thy Sacrament, O Lord which we have now received and the prayers of the blessed Abbot Giles effectually defend us: that we may both imitate the example of his conversation, and receive the succour of his intercession. Through.

For the SS. Martyrs. Postcommunion.

GRANT, we beseech thee, almighty God: that we growing in virtue may follow the faith of them whose memory by the partaking of this Sacrament we now recall. Through.

September 2.

St. Stephen

King, Confessor.

Simple.

Introit. Ps. 37, 30-31. Os justi.

THE mouth of the righteous is exercised in wisdom: and his tongue will be talking of judgment: the law of his God is in his heart. Ps. ibid., 1. Fret not thyself because of the ungodly: neither be thou envious against the evildoers. V. Glory.

Collect.

GRANT, we beseech thee, almighty God, unto thy Church: that like as thy blessed Confessor Stephen, while he reigned on earth, did spread abroad her faith; so she may be found worthy to have him for her glorious defender in the heavens. Through.

The Lesson from the book of Wisdom.

Ecclus. 31, 8-11.

BLESSED is the man that is found without blemish: and hath not gone after gold. Who is he, and we will call him blessed? for wonderful things hath he done among his people. Who hath been tried thereby, and found perfect? then let him glory. Who might offend, and hath not offended? or done evil, and hath not done it? His goods shall be established, and the congregation shall declare his alms.

Gradual. Ps. 92, 13-14. The righteous shall flourish like a palm-tree: and shall spread abroad like a cedar in Libanus in the house of the Lord. V. Ibid., 3. To tell of thy loving kindness early in the morning, and of thy truth in the night-season.

Alleluia, alleluia. V. James 1, 12. Blessed is the man that endureth temptation: for when he is tried, he shall receive the crown of life. Alleluia.

☩ The Continuation of the holy Gospel according to Luke.

Luke 19, 12.

AT that time: Jesus spake this parable unto his disciples: A certain nobleman went into a far country to receive for himself a kingdom, and to return. And he called his ten servants, and delivered them ten pounds, and said unto them: Occupy till I come. But his citizens hated him: and sent a message after him, saying: We will not have this man to reign over us. And it came to pass, that when he was returned, having received the kingdom: then he commanded these servants to be called unto him, to whom he had given the money, that he might know how much every man had gained by trading. Then came the first, saying: Lord, thy pound hath gained ten pounds. And he said unto him: Well, thou good servant, because thou hast been faithful in a very little, have thou authority over ten cities. And the second came, saying: Lord, thy pound hath gained five pounds. And he said likewise to him: Be thou also over five cities. And another came, saying: Lord, behold, here is thy pound, which I have kept laid up in a napkin: for I feared thee, because thou art an austere man: thou takest up that thou layedst not down, and reapest that thou didst not sow. And he saith unto him: Out of thine own mouth will I judge thee, thou wicked servant. Thou knewest that I was an austere man, taking up that I laid not down, and reaping that I did not sow: wherefore then gavest not thou my money into the bank, that at my coming I might have required mine own with usury? And he said unto them that stood by: Take from him the pound, and give it to him that hath ten pounds. And they said unto him: Lord, he hath ten pounds. For I say unto you: That unto every one which hath shall be given: and from him that hath not, even that he hath shall be taken away from him.

Offertory. Ps. 89, 25. My truth and my mercy shall be with him: and in my name shall his horn be exalted.

Secret.

ALMIGHTY God, mercifully look upon these our oblations: and grant; that we, who celebrate the mysteries of the Passion of the Lord, may likewise in our lives shew forth the same. Through.

Communion. Matt. 24, 46-47. Blessed is the servant whom his lord when he cometh shall find watching: verily I say unto you, he shall make him ruler over all his goods.

Postcommunion.

GRANT, we beseech thee, almighty God: that as thy blessed Confessor Stephen, for the propagation of thy faith, was counted worthy to pass from an earthly realm to the glory of thy heavenly kingdom; so we may follow his faith with due and meet devotion. Through.

September 3.

St. Pius X.

Pope and Confessor

Double.

Introit. Ps. 89, 20-22. Extuli.

I HAVE exalted one chosen out of the people, with my holy oil have I anointed him: with whom my hand shall be established, mine arm also shall strengthen him. Ps. ibid., 1. I will sing of the mercies of the Lord for ever: with my mouth will I make known thy faithfulness to all generations. V. Glory.

Collect.

O GOD, who for the defence of the Catholic faith, and the restoring of all things in Christ, didst endue thy Chief Bishop Saint Pius with heavenly wisdom and apostolic fortitude: mercifully grant; that we, following his teaching and example, may attain the rewards of everlasting felicity. Through.

The Lesson from the Epistle of blessed Paul the Apostle to the Thessalonians.

I Thess. 2, 2-8.

BRETHREN: We were bold in our God to speak unto you the gospel of God with much contention. For our exhortation was not of deceit, nor of uncleanness, nor in guile; but as we were allowed of God to be put in trust with the gospel, even so we speak; not as pleasing men, but God, which tryeth our hearts. For neither at any time used we flattering words, as ye know, nor a cloke of covetousness, God is witness, nor of men sought we glory, neither of you nor yet of others. When we might have been burdensome unto you as the Apostles of Christ, but we were gentle among you, even as a nurse cherisheth her children. So being affectionately desirous of you, we were willing to have imparted to you not the gospel of God only, but also our own souls, because ye were dear unto us.

Gradual. Ps. 40, 10-11. I have made known thy righteousness in the great congregation; lo, I have not refrained my lips: O Lord, and that thou knowest. ℣. I have not hid thy righteousness within my heart; my talk hath been of thy truth and thy salvation.

Alleluia, alleluia. ℣. Ps. 23, 5-6. Thou preparest a table before me, thou anointest my head with oil, my cup runneth over. Alleluia.

¶ In votive Masses after Septuagesima, omitting Alleluia and the Verse following, is said:

Tract. Ps. 132, 16-18. I will deck her priests with health, and her saints shall rejoice and sing. ℣. There shall I make the horn of David to flourish, I have ordained a lantern for mine Anointed. ℣. As for his enemies, I shall clothe them with shame, but upon himself shall his crown flourish.

In Easter Tide the Gradual is omitted, and in its place is said:

Alleluia, alleluia. ℣. Ps. 23, 5-6. Thou preparest a table before me, thou anointest my head with oil, my cup runneth over. Alleluia. ℣. Ps. 26, 8. Lord, I have loved the habitation of thy house: and the place where thine honour dwelleth. Alleluia.

✠ The Continuation of the holy Gospel according to John.

John 21, 15-17.

AT that time: Said Jesus to Simon Peter: Simon, son of Jonas, lovest thou me more than these? He saith unto him: Yea, Lord, thou knowest that I love thee. He saith unto him: Feed my lambs. He saith to him again the second time: Simon, son of Jonas, lovest thou me? He saith unto him: Yea, Lord, thou knowest that I love thee. He saith unto him: feed my sheep. He saith unto him the third time: Simon, son of Jonas, lovest thou me? Peter was grieved, because he said unto him the third time: Lovest thou me? and he said unto him: Lord, thou knowest all things; thou knowest that I love thee. Jesus saith unto him: Feed my sheep.

Offertory. Ps. 34, 12. Come, ye children, and hearken unto me; I will teach you the fear of the Lord.

Secret.

O LORD, we beseech thee, graciously to accept these our oblations, and grant unto us: that at the intercession of thy Chief Bishop Saint Pius we may perform these heavenly mysteries with unfeigned devotion, and receive the same with a faithful and true heart. Through.

Common Preface.

Communion. John 6, 56-57. My flesh is meat indeed, and my blood is drink indeed. He that eateth my flesh and drinketh my blood, dwelleth in me, and I in him.

Postcommunion.

O LORD our God, who hast refreshed us with the strength of this heavenly table, we beseech thee: that at the intercession of thy Chief Bishop Saint Pius; we may be made stedfast in the faith, and live in unity and godly love. Through.

September 5.

St. Lawrence Justinian

Bishop and Confessor

Simple.

The Mass Statuit ei, from the Common of a Confessor Bishop, p. [19].

Collect. C

GRANT, we beseech thee, almighty God: that we, devoutly observing this festival of blessed Lawrence, thy Confessor and Bishop, may hereby advance in true godliness and attain unto everlasting salvation. Through.

Secret. C

WE beseech thee, O Lord, that we, remembering with gladness the merits of thy Saints, may in all places feel the succour of their intercession. Through.

Postcommunion. C

GRANT, we beseech thee, almighty God: that we, shewing forth our thankfulness for the gifts which we have received, may, at the intercession of blessed Lawrence, thy Confessor and Bishop, obtain yet more abundant mercies. Through.

September 8.

THE NATIVITY OF THE B.V. MARY

Double of 2nd class.

Introit. Sedulius. Salve, sancta Parens.

HAIL, O Mother most holy, who didst give birth to the Monarch: reigning o'er heaven and earth, world without end. Ps. 45, 1. My heart is inditing of a good matter: I speak of the things which I have made unto the King. ℣. Glory.

Collect.

WE beseech thee, O Lord, to bestow on us thy servants the gift of thy heavenly grace: that as the child-bearing of the blessed Virgin was unto us the beginning of our salvation; so the devout observance of her Nativity may avail for the increasing of our peace. Through.

In private Masses only, Commemoration of St. Hadrian, M.

Collect.

GRANT, we beseech thee, almighty God: that we, who celebrate the heavenly birthday of blessed Hadrian, thy Martyr, may by his intercession be stablished in the love of thy name. Through.

The Lesson from the book of Wisdom.
Prov. 8, 22-35.

THE Lord possessed me in the beginning of his way, before his works of old. I was set up from everlasting, from the beginning, or ever the earth was. When there were no depths, I was brought forth: when there were no fountains abounding with water: before the mountains were settled: before the hills was I brought forth: while as yet he had not made the earth, nor the fields, nor the highest part of the dust of the world. When he prepared the heavens, I was there: when he set a compass upon the face of the depth: when he established the clouds above, when he strengthened the fountains of the deep: when he gave to the sea his decree, that the waters should not pass his commandment: when he appointed the foundations of the earth. Then I was by him, as one brought up with him: and I was daily his delight, rejoicing always before him: rejoicing in the habitable part of his earth: and my delights were with the sons of men. Now therefore hearken unto me, O ye children: for blessed are they that keep my ways. Hear instruction, and be wise, and refuse it not. Blessed is the man that heareth me, watching daily at my gates, waiting at the posts of my doors. For whoso findeth me findeth life, and shall obtain favour of the Lord.

Gradual. Blessed and venerable art thou, O Virgin Mary: who a maiden undefiled hast our Saviour for thy child. ℣. Virgin, Mother of God, the whole world cannot contain him, yet, made man for our sake, hidden he lay in thy womb.

Alleluia, alleluia. ℣. Blessed art thou, O holy Virgin Mary, and most worthy of all praise: for out of thee hath arisen the sun of righteousness, Christ our God. Alleluia.

✠ The Beginning of the holy Gospel according to Matthew.

Matt. 1, 1-16.

THE book of the generation of Jesus Christ, the son of David, the son of Abraham. Abraham begat Isaac. And Isaac begat Jacob. And Jacob begat Judas and his brethren. And Judas begat Phares and Zara of Thamar. And Phares begat Esrom. And Esrom begat Aram. And Aram begat Aminadab. And Aminadab begat Naasson. And Naasson begat Salmon. And Salmon begat Booz of Rachab. And Booz begat Obed of Ruth. And Obed begat Jesse. And Jesse begat David the king. And David the king begat Solomon of her that had been the wife of Urias. And Solomon begat Roboam. And Roboam begat Abia. And Abia begat Asa. And Asa begat Josaphat. And Josaphat begat Joram. And Joram begat Ozias. And Ozias begat Joatham. And Joatham begat Achaz. And Achaz begat Ezekias. And Ezekias begat Manasses. And Manasses begat Amon. And Amon begat Josias. And Josias begat Jechonias and his brethren, about the time they were carried away to Babylon. And after they were brought to Babylon: Jechonias begat Salathiel. And Salathiel begat Zorobabel. And Zorobabel begat Abiud. And Abiud begat Eliakim. And Eliakim begat Azor. And Azor begat Sadoc. And Sadoc begat Achim. And Achim begat Eliud. And Eliud begat Eleazar. And Eleazar begat Matthan. And Matthan begat Jacob. And Jacob begat Joseph the husband of Mary, of whom was born Jesus who is called Christ. Creed.

Offertory. Blessed art thou, O Virgin Mary, who didst bear the Creator of all things: thou broughtest forth him who made thee, and for ever remainest a Virgin.

Secret.

MAY the manhood of thine only-begotten Son, O Lord, avail for our succour: that, even as he, being born of a Virgin, destroyed not but hallowed the innocence of his Mother; so on this feast of her Nativity, he may deliver us from our offences, and render us an oblation acceptable unto thee, even Jesus Christ our Lord: Who liveth.

For St. Hadrian.   Secret.

WE beseech thee, O Lord, to accept our prayers and oblations: and graciously hearken unto us, whom thou dost cleanse by thy heavenly mysteries. Through.

Preface of the B.V.Mary, And that on the Nativity.

Communion. Blessed is the womb of the Virgin Mary, that bare the Son of the everlasting Father.

Postcommunion.

GRANT, we beseech thee, O Lord: that the Sacrament which we have received in the mysteries of this yearly festival; may both in this life and that which is to come be profitable unto us for the healing of our souls. Through.

For St. Hadrian.   Postcommunion.

GRANT, we beseech thee, O Lord our God: that like as we in this life do gladly honour the memory of thy Saints; so we may rejoice hereafter in their everlasting fellowship. Through.

September 9.

For St. Gorgonius

Martyr

The Mass Laetabitur, p. [7], with the following Prayers:

Collect. P

LET thy Saint Gorgonius, O Lord, gladden us by his intercession: and make us to rejoice in the devout observance of his festival. Through.

Secret. P

O LORD, let thy holy Martyr Gorgonius so intercede for us: that this oblation of our service may be acceptable unto thee. Through.

Postcommunion. P

GRANT, O God, that thy household may be quickened and refreshed by thine eternal goodness: and in thy Martyr Gorgonius be continually nourished with the sweet savour of Christ, thy Son. Who liveth and reigneth with thee.

September 10.

St. Nicholas of Tolentino

Confessor

Double.

The Mass Justus ut palma, p. [25].

Collect. C

ASSIST us mercifully, O Lord, in these our supplications, which we make before thee on the solemnity of blessed Nicholas, thy Confessor: that we, who put not our trust in our own righteousness, may be succoured by the prayers of him who found favour in thy sight. Through.

Secret. C

GRANT to us, we beseech thee, almighty God: that this oblation of our humble service may be acceptable in thy sight to the honour of thy Saints, and may cleanse us both in body and soul. Through.

Postcommunion. C

WE beseech thee, almighty God: that we, who have received this heavenly food, may at the intercession of blessed Nicholas, thy Confessor, be thereby defended against all adversities. Through.

September 11.

For SS. Protus and Hyacinth

Martyrs

The Mass Salus autem, p. [12], with the following Prayers:

Collect. P

O LORD, let the meritorious confession of thy blessed Martyrs, Protus and Hyacinth, avail for our protection: and let their loving intercession ever defend us. Through.

Secret. P

GRANT, we beseech thee, O Lord: that this oblation of our bounden service, which we offer unto thee for the commemoration of thy holy Martyrs, Protus and Hyacinth; may effectually avail for our healing unto everlasting salvation. Through.

Postcommunion. P

WE beseech thee, O Lord, that by the supplication of thy blessed Martyrs, Protus and Hyacinth: thy holy mysteries which we have here received may cleanse and purify our souls. Through.

September 12.

The Most Holy Name of Mary

Greater double.

Introit. Ps. 45, 13, 15-16. Vultum tuum.

THE rich among the people shall make their supplication before thee: the Virgins that be her fellows shall be brought unto the King: they that bear her company shall be brought unto thee with joy and gladness. Ps. Ibid. 1. My heart is inditing of a good matter: I speak of the things which I have made unto the King. ℣. Glory.

Collect.

GRANT, we beseech thee, almighty God: that we thy faithful people, who rejoice in the Name and protection of the most holy Virgin Mary, may by her loving intercession be delivered from all evils upon earth, and be worthy in heaven to attain unto everlasting felicity. Through.

The Lesson from the book of Wisdom.

Ecclus. 24, 17.

AS the vine I brought forth a pleasant savour: and my flowers are the fruit of honour and riches. I am the mother of fair love and fear, and knowledge, and holy hope. In me is all grace of the way and the truth: in me is all hope of life and of virtue. Come unto me, all ye that be desirous of me, and fill yourselves with my fruits. For my spirit is sweeter than honey, and mine inheritance than honey and the honeycomb. My memorial shall be unto everlasting generations. They that eat me shall yet be hungry: and they that drink me shall yet be thirsty. He that obeyeth me shall never be confounded: and they that work by me shall not do amiss. They that expound me shall have life everlasting.

Gradual. Blessed and venerable art thou, O Virgin Mary: who a maiden undefiled hast our Saviour for thy child. ℣. Virgin, Mother of God, the whole world cannot contain him, yet, made man for our sake, hidden he lay in thy womb.

Alleluia, alleluia. ℣. After child-birth thou remainedst a pure Virgin: Mother of God, intercede for us. Alleluia.

✠ The Continuation of the holy Gospel according to Luke.

Luke 1, 26-38.

AT that time: The Angel Gabriel was sent from God unto a city of Galilee named Nazareth, to a Virgin espoused to a man whose name was Joseph, of the house of David, and the Virgin's name was Mary. And the Angel came unto her, and said: Hail, full of grace; the Lord is with thee: blessed art thou among women. And when she saw him she was troubled at his saying: and cast in her mind what manner of salutation this should be. And the Angel said unto her: Fear not, Mary, for thou hast found favour with God, and behold, thou shalt conceive in thy womb, and bring forth a Son, and shalt call his name Jesus. He shall be great, and shall be called the Son of the Highest, and the Lord God shall give unto him the throne of his father David: and he shall reign over the house of Jacob for ever, and of his kingdom there shall be no end. Then said Mary unto the Angel: How shall this be, seeing I know not a man? And the Angel answered and said unto her: The Holy Ghost shall come upon thee, and the power of the Highest shall overshadow thee. Therefore also that Holy Thing which shall be born of thee shall be called the Son of God. And behold, thy cousin Elisabeth, she hath also conceived a son in her old age: and this is the sixth month with her who was called barren: for with God nothing shall be impossible. And Mary said: Behold the handmaid of the Lord, be it unto me according to thy word. Creed.

Offertory. Luke 1, 28 and 42. Hail Mary, full of grace; the Lord is with thee: blessed art thou among women, and blessed is the fruit of thy womb.

Secret.

THROUGH thy mercy, O Lord, and the intercession of blessed Mary ever Virgin, may this oblation avail for our prosperity and peace, both now and for ever. Through.

Preface of the B.V.Mary, And that on the Festival.

Communion. Blessed is the womb of the Virgin Mary, that bare the Son of the everlasting Father.

Postcommunion.

O LORD, who hast appointed these holy mysteries which we have here received to be the means of our salvation: grant, we beseech thee, that we, who have offered these our gifts unto thy majesty in honour of blessed Mary ever Virgin; may by her advocacy be at all times and in all places effectually defended. Through.

September 14.

The Exaltation of the Holy Cross

Greater double.

Introit. Gal. 6, 14. Nos autem.

BUT as for us, it behoveth us to glory in the Cross of our Lord Jesus Christ: in whom is our salvation, our life and resurrection: by whom we were saved and obtained our freedom. Ps. 67, 1. God be merciful unto us, and bless us: and shew us the light of his countenance, and be merciful unto us. ℣. Glory.

Collect.

O GOD, who on this day dost gladden us with the yearly solemnity of the Exaltation of the holy Cross: grant, we beseech thee; that we, who on earth have known the mystery of the redemption which thy Son hath wrought for us, may likewise attain unto the reward thereof in heaven. Through the same.

The Lesson from the Epistle of blessed Paul the Apostle to the Philippians.

Phil. 2, 5-11.

BRETHREN: Let this mind be in you, which was also in Christ Jesus: who, being in the form of God, thought it not robbery to be equal with God: but made himself of no reputation, and took upon him the form of a servant, and was made in the likeness of men. And being found in fashion as a man, he humbled himself, and became obedient unto death, even the death of the cross. Wherefore God also hath highly exalted him: and given him a name which is above every name: (Here genuflect) that at the name of Jesus every knee should bow, of things in heaven, and things in earth, and things under the earth: and that every tongue should confess that Jesus Christ is Lord, to the glory of God the Father.

Gradual. Ibid., 8-9. Christ for us became obedient unto death, even the death of the cross. ℣. Wherefore God also hath highly exalted him, and given him a name which is above every name.

Alleluia, alleluia. ℣. Sweetest wood, sweetest iron, sweetest weight is hung on thee: who alone wast counted worthy to bear the King of heaven, and the Lord. Alleluia.

✠ The Continuation of the holy Gospel according to John.

John 12, 31-36.

AT that time: Jesus said unto the multitudes of the Jews: Now is the judgment of this world: now shall the prince of this world be cast out. And I, if I be lifted up from the earth, will draw all men unto me. This he said, signifying what death he should die. The people answered him: We have heard out of the law that Christ abideth for ever: and how sayest thou: The Son of man must be lifted up? Who is this Son of man? Then Jesus said unto them: Yet a little while is the light with you. Walk while ye have the light, lest darkness come upon you: for he that walketh in darkness knoweth not whither he goeth. While ye have light, believe in the light, that ye may be the children of light. Creed.

Offertory. Protect, O Lord, thy people, by the sign of the holy Cross, from all the snares of every enemy: that we may render thee acceptable service, and that our sacrifice may be well pleasing unto thee, alleluia.

Secret.

O LORD our God, who dost fulfil us with the Body and Blood of Jesus Christ our Lord, through whom thou hast sanctified the standard of the Cross: we beseech thee; that as we have been counted worthy to venerate that Cross, so we may effectually be made partakers of its glory unto everlasting salvation. Through the same.

Preface of the Cross.

Communion. By the sign of the Cross deliver us from our enemies, O our God.

Postcommunion.

ASSIST us mercifully, O Lord our God: that we whom thou dost suffer to rejoice in honouring the holy Cross; may be defended by the perpetual succour of the same. Through.

¶ For Votive Masses the Mass Nos autem, p. [62], is said.

September 15.

THE SEVEN SORROWS OF THE BLESSED VIRGIN MARY

Double of 2nd class.

Introit. John 19, 25. Stabant.

THERE stood by the Cross of Jesus his Mother, and his Mother's sister, Mary the wife of Cleophas, and Salome, and Mary Magdalene. ℣. Ibid., 26-27. Woman, behold thy Son: said Jesus; and to the disciple: Behold thy Mother. ℣. Glory.

Collect.

O GOD, in whose passion according to the prophecy of Simeon the sword of sorrow did pierce the most loving soul of the glorious Virgin Mother Mary: mercifully grant; that we, who devoutly call to mind her sorrows, may obtain with gladness the benefits of thy passion: Who livest and reignest with God the Father.

In private Masses only Commemoration of St. Nicomede, Martyr.

Collect.

ASSIST, O Lord, thy people: that as they do profit by the glorious merits of blessed Nicomede thy Martyr, so his advocacy may at all times succour them to the obtaining of thy mercy. Through.

The Lesson from the book of Judith.

Jud. 13, 22-25.

THE Lord hath blessed thee in his power, because through thee he hath brought our enemies to nought. O daughter, blessed art thou of the most high God, above all the women upon the earth. And blessed be the Lord God which hath created the heavens and the earth: because he hath so magnified thy name this day, that this thy praise shall not depart from the heart of men, which remember the power of God for ever, for whom thou hast not spared thy life for the affliction of our nation, but hast revenged our ruin, walking a straight way before our God.

Gradual. Mournful and weeping art thou, O Virgin Mary, standing by the Cross of the Lord Jesus, thy Son, the Redeemer. ℣. Virgin, Mother of God, he, whom the whole world containeth not, endureth this torment of the cross, the author of life made man.

Alleluia, alleluia. ℣. There stood by the Cross of our Lord Jesus Christ holy Mary, Queen of heaven and Lady of the world, mournful and weeping.

Sequence. Stabat Mater dolorosa.

BY the Cross her station keeping,
Stood the mournful Mother weeping,
Where he hung, her dying Son.

Through her soul, of joy bereavéd,
Torn with anguish, deeply grievéd,
Lo! the piercing sword hath run.

O how sad and sore distresséd
Then was she, that Mother blesséd
Of the sole-begotten One!

Torn with grief and desolation,
Mother good, the bitter Passion
Saw she of her glorious Son.

Who, on Christ's dear Mother gazing,
Torn by anguish so amazing,
Born of woman, would not weep?

Who, on Christ's dear Mother thinking,
With her Son in sorrow sinking,
Would not share her sadness deep?

For his people's sin chastiséd,
She her Jesus saw despiséd,
Saw him by the scourges rent.

Saw her own sweet Offspring taken,
And in death by all forsaken
While his spirit forth he sent.

Mother, fount of love o'erflowing,
Ah, that I, thy sorrow knowing,
In thy grief may mourn with thee.

That my heart, fresh ardour gaining,
Love of Christ my God attaining,
Unto him may pleasing be.

Holy Mother, be there written
Every wound of Jesus smitten
In my heart, and there remain.

As thy Son through tribulation
Deigned to purchase my salvation,
Let me share with thee the pain.

Let me mourn with thee beside him
For the sins which crucified him,
While my life remains in me.

Take beneath the Cross my station,
Share with thee thy desolation,
Humbly this I ask of thee.

Virgin, virgins all excelling,
Spurn me not, my prayer repelling:
Make me weep and mourn with thee.

So Christ's death within me bearing,
Let me, in his Passion sharing,
Keep his wounds in memory.

Let the five wounds penetrate me:
May the Cross inebriate me,
And thy Son's most precious blood.

Lest I burn in hell's damnation,
Virgin, be my consolation
On the judgment day of God.

Christ, when this world's troubles leave me,
Through thy Mother then receive me
To the palm of victory.

When the bonds of flesh are riven,
Glory to my soul be given
In thy Paradise with thee.   Amen.
Alleluia.

✠ The Continuation of the holy Gospel according to John.
John 19, 25-27.

AT that time: There stood by the Cross of Jesus his Mother, and his Mother's sister, Mary, the wife of Cleophas, and Mary Magdalene. When Jesus therefore saw his Mother, and the disciple standing by, whom he loved, he saith unto his Mother: Woman, behold thy Son. Then saith he to the disciple: Behold thy Mother. And from that hour that disciple took her unto his own home.   Creed.

Offertory. Jer. 18, 20. Remember, O Virgin, Mother of God, when thou standest in the sight of the Lord, that thou speak good things for us, and that he may turn away his indignation from us.

Secret.

WE offer unto thee our prayers and sacrifices, O Lord Jesu Christ, humbly beseeching thee: that we, who in our prayers do recall the Piercing of the most loving soul of blessed Mary, thy Mother; may by the manifold and devout intercessions both of her and of the Saints that with her have stood beneath the Cross, through the merits of thy death, be made worthy to be partakers of the inheritance of thine elect: Who livest.

Feasts of September (16)

For St. Nicomede. Secret.

MERCIFULLY receive, O Lord, the gifts which we offer: and let the prayer of the blessed Martyr Nicomede commend them unto thy majesty. Through.

Preface of the B.V.Mary, And that in the Transfixion.

Communion. Happy the heart of the blessed Virgin Mary, which without death gained the palm of martyrdom beneath the Cross of the Lord.

Postcommunion.

O LORD Jesu Christ, let this sacrifice which we have here received in devout remembrance of the Piercing of thy Virgin Mother: obtain for us of thy mercy all such blessings as may effectually avail for our salvation: Who livest and reignest.

For St. Nicomede. Postcommunion.

CLEANSE us, O Lord, by this Sacrament which we have here received: that through the intercession of blessed Nicomede, thy Martyr, we may be delivered thereby from all our offences. Through.

¶ If on this day or on the following days an Ember Day occur, in all Masses except the Conventual Mass of the Feast, before the Commemoration of the Simples which occur a Commemoration is made of the Feria. Where there is the obligation of Choir, after Terce outside Choir a Mass of the Feast is read without Commemoration of the Ember Day; and in Choir after None a Mass is said of the Feria without Commemoration of the occurring Feast. Private Masses, however, may be said of the Feria also, with Commemoration of the occurring Office. On this day, however, and on the other days on which there occurs a Feast of the first or second class, in Choir a Conventual Mass of the Feast is said after Terce, and out of Choir after None a Mass of the Feria is read, which however, in this case cannot be said as a private Mass.

September 16.

SS. Cornelius, Pope, and Cyprian

Bishop, Martyrs.

Simple.

The Mass Intret, p. [9].

Collect. C

DEFEND us, O Lord, we beseech thee, who observe the feast of thy blessed Martyrs and Bishops Cornelius and Cyprian: and grant that by their meritorious supplication we may ever be holpen in thy sight. Through.

And Commemoration is made of SS. Euphemia, V., Lucy and Geminian, MM.

Collect. P

GRANT, O Lord, that our prayers in this time of our rejoicing may be brought to good effect: that as with yearly service we recall the day of the passion of thy holy Martyrs, Euphemia, Lucy and Geminian, so we may imitate the stedfastness of their faith. Through.

Secret. C

ASSIST us mercifully, O Lord, in these our supplications which we make before thee in remembrance of thy Saints: that we who trust not in our own righteousness may be succoured by the merits of them that have found favour in thy sight. Through.

For the Holy Martyrs. Secret.

GRACIOUSLY hearken, we beseech thee, O Lord, unto the prayers of thy people: and make us to rejoice in the intercession of those whose festival thou dost suffer us to celebrate. Through.

Postcommunion.

O LORD, who hast fulfilled us with these saving mysteries: we beseech thee that we may be aided by the prayers of those whose festival we celebrate. Through.

For the Holy Martyrs. Postcommunion.

O LORD, graciously hear our prayers: that we, who solemnly observe the feast of thy holy Martyrs Euphemia, Lucy and Geminian, may be succoured by their continual help. Through.

(For SS. Euphemia etc., the Mass Intret, p. [9], with Prayers as above, and Gospel from Mass Sapientiam, p. [11]).

In Scotland:

The same day, September 16.

St. Ninian

Bishop and Confessor

See Supplement.

September 17.

The Impression of the Holy Stigmata of St. Francis

Confessor

Double.

Introit. Gal. 6, 14. Mihi autem.

BUT God forbid that I should glory, save in the Cross of our Lord Jesus Christ: by whom the world is crucified unto me, and I unto the world. Ps. 142, 1. I cried unto the Lord with my voice: yea, even unto the Lord did I make my supplication. ℣. Glory.

Collect.

O LORD Jesu Christ, who, when the world was waxing cold, to the inflaming of our hearts with the fire of thy love didst in the flesh of the most blessed Francis renew the sacred Marks of thy passion: mercifully grant; that by his merits and prayers we may continually bear thy cross, and may bring forth fruits worthy of repentance: Who livest.

The Lesson from the Epistle of blessed Paul the Apostle to the Galatians.

Gal. 6, 14-18.

BRETHREN: God forbid that I should glory, save in the Cross of our Lord Jesus Christ: by whom the world is crucified unto me, and I unto the world. For in Christ Jesus neither circumcision availeth any thing, nor uncircumcision, but a new creature. And as many as walk according to this rule, peace be on them, and mercy, and upon the Israel of God. From henceforth let no man trouble me: for I bear in my body the marks of the Lord Jesus. Brethren, the grace of our Lord Jesus Christ be with your spirit. Amen.

Gradual. Ps. 37, 30-31. The mouth of the righteous is exercised in wisdom: and his tongue will be talking of judgment. ℣. The law of his God is in his heart: and his goings shall not slide.

Alleluia, alleluia. ℣. Francis, poor and lowly, enters heaven rich, he is honoured with celestial hymns. Alleluia.

✠ The Continuation of the holy Gospel according to Matthew.

Matt. 16, 24-27.

AT that time: Jesus said unto his disciples: If any man will come after me, let him deny himself, and take up his cross, and follow me. For whosoever will save his life shall lose it: and whosoever will lose his life for my sake shall find it. For what is a man profited, if he shall gain the whole world, and lose his own soul? Or what shall a man give in exchange for his soul? For the Son of man shall come in the glory of his Father with his Angels: and then he shall reward every man according to his works.

Offertory. Ps. 89, 25. My truth and my mercy shall be with him: and in my name shall his horn be exalted.

Secret.

SANCTIFY, O Lord, the gifts which we dedicate unto thee: and at the intercession of blessed Francis purify us from every stain of sin. Through.

Communion. Luke 12, 42. A faithful and wise servant, whom the lord hath made ruler over his household: to give them their portion of meat in due season.

Postcommunion.

O GOD, who in divers ways didst shew forth in blessed Francis, thy Confessor, the wondrous mysteries of the Cross: grant us, we beseech thee; ever to follow the pattern of his devotion, and continually thinking on the same thy Cross, thereby to be defended against all temptations. Through.

September 18.

St. Joseph of Cupertino

Confessor

Double.

Introit. Ecclus. 1, 14-15. Dilectio Dei.

THE love of God is honourable wisdom: and they, to whom she shall shew herself, love her by the sight and by the knowledge of her wondrous works. Ps. 84, 1. O how amiable are thy dwellings, thou Lord of hosts! my soul hath a desire and longing to enter into the courts of the Lord. ℣. Glory.

Collect.

O GOD, who didst ordain that thine only-begotten Son should be lifted up from the earth, that he might draw all things unto him: mercifully grant; that, by the merits and example of thy seraphic Confessor Joseph, we, being raised above all earthly desires, may be found worthy to attain unto him: Who liveth and reigneth with thee.

The Lesson from the Epistle of blessed Paul the Apostle to the Corinthians.

I Cor. 13, 1-8.

BRETHREN: Though I speak with the tongues of men and of Angels, and have not charity, I am become as sounding brass, or a tinkling cymbal. And though I have the gift of prophecy, and understand all mysteries, and all knowledge: and though I have all faith, so that I could remove mountains, and have not charity, I am nothing. And though I bestow all my goods to feed the poor, and though I give my body to be burned, and have not charity, it profiteth me nothing. Charity suffereth long, and is kind: charity envieth not, charity vaunteth not itself, is not puffed up, doth not behave itself unseemly, seeketh not her own, is not easily provoked, thinketh no evil, rejoiceth not in iniquity, but rejoiceth in the truth: beareth all things, believeth all things, hopeth all things, endureth all things. Charity never faileth: but whether there be prophecies, they shall fail, whether there be tongues, they shall cease, whether there be knowledge, it shall vanish away.

Gradual. Ps. 21, 4-5. Thou hast prevented him, O Lord, with the blessings of goodness: thou hast set a crown of pure gold upon his head. ℣. He asked life of thee, and thou gavest him a long life, even for ever and ever.

Alleluia, alleluia. ℣. Ecclus. 11, 13. The eye of God looked upon him for good, and set him up from his low estate, and lifted up his head. Alleluia.

☩ The Continuation of the holy Gospel according to Matthew.

Matt. 22, 1.

AT that time: Jesus spake unto the chief priests and Pharisees in parables, saying: The kingdom of heaven is like unto a certain king, who made a marriage for his son. And sent forth his servants to call them that were bidden to the wedding, and they would not come. Again, he sent forth other servants, saying: Tell them which are bidden: Behold, I have prepared my dinner, my oxen and my fatlings are killed, and all things are ready: come unto the marriage. But they made light of it, and went their ways, one to his farm, another to his merchandise: and the remnant took his servants, and entreated them spitefully, and slew them. But when the king heard thereof, he was wroth: and he sent forth his armies and destroyed those murderers, and burnt up their city. Then saith he to his servants: The wedding is ready, but they who were bidden were not worthy. Go ye therefore into the highways, and as many as ye shall find bid to the marriage. So those servants went out into the highways, and gathered together all, as many as they found, both bad and good: and the wedding was furnished with guests. And when the king came in to see the guests, he saw there a man which had not on a wedding-garment. And he saith unto him: Friend, how camest thou in hither, not having a wedding-garment? And he was speechless. Then said the king to the servants: Bind him hand and foot, and take him away, and cast him into outer darkness: there shall be weeping and gnashing of teeth. For many are called, but few are chosen. Creed.

Offertory. Ps. 35, 13. As for me, when they were sick, I put on sackcloth. I humbled my soul with fasting: and my prayer shall turn into mine own bosom.

Secret.

WE offer unto thee, O Lord, this our sacrifice of praise to the honour of thy Saints: whereby we trust to be delivered from all evils both in this life and in that which is to come. Through.

Communion. Ps. 69, 30-31. As for me, when I am poor and in heaviness: thy help, O God, shall lift me up. I will praise the name of God with a song: and magnify it with thanksgiving.

Postcommunion.

O LORD our God, who hast refreshed us with heavenly meat and drink, we humbly beseech thee: that we may be defended by the prayers of him in whose memory we have received the same. Through.

September 19.

SS. Januarius, Bishop, and his Companions

Martyrs

Introit. Ps. 37, 39. Salus autem justorum.

BUT the salvation of the righteous cometh of the Lord, who is also their strength in the time of trouble. Ps. ibid., 1. Fret not thyself because of the ungodly: neither be thou envious against the evil doers. ℣. Glory.

Collect.

O GOD, who makest us glad with the yearly solemnity of thy holy Martyrs Januarius and his Companions: mercifully grant; that as we do rejoice in their merits, so we may be enkindled by their example. Through.

The Lesson from the Epistle of blessed Paul the Apostle to the Hebrews.

Heb. 10, 32-38.

BRETHREN: Call to remembrance the former days, in which, after ye were illuminated, ye endured a great fight of afflictions: partly, whilst ye were made a gazingstock both by reproaches and afflictions, and partly, whilst ye became companions of them that were so used. For ye had compassion of me in my bonds, and took joyfully the spoiling of your goods, knowing in yourselves that we have in heaven a better and an enduring substance. Cast not away therefore your confidence, which hath great recompence of reward. For ye have need of patience: that, after ye have done the will of God, ye might receive the promise. For yet a little while, and he that shall come will come, and will not tarry. Now the just shall live by faith.

Gradual. Ps. 34, 18-19. The righteous cry, and the Lord heareth them: and delivereth them out of all their troubles. ℣. The Lord is nigh unto them that are of a contrite heart: and will save such as be of an humble spirit.

Alleluia, alleluia. ℣. The noble army of Martyrs praise thee, O Lord. Alleluia.

✠ The Continuation of the holy Gospel according to Matthew.

Matt. 24, 3-13.

AT that time: As Jesus sat upon the mount of Olives, the disciples came unto him privately, saying: Tell us, when shall these things be? and what shall be the sign of thy coming, and of the end of the world? And Jesus answered and said unto them: Take heed that no man deceive you. For many shall come in my name, saying: I am Christ: and shall deceive many. And ye shall hear of wars and rumours of wars. See that ye be not troubled. For all these things must come to pass, but the end is not yet. For nation shall arise against nation, and kingdom against kingdom, and there shall be famines, and pestilences, and earthquakes, in divers places. All these are the beginning of sorrows. Then shall they deliver you up to be afflicted, and shall kill you: and ye shall be hated of all nations for my name's sake. And then shall many be offended, and shall betray one another, and shall hate one another. And many false prophets shall rise, and shall deceive many. And because iniquity shall abound, the love of many shall wax cold. But he that shall endure unto the end, the same shall be saved.

Offertory. Wisd. 3, 1-3. The souls of the righteous are in the hand of God, and there shall no torment touch them. In the sight of the unwise they seemed to die: but they are in peace, alleluia.

Secret.

WE beseech thee, O Lord, mercifully to accept these our oblations: that at the intercession of thy holy Martyrs Januarius and his Companions we may be defended against all adversities. Through.

Communion. Matt. 10, 27. What I tell you in darkness, that speak ye in light, saith the Lord: and what ye hear in the ear, that preach ye upon the housetops.

Postcommunion.

O LORD, let this holy Communion cleanse us from every guilty stain: that at the intercession of thy holy Martyrs Januarius and his Companions we may thereby be made partakers of thy healing unto life eternal. Through.

September 20.

SS. Eustace and his Companions

Martyrs

Double.

The Mass Sapientiam, from the Common of many Martyrs, p. [11].

Collect.

O GOD, who dost vouchsafe unto us to celebrate the heavenly birthday of the holy Martyrs Eustace and his Companions: grant that we may rejoice in their perpetual fellowship in heaven. Through.

Secret.

WE beseech thee, O Lord, that the gifts which we offer unto thee of our bounden duty and service may be acceptable unto thee for the honour of thy Saints: and by thy mercy profitable unto us for our salvation. Through.

Postcommunion.

GRANT to us, we beseech thee, O Lord: at the intercession of thy holy Martyrs Eustace and his Companions; that we, who with our outward lips are partakers of this holy Sacrament, may inwardly receive the same in purity of heart. Through.

September 21.

ST. MATTHEW
APOSTLE AND EVANGELIST

Double of 2nd class.

¶ If on this day there occur an Ember Day, in Choir after Terce a Conventual Mass is said of the Feast; outside Choir after None a Mass is read of the Feria, of which, however, private Masses are forbidden.

Introit. Ps. 37, 30-31. Os justi.

THE mouth of the righteous is exercised in wisdom, and his tongue will be talking of judgment: the law of his God is in his heart. Ps. ibid., 1. Fret not thyself because of the ungodly: neither be thou envious against the evil doers. ℣. Glory.

Collect.

O ALMIGHTY God, who by thy blessed Son didst call Matthew from the receipt of custom to be an Apostle and Evangelist: grant us grace to forsake all covetous desires, and inordinate love of riches; and to follow the same thy Son Jesus Christ: Who liveth and reigneth with thee.

Or, Collect.

O LORD, let the prayers of thy blessed Apostle and Evangelist Matthew avail for our continual succour: that those things, which of our own power we cannot obtain, may through his intercession be granted unto us. Through.

The Lesson from the Epistle of blessed Paul the Apostle to the Corinthians.

II Cor. 4, 1-6.

BRETHREN: Seeing we have this ministry, as we have received mercy, we faint not: but have renounced the hidden things of dishonesty, not walking in craftiness, nor handling the word of God deceitfully: but by manifestation of the truth commending ourselves to every man's conscience in the sight of God. But if our Gospel be hid, it is hid to them that are lost: in whom the god of this world hath blinded the minds of them which believe not: lest the light of the glorious Gospel of Christ, who is the image of God, should shine unto them. For we preach not ourselves, but Christ Jesus the Lord: and ourselves your servants for Jesus' sake. For God, who commanded the light to shine out of darkness, hath shined in our hearts, to give the light of the knowledge of the glory of God, in the face of Jesus Christ.

Or:

The Lesson from the Prophet Ezekiel.

Ezek. 1, 10-14.

THE likeness of the faces of the four animals: they four had the face of a man, and the face of a lion, on the right side: and they four had the face of an ox on the left side, they four also had the face of an eagle. Thus were their faces, and their wings were stretched upward: two wings of every one were joined one to another, and two covered their bodies: and they went every one straight forward: whither the spirit was to go, they went, and they turned not when they went. As for the likeness of the living creatures, their appearance was like burning coals of fire and like the appearance of lamps. It went up and down among the living creatures, and the fire was bright, and out of the fire went forth lightning. And the living creatures ran and returned as the appearance of a flash of lightning.

Gradual. Ps. 112, 1-2. Blessed is the man that feareth the Lord: he hath great delight in his commandments. ℣. His seed shall be mighty upon earth: the generation of the faithful shall be blessed.

Alleluia, alleluia. ℣. The glorious company of the Apostles praise thee, O Lord. Alleluia.

✠ The Continuation of the holy Gospel according to Matthew.

Matt. 9, 9-13.

AT that time: Jesus saw a man named Matthew, sitting at the receipt of custom. And he saith unto him: Follow me. And he arose, and followed him. And it came to pass, as Jesus sat at meat in the house, behold, many publicans and sinners came, and sat down with him and his disciples. And when the Pharisees saw it, they said unto his disciples: Why eateth your Master with publicans and sinners? But when Jesus heard that, he said unto them: They that be whole need not a physician, but they that are sick. But go ye and learn what that meaneth: I will have mercy, and not sacrifice. For I am not come to call the righteous but sinners *[to repentance]. Creed.

Offertory. Ps. 21, 4-5. Thou hast set, O Lord, a crown of pure gold upon his head: he asked life of thee, and thou gavest it him, alleluia.

Secret.

O LORD, who dost instruct thy Church with the wondrous preaching of thy blessed Apostle and Evangelist Matthew: we beseech thee, that by his supplication her oblation may be commended unto thee. Through.

Preface of the Apostles.

Communion. Ps. 21, 6. His honour is great in thy salvation: glory and great worship shalt thou lay upon him, O Lord.

Postcommunion.

O LORD, who hast bestowed on us this holy Sacrament, we humbly beseech thee: that at the intercession of blessed Matthew, thine Apostle and Evangelist, the mysteries which we have celebrated to the increase of his glory may be profitable unto us for the healing of our souls. Through.

September 22.

St. Thomas of Villanova

Bishop and Confessor

Double.

Introit. Ecclus. 45, 24. Statuit ei.

THE Lord hath established a covenant of peace with him, and made him the chief of his people: that he should have the dignity of the priesthood for ever. Ps. 132, 1. Lord, remember David: and all his trouble. ℣. Glory.

Collect.

O GOD, who didst adorn thy blessed Bishop Thomas with wondrous gifts of mercy to the poor: we humbly beseech thee; that, at his intercession, thou wouldest pour forth on all who call upon thee the abundant riches of thy mercy. Through.

Commemoration of SS. Maurice and his Companions, Martyrs.

Collect.

GRANT, we beseech thee, almighty God: that the solemn festival of thy holy Martyrs Maurice and his Companions may bring gladness to our hearts: that as we trust in their intercession, so we may glory in their heavenly birth. Through.

The Lesson from the book of Wisdom.
Ecclus. 44, 16-45, 15.

BEHOLD, a great priest, who in his days pleased the Lord, and was found righteous: and in the time of wrath he was taken in exchange for the world. There was none like unto him, who kept the law of the Most High. Therefore by an oath the Lord assured him that he would increase him among his people. He established with him the blessing of all men and the covenant, and made it rest upon his head. He acknowledged him in his blessing: he preserved for him his mercy: so that he found favour in the sight of the Lord. He magnified him in the sight of kings: and gave unto him a crown of glory. An everlasting covenant he made with him, and gave him a great priesthood: and blessed him with glory. That he should execute the office of the priesthood, and have praise in his name, and offer unto him incense, and a sweet savour.

Gradual. Ecclus. 44, 16. Behold, a great priest, who in his days pleased the Lord. ℣. Ibid., 20. There was none like unto him to keep the law of the Most High.

Alleluia, alleluia. ℣. Ps. 110, 4. Thou art a priest for ever after the order of Melchisedech. Alleluia.

✠ The Continuation of the holy Gospel according to Matthew.
Matt. 25, 14-23.

AT that time: Jesus spake this parable unto his disciples: A man travelling into a far country called his own servants, and delivered unto them his goods. And unto one he gave five talents, to another two, and to another one, to every man according to his several ability, and straightway took his journey. Then he that had received the five talents went and traded with the same, and made them other five talents. And likewise he that had received two, he also gained other two. But he that had received one went and digged in the earth, and hid his lord's money. After a long time the lord of those servants cometh, and reckoneth with them. And so he that had received five talents came and brought other five talents, saying: Lord, thou deliveredst unto me five talents, behold, I have gained beside them five talents more. His lord said unto him: Well done, thou good and faithful servant, thou hast been faithful over a few things, I will make thee ruler over many things: enter thou into the joy of thy lord. He also that had received two talents came and said: Lord, thou deliveredst unto me two talents, behold, I have gained two other talents beside them. His lord said unto him: Well done, good and faithful servant, thou hast been faithful over a few things, I will make thee ruler over many things: enter thou into the joy of thy lord.

Offertory. Ps. 89, 21-22. I have found David my servant, with my holy oil have I anointed him: my hand shall hold him fast, and my arm shall strengthen him.

Secret.

WE beseech thee, O Lord, that our devout observance of the yearly solemnity of Saint Thomas, thy Confessor and Bishop, may render us acceptable unto thy loving kindness: that this service of propitiation, which we duly offer, may be profitable unto him for the reward of blessedness, and obtain for us the gifts of thy grace. Through.

For the Holy Martyrs.   Secret.

REGARD, we beseech thee, O Lord, the gifts which we offer unto thee in commemoration of thy holy Martyrs, Maurice and his Companions: and grant; that through the intercession of them, for whose sake they are acceptable unto thee, they may be profitable unto us for evermore. Through.

Communion. Luke 12, 42. A faithful and wise servant, whom his lord hath made ruler over his household: to give them their portion of meat in due season.

Postcommunion.

O GOD, who rewardest the souls of them that put their trust in thee: vouchsafe; that we, who keep the solemn festival of blessed Thomas, thy Confessor and Bishop, may by his prayers obtain thy merciful pardon. Through.

For the Holy Martyrs.   Postcommunion.

O LORD, who hast refreshed us with the gladness of thy heavenly sacraments: we humbly pray thee; that we may be protected by the succour of them in whose triumphs we glory. Through.

September 23.

St. Linus

Pope and Martyr

Simple.

The Mass Si diligis me, p. [2].

Collect.   C 1

O EVERLASTING Shepherd, look down in mercy on thy flock: and as thou didst choose blessed Linus thy Martyr and Chief Bishop to be pastor and ruler of thy Church; so at his intercession defend it with thy continual protection. Through.

Commemoration of St. Thecla, Virgin and Martyr.

Collect.   P

GRANT, we beseech thee, almighty God: that we, who celebrate the birthday of blessed Thecla, thy Virgin and Martyr; may both rejoice in her yearly solemnity, and likewise profit by the example of her faith. Through.

Secret.   C 1

WE beseech thee, O Lord, graciously enlighten thy Church by the gifts which we here offer: that in every place thy flock may increase and prosper, and the shepherds by thy governance may be made pleasing to thy name. Through.

For St. Thecla.   Secret. C

RECEIVE, O Lord, the gifts which we offer on the solemnity of blessed Thecla, thy Virgin and Martyr: through whose advocacy we trust to be delivered. Through.

Common Preface.

Postcommunion.   C 1

MERCIFUL Lord, we beseech thee to govern and preserve thy Church, which thou hast here refreshed with heavenly food: that by the guiding of thy mighty power it may serve thee in more abundant freedom, and ever keep thy true religion whole and undefiled. Through.

For St. Thecla.   Postcommunion. C

ASSIST us mercifully, O Lord, who have here received these holy mysteries: and at the intercession of blessed Thecla thy Virgin and Martyr, make us ever to rejoice in thy continual protection. Through.

(For St. Thecla, V.M., the Mass Loquebar, p. [28], except the Collect).

September 24.

Blessed Virgin Mary of Ransom

Greater double.

The Mass Salve, p. [41], except the Collect.

Collect. P

O GOD, who, through the most glorious Mother of thy Son, didst vouchsafe to increase thy Church with a new offspring for the delivering of the faithful of Christ from the power of the heathen: grant, we beseech thee; that we, who devoutly honour her for the institution of so great a work, may likewise, through her merits and intercession, be delivered from all our sins and from the captivity of the devil. Through the same.

The Creed is said.

Secret. C

THROUGH thy mercy, O Lord, and the intercession of blessed Mary ever Virgin, may this oblation avail for our prosperity and peace, both now and for ever. Through.

Preface of the B.V. Mary, And that on the. Festival.

Postcommunion.

O LORD, who hast appointed these holy mysteries which we have here received to be the means of our salvation: grant, we beseech thee, that we, who have offered these our gifts unto thy majesty in honour of blessed Mary ever Virgin; may by her advocacy be at all times and in all places effectually defended. Through.

September 26.

For SS. Cyprian and Justina

Virgin, Martyrs

The Mass Salus autem, p. [12], the Prayers excepted.

Collect. P

O LORD, let the intercession of thy blessed Martyrs, Cyprian and Justina, continually defend us: forasmuch as thou never failest to look with mercy on those to whom thou dost grant the succour of their assistance. Through.

Secret. P

WE beseech thee, O Lord, that the gifts which we offer unto thee of our bounden duty and service may be acceptable unto thee for the honour of thy Saints: and by thy mercy profitable unto us for our salvation. Through.

Postcommunion. P

GRANT to us, we beseech thee, O Lord: at the intercession of thy holy Martyrs, Cyprian and Justina; that we, who with our outward lips have partaken of this holy Sacrament, may inwardly receive the same in purity of heart. Through.

September 27.

SS. Cosmas and Damian

Martyrs

Simple.

Introit. Ecclus. 44, 15 and 14.

Sapientiam Sanctorum.

LET the people tell of the wisdom of the Saints, and let the Church shew forth their praise: their names shall live for evermore. Ps. 33, 1. Rejoice in the Lord, O ye righteous: for it becometh well the just to be thankful. V. Glory.

Collect.

GRANT, we beseech thee, almighty God: that we, who observe the heavenly birthday of thy holy Martyrs, Cosmas and Damian, may by their intercession be delivered from all evils that beset us. Through.

The Lesson from the book of Wisdom.
Wisd. 5, 16-20.

BUT the righteous live for evermore, their reward also is with the Lord, and the care of them is with the Most High. Therefore shall they receive a glorious kingdom, and a beautiful crown from the Lord's hand: for with his right hand shall he cover them, and with his arm shall he protect them. He shall take to him his jealousy for complete armour, and make the creature his weapon for the revenge of his enemies. He shall put on righteousness as a breastplate, and true judgment instead of an helmet. He shall take holiness for an invincible shield.

Gradual. Ps. 34, 18-19. The righteous cry, and the Lord heareth them: and delivereth them out of all their troubles. ℣. The Lord is nigh unto them that are of a contrite heart: and will save such as be of an humble spirit.

Alleluia, alleluia. ℣. This is the true brotherhood, which overcame the wickedness of the world: which followed Christ, gaining heaven's glorious realms. Alleluia.

✠ The Continuation of the Holy Gospel according to Luke.
Luke 6, 17-23.

AT that time: Jesus came down from the mountain, and stood in the plain, and the company of his disciples, and a great multitude of people out of all Judæa and Jerusalem, and from the sea coast of Tyre and Sidon which came to hear him, and to be healed of their diseases, and they that were vexed with unclean spirits: and they were healed. And the whole multitude sought to touch him: for there went virtue out of him, and healed them all. And he lifted up his eyes on his disciples, and said: Blessed be ye poor: for yours is the kingdom of God. Blessed are ye that hunger now: for ye shall be filled. Blessed are ye that weep now: for ye shall laugh. Blessed are ye, when men shall hate you, and when they shall separate you from their company, and shall reproach you, and cast out your name as evil, for the Son of man's sake. Rejoice ye in that day, and leap for joy: for, behold, your reward is great in heaven.

Offertory. Ps. 5, 12-13. All they that love thy name shall be joyful in thee: for thou, Lord, wilt give thy blessing unto the righteous: and with thy favourable kindness, O Lord, wilt thou defend us as with a shield.

Secret.

MAY the devout prayers of thy Saints never fail us, O Lord: that they may both render our oblations acceptable, and ever obtain for us thy merciful pardon. Through.

Communion. Ps. 79, 2 and 11. The dead bodies of thy servants, O Lord, have they given to be meat unto the fowls of the air, and the flesh of thy Saints unto the beasts of the land: according to the greatness of thy power preserve thou those that are appointed to die.

Postcommunion.

O LORD, who hast made us partakers of this heavenly banquet, and hast bestowed on us the succour of the intercession of thy Saints: we beseech thee; that we thy people may effectually be defended by the same. Through.

Feasts of September (28)

September 28.

St. Wenceslas

Duke, Martyr

Simple.

The Mass In virtute, p. [6], the Collect excepted.

Collect. P

O GOD, who through the victory of martyrdom didst translate blessed Wenceslas from his earthly principality to the glory of heaven: defend us through his prayers from all adversity; and grant us likewise to rejoice in his eternal fellowship. Through.

Secret. C

WE beseech thee, O Lord, to accept our prayers and oblations: and graciously hearken unto us, whom thou dost cleanse by thy heavenly mysteries. Through.

Postcommunion. C

GRANT, we beseech thee, O Lord our God: that like as we in this life do gladly honour the memory of thy Saints; so we may rejoice hereafter in their everlasting fellowship. Through.

September 29.

DEDICATION

OF

ST. MICHAEL THE ARCHANGEL

Double of 1st class.

Introit. Ps. 103, 20.

Benedicite Dominum.

O PRAISE the Lord, ye Angels of his: ye that excel in strength, ye that fulfil his commandment, and hearken unto the voice of his words. Ps. ibid., 1. Praise the Lord, O my soul: and all that is within me praise his holy name. ℣. Glory.

Collect.

O EVERLASTING God, who hast ordained and constituted the services of Angels and men in a wonderful order: mercifully grant; that as thy holy Angels alway do thee service in heaven, so by thy appointment they may succour and defend us on earth. Through.

Or, Collect.

O GOD, who dost ordain and constitute the services of Angels and men in a wonderful order: mercifully grant; that they, who alway stand before thee and do thee service in heaven, may likewise succour and defend our life on earth. Through.

The Lesson from the book of the Revelation of blessed John the Apostle.

Rev. 12, 7-12.

IN those days: There was war in heaven: Michael and his Angels fought against the dragon; and the dragon fought and his angels, and prevailed not; neither was their place found any more in heaven. And the great dragon was cast out, that old serpent, called the devil and Satan, which deceiveth the whole world: he was cast out into the earth, and his angels were cast out with him. And I heard a loud voice saying in heaven: Now is come salvation, and strength, and the kingdom of our God, and the power of his Christ: for the accuser of our brethren is cast down, which accused them before our God day and night. And they overcame him by the blood of the Lamb, and by the word of their testimony: and they loved not their lives unto the death. Therefore rejoice, ye heavens, and ye that dwell in them. Woe to the inhabiters of the earth, and of the sea: for the devil is come down unto you, having great wrath, because he knoweth that he hath but a short time.

Or:

The Lesson from the book of the Revelation of blessed John the Apostle.

Rev. 1, 1-5.

IN those days: God shewed the things which must shortly come to pass, and he sent and signified it by his Angel unto his servant John, who bare record of the word of God, and of the testimony of Jesus Christ, and of all things that he saw. Blessed is he that readeth, and they that hear the words of this prophecy: and keep those things which are written therein: for the time is at hand. John to the seven churches which are in Asia. Grace be unto you, and peace, from him which is, and which was, and which is to come, and from the seven spirits which are before his throne, and from Jesus Christ, who is the faithful witness, and the first begotten of the dead, and the prince of the kings of the earth, who loved us, and washed us from our sins in his own blood.

Gradual. Ps. 103, 20 and 1. O praise the Lord, ye Angels of his: ye that excel in strength, ye that fulfil his commandment. ℣. Praise the Lord, O my soul; and all that is within me praise his holy name.

Alleluia, alleluia. ℣. Holy Michael, Archangel, defend us in the battle: that we perish not in the dreadful judgment. Alleluia.

☩ The Continuation of the Holy Gospel according to Matthew.

Matt. 18, 1-10.

AT that time: The disciples came unto Jesus, saying: Who is the greatest in the kingdom of heaven? And Jesus called a little child unto him, and set him in the midst of them, and said: Verily I say unto you, Except ye be converted, and become as little children, ye shall not enter into the kingdom of heaven. Whosoever therefore shall humble himself as this little child, the same is greatest in the kingdom of heaven. And whoso shall receive one such little child in my name, receiveth me. But whoso shall offend one of these little ones which believe in me, it were better for him that a millstone were hanged about his neck, and that he were drowned in the depth of the sea. Woe unto the world because of offences! For it must needs be that offences come: but woe to that man by whom the offence cometh! Wherefore if thy hand or thy foot offend thee, cut them off, and cast them from thee: it is better for thee to enter into life halt or maimed, rather than having two hands or two feet to be cast into everlasting fire. And if thine eye offend thee, pluck it out, and cast it from thee: it is better for thee to enter into life with one eye, rather than having two eyes to be cast into hell-fire. Take heed that ye despise not one of these little ones: for I say unto you, That in heaven their Angels do always behold the face of my Father which is in heaven. Creed.

In Votive Masses after Septuagesima at the end of the following Offertory, Alleluia is omitted.

Offertory. Rev. 8, 3-4. An Angel stood by the altar of the temple, having a golden censer in his hand, and there was given unto him much incense: and the smoke of the incense ascended up before God, alleluia.

Secret.

WE offer thee, O Lord, this sacrifice of praise, humbly beseeching thee: that, by the prayers of the Angels interceding for us, thou wouldest both graciously accept the same, and grant that it may avail to our salvation. Through.

Common Preface, even if this Feast fall on Sunday.

Communion. Dan. 3, 37. O all ye Angels of the Lord, bless ye the Lord: sing ye praises, and magnify him above all for ever.

Postcommunion.

O LORD, forasmuch as we put our trust in the intercession of thy blessed Archangel Michael: we humbly beseech thee; that as with our outward lips we are made partakers of this holy Sacrament, so we may inwardly receive the benefit of the same. Through.

¶ In Votive Masses everything is said as above, but after Septuagesima the Gradual and Tract as in the Votive Mass of the Holy Angels, p. [52], and in Eastertide Mass is said as on May 8, p. 651.

September 30.

St. Jerome

Priest, Confessor and Doctor of the Church

Double.

Introit. Ecclus. 15, 5. In medio.

IN the midst of the Church he opened his mouth: and the Lord filled him with the spirit of wisdom and understanding: he clothed him with a robe of glory. Ps. 92, 1. It is a good thing to give thanks unto the Lord: and to sing praises unto thy name, O most Highest. ℣. Glory.

Collect.

O GOD, who for the expounding of the holy Scriptures didst bestow upon thy Church blessed Jerome, thy Confessor and most excellent Doctor: grant we beseech thee; that, by the intercession of his merits, we may through thine assistance be enabled to perform those things which he taught both by word and deed. Through.

The Lesson from the Epistle of blessed Paul the Apostle to Timothy.

II Tim. 4, 1-8.

DEARLY beloved: I charge thee before God, and the Lord Jesus Christ, who shall judge the quick and the dead at his appearing and his kingdom: preach the word, be instant in season, out of season: reprove, rebuke, exhort with all longsuffering and doctrine. For the time will come when they will not endure sound doctrine, but after their own lusts shall they heap to themselves teachers, having itching ears, and they shall turn away their ears from the truth, and shall be turned unto fables. But watch thou in all things, endure afflictions, do the work of an Evangelist, make full proof of thy ministry. For I am now ready to be offered, and the time of my departure is at hand. I have fought a good fight, I have finished my course, I have kept the faith. Henceforth there is laid up for me a crown of righteousness, which the Lord, the righteous judge, shall give me at that day: and not to me only, but unto all them also that love his appearing.

Gradual. Ps. 37, 30-31. The mouth of the righteous is exercised in wisdom, and his tongue will be talking of judgment. ℣. The law of his God is in his heart: and his goings shall not slide.

Alleluia, alleluia. ℣. Ecclus. 45, 9. The Lord loved him, and adorned him: he clothed him with a robe of glory. Alleluia.

✠ The Continuation of the Holy Gospel according to Matthew.

Matt. 5, 13-19.

AT that time: Jesus said unto his disciples: Ye are the salt of the earth. But if the salt have lost his savour, wherewith shall it be salted? It is thenceforth good for nothing, but to be cast out, and to be trodden under foot of men. Ye are the light of the world. A city that is set on an hill cannot be hid. Neither do men light a candle, and put it under a bushel, but on a candlestick, and it giveth light unto all that are in the house. Let your light so shine before men, that they may see your good works, and glorify your Father which is in heaven. Think not that I am come to destroy the law or the prophets: I am not come to destroy, but to fulfil. For verily I say unto you, Till heaven and earth pass, one jot or one tittle shall in no wise pass from the law, till all be fulfilled. Whosoever therefore shall break one of these least commandments, and shall teach men so, he shall be called the least in the kingdom of heaven: but whosoever shall do and teach them, the same shall be called great in the kingdom of heaven. Creed.

Offertory. Ps. 92, 13. The righteous shall flourish like a palm-tree: and shall spread abroad like a cedar in Libanus.

Secret.

GRANT us, we beseech thee, O Lord, through these heavenly gifts to serve thee in freedom of spirit: that these our oblations may, through the intercession of blessed Jerome, thy Confessor, avail for our healing, and bring us to everlasting glory. Through.

Communion. Luke 12, 42. A faithful and wise servant, whom his lord hath made ruler over his household: to give them their portion of meat in due season.

Postcommunion.

WE beseech thee, O Lord, that we whom thou hast fulfilled with heavenly food may through the intercession of blessed Jerome, thy Confessor, be found worthy to obtain the grace of thy loving kindness. Through.

FEASTS OF OCTOBER

October 1.

For St. Remigius

Bishop and Confessor

The Mass Statuit ei, from the Common of a Confessor Bishop, p. [19].

Collect. C

GRANT, we beseech thee, almighty God: that we, devoutly observing this festival of blessed Remigius, thy Confessor and Bishop, may hereby advance in true godliness and attain unto everlasting salvation. Through.

Secret. C

WE beseech thee, O Lord, that we, remembering with gladness the merits of thy Saints, may in all places feel the succour of their intercession. Through.

Postcommunion. C

GRANT, we beseech thee, almighty God: that we, shewing forth our thankfulness for the gifts which we have received, may, at the intercession of blessed Remigius, thy Confessor and Bishop, obtain yet more abundant mercies. Through.

October 2.

The Holy Guardian Angels

Greater double.

Introit. Ps. 103, 20. Benedicite.

O PRAISE the Lord, ye Angels of his: ye that excel in strength, ye that fulfil his commandment, and hearken unto the voice of his words. Ps. ibid., 1. Praise the Lord, O my soul: and all that is within me praise his holy name. ℣. Glory.

Collect.

O GOD, who of thy ineffable providence dost vouchsafe to send thy holy Angels to be our guardians: grant unto us thy humble servants; that we, being continually defended by their protection, may hereafter rejoice in their everlasting fellowship. Through.

The Lesson from the book Exodus.

Exod. 23, 20-23.

THUS saith the Lord God: Behold, I send an Angel before thee to keep thee in the way, and to bring thee into the place which I have prepared. Beware of him, and obey his voice, provoke him not: for he will not pardon your transgressions, for my name is in him. But if thou shalt indeed obey his voice, and do all that I speak, then I will be an enemy unto thine enemies, and an adversary unto thine adversaries: for mine Angel shall go before thee.

Gradual. Ps. 91, 11-12. God shall give his Angels charge over thee, to keep thee in all thy ways. ℣. They shall bear thee in their hands, that thou hurt not thy foot against a stone.

Alleluia, alleluia. ℣. Ps. 103, 21. O praise the Lord, all ye his hosts: ye servants of his that do his pleasure. Alleluia.

In Votive Masses after Septuagesima the Tract, and in Eastertide Alleluia, as in Votives of the Holy Angels, p. [52].

✠ The Continuation of the Holy Gospel according to Matthew.

Matt. 18, 1-10.

AT that time: The disciples came unto Jesus, saying: Who is the greatest in the kingdom of heaven? And Jesus called a little child unto him, and set him in the midst of them, and said: Verily I say unto you, Except ye be converted, and become as little children, ye shall not enter into the kingdom of heaven. Whosoever therefore shall humble himself as this little child, the same is greatest in the kingdom of heaven. And whoso shall receive one such little child in my name, receiveth me. But whoso shall offend one of these little ones which believe in me, it were better for him that a millstone were hanged about his neck, and that he were drowned in the depth of the sea. Woe unto the world because of offences! For it must needs be that offences come: but woe to that man by whom the offence cometh! Wherefore if thy hand or thy foot offend thee: cut them off, and cast them from thee: it is better for thee to enter into life halt or maimed, rather than having two hands or two feet to be cast into everlasting fire. And if thine eye offend thee, pluck it out, and cast it from thee: it is better for thee to enter into life with one eye, rather than having two eyes to be cast into hell-fire. Take heed that ye despise not one of these little ones: for I say unto you, That in heaven their Angels do always behold the face of my Father which is in heaven.

The Creed is not said.

Offertory. Ps. 103, 20 and 21. O praise the Lord, ye Angels of his: ye servants of his, that fulfil his commandment, and hearken unto the voice of his words.

Secret.

ACCEPT, O Lord, these our oblations, which we here present to the honour of thy holy Angels: and mercifully grant; that by their continual protection we may be delivered from present dangers and attain unto everlasting life. Through.

Communion. Dan. 3, 58. O all ye Angels of the Lord, bless ye the Lord: sing ye praises, and magnify him above all for ever.

Postcommunion.

O LORD, who on this festival of thy holy Angels, hast suffered us to receive in gladness thy heavenly mysteries: we beseech thee; that by their protection we may ever be delivered from the snares of our enemies, and defended against all adversities. Through.

October 3.

St. Theresa of the Infant Jesus

Virgin.

Double.

Introit. Cant. 4, 8-9.

COME from Libanus, my spouse, come from Libanus, come: thou hast wounded my heart, my sister, my spouse, thou hast wounded my heart. Ps. 113, 1. Praise the Lord, ye children: O praise the name of the Lord. ℣. Glory.

Collect.

O LORD, who hast said: Except ye become as little children, ye shall not enter into the kingdom of heaven: grant us, we beseech thee; so to follow the footsteps of Saint Theresa, thy Virgin, in humility and singleness of heart, that we may attain unto the rewards of everlasting life: Who livest.

The Lesson from the Prophet Isaiah.

Is. 66, 12-14.

THUS saith the Lord: Behold I will extend peace to her like a river, and the glory of the Gentiles like a flowing stream: then shall ye suck, ye shall be borne upon her sides, and be dandled upon her knees. As one whom his mother comforteth, so will I comfort you, and ye shall be comforted in Jerusalem. And when ye see this, your heart shall rejoice, and your bones shall flourish like an herb, and the hand of the Lord shall be known toward his servants.

Gradual. Matt. 11, 25. I thank thee, O Father, Lord of heaven and earth, because thou hast hid these things from the wise and prudent, and hast revealed them unto babes. ℣. Ps. 71, 5. O Lord, thou art my hope even from my youth.

Alleluia, alleluia. ℣. Ecclus. 39, 13-14. Bud forth as a rose growing by a brook of water: and give ye a sweet savour as frankincense: put forth flowers as a lily, spread abroad a sweet smell, and sing a song of praise: bless ye the Lord in all his works. Alleluia.

After Septuagesima, omitting Alleluia and the Verse following, is said:

Tract. Cant. 2, 11-12. Lo the winter is past, the rain is over, and gone. ℣. The flowers appear on the earth, the time of the singing of birds is come: and the voice of the turtle is heard in our land.

℣. Jerem. 31, 3. I have loved thee with an everlasting love: therefore with loving kindness have I drawn thee.

In Eastertide the Gradual is omitted, and in its place is said:

Alleluia, alleluia. ℣. Ecclus. 39, 13-14. Bud forth as a rose growing by a brook of water: and give ye a sweet savour as frankincense: put forth flowers as a lily, spread abroad a sweet smell, and sing a song of praise: bless ye the Lord in all his works. Alleluia. ℣. Ps. 34, 9; 100, 4. O taste and see how gracious the Lord is: his mercy is everlasting. Alleluia.

✠ The Continuation of the holy Gospel according to Matthew.

Matt. 18, 1-4.

AT that time: The disciples came unto Jesus, saying: Who is the greatest in the kingdom of heaven? And Jesus called a little child unto him, and set him in the midst of them, and said: Verily I say unto you, Except ye be converted, and become as little children, ye shall not enter into the kingdom of heaven. Whosoever therefore shall humble himself as this little child, the same is the greatest in the kingdom of heaven.

Offertory. Luke 1, 46-48 and 49. My soul doth magnify the Lord: and my spirit hath rejoiced in God my Saviour: for he hath regarded the lowliness of his handmaiden: he that is mighty hath done to me great things.

Secret.

WE beseech thee, O Lord, that the holy prayer of Saint Theresa, thy Virgin, may render our sacrifice pleasing unto thee: that, as it is solemnly offered in her honour, so it may be made acceptable by her merits. Through.

Communion. Deut. 32, 10-12. He led her about, he instructed her: he kept her as the apple of his eye. As an eagle spreadeth abroad her wings, so he took her, he bare her on his pinions. The Lord alone did lead her.

Postcommunion.

O LORD, let this heavenly mystery inflame us with that fire of love: wherewith thy holy Virgin Theresa dedicated herself unto thee, a victim of charity for all mankind. Through.

October 4.

St. Francis

Confessor

Greater double.

Introit. Gal. 6, 14. Mihi autem.

GOD forbid that I should glory, save in the Cross of our Lord Jesus Christ: by whom the world is crucified unto me, and I unto the world. Ps. 142, 1. I cried unto the Lord with my voice: yea, even unto the Lord did I make my supplication. ℣. Glory.

Collect.

O GOD, who by the merits of blessed Francis dost increase thy Church with a new offspring: vouchsafe unto us; that after his example, we may despise all things earthly, and ever rejoice in the partaking of thy heavenly bounty. Through.

The Lesson from the Epistle of blessed Paul the Apostle to the Galatians.

Gal. 6, 14-18.

BRETHREN: But God forbid that I should glory, save in the Cross of our Lord Jesus Christ: by whom the world is crucified unto me, and I unto the world. For in Christ Jesus neither circumcision availeth any thing, nor uncircumcision, but a new creature. And as many as walk according to this rule, peace be on them, and mercy, and upon the Israel of God. From henceforth let no man trouble me: for I bear in my body the marks of the Lord Jesus. Brethren, the grace of our Lord Jesus Christ be with your spirit. Amen.

Gradual. Ps. 37, 30-31. The mouth of the righteous is exercised in wisdom, and his tongue will be talking of judgment. ℣. The law of his God is in his heart: and his goings shall not slide.

Alleluia, alleluia. ℣. Francis, poor and lowly, entereth heaven rich, he is honoured with celestial hymns. Alleluia.

☩ The Continuation of the holy Gospel according to Matthew.

Matt. 11, 25-30.

AT that time: Jesus answered and said: I thank thee, O Father, Lord of heaven and earth, because thou hast hid these things from the wise and prudent, and hast revealed them unto babes. Even so, Father: for so it seemed good in thy sight. All things are delivered unto me of my Father. And no man knoweth the Son, but the Father: neither knoweth any man the Father, save the Son, and he to whomsoever the Son will reveal him. Come unto me, all ye that labour and are heavy laden, and I will give you rest. Take my yoke upon you, and learn of me, for I am meek and lowly in heart: and ye shall find rest unto your souls. For my yoke is easy, and my burden is light.

Offertory. Ps. 89, 25 My truth and my mercy shall be with him: and in my name shall his horn be exalted.

Secret.

SANCTIFY, O Lord, the gifts which we dedicate unto thee: and, at the intercession of blessed Francis, cleanse us from the defilements of all our iniquities. Through.

Communion. Luke 12, 42. A faithful and wise servant, whom his lord hath made ruler over his household: to give them their portion of meat in due season.

Postcommunion.

MULTIPLY, we beseech thee, O Lord, thy Church with thy heavenly grace: even as thou didst vouchsafe to illumine her with the glorious merits and example of thy blessed Confessor Francis. Through.

October 5.

For St. Placid and his Companions

Martyrs

The Mass Salus autem, p. [12], with Prayers as below.

Collect. P

O GOD, who dost vouchsafe unto us to celebrate the heavenly birthday of thy holy Martyrs Placid and his Companions: grant that we may rejoice in their perpetual fellowship in heaven. Through.

Secret. P

WE beseech thee, O Lord, that the gifts which we offer unto thee of our bounden duty and service may be acceptable unto thee for the honour of thy Saints: and by thy mercy profitable unto us for our salvation. Through.

Postcommunion. P

GRANT to us, we beseech thee, O Lord: at the intercession of thy holy Martyrs Placid and his Companions; that we, who with our outward lips are partakers of this holy Sacrament, may inwardly receive the same in purity of heart. Through.

October 6.

St. Bruno

Confessor

Double.

Introit. Ps. 37, 30-31. Os justi.

THE mouth of the righteous is exercised in wisdom: and his tongue will be talking of judgment: the law of his God is in his heart. Ps. ibid., 1. Fret not thyself because of the ungodly: neither be thou envious against the evil-doers. V. Glory.

Collect.

O LORD, we beseech thee, let the intercession of thy Confessor, Saint Bruno, avail for our succour: that we, who by our trespasses have grievously offended against thy majesty, may by his merits and prayers obtain the pardon of all our offences. Through.

The Lesson from the book of Wisdom.

Ecclus. 31, 8-11.

BLESSED is the man that is found without blemish: and hath not gone after gold. Who is he, and we will call him blessed? for wonderful things hath he done among his people. Who hath been tried thereby, and found perfect? then let him glory. Who might offend, and hath not offended? or done evil, and hath not done it? His goods shall be established, and the congregation shall declare his alms.

Gradual. Ps. 92, 13-14. The righteous shall flourish like a palm-tree: and shall spread abroad like a cedar in Libanus in the house of the Lord. V. Ibid., 3. To tell of thy loving kindness early in the morning, and of thy truth in the night-season.

Alleluia, alleluia. V. James 1, 12. Blessed is the man that endureth temptation: for when he is tried, he shall receive the crown of life. Alleluia.

✠ The Continuation of the holy Gospel according to Luke.

Luke 12, 35-40.

AT that time: Jesus said unto his disciples: Let your loins be girded about, and your lights burning, and ye yourselves like unto men that wait for their lord, when he will return from the wedding: that when he cometh and knocketh, they may open unto him immediately. Blessed are those servants, whom the lord when he cometh shall find watching: verily I say unto you, that he shall gird himself, and make them to sit down to meat and will come forth and serve them. And if he shall come in the second watch, or come in the third watch, and find them so, blessed are those servants. And this know, that if the good man of the house had known what hour the thief would come, he would have watched, and not have suffered his house to be broken through. Be ye therefore ready also: for the Son of man cometh at an hour when ye think not.

Offertory. Ps. 89, 25. My truth and my mercy shall be with him: and in my name shall his horn be exalted.

Secret.

WE offer thee, O Lord, this our sacrifice of praise to the honour of thy Saints: whereby we trust to be delivered from all evils both in this life and in that which is to come. Through.

Communion. Matt. 24, 46-47. Blessed is the servant whom his lord when he cometh shall find watching: verily I say unto you, he shall make him ruler over all his goods.

Postcommunion.

WE beseech thee, almighty God: that we, who have received this heavenly food, may at the intercession of blessed Bruno, thy Confessor, be thereby defended against all adversities. Through.

October 7.

THE MOST SACRED ROSARY OF THE BLESSED VIRGIN MARY

Double of 2nd class.

Introit. Gaudeamus omnes.

REJOICE we all in the Lord, keeping feast day in honour of the blessed Virgin Mary: in whose solemnity the Angels rejoice and glorify the Son of God. Ps. 45, 1. My heart is inditing of a good matter: I speak of the things which I have made unto the King. ℣. Glory.

Collect.

O GOD, whose only-begotten Son by his life, death and resurrection, hath purchased for us the rewards of eternal salvation: grant, we beseech thee; that we, recalling these mysteries in the most holy Rosary of the blessed Virgin Mary, may so follow the pattern of their teaching, that we finally be made partakers of thy heavenly promises. Through the same.

In private Masses only a Commemoration is made of St. Mark, Pope, C.

Collect.

O EVERLASTING Shepherd, look down in mercy on thy flock: and as thou didst choose blessed Mark thy Chief Bishop to be pastor and ruler of thy Church; so at his intercession defend it with thy continual protection. Through.

The Lesson from the book of Wisdom.

Prov. 8, 22.

THE Lord possessed me in the beginning of his way, before his works of old. I was set up from everlasting, from the beginning, or ever the earth was. When there were no depths, I was brought forth. Now therefore hearken unto me, O ye children: for blessed are they that keep my ways. Hear instruction, and be wise, and refuse it not. Blessed is the man that heareth me, watching daily at my gates, waiting at the posts of my doors. For whoso findeth me findeth life, and shall obtain favour of the Lord.

Gradual Ps. 45. Because of the word of truth, of meekness, and righteousness, and thy right hand shall teach thee terrible things. ℣. Hearken, O daughter, and consider, incline thine ear: so shall the King have pleasure in thy beauty.

Alleluia, alleluia. ℣. The solemnity of the glorious Virgin Mary of the seed of Abraham, sprung from the tribe of Juda, of David's noble stock. Alleluia.

☩ The Continuation of the holy Gospel according to Luke.

Luke 1, 26.

AT that time: The Angel Gabriel was sent from God unto a city of Galilee named Nazareth, to a Virgin espoused to a man whose name was Joseph, of the house of David, and the Virgin's name was Mary. And the Angel came in unto her, and said: Hail, full of grace, the Lord is with thee: blessed art thou among women. And when she saw him, she was troubled at his saying, and cast in her mind what manner of salutation this should be. And the Angel said unto her: Fear not, Mary, for thou hast found favour with God. And behold, thou shalt conceive in thy womb, and bring forth a Son, and shalt call his name Jesus. He shall be great, and shall be called the Son of the Highest, and the Lord God shall give unto him the throne of his father David: and he shall reign over the house of Jacob for ever, and of his kingdom there shall be no end. Then Mary said unto the Angel: How shall this be, seeing I know not a man? And the Angel answered and said unto her: The Holy Ghost shall come upon thee, and the power of the Highest shall overshadow thee. Therefore also that Holy Thing which shall be born of thee shall be called the Son of God. And behold, thy cousin Elisabeth, she hath also conceived a son in her old age: and this is the sixth month with her who was called barren: for with God nothing shall be impossible. And Mary said: Behold the handmaid of the Lord, be it unto me according to thy word. Creed.

Offertory. Ecclus. 24 and 39. In me is all grace of the way and of truth: in me is all hope of life and of virtue: I have budded forth as a rose growing by the brooks of water.

Secret.

GRANT, we beseech thee, O Lord, that we may be enabled to offer these our gifts according to thy will: and through the mysteries of the most sacred Rosary so to recall the life, the passion and the glory of thy only-begotten Son; that we may be made worthy to attain unto his promises: Who liveth and reigneth with thee.

For St. Mark. Secret.

WE beseech thee, O Lord, graciously enlighten thy Church by the gifts which we here offer: that in every place thy flock may increase and prosper, and the shepherds by thy governance may be made pleasing to thy name. Through.

Preface of the B.V. Mary, And that on the Festival.

Communion. Ecclus. 39. Put forth flowers as a lily, spread abroad a sweet smell, and bring forth leaves in grace, sing a song of praise, and bless the Lord in all his works.

Postcommunion.

WE beseech thee, O Lord, that we, who here celebrate the Rosary of thy most holy Mother, may in such wise be succoured by her prayers: that we may be partakers of the power of the mysteries which we therein recall; and obtain the effectual benefits of the sacraments which we have now received: Who livest.

For St. Mark. Postcommunion.

MERCIFUL Lord, we beseech thee to govern and preserve thy Church, which thou hast here refreshed with heavenly food: that by the guiding of thy mighty power it may serve thee in more abundant freedom, and ever keep thy true religion whole and undefiled. Through.

October 8.

St. Bridget

Widow

Double.

The Mass Cognovi, p. [36], the Collect and Epistle excepted.

Collect.

O LORD our God, who through thine only-begotten Son didst reveal unto blessed Bridget the secrets of heaven: grant, through her devout intercession; that we thy servants may continually rejoice in the revelation of thine everlasting glory. Through the same.

Feasts of October (9)   813

The Lesson from the Epistle of blessed Paul the Apostle to Timothy.

I Tim. 5, 3-10.

DEARLY beloved: Honour widows that are widows indeed. But if any widow have children or nephews: let them learn first to shew piety at home, and to requite their parents: for that is good and acceptable before God. Now she that is a widow indeed, and desolate, trusteth in God, and continueth in supplications and prayers night and day. But she that liveth in pleasure is dead while she liveth. And these things give in charge, that they may be blameless. But if any provide not for his own and specially for those of his own house, he hath denied the faith, and is worse than an infidel. Let not a widow be taken into the number under threescore years old, having been the wife of one man, well reported of for good works, if she have brought up children, if she have lodged strangers, if she have washed the saints' feet, if she have relieved the afflicted, if she have diligently followed every good work.

Secret.

GRANT, O Lord, that like as thy dedicated people do acknowledge that in tribulation they have been succoured by the merits of thy Saints: so this oblation, which they here offer unto thee in honour of the same, may be acceptable in thy sight. Through.

Postcommunion.

O LORD, who hast satisfied this thy family with thy sacred gifts: we beseech thee; that we may at all times be comforted by the intercession of her whose festival we celebrate. Through.

October 9.

St. John Leonardi

Confessor

Double.

Introit. Ecclus. 42, 15-16. In sermonibus.

IN the words of the Lord are his works: the sun that giveth light looketh upon all things, and his work is full of the glory of the Lord. Ps. 96, 1. O sing unto the Lord a new song: sing unto the Lord, all the whole earth. ℣. Glory.

Collect.

O GOD, who for the propagation of thy faith among the nations didst vouchsafe wondrously to raise up blessed John thy Confessor, and through him didst gather a new family in thy Church for the instructing of the faithful: grant unto us thy servants, so to profit by his teaching; that we may attain unto the rewards of everlasting life. Through.

Commemoration is made of SS. Denys, Bp., Rusticus and Eleutherius, Martyrs.

Collect.

O GOD, who on this day didst endue blessed Denys, thy Martyr and Bishop, with strength and constancy in his passion, and didst vouchsafe to join unto him Rusticus and Eleutherius for the preaching of thy glory to the Gentiles: grant us, we beseech thee; by their example, to despise for love of thee the prosperity of the world, and to fear none of its adversities. Through.

The Lesson from the Epistle of blessed Paul the Apostle to the Corinthians.

II Cor. 4, 1-6 and 15-18.

BRETHREN: Seeing we have this ministry, as we have received mercy, we faint not, but have renounced the hidden things of dishonesty, not walking in craftiness, nor handling the word of God deceitfully, but by manifestation of the truth commending ourselves to every man's conscience in the sight of God. But if our Gospel be hid: it is hid to them that are lost: in whom the god of this world hath blinded the minds of them which believe not, lest the light of the glorious Gospel of Christ, who is the image of God, should shine unto them. For we preach not ourselves, but Christ Jesus the Lord: and ourselves your servants for Jesus' sake: for God, who commanded the light to shine out of darkness, hath shined in our hearts to give the light of the knowledge of the glory of God in the face of Jesus Christ. For all things are for your sakes: that the abundant grace might through the thanksgiving of many redound to the glory of God. Wherefore we faint not: but though our outward man perish: yet the inward man is renewed day by day. For our light affliction, which is but for a moment, worketh for us a far more exceeding and eternal weight of glory, while we look not at the things which are seen, but at the things which are not seen. For the things which are seen are temporal: but the things which are not seen are eternal.

Gradual. Ps. 73, 21; 69, 10. My heart was grieved, and it went even through my reins: the zeal of thine house hath eaten me. ℣. Is. 49, 2. He hath made my mouth like a sharp sword: in the shadow of his hand hath he hid me and made me a polished shaft.

Alleluia, alleluia. ℣. Ps. 71, 7. I am become as it were a monster unto many: but my sure trust is in thee. Alleluia.

After Septuagesima, omitting Alleluia and the Verse following, is said:

℣. Ps. 55, 3-4 and 17. I mourn in my prayer and am vexed: the enemy crieth so, and the ungodly cometh on so fast. ℣. For they are minded to do me some mischief: so maliciously are they set against me. ℣. As for me, I will call upon God: and the Lord shall save me.

In Eastertide the Gradual is omitted, and in its place is said:

Alleluia, alleluia. ℣. Ps. 52, 10. Like a green olive-tree in the house of God, I have trusted in the tender mercy of God for ever and ever. Alleluia.

℣. Ps. 62, 8. In God is my health and my glory: the rock of my might, and in God is my trust. Alleluia.

✠ The Continuation of the holy Gospel according to Luke.

Luke 10, 1-9.

AT that time: The Lord appointed other seventy also: and sent them two and two before his face into every city and place whither he himself would come. Therefore said he unto them: The harvest truly is great, but the labourers are few. Pray ye therefore the Lord of the harvest, that he would send forth labourers into his harvest. Go your ways: behold, I send you forth as lambs among wolves. Carry neither purse, nor scrip, nor shoes, and salute no man by the way. And into whatsoever house ye enter, first say: Peace be to this house: and if the son of peace be there, your peace shall rest upon it: if not, it shall turn to you again. And in the same house remain, eating and drinking such things as they give: for the labourer is worthy of his hire. Go not from house to house. And into whatsoever city ye enter, and they receive you, eat such things as are set before you: and heal the sick that are therein, and say unto them: The kingdom of God is come nigh unto you.

Offertory. Col. 1, 25. I am made a minister of Christ according to the dispensation of God, which is given to me, to fulfil the word of God.

Secret.

RECEIVE, O Lord, the pure oblation of this saving victim: and vouchsafe; that at the intercession of blessed John thy Confessor, it may continually be offered in every place among the nations. Through.

For SS. Denys, Bp., Rusticus and Eleutherius, MM.

Secret.

GRACIOUSLY accept, we beseech thee, O Lord, the oblations of thy people for the honour of thy Saints: and sanctify us by their intercession. Through.

Communion. Phil. 3, 7. What things were gain to me, those I counted loss for Christ.

Postcommunion.

O LORD, who hast refreshed us with the sacred mysteries of thy precious Body and Blood, we entreat thee: that following the example of blessed John thy Confessor, we may study to confess that faith which he believed, and to perform those things which he taught: Who livest.

For SS. Denys, Bp., Rusticus and Eleutherius, MM.

Postcommunion.

WE beseech thee, O Lord, that we who have here received thy holy sacraments: may, at the intercession of thy blessed Martyrs Denys, Rusticus and Eleutherius, grow and increase toward the attainment of eternal redemption. Through.

The same day, October 9.

For SS. Denys, Bishop, Rusticus and Eleutherius

Martyrs

Introit. Ecclus. 44, 15 and 41.

Sapientiam Sanctorum.

LET the people tell of the wisdom of the Saints, and let the Church shew forth their praise: their names shall live for evermore. Ps. 33, 1. Rejoice in the Lord, O ye righteous: for it becometh well the just to be thankful. ℣. Glory.

Collect.

O GOD, who on this day didst endue blessed Denys, thy Martyr and Bishop, with strength and constancy in his passion, and didst vouchsafe to join unto him Rusticus and Eleutherius for the preaching of thy glory to the Gentiles: grant us, we beseech thee; by their example, to despise for love of thee the prosperity of the world, and to fear none of its adversities. Through.

The Lesson from the Acts of the Apostles.

Acts 17, 22-34.

IN those days: Paul stood in the midst of Mars' hill, and said: Ye men of Athens, I perceive that in all things ye are too superstitious. For as I passed by, and beheld your devotions, I found an altar with this inscription: To the Unknown God. Whom therefore ye ignorantly worship, him declare I unto you. God that made the world and all things therein, seeing that he is Lord of heaven and earth, dwelleth not in temples made with hands, neither is worshipped with men's hands, as though he needed any thing, seeing he giveth to all life, and breath, and all things: and hath made of one blood all nations of men for to dwell on all the face of the earth, and hath determined the times before appointed, and the bounds of their habitation, that they should seek the Lord, if haply they might feel after him, and find him, though he be not far from every one of us. For in him we live, and move, and have our being: as certain also of your own poets have said: For we are also his offspring. Forasmuch then as we are the offspring of God, we ought not to think that the Godhead is like unto gold, or silver, or stone, graven by art and man's device. And the times of this ignorance God winked at, but now commandeth all men every where to repent, because he hath appointed a day, in the which he will judge the world in righteousness by that man whom he hath ordained, whereof he hath given assurance unto all men, in that he hath raised him from the dead. And when they heard of the resurrection of the dead, some mocked: and others said: We will hear thee again of this matter. So Paul departed from among them. Howbeit certain men clave unto him, and believed: among the which was Dionysius the Areopagite, and a woman named Damaris, and others with them.

Gradual. Ps. 124, 7-8. Our soul is escaped even as a bird out of the snare of the fowler. ℣. The snare is broken, and we are delivered: our help is in the name of the Lord, who hath made heaven and earth.

Alleluia, alleluia. ℣. Ps. 68, 4. Let the righteous be glad and rejoice before God: let them also be merry and joyful. Alleluia.

✠ The Continuation of the holy Gospel according to Luke.

Luke 12, 1-8.

AT that time: Jesus said unto his disciples: Beware ye of the leaven of the Pharisees, which is hypocrisy. For there is nothing covered, that shall not be revealed: neither hid, that shall not be known. Therefore whatsoever ye have spoken in darkness shall be heard in the light: and that which ye have spoken in the ear in closets shall be proclaimed upon the housetops. And I say unto you, my friends: Be not afraid of them that kill the body, and after that have no more that they can do. But I will forewarn you whom ye shall fear: Fear him, which after he hath killed hath power to cast into hell. Yea, I say unto you: Fear him. Are not five sparrows sold for two farthings, and not one of them is forgotten before God? But even the very hairs of your head are all numbered. Fear not therefore: ye are of more value than many sparrows. Also I say unto you: Whosoever shall confess me before men, him shall the Son of man also confess before the Angels of God.

Offertory. Ps. 149, 5-6. Let the Saints be joyful with glory, let them rejoice in their beds: let the praises of God be in their mouth, alleluia.

Secret.

GRACIOUSLY accept, we beseech thee, O Lord, the oblations of thy people, for the honour of thy Saints: and sanctify us by their intercession. Through.

Communion. Luke 12, 4. And I say unto you, my friends: Be not afraid of them that persecute you.

Postcommunion.

WE beseech thee, O Lord, that we, who have here received thy holy sacraments: may, at the intercession of thy blessed Martyrs Denys, Rusticus and Eleutherius, grow and increase toward the attainment of eternal redemption. Through.

October 10.

St. Francis Borgia

Confessor

Simple.

The Mass Os justi, from the Common of Abbots, p. [26], the Prayers excepted.

Collect.   P

O LORD Jesu Christ, who art both the ensample and reward of true humility: we beseech thee; that as thou didst give grace to blessed Francis gloriously to imitate thee in contempt of earthly honour, so thou wouldest grant us to be partakers of his imitation of thee, and likewise of his glory: Who livest.

Secret.   P

WE beseech thee, O Lord, let Saint Francis intercede for us: that this sacrifice which we offer and present upon thy holy altar may be profitable for our salvation. Through.

Postcommunion.   P

LET this thy Sacrament which we have received, O Lord, and the prayers of blessed Francis, effectually defend us: that we may both imitate the example of his conversation, and receive the succour of his intercession. Through.

October 11.

THE MOTHERHOOD OF THE BLESSED VIRGIN MARY

Double of 2nd class.

Introit. Is. 7, 14. Ecce Virgo.

BEHOLD, a Virgin shall conceive and bear a Son, and his name shall be called Emmanuel. Ps. 98, 1. O sing unto the Lord a new song, for he hath done marvellous things. ℣. Glory.

Collect.

O GOD, who wast pleased that thy Word should take flesh of the womb of the Blessed Virgin Mary at the message of an Angel: grant to us thy humble servants; that we, believing her to be indeed the Mother of God, may by her intercession be holpen in thy sight. Through the same.

The Lesson from the book of Wisdom.

Ecclus. 24, 17-22.

AS the vine I brought forth a pleasant savour: and my flowers are the fruit of honour and riches. I am the mother of fair love, and fear, and knowledge, and holy hope. In me is all grace of the way and the truth: in me is all hope of life and of virtue. Come unto me, all ye that be desirous of me, and fill yourselves with my fruits. For my spirit is sweeter than honey, and mine inheritance than honey and the honeycomb. My memorial shall be unto everlasting generations. They that eat me shall yet be hungry: and they that drink me shall yet be thirsty. He that obeyeth me shall never be confounded: and they that work by me shall not do amiss. They that expound me shall have life everlasting.

Gradual. Is. 11, 1-2. There shall come forth a rod out of the stem of Jesse: and a branch shall rise up out of his roots. ℣. And the Spirit of the Lord shall rest upon him.

Alleluia, alleluia. ℣. Virgin, Mother of God, the whole world cannot contain him: yet, made man for our sakes, hidden he lay in thy womb. Alleluia.

✠ The Continuation of the holy Gospel according to Luke.

Luke 2, 43-51.

AT that time: As they returned, the Child Jesus tarried behind in Jerusalem, and Joseph and his Mother knew not of it. But they, supposing him to have been in the company, went a day's journey, and they sought him among their kinsfolk and acquaintance. And when they found him not, they turned back again to Jerusalem, seeking him. And it came to pass, that after three days they found him in the temple, sitting in the midst of the doctors, both hearing them and asking them questions. And all that heard him were astonished at his understanding and answers. And when they saw him, they were amazed. And his Mother said unto him: Son, why hast thou thus dealt with us? Behold, thy father and I have sought thee sorrowing. And he said unto them: How is it that ye sought me? Wist ye not that I must be about my Father's business? And they understood not the saying which he spake unto them. And he went down with them, and came to Nazareth: and was subject unto them. Creed.

Offertory. Matt. 1, 18. When Mary his Mother was espoused to Joseph, she was found with child of the Holy Ghost.

Secret.

THROUGH thy mercy, O Lord, and the intercession of blessed Mary ever Virgin, Mother of thine only-begotten Son, may this oblation avail for our prosperity and peace, both now and for ever. Through.

Preface of the B.V.Mary, And that on the Festival.

Communion. Blessed is the womb of the Virgin Mary, that bare the Son of the everlasting Father.

Postcommunion.

O LORD, let this holy Communion cleanse us from every guilty stain: that at the intercession of the blessed Virgin Mary, Mother of God, we may be made partakers thereby of thy healing unto life eternal. Through the same.

October 13.

St. Edward

King and Confessor

Double of 2nd class.

(or Greater double.)

(Outside England and Wales: Simple.)

The Mass Os justi (for a Confessor not a Bishop), p. [24], the Collect excepted.

Collect. P

O GOD, who didst bestow upon thy blessed Confessor King Edward the crown of everlasting glory: make us, we beseech thee; so to venerate him on earth, that we may be found worthy to reign with him in heaven. Through.

Secret. C

WE offer thee, O Lord, this our sacrifice of praise to the honour of thy Saints: whereby we trust to be delivered from all evils both in this life and in that which is to come. Through.

Postcommunion. C

O LORD our God, who hast refreshed us with heavenly meat and drink, we humbly beseech thee: that we may be defended by the prayers of him in whose memory we have received the same. Through.

October 14.

St. Callistus I

Pope and Martyr

Double.

Introit. John 21, 15-17. Si diligis me.

IF thou lovest me, Simon Peter, feed my lambs, feed my sheep. Ps. 30, 1. I will magnify thee, O Lord, for thou hast set me up, and not made my foes to triumph over me. ℣ Glory.

Collect.

O GOD, who seest that by reason of our infirmity we cannot always stand upright: through the examples of thy Saints mercifully restore us to the love of thee. Through.

The Lesson from the Epistle of blessed Peter the Apostle.

I Peter 5, 1-4 and 10-11.

DEARLY beloved: The elders which are among you I exhort, who am also an elder, and a witness of the sufferings of Christ, and also a partaker of the glory that shall be revealed: feed the flock of God which is among you, taking the oversight thereof, not by constraint, but willingly, not for filthy lucre, but of a ready mind; neither as being lords over God's heritage, but being ensamples to the flock. And when the chief Shepherd shall appear, ye shall receive a crown of glory that fadeth not away. Now the God of all grace, who hath called us unto his eternal glory by Christ Jesus, after that ye have suffered a while, make you perfect, stablish, strengthen, settle you. To him be glory and dominion for ever and ever. Amen.

Gradual. Ps. 107, 32 and 31. Let them exalt him in the congregation of the people: and praise him in the seat of the elders. ℣. O that men would praise the Lord for his goodness: and declare the wonders that he doeth for the children of men.

Alleluia, alleluia. ℣. Matt. 16, 18. Thou art Peter, and upon this rock I will build my Church. Alleluia.

✠ The Continuation of the holy Gospel according to Matthew.

Matt. 16, 13-19.

AT that time: Jesus came into the coasts of Cæsarea Philippi, and asked his disciples, saying: Whom do men say that I, the Son of man, am? And they said: Some say that thou art John the Baptist, some Elias, and others Jeremias, or one of the Prophets. He said unto them: But whom say ye that I am? And Simon Peter answered and said: Thou art the Christ, the Son of the living God. And Jesus answered and said unto him: Blessed art thou, Simon Bar-jona: for flesh and blood hath not revealed it unto thee, but my Father which is in heaven. And I say also unto thee, That thou art Peter, and upon this rock I will build my Church, and the gates of hell shall not prevail against it. And I will give unto thee the keys of the kingdom of heaven. And whatsoever thou shalt bind on earth, shall be bound in heaven: and whatsoever thou shalt loose on earth, shall be loosed in heaven.

Offertory. Jer. 1, 9-10. Behold, I have put my words in thy mouth: see, I have set thee over the nations and over the kingdoms, to pull down and to destroy, to build and to plant.

Secret.

O LORD, let this mystical oblation be profitable unto us: that it may both deliver us from our offences, and stablish us in everlasting salvation. Through.

Common Preface.

Communion. Matt. 16, 18. Thou art Peter, and upon this rock I will build my Church.

Postcommunion.

WE beseech thee, almighty God: that the gifts which we have hallowed may cleanse us from our iniquities, and bring forth in us the fruit of godly living. Through.

October 15.

St. Theresa

Virgin

Double.

The Mass Dilexisti, p. [31], the Collect excepted.

Collect. P.

GRACIOUSLY hear us, O God of our salvation: that, like as we do rejoice in the festival of blessed Theresa, thy Virgin: so we may be fed with the sustenance of her heavenly doctrine, and may learn to follow her example in godliness and charity. Through.

Secret. C

GRANT, O Lord, that like as thy dedicated people do acknowledge that in tribulation they have been succoured by the merits of thy Saints: so this oblation, which they here offer unto thee in honour of the same, may be acceptable in thy sight. Through.

October 16.

St. Hedwig

Widow

Simple.

The Mass Cognovi, p. [36], the Collect excepted.

Collect. P

O GOD, who didst teach blessed Hedwig to turn with her whole heart from the pomp of this world to the humble following of thy Cross: vouchsafe; that, by her merits and example, we may learn to tread under foot the transitory pleasures of the world, and in the embrace of thy Cross to overcome all things that may hurt us: Who livest and reignest with God the Father.

Secret. C

GRANT, O Lord, that like as thy faithful people do acknowledge that in tribulation they have been succoured by the merits of thy Saints: so this oblation, which they here offer unto thee in honour of the same, may be acceptable in thy sight. Through.

Postcommunion. C

O LORD, who hast satisfied this thy family with thy sacred gifts: we beseech thee that we may at all times be comforted by the intercession of her whose festival we celebrate. Through.

October 17.

St. Margaret Mary Alacoque

Virgin

Double.

Introit. Cant. 2, 3. *Sub umbra.*

I SAT down under the shadow of my beloved with great delight: and his fruit was sweet to my taste. Ps. 83, 1-2. O how amiable are thy dwellings, thou Lord of hosts! My soul hath a desire and longing to enter into the courts of the Lord. V. Glory.

Collect.

O LORD Jesu Christ, who unto blessed Margaret Mary, thy Virgin, didst wondrously reveal the unsearchable riches of thy Heart: grant us by her merits and example; that, loving thee in all and above all, we may be found worthy to obtain an everlasting habitation in the same thy Heart: Who livest and reignest with God the Father.

The Lesson from the Epistle of blessed Paul the Apostle to the Ephesians.

Eph. 3, 8-9 and 14-19.

BRETHREN: Unto me, who am less than the least of all saints, is this grace given, that I should preach among the Gentiles the unsearchable riches of Christ, and to make all men see what is the fellowship of the mystery, which from the beginning of the world hath been hid in God, who created all things. For this cause I bow my knees unto the Father of our Lord Jesus Christ, of whom the whole family in heaven and earth is named, that he would grant you, according to the riches of his glory, to be strengthened with might by his Spirit in the inner man: that Christ may dwell in your hearts by faith: that ye, being rooted and grounded in love, may be able to comprehend with all saints what is the breadth, and length, and depth, and height: and to know the love of Christ, which passeth knowledge, that ye might be filled with all the fulness of God.

Gradual. Cant. 8, 7. Many waters cannot quench love, neither can the floods drown it. ℣. Ps. 73, 26. My flesh and my heart faileth: but God is the strength of my heart, and my portion for ever.

Alleluia, alleluia. ℣. Cant. 7, 10. I am my beloved's, and his desire is toward me. Alleluia.

✠ The Continuation of the holy Gospel according to Matthew.

Matt. 11, 25-30.

AT that time: Jesus answered and said: I thank thee, O Father, Lord of heaven and earth, because thou hast hid these things from the wise and prudent, and hast revealed them unto babes. Even so, Father: for so it seemed good in thy sight. All things are delivered unto me of my Father. And no man knoweth the Son, but the Father: neither knoweth any man the Father save the Son, and he to whomsoever the Son will reveal him. Come unto me, all ye that labour and are heavy laden, and I will give you rest. Take my yoke upon you, and learn of me, for I am meek and lowly in heart: and ye shall find rest unto your souls. For my yoke is easy, and my burden is light.

Offertory. Zech. 9, 17. How great is his goodness, and how great is his beauty! Corn shall make the young men cheerful, and new wine the maids.

Secret.

O LORD, let the gifts of thy people be acceptable unto thee: and grant; that we may be inflamed by that divine fire sent forth from the Heart of thy Son, wherewith blessed Margaret Mary was vehemently enkindled. Through the same.

Communion. Cant. 6, 2. I am my beloved's, and my beloved is mine: he feedeth among the lilies.

Postcommunion.

GRANT to us, we beseech thee, O Lord Jesu, by the intercession of the blessed Virgin Margaret Mary: that we, who have received the mysteries of thy Body and Blood, may renounce the pomps and vanities of the world, and be worthy to be clothed with the meekness and humility of thy Heart: Who livest and reignest with God the Father.

October 18.

ST. LUKE THE EVANGELIST

Double of 2nd class.

Introit. Ps. 139, 17. Mihi autem.

RIGHT dear are thy friends unto me, O God, and held in highest honour: their rule and governance is exceeding stedfast. Ps. ibid., 1. O Lord, thou hast searched me out, and known me: thou knowest my down-sitting and mine up-rising. V. Glory.

Collect.

ALMIGHTY God, who calledst Luke the Physician, whose praise is in the Gospel, to be an Evangelist, and Physician of the soul: may it please thee; that, by the wholesome medicines of the doctrine delivered by him, all the diseases of our souls may be healed. Through the merits of thy Son Jesus Christ our Lord: Who liveth.

Or, Collect.

WE beseech thee, O Lord, that as thy holy Evangelist Luke for the honour of thy name continually did bear in his body the mortification of the cross: so he may ever intercede with thee on our behalf. Through.

The Lesson from the Epistle of blessed Paul the Apostle to Timothy.

II Tim. 4, 5-15.

DEARLY beloved: Watch thou in all things, endure afflictions, do the work of an Evangelist, make full proof of thy ministry. For I am now ready to be offered, and the time of my departure is at hand. I have fought a good fight, I have finished my course, I have kept the faith. Henceforth there is laid up for me a crown of righteousness, which the Lord, the righteous judge, shall give me at that day: and not to me only, but unto all them also that love his appearing. Do thy diligence to come shortly unto me: for Demas hath forsaken me, having loved this present world, and is departed unto Thessalonica: Crescens to Galatia, Titus unto Dalmatia. Only Luke is with me. Take Mark and bring him with thee: for he is profitable to me for the ministry. And Tychicus have I sent to Ephesus. The cloke that I left at Troas with Carpus, when thou comest, bring with thee; and the books, but especially the parchments. Alexander the coppersmith did me much evil: the Lord reward him according to his works. Of whom be thou ware also, for he hath greatly withstood our words.

Or:

The Lesson from the Epistle of blessed Paul the Apostle to the Corinthians.

II Cor. 8, 16-24.

BRETHREN: I give thanks to God, which put the same earnest care into the heart of Titus for you, for indeed he accepted the exhortation: but being more forward, of his own accord he went unto you. And we have sent with him the brother, whose praise is in the Gospel throughout all the churches: and not only, but who was also chosen of the churches to travel with us with this grace, which is administered by us to the glory of the same Lord, and declaration of your ready mind: avoiding this, that no man should blame us in this abundance which is administered by us. Providing for honest things, not only in the sight of the Lord, but also in the sight of men. And we have sent with them the brother, whom we have oftentimes proved diligent in many things: but now much more diligent, upon the great confidence which I have in you. Whether any do inquire of Titus, he is my partner and fellow-helper concerning you, or our brethren be inquired of, they are the Apostles of the churches, and the glory of Christ. Wherefore shew ye to them, and before the churches, the proof of your love, and of our boasting on your behalf.

Gradual. Ps. 19, 5 and 2. Their sound is gone out into all lands: and their words into the end of the world. ℣. The heavens declare the glory of God: and the firmament sheweth his handy-work.

Alleluia, alleluia. ℣. John 15, 16. I have chosen you out of the world, that ye should go and bring forth fruit: and that your fruit should remain. Alleluia.

✠ The Continuation of the holy Gospel according to Luke.

Luke 10, 1-9.

AT that time: The Lord appointed other seventy also: and sent them two and two before his face into every city and place whither he himself would come. Therefore said he unto them: The harvest truly is great, but the labourers are few. Pray ye therefore the Lord of the harvest, that he would send forth labourers into his harvest. Go your ways: behold, I send you forth as lambs among wolves. Carry neither purse, nor scrip, nor shoes, and salute no man by the way. And into whatsoever house ye enter, first say: Peace be to this house: and if the son of peace be there, your peace shall rest upon it: if not, it shall turn to you again. And in the same house remain, eating and drinking such things as they give: for the labourer is worthy of his hire.†

Go not from house to house. And into whatsoever city ye enter, and they receive you, eat such things as are set before you: and heal the sick that are therein, and say unto them: The kingdom of God is come nigh unto you.   Creed.

Offertory. Ps. 139, 17. Right dear are thy friends unto me, O God, and held in highest honour: their rule and governance is exceeding stedfast.

Secret.

GRANT us, O Lord, we beseech thee, by thy heavenly gifts to serve thee in perfect freedom: that, through the intercession of thy blessed Evangelist Luke, these our oblations may avail for the healing of our souls, and for the attainment of everlasting glory. Through.

Preface of the Apostles.

Communion. Matt. 19, 28. Ye which have followed me shall sit upon thrones, judging the twelve tribes of Israel.

Postcommunion.

GRANT, we beseech thee, almighty God: that these gifts which we have received from thy holy altar may, through the prayers of thy blessed Evangelist Luke, sanctify our souls, and avail for our protection. Through.

October 19.

St. Peter of Alcantara

Confessor

Double.

The Mass Justus ut palma, from the Common of a Confessor not a Bishop, p. [25], the Collect and Epistle excepted.

Collect.   P

O GOD, who didst vouchsafe to adorn blessed Peter, thy Confessor, with the gift of wondrous penitence and lofty contemplation: grant to us, we beseech thee; that through his prevailing merits we, being mortified in the flesh, may more readily attain unto heavenly things. Through.

The Lesson from the Epistle of blessed Paul the Apostle to the Philippians.

Phil. 3, 7.

BRETHREN: What things were gain to me, those I counted loss for Christ. Yea doubtless, and I count all things but loss for the excellency of the knowledge of Christ Jesus my Lord: for whom I have suffered the loss of all things, and do count them but dung, that I may win Christ, and be found in him, not having mine own righteousness, which is of the law, but that which is through the faith of Christ: the righteousness which is of God by faith, that I may know him, and the power of his resurrection, and the fellowship of his sufferings: being made conformable unto his death: if by any means I might attain unto the resurrection of the dead: not as though I had already attained, either were already perfect: but I follow after, if that I may apprehend that for which also I am apprehended of Christ Jesus.

Secret.

GRANT to us, we beseech thee, almighty God: that this oblation of our humble service may be acceptable in thy sight to the honour of thy Saints, and may cleanse us both in body and soul. Through.

Postcommunion.

WE beseech thee, almighty God: that we, who have received this heavenly food, may at the intercession of blessed Peter, thy Confessor, be thereby defended against all adversities. Through.

October 20.

St. John Cantius

Confessor

Double.

Introit. Ecclus. 18, 12-13. Miseratio.

THE mercy of man is toward his neighbour: but the mercy of the Lord is upon all flesh. He reproveth and nurtureth, and teacheth, and bringeth again as a shepherd his flock. Ps. 1, 1. Blessed is the man that hath not walked in the counsel of the ungodly, nor stood in the way of sinners, and hath not sat in the seat of the scornful. ℣. Glory.

Collect.

GRANT, we beseech thee, almighty God: that after the example of Saint John thy Confessor we, advancing in the knowledge of the Saints, and shewing mercy unto all men, may, by his merits, obtain thy pardon. Through.

The Lesson from the Epistle of blessed James the Apostle.

James 2, 12-17.

SO speak ye, and so do, as they that shall be judged by the law of liberty. For he shall have judgment without mercy, that hath shewed no mercy: and mercy rejoiceth against judgment. What doth it profit, my brethren, though a man say he hath faith, and have not works? Can faith save him? If a brother or sister be naked, and destitute of daily food, and one of you say unto them: Depart in peace, be ye warmed and filled: notwithstanding ye give them not those things which are needful to the body, what does it profit? Even so faith, if it hath not works, is dead, being alone.

Gradual. Ps. 107, 8-9. O that men would praise the Lord for his goodness: and declare the wonders that he doeth for the children of men! ℣. For he satisfieth the empty soul: and filleth the hungry soul with goodness.

Alleluia, alleluia. ℣. Prov. 31, 20. He opened his hand to the needy: and stretched out his hands to the poor. Alleluia.

☩ The Continuation of the holy Gospel according to Luke.

Luke 12, 35.

AT that time: Jesus said unto his disciples: Let your loins be girded about, and your lights burning, and ye yourselves like unto men that wait for their lord, when he will return from the wedding: that when he cometh and knocketh, they may open unto him immediately. Blessed are those servants, whom the lord when he cometh shall find watching: verily I say unto you, that he shall gird himself and make them to sit down to meat, and will come forth and serve them. And if he shall come in the second watch, or come in the third watch, and find them so, blessed are those servants. And this know, that if the good man of the house had known what hour the thief would come, he would have watched, and not have suffered his house to be broken through. Be ye therefore ready also: for the Son of man cometh at an hour when ye think not.

Offertory. Job 29, 14-16. I put on righteousness, and it clothed me, my judgment was as a robe and a diadem. I was eyes to the blind, and feet was I to the lame: I was a father to the poor.

Secret.

WE beseech thee, O Lord, through the merits of thy Confessor Saint John, graciously to accept these sacrifices: and grant; that we, loving thee above all things, and all men for thy sake, may please thee both in will and deed. Through.

Communion. Luke 6, 38. Give, and it shall be given unto you: good measure, pressed down, and shaken together, and running over, shall men give into your bosom.

Postcommunion.

O LORD, who hast fed us with the delights of thy precious Body and Blood, we humbly entreat thy mercy: that by the merits and example of Saint John, thy Confessor, we, following the example of his charity, may likewise be partakers of his glory: Who livest and reignest.

October 21.

For St. Hilarion

Abbot

The Mass Os justi, from the Common of an Abbot p. [26].

Collect.

O LORD, we beseech thee let the intercession of the blessed Abbot Hilarion commend us unto thee: that those things which for our own merits we cannot ask, we may through his advocacy obtain. Through.

Commemoration of SS. Ursula and Companions, Virgins and Martyrs.

Collect.

GRANT, we beseech thee, O Lord our God, that we may devoutly honour the triumph of thy holy Virgins and Martyrs Ursula and her Companions: and, although we cannot worthily shew forth their praise, yet we beseech thee to accept the worship we render in thine honour. Through.

Secret. C

WE beseech thee, O Lord, that thy holy Abbot Hilarion may intercede for us: that this sacrifice which we offer and present upon thy holy altar may be profitable unto us for our salvation. Through.

For SS. Ursula, etc. Secret. P

O LORD, we beseech thee, look down upon these gifts, which we offer on thine altars on this festival of thy holy Virgins and Martyrs Ursula and her Companions: that as by these blessed mysteries thou hast bestowed glory upon them; so likewise of thy bounty thou wouldest vouchsafe to us thy pardon. Through.

Postcommunion. C

LET thy Sacrament, O Lord, which we have now received and the prayers of the blessed Abbot Hilarion, effectually defend us: that we may both imitate the example of his conversation, and receive the succour of his intercession. Through.

For SS. Ursula, etc. Postcommunion. P

GRANT to us, we beseech thee, O Lord, at the intercession of thy holy Virgins and Martyrs Ursula and her Companions: that we, who with our outward lips are partakers of this holy Sacrament, may inwardly receive the same in purity of heart. Through.

(For SS. Ursula, etc., Mass Loquebar, p. [28], with Prayers as above.)

October 24.

St. Raphael the Archangel

Greater double.

Introit. Ps. 103, 20. Benedicite Dominum.

O PRAISE the Lord, ye Angels of his, ye that excel in strength: ye that fulfil his commandment, and hearken unto the voice of his words. Ps. ibid., 1. Praise the Lord, O my soul: and all that is within me praise his holy name. ℣. Glory.

Collect.

O GOD, who didst give blessed Raphael the Archangel unto thy servant Tobias for a companion on his way: grant to us thy servants; that we may ever be guarded by his protection and strengthened by his help. Through.

The Lesson from the book of Tobit.

Tobit 12, 7-15.

IN those days: The Angel Raphael said to Tobias: It is good to keep close the secret of a king: but it is honourable to reveal the works of God. Prayer is good with fasting, and it is better to give alms than to lay up gold: for alms doth deliver from death, and it shall purge away all sin. Those that do alms and righteousness shall be filled with life. But they that sin are enemies to their own life. Surely I will declare unto you the truth, and keep close nothing from you. When thou didst pray, and didst bury the dead, and when thou didst leave thy dinner, to go and cover the dead, I did bring thy prayer before the Lord. And because thou wast accepted with God, it was needful that temptation should try thee. And now God hath sent me to heal thee and Sara thy daughter-in-law. I am Raphael, one of the seven holy Angels, which go in and out before the glory of the Holy One.

Gradual. Tob. 8, 3. The Angel of the Lord, Raphael, took the devil and bound him. ℣. Ps. 147, 5. Great is our Lord, and great is his power.

Alleluia, alleluia. ℣. Ps. 138, 1-2. In the sight of the Angels will I sing praise unto thee: I will worship toward thy holy temple and praise thy name, O Lord. Alleluia.

✠ The Continuation of the holy Gospel according to John.

John 5, 1-4.

AT that time: There was a feast of the Jews: and Jesus went up to Jerusalem. Now there is at Jerusalem by the sheep-market a pool, which is called in the Hebrew tongue Bethesda, having five porches. In these lay a great multitude of impotent folk, of blind, halt, withered, waiting for the moving of the water. For an Angel went down at a certain season into the pool, and troubled the water. Whosoever then first after the troubling of the water stepped in was made whole of whatsoever disease he had.

The Creed is not said.

Offertory. Rev. 8, 3-4. An Angel stood by the altar of the temple, having a golden censer in his hand, and there was given unto him much incense: and the smoke of the incense ascended up before God.

Secret.

WE offer thee, O Lord, sacrifices of praise, humbly beseeching thee: that, by the prayers of the Angels interceding for us, thou wouldest both graciously accept the same, and grant that they may avail to our salvation. Through.

Communion. Dan. 3, 58. O all ye Angels of the Lord, bless ye the Lord: sing ye praises, and magnify him above all for ever.

Postcommunion.

VOUCHSAFE, O Lord God, to send thy holy Archangel Raphael to our aid: that, as we believe him ever to stand before thy majesty, so he may present our unworthy supplications for thy blessing. Through.

The last Sunday in October.

THE FEAST OF OUR LORD

JESUS CHRIST THE KING

Double of 1st class.

Introit. Rev. 5, 12; 1, 6. Dignus.

WORTHY is the Lamb that was slain to receive power, and riches, and wisdom, and strength, and honour. To him be glory and dominion for ever and ever. Ps. 72, 1. Give the King thy judgments, O God: and thy righteousness unto the King's Son. ℣. Glory.

Collect.

ALMIGHTY and everlasting God, who in thy beloved Son, the King of all, hast willed to make all things new: mercifully grant; that all the kindreds of the nations, now divided by the wounds of sin, may be made subject to his most gracious governance: Who liveth and reigneth with thee.

Commemoration is made of the Sunday occurring.

The Lesson from the Epistle of blessed Paul the Apostle to the Colossians.

Col. 1, 12-20.

BRETHREN: We give thanks unto God the Father, which hath made us meet to be partakers of the inheritance of the saints in light: who hath delivered us from the power of darkness, and hath translated us into the kingdom of his dear Son, in whom we have redemption through his blood, even the forgiveness of sins: who is the image of the invisible God, the firstborn of every creature: for by him were all things created, that are in heaven and that are in earth, visible and invisible, whether they be Thrones, or Dominions, or Principalities, or Powers: all things were created by him and for him: and he is before all things, and by him all things consist. And he is the head of the body, the Church, who is the beginning, the firstborn from the dead: that in all things he might have the pre-eminence; for it pleased the Father that in him should all fulness dwell; and having made peace through the blood of his cross, by him to reconcile all things unto himself, by him, I say, whether they be things in earth or things in heaven, in Christ Jesus our Lord.

Gradual. Ps. 72, 8 and 11. His dominion shall be from the one sea to the other, and from the flood unto the world's end. ℣. All kings shall fall down before him: all nations shall do him service.

Alleluia, alleluia. ℣. Dan. 7, 14. His dominion is an everlasting dominion, which shall not pass away: and his kingdom that which shall not be destroyed. Alleluia.

In Votive Masses after Septuagesima, omitting Alleluia and the Verse following, is said:

Tract. Ps. 89, 27-28 and 30. He shall call me: Thou art my Father: my God and my strong salvation. ℣. And I will make him my firstborn: higher than the kings of the earth. ℣. His seed also will I make to endure for ever: and his throne as the days of heaven.

In Eastertide the Gradual is omitted, and in its place is said:

Alleluia, alleluia. ℣. Dan. 7, 14. His dominion is an everlasting dominion, which shall not pass away: and his kingdom that which shall not be destroyed. Alleluia. ℣. Rev. 19, 16. He hath on his vesture and on his thigh a name written: King of kings and Lord of lords. Alleluia.

✠ The Continuation of the holy Gospel according to John.

John 18, 33-37.

AT that time: Pilate said unto Jesus: Art thou the King of the Jews? Jesus answered him: Sayest thou this thing of thyself, or did others tell it thee of me? Pilate answered: Am I a Jew? Thine own nation and the chief priests have delivered thee unto me: what hast thou done? Jesus answered: My kingdom is not of this world. If my kingdom were of this world, then would my servants fight, that I should not be delivered unto the Jews: but now is my kingdom not from hence. Pilate therefore said unto him: Art thou a King then? Jesus answered: Thou sayest that I am a King. To this end was I born, and for this cause came I into the world, that I should bear witness unto the truth: everyone that is of the truth heareth my voice. Creed.

Offertory. Ps. 2, 8. Desire of me, and I shall give thee the heathen for thine inheritance, and the utmost parts of the earth for thy possession.

Secret.

WE offer unto thee, O Lord, the victim who wrought the redemption of mankind: grant, we beseech thee; that he, whom we offer in this present sacrifice, may himself grant unto all nations the gifts of unity and peace, even Jesus Christ thy Son our Lord: Who liveth.

Commemoration of the Sunday occurring.

Proper Preface.

Communion. Ps. 29, 10-11. The Lord remaineth a King for ever: the Lord shall give his people the blessing of peace.

Postcommunion.

O LORD, who hast bestowed on us the food of everlasting life, we beseech thee: that as we now glory to fight beneath the banner of Christ the King; so with him enthroned in heaven, we may hereafter continually reign: Who liveth and reigneth with thee.

Commemoration of the Sunday occurring.

October 25.

For SS. Chrysanthus and Daria

Martyrs

The Mass Intret, p. [9], the Prayers, Epistle, and Gospel excepted.

Collect. P

O LORD, we beseech thee, let the prayers of thy blessed Martyrs Chrysanthus and Daria ever assist us: that, as we render them our humble service, so we may ever feel their loving succour. Through.

Epistle, Let us approve ourselves, as on the Feast of SS. Abdon and Sennen, July 30, p. 735.

Gospel, Woe unto you, No. 4, p. [14].

Secret. P

WE beseech thee, O Lord, that the sacrifice of thy people, which they solemnly offer on the birthday of thy holy Martyrs Chrysanthus and Daria, may be pleasing unto thee. Through.

Postcommunion. P

O LORD, who hast fulfilled us with gladness in these wondrous mysteries: grant, we beseech thee; that by the intercession of thy holy Martyrs Chrysanthus and Daria, we, who offer unto thee our temporal worship, may in our souls receive the benefit of the same. Through.

October 26.

For St. Evaristus

Pope and Martyr

The Mass Si diligis me, p. [2].

Collect. C1

O EVERLASTING Shepherd, look down in mercy on thy flock: and as thou didst choose blessed Evaristus thy Martyr and Chief Bishop to be pastor and ruler of thy Church; so at his intercession defend it with thy continual protection. Through.

Secret. C1

WE beseech thee, O Lord, graciously enlighten thy Church by the gifts which we here offer: that in every place thy flock may increase and prosper, and the shepherds by thy governance may be made pleasing to thy name. Through.

Postcommunion. C1

MERCIFUL Lord, we beseech thee to govern and preserve thy Church, which thou hast here refreshed with heavenly food: that by the guiding of thy mighty power it may serve thee in more abundant freedom, and ever keep thy true religion whole and undefiled. Through.

October 28.

SS. SIMON AND JUDE APOSTLES

Double of 2nd class.

Introit. Ps. 139, 17. *Mihi autem.*

RIGHT dear are thy friends unto me, O God, and held in highest honour: their rule and governance is exceeding stedfast. Ps. ibid., 1. O Lord, thou hast searched me out, and known me: thou knowest my down-sitting, and mine up-rising. ℣. Glory.

Collect.

O ALMIGHTY God, who hast built thy Church upon the foundation of the Apostles and Prophets, Jesus Christ himself being the head corner-stone: grant us so to be joined together in unity of spirit by their doctrine; that we may be made an holy temple acceptable unto thee. Through the same.

Or, Collect.

O GOD, who through thy blessed Apostles Simon and Jude hast vouchsafed unto us to attain unto the knowledge of thy name: grant that we, advancing in virtue, may celebrate their everlasting glory, and, celebrating their glory, may likewise thereby advance in virtue. Through.

The Lesson from the Epistle of blessed Jude the Apostle.

Jude, 1-8.

JUDE, the servant of Jesus Christ, and brother of James. To them that are sanctified by God the Father, and preserved in Jesus Christ, and called: mercy unto you, and peace, and love be multiplied. Beloved, when I gave all diligence to write unto you of the common salvation, it was needful for me to write unto you, and exhort you, that ye should earnestly contend for the faith which was once delivered unto the saints. For there are certain men crept in unawares, who were before of old ordained to this condemnation: ungodly men, turning the grace of our God into lasciviousness: and denying the only Lord God, and our Lord Jesus Christ. I will therefore put you in remembrance, though ye once knew this, how that the Lord, having saved the people out of the land of Egypt, afterward destroyed them that believed not. And the Angels which kept not their first estate, but left their own habitation, he hath reserved in everlasting chains under darkness unto the judgment of the great day. Even as Sodom and Gomorrha, and the cities about them in like manner giving themselves over to fornication, and going after strange flesh, are set forth for an example, suffering the vengeance of eternal fire. Likewise also these filthy dreamers defile the flesh, despise dominion, and speak evil of dignities.

Or:

The Lesson from the Epistle of blessed Paul the Apostle to the Ephesians.

Eph. 4, 7-13.

BRETHREN: Unto every one of us is given grace according to the measure of the gift of Christ. Wherefore he saith: When he ascended up on high, he led captivity captive: and gave gifts unto men. Now that he ascended, what is it but that he also descended first into the lower parts of the earth? He that descended is the same also that ascended up far above all heavens, that he might fill all things. And he gave some, apostles, and some evangelists, and some, pastors and teachers, for the perfecting of the saints, for the work of the ministry, for the edifying of the body of Christ: till we all come in the unity of the faith, and of the knowledge of the Son of God, unto a perfect man, unto the measure of the stature of the fulness of Christ.

Gradual. Ps. 45, 17-18. Thou shalt make them princes in all lands: they shall remember thy name, O Lord. ℣. Instead of thy fathers thou shalt have children: therefore shall the people give thanks unto thee.

Alleluia, alleluia. ℣. Ps. 139, 17. Right dear are thy friends unto me, O God, and held in highest honour: their rule and governance is exceeding stedfast. Alleluia.

✠ The Continuation of the holy Gospel according to John.

John 15, 17-25.

AT that time: Jesus said unto his disciples: These things I command you, that ye love one another. If the world hate you: ye know that it hated me before it hated you. If ye were of the world, the world would love his own: but because ye are not of the world, but I have chosen you out of the world, therefore the world hateth you. Remember the word that I said unto you: The servant is not greater than his lord. If they have persecuted me, they will also persecute you: if they have kept my saying, they will keep yours also. But all these things will they do unto you for my name's sake: because they know not him that sent me. If I had not come and spoken unto them, they had not had sin: but now they have no cloke for their sin. He that hateth me: hateth my Father also. If I had not done among them the works which none other man did, they had not had sin: but now have they both seen and hated both me and my Father. But this cometh to pass, that the word might be fulfilled that is written in their law: They hated me without a cause.*

But when the Comforter is come, whom I will send unto you from the Father, even the Spirit of truth, which proceedeth from the Father, he shall testify of me: and ye also shall bear witness, because ye have been with me from the beginning. Creed.

Offertory. Ps. 19, 5. Their sound is gone out into all lands: and their words into the ends of the world.

Secret.

WE beseech thee, O Lord: that as we venerate the everlasting glory of thy holy Apostles Simon and Jude; so, being cleansed by these sacred mysteries, we may more worthily celebrate the same. Through.

Preface of the Apostles.

Communion. Matt. 19, 28. Ye which have followed me shall sit upon thrones, judging the twelve tribes of Israel.

Postcommunion.

O LORD, who hast bestowed on us this holy Sacrament, we humbly pray thee: that at the intercession of thy blessed Apostles Simon and Jude, the mysteries which we celebrate in remembrance of their glorious passion may be profitable for the healing of our souls. Through.

FEASTS OF NOVEMBER

November 1.

THE FEAST OF

ALL SAINTS

Double of 1st class.

Introit. Gaudeamus.

REJOICE we all in the Lord, keeping feast day in honour of all the Saints: in whose solemnity the Angels rejoice, and glorify the Son of God. Ps. 33, 1. Rejoice in the Lord, O ye righteous: for it becometh well the just to be thankful. ℣. Glory.

Collect.

O ALMIGHTY God, who hast knit together thine elect in one communion and fellowship, in the mystical body of thy Son Christ our Lord: grant us grace so to follow thy blessed Saints in all virtuous and godly living; that we may come to those unspeakable joys, which thou hast prepared for them that unfeignedly love thee. Through the same.

Or, Collect.

ALMIGHTY and everlasting God, who in one solemnity hast given unto us to venerate the merits of all thy Saints: we beseech thee; that, at the intercession of so great a multitude, thou wouldest bestow on us, who call upon thee, the abundance of thy mercy. Through.

The Lesson from the book of the Revelation of blessed John the Apostle.

Rev. 7, 2-12.

IN those days: Behold, I John saw another Angel ascending from the East, having the seal of the living God: and he cried with a loud voice to the four Angels, to whom it was given to hurt the earth, and the sea, saying: Hurt not the earth, neither the sea, nor the trees, till we have sealed the servants of our God in their foreheads. And I heard the number of them which were sealed, and there were sealed an hundred and forty and four thousand, of all the tribes of the children of Israel. Of the tribe of Juda were sealed twelve thousand. Of the tribe of Reuben were sealed twelve thousand. Of the tribe of Gad were sealed twelve thousand. Of the tribe of Aser were sealed twelve thousand. Of the tribe of Nephthali were sealed twelve thousand. Of the tribe of Manasses were sealed twelve thousand. Of the tribe of Simeon were sealed twelve thousand. Of the tribe of Levi were sealed twelve thousand. Of the tribe of Issachar were sealed twelve thousand. Of the tribe of Zabulon were sealed twelve thousand. Of the tribe of Joseph were sealed twelve thousand. Of the tribe of Benjamin were sealed twelve thousand. After this I beheld, and lo, a great multitude, which no man could number, of all nations, and kindreds, and people, and tongues: stood before the throne, and before the Lamb, clothed with white robes, and palms in their hands: and cried with a loud voice, saying: Salvation to our God which sitteth upon the throne, and unto the Lamb. And all the Angels stood round about the throne, and about the elders, and the four beasts: and fell before the throne on their faces and worshipped God, saying: Amen. Blessing, and glory, and wisdom, and thanksgiving, and honour, and power, and might, be unto our God for ever and ever. Amen.

Gradual. Ps. 34, 10-11. O fear the Lord, all ye Saints of his: for they that fear him lack nothing. ℣. But they that seek the Lord shall want no manner of thing that is good.

Alleluia, alleluia. ℣. Matt. 11, 28. Come unto me all ye that travail and are heavy laden: and I will refresh you. Alleluia.

✠ The Continuation of the holy Gospel according to Matthew.

Matt. 5, 1-12.

AT that time: Jesus, seeing the multitudes, went up into a mountain, and when he was set, his disciples came unto him, and he opened his mouth, and taught them, saying: Blessed are the poor in spirit: for theirs is the kingdom of heaven. Blessed are they that mourn: for they shall be comforted. Blessed are the meek: for they shall inherit the earth. Blessed are they which do hunger and thirst after righteousness: for they shall be filled. Blessed are the merciful: for they shall obtain mercy. Blessed are the pure in heart: for they shall see God. Blessed are the peacemakers: for they shall be called the children of God. Blessed are they which are persecuted for righteousness' sake: for theirs is the kingdom of heaven. Blessed are ye, when men shall revile you, and persecute you, and shall say all manner of evil against you falsely for my sake: rejoice, and be exceeding glad, for great is your reward in heaven.*

For so persecuted they the prophets which were before you. Creed.

Offertory. Wisd. 3, 1-2. The souls of the righteous are in the hand of God, and there shall no torment touch them: in the sight of the unwise they seemed to die: but they are in peace, alleluia.

Secret.

WE offer unto thee, O Lord, these gifts of our bounden duty and service; that they may both be acceptable unto thee for the honour of all thy Saints, and through thy mercy profitable unto us for our salvation. Through.

Common Preface, even if this Feast fall on Sunday.

Communion. Matt. 5, 8-10. Blessed are the pure in heart, for they shall see God; blessed are the peacemakers, for they shall be called the children of God; blessed are they which are persecuted for righteousness' sake, for theirs is the kingdom of heaven.

Postcommunion.

GRANT, we beseech thee, O Lord, unto thy faithful people ever to rejoice in the veneration of all thy Saints: and to be defended by their perpetual supplication. Through.

Votive Mass of All Saints

Outside Eastertide:

Introit. Wisd. 3, 8. Judicant.

THE Saints judge the nations, and have dominion over the people: and their Lord shall reign for ever. Ps. 33, 1. Rejoice in the Lord, O ye righteous: for it becometh well the just to be thankful. ℣. Glory.

In Eastertide, Introit, Alleluia, Offertory and Communion from Mass Sancti, p. [17].

Collect.

GRANT, we beseech thee, almighty God: that the intercession of holy Mary, Mother of God, and of all the holy Apostles, Martyrs, Confessors and Virgins, and of all thine elect, may everywhere cause us to rejoice; that while we call to mind their merits, we may perceive their advocacy. Through the same.

The Epistle, Gradual, Alleluia, Gospel, Offertory and Communion as on the Feast, p. 834.

After Septuagesima Tract, They that sow, p. [10].

Secret.

MERCIFULLY receive, O Lord, these our oblations: and, at the intercession of blessed Mary ever Virgin with all thy Saints, defend us from all dangers. Through.

Postcommunion.

WE have received, O Lord, this heavenly Sacrament, recalling the memory of blessed Mary ever Virgin and of all thy Saints: grant, we beseech thee; that as we celebrate this mystery in time, so we may attain unto the fulness thereof in everlasting felicity. Through.

November 2.

Commemoration of all the Faithful Departed

See Masses of the Dead, pp. [101]-[103].

November 4.

St. Charles

Bishop and Confessor
Double.

Introit. Ecclus. 45, 24. Statuit ei.

THE Lord hath established a covenant of peace with him, and made him the chief of his people: that he should have the dignity of the priesthood for ever. Ps. 132, 1. Lord, remember David: and all his trouble. ℣. Glory.

Collect.

DEFEND, O Lord, thy Church by the continual protection of thy Confessor and Bishop Saint Charles: that as thou didst render him glorious by reason of his zeal for the flock committed to his charge; so his intercession may render us fervent in love toward thee. Through.

Commemoration of SS. Vitalis and Agricola, MM.

GRANT, we beseech thee, almighty God: that we, who devoutly observe the festival of thy holy Martyrs Vitalis and Agricola; may be holpen by their intercession before thee. Through.

The Lesson from the book of Wisdom.

Ecclus. 44, 16-25, 15.

BEHOLD, a great priest, who in his days pleased the Lord, and was found righteous: and in the time of wrath he was taken in exchange for the world. There was none like unto him, who kept the law of the Most High. Therefore by an oath the Lord assured him that he would increase him among his people. He established with him the blessing of all men and the covenant, and made it rest upon his head. He acknowledged him in his blessing: he preserved for him his mercy: so that he found favour in the sight of the Lord. He magnified him in the sight of kings: and gave unto him a crown of glory. An everlasting covenant he made with him, and gave him a great priesthood: and blessed him with glory. That he should execute the office of the priesthood, and have praise in his name, and offer unto him incense, and a sweet savour.

Gradual. Ecclus. 44, 16. Behold, a great priest, who in his days pleased the Lord. ℣. Ibid., 20. There was none like unto him to keep the law of the Most High.

Alleluia, alleluia. ℣. Ps. 110, 4. Thou art a priest for ever after the order of Melchisedech. Alleluia.

✠ The Continuation of the holy Gospel according to Matthew.

Matt. 25, 14-23.

AT that time: Jesus spake this parable unto his disciples: A man travelling into a far country called his own servants, and delivered unto them his goods. And unto one he gave five talents, to another two, and to another one, to every man according to his several ability, and straightway took his journey. Then he that had received the five talents went and traded with the same, and made them other five talents. And likewise he that had received two, he also gained other two. But he that had received one went and digged in the earth, and hid his lord's money. After a long time the lord of those servants cometh, and reckoneth with them. And so he that had received five talents came and brought other five talents, saying: Lord, thou deliveredst unto me five talents, behold, I have gained beside them five talents more. His lord said unto him: Well done, thou good and faithful servant, thou hast been faithful over a few things, I will make thee ruler over many things: enter thou into the joy of thy lord. He also that had received two talents came and said: Lord, thou deliveredst unto me two talents, behold, I have gained two other talents beside them. His lord said unto him: Well done, good and faithful servant, thou hast been faithful over a few things, I will make thee ruler over many things: enter thou into the joy of thy lord.

Offertory. Ps. 89, 21-22. I have found David my servant, with my holy oil have I anointed him: my hand shall hold him fast, and my arm shall strengthen him.

Secret.

WE beseech thee, O Lord, that we, remembering with gladness the merits of thy Saints, may in all places feel the succour of their intercession. Through.

For the SS. Martyrs. Secret.

WE beseech thee, O Lord, look favourably upon these our oblations: and, at the intercession of thy holy Martyrs Vitalis and Agricola, defend us from all dangers that beset us. Through.

Communion. Luke 12, 42. A faithful and wise servant, whom his lord hath made ruler over his household: to give them their portion of meat in due season.

Postcommunion.

GRANT, we beseech thee, almighty God: that we, shewing forth our thankfulness for the gifts which we have received, may, at the intercession of blessed Charles, thy Confessor and Bishop, obtain yet more abundant mercies. Through.

For the SS. Martyrs. Postcommunion.

O LORD, let this holy Communion cleanse us from every guilty stain: that, at the intercession of thy holy Martyrs Vitalis and Agricola, we may be made partakers thereby of thy healing unto life eternal. Through.

November 8.

For the Four Holy Crowned Martyrs

Martyrs

Introit. Ps. 79, 11, 12 and 10. Intret in conspectu.

LET the sorrowful sighing of the prisoners, O Lord, come before thee: reward thou our neighbours sevenfold into their bosom: avenge thou the blood of thy Saints that is shed. Ps. ibid. 1. O God, the heathen are come into thine inheritance: thy holy temple have they defiled: and made Jerusalem an heap of stones. ℣. Glory.

Collect.

GRANT, we beseech thee, almighty God: that, like as we have known thy glorious Martyrs to be stedfast in their confession of thy name: so we may feel the benefit of their loving intercession for us. Through.

The Lesson from the Epistle of blessed Paul the Apostle to the Hebrews.

Hebr. 11, 33-39.

BRETHREN: The Saints through faith subdued kingdoms, wrought righteousness, obtained promises, stopped the mouth of lions, quenched the violence of fire, escaped the edge of the sword, out of weakness were made strong, waxed valiant in fight, turned to flight the armies of the aliens: women received their dead raised to life again: and others were tortured, not accepting deliverance, that they might obtain a better resurrection: and others had trial of cruel mockings and scourgings, yea, moreover of bonds and imprisonment: they were stoned, they were sawn asunder, were tempted, were slain with the sword: they wandered about in sheepskins and goatskins, being destitute, afflicted, tormented: of whom the world was not worthy: they wandered in deserts, and in mountains, and in dens and caves of the earth. And these all, having obtained a good report through faith, were found in Christ Jesus our Lord.

Gradual. Exod. 15, 11. God is glorious in his holy ones, fearful in praises, doing wonders. ℣. ibid., 6. Thy right hand, O Lord, is become glorious in power: thy right hand hath dashed in pieces the enemy.

Alleluia, alleluia. ℣. Ecclus. 44, 14. The bodies of the Saints are buried in peace, but their name liveth for evermore. Alleluia.

☩ The Continuation of the holy Gospel according to Matthew.

Matt. 5, 1-12.

AT that time: Jesus, seeing the multitudes, went up into a mountain, and when he was set, his disciples came unto him, and he opened his mouth, and taught them, saying: Blessed are the poor in spirit: for theirs is the kingdom of heaven. Blessed are they that mourn: for they shall be comforted. Blessed are the meek: for they shall inherit the earth. Blessed are they which do hunger and thirst after righteousness: for they shall be filled. Blessed are the merciful: for they shall obtain mercy. Blessed are the pure in heart: for they shall see God. Blessed are the peacemakers: for they shall be called the children of God. Blessed are they which are persecuted for righteousness' sake: for theirs is the kingdom of heaven. Blessed are ye, when men shall revile you, and persecute you, and shall say all manner of evil against you falsely for my sake: rejoice, and be exceeding glad, for great is your reward in heaven.

Offertory. Ps. 68, 36. God is wonderful in his holy ones: even the God of Israel, he will give strength and power unto his people: blessed be God, alleluia.

Secret.

LET thy plenteous benediction descend, O Lord; that at the intercession of thy holy Martyrs these our oblations may thereby be rendered acceptable in thy sight, and become for us the Sacrament of our redemption. Through.

Communion. Wisd. 3, 4, 5 and 6. Though they be punished in the sight of men, yet hath God proved them: as gold in the furnace hath he tried them, and received them as a burnt offering.

Postcommunion.

O LORD, who hast here refreshed us with the gladness of thy heavenly mysteries: we humbly beseech thee; that as we glory in the triumph of thy Saints, so we may be protected by their succour. Through.

November 9.

DEDICATION OF THE ARCHBASILICA OF THE MOST HOLY SAVIOUR

Double of 2nd class.

The Mass **Terribilis**, p. [38].

The Creed is said.

Common Preface, even if this Feast fall on Sunday.

Commemoration (in low Mass only) of St. Theodore, Martyr, as below.

Collect. P

O GOD, who dost encompass and protect us by the glorious intercession of thy blessed Martyr Theodore: grant us both to profit by his example, and to be sustained by his intercession. Through.

Secret. P

ACCEPT, O Lord, the prayers of thy faithful people, and the oblations of their sacrifices: that at the intercession of thy blessed Martyr Theodore, we may through this our bounden duty and service enter into heavenly glory. Through.

Postcommunion. P

GRANT to us, we beseech thee, O Lord, at the intercession of thy blessed Martyr Theodore: that we who with our outward lips are made partakers of this holy Sacrament; may inwardly receive the same in purity of heart. Through.

November 10.

St. Andrew Avellino
Confessor
Double.

Introit. Ps. 37. 30-31. Os justi.

THE mouth of the righteous is exercised in wisdom: and his tongue will be talking of judgment: the law of his God is in his heart. Ps. ibid., 1. Fret not thyself because of the ungodly: neither be thou envious against the evildoers. V. Glory.

Collect.

O GOD, who didst inspire thy blessed Confessor Andrew with a firm purpose to increase daily in virtuous living, and didst wondrously dispose him to attain unto thee: grant us, by his merits and intercession, so to be partakers of that same grace; that we, ever following in the way of perfection, may attain with gladness to the fulness of thy glory. Through.

Commemoration is made of SS. Tryphon, Respicius and Nympha, Virgin, Martyrs.

Collect.

O LORD, we beseech thee, make us alway to observe the feast of thy holy Martyrs, Tryphon, Respicius and Nympha: and grant; that through their intercession we may feel the effectual succour of thy mercy. Through.

The Lesson from the book of Wisdom.
Ecclus. 31, 7-11.

BLESSED is the man that is found without blemish: and hath not gone after gold. Who is he, and we will call him blessed? for wonderful things hath he done among his people. Who hath been tried thereby, and found perfect? then let him glory. Who might offend, and hath not offended? or done evil, and hath not done it? His goods shall be established, and the congregation shall declare his alms.

Gradual. Ps. 92, 13-14. The righteous shall flourish like a palm-tree: and shall spread abroad like a cedar in Libanus in the house of the Lord. ℣. Ibid., 3. To tell of thy loving kindness early in the morning, and of thy truth in the night-season.

Alleluia, alleluia. ℣. James 1, 12. Blessed is the man that endureth temptation: for when he is tried, he shall receive the crown of life. Alleluia.

✠ The Continuation of the holy Gospel according to Luke.
Luke 12, 35-40.

AT that time: Jesus said unto his disciples: Let your loins be girded about, and your lights burning, and ye yourselves like unto men that wait for their lord, when he will return from the wedding: that when he cometh and knocketh, they may open unto him immediately. Blessed are those servants, whom the lord when he cometh shall find watching: verily I say unto you, that he shall gird himself, and make them to sit down to meat, and will come forth and serve them. And if he shall come in the second watch, or come in the third watch, and find them so, blessed are those servants. And this know, that if the good man of the house had known what hour the thief would come, he would have watched, and not have suffered his house to be broken through. Be ye therefore ready also: for the Son of man cometh at an hour when ye think not.

Offertory. Ps. 89, 25. My truth and my mercy shall be with him: and in my name shall his horn be exalted.

For the Martyrs.   Secret.

WE beseech thee, O Lord, that the gifts which we offer unto thee of our bounden duty and service may be acceptable unto thee for the honour of thy Saints: and by thy mercy profitable unto us for our salvation. Through.

Communion. Matt. 24, 46-47. Blessed is the servant whom his lord when he cometh shall find watching: verily I say unto you, he shall make him ruler over all his goods.

Postcommunion.

O LORD our God, who hast refreshed us with heavenly meat and drink, we humbly beseech thee: that we may be defended by the prayers of him in whose memory we have received the same. Through.

For the Martyrs.   Postcommunion.

GRANT to us, we beseech thee, O Lord: at the intercession of thy holy Martyrs Tryphon, Respicius and Nympha; that we, who with our outward lips are partakers of this holy Sacrament, may inwardly receive the same in purity of heart. Through.

November 11.

St. Martin

Bishop and Confessor.

Double.

Introit. Ecclus. 45, 30. Statuit ei.

THE Lord hath established a covenant of peace with him, and made him the chief of his people: that he should have the dignity of the priesthood for ever. Ps. 132, 1. Lord, remember David: and all his trouble. ℣. Glory.

Collect.

O GOD, who seest that by reason of our weakness we cannot but fall: mercifully grant; that, by the intercession of blessed Martin, thy Confessor and Bishop, we may be defended against all adversities. Through.

Commemoration of St. Mennas, Martyr.

Collect.

GRANT, we beseech thee, almighty God: that we, who celebrate the heavenly birthday of blessed Mennas, thy Martyr, may by his intercession be stablished in the love of thy name. Through.

The Lesson from the book of Wisdom.

Ecclus. 44, 16.

BEHOLD, a great priest, who in his days pleased the Lord, and was found righteous: and in the time of wrath he was taken in exchange for the world. There was none like unto him, who kept the law of the Most High. Therefore by an oath the Lord assured him that he would increase him among his people. He established with him the blessing of all men and the covenant, and made it rest upon his head. He acknowledged him in his blessing: he preserved for him his mercy: so that he found favour in the sight of the Lord. He magnified him in the sight of kings, and gave unto him a crown of glory. An everlasting covenant he made with him, and gave him a great priesthood, and blessed him with glory. That he should execute the office of the priesthood, and bless the people in his name, and offer unto him incense, and a sweet savour.

Gradual. Ecclus. 44, 16. Behold a great priest, who in his days pleased God. ℣. There was none found like unto him, to keep the law of the most High.

Alleluia, alleluia. ℣. The blessed man, Saint Martin, Bishop of the city of Tours, entered into rest: Angels and Archangels, Thrones, Dominations and Virtues received him. Alleluia.

☩ The Continuation of the holy Gospel according to Luke.

Luke 11, 33-36.

AT that time: Jesus said unto his disciples: No man, when he hath lighted a candle, putteth it in a secret place, neither under a bushel: but on a candlestick, that they which come in may see the light. The light of the body is the eye. Therefore when thine eye is single, thy whole body also is full of light: but when thine eye is evil, thy body also is full of darkness. Take heed therefore that the light which is in thee be not darkness. If thy whole body therefore be full of light, having no part dark, the whole shall be full of light, as when the bright shining of a candle doth give thee light.

Offertory. Ps. 89, 25. My truth and my mercy shall be with him: and in my name shall his horn be exalted.

Secret.

SANCTIFY, we beseech thee, O Lord God, these gifts which we offer on the solemnity of thy holy Bishop Martin: that our life may ever thereby be directed both in prosperity and adversity. Through.

For St. Mennas.   Secret.

WE beseech thee, O Lord, to accept our prayers and oblations: and graciously hearken unto us, whom thou dost cleanse by thy heavenly mysteries. Through.

Communion. Matt. 24, 46-47. Blessed is the servant, whom his lord when he cometh shall find watching: verily I say unto you, that he shall make him ruler over all his goods.

Postcommunion.

GRANT, we beseech thee, O Lord our God: that this Sacrament, which we have now received in honour of the festival of thy Saints, may through their intercession be profitable for our salvation. Through.

For St. Mennas.   Postcommunion.

GRANT, we beseech thee, O Lord our God: that like as we in this life do gladly honour the memory of thy Saints; so we may rejoice hereafter in their everlasting fellowship. Through.

November 12.

St. Martin, I.

Pope and Martyr

Simple.

The Mass Si diligis me, p. [2].

Collect.   C 1

O EVERLASTING Shepherd, look down in mercy on thy flock: and as thou didst choose blessed Martin thy Martyr and Chief Bishop to be pastor and ruler of thy Church; so at his intercession defend it with thy continual protection. Through.

Secret.   C 1

WE beseech thee, O Lord, graciously enlighten thy Church by the gifts which we here offer: that in every place thy flock may increase and prosper, and the shepherds by thy governance may be made pleasing to thy name. Through.

Postcommunion.   C 1

MERCIFUL Lord, we beseech thee to govern and preserve thy Church, which thou hast here refreshed with heavenly food: that by the guiding of thy mighty power it may serve thee in more abundant freedom, and ever keep thy true religion whole and undefiled. Through.

November 13.

St. Didacus

Confessor.

Simple.

The Mass Justus ut palma, p. [25], the Collect excepted.

Collect.   P

ALMIGHTY and everlasting God, who of thy wondrous providence dost choose the weak things of the world to confound the strong: mercifully grant unto us thy humble servants; that by the faithful prayers of blessed Didacus, thy Confessor, we may be found worthy to be exalted to the everlasting glory of heaven. Through.

Secret.   C

GRANT to us, we beseech thee, almighty God: that this oblation of our humble service may be acceptable in thy sight to the honour of thy Saints, and may cleanse us both in body and soul. Through.

Postcommunion.

WE beseech, thee, almighty God: that we, who have received this heavenly food, may at the intercession of blessed Didacus, thy Confessor, be thereby defended against all adversities. Through.

November 14.

St. Josaphat

Bishop and Martyr

Double.

Introit Gaudeamus.

REJOICE we all in the Lord, keeping feast day in honour of blessed Josaphat the Martyr: in whose passion the Angels rejoice, and glorify the Son of God. Ps. 33, 1. Rejoice in the Lord, O ye righteous: for it becometh well the just to be thankful. ℣. Glory.

Collect.

STIR up, O Lord, we beseech thee, in thy Church the Spirit, wherewith blessed Josaphat, thy Martyr and Bishop, was filled, when he laid down his life for the sheep: that at his intercession, we also, being moved and strengthened by the same Spirit, may not fear to lay down our lives for our brethren. Through . . . in the unity of the same Holy Spirit.

The Lesson from the Epistle of blessed Paul the Apostle to the Hebrews.

Heb. 5, 1-6.

BRETHREN: Every high priest taken from among men is ordained for men in things pertaining to God: that he may offer both gifts and sacrifices for sins: who can have compassion on the ignorant, and on them that are out of the way: for that he himself also is compassed with infirmity: and by reason hereof he ought, as for the people, so also for himself to offer for sins. And no man taketh this honour unto himself, but he that is called of God, as was Aaron. So also Christ glorified not himself to be made an high priest: but he that said unto him: Thou art my Son, to-day have I begotten thee. As he saith also in another place: Thou art a priest for ever after the order of Melchisedec.

Gradual. Ps. 89, 21-23. I have found David my servant, with my holy oil have I anointed him: my hand shall hold him fast, and my arm shall strengthen him. ℣. The enemy shall not be able to do him violence, the son of wickedness shall not hurt him.

Alleluia, alleluia. ℣. This is a priest whom the Lord hath crowned. Alleluia.

✠ *The Continuation of the holy Gospel according to John.*

John 10, 11-16.

AT that time: Jesus said unto the Pharisees: I am the good shepherd. The good shepherd giveth his life for the sheep. But he that is an hireling, and not the shepherd, whose own the sheep are not, seeth the wolf coming, and leaveth the sheep, and fleeth: and the wolf catcheth them, and scattereth the sheep; the hireling fleeth, because he is an hireling, and careth not for the sheep. I am the good shepherd: and know my sheep, and am known of mine. As the Father knoweth me, even so know I the Father, and I lay down my life for the sheep. And other sheep I have, which are not of this fold: them also must I bring, and they shall hear my voice, and there shall be one fold, and one shepherd.

Offertory. John 15, 13. Greater love hath no man than this, that a man lay down his life for his friends.

Secret.

MOST merciful God, pour forth upon these gifts thy benediction: that like as Saint Josaphat, thy Martyr and Bishop, maintained thy faith even to the shedding of his blood, so we may be strengthened in the same. Through.

Communion. John 10, 14. I am the good shepherd: and know my sheep, and am known of mine.

Postcommunion.

WE beseech thee, O Lord, that like as this heavenly banquet sustained the life of blessed Josaphat, thy Martyr and Bishop, to win the victory for the honour of thy Church: so it may ever bestow the spirit of constancy upon the hearts of us thy servants. Through.

November 15.

St. Albert the Great

Bishop, Confessor
and Doctor of the Church

Double.

Introit. Ecclus. 15, 5. In medio.

IN the midst of the Church he opened his mouth: and the Lord filled him with the spirit of wisdom and understanding: he clothed him with a robe of glory. Ps. 92, 1. It is a good thing to give thanks unto the Lord: and to sing praises unto thy name, O most Highest. ℣. Glory.

Collect.

O GOD, who through blessed Albert, thy Bishop and Doctor, didst bring the wisdom of man into captivity to the obedience of faith, and by reason of his labours didst make him to be great: grant us, we beseech thee, so to follow his doctrine and holy life; that we may attain unto the fruition of thy perfect light in heaven. Through.

The Lesson from the Epistle of blessed Paul the Apostle to Timothy.

II. Tim. 4, 1-8.

DEARLY beloved: I charge thee before God, and the Lord Jesus Christ, who shall judge the quick and the dead at his appearing and his kingdom: preach the word, be instant in season, out of season: reprove, rebuke, exhort with all longsuffering and doctrine. For the time will come when they will not endure sound doctrine, but after their own lusts shall they heap to themselves teachers, having itching ears, and they shall turn away their ears from the truth, and shall be turned unto fables. But watch thou in all things, endure afflictions, do the work of an Evangelist, make full proof of thy ministry. For I am now ready to be offered, and the time of my departure is at hand. I have fought a good fight, I have finished my course, I have kept the faith. Henceforth there is laid up for me a crown of righteousness, which the Lord, the righteous judge, shall give me at that day: and not to me only, but unto all them also that love his appearing.

Gradual. Ps. 37, 30-31. The mouth of the righteous is exercised in wisdom, and his tongue will be talking of judgment. ℣. The law of his God is in his heart: and his goings shall not slide.

Alleluia, alleluia. ℣. Ecclus. 45, 9. The Lord loved him, and adorned him: he clothed him with a robe of glory. Alleluia.

☩ The Continuation of the holy Gospel according to Matthew.

Matt. 5, 13-19.

AT that time: Jesus said unto his disciples: Ye are the salt of the earth. But if the salt have lost his savour, wherewith shall it be salted? It is thenceforth good for nothing, but to be cast out, and to be trodden under foot of men. Ye are the light of the world. A city that is set on an hill cannot be hid. Neither do men light a candle, and put it under a bushel, but on a candlestick, and it giveth light unto all that are in the house. Let your light so shine before men, that they may see your good works, and glorify your Father which is in heaven. Think not that I am come to destroy the law or the prophets: I am not come to destroy, but to fulfil. For verily I say unto you, Till heaven and earth pass, one jot or one tittle shall in no wise pass from the law, till all be fulfilled. Whosoever therefore shall break one of these least commandments, and shall teach men so, he shall be called the least in the kingdom of heaven: but whosoever shall do and teach them, the same shall be called great in the kingdom of heaven. Creed.

Offertory. Ps. 92, 13. The righteous shall flourish like a palm-tree: and shall spread abroad like a cedar in Libanus.

Secret.

LOOK favourably, we beseech thee, O Lord, upon these our oblations: that, as we celebrate the mystery of the passion of thy Son our Lord, so with devout affection we may attain thereunto by the intercession and example of blessed Albert. Through the same.

Communion. Luke 12, 42. A faithful and wise servant, whom his lord hath made ruler over his household: to give them their portion of meat in due season.

Postcommunion.

DEFEND us, O Lord, by these holy mysteries, which we have now received, from the assaults of our enemies: and, at the intercession of blessed Albert thy Confessor and Bishop, grant us to be preserved in thy perpetual peace. Through.

November 16.

St. Gertrude

Virgin

Double.

The Mass Dilexisti, p. [31], the Collect excepted.

Collect.

O GOD, who in the heart of blessed Gertrude thy Virgin didst prepare a mansion acceptable unto thyself: we beseech thee by her merits and intercession mercifully to cleanse our hearts from all defilement; that we may rejoice in her everlasting fellowship in heaven. Through.

Secret.

GRANT, O Lord, that like as thy dedicated people do acknowledge that in tribulation they have been succoured by the merits of thy Saints: so this oblation, which they offer unto thee in honour of the same, may be acceptable in thy sight. Through.

Postcommunion.

O LORD, who hast satisfied this thy family with thy sacred gifts: we beseech thee, that we may at all times be comforted by the intercession of her whose festival we celebrate. Through.

In Scotland: the same day.

St. Margaret

Queen and Widow

See Supplement.

November 17.

St. Gregory Thaumaturgus

Bishop and Confessor

Simple.

Introit. Ecclus. 45, 24. Statuit ei.

THE Lord hath established a covenant of peace with him, and made him the chief of his people: that he should have the dignity of the priesthood for ever. Ps. 132, 1. Lord remember David: and all his trouble. ℣. Glory.

Collect.

GRANT, we beseech thee, almighty God: that we, devoutly observing this festival of blessed Gregory, thy Confessor and Bishop, may hereby advance in true godliness and attain unto everlasting salvation. Through.

The Lesson from the book of Wisdom.

Ecclus. 44, 16-25, 15.

BEHOLD, a great priest, who in his days pleased the Lord, and was found righteous: and in the time of wrath he was taken in exchange for the world. There was none like unto him, who kept the law of the Most High. Therefore by an oath the Lord assured him that he would increase him among his people. He established with him the blessing of all men and the covenant, and made it rest upon his head. He acknowledged him in his blessing: he preserved for him his mercy: so that he found favour in the sight of the Lord. He magnified him in the sight of kings: and gave unto him a crown of glory. An everlasting covenant he made with him, and gave him a great priesthood: and blessed him with glory. That he should execute the office of the priesthood, and have praise in his name, and offer unto him incense, and a sweet savour.

Gradual. Ecclus. 44, 16. Behold, a great priest, who in his days pleased the Lord. ℣. Ibid., 20. There was none like unto him to keep the law of the Most High.

Alleluia, alleluia. ℣. Ps. 110, 4. Thou art a priest for ever after the order of Melchisedech. Alleluia.

✠ The Continuation of the holy Gospel according to Mark.

Mark 11, 22-24.

AT that time: Jesus, answering his disciples, saith unto them: Have faith in God. For verily I say unto you, That whosoever shall say unto this mountain: Be thou removed, and be thou cast into the sea, and shall not doubt in his heart, but shall believe that those things which he saith shall come to pass, he shall have whatsoever he saith. Therefore I say unto you: What things soever ye desire, when ye pray, believe that ye receive them, and ye shall have them.

Offertory. Ps. 89, 21-22. I have found David my servant, with my holy oil have I anointed him: my hand shall hold him fast, and my arm shall strengthen him.

Secret.

WE beseech thee, O Lord, that we, remembering with gladness the merits of thy Saints, may in all places feel the succour of their intercession. Through.

Communion. Luke 12, 42. A faithful and wise servant, whom his lord hath made ruler over his household: to give them their portion of meat in due season.

Postcommunion.

GRANT, we beseech thee, almighty God: that we, shewing forth our thankfulness for the gifts which we have received, may, at the intercession of blessed Gregory, thy Confessor and Bishop, obtain yet more abundant mercies. Through.

November 18.

Dedication of the Basilicas of SS. Peter and Paul

Apostles

Greater double.

The Mass Terribilis, p. [38], and the Creed is said.

Common Preface, even if this Feast fall on Sunday.

November 19.

St. Elizabeth

Widow

Double.

Introit. Ps. 119, 75 and 120.

Cognovi, Domine.

I KNOW, O Lord, that thy judgments are right, and that thou of very faithfulness hast caused me to be troubled: my flesh trembleth for fear of thee, and I am afraid of thy judgments. Ps. ibid., 1. Blessed are those that are undefiled in the way, and walk in the law of the Lord. ℣. Glory.

Collect.

O MERCIFUL God, enlighten the hearts of thy faithful people: and by the glorious prayers of blessed Elizabeth; make us to despise the prosperity of this world, and evermore to rejoice in thy heavenly comfort. Through.

Commemoration of St. Pontian, Pope and Martyr.

Collect.

O EVERLASTING Shepherd, look down in mercy on thy flock: and as thou didst choose blessed Pontian thy Martyr and Chief Bishop to be pastor and ruler of thy Church; so at his intercession defend it with thy continual protection. Through.

The Lesson from the book of Wisdom.

Prov. 31, 10-31.

WHO can find a virtuous woman? For her price is far above rubies. The heart of her husband doth safely trust in her, so that he shall have no need of spoil. She will do him good and not evil all the days of her life. She seeketh wool, and flax, and worketh willingly with her hands. She is like the merchants' ships, she bringeth her food from afar. She riseth also while it is yet night, and giveth meat to her household, and a portion to her maidens. She considereth a field, and buyeth it: with the fruit of her hands she planteth a vine-yard. She girdeth her loins with strength, and strengtheneth her arms. She perceiveth that her merchandise is good: her candle goeth not out by night. She layeth her hands to the spindle, and her hands hold the distaff. She stretcheth out her hand to the poor, yea, she reacheth forth her hands to the needy. She is not afraid of the snow for her household: for all her household are clothed with scarlet. She maketh herself coverings of tapestry: her clothing is silk and purple. Her husband is known in the gates, when he sitteth among the elders of the land. She maketh fine linen, and selleth it, and delivereth girdles unto the merchant. Strength and honour are her clothing, and she shall rejoice in time to come. She openeth her mouth with wisdom, and in her tongue is the law of kindness. She looketh well to the ways of her household, and eateth not the bread of idleness. Her children arise up, and call her blessed: her husband also, and he praiseth her. Many daughters have done virtuously, but thou excellest them all. Favour is deceitful, and beauty is vain: but a woman that feareth the Lord, she shall be praised. Give her of the fruit of her hands: and let her own works praise her in the gates.

Gradual. Ps. 45, 3 and 5. Full of grace are thy lips: therefore God hath blessed thee for ever. ℣. Because of the word of truth, of meekness, and righteousness: and thy right hand shall teach thee terrible things.

Alleluia, alleluia. ℣. Ibid., 3. In thy comeliness and in thy beauty go forth, ride prosperously, and reign. Alleluia.

✠ The Continuation of the holy Gospel according to Matthew.

Matt. 13, 44-52.

AT that time: Jesus spake this parable unto his disciples. The kingdom of heaven is like unto treasure hid in a field: the which when a man hath found, he hideth, and for joy thereof goeth and selleth all that he hath, and buyeth that field. Again, the kingdom of heaven is like unto a merchant man, seeking goodly pearls. Who, when he had found one pearl of great price, went and sold all that he had, and bought it. Again, the kingdom of heaven is like unto a net, that was cast into the sea, and gathered of every kind. Which, when it was full, they drew to shore, and sat down, and gathered the good into vessels, but cast the bad away. So shall it be at the end of the world: the Angels shall come forth, and sever the wicked from among the just, and shall cast them into the furnace of fire: there shall be wailing and gnashing of teeth. Jesus saith unto them: Have ye understood all these things? They say unto him: Yea, Lord. Then said he unto them: Therefore every scribe which is instructed unto the kingdom of heaven is like unto a man that is an householder, which bringeth forth out of his treasure things new and old.

Offertory. Ps. 45, 3. Full of grace are thy lips: therefore God hath blessed thee for ever, and world without end.

Secret.

GRANT, O Lord, that like as thy faithful people do acknowledge that in tribulation they have been succoured by the merits of thy Saints: so this oblation, which they here do offer unto thee in honour of the same, may be acceptable in thy sight. Through.

For St. Pontian. Secret.

WE beseech thee, O Lord, graciously enlighten thy Church by the gifts which we here offer: that in every place thy flock may increase and prosper, and the shepherds by thy governance may be made pleasing to thy name. Through.

Common Preface.

Communion. Ps. 45, 8. Thou hast loved righteousness, and hated iniquity: therefore God, even thy God, hath anointed thee with the oil of gladness above thy fellows.

Postcommunion.

O LORD, who hast satisfied this thy family with thy sacred gifts: we beseech thee, that we may at all times be comforted by her whose festival we celebrate. Through.

For St. Pontian. Postcommunion.

MERCIFUL Lord, we beseech thee to govern and preserve thy Church, which thou hast here refreshed with heavenly food: that by the guiding of thy mighty power it may serve thee in more abundant freedom, and ever keep thy true religion whole and undefiled. Through.

November 20.

St. Felix of Valois

Confessor

Double.

The Mass Justus ut palma, p. [25], the Collect excepted.

Collect. P

O GOD, who by a sign from heaven didst vouchsafe to call blessed Felix, thy Confessor, from the desert to the work of ransoming captives: grant, we beseech thee; that through thy grace we may, at his intercession, be delivered from the captivity of our sins, and finally be brought unto our heavenly country. Through.

Secret. C

GRANT to us, we beseech thee, almighty God: that this oblation of our humble service may be acceptable in thy sight to the honour of thy Saints, and may cleanse us both in body and soul. Through.

Postcommunion. C

WE beseech thee, almighty God: that we, who have received this heavenly food, may, at the intercession of blessed Felix, thy Confessor, be thereby defended against all adversities. Through.

November 21.

The Presentation of the Blessed Virgin Mary

Greater double.

The Mass Salve, p. [41], the Collect excepted:

Collect. P

O GOD, who on this day didst vouchsafe that blessed Mary ever Virgin, the dwelling-place of the Holy Ghost, should be presented in the temple: grant, we beseech thee; that at her intercession we may be found worthy to be presented unto thee in the temple of thy glory. Through ... in the unity of the same Holy Ghost.

The Creed is said.

Secret. C

THROUGH thy mercy, O Lord, and the intercession of blessed Mary ever Virgin, may this oblation avail for our prosperity and peace, both now and for ever. Through.

Preface of the B.V.Mary, And that in the Presentation.

Postcommunion. C

O LORD, who hast appointed these holy mysteries, which we have here received, to be the means of our salvation: grant, we beseech thee that we who have offered these our gifts unto thy majesty in honour of blessed Mary ever Virgin; may by her advocacy be at all times and in all places effectually defended.

November 22.

St. Cecilia

Virgin and Martyr

Double.

Introit. Ps. 119, 46-47. Loquebar.

I WILL speak of thy testimonies, even before kings, and will not be ashamed: and my delight shall be in thy commandments, which I have loved exceedingly. Ps. ibid., 1. Blessed are those that are undefiled in the way: and walk in the law of the Lord. ℣. Glory.

Collect.

O GOD, who makest us glad with the yearly solemnity of blessed Cecilia, thy Virgin and Martyr: grant, that as we do venerate her in our outward service, so we may follow the example of her godly conversation. Through.

The Lesson from the book of Wisdom.
Ecclus. 51, 9-12.

O LORD my God, I lifted up my supplication from the earth, and I prayed for deliverance from death. I called upon the Lord, the Father of my Lord, that he would not leave me in the days of my trouble, and in the time of the proud, when there was no help. I will praise thy name continually, and will sing praise with thanksgiving, and so my prayer was heard. For thou savedst me from destruction, and deliveredst me from the evil time. Therefore will I give thanks, and praise thee, O Lord our God.

Gradual. Ps. 45, 11-12. Hearken, O daughter, and consider, incline thine ear: so shall the King have pleasure in thy beauty. ℣. In thy comeliness and in thy beauty go forth, proceed prosperously and reign.

Alleluia, alleluia. ℣. Matt. 25, 4 and 6. The five wise virgins took oil in their vessels with their lamps: and at midnight there was a cry made: Behold, the bridegroom cometh: go ye out to meet Christ the Lord. Alleluia.

✠ The Continuation of the holy Gospel according to Matthew.
Matt. 25, 1-13.

AT that time: Jesus spake this parable unto his disciples: The kingdom of heaven shall be likened unto ten virgins: which took their lamps, and went forth to meet the bridegroom. And five of them were wise, and five were foolish: they that were foolish took their lamps, and took no oil with them: but the wise took oil in their vessels with their lamps. While the bridegroom tarried, they all slumbered and slept. And at midnight there was a cry made: Behold, the bridegroom cometh, go ye out to meet him. Then all those virgins arose, and trimmed their lamps. And the foolish said unto the wise: Give us of your oil: for our lamps are gone out. But the wise answered, saying: Not so, lest there be not enough for us and you, but go ye rather to them that sell, and buy for yourselves. And while they went to buy, the bridegroom came: and they that were ready went in with him to the marriage, and the door was shut. Afterward came also the other virgins, saying: Lord, Lord, open to us. But he answered and said: Verily I say unto you, I know you not. Watch therefore, for ye know neither the day nor the hour* [wherein the Son of Man cometh].

Offertory. Ps. 45, 15-16. The Virgins that be her fellows shall be brought unto the King: they that bear her company shall be brought unto thee with joy and gladness: and shall enter into the palace of the Lord the King.

Secret.

WE beseech thee, O Lord: that this sacrifice of atonement and praise may at the intercession of blessed Cecilia, thy Virgin and Martyr, ever render us worthy of thy loving-kindness. Through.

Communion. Ps. 119, 80. Let the proud be confounded, for they go wickedly about to destroy me: but I will be occupied in thy commandments and in thy statutes, that I be not ashamed.

Postcommunion.

O LORD, who hast satisfied this thy family with thy sacred gifts: we beseech thee, that we may at all times be comforted by the intercession of her whose festival we celebrate. Through.

November 23.

St. Clement I

Pope and Martyr

Double.

Introit. Is. 59, 21; 56, 7.   Dicit Dominus.

THE Lord saith: My words, which I have put in thy mouth, shall not depart out of thy mouth: and thy gifts shall be accepted upon mine altar. Ps. 112, 1. Blessed is the man that feareth the Lord: he hath great delight in his commandments. ℣. Glory.

Collect.

O EVERLASTING Shepherd, look down in mercy on thy flock: and as thou didst choose blessed Clement thy Martyr and Chief Bishop to be pastor and ruler of thy Church; so at his intercession defend it with thy continual protection. Through.

Commemoration of St. Felicity, Martyr.

Collect.

GRANT, we beseech thee, almighty God: that we, who celebrate the festival of blessed Felicity, thy Martyr, may by her merits and prayers be continually defended. Through.

The Lesson from the Epistle of blessed Paul the Apostle to the Philippians.

Phil. 3, 17-21; 4, 1.

BRETHREN: Be followers together of me, and mark them which walk so as ye have us for an ensample. For many walk, of whom I have told you often, (and now tell you even weeping,) that they are the enemies of the Cross of Christ: whose end is destruction: whose god is their belly: and whose glory is in their shame, who mind earthly things. For our conversation is in heaven: from whence also we look for the Saviour, the Lord Jesus Christ, who shall change our vile body, that it may be fashioned like unto his glorious body, according to the working whereby he is able even to subdue all things unto himself. Therefore, my brethren dearly beloved and longed for, my joy and crown: so stand fast in the Lord, my dearly beloved. I beseech Euodias, and beseech Syntyche, that they be of the same mind in the Lord. And I entreat thee also, true yoke-fellow, help those women which laboured with me in the Gospel, with Clement also, and with other my fellow labourers, whose names are in the book of life.

Gradual. Ps. 107, 32 and 31. Let them exalt him in the congregation of the people: and praise him in the seat of the elders. ℣. O that men would praise the Lord for his goodness; and declare the wonders that he doeth for the children of men.

Alleluia, alleluia. ℣. Matt. 16, 18. Thou art Peter, and upon this rock I will build my Church. Alleluia.

✠ The Continuation of the holy Gospel according to Matthew.

Matt. 16, 13-19.

AT that time: Jesus came into the coasts of Cæsarea Philippi, and asked his disciples, saying: Whom do men say that I, the Son of man, am? And they said: Some say that thou art John the Baptist, some Elias, and others Jeremias, or one of the Prophets. He saith unto them: But whom say ye that I am? And Simon Peter answered and said: Thou art the Christ, the son of the living God. And Jesus answered and said unto him: Blessed art thou, Simon Bar-jona: for flesh and blood hath not revealed it unto thee, but my Father which is in heaven. And I say also unto thee, That thou art Peter, and upon this rock I will build my Church, and the gates of hell shall not prevail against it. And I will give unto thee the keys of the kingdom of heaven. And whatsoever thou shalt bind on earth, shall be bound in heaven: and whatsoever thou shalt loose on earth, shall be loosed in heaven.

Offertory. Jer. 1, 9-10. Behold, I have put my words in thy mouth: see, I have set thee over the nations and over the kingdoms, to pull down and to destroy, to build and to plant.

Secret.

WE beseech thee, O Lord, graciously enlighten thy Church by the gifts which we here offer: that in every place thy flock may increase and prosper, and the shepherds by thy governance may be made pleasing to thy name. Through.

For St. Felicity. Secret.

GRACIOUSLY hearken, O Lord, to the prayers of thy people: and make us to rejoice in the intercession of her whose festival thou dost cause us to celebrate. Through.

Common Preface.

Communion. Matt. 16, 18. Thou art Peter, and upon this rock I will build my Church.

Postcommunion.

MERCIFUL Lord, we beseech thee to govern and preserve thy Church, which thou hast here refreshed with heavenly food: that by the guiding of thy mighty power it may serve thee in more abundant freedom, and ever keep thy true religion whole and undefiled. Through.

For St. Felicity. Postcommunion.

WE humbly beseech thee, almighty God: that at the intercession of thy Saints thou wouldest multiply thy gifts within us, and dispose our times according to thy will. Through.

November 24.

St. John of the Cross

Confessor and Doctor of the Church

Double.

Introit. Ecclus. 15, 5. In medio.

IN the midst of the Church he opened his mouth: and the Lord filled him with the spirit of wisdom and understanding: he clothed him with a robe of glory. Ps. 92, 1. It is a good thing to give thanks unto the Lord: and to sing praises unto thy name, O most Highest. ℣. Glory.

Collect.

O GOD, who didst endue blessed John, thy Confessor and Doctor, with wondrous love of perfect self-denial and of carrying thy Cross: vouchsafe; that we, cleaving stedfastly to his example, may attain unto everlasting glory. Through.

And Commemoration is made of St. Chrysogonus, Martyr.

Collect.

ASSIST us mercifully, O Lord, in these our supplication: that we, who acknowledge ourselves to be guilty by reason of our iniquities, may by the intercession of thy blessed Martyr Chrysogonus obtain our deliverance. Through.

The Lesson from the Epistle of blessed Paul the Apostle to Timothy.

II Tim. 4, 1-8.

DEARLY beloved: I charge thee before God, and the Lord Jesus Christ, who shall judge the quick and the dead at his appearing and his kingdom: preach the word, be instant in season, out of season: reprove, rebuke, exhort with all longsuffering and doctrine. For the time will come when they will not endure sound doctrine, but after their own lusts shall they heap to themselves teachers, having itching ears, and they shall turn away their ears from the truth, and shall be turned unto fables. But watch thou in all things, endure afflictions, do the work of an Evangelist, make full proof of thy ministry. For I am now ready to be offered, and the time of my departure is at hand. I have fought a good fight, I have finished my course, I have kept the faith. Henceforth there is laid up for me a crown of righteousness, which the Lord, the righteous judge, shall give me at that day: and not to me only, but unto all them also that love his appearing.

Gradual. Ps. 37, 30-31. The mouth of the righteous is exercised in wisdom, and his tongue will be talking of judgment. ℣. The law of his God is in his heart: and his goings shall not slide.

Alleluia, alleluia. ℣. Ecclus 45, 9. The Lord loved him, and adorned him: he clothed him with a robe of glory. Alleluia.

✠ The Continuation of the holy Gospel according to Matthew.

Matt. 5, 13-19.

AT that time: Jesus said unto his disciples: Ye are the salt of the earth. But if the salt have lost his savour, wherewith shall it be salted? It is thenceforth good for nothing, but to be cast out, and to be trodden under foot of men. Ye are the light of the world. A city that is set on an hill cannot be hid. Neither do men light a candle, and put it under a bushel, but on a candlestick, and it giveth light unto all that are in the house. Let your light so shine before men, that they may see your good works, and glorify your Father which is in heaven. Think not that I am come to destroy the law or the prophets: I am not come to destroy, but to fulfil. For verily I say unto you, Till heaven and earth pass, one jot or one tittle shall in no wise pass from the law, till all be fulfilled. Whosoever therefore shall break one of these least commandments, and shall teach men so, he shall be called the least in the kingdom of heaven: but whosoever shall do and teach them, the same shall be called great in the kingdom of heaven. Creed.

Offertory. Ps. 92, 13. The righteous shall flourish like a palm-tree: and shall spread abroad like a cedar in Libanus.

Secret.

MAY the devout prayers of thy Bishop and Doctor, Saint John, continually succour us, O Lord: that they may render our oblations acceptable in thy sight; and ever obtain for us thy merciful pardon. Through.

For St. Chrysogonus.   Secret.

WE beseech thee, O Lord, mercifully to accept these our oblations: that at the intercession of thy blessed Martyr Chrysogonus we may be defended against all dangers. Through.

Communion. Luke 12, 42. A faithful and wise servant, whom his lord hath made ruler over his household: to give them their portion of meat in due season.

Postcommunion.

WE beseech thee, O Lord, that blessed John, thy Bishop and most excellent Doctor, may ever stand before thee as our advocate: that this sacrifice of thine ordinance may effectually avail for our salvation. Through.

For St. Chrysogonus.   Postcommunion.

GRANT, O Lord, that by this holy Sacrament, which we have here received, we may both be cleansed from our secret faults, and delivered from all the crafts and assaults of our enemies.

November 25.

St. Catharine

Virgin and Martyr.

Double.

The Mass Loquebar, p. [28], except the Collect.

Collect.

O GOD, who didst give the law to Moses on the height of Mount Sinai, and in the same place didst through thy Angels wondrously bestow the body of blessed Catharine thy Virgin and Martyr: grant, we beseech thee; that by her merits and intercession we may be enabled to attain unto that mount which is Christ: Who liveth and reigneth with thee.

Secret.

RECEIVE, O Lord, the gifts which we offer on the solemnity of blessed Catharine thy Virgin and Martyr: through whose advocacy we trust to be delivered. Through.

Postcommunion.

ASSIST us mercifully, O Lord, who have here received these holy mysteries: and at the intercession of blessed Catharine, thy Virgin and Martyr, make us ever to rejoice in thy continual protection. Through.

November 26.

St. Silvester

Abbot

Double.

Introit. Ps. 37, 30-31. Os justi.

THE mouth of the righteous is exercised in wisdom, and his tongue will be talking of judgment: the law of his God is in his heart. Ps. ibid., 1. Fret not thyself because of the ungodly: neither be thou envious against the evil doers. ℣. Glory.

Collect.

MOST merciful God, who didst vouchsafe to call thy blessed Abbot Silvester, devoutly meditating at an open tomb upon the vanity of this world, unto the desert, and to adorn him with wondrous virtue and godly living: we humbly beseech thee; that following his example, we may despise the things on earth, and attain unto the fruition of thine eternal fellowship. Through.

And Commemoration is made of St. Peter of Alexandria, Bishop and Martyr.

Collect.

ALMIGHTY God, mercifully look upon our infirmities: and whereas we are sore afflicted by the burden of our sins, let the glorious intercession of blessed Peter thy Martyr and Bishop be our succour and defence. Through.

The Lesson from the book of Wisdom.

Ecclus. 45, 1-6.

BELOVED of God and men, whose memorial is blessed. He made him like to the glorious saints, and magnified him so that his enemies stood in fear of him. By his words he caused the wonders to cease, and he made him glorious in the sight of kings, and gave him a commandment for his people, and shewed him his glory. He sanctified him in his faithfulness and meekness, and chose him out of all men. He made him to hear his voice, and brought him into the dark cloud, and gave him commandments before his face, even the law of life and knowledge.

Gradual. Ps. 21, 4-5. Thou hast prevented him, O Lord, with the blessings of goodness: thou hast set a crown of pure gold upon his head. ℣. He asked life of thee, and thou gavest him a long life, even for ever and ever.

Alleluia, alleluia. ℣. Ps. 92, 13. The righteous shall flourish like a palm-tree: and shall spread abroad like a cedar in Libanus. Alleluia.

☩ The Continuation of the holy Gospel according to Matthew.

Matt. 19, 27-29.

AT that time: Peter said unto Jesus: Behold, we have forsaken all, and followed thee: what shall we have therefore? And Jesus said unto them: Verily I say unto you, That ye which have followed me, in the regeneration when the Son of man shall sit in the throne of his glory, ye also shall sit upon twelve thrones, judging the twelve tribes of Israel. And every one that hath forsaken houses, or brethren, or sisters, or father, or mother, or wife, or children, or lands, for my name's sake, shall receive an hundredfold, and shall inherit everlasting life.

Offertory. Ps. 21, 3-4. Thou hast given him his heart's desire, O Lord, and hast not denied him the request of his lips: thou hast set a crown of pure gold upon his head.

Secret.

WE beseech thee, O Lord: that, as we present these our offerings to thy divine majesty with reverence and godly fear; so, with devout preparation of mind and in purity of heart we, being made imitators of thy blessed Abbot Silvester, may be worthy to receive in holiness the Body and Blood of thy Son: Who liveth and reigneth with thee.

For St. Peter. Secret.

WE beseech thee, O Lord, mercifully to accept this our sacrifice which we offer unto thee, pleading the merits of blessed Peter thy Martyr and Bishop: that the same may avail for our perpetual succour. Through.

Communion. Luke 12, 42. A faithful and wise servant, whom his lord hath made ruler over his household, to give them their portion of meat in due season.

Postcommunion.

O LORD, who hast refreshed us with this heavenly banquet, we beseech thee to grant: that we may so walk in the footsteps of thy holy Abbot Silvester; that we may win an abundant reward with thy Saints in the kingdom of thy glory. Through.

For St. Peter. Postcommunion.

WE beseech thee, O Lord our God, that like as we whom thou hast refreshed by the partaking of thy sacred gift do offer unto thee our outward worship: so, at the intercession of blessed Peter thy Martyr and Bishop, we may inwardly be profited thereby to our salvation. Through.

FEASTS PROPER
TO
ENGLAND AND WALES

The numbers preceding Feasts in this Supplement indicate the *districts* in which they are to be observed, as follows:—

COUNTIES of ENGLAND and WALES

Bedfordshire - - - - -	11
Berkshire - - - - -	16
Buckinghamshire - - - -	11
Cambridgeshire - - - -	11
Cheshire - - - - -	8
Cornwall - - - - -	18
Cumberland - - - - -	2
Derbyshire - - - - -	7
Devonshire - - - - -	18
Dorsetshire - - - - -	18
Durham - - - - -	1
Essex - - - - -	15
Glamorganshire - - - -	12
Gloucestershire - - - -	13
Hampshire - - - - -	16
Herefordshire - - - -	12
Hertfordshire - - - -	14
Huntingdonshire - - - -	11
Isle of Man - - - -	6
Isle of Wight - - - -	16
Kent - - - - -	17
Lancashire	
North of Ribble - - - -	2
Hundreds of Salford and Blackburn - - - -	5
Remainder of County - -	6
Leicestershire - - - -	7
Lincolnshire - - - - -	7
London	
North of Thames - - -	14
South of Thames - - -	17
Middlesex - - - - -	14
Monmouthshire - - - -	12
Norfolk - - - - -	11
Northamptonshire - - - -	11
Northumberland - - - -	1
Nottinghamshire - - - -	7
Oxfordshire - - - - -	10
Rutlandshire - - - - -	7
Shropshire - - - - -	8
Somersetshire - - - -	13
Staffordshire - - - - -	10
Suffolk - - - - -	11
Surrey - - - - -	17
Sussex - - - - -	17
Wales (except Glamorganshire)	9
Warwickshire - - - -	10
Westmorland - - - -	2
Wiltshire - - - - -	13
Worcestershire - - - -	10
Yorkshire	
East Riding - - - -	3
North Riding - - - -	3
West Riding - - - -	4

CALENDAR
FOR
ENGLAND AND WALES

† Feasts peculiar to the Calendar of the Book of Common Prayer.

JANUARY

† 8 St. Lucian, Priest, Mart.
12 17: Com. St. Benedict Biscop, Abb.
14 5, 6, 9: St. Kentigern, Bp. and Conf., double. (6 gr. d.)
16 11: St. Fursey, Abb., double. Com. St. Marcellus I, Pope and Mart.
19 10, 11, 13: St. Wolstan, Bp. and Conf., double.
    2: St. Kentigern, Bp. and Conf., double.
    6: St. Benedict Biscop, Abb., double. Com. SS. Marius and Comp. MM. and St. Canute, King, Mart.

FEBRUARY

1 9, 12: St. Brigid, Virg., double. 16: Com. same. Com. St. Ignatius, Bp. and Mart.
3 14, 17: St. Lawrence, Bp. and Conf., double.
   8, 10: St. Werburgh, Virg., double. Com. St. Blasius, Bp. and Mart.
4 1: Bb. Thomas Plumtree and Comp. MM., double. Com. St. Andrew Corsini, Bp. and Conf.
9 12: St. Teilo, Bp. and Conf., double. Com. St. Cyril, Bp. of Alexandria, Conf. and Doct. of the Ch.
13 1: St. Benedict Biscop, Abb., double.
16 7, 11: St. Gilbert, Conf., double.
17 2: St. Finan, Bp. and Conf., double.
23 8: St. Milburga, Virg., double. Com. St. Peter Damian, Bp., Conf. and Doct. of the Ch.
24 (Leap year—25) 7: Com. St. Ethelbert, King, Conf.
25 (Leap year—26) 14, 17: St. Ethelbert, King, Conf., double.
    18: St. Walburga, Virg., double.
26 (Leap year—27) 11: The same.
28 (Leap year—29) 10: St. Oswald, Bp. and Conf., double.

MARCH

1 9, 12: St. David, Bp. and Conf., Principal Patron of Wales, double I class.
   14, 16: The same, double.
2 1, 3, 4, 5, 6, 7, 8: St. Chad, Bp. and Conf., double.
   10: The same, double I class.
3 1, 3, 6: St. Aelred, Abb., double. 7: The same, Com.
8 11: St. Felix, Bp. and Conf., greater double. Com. St. John of God, Conf.
11 15: Bl. John Larke, Mart., double.
12 In all England and Wales: St. Gregory I, Pope, Conf. and Doct. of the Ch., greater double. (1, 2, 6, 7, 8: double).
13 10: Bl. Agnellus of Pisa, Conf., double.
17 7, 9, 10, 12, 14, 16: St. Patrick, Bp. and Conf., greater double.
18 18: St. Edward, King, Mart., double. Com. St. Cyril, Bp. of Jerusalem, Conf. and Doct. of the Ch.
20 1: St. Cuthbert, Bp. and Conf., double I class; 2: greater double: 6, 8: double.
28 18: Com. St. Stephen, Abb., and St. John of Capistrano, Conf.
30 10: St. Osburga, Virg., double.

APRIL

2 11: Bl. John Payne, Mart., double. Com St. Francis de Paula, Conf.
3 15: Bl. John Payne, Mart., double.
   10, 14, 17: St. Richard, Bp. and Conf., double.
† 4 St. Ambrose, B.C.D.
17 14: St. Stephen, Abb., simple. Com. St. Anicetus, Pope and Mart.
19 13, 14, 16, 17: St. Alphege, Bp. and Mart., double.
21 9: St. Beuno, Abb., double. Com. St. Anselm, Bp., Conf and Doct of the Ch.
23 In all England: St. George, Martyr, Principal Patron of England, double I class. Wales: St. George, Mart., greater double.
24 14, 15: St. Mellitus, Bp. and Conf., greater double.
    17: The same, double. 1: St. Egbert, Conf., double. Com. St. Fidelis, Mart.
27 6: St. Maughold, Bp. and Conf., double. Com. St. Peter Canisius, Conf., Doct.

Calendar

MAY

4   In all England and Wales: Bl. Martyrs of England and Wales, greater double. Com. St. Monica, Widow.
6   1: Com. St. Eadbert, Bp. and Conf.
7   1: St. John of Beverley, Bp. and Conf., double. Com. St. Stanislas, Bp. and Mart.
11 17: Com. St. Erconwald, Bp. and Conf.
    3, 4: Com. Bl. John Rochester and James Walworth and Comp., MM.
12 14: Bl. Carthusian MM., double.
    15: Bl. John Houghton, Mart., double.
    9: St. Asaph, Bp. and Conf., double.
13 14, 15: St. Erconwald, Bp. and Conf., greater double. Com. St. Robert Bellarmine, Bp., Conf. and Doct. of the Church.
14 14: Bl. Richard Reynolds, Mart., double. Com. St. Boniface, Mart.
16 10, 11, 17: St. Simon Stock, Conf., double. Com. St. Ubald, Bp. and Conf.
19 10, 14: greater double; 13, 15, 17: double. St. Dunstan, Bp. and Conf. Com. St. Peter Celestine, Pope and Conf.
20 11, 12: St. Ethelbert, King, Mart., double. Com. St. Bernardine of Siena, Conf.
21 15: Bl. John Haile, Mart., double.
24 5, 9: B.V.M. Help of Christians, double I class.
25 13, 18: St. Aldhelm, Bp. and Conf., double. Com. St. Gregory VII, Pope and Conf. and St. Urban I, Pope and Mart.
26 In all England and Wales: St. Augustine, Bp. and Conf., Apostle of the English, double II class. Com. St. Philip Neri, Conf.
27 St. Venerable Bede, Conf. and Doct. of the Ch. 1: double II class; 8, 11, 12, 13, 14, 16, 17: greater double. Com. St. John I, Pope and Mart.
28 10, 13, 14, 15, 16: Bl. Margaret Pole, Widow, double.
    17: St. Aldhelm, Bp. and Conf., simple. Elsewhere: Feria.
30 14, 16: St. Eleutherius, Pope and Mart., double. Com. St. Felix I Pope and Mart.
    10: Tues. in 4th week after Oct. of Easter: Translation of St. Chad, Bp. and Conf., double II class.

JUNE

1   1, 9, 12: B.V. Mary, Mediatrix of all graces, greater double. Com. St. Angela Merici, Virg. †St. Nicomede, Mart.
5   18: St. Boniface, Bp. and Mart., Patron, double I class.
7   1: St. Robert, Abb., double.
    18: St. Willibald, Bp. and Conf., double.
8   2, 3, 4, 5, 6: St. William, Bp. and Conf., double: 1: simple; 7; Com.
9   15, 16: Translation of St. Edmund, Bp. and Conf., greater double. Com. SS. Primus and Felician, MM.
10 14, 15: St. Margaret, Queen, Widow, double.
17 7, 11, 15: St. Botulph, Abbot, double.
19 10: Bb. Sebastian and Humphrey, MM., double. Com. St. Juliana de Falconeri, Virg. and SS. Gervase and Protase, MM.
†20 Transl. of St. Edward, King, M.
22 In all England and Wales: St. Alban, Protomartyr of Britain, greater double. Com. St. Paulinus, Bp. and Conf.
23 1, 6, 10, 11, 14: St. Etheldreda, Virg., double. Com. Vigil of St. John Baptist.
27 3, 4: B.V. Mary of Perpetual Succour, double I class.

JULY

3   12: SS. Julius and Aaron, Martyrs, double. Com. St. Leo II, Pope and Conf.
4   18: Bl. John Cornelius and Comp. and Hugh Green, MM., double. †Transl. of St. Martin, B.C.
7   Cities of Canterbury and Portsmouth: Transl. of S. Thomas of Canterbury, Bp. and Mart., greater double. Com. SS. Cyril and Methodius, Bpp. and CC.
    10: Com. St. Hedda, Bp. and Conf.
9   In all England and Wales: SS. John Fisher, Bp. and Thomas More, MM., double I class.
11 10: Bl. Adrian Fortescue Mart., double.
    13: Bl. Oliver Plunket, Bp. and Mart., greater double. Com. St. Pius I, Pope and Mart.
15 16 (double), 17 (simple): St. Swithun, Bp. and Conf. Com. St. Henry, Emperor, Conf.
16 16: Com St. Helerius, Mart.
17 9, 12: B.V. Mary in Porticu, greater double. Com. St. Alexius, Conf.
    10, 13: Com. St. Kenelm, King, Mart.
28 12: St. Samson, Bp. and Conf., double. Com. SS. Nazarius and others, MM.
30 11: Bl. Everard Hanse, Mart., double.
    9, 12: Bl. Edward Powell and Comp. MM., greater double.
    18: St. Germanus, Bp. and Conf., double. Com. SS. Abdon and Sennen, MM.
31 16: Com. St. Germanus, Bp. and Conf.

AUGUST

3   9, 12: St. Germanus, Bp. and Conf., double. Com. Finding of St. Stephen, Protomart.
5   7: Com. St. Oswald, King, Mart.
8   14: St. Oswald, King, Mart., double. Com. SS. Cyriacus, Largus and Smaragdus, MM.

9 1, 2, 3, 8: St. Oswald, King, Mart., double. Com. St. John Mary Vianney, Conf. (exc. 2), Vigil of St. Lawrence and (2 only): St. Romanus, Mart.
11 2: St. John Mary Vianney, Conf., double.
    6: St. Oswald, King, Mart., double.
    14: St. Germanus, Bp. and Conf., double. Com. SS. Tiburtius and Susanna, Virg., MM.
18 15: double I class; 5: double; 6: simple. St. Helen, Empress, Widow. Com. St. Agapitus, Mart.
26 1, 3, 4: Bl. Thomas Percy, Mart., double.
    10: Bl. John Wall, Mart., double. Com. St. Zephyrinus, Pope and Mart.
31 1, 2, 3, 6, 8, 11, 16: St. Aidan, Bp. and Conf., double. Com. St. Raymund Nonnatus, Conf.

SEPTEMBER

1 7: Bl. Hugh More, Mart., double. Com. St. Giles, Ab. and the holy twelve Brethren MM.
   10: St. Giles, Abb., double. Com. the holy twelve Brethren MM.
   15: St. Sebbi, King, Conf., double. Com. St. Giles, Abb. and the holy twelve Brethren, MM.
4 15: SS. Hildelitha and Cuthberga VV., double. Com. St. Pius X, P.C.
   1: Translation of St. Cuthbert, Bp. and Conf., greater double.
6 2: St. Begh, Virg., double.
† 7 St. Evurtius, BC.
11 9: St. Deiniol, Bp. and Conf., double. Com. SS. Protus and Hyacinth MM.
16 1, 2: St. Ninian, Bp. and Conf., double. Com. SS. Cornelius, P. and Cyprian Bp., MM. and St. Euphemia, Virg. and others MM.
    13: Com. St. Edith, Virg.
†17 St. Lambert, B.M.
19 5, 14, 15, 17: St. Theodore, Bp. and Conf., double. Com. SS. Januarius and Comp., MM.
    1: Com St. Theodore.
25 9, 12: St. Cadoc, Bp. and Mart., double.
26 2: St. Theodore, Bp. and Conf., double. Com. SS. Cyprian and Justina, Virg., MM.
30 7, 17: Com. St. Honorius, Bp. and Conf.

OCTOBER

3 8: St. Thomas of Hereford, Bp. and Conf., double. Com. St. Teresa of the Infant Jesus, Virg., double.
   10: St. Teresa, Virg., double. Com St. Thomas.
5 5 (double); 12 (greater double): St. Thomas of Hereford, Bp. and Conf. Com. SS. Placid and Comp. MM.
† 6 St. Faith, V.M.
8 13: Com St. Keyna, Virg.

10 1, 2, 3, 4, 6, 7, 17: St. Paulinus, Bp. and Conf., double. Com. St. Francis Borgia, Conf.
12 1, 2, 6, 8, 10, 11, 17: St. Wilfrid, Bp. and Conf., double.
    3, 4, 16: the same, greater double. 7: the same, Com.
13 In England and Wales: St. Edward, King, Conf., double II class.
    City of Westminster: double I class. 14 (outside City), 15: greater double.
16 9: Bl. Richard Gwyn, M., double.
19 10: St. Frideswide, Virg., greater double. Com. St. Peter of Alcantara, Conf.
21 3: St. John of Bridlington, Conf., double. Com. St. Hilarion, Abb, and SS. Ursula and Comp. VV. and MM.
22 14: St. Thomas of Hereford, Bp. and Conf., double.
24 16: Com. St. Maglorius (Malo) Bp. and Conf.
25 4, 6: St. John of Beverley, Bp. and Conf., double. Com SS. Chrysanthus and Daria, MM. 3: the same, greater double. † St. Crispin, Mart.
26 2: St. Eata, Bp. and Conf., double. Com. St. Evaristus, Pope and Mart.
29 14: Bl. Martyrs of Douai, double.
30 1: The same, greater double.

NOVEMBER

3 8, 9: St. Winifred, Virg., greater double.
5 1, 2, 6, 9, 10, 12, 14, 15, 16: Sacred Relics, greater double.
6 12: St. Illtyd, Abb., greater double. † St. Leonard, Abb.
7 1: St. Willibrord, Bp. and Conf., simple.
10 17: St. Justus, Bp. and Conf., double. Com. St. Andrew Avellini, Conf. and SS. Tryphon and others, MM.
†13 St. Britius, B.C.
14 12: St. Dubritius (Dyfrig), Bp. and Conf., double. Com. St. Josaphat, Bp. and Mart.
    16: Com. Bl. Hugh Cook and Comp. MM.
15 13: Bl. Richard Whiting, Abb. and Comp. MM., double. Com. St. Albert the Great, Bp., Conf. and Doct. of the Ch. † St. Machutus B.C.
16 All England (exc. 1, 2, 7 and Herefordshire): St. Edmund, Bp. and Conf., greater double. Com. St. Gertrude, Virg.
17 10, 11, 13, 14: St. Hugh, Bp. and Conf., double.
    7: the same, double II class.
    3: St. Hilda, Virg., double. Com. St. Gregory Thaumaturgus, Bp. and Conf.
20 11, 14: St. Edmund, King Mart., greater double. Com. St. Felix de Valois, Conf.
27 13: Com. St. Cungar, Abb.

Calendar

29   2, 6, 11, 14, 18: **Bl. Cuthbert Mayne**, Mart., double. Com. St. Saturninus, Mart. In Advent, com. feria.

DECEMBER

1   7: **Bl. Ralph Sherwine**, Mart., double.
    10: **Bl. Martyrs of University of Oxford**, double.
    11, 16: **Bl. Edmund Campion and Comp. MM.**, double.
    14: **Bl. Richard Whiting and Comp. MM.**, double.
    15: **Bl. John Beche**, Mart., double.

4   13, 14, 18: **St. Osmund**, Bp. and Conf., double. Com. Feria and St. Peter Chrysologus, Bp., Conf. and Doct. of the Ch.

5   10, 16: **St. Birinus**, Bp. and Conf., double. Com. Feria and St. Sabbas, Ab.

10   3: Translation of the holy House of the B.V.M., greater double. Com. Feria and St. Melchiades, Pope and Mart.

    9: **Bl. John Roberts**, Mart., double. Com. feria and S. Melchiades, Pope, M.

29   In all England and Wales: **St. Thomas of Canterbury**, Bp. and Mart., double II class. (11: double I class). Com. Octave of the Nativity.

30   10: **St. Egwin**, Bp and Conf., double. Com. Oct. of the Nativity.

MASSES of SAINTS

PROPER TO

ENGLAND AND WALES

FEASTS OF NOVEMBER
2, 6, 11, 14, 18

November 29.

Blessed Cuthbert Maine

Martyr

Double.

The Mass In virtute, p. [6], except the Collect and the Epistle.

Collect.

O GOD, who for the salvation of souls didst grant unto blessed Cuthbert before the other students of the Seminaries, to run the way of torments: mercifully grant unto us; that kindled by the same zeal for souls, we may not fear to lay down our lives for others. Through.

Commemoration of the Feria in Advent, p. 546, and of St. Saturninus, p. 549.

The Lesson from the Epistle of blessed James the Apostle.

James 1, 2-12.

DEARLY beloved: Count it all joy when ye fall into divers temptations: knowing this, that the trying of your faith worketh patience. But let patience have her perfect work: that ye may be perfect and entire, wanting nothing. If any of you lack wisdom, let him ask of God, that giveth to all men liberally, and upbraideth not: and it shall be given him. But let him ask in faith, nothing wavering: for he that wavereth is like a wave of the sea driven with the wind and tossed. For let not that man think that he shall receive any thing of the Lord. A double minded man is unstable in all his ways. Let the brother of low degree rejoice in that he is exalted: but the rich, in that he is made low, because as the flower of the grass he shall pass away: for the sun is no sooner risen with a burning heat, but it withereth the grass, and the flower thereof faileth, and the grace of the fashion of it perisheth: so also shall the rich man fade away in his ways. Blessed is the man that endureth temptation: for when he is tried, he shall receive the crown of life, which the Lord hath promised to them that love him.

Secret.

WE beseech thee, O Lord, to accept our prayers and oblations: and graciously hearken unto us, whom thou dost cleanse by thy heavenly mysteries. Through.

Postcommunion.

GRANT, we beseech thee, O Lord our God: that as we in this life do gladly honour the memory of thy Saints, so we may rejoice to behold them for ever. Through.

FEASTS OF DECEMBER

14

December 1.

Blessed Richard Whiting, Hugh Faringdon and John Beche

Abbots with their Companions,

Martyrs

Double.

Introit. Ps. 80, 8. Vineam.

THOU hast brought a vine out of Egypt: thou hast cast out the heathen and planted it. The hills were covered with the shadow of it: and the boughs thereof were like the goodly cedar-trees. Ps. ibid., 1. Hear, O thou Shepherd of Israel, thou that leadest Joseph like a sheep. ℣. Glory.

Collect.

GRANT, we beseech thee, almighty God: that we, who know these glorious Abbots and their Companions to have been Martyrs for the unity of thy Church and valiant in their confession; may perceive their loving intercession for us with thee. Through.

In Advent, Commemoration of the Feria.

The Lesson from the Prophet Jeremiah.

Lamentations 5, 1-7.

REMEMBER, O Lord, what is come upon us: consider, and behold our reproach. Our inheritance is turned to strangers, our houses to aliens. We are orphans and fatherless, our mothers are as widows. We have drunken our water for money: our wood is sold unto us. Our necks are under persecution: we labour, and have no rest. We have given the hand to the Egyptians, and to the Assyrians, to be satisfied with bread. Our fathers have sinned, and are not: and we have borne their iniquities.

Gradual. Is. 51, 3. The Lord shall comfort Sion: he will comfort all her waste places; and he will make her wilderness like Eden, and her desert like the garden of the Lord. ℣. Joy and gladness shall be found therein, thanksgiving and the voice of melody.

Alleluia, alleluia. ℣. The noble army of Martyrs praise thee, O Lord. Alleluia.

✠ The Continuation of the holy Gospel according to Matthew.

Matt. 16, 13-18.

AT that time: Jesus saith unto his disciples: But whom say ye that I am? And Simon Peter answered and said: Thou art the Christ, the Son of the living God. And Jesus answered and said unto him: Blessed art thou, Simon Barjona: for flesh and blood hath not revealed it unto thee, but my Father who is in heaven. And I say also unto thee. That thou art Peter, and upon this rock I will build my Church, and the gates of hell shall not prevail against it.

Offertory. Is. 51, 1-2. Look unto the rock whence ye are hewn. Look unto Abraham your father: for I called him alone, and blessed him, and increased him.

Secret.

WE beseech thee, O Lord, that the confession of thy blessed Abbots and Martyrs, Richard, Hugh, John and their Companions, may be pleasing unto thee: and both commend our gifts, and ever implore for us thy pardon. Through.

In Advent, Commemoration of the Feria.

Communion. Ps. 80, 14-15. Look down from heaven: behold, and visit this vine; and the place of the vineyard that thy right hand hath planted.

Postcommunion.

WE beseech thee, O Lord, that the holy sacraments which we have received may, through the prayers of thy blessed Martyrs Richard, Hugh, John, and their Companions, increase in us both contempt of the world, and stedfastness in the faith. Through.

In Advent, Commemoration of the Feria, p. 546.

10

The same day, December 1.

Blessed Martyrs of the University of Oxford

Double.

The Mass Intret, p. [9], except the Prayers and Epistle.

Collect. P

O GOD, who didst strengthen thy blessed Martyrs Edmund and his Companions with invincible courage for the defence of the true faith and the primacy of the Apostolic See: hearken, we beseech thee, to their prayers; and succour our infirmity, that we being stedfast in the faith may be able to resist the adversary even to the end. Through.

In Advent, Commemoration of the Feria, p. 546.

The Lesson from the book of the Revelation of blessed John the Apostle.

Rev. 7, 13.

IN those days: One of the elders answered, saying unto me: What are these which are arrayed in white robes? and whence came they? And I said unto him: Sir, thou knowest. And he said to me: These are they which came out of great tribulation, and have washed their robes, and made them white in the blood of the Lamb. Therefore are they before the throne of God, and serve him day and night in his temple: and he that sitteth on the throne shall dwell among them: they shall hunger no more, neither thirst any more, neither shall the sun light on them, nor any heat: for the Lamb which is in the midst of the throne shall feed them, and shall lead them unto living fountains of waters: and God shall wipe away all tears from their eyes.

Secret. P

MAY the gifts of thy people, O Lord, become more acceptable to thee through the commemoration of thy blessed Martyrs: and by this holy oblation and partaking avail for our salvation unto everlasting life. Through.

Postcommunion. P

O LORD Jesu Christ, whom we proclaim glorious in the charity of thy blessed Martyrs: grant, we beseech thee, through their prayers; that we may ever abide in thy love: Who livest.

11, 16

The same day, December 1.

Blessed Edmund Campion and Companions

Martyrs.

Double.

The Mass Intret, p. [9], with Collect and Epistle as below.

Collect. P

O LORD Jesu Christ, who in the likeness of thy Passion didst adorn blessed Edmund and his Companions thy Priests with betrayal, torments and a shameful death: grant that by their merits and intercession we, constantly bearing thy Cross; may attain unto the crown of eternal glory. Through.

In Advent, Commemoration of the Feria, p. 546.

The Lesson from the Epistle of blessed Paul the Apostle to the Hebrews.

Heb. 11, 33.

BRETHREN: The saints through faith subdued kingdoms, wrought righteousness, obtained promises, stopped the mouths of lions, quenched the violence of fire, escaped the edge of the sword, out of weakness were made strong, waxed valiant in fight, turned to flight the armies of the aliens: women received their dead raised to life again: and others were tortured, not accepting deliverance, that they might obtain a better resurrection: and others had trial of cruel mockings and scourgings, yea, moreover of bonds and imprisonment: they were stoned, they were sawn asunder, were tempted, were slain with the sword: they wandered about in sheepskins and goatskins, being destitute, afflicted, tormented: (of whom the world was not worthy:) they wandered in deserts, and in mountains, and in dens and caves of the earth. And these all obtained a good report through faith, and were found in Christ Jesus our Lord.

15

December 1.

Blessed John Beche

Abbot, and Companions, Martyrs

Double.

Mass as on p. 863, substituting Abbot John and his Companions.

7

The same day, December 1.

Blessed Ralph Sherwine

Martyr

Double.

Mass In virtute, p. [6].

13, 14, 18

December 4.

St. Osmund

Bishop and Confessor

Double.

The Mass Statuit, for a Confessor Bishop p. [19], the Prayers excepted. The Creed is not said.

Collect. P

ALMIGHTY and everlasting God, who on this day dost gladden us with the feast of blessed Osmund thy Confessor and Bishop: we humbly beseech thy mercy; that we, who devoutly celebrate his festival, may by his gracious intercession, attain unto the glory (13: rewards) of everlasting life. Through.

Commemoration of St. Peter Chrysologus, B.C.D., and the Feria, p. 546.

14, 18

Secret. P

SANCTIFY, O Lord, we beseech thee, by the bounteous merits and intercession of thy Confessor Osmund, these our oblations: that they may be changed into the body and blood of thy Son our Lord Jesus Christ, and be profitable for the salvation of our souls. Through the same.

Postcommunion. P

WE humbly beseech thee, O Lord, that we who have received these sacred gifts: may be so strengthened by the power of the same, that following the example of blessed Osmund thy Confessor and Bishop; we may attain to everlasting felicity. Through.

13

The Mass as above, except the following:

Gradual. Ps. 110, 4. The Lord sware and will not repent: Thou art a priest for ever after the order of Melchisedech. ℣. Ibid., 1. The Lord said unto my Lord: Sit thou at my right hand.

Alleluia, alleluia. ℣. Hos. 14. The just shall grow as the lily: and flourish for ever before the Lord. Alleluia.

Secret.

WE beseech thee, O Lord, mercifully hearken unto these our supplications: and, at the intercession of blessed Osmund on our behalf, grant that we who minister these heavenly sacraments may be free from all sin; that, through thy purifying grace, we may be cleansed by those same mysteries which we serve. Through.

Communion. Matt. 25. Lord, thou deliveredst unto me five talents: behold I have gained beside them five talents more. Well done, thou good and faithful servant, thou hast been faithful over a few things, I will make thee ruler over many things, enter thou into the joy of thy lord.

Postcommunion.

GRANT, we beseech thee, O Lord our God: that, being cleansed by divine mysteries, we who have tasted of holy things may, at the intercession of blessed Osmund thy Confessor and Bishop, attain unto the fulness of this heavenly Sacrament. Through.

10, 16.

December 5.

St. Birinus
Bishop and Confessor
Double.

The Mass *Statuit*, for a Confessor Bishop p. [19], with Commemoration of the Feria, p. 546, and of St. Sabbas, p. 555.

3

December 10.

Translation of the Holy House of the Blessed Virgin Mary
Greater double.

Introit. Gen. 28, 17. Terribilis est.

HOW dreadful is this place: this is the house of God and the gate of heaven: and it shall be called the palace of God. Ps. 84, 1. O how amiable are thy dwellings: thou Lord of hosts! My soul hath a desire and longing to enter into the courts of the Lord. ℣. Glory.

Collect.

O GOD, who through the mystery of the Word made flesh didst in thy mercy sanctify the house of the blessed Virgin Mary, and wondrously place it in the bosom of thy Church: grant; that we, being made separate from the tabernacles of sinners, may become worthy to dwell in thy holy house. Through the same.

Commemoration of the Feria, p. 546.

The Lesson from the book of Wisdom.
Ecclus. 24, 7.

IN all things I sought rest, and in the inheritance of the Lord shall I abide. So the Creator of all things gave me a commandment: and he that made me caused my tabernacle to rest, and said: Let thy dwelling be in Jacob, and thine inheritance in Israel: and take root in my elect. And so was I established in Sion, likewise in the beloved city he gave me rest, and in Jerusalem was my power. And I took root in an honourable people, even in the portion of the Lord's inheritance, and my abode is in the full assembly of the Saints. I was exalted like a cedar in Libanus, and as a cypress tree upon the mountains of Hermon; I was exalted like a palm tree in En-gaddi, and as a rose plant in Jericho; as a fair olive tree in a pleasant field, and grew up as a plane tree by the water in the streets. I gave a sweet smell like cinnamon and aspálathus: and I yielded a pleasant odour like the best myrrh.

Gradual. Ps. 27, 4. One thing have I desired of the Lord which I will require, that I may dwell in the house of the Lord all the days of my life. ℣. That I may behold the fair beauty of the Lord, and visit his temple.

Alleluia, alleluia. ℣. Ps. 84, 4. Blessed are they that dwell in thy house, O Lord: they shall praise thee for ever and ever. Alleluia.

☩ The Continuation of the holy Gospel according to Luke.

Luke 1, 26.

AT that time: The Angel Gabriel was sent from God unto a city of Galilee named Nazareth, to a Virgin espoused to a man whose name was Joseph, of the house of David, and the Virgin's name was Mary. And the Angel came in unto her, and said: Hail, full of grace: the Lord is with thee: blessed art thou among women. And when she saw him, she was troubled at his saying, and cast in her mind what manner of salutation this should be. And the Angel said unto her: Fear not, Mary, for thou hast found favour with God. And behold, thou shalt conceive in thy womb and bring forth a Son, and shalt call his name Jesus. He shall be great, and shall be called the Son of the Highest, and the Lord God shall give unto him the throne of his father David: and he shall reign over the house of Jacob for ever; and of his kingdom there shall be no end. Then said Mary unto the Angel: How shall this be, seeing I know not a man? And the Angel answered and said unto her: The Holy Ghost shall come upon thee, and the power of the Highest shall overshadow thee. Therefore also that Holy Thing which shall be born of thee shall be called the Son of God. And behold, thy cousin Elisabeth, she hath also conceived a son in her old age: and this is the sixth month with her who was called barren: for with God nothing shall be impossible. And Mary said: Behold the handmaid of the Lord, be it unto me according to thy word. Creed.

Offertory. Ps. 5, 7. I will come into thy house: I will worship toward thy holy temple, and I will confess thy name.

Secret.

ACCEPT, we beseech thee, O Lord, the gifts which we duly offer unto thee in this sacred house: and grant, by the pleading of the merits of blessed Mary the Virgin, that they may avail for our help unto salvation. Through.

Preface of the B.V. Mary, And that on the Festival.

Communion. Prov. 8. Blessed is the man that heareth me, watching daily at my gates, guarding the posts of my doors. For whoso findeth me, findeth life, and shall obtain salvation from the Lord.

Postcommunion.

WE beseech thee, O Lord our God: that through the intercession of blessed Mary ever Virgin, these most holy mysteries, which thou hast bestowed upon us as a defence for our regenerated nature, may avail for our healing both now and in the world to come. Through.

9: The same day, December 10.

Blessed John Roberts

Martyr.

Double.

The Mass In virtute, p. [6], except:

Collect. P

O GOD, who didst make blessed John to labour valiantly for the defence and freedom of thy Church, and didst reward him with the palm of martyrdom: grant us, through his example and intercession; that we may both live and die in loving obedience to the same Holy See. Through.

Commemoration of Feria, p. 546 and S. Melchiades, P.M., p. 560.

All England and Wales:
December 29.

St. Thomas of Canterbury

Bishop and Martyr

Double of 2nd class (11: double of 1st cl.)

Mass as on p. 34.

10

December 30.

St. Egwin

Bishop and Confessor

Double.

The Mass Statuit, for a Confessor Bishop, p. [19], except:

Collect.

O GOD, who on this day didst translate the soul of blessed Egwin thy Confessor and Bishop unto everlasting joys: grant unto us through his prayers; humbly to press onward to the place whither that glorious shepherd, led by thee, is gone before. Through.

Commemoration of the Octave. And the Creed is said.

Preface and Canon of the Nativity.

FEASTS OF JANUARY

17

January 12.

Commemoration of St. Benedict Biscop

Abbot

The Mass Os justi, for an Abbot p. [26], the Collect excepted.

Collect. P

O GOD, by whose gift the blessed Abbot Benedict left all things that he might become perfect: vouchsafe unto all who have entered upon the path of evangelical perfection; that they may neither look back, nor linger on the way, but pressing on towards thee without stumbling, may lay hold of everlasting life. Through.

Secret. C

WE beseech thee, O Lord, that thy holy Abbot Benedict may intercede for us: that this sacrifice which we offer and present upon thy holy altar may be profitable unto us for our salvation. Through.

Postcommunion. C

LET thy Sacrament, O Lord, which we have now received, and the prayers of the blessed Abbot Benedict, defend us: that we may both imitate the example of his conversation and receive the succour of his intercession. Through.

5, 6, 9

January 14.

St. Kentigern

Bishop and Confessor

Double.

The Mass Statuit, for a Confessor Bishop, p. [19], the Prayers excepted.

Collect. P

O GOD, who wast pleased that through blessed Kentigern, thy Confessor and Bishop, the light of the true faith should shine upon the barbarian people: grant, we beseech thee; that we, faithfully following that which he preached and taught, may attain unto the glory of everlasting brightness. Through.

Commemoration of St. Hilary, B.C.D., p. 564.

The Creed is not said.

Secret. P

SANCTIFY, O Lord, we beseech thee, the gift which we offer to thy majesty in honour of Saint Kentigern, thy Bishop: that the same may be acceptable unto thee, and profitable for our salvation. Through.

Postcommunion. P

O LORD, who hast refreshed us with these heavenly mysteries, which on the solemnity of Saint Kentigern thy Bishop we have offered unto thy majesty: we humbly beseech thee; that through him and with him we may rejoice in everlasting felicity. Through.

11

January 16.
St. Fursey
Abbot
Double.

The Mass Os justi, for an Abbot, p. [26].

Commemoration of St. Marcellus I, P.M. p. 567.

2

January 19.
St. Kentigern
Bishop and Confessor
Double.

Mass as on January 14th above.

Commemoration of SS. Marius, etc., MM., and of St. Canute, K.M., p. 571.

6

The same day, January 19.
St. Benedict Biscop
Bishop and Abbot
Double.

Mass as on January 12th above.

10, 11, 13

The same day, January 19.
St. Wulfstan
Bishop and Confessor
Double.

The Mass Sacerdotes tui, p. [20], the Prayers excepted.

Collect. P

POUR forth upon us, O Lord, the Spirit of thy charity: that by the intercession of blessed Wulfstan, thy Confessor and Bishop, we may be worthy to taste of thy sweetness in everlasting felicity. Through ... in the unity of the same Holy Spirit.

Commemoration of SS. Marius, etc., MM, and of St. Canute, K.M. p. 571.

Secret. P

RECEIVE, we beseech thee, O Lord, the gift which we thy family humbly offer: and through the intercession of blessed Wulfstan, mercifully grant unto us those things for which our guilty conscience dares not hope. Through.

Postcommunion. P

O LORD, who hast fulfilled us with the mystery of thy salvation, we humbly entreat thy mercy: that he whom thou hast given to be our advocate and guide may never fail to pray for us. Through.

FEASTS OF FEBRUARY
9, 12, 16

February 1.
St. Brigid
Virgin
Double.

16: Commemoration only.

The Mass Dilexisti, p. [44], except:

Collect.

O GOD, who on this day dost make us to rejoice in the yearly festival of blessed Brigid thy Virgin: mercifully grant; that we who are enlightened by the example of her purity may be aided by her merits. Through.

Commemoration of St. Ignatius, B.M., p. 585.

14, 17
February 3.
St. Lawrence
Bishop and Confessor
Double.

The Mass Sacerdotes tui, for a Confessor Bishop, p. [20], with Commemoration of St. Blasius, B.M., p. 591.

8, 10
The same day, February 3.
St. Werburgh
Virgin
Double.

The Mass Dilexisti, p. [31], with Commemoration of St. Blasius, p. 591.

1
February 4.
Blessed Thomas Plumtree and Companions
Martyrs
Double.

The Mass Intret, p. [9], with Collect from Mass Salus autem p. [12].

Commemoration of St. Andrew Corsini, B.C., p. 592.

12
February 9.
St. Teilo
Bishop and Confessor
Double.

The Mass Statuit, for a Confessor Bishop, p. [19].

Commemoration of St. Cyril of Alexandria, B.C.D., and St. Apollonia, V.M., p. 596.

In Lent, Commemoration of the Feria and St. Cyril only.

The Creed is not said.

Feb. 13-17. In Lent, Commemoration of the Feria.

1
February 13.
St. Benedict Biscop
Abbot
Double.

Mass as on January 12, p. 867.

7, 11
February 16.
St. Gilbert
Confessor.
Double.

The Mass Justus ut palma, p. [25].

2
February 17.
St. Finan
Bishop and Confessor
Double.

The Mass Statuit, for a Confessor Bishop, p. [19].

8
February 23.
St. Milburga
Virgin
Double.

The Mass Dilexisti, p. [31].
In Lent, Commemoration of the Feria.

7
February 24.
(or 25 in Leap Year.)
Commemoration of St. Ethelbert
King and Confessor
Prayers as below, February 25.

18
February 25 (or 26).
St. Walburga
Virgin
Double.

The Mass Dilexisti, p. [31], except:

Collect.

O GOD, who among the countless gifts of thy grace dost work thy wonders even in the weakness of women: mercifully grant; that we, who are not only enlightened by the example of the chastity of blessed Walburga thy Virgin but also gladdened by the glory of her miracles, may perceive her to be our advocate at thy mercy-seat. Through.

In Lent, Commemoration of the Feria.

14, 17
February 25 (or 26).

11
February 26 (or 27).
St. Ethelbert
King and Confessor
Double.

The Mass Os justi, for a Confessor not a Bishop, p. [24], the Collect excepted.

Collect. P

O GOD, who didst crown the blessed King Ethelbert with the glory of eternity: make us we beseech thee, so to venerate him upon earth, that we may reign with him in heaven. Through.

In Lent, Commemoration of the Feria.

Secret. C

WE offer thee, O Lord, this sacrifice of praise in commemoration of thy Saints: whereby we trust to be delivered from evil both present and to come. Through.

Postcommunion. C

O LORD, our God, who hast refreshed us with heavenly meat and drink, we humbly beseech thee: that we may be defended by the prayers of him in whose memory we have received the same. Through.

10
February 28 (or 29).
St. Oswald
Bishop and Confessor
Double.

The Mass Statuit, for a Confessor Bishop, p. [19].

In Lent, Commemoration of the Feria.

FEASTS OF MARCH

9, 12, 14, 16
March 1.
St. David
Bishop and Confessor

14, 16
Double.

9, 12
Double of 1st class. (Patron of Wales.)

The Mass Statuit, for a Confessor Bishop, p. [19], the Collect excepted.

Collect. P

GRANT to us, almighty God: that the gracious intercession of blessed David, thy Confessor and Bishop, may protect us; that as we celebrate his festival, so we may imitate his stedfastness in the defence of the catholic faith. Through.

In Lent, Commemoration of the Feria.
9, 12: The Creed is said.

Secret. C

WE beseech thee, O Lord, that we, remembering with gladness the merits of thy Saints, may in all places feel the succour of their intercession. Through.

Postcommunion. C

GRANT, we beseech thee, almighty God: that we, shewing forth our thankfulness for the gifts which we have received, may, at the intercession of blessed David, thy Confessor and Bishop, obtain yet more abundant mercies. Through.

1, 3, 4, 5, 6, 7, 8, 10
March 2.
St. Chad
Bishop and Confessor

Double.

1: Simple.

10: Double of 1st class.   Creed.

The Mass Sacerdotes tui, for a Confessor Bishop, p. [20], the Prayers excepted.

Collect.   P

ALMIGHTY and everlasting God, who on this day dost gladden us by the festival of blessed Chad, thy Confessor and Bishop: we humbly beseech thy mercy; that we who devoutly celebrate his festival, may by his loving advocacy obtain the reward of everlasting life. Through.

In Lent, Commemoration of the Feria.

Secret.   P

WE beseech thee, O Lord, mercifully hearken unto our supplications: and at the intercession of blessed Chad thy Confessor and Bishop on our behalf, grant that we who minister thy heavenly sacraments may be free from all sin; that through thy purifying grace we may be cleansed by those same mysteries which we serve.   Through.

In Lent, Commemoration of the Feria.

Postcommunion.   P

GRANT, we beseech thee, O Lord our God: that being cleansed by these heavenly mysteries, we who have tasted of holy things, may at the intercession of blessed Chad thy Confessor and Bishop, attain to the fulness of this heavenly Sacrament.   Through.

In Lent, Commemoration of the Feria.

1, 3, 6, 7
March 3.
St. Aelred
Abbot

Double.

In Lent, Commemoration of the Feria..

The Mass Os justi, for an Abbot, p. [26], the Collect excepted.

7: Commemoration.

Mass of the Feria, with Commemoration of the Feast.

Collect.   P

ALMIGHTY and everlasting God, who ceasest not to instruct the children of thy Church, and likewise failest not to help them: grant to thy faithful, at the intercession of thy blessed Abbot Aelred, that, as thou hast given him unto them to be a minister of everlasting salvation, so they may by thy mercy be enabled to know the things that be right, and also have power to fulfil the same.   Through.

Secret.   C

WE beseech thee, O Lord, that thy holy Abbot Aelred, may intercede for us: that this sacrifice which we offer and present upon thy holy altar may be profitable unto us for our salvation. Through.

Postcommunion.   C

LET thy Sacrament, O Lord, which we have now received, and the prayers of the blessed Abbot Aelred effectually defend us: that we may both imitate the example of his conversation, and receive the succour of his intercession.   Through.

11
March 8.
St. Felix
Bishop and Confessor

Double.

The Mass Statuit, for a Confessor Bishop, p. [19].

Commemoration of the Feria and of St. John of God, C., p. 610.

15
March 11.
Blessed John Larke
Martyr

Double.

The Mass Laetabitur, p. [7], except the Epistle.

Commemoration of the Feria.

The Lesson from the Epistle of blessed Peter the Apostle.

I Pet. 4, 13-19.

DEARLY beloved: Rejoice, inasmuch as ye are partakers of Christ's sufferings; that, when his glory shall be revealed, ye may be glad also with exceeding joy. If ye be reproached for the name of Christ, happy are ye: for the spirit of glory and of God resteth upon you. But let none of you suffer as a murderer, or as a thief, or as an evildoer, or as a busybody in other men's matters. Yet if any man suffer as a Christian, let him not be ashamed: but let him glorify God on this behalf. For the time is come that judgment must begin at the house of God. And if it first begin at us: what shall the end be of them that obey not the gospel of God? And if the righteous scarcely be saved, where shall the ungodly and the sinner appear? Wherefore let them that suffer according to the will of God commit the keeping of their souls to him in well doing, as unto a faithful Creator.

10
March 13.
Blessed Agnellus of Pisa
Confessor

Double.

The Mass Os justi, for a Confessor not a Bishop, p. [24], except:

Collect.

O LORD Jesu Christ, who didst cause blessed Agnellus to leave the enticements of the world, and to turn to the following of thy Cross: make us so to follow in his footsteps; that we may be worthy to win the crown of glory which he hath received in heaven. Through.

Commemoration of the Feria.

18
March 18.
St. Edward
King and Martyr

Double.

The Mass Laetabitur, p. [7], the Collect and Gospel excepted.

Collect.

O GOD, the triumphant ruler of an everlasting kingdom, mercifully behold this thy family who celebrate the memory of blessed Edward, thy King and Martyr: and, by his merits and intercession, vouchsafe; that they who glory in his triumph may also attain unto his rewards. Through.

Commemoration is made of the Feria and of St. Cyril of Jerusalem, B.C.D., p. 613.

✠ The Continuation of the holy Gospel according to Matthew.

Matt. 16, 24-27.

AT that time; Jesus said unto his disciples: If any man will come after me, let him deny himself, and take up his cross, and follow me. For whosoever will save his life shall lose it: and whosoever will lose his life for my sake shall find it. For what is a man profited, if he shall gain the whole world, and lose his own soul? Or what shall a man give in exchange for his soul? For the Son of man shall come in the glory of his Father with his Angels: and then he shall reward every man according to his works.

The Creed is not said.

Secret. C

GRANT, O Lord, that this our bounden service may be acceptable in thy sight: that these our oblations may, by the prayers of him on whose solemnity they are offered, be made profitable unto our salvation. Through.

Commemoration of the Feria and St. Cyril, p. 614.

Postcommunion. C

WE beseech thee, O Lord our God, that as we, whom thou hast refreshed by the partaking of thy sacred gift, offer unto thee our worship: so by the intercession of blessed Edward thy Martyr, we may perceive the benefit of the same. Through.

Commemoration of the Feria and St. Cyril, p. 614.

1, 2, 6, 8
March 20.

St. Cuthbert

Bishop and Confessor

1: Double of 1st class. Creed.

2: Greater double.

6, 8: Double.

The Mass **Sacerdotes tui**, for a Confessor Bishop, p. [20], the Prayers excepted.

Collect. P

O GOD, who dost make thy Saints glorious by the inestimable gift of thy grace: grant, we beseech thee; that at the intercession of blessed Cuthbert, thy Confessor and Bishop, we may be found worthy to attain to the perfection of all virtue. Through.

Commemoration of the Feria.

Secret. P

ACCEPT, we beseech thee, O Lord, the sacrifice of man's redemption: and at the intercession of blessed Cuthbert thy Confessor and Bishop, mercifully grant us health of body and soul. Through.

Commemoration of the Feria.

Postcommunion. P

WE beseech thee, O Lord, that thy holy things which we have received may protect us by their power: and at the intercession of blessed Cuthbert, thy Confessor and Bishop, whose life shone forth in glory, guard us in peace and holiness. Through.

Commemoration of the Feria.

18
March 28.

For St. Stephen

Abbot

Simple.

The Mass **Os justi**, for an Abbot, p. [26], the Collect excepted.

In Lent, Mass of the Feria, with Commemoration of St. Stephen, Abbot, as below, and of St. John of Capistrano, Conf., p. 622.

Collect.

O GOD, by whose gift the blessed Abbot Stephen forsook all things that he might become perfect: grant unto all who have entered upon the path of evangelical perfection; that they may neither look back nor falter in the way, but pressing on towards thee without offence, may lay hold of everlasting life to which they have been called. Through.

Secret. C

O LORD, we beseech thee, let thy holy Abbot Stephen intercede for us: that this sacrifice which we offer and present upon thy holy altar may be profitable unto us for our salvation. Through.

Postcommunion. C

LET thy Sacrament, O Lord, which we have now received, and the prayers of thy blessed Abbot Stephen, effectually defend us: that we may both imitate the example of his conversation, and receive the succour of his intercession. Through.

10

March 30.
St. Osburga
Virgin
Double.

The Mass Dilexisti, p. [31]. Commemoration of the Feria.

FEASTS OF APRIL

11

April 2.
Blessed John Payne
Martyr
Double.

The Mass In virtute, p. [6]. Commemoration of the Feria and of St. Francis de Paula, C., p. 625.

15

April 3.
Blessed John Payne
Martyr
Double.

Mass as above, except the following:

Collect. P

O GOD, who didst make blessed John to triumph in the power of the most holy name of Jesus: make us by his intercession so to be strengthened in the love of thy name; that we may never be separated by any temptations from thee. Through.

10, 14, 17

April 3.
St Richard
Bishop and Confessor
Double.

The Mass Statuit, for a Confessor Bishop, p. [19], the Prayers excepted.

Collect. P

O GOD, who by the merits of blessed Richard, thy Confessor and Bishop, didst illumine thy Church with wondrous miracles: grant through his intercession; that we thy servants may attain unto the glory of everlasting felicity. Through.

In Lent, Commemoration of the Feria.

Secret. P

GRANT, we beseech thee, O merciful God: that at the intercession of blessed Richard, thy Confessor and Bishop, the gifts which we offer in the sight of thy majesty may obtain for us grace to serve thee in this life, and bring us in the end to everlasting glory. Through.

In Lent, Commemoration of the Feria.

Postcommunion. P

O LORD, who didst make blessed Richard a faithful steward of these most holy mysteries: grant, we beseech thee; that the same may accomplish in us, who have received them, the effectual work of our salvation. Through.

In Lent, Commemoration of the Feria.

14
April 17.
St. Stephen
Abbot
Simple.

Mass as on March 28, p. 874.

Commemoration of St. Anicetus, P.M. p. 631.

Preface of Easter.

13, 14, 16, 17
April 19.
St. Alphege
Bishop and Martyr
Double.

The Mass Protexisti, p. [15], the Collect and Epistle excepted.

Collect. P

O GOD, who didst adorn blessed Alphege (13: thy Bishop, elsewhere: most devout Confessor of thy name,) with the dignity of the priesthood and the palm of martyrdom: mercifully grant; that we may be so aided by his intercession before thee, that we may be enabled to rejoice with him in everlasting felicity. Through.

The Lesson from the Epistle of blessed Paul the Apostle to the Hebrews.

Heb. 5, 1-4.

BRETHREN: Every high priest taken from among men is ordained for men in things pertaining to God, that he may offer both gifts and sacrifices for sins: who can have compassion on the ignorant, and on them that are out of the way: for that he himself also is compassed with infirmity. And by reason hereof he ought, as for the people, so also for himself, to offer for sins. And no man taketh this honour to himself, but he that is called of God, as was Aaron.

14, 16, 17
Secret. C

WE beseech thee, O Lord, mercifully to accept this our sacrifice, which we offer unto thee, pleading the merits of blessed Alphege, thy Martyr and Bishop: that the same may effectually avail for our perpetual succour. Through.

Postcommunion. C

WE beseech thee, O Lord, our God, that as we, whom thou hast refreshed by the partaking of thy sacred gift, offer unto thee our worship: so by the intercession of blessed Alphege, thy Martyr and Bishop, we may perceive the benefit of the same. Through.

13
Secret and Postcommunion as below:

Secret. P

BLESS and thyself receive, O Lord, these gifts which we set upon thine altar: that by the intercession of blessed Alphege, thy Martyr and Bishop, they may effectually avail for our salvation both of soul and body. Through.

Postcommunion. P

O LORD, who hast bestowed on us this Sacrament, we humbly entreat thy mercy: that at the intercession of blessed Alphege, thy Martyr and Bishop, the mysteries which we celebrate in time we may receive unto life eternal. Through.

9
April 21.
St. Beuno
Abbot
Double.

The Mass Os justi, for an Abbot, p. [26].

Commemoration of St. Anselm, B.C.D. p. 631.

The Creed is not said.

(All England and Wales.)
April 23.
St. George
Martyr
Principal Patron of England
England: Double of 1st class.
Wales: Greater double.
Mass as on p. 633.

14, 15, 17
April 24.
St. Mellitus
Bishop and Confessor
14: Greater double. (15, 17: Double).

The Mass Statuit, for a Confessor Bishop, p. [19], with Prayers as below, and Commemoration of St. Fidelis, M., p. 634.

Collect. C 2

WE beseech thee, O Lord, graciously to hear the prayers which we offer unto thee on the solemnity of blessed Mellitus, thy Confessor and Bishop: that, as he was found worthy to do thee faithful service, so by his merits and intercession we may be absolved from all our sins. Through.

14, 15
Secret. C 2

WE beseech thee, O Lord, that our devout observance of the yearly solemnity of blessed Mellitus, thy Confessor and Bishop, may render us acceptable unto thy lovingkindness: that this service of propitiation, which we duly offer, may be profitable unto him for the reward of blessedness, and obtain for us the gifts of thy grace. Through.

Postcommunion. C 2

O GOD, who rewardest the souls of them that put their trust in thee: vouchsafe; that we who keep the solemn festival of blessed Mellitus, thy Confessor and Bishop, may by his prayers obtain thy merciful pardon. Through.

17
Secret. C 1

WE beseech thee, O Lord, that we, remembering with gladness the merits of thy Saints, may in all places feel the succour of their intercession. Through.

Postcommunion. C 1

GRANT we beseech thee, almighty God, that we, shewing forth our thankfulness for the gifts which we have received: may, at the intercession of blessed Mellitus, thy Confessor and Bishop, obtain yet more abundant mercies. Through.

1
April 24.
St. Egbert
Confessor
Double.

The Mass Os justi, for a Confessor not a Bishop, p. [24] except:

Collect. P

O GOD, by whose Spirit blessed Egbert, thirsting for salvation, did send forth the divers heralds of the faith for the work of the Gospel: direct, we beseech thee, at the intercession of his merits, the hearts of thy servants unto thee; that being filled with the fervour of thy Spirit, they may be found stedfast in faith and fruitful in work. Through... in the unity of the same holy Spirit.

Commemoration of St. Fidelis, M., p. 634.

Gospel The Lord appointed, as on Feast of St. Mark, p. 636.

6

April 27.

St. Maughold

Bishop and Confessor

Double.

The Mass Statuit, for a Confessor Bishop, p. [19].

Commemoration of St. Peter Canisius, C.D., p. 638.

The Creed is not said.

FEASTS OF MAY

All England and Wales:

May 4

Blessed Martyrs of England and Wales

Greater double.

Introit. Ps. 79, 1. Deus venerunt.

O GOD, the heathen are come into thine inheritance, thy holy temple have they defiled: and made Jerusalem an heap of stones, alleluia, alleluia. Ps. ibid., 2. The dead bodies of thy servants have they given to be meat unto the fowls of the air, and the flesh of thy saints unto the beasts of the land. ℣. Glory.

Collect.

O GOD, who from among all estates of the English people didst raise up thy blessed Martyrs, John the Bishop, Thomas, and their Companions to be defenders of the true faith and the supreme priesthood: grant through their merits and prayers; that by the profession of that same faith, we may all, as thy Son prayed, be made and continue one: Who with thee.

And Commemoration is made, in Low Masses only, of St. Monica, W.

Collect.

O GOD, the comforter of them that mourn and the salvation of them that hope in thee, who didst mercifully accept the loving tears of blessed Monica for the conversion of Augustine her son: grant to us by the intercession of them both; that we may bewail our sins, and obtain the abundant pardon of thy grace.

Another Collect, to be said in all Masses today, even if a Double of the 1st class be celebrated.

O GOD, who from the beginning of our infant Church didst make us the dowry of the Blessed Virgin Mary, and subject unto Peter the Prince of the Apostles: mercifully grant; that, in the stedfastness of the catholic faith, we may be enabled constantly to love the same most blessed Virgin, and to remain in the obedience of Peter. Through.

The Lesson from the Epistle of blessed Paul the Apostle to the Hebrews.

Heb. 12, 1-10.

SEEING we are compassed about with so great a cloud of witnesses, let us lay aside every weight, and the sin which doth so easily beset us, and let us run with patience the race that is set before us: looking unto Jesus the author and finisher of our faith, who for the joy that was set before him endured the cross, despising the shame, and is set down at the right hand of the throne of God. For consider him that endured such contradiction of sinners against himself: lest ye be wearied and faint in your minds. Ye have not yet resisted unto blood, fighting against sin: and ye have forgotten the exhortation which speaketh unto you as unto children: My son, despise not thou the chastening of the Lord, nor faint when thou art rebuked of him. For whom the Lord loveth he chasteneth: and scourgeth every son whom he receiveth. If ye endure chastening, God dealeth with you as with sons: for what son is he whom the father chasteneth not? But if ye be without chastisement, whereof all are partakers: then are ye bastards, and not sons. Furthermore we have had fathers of our flesh which corrected us, and we gave them reverence: shall we not much rather be in subjection unto the Father of spirits and live? For they verily for a few days chastened us after their own pleasure: but he for our profit, that we might be partakers of his holiness.

Alleluia, alleluia. ℣. Thy Saints, O Lord, shall grow as the lily, and as the odour of balsam shall they be before thee. Alleluia. ℣. Ps. 116, 15. Right dear in the sight of the Lord is the death of his Saints. Alleluia.

Out of Eastertide is said:

Gradual. Ps. 79, 3-4. Their blood have they shed like water on every side of Jerusalem, and there was no man to bury them: we are become an open shame to our enemies, a very scorn and derision unto them that are round about us. ℣. O remember not our old sins, but have mercy upon us, and that soon.

Alleluia, alleluia. ℣. Ibid., 13. So we that are thy people and the sheep of thy pasture, shall give thee thanks for ever. Alleluia.

✠ The Continuation of the holy Gospel according to John.

John 10, 24-30.

AT that time: Jesus walked in the temple in Solomon's porch. Then came the Jews round about him, and said unto him: How long dost thou make us to doubt? If thou be the Christ, tell us plainly. Jesus answered them: I told you, and ye believe not; the works that I do in my Father's name, they bear witness of me; but ye believe not, because ye are not of my sheep. My sheep hear my voice: and I know them, and they follow me: and I give unto them eternal life: and they shall never perish, and no man is able to pluck them out of my Father's hand. I and my Father are one.

Offertory. Baruch 3, 5-6. Remember not the iniquities of our forefathers, but think upon thy power and thy name now at this time: for thou art the Lord our God, and thee, O Lord, will we praise, alleluia.

Secret.

GRACIOUSLY hearken, O Lord, unto the voices of thy blessed Martyrs who cry from beneath thine altar, and mercifully regard our oblations. Through.

For St. Monica. Secret.

GRANT, O Lord, that like as thy faithful people do acknowledge that in tribulation they have been succoured by the merits of thy Saints: so this oblation, which they here do offer unto thee in honour of the same, may be acceptable in thy sight.

Another Secret to be said.

MOST gracious God, whose mercies are without number, graciously regard the oblation of this spotless host, at the intercession of the blessed Virgin Mary with Peter, Prince of the Apostles: and so illumine the mind of this people and inflame their hearts, that they may constantly perserve in that faith which worketh charity. Through.

Communion. Rev. 6, 9-11. Under the altar of God I heard the voice of them that were slain, saying: Wherefore dost thou not avenge our blood? And they received a divine answer: Rest yet for a little season, till the number of your brethren be fulfilled, alleluia.

Postcommunion.

O LORD, our God, who hast refreshed us with this heavenly banquet: we beseech thee; that by the intercession of thy blessed Martyrs, we may be made worthy to attain unto their fellowship. Through.

For St. Monica.   Postcommunion.

O LORD, who hast satisfied this thy family with thy sacred gifts; we beseech thee; that we may at all times be comforted by the intercession of her whose festival we celebrate.

Another Postcommunion to be said.

O GOD, who of old didst make our nation, the dowry of the blessed Virgin Mary, glorious by reason of its faithfulness unto Peter the Apostle: by the power of this sacrifice; strengthen it in the love of the same blessed Virgin Mary, and in obedience to the Apostolic See. Through.

1

May 6.

For Commemoration of St. Eadbert

Bishop and Confessor

The Mass Statuit, for a Confessor Bishop, p. [19].

1

May 7.

St. John of Beverly

Bishop and Confessor

Double.

The Mass Sacerdotes tui, for a Confessor Bishop, p. [24], except the following:

Collect.

O GOD, who hast hallowed this day by the festivity of blessed John, thy Confessor and Bishop: grant unto thy Church worthily to rejoice in his solemnity; that by his example and merits we may obtain the succour of thy mercy. Through.

Commemoration of St. Stanislaus, B.M., p. 650.

Secret.

MAY thy merciful kindness, O God, receive at our hands the gift which we offer: and by the prayers of thy holy Confessor and Bishop John absolve us from all our sins. Through.

Postcommunion.

O LORD, who hast sanctified us by these saving mysteries, we beseech thee: that as thou hast given unto us blessed John thy Confessor and Bishop for our advocate and guide, so we may ever be succoured by his intercession. Through.

17

May 11.

For Commemoration (in Low Mass) of St. Erconwald, B.C., the prayers as on 13th, p. 882.

3, 4

The same day, May 11.

For Blessed John Rochester, James Walworth, Carthusian Monks and Companions

Martyrs

Mass as for Bl. Carthusian, MM., below, but in Collect and Postcommunion after John add James.

14

May 12.

The Blessed Carthusian Martyrs

Double.

The Mass Sancti tui, p. [17], with the following exceptions:

Collect.

MAY the holy solemnity of blessed John [3, 4: James] and his Companions magnify thee, O Lord: wherein by thine unspeakable providence; thou hast both bestowed upon them everlasting glory and upon us thy succour. Through.

Commemoration of SS. Nereus and Companions, MM., p. 657.

The Lesson from the Epistle of blessed Peter the Apostle.

I Pet. 4, 13-19.

DEARLY beloved: Rejoice, inasmuch as ye are partakers of Christ's sufferings; that, when his glory shall be revealed, ye may be glad also with exceeding joy. If ye be reproached for the name of Christ, happy are ye: for the spirit of glory and of God resteth upon you. But let none of you suffer as a murderer, or as a thief, or as an evildoer, or as a busybody in other men's matters. Yet if any man suffer as a Christian, let him not be ashamed: but let him glorify God on this behalf. For the time is come that judgment must begin at the house of God. And if it first begin at us: what shall the end be of them that obey not the gospel of God? And if the righteous scarcely be saved, where shall the ungodly and the sinner appear? Wherefore let them that suffer according to the will of God commit the keeping of their souls to him in well doing, as unto a faithful Creator.

✠ The Continuation of the holy Gospel according to Matthew.

Matt. 10, 34.

AT that time: Jesus said unto his disciples: Think not that I am come to send peace on earth: I came not to send peace, but a sword. For I am come to set a man at variance against his father, and the daughter against her mother, and the daughter in law against her mother in law: and a man's foes shall be they of his own household. He that loveth father or mother more than me is not worthy of me: and he that loveth son or daughter more than me is not worthy of me. And he that taketh not his cross, and followeth after me, is not worthy of me. He that findeth his life shall lose it: and he that loseth his life for my sake shall find it.

He that receiveth you receiveth me: and he that receiveth me receiveth him that sent me. He that receiveth a prophet in the name of a prophet shall receive a prophet's reward: and he that receiveth a righteous man in the name of a righteous man shall receive a righteous man's reward. And whosoever shall give to drink unto one of these little ones a cup of cold water only in the name of a disciple: verily I say unto you he shall in no wise lose his reward.

Secret.

O LORD, who in this sacrifice hast given unto us the beginning of all martyrdom; we offer unto thee the same in honour of the precious death of thy Saints. Through.

Postcommunion.

MAY this thy Sacrament, O Lord, be unto us a pledge of everlasting blessedness: which we ask through the merits of thy blessed Martyrs, John [3, 4: James] and his Companions. Through.

15

The same day, May 12.

Blessed John Houghton

Martyr

Double.

Mass as for the Bl. Carthusian Martyrs, except the following: Introit, Alleluia and Communion from Mass Protexisti, p. [15]. In Collect say: blessed John thy Martyr, in Postcommunion: blessed John.

9

The same day, May 12.

St. Asaph

Bishop and Confessor

Double.

The Mass Sacerdotes tui, p. [20].

14, 15

May 13.

St. Erconwald

Bishop and Confessor

Greater double.

The Mass Sacerdotes tui, p. [20], excepting the Prayers, as below:

Collect. P

ALMIGHTY and everlasting God, who on this day dost gladden us with the feast of blessed Erconwald, thy Confessor and Bishop: we humbly beseech thy mercy; that we, who now honour his festival, may by his loving advocacy obtain the reward of everlasting life. Through.

14, 15: Commemoration of St. Robert Bellarmine, B.C.D., p. 658.

The Creed is not said.

Secret. P

BE favourable, we beseech thee, O Lord, unto our supplications: and, at the intercession of blessed Erconwald, thy Confessor and Bishop, grant that we, who minister thy heavenly sacraments, may be free from all sins; that through thy purifying grace, for the mysteries wherein we serve thee may avail for the healing of our souls. Through.

Postcommunion. P

GRANT, we beseech thee, almighty God: that by the cleansing power of these heavenly mysteries, we, who have been partakers of holy things, may, at the intercession of blessed Erconwald, thy Confessor and Bishop, attain to the fulfilment of thy sacraments in heaven.

14

May 14.

Blessed Richard Reynolds

Martyr

Double.

The Mass Laetabitur, p. [7], with Paschal rite, excepting:

Collect. P

O GOD, who in thy goodness didst set blessed Richard among the noble Martyrs of the Apostolic See: grant to us, by his example and intercession; that we may most lovingly live and most devotedly die in faithful obedience to that same Holy See. Through.

Commemoration is made of S. Boniface, M., p. 659.

Epistle, Rejoice inasmuch as, p. 958.

Alleluia, alleluia. Ps. 89. O Lord, the very heavens shall praise thy wondrous works; and thy truth in the congregation of thy saints. Alleluia. ℣. Ps. 21. Thou hast set, O Lord, a crown of pure gold upon his head, alleluia.

☩ The Continuation of the holy Gospel according to John.

John 12, 24.

AT that time: Jesus said unto his disciples: Verily, verily, I say unto you, except a corn of wheat fall into the ground and die, it abideth alone: but if it die, it bringeth forth much fruit. He that loveth his life shall lose it: and he that hateth his life in this world shall keep it unto life eternal. If any man serve me, let him follow me: and where I am, there shall also my servant be. If any man serve me, him will my Father honour.

Secret. C 4

GRANT, O Lord, that this our bounden service may be acceptable in thy sight: that these our oblations may, by the prayers of him on whose solemnity they are offered, be made profitable unto our salvation. Through.

Commemoration of St. Boniface, M., p. 659.

Postcommunion C 4

WE beseech thee, O Lord, that as we, whom thou hast refreshed by the partaking of thy sacred gift, offer unto thee our worship: so by the intercession of blessed Richard, thy Martyr, we may perceive the benefits of the same. Through.

For St. Boniface, M.

Postcommunion. C 3

GRANT, we beseech thee, O Lord our God: that as we in this life gladly honour the memory of thy Saints; so we may rejoice to behold them for ever. Through.

10, 11, 17
May 16.

St. Simon Stock

Confessor

Double.

The Mass Os justi, for a Confessor not a Bishop, p. [24], the Collect excepted.

Collect. P

O LORD, let the people, that is dedicated unto thee and to the Virgin Mother, rejoice in the solemnity of blessed Simon: that as through him they have obtained a token of thy mighty protection, so they may attain unto the gifts of eternal predestination. Through.

Commemoration of St. Ubald, B.C., p. 660.

Secret. C

GRANT, we beseech thee, O Lord, that we who, trusting in this our sacrifice of praise, offer it before thee to the honour of thy Saints: may by the same be delivered from all evils both in this life and in that which is to come. Through.

Postcommunion. C

O LORD, our God, who hast refreshed us with heavenly meat and drink, we humbly beseech thee: that we may be defended by the prayers of him in whose memory we have received the same. Through.

10, 13, 14, 15, 17
May 19.

St. Dunstan

Greater double (or double).

The Mass Sacerdotes tui, p. [20], the Prayers excepted.

Collect. P

O GOD, who hast exalted blessed Dunstan, thy Bishop, to thy heavenly kingdom: grant that through his glorious merits we may attain unto everlasting felicity. Through.

Commemoration of St. Peter Celestine, P.C., and St. Pudentiana, Virgin, p. 662.

Secret. P

ACCEPT, O Lord, we beseech thee; the gifts of thy humble servants, which we offer unto thee on the solemnity of blessed Dunstan, thy Confessor and Bishop, entreating thee: that by the succour of his heavenly advocacy, we may be found worthy to be defended from the snares of all our enemies. Through.

Common Preface.

Postcommunion. P

WE beseech thee, O Lord, that as we have received thy sacraments in honour of blessed Dunstan, thy Confessor and Bishop: so we may be ever succoured by his intercession. Through.

11, 12
May 20
St. Ethelbert
King and Martyr
Double.

The Mass Protexisti, p. [15].

Commemoration of St. Bernardine, C., p. 664.

15
May 21.
Blessed John Haile
Martyr
Double.

The Mass Protexisti, p. [15].

8, 9
May 24.
The Blessed Virgin Mary under the title Help of Christians
Greater double.

The Mass Salve, p. [41], as in the Common of Feasts of B.V.M., except the Prayers:

Collect. P

ALMIGHTY and merciful God, who for the defence of the Christian people didst in the most blessed Virgin Mary wondrously establish a perpetual succour: mercifully grant; that we, being strengthened by her sure protection as we strive in life, may in death have strength to win the victory over the malicious enemy. Through.

The Creed is said.

Secret. P

WE offer unto thee, O Lord, this sacrifice of propitiation for the triumph of the Christian religion: and may the Virgin our helper, through whom so great a victory was won, obtain that it may avail for our succour. Through.

Postcommunion. P

ASSIST, O Lord, the peoples, who are refreshed by the partaking of thy Body and Blood: that by the help of thy most holy Mother, they may be delivered from all evil and danger, and be preserved in all good works: Who livest.

13, 18
May 25.
St. Aldhelm
Bishop and Confessor
Double.

The Mass Statuit, p. [19], the Prayers excepted.

Collect. P

O GOD, who on this day didst exalt thy holy Bishop Aldhelm to everlasting felicity: we beseech thee, that by his merits (17, 18: and prayers) thy mercy may lead us to the same. Through.

Commemoration of St. Gregory VII, P.C., and St. Urban, P.M., p. 665.

Secret. P

WE beseech thee, O Lord, that this our oblation may be rendered pleasing unto thee by the prayers of him for whose festival it is offered. Through.

Preface of the Season.

Postcommunion. P

ASSIST us mercifully, we beseech thee, O Lord, who now celebrate the solemnity of thy blessed (13: holy) Bishop Aldhelm: and by his merits grant to us the joys of (13: life in) heaven. Through.

May 26.

In all England and Wales.

ST. AUGUSTINE, BISHOP AND CONFESSOR,

APOSTLE OF ENGLAND

Double of 2nd class.

Introit. Ps. 132, 9-10. Sacerdotes tui.

LET thy priests, O Lord, be clothed with righteousness: and let thy saints sing with joyfulness: for thy servant David's sake, turn not away the presence of thine Anointed. (E.T. Alleluia, alleluia.) Ps. ibid., 1. Lord, remember David: and all his trouble. ℣. Glory.

Collect.

O GOD, who didst give the blessed Bishop Augustine to be the first Teacher of the English people: grant us, we beseech thee; that we who proclaim his merits on earth may perceive his intercession in heaven. Through.

And Commemoration is made, in Low Masses, of St. Philip Neri, C., only.

Collect.

O GOD, who hast exalted blessed Philip, thy Confessor, to the glory of thy Saints: mercifully grant; that we who rejoice in his solemnity may follow him in all virtuous and godly living. Through.

The Lesson from the Epistle of blessed Paul the Apostle to the Hebrews.

Heb. 7. 23-27.

BRETHREN: They were many priests, because they were not suffered to continue by reason of death: but Jesus, because he continueth ever, hath an unchangeable priesthood. Wherefore he is able also to save them to the uttermost that come unto God by him: seeing he ever liveth to make intercession for them. For such an high priest became us, who is holy, harmless, undefiled, separate from sinners, and made higher than the heavens: who needeth not daily, as those high priests, to offer up sacrifice, first for his own sins, and then for the people's: for this he did once, when he offered up himself, Jesus Christ our Lord.

Gradual. Ps. 132, 16-17. I will deck her priests with health: and her saints shall rejoice and sing. ℣. There shall I make the horn of David to flourish: I have ordained a lantern for mine Anointed.

Alleluia, alleluia. ℣. Ps. 110, 4. The Lord sware, and will not repent: Thou art a priest for ever after the order of Melchisedech. Alleluia.

In Eastertide the Gradual is omitted, and in its place is said:

Alleluia, alleluia. ℣. Ps. 110, 4. The Lord sware, and will not repent: Thou art a priest for ever after the order of Melchisedech. Alleluia. ℣. Ecclus. 45, 7. The Lord loved him, and adorned him: he clothed him with a robe of glory. Alleluia.

☩ The Continuation of the holy Gospel according to Luke.

Luke 10. 1-9.

AT that time: The Lord appointed other seventy also: and sent them two and two before his face into every city and place whither he himself would come. Therefore said he unto them: The harvest truly is great, but the labourers are few. Pray ye therefore the Lord of the harvest, that he would send forth labourers into his harvest. Go your ways: behold, I send you forth as lambs among wolves. Carry neither purse nor scrip, nor shoes; and salute no man by the way. And into whatsoever house ye enter, first say: Peace be to this house: and if the son of peace be there, your peace shall rest upon it: if not, it shall turn to you again. And in the same house remain, eating and drinking such things as they give: for the labourer is worthy of his hire. Go not from house to house. And into whatsoever city ye enter, and they receive you, eat such things as are set before you: and heal the sick that are therein, and say unto them: The kingdom of God is come nigh unto you.

Offertory. Ps. 89, 24. My truth and my mercy shall be with him: and in my name shall his horn be exalted. (E.T. Alleluia.)

Secret.

WE beseech thee, O Lord, that the gifts which we offer may be acceptable unto thee: whereby we venerate the merits of blessed Augustine, thy Confessor and Bishop, and likewise call to remembrance the tokens of our life and freedom. Through.

For St. Philip.   Secret.

WE beseech thee, O Lord, favourably to regard these present sacrifices; and grant; that the Holy Spirit may inflame us with that fire, wherewith he wondrously penetrated the heart of blessed Philip. Through ... in the unity of the same Holy Spirit.

Communion. Matt. 24, 46-47. Blessed is the servant, whom the lord when he cometh shall find watching: verily I say unto you, He shall make him ruler over all his goods. (E.T. Alleluia.)

Postcommunion.

WE beseech thee, O Lord, that we, being nourished by thy holy mysteries, which we have received on the solemnity of blessed Augustine, thy Confessor and Bishop: may continually be satisfied and evermore desire to be fulfilled with the same. Through.

For St. Philip.   Postcommunion.

O LORD, who hast fulfilled us with thy heavenly delight: we beseech thee; that by the merits of thy blessed Confessor Philip, and by following him, we may ever earnestly seek after those things whereby we truly live. Through.

15: Epistle, We were bold as in Missal, May 28, p.669.

1, 10, 11: Mass as in Missal, May 28, p. 669.

17
May 28.
St. Aldhelm
Bishop and Confessor
Simple.

Mass as on May 25, p. 884, without any Commemoration.

10, 13, 14, 15, 16
The same day, May 28.
Blessed Margaret Pole
Countess and Martyr
Double.

The Mass Me exspectaverunt from the Common of a Martyr not a Virgin, p. [34], except the Introit and Collect.

Introit. Ps. 119, 46-47. Loquebar.

I WILL speak of thy testimonies, even before kings, and will not be ashamed: and my delight shall be in thy commandments, which I have loved exceedingly. (E.T. Alleluia, alleluia.) Ps. ibid. Blessed are those that are undefiled in the way: and walk in the law of the Lord. ℣. Glory.

Collect. P

O GOD, who didst adorn the life of blessed Margaret, wondrous in virtue, with the crown of martyrdom: grant by her merits and intercession; that we, being affrighted by no adversity, may have power to dedicate our life and death to thy service. Through.

13

Collect. P

O GOD, the author and giver of all good things, who, that thou mightest stir up mankind to confess thy name, didst even in the frailty of woman bring martyrdom to perfection: grant, we beseech thee, that thy Church, being admonished by the example of blessed Margaret thy Martyr, may not fear to suffer for thee, and may seek after the glory of thy heavenly reward. Through.

Secret. C

RECEIVE, O Lord, the gifts which we offer on the solemnity of blessed Margaret, thy Martyr; through whose advocacy we trust to be delivered. Through.

Postcommunion. C

MAY the mysteries which we have received avail for our succour, O Lord: and at the intercession of blessed Margaret, thy Martyr, cause us to rejoice in thy continual protection. Through.

14, 16
May 30.
St. Eleutherius
Pope and Martyr
Double.

2nd Prayers from Mass Si diligis me, p. [2].

Commemoration of St. Felix, P.M., with 2nd Prayers from Mass Si diligis me, p. [2].

Common Preface (or of the Season).

10

Tuesday within the 4th week after the Octave of Easter.

Translation of St. Chad
Bishop and Confessor
Double of 2nd class.

Mass as on the Feast, March 2, p. 872.

FEASTS OF JUNE
1, 9, 12
June 1.

Blessed Virgin Mary, Mediatrix of all Graces
Greater double.

Introit. Heb. 4, 16. Adeamus.

LET us come boldly unto the throne of grace, that we may obtain mercy, and find grace to help in time of need. (E.T. Alleluia, alleluia.) Ps. 121, 1. I will life up mine eyes unto the hills: from whence cometh my help. ℣. Glory.

Collect.

O LORD Jesu Christ, our Mediator with the Father, who didst vouchsafe to appoint the most blessed Virgin Mary, thy mother, to be our mother also, and our Mediatrix with thee: mercifully grant; that whosoever cometh to thee to ask for benefits, may rejoice in the obtaining through her of all his petitions; Who livest and reignest with the same God the Father.

Commemoration of St. Angela, V., p. 673.

Feasts of May (28, 30), June (1, 5)   889

The Lesson from the Prophet Isaiah.

Is. 55. 1-5.

HO, everyone that thirsteth, come ye to the waters, and he that hath no money; come ye, buy, and eat: yea, come, buy wine and milk without money and without price. Wherefore do ye spend money for that which is not bread, and your labour for that which satisfieth not? Hearken diligently unto me, and eat ye that which is good, and let your soul delight itself in fatness. Incline your ear, and come unto me; hear, and your soul shall live. Behold, thou shalt call a nation that thou knowest not: and nations that knew not thee shall run unto thee because of the Lord thy God, and for the holy one of Israel, for he hath glorified thee.

Gradual. Ecclus. 24. In me is all grace of the way and the truth, in me is all hope of life and virtue. ℣. Come unto me all ye that be desirous of me, and fill yourselves with my fruits.

Alleluia, alleluia. ℣. Hail, Mother of mercy, Mother of hope and grace, O Mary. Alleluia.

In Easter Tide the Gradual is omitted, and in its place is said:

Alleluia, alleluia. ℣. Is. 60. Lift up thine eyes round about, and see: all they gather themselves together, they come to thee. Alleluia. ℣. Thy sons shall come from afar, and thy daughters shall be nursed at thy side. Alleluia.

✠ The Continuation of the holy Gospel according to John.

John 19. 25-27.

AT that time: There stood by the Cross of Jesus his mother, and his mother's sister, Mary the wife of Cleophas, and Mary Magdalene. When Jesus therefore saw his mother, and the disciple standing by, whom he loved, he saith unto his mother: Woman, behold thy son. Then saith he to the disciple: Behold thy mother. And from that hour that disciple took her unto his own home. Creed.

Offertory. Jerem. 18, 20. Remember, O Virgin Mary, in the sight of God, that thou speak good things for us, and that thou turn away his indignation from us. (E.T. Alleluia.)

Secret.

THROUGH the prayers of thy Mother and our Mediatrix we beseech thee, O Lord, that this sacrifice and oblation may by the bounty of thy grace render us ourselves an eternal offering unto thee: Who livest.

Commemoration, as above.

Preface of the B.V.M., And that on the Festival.

Communion. Esther 15, 14. Exceeding wonderful art thou, O Mary, and thy countenance is full of graces. (E.T. Alleluia.)

Postcommunion.

LET the prayer of blessed Mary, thy Mother and our Mediatrix, assist us, O Lord: that through this holy Communion we may by the bounty of thy grace be profited unto the increase of eternal redemption: Who livest.

Commemoration, as above.

18

June 5.

St. Boniface

Bishop and Martyr

(Patron)

Double of 1st class.

All as in Missal, June 5, p. 677, except the following Introit:

Introit. Gaudeamus.

REJOICE we all in the Lord, keeping feast-day in honour of blessed Boniface the Martyr: in whose passion the Angels rejoice, and glorify the Son of God. (E.T. Alleluia, alleluia.) Ps. 33, 1. Rejoice in the Lord, O ye righteous: for it becometh well the just to be thankful. ℣. Glory.

And the Creed is said.

18

June 7.

St. Willibald

Bishop and Confessor

Double.

The Mass Sacerdotes, for a Confessor Bishop, p. [20].

1

The same day, June 7.

St. Robert

Abbot

Double.

The Mass Os justi, for an Abbot, p. [26].

1, 2, 3, 4, 5, 6, 7

June 8.

St. William

Bishop and Confessor

1, 2, 3, 4, 5: Double.

7: Commemoration.

1: Simple.

The Mass Sacerdotes tui, p. [20], the Prayers excepted.

Collect.   P

O GOD, who makest us glad by the merits and intercession of blessed William, thy Confessor and Bishop: mercifully grant, that we, who ask thy bounty, may by the gift of thy grace obtain the same. Through.

Secret.   P

SANCTIFY, O Lord, these our oblations: and, at the intercession of blessed William, thy Confessor and Bishop, cleanse us thereby from the defilements of our iniquities. Through.

Postcommunion.   P

WE humbly beseech thee, almighty God: that as thou dost refresh us with thy sacraments, so at the intercession of blessed William, thy Confessor and Bishop, thou wouldest vouchsafe unto us to do thee worthy and acceptable service. Through.

15, 16

June 9.

Translation of St. Edmund

Bishop and Confessor

Greater double.

The Mass Gaudeamus, as on November 16, except the following:

Collect.

O GOD, who dost vouchsafe unto us to celebrate the Translation of blessed Edmund thy Confessor and Bishop: grant to us by his merits and prayers; that we, being set free from the slavery of sin, may be enabled to attain unto the joys of the heavenly kingdom. Through.

Commemoration of SS. Primus, etc., MM., p. 679.

In Easter Tide, instead of the Gradual, is said:

Alleluia, alleluia. ℣. Ps. 110, 4. Thou art a priest for ever after the order of Melchisedech. Alleluia. ℣. This is the priest whom the Lord hath crowned. Alleluia.

Secret. P

SANCTIFY these gifts, O Lord, by thy benediction, and vouchsafe: that at the intercession of blessed Edmund thy Confessor and Bishop they may avail for our salvation. Through.

Postcommunion. P

O LORD, who hast refreshed us with the mysteries of thy body and blood, we humbly beseech thee: that as thou didst translate blessed Edmund, thy Confessor and Bishop from this world unto celestial glory, so we, who celebrate his translation, may be worthy to be partakers of that same glory: Who livest.

7, 11, 15

June 17.

St. Botulph

Abbot

The Mass Os justi, for an Abbot, p. [26].

10

June 19.

Blessed Sebastian Newdigate and Humphrey Middlemore

Martyrs

Double.

The Mass Intret, p. [9], with Prayers, Epistle and Gospel as on May 12, p. 880, changing the names John, James and their Companions into Sebastian and Humphrey.

Commemoration of St. Juliana de Falconeri, V., and SS. Gervase and Protase, MM., p. 688.

June 22.

(In all England and Wales.)

St. Alban, First Martyr of Britain

Greater double.

Introit. Ps. 21, 1. In virtute tua.

THE just shall rejoice in thy strength, O Lord: exceeding glad shall he be of thy salvation: thou hast given him his heart's desire. Ps. ibid., 2. For thou hast prevented him with the blessings of goodness: thou hast set a crown of pure gold upon his head. ℣. Glory.

Collect.

O GOD, who hast hallowed this day by the martyrdom of blessed Alban: grant, we beseech thee; that as year by year we rejoice to pay him honour, so we may be defended by his continual help. Through.

And Commemoration is made, in Low Masses only, of St. Paulinus, B.C.

Collect.

O GOD, who hast promised them that leave all things in this world for thee to receive an hundred-fold and life eternal in the world to come: mercifully grant; that, following in the footsteps of thy holy Bishop Paulinus, we may be enabled to despise things earthly, and to desire only those things that are heavenly: Who livest and reignest with God the Father.

The Lesson from the book of Wisdom.

Wisd. 10, 10-14.

THE Lord guided the just in right paths, shewed him the kingdom of God, and gave him knowledge of holy things: made him rich in his travails, and multiplied the fruit of his labours. In the covetousness of such as oppressed him he stood by him, and made him rich. He defended him from his enemies, and kept him safe from those that lay in wait, and in a sore conflict he gave him the victory, that he might know that wisdom is stronger than all. When the just was sold, she forsook him not, but delivered him from sin she went down with him into the pit, and left him not in bonds, till she brought him the sceptre of the kingdom, and power against those that oppressed him: as for them that had accused him, she shewed them to be liars, and the Lord our God gave him perpetual glory.

Gradual. Ps. 112, 1-2. Blessed is the man that feareth the Lord: he hath great delight in his commandments. ℣. His seed shall be mighty upon earth: the generation of the faithful shall be blessed.

Alleluia, alleluia. ℣. Ps. 21, 3. Thou hast set, O Lord, a crown of pure gold upon his head. Alleluia.

✠ The Continuation of the holy Gospel according to Matthew.

Matt. 16, 24-27.

AT that time: Jesus said unto his disciples: If any man will come after me, let him deny himself, and take up his cross, and follow me. For whosoever will save his life shall lose it; and whosoever will lose his life for my sake shall find it. For what is a man profited, if he shall gain the whole world, and lose his own soul? Or what shall a man give in exchange for his soul? For the Son of man shall come in the glory of his Father with his Angels: and then he shall reward every man according to his works.

Offertory. Ps. 8, 5-6. Thou hast crowned him with glory and worship, and hast made him to have dominion of the work of thy hands, O Lord.

Secret.

WE beseech thee, O Lord, that like as in the veneration of blessed Alban, thy Martyr, we do shew forth thy wonders: so through this bounden service of propitiation he may be a faithful intercessor for us in the sight of thy mercy. Through.

For St. Paulinus. Secret.

GRANT, O Lord, that after the example of thy holy Bishop Paulinus, we may join the sacrifice of perfect charity to the oblation of the altar: and by zeal in well-doing be found worthy of thy everlasting mercy. Through.

Communion. Matt. 16, 24. If any man will come after me, let him deny himself, and take up his cross, and follow me.

Postcommunion.

LET blessed Alban, we pray thee, O Lord, ever beseech thy divine majesty: that this holy Sacrament may effectually cleanse us from our iniquities, [and preserve in us thy most excellent gift of charity.] Through.

13: The words in brackets are omitted.

For St. Paulinus. Postcommunion.

GRANT us, O Lord, through these sacred mysteries that love of godliness and humility which thy holy Bishop Paulinus drew from this heavenly fountain: and at his intercession pour forth on all who call upon thee the riches of thy bounteous grace. Through.

2, 3, 5, 6, 9, 12: The following Gospel is read:

✠ The Continuation of the holy Gospel according to Luke.

Luke 14, 26-33.

AT that time: Jesus said unto the multitudes: If any man come to me, and hate not his father, and mother, and wife, and children, and brethren, and sisters, yea, and his own life also, he cannot be my disciple. And whosoever doth not bear his cross, and come after me, cannot be my disciple. For which of you, intending to build a tower, sitteth not down first, and counteth the cost, whether he have sufficient to finish it; lest haply, after he hath laid the foundation, and is not able to finish it, all that behold it begin to mock him, saying: This man began to build, and was not able to finish? Or what king, going to make war against another king, sitteth not down first, and consulteth whether he be able with ten thousand to meet him that cometh against him with twenty thousand? Or else, while the other is yet a great way off, he sendeth an ambassage, and desireth conditions of peace. So likewise, whosoever he be of you that forsaketh not all that he hath, he cannot be my disciple.

10, 13: The following Gospel is read:

✠ The Continuation of the holy Gospel according to Matthew.

Matt. 10, 34-39.

AT that time: Jesus said unto his disciples: Think not that I am come to send peace on earth: I came not to send peace, but a sword. For I am come to set a man at variance against his father, and the daughter against her mother, and the daughter-in-law against her mother-in-law: and a man's foes shall be they of his own household. He that loveth father or mother more than me is not worthy of me: and he that loveth son or daughter more than me is not worthy of me. And he that taketh not his cross, and followeth after me, is not worthy of me. He that findeth his life shall lose it: and he that loseth his life for my sake shall find it. He that receiveth you receiveth me: and he that receiveth me receiveth him that sent me. He that receiveth a prophet in the name of a prophet shall receive a prophet's reward: and he that receiveth a righteous man in the name of a righteous man shall receive a righteous man's reward. And whosoever shall give to drink unto one of these little ones a cup of cold water only in the name of a disciple: verily I say unto you he shall in no wise lose his reward.

1, 6, 10, 11, 14

June 23.

St. Etheldreda

Virgin

Double.

The Mass Dilexisti, p. [31], excepting the Collect.

Collect. P

O GOD, who makest us glad with the yearly solemnity of blessed Etheldreda, thy Virgin: mercifully grant; that as we are enlightened by the example of her purity so we may be succoured by her prayers. Through.

Commemoration of the Vigil of St. John Baptist, p. 693.

Secret. C

GRANT, O Lord, that as thy dedicated people acknowledge that in tribulation they have been succoured by the merits of thy Saints: so this oblation, which they offer unto thee in honour of the same, may be acceptable in thy sight. Through.

Postcommunion. C

O LORD, who hast satisfied thy family with sacred gifts: we beseech thee; that we may at all times be comforted by the intercession of her whose festival we celebrate. Through.

3, 4
June 27.
Blessed Virgin Mary of Perpetual Succour

Double of 1st class.

Introit. Gaudeamus.

REJOICE we all in the Lord, keeping feast day in honour of the blessed Virgin Mary: in whose solemnity the Angels rejoice and glorify the Son of God. Ps. 45, 1. My heart is inditing of a good matter: I speak of the things which I have made unto the King. ℣. Glory.

Collect.

ALMIGHTY and merciful God who hast granted unto us to venerate the Image of thy Mother under the special title of Perpetual succour: mercifully grant; that amid all the changes of this way and life we may be so defended by the continual protection of the same Immaculate and ever Virgin Mary, that we may be found worthy to attain unto the rewards of thy eternal redemption: Who livest.

The Lesson from the book of Wisdom.
Ecclus. 24, 17-22.

AS the vine, I brought forth a pleasant savour: and my flowers are the fruit of honour and riches. I am the mother of fair love, and fear, and knowledge and holy hope. In me is all grace of the way and the truth: in me is all hope of life and of virtue. Come unto me, all ye that be desirous of me, and fill yourselves with my fruits. For my spirit is sweeter than honey, and mine inheritance than honey and the honeycomb. My memorial shall be unto everlasting generations. They that eat me shall yet be hungry: and they that drink me shall yet be thirsty. He that obeyeth me shall never be confounded: and they that work by me shall not do amiss. They that expound me shall have life everlasting.

Gradual. Cant. 6, 10. All comely and sweet art thou, O daughter of Sion, fair as the moon, bright as the sun, terrible as an army arrayed with banners. ℣. Judith 13. The Lord hath blessed thee by his power, because through thee he hath brought our enemies to nought.

Alleluia, alleluia. ℣. Luke 1, 28. Hail, Mary, full of grace, the Lord is with thee: blessed art thou among women. Alleluia.

✠ The Continuation of the holy Gospel according to John.

John 19, 25-27.

AT that time: There stood by the Cross of Jesus his mother and his mother's sister, Mary, the wife of Cleophas, and Mary Magdalene. When Jesus therefore saw his mother, and the disciple standing by, whom he loved, he saith unto his mother: Woman, behold thy son. Then saith he to the disciple: Behold thy mother. And from that hour that disciple took her unto his own home. Creed.

Offertory. Jerem. 18, 20. Remember, O Virgin Mary, in the sight of God, that thou speak good things for us, and that he may turn away his indignation from us.

Secret.

THROUGH thy mercy, O Lord, and the intercession of the blessed Virgin and Mother Mary, may this oblation avail for our prosperity and peace, both now and for evermore.. Through.

Preface of the B.V.M., And that on the Festival.

Communion. Queen of the world most worthy, Mary Virgin perpetual, intercede for our peace and salvation, who didst bring forth Christ the Lord, the Saviour of all.

Postcommunion.

WE beseech thee, O Lord, let the venerable intercession of thy immaculate Mother and ever Virgin Mary bring us help: that we, who have received perpetual benefits, being delivered from all dangers, may be made of one heart and mind: Who livest and reignest with God the Father.

FEASTS OF JULY

12

July 3.

SS. Julius and Aaron

Martyrs

Double.

The Mass Salus, p. [12].

Commemoration of St. Leo II, P.C., p. 709.

Common Preface.

18

July 4.

Blessed John Cornelius and Companions, and Hugh Green,

Martyrs

Double.

The Mass Salus autem, p. [12], the Collect excepted.

Collect. P

ALMIGHTY and everlasting God, who by thy grace didst strengthen thy blessed Martyrs John and his Companions, striving even unto death in defence of the catholic faith: vouchsafe; that we also, being shaken by no temptations, may be found stedfast in the same faith. Through.

10

July 7.

For Commemoration of St. Hedda

Bishop and Confessor

Prayers from Mass Statuit, for a Confessor Bishop, p. [19].

The same day, July 7.

Cities of Canterbury and Portsmouth.

Translation of St. Thomas of Canterbury

Bishop and Martyr

Greater double.

The Mass as on December 29th, p. 34, except the Prayers.

Collect. P

O GOD, who dost vouchsafe unto us to celebrate the translation of blessed Thomas thy Martyr and Bishop: we humbly entreat thee; that by his merits and prayers we may be translated from vice to virtue, and from prison to thy kingdom. Through.

Commemoration of SS. Cyril and Methodius, BB., CC., p. 711.

The Creed is not said.

Secret. P

O GOD, who by thy heavenly benediction dost change bread and wine into thy Body and Blood: grant unto us by the merits of blessed Thomas, thy Martyr and Bishop; that being restored to thy mercy we may be conformed to thy good pleasure: Who livest and reignest with God the Father.

Common Preface.

Postcommunion. P

O GOD, who didst translate blessed Thomas, thy Martyr and Bishop from torment unto gladness: grant, we beseech thee; that we, who venerate his translation on earth, may through his advocacy be translated unto heaven. Through.

(In all England and Wales.)

July 9.

SS. JOHN FISHER, Bishop
AND
THOMAS MORE, Martyrs

Double of 1st class.

Introit. Ps. 34, 19. Multae tribulationes.

GREAT are the troubles of the righteous, but the Lord delivereth them out of all: the Lord keepeth all their bones: so that not one of them is broken. (E.T. Alleluia, alleluia.) Ps. ibid., 1. I will always give thanks unto the Lord: his praise shall ever be in my mouth. ℣. Glory.

Collect.

O GOD, who from among the English people didst raise up thy blessed Martyrs John and Thomas to be defenders of the true faith and the primacy of the Roman Church: grant through their merits and prayers; that, by the profession of the same faith we may all in Christ be made and continue one. Through the same.

The Lesson from the book of the Maccabees.

II Macc. 6, 18-28.

IN those days: Eleazar, one of the principal scribes, an aged man, and of a well-favoured countenance, was constrained to open his mouth, and to eat swine's flesh. But he, choosing rather to die gloriously, than to live stained with such an abomination, spit it forth, and came of his own accord to the torment: as it behoved them to come, that are resolute to stand out against such things, as are not lawful for love of life to be tasted. But they that had the charge of that wicked feast, for the old acquaintance they had with the man, taking him aside, besought him to bring flesh of his own provision, such as was lawful for him to use, and make as if he did eat of the flesh taken from the sacrifice commanded by the king, that in so doing he might be delivered from death: and for the old friendship with them find favour. But he began to consider discreetly, and as became his age, and the excellency of his ancient years, and the honour of his gray head, whereunto he was come, and his most honest education from a child, or rather the holy law made and given by God: therefore he answered accordingly, and willed them straightways to send him to the grave. For it becometh not our age, said he, in any wise to dissemble, whereby many young persons might think that Eleazar, being fourscore years old and ten, were now gone to a strange religion, and so they through mine hypocrisy, and desire to live a little time and a moment longer, should be deceived by me: and I get a stain to mine old age, and make it abominable. For though for the present time I should be delivered from the punishment of men, yet should I not escape the hand of the Almighty, neither alive nor dead. Wherefore now, manfully changing this life, I will shew myself such an one of mine age requireth, and leave a notable example to such as be young to die willingly and courageously for the honourable and holy laws. And when he had said these words, immediately he went to the torment.

Gradual. Ps. 34, 5. Come unto him and be enlightened, and your faces shall not be ashamed. ℣. Ibid., 15. The eyes of the Lord are over the righteous, and his ears are open unto their prayers.

Alleluia, alleluia. ℣. John 17, 3. This is life eternal, that they may know thee the only true God, and Jesus Christ, whom thou hast sent. Alleluia.

In Votive Masses in Eastertide is said:

Alleluia, alleluia. ℣. John 17, 3. This is life eternal that they may know thee the only true God, and Jesus Christ, whom thou hast sent. Alleluia. ℣. Ps. 34, 10. Come unto him and be enlightened, and your faces shall not be ashamed. Alleluia.

After Septuagesima, Alleluia, and the Verse following are omitted, and in place thereof is said: Tract. Ps. 126, p. [10].

☩ The Continuation of the holy Gospel according to John.

John 10, 23-30.

AT that time: Jesus walked in the temple in Solomon's porch. Then came the Jews round about him, and said unto him: How long dost thou make us to doubt? If thou be the Christ tell us plainly. Jesus answered them: I told you, and ye believed not. The works that I do in my Father's name, they bear witness of me. But ye believe not, because ye are not of my sheep. My sheep hear my voice, and I know them, and they follow me: and I give unto them eternal life, and they shall never perish, neither shall any man pluck them out of my hand. My Father, which gave them me, is greater than all, and no man is able to pluck them out of my Father's hand. I and my Father are one.

Offertory. Ps. 68, 35. God is wonderful in his saints: even the God of Israel, he will give strength and power to his people: blessed be God. (E.T. Alleluia.)

Secret.

WE beseech thee, O Lord, mercifully regard our oblations: and through the intercession and prayers of thy Martyrs grant us the gifts of thy grace. Through.

Communion. John 10, 27-28. My sheep hear my voice and I know them, and they follow me: and I give unto them eternal life, and they shall never perish. (E.T. Alleluia.)

Postcommunion.

O LORD our God, who hast refreshed us with this heavenly banquet, we beseech thee: that at the intercession of thy blessed Martyrs, John and Thomas, we may be made worthy to attain unto their fellowship. Through.

Votive Mass in honour of St. John Fisher

Bishop and Martyr

The Mass Statuit from the Common of one Martyr, p. [4], with the Prayers as follows:

Collect.

O GOD, who on thy blessed Bishop John didst bestow grace valiantly to lay down his life for truth and justice: grant us by his intercession and example; so to lose our life for Christ in this world, that we may be counted worthy to find it in heaven. Through the same.

Secret.

MOST merciful God, pour forth upon these gifts thy benediction: that as blessed John, thy Martyr and Bishop, maintained the faith even to the shedding of his blood, so we may be strengthened in the same. Through.

Postcommunion.

O LORD, let this heavenly table bestow on us that spirit of fortitude: wherewith the life of blessed John, thy Martyr and Bishop, was continually sustained, that he might win the victory for the honour of the Church. Through.

Votive Mass in honour of St. Thomas More

Martyr

The Mass In virtue, p. [6], except the following:

Collect.

O GOD, who didst grant unto blessed Thomas thy Martyr amid the enticements of the world and the pains of prison and death to embrace thy Cross with a stout and cheerful heart: grant, we beseech thee, by his intercession and example; that, striving eagerly for faith and justice, we may be found worthy to attain with gladness to everlasting joys. Through.

The Epistle Eleazar, as above.

Secret.

WE beseech thee, almighty God, mercifully regard this sacrifice of our redemption: and at the intercession of blessed Thomas, thy Martyr, graciously accept it for this thy family. Through.

Postcommunion.

LET the homage of our service be pleasing unto thee, almighty God: that, at the intercession of blessed Thomas thy Martyr, we may perceive these holy things of which we have partaken to be profitable unto us for the obtaining of the rewards of everlasting life. Through.

10

July 11.

Blessed Hadrian Fortescue

Martyr

Double.

Introit. Wisd. 10, 13-14. Venditum.

WHEN the righteous was sold, the Lord forsook him not, but delivered him from sinners; and left him not in bonds, till he brought him the sceptre of the kingdom. Ps. 37. The Lord knoweth the days of the godly; and their inheritance shall be for ever. ℣. Glory.

Collect.

POUR forth upon us, O Lord, we beseech thee, the spirit of constancy and fortitude wherewith thou didst strengthen thy blessed Martyr Hadrian for the defence of the Catholic faith: that we, being filled therewith, may be worthy to attain to the fellowship of his glory in heaven: in whose triumphal passion we rejoice on earth. Through.

Commemoration of St. Pius I, P.M., p. 714.

The Epistle, Count it all joy, p. [8].

Gradual. Ps. 79, 1-3. O God, the heathen are come into thine inheritance, thine holy temple have they defiled: and made Jerusalem an heap of stones. ℣. The blood of thy servants have they shed like water, and there was no man to bury them. Alleluia, alleluia. ℣. Ps. 37, 39-40. But the salvation of the righteous is of the Lord, and he will save them that put their trust in him. Alleluia.

The Gospel, Think not, as in the Mass In virtue, p. [6].

Offertory. Wisd. 10, 12-14. In a sore conflict he gave him the victory. He gave him perpetual glory.

Secret.

MAY the Holy Ghost, O Lord, pour his blessing upon our gifts: and make us stedfast in that faith, whereto blessed Hadrian thy Martyr bare witness both by the word of his mouth and the shedding of his blood. Through ... in the unity of the same Holy Ghost.

Common Preface.

Communion. John 15, 13 Greater love hath no man than this, that a man lay down his life for his friends.

Postcommunion.

GRANT us, O Lord, through these holy mysteries which we have received, to imitate the zeal and constancy of blessed Hadrian: who by the example of his courage and by his martyrdom hath kindled us to desire the things eternal. Through.

13

The same day, July 11.

Blessed Oliver Plunket

Bishop and Martyr

Greater double.

The Mass Statuit, for a Martyr Bishop, p. [4], except the Prayers.

Collect. P

O GOD, who for the defence of the Catholic faith didst endue blessed Oliver, thy Martyr and Bishop, with wondrous strength of spirit: grant unto us by his intercession and example; that we may imitate his constancy in faith, and in danger perceive his advocacy. Through.

Commemoration of St. Pius I, P.M., p. 714.

Secret. P

MOST merciful God, pour forth thy blessing upon these thy gifts, and confirm us in that faith to which by cruel torments blessed Oliver, thy Martyr and Bishop, bore witness. Through.

Common Preface.

Postcommunion. P

O LORD, let this heavenly table bestow on us that spirit of fortitude; wherewith the life of blessed Oliver, thy Martyr and Bishop, was continually sustained that he might win the victory for the honour of thy Church. Through.

16, 17

July 15.

St. Swithun

Bishop and Confessor

16: Double (17: Simple).

The Mass Sacerdotes tui, for a Confessor Bishop, p. [20], the Prayers excepted.

Collect. P

ALMIGHTY and everlasting God: who hast made this day honourable unto us by reason of the festival of blessed Swithun, thy Confessor and Bishop: give joy unto thy Church upon this day; that we who celebrate his solemnity on earth may be aided by his intercession in heaven. Through.

Commemoration of St. Henry, Emperor, p. 718.

Secret. P

WE beseech thee, O Lord, look mercifully upon thy people who on this festival of blessed Swithun, thy Confessor and Bishop, do gladly draw near unto thy sacraments; and grant, that by his intercession, the gifts which they have offered to the honour of thy name may be profitable unto all for their forgiveness. Through.

Commemoration of St. Henry, Emperor, p. 718.

Postcommunion. P

O LORD, who hast bestowed upon us this pledge of everlasting life, we humbly implore thee: that at the intercession of blessed Swithun thy Confessor and Bishop, we who have tasted of this Sacrament beneath a figure, may partake of the fulness thereof hereafter face to face. Through.

Commemoration of St. Henry, Emperor, p. 718.

16
July 16.
Commemoration of St. Helier
Martyr
Collect.

GRANT us we beseech thee, O Lord, through the merits and intercession of thy holy Martyr Helier, to overcome the adversities of this failing world: and to attain with gladness to the fellowship of the heavenly city. Through.

Secret and Postcommunion from Mass Laetabitur, p. [7].

10, 13
July 17.
Commemoration of St. Kenelm
King and Martyr

10: Prayers from the Mass In virtute, p. [6].

13
Collect. P

ALMIGHTY and merciful God, who on this day hast given to us wondrous joy in the solemnity of blessed Kenelm, thy King and Martyr: graciously hearken to the prayers of thy faithful people and vouchsafe; that we, who this day celebrate his feast, may ever be aided by his merits and prayers. Through.

Secret. P

LOOK down, O Lord, on these our oblations: and through the advocacy of blessed Kenelm thy Martyr, whose venerable festival we celebrate, may they bestow upon the faithful pardon unto salvation, and the rewards of everlasting life. Through.

Postcommunion. P

WE beseech thee, O Lord, that thy people who celebrate the birthday of blessed Kenelm may thereby obtain joy and gladness: and make them to be numbered in thine eternal fellowship, whom thou hast renewed by the food of this heavenly table. Through.

9, 12
July 17.
Appearing of the Sacred Image of St. Mary in Porticu
Greater double.

Introit. Cant. 6, 10.

WHO is she that proceedeth forth as the rising dawn, fair as the moon, bright as the sun, terrible as an army arrayed with banners. Ps. 19, 1. The heavens declare the glory of God, and the firmament sheweth his handy-work. ℣. Glory.

Feasts of July (16, 17)

Collect.

O GOD, who hast given the Mother of thy beloved Son for our Mother also, and didst vouchsafe to glorify her beauteous Image by a wonderful appearing: grant, we beseech thee; that by the intercession of the same Virgin we, being delivered from every assault of perdition, may be enabled to live according to thy heart, and to attain with gladness to our heavenly country. Through the same.

Commemoration of St. Alexius, C. p. 719.

The Lesson from the book of Wisdom. Ecclus. 24, 7-15.

IN all things I sought rest, and in the inheritance of the Lord shall I abide. So the Creator of all things gave me a commandment: and he that made me caused my tabernacle to rest, and said: Let thy dwelling be in Jacob, and thine inheritance in Israel: and take root in my elect. And so was I established in Sion, likewise in the beloved city he gave me rest, and in Jerusalem was my power. And I took root in an honourable people, even in the portion of the Lord's inheritance, and my abode is in the full assembly of the Saints. I was exalted like a cedar in Libanus, and as a cypress tree upon the mountains of Hermon; I was exalted like a palm tree in En-gaddi, and as a rose plant in Jericho: as a fair olive tree in a pleasant field, and grew up as a plane tree by the water in the streets. I gave a sweet smell like cinnamon and aspálathus: and I yielded a pleasant odour like the best myrrh.

Gradual. Ps. 45, 12-14. All the rich among the people shall entreat thy countenance; the Virgins that be her fellows shall bear her company, and shall be brought unto thee with joy and gladness. ℣. Judith 13, 19. For the Lord hath so magnified thy name this day, that thy praise shall not depart from the mouth of men.

Alleluia, alleluia. ℣. Esther 15. And do thou call upon the Lord, and speak unto the King for us, and deliver us from death. Alleluia.

☩ The Continuation of the holy Gospel according to Luke.

Luke 11, 27-28.

AT that time: As Jesus spake to the multitudes, a certain woman of the company lifted up her voice, and said unto him: Blessed is the womb that bare thee, and the paps which thou hast sucked. But he said: Yea, rather, blessed are they that hear the word of God, and keep it. Creed.

Offertory. Remember, O Virgin Mother, in the sight of the Lord, that thou speak good things for us, and that he may turn away his indignation from us.

Secret.

ACCEPT, we beseech thee, O Lord, the gifts which we duly offer in this sacred commemoration: and through the interceding merits of the blessed Virgin Mary grant that they may avail for our succour and salvation. Through.

Preface of the B.V. Mary, And that on the Festival.

Communion. Queen of the world most worthy, Mary, Virgin perpetual, intercede for our peace and salvation, who didst bring forth Christ the Lord, the Saviour of all.

Postcommunion.

WE have received, O Lord, this Sacrament in due observance of this yearly festival: grant, we beseech thee; that at the intercession of blessed Mary ever Virgin it may bestow on us healing both in this life and for evermore. Through.

12
July 28.
St. Samson
Bishop and Confessor
Double.

The Mass Statuit, for a Confessor Bishop, p. [19].

9, 12
July 30.
Blessed Edward Powell, Richard Featherstone and Companions
Martyrs
Double.

The Mass Intret, p. [9], with Prayers from Mass Sapientiam, p. [11] and Epistle No. 4, Let us approve, as on the Feast of SS. Abdon and Sennen, MM., July 30, p. 735.

Commem. of the SS. Martyrs, p. 735.

11
July 30.
Blessed Everard Hanse
Martyr
Double.

The Mass Laetabitur, p. [7].

Commem. of the SS. Martyrs, p. 735.

18
July 30.

16
Commemoration, July 31.

9, 12
August 3.
St. Germanus
Bishop and Confessor
Double.

The Mass Sacerdotes tui, p. [20].

FEASTS OF AUGUST

7
August 5.
For Commemoration of St. Oswald
King and Martyr
Prayers from following Mass.

1, 2, 3, 6, 8, 14
August 8, 9 or 11.
St. Oswald
King and Martyr
Double.

14
August 8.
Introit. Ps. 21, 1. In virtute tua.

THE just shall rejoice in thy strength, O Lord: exceeding glad shall he be of thy salvation: thou hast given him his heart's desire. Ps. ibid., 2. For thou hast prevented him with the blessings of goodness: and hast set a crown of pure gold upon his head. ℣. Glory.

Collect.

ALMIGHTY and everlasting God, who by the martyrdom of blessed King Oswald hast sanctified this day with holy joy and gladness: pour into our hearts such abundant increase of thy love; that we, who honour his glorious battle for the faith, may imitate his constancy even unto death. Through.

Commemoration of SS. Cyriacus, Largus and Smaragdus, p. 748.

The Lesson from the book of Wisdom.
Wisd. 10, 10-14.

THE Lord guided the just in right paths, shewed him the kingdom of God, and gave him knowledge of holy things: made him rich in his travails, and multiplied the fruit of his labours. In the covetousness of such as oppressed him he stood by him, and made him rich. He defended him from his enemies, and kept him safe from those that lay in wait, and in a sore conflict he gave him the victory, that he might know that wisdom is stronger than all. When the just was sold, she forsook him not, but delivered him from sin: she went down with him into the pit, and left him not in bonds, till she brought him the sceptre of the kingdom, and power against those that oppressed him: as for them that had accused him, she shewed them to be liars, and gave him perpetual glory, even he, the Lord our God.

Gradual. Ps. 112, 1-2. Blessed is the man that feareth the Lord: he hath great delight in his commandments. ℣. His seed shall be mighty upon earth: the generation of the faithful shall be blessed.

Alleluia, alleluia. ℣. Ps. 21, 4. Thou hast set, O Lord, a crown of pure gold upon his head. Alleluia.

✠ The Continuation of the holy Gospel according to Matthew.

Matt. 16, 24-27.

AT that time: Jesus said unto his disciples: If any man will come after me, let him deny himself, and follow me. For whosoever will save his life shall lose it: and whosoever will lose his life for my sake shall find it. For what is a man profited, if he shall gain the whole world, and lose his own soul? Or what shall a man give in exchange for his soul? For the Son of man shall come in the glory of his Father with his Angels: and then he shall reward every man according to his works.

Offertory. Ps. 8, 6-7. Thou hast crowned him with glory and worship: thou hast made him to have dominion of the works of thy hands, O Lord.

Secret. C 3

WE beseech thee, O Lord, to accept our prayers and oblations: and graciously hearken unto us, whom thou dost cleanse by thy heavenly mysteries. Through.

Commemoration of SS. Cyriacus, etc., MM., p. 749.

Communion. Matt. 16, 24. He that will come after me, let him deny himself, and take up his cross, and follow me.

Postcommunion. C 3

GRANT, we beseech thee, O Lord our God: that as we in this life gladly honour the memory of thy Saints; so we may rejoice to behold them for ever. Through.

Commemoration of the SS. Martyrs, p. 749.

1

August 9.

Mass as above, except the following:

Commemoration of St. John Mary Vianney and the Vigil of St. Lawrence as on August 9th in Mass of Feast, p. 749.

Secret. P

MERCIFULLY receive, we beseech thee, O Lord, the gifts which we here offer to thy majesty in commemoration of Saint Oswald thy Martyr: and by thy grace inspire us with that fervent love which burned in him. Through.

England and Wales

Postcommunion. P

ALMIGHTY God, who hast renewed us with the food of life: we beseech thee; that, as we celebrate in solemn festival the glorious conflict of Saint Oswald thy Martyr, so through his intercession we may be assured of thy merciful goodness towards us. Through.

2
August 9.

All as on August 8, except the following:

Commemoration of the Vigil of St. Lawrence and St. Romanus, M., only, p. 751.

Secret. C 4

GRANT, O Lord, that this our bounden duty may be acceptable in thy sight: that these our oblations may, by the prayers of him on whose solemnity they are offered, be made profitable unto our salvation. Through.

Postcommunion. C 4

WE beseech thee, O Lord, that as we, whom thou hast refreshed by the partaking of thy sacred gift, offer unto thee our worship: so, by the intercession of blessed Oswald thy Martyr, we may perceive the benefit of the same. Through.

3, 8

Mass as on August 8, except the following:

Commemoration of St. John Mary Vianney, C., and the Vigil of St. Lawrence, p. 749. But for the Vigil the Postcommunion We beseech thee, (C4) is said, as immediately above, substituting Lawrence for Oswald.

6
August 11.

Mass as on August 8th, but Commemoration is made of SS. Tiburtius and Susanna, V., MM., p. 754.

14

The same day, August 11.

St. Germanus

Bishop and Confessor

Double.

The Mass Sacerdotes tui, p. [20].

Commemoration of SS. Tiburtius and Susanna, V., MM., p. 754.

2

The same day, August 11.

St. John Mary Vianney

Confessor

Double.

The Mass Os justi, for a Confessor not a Bishop, p. [24], with the Prayers as below:

Collect. P

ALMIGHTY and merciful God, who didst make Saint John Mary wondrous in pastoral zeal and in continual fervour of prayer and penance: grant, we beseech thee, that by his example and intercession we may be enabled to gain the souls of our brethren for Christ, and with them to attain to eternal glory. Through the same.

Commemoration of SS. Tiburtius and Susanna, MM., p. 754.

Secret. P

ALMIGHTY and everlasting God, let the invisible fulness of the Holy Ghost descend upon this spotless sacrifice: and grant; that at the intercession of Saint John Mary we may ever draw near with chaste bodies and pure hearts to this great mystery. Through... in the unity of the same Holy Ghost.

Postcommunion.

O LORD, who hast refreshed us with the food of Angels, we beseech thee: that like as Saint John Mary in the strength of this bread endured all adversities with unbroken constancy; so we, aided by his merits and following his example, may go from strength to strength, and be brought with gladness unto thee. Through.

5: D.   6: Sp.   15: D. 1st class.

August 18.

St. Helen
Empress, Widow

Introit. Gal. 6, 14. Mihi autem.

BUT God forbid that I should glory, save in the Cross of our Lord Jesus Christ: by whom the world is crucified unto me, and I unto the world. Ps. 23, 4. Thy rod and thy staff comfort me. ℣. Glory.

Collect.

O LORD Jesu Christ, who didst reveal unto blessed Helen the place where thy Cross lay hid, that through her thou mightest enrich thy Church with this precious treasure: grant unto us at her intercession; that by the ransom of the life-giving tree we may attain unto the rewards of everlasting life: Who livest.

5, 6: Commemoration of St. Agapitus, M., p. 760.

The Lesson from the book of Wisdom. Prov. 31, 10-31.

WHO can find a virtuous woman? For her price is far above rubies. The heart of her husband doth safely trust in her, so that he shall have no need of spoil. She will do him good and not evil all the days of her life. She seeketh wool, and flax, and worketh willingly with her hands. She is like the merchants' ships, she bringeth her food from afar. She riseth also while it is yet night, and giveth meat to her household, and a portion to her maidens. She considereth a field, and buyeth it: with the fruit of her hands she planteth a vine-yard. She girdeth her loins with strength, and strengtheneth her arms. She perceiveth that her merchandise is good: her candle goeth not out by night. She layeth her hands to the spindle, and her hands hold the distaff. She stretcheth out her hand to the poor, yea, she reacheth forth her hands to the needy. She is not afraid of the snow for her household: for all her household are clothed with scarlet. She maketh herself coverings of tapestry: her clothing is silk and purple. Her husband is known in the gates, when he sitteth among the elders of the land. She maketh fine linen, and selleth it, and delivereth girdles unto the merchant. Strength and honour are her clothing, and she shall rejoice in time to come. She openeth her mouth with wisdom, and in her tongue is the law of kindness. She looketh well to the ways of her household, and eateth not the bread of idleness. Her children arise up, and call her blessed: her husband also, and he praiseth her. Many daughters have done virtuously, but thou excellest them all. Favour is deceitful, and beauty is vain: but a woman that feareth the Lord, she shall be praised. Give her of the fruit of her hands: and let her own works praise her in the gates.

Gradual. Ps. 45, 13, 10 and 15-16. The rich among the people shall make their supplication before thee: Kings' daughters were among thine honourable women. ℣. The Virgins that be her fellows shall be brought unto the King: they that bear her company shall be brought unto thee. ℣. With joy and gladness shall they be brought: they shall enter the palace of the King.

Alleluia, alleluia. ℣. Ps. 112, 9. He hath dispersed abroad; he hath given to the poor: his righteousness remaineth for ever. Alleluia.

✠ The Continuation of the holy Gospel according to Matthew.

Matt. 13, 44-52.

AT that time: Jesus spake this parable unto his disciples: The kingdom of heaven is like unto treasure hid in a field: the which when a man hath found, he hideth, and for joy thereof goeth and selleth all that he hath, and buyeth that field. Again, the kingdom of heaven is like unto a merchant man, seeking goodly pearls. Who, when he had found one pearl of great price, went and sold all that he had, and bought it. Again, the kingdom of heaven is like unto a net, that was cast into the sea, and gathered of every kind. Which, when it was full, they drew to shore, and sat down, and gathered the good into vessels, but cast the bad away. So shall it be at the end of the world: the Angels shall come forth, and sever the wicked from among the just, and shall cast them into the furnace of fire: there shall be wailing and gnashing of teeth. Jesus saith unto them: Have ye understood all these things? They say unto him: Yea, Lord. Then said he unto them: Therefore every scribe which is instructed unto the kingdom of heaven is like unto a man that is an householder, which bringeth forth out of his treasure things new and old.

15: The Creed is said.

Offertory. I Cor. 2, 2. For I determined not to know any thing, save Jesus Christ, and him crucified.

Secret.

THROUGH these sacred mysteries vouchsafe unto us, O Lord: that as in thy mercy thou didst grant unto blessed Helen ever to carry thy Son crucified in her heart; so we may likewise continually bear him in our hearts: Who liveth and reigneth with thee.

Communion. Song of Sol. 7, 8. I will go up to the palm-tree, I will take hold of the boughs thereof.

Postcommunion.

GRANT unto us, O merciful God: that we who have been refreshed by the benefits of thy life-giving Cross on earth; may through the intercession of blessed Helen attain unto the eternal fruition of the same in heaven: Who livest.

1, 3, 4

August 26.

Blessed Thomas Percy

Martyr

Double.

The Mass as on Feast of Blessed Hadrian Fortescue, July 11, p. 898 substituting Thomas for Hadrian.

10

The same day, August 26.

Blessed John Wall

Martyr

Double.

The Mass In virtute, p. [6], with Prayers as below.

Collect.

POUR forth upon us, O Lord, we beseech thee, the spirit of constancy and fortitude, wherewith thou didst strengthen thy blessed Martyr John for the defence of the Catholic faith: that we, being filled therewith, may be worthy to attain to the fellowship of his glory in heaven, in whose triumphal passion we rejoice on earth. Through.

Commemoration of St. Zephyrinus, P.M., p. 770.

Secret.

MAY the Holy Ghost, O Lord, pour his blessing upon our gifts: and make us stedfast in that faith, whereto blessed John thy Martyr bare witness both by the word of his mouth and the shedding of his blood. Through... in the unity of the same Holy Ghost.

Postcommunion.

GRANT us, O Lord, through the holy mysteries which we have received, to imitate the zeal and constancy of blessed John: who by the example of his courage hath kindled us, and by his martyrdom hath strengthened us to desire the things eternal. Through.

1, 2, 3, 6, 8, 11, 16

August 31.

St. Aidan

Bishop and Confessor

Double.

The Mass Statuit, for a Confessor Bishop, p. [19].

Commemoration of St. Raymund Nonnatus, C., p. 776.

FEASTS OF SEPTEMBER

7

September 1.

Blessed Hugh More

Martyr

Double.

Introit. Ps. 27, 10.

MY father and my mother have forsaken me: but the Lord hath raised me up. Ps. ibid., 1. The Lord is my light and my salvation, whom then shall I fear? ℣. Glory.

Collect.

O GOD, who didst make blessed Hugh to overcome cruel torments: mercifully grant; that we, being stirred up by the love of our fatherland in heaven, may be enabled to set things heavenly before things earthly. Through.

Commemoration of St. Giles, Ab., and the SS. Martyrs, p. 776.

The Epistle, Gradual and Gospel from the Mass In virtute, p. [6].

Offertory. Numb. 18, 20. I am thy portion and thine inheritance among the children of Israel.

Secret.

WE beseech thee, O Lord, that the gifts which we humbly offer unto thee may at the intercession of blessed Hugh thy Martyr be pleasing to thy majesty; and graciously make them to be profitable unto us. Through.

Communion. Rev. 3, 21. To him that overcometh will I grant to sit in my throne.

Postcommunion.

O LORD, who hast sanctified us with this heavenly mystery, we beseech thee: that being taught by the example and supported by the prayer of blessed Hugh; we may never be afraid of any threats, and may boldly confess our faith. Through.

15

The same day, September 1.

St. Sebbe

King and Confessor

Double.

The Mass Justus ut palma, p. [25], except the following:

Collect.

O GOD, who didst teach blessed Sebbe to lay down an earthly princedom for a heavenly realm: make us, we beseech thee, by following his example to shun the enticements of this world, and with pure hearts to attain unto thee. Through.

Commemoration of St. Giles, Ab., and the SS. Martyrs, p. 776.

The Lesson from the Epistle of blessed Paul the Apostle to the Philippians.

Phil. 3, 7-12.

BRETHREN: What things were gain to me, those I counted loss for Christ. Yea doubtless, and I count all things but loss for the excellency of the knowledge of Christ Jesus my Lord: for whom I have suffered the loss of all things, and do count them but dung, that I may win Christ and be found in him, not having mine own righteousness which is of the law, but that which is through the faith of Christ: the righteousness which is of God by faith, that I may know him, and the power of his resurrection, and the fellowship of his sufferings: being made comformable unto his death: if by any means I might attain unto the resurrection of the dead: not as though I had already attained, either were already perfect; but I follow after, if that I may apprehend that for which also I am apprehended of Christ Jesus.

Gospel, If any man come to me, p. [4].

15

September 4.

SS. Hildelitha and Cuthberga

Virgins

Double.

Introit. Ps. 147, 13. Virgines.

LET the Virgins praise the name of the Lord: for his name only is exalted: his praise is above heaven and earth. Ps. ibid., 1. O praise the Lord of heaven: praise him in the height. ℣. Glory.

Collect.

O GOD, who didst abundantly adorn thine handmaids Hildelitha and Cuthberga with the gifts of wondrous purity: grant to us thy servants, by the merit of their intercession, health of body and soul; that as their festival is celebrated by us on earth, so through their advocacy our desire may ever turn to thee in heaven. Through.

The Epistle, Concerning virgins, p. [33].

Gradual. Ps. 45, 2. Thou art fairer than the children of men: full of grace are thy lips. ℣. Ibid., 9. Kings' daughters were among thine honourable women: upon thy right hand did stand the queen in a vesture of gold. Alleluia, alleluia. ℣. Wisd. 4. O how beautiful is the chaste generation with its glory. Alleluia.

The Gospel, The kingdom of heaven shall be likened to ten virgins, p. [32].

Offertory. Ps. 34. Draw nigh unto the Lord and be enlightened: and your faces shall not be ashamed.

Secret.

O MERCIFUL God, let the advocacy of thy blessed Virgins Hildelitha and Cuthberga commend us to thy majesty, as we offer to thee the sacrifice of praise: who in their virginity made ready a dwelling-place pleasing unto thee by works agreeable to the same. Through.

Communion. Matt. 25. The bridegroom came: and the virgins that were ready went in with him to the marriage, and the door was shut.

Postcommunion.

O LORD, let the sacred partaking of thy Body and Blood, at the intercession of thy blessed Virgins Hildelitha and Cuthberga, turn us from all things transitory: that we may be able on earth to grow in sincerity and love, and in heaven to rejoice in the perpetual vision of thyself: Who livest.

1

The same day, September 4.

Translation of St. Cuthbert

Bishop and Confessor

Greater double.

The Mass Sacerdotes, for a Confessor Bishop, p. [20], except the Prayers.

Collect.

GRANT to us, we beseech thee, almighty and merciful God: that we, who venerate the day of the translation of blessed Cuthbert thy Confessor and Bishop, may through his intercession obtain the benefit of thy loving-kindness. Through.

Secret.

SANCTIFY, we beseech thee, O Lord, these gifts by the intercession of blessed Cuthbert, thy Confessor and Bishop, and graciously cleanse us thy servants from the stains of all our sins. Through.

Postcommunion.

WE beseech thee, O Lord: let blessed Cuthbert, thy Confessor and Bishop, whose translation we celebrate this day, obtain for us by his prayers and intercession, that this Communion may render us well-pleasing unto thee. Through.

2

September 6.

St. Begh

Virgin

Double.

The Mass Dilexisti, p. [31].

9

September 11.

St. Deiniol

Bishop and Confessor

Double.

The Mass Statuit, for a Confessor Bishop, p. [19].

Commemoration of SS. Protus and Hyacinth, MM., p. 783.

1, 2

September 16.

St. Ninian

Bishop and Confessor

Double.

The Mass Sacerdotes tui, for a Confessor Bishop, p. [20].

Commemoration of SS. Cornelius, P., and Cyprian, B., MM., p. 789.

13

The same day, September 16.

For Commemoration of St. Edith

Virgin

Collect.

O GOD, who didst will that thy Son, our Lord, should be born of a Virgin, and didst thereby give unto thy faithful a pattern of chastity: grant to us through the prayers of Saint Edith thy Virgin; such piety as may win for us the felicity which thou hast promised. Through the same.

Secret.

LET thy benediction, O Lord, we beseech thee, descend upon this our oblation: and may Saint Edith obtain of thee, that we ourselves may be made a sacrifice acceptable unto thee. Through.

Postcommunion.

O LORD, let the partaking of this spiritual table avail to us for salvation of body and soul, and may the supplication of Saint Edith thy Virgin commend us unto thee. Through.

September 19.

1

Commemoration.

5, 14, 15, 17

Double.

2

September 26.

St. Theodore

Bishop and Confessor

Double.

The Mass Statuit, for a Confessor Bishop, p. [19].

Com. of SS. Cyprian, etc., MM., p. 799.

9, 12

September 25.

St. Cadoc

Bishop and Martyr

Double.

The Mass Statuit, for a Martyr Bishop, p. [4].

7, 17

September 30.

For Commemoration of St. Honorius

Bishop and Confessor

Prayers from Mass Statuit, for a Confessor Bishop, p. [19].

FEASTS OF OCTOBER

October 3 or 5 or 22.

8: [3rd].

10: [Commemoration 3rd].

5, 12: [5th].

14: [22nd].

St. Thomas of Hereford

Bishop and Confessor

Double.

The Mass Sacerdotes tui, for a Confessor Bishop, p. [20], the Collect excepted.

Collect.

O GOD, who didst adorn thy Church with the angelic purity and glorious virtues of the blessed Bishop Thomas: grant unto us thy servants; that, by his prevailing merits, we may with him be made worthy to be joined unto the companies of Angels. Through.

Secret.

WE beseech thee, O Lord, that our devout observance of the yearly solemnity of Saint Thomas, thy Confessor and Bishop, may render us acceptable unto thy loving-kindness: that this service of propitiation, which we duly offer, may be profitable unto him for the reward of blessedness, and obtain for us the gifts of thy grace. Through.

Postcommunion.

O GOD, who rewardest the souls of them that put their trust in thee: vouchsafe; that we who keep the solemn festival of blessed Thomas, thy Confessor and Bishop, may by his prayers obtain thy merciful pardon. Through.

13
October 8.
For Commemoration of St. Keyna
Virgin
Collect.

GRACIOUSLY hear us, O God of our salvation: that, as we rejoice in the festival of blessed Keyna thy Virgin; so we may be instructed in all godly and devout affection. Through.

Secret.

GRACIOUSLY receive, O Lord, through the merits of blessed Keyna thy Virgin, the sacrifices which we offer unto thee: and grant that they may avail for our continual help. Through.

Postcommunion.

O LORD our God, who hast fulfilled us with the bounty of thy heavenly gift: we beseech thee, that, at the intercession of blessed Keyna, thy Virgin, we may ever live by the partaking of the same. Through.

October 10.
1, 2, 3, 4, 6, 7, 17
St. Paulinus
Bishop and Confessor
Double.
(7: Sp.)

The Mass Statuit, p. [19].

Commemoration of St. Francis Borgia, C., p. 817.

15
October 12.
St. Ethelburga
Virgin
Double.

The Mass Vultum, p. [33], except the Collect.

O GOD, who makest us glad with the yearly solemnity of blessed Ethelburga, thy Virgin: mercifully grant; that as we are illumined by the example of her purity, so we may likewise be aided by her merits. Through.

The same day, October 12.
1, 2, 3, 4, 6, 7, 8, 10, 11, 16, 17
St. Wilfrid
Bishop and Confessor
Double.
(3, 4, 16: Greater double. 7: Sp.)

The Mass Sacerdotes tui, for a Confessor Bishop, p. [20], the Prayers excepted.

Collect.   P

O GOD, by whose grace thy blessed Bishop Wilfrid did wondrously shine forth with the glorious tokens of his merits: mercifully grant unto us; that we, who by his doctrine are taught to seek after things heavenly, may ever be defended by his intercession. Through.

Secret.   P

CLEANSE, we beseech thee, almighty God, the hearts of thy family by the enlightening of thy Holy Spirit: that through the intercession of blessed Wilfrid, thy Confessor and Bishop, this offering of our bounden duty and service may be rendered acceptable unto thee. Through... in the unity of the same Holy Spirit.

Postcommunion.   P

O LORD, who hast fulfilled us with the food of eternal redemption, we humbly beseech thy mercy: that by the interceding merits of blessed Wilfrid, thy Confessor and Bishop, we may receive the gift of everlasting salvation. Through.

October 13.

England and Wales.

St. Edward

King and Confessor

Double of 2nd class.

14, 15

Greater double.

The Mass as on p. 819.

9

October 16.

Blessed Richard Gwyn

Martyr

Double.

The Mass Laetabitur, p. [7], except:

Collect. P

O GOD, who didst raise up thy blessed Martyr Richard to be a teacher of the young and a defender of the Catholic faith: grant, we beseech thee; that we, being strengthened through his example in the same, may attain unto thee in everlasting felicity. Through.

10

October 19.

St. Frideswide

Virgin

Greater double.

The Mass Dilexisti, p. [31], the Prayers excepted.

Collect. P

ALMIGHTY and everlasting God, the author of all goodness and the lover of virgin purity: grant us, we beseech thee; that, like as thy Virgin Frideswide was pleasing unto thee by reason of her chastity of life; so through her merits we may find favour in thy sight. Through.

Commemoration is made of St. Peter Alcantara, C., p. 824.

Secret. P

WE offer thee, O Lord, our prayers and gifts with gladness in honour of Saint Frideswide thy Virgin: that we may be enabled worthily to perform the same, and to obtain thine everlasting healing. Through.

Postcommunion. P

WE beseech thee, O Lord, that the mysteries which we have received may be profitable unto us: that, through the intercession of thy blessed Virgin Frideswide, they may both deliver us from our sins, and obtain for us thy gracious protection. Through.

3

October 21.

St. John of Bridlington

Confessor

Double.

The Mass Os justi, for a Confessor not a Bishop, p. [24], except:

Collect. P

O GOD, who didst make blessed John thy Confessor to be numbered with thy Saints: mercifully grant; that we, who celebrate the festival of his commemoration, may likewise follow the example of his life. Through.

14
October 22.
St. Thomas of Hereford
Bishop and Confessor
Double.
Mass as on October 3, p. 910.

16
October 24.
For Commemoration of St. Maglorious (Malo)
Bishop and Confessor
Prayers from Mass Sacerdotes, for a Confessor Bishop, p. [20].

3, 4, 6
October 25.
St. John of Beverley
Bishop and Confessor
Double.

3
Greater double.
All as on May 7, p. 880.
Commemoration of SS. Chrysanthus and Daria, MM., p. 830.

2
October 26.
St. Eata
Bishop and Confessor
Double.
The Mass Statuit, for a Confessor Bishop, p. [19].
Commemoration of St. Evaristus, P.M., p. 831.

October 29 or 30.
The Blessed Martyrs of Douai
14: [29th] Double.
1: [30th] Greater double.
The Mass Deus venerunt, as on May 4, the Collect and Gospel excepted.

Collect.   P

STIR up in us, O Lord, the Spirit whom thy blessed Martyrs of Douai served: that we, being filled with the same, may study to love that which they loved, and to perform in deed that which they taught. Through ... in the unity of the same Holy Spirit.

The Gospel, Beware ye of the leaven, p. [13].

Secret.   P
(as on May 4.)

GRACIOUSLY hearken, O Lord, unto the voices of thy blessed Martyrs who cry from beneath thine altar, and mercifully regard our oblations.   Through.

Postcommunion.   P
(as on May 4.)

O LORD our God, who hast refreshed us with this heavenly banquet: we beseech thee, that by the intercession of thy blessed Martyrs, we may be made worthy to attain unto their fellowship. Through.

FEASTS OF NOVEMBER
8, 9
November 3.
St. Winifred
Virgin and Martyr
Greater double.
The Mass Me exspectaverunt, p. [29] except the Prayers as below, and Gospel from Mass Loquebar, p. [28].

Collect. P

ALMIGHTY and everlasting God, who didst bestow on blessed Winifred the reward of virgin purity: make us, we beseech thee, by her intercession to lay aside the enticements of the world; and with her to attain unto the abode of everlasting glory. Through.

Secret. P

MERCIFULLY regard, O Lord, the oblations which we present unto thee: and at the intercession of blessed Winifred, thy Virgin and Martyr, loose the bonds of our sins. Through.

Postcommunion. P

WE beseech thee, O merciful God, let this our bounden service be pleasing unto thee: that the most holy mysteries which we have received, may at the intercession of blessed Winifred, thy Virgin and Martyr, both win for us thy grace, and also bestow on us the joy of everlasting felicity. Through.

1, 2, 6, 9, 10, 12, 14, 15, 16

November 5.

The Sacred Relics

Greater double.

Introit. Ps. 34, 19. Multae tribulationes.

GREAT are the troubles of the righteous, but the Lord delivereth him out of all: he keepeth all his bones: so that not one of them is broken. Ps. ibid., 1. I will alway give thanks unto the Lord: his praise shall ever be in my mouth. ℣. Glory.

Collect.

O LORD, who in the relics of thy Saints dost perform thy marvellous works: increase in us our faith in the resurrection; that as in their ashes we venerate the pledges of immortal glory, so by thee we may be made partakers of the same. Through.

The Lesson from the book of Wisdom.

Ecclus. 44, 10-15.

THESE were merciful men, whose righteousness hath not been forgotten: with their seed shall continually remain a good inheritance, and their children are within the covenant: their seed standeth fast, and their children for their sakes: their seed shall remain for ever, and their glory shall not be blotted out. Their bodies are buried in peace, but their name liveth for evermore. The people will tell of their wisdom and the Church will shew forth their praise.

Gradual. Ps. 149, 5. The Saints shall be joyful in glory: they shall rejoice in their beds. ℣. Ibid., 1. O sing unto the Lord a new song; let the congregation of Saints praise him.

Alleluia, alleluia. ℣. Ps. 68, 3. Let the righteous be glad and rejoice before God: let them also be merry and joyful. Alleluia.

✠ The Continuation of the holy Gospel according to Luke.

Luke 6, 17-23.

AT that time: Jesus came down from the mountain, and stood in the plain, and the company of his disciples, and a great multitude of people out of all Judæa and Jerusalem, and from the coast of Tyre and Sidon, which came to hear him, and to be healed of their diseases, and they that were vexed with unclean spirits. And they were healed. And the whole multitude sought to touch him: for there went virtue out of him, and healed them all. And he lifted up his eyes on his disciples, and said: Blessed be ye poor: for yours is the kingdom of God.

Blessed are ye that hunger now: for ye shall be filled. Blessed are ye that weep now: for ye shall laugh. Blessed are ye, when men shall hate you, and when they shall separate you from their company, and shall reproach you, and cast out your name as evil, for the Son of man's sake. Rejoice ye in that day, and leap for joy: for behold your reward is great in heaven.

Offertory. Ps. 68, 35. God is wonderful in his Saints: even the God of Israel he will give strength and power unto his people: blessed be God, alleluia.

Secret.

WE humbly entreat thy mercy, O Lord: that by the merits and intercession of thy Saints, whose relics we venerate, the sacrifice which we offer may do away our offences. Through.

Communion. Ps. 33, 1. Rejoice in the Lord, O ye righteous: for it becometh well the just to be thankful.

Postcommunion.

MULTIPLY upon us, O Lord, we beseech thee, thy loving-kindness through these holy gifts which we have received: that as we rejoice with godly devotion in the solemnity of thy Saints, whose relics we now honour, so by thy bounty we may enjoy their everlasting fellowship. Through.

12

November 6.

St. Illtyd

Abbot

Double.

The Mass Os justi, for an Abbot, p. [26].

1

November 7.

St. Willibrord

Bishop and Confessor

Simple.

The Mass Statuit, for a Confessor Bishop, p. [19], except:

Collect.   P

O GOD, who to proclaim thy glory among the nations, didst vouchsafe to send forth blessed Willibrord, thy Confessor and Bishop: grant through his merits and prayers; that those things which thou commandest us to do, we may by thy mercy have power to fulfil. Through.

17

November 10.

St. Justus

Bishop and Confessor

Double.

The Mass Statuit, for a Confessor Bishop, p. [19], with the following Collect:

Collect.   P

GRACIOUSLY hearken unto thy people, O Lord, whose hearts are devoted unto thee, and protect them through the supplication of blessed Justus, the Confessor and Bishop: that they may desire those things which they devoutly believe, and may surely attain unto those things for which they justly hope. Through.

Commemoration of St. Andrew and SS. Tryphon, etc, p. 839.

Secret.   C

WE beseech thee, O Lord, that, remembering with gladness the merits of thy Saints, we may in all places feel the succour of their intercession. Through.

Postcommunion. C

GRANT, we beseech thee, almighty God: that we, shewing forth our thankfulness for the gifts which we have received, may, at the intercession of blessed Justus, thy Confessor and Bishop, obtain yet more abundant mercies. Through.

12

November 14.

St. Dubritius

Bishop and Confessor

Double.

The Mass Statuit, for a Confessor Bishop, p. [19].

Commemoration of St. Josaphat, B.M., p. 843.

16

The same day, November 14.

For Commemoration of Blessed Hugh Cook and his Companions

Martyrs

Collect. P

O GOD, who didst strengthen thy blessed Martyrs Hugh and his Companions with invincible courage for the defence of the true faith and the primacy of the Apostolic see: hearken, we beseech thee, to their prayers; and succour our infirmity, that we being stedfast in the faith may be able to resist the adversary even to the end. Through.

Secret. P

MAY the gifts of thy people, O Lord, become more acceptable to thee through the commemoration of thy blessed Martyrs: and by this holy oblation and partaking avail for our salvation unto everlasting life. Through.

Postcommunion. P

O LORD Jesu Christ, whom we proclaim glorious in the charity of thy blessed Martyrs: grant, we beseech thee, through their prayers; that we may ever abide in thy love: Who livest.

13

November 15.

Blessed Richard Whiting and his Companions

Martyrs.

Double.

The Mass Salus, p. [12], except the Prayers.

Commemoration of St. Albert, B.C.D., p. 844.

No Creed.

Collect. P

ALMIGHTY and everlasting God, who didst give to thy holy Martyrs Richard and his Companions both patience in suffering and a blessed triumph in their warfare: grant to us, who live beneath their patronage, that we may be preserved in perpetual safety and may rejoice in the work of our salvation. Through.

Secret. P

MAY this victim, O Lord, to be hallowed in celebration of this precious martyrdom, obtain for us thy mercy; that it may both purify our hearts and render the prayers of thy servants acceptable to thee. Through.

Postcommunion. P

O LORD, who hast bestowed on us the grace of this sacred gift, we beseech thee: that through the supplication of thy holy Martyrs on our behalf, we may perceive in our souls the effects of that divine power which in our bodies we have received. Through.

Everywhere (except 1, 2, 7, 9, 12).

November 16.

St. Edmund

Bishop and Confessor

Greater double.

The Mass Statuit, for a Confessor Bishop, p. [19], except the Prayers as below:

14, 15, 16: Mass is said as follows:

Introit. Gaudeamus.

REJOICE we all in the Lord, keeping feast day in honour of blessed Edmund: in whose solemnity the Angels rejoice, and glorify the Son of God. Ps. 33, 1. Rejoice in the Lord, O ye righteous: for it becometh well the just to be thankful. ℣. Glory.

Collect.

O GOD, who in the counsels of thine abundant goodness didst adorn thy Church with the merits of the wondrous life of blessed Edmund, thy Confessor and Bishop, and gladden her by his glorious miracles: mercifully grant unto us thy servants; that by his example we may learn to amend our lives, and by his advocacy be defended against all adversities. Through.

And Commemoration is made of St. Gertrude, V., p. 845.

Collect.

O GOD, who in the heart of blessed Gertrude thy Virgin didst prepare a mansion acceptable unto thyself: we beseech thee by her merits and intercession mercifully to cleanse our hearts from all defilement; that we may rejoice in her everlasting fellowship. Through.

The Lesson from the book of Wisdom.

Ecclus. 50, 1-11.

BEHOLD a great priest, who in his life repaired the house again, and in his days took care of the temple that it should not fall. He fortified the city against besieging; how was he honoured in the midst of the people in his coming out of the sanctuary! He was as the morning star in the midst of a cloud, and as the moon at the full; as the sun shining upon the temple of the Most High. And as the rainbow giving light in the bright clouds, and as the flower of roses in the spring of the year, as lilies by the rivers of waters, as fire and incense in the censer. And as a vessel of beaten gold set with all manner of precious stones. And as a fair olive tree budding forth fruit, and as a cypress tree which groweth up to the clouds. When he put on the robe of honour and was clothed with the perfection of glory.

Gradual. Ps. 21, 3-4. Thou hast prevented him, O Lord, with the blessings of goodness: thou hast set a crown of pure gold upon his head. ℣. He asked life of thee, and thou gavest him a long life, even for ever and ever.

Alleluia, alleluia. ℣. Edmund, poor and lowly, enters heaven rich, he is honoured with celestial hymns. Alleluia.

✠ The Continuation of the holy Gospel according to Matthew.

Matt. 25, 14-23.

AT that time: Jesus spake this parable unto his disciples: A man travelling into a far country, called his own servants, and delivered unto them his goods. And unto one he gave five talents, to another two, and to another one, to every man according to his several ability, and staightway took his journey. Then he that had received the five talents went and traded with the same, and made them other five talents. And likewise he that had received two, he also gained other two. But he that had received one, went and digged in the earth, and hid his lord's money. After a long time the lord of those servants cometh, and reckoned with them. And so he that had received five talents came and brought other five talents, saying: Lord, thou deliveredst unto me five talents, behold, I have gained beside them five talents more. His lord said unto him: Well done, thou good and faithful servant, thou hast been faithful over a few things, I will make thee ruler over many things: enter thou into the joy of thy Lord. He also that had received two talents came and said: Lord, thou deliveredst unto me two talents, behold, I have gained two other talents beside them. His lord said unto him: Well done, good and faithful servant, thou hast been faithful over a few things, I will make thee ruler over many things: enter thou into the joy of thy lord.

Offertory. Ps. 89, 24. My truth and my mercy shall be with him and in my name shall his horn be exalted.

Secret. P

WE beseech thee, O Lord, that the gifts now to be offered may be made acceptable unto thee through the prayers of blessed Edmund, thy Confessor and Bishop: and that the oblation thereof may be profitable for our salvation. Through.

For St. Gertrude. Secret.

GRANT, O Lord, that like as thy dedicated people do acknowledge that in tribulation they have been succoured by the merits of thy Saints; so this oblation, which we offer unto thee in honour of the same, may be acceptable in thy sight. Through.

Communion. Matt. 24, 46-47. Blessed is the servant, whom the lord when he cometh shall find watching: verily I say unto you, that he shall make him ruler over all his goods.

Postcommunion. P

WE beseech thee, O Lord, strengthen our souls by the sacraments which we have received: that as thou hast vouchsafed to confirm them by the wondrous miracles of blessed Edmund, thy Confessor and Bishop, so also thou wouldest vouchsafe to succour us by his intercession, and to enlighten us by his example. Through.

For St. Gertrude. Postcommunion.

O LORD, who hast satisfied this thy family with thy sacred gifts: we beseech thee, that we may at all times be comforted by the intercession of her whose festival we celebrate. Through.

7, 10, 11, 13, 14.
November 17.
St. Hugh
Bishop and Confessor
Double.

The Mass Sacerdotes tui, for a Confessor Bishop p. [19], the Prayers excepted.

Collect, P

O GOD, who didst wondrously adorn blessed Hugh, thy Confessor and Bishop, with pre-eminent merits and glorious miracles: mercifully grant; that we may be stirred up by his example and enlightened by his virtues. Through.

Commemoration of St. Gregory Thaumaturgus, B.C., p. 846.

Secret. P

WE beseech thee, O Lord, that blessed Hugh, thy Confessor and Bishop, may commend the gifts which we offer: that we, being aided by his merits, may obtain both grace and glory. Through.

Feasts of November (17, 20, 27)

Postcommunion. P

WE beseech thee, O Lord, that blessed Hugh, thy Confessor and Bishop, may render the performance of our service acceptable unto thee: lest our guilt put far from us the benefit of this heavenly Sacrament. Through.

3
The same day, **November 17.**
St. Hilda
Virgin.
Double.

The Mass Dilexisti, p. [31], except the Prayers and Gradual.

Collect. P

GRANT, we beseech thee almighty God: that we, who rejoice in the yearly solemnity of blessed Hilda, thy Virgin, may by her intercession be led from our old nature to newness of life. Through.

Commemoration of St. Gregory, B.C., p. 846.

Gradual. Ps. 45. Thou hast loved righteousness and hated iniquity. V. Therefore God, even thy God, hath anointed thee with the oil of gladness.

Alleluia, alleluia. V. II Cor. 11. For I am jealous over you with godly jealousy: for I have espoused you to one husband, that I may present you as a chaste virgin to Christ. Alleluia.

For St. Hilda. Secret.

WE bring these our sacrifices, O Lord, to be offered unto thee: beseeching thee, that through the merits of blessed Hilda we, being reconciled thereby to thy mercy, may be made a living sacrifice, acceptable unto thee. Through.

Postcommunion. P

O LORD, through whom we have received the benediction of this heavenly banquet, we entreat thee: that as to us it is thy sacrament, so at the intercession of blessed Hilda, thy Virgin, it may effectually avail for our salvation. Through.

11, 14.
November 20.
St. Edmund
King and Martyr
Greater double.

The Mass In virtute, p. [6], the Prayers excepted.

Collect. P

O GOD of unspeakable mercy, who didst give the most blessed King Edmund grace to overcome the enemy by dying for thy name: mercifully grant unto us thy servants; that by his intercession they may be worthy to vanquish and subdue the temptations of their ancient foe. Through.

Commemoration of St. Felix, C., p. 849.

Secret. P

WE beseech thee, almighty God, mercifully look upon this sacrifice of our redemption: and at the intercession of blessed Edmund, thy King and Martyr, graciously accept it for this thy family. Through.

Postcommunion. P

LET the performance of our bounden duty and service be acceptable unto thee, almighty God: that these holy mysteries, which we have received may, at the intercession of blessed Edmund, thy King and Martyr, be profitable unto us for the attainment of the rewards of everlasting life. Through.

13
November 27.
For St. Cungar
Abbot

The Mass Os justi, for an Abbot, p. [26].

OTHER FEASTS

Contained in the Calendar of the Book of Common Prayer, but for which no Mass is provided in the Proper of Saints.

In each case a Mass given in the appropriate Common may be used, where these Feasts are observed.

January 8.	St. Lucian, Priest and Martyr.
April 4.	St. Ambrose, Bishop, Confessor and Doctor.
June 1.	St. Nicomede, Martyr.
June 20.	Translation of St. Edward, King and Martyr.
July 4.	Translation of St. Martin, Bishop and Confessor.
September 7.	St. Enurchus (Evurtius), Bishop and Confessor.
September 17.	St. Lambert, Bishop and Martyr.
October 6.	St. Faith, Virgin and Martyr.
October 25.	St. Crispin, Martyr.
November 6.	St. Leonard, Abbot.
November 13.	St. Britius, Bishop and Confessor.
November 15.	St. Machutus, Bishop and Confessor.

The appropriate Common is also used for any Patronal or Titular Feast, for which no Mass is provided in the Proper of Saints.

MASSES PROPER FOR SCOTLAND

The numbers preceding local Feasts in this Proper indicate the Dioceses or districts in which they are to be observed, as follows:

19: Aberdeen and Orkney; Moray; *Kincardineshire.*

20: Argyll and the Isles.

21: Edinburgh (*with S. Fife—right of the river Eden.*)

22: Glasgow and Galloway.

23: St. Andrew's (*except S. Fife*), Dunkeld and Dunblane; Brechin (*except Kincardineshire*).

CALENDAR

JANUARY

14 In all Scotland: St. Kentigern, Bp. and Conf., double. Com. St. Hilary, Bp., Conf. and Doct. of the Ch., and St. Felix, Priest and Mart. Glasgow and Dumbartonshire: double I class.
19 19: St. Nathalan, Bp. and Conf., double.
    23: St. Fillan, Abbot, double. Com. SS. Marius and Comp., MM., and St. Canute, King, Mart.

FEBRUARY

17 20: St. Finan, Bp. and Conf., double.
18 20: St. Colman, Bp. and Conf., **double**. Com. Feria and St. Simeon Bp. and Mart.

MARCH

8 19: St. Duthac, Bp. and Conf., double. Com. Feria and St. John of God, Conf.
10 In all Scotland: Bl. John Ogilvie, Mart., greater double. Com. Feria and the Holy Forty Martyrs.
11 20: St. Constantine, Mart., double.
17 In all Scotland: St. Patrick, Bp. and Conf., greater double. Glasgow and Dumbartonshire: double II class.
20 21: St. Cuthbert, Bp. and Conf., double.

APRIL

16 19: St. Magnus, Mart., double.
17 20: SS. Donnan and Comp. MM., double. Com. St. Anicetus, Pope, Mart.

21 19: St. Malrubius, Abbot, double. Com. St. Anselm, Bp., Conf. and Doct. of the Ch.
24 20: St. Egbert, Conf., double. Com. St. Fidelis of Sigmaringa, Mart.

MAY

9 21: Translation of St. Andrew Ap., greater double. Com. St. Gregory Nazianzen, Bp., Conf. and Doct. of the Ch.

JUNE

9 In all Scotland: St. Columba, Abbot, double. Com. SS. Primus and Felician, MM. (20, 23: double I class).
10 In all Scotland: Feria.
25 20: St. Luan, Abbot, double. Com. St. William, Abbot.

JULY

7 19: St. Palladius, Bp. and Conf., double. Com. SS. Cyril and Methodius, Bpp. and CC.
9 19: B.V. Mary of Succour (Our Lady of Aberdeen), double I class.
11 19, 20: St. Drostan, Abbot, double. Com. St. Pius I, Pope and Mart.

AUGUST

9 20: St. Oswald, King and Mart., double. Com. St. John Mary Vianney, Conf., and Vigil of St. Lawrence.
11 20, 21, 23: St. Blaan, Bp. and Conf., double. Com. SS. Tiburtius and Susanna, Virg., MM.
31 20: St. Aidan, Bp. and Conf., double. Com. St. Raymund Nonnatus, Conf.

SEPTEMBER

1   21: St. Giles, Abbot, double. Com. the twelve H. Brethren, MM.
15   Renfrewshire: St. Mirin, Bp. and Conf., double I class.
16   Renfrewshire: VII Sorrows of B.V. Mary, double II class. Com. S. Ninian, Bp., Conf. Rest of Scotland: St. Ninian, Bp. and Conf., double. Com. SS. Cornelius, Pope and Cyprian Bp., MM., and SS. Euphemia, Virg. and Comp., MM. Cos, Ayr, Dumfries, Kirkcudbright, Wigtown: double I class.
23   20: St. Adamnan, Abbot, double. Com. St. Linus, Pope and Mart., and St. Thecla, Virg. and Mart.

OCTOBER

12   20, 21: St. Kenneth (Canice), Abbot, double.
13   19: St. Comgan, Abbot, double. Com. St. Edward, King and Conf.
26   19: St. Bean, Bp. and Conf., double. Com. St. Evaristus, Pope and Mart.

NOVEMBER

12   19: St. Machar, Bp. and Conf., double. Com. St. Martin I, Pope and Mart.
16   In all Scotland: St. Margaret, Queen of Scotland, Widow, Secondary Patron of Scotland: double II class. Com. St. Gertrude, Virg.
27   19, 23: St. Fergust, Bp. and Conf., double.
30   In all Scotland: St. Andrew, Apostle, PRINCIPAL PATRON of Scotland, double I class.

MASSES OF THE SAINTS

PROPER TO

SCOTLAND

In all Scotland.

November 30.

ST. ANDREW

Apostle

Principal Patron of Scotland.

Double of 1st class.

Mass as in the Missal, p. 550.

In all Scotland.

January 14.

St. Kentigern

Bishop and Confessor

Double.

The Mass Statuit, for a Confessor Bishop, p. [19], except the following Prayers:

Collect.

O GOD, who through blessed Kentigern thy Confessor and Bishop didst cause the light of the true faith to shine forth: grant, we beseech thee; that as we devoutly celebrate his festival, so faithfully following his doctrine, we may attain unto the brightness of everlasting glory. Through.

And Commemoration is made of St. Hilary, B.C.D.

Collect.

O GOD, who didst send blessed Hilary thy Doctor to guide thy people in the way of everlasting salvation: grant, we beseech thee; that as we have learned of him the doctrine of life on earth, so we may be found worthy to have him for our advocate in heaven. (Through.)

Then of St. Felix, M.

Collect.

GRANT, we beseech thee, almighty God, that by the examples of thy Saints we may so learn to amend our lives: that as we celebrate their festival, so we may likewise follow them in godliness and virtue. Through.

22: The Creed is said.

Secret. P

SANCTIFY, O Lord, we beseech thee, this gift which we offer to thy majesty in honour of thy Bishop, Saint Kentigern; that the same may be acceptable unto thee, and profitable for our salvation. Through.

For St. Hilary. Secret.

MAY the devout prayers of thy Bishop and Doctor Saint Hilary never fail to succour us, O Lord: that they may render our oblations acceptable in thy sight and ever obtain for us thy merciful pardon. (Through.)

For St. Felix. Secret

WE beseech thee, O Lord, mercifully to accept this our sacrifice, which we offer unto thee, pleading the merits of blessed Felix thy Martyr: that the same may avail for our perpetul succour. Through.

Postcommunion. P

O LORD, who hast refreshed us with these heavenly mysteries, which on the solemnity of Saint Kentigern thy Bishop we have offered unto thy majesty: we humbly beseech thee; that with him we may rejoice in everlasting felicity. Through.

For St. Hilary. Postcommunion.

WE beseech thee, O Lord, that blessed Hilary, thy Bishop and illustrious Doctor, may ever stand before thee as our advocate: that this sacrifice of thine ordinance may effectually avail for our salvation. (Through.)

For St. Felix. Postcommunion.

O LORD, who hast fulfilled us with these saving mysteries: we beseech thee; that, as we celebrate the festival of thy blessed Martyr Felix, so we may be succoured by his prayers. Through.

19

January 19.

St. Nathalan

Bishop and Confessor

Double.

The Mass Statuit, p. [19], except the following Collect:

Collect. P

MAKE us, O Lord, continually to cleave unto thee with devout hearts and minds; that by the intercession of blessed Nathalan, thy Confessor and Bishop; we may be worthy to sing perpetual praises to thee in glory. Through.

23

The same day, January 19.

St. Fillan

Abbot

The Mass Os justi, from the Common of Abbots, p. [26].

20

February 17.

St. Finan

Bishop and Confessor

Double.

The Mass Statuit, from the Common of a Confessor Bishop, p. [19], except the following Collect:

Collect. P

WE beseech thee, O Lord, mercifully pour into our hearts the glory of thy praise: that, at the intercession of blessed Finan thy Confessor and Bishop, we may be made worthy to attain unto the same thine ineffable glory. Through.

20

February 18.

St. Colman

Bishop and Confessor

Double.

The Mass Statuit, for a Confessor Bishop, p. [19], except the following Collect:

Collect.   P

GRANT to us, we beseech thee, almighty God, ever to persevere in thy holy service: and through the devout intercession of blessed Colman thy Confessor and Bishop, worthily to serve thee in thy glory. Through.

Commemoration of St. Simeon, B.M., p. 602.

19

March 8.

St. Duthac

Bishop and Confessor

Double.

The Mass Sacerdotes tui, p. [20], except the following Collect:

Collect.   P

O LORD God almighty, who dost hearken unto those, unworthy though they be, who cry to thee: hearken unto us thy servants; that at the intercession of blessed Duthac, thy Confessor and Bishop, we may be worthy through thy mercy to have our dwelling place with thee. Through.

Commemoration of St. John of God, C., p. 610.

In all Scotland.

March 10.

Blessed John Ogilvie

Martyr

Greater double.

Introit. Col. 1, 24. Gaudeo.

I REJOICE in my sufferings for you, and fill up that which is behind of the afflictions of Christ in my flesh, for his body's sake, which is the Church. Ps. 27, 1. The Lord is my light and my salvation, whom then shall I fear? ℣. Glory be.

Collect.

ALMIGHTY and everlasting God, who didst make blessed John thy Martyr an invincible defender of the Catholic faith: grant unto us by his intercession, that we may daily increase in faith, hope and charity more and more. Through.

Then Commemoration of the Feria.

Then of the Holy Forty Martyrs.

Collect.

GRANT, we beseech thee, almighty God: that like as we have known thy glorious Martyrs to be constant in their confession, so we may feel the succour of their loving intercession. Through.

The Lesson from the Epistle of blessed Paul the Apostle to the Corinthians.

II Cor. 1, 3-7.

BRETHREN: Blessed be God, even the Father of our Lord Jesus Christ, the Father of mercies, and the God of all comfort: Who comforteth us in all our tribulation: that we may be able to comfort them which are in any trouble, by the comfort wherewith we ourselves are comforted of God. For as the sufferings of Christ abound in us; so our consolation also aboundeth by Christ. And whether we be afflicted, it is for your consolation and salvation, which is effectual in the enduring of the same sufferings which we also suffer: or whether we be comforted, it is for your consolation and salvation: and our hope of you is stedfast, knowing that as ye are partakers of the sufferings, so shall ye be also of the consolation in Christ Jesu our Lord.

Gradual. Ps. 76, 4-7. I thought upon God and was comforted, mine eyes prevent the night-watches; and in the night I commune with mine own heart. ℣. Rom. 8, 18. I reckon that the sufferings of this present time are not worthy to be compared with the glory which shall be revealed in us.

Tract. Rom. 8, 35-37. Who then shall separate us from the love of Christ? shall tribulation? or distress? or persecution? or famine? or nakedness? or peril? or sword? ℣. As it is written: for thy sake we are killed all the day long, we are accounted as sheep for the slaughter. ℣. Nay, in all these things we are more than conquerors through him that loved us.

☩ The Continuation of the holy Gospel according to John.

John 12, 24-26.

AT that time: Jesus said unto his disciples: Verily, verily, I say unto you, except a corn of wheat fall into the ground and die, it abideth alone: but if it die, it bringeth forth much fruit. He that loveth his life shall lose it, and he that hateth his life in this world shall keep it unto life eternal. If any man serve me, let him follow me, and where I am, there shall also my servant be. If any man serve me, him will my Father honour.

Offertory. II Tim. 2, 9-10. I labour in the Gospel, as an evildoer, even unto bonds, but the word of God is not bound, therefore I endure all things for the elect's sakes.

Secret.

LET this oblation of our bounden service, O Lord, be acceptable unto thee: that, through the intercession of blessed John thy Martyr it may by thy mercy avail for our sanctification. Through.

2nd Secret of the Feria.

Then of the SS. Martyrs.

Secret.

REGARD, O Lord, the prayers and oblations of thy faithful people: that they may be acceptable unto thee for the festival of thy Saints, and bestow on us the succour of thy mercy. Through.

Communion. Matt. 16, 18. The Lord said unto Simon: Thou art Peter, and upon this rock I will build my Church, and the gates of hell shall not prevail against it.

Postcommunion.

WE humbly beseech thee, O Lord, that we, who have received this heavenly nourishment, may together with blessed John be worthy to be made partakers of thine everlasting glory. Through.

2nd Postcommunion of the Feria.

Then for the SS. Martyrs.

Postcommunion.

GRANT, O Lord, we beseech thee, that the intercession of thy Saints may so render us acceptable unto thee: that this temporal celebration may avail unto us for the attainment of eternal salvation. Through.

19

March 11.

St. Constantine

Martyr

Double.

The Mass In virtue, p. [6], except the following:

Collect.

O GOD, who didst wondrously adorn blessed Constantine, thy King and Martyr, with the glorious triumph of his passion: grant to us, we beseech thee; by following his example to despise earthly glory, and continually to love the things of heaven. Through.

Commemoration of the Feria.

Gospel The kingdom of heaven, as in the Missal for Septuagesima Sunday, p. 58.

In all Scotland.

March 17.

St. Patrick

Bishop and Confessor

Greater double.

(22: Double 2nd class.)

Introit. Gen. 12, 1-2. Egredere.

GET thee out of thy country, and from thy kindred, and from thy father's house, and come into the land, that I will show thee. And I will make of thee a great nation. Ps. 105, 1. O give thanks unto the Lord, and call upon his name: tell the people what things he hath done. ℣. Glory be.

Collect.

O GOD, who for the preaching of thy glory unto the nations wast pleased to send forth blessed Patrick, thy Confessor and Bishop: grant by his merits and intercession; that we may through thy mercy be enabled to accomplish those things which thou commandest us to do. Through.

Commemoration of the Feria.

The Lesson from the Epistle of blessed Paul the Apostle to the Romans.

Rom. 10, 10-18.

BRETHREN: For with the heart man believeth unto righteousness: and with the mouth confession is made unto salvation. For the scripture saith: Whosoever believeth on him shall not be ashamed. For there is no difference between the Jews and the Greek: for the same Lord over all is rich unto all that call upon him. For whosoever shall call upon the name of the Lord, shall be saved. How then shall they call on him, in whom they have not believed? And how shall they believe in him, of whom they have not heard? And how shall they hear without a preacher? And how shall they preach, except they be sent? as it is written: How beautiful are the feet of them that preach the gospel of peace, and bring glad tidings of good things! But they have not all obeyed the Gospel. For Esaias saith: Lord, who hath believed our report? So then faith cometh by hearing, and hearing by the word of God. But I say: Have they not heard? Yes verily, their sound went into all the earth, and their words unto the ends of the world.

Gradual. Ps. 105, 17 and 19. He sent a man before them: even Joseph, who was sold to be a bond-servant. ℣. Until the time came that his cause was known. The word of the Lord tried him.

Tract. Is. 42, 6-8. I the Lord have called thee in righteousness, and will hold thine hand, and will keep thee. And give thee for a covenant of the people, for a light of the Gentiles. ℣. To open the blind eyes, to bring out the prisoners from the prison, and them that sit in darkness out of the prison house. ℣. I am the Lord, that is my name: and my glory will I not give to another, neither my praise to graven images.

In votive Masses throughout the year, the Tract being omitted, there is said:

Alleluia, alleluia. ℣. Ps. 105, 21. He made him Lord of his house and ruler of all his substance. Alleluia.

In Easter Tide, in place of the Gradual, is said:

Alleluia, alleluia. ℣. Ps. 105, 21. He made him Lord of his house and ruler of all his substance. Alleluia. ℣. Ibid., 24. And he increased his people exceedingly: and made them stronger than their enemies. Alleluia.

✠ The Continuation of the holy Gospel according to Luke.

Luke 10, 1-9.

AT that time: the Lord appointed other seventy also: and sent them two and two before his face into every city and place, whither he himself would come. Therefore said he unto them: The harvest truly is great, but the labourers are few. Pray ye therefore the Lord of the harvest, that he would send forth labourers into his harvest. Go your ways: behold I send you forth as lambs among wolves. Carry neither purse, nor scrip, nor shoes: and salute no man by the way. And into whatsoever house ye enter, first say: Peace be to this house: and if the son of peace be there, your peace shall rest upon it: if not, it shall turn to you again. And in the same house remain, eating and drinking such things as they give: for the labourer is worthy of his hire. Go not from house to house. And into whatsoever city ye enter, and they receive you, eat such things as are set before you. And heal the sick that are therein, and say unto them: The kingdom of God is come nigh unto you.

Offertory. Gen. 15, 5. He brought him forth abroad, and said: Look now toward heaven, and tell the stars, if thou be able to number them. And he said unto him: So shall thy seed be.

Secret.

O LORD of hosts, let this pure oblation be acceptable unto thee: which, through the labours of blessed Patrick, thou didst will should be offered to thy great name among the Gentiles, from the rising of the sun even unto the going down of the same. Through.

Commemoration of the Feria.

Communion. Judith 15. The hand of the Lord hath strengthened thee, and therefore thou shalt be blessed for ever.

Postcommunion.

O GOD, who didst ordain the Sacrament of thy Body and Blood for a pledge of charity among all nations: mercifully grant that they, whom thou hast hallowed by this heavenly mystery, may, at the intercession of blessed Patrick, be knit together more closely day by day in bonds of peace and concord: Who livest and reignest with God the Father.

Commemoration of the Feria.

21

March 20.

St. Cuthbert

Bishop and Confessor

Double.

The Mass Sacerdotes tui, p. [20], except the following:

Collect. P

O GOD, who dost make thy Saints glorious by the inestimable gift of thy grace: grant, we beseech thee; that at the intercession of blessed Cuthbert, thy Confessor and Bishop, we may be found worthy to attain to the perfection of all virtue. Through.

Commemoration of the Feria.

✠ The Continuation of the holy Gospel according to Matthew.

Matt. 9, 35-38.

AT that time: Jesus went about all the cities and villages, teaching in their synagogues, and preaching the Gospel of the kingdom, and healing every sickness and every disease among the people. But when he saw the multitudes, he was moved with compassion on them: because they fainted, and were scattered abroad, as sheep having no shepherd. Then saith he unto his disciples: The harvest truly is plenteous, but the labourers are few. Pray ye therefore the Lord of the harvest, that he will send forth labourers into his harvest.

Secret. P

ACCEPT, we beseech thee, O Lord, the sacrifice of man's redemption: and at the intercession of blessed Cuthbert, thy Confessor and Bishop, mercifully grant us health of body and soul. Through.

Commemoration of the Feria.

Postcommunion. P

WE beseech thee, O Lord, that thy holy gifts which we have here received may ever protect us by thy power: and, at the intercession of blessed Cuthbert thy Confessor and Bishop, guard us in peace and holiness. Through.

Commemoration of the Feria.

19

April 16.

St. Magnus

Martyr

Double.

The Mass Protexisti, p. [15], except the following:

Collect. P

PROTECT us, O Lord, by the glorious merits of Saint Magnus: and grant that we, proclaiming the works of thy majesty, may thereby obtain thy succour both in this world and in that which is to come. Through.

The Lesson from the book of Wisdom.

Wisd. 4, 7-15.

THOUGH the righteous be prevented with death, yet shall he be in rest. For honourable age is not that which standeth in length of time, nor that is measured by number of years. But wisdom is the gray hair unto men, and an unspotted life is old age. He pleased God, and was beloved of him: so that living among sinners he was translated. Yea, speedily was he taken away, lest that wickedness should alter his understanding, or deceit beguile his soul. For the bewitching of naughtiness doth obscure things that are honest; and the wandering of concupiscence doth undermine the simple mind. He, being made perfect in a short time, fulfilled a long time: For his soul pleased the Lord: therefore hasted he to take him away from among the wicked. This the people saw, and understood it not, neither laid they up this in their minds: that his grace and mercy is with his saints, and that he hath respect unto his chosen.

Gospel Think not, from the Mass In virtute, p. [6].

Secret. P

WE beseech thee, O Lord, look upon these our oblations in thy tender mercy: that they may be filled with the benediction of thy Holy Spirit, and may pour into our hearts that fervent love, whereby thy holy Martyr Magnus overcame all his bodily torments. Through ... in the unity of the same Holy Spirit.

Postcommunion. P

WE have received, O Lord, these heavenly sacraments on the feast of thy holy Martyr Magnus: by whose prayers, we beseech thee, vouchsafe; that we who now celebrate these temporal mysteries, may attain unto the fulness thereof in everlasting felicity. Through.

20
April 17.
St. Donnan and Companions
Martyrs

Double.

The Mass Sancti tui, from the Common of Martyrs in E.T. (2nd place), p. [17], except the following Collect:

Collect. P

ALMIGHTY and everlasting God, remember not, we beseech thee, the offences of our youth, who lift up our souls to thee: and at the intercession of thy blessed Martyrs Donnan and his Companions; vouchsafe mercifully to pardon whatsoever through our neglect we have done amiss. Through.

Commemoration of St. Anicetus, P.M., p. 631.

Preface of Easter.

19
April 21.
St. Malrubius
Abbot

The Mass Os justi, from the Common of Abbots, p. [26].

Commemoration of St. Anselm, B.C.D., p. 631.

The Creed is not said.

20
April 24.
St. Egbert
Confessor

Double.

The Mass Os justi, from the Common of a Confessor not a Bishop, p. [24], except the following:

Introit. John 8, 56. Pater vester.

YOUR father rejoiced to see my day: and he saw it, and was glad, alleluia, alleluia. Ps. 4, 9-10. I will lay me down in peace and take my rest: for it is thou, Lord, only, that makest me dwell in safety. ℣. Glory be.

Collect. P

O GOD, who makest us to rejoice in the yearly festival of blessed Egbert thy Confessor: turn, we beseech thee, through the pleading of his merits the hearts of thy servants unto thee: that they, being enkindled by the fire of thy Spirit may be found stedfast in faith and fruitful in good works. Through ... in the unity of the same Holy Spirit.

Commemoration of St. Fidelis, M., p. 634.

Epistle Though I speak, as in the Missal for Quinquagesima Sunday, p. 61.

Gospel Jesus seeing, as on the Feast of All Saints, November 1st, p. 834.

Secret.

GRANT, we beseech thee, O Lord, ever to rejoice in these paschal mysteries: that the continual working of our redemption may become to us the cause of everlasting gladness. Through.

Postcommunion.

POUR into our hearts, O Lord, the Spirit of thy love: that we whom thou hast fulfilled with this paschal Sacrament may of thy goodness be made of one heart and mind. Through... in the unity of the same Holy Spirit.

21

May 9.

Translation of St. Andrew

Apostle

Greater double.

Introit. Ps. 139, 17. Mihi autem.

RIGHT dear are thy friends unto me, O God, and held in highest honour: their rule and governance is exceeding stedfast, alleluia, alleluia. Ps. ibid., 1. O Lord, thou hast searched me out, and known me: thou knowest my down-sitting and mine up-rising. ℣. Glory.

Collect.

O GOD, who makest us to celebrate with gladness the Translation of thy blessed Apostle Andrew: vouchsafe through his intercession to translate us to the vision of thy glory. Through.

Commemoration of St. Gregory Nazianzen, B.C.D., p. 652.

The Lesson from the Acts of the Apostles.

Acts 5, 12-16, 40-42.

IN those days: By the hands of the Apostles were many signs and wonders wrought among the people. And they were all with one accord in Solomon's porch. And of the rest durst no man join himself to them: but the people magnified them. And believers were the more added to the Lord, multitudes both of men and women, insomuch that they brought forth the sick into the streets, and laid them on beds and couches, that at the least the shadow of Peter passing by might overshadow some of them. There came also a multitude out of the cities round about unto Jerusalem, bringing sick folks, and them which were vexed with unclean spirits: and they were healed every one. And when they had called the Apostles, and beaten them, they commanded that they should not speak in the name of Jesus, and let them go. And they departed from the presence of the council, rejoicing that they were counted worthy to suffer for his name. And daily in the temple, and in every house they ceased not to preach and to teach Christ Jesus.

Alleluia, alleluia. ℣. The Lord loved Andrew as a sweet savour. Alleluia. ℣. Ps. 118, 16. The right hand of the Lord hath the pre-eminence; the right hand of the Lord hath exalted me. Alleluia.

✠ The Continuation of the holy Gospel according to Matthew.

Matt. 4, 18-22.

AT that time: Jesus walking by the sea of Galilee, saw two brethren, Simon called Peter, and Andrew his brother, casting a net into the sea (for they were fishers), and he saith unto them: Follow me, and I will make you fishers of men. And they straightway left their nets, and followed him. And going on from thence he saw other two brethren, James the son of Zebedee, and John his brother, in a ship with Zebedee their father, mending their nets: and he called them. And they immediately left the ship and their father, and followed him.

The Creed is not said.

Offertory. Ps. 89, 6. O Lord, the very heavens shall proclaim thy wondrous works: and thy truth in the congregation of the saints, alleluia, alleluia.

Secret.

LET this oblation, O Lord, which we offer on the Translation of thy holy Apostle Andrew, render us acceptable to thy mercy, that as he hath won the reward of everlasting felicity, so we may obtain thy mercy and grace. Through.

2nd Secret of St. Gregory, p. 653.

Preface of the Apostles.

Communion. John 15, 5. I am the vine, ye are the branches: he that abideth in me, and I in him, the same bringeth forth much fruit, alleluia, alleluia.

Postcommunion.

WE beseech thee, O Lord, that the prayers of Saint Andrew may obtain for us the succour of thy grace: that we who devoutly celebrate his Translation may be made partakers of his everlasting fellowship. Through.

2nd Postcommunion of St. Gregory, p. 653.

In all Scotland.
June 9.
St. Columba
Abbot
Double.

19, 23
Double of 1st class.

Introit. Ps. 139, 9-10. Si sumpsero.

IF I take the wings of the morning, and remain in the uttermost parts of the sea: even there also shall thy hand lead me, and thy right hand shall hold me. Ps. ibid., 1-2. O Lord, thou hast searched me out and known me: thou knowest my down-sitting and mine up-rising. ℣. Glory be.

Collect.

WE beseech thee, O Lord, pour into our hearts the longing for heavenly glory, and grant that we may bear sheaves of righteousness to that place: where thy holy Abbot Columba shines in brightness with thee. Through.

Then Commemoration is made of SS. Primus and Felician, MM.:

Collect.

O LORD, we beseech thee make us alway to observe the festival of thy holy Martyrs Primus and Felician: that through their prayers we may feel the effectual succour of their protection. Through.

The Lesson from the Prophet Isaiah.

Is. 42, 1-12.

BEHOLD my servant, whom I uphold: mine elect, in whom my soul delighteth; I have put my spirit upon him, he shall bring forth judgment to the Gentiles. He shall not cry, nor lift up, nor cause his voice to be heard in the street. A bruised reed shall he not break, and the smoking flax shall he not quench: he shall bring forth judgment unto truth. He shall not fail nor be discouraged, till he have set judgment in the earth: and the isles shall wait for his law. Thus said God the Lord, he that created the heavens, and stretched them out: he that spread forth the earth, and that which cometh out of it: he that giveth breath unto the people upon it, and spirit to them that walk therein. I the Lord have called thee in righteousness, and will hold thine hand, and will keep thee. And give thee for a covenant of the people, for a light of the Gentiles. To open the blind eyes, to bring out the prisoners from the prison, and them that sit in darkness out of the prison house. I am the Lord, that is my name: and my glory will I not give to another, neither my praise to graven images. Behold, the former things are come to pass: and new things do I declare: before they spring forth, I tell you of them. Sing unto the Lord a new song, and his praise from the end of the earth: ye that go down to the sea, and all that is therein: the isles, and the inhabitants thereof. Let the wilderness and the cities thereof lift up their voice: the villages that Kedar doth inhabit: let the inhabitants of the rock sing, let them shout from the top of the mountains. Let them give glory unto the Lord, and declare his praise in the islands.

Gradual. Wisd. 11, 1. The Lord prospered the works of his servants in the hand of the holy prophet. ℣. Ibid., 2. They went through the wilderness that was not inhabited, and pitched tents in places where there lay no way.

Alleluia, alleluia. ℣. Is. 52, 7. How beautiful upon the mountains are the feet of him that bringeth good tidings, that publisheth peace, that bringeth good tidings of good, that publisheth salvation. Alleluia.

In Easter Tide, the Gradual being omitted, is said:

Alleluia, alleluia. ℣. How beautiful... Alleluia. ℣. He shall set judgment in the earth, and the isles shall wait for his law. Alleluia.

In votive Masses after Septuagesima, Alleluia and the Verse following being omitted, is said:

Tract. Ps. 139, 9-12. I take the wings of the morning, and remain in the uttermost parts of the sea. ℣. Even there also shall thy hand lead me: and thy right hand shall hold me. ℣. If I say: Peradventure the darkness shall cover me: then shall my night be turned to day. ℣. Yea, the darkness is no darkness with thee, but the night is as clear as the day: the darkness and light to thee are both alike.

☩ The Continuation of the holy Gospel according to Matthew.

Matt. 9, 35-38; 10, 1-16.

AT that time: Jesus went about all the cities and villages, teaching in their synagogues, and preaching the gospel of the kingdom, and healing every sickness and every disease among the people. But when he saw the multitudes, he was moved with compassion on them: because they fainted, and were scattered abroad, as sheep having no shepherd. Then saith he unto his disciples: The harvest truly is plenteous, but the labourers are few. Pray ye therefore the Lord of the harvest, that he will send forth labourers into his harvest. And when he had called unto him his twelve disciples, he gave them power against unclean spirits, to cast them out, and to heal all manner of sickness and all manner of disease. Now the names of the twelve Apostles are these: The first: Simon, who is called Peter, and Andrew his brother, James the son of Zebedee, and John his brother, Philip, and Bartholomew, Thomas, and Matthew the publican, James the son of Alphæus, and Lebbæus, whose surname was Thaddæus, Simon the Canaanite, and Judas Iscariot, who also betrayed him. These twelve Jesus sent forth, and commanded them, saying: Go not into the way of the Gentiles, and into any city of the Samaritans enter ye not: But go rather to the lost sheep of the house of Israel. And as ye go, preach, saying: The kingdom of heaven is at hand. Heal the sick, cleanse the lepers, raise the dead, cast out devils: freely ye have received, freely give. Provide neither gold, nor silver, nor brass in your purses. Nor scrip for your journey, neither two coats, neither shoes, nor yet staves: for the workman is worthy of his meat. And into whatsoever city or town ye shall enter, enquire who in it is worthy: and there abide till ye go thence. And when ye come into an house, salute it. And if the house be worthy, let your peace come upon it: but if it be not worthy, let your peace return to you. And whosoever shall not receive you, nor hear your words: when ye depart out of that house or city, shake off the dust of your feet. Verily I say unto you: it shall be more tolerable for the land of Sodom and Gomorrha in the day of judgment, than for that city. Behold, I send you forth as sheep in the midst of wolves. Be ye therefore wise as serpents, and harmless as doves.

Offertory. Ecclus. 50, 11-12. When he went up to the holy altar, he made the garment of holiness honourable: and he himself stood by the altar compassed with his brethren round about, and the oblations of the Lord in their hands. (E.T. Alleluia.)

Secret.

WE beseech thee, O Lord, graciously accept these our oblations: and, that we may do thee worthy service at thy altars, guard us evermore by the intercession of thy holy Abbot Columba. Through.

For the SS. Martyrs. Secret.

WE beseech thee, O Lord, that the oblation to be consecrated on the day of the precious death of thy Martyrs may be acceptable unto thee: for the cleansing of our sins, and for the commending to thee of the prayers of thy servants. Through.

Communion. I Kings 19, 8. He did eat and drink, and went in the strength of that meat unto the mount of God. (E.T. Alleluia.)

Postcommunion.

O LORD, who hast refreshed us in this life by the partaking of thy Body and Blood, we beseech thee: that at the intercession of blessed Columba we may be fulfilled with the everlasting fruition of thy Godhead: Who livest and reignest with God the Father.

For the SS. Martyrs. Postcommunion.

WE beseech thee, O Lord, that the solemn festival of thy holy Martyrs Primus and Felician, which we have celebrated in these heavenly mysteries, may obtain for us the abundance of thy mercy and forgiveness. Through.

†For another Collect, Epistle and Gospel, see p. 944.

20

June 25.

St. Luan

Abbot

Double.

The Mass Os justi, from the Common of Abbots, p. [26], except the following Collect:

Collect.

ALMIGHTY and merciful God, graciously hearken unto the prayers of them that call upon thee: that, at the intercession of thy blessed Abbot Luan, thou wouldest vouchsafe to pour thy grace into our hearts; that we, obtaining the pardon of our offences, may enter into everlasting rest. Through.

And Commemoration is made of St. William, Abbot.

Collect.

O GOD, who in thy Saints hast appointed for our infirmity a pattern and protection in treading the way of salvation: grant us so to venerate the merits of thy blessed Abbot William; that we may ever receive the succour of his intercession, and follow in his footsteps. Through.

Secret. C

O LORD, we beseech thee, let thy holy Abbot Luan intercede for us: that this sacrifice which we offer and present upon thy holy altar may be profitable unto us for our salvation. Through.

For St. William. Secret

WE offer thee, O Lord, this our sacrifice of praise to the honour of thy Saints: whereby we trust to be delivered from all evils both in this life and in that which is to come. Through.

Postcommunion. C

LET thy Sacrament, O Lord, which we have now received, and the prayers of thy blessed Abbot Luan, effectually defend us: that we may both imitate the example of his conversation, and receive the succour of his intercession. Through.

For St. William. Postcommunion.

O LORD our God, who hast refreshed us with heavenly meat and drink, we humbly beseech thee: that we may be defended by the prayers of him in whose memory we have received the same. Through.

19

July 7.

St. Palladius

Bishop and Confessor

Double.

The Mass Statuit, p. [19], except the following Prayers:

Collect. P

O GOD, who to the people of the Scots didst send thy blessed Bishop Palladius to be an Apostle of the Catholic faith: grant to us, we beseech thee; that, by his intercession, we may attain unto thine ineffable mercy, and of thy bountiful goodness come to enjoy everlasting life. Through.

Commemoration of SS. Cyril and Methodius, BB., CC., p. 711.

Secret. P

SANCTIFY, we beseech thee, O Lord, these our gifts which we offer in commemoration of thy blessed Bishop and Confessor Palladius: that they may be profitable for the salvation of our souls. Through.

Postcommunion. P

O LORD, who hast bestowed on us thy sacred gifts, we humbly beseech thee: that we, being strengthened by their power, may follow the example of blessed Palladius thy Bishop and Confessor, and attain unto everlasting felicity. Through.

19

July 9.

Blessed Virgin Mary of Succour

(Our Lady of Aberdeen.)

Double of 1st class.

The Mass Salve, p. [41].

And the Creed is said.

Preface of the B.V.M. And that on the Festival.

19, 20

July 11.

St. Drostan

Abbot

Double.

The Mass Os justi, from the Common of Abbots, p. [26], except the following Collect:

Collect. P

O GOD, who didst adorn blessed Drostan thy Confessor and Abbot with singular gifts of thy grace: grant, we beseech thee; that in heaven we may enjoy eternally those rewards which thou hast bestowed on him. Through.

Commemoration of St. Pius I, P.M., p. 714.

Common Preface.

19

August 9.

St. Oswald

King and Martyr

Double.

The Mass In virtute, p. [6], except the following:

Collect. P

ALMIGHTY and everlasting God, who by the martyrdom of blessed King Oswald hast hallowed this day with holy joy and gladness: grant unto our hearts the increase of thy charity; that we, who honour his glorious battle for the faith, may imitate his constancy even unto death. Through.

Commemoration of St. John Mary and Vigil of St. Lawrence only, p. 749.

Epistle Though the righteous, as on the Feast of St. Magnus, p. 929.

✠ The Continuation of the holy Gospel according to John.

John 15, 12-21.

AT that time: Jesus said unto his disciples: This is my commandment, That ye love one another, as I have loved you. Greater love hath no man than this, that a man lay down his life for his friends. Ye are my friends, if ye do whatsoever I command you. Henceforth I call you not servants; for the servant knoweth not what his lord doeth: but I have called you friends; for all things that I have heard of my Father I have made known unto you. Ye have not chosen me, but I have chosen you, and ordained you, that ye should go and bring forth fruit, and that your fruit should remain: that whatsoever ye shall ask of the Father in my name, he may give it you. These things I command you, that ye love one another. If the world hate you, ye know that it hated me before it hated you. If ye were of the world, the world would love his own: but because ye are not of the world, but I have chosen you out of the world, therefore the world hateth you. Remember the word that I said unto you, The servant is not greater than his lord. If they have persecuted me, they will also persecute you; if they have kept my saying, they will keep yours also. But all these things will they do unto you for my name's sake, because they know not him that sent me.

Secret. P

MERCIFULLY receive, we beseech thee, O Lord, the gifts which we offer to thy majesty in commemoration of Saint Oswald thy Martyr: and graciously inspire us with that fervent love which burned in him. Through.

Postcommunion. P

ALMIGHTY God, who hast renewed us with the food of life, we beseech thee: that through the intercession of Saint Oswald thy Martyr, whose glorious conflict we celebrate in solemn festival, we may know the abundance of thy mercy toward us. Through.

20, 21, 23
August 11.
St. Blaan
Bishop and Confessor

Double.

The Mass Statuit, p. [19], except the following Collect:

Collect. P

GRANT, we beseech thee, almighty and merciful God: that we, being aided by the intercession of thy blessed Confessor and Bishop Blaan, may serve thee with pure hearts and minds. Through.

Commemoration of SS. Tiburtius and Susanna, V., MM., p. 754.

Secret. C

WE beseech thee, O Lord, that we, remembering with gladness the merits of thy Saints, may in all places feel the succour of their intercession. Through.

Postcommunion. C

GRANT, we beseech thee, almighty God: that we, shewing forth our thankfulness for the gifts which we have received, may at the intercession of thy blessed Confessor and Bishop Blaan obtain yet more abundant benefits. Through.

20
August 31.
St. Aidan
Bishop and Confessor

Double.

The Mass Statuit, p. [19], except the following:

Collect. P

O GOD, who didst raise blessed Aidan thy Confessor and Bishop to the glory of everlasting felicity: grant, we beseech thee; that we thy servants may through thy mercy obtain in heaven those good things which he valiantly maintained and taught on earth. Through.

Commemoration of St. Raymond Nonnatus, C., p. 776.

Gospel The Lord appointed as below for the Feast of Saint Ninian, Bishop and Confessor, p. 938.

21
September 1.
St. Giles
Abbot

Double.

All as in the Missal on this day.

Renfrewshire
September 15.
St. Mirin
Bishop and Confessor

Double of 1st class.

The Mass Statuit, p. [19]; and the Creed is said.

In all Scotland
September 16.
St. Ninian
Bishop and Confessor

Double.

(Cos, Ayr, Dumfries, Kirkcudbright, Wigtown: Double 1st class.)

Introit. Ecclus. 45, 39. Statuit.

THE Lord established with him a covenant of peace, and made him the chief of his people: that he should have the dignity of the priesthood for ever. Ps. 132, 1. Lord, remember David: and all his trouble. ℣. Glory.

Collect.

O GOD, who through the teaching of thy Bishop and Confessor Saint Ninian, didst bring the peoples of the Picts and Britons to the knowledge of thy faith: mercifully grant; that we, who by his teaching are illumined with the light of thy truth; may through his intercession attain unto the joys of heavenly life. Through.

Then, on Ember Wednesday, Commemoration of the Feria.

Then of SS. Cornelius, Pope, and Cyprian, MM.

Collect.

DEFEND us, O Lord, we beseech thee, who observe the feast of thy blessed Martyrs Cornelius and Cyprian: and grant that by their meritorious supplication we may ever be holpen in thy sight.

Then, unless it be Ember Wednesday, Commemoration of SS. Euphemia, V., Lucy and Geminian, MM.

Collect.

GRANT, O Lord, that our prayers in this time of rejoicing may be brought to good effect: that as with yearly service we recll the day of the passion of thy holy Martyrs, Euphemia, Lucy and Geminian; so we may imitate the stedfastness of their faith. Through.

The Lesson from the book of Wisdom.
Ecclus. 44, 19-45, 16.

BEHOLD a great priest who in his days pleased God, and was found righteous, and in the time of wrath he was taken in exchange for the world. There was none like unto him, who kept the law of the Most High. Therefore by an oath the Lord assured him that he would increase him among his people. He established him with the blessing of all men and the covenant, and made it rest upon his head. He acknowledged him in his blessing: he preserved for him his mercy: so that he found favour in the sight of the Lord. He magnified him in the sight of kings, and gave unto him a crown of glory. An everlasting covenant he made with him, and gave him a great priesthood, and blessed him with glory. That he should execute the office of the priesthood, and have glory in his name; and offer unto him incense, and a sweet savour.

Gradual. Ecclus. 44, 16. Behold a great priest who in his days pleased God. ℣. Ibid., 20. There was none found like unto him, to keep the law of the most High.

Alleluia, alleluia. ℣. Ps. 110, 4. Thou art a priest for ever, after the order of Melchisedech. Alleluia.

✠ The Continuation of the holy Gospel according to Luke.
Luke 10, 1-9.

AT that time: The Lord appointed other seventy also: and sent them two and two before his face into every city and place whither he himself would come. Therefore said he unto them: The harvest truly is great, but the labourers are few. Pray ye therefore the Lord of the harvest, that he would send forth labourers into his harvest. Go your ways: behold, I send you forth as lambs among wolves. Carry neither purse, nor scrip, nor shoes; and salute no man by the way. And into whatsoever house ye enter, first say: Peace be to this house: and if the son of peace be there, your peace shall rest upon it: if not, it shall turn to you again. And in the same house remain, eating and drinking such things as they give: for the labourer is worthy of his hire. Go not from house to house. And into whatsoever city ye enter, and they receive you, eat such things as are set before you: and heal the sick that are therein, and say unto them: The kingdom of God is come nigh unto you.

Offertory. Ps. 89, 21-22. I have found David my servant, with my holy oil have I anointed him: my hand shall hold him fast and mine arm shall strengthen him.

Secret.

LET the yearly festival of thy holy Bishop Ninian render these oblations of our bounden service acceptable unto thee, O Lord: that we, being defended by his constant supplication, may be worthy to obtain pardon of all our offences and the fellowship of everlasting bliss. Through.

Then, on Ember Wednesday, Commemoration of the Feria.

For SS. Cornelius and Cyprian, MM.

Secret.

ASSIST us mercifully, O Lord, in these our supplications which we make before thee in remembrance of thy Saints: that we who trust not in our own righteousness may be succoured by the merits of them that have found favour in thy sight. (Through.)

Except on Ember Wednesday:

For SS. Euphemia, etc. Secret.

GRACIOUSLY hearken, we beseech thee, O Lord, unto the prayers of thy people: and make us to rejoice in the intercession of those whose festival thou dost suffer us to celebrate. Through.

Communion. Luke 12, 42. A faithful and wise servant, whom his lord hath made ruler over his household: to give them their portion of meat in due season.

Postcommunion.

O LORD, who hast refreshed us with the sacraments of the food of life: protect us by the glorious intercession of thy holy Confessor and Bishop Ninian; and grant that we may attain unto the everlasting banquet of thy heavenly table. Through.

Then, on Ember Wednesday, Commemoration of the Feria.

For SS. Cornelius and Cyprian, MM.

Postcommunion.

O LORD, who hast fulfilled us with these saving mysteries: we beseech thee that we may be aided by the prayers of those whose festival we celebrate. (Through.)

Except on Ember Wednesday:

For St. Euphemia, etc. Postcommunion.

O LORD, graciously hear our prayers: that we, who solemnly observe the feast of thy holy Martyrs, Euphemia, Lucy and Geminian, may be succoured by their continual help. Through.

†For another Collect, Epistle and Gospel, see p. 944.

20

September 23.

St. Adamnan

Abbot

Double.

The Mass Os justi, from the Common of Abbots, p. [26], except the following Collect:

Collect. P

O GOD, who makest this day joyful to the honour of blessed Adamnan thy Confessor and Abbot: grant us, we beseech thee, through his intercession and merits; to rejoice before the face of thy divine majesty in everlasting glory. Through.

Commemoration of St. Linus, P.M., and St. Thecla, V.M., p. 798.

Common Preface.

19, 21

October 12.

St. Kenneth

Abbot

Double.

The Mass Os justi, from the Common of Abbots, p. [26], except the following Prayers:

Collect. P

ALMIGHTY God, whose service is full and perfect felicity: vouchsafe, we beseech thee; that after the example of blessed Kenneth, we, being subject one to another in the faith of Christ, as sons of obedience, may with unfeigned love serve thee in holiness and righteousness. Through.

Secret. P

ACCEPT, O Lord, we beseech thee, these our prayers and sacrifices, which we offer unto thee: and vouchsafe; that after the example of blessed Kenneth, we, mortifying by the spirit the desires of the flesh, may serve thee alone. Through.

Postcommunion. P

O GOD of our heart, and our portion for ever: grant unto us, at the intercession of blessed Kenneth; that through the partaking of this Sacrament, we may cleave to thee alone on earth, from whom we hope for an eternal heritage in heaven. Through.

19

October 13.

St. Comgan

Abbot

Double.

The Mass Os justi, from the Common of Abbots, p. [26], except the following Collect:

Collect. P

O GOD, who didst adorn blessed Comgan thy Abbot with glorious miracles: vouchsafe, we beseech thee; that we, being succoured by his merits and intercession, may be worthy to attain unto everlasting felicity. Through.

Commemoration of St. Edward, K.C., p. 819.

19

October 26.

St. Bean

Bishop and Confessor

Double.

The Mass Statuit, for a Confessor Bishop, p. [19], except the following Collect:

Collect. P

O GOD, who art nigh unto all them that call upon thee in truth: teach us through the intercession of Saint Bean, thy Confessor and Bishop, to call upon thee in sincerity of heart; that we may be worthy to be heard by thee. Through.

Commemoration of St. Evaristus, P.M., p. 831.

19

November 12.

St. Machar

Bishop and Confessor

Double.

The Mass Statuit, for a Confessor Bishop, p. [19], except the following Prayers:

Collect.   P

O GOD, who didst set blessed Machar thy Confessor and Bishop to be pastor and ruler of thy Church: grant, we beseech thee; that we, who observe his heavenly birthday, may lose not the hope of everlasting felicity. Through.

Commemoration of St. Martin I, P.M., p. 842.

Secret.   P

CLEANSE, we beseech thee, almighty God, the hearts of this thy family by the light of thy Holy Spirit: that, through the intercession of blessed Machar thy Confessor and Bishop, these offerings of our bounden duty and service may be made acceptable unto thee. Through... in the unity of the same Holy Spirit.

Common Preface.

Postcommunion.   P

O LORD, who hast fulfilled us with the food of our redemption, we humbly implore thy mercy: that, by the merits and intercession of blessed Machar thy Confessor and Bishop, we may obtain the gifts of everlasting salvation. Through.

In all Scotland:

November 16.

ST. MARGARET, QUEEN and WIDOW

Secondary Patron of Scotland.

Double of the 2nd class.

Introit. I Tim. 5, 10. In operibus.

WELL reported of for good works, she hath brought up children, she hath lodged strangers, she hath washed the saints' feet, she hath relieved the afflicted, she hath diligently followed every good work. Ps. 41, 1. Blessed is he that considereth the poor and needy: the Lord shall deliver him in the day of trouble. ℣. Glory.

Collect.

O GOD, who didst call thy servant Queen Margaret to an earthly throne that she might advance thy heavenly kingdom, and didst endue her with zeal for thy Church and charity towards thy people: mercifully grant that we who commemorate her example may be fruitful in good works, and attain to the glorious fellowship of thy Saints. Through.

or

Collect.

O GOD, who didst make the blessed Queen Margaret wondrous by reason of her abounding charity toward the poor: grant, that by her intercession and example thy charity may continually be increased within our hearts. Through.

Then, in low Masses, Commemoration is made of St. Gertrude, V.

Collect.

O GOD, who in the heart of blessed Gertrude, thy Virgin, didst prepare a mansion acceptable unto thyself: we beseech thee by her merits and intercession mercifully to cleanse our hearts from all defilement; that we may rejoice in her everlasting fellowship in heaven. Through.

The Lesson from the book of Wisdom. Prov. 31, 10-31.

WHO can find a virtuous woman? For her price is far above rubies. The heart of her husband doth safely trust in her, so that he shall have no need of spoil. She will do him good and not evil, all the days of her life. She seeketh wool and flax, and worketh willingly with her hands. She is like the merchants' ships, she bringeth her food from afar. She riseth also while it is night, and giveth meat to her household, and a portion to her maidens. She considereth a field, and buyeth it; with the fruit of her hands she planteth a vineyard. She girdeth her loins with strength, and strengtheneth her arms. She perceiveth that her merchandise is good: her candle goeth not out by night. She layeth her hands to the spindle, and her hands hold the distaff. She stretcheth out her hand to the poor, yea, she reacheth forth her hands to the needy. She is not afraid of the snow for her household: for all her household are clothed with scarlet. She maketh herself coverings of tapestry: her clothing is silk and purple. Her husband is known in the gates, when he sitteth among the elders of the land. She maketh fine linen, and selleth it, and delivereth girdles to the merchant. Strength and honour are her clothing, and she shall rejoice in time to come. She openeth her mouth with wisdom, and in her tongue is the law of kindness. She looketh well to the ways of her household, and eateth not the bread of idleness. Her children arise up, and call her blessed: her husband also, and he praiseth her. Many daughters have done virtuously: but thou excellest them all. Favour is deceitful, and beauty is vain: but a woman that feareth the Lord, she shall be praised. Give her of the fruit of her hands: and let her own works praise her in the gates.

Gradual. Eccl. 26, 21-22. As the sun when it ariseth in the high heaven: so is the beauty of a good wife in the ordering of her house. ℣. As the clear light is upon the holy candlestick: so is the beauty of the face in ripe age.

Alleluia, alleluia. ℣. Ps. 45, 10. Upon thy right hand did stand the queen in a vesture of gold: wrought about with divers colours. Alleluia.

In votive Masses after Septuagesima, Alleluia and the Verse following being omitted, is said:

Tract. Ps. 41, 1. The Lord comforted him when he lay sick upon his bed: thou madest all his bed in his sickness. ℣. Ps. 112, 9. He hath dispersed abroad, he hath given to the poor: his righteousness remaineth for ever: his horn shall be exalted in glory. ℣. Ibid., 2. His seed shall be mighty upon earth: the generation of the faithful shall be blessed.

In Easter Tide, instead of the Gradual, is said:

Alleluia, alleluia. ℣. Ps. 45, 10; 14-15. At thy right hand stood the queen in a vesture of gold: wrought about with divers colours. Alleluia. ℣. The king's daughter is all glorious within: her clothing is of wrought gold. Alleluia.

✠ The Continuation of the holy Gospel according to Matthew.

Matt. 13, 44-53.

AT that time: Spake Jesus this parable unto his disciples: The kingdom of heaven is like unto treasure hid in a field: the which when a man hath found, he hideth, and for joy thereof goeth and selleth all that he hath, and buyeth that field. Again the kingdom of heaven is like unto a merchant-man, seeking goodly pearls. Who, when he had found one pearl of great price, went and sold all that he had, and bought it.†

Again, the kingdom of heaven is like unto a net, that was cast into the sea, and gathered of every kind. Which, when it was full, they drew to shore, and set down, and gathered the good into vessels, but cast the bad away. So shall it be at the end of the world: the Angels shall come forth, and sever the wicked from among the just, and shall cast them into the furnace of fire: there shall be wailing and gnashing of teeth. Jesus saith unto them: Have ye understood all these things? They say unto him: Yea, Lord. Then said he unto them: Therefore every scribe which is instructed unto the kingdom of heaven is like unto a man that is an householder, which bringeth forth out of his treasure things new and old.

Offertory. Ps. 45, 11-12. Hearken, O daughter, and consider, incline thine ear: forget also thine own people, and thy father's house. So shall the king have pleasure in thy beauty: for he is thy Lord God, and worship thou him.

Secret.

GRANT to us, O Lord, we beseech thee, through these holy sacrifices, to seek evermore thy kingdom and its righteousness: for the attaining whereof the holy queen Margaret despised the vain pomps and enticements of an earthly realm. Through.

For St. Gertrude. Secret.

GRANT, O Lord, that like as thy dedicated people do acknowledge that in tribulation they have been succoured by the merits of thy Saints: so this oblation, which they offer unto thee in honour of the same, may be acceptable in thy sight. Through.

Communion. Prov. 31, 28. Her children arise up, and call her blessed: her husband also, and he praiseth her.

Postcommunion.

POUR upon us, O Lord, through the power of this sacrament, the holy sweetness of thy love: that, at the intercession of blessed Margaret, we may overcome all the hindrances of the world, and with her be found worthy to cleave to thee alone. Through.

For St. Gertrude. Postcommunion.

O LORD, who hast satisfied this thy family with thy sacred gifts: we may at all times be comforted by the intercession of her whose festival we celebrate. Through.

19, 23

November 27.

St. Fergus

Bishop and Confessor

Double.

The Mass Statuit, for a Confessor Bishop, p. [19], except the following Collect:

Collect. P

ALMIGHTY and everlasting God, make us, by the merits of Saint Fergus, thy Confessor and Bishop, to abide stedfast in faith and fruitful in good works: that through right faith we may by thy mercy attain unto everlasting life. Through.

† Another Collect, Epistle and Gospel for St. Kentigern (Jan. 14), St. Patrick (March 17), St. Columba (June 9), and St. Ninian (Sept. 16):

Collect.

O GOD, who by the preaching of thy blessed servant Saint N. didst cause the light of the Gospel to shine in this our land (or in these islands): grant, we beseech thee; that, having his life and labours in remembrance, we may shew forth our thankfulness unto thee for the same by following the example of his zeal and patience. Through.

The Lesson from the Epistle of blessed Paul the Apostle to the Thessolonians.

I Thess. 2, 2-12.

BRETHREN: We were bold in our God to speak unto you the Gospel of God with much contention. For our exhortation was not of deceit, nor of uncleanness, nor in guile: but as we were approved of God to be put in trust with the Gospel, even so we speak; not as pleasing men, but God, which trieth our hearts. For neither at any time used we flattering words, as ye know, nor a cloke of covetousness: God is witness: nor of men sought we glory, neither of you, nor yet of others, when we might have been burdensome, as the Apostles of Christ. But we were gentle among you, even as a nurse cherisheth her children: so being affectionately desirous of you, we were willing to have imparted unto you, not the Gospel of God only, but also our own souls, because ye were dear unto us. For ye remember, brethren, our labour and travail: for labouring night and day, because we would not be chargeable unto any of you, we preached unto you the Gospel of God. Ye are witnesses, and God also, how holily and justly and unblameably we behaved ourselves among you that believe: as ye know how we exhorted and comforted and charged every one of you, as a father doth his children, that ye would walk worthy of God, who hath called you unto his kingdom and glory.

☩ The Continuation of the holy Gospel according to Matthew.

Matt. 28, 16-20.

AT that time: The eleven disciples went away into Galilee, unto a mountain where Jesus had appointed them. And when they saw him, they worshipped him: but some doubted. And Jesus came and spake unto them, saying: All power is given unto me in heaven and in earth. Go ye therefore, and teach all nations, baptizing them in the name of the Father, and of the Son, and of the Holy Ghost: teaching them to observe all things whatsoever I have commanded you: and, lo, I am with you alway, even unto the end of the world. Amen.

THE COMMON OF SAINTS

FOR THE VIGILS OF APOSTLES

(Mass formerly in use.)

Introit. Ps. 52, 10-11. Ego autem.

AS for me, I am like a green olive-tree in the house of the Lord, my trust is in the tender mercy of my God: and I will hope in thy name, for thy saints like it well. Ps. ibid., 3. Why boastest thou thyself, thou tyrant: that thou canst do mischief? ℣. Glory.

Glória in excélsis is not said.

Collect.

GRANT, we beseech thee, almighty God: that as we now prevent the feast of blessed N. thine Apostle; so by the devout observance of the same we may increase in godliness to the attainment of everlasting salvation. Through.

¶ If, however, the preceding Collect has already been said in the Mass, or for the Commemoration of a Confessor Bishop, then the following is to be said:

Collect.

WE beseech thee, almighty God: that as we do prevent the festival of blessed N. thine Apostle, so he may implore thy mercy for us; that we being delivered from our iniquities, may likewise be defended against all adversities. Through.

The Lesson from the book of Wisdom.

Ecclus. 44, 22-24; 45, 2-4 and 6-9.

THE blessing of the Lord was upon the head of the righteous. Therefore did the Lord give him an heritage, and divided his portions; among the twelve tribes did he part them: and he found favour in the sight of all flesh. And he magnified him so that his enemies stood in fear of him. By his words he caused the wonders to cease, and he made him glorious in the sight of kings, and gave him a commandment for his people, and shewed him his glory. He sanctified him in his faithfulness and meekness, and chose him out of all men. And he gave him commandments before his face, even the law of life and knowledge, and made him to be exalted. An everlasting covenant he made with him, and girded him about with the girdle of righteousness: and the Lord crowned him with a crown of glory.

Gradual. Ps. 92, 13-14. The righteous shall flourish like a palm-tree: and shall spread abroad like a cedar in Libanus in the house of the Lord. ℣. Ibid., 3. To tell of thy loving kindness early in the morning, and of thy truth in the night-season.

☩ The Continuation of the holy Gospel according to John.

John 15, 12-16.

AT that time: Jesus said unto his disciples: This is my commandment, That ye love one another, as I have loved you. Greater love hath no man than this, that a man lay down his life for his friends. Ye are my friends, if ye do whatsoever I command you. Henceforth I call you not servants: for the servant knoweth not what his lord doeth. But I have called you friends: for all things that I have heard of my Father I have made known unto you. Ye have not chosen me: but I have chosen you, and ordained you, that ye should go and bring forth fruit: and that your fruit should remain: that whatsoever ye shall ask of the Father in my name, he may give it you.

Offertory. Ps. 8, 6-7. Thou hast crowned him with glory and worship: thou hast made him to have dominion of the works of thy hands, O Lord.

Secret.

O LORD, who didst exalt blessed N. to be numbered among thine Apostles: we beseech thee; that we thy people, who, awaiting his heavenly birthday, do offer unto thee these holy mysteries, may be assisted by his intercession both in the making of our supplications before thee, and in the obtaining of all that we desire. Through.

Communion. Ps. 21, 6. His honour is great in thy salvation: glory and great worship shalt thou lay upon him, O Lord.

Postcommunion.

WE beseech thee, O Lord, mercifully to hear the supplication of thy holy Apostle N.: that we may thereby obtain the pardon of our sins, and the healing gifts of everlasting life. Through.

¶ In each Common the Epistles and Gospels which are given, either in the Masses themselves or at the end of the whole Common, may be said in any Mass of the same Common; provided only that a particular Mass to be said in its place or a particular Epistle or Gospel be not assigned in the Missal.

COMMON OF ONE OR MORE SUPREME PONTIFFS

Introit. John 21, 15-17. Si diligis me.

IF thou lovest me, Simon Peter, feed my lambs, feed my sheep. (E.T. Alleluia, alleluia.) Ps. 30, 1. I will magnify thee, O Lord, for thou hast set me up, and not made my foes to triumph over me. ℣. Glory.

Collect.

O EVERLASTING Shepherd, look down in mercy on thy flock: and as thou didst choose blessed N. thy (Martyr and) Chief Bishop to be pastor and ruler of thy Church; so at his intercession defend it with thy continual protection. Through.

If Commemoration is to be made of another Supreme Pontiff, then is said the following:

Collect.

O GOD, who dost deliver thy Church, built on the sure foundation of the apostolic rock, from the terror of the gates of hell: grant we beseech thee, that at the intercession of blessed N. thy (Martyr and) Chief Bishop, it may abide in thy truth; and be defended in continual safety. Through.

The Lesson from the Epistle of blessed Peter the Apostle.

I Peter 5, 1-4 and 10-11.

DEARLY beloved: The elders which are among you I exhort, who am also an elder, and a witness of the sufferings of Christ, and also a partaker of the glory that shall be revealed: feed the flock of God which is among you, taking the oversight thereof, not by constraint, but willingly, not for filthy lucre, but of a ready mind; neither as being lords over God's heritage, but being ensamples to the flock. And when the chief Shepherd shall appear, ye shall receive a crown of glory that fadeth not away. Now the God of all grace, who hath called us unto his eternal

Common of Supreme Pontiffs [3]

glory by Christ Jesus, after that ye have suffered a while, make you perfect, stablish, strengthen, settle you. To him be glory and dominion for ever and ever. Amen.

Gradual. Ps. 107, 32 and 31. Let them exalt him in the congregation of the people: and praise him in the seat of the elders. ℣. O that men would praise the Lord for his goodness; and declare the wonders that he doeth for the children of men.

Alleluia, alleluia. ℣. Matt. 16, 18. Thou art Peter, and upon this rock I will build my Church. Alleluia.

After Septuagesima, omitting Alleluia and the Verse following, is said:

Tract. Ps. 40, 10-11. I have declared thy righteousness in the great congregation, lo, I will not refrain my lips, O Lord, and that thou knowest. ℣. I have not hid thy righteousness within my heart: my talk hath been of thy truth and thy salvation. ℣. I have not kept back thy loving mercy and truth from the great congregation.

In Eastertide the Gradual is omitted, and in its place is said:

Alleluia, alleluia. ℣. Matt. 16, 18. Thou art Peter, and upon this rock I will build my Church. Alleluia. ℣. Ps. 45, 17, 18. Thou shalt make them princes in all lands: they shall remember thy name, O Lord. Alleluia.

✠ The Continuation of the holy Gospel according to Matthew.

Matt. 16, 13-19.

AT that time: Jesus came into the coasts of Cæsarea Philippi, and asked his disciples, saying: Whom do men say that I, the Son of man, am? And they said: Some say that thou art John the Baptist, some Elias, and others Jeremias, or one of the Prophets. He saith unto them: But whom say ye that I am? And Simon Peter answered and said: Thou art Christ, the son of the living God. And Jesus answered and said unto him: Blessed art thou, Simon Bar-jona: for flesh and blood hath not revealed it unto thee, but my Father which is in heaven. And I say also unto thee, That thou art Peter, and upon this rock I will build my Church, and the gates of hell shall not prevail against it. And I will give unto thee the keys of the kingdom of heaven. And whatsoever thou shalt bind on earth, shall be bound in heaven: and whatsoever thou shalt loose on earth, shall be loosed in heaven.

Offertory. Jer. 1, 9-10. Behold, I have put my words in thy mouth: see, I have set thee over the nations and over the kingdoms, to pull down and to destroy, to build and to plant. (E.T. Alleluia.)

Secret.

WE beseech thee, O Lord, graciously enlighten thy Church by the gifts which we here offer: that in every place thy flock may increase and prosper, and the shepherds by thy governance may be made pleasing to thy name. Through.

Another Secret, as above.

GRACIOUSLY receive, O Lord, the gifts which we with gladness offer unto thee, and grant: that at the intercession of blessed N. thy Church, rejoicing in purity of faith, may serve thee in all godly quietness. Through.

Common Preface (or of the Season).

Communion. Matt. 16, 18. Thou art Peter, and upon this rock I will build my Church. (E.T. Alleluia.)

Postcommunion.

MERCIFUL Lord, we beseech thee to govern and preserve thy Church, which thou dost here refresh with heavenly food: that by the guiding of thy mighty power it may serve thee in more abundant freedom, and ever keep thy true religion whole and undefiled. Through.

Another Postcommunion, as above.

MULTIPLY, we beseech thee, O Lord, in thy Church the spirit of grace, which thou hast given: that through the prayers of blessed N. thy (Martyr and) Chief Bishop neither the obedience of the flock may be wanting to the shepherd, nor the care of the shepherd to the flock. Through.

THE COMMON OF ONE MARTYR OUT OF EASTERTIDE

I
For a Martyr Bishop

Introit. Ecclus. 45, 30. Statuit ei.

THE Lord made a covenant of peace with him, that he should be the chief of his people: and that he should have the dignity of the priesthood for ever. Ps. 132, 1. Lord, remember David: and all his troubles. ℣. Glory.

Collect.

ALMIGHTY God, mercifully look upon our infirmities: and whereas we are sore afflicted by the burden of our sins, let the glorious intercession of blessed N. thy Martyr and Bishop be our succour and defence. Through.

The Lesson from the Epistle of blessed James the Apostle.

James 1, 12-18.

DEARLY beloved: Blessed is the man that endureth temptation: for when he is tried, he shall receive the crown of life, which the Lord hath promised to them that love him. Let no man say when he is tempted, I am tempted of God: for God cannot be tempted with evil: neither tempteth he any man. But every man is tempted, when he is drawn away of his own lust, and enticed. Then when lust hath conceived, it bringeth forth sin: and sin, when it is finished, bringeth forth death. Do not err, my beloved brethren. Every good gift and every perfect gift is from above, and cometh down from the Father of lights, with whom is no variableness, neither shadow of turning. Of his own will begat he us with the word of truth, that we should be a kind of firstfruits of his creatures.

Gradual. Ps. 89, 21-23. I have found David my servant, with my holy oil have I anointed him: my hand shall hold him fast, and my arm shall strengthen him. ℣. The enemy shall not be able to do him violence, the son of wickedness shall not hurt him.

Alleluia, alleluia. ℣. Ps. 110, 4. Thou art a priest for ever, after the order of Melchisedech. Alleluia.

After Septuagesima, omitting Alleluia and the Verse following, is said:

Tract. Ps. 21, 3-4. Thou hast given him his heart's desire: and hast not denied him the request of his lips. ℣. For thou hast prevented him with the blessings of goodness. ℣. And hast set a crown of pure gold upon his head.

✠ *The Continuation of the holy Gospel according to Luke.*

Luke 14, 26-33.

AT that time: Jesus said unto the multitudes: If any man come to me, and hate not his father, and mother, and wife, and children, and brethren, and sisters, yea, and his own life also, he cannot be my disciple. And whosoever doth not bear his cross, and come after me, cannot be my disciple. For which of you, intending to build a tower, sitteth not down first, and counteth the cost, whether he have sufficient to finish it; lest haply, after he hath laid the foundation, and is not able to finish it, all that behold it begin to mock him, saying: This man began to build, and was not able to finish? Or what king, going to make war against another king, sitteth not down first, and consulteth whether he be able with ten thousand to meet him that cometh against him with twenty thousand? Or else, while the other is yet a great way off, he sendeth an ambassage, and desireth conditions of peace. So likewise, whosoever he be of you that forsaketh not all that he hath, he cannot be my disciple.

Offertory. Ps. 89, 25. My truth and my mercy shall be with him: and in my name shall his horn be exalted.

Secret.

WE beseech thee, O Lord, mercifully to accept this our sacrifice which we offer unto thee, pleading the merits of blessed N. thy Martyr and Bishop: that the same may avail for our perpetual succour. Through.

Communion. Ps. 89, 36-38. I have sworn once by my holiness: His seed shall endure for ever: and his seat is like as the sun before me; he shall stand fast for evermore as the moon, and as the faithful witness in heaven.

Postcommunion.

WE beseech thee, O Lord our God, that like as we whom thou hast refreshed by the partaking of thy sacred gift do offer unto thee our outward worship: so, at the intercession of blessed N. thy Martyr and Bishop, we may inwardly be profited thereby to our salvation. Through.

II
For a Martyr Bishop
Another Mass.

Introit. Dan. 3, 84 and 87. Sacerdotes Dei.

O YE priests of the Lord, bless ye the Lord: O ye holy and humble men of heart, praise God. Ibid., 1. O all ye works of the Lord, bless ye the Lord: praise him and magnify him for ever. V. Glory.

Collect.

O GOD, who makest us glad with the yearly solemnity of blessed N. thy Martyr and Bishop: mercifully grant; that, as we now celebrate his heavenly birthday, so we may likewise rejoice in his protection. Through.

The Lesson from the Epistle of blessed Paul the Apostle to the Corinthians.

II Cor. 1, 3-7.

BRETHREN: Blessed be God, even the Father of our Lord Jesus Christ, the Father of mercies, and the God of all comfort, who comforteth us in all our tribulation: that we may be able to comfort them which are in trouble, by the comfort wherewith we ourselves are comforted of God. For as the sufferings of Christ abound in us: so our consolation also aboundeth by Christ. And whether we be afflicted, it is for your consolation and salvation, which is effectual in the enduring of the same sufferings which we also suffer: or whether we be comforted, it is for your consolation and salvation: and our hope of you is steadfast, knowing, that as ye are partakers of the sufferings, so shall ye be also of the consolation: in Christ Jesus our Lord.

Gradual. Ps. 8, 6-7. Thou hast crowned him with glory and worship. V. Thou hast made him to have dominion of the works of thy hands, O Lord.

Alleluia, alleluia. V. This is a priest whom the Lord hath crowned. Alleluia.

After Septuagesima, omitting Alleluia and the Verse following, is said:

Tract. Ps. 112, 1-3. Blessed is the man that feareth the Lord: he hath great delight in his commandments. V. His seed shall be mighty upon earth: the generation of the faithful shall be blessed. V. Riches and plenteousness shall be in his house: and his righteousness endureth for ever.

✠ The Continuation of the holy Gospel according to Matthew.

Matt. 16, 24-27.

AT that time: Jesus said unto his disciples: If any man will come after me, let him deny himself, and take up his cross, and follow me. For whosoever will save his life shall lose it: and whosoever will lose his life for my sake shall find it. For what is a man profited, if he shall gain the whole world, and lose his own soul? Or what shall a man give in exchange for his soul? For the Son of man shall come in the glory of his Father with his Angels: and then he shall reward every man according to his works.

Offertory. Ps. 89, 21-22. I have found David my servant, with my holy oil have I anointed him: my hand shall hold him fast, and my arm shall strengthen him.

Secret.

SANCTIFY, O Lord, the gifts which we dedicate to thee: that at the intercession of blessed N. thy Martyr and Bishop they may obtain for us thy gracious favour. Through.

Communion. Ps. 21, 4. Thou hast set, O Lord, a crown of pure gold upon his head.

Postcommunion.

O LORD, let this holy Communion cleanse us from every guilty stain: that at the intercession of blessed N., thy Martyr and Bishop we may be made partakers thereby of thy healing unto life eternal. Through.

III
For a Martyr not a Bishop

Introit. Ps. 21, 1-2. In virtute tua.

THE just shall rejoice in thy strength, O Lord: exceeding glad shall he be of thy salvation: thou hast given him his heart's desire. Ps. ibid., 4. For thou hast prevented him with the blessings of goodness: and hast set a crown of pure gold upon his head. ℣. Glory.

Collect.

GRANT, we beseech thee, almighty God: that we, who celebrate the heavenly birthday of blessed N., thy Martyr, may by his intercession be stablished in the love of thy name. Through.

The Lesson from the book of Wisdom.

Wisd. 10, 10-14.

THE Lord guided the just in right paths, shewed him the kingdom of God, and gave him knowledge of holy things: made him rich in his travails, and multiplied the fruit of his labours. In the covetousness of such as oppressed him he stood by him, and made him rich. He defended him from his enemies, and kept him safe from those that lay in wait, and in a sore conflict he gave him the victory, that he might know that wisdom is stronger than all. When the just was sold, she forsook him not, but delivered him from sin: she went down with him into the pit, and left him not in bonds, till she brought him the sceptre of the kingdom, and power against those that oppressed him: as for them that had accused him, he shewed them to be liars, and gave him perpetual glory, even he, the Lord our God.

Gradual. Ps. 112, 1-2. Blessed is the man that feareth the Lord: he hath great delight in his commandments. ℣. His seed shall be mighty upon earth: the generation of the faithful shall be blessed.

Alleluia, alleluia. ℣. Ps. 21, 4. Thou hast set, O Lord, a crown of pure gold upon his head. Alleluia.

After Septuagesima, omitting Alleluia and the Verse following, is said:

Tract. Ps. 21, 3-4. Thou hast given him his heart's desire: and hast not denied him the request of his lips. ℣. For thou

The Common of one Martyr out of Eastertide

hast prevented him with the blessings of goodness. ℣. And hast set a crown of pure gold upon his head.

✠ The Continuation of the holy Gospel according to Matthew.

Matt. 10, 34-42.

AT that time: Jesus said unto his disciples: Think not that I am come to send peace on earth: I came not to send peace, but a sword. For I am come to set a man at variance against his father, and the daughter against her mother, and the daughter in law against her mother in law: and a man's foes shall be they of his own household. He that loveth father or mother more than me is not worthy of me: and he that loveth son or daughter more than me is not worthy of me. And he that taketh not his cross, and followeth after me, is not worthy of me. He that findeth his life shall lose it: and he that loseth his life for my sake shall find it. He that receiveth you receiveth me: and he that receiveth me receiveth him that sent me. He that receiveth a prophet in the name of a prophet shall receive a prophet's reward: and he that receiveth a righteous man in the name of a righteous man shall receive a righteous man's reward. And whosoever shall give to drink unto one of these little ones a cup of cold water only in the name of a disciple: verily I say unto you he shall in no wise lose his reward.

Offertory. Ps. 8, 6-7. Thou hast crowned him with glory and worship: thou hast made him to have dominion of the works of thy hands, O Lord.

Secret.

WE beseech thee, O Lord, to accept our prayers and oblations: and graciously hearken unto us, whom thou dost cleanse by thy heavenly mysteries. Through.

Communion. Matt. 16, 24. If any man will come after me, let him deny himself, and take up his cross, and follow me.

Postcommunion.

GRANT, we beseech thee, O Lord our God: that like as we in this life do gladly honour the memory of thy Saints; so we may rejoice hereafter in their everlasting fellowship. Through.

IV

For a Martyr not a Bishop

Another Mass.

Introit. Ps. 64, 11. Laetabitur.

THE righteous shall rejoice in the Lord, and put his trust in him: and all they that are true of heart shall be glad. Ps. ibid., 2. Hear my voice, O God, in my prayer: preserve my life from fear of the enemy. ℣. Glory.

Collect.

GRANT, we beseech thee, almighty God: that, at the intercession of blessed N. thy Martyr, we may be delivered from all adversities which may happen to the body, and from all evil thoughts which may assault and hurt the soul. Through.

The Lesson from the Epistle of blessed Paul the Apostle to Timothy.

II Tim. 2, 8-10; 3, 10-12.

DEARLY beloved: Remember that Jesus Christ of the seed of David was raised from the dead according to my Gospel: wherein I suffer trouble, as an evildoer, even unto bonds: but the word of God is not bound. Therefore I endure all things for the elect's sakes, that they may also obtain the salvation which is in Christ Jesus with eternal glory. But thou hast fully known my doctrine, manner of life, purpose, faith, longsuffering, charity, patience, persecutions, afflictions: which came unto me at Antioch, at Iconium, at Lystra: what persecutions I endured, but out of them all the Lord delivered me. Yea, and all that will live godly in Christ Jesus shall suffer persecution.

Gradual. Ps. 37, 24. Though the righteous fall, he shall not be cast away: for the Lord upholdeth him with his hand. ℣. Ibid., 26. He is ever merciful, and lendeth: and his seed is blessed.

Alleluia, alleluia. ℣. John 8, 12. He that followeth me shall not walk in darkness: but shall have the light of eternal life. Alleluia.

After Septuagesima, omitting Alleluia and the Verse following, is said:

Tract. Ps. 112, 1-3. Blessed is the man that feareth the Lord: he hath great delight in his commandments. ℣. His seed shall be mighty upon earth: the generation of the faithful shall be blessed. ℣. Riches and plenteousness shall be in his house: and his righteousness endureth for ever.

☩ The Continuation of the Holy Gospel according to Matthew.

Matt. 10, 26-32.

AT that time: Jesus said unto his disciples: There is nothing covered, that shall not be revealed: and hid, that shall not be known. What I tell you in darkness, that speak ye in light: and what ye hear in the ear, that preach ye upon the housetops. And fear not them which kill the body, but are not able to kill the soul: but rather fear him which is able to destroy both soul and body in hell. Are not two sparrows sold for a farthing: and one of them shall not fall on the ground without your Father? But the very hairs of your head are all numbered. Fear ye not therefore: ye are of more value than many sparrows. Whosoever therefore shall confess me before men, him will I confess also before my Father which is in heaven.

After Septuagesima Alleluia at the end of the following Offertory is omitted:

Offertory. Ps. 21, 4-5. Thou hast set, O Lord, a crown of pure gold upon his head: he asked life of thee, and thou gavest it him, alleluia.

Secret.

LET this our bounden duty and service be acceptable in thy sight, O Lord: and through the supplication of him for whose solemnity it is offered, let it avail for our salvation. Through.

Communion. John 12, 26. If any man serve me, let him follow me; and where I am, there shall also my servant be.

Postcommunion.

WE beseech thee, O Lord our God, that like as we, whom thou hast refreshed by the partaking of thy sacred gift, do offer unto thee our outward worship: so at the intercession of blessed N. thy Martyr, we may inwardly be profited thereby to our salvation. Through.

Other Epistles and another Gospel in the Common of One Martyr outside Eastertide:

The Lesson from the Epistle of blessed James the Apostle.

James 1, 2-12.

DEARLY beloved: Count it all joy when ye fall into divers temptations: knowing this, that the trying of your faith worketh patience. But let patience have her perfect work: that ye may be perfect and entire, wanting nothing. If any of you lack wisdom, let him ask of God, that giveth to all men liberally, and upbraideth not: and it shall be given him. But let him ask in faith, nothing wavering: for he that wavereth is like a wave of the sea driven with the wind and tossed. For let not that man think that he shall receive any thing of the Lord. A double minded man is unstable in all his ways. Let the brother of low degree rejoice in that he is exalted: but the rich, in that he is made low, because as the flower of the grass he shall pass away: for the sun is no sooner risen with a burning heat, but it withereth the grass, and the flower thereof faileth, and the grace of the fashion of it perisheth: so also shall the rich man fade away in his ways. Blessed is the man that endureth temptation: for when he is tried, he shall receive the crown of life, which the Lord hath promised to them that love him.

The Lesson from the Epistle of blessed Peter the Apostle.

I Peter 4, 13.

DEARLY beloved: Rejoice, inasmuch as ye are partakers of Christ's sufferings: that, when his glory shall be revealed, ye may be glad also with exceeding joy. If ye be reproached for the name of Christ, happy are ye: for the spirit of glory and of God resteth upon you. But let none of you suffer as a murderer, or as a thief, or as an evildoer, or as a busybody in other men's matters. Yet if any man suffer as a Christian, let him not be ashamed: but let him glorify God on this behalf. For the time is come that judgment must begin at the house of God. And if it first begin at us: what shall be the end of them that obey not the gospel of God? And if the righteous scarcely be saved, where shall the ungodly and the sinner appear? Wherefore let them that suffer according to the will of God commit the keeping of their souls to him in well doing, as unto a faithful Creator.

Gospel Except a corn of wheat, as on the Feast of St. Lawrence, M., August 10.

THE COMMON OF MANY MARTYRS OUT OF EASTERTIDE

I

For many Martyrs

Introit. Ps. 79, 11, 12 and 10. Intret in conspectu.

LET the sorrowful sighing of the prisoners, O Lord, come before thee: reward thou our neighbours sevenfold into their bosom: avenge thou the blood of thy Saints that is shed. Ps. ibid. 1. O God, the heathen are come into thine inheritance: thy holy temple have they defiled: and made Jerusalem an heap of stones. ℣. Glory.

For many Martyr Bishops. Collect.

DEFEND us, O Lord, we beseech thee, who observe the feast of thy blessed Martyrs and Bishops N. and N.: and grant that by their meritorious supplication we may ever be holpen in thy sight. Through.

If they were not Bishops, the Prayers of the following Mass are said.

The Lesson from the book of Wisdom.

Wisd. 3, 1-8.

THE souls of the righteous are in the hand of God, and there shall no torment touch them. In the sight of the unwise they seemed to die: and their departure is taken for misery: and their going from us to be utter destruction: but they are in peace. For though they be punished in the sight of men, yet is their hope full of immortality. And having been a little chastised, they shall be greatly rewarded: for God proved them, and found them worthy for himself. As gold in the furnace hath he tried them, and received them as a burnt offering. And in the time of their visitation they shall shine, and run to and fro like sparks among the stubble. They shall judge the nations, and have dominion over the people, and their Lord shall reign for ever.

Gradual. Exod. 15, 11. God is glorious in his holy ones, fearful in praises, doing wonders. ℣. ibid., 6. Thy right hand, O Lord, is become glorious in power: thy right hand hath dashed in pieces the enemy.

Alleluia, alleluia. ℣. Ecclus. 44, 14. The bodies of the Saints are buried in peace, but their name liveth for evermore. Alleluia.

After Septuagesima, omitting Alleluia and the Verse following, is said:

Tract. Ps. 126, 5-6. They that sow in tears, shall reap in joy. ℣. He that now goeth on his way weeping, and beareth forth good seed. ℣. Shall doubtless come again with joy, and bring his sheaves with him.

☩ The Continuation of the Holy Gospel according to Luke.

Luke 21, 9-19.

AT that time: Jesus said unto his disciples: When ye shall hear of wars and commotions, be not terrified: for these things must first come to pass, but the end is not by and by. Then said he unto them: Nation shall rise again nation, and kingdom against kingdom. And great earthquakes shall be in divers places, and famines, and pestilences, and fearful sights and great signs shall there be from heaven. But before all these, they shall lay their hands on you, and persecute you, delivering you up to the synagogues, and into prisons, being brought before kings and rulers for my name's sake: and it shall turn to you for a testimony. Settle it therefore in your hearts, not to meditate before what ye shall answer. For I will give you a mouth and wisdom, which all your adversaries shall not be able to gainsay nor resist. And ye shall be betrayed both by parents, and brethren, and kinsfolks, and friends, and some of you shall they cause to be put to death: and ye shall be hated of all men for my name's sake: but there shall not an hair of your head perish. In your patience possess ye your souls.

After Septuagesima Alleluia at the end of the following Offertory is omitted.

Offertory. Ps. 68, 36. God is wonderful in his holy ones: even the God of Israel, he will give strength and power unto his people: blessed be God, alleluia.

1. For many Martyr Bishops.   Secret.

ASSIST us mercifully, O Lord, in these our supplications which we make before thee in remembrance of thy Saints: that we who trust not in our own righteousness may be succoured by the merits of them that have found favour in thy sight. Through.

2. For many Martyrs only. Secret of the following Mass.

Communion. Wisd. 3, 4, 5 and 6. Though they be punished in the sight of men, yet hath God proved them: as gold in the furnace hath he tried them, and received them as a burnt offering.

1. For many Martyr Bishops. Postcommunion.

O LORD, who hast fulfilled us with these saving mysteries: we beseech thee that we may be aided by the prayers of those whose festival we celebrate. Through.

2. For many Martyrs only. Postcommunion of the following Mass.

II

For many Martyrs

Another Mass.

Introit. Ecclus. 44, 15 and 14. Sapientiam Sanctorum.

LET the people tell of the wisdom of the Saints, and let the Church shew forth their praise: their names shall live for evermore. Ps. 33, 1. Rejoice in the Lord, O ye righteous: for it becometh well the just to be thankful. ℣. Glory.

Collect.

O GOD, who dost vouchsafe unto us to celebrate the heavenly birthday of thy holy Martyrs N. and N.: grant that we may rejoice in their perpetual fellowship in heaven. Through.

If they were Bishops, let the Prayers of the preceding Mass be said, which is also to be observed in those that follow.

The Lesson from the book of Wisdom.
Wisd. 5, 16-20.

BUT the righteous live for evermore, their reward also is with the Lord, and the care of them is with the Most High. Therefore shall they receive a glorious kingdom, and a beautiful crown from the Lord's hand: for with his right hand shall he cover them, and with his arm shall he protect them. He shall take to him his jealousy for complete armour, and make the creature his weapon for the revenge of his enemies. He shall put on righteousness as a breastplate, and true judgment instead of an helmet. He shall take holiness for an invincible shield.

Gradual. Ps. 124, 7-8. Our soul is escaped even as a bird out of the snare of the fowler. ℣. The snare is broken, and we are delivered: our help standeth in the name of the Lord, who hath made heaven and earth.

Alleluia, alleluia. ℣. Ps. 68, 4. Let the righteous be glad and rejoice before God: let them also be merry and joyful. Alleluia.

After Septuagesima, omitting Alleluia and the Verse following, is said:

Tract. Ps. 126, 5-6. They that sow in tears, shall reap in joy. ℣. He that now goeth on his way weeping, and beareth forth good seed. ℣. Shall doubtless come again with joy, and bring his sheaves with him.

✠ The Continuation of the Holy Gospel according to Luke.

Luke 6, 17-23.

AT that time: Jesus came down from the mountain, and stood in the plain, and the company of his disciples, and a great multitude of people out of all Judæa and Jerusalem, and from the sea coast of Tyre and Sidon which came to hear him, and to be healed of their diseases, and they that were vexed with unclean spirits: and they were healed. And the whole multitude sought to touch him: for there went virtue out of him, and healed them all. And he lifted up his eyes on his disciples, and said: Blessed be ye poor: for yours is the kingdom of God. Blessed are ye that hunger now: for ye shall be filled. Blessed are ye that weep now: for ye shall laugh. Blessed are ye, when men shall hate you, and when they shall separate you from their company, and shall reproach you, and cast out your name as evil, for the Son of man's sake. Rejoice ye in that day, and leap for joy: for, behold, your reward is great in heaven.

After Septuagesima **Alleluia** at the end of the following Offertory is omitted.

Offertory. Ps. 149, 5-6. Let the Saints be joyful with glory, let them rejoice in their beds: let the praises of God be in their mouth, alleluia.

Secret.

WE beseech thee, O Lord, that the gifts which we offer unto thee of our bounden duty and service may be acceptable unto thee for the honour of thy Saints: and by thy mercy profitable unto us for our salvation. Through.

Communion. Luke 12, 4. I say unto you, my friends: Be not afraid of them that persecute you.

Postcommunion.

GRANT to us, we beseech thee, O Lord: at the intercession of thy holy Martyrs N. and N.; that we, who with our outward lips are partakers of this holy Sacrament, may inwardly receive the same in purity of heart. Through.

III

For many Martyrs

A Third Mass.

Introit. Ps. 37, 39. Salus autem justorum.

BUT the salvation of the righteous cometh of the Lord: who is also their strength in the time of trouble. Ps. ibid., 1. Fret not thyself because of the ungodly: neither be thou envious against the evil doers. ℣. Glory.

Collect.

O GOD, who makest us glad with the yearly solemnity of thy holy Martyrs N. and N.: mercifully grant; that as we do rejoice in their merits, so we may be enkindled by their example. Through.

The Lesson from the Epistle of blessed Paul the Apostle to the Hebrews.

Heb. 10, 32-38.

BRETHREN: Call to remembrance the former days, in which, after ye were illuminated, ye endured a great fight of afflictions: partly, whilst ye were made a gazingstock both by reproaches and afflictions, and partly, whilst ye became companions of them that were so used. For ye had compassion of me in my bonds, and took joyfully the spoiling of your goods, knowing in yourselves that we have in heaven a better and an enduring substance. Cast not away therefore your confidence, which hath great recompence of reward. For ye have need of patience: that, after ye have done the will of God, ye might receive the promise. For yet a little while, and he that shall come will come, and will not tarry. Now the just shall live by faith.

Gradual. Ps. 34, 18-19. The righteous cry, and the Lord heareth them: and delivereth them out of all their troubles. ℣. The Lord is nigh unto them that are of a contrite heart: and will save such as be of an humble spirit.

Alleluia, alleluia. ℣. The noble army of Martyrs praise thee, O Lord. Alleluia.

After Septuagesima, omitting Alleluia and the Verse following, is said:

Tract. Ps. 126, 5-6. They that sow in tears, shall reap in joy. ℣. He that now goeth on his way weeping, and beareth forth good seed. ℣. Shall doubtless come again with joy, and bring his sheaves with him.

✠ The Continuation of the Holy Gospel according to Luke.

Luke 12, 1-8.

AT that time: Jesus said unto his disciples: Beware ye of the leaven of the Pharisees, which is hypocrisy. For there is nothing covered, that shall not be revealed: neither hid, that shall not be known. Therefore whatsoever ye have spoken in darkness shall be heard in the light: and that which ye have spoken in the ear in closets shall be proclaimed upon the housetops. And I say unto you my friends; Be not afraid of them that kill the body, and after that have no more that they can do. But I will forewarn you whom ye shall fear: fear him, which after he hath killed hath power to cast into hell. Yea, I say unto you: fear him. Are not five sparrows sold for two farthings, and not one of them is forgotten before God? But even the very hairs of your head are all numbered. Fear not therefore: ye are of more value than many sparrows. Also I say unto you: Whosoever shall confess me before men, him shall the Son of man also confess before the Angels of God.

After Septuagesima Alleluia at the end of the following Offertory is omitted:

Offertory. Wisd. 3, 1, 2 and 3. The souls of the righteous are in the hand of God, and there shall no torment touch them. In the sight of the unwise they seemed to die: but they are in peace, alleluia.

Secret.

WE beseech thee, O Lord, mercifully to accept these our oblations: that at the intercession of thy holy Martyrs N. and N. we may be defended against all adversities. Through.

Communion. Matt. 10, 27. What I tell you in darkness, that speak ye in light, saith the Lord: and what ye hear in the ear, that preach ye upon the housetops.

Postcommunion.

O LORD, let this holy Communion cleanse us from every guilty stain: that at the intercession of thy holy Martyrs N. and N. we may thereby be made partakers of thy healing unto life eternal. Through.

Other Epistles and Gospels for many Martyrs.

1. Epistle God rendered to the righteous, as on the Feast of SS. Nazarius and his Companions, MM., July 28.

2. The Lesson from the Epistle of blessed Paul the Apostle to the Romans.

Rom. 5, 1-5.

BRETHREN: Being justified by faith, we have peace with God through our Lord Jesus Christ: by whom also we have access by faith into this grace wherein we stand, and rejoice in hope of the glory of God. And not only so, but we glory in tribulations also: knowing that tribulation worketh patience and patience, experience, and experience, hope, and hope maketh not ashamed: because the love of God is shed abroad in our hearts by the Holy Ghost which is given unto us.

3. Epistle I reckon that the sufferings, as on the fourth Sunday after Trinity.

4. Epistle Let us approve ourselves, as on the Feast of SS. Abdon and Sennen, MM., July 30.

5. Epistle The Saints through faith, as on the Feast of SS. Fabian, Pope and Sebastian, MM., January 20.

6. The Lesson from the book of the Revelation of blessed John the Apostle.

Rev. 7, 13-17.

IN those days: One of the elders answered, saying unto me: What are these which are arrayed in white robes? and whence came they? And I said unto him: Sir, thou knowest. And he said to me: These are they which came out of great tribulation, and have washed their robes, and made them white in the blood of the Lamb. Therefore are they before the throne of God, and serve him day and night in his temple: and he that sitteth on the throne shall dwell among them: they shall hunger no more, neither thirst any more, neither shall the sun light on them, nor any heat: for the Lamb which is in the midst of the throne shall feed them, and shall lead them unto living fountains of waters: and God shall wipe away all tears from their eyes.

1. ✠ The Continuation of the holy Gospel according to Matthew.

Matt. 24, 3-13.

AT that time: As Jesus sat upon the mount of Olives, the disciples came unto him privately, saying: Tell us, when shall these things be? and what shall be the sign of thy coming, and of the end of the world? And Jesus answered and said unto them: Take heed that no man deceive you. For many shall come in my name, saying: I am Christ: and shall deceive many. And ye shall hear of wars and rumours of wars. See that ye be not troubled. For all these things must come to pass, but the end is not yet. For nation shall arise against nation, and kingdom against kingdom, and there shall be famines, and pestilences, and earthquakes, in divers places. All these are the beginning of sorrows. Then shall they deliver you up to be afflicted, and shall kill you: and ye shall be hated of all nations for my name's sake. And then shall many be offended, and shall betray one another, and shall hate one another. And many false prophets shall rise, and shall deceive many. And because iniquity shall abound, the love of many shall wax cold. But he that shall endure unto the end, the same shall be saved.

2. Gospel Jesus, seeing the multitudes, as on the Feast of All Saints, November 1.

3. Gospel I thank thee, O Father, as on the Feast of St. Francis, C., October 4.

4. ✠ The Continuation of the holy Gospel according to Luke.

Luke 11, 47-51.

AT that time: Jesus said unto the scribes and Pharisees: Woe unto you, for ye build the sepulchres of the prophets: and your fathers killed them. Truly ye bear witness that ye allow the deeds of your fathers: for they indeed killed them, and ye build their sepulchres. Therefore also said the wisdom of God: I will send them prophets and apostles, and some of them they shall slay and persecute: that the blood of all the prophets, which was shed from the foundation of the world, may be required of this generation, from the blood of Abel unto the blood of Zacharias, which perished between the altar and the temple. Verily I say unto you, it shall be required of this generation.

5. ✠ The Continuation of the holy Gospel according to Luke.

Luke 10, 16-20.

AT that time: Jesus said unto his disciples: He that heareth you heareth me: and he that despiseth you despiseth me. And he that despiseth me despiseth him that sent me. And the seventy returned again with joy, saying: Lord, even the devils are subject unto us through thy name. And he said unto them: I beheld Satan as lightning fall from heaven. Behold, I give unto you power to tread on serpents and scorpions, and over all the power of the enemy: and nothing shall by any means hurt you. Notwithstanding in this rejoice not, that the spirits are subject unto you: but rather rejoice, because your names are written in heaven.

THE COMMON OF MARTYRS IN EASTERTIDE

I

For one Martyr

Introit. Ps. 64, 3. Protexisti.

THOU hast hidden me, O God, from the gathering together of the froward, alleluia: and from the insurrection of wicked doers, alleluia, alleluia. Ps. ibid., 2. Hear my voice, O God, in my prayer: preserve my life from fear of the enemy. ℣. Glory.

1. For a Martyr Bishop. Collect.

ALMIGHTY God, mercifully look upon our infirmities: and whereas we are sore afflicted by the burden of our sins, let the glorious intercession of blessed N. thy Martyr and Bishop be our succour and defence. Through.

2. For a Martyr Bishop. Another Collect.

O GOD, who makest us glad with the yearly solemnity of blessed N., thy Martyr and Bishop: mercifully grant; that as we now celebrate his heavenly birthday, so we may likewise rejoice in his protection. Through.

3. For a Martyr only. Collect.

GRANT, we beseech thee, almighty God: that we, who celebrate the heavenly birthday of blessed N., thy Martyr; may by his intercession be stablished in the love of thy name. Through.

4. For a Martyr only. Another Collect.

GRANT, we beseech thee, almighty God: that at the intercession of blessed N., thy Martyr, we may be delivered from all adversities which may happen to the body, and from all evil thoughts which may assault and hurt the soul. Through.

The Lesson from the book of Wisdom.
Wisd. 5, 1-5.

THE righteous shall stand in great boldness before the face of such as have afflicted them, and made no account of their labours. When they see it they shall be troubled with terrible fear, and shall be amazed at the strangeness of their salvation, so far beyond all that they looked for, and they repenting and groaning for anguish of spirit shall say within themselves: These were they, whom we had sometime in derision, and a proverb of reproach. We fools accounted their life madness, and their end to be without honour: how are they numbered among the children of God, and their lot is among the Saints.

Or the Epistle of Blessed Paul the Apostle to Timothy, Remember, as in the Mass Laetabitur, p. [7].

Alleluia, alleluia. ℣. Ps. 89, 6. O Lord, the very heavens shall praise thy wondrous works: and thy truth in the congregation of the saints. Alleluia. ℣. Ps. 21, 4. Thou hast set, O Lord, a crown of pure gold upon his head. Alleluia.

✠ The Continuation of the holy Gospel according to John.
John 15, 1-7.

AT that time: Jesus said unto his disciples: I am the true vine: and my Father is the husbandman. Every branch in me that beareth not fruit he taketh away: and every branch that beareth fruit, he purgeth it, that it may bring forth more fruit. Now ye are clean through the word which I have spoken unto you. Abide in me: and I in you. As the branch cannot bear fruit of itself, except it abide in the vine: no more can ye, except ye abide in me. I am the vine, ye are the branches: he that abideth in me, and I in him, the same bringeth forth much fruit: for without me ye can do nothing. If a man abide not in me, he is cast forth as a branch, and is withered, and men gather them, and cast them into the fire, and they are burned. If ye abide in me, and my words abide in you: ye shall ask what ye will, and it shall be done unto you.

Offertory. Ps. 89, 6. O Lord, the very heavens shall praise thy wondrous works: and thy truth in the congregation of the saints, alleluia, alleluia.

1. For a Martyr Bishop. Secret.

WE beseech thee, O Lord, mercifully to accept this our sacrifice, which we offer unto thee, pleading the merits of blessed N., thy Martyr and Bishop: that the same may effectually avail for our perpetual succour. Through.

2. For a Martyr Bishop. Another Secret.

SANCTIFY, O Lord, the gifts which we dedicate to thee: that, at the intercession of blessed N., thy Martyr and Bishop, they may obtain for us thy gracious favour. Through.

3. For a Martyr only. Secret.

WE beseech thee, O Lord, to accept our prayers and oblations: and graciously hearken unto us whom thou dost cleanse by thy heavenly mysteries. Through.

4. For a Martyr only. Another Secret.

LET this our bounden duty and service be acceptable in thy sight, O Lord: and through the supplication of him for whose solemnity it is offered, let it avail for our salvation. Through.

Communion. Ps. 64, 11. The righteous shall rejoice in the Lord, and put his trust in him: and all they that are true of heart shall be glad, alleluia, alleluia.

1. For a Martyr Bishop. Postcommunion.

WE beseech thee, O Lord our God, that like as we, whom thou hast refreshed by the partaking of thy sacred gift, do offer unto thee our outward worship: so, at the intercession of blessed N. thy Martyr and Bishop, we may be inwardly profited thereby to our salvation. Through.

2. For a Martyr Bishop. Another Postcommunion.

O LORD, let this holy Communion cleanse us from every guilty stain: that, at the intercession of blessed N. thy Martyr and Bishop, we may be made partakers thereby of thy healing unto life eternal. Through.

3. For a Martyr only. Postcommunion.

GRANT, we beseech thee, O Lord our God: that like as we in this life do gladly honour the memory of thy Saints; so we may rejoice hereafter in their everlasting fellowship. Through.

4. For a Martyr only. Another Postcommunion.

WE beseech thee, O Lord our God: that like as we, whom thou hast refreshed by the partaking of thy sacred gift, do offer unto thee our outward worship; so, at the intercession of blessed N. thy Martyr, we may inwardly be profited thereby to our salvation. Through.

¶ The first Epistle and the Gospel of the above Mass may be said also in the following Mass, and those in the following may be said in the above, provided a special Epistle or Gospel be not appointed in the Missal.

II
For many Martyrs
Introit. Ps. 145, 10-11. Sancti tui.

THY Saints give thanks unto thee, O Lord: they shew the glory of thy kingdom, alleluia, alleluia. Ps. ibid., 1. I will magnify thee, O God, my King: and I will praise thy name for ever and ever. ℣. Glory.

1. For many Martyr Bishops. Collect.

DEFEND us, O Lord, we beseech thee, who observe the feast of thy blessed Martyrs and Bishops N. and N.: and grant that by their meritorious supplication we may ever be holpen in thy sight. Through.

2. For many Martyrs only. Collect.

O GOD, who dost vouchsafe unto us to celebrate the heavenly birthday of thy holy Martyrs N. and N.: grant that we may rejoice in their perpetual fellowship in heaven. Through.

3. For many Martyrs. Another Collect.

O GOD, who makest us glad with the yearly solemnity of thy holy Martyrs N. and N.: mercifully grant that as we do rejoice in their merits, so we may be enkindled by their example. Through.

The Lesson from the Epistle of blessed Peter the Apostle.

I Peter 1, 3-7.

BLESSED be the God and Father of our Lord Jesus Christ, which according to his abundant mercy hath begotten us again unto a lively hope by the resurrection of Jesus Christ from the dead, to an inheritance incorruptible, and undefiled, and that fadeth not away, reserved in heaven for you, who are kept by the power of God through faith unto salvation ready to be revealed in the last time. Wherein ye greatly rejoice, though now for a season, if need be, ye are in heaviness through manifold temptations: that the trial of your faith, being much more precious than of gold that perisheth, though it be tried with fire, might be found unto praise and honour and glory at the appearing of Jesus Christ our Lord.

Alleluia, alleluia. ℣. Thy Saints, O Lord, shall grow as the lily, and as the odour of balsam shall they be before thee. Alleluia. ℣. Ps. 116, 15. Right dear in the sight of the Lord is the death of his Saints. Alleluia.

☩ The Continuation of the holy Gospel according to John.

John 15, 5-11.

AT that time: Jesus said unto his disciples: I am the vine, ye are the branches: he that abideth in me, and I in him, the same bringeth forth much fruit: for without me ye can do nothing. If a man abide not in me, he is cast forth as a branch, and is withered, and men gather them, and cast them into the fire, and they are burned. If ye abide in me, and my words abide in you: ye shall ask what ye will, and it shall be done unto you. Herein is my Father glorified, that ye bear much fruit, so shall ye be my disciples. As the Father hath loved me, so have I loved you. Continue ye in my love. If ye keep my commandments, ye shall abide in my love, even as I have kept my Father's commandments, and abide in his love. These things have I spoken unto you: that my joy might remain in you, and that your joy might be full.

Offertory. Ps. 32, 11. Be glad, O ye righteous, and rejoice in the Lord: and be joyful, all ye that are true of heart, alleluia, alleluia.

The Common of many Martyrs in Eastertide

1. *For many Martyr Bishops. Secret.*

ASSIST us mercifully, O Lord, in these our supplications, which we make before thee in remembrance of thy Saints: that we who trust not in our own righteousness may be succoured by the merits of them that have found favour in thy sight. Through.

2. *For many Martyrs only. Secret.*

WE beseech thee, O Lord, that the gifts which we offer unto thee of our bounden duty and service may be acceptable unto thee for the honour of thy Saints: and by thy mercy profitable unto us for our salvation. Through.

3. *For many Martyrs. Another Secret.*

WE beseech thee, O Lord, mercifully to accept these our oblations: that at the intercession of thy holy Martyrs N. and N. we may be defended against all adversities. Through.

Communion. Ps. 33, 1. Rejoice in the Lord, O ye righteous, alleluia: for it becometh well the just to be thankful, alleluia.

1. *For Martyr Bishops. Postcommunion.*

O LORD, who hast fulfilled us with these saving mysteries: we beseech thee that we may be aided by the prayers of those whose festival we celebrate. Through.

2. *For many Martyrs only. Another Postcommunion.*

GRANT to us, we beseech thee, O Lord: at the intercession of thy holy Martyrs N. and N.; that we, who with our outward lips are partakers of this holy Sacrament, may inwardly receive the same in purity of heart. Through.

3. *For many Martyrs only. Another Postcommunion.*

O LORD, let this holy Communion cleanse us from every guilty stain: that, at the intercession of thy holy Martyrs N. and N., we may thereby be made partakers of thy healing unto life eternal. Through.

In the Common of Martyrs in Eastertide, another Epistle and Gospel:

The Lesson from the book of the Revelation of blessed John the Apostle:

Rev. 19, 1-9.

IN those days: After these things I, John, heard a great voice of much people in heaven, saying: Alleluia: salvation, and glory, and honour, and power unto the Lord our God: for true and righteous are his judgments, for he hath judged the great whore, which did corrupt the earth with her fornication, and hath avenged the blood of his servants at her hand. And again they said: Alleluia. And her smoke rose up for ever and ever. And the four and twenty elders and the four beasts fell down and worshipped God that sat on the throne, saying: Amen, Alleluia. And a voice came out of the throne, saying: Praise our God, all ye his servants, and ye that fear him, both small and great. And I heard as it were the voice of a great multitude, and as the voice of many waters, and as the voice of mighty thunderings, saying: Alleluia: for the Lord God omnipotent reigneth. Let us be glad and rejoice, and give honour to him: for the marriage of the Lamb is come, and his wife hath made herself ready. And to her was granted that she should be arrayed in fine linen, clean and white. For the fine linen is the righteousness of saints. And he saith unto me: Write: Blessed are they which are called unto the marriage supper of the Lamb.

✠ The Continuation of the holy Gospel according to John.

John 16, 20-22.

AT that time: Jesus said unto his disciples: Verily, verily I say unto you: that ye shall weep and lament, but the world shall rejoice: and ye shall be sorrowful, but your sorrow shall be turned into joy. A woman, when she is in travail, hath sorrow, because her hour is come: but as soon as she is delivered of the child, she remembereth no more the anguish for joy: that a man is born into the world. And ye now therefore have sorrow, but I will see you again, and your heart shall rejoice: and your joy no man taketh from you.

¶ In the Common of Confessors, and Virgins, and in other Masses of Eastertide, all is said as in the rest of the year, a double Alleluia being added in the Introit before the Psalm, and at the end of the Offertory and Communion one Alleluia, where it is not given; and the Gradual being omitted, two ℣℣. are said with four Alleluias, as is set down in their places.

THE COMMON OF A CONFESSOR BISHOP

I

For a Confessor Bishop

Introit. Ecclus. 45, 24. Statuit ei.

THE Lord hath established a covenant of peace with him, and made him the chief of his people: that he should have the dignity of the priesthood for ever. (E.T. Alleluia, alleluia.) Ps. 132, 1. Lord, remember David: and all his trouble. ℣. Glory.

Collect.

GRANT, we beseech thee, almighty God: that we, devoutly observing this festival of blessed N., thy Confessor and Bishop, may hereby advance in true godliness and attain unto everlasting salvation. Through.

The Lesson from the book of Wisdom.

Ecclus. 44, 16-45, 15.

BEHOLD, a great priest, who in his days pleased the Lord, and was found righteous: and in the time of wrath he was taken in exchange for the world. There was none like unto him, who kept the law of the Most High. Therefore by an oath the Lord assured him that he would increase him among his people. He established with him the blessing of all men and the covenant, and made it rest upon his head. He acknowledged him in his blessing: he preserved for him his mercy: so that he found favour in the sight of the Lord. He magnified him in the sight of kings: and gave unto him a crown of glory. An everlasting covenant he made with him, and gave him a great priesthood: and blessed him with glory. That he should execute the office of the priesthood, and have praise in his name, and offer unto him incense, and a sweet savour.

Gradual. Ecclus. 44, 16. Behold, a great priest, who in his days pleased the Lord. ℣. Ibid., 20. There was none like unto him to keep the law of the Most High.

Alleluia, alleluia. ℣. Ps. 110, 4. Thou art a priest for ever after the order of Melchisedech. Alleluia.

After Septuagesima, omitting Alleluia and the Verse following, is said:

Tract. Ps. 112, 1-3. Blessed is the man that feareth the Lord: he hath great delight in his commandments. ℣. His seed shall be mighty upon earth: the generation of the faithful shall be blessed. ℣. Riches and plenteousness shall be in his house: and his righteousness endureth for ever.

In Eastertide the Gradual is omitted, and in its place is said:

Alleluia, alleluia. ℣. Ps. 110, 4. Thou art a priest for ever after the order of Melchisedech. Alleluia. ℣. This is a priest whom the Lord hath crowned. Alleluia.

✠ The Continuation of the holy Gospel according to Matthew.

Matt. 25, 14-23.

AT that time: Jesus spake this parable unto his disciples: A man travelling into a far country called his own servants, and delivered unto them his goods. And unto one he gave five talents, to another two, and to another one, to every man according to his several ability, and straightway took his journey. Then he that had received the five talents went and traded with the same, and made them other five talents. And likewise he that had received two, he also gained other two. But he that had received one went and digged in the earth, and hid his lord's money. After a long time the lord of those servants cometh, and reckoneth with them. And so he that had received five talents came and brought other five talents, saying: Lord, thou deliveredst unto me five talents, behold, I have gained beside them five talents more. His lord said unto him: Well done, thou good and faithful servant, thou hast been faithful over a few things, I will make thee ruler over many things: enter thou into the joy of thy lord. He also that had received two talents came and said: Lord, thou deliveredst unto me two talents, behold, I have gained two other talents beside them. His lord said unto him: Well done, good and faithful servant, thou hast been faithful over a few things, I will make thee ruler over many things: enter thou into the joy of thy lord.

Offertory. Ps. 89, 21-22. I have found David my servant, with my holy oil have I anointed him: my hand shall hold him fast, and my arm shall strengthen him. (E.T. Alleluia.)

Secret.

WE beseech thee, O Lord, that we, remembering with gladness the merits of thy Saints, may in all places feel the succour of their intercession. Through.

Communion. Luke 12, 42. A faithful and wise servant, whom his lord hath made ruler over his household: to give them their portion of meat in due season. (E.T. Alleluia.)

Postcommunion.

GRANT, we beseech thee, almighty God: that we, shewing forth our thankfulness for the gifts which we have received, may, at the intercession of blessed N., thy Confessor and Bishop, obtain yet more abundant mercies. Through.

II

For a Confessor Bishop

Another Mass.

Introit. Ps. 132, 9-10. Sacerdotes tui.

LET thy priests, O Lord, be clothed with righteousness, and let thy saints sing with joyfulness: for thy servant David's sake, turn not away the presence of thine Anointed. (E.T. Alleluia, alleluia.) Ps. ibid., 1. Lord, remember David: and all his trouble. ℣. Glory.

Collect.

WE beseech thee, O Lord, graciously to hear the prayers which we offer unto thee on the solemnity of blessed N., thy Confessor and Bishop: that, like as he was found worthy to do thee faithful service, so by his merits and intercession we may be absolved from all our sins. Through.

The Common of a Confessor Bishop

The Lesson from the Epistle of blessed Paul the Apostle to the Hebrews.

Heb. 7, 23-27.

BRETHREN: They were many priests, because they were not suffered to continue by reason of death: but Jesus, because he continueth ever, hath an unchangeable priesthood. Wherefore he is able also to save them to the uttermost that come unto God by him: seeing he ever liveth to make intercession for them. For such an high priest became us, who is holy, harmless, undefiled, separate from sinners, and made higher than the heavens: who needeth not daily, as those high priests, to offer up sacrifice, first for his own sins, and then for the people's: for this he did once, when he offered up himself, Jesus Christ, our Lord.

Gradual. Ps. 132, 16-17. I will deck her priests with health: and her saints shall rejoice and sing. ℣. There shall I make the horn of David to flourish: I have ordained a lantern for mine Anointed.

Alleluia, alleluia. ℣. Ps. 110, 4. The Lord sware, and will not repent: Thou art a priest for ever after the order of Melchisedech. Alleluia.

After Septuagesima, omitting Alleluia and the Verse following, is said:

Tract. Ps. 112, 1-3. Blessed is the man that feareth the Lord: he hath great delight in his commandments. ℣. His seed shall be mighty upon earth: the generation of the faithful shall be blessed. ℣. Riches and plenteousness shall be in his house: and his righteousness endureth for ever.

In Eastertide the Gradual is omitted, and in its place is said:

Alleluia, alleluia. ℣. Ps. 110, 4. The Lord sware, and will not repent: Thou art a priest for ever after the order of Melchisedech. Alleluia. ℣. Ecclus. 45, 9. The Lord loved him, and adorned him: he clothed him with a robe of glory. Alleluia.

✠ The Continuation of the holy Gospel according to Matthew.

Matt. 24, 42-47.

AT that time: Jesus said unto his disciples: Watch, for ye know not what hour your Lord doth come. But know this, that if the goodman of the house had known in what watch the thief would come, he would have watched, and would not have suffered his house to be broken up. Therefore be ye also ready: for in such an hour as ye think not the Son of man cometh. Who then is a faithful and wise servant, whom his lord hath made ruler over his household, to give them meat in due season? Blessed is that servant, whom his lord when he cometh shall find so doing. Verily I say unto you, that he shall make him ruler over all his goods.

Offertory. Ps. 89, 25. My truth and my mercy shall be with him: and in my name shall his horn be exalted. (E.T. Alleluia.)

Secret.

WE beseech thee, O Lord, that our devout observance of the yearly solemnity of blessed N., thy Confessor and Bishop, may render us acceptable unto thy loving kindness: that this service of propitiation, which we duly offer, may be profitable unto him for the reward of blessedness, and obtain for us the gifts of thy grace. Through.

Communion. Matt. 24, 46-47. Blessed is the servant, whom his lord when he cometh shall find watching: verily I say unto you, he shall make him ruler over all his goods. (E.T. Alleluia.)

Postcommunion.

O GOD, who rewardest the souls of them that put their trust in thee: vouchsafe; that we, who keep the solemn feast of blessed N., thy Confessor and Bishop, may by his prayers obtain thy merciful pardon. Through.

¶ Other Epistles and Gospels for a Confessor Bishop:

1. Epistle Every high priest, as on the Anniversary of the Consecration or Election of a Bishop.

2. Epistle Remember them as on the Feast of St. Nicholas, Bp. and Conf., December 6.

1. Gospel No man, when he hath lighted, as on the Feast of St. Martin, Bp. and Conf., November 11.

2. Gospel Take ye heed, as on the Anniversary of the Consecration or election of a Bishop.

THE COMMON OF DOCTORS

Introit. Ecclus. 15, 5. In medio.

IN the midst of the Church he opened his mouth: and the Lord filled him with the spirit of wisdom and understanding: he clothed him with a robe of glory. (E.T. Alleluia, alleluia.) Ps. 92, 2. It is a good thing to give thanks unto the Lord: and to sing praises unto thy name, O most Highest. ℣. Glory.

Collect.

O GOD, who didst send blessed N. thy Doctor to guide thy people in the way of everlasting salvation: grant, we beseech thee; that as we have learned of him the doctrine of life on earth, so we may be found worthy to have him for our advocate in heaven. Through.

The Lesson from the Epistle of blessed Paul the Apostle to Timothy.

II Tim. 4, 1-8.

DEARLY beloved: I charge thee before God, and the Lord Jesus Christ, who shall judge the quick and the dead at his appearing and his kingdom: preach the word, be instant in season, out of season: reprove, rebuke, exhort with all longsuffering and doctrine. For the time will come when they will not endure sound doctrine, but after their own lusts shall they heap to themselves teachers, having itching ears, and they shall turn away their ears from the truth, and shall be turned unto fables. But watch thou in all things, endure afflictions, do the work of an Evangelist, make full proof of thy ministry. For I am now ready to be offered, and the time of my departure is at hand. I have fought a good fight, I have finished my course, I have kept the faith. Henceforth there is laid up for me a crown of righteousness, which the Lord, the righteous judge, shall give me at that day: and not to me only, but unto all them also that love his appearing.

Gradual. Ps. 37, 30-31. The mouth of the righteous is exercised in wisdom, and his tongue will be talking of judgment. ℣. The law of his God is in his heart: and his goings shall not slide.

Alleluia, alleluia. ℣. Ecclus. 45, 9. The Lord loved him, and adorned him: he clothed him with a robe of glory. Alleluia.

After Septuagesima, omitting Alleluia and the Verse following, is said:

Tract. Ps. 112, 1-3. Blessed is the man that feareth the Lord: he hath great delight in his commandments. ℣. His seed shall be mighty upon earth: the generation of the faithful shall be blessed. ℣. Riches and plenteousness shall be in his house: and his righteousness endureth for ever.

In Eastertide the Gradual is omitted, and in its place is said:

Alleluia, alleluia. ℣. Ecclus. 45, 9. The Lord loved him, and adorned him: he clothed him with a robe of glory. Alleluia. ℣. Hos. 14, 6. The righteous shall grow as the lily: and flourish for ever before the Lord. Alleluia.

☩ The Continuation of the holy Gospel according to Matthew.

Matt. 5, 13-19.

AT that time: Jesus said unto his disciples: Ye are the salt of the earth. But if the salt have lost his savour, wherewith shall it be salted? It is thenceforth good for nothing, but to be cast out, and to be trodden under foot of men. Ye are the light of the world. A city that is set on an hill cannot be hid. Neither do men light a candle, and put it under a bushel, but on a candlestick, and it giveth light unto all that are in the house. Let your light so shine before men, that they may see your good works, and glorify your Father which is in heaven. Think not that I am come to destroy the law, or the prophets: I am not come to destroy, but to fulfil. For verily I say unto you, Till heaven and earth pass, one jot or one tittle shall in no wise pass from the law, till all be fulfilled. Whosoever therefore shall break one of these least commandments, and shall teach men so, he shall be called the least in the kingdom of heaven: but whosoever shall do and teach them, the same shall be called great in the kingdom of heaven. Creed.

Offertory. Ps. 92, 13. The righteous shall flourish like a palm-tree: and shall spread abroad like a cedar in Libanus. (E.T. Alleluia.)

1. For a Doctor and Bishop. Secret.

MAY the devout prayers of thy Bishop and Doctor, Saint N., continually succour us, O Lord: that they may render our oblations acceptable in thy sight; and ever obtain for us thy merciful pardon. Through.

2. For a Doctor not a Bishop. Secret.

MAY the devout prayers of thy Confessor and Doctor, Saint N., continually succour us, O Lord: that they may render our oblations acceptable in thy sight; and ever obtain for us thy merciful pardon. Through.

Communion. Luke 12, 42. A faithful and wise servant, whom his lord hath made ruler over his household: to give them their portion of meat in due season. (E.T. Alleluia.)

1. For a Doctor and Bishop.

Postcommunion.

WE beseech thee, O Lord, that blessed N., thy Bishop and most excellent Doctor, may ever stand before thee as our advocate: that this sacrifice of thine ordinance may effectually avail for our salvation. Through.

2. For a Doctor not a Bishop.

Postcommunion.

WE beseech thee, O Lord, that blessed N., thy Confessor and most excellent Doctor, may ever stand before thee as our advocate: that this sacrifice of thine ordinance may effectually avail for our salvation. Through.

¶ Another Epistle for Doctors: The righteous will give his heart, as on the Feast of St. Cyril, March 18.

COMMON OF A CONFESSOR NOT A BISHOP

I

For a Confessor not a Bishop

Introit. Ps. 37, 30-31. Os justi.

THE mouth of the righteous is exercised in wisdom: and his tongue will be talking of judgment: the law of his God is in his heart. (E.T. Alleluia, alleluia.) Ps. ibid., 1. Fret not thyself because of the ungodly: neither be thou envious against the evildoers. ℣. Glory.

Collect.

O GOD, who dost make us to rejoice in the yearly solemnity of blessed N. thy Confessor: mercifully grant; that, as we now observe his heavenly birthday, so we may follow the example of his life. Through.

The Lesson from the book of Wisdom.

Ecclus. 31, 8-11.

BLESSED is the man that is found without blemish: and hath not gone after gold. Who is he, and we will call him blessed? for wonderful things hath he done among his people. Who hath been tried thereby, and found perfect? then let him glory. Who might offend, and hath not offended? or done evil, and hath not done it? His goods shall be established, and the congregation shall declare his alms.

Gradual. Ps. 92, 13-14. The righteous shall flourish like a palm-tree: and shall spread abroad like a cedar in Libanus in the house of the Lord. ℣. Ibid., 3. To tell of thy loving kindness early in the morning, and of thy truth in the night-season.

Alleluia, alleluia. ℣. James 1, 12. Blessed is the man that endureth temptation: for when he is tried, he shall receive the crown of life. Alleluia.

After Septuagesima, omitting Alleluia and the Verse following, is said:

Tract. Ps. 112, 1-3. Blessed is the man that feareth the Lord: he hath great delight in his commandments. ℣. His seed shall be mighty upon earth: the generation of the faithful shall be blessed. ℣. Riches and plenteousness shall be in his house: and his righteousness endureth for ever.

In Eastertide the Gradual is omitted, and in its place is said:

Alleluia, alleluia. ℣. James 1, 12. Blessed is the man that endureth temptation: for when he is tried, he shall receive the crown of life. Alleluia. ℣. Ecclus. 45, 7. The Lord loved him, and adorned him: he clothed him with a robe of glory. Alleluia.

✠ The Continuation of the holy Gospel according to Luke.

Luke 12, 35-40.

AT that time: Jesus said unto his disciples: Let your loins be girded about, and your lights burning, and ye yourselves like unto men that wait for their lord, when he will return from the wedding: that when he cometh and knocketh, they may open unto him immediately.

Blessed are those servants, whom the lord when he cometh shall find watching: verily I say unto you, that he shall gird himself, and make them to sit down to meat, and will come forth and serve them. And if he shall come in the second watch, or come in the third watch, and find them so, blessed are those servants. And this know, that if the good man of the house had known what hour the thief would come, he would have watched, and not have suffered his house to be broken through. Be ye therefore ready also: for the Son of man cometh at an hour when ye think not.

Offertory. Ps. 89, 25. My truth and my mercy shall be with him: and in my name shall his horn be exalted. (E.T. Alleluia.)

Secret.

WE offer thee, O Lord, this our sacrifice of praise to the honour of thy Saints: whereby we trust to be delivered from all evils both in this life and in that which is to come. Through.

Communion. Matt. 24, 46-47. Blessed is the servant whom his lord when he cometh shall find watching: verily I say unto you, he shall make him ruler over all his goods. (E.T. Alleluia.)

Postcommunion.

O LORD our God, who hast refreshed us with heavenly meat and drink, we humbly beseech thee: that we may be defended by the prayers of him in whose memory we have received the same. Through.

II

For a Confessor not a Bishop

Another Mass.

Introit. Ps. 92, 13-14. Justus ut palma.

THE righteous shall flourish like a palm-tree: and shall spread abroad like a cedar in Libanus: such as are planted in the house of the Lord: in the courts of the house of our God. (E.T. Alleluia, alleluia.) Ps. ibid., 1. It is a good thing to give thanks unto the Lord: and to sing praises unto thy name, O most Highest. ℣. Glory.

Collect.

ASSIST us mercifully, O Lord, in these our supplications, which we make before thee on the solemnity of blessed N., thy Confessor: that we, who put not our trust in our own righteousness, may be succoured by the prayers of him who found favour in thy sight. Through.

The Lesson from the Epistle of blessed Paul the Apostle to the Corinthians.

I Cor. 4, 9-14.

BRETHREN: We are made a spectacle unto the world, and to Angels, and to men. We are fools for Christ's sake, but ye are wise in Christ: we are weak, but ye are strong: ye are honourable, but we are despised. Even unto this present hour we both hunger, and thirst, and are naked, and are buffeted, and have no certain dwelling-place, and labour, working with our own hands: being reviled, we bless: being persecuted, we suffer it: being defamed, we intreat: we are made as the filth of the world, and are the offscouring of all things unto this day. I write not these things to shame you, but as my beloved sons I warn you: in Christ Jesus our Lord.

Gradual. Ps. 37, 30-31. The mouth of the righteous is exercised in wisdom, and his tongue will be talking of judgment. ℣. The law of his God is in his heart: and his goings shall not slide.

Alleluia, alleluia. ℣. Ps. 112, 1. Blessed is the man that feareth the Lord: he hath great delight in his commandments. Alleluia.

After Septuagesima, omitting Alleluia and the Verse following, is said:

Tract. Ps. 112, 1-3. Blessed is the man that feareth the Lord: he hath great delight in his commandments. ℣. His seed shall be mighty upon earth: the generation of the faithful shall be blessed. ℣. Riches and plenteousness shall be in his house: and his righteousness endureth for ever.

In Eastertide the Gradual is omitted, and in its place is said:

Alleluia, alleluia. ℣. Ps. 112, 1. Blessed is the man that feareth the Lord: he hath great delight in his commandments. Alleluia. ℣. Hos. 14, 4. The righteous shall grow as the lily: and flourish for ever before the Lord. Alleluia.

✠ The Continuation of the holy Gospel according to Luke.

Luke 12, 32-34.

AT that time: Jesus said unto his disciples: Fear not, little flock, for it is your Father's good pleasure to give you the kingdom. Sell that ye have, and give alms. Provide yourselves bags which wax not old, a treasure in the heavens that faileth not: where no thief approacheth, neither moth corrupteth. For where your treasure is, there will your heart be also.

Offertory. Ps. 21, 2-3. The just shall rejoice in thy strength, O Lord, exceeding glad shall he be of thy salvation: thou hast given him his heart's desire. (E.T. Alleluia.)

Secret.

GRANT to us, we beseech thee, almighty God: that this oblation of our humble service may be acceptable in thy sight to the honour of thy Saints, and may cleanse us both in body and soul. Through.

Communion. Matt. 19, 28-29. Verily I say unto you: that ye which have forsaken all, and followed me, shall receive an hundredfold, and shall inherit everlasting life. (E.T. Alleluia.)

Postcommunion.

WE beseech thee, almighty God: that we, who have received this heavenly food, may at the intercession of blessed N., thy Confessor, be thereby defended against all adversities. Through.

Another Epistle and Gospel for a Confessor not a Bishop:

Epistle What things were gain, as on the Feast of St. Francis de Paula, Conf. April 2.

Gospel A certain nobleman, as on the Feast of St. Louis, King, Conf., August 25.

THE COMMON OF ABBOTS

Introit. Ps. 37, 30-31. Os justi.

THE mouth of the righteous is exercised in wisdom, and his tongue will be talking of judgment: the law of his God is in his heart. (E.T. Alleluia, alleluia.) Ps. ibid., 1. Fret not thyself because of the ungodly: neither be thou envious against the evil doers. ℣. Glory.

Collect.

O LORD, we beseech thee, let the intercession of thy blessed Abbot N. commend us unto thee: that those things which for our own merits we cannot ask, we may through his advocacy obtain. Through Jesus Christ thy Son our Lord: Who liveth.

The Common of Abbots

The Lesson from the book of Wisdom.
Ecclus. 45, 1-6.

BELOVED of God and men, whose memorial is blessed. He made him like to the glorious saints, and magnified him so that his enemies stood in fear of him. By his words he caused the wonders to cease, and he made him glorious in the sight of kings, and gave him a commandment for his people, and shewed him his glory. He sanctified him in his faithfulness and meekness, and chose him out of all men. He made him to hear his voice, and brought him into the dark cloud, and gave him commandments before his face, even the law of life and knowledge.

Gradual. Ps. 21, 4-5. Thou hast prevented him, O Lord, with the blessings of goodness: thou hast set a crown of pure gold upon his head. ℣. He asked life of thee, and thou gavest him a long life, even for ever and ever.

Alleluia, alleluia. ℣. Ps. 92, 13. The righteous shall flourish like a palm-tree: and shall spread abroad like a cedar in Libanus. Alleluia.

After Septuagesima, omitting Alleluia and the Verse following, is said:

Tract. Ps. 112, 1-3. Blessed is the man that feareth the Lord: he hath great delight in his commandments. ℣. His seed shall be mighty upon earth: the generation of the faithful shall be blessed. ℣. Riches and plenteousness shall be in his house: and his righteousness endureth for ever.

In Eastertide the Gradual is omitted, and in its place is said:

Alleluia, alleluia. ℣. Ps. 92, 13. The righteous shall flourish like a palm-tree: and shall spread abroad like a cedar in Libanus. Alleluia. ℣. Hos. 14, 6. The righteous shall grow as the lily: and flourish for ever before the Lord. Alleluia.

☩ The Continuation of the holy Gospel according to Matthew.
Matt. 19, 27-29.

AT that time: Peter said unto Jesus: Behold, we have forsaken all, and followed thee: what shall we have therefore? And Jesus said unto them: Verily I say unto you, That ye which have followed me, in the regeneration when the Son of man shall sit in the throne of his glory, ye also shall sit upon twelve thrones, judging the twelve tribes of Israel. And every one that hath forsaken houses, or brethren, or sisters, or father, or mother, or wife, or children, or lands, for my name's sake, shall receive an hundredfold, and shall inherit everlasting life.

Offertory. Ps. 21, 3-4. Thou hast given him his heart's desire, O Lord, and hast not denied him the request of his lips: thou hast set a crown of pure gold upon his head. (E.T. Alleluia.)

Secret.

O LORD, we beseech thee, let thy holy Abbot N. intercede for us: that this sacrifice which we offer and present upon thy holy altar may be profitable unto us for our salvation. Through.

Communion. Luke 12, 42. A faithful and wise servant, whom his lord hath made ruler over his household, to give them their portion of meat in due season. (E.T. Alleluia.)

Postcommunion.

LET thy Sacrament, O Lord, which we have now received, and the prayers of thy blessed Abbot N., effectually defend us: that we may both imitate the example of his conversation, and receive the succour of his intercession. Through.

COMMON OF VIRGINS

I
For a Virgin and Martyr

Introit. Ps. 119, 46-47. Loquebar.

I WILL speak of thy testimonies, even before kings, and will not be ashamed: and my delight shall be in thy commandments, which I have loved exceedingly. (E.T. Alleluia, alleluia.) Ps. ibid., 1. Blessed are those that are undefiled in the way: and walk in the law of the Lord. ℣. Glory.

Collect.

O GOD, who among the manifold works of thy power hast bestowed even upon the weakness of women the victory of martyrdom: mercifully grant; that we, who this day celebrate the heavenly birth of blessed N. thy Virgin and Martyr, may by her example be drawn nearer unto thee. Through.

The Lesson from the book of Wisdom.
Ecclus. 51, 1-8 and 12.

I WILL thank thee, O Lord and king, and praise thee, O God my Saviour. I do give praise unto thy name: for thou art my defender and helper, and hast preserved my body from destruction, and from the snare of the slanderous tongue, and from the lips that forge lies, and hast been mine helper against mine adversaries. And hast delivered me, according to the multitude of thy mercies and greatness of thy name, from the teeth of them that were ready to devour me, and out of the hands of such as sought after my life, and from the manifold afflictions which I had: from the choking of fire on every side, and from the midst of the fire which I kindled not: from the depth of the belly of hell, from an unclean tongue, and from lying words. By an accusation to the king from an unrighteous tongue my soul drew near even unto death: but thou deliverest such as wait for thee, and savest them out of the hands of their enemies, O Lord our God.

Gradual. Ps. 45, 8. Thou hast loved righteousness, and hated iniquity. ℣. Therefore God, even thy God, hath anointed thee with the oil of gladness.

Alleluia, alleluia. ℣. Ibid., 15-16. The Virgins that be her fellows shall be brought unto the King: they that bear her company shall be brought unto thee with joy. Alleluia.

After Septuagesima, omitting Alleluia and the Verse following, is said:

Tract. Come, thou Bride of Christ, receive the crown, which the Lord hath prepared for thee for ever: for whose love thou didst shed thy blood. ℣. Ps. 45, 8 and 5. Thou hast loved righteousness, and hated iniquity: therefore God, even thy God, hath anointed thee with the oil of gladness above thy fellows. ℣. In thy comeliness and in thy beauty go forth, ride prosperously and reign.

In Eastertide the Gradual is omitted, and in its place is said:

Alleluia, alleluia. ℣. Ps. 45, 15 and 16. The Virgins that be her fellows shall be brought unto the King: they that bear her company shall be brought unto thee with joy. Alleluia. ℣. Ibid., 5. In thy comeliness and beauty go forth, ride prosperously and reign. Alleluia.

✠ The Continuation of the holy Gospel according to Matthew.
Matt. 25, 1-13.

AT that time: Jesus spake this parable unto his disciples: The kingdom of heaven shall be likened unto ten virgins:

which took their lamps, and went forth to meet the bridegroom. And five of them were wise, and five were foolish: they that were foolish took their lamps, and took no oil with them: but the wise took oil in their vessels with their lamps. While the bridegroom tarried, they all slumbered and slept. And at midnight there was a cry made: Behold, the bridegroom cometh, go ye out to meet him. Then all those virgins arose, and trimmed their lamps. And the foolish said unto the wise: Give us of your oil: for our lamps are gone out. But the wise answered, saying: Not so, lest there be not enough for us and you, but go ye rather to them that sell, and buy for yourselves. And while they went to buy, the bridegroom came: and they that were ready went in with him to the marriage, and the door was shut. Afterward came also the other virgins, saying: Lord, Lord, open to us. But he answered and said: Verily I say unto you, I know you not. Watch therefore, for ye know neither the day nor the hour* [wherein the Son of Man cometh].

Offertory. Ps. 45, 15-16. The Virgins that be her fellows shall be brought unto the King: they that bear her company shall be brought unto thee with joy and gladness: and shall enter into the palace of the Lord the King. (E.T. Alleluia.)

Secret.

RECEIVE, O Lord, the gifts which we offer on the solemnity of blessed N., thy Virgin and Martyr: through whose advocacy we trust to be delivered. Through.

Communion. Ps. 119, 78 and 80. Let the proud be confounded, for they go wickedly about to destroy me: but I will be occupied in thy commandments and in thy statutes, that I be not ashamed. (E.T. Alleluia.)

Postcommunion.

ASSIST us mercifully, O Lord, who have here received these holy mysteries: and at the intercession of blessed N., thy Virgin and Martyr, make us ever to rejoice in thy continual protection. Through.

II

For a Virgin and Martyr

Another Mass.

Introit. Ps. 119, 95-96. Me exspectaverunt.

THE ungodly laid wait for me to destroy me: O Lord, I will consider thy testimonies: I see that all things come to an end: but thy commandment is exceeding broad. (E.T. Alleluia, alleluia.) Ps. ibid., 1. Blessed are those that are undefiled in the way: and walk in the law of the Lord. ℣. Glory.

Collect.

WE beseech thee, O Lord, that, like as blessed N., thy Virgin and Martyr, by the merit of her chastity, and by her confession of thy power, was ever found acceptable in thy sight: so she may effectually intercede for our forgiveness. Through.

The Lesson from the book of Wisdom.

Ecclus. 51, 9-12.

O LORD my God, I lifted up my suplication from the earth, and prayed for deliverance from death. I called upon the Lord, the Father of my Lord, that he would not leave me in the day of my trouble, and in the time of the proud, when there was no help. I will praise thy name continually, and will sing praise with thanksgiving, and so my prayer was heard. For thou savedst me from destruction, and deliveredst me from the evil time. Therefore will I give thanks, and praise thee, O Lord our God.

Gradual. Ps. 46, 6 and 5. God shall help her with his countenance: God is in the midst of her, therefore shall she not be removed. ℣. The rivers of the flood thereof shall make glad the city of God: the holy place of the tabernacle of the Most Highest.

Alleluia, alleluia. ℣. This is a wise Virgin, and one of the number of the prudent. Alleluia.

After Septuagesima, omitting Alleluia and the Verse following, is said:

Tract. Come, thou Bride of Christ, receive the crown which the Lord hath prepared for thee for ever: for whose love thou didst shed thy blood. ℣. Ps. 45, 8 and 5. Thou hast loved righteousness, and hated iniquity: therefore God, even thy God, hath anointed thee with the oil of gladness above thy fellows. ℣. In thy comeliness and in thy beauty go forth, ride prosperously and reign.

In Eastertide the Gradual is omitted, and in its place is said:

Alleluia, alleluia. ℣. This is a wise Virgin, and one of the number of the prudent. Alleluia. ℣. Wisd. 4, 1. O how beautiful is the chaste generation with its glory. Alleluia.

✠ The Continuation of the holy Gospel according to Matthew.

Matt. 13, 44-52.

AT that time: Jesus spake this parable unto his disciples: The kingdom of heaven is like unto treasure hid in a field: the which when a man hath found, he hideth, and for joy thereof goeth and selleth all that he hath, and buyeth that field. Again, the kingdom of heaven is like unto a merchant man, seeking goodly pearls. Who, when he had found one pearl of great price, went and sold all that he had, and bought it. Again, the kingdom of heaven is like unto a net that was cast into the sea, and gathered of every kind. Which, when it was full, they drew to shore, and sat down, and gathered the good into vessels, but cast the bad away. So shall it be at the end of the world: the Angels shall come forth, and sever the wicked from among the just, and shall cast them into the furnace of fire: there shall be wailing and gnashing of teeth. Jesus said unto them: Have ye understood all these things? They say unto him: Yea, Lord. Then said he unto them: Therefore every scribe which is instructed unto the kingdom of heaven is like unto a man that is an householder, which bringeth forth out of his treasure things new and old.

Offertory. Ps. 45, 3. Full of grace are thy lips: therefore God hath blessed thee for ever, and world without end. (E.T. Alleluia.)

Secret.

GRACIOUSLY receive, O Lord, through the merits of blessed N., thy Virgin and Martyr, the sacrifices which we offer unto thee: and grant that they may avail for our continual help. Through.

Communion. Ps. 119, 121, 122 and 128. I deal with the thing that is lawful and right, O Lord, let the proud do me no wrong: I hold straight all thy commandments, and all false ways I utterly abhor. (E.T. Alleluia.)

Postcommunion.

O LORD our God, who hast fulfilled us with the bounty of thy heavenly gift: we beseech thee that, at the intercession of blessed N., thy Virgin and Martyr, we may ever live by the partaking of the same. Through.

¶ Another Gospel:

✠ The Continuation of the holy Gospel according to Matthew.

Matt. 19, 3-12.

AT that time: The Pharisees came unto Jesus, tempting him, and saying unto him: Is it lawful for a man to put away his wife for every cause? And he answered and said unto them: Have ye not read, that he which made them at the beginning made them male and female? and said: For this cause shall a man leave father and mother, and shall cleave to his wife, and they twain shall be one flesh. Wherefore they are no more twain, but one flesh. What therefore God hath joined together, let not man put asunder. They say unto him: Why did Moses then command to give a writing of divorcement, and to put her away? He saith unto them: Moses because of the hardness of your hearts suffered you to put away your wives: but from the beginning it was not so. And I say unto you, Whosoever shall put away his wife, except it be for fornication, and shall marry another, committeth adultery: and whoso marrieth her which is put away doth commit adultery. His disciples say unto him: If the case of the man be so with his wife, it is not good to marry. But he said unto them: All men cannot receive this saying, save they to whom it is given. For there are some eunuchs, which were so born from their mother's womb; and there are some eunuchs, which were made eunuchs of men; and there be eunuchs, which have made themselves eunuchs for the kingdom of heaven's sake. He that is able to receive it, let him receive it.

¶ For many Virgin Martyrs Mass is said as above, with the Epistle Concerning virgins, from the Mass Vultum tuum from the Common of Virgins IV p. [33] and the Prayers as below:

Collect.

GRANT, we beseech thee, O Lord our God, that we may never cease to venerate the triumph of thy holy Virgins and Martyrs N. and N.: and though we cannot worthily shew forth their praises, yet we beseech thee to accept the worship we render in their honour. Through.

Secret.

O LORD, we beseech thee, look down upon these gifts, which we offer on thine altars on this festival of thy holy Virgins and Martyrs N. and N.: that as by these blessed mysteries thou hast bestowed glory upon them, so likewise of thy bounty thou wouldest vouchsafe to us thy pardon. Through.

Postcommunion.

GRANT to us, we beseech thee, O Lord, at the intercession of thy holy Virgins and Martyrs N. and N.: that we, who with our outward lips are partakers of this holy Sacrament, may inwardly receive the same in purity of heart. Through.

III

For a Virgin only

Introit. Ps. 45, 8. Dilexisti.

THOU hast loved righteousness, and hated iniquity: therefore God, even thy God, hath anointed thee with the oil of gladness above thy fellows. (E.T. Alleluia, alleluia.) Ps. ibid., 1. My heart is inditing of a good matter: I speak of the things which I have made unto the King. ℣. Glory.

Collect.

GRACIOUSLY hear us, O God of our salvation: that, like as we do rejoice in the festival of blessed N., thy Virgin; so we may learn to follow her example in godliness and charity. Through.

The Lesson from the Epistle of blessed Paul the Apostle to the Corinthians.

II Cor. 10, 17-18; 11, 1-2.

BRETHREN: He that glorieth, let him glory in the Lord. For not he that commendeth himself is approved; but whom the Lord commendeth. Would to

God ye could bear with me a little in my folly, and indeed bear with me: for I am jealous over you with godly jealousy. For I have espoused you to one husband, that I may present you as a chaste virgin to Christ.

Gradual. Ps. 45, 5. In thy comeliness and in thy beauty go forth, ride prosperously and reign. ℣. Because of the word of truth, of meekness, and righteousness: and thy right hand shall teach thee terrible things.

Alleluia, alleluia. ℣. Ibid., 15-16. The Virgins that be her fellows shall be brought unto the King: they that bear her company shall be brought unto thee with joy. Alleluia.

After Septuagesima, omitting Alleluia and the Verse following, is said:

Tract. Ps. 45, 11-12. Hearken O daughter, and consider, incline thine ear: so shall the King have pleasure in thy beauty. ℣. Ibid., 13 and 10. The rich among the people shall make their supplication before thee: kings' daughters were among thy honourable women. ℣. Ibid., 15-16. The Virgins that be her fellows shall be brought unto the King: they that bear her company shall be brought unto thee. ℣. With joy and gladness shall they be brought: and shall enter into the King's palace.

In Eastertide the Gradual is omitted, and in its place is said:

Alleluia, alleluia. ℣. Ibid., 15-16. The Virgins that be her fellows shall be brought unto the King: they that bear her company shall be brought unto thee with joy. Alleluia. ℣. Ibid., 5. In thy comeliness and in thy beauty go forth, ride prosperously and reign. Alleluia.

✠ The Continuation of the holy Gospel according to Matthew.
Matt. 25, 1-13.

AT that time: Jesus spake this parable unto his disciples: The kingdom of heaven shall be likened unto ten virgins, which took their lamps, and went forth to meet the bridegroom. And five of them were wise, and five were foolish: they that were foolish took their lamps, and took no oil with them: but the wise took oil in their vessels with their lamps. While the bridegroom tarried, they all slumbered and slept. And at midnight there was a cry made: Behold, the bridegroom cometh; go ye out to meet him. Then all those virgins arose, and trimmed their lamps. And the foolish said unto the wise: Give us of your oil: for our lamps are gone out. But the wise answered, saying: Not so, lest there be not enough for us and you, but go ye rather to them that sell, and buy for yourselves. And while they went to buy, the bridegroom came: and they that were ready went in with him to the marriage, and the door was shut. Afterward came also the other virgins, saying: Lord, Lord, open to us. But he answered and said: Verily I say unto you, I know you not. Watch therefore, for ye know neither the day nor the hour* [wherein the Son of man cometh].

Offertory. Ps. 45, 10. Kings' daughters were among thy honourable women, upon thy right hand did stand the queen in a vesture of gold, wrought about with divers colours. (E.T. Alleluia.)

Secret.

GRANT, O Lord, that like as thy dedicated people do acknowledge that in tribulation they have been succoured by the merits of thy Saints: so this oblation, which they offer unto thee in honour of the same, may be acceptable in thy sight. Through.

Communion. Matt. 25, 4 and 6. The five wise virgins took oil in their vessels with their lamps: and at midnight there was a cry made: Behold the bridegroom cometh: go ye out to meet Christ the Lord. (E.T. Alleluia.)

Postcommunion.

O LORD, who hast satisfied this thy family with thy sacred gifts: we beseech thee; that we may at all times be comforted by the intercession of her whose festival we celebrate. Through.

IV

For a Virgin only

Another Mass.

Introit. Ps. 45, 13, 15-16. Vultum tuum.

THE rich also among the people shall make their supplications before thee: the Virgins that be her fellows shall be brought unto the King: they that bear her company shall be brought unto thee with joy and gladness. (E.T. Alleluia, alleluia.) Ps. ibid., 1. My heart is inditing of a good matter: I speak of the things which I have made unto the King. ℣. Glory.

Collect.

GRACIOUSLY hear us, O God of our salvation: that, like as we do rejoice in the festival of blessed N., thy Virgin, so we may learn to follow her example in godliness and charity. Through.

The Lesson from the Epistle of blessed Paul the Apostle to the Corinthians.

1 Cor. 7, 25-34.

BRETHREN: Concerning virgins I have no commandment of the Lord: yet I give my judgment, as one that hath obtained mercy of the Lord to be faithful. I suppose therefore that this is good for the present distress, I say, that it is good for a man so to be. Art thou bound unto a wife? seek not to be loosed. Art thou loosed from a wife? seek not a wife. But and if thou marry, thou hast not sinned. And if a virgin marry, she hath not sinned: nevertheless such shall have trouble in the flesh. But I spare you. But this I say, brethren: The time is short: it remaineth, that both they that have wives be as though they had none; and they that weep, as though they wept not; and they that rejoice, as though they rejoiced not; and they that buy, as though they possessed not; and they that use this world, as not abusing it; for the fashion of this world passeth away. But I would have you without carefulness. He that is unmarried careth for the things that belong to the Lord, how he may please the Lord. But he that is married careth for the things that are of the world, how he may please his wife. There is difference also between a wife and a virgin. The unmarried woman careth for the things of the Lord, that she may be holy both in body and in spirit: in Christ Jesus our Lord.

Gradual. Ps. 45, 12 and 11. The King shall have pleasure in thy beauty, for he is thy Lord God. ℣. Hearken, O daughter, and consider, incline thine ear.

Alleluia, alleluia. ℣. This is a wise Virgin, and one of the number of the prudent. Alleluia.

After Septuagesima, omitting Alleluia and the Verse following, is said:

Tract. Ps. 45, 12, 13 and 10. The King shall have pleasure in thy beauty. ℣. The rich also among the people shall make their supplication before thee: kings' daughters were among thy honourable women. ℣. Ibid., 15-16. The Virgins that be her fellows shall be brought unto the King: they that bear her company shall be brought unto thee. ℣. With joy and gladness shall they be brought: and shall enter into the King's palace.

In Eastertide the Gradual is omitted, and in its place is said:

Alleluia, alleluia. ℣. This is a wise Virgin, and one of the number of the prudent. Alleluia. ℣. Wisd. 4, 1. O how beautiful is the chaste generation with its glory. Alleluia.

✠ The Continuation of the holy Gospel according to Matthew.

Matt. 13, 44-52.

AT that time: Jesus spake this parable unto his disciples: The kingdom of heaven is like unto treasure hid in a field: the which when a man hath found, he hideth, and for joy thereof goeth and selleth all that he hath, and buyeth that field. Again, the kingdom of heaven is like unto a merchant man, seeking goodly pearls. Who, when he had found one pearl of great price, went and sold all that he had, and bought it. Again, the kingdom of heaven is like unto a net, that was cast into the sea, and gathered of every kind. Which, when it was full, they drew to shore, and sat down, and gathered the good into vessels, but cast the bad away. So shall it be at the end of the world: the Angels shall come forth, and sever the wicked from among the just, and shall cast them into the furnace of fire: there shall be wailing and gnashing of teeth. Jesus saith unto them: Have ye understood all these things? They say unto him: Yea, Lord. Then said he unto them: Therefore every scribe which is instructed unto the kingdom of heaven is like unto a man that is an householder, which bringeth forth out of his treasure things new and old.

Or the Gospel The kingdom of heaven shall be likened unto ten virgins, as above p. [28].

Offertory. Ps. 45, 15-16. The Virgins that be her fellows shall be brought unto the King: they that bear her company shall be brought unto thee with joy and gladness: and shall enter into the palace of the Lord the King. (E.T. Alleluia.)

Secret.

GRANT, O Lord, that like as thy dedicated people do acknowledge that in tribulation they have been succoured by the merits of thy Saints: so this oblation, which they offer unto thee in honour of the same, may be acceptable in thy sight. Through.

Communion. Matt. 13, 45-46. The kingdom of heaven is like unto a merchant man, seeking goodly pearls: who when he had found one pearl of great price, gave all that he had, and bought it. (E.T. Alleluia.)

Postcommunion.

O LORD, who hast satisfied this thy family with thy sacred gifts: we beseech thee; that we may at all times be comforted by the intercession of her whose festival we celebrate. Through.

THE COMMON OF THOSE WHO ARE NOT VIRGINS

I

For a Martyr not a Virgin

Introit. Ps. 119, 95-96. Me exspectaverunt.

THE ungodly laid wait for me to destroy me: O Lord, I will consider thy testimonies: I see that all things come to an end: but thy commandment is exceeding broad. (E.T. Alleluia, alleluia.) Ps. ibid., 1. Blessed are those that are undefiled in the way: and walk in the law of the Lord. ℣. Glory.

Collect.

O GOD, who among the manifold works of thy power hast bestowed even upon the weakness of women the victory of martyrdom: mercifully grant: that we, who celebrate the birthday of blessed N. thy Martyr, may by her example draw nearer unto thee. Through.

For a Martyr not a Virgin

The Lesson from the book of Wisdom.

Ecclus. 51, 1-8 and 12.

I WILL thank thee, O Lord and King, and praise thee, O God my Saviour. I do give praise unto thy name: for thou art my defender and helper, and hast preserved my body from destruction, and from the snare of the slanderous tongue, and from the lips that forge lies, and hast been mine helper against mine adversaries. And hast delivered me, according to the multitude of thy mercies and greatness of thy name, from the teeth of them that were ready to devour me, and out of the hands of such as sought after my life, and from the manifold afflictions which I had: from the choking of fire on every side, and from the midst of the fire which I kindled not: from the depth of the belly of hell, from an unclean tongue, and from lying words. By an accusation to the king from an unrighteous tongue my soul drew near even unto death: but thou deliverest such as wait for thee, and savest them out of the hands of the enemies, O Lord our God.

Gradual. Ps. 45, 8. Thou hast loved righteousness and hated iniquity. ℣. Therefore God, even thy God, hath anointed thee with the oil of gladness.

Alleluia, alleluia. ℣. Ibid., 5. In thy comeliness and in thy beauty go forth, ride prosperously and reign. Alleluia.

After Septuagesima, omitting Alleluia and the Verse following, is said:

Tract. Come, thou Bride of Christ, receive the crown which the Lord hath prepared for thee for ever: for whose love thou didst shed thy blood. ℣. Ps. 45, 8 and 5. Thou hast loved righteousness and hated iniquity: therefore God, even thy God, hath anointed thee with the oil of gladness, above thy fellows. ℣. In thy comeliness and in thy beauty go forth, ride prosperously and reign.

In Eastertide the Gradual is omitted, and in its place is said:

Alleluia, alleluia. ℣. Ps. 45, 5. In thy comeliness and in thy beauty go forth, ride prosperously and reign. Alleluia. ℣. Because of the word of truth, of meekness, and righteousness: and thy right hand shall teach thee terrible things. Alleluia.

✠ The Continuation of the holy Gospel according to Matthew.

Matt. 13, 44-52.

AT that time: Jesus spake this parable unto his disciples: The kingdom of heaven is like unto treasure hid in a field: the which when a man hath found, he hideth, and for joy thereof goeth and selleth all that he hath, and buyeth that field. Again, the kingdom of heaven is like unto a merchant man, seeking goodly pearls. Who, when he had found one pearl of great price, went and sold all that he had, and bought it. Again, the kingdom of heaven is like unto a net, that was cast into the sea, and gathered of every kind. Which, when it was full, they drew to shore, and sat down, and gathered the good into vessels, but cast the bad away. So shall it be at the end of the world: the Angels shall come forth, and sever the wicked from among the just, and shall cast them into the furnace of fire: there shall be wailing and gnashing of teeth. Jesus saith unto them: Have ye understood all these things? They say unto him: Yea, Lord. Then said he unto them: Therefore every scribe which is instructed unto the kingdom of heaven is like unto a man that is an householder, which bringeth forth out of his treasure things new and old.

After Septuagesima Alleluia at the end of the following Offertory is omitted:

Offertory. Ps. 45, 3. Full of grace are thy lips: therefore God hath blessed thee for ever, and world without end, alleluia.

Secret.

RECEIVE, O Lord, the gifts which we offer on the solemnity of blessed N., thy Martyr: through whose advocacy we trust to be delivered. Through.

Communion. Ps. 119, 161-162. Princes have persecuted me without a cause: but my heart standeth in awe of thy word: I am as glad of thy word, as one that findeth great spoils. (E.T. Alleluia.)

Postcommunion.

ASSIST us mercifully, O Lord, who have here received these holy mysteries: and, at the intercession of blessed N., thy Martyr, make us thereby to rejoice in thy continual protection. Through.

¶ For many Martyrs, who are not Virgins, Mass is to be said as above, with the Prayers as below:

Collect.

GRANT, we beseech thee, O Lord our God, that we may never cease to venerate the triumph of thy holy Martyrs N. and N.: and, although we cannot worthily shew forth their praises, yet we beseech thee to accept the worship we render in their honour. Through.

Secret.

O LORD, we beseech thee, look down upon these gifts, which we offer on thine altars on this festival of thy holy Martyrs N. and N.: that as by these blessed mysteries thou hast bestowed glory upon them, so likewise of thy bounty thou wouldest vouchsafe us thy pardon. Through.

Postcommunion.

GRANT to us, we beseech thee, O Lord, at the intercession of thy holy Martyrs N. and N.: that we, who with our outward lips are partakers of this holy Sacrament, may inwardly receive the same in purity of heart. Through.

II

For one neither Virgin nor Martyr

Introit. Ps. 119, 75 and 120.
Cognovi, Domine.

I KNOW, O Lord, that thy judgments are right, and that thou of very faithfulness hast caused me to be troubled: my flesh trembleth for fear of thee, and I am afraid of thy judgments. (E.T. Alleluia, alleluia.) Ps. ibid., 1. Blessed are those that are undefiled in the way, and walk in the law of the Lord. ℣. Glory.

Collect.

GRACIOUSLY hear us, O God of our salvation: that, like as we do rejoice in the festival of blessed N., so we may learn to follow her example in godliness and charity. Through.

The Lesson from the book of Wisdom.

Prov. 31, 10-31.

WHO can find a virtuous woman? For her price is far above rubies. The heart of her husband doth safely trust in her, so that he shall have no need of spoil. She will do him good and not evil all the days of her life. She seeketh wool, and flax, and worketh willingly with her hands. She is like the merchants' ships, she bringeth her food from afar. She riseth also while it is yet night, and giveth meat to her household, and a portion to her maidens. She considereth a field, and buyeth it: with the fruit of her hands she planteth a vine-yard. She girdeth her

For one neither Virgin nor Martyr

loins with strength, and strengtheneth her arms. She perceiveth that her merchandise is good: her candle goeth not out by night. She layeth her hands to the spindle, and her hands hold the distaff. She stretcheth out her hand to the poor, yea, she reacheth forth her hands to the needy. She is not afraid of the snow for her household: for all her household are clothed with scarlet. She maketh herself coverings of tapestry: her clothing is silk and purple. Her husband is known in the gates, when he sitteth among the elders of the land. She maketh fine linen, and selleth it, and delivereth girdles unto the merchant. Strength and honour are her clothing, and she shall rejoice in time to come. She openeth her mouth with wisdom, and in her tongue is the law of kindness. She looketh well to the ways of her household, and eateth not the bread of idleness. Her children arise up, and call her blessed: her husband also, and he praiseth her. Many daughters have done virtuously, but thou excellest them all. Favour is deceitful, and beauty is vain: but a woman that feareth the Lord, she shall be praised. Give her of the fruit of her hands: and let her own works praise her in the gates.

Gradual. Ps. 45, 3 and 5. Full of grace are thy lips: therefore God hath blessed thee for ever. ℣. Because of the word of truth, of meekness, and righteousness: and thy right hand shall teach thee terrible things.

Alleluia, alleluia. ℣. Ibid., 3. In thy comeliness and in thy beauty go forth, ride prosperously, and reign. Alleluia.

After Septuagesima, omitting Alleluia and the Verse following, is said:

Tract. Come, thou Bride of Christ, receive the crown, which the Lord hath prepared for thee for ever. ℣. Ps. 45, 8 and 5. Thou hast loved righteousness, and hated iniquity: therefore God, even thy God, hath anointed thee with the oil of gladness above thy fellows. ℣. In thy comeliness and in thy beauty go forth, ride prosperously, and reign.

In Eastertide the Gradual is omitted, and in its place is said:

Alleluia, alleluia. ℣. Ps. 45, 5. In thy comeliness and in thy beauty go forth, ride prosperously, and reign. Alleluia. ℣. Because of the word of truth, of meekness, and righteousness: and thy right hand shall teach thee terrible things. Alleluia.

✠ The Continuation of the holy Gospel according to Matthew.

Matt. 13, 44-52.

AT that time: Jesus spake this parable unto his disciples: The kingdom of heaven is like unto treasure hid in a field: the which when a man hath found, he hideth, and for joy thereof goeth and selleth all that he hath, and buyeth that field. Again, the kingdom of heaven is like unto a merchant man, seeking goodly pearls. Who, when he had found one pearl of great price, went and sold all that he had, and bought it. Again, the kingdom of heaven is like unto a net, that was cast into the sea, and gathered of every kind. Which, when it was full, they drew to shore, and sat down, and gathered the good into vessels, but cast the bad away. So shall it be at the end of the world: the Angels shall come forth, and sever the wicked from among the just, and shall cast them into the furnace of fire: there shall be wailing and gnashing of teeth. Jesus saith unto them: Have ye understood all these things? They say unto him: Yea, Lord. Then said he unto them: Therefore every scribe which is instructed unto the kingdom of heaven is like unto a man that is an householder, which bringeth forth out of his treasure things new and old.

Offertory. Ps. 45, 3. Full of grace are thy lips: therefore God hath blessed thee for ever, and world without end. (E.T. Alleluia.)

Secret.

GRANT, O Lord, that like as thy dedicated people do acknowledge that in tribulation they have been succoured by the merits of thy Saints: so this oblation, which they here offer unto thee in honour of the same, may be acceptable in thy sight. Through.

Communion. Ps. 45, 8. Thou hast loved righteousness, and hated iniquity: therefore God, even thy God, hath anointed thee with the oil of gladness above thy fellows. (E.T. Alleluia.)

Postcommunion.

O LORD, who hast satisfied this thy family with thy sacred gifts: we beseech thee that we may at all times be comforted by the intercession of her whose festival we celebrate. Through.

¶ Another Epistle for a Widow:

The Lesson from the Epistle of blessed Paul the Apostle to Timothy.

I Tim. 5, 3-10.

DEARLY beloved: Honour widows that are widows indeed. But if any widow have children or nephews: let them learn first to shew piety at home, and to requite their parents: for that is good and acceptable before God. Now she that is a widow indeed, and desolate, trusteth in God, and continueth in supplications and prayers night and day. But she that liveth in pleasure is dead while she liveth. And these things give in charge, that they may be blameless. But if any provide not for his own and specially for those of his own house, he hath denied the faith, and is worse than an infidel. Let not a widow be taken into the number under threescore years old, having been the wife of one man, well reported of for good works, if she have brought up children, if she have lodged strangers, if she have washed the saints' feet, if she have relieved the afflicted, if she have diligently followed every good work.

COMMON OF THE DEDICATION OF A CHURCH

Introit. Gen. 28, 17. Terribilis est.

HOW dreadful is this place: this is the house of God, and the gate of heaven: and men shall call it the palace of God. (E.T. Alleluia, alleluia.) Ps. 84, 2-3. O how amiable are thy dwellings, thou Lord of hosts! My soul hath a desire and longing to enter into the courts of the Lord. ℣. Glory.

1. Collect.

O GOD, who year by year renewest unto us the day of consecration of this thy holy temple, and dost ever bring us again in safety to thy sacred mysteries: graciously hear the prayers of thy people, and grant; that whosoever entereth this temple to ask thy blessings may rejoice in the obtaining of all his petitions. Through.

¶ On the day itself of the Dedication of a Church, and when the Collect is to be varied, is said the following:

Common of the Dedication of a Church

2. Collect.

O GOD, who, thyself invisible, containest all things, but dost for the salvation of mankind shew forth visibly the signs of thy power: enlighten this temple with the power of thine indwelling, and grant; that all they, who come together here to ask thy mercy, may, in whatsoever tribulations they call upon thee, obtain the blessings of thy consolation. Through.

The Lesson from the book of the Revelation of blessed John the Apostle.

Rev. 21, 2-5.

IN those days: I saw the holy city, new Jerusalem, coming down from God out of heaven, prepared as a bride adorned for her husband. And I heard a great voice out of heaven saying: Behold, the tabernacle of God is with men, and he will dwell with them. And they shall be his people, and God himself shall be with them, and be their God: and God shall wipe away all tears from their eyes: and there shall be no more death, neither sorrow, nor crying, neither shall there be any more pain, for the former things are passed away. And he that sat upon the throne said: Behold, I make all things new.

Gradual. This dwelling is God's handywork, it is a mystery beyond all price, and beyond reproof. ℣. O God, before whom standeth the choir of Angels, graciously hear the prayers of thy servants.

Alleluia, alleluia. ℣. Ps. 138, 2. I will worship toward thy holy temple: and praise thy name. Alleluia.

After Septuagesima, omitting Alleluia and the verse following, is said:

Tract. Ps. 125, 1-2. They that put their trust in the Lord shall be even as the mount Sion: which may not be removed, but standeth fast for ever. ℣. The hills stand about Jerusalem, even so standeth the Lord round about his people, from this time forth for evermore.

In Eastertide the Gradual is omitted, and in its place is said:

Alleluia, alleluia. ℣. Ps. 138, 2. I will worship toward thy holy temple: and praise thy name. Alleluia. ℣. The house of the Lord is well founded upon a sure rock. Alleluia.

✠ The Continuation of the holy Gospel according to Luke.

Luke 19, 1-10.

AT that time: Jesus entered and passed through Jericho. And, behold, there was a man named Zacchæus, which was the chief among the publicans, and he was rich: and he sought to see Jesus who he was: and could not for the press, because he was little of stature. And he ran before, and climbed up into a sycamore tree to see him; for he was to pass that way. And when Jesus came to the place, he looked up, and saw him, and said unto him: Zacchæus, make haste, and come down; for to day I must abide at thy house. And he made haste and came down, and received him joyfully. And when they saw it, they all murmured, saying, That he was gone to be guest with a man that is a sinner. And Zacchæus stood, and said unto the Lord: Behold, Lord, the half of my goods I give to the poor: and if I have taken any thing from any man by false accusation, I restore him fourfold. And Jesus said unto him: This day is salvation come to this house: forsomuch as he also is a son of Abraham. For the Son of man is come to seek and to save that which was lost. Creed.

After Septuagesima Alleluia at the end of the following Offertory is omitted:

Common of the Dedication of a Church

Offertory. I Chron. 29, 17 and 18. O Lord God, in the uprightness of mine heart I have willingly offered all these things; and now have I seen with joy thy people which are present here: O God of Israel, keep this in the imagination of the thoughts of their heart, alleluia.

In the dedicated Church itself.

1. Secret.

O LORD, we beseech thee, mercifully hear our prayers: that all we, who are gathered within the precincts of this temple, whose dedication year by year we celebrate, may perfectly serve thee, both in body and soul: that, like as we do here present our offerings unto thee, so we may by thee be enabled to attain unto the rewards of everlasting felicity. Through.

Outside the dedicated Church itself.

1. Secret.

O LORD, we beseech thee, mercifully hear our prayers: that, like as we do here present our offerings unto thee, so we may by thee be enabled to attain unto the rewards of everlasting felicity. Through.

On the day itself of the Dedication of a Church, and when the Secret is to be varied, is said the following:

2. Secret.

O GOD, who art the author of the gifts to be consecrated unto thee, pour forth upon this house of prayer thy blessing: that all who shall call upon thy name therein may perceive the succour of thy defence. Through.

The common Preface, or that of the Season occurring.

Communion. Matt. 21, 13. My house shall be called the house of prayer, saith the Lord: in it every one that asketh receiveth; and he that seeketh findeth: and to him that knocketh it shall be opened. (E.T. Alleluia.)

1. Postcommunion.

O GOD, who of elect and living stones dost fashion for thy majesty an everlasting habitation: assist the supplications of us thy people; that, like as thy Church increaseth in visible habitations, so it may advance toward the attainment of all inward and spiritual perfection. Through.

¶ On the day itself of the Dedication of a Church, or where the Postcommunion is to be varied, is said the following:

2. Postcommunion.

WE beseech thee, almighty God: that in this place, which we, though unworthy, have dedicated to thy name, thou wouldest incline thy merciful ears to all that call upon thee. Through Jesus Christ thy Son our Lord: Who liveth and reigneth with thee in the unity of the Holy Ghost...

¶ On the day of the Dedication itself, Mass is said as above with the second Prayers; and the Collect of the Mystery or Saint in whose honour the Church is dedicated is added to the first under one conclusion.

¶ On the day of the Dedication of an Altar, Mass is said as on the Dedication of a Church, except the Prayers following: to which likewise in the case of a fixed Altar the prayers of the Mystery or Saint in whose honour the Altar is dedicated are added under one conclusion.

Collect.

O GOD who, from the whole assembly of thy Saints, dost prepare for thyself an everlasting habitation: grant to this building the abundance of thy heavenly grace; that like as we do here venerate with devout affection the relics of thy Saints, so we may ever be aided by their merits. Through.

Secret.

WE beseech thee, O Lord our God, let thy Holy Spirit come down upon this altar: that he may sanctify the gifts of thy people, and graciously cleanse the hearts of them that receive the same. Through ... in the the unity of the same Holy Spirit.

Postcommunion.

ALMIGHTY and everlasting God, sanctify with the power of thy heavenly benediction this altar, which we have dedicated to the honour of thy name: and shew forth upon all that put their trust in thee the bounty of thy succour; that they may here obtain the grace of thy sacraments and the fulfilment of their desires. Through.

COMMON OF FEASTS OF THE BLESSED VIRGIN MARY

Introit. Sedulius. Salve, sancta Parens.

HAIL, O Mother most holy, who didst give birth to the Monarch: reigning o'er heaven and earth, world without end. (E.T. Alleluia, alleluia.) Ps. 45, 1. My heart is inditing of a good matter: I speak of the things which I have made unto the King. ℣. Glory.

Collect.

GRANT, we beseech thee, O Lord God, that we thy servants may enjoy perpetual health of body and soul: and, at the glorious intercession of blessed Mary ever Virgin, be delivered from our present sadness, and rejoice in everlasting gladness. Through.

The Lesson from the book of Wisdom.

Ecclus. 24, 9-12.

HE created me from the beginning before the world, and I shall never fail, in the holy tabernacle I served before him. And so was I established in Sion, likewise in the beloved city he gave me rest, and in Jerusalem was my power. And I took root in an honourable people, even in the portion of the Lord's inheritance, and my abode is in the company of the saints.

Gradual. Blessed and venerable art thou, O Virgin Mary: who a maiden undefiled hast our Saviour for thy child. ℣. Virgin, Mother of God, the whole world cannot contain him, yet, made man for our sakes, hidden he lay in thy womb.

Alleluia, alleluia. ℣. After child-bearing thou remainedst a pure Virgin; Mother of God, intercede for us. Alleluia.

In Advent, in place of the preceding Verse is said:

Alleluia, alleluia. ℣. Luke 1, 28. Hail, Mary, full of grace: the Lord is with thee: blessed art thou among women. Alleluia.

After Septuagesima, omitting Alleluia and the Verse following, is said:

Tract. Rejoice, O Virgin Mary, thou alone all heresies didst slay. ℣. Thou the Archangel Gabriel's message didst obey. ℣. He who is God and man was born thy Son: yet art thou still a Maid, O spotless one. ℣. Mother of God, intercede for us.

In Eastertide the Gradual is omitted, and in its place is said:

Alleluia, alleluia. ℣. Num. 17, 8. Now hath blossomed Jesse's rod: a Virgin beareth man and God: God restoreth peace to men, high and low are one again. Alleluia.

℣. Luke 1. Hail, Mary, full of grace, the Lord is with thee: blessed art thou among women. Alleluia.

✠ The Continuation of the holy Gospel according to Luke.

Luke 11, 27-28.

AT that time: As Jesus spake to the multitudes, a certain woman of the company lifted up her voice, and said unto him: Blessed is the womb that bare thee, and the paps which thou hast sucked. But he said: Yea rather, blessed are they that hear the word of God, and keep it. Creed.

Offertory. Luke 1, 28 and 42. Hail, Mary, full of grace; the Lord is with thee: blessed art thou among women, and blessed is the fruit of thy womb. (E.T. Alleluia.)

Secret.

THROUGH thy mercy, O Lord, and the intercession of blessed Mary ever Virgin, may this oblation avail for our prosperity and peace, both now and for ever. Through.

Preface of B.V.M. In the Festival.

Communion. Blessed is the womb of the Virgin Mary, that bare the Son of the everlasting Father. (E.T. Alleluia.)

Postcommunion.

O LORD, who hast appointed these holy mysteries which we have here received to be the means of our salvation: grant, we beseech thee, that we, who have offered these our gifts unto thy majesty in honour of blessed Mary ever Virgin; may by her advocacy be at all times and in all places effectually defended. Through.

MASSES OF SAINT MARY ON SATURDAY

WHICH MAY ALSO BE SAID ON OTHER DAYS AS VOTIVES, ACCORDING TO THE SEASON.

N.B. In Masses of the B.V. Mary one Collect only is said, unless a Commemoration is to be made. (But in private Masses three Prayers may be said.)

I

In Advent till December 23rd inclusive.

Introit. Is. 45, 8. Rorate.

DROP down, ye heavens, from above, and let the skies pour down righteousness: let the earth open, and bring forth a Saviour. Ps. 85, 1. Lord, thou art become gracious unto thy land: thou hast turned away the captivity of Jacob. ℣. Glory.

On Saturday Glória in excélsis is said.

Collect.

O GOD, who wast pleased that thy Word should take flesh of the womb of the Blessed Virgin Mary at the message of an Angel: grant to us thy humble servants; that we, believing her to be indeed the Mother of God; may by her intercession be holpen in thy sight. Through the same.

2nd Collect of the Feria of Advent.

[3rd of the Holy Spirit.]

Collect.

GOD, who didst teach the hearts of thy faithful people, by the sending to them the light of thy Holy Spirit: grant us by the same Spirit to have a right judgment in all things; and evermore to rejoice in his holy comfort. Through ... in the unity of the same Holy Spirit.

The Lesson from the Prophet Isaiah.

Is. 7, 10-15.

IN those days: The Lord spake unto Ahaz, saying: Ask thee a sign of the Lord thy God, ask it either in the depth, or in the height above. But Ahaz said: I will not ask, neither will I tempt the Lord. And he said: Hear ye now, O house of David: Is it a small thing for you to weary men, but will ye weary my God also? Therefore the Lord himself shall give you a sign. Behold, a Virgin shall conceive, and bear a son, and shall call his name Emmanuel. Butter and honey shall he eat, that he may know to refuse the evil, and choose the good.

Gradual. Ps. 24, 7. Lift up your heads, O ye gates: and be ye lift up, ye everlasting doors: and the King of glory shall come in. ℣. Who shall ascend into the hill of the Lord? or who shall rise up in his holy place? Even he that hath clean hands, and a pure heart.

Alleluia, alleluia. ℣. Luke 1, 28. Hail, Mary, full of grace; the Lord is with thee: blessed art thou among women. Alleluia.

✠ The Continuation of the holy Gospel according to Luke.

Luke, 1, 26-38.

AT that time: The Angel Gabriel was sent from God unto a city of Galilee named Nazareth, to a Virgin espoused to a man whose name was Joseph, of the house of David, and the Virgin's name was Mary. And the Angel came in unto her, and said: Hail, thou that art highly favoured: the Lord is with thee: blessed art thou among women. And when she saw him she was troubled at his saying, and cast in her mind what manner of salutation this should be. And the Angel said unto her: Fear not, Mary, for thou hast found favour with God. And behold, thou shalt conceive in thy womb, and bring forth a Son, and shalt call his name Jesus. He shall be great, and shall be called the Son of the Highest, and the Lord God shall give unto him the throne of his father David: and he shall reign over the house of Jacob for ever; and of his kingdom there shall be no end. Then said Mary unto the Angel: How shall this be, seeing I know not a man? And the Angel answered and said unto her: The Holy Ghost shall come upon thee, and the power of the Highest shall overshadow thee. Therefore also that Holy Thing which shall be born of thee shall be called the Son of God. And behold, thy cousin Elisabeth, she hath also conceived a son in her old age: and this is the sixth month with her who was called barren: for with God nothing shall be impossible. And Mary said: Behold the handmaid of the Lord, be it unto me according to thy word.

Offertory. Luke 1, 28 and 42. Hail, Mary, full of grace; the Lord is with thee: blessed art thou among women, and blessed is the fruit of thy womb.

Secret.

STABLISH in our hearts, we beseech thee, O Lord, the mysteries of the true faith: that like as we acknowledge thy Son conceived of a Virgin to be very God and very man; so by the power of his Resurrection, we may be found worthy to attain unto everlasting gladness Through the same.

2nd Secret of the Feria.
[3rd of the Holy Spirit.]

Secret.

SANCTIFY, we beseech thee, O Lord, the gifts which we offer: and cleanse our hearts by the enlightening of the Holy Spirit. Through ... in the unity of the same Holy Spirit.

Preface of the Blessed Virgin Mary In the Veneration.

Communion. Is. 7, 14. Behold, a Virgin shall conceive, and bear a Son: and his name shall be called Emmanuel.

Postcommunion.

WE beseech thee, O Lord, pour thy grace into our hearts: that, as we have known the incarnation of Christ thy Son by the message of an Angel; so through his passion and cross we may be brought unto the glory of his resurrection. Through the same.

2nd Postcommunion of Advent.

[3rd of the Holy Spirit.]

Postcommunion.

POUR thy Holy Spirit upon us, O Lord, and cleanse our hearts: that they may be made fruitful by the inward sprinkling of his dew. Through... in the unity of the same Holy Spirit.

II

From Saturday after the Feast of the Circumcision (or in Votive Masses, from Dec. 26) until Feb. 1, inclusive.

Introit. Ps. 45, 13, 15 and 16.

Vultum tuum.

THE rich also among the people shall make their supplication before thee: the Virgins that be her fellows shall be brought unto the King: they that bear her company shall be brought unto thee with joy and gladness. Ps. ibid. My heart is inditing of a good matter: I speak of the things which I have made unto the King. ℣. Glory.

On Saturday Glória in excélsis is said.

Collect.

O GOD, who by the child-bearing of the blessed Virgin Mary hast bestowed upon mankind the rewards of eternal salvation: grant, we beseech thee; that we may know the succour of her intercession for us, through whom we have been found worthy to receive the author of life, even Jesus Christ thy Son our Lord: Who liveth and reigneth with thee.

[2nd Collect of the Holy Spirit, 3rd against the persecutors of the Church or for the Chief Bishop, p. [45].]

The Lesson from the Epistle of blessed Paul the Apostle to Titus.

Tit. 3, 4-7.

DEARLY beloved: The kindness and love of God our Saviour toward man appeared: not by works of righteousness which we have done, but according to his mercy he saved us, by the washing of regeneration, and renewing of the Holy Ghost, which he shed on us abundantly through Jesus Christ our Saviour: that being justified by his grace, we should be made heirs according to the hope of eternal life: in Christ Jesus our Lord.

Gradual. Ps. 45, 3 and 2. Thou art fairer than the children of men: full of grace are thy lips. ℣. Ibid., 2. My heart is inditing of a good matter: I speak of the things which I have made unto the King: my tongue is the pen of a ready writer.

Alleluia, alleluia. ℣. After child-bearing thou remainedst a pure Virgin: Mother of God, intercede for us. Alleluia.

After Septuagesima, omitting Alleluia and the Verse following, is said:

Tract. Rejoice, O Virgin Mary, thou alone all heresies didst slay. ℣. Thou the Archangel Gabriel's message didst obey. ℣. He who is God and man was born thy Son: yet art thou still a Maid, O spotless one. ℣. Mother of God, intercede for us.

✠ The Continuation of the holy Gospel according to Luke.

Luke 2, 15-20.

AT that time: The shepherds said one to another: Let us now go even unto Bethlehem, and see this thing which is come to pass, which the Lord hath made

Masses of Saint Mary on Saturday

known unto us. And they came with haste: and found Mary, and Joseph, and the Babe lying in a manger. And when they had seen it, they made known abroad the saying which was told them concerning this Child. And all they that heard it wondered at those things which were told them by the shepherds. But Mary kept all these things, and pondered them in her heart. And the shepherds returned, glorifying and praising God for all the things that they had heard and seen, as it was told unto them.

Offertory. Happy indeed art thou, O sacred Virgin Mary, and most worthy of all praise: for out of thee arose the sun of righteousness, Christ our God.

Secret.

THROUGH thy mercy, O Lord, and the intercession of blessed Mary, ever Virgin, may this oblation avail for our prosperity and peace, both now and for ever. Through.

[2nd Secret of the Holy Spirit, 3rd against the persecutors of the Church or for the Chief Bishop, as below.]

Preface of the Blessed Virgin Mary In the Veneration.

Communion. Blessed is the womb of the Virgin Mary, that bare the Son of the everlasting Father.

Postcommunion.

O LORD, let this holy Communion cleanse us from every guilty stain: that at the intercession of the blessed Virgin Mary, Mother of God, we may be made partakers thereby of thy healing unto life eternal. Through.

[2nd Postcommunion of the Holy Spirit, 3rd against the persecutors of the Church or for the Chief Bishop, as below.]

PRAYERS.

Which may be said ad libitum in private Masses of Saint Mary on Saturday, and in private Votive Masses of the blessed Virgin Mary.

2nd of the Holy Spirit.

Collect.

GOD, who didst teach the hearts of thy faithful people, by the sending to them the light of thy Holy Spirit: grant us by the same Spirit to have a right judgment in all things; and evermore to rejoice in his holy comfort. (Through... in the unity of the same Holy Spirit.)

Secret.

SANCTIFY, we beseech thee, O Lord, the gifts which we offer: and cleanse our hearts by the enlightening of the Holy Spirit. (Through... in the unity of the same Holy Spirit.)

Postcommunion.

POUR thy Holy Spirit upon us, O Lord, and cleanse our hearts: that they may be made fruitful by the inward sprinkling of his dew. (Through... in the unity of the same Holy Spirit.)

3rd against the persecutors of the Church.

Collect.

WE beseech thee, O Lord, mercifully to hear the prayers of thy Church: that all adversities and errors being done away, it may serve thee in freedom and safety. Through.

Secret.

DEFEND us, O Lord, who wait upon thy mysteries: that we, cleaving fast to things heavenly, may serve thee both in body and soul. Through.

Masses of Saint Mary on Saturday

Postcommunion.

WE beseech thee, O Lord our God: that we whom thou makest to rejoice in the partaking of heavenly things may by thee be defended against all earthly perils. Through.

Or 3rd for the Chief Bishop.
Collect.

O GOD, the pastor and governor of all the faithful, mercifully look upon thy servant N., whom thou hast chosen to be pastor and ruler of thy Church: grant unto him, we beseech thee, to be in word and conversation a wholesome example to the people committed to his charge; that he with them may attain unto everlasting life. Through.

Secret.

LOOK favourably, we beseech thee, O Lord, upon the gifts which we offer: and guide with thy continual protection thy servant N., whom thou hast chosen to be pastor and ruler of thy Church. Through.

Postcommunion.

DEFEND us, O Lord, we beseech thee, who have here received these heavenly mysteries: and grant that thy servant N., whom thou hast chosen to be pastor and ruler of thy Church, together with the flock committed to his charge, may thereby be strengthened and preserved against all adversities. Through.

III

From the Saturday after the Purification of the Blessed Virgin Mary to the Saturday after Sexagesima Sunday, or in Votive Masses till the Saturday after Passion Sunday, inclusive, according to the Rubrics.

Introit. Sedulius. Salve, sancta Parens.

HAIL, O Mother most holy, who didst give birth to the Monarch: reigning o'er heaven and earth, world without end. Ps. 45, 1. My heart is inditing of a good matter: I speak of the things which I have made unto the King. ℣. Glory.

On Saturday Glória in excélsis is said.

Collect.

GRANT, we beseech thee, O Lord God, that we thy servants may rejoice in perpetual health of body and soul: and, at the glorious intercession of blessed Mary ever Virgin, be delivered from our present sadness, and attain in the end unto everlasting gladness. Through.

[2nd Collect of the Holy Spirit, 3rd against the persecutors of the Church or for the Chief Bishop p. [45].]

The Lesson from the book of Wisdom.

Ecclus. 24, 9-12.

HE created me from the beginning before the world, and I shall never fail, in the holy tabernacle I served before him. And so was I established in Sion, likewise in the beloved city he gave me rest, and in Jerusalem was my power. And I took root in an honourable people, even in the portion of the Lord's inheritance, and my abode is in the company of the saints.

Gradual. Blessed and venerable art thou, O Virgin Mary: who a maiden undefiled hast our Saviour for thy child. ℣. Virgin Mother of God, the whole world cannot contain him: yet made man for our sake, hidden he lay in thy womb.

Alleluia, alleluia. ℣. Num. 17, 8. Now hath blossomed Jesse's rod: a Virgin bears both man and God: God restoreth peace to men, high and low are one again. Alleluia.

After Septuagesima, omitting Alleluia and the verse following, is said:

Tract. Rejoice, O Virgin Mary, thou alone all heresies didst slay. ℣. Thou the Archangel Gabriel's message didst obey. ℣. He who is God and man was born thy Son: yet art thou still a Maid, O spotless one. ℣. Mother of God, intercede for us.

✠ The Continuation of the holy Gospel according to Luke.

Luke 11, 27-28.

AT that time: As Jesus spake to the multitudes, a certain woman of the company lifted up her voice, and said unto him: Blessed is the womb that bare thee, and the paps which thou hast sucked. But he said: Yea rather, blessed are they that hear the word of God, and keep it.

Offertory. Happy indeed art thou, O sacred Virgin Mary, and most worthy of all praise: for out of thee arose the sun of righteousness, Christ our God.

Secret.

THROUGH thy mercy, O Lord, and the intercession of blessed Mary ever Virgin, may this oblation avail for our prosperity and peace, both now and ever. Through.

[2nd Secret of the Holy Spirit, 3rd against the persecutors of the Church or for the Chief Bishop, p. [45].]

Preface of the Blessed Virgin Mary In the Veneration.

Communion. Blessed is the womb of the Virgin Mary, that bare the Son of the everlasting Father.

Postcommunion.

O LORD, who hast appointed these holy mysteries which we have here received to be the means of our salvation: grant, we beseech thee, that we, who have offered these our gifts unto thy majesty in honour of blessed Mary ever Virgin; may by her advocacy be at all times and in all places effectually defended. Through.

[2nd Postcommunion of the Holy Spirit, 3rd against the persecutors of the Church or for the Chief Bishop, p. [45].]

IV

From the Saturday after Low Sunday until Saturday after the Fourth Sunday after Easter; or in votive Masses from Wednesday after Easter till Saturday in the Octave of Pentecost, inclusive, according to the Rubrics.

Introit. Sedulius. Salve, sancta Parens.

HAIL, O Mother most holy, who didst give birth to the Monarch: reigning o'er heaven and earth, world without end, alleluia, alleluia. Ps. 45, 1. My heart is inditing of a good matter: I speak of the things which I have made unto the King. ℣. Glory.

On Saturday Glória in excélsis is said.

Collect.

GRANT, we beseech thee, O Lord God, that we thy servants may rejoice in perpetual health of body and soul: and, at the glorious intercession of blessed Mary ever Virgin, be delivered from our present sadness, and attain in the end unto everlasting gladness. Through.

[2nd Collect of the Holy Spirit, 3rd against the persecutors of the Church or for the Chief Bishop, p. [45].]

The Lesson from the book of Wisdom.

Ecclus. 24, 9-12.

HE created me from the beginning before the world, and I shall never fail, in the holy tabernacle I served before him. And so was I established in Sion. Likewise in the beloved city he gave me rest, and in Jerusalem was my power. And I took root in an honourable people, even in the portion of the Lord's inheritance, and my abode is in the company of the saints.

Alleluia, alleluia. ℣. Num. 17, 8. Now hath blossomed Jesse's rod: a Virgin bears both man and God: God restoreth peace to men, high and low are one again. Alleluia. ℣. Luke 1, 28. Hail, Mary, full of grace; the Lord is with thee: blessed art thou among women. Alleluia.

✠ The Continuation of the holy Gospel according to John.

John 19, 25-27.

AT that time: There stood by the Cross of Jesus his mother, and his mother's sister, Mary the wife of Cleophas, and Mary Magdalene. When Jesus therefore saw his mother, and the disciple standing by, whom he loved, he saith unto his mother: Woman, behold thy son. Then saith he to the disciple: Behold thy mother. And from that hour that disciple took her unto his own home.

Offertory. Blessed art thou, O Virgin Mary, who didst bear the Creator of all things: thou broughtest forth him who made thee, and for ever remainest a Virgin, alleluia.

Secret.

THROUGH thy mercy, O Lord, and the intercession of blessed Mary ever Virgin, may this oblation avail for our prosperity and peace, both now and ever. Through.

[2nd Secret of the Holy Spirit, 3rd against the persecutors of the Church or for the Pope, p. [45].]

Preface of the Blessed Virgin Mary In the Veneration.

Communion. Blessed is the womb of the Virgin Mary, that bare the Son of the everlasting Father, alleluia.

Postcommunion.

O LORD, who hast appointed these holy mysteries which we have here received to be the means of our salvation: grant, we beseech thee, that we, who have offered these our gifts unto thy majesty in honour of blessed Mary ever Virgin; may by her advocacy be at all times and in all places effectually defended. Through.

[2nd Postcommunion of the Holy Spirit, 3rd against the persecutors of the Church or for the Chief Bishop, p. [45].]

V

From the Saturday, or, in Votive Masses, from the Monday after the Feast of the Most Holy Trinity, until the Saturday before the First Sunday in Advent inclusive.

Introit. Sedulius. Salve, sancta Parens.

HAIL, O Mother, most holy, who didst give birth to the Monarch: reigning o'er heaven and earth, world without end. Ps. 45, 1. My heart is inditing of a good matter: I speak of the things which I have made unto the King. ℣. Glory.

On Saturday Glória in excélsis is said.

Collect.

GRANT, we beseech thee, O Lord God, that we thy servants may rejoice in perpetual health of body and soul: and through the glorious intercession of blessed Mary ever Virgin, be delivered from our present sadness, and attain in the end unto everlasting gladness. Through.

Masses of Saint Mary on Saturday

2nd of the Holy Spirit.
Collect.

GOD, who didst teach the hearts of thy faithful people, by the sending to them the light of thy Holy Spirit: grant us by the same Spirit to have a right judgment in all things; and evermore to rejoice in his holy comfort. (Through ... in the unity of the same Holy Spirit.)

3rd against the persecutors of the Church.
Collect.

WE beseech thee, O Lord, mercifully to hear the prayers of thy Church: that all adversities and errors being done away, it may serve thee in freedom and safety. Through.

Or 3rd for the Chief Bishop.
Collect.

O GOD, the pastor and ruler of all the faithful, mercifully look upon thy servant N., whom thou hast chosen to be pastor and ruler of thy Church: grant unto him, we beseech thee, to be in word and conversation a wholesome example to the people committed to his charge; that he with them may attain unto everlasting life. Through.

The Lesson from the book of Wisdom.
Ecclus. 24, 9-12.

HE created me from the beginning before the world, and I shall never fail, in the holy tabernacle I served before him. And so was I established in Sion, likewise in the beloved city he gave me rest, and in Jerusalem was my power. And I took root in an honourable people, even in the portion of the Lord's inheritance, and my abode is in the company of the saints.

Gradual. Blessed and venerable art thou, O Virgin Mary: who a maiden undefiled hast our Saviour for thy child. ℣. Virgin Mother of God, the whole world cannot contain him, yet made man for our sake, hidden he lay in thy womb.

Alleluia, alleluia. ℣. After childbirth, thou didst remain a pure Virgin: Mother of God, intercede for us. Alleluia.

✠ The Continuation of the holy Gospel according to Luke.
Luke 11, 27-28.

AT that time: As Jesus spake to the multitudes, a certain woman of the company lifted up her voice, and said unto him: Blessed is the womb that bare thee, and the paps which thou hast sucked. But he said: Yea rather, blessed are they that hear the word of God, and keep it.

Offertory. Luke 1, 28 and 42. Hail, Mary, full of grace; the Lord is with thee: blessed art thou among women, and blessed is the fruit of thy womb.

Secret.

THROUGH thy mercy, O Lord, and the intercession of blessed Mary ever Virgin, may this oblation avail for our prosperity and peace, both now and ever. Through.

2nd of the Holy Spirit. Secret.

SANCTIFY, we beseech thee, O Lord, the gifts which we offer: and cleanse our hearts by the enlightening of the Holy Spirit. (Through ... in the unity of the same Holy Spirit.)

3rd against the persecutors of the Church.
Secret.

DEFEND us, O Lord, who wait upon thy mysteries: that we, cleaving fast to things heavenly, may serve thee both in body and soul. Through.

D

Or 3rd for the Chief Bishop. Secret.

LOOK favourably, we beseech thee, O Lord, upon the gifts which we offer: and guide with thy continual protection thy servant N., whom thou hast been pleased to set as pastor over thy Church. Through.

Preface of the Blessed Virgin Mary In the Veneration.

Communion. Blessed is the womb of the Virgin Mary, that bare the Son of the everlasting Father.

Postcommunion.

O LORD, who hast appointed these holy mysteries which we have here received to be the means of our salvation: grant, we beseech thee, that we, who have offered these our gifts unto thy majesty in honour of blessed Mary ever Virgin; may by her advocacy be at all times and in all places effectually defended. Through.

2nd of the Holy Spirit. Postcommunion.

POUR thy Holy Spirit upon us, O Lord, and cleanse our hearts: that they may be made fruitful by the inward sprinkling of his dew. (Through... in the unity of the same Holy Spirit.)

3rd against the persecutors of the Church.

Postcommunion.

WE beseech thee, O Lord our God: that we, whom thou makest to rejoice in the partaking of heavenly things, may by thee be defended against all earthly perils. Through.

Or 3rd for the Chief Bishop.
Postcommunion.

DEFEND us, O Lord, we beseech thee, who have here received these heavenly mysteries: and grant that thy servant N., whom thou hast chosen to be pastor and ruler of thy Church, together with the flock committed to his charge, may thereby be strengthened and preserved against all adversities. Through.

N.B. The 2nd and 3rd Prayers given above may be said ad lib in private Masses only.

VOTIVE MASSES

I
VOTIVE MASSES

WHICH MAY BE SAID IN PLACE OF THE CONVENTUAL MASS OF A COMMON FERIA IN CHOIR.

¶ On all week-days when the Office is of the Feria (excepting the Ferias of Advent and Lent, the Ember-days, the Rogation-days, and Vigils) and Mass of the Dead is not to be said according to the Rubrics; for the Conventual Mass one of the following Votive Masses may be said as arranged for the days of the week, and in them a Commemoration is made of the Feria whereof the Office is said.

MONDAY.
Mass of the Holy Trinity

Introit. Tobit 12, 6. Benedicta sit.

BLESSED be the holy Trinity and the undivided Unity: we will praise and glorify him, because he hath shewed his mercy upon us. (E.T. Alleluia, alleluia.) Ps. 8, 1. O Lord our Governour: how excellent is thy name in all the world! ℣. Glory.

Collect.

ALMIGHTY and everlasting God, who hast given unto us thy servants grace by the confession of a true faith to acknowledge the glory of the eternal Trinity, and in the power of the Majesty to worship the Unity: we beseech thee; that thou wouldest keep us stedfast in this faith, and evermore defend us from all adversities. Through.

The Lesson from the Epistle of blessed Paul the Apostle to the Corinthians.

II Cor. 13, 11 and 13.

BRETHREN: Rejoice, be perfect, be of good comfort, be of one mind, live in peace, and the God of love and peace shall be with you. The grace of the Lord Jesus Christ, and the love of God, and the communion of the Holy Ghost, be with you all. Amen.

Gradual. Dan. 3, 55-56. Blessed art thou, O Lord, that beholdest the depths, and sittest upon the Cherubim. ℣. Blessed art thou, O Lord, in the firmament of heaven, and worthy to be praised for ever.

Alleluia, alleluia. ℣. Dan. 3, 52. Blessed art thou, O Lord God of our fathers, and worthy to be praised for ever. Alleluia.

After Septuagesima, omitting Alleluia and the Verse following is said:

Tract. Thee, O God, the unbegotten Father, thee the only-begotten Son, thee the Holy Ghost the Comforter, the holy and undivided Trinity, we glorify, praise, and bless with our whole heart. ℣. For thou art great, and doest wondrous things: thou art God alone. ℣. To thee be praise, to thee be glory, to thee be thanksgiving, for ever and ever, O blessed Trinity.

In Eastertide the Gradual is omitted, and in its place is said:

Alleluia, alleluia. ℣. Dan. 3, 52. Blessed art thou, O Lord God of our fathers, and worthy to be praised for ever. Alleluia. ℣. Let us bless the Father, and the Son, with the Holy Ghost. Alleluia.

✠ The Continuation of the holy Gospel according to John.

John 15, 26-27; 16, 1-4.

AT that time: Jesus said unto his disciples: When the Comforter is come, whom I will send unto you from the Father, even the Spirit of truth, which proceedeth from the Father, he shall testify of me: and ye also shall bear witness, because ye have been with me from the beginning. These things have I spoken unto you, that ye should not be offended. They shall put you out of the synagogues: yea, the time cometh, that whosoever killeth you will think that he doeth God service. And these things will they do unto you, because they have not known the Father, nor me. But these things have I told you, that when the time shall come, ye may remember that I told you of them.

Offertory. Tobit 12, 6. Blessed be God the Father, and the only-begotten Son of God, and the Holy Spirit: because he hath shewed his mercy upon us. (E.T. Alleluia.)

Secret.

SANCTIFY, we beseech thee, O Lord our God, the sacrifice, which we here offer, by the invocation of thy holy name: that through the same we may ourselves be made a perfect gift unto thee for evermore. Through.

Preface of the Most Holy Trinity.

Communion. Tobit 12, 6. We bless the God of heaven, and will praise him in the sight of all that live: because he hath shewed his mercy upon us. (E.T. Alleluia.)

Postcommunion.

GRANT, O Lord our God, that we who have received this holy Sacrament, and who acknowledge the holy and everlasting Trinity to be likewise the undivided Unity: may be defended thereby from all evils both in body and soul. Through.

TUESDAY.
Mass of the Angels

Introit. Ps. 103, 20. Benedicite Dominum.

O PRAISE the Lord, ye Angels of his, ye that excel in strength: ye that fulfil his commandment, and hearken unto the voice of his words. (E.T. Alleluia, alleluia.) Ps. ibid., 1. Praise the Lord, O my soul: and all that is within me praise his holy name. ℣. Glory.

Glória in excélsis is always said.

Collect.

O EVERLASTING God, who hast ordained and constituted the services of Angels and men in a wonderful order: mercifully grant; that as thy holy Angels alway do thee service in heaven, so by thy appointment they may succour and defend us on earth. Through.

Or

Collect.

O GOD, who dost ordain the services of Angels and men in a wonderful order: mercifully grant; that they, who alway stand before thee and do thee service in heaven, may likewise succour and defend our life on earth. Through.

The Lesson from the book of the Revelation of blessed John the Apostle.

Rev. 5, 11-14.

IN those days: I heard the voice of many Angels round about the throne and the beasts and the elders: and the number of them was ten thousand times ten thousand, and thousands of thousands, saying with a loud voice: Worthy is the Lamb that was slain to receive power, and riches, and wisdom, and strength, and honour, and glory, and blessing. And every creature which is in heaven, and on the earth, and under the earth, and such as are in the sea, and all that are in them: heard I saying: Blessing, and honour, and glory, and power: be unto him that sitteth upon the throne, and unto the Lamb for ever and ever. And the four beasts said: Amen. And the four and twenty elders fell down: and worshipped him that liveth for ever and ever.

Gradual. Ps. 148, 1-2. O praise the Lord of heaven: praise him in the height. ℣. Praise him, all ye Angels of his: praise him, all his host.

Alleluia, alleluia. ℣. Ps. 138, 1-2. In the presence of the Angels will I sing praise unto thee: I will worship toward thy holy temple, and praise thy name. Alleluia.

After Septuagesima, omitting Alleluia and the Verse following is said:

Tract. Ps. 103, 20. O praise the Lord, ye Angels of his: ye that excel in strength, ye that fulfil that commandment. ℣. Ibid., 21-22. O praise the Lord, all ye his hosts: ye servants of his that do his pleasure. ℣. O speak good of the Lord, all ye works of his: in all places of his dominion, praise thou the Lord, O my soul.

In Eastertide the Gradual is omitted, and in its place is said:

Alleluia, alleluia. ℣. Ps. 138, 1-2. In the presence of the Angels will I sing praise unto thee: I will worship toward thy holy temple, and praise thy name. Alleluia. ℣. Matt. 28, 2. The Angel of the Lord descended from heaven, and came and rolled back the stone, and sat upon it. Alleluia.

✠ The Continuation of the holy Gospel according to John.

John 1, 47-51.

AT that time: Jesus saw Nathanael coming to him, and saith of him: Behold an Israelite indeed, in whom is no guile. Nathanael saith unto him: Whence knowest thou me? Jesus answered and said unto him: Before that Philip called thee, when thou wast under the fig tree, I saw thee. Nathanael answered and saith unto him: Rabbi, thou art the Son of God, thou art the King of Israel. Jesus answered and said unto him: Because I said unto thee: I saw thee under the fig tree, believest thou? thou shalt see greater things than these. And he saith unto him: Verily, verily, I say unto you, Hereafter ye shall see heaven open, and the Angels of God ascending and descending upon the Son of man.

Offertory. Rev. 8, 3-4. An Angel stood at the altar of the temple, having a golden censer in his hand: and there was given unto him much incense: and the smoke of the incense ascended up before God. (E.T. Alleluia.)

Secret.

WE offer thee, O Lord, sacrifices of praise, humbly beseeching thee: that, by the prayers of the Angels interceding for us, thou wouldest both graciously accept the same, and grant that they may avail to our salvation. Through.

Communion. Angels, Archangels, Thrones and Dominations, Principalities and Powers, Virtues of heaven, Cherubim and Seraphim, bless ye the Lord for ever. (E.T. Alleluia.)

Postcommunion.

O LORD, who hast vouchsafed to accept this frailty of our service, and hast filled us with thy heavenly benediction, we humbly beseech thee: that the succour of thy holy Angels and Archangels may effectually avail for our assistance. Through.

WEDNESDAY.
Mass of Saint Joseph

Introit. Ps. 33, 20-21. Adjutor et protector.

THE Lord is our help and our shield: our heart shall rejoice in him, because we have hoped in his holy name. (E.T. Alleluia, alleluia.) Ps. 80, 1. Hear, O thou Shepherd of Israel, thou that leadest Joseph like a sheep. ℣. Glory.

Votive Mass of Saint Joseph

Collect.

O GOD, who by thy ineffable providence didst vouchsafe to choose blessed Joseph to be the spouse of thy most holy Mother: grant, we beseech thee; that we who venerate him as our protector on earth may be worthy to have him for our advocate in heaven: Who livest and reignest.

The Lesson from the book of Genesis.
Gen. 49, 22-26.

JOSEPH is a fruitful bough, even a fruitful bough by a well: whose branches run over the wall. The archers have sorely grieved him, and shot at him, and hated him. But his bow abode in strength, and the arms of his hands were made strong by the hands of the mighty God of Jacob; from thence is the shepherd, the stone of Israel. Even by the God of thy Father, who shall help thee, and by the Almighty, who shall bless thee with blessings of heaven above, blessings of the deep that lieth under, blessings of the breasts, and of the womb. The blessings of thy father have prevailed above the blessings of my progenitors unto the utmost bound of the everlasting hills: they shall be on the head of Joseph, and on the crown of the head of him that was separate from his brethren.

Gradual. Ps. 21, 4-5. Thou hast prevented him, O Lord, with the blessings of goodness: and hast set a crown of pure gold upon his head. ℣. He asked life of thee, and thou gavest him a long life, even for ever and ever.

Alleluia, alleluia. ℣. Grant us, O Joseph, to walk in innocency: and ever to be safe under thy protection. Alleluia.

After Septuagesima, omitting Alleluia and the Verse following is said:

Tract. Ps. 112, 1-3. Blessed is the man that feareth the Lord: he hath great delight in his commandments. ℣. His seed shall be mighty upon earth: the generation of the faithful shall be blessed. ℣. Riches and plenteousness shall be in his house: and his righteousness endureth for ever.

In Eastertide the Gradual is omitted, and in its place is said:

Alleluia, alleluia. ℣. From whatsoever tribulation they shall cry unto me, I will hear them, and I will be their protector for ever. Alleluia. ℣. Grant us, O Joseph, to walk in innocency: and ever to be safe under thy protection. Alleluia.

✠ The Continuation of the holy Gospel according to Luke.
Luke 3, 21-23.

AT that time: It came to pass, when all the people were baptized, that Jesus also being baptized, and praying, the heaven was opened: and the Holy Ghost descended in a bodily shape like a dove upon him: and a voice came from heaven, which said: Thou art my beloved Son, in thee I am well pleased. And Jesus himself began to be about thirty years of age, being, as was supposed, the son of Joseph.

Offertory. Ps. 147, 12-13. Praise the Lord, O Jerusalem: for he hath made fast the bars of thy gates, and hath blessed thy children within thee. (E.T. Alleluia.)

Secret.

O LORD, forasmuch as we put our trust in the advocacy of the spouse of thy most holy Mother, we entreat thy mercy: that thou wouldest make our hearts to despise all earthly things, and to love thee the true God with perfect charity: Who livest and reignest.

Preface of St. Joseph In the Veneration.

Communion. Matt. 1, 16. Jacob begat Joseph the husband of Mary, of whom was born Jesus, who is called Christ. (E.T. Alleluia.)

Postcommunion.

WE beseech thee, O Lord our God: that we whom thou hast refreshed with the river of thy heavenly bounty, may by thee be enabled so to rejoice in the protection of blessed Joseph; that, by his merits and intercession, we may be made partakers of thy heavenly glory. Through.

ALSO ON WEDNESDAY.

Mass of SS. Peter and Paul the Apostles

Out of Eastertide.

Introit. Ps. 139, 17. Mihi autem nimis.

RIGHT dear are thy friends unto me, O God, their rule and governance is exceeding steadfast. Ps. ibid., 1. O Lord, thou hast searched me out and known me: thou knowest my down-sitting, and mine up-rising. ℣. Glory.

In Eastertide.

Introit. Ps. 64, 3. Protexisti.

THOU hast hidden me, O God, from the gathering together of the froward, alleluia: and from the insurrection of wicked doers, alleluia, alleluia. Ps. ibid., 1. Hear my voice, O God, in my prayer: preserve my life from fear of the enemy. ℣. Glory.

Collect.

O GOD, who by thy right hand didst raise up blessed Peter lest he should sink when he walked upon the waves, and didst thrice in shipwreck deliver his fellow-apostle Paul from the depths of the sea: mercifully hear us, and grant; that, by the merits of them both, we may be brought unto the glory of everlasting life: Who livest and reignest.

The Lesson from the Acts of the Apostles.

Acts 5, 12-16.

IN those days: By the hands of the Apostles were many signs and wonders wrought among the people. And they were all with one accord in Solomon's porch. And of the rest durst no man join himself to them: but the people magnified them. And believers were the more added to the Lord, multitudes both of men and women, insomuch that they brought forth the sick into the streets, and laid them on beds and couches, that at the least the shadow of Peter passing by might overshadow some of them. There came also a multitude out of the cities round about unto Jerusalem, bringing sick folks, and them which were vexed with unclean spirits: and they were healed every one.

Gradual. Ps. 45, 17-18. Thou shalt make them princes in all lands: they shall remember thy name, O Lord. ℣. Instead of thy fathers thou shalt have children: therefore shall the people give thanks unto thee.

Alleluia, alleluia. ℣. Ps. 139, 17. Right dear are thy friends unto me, O God: their rule and governance is exceeding steadfast. Alleluia.

After Septuagesima, omitting Alleluia and the Verse following, is said:

Tract. Ps. 126, 5-6. They that sow in tears shall reap in joy. ℣. He that now goeth on his way weeping, and beareth forth good seed. ℣. Shall doubtless come again with joy, and bring his sheaves with him.

In Eastertide the Gradual is omitted, and in its place is said:

Alleluia, alleluia. ℣. Ps. 89, 6. O Lord, the very heavens shall praise thy wondrous works: and thy truth in the congregation of the saints. Alleluia. ℣. Ps. 21, 4. Thou hast set, O Lord, a crown of pure gold upon his head. Alleluia.

✠ The Continuation of the holy Gospel according to Matthew.

Matt. 19, 27-29.

AT that time: Peter said unto Jesus, Behold, we have forsaken all, and followed thee: what shall we have therefore? And Jesus said unto them: Verily I say unto you, That ye which have followed me, in the regeneration when the Son of man shall sit in the throne of his glory, ye also shall sit upon twelve thrones, judging the twelve tribes of Israel. And every one that hath forsaken houses, or brethren, or sisters, or father, or mother, or wife, or children, or lands, for my name's sake, shall receive an hundredfold, and shall inherit everlasting life.

Offertory. Ps. 19, 5. Their sound is gone out into all lands: and their words into the ends of the world.

But in Eastertide the following is said:

Offertory. Ps. 89, 6. O Lord, the very heavens shall praise thy wondrous works: and thy truth in the congregation of the saints, alleluia, alleluia.

Secret.

WE offer thee, O Lord, our prayers and gifts: and that they may be acceptable in thy sight, grant that we may be aided by the prayers of thine Apostles Peter and Paul. Through.

Preface of the Apostles.

Communion. Matt. 19, 28. Ye which have followed me, shall sit upon thrones, judging the twelve tribes of Israel.

But in Eastertide the following is said:

Communion. Ps. 64, 11. The righteous shall rejoice in the Lord, and put his trust in him: and all they that are true of heart shall be glad, alleluia, alleluia.

Postcommunion.

DEFEND, O Lord, thy people: that we, who put our trust in the advocacy of thine Apostles Peter and Paul, may be preserved by thy perpetual and ready help. Through.

ALSO ON WEDNESDAY.

Mass of all the Holy Apostles

Out of Eastertide.

Introit. Ps. 139, 17. Mihi autem.

RIGHT dear are thy friends unto me, O God, and held in highest honour: their rule and governance is exceeding steadfast. Ps. ibid., 1. O Lord, thou hast searched me out, and known me: thou knowest my down-sitting, and mine up-rising. ℣. Glory.

In Eastertide.

Introit. Ps. 64, 3. Protexisti.

THOU hast hidden me, O God, from the gathering together of the froward, alleluia: and from the insurrection of wicked doers, alleluia, alleluia. Ps. ibid., 1. Hear my voice, O God, in my prayer: preserve my life from fear of the enemy. ℣. Glory.

Votive Mass of all the Holy Apostles

1.   For all the holy Apostles. Collect.

O GOD, who through thy blessed Apostles hast vouchsafed to us to come unto the knowledge of thy name: grant unto us; that by advancing in virtue, we may celebrate their everlasting glory, and likewise by celebrating their glory may advance in virtue. Through.

2.   For one holy Apostle. Collect.

O LORD, we humbly beseech thy majesty: that as thou didst send forth thy blessed Apostle N. for the teaching and governance of thy Church; so we may ever feel the succour of his intercession in thy sight. Through.

The Lesson from the Epistle of blessed Paul the Apostle to the Ephesians.
Eph. 4, 7-13.

BRETHREN: Unto everyone of us is given grace, according to the measure of the gift of Christ. Wherefore he saith: When he ascended up on high, he led captivity captive, and gave gifts unto men. Now that he ascended, what is it but that he also descended first into the lower parts of the earth? He that descended is the same also that ascended up far above all heavens, that he might fill all things. And he gave some Apostles, and some Prophets, and some Evangelists, and some Pastors and Teachers for the perfecting of the saints, for the work of the ministry, for the edifying of the body of Christ: till we all come in the unity of the faith, and of the knowledge of the Son of God, unto a perfect man, unto the measure of the stature of the fulness of Christ.

Gradual. Ps. 45, 17-18. Thou shalt make them princes in all lands: they shall remember thy name, O Lord. ℣. Instead of thy fathers thou shalt have children: therefore shall the people give thanks unto thee.

Alleluia, alleluia. Ps. 139, 17. Right dear are thy friends unto me, O God, and held in highest honour: their rule and governance is exceeding steadfast. Alleluia.

After Septuagesima, omitting Alleluia and the Verse following, is said:

Tract. Ps. 126, 5-6. They that sow in tears: shall reap in joy. ℣. He that now goeth on his way weeping, and beareth forth good seed, ℣. Shall doubtless come again with joy, and bring his sheaves with him.

In Eastertide the Gradual is omitted, and in its place is said:

Alleluia, alleluia. ℣. Ps. 89, 6. O Lord, the very heavens shall praise thy wondrous works: and thy truth in the congregation of the saints. Alleluia. ℣. John 15, 16. I have chosen you out of the world, that ye should go and bring forth fruit, and that your fruit should remain. Alleluia.

✠ The Continuation of the holy Gospel according to Matthew.
Matt. 19, 27-29.

AT that time: Peter said unto Jesus: Behold, we have forsaken all, and followed thee: what shall we have therefore? And Jesus said unto them: Verily I say unto you, That ye which have followed me, in the regeneration when the Son of man shall sit in the throne of his glory, ye also shall sit upon twelve thrones, judging the twelve tribes of Israel. And every one that hath forsaken houses, or brethren, or sisters, or father, or mother, or wife, or children, or lands, for my name's sake, shall receive an hundredfold, and shall inherit everlasting life.

Offertory. Ps. 19, 5. Their sound is gone out into all lands: and their words into the ends of the world.

But in Eastertide is said the following:

Offertory. Ps. 45, 17-18. Thou shalt make them princes in all lands: they shall remember thy name, O Lord, from one generation to another, alleluia, alleluia.

1. For all the holy Apostles. Secret.

WE beseech thee O Lord: that we who venerate the everlasting glory of thy holy Apostles; may in such wise be cleansed by thy holy mysteries, that we may more worthily celebrate the same. Through.

2. For one holy Apostle. Secret.

WE beseech thee, O Lord, that the holy prayer of blessed N. thine Apostle, may render our sacrifice pleasing unto thee: that as it is solemnly offered in his honour, so it may be made acceptable by his merits. Through.

Preface of the Apostles.

Communion. Matt. 19, 28. Ye which have followed me shall sit upon thrones, judging the twelve tribes of Israel.

But in Eastertide is said the following:

Communion. Ps. 19, 5. Their sound is gone out into all lands: and their words into the ends of the world, alleluia, alleluia.

1. For all the holy Apostles. Postcommunion.

O LORD, who hast bestowed on us these thy sacraments, we humbly pray thee: that, at the intercession of thy blessed Apostles; the mysteries which we celebrate in honour of their glorious passion may be profitable unto us for the healing of our souls. Through.

2. For one holy Apostle. Postcommunion.

WE beseech thee, O Lord: that these heavenly mysteries, which we have joyfully received on this commemoration of blessed N., thine Apostle; may effectually avail for the glory of thy Saints, and the forgiveness of our sins. Through.

¶ Also on Wednesday, the conventual Mass may be said of the principal patron of the Town, City, Diocese, Province, and Nation, or else of the Titular Saint of the Church, and of the Title or Holy Founder of the Order or Congregation.

THURSDAY.

Mass of the Holy Ghost

Introit. Wisd. 1, 7. Spiritus Domini.

THE Spirit of the Lord hath filled the whole world: and that which containeth all things hath knowledge of the voice. (E.T. Alleluia, alleluia.) ℣. Ps. 68, 1. Let God arise, and let his enemies be scattered: let them also that hate him flee before him. ℣. Glory.

Collect.

GOD, who didst teach the hearts of thy faithful people, by the sending to them the light of thy Holy Spirit: grant us by the same Spirit to have a right judgment in all things; and evermore to rejoice in his holy comfort. Through... in the unity of the same Holy Spirit.

The Lesson from the Acts of the Apostles.

Acts 8, 14-17.

IN those days: When the Apostles, which were at Jerusalem, heard that Samaria had received the word of God, they sent unto them Peter and John. Who, when they were come down, prayed for them, that they might receive the Holy Ghost: for as yet he was fallen upon none of them, only they were baptized in the Name of the Lord Jesus. Then laid they their hands on them, and they received the Holy Ghost.

Gradual. Ps. 33, 12 and 6. Blessed are the people, whose God is the Lord: and blessed are the folk, that the Lord hath chosen to him to be his inheritance. ℣. By the word of the Lord were the heavens made: and all the hosts of them by the breath of his mouth.

Alleluia, alleluia. (Here genuflect.) ℣. Come, Holy Ghost, fill the hearts of thy faithful: and kindle in them the fire of thy love. Alleluia.

After Septuagesima, omitting Alleluia and the Verse following, is said:

Tract. Ps. 104, 30. Send forth thy Spirit and they shall be made: and thou shalt renew the face of the earth. ℣. O how good and sweet, O Lord, is thy Spirit within us. (Here genuflect.) ℣. Come, Holy Ghost, fill the hearts of thy faithful: and kindle in them the fire of thy love.

In Eastertide the Gradual is omitted, and in its place is said:

Alleluia, alleluia. ℣. Ps. 104, 30. Send forth thy Spirit and they shall be made: and thou shalt renew the face of the earth. Alleluia. (Here genuflect.) ℣. Come, Holy Ghost, fill the hearts of thy faithful: and kindle in them the fire of thy love. Alleluia.

☩ The Continuation of the holy Gospel according to John.

John 14, 23-31.

AT that time: Jesus said unto his disciples: If a man love me, he will keep my words, and my Father will love him, and we will come unto him, and make our abode with him: he that loveth me not keepeth not my sayings. And the word which ye hear is not mine: but the Father's which sent me. These things have I spoken unto you, being yet present with you. But the Comforter, which is the Holy Ghost, whom the Father will send in my name, he shall teach you all things, and bring all things to your remembrance, whatsoever I have said unto you. Peace I leave with you, my peace I give unto you: not as the world giveth, give I unto you. Let not your heart be troubled, neither let it be afraid. Ye have heard how I said unto you: I go away, and come again unto you. If ye loved me, ye would rejoice, because I said, I go unto the Father: for my Father is greater than I. And now I have told you before it come to pass: that when it is come to pass, ye might believe. Hereafter I will not talk much with you. For the prince of this world cometh, and hath nothing in me. But that the world may know that I love the Father, and as the Father gave me commandment, even so I do.

Offertory. Ps. 68, 29-30. Stablish the thing, O God, that thou hast wrought in us: for thy temple's sake at Jerusalem shall kings bring presents unto thee. (E.T. Alleluia.)

Secret.

SANCTIFY, we beseech thee, O Lord, the gifts which we offer: and cleanse our hearts by the enlightening of the Holy Spirit. Through ... in the unity of the same Holy Spirit.

Preface of the Holy Ghost.

Communion. Acts 2, 2 and 4. Suddenly there came a sound from heaven as of a rushing mighty wind, where they were sitting: and they were all filled with the Holy Ghost, speaking the wonderful works of God. (E.T. Alleluia.)

Postcommunion.

POUR thy Holy Spirit upon us, O Lord, and cleanse our hearts: that through the inward dew of his blessing they may bring forth fruit unto thee. Through ... in the unity of the same Holy Spirit.

ALSO ON THURSDAY.

Mass of the Most Holy Sacrament of the Eucharist

Introit. Ps. 81, 17. Cibavit eos.

HE fed them with the finest wheat-flour: and with honey out of the stony rock hath he satisfied them. (E.T. Alleluia, alleluia.) Ps. ibid., 1. Sing we merrily unto God our strength: make a cheerful noise unto the God of Jacob. ℣. Glory.

Votive Mass of the Most Holy Sacrament of the Eucharist

Collect.

O GOD, who in a wonderful Sacrament hast left us a memorial of thy Passion: grant that we may so reverence the sacred mysteries of thy Body and Blood: that we may ever enjoy within ourselves the fruit of thy redemption: Who livest and reignest.

(Another version.)

O GOD, who under a wonderful Sacrament hast left unto us a memorial of thy Passion: grant us, we beseech thee, so to venerate the sacred mysteries of thy Body and Blood; that we may ever perceive within ourselves the fruit of thy redemption: Who livest and reignest.

The Lesson from the Epistle of blessed Paul the Apostle to the Corinthians.
I Cor. 11, 23-29.

BRETHREN: I have received of the Lord that which also I delivered unto you, That the Lord Jesus the same night in which he was betrayed took bread: and when he had given thanks, he brake it, and said: Take, eat: this is my body, which is broken for you: this do in remembrance of me. After the same manner also he took the cup, when he had supped, saying: This cup is the new testament in my blood: this do ye, as oft as ye drink it, in remembrance of me. For as often as ye eat this bread, and drink this cup, ye do shew the Lord's death till he come. Wherefore whosoever shall eat this bread, or drink this cup of the Lord, unworthily, shall be guilty of the body and blood of the Lord. But let a man examine himself: and so let him eat of that bread, and drink of that cup. For he that eateth and drinketh unworthily, eateth and drinketh judgment to himself, not discerning the Lord's body.

Gradual. Ps. 145, 15-16. The eyes of all wait upon thee, O Lord: and thou givest them their meat in due season. ℣. Thou openest thine hand: and fillest all things living with plenteousness.

Alleluia, alleluia. ℣. John 6, 56-57. My flesh is meat indeed, and my blood is drink indeed: he that eateth my flesh, and drinketh my blood, dwelleth in me, and I in him. Alleluia.

After Septuagesima, omitting Alleluia and the Verse following, is said:

Tract. Mal. 1, 11. From the rising of the sun even unto the going down of the same, my name shall be great among the Gentiles; ℣. And in every place incense shall be offered unto my name, and a pure offering: for my name shall be great among the heathen. ℣. Prov. 9, 5. Come, eat of my bread: and drink of the wine which I have mingled.

In Eastertide the Gradual is omitted, and in its place is said:

Alleluia, alleluia. ℣. Luke 24, 35. The Lord Jesus was known of the disciples in breaking of bread. Alleluia. ℣. John 6, 56-57. My flesh is meat indeed: he that eateth my flesh, and drinketh my blood, dwelleth in me, and I in him. Alleluia.

✠ The Continuation of the holy Gospel according to John.
John 6, 55-59.

AT that time: Jesus said unto the multitudes of the Jews: My flesh is meat indeed, and my blood is drink indeed. He that eateth my flesh, and drinketh my blood, dwelleth in me, and I in him. As the living Father hath sent me, and I live by the Father. so he that eateth me, even he shall live by me. This is that bread which came down from heaven. Not as your fathers did eat manna, and are dead. He that eateth of this bread shall live for ever.

Offertory. Lev. 21, 6. The priests of the Lord do offer the offerings of the Lord, made by fire, and the bread of their God:

Votive Mass of Christ the Eternal High Priest

and therefore they shall be holy unto their God, and shall not profane his name. (E.T. Alleluia.)

Secret.

GRACIOUSLY grant, we beseech thee, O Lord, unto thy Church the gifts of unity and peace: which are shewn forth in a mystery in the gifts we here offer. Through.

Common Preface (or of the Season).

Communion. I Cor. 11, 26-27. As often as ye do eat this bread, and drink this cup, ye do shew the Lord's death till he come: wherefore whosoever shall eat this bread, or drink this cup of the Lord, unworthily, shall be guilty of the body and blood of the Lord. (E.T. Alleluia.)

Postcommunion.

WE beseech thee, O Lord: that like as the receiving of thy precious Body and Blood in this life doth foreshadow the everlasting fruition of thy Godhead, so thou wouldest vouchsafe unto us to be fulfilled with the same: Who livest and reignest.

ALSO ON THURSDAY.
Mass of Our Lord Jesus Christ the Eternal High Priest

Introit. Ps. 110, 4. Juravit Dominus.

THE Lord sware, and will not repent: Thou art a priest for ever after the order of Melchisedech. (E.T. Alleluia, alleluia.) Ps. ibid., 1. The Lord said unto my lord: Sit thou on my right hand. ℣. Glory.

Collect.

O GOD, who, for the glory of thy majesty and the salvation of mankind, didst make thine Only-begotten Son to be an High Priest for ever: vouchsafe; that they, whom he hath chosen to be the ministers and stewards of his mysteries, may ever be found faithful in fulfilling the ministry they have received. Through the same.

The Lesson from the Epistle of blessed Paul the Apostle to the Hebrews.

Heb. 5, 1-11.

BRETHREN: Every high priest taken from among men, is ordained for men in things pertaining to God, that he may offer both gifts and sacrifices for sins: who can have compassion on the ignorant, and on them that are out of the way: for that he himself also is compassed with infirmity: and by reason hereof he ought, as for the people, so also for himself, to offer for sins. And no man taketh this honour unto himself, but he that is called of God, as was Aaron. So also Christ glorified not himself to be made an high priest, but he that said unto him: Thou art my Son; to-day have I begotten thee. As he saith also in another place: Thou art a Priest for ever after the order of Melchisedech. Who in the days of his flesh, when he had offered up prayers and supplications, with strong crying and tears, unto him that was able to save him from death, and was heard in that he feared: though he were the Son of God, yet learned he obedience by the things which he suffered: and being made perfect, he became the author of eternal salvation unto all them that obey him, called of God an high priest after the order of Melchisedech. Of whom we have many things to say, and hard to be uttered.

Gradual. Luke 4, 16. The Spirit of the Lord is upon me: because he hath anointed me. ℣. He hath sent me to preach the gospel to the poor, to heal the broken-hearted.

Alleluia, alleluia. ℣. Heb. 7, 24. But Jesus, because he continueth ever, hath an unchangeable priesthood. Alleluia.

[62] Votive Mass of the Holy Cross

After Septuagesima, omitting Alleluia and the Verse following, is said:

Tract. Ps. 10, 13 and 15. Arise, O Lord God, and lift up thine hand: forget not the poor. ℣. See, for thou beholdest labour and sorrow. ℣. The poor committeth himself unto thee: for thou art the helper of the fatherless.

In Eastertide the Gradual is omitted, and in its place is said:

Alleluia, alleluia. ℣. Heb. 7, 24. But Jesus, because he continueth ever, hath an unchangeable priesthood. Alleluia. ℣. Luke 4, 18. The Spirit of the Lord is upon me; because he hath anointed me to preach the gospel to the poor, he hath sent me to heal the broken-hearted. Alleluia.

✠ The Continuation of the holy Gospel according to Luke.

Luke 22, 14-20.

AT that time: Jesus sat down, and the twelve Apostles with him. And he said unto them: With desire I have desired to eat this passover with you, before I suffer. For I say unto you, I will not any more eat thereof, until it be fulfilled in the kingdom of God. And he took the cup, and gave thanks, and said: Take this, and divide it among yourselves. For I say unto you, I will not drink of the fruit of the vine, until the kingdom of God shall come. And he took bread, and gave thanks, and brake it, and gave unto them, saying: This is my body, which is given for you: this do in remembrance of me. Likewise also the cup after supper, saying: This cup is the new testament in my blood, which is shed for you.

Offertory. Heb. 10, 12 and 14. Christ, after he had offered one sacrifice for sins, for ever sat down on the right hand of God: for by one offering he hath perfected for ever them that are sanctified. (E.T. Alleluia.)

Secret.

MAY Jesus Christ our Mediator render these gifts acceptable unto thee, O Lord: and present us together with himself a sacrifice well-pleasing unto thee: Who with thee.

Preface of the Cross.

Communion. I Cor. 11, 24-25. This is my body, which is given for you: this cup is the new testament in my blood, saith the Lord: do this, as oft as ye partake, in remembrance of me. (E.T. Alleluia.)

Postcommunion.

QUICKEN us, we beseech thee O Lord, by the heavenly victim which we have offered and received: that, being united to thee in perpetual charity, we may bring forth fruit that abideth for ever. Through.

FRIDAY.

Mass of the Holy Cross

Introit. Gal. 6, 14. Nos autem gloriari.

BUT as for us, it behoveth us to glory in the Cross of our Lord Jesus Christ: in whom is our salvation, life and resurrection: by whom we are saved and set free. (E.T. Alleluia, alleluia.) Ps. 67, 1. God be merciful unto us, and bless us: and shew us the light of his countenance, and be merciful unto us. ℣. Glory.

Out of Eastertide.

Collect.

O GOD, who by the precious blood of thine only-begotten Son hast vouchsafed to sanctify the standard of the life-giving Cross: grant, we beseech thee; that they who rejoice in honouring the same holy cross may likewise evermore rejoice in thy protection. Through the same.

Votive Mass of the Holy Cross

In Eastertide.
Collect.

O GOD, who for our sakes didst send thy Son to suffer death upon the Cross, that thou mightest drive far from us the power of the enemy: grant to us thy servants; that we may attain unto his resurrection. Through the same.

The Lesson from the Epistle of blessed Paul the Apostle to the Philippians.

Phil. 2, 8-11.

BRETHREN: Christ for us became obedient unto death, even the death of the cross. Wherefore God also hath highly exalted him, and given him a name which is above every name: (here genuflect) that at the name of Jesus every knee should bow, of things in heaven, and things in earth, and things under the earth, and that every tongue should confess that Jesus Christ is Lord, to the glory of God the Father.

Gradual. Ibid., 8-9. Christ for us became obedient unto death, even the death of the cross. ℣. Wherefore God also hath highly exalted him, and given him a name which is above every name.

Alleluia, alleluia. ℣. Sweetest wood, and sweetest iron, sweetest weight is hung on thee: thou alone wast counted worthy to bear the King of heaven and the Lord. Alleluia.

After Septuagesima, omitting Alleluia and the Verse following, is said:

Tract. We adore thee, O Christ, and we bless thee: because by thy Cross thou hast redeemed the world. ℣. We adore thy Cross, O Lord, we commemorate thy glorious passion: have mercy on us, thou who didst suffer for us. ℣. O blessed Cross, which alone wast worthy to sustain the King of heaven and the Lord.

In Eastertide the Gradual is omitted, and in its place is said:

Alleluia, alleluia. ℣. Ps. 96, 10. Tell it out among the heathen that the Lord hath reigned from the tree. Alleluia. ℣. Sweetest wood, and sweetest iron, sweetest weight is hung on thee: which alone wast worthy to sustain the King of heaven and the Lord. Alleluia.

✠ The Continuation of the holy Gospel according to Matthew.

Matt. 20, 17-19.

AT that time: Jesus took the twelve disciples apart, and said unto them: Behold, we go up to Jerusalem, and the Son of man shall be betrayed unto the chief priests and unto the scribes, and they shall condemn him to death, and shall deliver him to the Gentiles to mock, and to scourge, and to crucify him, and the third day he shall rise again.

Offertory. Protect thy people, O Lord, by the sign of the holy Cross, from all the snares of their enemies: that we may render thee pleasing service, and that our sacrifice may be acceptable unto thee. (E.T. Alleluia.)

Secret.

WE beseech thee, O Lord: that as this oblation hath upon the altar of the Cross taken away the sin of the whole world, so likewise it may cleanse us from all our sins. Through the same.

Preface of the Cross.

Communion. By the sign of the Cross deliver us from our enemies, O our God. (E.T. Alleluia.)

Postcommunion.

ASSIST us mercifully, O Lord our God: that, like as thou dost vouchsafe unto us to rejoice in honouring the holy Cross, so we may be defended by the perpetual succour of the same. Through.

ALSO ON FRIDAY.

Mass of the Passion of the Lord

Introit. Phil. 2, 8-9. Humiliavit.

THE Lord Jesus Christ humbled himself unto death, even the death of the Cross: wherefore God also hath highly exalted him, and given him a name which is above every name. (E.T. Alleluia, alleluia.) Ps. 89, 1. My song shall be alway of the loving-kindness of the Lord: from one generation to another. ℣. Glory.

Collect.

O LORD Jesu Christ, who from the bosom of the Father in heaven didst come down to earth, and shed thy precious blood for the remission of our sins: we humbly beseech thee; that in the day of judgment we may be found worthy to stand at thy right hand and hear thee say: Come, ye blessed ones: Who with the same God the Father and the Holy Spirit, livest and reignest one God, world without end.

The Lesson from the Prophet Zechariah.
Zech. 12, 10-11; 13, 6-7.

THUS saith the Lord: I will pour upon the house of David, and upon the inhabitants of Jerusalem, the spirit of grace and of supplications: and they shall look upon me whom they have pierced: and they shall mourn for him, as one mourneth for his only son, and shall be in bitterness for him, as one that is in bitterness for his first-born. In that day there shall be a great mourning in Jerusalem, and one shall say unto him: What are these wounds in thine hands? Then he shall answer: Those with which I was wounded in the house of my friends. Awake, O sword, against my shepherd, and against the man that is my fellow, saith the Lord of hosts: smite the shepherd, and the sheep shall be scattered: saith the Lord almighty.

Gradual. Ps. 69, 21. Thy rebuke hath broken my heart, I am full of heaviness: I looked for some to have pity on me, but there was no man: neither found I any to comfort me. ℣. They gave me gall to eat, and when I was thirsty they gave me vinegar to drink.

Alleluia, alleluia. ℣. Hail, our King: thou alone didst pity our transgressions: obedient to the Father, thou wast led to be crucified, even as a meek lamb to the slaughter. Alleluia.

After Septuagesima, omitting Alleluia and the Verse following, is said:

Tract. Is. 53, 4-5. Surely he hath borne our griefs, and carried our sorrows. ℣. Yet we did esteem him stricken, smitten of God, and afflicted. ℣. But he was wounded for our transgressions, he was bruised for our iniquities. ℣. The chastisement of our peace was upon him: and with his stripes we are healed.

In Eastertide the Gradual is omitted, and in its place is said:

Alleluia, alleluia. ℣. Hail, our King: Thou alone didst pity our transgressions: obedient to the Father, thou wast led to be crucified, even as a meek lamb to the slaughter. Alleluia. ℣. To thee be glory, hosanna: to thee triumph and victory: to thee the crown of highest praise and honour. Alleluia.

✠ The Continuation of the holy Gospel according to John.
John 19, 28-35.

AT that time: Jesus knowing that all things were now accomplished, that the Scripture might be fulfilled, saith: I thirst. Now there was set a vessel full of vinegar. And they filled a sponge with vinegar, and put it upon hyssop, and put it to his mouth. When Jesus therefore had received the vinegar, he said: It is finished. And he bowed his head, and gave up the ghost. The Jews therefore, (because it was the Preparation), that the bodies should not remain upon the cross on the sabbath-day, (for that sabbath-day was an high-day,) besought Pilate that their legs might be broken, and that they might be taken away. Then came the soldiers: and brake the legs of the first, and of the other which was crucified with him. But when they came to Jesus, and saw that he was dead already, they brake not his legs, but one of the soldiers with a spear pierced his side, and forthwith came there out blood and water. And he that saw it bare record: and his record is true.

Offertory. Wicked men rose up against me: without mercy they sought to kill me: and they did not spare to spit in my face: they wounded me with their spears, and all my bones are broken. (E.T. Alleluia.)

Secret.

MAY the sacrifice which we offer unto thee, O Lord, through the pleading of the passion of thine only-begotten Son, evermore quicken and defend us: Who with thee liveth.

Preface of the Cross.

Communion. Ps. 22, 17-18. They pierced my hands and my feet: they may tell all my bones. (E.T. Alleluia.)

Postcommunion.

O LORD Jesu Christ, Son of the living God, who at the sixth hour for the redemption of the world wast lifted up upon the Cross of shame, and didst shed thy precious blood for the remission of our sins: we humbly beseech thee; that after our passing hence thou wouldest grant unto us joyfully to enter the gates of paradise: Who livest and reignest.

¶ On Saturday Mass is said of St. Mary, as above, p. [42]-[50].

¶ Outside the Conventual Mass, on any free day, the Votive Masses may be said which are assigned to the days of the week in place of the Conventual Mass, as above. Likewise Votive Masses may be said of the Immaculate Conception and of the Seven Sorrows, B.V.M., and also of all canonized Saints in the Roman Martyrology, for whom the Mass will either be proper, if there is one, or from the Common, with the necessary changes as given in the Proper. But if they are not in the Kalendar, everything is said of the Common ad lib. Moreover, according to the different cases, Votive Masses may be said for various objects as below, noting, however, that Masses on the day of election and coronation of the Pope, and on the anniversary of those days, as also on the anniversary of the election and consecration of the Bishop, cannot be said as private Masses, but a Commemoration is made of them.

II

VOTIVE MASSES FOR VARIOUS OBJECTS

Mass for the Election of the Chief Bishop

Mass is said of the Holy Ghost, as above, p. [58], or as follows:

Introit. I Sam. 2, 35. Suscitabo.

I WILL raise me up a faithful priest, that shall do according to that which is in mine heart and in my mind: and I will build him a sure house, and he shall walk before mine Anointed for ever. (E.T. Alleluia, alleluia.) Ps. 132, 1. Lord, remember David: and all his trouble. ℣. Glory.

Collect.

WE humbly beseech thee, O Lord: that of thy unbounded mercy thou wouldest grant unto the holy Roman Church a Pontiff; who by his tender care towards us may ever find favour in thy sight, and, studying to preserve thy people in safety, may ever be honoured by us to the glory of thy name. Through.

The Lesson from the Epistle of blessed Paul the Apostle to the Hebrews.

Heb. 4, 16; 5, 1-7.

BRETHREN: Let us come boldly unto the throne of grace, that we may obtain mercy, and find grace to help in time of need. For every high priest taken from among men is ordained for men in things pertaining to God, that he may offer both gifts and sacrifices for sins: who can have compassion on the ignorant, and on them that are out of the way, for that he himself also is compassed with infirmity: and by reason hereof he ought, as for the people, so also for himself, to offer for sins. And no man taketh this honour unto himself, but he that is called of God, as was Aaron. So also Christ glorified not himself to be made an high priest, but he that said unto him: Thou art my Son, to-day have I begotten thee. As he saith also in another place: Thou art a priest for ever after the order of Melchisedech. Who in the days of his flesh, when he had offered up prayers and supplications with strong crying and tears unto him that was able to save him from death, was heard in that he feared.

Gradual. Lev. 21, 10. The high priest, the priest great among his brethren, upon whose head the anointing oil hath been poured, and whose hands have been consecrated for the priesthood, and that hath been clothed with the holy garments: ought in all things to be made like unto his brethren. ℣. Heb. 2, 17. That he might be a merciful and faithful high priest in things pertaining to God: to make reconciliation for the sins of the people.

Alleluia, alleluia. ℣. Lev. 21, 8. Let the priest be holy, for I the Lord which sanctify you am holy. Alleluia.

After Septuagesima, omitting Alleluia and the Verse following, is said:

Tract. Ps. 132, 8-10. Arise, O Lord, into thy resting-place: thou, and the ark of thy strength. ℣. Let thy priests be clothed with righteousness, and let thy saints sing with joyfulness. ℣. For thy servant David's sake, turn not away the presence of thine Anointed.

Votive Mass on the Election and Coronation of the Chief Bishop

In Eastertide the Gradual is omitted, and in its place is said:

Alleluia, alleluia. ℣. Lev. 21, 8. Let the priest be holy, for I the Lord which sanctify you am holy. Alleluia. ℣. John 10, 14. I am the good shepherd: and know my sheep, and am known of mine. Alleluia.

✠ The Continuation of the holy Gospel according to John.

John 14. 15-21.

AT that time: Jesus said unto his disciples: If ye love me, keep my commandments. And I will pray the Father, and he shall give you another Comforter, that he may abide with you for ever, even the Spirit of truth, whom the world cannot receive, because it seeth him not, neither knoweth him. But ye know him; for he dwelleth with you, and shall be in you. I will not leave you comfortless: I will come to you. Yet a little while; and the world seeth me no more. But ye see me, because I live, ye shall live also. At that day ye shall know that I am in my Father, and ye in me, and I in you. He that hath my commandments, and keepeth them: he it is that loveth me. And he that loveth me shall be loved of my Father: and I will love him, and will manifest myself to him.

Offertory. I Esdr. 5, 40. They shall not be partakers of the holy things, till there arise up an high priest clothed with doctrine and truth. (E.T. Alleluia.)

Secret.

LET the abundance of thy mercy assist us, O Lord: that by the sacred gifts which we devoutly offer unto thee, we may rejoice to have a Pontiff pleasing in the sight of thy majesty to be the governour of our holy mother the Church. Through.

Communion. Exod. 29, 29-30. The high priest, that shall be appointed, shall put on the holy garments, and he shall come into the tabernacle of the congregation, to minister in the holy place. (E.T. Alleluia.)

Postcommunion.

MAKE us, O Lord, whom thou hast refreshed with the sacrament of thy precious Body and Blood, to rejoice in the wondrous grace of thy majesty: that we may obtain a Pontiff meet to instruct thy people in all godliness, and pour forth upon the minds of thy faithful the savour of spiritual sweetness: Who livest.

On the day of the Election and Coronation of the Chief Bishop

And on the Anniversary of those days

¶ On the day of the Creation or Coronation of a Pope, and on the Anniversary of those days, the following Mass is sung, as a solemn votive:

The Mass Statuit ei, as on the Feast of S. Peter's Chair at Rome, Jan. 18th, with the following exceptions.

Collect.

O GOD, the pastor and ruler of all the faithful, mercifully look upon thy servant N., whom thou hast been pleased to set as pastor over thy Church: grant unto him, we beseech thee, to be in word and conversation a wholesome example to the people committed to his charge; that he with them may attain at last to the crown of everlasting life. Through.

Secret.

WE beseech thee, O Lord, mercifully to accept these our oblations: granting unto N., thy servant, that like as thou hast chosen him to be pastor and ruler of thy Church, so he may be governed evermore by thy defence. Through.

Votive Mass on Anniversary of Election and Consecration of a Bishop

Postcommunion.

DEFEND us, O Lord, we beseech thee, who have here received these heavenly mysteries: and grant that thy servant N., whom thou hast chosen to be pastor and ruler of thy Church; together with the flock committed to his charge, may thereby be preserved and strengthened against all adversities. Through.

At the Consecration of a Bishop

¶Mass is said of the Office of the day, but under one conclusion with the first Collect: the following prayers are added; and Infra actionem the Hanc igituris said as below.

Collect.

GIVE ear, O Almighty God, to our supplications: that what is to be performed by our unworthy ministry may be fulfilled by thine effectual power. Through.

Secret.

The consecrator says:

RECEIVE, O Lord, the offerings which we present unto thee for this thy servant: that thou wouldest mercifully preserve in him the gifts which thou hast bestowed. Through.

The consecrated Bishop says:

RECEIVE, O Lord, the offerings which we present unto thee for me thy servant: that thou wouldest mercifully preserve in me the gifts which thou hast bestowed. Through.

Infra actionem.

The consecrator says:

THIS oblation, therefore, of our bounden duty and service, and also of thy whole family, which we present to thee also on behalf of this thy servant whom thou hast vouchsafed to advance to the order of Bishops, we beseech thee, O Lord, that thou wouldst graciously receive: and mercifully preserve in him the gifts thou hast bestowed: that by divine working he may accomplish that which by divine bounty he has received: and do thou order our days in thy peace, and bid us to be delivered from eternal damnation, and to be numbered in the flock of thine elect. Through Christ our Lord. Amen.

The consecrated Bishop says the same with the necessary alterations.

Postcommunion.

WE pray thee, O Lord, to accomplish in us the perfect healing of thy mercy: and of thy goodness, so work in us and comfort us; that we may in all things be enabled to be pleasing unto Thee. Through.

On the Anniversary of the Election and Consecration of a Bishop

On the anniversary of the election or translation of a Bishop, and also of his consecration, in cathedral and collegiate churches of the diocese, upon the reception of the Bishop's mandate, the following Mass is said, as a solemn votive.

The Mass Sacerdotes tui, as in the Common of a Confessor Bishop, p. [19], with the following exceptions:

Collect.

O GOD, the pastor and ruler of all the faithful, mercifully look upon thy servant N., whom thou hast chosen to be pastor and ruler of the Church of N.: grant unto him, we beseech thee, to be in word and conversation a wholesome example to the people committed to his charge; that he with them may attain at last to the crown of everlasting life. Through.

The Epistle Every high priest, p. [89].

The Gospel Take ye heed, p.[89].

The Creed is said.

Secret.

WE beseech thee, O Lord, mercifully to accept these our oblations: granting unto N., thy servant, that like as thou hast chosen him to be pastor and ruler of the Church of N.; so he may be governed evermore by thy defence. Through.

Postcommunion.

DEFEND us, O Lord, we beseech thee, who have here received these heavenly mysteries: and grant that thy servant, N., whom thou hast chosen to be pastor and ruler of the Church of N.: together with the flock committed to his charge, may thereby be preserved and strengthened against all adversities. Through.

At the Conferring of Holy Orders

On the Ember Saturdays or on the Saturday in the fourth week of Lent, Mass is said of the Saturday, on other days of the Day; but under one conclusion with the first Collect the following are added:

Collect.

WE beseech thee, O Lord, to hear the prayers of them that call upon thee, and guard with thy never-failing protection those who wait upon thee with devout hearts: that being hindered by no distress we may ever in thy worship render unto thee a service of perfect freedom. Through.

Secret.

WE beseech thee, O Lord, so to work by thy mysteries: that we may offer thee these gifts with worthy hearts. Through.

Postcommunion.

GRACIOUSLY sustain, we beseech thee, O Lord, by thy continual help those whom thou dost refresh with thy sacraments: that we may obtain the fruit of thy redemption both in thy mysteries and in our lives: Who livest.

Mass for Bridegroom and Bride

¶ If the solemn blessing of a Marriage, within Mass, is to be performed on a Sunday or Feast of precept, even suppressed, or a Double of the First or Second Class, or within the Octaves of Easter or Pentecost, or on privileged Ferias and Vigils, Mass of the Day is said, with Glória in excélsis, and Creed if the Mass require them, with Commemoration of the following Mass for Bridegroom and Bride, and the other things that belong. On other days (except the Commemoration of All the Faithful Departed, on which both the votive Mass and the solemn nuptial benediction are forbidden) the following Mass is said, even if a greater or lesser double occur.

Introit. Tob. 7, 15; 8, 19. Deus Israel.

THE God of Israel make you one: and may he be with you, even as he had mercy of two that were the only-begotten of their fathers: and now, O Lord, grant them to bless thee yet more abundantly. (E.T.Alleluia, alleluia.) Ps. 128, 1. Blessed are all they that fear the Lord: and walk in his ways. ℣.Glory.

Collect.

GRACIOUSLY hear us, almighty and merciful God: that whatsoever is now done by our office and ministry, may be fulfilled with the abundance of thy benediction. Through.

Votive Mass for Bridegroom and Bride

The Lesson from the Epistle of blessed Paul the Apostle to the Ephesians.

Ephes. 5, 22-33.

BRETHREN: Let the wives submit themselves unto their own husbands, as unto the Lord: for the husband is the head of the wife, even as Christ is the head of the Church: and he is the saviour of the body. Therefore as the Church is subject unto Christ, so let the wives be to their own husbands in every thing. Husbands, love your wives, even as Christ also loved the Church, and gave himself for it, that he might sanctify and cleanse it with the washing of water by the word, that he might present it to himself a glorious Church, not having spot, or wrinkle, or any such thing, but that it should be holy and without blemish. So ought men to love their wives as their own bodies. He that loveth his wife loveth himself. For no man ever yet hated his own flesh, but nourisheth and cherisheth it, even as the Lord the Church: for we are members of his body, of his flesh, and of his bones. For this cause shall a man leave his father and mother, and shall be joined unto his wife: and they two shall be one flesh. This is a great mystery, but I speak concerning Christ and the Church. Nevertheless, let every one of you in particular so love his wife even as himself: and the wife see that she reverence her husband.

Gradual. Ps. 128, 3. Thy wife shall be as the fruitful vine upon the walls of thine house. ℣. Thy children like the olive-branches round about thy table.

Alleluia, alleluia. ℣. Ps. 20, 3. The Lord send you help from the sanctuary: and strengthen you out of Sion. Alleluia.

After Septuagesima, omitting Alleluia and the Verse following, is said:

Tract. Ps. 128, 4-6. Lo, thus shall the man be blessed, that feareth the Lord. ℣. The Lord from out of Sion shall so bless thee: that thou shalt see Jerusalem in prosperity all thy life long. ℣. Yea, that thou shalt see thy children's children: and peace upon Israel.

In Eastertide the Gradual is omitted, and in its place is said:

Alleluia, alleluia. ℣. Ps. 20, 3. The Lord send you help from the sanctuary: and strengthen you out of Sion. Alleluia. ℣. Ps. 134, 3. The Lord that made heaven and earth: give you blessing out of Sion. Alleluia.

✠ The Continuation of the holy Gospel according to Matthew.

Matt. 19, 3-6.

AT that time: The Pharisees came unto Jesus, tempting him, and saying unto him: Is it lawful for a man to put away his wife for every cause? And he answered and said unto them: Have ye not read, that he which made them at the beginning made them male and female? and said: For this cause shall a man leave father and mother, and shall cleave to his wife, and they twain shall be one flesh. Wherefore they are no more twain, but one flesh. What therefore God hath joined together, let not man put asunder.

Offertory. Ps. 31, 15-16. My hope hath been in thee, O Lord: I have said, Thou art my God: My time is in thy hand. (E.T. Alleluia.)

Secret.

O LORD, we beseech thee, to accept these our gifts which we offer unto thee in commemoration of this sacred ordinance of matrimony: that this work begun by the bounty of thy goodness may be disposed according to thy will. Through.

Votive Mass for Bridegroom and Bride

¶ Our Father being said, the Priest, before he says Deliver us, stands at the Epistle corner, and, turning towards the Bridegroom and Bride kneeling before the Altar, says the following Prayers over them:

Let us pray. *Collect.*

MERCIFULLY hearken, O Lord, to these our supplications, and graciously prosper this thine institution, which thou hast ordained for the propagation of mankind: that those who are joined together by thine authority may be preserved by thy continual help. Through.

Let us pray. *Collect.*

O GOD, who by thy mighty power hast made all things of nothing: who also (after the first beginnings of the world were set in order) didst create for man, made after the image of God, woman to be an inseparable helpmeet, insomuch that thou didst cause the body of woman to take her origin from the flesh of man, and didst teach that it should never be lawful to put asunder what thou wast pleased at the beginning to make one: O God, who didst consecrate the bond of Matrimony to such an excellent mystery, that in the covenant of wedlock thou didst foreshadow the sacrament of Christ and his Church: O God, through whom woman is joined to man, and mankind in the beginning was endowed with that blessing, which alone hath not been taken away either by the punishment of original sin or by the judgement of the flood: look mercifully upon this thine handmaid, who, coming to be joined in Matrimony, seeketh thy protection and defence: may the bond of love and peace abide in her: may she be wedded faithful and chaste in Christ, and ever be a follower of holy matrons: may she be loving to her husband, as Rachel: wise, as Rebecca: may she be faithful and live long, as Sara: let the father of lies have no dominion over her by reason of her transgression: may she continue stedfast in the faith and the commandments: may she cleave to one husband, and flee unlawful communications: may she strengthen her infirmity by the spirit of discipline: may she be grave and modest, honourable and chaste, instructed in heavenly doctrine: may she be fruitful in offspring, approved and without offence: may she attain unto the rest of the Blessed and unto the heavenly realms: and may they both see their children's children, even unto the third and fourth generation, and come to the old age which they desire. Through the same.

¶ Then the Priest, turning back to the middle of the Altar, says Deliver us and the rest as usual; and after he has received the Blood, communicates the Bridegroom and Bride; and proceeds with the Mass.

Communion. Ps. 128, 4 and 6. Lo, thus shall the man be blessed, that feareth the Lord: yea, thou shalt see thy children's children: and peace upon Israel. (E.T. Alleluia.)

Postcommunion.

WE beseech thee, almighty God: let thy gracious favour accompany the ordinance of thy loving providence; that those whom thou hast joined together in lawful union, may by thy protection live in lasting peace. Through.

¶ Having said Let us bless the Lord, or if the Mass of the Day require it, Ite, Missa est, before blessing the people, the Priest turns to the Bridegroom and Bride and says:

THE God of Abraham, the God of Isaac and the God of Jacob be with you: and may he fulfil his blessing upon you: that ye may see your children's children unto the third and fourth generation, and thereafter may have eternal life without end: through the help of our Lord Jesus Christ, who with the Father and the Holy Ghost liveth and reigneth God, throughout all ages, world without end. ℟. Amen.

¶ The Priest shall solemnly charge them that they shall be faithful to each other; that they shall remain chaste at the time of prayer, and especially during fasts and solemnities; that they shall love each other, and remain in the fear of God. Then he sprinkles them with blessed water, and, having said Pláceat tibi, gives the blessing, and reads the Gospel of St. John as usual, or another according to the Rubrics.

Mass for the Propagation of the Faith

Introit. Ps. 67, 2-3. Deus misereatur.

GOD be merciful unto us, and bless us: and shew us the light of his countenance, and be merciful unto us: that thy way may be known upon earth, thy saving health among all nations. (E.T. Alleluia, alleluia.) Ps. ibid., 4. Let the people praise thee, O God: yea, let all the people praise thee. ℣. Glory.

Collect.

O GOD, who wouldest that all men should be saved, and come to the knowledge of the truth: send forth, we beseech thee, labourers into thy harvest, and enable them to speak thy word with all boldness; that thy word may run and be glorified, and that all nations may know thee, the one true God, and him whom thou hast sent, even Jesus Christ thy Son our Lord: Who liveth and reigneth with thee.

The Lesson from the book of Wisdom.
Ecclus. 36, 1-8 and 15-17.

HAVE mercy upon us, O Lord God of all, and behold us, and send thy fear upon all the nations that seek not after thee. Lift up thy hand against the strange nations, and let them see thy power. As thou wast sanctified in us before them, so be thou magnified among them before us, and let them know thee, as we have known thee, that there is no God, but only thou, O God. Shew new signs, and make other strange wonders. Glorify thy hand and thy right arm, that they may set forth thy wondrous works. Raise up indignation, and pour out wrath. Take away the adversary, and destroy the enemy. Make the time short, remember the covenant, and let them declare thy wonderful works. Give testimony unto those that thou hast possessed from the beginning, and raise up prophets that have been in thy name. Reward them that wait for thee, and let thy prophets be found faithful: O Lord, hear the prayer of thy servants, according to the blessing of Aaron over thy people, that all they which dwell upon the earth may know that thou art the Lord, the eternal God.

Gradual. Ps. 67, 6-8. Let the people praise thee, O God, let all the people praise thee: then shall the earth bring forth her increase. ℣. God shall bless us: and all the ends of the world shall fear him.

Alleluia, alleluia. ℣. Ps. 100, 1. O be joyful in the Lord, all ye lands: serve the Lord with gladness, and come before his presence with a song. Alleluia.

After Septuagesima, omitting Alleluia and the Verse following, is said:

Tract. Ps. 96, 3-5. Declare the honour of the Lord unto the heathen, and his wonders unto all people. ℣. For the Lord is great, and cannot worthily be praised: he is more to be feared than all gods. ℣. As for all the gods of the heathen, they are but idols: but it is the Lord that made the heavens.

In Eastertide the Gradual is omitted, and in its place is said:

Alleluia, alleluia. ℣. Ps. 100, 1-2. O be joyful in the Lord, all ye lands: serve the

Lord with gladness: and come before his presence with a song. Alleluia. ℣. Be ye sure that the Lord he is God: it is he that hath made us, and not we ourselves. Alleluia.

☩ The Continuation of the holy Gospel according to Matthew.

Matt. 9, 35-38.

AT that time: Jesus went about all the cities and villages, teaching in their synagogues, and preaching the Gospel of the kingdom, and healing every sickness and every disease among the people. But when he saw the multitudes, he was moved with compassion on them: because they fainted, and were scattered abroad, as sheep having no shepherd. Then saith he unto his disciples: The harvest truly is plenteous, but the labourers are few. Pray ye therefore the Lord of the harvest, that he will send forth labourers into his harvest.

Offertory. Ps. 96, 7-9. Ascribe unto the Lord, O ye kindreds of the people, ascribe unto the Lord worship and power, ascribe unto the Lord the honour due unto his name: bring presents, and come into his courts: O worship the Lord in the beauty of holiness. (E.T. Alleluia.)

Secret.

BEHOLD, O God our defender, and look upon the face of thine Anointed, who gave himself a ransom for all: and grant; that, from the rising of the sun even unto the going down of the same, thy name may be great among the Gentiles, and that in every place a pure oblation may be sacrificed and offered unto thy name. Through the same.

Communion. Ps. 117, 1-2. O praise the Lord, all ye heathen: praise him, all ye nations: for his merciful kindness is ever more and more towards us, and the truth of the Lord endureth for ever. (E.T. Alleluia.)

Postcommunion.

WE beseech thee, O Lord: that as thou hast fed us with the gift of our redemption; so also this means of eternal salvation may ever avail for the furtherance of the true faith. Through.

Another Epistle:

The Lesson from the Epistle of blessed Paul the Apostle to Timothy.

I Tim. 2, 1-7.

I EXHORT that, first of all, supplications, prayers, intercessions, and giving of thanks, be made for all men: for kings, and for all that are in authority, that we may lead a quiet and peaceable life in all godliness and honesty; for this is good and acceptable in the sight of God our Saviour, who will have all men to be saved, and to come unto the knowledge of the truth. For there is one God, and one mediator between God and men, the man Christ Jesus: who gave himself a ransom for all, to be testified in due time: whereunto I am ordained a preacher, and an apostle, (I speak the truth in Christ, and lie not), a teacher of the Gentiles in faith and verity.

Mass against the Heathen

Introit. Ps. 44, 23-24 and 25-26. Exsurge.

UP, Lord, why sleepest thou? awake, and be not absent from us for ever: wherefore hidest thou thy face, and forgettest our trouble? Our belly cleaveth unto the ground: arise, Lord, help us and deliver us. (E.T. Alleluia, alleluia.) Ps. ibid., 1. We have heard with our ears, O God: our fathers have told us. ℣. Glory.

Collect.

ALMIGHTY and everlasting God, in whose hand is the dominion of all kings and the governance of all kingdoms: look down and succour the Christian people; that the nations of the heathen, who trust in their own fierceness, may be confounded by the strength of thy right hand. Through.

Votive Mass against the Heathen

The Lesson from the book of Esther.
Esther 13, 8-11 and 15-17.

IN those days: Mardocheus made his prayer unto the Lord, saying: O Lord, Lord, the King almighty, for the whole world is in thy power, and if thou hast appointed to save Israel, there is no man that can gainsay thee. For thou hast made heaven and earth, and all the wondrous things under the heaven. Thou art Lord of all things, and there is no man that can resist thee, which art the Lord. And now, O Lord God and King, spare thy people, for their eyes are upon us to bring us to nought, yea, they desire to destroy the inheritance, that hath been thine from the beginning. Despise not the portion, which thou hast delivered out of Egypt for thine own self. Hear my prayer, and be merciful unto thine inheritance, turn our sorrow into joy, that we may live, O Lord, and praise thy name, and destroy not the mouths of them that praise thee, O Lord our God.

Gradual. Ps. 83, 19 and 14. Let the nations know that thou, whose name is Jehovah: art only the most Highest over all the earth. ℣. O my God, make them like unto a wheel, and as the stubble before the wind.

Alleluia, alleluia. ℣. Ps. 80, 3. Stir up thy strength, O Lord, and come, and help us. Alleluia.

After Septuagesima, omitting Alleluia and the Verse following, is said:

Tract. Ps. 79, 9-11. Help us, O God of our salvation: and for the glory of thy name, O Lord, deliver us: and be merciful unto our sins, for thy name's sake. ℣. Wherefore do the heathen say: Where is now their God? ℣. O let the vengeance of thy servants' blood that is shed: be openly shewed upon the heathen in our sight: O let the sorrowful sighing of the prisoners come before thee.

In Eastertide the Gradual is omitted, and in its place is said:

Alleluia, alleluia. ℣. Ps. 80, 3. Stir up thy strength, O Lord, and come, and help us. Alleluia. ℣. Ibid., 15-16. Turn thee again, thou God of hosts, look down from heaven, behold, and visit this vine: and the place of the vineyard that thy right hand hath planted. Alleluia.

✠ The Continuation of the holy Gospel according to Luke.
Luke 11, 5-13.

AT that time: Jesus said unto his disciples: Which of you shall have a friend, and shall go unto him at midnight, and say unto him: Friend, lend me three loaves, for a friend of mine in his journey is come to me, and I have nothing to set before him: and he from within shall answer and say: Trouble me not, the door is now shut, and my children are with me in bed, I cannot rise and give thee. I say unto you, though he will not rise and give him, because he is his friend, yet because of his importunity he will rise and give him as many as he needeth. And I say unto you: Ask, and it shall be given you; seek, and ye shall find; knock, and it shall be opened unto you. For every one that asketh receiveth; and he that seeketh findeth; and to him that knocketh it shall be opened. If a son shall ask bread of any of you that is a father: will he give him a stone? Or if he ask a fish: will he for a fish give him a serpent? Or if he shall ask an egg: will he offer him a scorpion? If ye then, being evil, know how to give good gifts unto your children: how much more shall your heavenly Father give the Holy Spirit to them that ask him?

Offertory. Ps. 18, 28 and 32. Thou shalt save the people that are in adversity: and shalt bring down the high looks of the proud: for who is God, but thou, O Lord? (E.T. Alleluia.)

Votive Mass for the ending of Schism

Secret.

GIVE heed, O Lord, to the sacrifice which we offer: that thou wouldest deliver them that fight for thee from all the wickedness of the heathen, and stablish them with the protection of thy sure defence. Through.

Communion. Ps. 119, 81, 84 and 86. My soul hath longed for thy salvation, and I have a good hope because of thy word: when wilt thou be avenged of them that persecute me? They persecute me falsely, be thou my help, O Lord my God. (E.T. Alleluia.)

Postcommunion.

BEHOLD, O God our defender, and protect against the assaults of the heathen them that fight for thee: that they may be delivered from all distress, and serve thee with a quiet mind. Through.

Mass for the ending of Schism

Introit. Ps. 106, 47. Salvos nos fac.

DELIVER us, O Lord our God, and gather us from among the heathen: that we may give thanks unto thy holy name, and make our boast of thy praise. (E.T. Alleluia, alleluia.) Ps. ibid., 1. O give thanks unto the Lord, for he is gracious: and his mercy endureth for ever. ℣. Glory.

Collect.

O GOD, who dost bring into the way of truth them that have gone astray, dost gather together them that are scattered abroad, and preserve them that thou hast gathered: we beseech thee, of thy mercy, to pour out upon the Christian people the grace of thy unity; that, all division being done away, they may be joined to the true shepherd of thy Church, and do thee worthy service. Through.

The Lesson from the Epistle of blessed Paul the Apostle to the Ephesians.

Ephes. 4, 1-7 and 13-21.

BRETHREN: I beseech you that ye walk worthy of the vocation wherewith ye are called, with all lowliness and meekness, with long suffering, forbearing one another in love, endeavouring to keep the unity of the spirit in the bond of peace. There is one body, and one spirit, even as ye are called in one hope of your calling. One Lord, one faith, one baptism. One God and Father of all, who is above all, and through all, and in you all. But unto every one of us is given grace according to the measure of the gift of Christ: till we all come in the unity of the faith, and of the knowledge of the Son of God, unto a perfect man, unto the measure of the stature of the fulness of Christ: that we henceforth be no more children, tossed to and fro, and carried about with every wind of doctrine, by the sleight of men, and cunning craftiness, whereby they lie in wait to deceive. But speaking the truth in love, may grow up into him in all things, which is the head, even Christ: from whom the whole body fitly joined together and completed by that which every joint supplieth, according to the effectual working in the measure of every part, maketh increase of the body unto the edifying of itself in love. This I say therefore, and testify in the Lord, that ye henceforth walk not as other Gentiles walk, in the vanity of their mind, having the understanding darkened, being alienated from the life of God through the ignorance that is in them, because of the blindness of their heart, who being past feeling have given themselves over unto lasciviousness, to work all uncleanness with greediness. But ye have not so learned Christ: if so be that ye have heard him, and have been taught by him as the truth is in Christ Jesus our Lord.

Gradual. Ps. 122, 6-7. O pray for the peace of Jerusalem: they shall prosper that love thee. ℣. Peace be within thy walls: and plenteousness within thy palaces.

Alleluia, alleluia. ℣. Ps. 147, 12. Praise the Lord, O Jerusalem: praise thy God, O Sion. Alleluia.

After Septuagesima, omitting Alleluia and the Verse following, is said:

Tract. Ps. 76, 2-4. In Jewry is God known, his name is great in Israel. ℣. At Salem is his tabernacle, and his dwelling in Sion. ℣. There brake he the arrows of the bow, the shield, the sword, and the battle.

In Eastertide the Gradual is omitted, and in its place is said:

Alleluia, alleluia. ℣. Ps. 147, 12. Praise the Lord, O Jerusalem: praise thy God, O Sion. Alleluia. ℣. Ibid., 14. He maketh peace in thy borders, and filleth thee with the flour of wheat. Alleluia.

✠ The Continuation of the holy Gospel according to John.

John 17, 1 and 11-23.

AT that time: Jesus lifted up his eyes unto heaven and said: Holy Father, keep through thine own name those whom thou hast given me: that they may be one, as we are. While I was with them in the world, I kept them in thy name. Those that thou gavest me I have kept: and none of them is lost, but the son of perdition, that the Scripture might be fulfilled. And now come I to thee: and these things I speak in the world, that they might have my joy fulfilled in themselves. I have given them thy word, and the world hath hated them, because they are not of the world, even as I am not of the world. I pray not that thou shouldest take them out of the world, but that thou shouldest keep them from the evil. They are not of the world, even as I am not of the world. Sanctify them through thy truth. Thy word is truth. As thou hast sent me into the world, even so have I also sent them into the world. And for their sakes I sanctify myself, that they also might be sanctified through the truth. Neither pray I for these alone, but for them also which shall believe on me through their word: that they all may be one, as thou, Father, art in me, and I in thee, that they also may be one in us: that the world may believe that thou hast sent me. And the glory which thou gavest me I have given them, that they may be one, even as we are one. I in them and thou in me, that they may be made perfect in one.

Offertory. Rom. 15, 5-6. God grant you to be likeminded one towards another: that ye may with one mind and one mouth glorify our God. (E.T. Alleluia.)

Secret.

SANCTIFY, O Lord, these oblations which we present unto thee for the union of the Christian people: and grant us thereby in thy Church the gifts of unity and peace. Through.

Communion. I Cor. 10, 17. We being many are one bread, and one body, for we are all partakers of one bread and one cup. (E.T. Alleluia.)

Postcommunion.

LET this holy Communion, O Lord: which we have received in token of the union in thee of thy faithful people; likewise work effectually to the unity of thy Church. Through.

Mass in time of War

Introit. Ps. 25, 6, 3 and 22. Reminiscere.

CALL to remembrance, O Lord, thy tender mercies, and thy loving kindnesses, which have been ever of old: neither let our enemies triumph over us: deliver us, O God of Israel, out of all our troubles. (E.T. Alleluia, alleluia) Ps. ibid., 1-2. Unto thee, O Lord, will I lift up my soul: my God, I have put my trust in thee, O let me not be confounded. ℣. Glory.

Collect.

O GOD, who makest wars to cease, and by thy mighty arm dost overthrow the adversaries of them that put their trust in thee: come to the help of thy servants who implore thy mercy; that the fierceness of our enemies being overthrown, we may evermore praise thee with thanksgiving. Through.

The Lesson from the Prophet Jeremiah.

Jer. 42, 1-2 and 7-12.

IN those days: All the captains of the forces came near: and said unto Jeremiah the Prophet: Pray for us unto the Lord thy God. And the word of the Lord came unto Jeremiah. Then called he all the captains of the forces which were with him, and all the people from the least even to the greatest. And said unto them: Thus saith the Lord, the God of Israel, unto whom ye sent me to present your supplication before him: If ye will still abide in this land, then will I build you, and not pull you down; and I will plant you, and not pluck you up: for I repent me of the evil that I have done unto you. Be not afraid of the king of Babylon, of whom ye are afraid; be not afraid of him, saith the Lord: for I am with you to save you, and to deliver you from his hand. And I will shew mercies unto you, that he may have mercy upon you, and cause you to return to your own land: saith the Lord almighty.

Gradual. Ps. 77, 15-16. Thou art the God that doest wonders: and hast declared thy power among the people. ℣. Thou hast mightily delivered thy people, even the sons of Jacob and Joseph.

Alleluia, alleluia. ℣. Ps. 59, 2. Deliver me from mine enemies, O God: defend me from them that rise up against me. Alleluia.

After Septuagesima, omitting Alleluia and the Verse following, is said:

Tract. Ps. 103, 10. O Lord, deal not with us after our sins which we have committed: nor reward us according to our wickednesses. ℣. Ps. 79, 8-9. Lord, remember not our old sins: but have mercy upon us, and that soon, for we are come to great misery. ℣. Help us, O God of our salvation: and for the glory of thy name, O Lord, deliver us: and be merciful unto our sins, for thy name's sake.

In Eastertide the Gradual is omitted, and in its place is said:

Alleluia, alleluia. ℣. Ps. 59, 2. Deliver me from mine enemies, O God: defend me from them that rise up against me. Alleluia. ℣. Ps. ibid., 17. As for me, I will sing of thy power: and will praise thy mercy betimes in the morning. Alleluia.

✠ The Continuation of the holy Gospel according to Matthew.

Matt. 24, 3-8.

AT that time: The disciples came unto Jesus privately, saying: Tell us, when shall these things be? and what shall be the sign of thy coming, and of the end of the world? And Jesus answered and said unto them: Take heed that no man deceive you. For many shall come in my name, saying: I am Christ; and shall deceive many. And ye shall hear of wars and rumours of wars. See that ye be not troubled. For all these things must come to pass, but the end is not yet. For nation shall rise against nation, and kingdom against kingdom, and there shall be famines, and pestilences, and earthquakes in divers places. All these are the beginning of sorrows.

Offertory. Ps. 18, 28 and 32. Thou shalt save the people that are in adversity, O Lord, and shalt bring down the high looks of the proud: for who is God, but the Lord? (E.T. Alleluia.)

Secret.

MERCIFULLY give heed to the sacrifice which we offer, O Lord: that we, being preserved from all the wickedness of war, may ever be stablished with the protection of thy sure defence. Through.

Communion. Ps. 31, 3. Bow down thine ear: make haste to deliver us. (E.T. Alleluia.)

Postcommunion.

O GOD, the ruler of all kings and kingdoms, who dost heal us by thy chastisement, and by pardon dost preserve us: shew forth upon us thy mercy; that peace and quietness being restored by thy power, we may use the same for our healing and correction. Through.

Mass for Peace

Introit. Ecclus. 36, 18. Da pacem.

GIVE peace, O Lord, to them that wait for thee, and let thy prophets be found faithful: hear the prayers of thy servant, and of thy people Israel. (E.T. Alleluia, alleluia.) Ps. 122, 1. I was glad when they said unto me: we will go into the house of the Lord. ℣. Glory.

Collect.

O GOD, from whom all holy desires, all good counsels, and all just works do proceed: give unto thy servants that peace which the world cannot give; that both our hearts may be set to obey thy commandments, and also that by thee we being defended from the fear of our enemies may pass our time in rest and quietness. Through.

The Lesson from the book of the Maccabees.

II Macc. 1, 1-5.

THE brethren, the Jews that be at Jesusalem and in the land of Judea, wish unto the brethren, the Jews that are throughout Egypt, health and peace. God be gracious unto you, and remember his covenant that he made with Abraham, Isaac, and Jacob, his faithful servants; and give you all an heart to serve him, and to do his will, with a good courage and a willing mind. And open your hearts in his law and commandments, and send you peace. And hear your prayers, and be at one with you, and never forsake you in time of trouble, he, the Lord our God.

Gradual. Ps. 122, 6-7. O pray for the peace of Jerusalem: they shall prosper that love thee. ℣. Peace be within thy walls, and plenteousness within thy palaces.

Alleluia, alleluia. ℣. Ps. 147, 12. Praise the Lord, O Jerusalem: praise thy God, O Sion. Alleluia.

After Septuagesima, omitting Alleluia and the Verse following, is said:

Tract. Ps. 76, 2-4. In Jewry is God known, his Name is great in Israel. ℣. At Salem is his tabernacle, and his dwelling in Sion. ℣. There brake he the arrows of the bow, the shield, the sword, and the battle.

In Eastertide the Gradual is omitted, and in its place is said:

Alleluia, alleluia. ℣. Ps. 147, 12. Praise the Lord, O Jerusalem: praise thy God, O Sion. Alleluia. ℣. Ibid., 14. He maketh peace in thy borders, and filleth thee with the flour of wheat. Alleluia.

✠ The Continuation of the holy Gospel according to John.

John 20, 19-23.

AT that time: The same day at evening, being the first day of the week, when the doors were shut where the disciples were assembled for fear of the Jews: came Jesus and stood in the midst, and saith unto them: Peace be unto you. And when he had so said, he shewed unto them his hands and his side. Then were the disciples glad, when they saw the Lord. Then said Jesus to them again: Peace be unto you. As my Father hath sent me, even so send I you. And when he had said this, he breathed on them, and saith unto them: Receive ye the Holy Ghost: whosesoever sins ye remit, they are remitted unto them: and whosesoever sins ye retain, they are retained.

Offertory. Ps. 135, 3 and 6. O praise the Lord, for he is gracious: O sing praises unto his name, for he is lovely: whatsoever the Lord pleased, that did he in heaven, and in earth. (E.T. Alleluia.)

Secret.

O GOD, who sufferest not any terror to confound the nations that put their trust in thee: vouchsafe to accept the prayers and oblations of the people of thine inheritance; that by thy mercy all Christian lands may be established in peace, and preserved from the fear of their enemies. Through.

Communion. John 14, 27. Peace I leave with you: my peace I give unto you, saith the Lord. (E.T. Alleluia.)

Postcommunion.

O GOD, who art the author of peace and lover of concord, in knowledge of whom standeth our eternal life, whose service is perfect freedom: defend us thy humble servants in all assaults of our enemies; that we, surely trusting in thy defence, may not fear the power of any adversaries. Through.

Mass for Protection against Disease

Introit. II Sam. 24, 16. Recordare.

BE mindful of thy covenant, O Lord, and say to the destroying Angel: Stay now thy hand, and let not the land be made desolate, and destroy not every living thing. (E.T. Alleluia, alleluia.) Ps. 80, 2. Hear, O thou Shepherd of Israel: thou that leadest Joseph like a sheep. ℣. Glory.

Collect.

O GOD, who wouldest not the death of a sinner, but rather that he should repent: look down in mercy on thy people who turn again to thee; that they, being ever steadfast in thy service, may by thy mercy be delivered from the scourges of thy wrath. Through.

The Lesson from the book of Samuel.

II Sam. 24, 15-19 and 25.

IN those days: The Lord sent a pestilence upon Israel from the morning even to the time appointed, and there died of the people from Dan even to Beer-sheba seventy thousand men. And when the Angel stretched out his hand upon Jerusalem to destroy it, the Lord repented him of the evil, and said to the Angel that destroyed the people: It is enough; stay now thine hand. And the Angel of the Lord was by the threshingplace of Araunah the Jebusite. And David spake unto the Lord when he saw the Angel that smote the people, and said: Lo, I have sinned, and I have done wickedly: but these sheep, what have they done? Let thine hand, I pray thee, be against me, and against my father's house. And Gad came that day to David, and said unto him: Go up, rear an altar unto the Lord in the threshingfloor of Araunah the Jebusite.

And David, according to the saying of Gad, went up as the Lord commanded. And David built there an altar unto the Lord, and offered burnt offerings and peace offerings: so the Lord was intreated for the land, and the plague was stayed from Israel.

Gradual. Ps. 107, 20-21. The Lord sent his word, and healed them: and they were saved from their destruction. ℣. O that men would therefore praise the Lord for his goodness: and declare the wonders that he doeth for the children of men.

Alleluia, alleluia. ℣. Ps. 69, 2. Save me, O God, for the waters are come in, even unto my soul. Alleluia.

After Septuagesima, omitting Alleluia and the Verse following, is said:

Tract. Ps. 103, 10. O Lord, deal not with us after our sins which we have committed: nor reward us according to our wickednesses. ℣. Ps. 79, 8-9. Lord, remember not our old sins: but have mercy upon us, and that soon, for we are come to great misery. ℣. Help us, O God of our salvation: and for the glory of thy name, O Lord, deliver us, and be merciful unto our sins, for thy name's sake.

In Eastertide the Gradual is omitted, and in its place is said:

Alleluia, alleluia. ℣. Ps. 69, 2. Save me, O God, for the waters are come in, even unto my soul. Alleluia. ℣. Zech. 8, 7 and 8. I will save my people Israel in the evil day, and I will be their God, in truth and in righteousness. Alleluia.

☩ The Continuation of the holy Gospel according to Luke.

Luke 4, 38-44.

AT that time: Jesus arose out of the synagogue, and entered into Simon's house. And Simon's wife's mother was taken with a great fever: and they besought him for her. And he stood over her, and rebuked the fever: and it left her. And immediately she arose and ministered unto them. Now when the sun was setting, all they that had any sick with divers diseases brought them unto him. And he laid his hands on every one of them, and healed them. And devils also came out of many, crying out, and saying: Thou art Christ the Son of God: and he rebuking them suffered them not to speak, for they knew that he was Christ. And when it was day, he departed and went into a desert place, and the people sought him, and came unto him, and stayed him, that he should not depart from them. And he said unto them: I must preach the kingdom of God to other cities also: for therefore am I sent. And he preached in the synagogues of Galilee.

Offertory. Num. 16, 48. The high priest stood between the dead and the living, having a golden censer in his hand: and he made an offering of incense, and appeased the anger of God, and the plague from the Lord was stayed. (E.T. Alleluia.)

Secret.

WE beseech thee, O Lord, that this sacrifice which we here offer may be our succour: that by the power thereof we may be loosed from every error, and delivered from all the assaults of destruction. Through.

Communion. Luke 6, 17-19. A multitude of sick folk, and they that were vexed with unclean spirits, came to him: for there went virtue out of him, and healed them all. (E.T. Alleluia.)

Postcommunion.

HEAR us, O God of our salvation: that we thy people, being delivered from the terrors of thy wrath, may by the bountiful goodness of thy mercy abide in peace and quietness. Through.

Mass to ask the Grace of the Holy Ghost

Mass is said of the Holy Ghost, as on p. [58], with the Prayers as below.

Collect.

ALMIGHTY God, unto whom all hearts be open, all desires known, and from whom no secrets are hid: cleanse the thoughts of our hearts by the inspiration of thy Holy Spirit; that we may perfectly love thee, and worthily magnify thy holy name. Through.... in the unity of the same Holy Spirit.

Secret.

WE beseech thee, O Lord, that this oblation may cleanse the stains of our hearts: that they may be made a dwellingplace meet for thy Holy Spirit. Through ... in the unity of the same Holy Spirit.

Postcommunion.

GRANT, we beseech thee, almighty God, that we thy servants, ever seeking diligently thy Holy Spirit, may be made partakers of the same: that through his grace we may be delivered from all temptations, and be found worthy to obtain the remission of our sins. Through ... in the unity of the same Holy Spirit.

Mass for the Remission of Sins

Introit. Wisd. 11, 24, 25 and 27.

Misereris omnium.

THOU hast mercy upon all, O Lord, and hatest nothing that thou hast made: and winkest at the sins of men because they should amend, and sparest them: for thou art the Lord our God. (E.T. Alleluia, alleluia.) Ps. 57, 2. Be merciful unto me, O God, be merciful unto me: for my soul trusteth in thee. ℣. Glory.

Collect.

WE beseech thee, O Lord, mercifully to hear the prayers of thy humble servants, and to forgive the sins of them that confess the same unto thee: that they may obtain of thy loving kindness pardon and peace. Through.

The Lesson from the Epistle of blessed Paul the Apostle to the Romans.

Rom. 7, 22-25.

BRETHREN: I delight in the law of God after the inward man: but I see another law in my members, warring against the law of my mind, and bringing me into captivity to the law of sin which is in my members. O wretched man that I am, who shall deliver me from the body of this death? I thank God through Jesus Christ our Lord.

Gradual. Ps. 79, 9-10. Be merciful, O Lord, unto our sins. Wherefore do the heathen say: Where is now their God? ℣. Ibid., 9. Help us, O God of our salvation: and for the glory of thy name, O Lord, deliver us.

Alleluia, alleluia. ℣. Ps. 7, 12. God is a righteous judge, strong and patient: and God is provoked every day. Alleluia.

After Septuagesima, omitting Alleluia and the Verse following, is said:

Tract. Ps. 130, 1-4. Out of the deep have I called unto thee, O Lord: Lord, hear my voice. ℣. O let thine ears consider well the prayer of thy servant. ℣. If thou, Lord, wilt be extreme to mark what is done amiss: O Lord, who may abide it? ℣. For there is mercy with thee: therefore shalt thou be feared, O Lord.

In Eastertide the Gradual is omitted, and in its place is said:

Alleluia, alleluia. ℣. Ps. 7, 12. God is a righteous judge, strong, and patient: and God is provoked every day. Alleluia.

℣. Ps. 51, 10. Thou shalt make me hear of joy and gladness: that the bones which thou hast broken may rejoice. Alleluia.

✠ The Continuation of the holy Gospel according to Luke.

Luke 11, 9-13.

AT that time: Jesus said unto his disciples: Ask, and it shall be given you; seek, and ye shall find; knock, and it shall be opened unto you. For every one that asketh receiveth; and he that seeketh findeth; and to him that knocketh it shall be opened. If a son shall ask bread of any of you that is a father: will he give him a stone, or if he ask a fish: will he for a fish give him a serpent? or if he shall ask an egg: will he offer him a scorpion? If ye then, being evil, know how to give good gifts unto your children: how much more shall your heavenly Father give the Holy Spirit to them that ask him?

Offertory. Ps. 102, 2. Hear my prayer, O Lord: and let my crying come unto thee. (E.T. Alleluia.)

Secret.

WE offer unto thee, O Lord, these sacrifices of propitiation and praise: beseeching thee mercifully to absolve our offences, and to guide the hearts of them that go astray. Through.

Communion. Luke 11, 9-10. Ask, and ye shall receive; seek, and ye shall find; knock, and it shall be opened unto you. For every one that asketh receiveth; and he that seeketh findeth; and to him that knocketh it shall be opened. (E.T. Alleluia.)

Postcommunion.

GRANT unto us, O everlasting Saviour: that we, who have received these thy gifts to the remission of our sins, may hereafter flee from all transgressions. Through.

Mass for Pilgrims and Travellers

Introit. Ps. 26, 11-12. Redime me.

DELIVER me, O Lord, and be merciful unto me: my foot standeth right: I will praise the Lord in the congregations. (E.T. Alleluia, alleluia.) Ps. ibid., 1. Be thou my judge, O Lord, for I have walked innocently: my trust hath been also in the Lord, therefore shall I not fall. ℣. Glory.

Collect.

ASSIST us mercifully, O Lord, in these our supplications and prayers: and dispose the way of thy servants towards the attainment of everlasting salvation; that, among all the changes and chances of this mortal life, they may ever be defended by thy most gracious and ready help. Through.

The Lesson from the book Genesis.

Gen. 28, 10-12, 13-15, 18 and 20-22.

IN those days: Jacob went out from Beer-sheba, and went toward Haran. And he lighted upon a certain place, and tarried there all night, because the sun was set, and he took of the stones of that place, and put them for his pillows, and lay down in that place to sleep. And he dreamed, and, behold the Lord said: I am the Lord God of Abraham thy father, and the God of Isaac: the land whereon thou liest to thee will I give it, and to thy seed. And thy seed shall be as the dust of the earth: and thou shalt spread abroad to the west, and to the east, and to the north, and to the south: and in thee and in thy seed shall all the families of the earth be blessed. And, behold, I am with thee, and will keep thee in all places whither thou goest, and will bring thee again into this land, for I will not leave thee, until I have done that which I have spoken to thee of. And Jacob rose up early in the morning, and took the stone that he had put for his

Votive Mass for Pilgrims and Travellers

pillows, and set it up for a pillar, and poured oil upon the top of it. And Jacob vowed a vow, saying: If God will be with me, and will keep me in this way that I go, and will give me bread to eat, and raiment to put on, so that I come again to my father's house in peace: then shall the Lord be my God, and this stone, which I have set for a pillar, shall be God's house: and of all that thou shalt give me I will surely give the tenth unto thee.

Gradual. Ps. 23, 4. Yea, though I walk through the valley of the shadow of death, I will fear no evil, for thou art with me, O Lord. ℣. Thy rod and thy staff comfort me.

Alleluia, alleluia. ℣. Ps. 119, 133. Order my steps in thy word: and so shall no wickedness have dominion over me. Alleluia.

After Septuagesima, omitting Alleluia and the Verse following, is said:

Tract. Ps. 91, 11-13. God shall give his Angels charge over thee, to keep thee in all thy ways. ℣. They shall bear thee in their hands, that thou hurt not thy foot against a stone. ℣. Thou shalt go upon the lion and adder, the young lion and the dragon shalt thou tread under thy feet.

In Eastertide the Gradual is omitted, and in its place is said:

Alleluia, alleluia. ℣. Ps. 119, 133. Order my steps in thy word: and so shall no wickedness have dominion over me. Alleluia. ℣. Ps. 122, 1. I was glad when they said unto me: We will go into the house of the Lord. Alleluia.

✠ The Continuation of the holy Gospel according to Matthew.

Matt. 10, 7-14.

AT that time: Jesus said unto his disciples: As ye go, preach, saying: The kingdom of heaven is at hand. Heal the sick, cleanse the lepers, raise the dead, cast out devils: freely ye have received, freely give. Provide neither gold, nor silver, nor brass in your purses: nor scrip for your journey, neither two coats, neither shoes, nor yet staves: for the workman is worthy of his meat. And into whatsoever city or town ye shall enter, enquire who in it is worthy: and there abide till ye go thence. And when ye come into an house, salute it. And if the house be worthy, let your peace come upon it: but if it be not worthy, let your peace return to you. And whosoever shall not receive you, nor hear your words: when ye depart out of that house or city, shake off the dust of your feet.

Offertory. Ps. 17, 5-7. O hold thou up my goings in thy paths, that my footsteps slip not: incline thine ear to me, and hearken unto my words: shew thy marvellous loving-kindness, thou that art the Saviour of them which put their trust in thee, O Lord. (E.T. Alleluia.)

Secret.

BE favourable unto our supplications, O Lord, and graciously accept these oblations which we offer unto thee on behalf of thy servants: that in their journey thou wouldest vouchsafe to be their companion and guide; and that thy grace may so prevent and follow them, that by the succour of thy mercy we may rejoice in their effectual deliverance from all perils. Through.

Communion. Ps. 119, 4-5. Thou hast charged that we shall diligently keep thy commandments: O that my ways were made so direct, that I might keep thy statutes. (E.T. Alleluia.)

Postcommunion.

LET this holy Sacrament, O Lord, which we have now received, preserve thy servants who put their trust in thee: and defend them against all the assaults of their enemies. Through.

Mass for the Sick

Introit. Ps. 54, 1-2. Exaudi, Deus.

HEAR my prayer, O God, and hide not thyself from my petition: take heed unto me, and hear me. (E.T. Alleluia, alleluia.) Ps. ibid., 3-4. I mourn in my prayer, and am vexed: the enemy crieth so, and the ungodly cometh on so fast. ℣. Glory.

1. For several sick persons.

Collect.

ALMIGHTY and everlasting God, the eternal salvation of them that believe: graciously hear us, who implore the aid of thy mercy for thy servants in their sickness; that they, being restored to health, may render thanks unto thee in thy Church. Through.

2. For one sick person.

Collect.

ALMIGHTY and everlasting God, the eternal salvation of them that believe: graciously hear us who implore the aid of thy mercy for thy servant in his (her) sickness; that he (she), being restored to health, may render thanks unto thee in thy Church. Through.

3. For a sick person, who is near to death, is said the following:

Collect.

ALMIGHTY and merciful God, who hast bestowed upon mankind the healing grace of salvation and the rewards of eternal life: look mercifully upon thy servant (handmaid), lying under thy hand in great weakness of body, and comfort again the soul which thou hast created; that in the hour of his (her) departure he (she) may be found worthy to be presented without spot by the hands of the holy Angels unto thee, his (her) Creator. Through.

The Lesson from the Epistle of blessed James the Apostle.

James 5, 14-16.

DEARLY beloved: Is any among you afflicted? let him pray. Is any merry? let him sing psalms. Is any sick among you? let him call for the elders of the Church, and let them pray over him, anointing him with oil in the name of the Lord: and the prayer of faith shall save the sick, and the Lord shall raise him up: and if he have committed sins, they shall be forgiven him. Confess your faults one to another, and pray one for another, that ye may be healed.

Gradual. Ps. 6, 3-4. Have mercy upon me, O Lord, for I am weak: O Lord, heal me. ℣. All my bones are vexed: my soul also is sore troubled.

Alleluia, alleluia. ℣. Ps. 102, 1. Hear my prayer, O Lord: and let my crying come unto thee. Alleluia.

After Septuagesima, omitting Alleluia and the Verse following, is said:

Tract. Ps. 31, 10-11. Have mercy upon me, O Lord, for I am in trouble: and mine eye is consumed for very heaviness, yea, my soul and my body. ℣. For my life is waxen old with heaviness, and my years with mourning. ℣. My strength faileth me, because of mine iniquity: and my bones are consumed.

In Eastertide the Gradual is omitted, and in its place is said:

Alleluia, alleluia. ℣. Ps. 102, 1. Hear my prayer, O Lord: and let my crying come unto thee. Alleluia. ℣. Ps. 28, 7. My heart hath trusted in God, and I am helped: therefore my heart danceth for joy, and in my song will I praise him. Alleluia.

Votive Mass for the Sick

✠ The Continuation of the holy Gospel according to Matthew.

Matt. 8, 5-13.

AT that time: When Jesus was entered into Capernaum, there came unto him a centurion, beseeching him, and saying: Lord, my servant lieth at home sick of the palsy, grievously tormented. And Jesus saith unto him: I will come and heal him. The centurion answered and said: Lord, I am not worthy that thou shouldest come under my roof: but speak the word only, and my servant shall be healed. For I am a man under authority, having soldiers under me, and I say to this man: Go, and he goeth; and to another: Come, and he cometh; and to my servant: Do this, and he doeth it. When Jesus heard it, he marvelled, and said to them that followed: Verily I say unto you, I have not found so great faith, no, not in Israel. And I say unto you, that many shall come from the east and west, and shall sit down with Abraham, and Isaac, and Jacob, in the kingdom of heaven: but the children of the kingdom shall be cast out into outer darkness: there shall be weeping and gnashing of teeth. And Jesus said unto the centurion: Go thy way, and as thou hast believed, so be it done unto thee. And his servant was healed in the self-same hour.

Offertory. Ps. 55, 1-2. Hear my prayer, O God, and hide not thyself from my petition: take heed unto me, and hear me. (E.T. Alleluia.)

1. For several sick persons.

Secret.

O GOD, by whose ordinance the moments of our lives are numbered: receive the prayers and oblations of thy servants, for whom in their sickness we implore thy mercy; that we, who are now afraid by reason of their peril, may yet rejoice in their deliverance. Through.

2. For one sick person.

Secret.

O GOD, by whose ordinance the moments of our lives are numbered: receive the prayers and oblations of thy servant, for whom in his (her) sickness we implore thy mercy: that we, who are now afraid by reason of his (her) peril, may yet rejoice in his (her) deliverance. Through.

3. For a sick person, who is near to death, is said the following:

Secret.

ACCEPT, O Lord, we pray thee, the sacrifice which we offer for thy servant (handmaid) in this hour of his (her) dissolution: and grant, that all his (her) sins being thereby purged and done away; he (she), who in this life is chastened by the visitation of thy wrath, may in the life to come obtain eternal rest. Through.

Communion. Ps. 31, 17-18. Shew thy servant the light of thy countenance, and save me for thy mercy's sake: let me not be confounded, O Lord, for I have called upon thee. (E.T. Alleluia.)

1. For several sick persons.

Postcommunion.

O GOD, who art the only assistance of our mortal frailty: shew forth, we pray thee, upon thy servants in their sickness the might of thy succour; that they, being delivered by the help of thy mercy, may be found worthy to be restored in safety to thy holy Church. Through.

2. For one sick person.

Postcommunion.

O GOD, who art the only assistance of our mortal frailty: shew forth, we pray thee, upon thy servant in his (her) sickness the might of thy succour; that he (she), being delivered by the help of thy mercy, may be found worthy to be restored in safety to thy holy Church. Through.

3. For a sick person, who is near to death, is said the following:

Postcommunion.

ALMIGHTY God, we beseech thy mercy, that by the power of this sacrament thou wouldest vouchsafe to strengthen thy servant (handmaid) in thy grace: that in the hour of his (her) death the adversary may not prevail against him (her); but that with thy Angels he (she) may be found worthy to enter into life. Through.

Another Collect, Epistle and Gospel:

Collect.

ALMIGHTY, everliving God, Maker of mankind, who dost correct those whom thou dost love, and chastise every one whom thou dost receive: we beseech thee to have mercy upon this thy servant visited with thine hand, and to grant that he (she) may take his (her) sickness patiently, and recover his (her) bodily health (if it be thy gracious will;) and whensoever his (her) soul shall depart from the body, it may be without spot presented unto thee. Through.

The Lesson from the Epistle of blessed Paul the Apostle to the Hebrews.

Heb. 12, 5-6.

MY son: Despise not thou the chastening of the Lord, nor faint when thou art rebuked of him. For whom the Lord loveth he chasteneth; and scourgeth every son whom he receiveth.

☩ The Continuation of the holy Gospel according to John.

John 5. 24.

AT that time: Jesus said unto his disciples: Verily, verily I say unto you, he that heareth my word, and believeth on him that sent me, hath everlasting life, and shall not come into condemnation; but is passed from death unto life.

Mass to ask the Grace of a Good Death

Introit. Ps. 13, 4. Illumina oculos.

LIGHTEN mine eyes that I sleep not in death, lest mine enemy say: I have prevailed against him. (E.T. Alleluia, alleluia.) Ps. ibid., 1. How long wilt thou forget me, O Lord, for ever? How long wilt thou hide thy face from me? ℣. Glory.

Collect.

ALMIGHTY and merciful God, who hast bestowed upon mankind both means for the attainment of salvation, and also the rewards of eternal life: look down in mercy on us thy servants, and comfort again the souls which thou hast created; that in the hour of their departure they may be found worthy to be presented by the hands of thy holy Angels pure and without spot unto thee their Creator. Through.

The Lesson from the Epistle of blessed Paul the Apostle to the Romans.

Rom. 14, 7-12.

BRETHREN: None of us liveth to himself, and no man dieth to himself. For whether we live, we live unto the Lord: and whether we die, we die unto the Lord. Whether we live therefore or die, we are the Lord's. For to this end Christ both died, and rose, and revived: that he might be Lord both of the dead and living. But why dost thou judge thy brother? or why dost thou set at nought thy brother? for we shall all stand before the judgment seat of Christ. For it is written: As I live saith the Lord, every knee shall bow to me: and every tongue shall confess to God. So then every one of us shall give account of himself to God.

Gradual. Ps. 23, 4. Though I walk through the valley of the shadow of death, I will fear no evil: for thou art with me, O Lord. ℣. Thy rod and thy staff comfort me.

Alleluia, alleluia. ℣. Ps. 31, 1-2. In thee, O Lord, have I put my trust, let me never be put to confusion: save me and deliver me in thy righteousness: bow down thine ear to me, make haste to deliver me. Alleluia.

After Septuagesima, omitting Alleluia and the Verse following, is said:

Tract. Ps. 25, 17-18 and 1-4. O Lord, bring thou me out of my troubles: look upon my adversity and misery: and forgive me all my sin. ℣. Unto thee, O Lord, will I lift up my soul: my God, I have put my trust in thee: O let me not be confounded: neither let mine enemies triumph over me. ℣. For all they that hope in thee shall not be ashamed: but such as transgress without a cause shall be put to confusion.

In Eastertide the Gradual is omitted, and in its place is said:

Alleluia, alleluia. ℣. Ps. 114, 1. When Israel came out of Egypt, and the house of Jacob from among the strange people. Alleluia. ℣. Ps. 108, 1. O God, my heart is ready, my heart is ready: I will sing and give praise unto thee, my glory. Alleluia.

✠ The Continuation of the holy Gospel according to Luke.

Luke 21, 34-36.

AT that time: Jesus said unto his disciples: Take heed to yourselves, lest at any time your hearts be overcharged with surfeiting, and drunkenness, and cares of this life: and so that day come upon you unawares: for as a snare shall it come on all them that dwell on the face of the whole earth. Watch ye therefore, and pray always, that ye may be accounted worthy to escape all these things that shall come to pass, and to stand before the Son of man.

Offertory. Ps. 31, 15-16. My hope hath been in thee, O Lord; I have said: Thou art my God, my time is in thy hand. (E.T. Alleluia.)

Secret.

ACCEPT, O Lord, we pray thee, the sacrifice which we offer for the hour of our dissolution, and grant: that all our sins being thereby purged and done away; we, who in this life are chastened by the visitation of thy wrath, may in the life to come obtain eternal rest. Through.

Communion. Ps. 71, 16-18. O Lord, I will make mention of thy righteousness only: thou O God, hast taught me from my youth up until now: forsake me not, O God, in mine old age, when I am grayheaded. (E.T. Alleluia.)

Postcommunion.

ALMIGHTY God, we beseech thy mercy, that by the power of this sacrament thou wouldest vouchsafe to strengthen us thy servants in thy grace: that in the hour of our death the adversary may not prevail against us; but with thy Angels we may be found worthy to enter into life. Through.

Mass for any Necessity

Introit. Salus populi.

I AM the salvation of my people, saith the Lord: out of whatsoever tribulation they shall cry unto me, I will hear them: and I will be their Lord for ever. (E.T. Alleluia, alleluia.) Ps. 78, 1. Hear my law, O my people: incline your ears unto the words of my mouth. ℣. Glory.

Collect.

GRACIOUSLY shew forth upon us, O Lord, thy unspeakable mercy: that we, being set free from all our sins; may likewise be delivered from the punishment which for the same we deserve. Through.

The Lesson from the Prophet Jeremiah.

Jer. 14, 7-9.

O LORD, though our iniquities testify against us: do thou it for thy name's sake, for our backslidings are many: we have sinned against thee. O the hope of Israel, the Saviour thereof in time of trouble. Yet thou, O Lord, art in the midst of us, and we are called by thy name, leave us not, O Lord our God.

Gradual. Ps. 44, 8-9. It is thou, O Lord, that savest us from our enemies: and puttest them to confusion that hate us. ℣. We make our boast of God all day long: and will praise thy name for ever.

Alleluia, alleluia. ℣. Ps. 79, 9-10. Be merciful, O Lord, unto our sins: wherefore do the heathen say: Where is now their God? Alleluia.

After Septuagesima, omitting Alleluia and the Verse following, is said:

Tract. Ps. 25, 17-18 and 1-4. O Lord, bring thou me out of my troubles: look upon my adversity and misery: and forgive me all my sin. ℣. Unto thee, O Lord, will I lift up my soul: my God, I have put my trust in thee, O let me not be confounded: neither let mine enemies triumph over me. ℣. For all they that hope in thee shall not be ashamed: but such as transgress without a cause shall be put to confusion.

In Eastertide the Gradual is omitted, and in its place is said:

Alleluia, alleluia. ℣. Ps. 79, 9-10. Be merciful, O Lord, unto our sins: wherefore do the heathen say: Where is now their God? Alleluia. ℣. Ps. 31, 8. I will be glad, and rejoice in thy mercy, for thou hast considered my trouble: and hast known my soul in adversities. Alleluia.

✠ The Continuation of the holy Gospel according to Mark.

Mark 11, 22-26.

AT that time: Jesus said unto his disciples: Have faith in God. For verily I say unto you, that whosoever shall say unto this mountain: Be thou removed, and be thou cast into the sea, and shall not doubt in his heart, but shall believe that those things which he saith shall come to pass, he shall have whatsoever he saith. Therefore I say unto you: What things soever ye desire, when ye pray, believe that ye receive them, and ye shall have them. And when ye stand praying, forgive, if ye have ought against any: that your Father also which is in heaven may forgive you your trespasses. But if ye do not forgive: neither will your Father which is in heaven forgive your trespasses.

Offertory. Ps. 138, 7 Though I walk in the midst of trouble, yet shalt thou refresh me, O Lord: thou shalt stretch forth thy hand upon the furiousness of mine enemies, and thy right hand shall save me. (E.T. Alleluia.)

Secret.

WE beseech thee, O Lord, that the gift which we here offer may cleanse our hearts: and make us worthy to be partakers of this holy Communion. Through.

Communion. Ps. 119, 49-50. Think upon thy servant, O Lord, as concerning thy word, wherein thou hast caused me to put my trust: the same is my comfort in my trouble. (E.T. Alleluia.)

Postcommunion.

GRANT, we beseech thee, O Lord: that we, who have tasted of these holy mysteries, being cleansed thereby from all earthly affections, may be brought unto the fulfilment of this heavenly Sacrament. Through.

Mass for giving of Thanks

¶ The Mass of the Most Holy Trinity, or of the Holy Spirit, or of the blessed Virgin Mary, or of any canonized Saint in the Martyrology, is said, with the addition of the following Prayers, under one conclusion, even in private Masses.

Collect.

O GOD, of whose mercies there is no number, and of whose goodness the treasure is infinite: we render thanks to thy most gracious majesty for the gifts thou hast bestowed upon us, alway beseeching thy mercy; that as thou grantest the petitions of them that ask thee, thou wilt never forsake them, but wilt prepare them for rewards that are to come. Through.

Secret.

O LORD, who hast vouchsafed to hear the prayers of thy servants, and hast preserved them from all perils, accept the savour of this sacrifice of thanksgiving, and grant: that they being defended hereafter against all adversities; may devoutly serve thee more and more, and continually increase in thy love. Through.

Postcommunion.

O GOD, who sufferest none that putteth his trust in thee to be afflicted above that he is able to bear, but dost ever incline thyself in mercy to our prayers: we give thee thanks for that thou hast vouchsafed to receive our vows and supplications, most humbly beseeching thee; that by the gifts whereof we have partaken we may be made worthy to be delivered from all adversities. Through.

The Lesson from the Epistle of blessed Paul the Apostle to the Hebrews.

Heb. 5, 1-4.

BRETHREN: Every high priest taken from among men is ordained for men in things pertaining to God, that he may offer both gifts and sacrifices for sins; who can have compassion on the ignorant, and on them that are out of the way: for that he himself also is compassed with infirmity: and by reason hereof he ought, as for the people, so also for himself, to offer for sins. And no man taketh this honour unto himself, but he that is called of God, as was Aaron.

✠ The Continuation of the holy Gospel according to Mark.

Mark 13, 33-37.

AT that time: Jesus said unto his disciples: Take ye heed, watch and pray: for ye know not when the time is. It is as when a man, taking a far journey, left his house and gave authority to his servants, and to every man his work, and commanded the porter to watch. Watch ye therefore (for ye know not when the master of the house cometh: at even or at midnight, or at the cock-crowing, or in the morning) lest coming suddenly he find you sleeping. And what I say unto you, I say unto all: Watch.

VARIOUS PRAYERS
TO BE SAID AT CHOICE ACCORDING TO THE RUBRICS

1. To ask the Prayers of the Saints

Collect.

GRANT, we beseech thee, almighty God: that the intercession of holy Mary, Mother of God, and of all the holy Apostles, Martyrs, Confessors and Virgins, and of all thy elect, may everywhere cause us to rejoice; that while we call to mind their merits, we may perceive their advocacy. Through the same.

Secret.

ACCEPT, O Lord, the gifts we offer: and, at the intercession of blessed Mary ever Virgin with all thy Saints, defend us from all perils. Through.

Postcommunion.

GRANT, we beseech thee, O Lord, that we, who have received these heavenly sacraments in veneration of the memory of blessed Mary ever Virgin and of all thy Saints; may attain in everlasting joys the fulfilment of our service in this life. Through.

2. Another for the Same

Collect.

DEFEND us, O Lord, we beseech thee, from all dangers of body and soul: and at the intercession of the blessed and glorious ever Virgin Mary, Mother of God, of blessed Joseph, of thy blessed Apostles Peter and Paul, of blessed N., and of all the Saints, grant us thy saving health and peace; that, all adversities and errors being done away, thy Church may serve thee in freedom and quietness. Through the same.

¶ In this Collect and its Postcommunion, where the letter N. occurs, the Titular Saint of the Church is mentioned, provided the title be not that of a Divine Person or of a mystery of our Lord, or that the Mass is not being said of the title itself, or a commemoration of it is not being made, or it is not already mentioned in the Collect; and the names of the Holy Angels and of St. John Baptist are placed before that of St. Joseph. In all these cases the words blessed N. are omitted. If the Mass or the Commemoration be of St. Joseph or of the Holy Apostles Peter and Paul, in the Collect and Postcommunion the words which refer to them are omitted.

¶ If the Mass or Commemoration be of Saint Mary, the words referring to her are omitted here.

Secret.

GRACIOUSLY hear us, O God of our salvation: and by the power of this Sacrament defend us from all enemies of body and soul; granting us grace in this world, and glory in that which is to come. Through.

Postcommunion.

LET the gifts, O Lord, which we have now offered in these holy mysteries, evermore cleanse and defend us: that at the intercession of the blessed Virgin Mary, Mother of God, of blessed Joseph, of thy blessed Apostles Peter and Paul, of blessed N. and of all the Saints; we may thereby be set free from all our iniquities, and delivered from all adversities. Through the same.

3. For all Estates of Men in the Church
Collect.

ALMIGHTY and everlasting God, by whose Spirit the whole body of the Church is governed and sanctified: receive our supplications and prayers, which we offer before thee for all estates of men in thy holy Church; that every member of the same in his vocation and ministry may truly and godly serve thee. Through ... in the unity of the same Holy Spirit.

Secret.

GRANT unto thy servants, O Lord, the pardon of their sins, comfort in their life, and thy continual governance: so that they, serving thee aright, may continually obtain thy mercy. Through.

Postcommunion.

DELIVER, O Lord, we beseech thee, thy servants who call upon thee from all sin, and from every foe: that they, walking in godly conversation, may be hurt by no adversity. Through.

4. For the Pope
Collect.

O GOD, the pastor and ruler of all the faithful, look down in mercy on thy servant N., whom thou hast chosen to be pastor and ruler of thy Church: grant him, we beseech thee, to be in word and conversation a wholesome example to the people committed to his charge; that he with them may attain everlasting life. Through.

Secret.

LOOK favourably, we beseech thee, O Lord, upon the gifts which we offer: and guide with thy continual protection thy servant N., whom thou hast chosen to be pastor and ruler of thy Church. Through.

Postcommunion.

DEFEND us, O Lord, we beseech thee, who have here received these heavenly mysteries: and grant that thy servant N., whom thou hast chosen to be pastor and ruler of thy Church, together with the flock committed to his charge, may thereby be strengthened and preserved against all adversities. Through.

5. For the Emperor
Collect.

O GOD, the protector of all kingdoms, and specially of the Christian empire: grant unto thy servant, our emperor N., to labour with wisdom for the triumph of virtue, that he who by thy institution is a prince, may ever by thy gift be powerful. Through.

If he is not crowned, say Emperor-elect.

Secret.

RECEIVE, O Lord, the prayers and offerings of thy Church, that calleth upon thee for the safety of thy servant: and for the protection of the faithful peoples perform with thy mighty arm thy wondrous works of old, that they may overcome the enemies of peace, and serve thee in freedom and safety. Through.

Postcommunion.

O GOD, who didst prepare the Roman empire for the preaching of the Gospel of the eternal King: defend thy servant, our emperor N., with thy heavenly armour, that the peace of the churches may be troubled by no war nor tumult. Through.

6. For the King

Collect.

ALMIGHTY God, we pray for thy servant N. our King, now by thy mercy reigning over us: adorn him yet more with every virtue, remove all evil from his path; that he may come at last in grace to thee, who art the way, the truth, and the life. Through.

Secret.

SANCTIFY, we beseech thee, O Lord, the gifts which we offer: that they may be made unto us the Body and Blood of thine only-begotten Son; and of thy great goodness grant that they may at all times be profitable unto our King, both for the obtaining of health of body and soul, and for the fulfilling of the charge committed unto him. Through.

Postcommunion.

LET this saving oblation, O Lord, keep thy servant, N., our King, from all adversity: that he may preserve peace and tranquillity for thy Church; and after the course of this life may attain unto his eternal inheritance. Through.

7. For Prelates and Congregations committed to their charge

Collect.

ALMIGHTY and everlasting God, who alone workest great marvels: send down upon our Bishops, and all Congregations committed to their charge, the healthful spirit of thy grace; and, that they may truly please thee, pour upon them the continual dew of thy blessing. Through.

Secret.

LOOK down, O Lord, in mercy on the sacrifices of thy servants, which we devoutly celebrate for them unto the honour of thy name: that they may perceive the same to be profitable for the healing of their souls. Through.

Postcommunion.

ASSIST, O Lord, with thy continual protection those whom thou dost refresh with this heavenly gift: and grant that, as thou never failest to comfort them, so thou wouldest make them worthy of everlasting redemption. Through.

8. For the Congregation and Family

Collect.

WE beseech thee, O Lord, at the intercession of blessed Mary ever Virgin, to defend this thy family from all adversities: that they, devoutly serving thee with all their hearts, may by thy mercy be protected from the assaults of their enemies. Through.

Secret.

ALMIGHTY God, we beseech thee to accept this our bounden service: that by the power of this Sacrament we thy servants may be protected against all adversities. Through.

Postcommunion.

GRANT, we beseech thee, O merciful God: that we who have here received the gifts of our redemption; may through the celebration of the same obtain the help of thy defence against all adversities. Through.

Various Prayers [93]

9. For the Preservation of Concord in the Congregation
Collect.

O GOD, who art the author of peace and lover of charity: grant unto thy servants that true unity which is according to thy will; that we may be delivered from all the temptations which beset us. Through.

Secret.

WE beseech thee, O Lord, mercifully to accept these sacrifices: and grant that we, who pray to be absolved from our own offences, be not burdened with the sins of other men. Through.

Postcommunion.

POUR forth upon us, O Lord, the Spirit of thy charity: that as thou hast fulfilled us with one heavenly bread, so of thy goodness thou wouldest make us to be of one heart and mind. Through ... in the unity of the same Holy Spirit.

10. Against the Persecutors of the Church
Collect

WE beseech thee, O Lord, mercifully to hear the prayers of thy Church: that all adversities and errors being done away, it may serve thee in freedom and quietness. Through.

Secret.

DEFEND us, O Lord, who wait upon thy mysteries: that we cleaving fast to things heavenly may serve thee both in body and soul. Through.

Postcommunion.

WE beseech thee, O Lord our God: that we, whom thou makest to rejoice in the partaking of heavenly things, may by thee be defended against all earthly perils. Through.

11. Against Persecutors and Malefactors
Collect.

WE beseech thee, O Lord, to bring down the pride of our enemies: and by the right hand of thy power destroy their obstinacy. Through.

Secret.

GRANT, O Lord, that by the power of this mystery we may be cleansed from our secret faults, and delivered from the snares of our enemies. Through.

Postcommunion.

BEHOLD, O God our defender, and protect us against the dangers of our enemies: that we may be delivered from all distress, and serve thee in freedom of spirit. Through.

12. For any Necessity
Collect.

O GOD, our refuge and strength, who art the author of all godliness: be ready, we beseech thee, to hear the devout prayers of thy Church; and grant that those things which we ask faithfully we may obtain effectually. Through.

Secret.

GRANT, O merciful God: that this saving oblation may continually deliver us from our sins, and shield us from all adversities. Through.

Postcommunion.

O LORD, who hast bestowed on us the gifts of this sacred mystery, we humbly beseech thee: that those things which thou hast commanded us to do in remembrance of thee may be profitable for the succour of our infirmity: Who livest and reignest with God the Father.

13. In any Calamity
Collect.

ALMIGHTY God, despise not thy people who cry to thee in their affliction: but for the glory of thy name mercifully assist them in their tribulation. Through.

Secret.

MERCIFULLY accept, O Lord, these sacrifices, which thou hast ordained to be the propitiation of our sins, and the means whereby of thy loving mercy we are restored to salvation. Through.

Postcommunion.

WE beseech thee, O Lord, mercifully look upon our tribulation: and turn from us the fury of thine anger, which we most righteously deserve. Through.

14. In time of Famine
Collect.

GRANT to us, we beseech thee, O Lord, the fulfilment of our devout supplications, and graciously turn away this famine; that the hearts of men may know that in thine anger thou sendest forth thy scourges, and in thy mercy makest them to cease. Through.

Secret.

O GOD, who dost sustain the twofold nature of man by the food of the gifts we offer, and by this Sacrament dost renew the same: grant, we beseech thee; that these thy gifts may never be lacking for our assistance both in body and soul. Through.

Postcommunion.

O LORD, support us, we beseech thee, with temporal food: even as thou dost vouchsafe to dwell in us in everlasting mysteries. Through.

15. In time of Earthquake
Collect

ALMIGHTY and everlasting God, who lookest upon the earth, and makest it to tremble: spare them that fear thee, be merciful to them that call upon thee: that whereas we are sore afraid for thy wrath that shaketh the foundations of the earth, we may likewise feel thy mercy when thou healest the sores thereof. Through.

Secret.

O GOD, who hast laid the foundations of the earth that they should never be moved, receive the prayers and oblations of thy people: put far from us the present perils of earthquake, and turn the terrors of thy divine anger into a wholesome medicine for the safety of mankind; that they who are of the earth, and shall return to earth, may rejoice to be made citizens of heaven by holy conversation. Through.

Postcommunion.

PROTECT us, O Lord, we beseech thee, who receive thy holy gifts: and by thy heavenly bounty stablish the earth which we see trembling for our sins; that the hearts of men may know that in thine anger thou sendest forth thy scourges, and in thy mercy makest them to cease. Through.

16. For Rain
Collect.

O GOD, in whom we live and move, and have our being: grant us such a seasonable rain; that we, receiving those things that be requisite for our necessities in this life, may the more confidently seek the things that are eternal. Through.

Secret.

WE beseech thee, O Lord, mercifully to receive the gifts which we offer: and send unto us a seasonable rain that may suffice for our necessities. Through.

Postcommunion.

GRANT us, O Lord, we beseech thee, a refreshing rain: and graciously water the parched face of the earth by showers from heaven. Through.

17. For Fine Weather
Collect.

GRACIOUSLY hear us, O Lord, who call upon thee: and grant fair weather in answer to our prayers; that we, who are justly afflicted for our sins, may by thy preventing mercy feel thy pity. Through.

Secret.

LORD, we pray thee, that thy grace may alway prevent and follow us: and graciously accept these oblations which for our sins we bring for consecration unto thy name; that, through the intercession of thy Saints, they may be profitable for the safety of us all. Through.

Postcommunion.

ALMIGHTY God, we humbly beseech thy mercy: that thou wouldest assuage this plague of immoderate rains, and vouchsafe to shew forth on us the gladness of thy countenance. Through.

18. Against Storms
Collect.

WE beseech thee, O Lord, that all spiritual wickedness may be driven far from thy house: and that the malignity of the tempests of the air be likewise dispelled. Through.

Secret.

WE offer unto thee, O Lord, our praises and gifts, rendering thanks for the blessings bestowed upon us, and ever humbly praying for the continuance of the same. Through.

Postcommunion.

ALMIGHTY and everlasting God, who dost heal us by thy chastisement, and preserve us by thy pardon: grant unto thy suppliant people; that in tranquillity of weather we may rejoice in the comfort we have ever desired, and may alway make use of thy bountiful goodness. Through.

19. Against Cattle Disease
Collect

O GOD, who even by the dumb beasts hast brought comfort to man's labour: we humbly beseech thee; that forasmuch as without them the sustenance of man cannot but fail, so thou wouldest preserve them for our enjoyment. Through.

Secret.

LOOK mercifully, O Lord, upon the sacrifices which we offer: and of thy mercy grant us thy help in our time. Through.

Postcommunion.

GRANT, O Lord, that thy faithful people, being filled with thy blessing, may be preserved both in body and soul: that they may render unto thee worthy service, and evermore receive the benefits of thy mercy. Through.

Various Prayers

20. For the Priest Himself
Collect.

ALMIGHTY and merciful God, graciously hearken unto my humble prayers: and make me thy servant, to whom for no merits of my own but by the boundless compassion of thy bounty thou hast vouchsafed to serve thee in these heavenly mysteries, a worthy minister at thy sacred altars; that the words which I utter with my lips may by thy sanctifying power be brought to good effect. Through.

Secret.

CLEANSE me, O Lord, by the power of this Sacrament, from all the stains of my sins: and grant; that with the help of thy grace I may be made worthy thereby to fulfil the ministry committed to my charge. Through.

Postcommunion.

ALMIGHTY and everlasting God, who hast vouchsafed to me, a sinner, to stand before thy sacred altars, and to praise the power of thy holy name: mercifully grant to me through the mystery of this Sacrament the pardon of my sins; that I may offer unto thy majesty true and worthy service. Through.

21. To ask for Tears
Collect.

ALMIGHTY and most merciful God, who didst bring forth living water from the rock for thy thirsting people: draw out from our stony hearts the tears of repentance; that we, worthily lamenting our sins, may of thy mercy obtain forgiveness of the same. Through.

Secret.

O LORD God, we beseech thee, look down in mercy on this oblation, which we offer to thy majesty for our sins: and draw forth from our eyes such streams of tears, as shall quench the burning flames which we most righteously deserve. Through.

Postcommunion.

O LORD God, mercifully pour the grace of thy Holy Spirit into our heart: that we may be enabled thereby with tears of sorrow to wash away the defilements of our sins; that like as we do desire thy merciful pardon, so of thy bountiful goodness we may effectually receive the same. Through ... in the unity of the same Holy Spirit.

22. For the Remission of Sins
Collect.

O GOD, who dost not cast out sinners, and of thy loving mercy sparest them that are penitent, howsoever they sin against thee: mercifully incline to the prayers of thy humble servants, and enlighten our hearts; that we may be enabled to fulfil all that thou dost command. Through.

Secret.

LET this present sacrifice, O Lord, which we offer to thee for our offences, be made a gift acceptable in thy sight: and avail for salvation both to the living and the dead. Through.

Postcommunion.

ALMIGHTY God, graciously hear the prayers of this thy family: and grant; that, like as we have received these holy mysteries from thee, so of thy bounty they may be preserved pure and undefiled within us. Through.

23. For Public Penitents

Collect.

ALMIGHTY and everlasting God, of thy great goodness forgive the sins of thy servants who confess the same to thee: that they whose consciences by sin are accused may not be delivered unto punishment, but may obtain of thy loving mercy pardon and forgiveness. Through.

Secret.

GRANT, we beseech thee, almighty and merciful God: that this saving oblation may continually deliver thy servants from their offences, and defend them against all adversities. Through.

Postcommunion.

ALMIGHTY and merciful God, who wouldest not the death of sinners, but rather that they should repent, and confess to thee, and amend their lives: look down upon these thy servants; and through these holy sacraments which we have received turn from them thy wrathful indignation, and grant them forgiveness of all their sins. Through.

24. For the Tempted and Troubled

Collect.

O GOD, who dost justify the wicked, and wouldest not the death of a sinner, we humbly beseech thy majesty: that thy servants who put their trust and confidence in thy mercy may be defended by the loving-kindness of thy heavenly succour, and preserved by thy continual help; that in all temptations they may steadfastly cleave unto thy service. Through.

Secret.

WE beseech thee, O Lord, that by the power of this mystery thou wouldest cleanse us from our faults and absolve thy servants from all their offences. Through.

Postcommunion.

GRANT, we beseech thee, O Lord, that the sacraments which we have received may purify our hearts: and that thy servants may be delivered from all transgression; that whereas their consciences are bound by reason of their guilt, they may receive with gladness the plenteous healing of thy heavenly power. Through.

25. To Repel Evil Thoughts

Collect.

ALMIGHTY and most merciful God, graciously regard our prayers: and deliver our hearts from the temptations of evil thoughts; that we may be found worthy to be made a dwelling-place acceptable to thy Holy Spirit. Through ... in the unity of the same Holy Spirit.

Secret.

WE here present unto thee, O Lord, these offerings for our salvation: that the thoughts of our hearts being purged from all uncleanness and preserved from harm, we may be enlightened by the grace of thy Holy Spirit. Through ... in the unity of the same Holy Spirit.

Postcommunion.

O GOD, who lightenest every man that cometh into this world: lighten, we beseech thee, our hearts with the brightness of thy grace; that we may ever be enabled to think such things as be good and pleasing to thy majesty, and that we may love thee with an unfeigned heart. Through.

26. To obtain the Grace of Continence
Collect.

KINDLE, O Lord, with the fire of the Holy Spirit our reins and our hearts: that we, serving thee in pureness both of body and soul, may be found pleasing in thy sight. Through ... in the unity of the same Holy Spirit.

Secret.

SMITE asunder, O Lord, the chains of our sins: that we who seek to offer unto thee the sacrifice of praise in perfect freedom and in innocency of heart, may be restored by thee unto our first estate; that like as thou hast saved us by thy grace, so by thy pardon thou wouldest restore us again unto salvation. Through.

Postcommunion.

ASSIST us, O Lord, our helper and defender: that our heart and flesh being renewed by the strength of continence and the newness of chastity, we who have offered unto thy majesty this sacrifice may be cleansed thereby from all temptations. Through.

27. To obtain the Grace of Humility
Collect.

O GOD, who resistest the proud, and givest grace unto the humble: grant to us the virtue of true humility, after the pattern wherewith thine only-begotten Son manifested himself unto thy faithful people; that we may in no wise exalt ourselves to provoke thine anger, but may in lowliness of heart obtain thy grace. Through the same.

Secret.

WE beseech thee, O Lord, that this oblation may obtain for us the grace of true humility: and likewise take from our hearts the lust of the flesh, the lust of the eyes, and the pride of life; that living soberly, righteously and godly, we may attain unto the rewards of everlasting life. Through.

Postcommunion.

O LORD, let this Sacrament which we have received, cleanse us from every stain of sin: that we, shewing forth humility, may be brought thereby unto thy heavenly kingdom. Through.

28. To obtain the Grace of Patience
Collect.

O GOD, who by the long-suffering of thine only begotten Son didst tread down the pride of our ancient enemy: grant us, we beseech thee, so rightly to call to mind the sufferings which of his goodness he bare for our sakes; that after his example we may patiently endure all our troubles and adversities. Through the same.

Secret.

WE beseech thee, O Lord, graciously to receive our gifts and oblations: which we devoutly offer to thy majesty, beseeching thee that thou wouldest vouchsafe to bestow upon us the gift of patience. Through.

Postcommunion.

WE beseech thee, O Lord, that we who have received these sacred mysteries may be restored thereby unto the grace from which we have fallen: that by thy continual protection both here and ever we may be enabled to endure patiently in all adversities. Through.

29. To obtain the Grace of Charity
Collect.

O GOD, who makest all things work together for good to them that love thee: pour into our hearts the steadfast affection of thy charity; that as thou dost put into our minds good desires, so we may not be turned from the same by any temptations. Through.

Secret.

O GOD, who by thy sacraments and commandments dost renew us after thy likeness: stablish our goings in thy paths; that like as thou hast vouchsafed unto us the hope of obtaining thy gift of charity, so by these sacrifices which we offer thou wouldest make us effectually to be partakers of the same. Through.

Postcommunion.

WE beseech thee, O Lord, that the grace of the Holy Spirit may enlighten our hearts: that they may be abundantly renewed in the sweetness of perfect charity. Through... in the unity of the same Holy Spirit.

30. For Devoted Friends
Collect.

O GOD, who by the grace of thy Holy Spirit hast endued the hearts of thy faithful people with the gift of charity: grant to thy servants and handmaids, for whom we implore thy mercy, safety of body and soul; that they may love thee with all their strength, and with pure affection perform such things as are acceptable unto thee. Through... in the unity of the same Holy Spirit.

Secret.

WE beseech thee, O Lord, to have compassion upon thy servants and handmaids, for whom we offer unto thy majesty this sacrifice of praise: that through these holy gifts they may obtain the grace of thy heavenly benediction, and attain unto the glory of everlasting felicity. Through.

Postcommunion.

O LORD, who dost make us to taste of these heavenly mysteries, we humbly beseech thee: that like as we have offered these sacraments of salvation for the advancement in charity of thy servants and handmaids; so they may be profitable unto them for their prosperity and peace. Through.

31. For Enemies
Collect.

O GOD, who art the lover of peace, and preserver of charity: grant unto all our enemies true peace and charity; and vouchsafe unto them remission of all their sins, and by thy mighty power deliver us from their snares. Through.

Secret.

WE beseech thee, O Lord, graciously to accept the gifts which we offer: that by thy mercy we may be delivered from our enemies, and that they may receive of thee the pardon of their offences. Through.

Postcommunion.

O LORD, let this holy Communion, deliver us from our offences: and defend us against the snares of our enemies. Through.

32. For a Prisoner or Captive
Collect.

O GOD, who didst deliver blessed Peter the Apostle from his chains, and suffer him to depart unhurt: loose the chains of thy servant who now lieth in captivity; and by the merits of the same thine Apostle suffer him to depart unhurt. Through.

Secret.

LET thy plenteous benediction, O Lord, descend upon these sacrifices: that they may loose the chains of this thy servant in captivity, and make us speedily to rejoice in his deliverance. Through.

Postcommunion.

O LORD, we beseech thee, graciously hear our prayers: and by these sacraments which we have received deliver thy servant from the chains of his captivity. Through.

Various Prayers

33. For those at Sea
Collect.

O GOD, who didst guide our fathers through the Red Sea, and didst bring them through the deep waters, singing praises to thy name: we humbly beseech thee; that thou wouldest defend thy servants now travelling by sea from all adversity, so that they, voyaging in tranquillity, may be brought by thee unto the haven where they would be. Through.

Secret.

WE beseech thee, O Lord, to receive the prayers of thy servants, with our sacrifices and oblations: that they for whom we celebrate these mysteries may be defended by thee against all adversities. Through.

Postcommunion.

O LORD, who hast sanctified us with these heavenly mysteries, we humbly entreat and beseech thy majesty: that as thou dost suffer us to call to remembrance thy servants by means of these thy heavenly gifts; so through the wood of the holy Cross thou wouldest absolve them from their sins, and in thy mercy deliver them from all perils and dangers. Through.

34. For the safety of the Living
Collect.

STRETCH forth, O Lord, upon thy faithful people the right hand of thy heavenly succour: that they, seeking thee with their whole heart, may be found worthy to obtain those things which they ask according to thy will. Through.

Secret.

WE beseech thee, O Lord, to have compassion on our prayers, and graciously to accept these oblations of thy faithful people, which we present before thee for their safety: and that none may pray amiss or fail in his petition; grant that those things which we ask faithfully, we may obtain effectually. Through.

Postcommunion.

GRANT, we beseech thee, O Lord, unto thy faithful people steadfastness in faith and singleness of heart: that they, being stablished in thy love, may not by any temptations be parted from the fulness of the same. Through.

35. For the Living and Departed
Collect.

ALMIGHTY and everlasting God, who hast dominion both of the quick and the dead, and hast mercy upon all men whom by reason of their faith and works thou dost foreknow: we humbly beseech thee; that those for whom we are minded to pour forth our prayers, whether in this present world they still be held in the flesh, or being delivered from the body have passed to that which is to come, may at the intercession of all thy Saints obtain of thy bountiful goodness the remission of all their sins. Through.

Secret.

O GOD, to whom alone is known the number of the elect, whom thou hast appointed unto heavenly felicity: grant, we beseech thee; that at the intercession of all thy Saints, the names of all those who have been commended to our prayers, and of all thy faithful people, may ever remain written in the book of those that are predestinated to everlasting blessedness. Through.

Postcommunion.

ALMIGHTY and merciful God, cleanse us, we pray thee, by the mysteries which we have received: and, at the intercession of all thy Saints, grant; that this thy Sacrament may bring upon us not guilt to our punishment but pardon to our salvation: that it may cleanse the guilty and confirm the feeble, that it may strengthen us against every danger of the world: and obtain for thy faithful people both quick and dead the remission of all their sins. Through.

MASSES OF THE DEAD

¶ The Sequence Dies irae must be said in the first (or chief) Mass of All Souls' Day, and on the Day of Death or Burial: on other occasions it may be omitted.

¶ For a departed Bishop or Priest, as well on the Day of Burial as on the Anniversary, the first Mass is said of those which are appointed below on the Commemoration of All the Faithful Departed, with the proper Prayers given among the Various Prayers, p. [112].

November 2,
or, if it fall on Sunday, November 3.

THE COMMEMORATION OF ALL THE FAITHFUL DEPARTED

Double.

¶ On this day any Priest may celebrate three Masses. He, however, who only celebrates one Mass, reads the first: he who celebrates Mass with chant does likewise, but he may anticipate the second and third.

At the First Mass

Introit. II Esdr. 2, 34-35. Requiem aeternam.

REST eternal grant unto them, O Lord: and let light perpetual shine upon them. Ps. 65, 1-2. Thou, O God, art praised in Sion, and unto thee shall the vow be performed in Jerusalem: thou that hearest the prayer, unto thee shall all flesh come.

Rest eternal is immediately repeated as far as the Psalm.

Collect.

O GOD, the Creator and Redeemer of all the faithful: grant unto the souls of thy servants and handmaids the remission of all their sins; that as they have ever desired thy merciful pardon, so by the supplications of their brethren they may receive the same: Who livest and reignest with God the Father.

The Lesson from the Epistle of blessed Paul the Apostle to the Corinthians.

I Cor. 15, 51-57.

BRETHREN: Behold, I shew you a mystery: We shall not all sleep, but we shall all be changed. In a moment, in the twinkling of an eye, at the last trump: for the trumpet shall sound, and the dead shall be raised incorruptible: and we shall be changed. For this corruptible must put on incorruption: and this mortal must put on immortality. So when this corruptible shall have put on incorruption, and this mortal shall have put on immortality, then shall be brought to pass the saying that is written: Death is swallowed up in victory. O death, where is thy sting? O grave, where is thy victory? The sting of death is sin: and the strength of sin is the law. But thanks be to God, which giveth us the victory through our Lord Jesus Christ.

Gradual. II Esdr. 2, 34-35. Rest eternal grant unto them, O Lord: and let light perpetual shine upon them. ℣. Ps. 112, 7. The righteous shall be had in everlasting remembrance: he will not be afraid of any evil tidings.

Tract. Absolve, O Lord, the souls of all the faithful departed from every bond of sin. ℣. And by the help of thy grace may they be worthy to escape the avenging judgment. ℣. And enjoy the bliss of everlasting light.

Sequence.   Dies irae.

DAY of wrath and doom impending,
 David's word with Sibyl's blending:
Heaven and earth in ashes ending.

Oh, what fear man's bosom rendeth,
 When from heaven the judge descendeth,
 On whose sentence all dependeth!

Wondrous sound the trumpet flingeth,
 Through earth's sepulchres it ringeth,
 All before the throne it bringeth.

Death is struck, and nature quaking,
 All creation is awaking,
 To its judge an answer making.

Lo! the book exactly worded,
 Wherein all hath been recorded,
 Thence shall judgment be awarded.

When the judge his seat attaineth,
 And each hidden deed arraigneth,
 Nothing unavenged remaineth.

What shall I, frail man, be pleading?
 Who for me be interceding,
 When the just are mercy needing?

King of majesty tremendous,
 Who dost free salvation send us,
 Fount of pity, then befriend us.

Think, kind Jesu, my salvation
 Caused thy wondrous Incarnation:
 Leave me not to reprobation.

Faint and weary thou hast sought me:
 On the Cross of suffering bought me:
 Shall such grace be vainly brought me?

Righteous judge, for sin's pollution
 Grant thy gift of absolution
 Ere that day of retribution.

Guilty, now I pour my moaning:
 All my shame with anguish owning:
 Spare, O God, thy suppliant groaning.

Through the sinful Mary shriven,
 Through the dying thief forgiven,
 Thou to me a hope hast given.

Worthless are my prayers and sighing:
 Yet, good Lord, in grace complying,
 Rescue me from fires undying.

With thy sheep a place provide me,
 From the goats afar divide me,
 To thy right hand do thou guide me.

When the wicked are confounded,
 Doomed to flames of woe unbounded,
 Call me, with thy Saints surrounded.

Low I kneel, with heart submission,
 See, like ashes, my contrition:
 Help me in my last condition.

Ah! that day of tears and mourning,
 From the dust of earth returning,
 Man for judgment must prepare him.

Spare, O God, in mercy spare him:
 Lord, all-pitying, Jesu blest,
 Grant them thine eternal rest.   Amen.

☩ The Continuation of the holy Gospel according to John.

John 5, 25-29.

AT that time: Jesus, said to the multitude of the Jews: Verily, verily, I say unto you, The hour is coming, and now is, when the dead shall hear the voice of the Son of God: and they that hear shall live. For as the Father hath life in himself, so hath he given to the Son to have life in himself: and hath given him authority to execute judgment also, because he is the Son of man. Marvel not at this, for the hour is coming, in the which all that are in the graves shall hear his voice: and shall come forth, they that have done good, unto the resurrection of life: and they that have done evil, unto the resurrection of judgment.

Masses of the Dead [103]

Offertory. O Lord Jesu Christ, King of glory, deliver the souls of all the faithful departed from the pains of hell and from the depths of the pit: deliver them from the lion's mouth, that hell devour them not, that they fall not into darkness: but let the standard-bearer, Saint Michael, bring them into the holy light: *Which of old thou didst promise unto Abraham and his seed. ℣. We offer unto thee, O Lord, sacrifices of prayer and praise: do thou receive them for the souls of those whose memory we this day recall: make them, O Lord, to pass from death unto life. Which of old thou didst promise unto Abraham and his seed.

Secret.

WE beseech thee, O Lord, look favourably upon the sacrifices which we offer unto thee for the souls of thy servants and handmaids: that, as thou hast bestowed on them grace to profess the Christian faith, so thou wouldest grant them the reward of the same. Through.

Preface of the Dead.

¶ At the first and second Mass, if the Priest is to say another at once, having received the divine Blood, he does not purify nor wipe the Chalice, but places it on the Corporal and covers it with the Pall; then with hands joined he says in the midst of the Altar: Quod ore súmpsimus, etc. and then he washes his fingers in a vessel made ready with water, saying: Corpus tuum, Dómine, etc., and wipes them. Having done this, he again arranges the Chalice, which is still on the Corporal, and taking off the Pall he covers it as usual, viz., first with the linen Purificator, then with the Paten containing the Host which is to be consecrated and the Pall, and lastly the Veil.

But if he is to celebrate again after an interval, then in the first (and second) Mass he takes the ablutions as usual, but in water only.

Communion. II Esdr. 2, 35 and 34. Let light eternal shine upon them, O Lord: * With thy Saints for evermore: for thou art gracious. ℣. Rest eternal grant unto them, O Lord: and let light perpetual shine upon them. With thy Saints for evermore: for thou art gracious.

Postcommunion.

O LORD, we beseech thee, let these our supplications be acceptable in thy sight: that the souls of thy servants and handmaids, being delivered from all their sins, may be made partakers of thy heavenly redemption: Who livest and reignest with God the Father.

¶ The Priest must say the Confession before the Masses which follow. Moreover, at the end of each Mass, The Lord be with you having been said, there is said: May they rest in peace. ℟. Amen.

¶ The blessing is not given: but Pláceat tibi is said secretly, and the Altar kissed. Then follows the Gospel of St. John, In the beginning, etc., as usual.

At the Second Mass

Introit. II Esdr. 2, 34-35. Requiem aeternam.

REST eternal grant unto them, O Lord: and let light perpetual shine upon them. Ps. 65, 1-2. Thou, O God, art praised in Sion, and unto thee shall the vow be performed in Jerusalem: thou that hearest the prayer, unto thee shall all flesh come. Rest eternal.

Collect.

O GOD, the Lord of mercy and compassion: grant unto the souls of thy servants and handmaids a place of refreshing, the blessedness of rest, and the brightness of thine everlasting light. Through.

The Lesson from the book of the Maccabees.

II Mac. 12, 43-46.

IN those days: The most valiant man Judas, when he had made a gathering throughout the company to the sum of two thousand drachms of silver, sent it to Jerusalem, to offer a sin-offering, doing therein very well and honestly, in that he was mindful of the resurrection, (for if he had not hoped that they that were slain should have risen again, it had been superfluous and vain to pray for the dead): and also in that he perceived that there was great favour laid up for those that died godly. It is therefore an holy and salutary thought to pray for the dead, that they may be loosed from sins.

Gradual. II Esdr. 2, 34-35. Rest eternal grant unto them, O Lord: and let light perpetual shine upon them. ℣. Ps. 112, 7. The righteous shall be had in everlasting remembrance: he will not be afraid of any evil tidings.

Tract. Absolve, O Lord, the souls of all the faithful departed from every bond of sin. ℣. And by the help of thy grace may they be worthy to escape the avenging judgment. ℣. And enjoy the bliss of everlasting light.

☩ The Continuation of the holy Gospel according to John.

John 6, 37-40.

AT that time: Jesus said to the multitudes of the Jews: All that the Father giveth me shall come to me: and him that cometh to me I will in no wise cast out: for I came down from heaven, not to do mine own will, but the will of him that sent me. And this is the Father's will which hath sent me: that of all which he hath given me I should lose nothing, but should raise it up again at the last day. And this is the will of him that sent me: that every one which seeth the Son, and believeth on him, may have everlasting life, and I will raise him up at the last day.

Offertory. O Lord Jesu Christ, King of glory, deliver the souls of all the faithful departed from the pains of hell and from the depths of the pit: deliver them from the lion's mouth, that hell devour them not, that they fall not into darkness: but let the standard-bearer, Saint Michael, bring them into the holy light: * Which of old thou didst promise unto Abraham and his seed. ℣. We offer unto thee, O Lord, sacrifices of prayer and praise: do thou receive them for the souls of those whose memory we this day recall: make them, O Lord, to pass from death unto life. Which of old thou didst promise unto Abraham and his seed.

¶ At the second and third Mass the Priest, if he has celebrated the first Mass, when he comes to the Offertory, takes off the Veil from the Chalice, which he places a little way towards the Epistle side, but not outside the Corporal: and having offered the Host he does not wipe the Chalice with the Purificator, but leaving it within the Corporal, slightly raises it, and carefully pours wine and water into it, and offers the Chalice as usual, but without wiping it at all inside.

Secret.

BE favourable, O Lord, to our supplications for the souls of thy servants and handmaids, for which we offer unto thee this sacrifice of praise: that thou wouldest vouchsafe to join them to the fellowship of thy Saints. Through.

Preface of the Dead.

Communion. II Esdr. 2, 35 and 34. Let light eternal shine upon them, O Lord: * With thy Saints for evermore: for thou art

Masses of the Dead [105]

gracious. ℣. Rest eternal grant unto them, O Lord: and let light perpetual shine upon them. With thy Saints for evermore: for thou art gracious.

Postcommunion.

GRANT, we beseech thee, O Lord: that the souls of thy servants and handmaids, being by this sacrifice cleansed from sin, may obtain thy pardon and everlasting rest. Through.

At the Third Mass

Introit. II Esdr. 2, 34-35. Requiem aeternam.

REST eternal grant unto them, O Lord: and let light perpetual shine upon them. Ps. 65, 1-2. Thou, O God, art praised in Sion, and unto thee shall the vow be performed in Jerusalem: thou that hearest the prayer, unto thee shall all flesh come. Rest eternal.

Collect.

O GOD, the giver of pardon and lover of man's salvation: we beseech thee mercifully to grant; that the souls of thy servants and handmaids, who have passed out of this world, may, at the intercession of blessed Mary ever Virgin and of all thy Saints, be made partakers of thine everlasting gladness. Through.

The Lesson from the book of the Revelation of blessed John the Apostle.
Rev. 14, 13.

IN those days: I heard a voice from heaven saying unto me: Write: Blessed are the dead which die in the Lord from henceforth. Yea, saith the Spirit, that they may rest from their labours: and their works do follow them.

Gradual. II Esdr. 2, 34-35. Rest eternal grant unto them, O Lord: and let light perpetual shine upon them. Ps. 112, 7. The righteous shall be had in everlasting remembrance: he will not be afraid of any evil tidings.

Tract. Absolve, O Lord, the souls of all the faithful departed from every bond of sin. ℣. And by the help of thy grace may they be worthy to escape the avenging judgment. ℣. And enjoy the bliss of everlasting light.

✠ The Continuation of the holy Gospel according to John.
John 6, 51-55.

AT that time: Jesus said to the multitudes of the Jews: I am the living bread which came down from heaven. If any man eat of this bread, he shall live for ever: and the bread that I will give is my flesh, which I will give for the life of the world. The Jews therefore strove among themselves, saying: How can this man give us his flesh to eat? Then Jesus said unto them: Verily, verily, I say unto you: Except ye eat the flesh of the Son of man, and drink his blood, ye have no life in you. Whoso eateth my flesh and drinketh my blood, hath eternal life: and I will raise him up at the last day.

Offertory. O Lord Jesu Christ, King of glory, deliver the souls of all the faithful departed from the pains of hell and from the depths of the pit: deliver them from the lion's mouth, that hell devour them not, that they fall not into darkness: but let the standard-bearer, Saint Michael, bring them into the holy light: * Which of old thou didst promise unto Abraham and his seed. ℣. We offer unto thee, O Lord, sacrifices of prayer and praise: do thou receive them for the souls of those whose memory we this day recall: make them, O Lord, to pass from death unto life. Which of old thou didst promise unto Abraham and his seed.

Masses of the Dead

Secret.

O GOD, whose mercies are without number, graciously receive our humble prayers: and through these sacraments of our salvation grant unto the souls of all the faithful departed, to whom thou hast given grace to confess thy holy name, the remission of all their sins. Through.

Preface of the Dead.

Communion. II Esdr. 2, 35 and 34. Let light eternal shine upon them, O Lord: * With thy Saints for evermore: for thou art gracious. ℣. Rest eternal grant unto them, O Lord: and let light perpetual shine upon them. With thy Saints for evermore: for thou art gracious.

Postcommunion.

GRANT, we beseech thee, almighty and merciful God: that the souls of thy servants and handmaids, for whom we have offered unto thy majesty this sacrifice of praise; may through the power of this sacrament be cleansed from all their sins, and by thy mercy obtain the blessedness of everlasting light. Through.

On the day of Death or Burial of a Departed Person

Introit. II Esdr. 2, 34-35. Requiem aeternam.

REST eternal grant unto them, O Lord: and let light perpetual shine upon them. Ps. 65, 1-2. Thou, O God, art praised in Sion, and unto thee shall the vow be performed in Jerusalem: thou that hearest the prayer, unto thee shall all flesh come. Rest eternal.

Collect.

O GOD, whose nature and property is ever to have mercy and to forgive, receive our humble petitions for the soul of thy servant N., (handmaid N.,) which thou hast this day commanded to depart from this world: deliver it not into the hands of the enemy, neither forget it at the last, but command it to be received by thy holy Angels, and brought unto the country of paradise; that forasmuch as he (she) hoped and believed in thee, he (she) may not undergo the pains of hell, but may be made partaker of everlasting felicity. Through.

On the 3rd, 7th and 30th Day.

Collect.

WE beseech thee, O Lord, that thou wouldest vouchsafe to grant unto the soul of thy servant N. (handmaid N.), whose burial three (or seven or thirty) days since we now commemorate, the fellowship of thy Saints and elect: and that thou wouldest pour upon it the continual dew of thy mercy. Through.

The Lesson from the Epistle of blessed Paul the Apostle to the Thessalonians.
I Thess. 4, 13-18.

BRETHREN: We would not have you to be ignorant concerning them which are asleep, that ye sorrow not, even as others which have no hope. For if we believe that Jesus died and rose again: even so them also which sleep in Jesus will God bring with him. For this we say unto you by the word of the Lord, that we which are alive and remain unto the coming of the Lord shall not prevent them which are asleep. For the Lord himself shall descend from heaven with a shout, with the voice of the Archangel, and with the trump of God: and the dead in Christ shall rise first. Then we which are alive and remain shall be caught up together with them in the clouds, to meet the Lord in the air, and so shall we ever be with the Lord. Wherefore comfort one another with these words.

Gradual. II Esdr. 2, 34-35. Rest eternal grant unto them, O Lord: and let light perpetual shine upon them. ℣. Ps. 112, 7. The righteous shall be had in everlasting remembrance: he will not be afraid of any evil tidings.

Masses of the Dead

Tract. Absolve, O Lord, the souls of all the faithful departed from every bond of sin. ℣. And by the help of thy grace may they be worthy to escape the avenging judgment. ℣. And enjoy the bliss of everlasting light.

Sequence.   Dies irae.

DAY of wrath and doom impending,
David's word with Sibyl's blending!
Heaven and earth in ashes ending!

Oh, what fear man's bosom rendeth
When from heaven the judge descendeth,
On whose sentence all dependeth!

Wondrous sound the trumpet flingeth,
Through earth's sepulchres it ringeth,
All before the throne it bringeth.

Death is struck, and nature quaking,
All creation is awaking,
To its judge an answer making.

Lo! the book exactly worded,
Wherein all hath been recorded;
Thence shall judgment be awarded.

When the judge his seat attaineth,
And each hidden deed arraigneth,
Nothing unavenged remaineth.

What shall I, frail man, be pleading?
Who for me be interceding,
When the just are mercy needing?

King of majesty tremendous,
Who dost free salvation send us,
Fount of pity, then befriend us!

Think, kind Jesu!—my salvation
Caused thy wondrous Incarnation;
Leave me not to reprobation.

Faint and weary thou hast sought me,
On the Cross of suffering bought me;
Shall such grace be vainly brought me?

Righteous judge! for sin's pollution
Grant thy gift of absolution,
Ere that day of retribution.

Guilty, now I pour my moaning,
All my shame with anguish owning;
Spare, O God, thy suppliant groaning!

Through the sinful Mary shriven,
Through the dying thief forgiven,
Thou to me a hope hast given.

Worthless are my prayers and sighing,
Yet, good Lord, in grace complying,
Rescue me from fires undying.

With thy sheep a place provide me,
From the goats afar divide me,
To thy right hand do thou guide me.

When the wicked are confounded,
Doomed to flames of woe unbounded,
Call me, with thy Saints surrounded.

Low I kneel, with heart-submission;
See, like ashes, my contrition!
Help me in my last condition!

Ah! that day of tears and mourning!
From the dust of earth returning,
Man for judgment must prepare him;

Spare, O God, in mercy spare him!
Lord, all-pitying, Jesu blest,
Grant them thine eternal rest.   Amen.

✠ The Continuation of the holy Gospel according to John.

John 11, 21-27.

AT that time, Martha said unto Jesus: Lord, if thou hadst been here, my brother had not died: but I know, that even now, whatsoever thou wilt ask of God, God will give it thee. Jesus saith unto her: Thy brother shall rise again. Martha saith unto him: I know that he shall rise again in the resurrection at the last day. Jesus said unto her: I am the resurrection, and the life: he that believeth in me, though he were dead, yet shall he live: and whosoever liveth and believeth in me shall never die. Believest thou this? She saith unto him: Yea, Lord, I believe that thou art the Christ, the Son of God, which should come into the world.

Offertory. O Lord Jesu Christ, King of glory, deliver the souls of all the faithful departed from the pains of hell and from the depths of the pit: deliver them from the lion's mouth, that hell devour them not, that they fall not into darkness: but let the standard-bearer, Saint Michael, bring them into the holy light: * Which of old thou didst promise unto Abraham and his seed. ℣. We offer unto thee, O Lord, sacrifices of prayer and praise: do thou receive them for the souls of those whose memory we this day recall: make them, O Lord, to pass from death unto life. Which of old thou didst promise unto Abraham and his seed.

Secret.

WE beseech thee, O Lord, to have mercy upon the soul of thy servant N., (handmaid N.,) for which we offer unto thee this sacrifice of praise, humbly entreating thy majesty: that, through this our bounden duty and service, it may be worthy to attain unto everlasting rest. Through.

On the 3rd, 7th and 30th Day.

Secret.

WE beseech thee, O Lord, graciously to regard the gifts which we offer unto thee for the soul of thy servant N., (handmaid N.,) that, being cleansed by the healing of thy heavenly grace, it may rest in thy mercy. Through.

Preface of the Dead.

Communion. II Esdr. 2, 35 and 34. Let light eternal shine upon them, O Lord: * With thy Saints for evermore: for thou art gracious. ℣. Rest eternal grant unto them, O Lord: and let light perpetual shine upon them. With thy Saints for evermore: for thou art gracious.

Postcommunion.

GRANT, we beseech thee, almighty God: that the soul of thy servant N. (handmaid N.) which today hath passed from this world, being by this sacrifice cleansed and delivered from sins, may obtain thy pardon and everlasting rest. Through.

On the 3rd, 7th and 30th Day.

Postcommunion.

RECEIVE, O Lord, our prayers for the soul of thy servant N. (handmaid N.): that whatsoever defilements it may have contracted in the midst of this earthly life, may by thy merciful forgiveness be done away. Through.

¶ On the 3rd, 7th and 30th day after the burial of the Departed Mass is said as above with the Prayers there noted.

On the Anniversary of the Departed

Introit. II Esdr. 2, 34-35. Requiem aeternam.

REST eternal grant unto them, O Lord: and let light perpetual shine upon them. Ps. 65, 1-2. Thou, O God, art praised in Sion, and unto thee shall the vow be performed in Jerusalem: thou that hearest the prayer, unto thee shall all flesh come. Rest eternal.

Collect.

O GOD, the Lord of mercy and compassion: grant unto the soul of thy servant N. (handmaid N., or souls of thy servants and handmaids), the anniversary of whose burial we now commemorate, a place of refreshing, the blessedness of rest, and the brightness of thine everlasting light. Through.

Masses of the Dead

The Lesson from the book of the Maccabees.
II Macc. 12, 43-46.

IN those days: The most valiant man Judas, when he had made a gathering throughout the company to the sum of two thousand drachms of silver, sent it to Jerusalem, to offer a sin-offering, doing therein very well and honestly, in that he was mindful of the resurrection, (for if he had not hoped that they that were slain should have risen again, it had been superfluous and vain to pray for the dead): and also in that he perceived that there was great favour laid up for those that died godly. It is therefore an holy and salutary thought to pray for the dead, that they may be loosed from sins.

Gradual. II Esdr. 2, 34-35. Rest eternal grant unto them, O Lord: and let light perpetual shine upon them. ℣. Ps. 112, 7. The righteous shall be had in everlasting remembrance: he will not be afraid of any evil tidings.

Tract. Absolve, O Lord, the souls of all the faithful departed from every bond of sin. ℣. And by the help of thy grace may they be worthy to escape the avenging judgment. ℣. And enjoy the bliss of everlasting light.

The Sequence Dies irae p. [102] may be said or omitted.

✠ The Continuation of the holy Gospel according to John.
John 6, 37-40.

AT that time: Jesus said to the multitudes of the Jews: All that the Father giveth me shall come to me: and him that cometh to me I will in no wise cast out: for I came down from heaven, not to do mine own will, but the will of him that sent me. And this is the Father's will which hath sent me: that of all which he hath given me I should lose nothing, but should raise it up again at the last day. And this is the will of him that sent me: that everyone which seeth the Son, and believeth on him, may have everlasting life, and I will raise him up at the last day.

Offertory. O Lord Jesu Christ, King of glory, deliver the souls of all the faithful departed from the pains of hell and from the depths of the pit: deliver them from the lion's mouth, that hell devour them not, that they fall not into darkness: but let the standard-bearer, Saint Michael, bring them into the holy light: * Which of old thou didst promise unto Abraham and his seed. ℣. We offer unto thee, O Lord, sacrifices of prayer and praise: do thou receive them for the souls of those whose memory we this day recall: make them, O Lord, to pass from death unto life. Which of old thou didst promise unto Abraham and his seed.

Secret.

BE favourable, O Lord, to our supplications for the soul of thy servant N. (handmaid N., or souls of thy servants and handmaids), whose anniversary is kept this day: for which we offer unto thee this sacrifice of praise; that thou wouldest vouchsafe to join it (them) to the fellowship of thy Saints.   Through.

Preface of the Dead.

Communion. II Esdr. 2, 35 and 34. Let light eternal shine upon them, O Lord: * With thy Saints for evermore: for thou art gracious. ℣. Rest eternal grant unto them, O Lord: and let light perpetual shine upon them. With thy Saints for evermore: for thou art gracious.

Postcommunion.

GRANT, we beseech thee, O Lord: that the soul of thy servant N. (handmaid N., or souls of thy servants and handmaids), the anniversary of whose burial we commemorate; being by this sacrifice cleansed from sin, may obtain thy pardon and everlasting rest.   Through.

In Daily Masses of the Dead

Introit. II Esdr. 2, 34-35. Requiem aeternam.

REST eternal grant unto them, O Lord: and let light perpetual shine upon them. Ps. 65, 1-2. Thou, O God, art praised in Sion, and unto thee shall the vow be performed in Jerusalem: thou that hearest the prayer, unto thee shall all flesh come. Rest eternal.

¶ If the Mass be applied for the Departed in general the Prayer O God the Creator is said; but if for Departed persons definitely named, the appropriate Prayer from Various Prayers is said: (if the name be missing or unknown, the Collect O God the giver is said).

In sung Masses one Collect only is to be said: in read Masses three Collects may be said ad libitum.

For departed Bishops or Priests. Collect.

O GOD, who didst cause thy servants to enjoy the dignity of the priesthood, and some to be Bishops after the order of thine Apostles: grant, we beseech thee; that in heaven they may be joined unto the company of their brethren for evermore. Through.

For departed brethren, kinsfolk, and benefactors. Collect.

O GOD, the given of pardon and lover of man's salvation: we beseech thee mercifully to grant; that the brethren, kinsfolk, and benefactors of our congregation who have passed out of this world, may at the intercession of blessed Mary ever Virgin and of all thy Saints be made partakers of thine everlasting gladness. (Through).

For all the faithful departed. Collect.

O GOD, the Creator and Redeemer of all the faithful: grant unto the souls of thy servants and handmaids the remission of all their sins; that as they have ever desired thy merciful pardon, so by the supplications of their brethren they may receive the same: Who livest and reignest with God the Father.

The Lesson from the book of the Revelation of blessed John the Apostle.
Rev. 14, 13.

IN those days: I heard a voice from heaven saying unto me: Write: Blessed are the dead which die in the Lord from henceforth. Yea, saith the Spirit, that they may rest from their labours: and their works do follow them.

Gradual. II Esdras 2, 34-34. Rest eternal grant unto them, O Lord: and let light perpetual shine upon them. Ps. 112, 7. The righteous shall be had in everlasting remembrance: he will not be afraid of any evil tidings.

Tract. Absolve, O Lord, the souls of all the faithful departed from every bond of sin. ℣. And by the help of thy grace may they be worthy to escape the avenging judgment. ℣. And enjoy the bliss of everlasting light.

Sequence, Dies irae, p. [102], may be said or omitted both in sung and read Masses.

✠ The Continuation of the holy Gospel according to John.
John 6, 51-55.

AT that time: Jesus said to the multitudes of the Jews: I am the living bread which came down from heaven. If any man eat of this bread, he shall live for ever: and the bread that I will give is my flesh, which I will give for the life of the world. The Jews therefore strove among themselves, saying: How can this man give us his flesh to eat? Then Jesus said unto them: Verily, verily, I say unto you: Except ye eat the flesh of the Son of man, and drink his blood, ye have no life in you. Whoso eateth my flesh, and drinketh my blood, hath eternal life: and I will raise him up at the last day.

Offertory. O Lord Jesu Christ, King of glory, deliver the souls of all the faithful departed from the pains of hell and from the depths of the pit: deliver them from the lion's mouth, that hell devour them not, that they fall not into darkness: but let the standard-bearer, Saint Michael, bring them into the holy light: * Which of old thou didst promise unto Abraham and his seed. ℣. We offer unto thee, O Lord, sacrifices of prayer and praise: do thou receive them for the souls of those whose memory we this day recall: make them, O Lord, to pass from death unto life. Which of old thou didst promise unto Abraham and his seed.

For departed Bishops or Priests.   Secret.

ACCEPT, O Lord, we beseech thee, the sacrifice which we offer to thee for the souls of thy servants, Bishops or Priests: that forasmuch as in this life thou didst bestow on them the dignity of Bishop or Priest, so thou wouldest bid them be joined unto the fellowship of thy Saints in the heavenly kingdom. Through.

For departed brethren, kinsfolk, and benefactors. Secret.

O GOD, whose mercies are without number, graciously receive our humble prayers: and through these sacraments of our salvation grant unto the souls of our brethren, kinsfolk, and benefactors, to whom thou hast given grace to confess thy holy name, the remission of all their sins. (Through).

For all the faithful departed.   Secret.

WE beseech thee, O Lord, look favourably upon the sacrifices which we offer unto thee for the souls of thy servants and handmaids: that as thou hast bestowed on them grace to confess the Christian faith, so thou wouldest grant them the reward of the same. Through

Preface of the Dead.

Communion. II Esdr. 2, 35 and 34. Let light eternal shine upon them, O Lord: * With thy Saints for evermore: for thou art gracious. ℣. Rest eternal grant unto them, O Lord: and let light perpetual shine upon them. With thy Saints for evermore: for thou art gracious.

For departed Bishops or Priests.

Postcommunion.

WE beseech thee, O Lord, that the prayers which we offer unto thee for the souls of thy servants, Bishops or Priests may effectually obtain for them thy gracious pardon: that by thy mercy they may enter into the eternal fellowship of him in whom they have ever put their hope and confidence. Through.

For departed brethren, kinsfolk, and benefactors. Postcommunion.

GRANT, we beseech thee, almighty and merciful God: that the souls of our brethren, kinsfolk, and benefactors, for whom we have offered unto thy majesty this sacrifice of praise; may through the power of this sacrament be cleansed from all their sins, and by thy mercy obtain the blessedness of everlasting light. (Through).

For all the faithful departed.

Postcommunion.

O LORD, we beseech thee, let our supplications be acceptable in thy sight: that the souls of thy servants and handmaids, being delivered from all their sins, may be made partakers of thy heavenly redemption: Who livest and reignest with God the Father.

VARIOUS PRAYERS FOR THE DEAD

1. For a Departed Pope

Collect.

O GOD, who of thy unspeakable providence didst vouchsafe to number thy servant N. in the company of thy high Priests: grant, we beseech thee; that like as he did fulfil on earth the office of thine only-begotten Son, so he may be joined unto the everlasting fellowship of thy holy Pontiffs in heaven. Through the same.

Secret.

ACCEPT, O Lord, we beseech thee, these our sacrifices for the soul of thy servant N., thy Supreme Pontiff: that forasmuch as in this life thou didst bestow on him the dignity of a Bishop, so thou wouldest bid him to be joined unto the fellowship of thy Saints in the heavenly kingdom. Through.

Postcommunion.

WE beseech thee, O Lord, that the prayers which we offer unto thee for the soul of thy servant N. the Supreme Pontiff may effectually obtain for him thy gracious pardon: that by thy mercy he may attain unto the eternal fellowship of him in whom he has ever put his hope and confidence. Through.

2. For a Departed Bishop

Collect.

O GOD, who didst cause thy servant N. to enjoy the dignity of a Bishop in the apostolic Priesthood: grant, we beseech thee; that in heaven he may be joined unto the company of his brethren for evermore. Through.

Secret.

ACCEPT, O Lord, we beseech thee, the sacrifice which we offer to thee for the soul of thy servant and Bishop N.: that forasmuch as in this life thou didst bestow on him the dignity of a Bishop, so thou wouldest bid him to be joined unto the fellowship of thy Saints in the heavenly kingdom. Through.

Postcommunion.

WE beseech thee, O Lord, that the prayers which we offer unto thee for the soul of thy servant and Bishop N. may effectually obtain for him thy gracious pardon: that by thy mercy he may attain unto the eternal fellowship of him in whom he has ever put his hope and confidence. Through.

3. For a Cardinal Bishop Departed

Collect.

O GOD, who didst cause thy servant N. the Cardinal Bishop to enjoy the dignity of a Bishop in the apostolic Priesthood: grant, we beseech thee, that in heaven he may be joined unto the company of his brethren for evermore. Through.

Secret.

ACCEPT, O Lord, we beseech thee, the sacrifice which we offer to thee for the soul of thy servant N. the Cardinal Bishop: that forasmuch as in this life thou didst bestow on him the dignity of a Bishop, so thou wouldest bid him to be joined unto the fellowship of thy Saints in the heavenly kingdom. Through.

Postcommunion.

WE beseech thee, O Lord, that the prayers which we offer unto thee for the soul of thy servant N. the Cardinal Bishop may effectually obtain for him thy gracious pardon: that by thy mercy he may attain unto the eternal fellowship of him in whom he has ever put his hope and confidence. Through.

Various Prayers for the Dead

3.* For a Cardinal who enjoyed the Dignity of a Bishop

The Prayers as above, substituting the words Cardinal Priest for Cardinal Bishop.

4. For a Cardinal Priest

who was not a Bishop, and for a Cardinal Deacon who had the dignity of a Priest.

The Prayers for a Cardinal Bishop are said with the necessary changes.

5. For a Cardinal Deacon

who was not a Priest.

The Prayers No. 9, with the addition Cardinal Deacon after N.

6. For a Departed Bishop

Another Collect.

GRANT unto us, O Lord, that the soul of thy servant and Bishop N. (souls of thy servants and Bishops N. and N.), which thou hast delivered from the toil and conflict of this world, may by thee be made partaker(s) of the fellowship of thy Saints.

Secret.

GRANT unto us, we beseech thee, O Lord: that like as by the offering of this oblation thou didst grant unto the whole world remission of sins, so the soul of thy servant and Bishop N. (souls of thy servants and Bishops N. and N.) may be profited by the same. Through.

Postcommunion.

WE beseech thee, almighty God, that the soul of thy servant and Bishop N., (souls of thy servants and Bishops N. and N.) being by this sacrifice cleansed from every stain of sin, may be found worthy to obtain thy pardon and everlasting refreshment. Through.

7. For a Departed Priest

To be said in the plural if necessary.

Collect.

O GOD, who didst cause thy servant N. to enjoy the dignity of a Priest in the apostolic Priesthood: grant, we beseech thee, that in heaven he may be joined unto the company of his brethren for evermore. Through.

Secret.

ACCEPT, O Lord, we beseech thee, the sacrifice which we offer to thee for the soul of thy servant and Priest N.: that forasmuch as in this life thou didst bestow on him the dignity of a Priest, so thou wouldest bid him to be joined unto the fellowship of thy Saints in thy heavenly kingdom. Through.

Postcommunion.

WE beseech thee, O Lord, that the prayers which we offer unto thee for the soul of thy servant and Priest N. may effectually obtain for him thy gracious pardon: that by thy mercy he may attain unto the eternal fellowship of him in whom he has ever put his hope and confidence. Through.

8. For a Departed Priest

To be said in the plural if necessary.

Collect.

GRANT, we beseech thee, O Lord: that the soul of thy servant N. (souls of thy servants N. and N.): whom while he (they) lived in this world thou didst adorn with thy holy gifts; may ever rejoice in the glory of thy heavenly abode. Through.

Secret.

RECEIVE, O Lord, we beseech thee, these sacrifices, which we offer for the soul of N. thy servant and Priest (souls of N. and N. thy servants and Priests): that as thou hast given him (them) the dignity of the Priesthood, thou wouldest also give him (them) the reward of the same. Through.

Postcommunion.

GRANT, we beseech thee, almighty God: that the soul of N. thy servant and Priest (souls of N. and N. thy servants and Priests), may by thee be made partaker(s) of everlasting gladness in the congregation of the Just. Through.

9. For a Man Departed

To be said in the plural if necessary.

Collect.

INCLINE thine ear, O Lord, unto the prayers wherewith we humbly entreat thy mercy: that thou wouldest set the soul of thy servant N. (souls of thy servants N. and N.), which thou hast bidden depart this life, may by thee be set in the abode of peace and light; and be made partaker(s) of the fellowship of thy Saints. Through.

Secret.

GRANT to us, we beseech thee, O Lord: that like as by the offering of this oblation thou didst bestow upon the whole world remission of sins: so the soul of thy servant N. (souls of thy servants N. and N.) may be profited by the same. Through.

Postcommunion.

ABSOLVE, O Lord, we beseech thee, the soul of thy servant N. (souls of thy servants N. and N.) from every bond of sin: that in the glory of the resurrection he (they) may be raised up amid thy Saints and elect unto newness of life. Through.

10. For a Woman Departed

To be said in the plural if necessary.

Collect.

WE beseech thee, O Lord, of thy loving-kindness to have mercy on the soul of thy handmaid N. (souls of thy handmaids N. and N.): that being purged from all the defilements of our mortal nature, she (they) may be restored to the portion of everlasting salvation. Through.

Secret.

WE beseech thee, O Lord, that by these sacrifices, whereby alone we have deliverance from our sins, the soul of thy handmaid N. (souls of thy handmaids N. and N.) may be absolved from all her (their) offences: that through this our bounden duty of propitiation she (they) may obtain thine everlasting mercy. Through.

Postcommunion.

WE beseech thee, O Lord, that the soul of thine handmaid N. (souls of thy handmaids N. and N.), who in this sacrament received the pledge of thy never-failing mercy; may be made partaker(s) of thine everlasting light. Through.

11. For a Father and Mother

Collect.

O GOD, who hast bidden us to honour our father and our mother: of thy loving-kindness have mercy on the souls of my father and mother (of our parents) and forgive them their sins; and grant that I (we) may behold them in the joy of thine eternal glory. Through.

Secret.

RECEIVE, O Lord, the sacrifice which I offer unto thee for the souls of my father and mother (of our parents): and grant them in the land of the living everlasting blessedness; and join me (us) with them in the felicity of thy Saints. Through.

Postcommunion.

WE beseech thee, O Lord, that this partaking of thy heavenly Sacrament may obtain for the souls of my father and mother (of our parents) rest and light perpetual: and that with them I (we) may receive the crown of thy everlasting grace. Through.

12. For a Father only
Collect.

O GOD, who hast bidden us to honour our father and our mother: of thy loving-kindness have mercy on the soul of my (our) father and forgive him his sins; and grant that I (we) may behold him in the joy of thine eternal glory. Through.

Secret.

RECEIVE, O Lord, the sacrifice which I offer unto thee for the soul of my (our) father: and grant him in the land of the living everlasting blessedness; and join me (us) with him in the felicity of thy Saints. Through.

Postcommunion.

WE beseech thee, O Lord, that this partaking of thy heavenly Sacrament may obtain for the soul of my (our) father rest and light perpetual; and that with him I (we) may receive the crown of thy everlasting grace. Through.

13. For a Mother only
Collect.

O GOD, who hast bidden us to honour our father and our mother: of thy loving-kindness have mercy on the soul of my (our) mother and forgive her her sins; and grant that I (we) may behold her in the joy of thine eternal glory. Through.

Secret.

RECEIVE, O Lord, the sacrifice which I offer unto thee for the soul of my (our) mother: and grant her in the land of the living everlasting blessedness; and join me (us) with her in the felicity of thy Saints. Through.

Postcommunion.

WE beseech thee, O Lord, that this partaking of thy heavenly Sacrament may obtain for the soul of my (our) mother rest and light perpetual: and that with her I (we) may receive the crown of thy everlasting grace. Through.

14. For Departed Brethren, Kinsfolk and Benefactors
Collect.

O GOD, the giver of pardon and lover of man's salvation: we beseech thee mercifully to grant; that the brethren, kinsfolk and benefactors of our congregation who have passed out of this world, may at the intercession of blessed Mary, ever Virgin, and of all thy Saints be made partakers of thine everlasting gladness. Through.

Secret.

O GOD, whose mercies are without number, graciously receive our humble prayers: and through these sacraments of our salvation grant unto the souls of our brethren, kinsfolk, and benefactors, to whom thou hast given grace to confess thy holy name, the remission of all their sins. Through.

Postcommunion.

GRANT, we beseech thee, almighty and merciful God: that the souls of our brethren, kinsfolk, and benefactors, for whom we have offered unto thy majesty this sacrifice of praise; may through the power of this sacrament be cleansed from all their sins, and by thy mercy obtain the blessedness of everlasting light. Through.

15. For those who rest in a Cemetery

Collect.

O GOD, through whose mercy the souls of the faithful are at rest: mercifully grant to thy servants and handmaids, and to all that here and in all places do rest in Christ, the remission of their sins; that being delivered from all their iniquities, they may rejoice with thee for evermore. Through the same.

Secret.

GRACIOUSLY receive, O Lord, this sacrifice which we offer for the souls of thy servants and handmaids, and of all Christian people who here and in all places are asleep in Christ: that by this wondrous sacrifice they may be delivered from the dread bonds of death, and be found worthy to enter into everlasting life. Through the same.

Postcommunion.

O GOD, the light of the souls of the faithful, mercifully assist our supplications: and grant unto thy servants and handmaids, whose bodies both here and in all places do rest in Christ, a place of refreshing, the blessedness of thy rest and the glory of everlasting light. Through the same.

16. For many persons Departed

Collect.

O GOD, whose nature and property is ever to have mercy and to forgive: have compassion upon the souls of thy servants and handmaids, and forgive them all their sins; that being delivered from the bonds of this our mortal nature, they may be found worthy to enter into everlasting life. Through.

Secret.

GRANT to us, we beseech thee, O Lord, that like as by the offering of this oblation thou didst bestow upon the whole world remission of sins: so the souls of thy servants and handmaids may be profited by the same. Through.

Postcommunion.

O GOD, to whom alone it belongeth to bestow healing after death: grant, we beseech thee; that the souls of thy servants and handmaids, being cleansed from the defilements of this earthly life, may be numbered in the portion of thy redeemed: Who livest and reignest.

17. Other prayers for many persons Departed

Collect.

GRANT, O Lord, we pray thee, to the souls of thy servants and handmaids thy perpetual mercy: that as they hoped and believed in thee, so it may be profitable unto them for evermore. Through.

Secret.

WE beseech thee, O Lord, mercifully to look upon these our gifts: that these things which we humbly offer to the glory of thy name, may be profitable unto them that are departed for the forgiveness of their sins. Through.

Postcommunion.

WE humbly offer unto thee, O Lord, our prayers for the souls of thy servants and handmaids: beseeching thee; that whatsoever defilements they may have contracted in their earthly conversation being pardoned by thy goodness, they may be made partakers of the gladness of thy redeemed. Through.

THE RITE OF ABSOLUTION AT FUNERALS

WHEN THE BODY OF THE DEPARTED IS PRESENT.

From The English Ritual.

¶ Mass being ended, if the Absolution is to be made, the Celebrant retires to the Epistle corner, where he takes off his chasuble and maniple, and puts on a black cope. The Subdeacon, between two Acolytes with lighted candles, carries the cross as in Processions, two other Acolytes preceding them, one with the thurible and incense-boat, the other with the holy-water bason and sprinkler. The Celebrant follows, having first made a reverence to the Altar, with the Deacon on his left. The Subdeacon with the Cross takes his stand at the feet of the bier or catafalque opposite the Altar, between the aforesaid Acolytes holding candles, while the Celebrant stands on the other side at the head of the place between the Altar and the bier, turning a little towards the Epistle corner, so that he looks towards the Subdeacon's Cross; on his left the Deacon, and near him the two other Acolytes carrying the thurible and holy-water bason. Then, an Acolyte or Clerk holding the book, the Celebrant says at once the following Collect (no change of number or gender being made, even if it is said for many persons or a woman).

Collect.

ENTER not into judgment with thy servant, O Lord, for in thy sight shall no man living be justified, except thou grant unto him remission of all his sins. Therefore, we beseech thee, let not the sentence of thy judgment fall upon him, whom the faithful prayer of Christian people commendeth unto thee: but by the succour of thy grace let him, who, while he lived, was sealed with the sign of the Holy Trinity be found worthy to escape the avenging judgment: Who livest and reignest world without end. ℟. Amen.

Then, the Cantor beginning, the Clergy standing around sing the following Responsory:

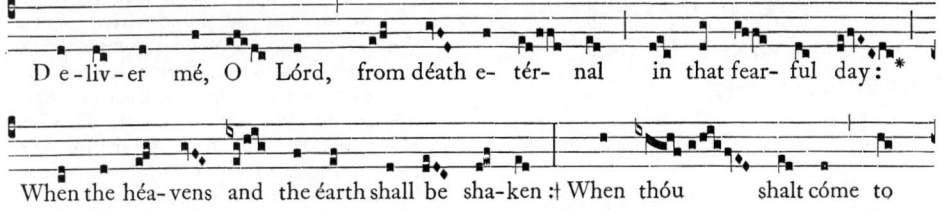

D e-liv-er mé, O Lórd, from déath e- tér- nal in that fear- ful day: *
When the héa-vens and the éarth shall be sha-ken :† When thóu shalt cóme to

Absolution at Funerals

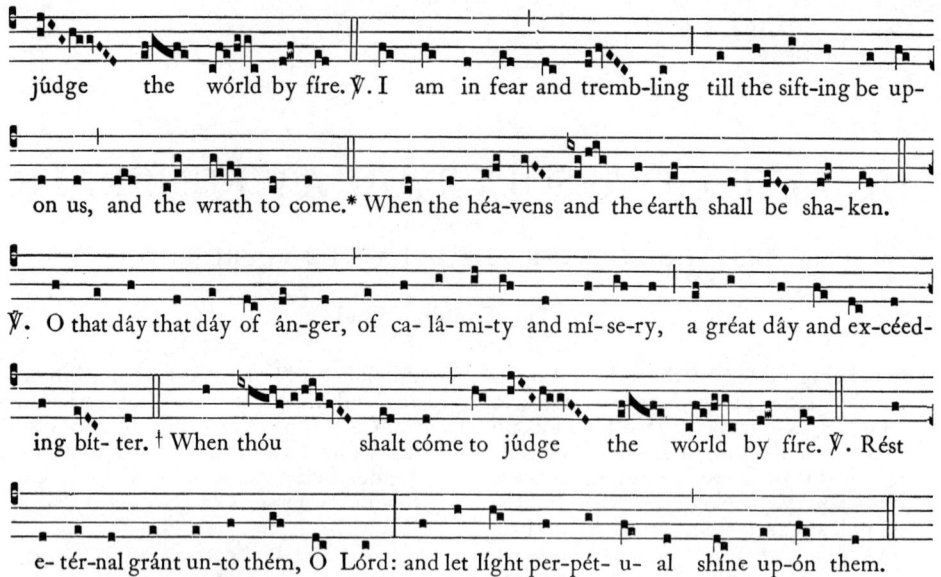

judge the world by fire. ℣. I am in fear and trembling till the sifting be upon us, and the wrath to come.* When the heavens and the earth shall be shaken.

℣. O that day that day of anger, of calamity and misery, a great day and exceeding bitter. † When thou shalt come to judge the world by fire. ℣. Rest eternal grant unto them, O Lord: and let light perpetual shine upon them.

Deliver me, O Lord, is repeated as far as the ℣. I am in fear exclusive.

¶ While the aforesaid Responsory is being repeated, the Priest, the Deacon ministering, takes incense from the boat and puts it into the censer, blessing it in the usual manner. The Responsory ended, a Cantor with the first Choir says:

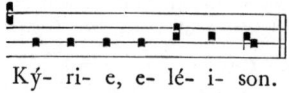
Ký-ri-e, e-lé-i-son.

And the second Choir answers:

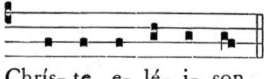
Chrís-te, e-lé-i-son.

Then all together say:

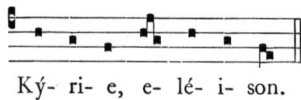
Ký-ri-e, e-lé-i-son.

Then the Priest says in a loud voice:

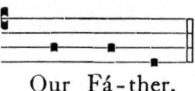
Our Fá-ther.

¶ And it is continued secretly by all. Meanwhile the Priest receives the sprinkler from the hand of the Deacon, and makes a reverence to the Altar; the Deacon accompanying him on his right, and holding the foreedge of the Cope, he goes around the bier, sprinkling the body of the departed with holy water, thrice on the left side of the corpse and thrice on the right. When he passes in front of the Cross he bows low, while the Deacon genuflects: afterwards he receives the thurible from the Deacon, and censes the bier in the same manner as he has sprinkled it. Having returned to his first position, the Deacon holding the book open before him, he says with joined hands:

Absolution at Funerals [119]

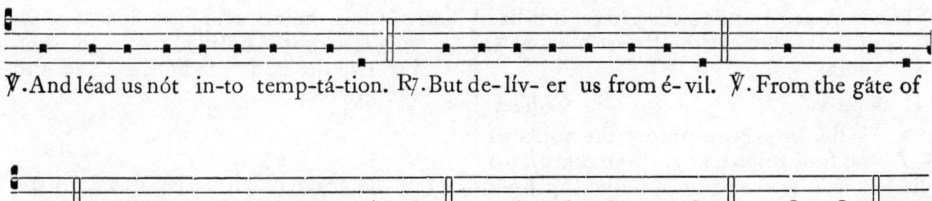

℣. And léad us nót in-to temp-tá-tion. ℟. But de-lív-er us from é-vil. ℣. From the gáte of héll. ℟. De-lív-er her soul, O Lórd. ℣. May she rést in péace. ℟. A-men.
                       his soul,   he
                       their souls,   they

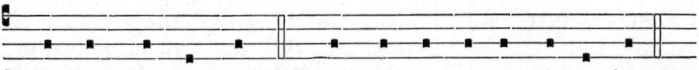

℣. O Lórd, héar my práyer. ℟. And lét my cry come ún-to thee.

℣. The Lord be with you.
℟. And with thy spirit.

Let us pray.   Collect.

O GOD, whose nature and property is ever to have mercy and to forgive, receive our humble petitions for the soul of thy servant N. (handmaid N.), which thou hast this day commanded to depart from this world: deliver it not into the hands of the enemy, neither forget it at the last, but command it to be received by thy holy Angels, and brought unto the country of paradise; that forasmuch as he (she) hoped and believed in thee, he (she) may not undergo the pains of hell, but may be made partaker of everlasting felicity. Through Christ our Lord. ℟. Amen.

If the departed be a Priest, there shall be said in the Prayer: for the soul of thy servant N. the Priest, which, etc.

The Collect being ended, the body is borne to the grave, if it is then to be borne; and while it is borne, or in the same place if it be not then borne, the Clerks sing the Antiphon:

In Paradisum.

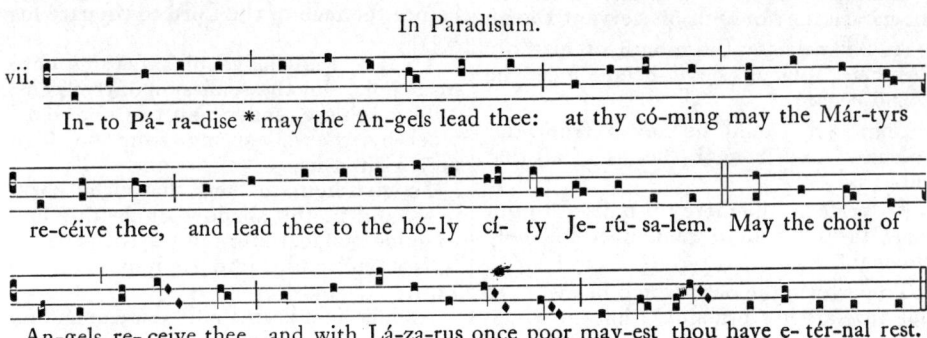

In-to Pá-ra-dise * may the An-gels lead thee: at thy có-ming may the Már-tyrs re-céive thee, and lead thee to the hó-ly cí-ty Je-rú-sa-lem. May the choir of An-gels re-ceive thee, and with Lá-za-rus once poor may-est thou have e-tér-nal rest.

Absolution at Funerals

When they are come to the grave, if it has not been blessed, the Priest blesses it, saying:

Let us pray.   Collect.

O GOD, by whose mercy the souls of the faithful are at rest, vouchsafe to ble✠ss this grave, and appoint thy holy Angel to guard it: and do thou absolve from every bond of sin the souls of them whose bodies are buried therein: that in thee and with thy Saints they may rejoice everlastingly. Through Christ our Lord. ℟. Amen.

If the grave is to serve for one person only, there shall be said:

The soul of him (her), whose body is buried therein.... he (she) may rejoice.

The Collect being said, the Priest shall sprinkle with holy water and then incense the body of the departed and the grave.

But, if the grave be already blessed, or the cemetery consecrated, this prayer and the sprinkling and censing of the body and grave are omitted.

Then, even if the body be not straightway borne to the grave, the Priest shall proceed with the Office, as below, which is never omitted; and shall intone the Antiphon:

I am. Cant. Bles-sed be the Lord God of Is- ra- el: for he hath vi- si-ted and

re-deem-ed his peo- ple. And hath rai-sed up.

Song of Zacharias.

Benedictus. Luke 1, 68-79.

BLESSED be the Lord God of Israel:* for he hath visited, and redeemed his people;

And hath raised up a mighty salvation for us:* in the house of his servant David;

As he spake by the mouth of his holy Prophets:* which have been since the world began;

That we should be saved from our enemies:* and from the hands of all that hate us;

To perform the mercy promised to our forefathers:* and to remember his holy covenant;

To perform the oath which he sware to our forefather Abraham:* that he would give us;

That we being delivered out of the hands of our enemies:* might serve him without fear;

In holiness and righteousness before him:* all the days of our life;

And thou, child, shalt be called the Prophet of the Highest:* for thou shalt go before the face of the Lord to prepare his ways;

To give knowledge of salvation unto his people:* for the remission of their sins;

Through the tender mercy of our God:* whereby the day-spring from on high hath visited us;

To give light to them that sit in darkness, and in the shadow of death:* and to guide our feet into the way of peace.

Rest eternal:* grant to him (her), O Lord.

And let light perpetual:* shine upon him (her).

Absolution at Funerals [121]

And the Antiphon is repeated:

I am the re-sur-réc-tion and the life: he that be-líe-veth in me, though he were

dead, yet shall he live: and who-so lí-veth and be-líe-veth in me, shall né-ver die.

Afterwards the Priest says: The Choir continues: Priest:

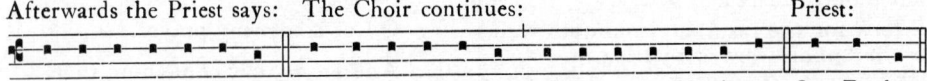
Ký-ri-e, e-lé-i-son. Chri-ste, e-lé-i-son. Ký-ri-e, e-lé-i-son. Our Fa-ther.

Meanwhile he sprinkles the body without going round.

℣. And lead us not into temptation.

℟. But deliver us from evil.

℣. From the gate of hell.

℟. Deliver his (her) soul, O Lord.

℣. May he (she) rest in peace.

℟. Amen.

℣. O Lord, hear my prayer.

℟. And let my cry come unto thee.

℣. The Lord be with you.

℟. And with thy spirit.

Let us pray. Collect.

GRANT, we beseech thee, O Lord, this mercy to thy servant (handmaid) departed: that, forasmuch as he (she) desired to do thy will, he (she) may not suffer the punishment of his (her) misdeeds: but that, even as true faith joined him (her) to the company of the faithful here below, so in heaven thy mercy may number him (her) among the angelic choirs. Through Christ our Lord. ℟. Amen.

Then the Celebrant, making a Cross with his right hand over the bier, says:

℣. Rest eternal grant unto him (her), O Lord.

℟. And let light perpetual shine upon him (her).

And, the Cantors having said:

he
℣. May she rest in peace. ℟. A-men.
they

The Celebrant says on one note:

℣. May his (her) soul, and the souls of all the faithful departed, through the mercy of God rest in peace.
℟. Amen.

While they return from the grave to the church, or from the church to the sacristy, the Cross going before, the Celebrant begins without chant the Antiphon, If thou, Lord, and with the clergy recites the following Psalm:

Absolution at Funerals

Psalm 130.   De profundis.

OUT of the deep have I called unto thee, O Lord:* Lord, hear my voice.

O let thine ears consider well:* the voice of my complaint.

If thou, Lord, wilt be extreme to mark what is done amiss:* O Lord, who may abide it?

For there is mercy with thee:* therefore shalt thou be feared.

I look for the Lord, my soul doth wait for him:* in his word is my trust.

My soul fleeth unto the Lord:* before the morning watch, I say, before the morning watch.

O Israel, trust in the Lord, for with the Lord there is mercy:* and with him is plenteous redemption.

And he shall redeem Israel:* from all his sins.

Rest eternal:* grant unto them, O Lord.

And let light perpetual:* shine upon them.

And the whole Antiphon is repeated by all: If thou, Lord, wilt be extreme to mark what is done amiss: O Lord, who may abide it? Then in the sacristy the Priest, before he puts off the vestments, says the following prayers:

      Kýrie, eléison.
      Christe, eléison.
      Kýrie, eléison.

Our Father secretly as far as

℣. And lead us not into temptation.

℟. But deliver us from evil.

℣. From the gate of hell.

℟. Deliver their souls, O Lord.

℣. May they rest in peace.

℟. Amen.

℣. O Lord, hear my prayer.

℟. And let my cry come unto thee.

℣. The Lord be with you.

℟. And with thy spirit.

Let us pray.   Collect.

O GOD, the Creator and Redeemer of all the faithful: grant unto the souls of thy servants and handmaids the remission of all their sins; that as they have ever desired thy merciful pardon, so through the supplications of their brethren they may obtain the same: Who livest and reignest world without end. ℟. Amen.

℣. Rest eternal grant unto them, O Lord.

℟. And let light perpetual shine upon them.

℣. May they rest in peace.

℟. Amen.

THE RITE OF ABSOLUTION WHEN THE BODY OF THE DEPARTED IS ABSENT

From The English Ritual.

¶ At the end of Mass, if the Absolution is to be made, the Celebrant retires to the Epistle Corner, where he takes off his chasuble and maniple, and puts on a black cope. The Subdeacon between two Acolytes with lighted candles, carries the Cross as in processions, two other Acolytes preceding them, one with the thurible and incense-boat, the other with the holy-water bason and sprinkler. The Celebrant follows, having first made a reverence to the Altar, with the Deacon on his left. The Subdeacon with the Cross takes his stand at the feet of the bier or catafalque opposite the altar, between the aforesaid Acolytes holding candles, while the Celebrant stands on the other side at the head of the place between the Altar and the bier, turning a little towards the Epistle corner, so that he looks towards the Subdeacon's Cross; on his left the Deacon, and near him the two other Acolytes carrying the thurible and vessel of blessed water.

Then, the Prayer Enter not, etc. being omitted, the Clergy standing around sing the following Responsory (as above, p. [117]):

DELIVER me, O Lord,* from death eternal in that fearful day: *When the heavens and the earth shall be shaken: *When thou shalt come to judge the world by fire. ℣. I am in fear and trembling till the sifting be upon us, and the wrath to come. When the heavens and the earth shall be shaken. ℣. O that day, that day of anger, of calamity and misery, a great day and exceeding bitter. When thou shalt come to judge the world by fire. ℣. Rest eternal grant unto them, O Lord: and let light perpetual shine upon them.

Repeat ℟. Deliver me, up to the first ℣. I am in fear exclusive.

¶ Towards the end of the Responsory the Celebrant puts incense into the thurible, blessing it as usual, the Deacon ministering the boat. The Responsory ended, a Cantor with the first Choir says:

> Kýrie, eléison,

and the second Choir answers:

> Christe, eléison.

Then all together say:

> Kýrie, eléison.

Then the Priest says in a loud voice:

> Our Father.

¶ And it is said secretly by all. Meanwhile the Priest receives the sprinkler from the hand of the Deacon, and makes a reverence to the Altar; the Deacon accompanying him on his right, and holding the fore-edge of the Cope, he goes around the bier, sprinkling it with holy water, thrice on the right side and thrice on the left. When he passes in front of the Cross he bows low, while the Deacon genuflects: afterwards he receives the thurible from the Deacon, and censes the bier in the same manner as he has sprinkled it. Having returned to his first position, the Deacon holding the book, he says with joined hands:

℣. And lead us not into temptation.
℟. But deliver us from evil.

℣. From the gate of hell.
℟. Deliver his (her) soul, (their souls), O Lord.
℣. May he (she) (they) rest in peace.
℟. Amen.
℣. O Lord, hear my prayer.
℟. And let my cry come unto thee.
℣. The Lord be with you.
℟. And with thy spirit.

Let us pray.   Collect.

ABSOLVE, O Lord, we beseech thee, the soul of thy servant N. (handmaid N., or souls of thy servants and handmaids) from every bond of sin: that in the glory of the resurrection he (she) (they) may be raised up amid thy Saints and elect unto newness of life. Through Christ our Lord. ℟. Amen.

¶ In place of the preceding Collect the Celebrant may say the Collect which was said in the Mass, or any other suitable one.

¶ Then the Celebrant, making a cross with his right hand over the bier, says:

℣. Rest eternal grant unto him (her) (them), O Lord.
℟. And let light perpetual shine upon him (her) (them).

And the Cantors having sung:

℣. May they rest in peace.
℟. Amen.

The Celebrant, again making the sign of the Cross over the bier, says without inflexion:

MAY his (her) soul (their souls) and the souls of all the faithful departed through the mercy of God rest in peace. ℟. Amen.

While they return to the Sacristy, the Psalm De profúndis and the rest are recited as on p. [122].

If the Absolution has been performed for all the faithful departed, the Verse May their souls, the Antiphon If thou, Lord and the Psalm with the prayers are not said.

THE ORDER FOR BLESSING OF WATER

¶ On Sunday, the salt and the water to be blessed being made ready in the Sacristy, the Priest who is about to celebrate the Mass, or another deputed for the purpose, vested in alb or surplice with a stole, first says:

℣. Our help is in the name of the Lord.

℟. Who hath made heaven and earth.

Then he straightway begins the exorcism of the salt.

I ADJURE thee, O creature of salt, by the living ✠ God, by the true ✠ God, by the holy ✠ God: by God who commanded thee to be cast by the prophet Eliseus into the water to heal the barrenness thereof: that thou become salt exorcised for the health of them that believe: be thou to all them that take of thee for healing of soul and body: let all vain imaginations, wickedness, and subtlety of the wiles of the devil, and every unclean spirit flee and depart from the place where thou shalt be sprinkled, adjured by him who shall come to judge the quick and the dead, and the world by fire. ℟. Amen.

The Order for Blessing of Water

Let us pray.   Collect.

ALMIGHTY and everlasting God, we humbly beseech thine infinite mercy: that thou wouldest vouchsafe of thy loving kindness to ble ✠ ss and sancti ✠ fy this creature of salt, which thou hast given for the use of mankind: that it may avail unto all that take of it for health of body and soul; and let all such things as shall be touched or sprinkled therewith be free from all uncleanness, and from all assaults of spiritual wickedness. Through. ℟. Amen.

Exorcism of the water: and straightway is said:

I ADJURE thee, O creature of water, in the name of God ✠ the Father almighty, in the name of Jesus ✠ Christ his Son, our Lord, and by the power of the Holy ✠ Ghost: that thou become water exorcised for the putting to flight of all the power of the enemy, and that thou be enabled to root out and expel the enemy himself with his apostate angels, by the power of the same Jesus Christ our Lord: who shall come to judge the quick and the dead, and the world by fire. ℟. Amen.

Let us pray.   Collect.

O GOD, who for the salvation of mankind, hast ordained in thy chiefest sacraments the use of the substance of water, mercifully assist us who call upon thee, and pour the power of thy bene ✠ diction upon this element, made ready by divers cleansings: that this thy creature, in the service of thy mysteries, may effectually receive thy divine grace for the casting forth of devils and the healing of diseases; that whatsoever in the dwellings or abodes of thy faithful people shall be sprinkled with this water may be free from all uncleanness and delivered from all evil: let not the spirit of pestilence abide therein, nor the breath of corruption; let all the snares of the unseen enemy depart from thence: and let all such things as are contrary to the health and peace of them that dwell therein be put to flight by the sprinkling of this water; that, as through the invocation of thy holy name we entreat for them thy saving health, so they may be defended against all assaults. Through. ℟. Amen.

Here he thrice casts the salt into the water in the form of a cross, saying once:

LET this commingling of salt and water be wrought in the Name of the Fa ✠ ther, and of the So ✠ n, and of the Holy ✠ Ghost. ℟. Amen.

℣. The Lord be with you.

℟. And with thy spirit.

Let us pray.   Collect.

O GOD, who art the author of strength invincible, the King of the empire that none may overcome, who art ever glorious in thy triumphs: who dost quell the might of the dominion that is against thee, who rulest the raging of the fierce enemy, who dost overthrow by thy power the wickedness of thy foes: we entreat thee, O Lord, and beseech thee in fear and lowliness: that thou wouldest graciously behold this creature of salt and water, and mercifully enlighten and sanctify it with the dew of thy lovingkindness; that, wheresoever it shall be sprinkled, all the snares of the unclean spirit may through the invocation of thy holy name be driven away, and the dread of the poisonous serpent be cast forth: and in all places let the presence of the Holy Ghost be vouchsafed unto us who call upon thy mercy. Through ... in the unity of the same Holy Ghost. ℟. Amen.

¶ The blessing being ended, the Priest who is to celebrate, vested in a cope of the colour of the Office, goes to the Altar, and there, kneeling at the steps with the ministers, even in Eastertide, he receives from the Deacon the sprinkler and first sprinkles the Altar thrice, then himself, and rises and sprinkles the ministers, beginning the Antiphon, Thou shalt purge me, and the Choir continues: O Lord, with hyssop, etc., as below. Meanwhile the Celebrant sprinkles the Clergy, then the people, saying in a low voice, with the ministers, the Psalm Miserére mei, Deus.

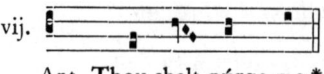

Ant. Thou shalt púrge me,*

O Lord, with hyssop, and I shall be clean: thou shalt wash me, and I shall be whiter than snow. Ps. 51, 1. Have mercy upon me, O God, after thy great goodness. ℣. Glory be to the Father.

And the Antiphon Thou shalt purge me is repeated.

¶ This Antiphon is said in the aforementioned manner at the sprinkling of holy water on Sundays throughout the year, except on Passion Sunday and Palm Sunday on which Glory be is not said, but after the Psalm Miserére the Antiphon Thou shalt purge me is at once repeated. Excepting also in Eastertide, that is from Easter-day to Pentecost inclusive, at which season the following is chanted:

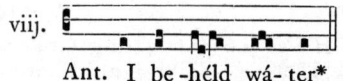

Ant. I be-héld wá-ter*

issuing out from the temple, on the right side, alleluia: and all to whom that water came were saved, and they shall say: alleluia, alleluia.

Ps. 118, 1. O give thanks unto the Lord, for he is gracious: because his mercy endureth for ever. ℣. Glory be.

The Antiphon is repeated, I beheld water.

¶ On Trinity Sunday the Antiphon, Thou shalt purge me is resumed.

¶ On the holy days of Easter and Pentecost, where there is a baptismal Font, the sprinkling is done with water blessed the day before in the Font of Baptism, and taken before the infusion of the Oil and Chrism.

¶ The Antiphon being concluded in the aforementioned manner, the Priest who has sprinkled the water returns to the Altar, and standing before the steps of the Altar with joined hands, shall say:

℣. O Lord, shew thy mercy upon us. (E.T. Alleluia.)

℟. And grant us thy salvation. (E.T. Alleluia.)

℣. O Lord, hear my prayer.

℟. And let my cry come unto thee.

℣. The Lord be with you.

℟. And with thy spirit.

Let us pray. Collect.

GRACIOUSLY hear us, O Lord holy Father almighty, everlasting God: and vouchsafe to send thy holy Angel from heaven; to guard and cherish, protect, visit and defend all who dwell in this place. Through Christ our Lord. ℟. Amen.

VARIOUS BENEDICTIONS

The Blessing of a Lamb at Easter

℣. Our help is in the Name of the Lord.

℟. Who hath made heaven and earth.

℣. The Lord be with you.

℟. And with thy spirit.

Let us pray.

O GOD, who by thy servant Moses, when thou didst set free thy people from Egypt, didst bid a lamb to be slain as a type of our Lord Jesus Christ, and didst command both the door-posts of the houses to be sprinkled with its blood: vouchsafe so to bl✠ss and sancti✠fy this creature of flesh, which we thy servants desire to receive to thy praise, by the resurrection of the same our Lord Jesus Christ: Who liveth and reigneth with thee, world without end. ℟. Amen.

And let it be sprinkled with holy water.

The Blessing of Eggs

℣. Our help.

℣. The Lord be with you.

Let us pray.

WE beseech thee, O Lord, that the grace of thy bless✠ing may come upon these eggs thy creatures: that they may be wholesome food to thy faithful people taking them and rendering thanks to thee for the resurrection of our Lord Jesus Christ: Who liveth and reigneth with thee, world without end. ℟. Amen.

And let them be sprinkled with holy water.

The Blessing of Bread

℣. Our help.

℣. The Lord be with you.

Let us pray.

O LORD, holy Father almighty, everlasting God, vouchsafe to bl✠ess this bread with thy holy spiritual benediction: that it may be to all that partake of it health of mind and body, and a defence against all diseases and every snare of the enemy. Through Jesus Christ thy Son our Lord, the living bread, who came down from heaven, and giveth life and salvation to the world: and liveth and reigneth with thee in the unity of the Holy Spirit, God: world without end. ℟. Amen.

And let it be sprinkled with holy water.

The Blessing of New Fruits

℣. Our help.

℣. The Lord be with you.

Let us pray.

BLESS, ✠ O Lord, these new fruits of N., and grant: that those who eat of them in thy holy name may obtain health of mind and body. Through Christ, our Lord. ℟. Amen.

And let them be sprinkled with holy water.

The Blessing of any Food

℣. Our help.

℣. The Lord be with you.

Let us pray.

BLESS, ✠ O Lord, this creature of N., that it may be a wholesome remedy for mankind: and grant by the invocation of thy holy name, that whosoever shall partake thereof may receive health of body and preservation of soul. Through Christ our Lord. ℟. Amen.

And let it be sprinkled with holy water.

The Blessing of Candles

℣. Our help.

℣. The Lord be with you.

Let us pray.

O LORD Jesu Christ, Son of the living God, bl✠ess these candles at our supplication: pour upon them, O Lord, by the virtue of the holy Cr✠oss, thy heavenly blessing, who hast bestowed them upon the human race to dispel the darkness: may they by the sign of the holy Cr✠oss receive thy benediction, in such wise that, in whatsoever place they be lighted or set up, the powers of darkness may depart and tremble, and in terror flee with all their ministers from those habitations: and may not venture more to disquiet or molest them who serve thee, the almighty God: Who livest and reignest for ever and ever. ℟. Amen.

And let them be sprinkled with holy water.

BLESSINGS

TO BE PERFORMED BY BISHOPS OR OTHERS HAVING THE FACULTY

Blessing of Sacerdotal Vestments in General

℣. Our help.

℣. The Lord be with you.

Let us pray.

ALMIGHTY, everlasting God, who by thy servant Moses didst decree that high-priestly and priestly and levitical vestments should be made for the fulfilment of their ministry in thy presence, to the honour and glory of thy name: graciously assist our supplications: that thou wouldest vouchsafe to pour out the showers of thy grace, and by thy mighty benediction through our lowly service to puri✠fy, bl✠ess, and, conse✠crate these priestly vestments: that they may be rendered fit for thy divine service and thy holy mysteries, and blessed: and also may thy Bishops, Priests and Levites, clothed in these holy garments, be counted worthy to be strengthened and defended against all assaults or temptations of malignant spirits: and make them worthily and meetly to serve and cleave unto thy mysteries, and therein to persevere devoutly and acceptably unto thee. Through Christ our Lord. ℟. Amen.

Let us pray.

O GOD, the creator and sanctifier of all things, who dost triumph in might invincible: graciously give heed to our prayers, and vouchsafe with thine own countenance to bl✠ess, sancti✠fy, and conse✠crate these garments of the levitical, priestly and pontifical dignity for the use of thy ministers: and vouchsafe to render all who use them meet for thy mysteries, that they, doing thee devout and laudable service, may be found acceptable unto thee. Through Christ our Lord. ℟. Amen.

Let us pray.

O LORD God almighty, who didst bid thy servant Moses make for the High-priests, Priests, and Levites vestments needful for the service of the tabernacle of the covenant, and didst replenish him with the spirit of wisdom for the accomplishment of the same: vouchsafe to bl✠ess, sancti✠fy, and conse✠crate these vestments for the service and worship of thy mysteries: and vouchsafe that the ministers of thine altar who shall be clothed in them may be meetly filled with the grace of thy sevenfold Spirit, with the garment of chastity, and with the fruit of good works in their ministry, which may win for them the bliss of everlasting life. Through Christ our Lord. ℟. Amen.

And let them be sprinkled with holy water.

Blessing of Altar-cloths or Altar-linen

℣. Our help.

℟. The Lord be with you.

Let us pray.

O LORD, graciously hear our prayers, and vouchsafe to bl✠ess and sancti✠fy this linen prepared for the service of thy holy Altar. Through Christ our Lord. ℟. Amen.

Let us pray.

O LORD, God almighty, who for forty days didst teach thy servant Moses to make ornaments and linen: the which also Miriam wove and made for the service of the tabernacle of the covenant: vouchsafe to bl✠ess, sancti✠fy and conse✠crate these linen cloths for the covering and enveloping of the Altar of thy most glorious Son, our Lord Jesus Christ: Who with thee liveth and reigneth in the unity of the Holy Spirit, God: world without end. ℟. Amen.

And let them be sprinkled with holy water.

Blessing of Corporals

℣. Our help.

℟. The Lord be with you.

Let us pray.

MOST gracious Lord, whose power is unspeakable, and whose mysteries are celebrated with hidden wonders: grant, we beseech thee, that this linen cloth may be sancti✠fied by thy merciful bene✠diction, that thereon may be consecrated the Body and Blood of our Lord and God Jesus Christ, thy Son: Who with thee liveth and reigneth in the unity of the Holy Spirit, God: world without end. ℟. Amen.

Let us pray.

ALMIGHTY everlasting God, vouchsafe to bl✠ess, sancti✠fy and conse✠crate this linen cloth, that it may cover and envelop the Body and Blood of thy Son our Lord Jesus Christ: Who with thee liveth and reigneth in the unity of the Holy Spirit, God: world without end. ℟. Amen.

Let us pray.

ALMIGHTY God, shed upon our hands the help of thy blessing: that through our bene✠diction this linen cloth may be sanctified, and may be made by the grace of thy Holy Spirit a new winding-sheet for the Body and Blood of our Redeemer. Through the same Jesus Christ thy Son our Lord: Who with thee liveth and reigneth in the unity of the same Holy Spirit, God: world without end. ℟. Amen.

And let them be sprinkled with holy water.

Blessing of a Tabernacle or Vessel for reserving the most holy Eucharist.

℣. Our help is in the name of the Lord.

℟. Who hath made heaven and earth.

℣. The Lord be with you.

℟. And with thy spirit.

Let us pray.

ALMIGHTY everlasting God, we humbly beseech thy majesty: that thou wouldest vouchsafe to hallow with the grace of thy bene✠diction this vessel fashioned to contain the Body of thy Son our Lord Jesus Christ. Through the same.

And let it be sprinkled with holy water.

ALPHABETICAL INDEX OF ALL FEASTS

NOTE. Feasts only observed locally in England, Wales or Scotland are printed in *italics*.

FEASTS OF OUR LORD JESUS CHRIST

	PAGE
Ascension	441
Ascension. Vigil. Baptism. Jan. 13	439
Christ, O.L. The King, The last Sunday of October	829
Circumcision. Jan. 1	39
Corpus Christi	465
Dedication of Archbasilica of St. Saviour. Nov. 9	839
Dedication of Basilicas of SS. Peter and Paul, App. Nov. 18	847
Easter Day	415
Epiphany. Jan. 6	43
Exaltation of the Holy Cross. Sept. 14	785
Holy Family, Jesu, Mary, Joseph. Sunday after the Epiphany	45
Invention of the Holy Cross. May 3	646
Most Holy Trinity	463
Most Precious Blood. July 1	706
Most Sacred Heart. Friday in the week after Corpus Christi	469
Name of Jesus. Sunday between Circumcision and Epiphany, or Jan. 2	41
Nativity. Dec. 25	16
„ Vigil. Dec. 24	14
„ Octave. Jan. 1	39
Pentecost	446
„ Vigil	444
Resurrection	415
Transfiguration. Aug. 6	745

FEASTS OF THE BLESSED VIRGIN MARY

Annunciation. Mar. 25	619
Appearing of B.V.M. Immaculate. Feb. 11	598
Assumption. Aug. 15	757
„ Vigil. Aug. 14	755
Dedication of the Snows. Aug. 5	743
Help of Christians. May 24	884
Holy House. Dec. 10	866
Immaculate Conception. Dec. 8	559
Immaculate Heart. Aug. 22	764
Mediatrix of all graces. June 1	888
Motherhood. Oct. 11	818
Of Mt. Carmel. July 16	718
Nativity. Sept. 8	781
Name of Mary. Sept. 12	784
Perpetual Succour. June 27	894
Porticu, in. July 17	900
Presentation. Nov. 21	849
Purification. Feb. 2	587
Queen. May 31	672
Of Ransom. Sept. 24	799
Rosary. Oct. 7	811
Seven Sorrows. Friday after Passion Sunday	623
Seven Sorrows. Sept. 15	787
Succour (of Aberdeen). July 9	935
Visitation. July 2	708

FEASTS OF THE SAINTS

A

Abdon and Sennen, MM. July 30	735
Adamnan, Ab. Sept. 23	940
Aelred, Ab. March 3	872
Agapitus, M. Aug. 18	760
Agatha, V.M. Feb. 5	592
Agnellus of Pisa, C. March 13	873
Agnes, V.M. Jan. 21	573
Agnes, Secundo. Jan. 28	582
Aidan, B.C. Aug. 31	907, 937
Alban, M. June 22	891
Albert the Great, B.C. Nov. 15	844
Aldhelm, B.C. May 25 or 28	884, 887
Alexander I, Pope and Comp., MM. May 3	646
Alexius, C. July 17	719
All Saints. Nov. 1	834

Alphabetical Index of all Feasts

	PAGE
All Souls. Nov. 2	836
Aloysius Gonzaga, C. June 21	690
Alphege, B.M. Apr. 19	876
Alphonsus Liguori, B.C.D. Aug. 2	739
Ambrose, B.C.D. Dec. 7	557
Ambrose, B.C.D. Apr. 4	920
Anacletus, Pope, M. July 13	716
Anastasia, M. Dec. 25	19
Anastasius and Vincent, MM. Jan. 22	575
Andrew, Ap. Nov. 30	550
Andrew. Translation. May 9	931
Andrew Avellino, C. Nov. 10	839
Andrew Corsini, B.C. Feb. 4	592
Angela Merici, V. June 1	673
Angels, Guardian. Oct. 2	805
Anicetus, Pope, M. Apr. 17	631
Anne, Mother B.V.M. July 26	731
Anselm, B.C.D. Apr. 21	631
Antoninus, B.C. May 10	653
Antony, Ab. Jan. 17	568
Antony Mary Zaccaria, C. July 5	710
Antony of Padua, C.D. June 13	683
Apollinaris, B.M. July 23	727
Apollonia, V.M. Feb. 9	596
Asaph, B.C. May 12	882
Athanasius, B.C.D. May 2	644
Augustine, B.C. May 26	886
Augustine, B.C. May 28	669
Augustine, B.C.D. Aug. 28	771

B

Barbara, V.M. Dec. 4	553
Barnabas, Ap. June 11	680
Bartholomew, Ap. Aug. 24	767
Basil the Great, B.C.D. June 14	685
Basilides and Comp., MM. June 12	682
Bean, Ab. Oct. 26	940
Bede, Ven., C.D. May 27	667
Bee (Begh), V. Sept. 6	909
Benedict, Ab. Mar. 21	616
Benedict Biscop, Ab. Jan. 12 or 19, or Feb. 12	868
Bernard, Ab., D. Aug. 20	761
Bernardine of Siena, C. May 20	664
Beuno, Ab. Apr. 21	876
Bibiana, V.M. Dec. 2	552
Birinus, B.C. Dec. 5	886
Blaan, B.C. Aug. 11	937
Blasius, B.M. Feb. 3	591
Bonaventura, B.C.D. July 14	716
Boniface (Winfrid), B.M. June 5	677
Boniface, M. May 14	659
Botolph, Ab.C. June 17	891
Bridget, V. Feb. 1	869
Bridget, W. Oct. 8	812
Britius, B.C. Nov. 13	920
Bruno, C. Oct. 6	809

C

	PAGE
Cadoc, B.M. Sept. 25	910
Cajetan, C. Aug. 7	746
Callistus, Pope, M. Oct. 14	819
Camillus of Lellis, C. July 18	720
Canute, K.M. Jan. 19	571
Carthusian Martyrs. May 12	880
Casimir, C. Mar. 4	608
Catherine, V.M. Nov. 25	854
Catherine of Siena, V. Apr. 30	641
Cecilia, V.M. Nov. 22	849
Chad, B.C. Mar. 2	872
Chad, B.C. Translation. Tuesday in 4th week after Octave of Easter	888
Chair of St. Peter at Rome. Jan. 18	569
Chair of St. Peter at Antioch. Feb. 22	602
Charles Borromeo, B.C. Nov. 4	836
Christina, V.M. July 24	728
Christopher, M. July 25	729
Chrysanthus and Daria, MM. Oct. 25	830
Chrysogonus, M. Nov. 24	852
Clare, V. Aug. 12	754
Clement I, Pope, M. Nov. 23	851
Cletus and Marcellinus, BB., MM. Apr. 26	637
Colman, B.C. Feb. 18	925
Columba, Ab. June 9	932
Comgan, Ab. Nov. 27	940
Commemoration of All the Faithful Departed. Nov. 2	836
Constantine, M. Mar. 11	926
Cornelius and Cyprian, BB., MM. Sept. 16	789
Cosmas and Damian, MM. Sept. 27	799
Cungar, Ab. Nov. 27	919
Cuthbert, B.C. Mar. 20	874, 928
Cuthbert, B.C.. Translation. Sept. 4	909
Cuthbert Maine, M. Nov. 29	862
Cyprian, B.M. Sept. 26	799
Cyprian and Justina, MM. Sept. 26	799
Cyriacus and Comp., MM. Aug. 8	748
Cyril of Alexandria, B.C.D. Feb. 9	596
Cyril of Jerusalem, B.C.D. Mar. 18	613
Cyril and Methodius, BB.CC. July 7	711

D

Damasus I, Pope, C. Dec. 11	561
David, B.C. Mar. 1	871
Deiniol, B.C. Sept. 11	909
Denys and Comp., MM. Oct. 9	815
Didacus (Diego), C. Nov. 13	847
Dominic, C. Aug. 4	742
Donatus, B.M. Aug. 7	746
Donnan and Comp., MM. Apr. 17	930
Dorothy, V.M. Feb. 6	594
Douai Martyrs. Oct. 29	936

1*

Alphabetical Index of all Feasts

	PAGE
Drostan, Ab. July 11	936
Dunstan, B.C. May 19	883
Duthac, Ab. Mar. 8	925
Dubritius (Dyfrig), B.C. Nov. 14	916

E

Eata, B.C. Oct. 26	913
Eadbert, B.C. May 6	880
Edith, V. Sept. 16	909
Edmund, B.C., Translation of. June 9	890
Edmund, B.C. Nov. 16	917
Edmund, K.M. Nov. 20	919
Edmund Campion and Comp., MM. Dec. 1	864
Edward, K.C. Oct. 13	819
Edward, K.M. Mar. 18	873
Edward, K.M. Translation. June 20	920
Edward Powell and Comp., MM. July 30	902
Egbert, C. Apr. 24	877, 930
Egwin, B.C. Dec. 30	868
Eleutherius, Pope, M. May 26	665, 888
Elizabeth of Portugal, Q.W. July 8	712
Elizabeth of Hungary, W. Nov. 19	847
Emerentiana, V.M. Jan. 23	575
England and Wales, Martyrs of. May 4	878
Enurchus, B.C. Sept. 7	920
Ephraem Syrus, De., C.D. June 18	687
Erconwald, B.C. May 11 or 13	882
Ethelbert, K.C. Feb. 25 or 26	870
Ethelbert, K.M. May 20	854
Ethelburga, V. Oct. 12	911
Etheldreda, V. June 23	892
Etheldreda, V. Translation. Oct. 17	920
Euphemia and Comp., MM. Sept. 16	789
Eusebius, B.M. Dec. 16	562
Eusebius, C. Aug. 14	755
Eustace and Comp., MM. Sept. 20	794
Everard Hanse, M. July 30	902
Evaristus, Pope, M. Oct. 26	831
Evurtius, B.C. Sept. 7	920

F

Fabian, Pope, and Sebastian, MM. Jan. 20	572
Faith, V.M. Oct. 6	920
Faustinus and Jovita, MM. Feb. 15	602
Felicity, M. Nov. 23	851
Felix, B.C. Mar. 8	873
Felix I, Pope, M. May 30	670
Felix II, Pope and Comp., MM. July 29	735
Felix, P.M. Jan. 14	564
Felix and Adauctus, MM. Aug. 30	774
Felix of Valois, C. Nov. 20	848
Fillan, Ab. Jan. 19	924
Fidelis of Sigmaringen, M. Apr. 24	634
Finan, B.C. Feb. 17	924
Forty Martyrs of Sebaste. Mar. 10	611

	PAGE
Four Crowned Martyrs. Nov. 8	837
Frances of Rome, W. Mar. 9	611
Francis, C. Oct. 4	808
Francis, C. Stigmata. Sept. 17	790
Francis, Borgia, C. Oct. 10	817
Francis, Caracciolo, C. June 4	675
Francis of Paula, C. Apr. 2	625
Francis de Sales, B.C.D. Jan. 29	583
Francis Xavier, C. Dec. 3	552
Frideswide, V. Oct. 19	912
Fursey, Ab. Jan. 16	869

G

Gabriel, Archangel. Mar. 24	617
Gabriel of the Sorrowful Virgin, C. Feb. 27 or 28	606
George, M. Apr. 23	633
German, B.C. July 30 or 31, Aug. 3 or 11	902
Gertrude, V. Nov. 16	845
Gervasius and Protasius, MM. June 19	689
Gilbert, C. Feb. 16	870
Giles, Ab. Sept. 1	776
Gordian and Epimachus, MM. May 10	653
Gorgonius, M. Sept. 9	782
Gregory I, Pope, C.D. Mar. 12	612
Gregory VII, Pope, C. May 25	665
Gregory Nazianzen, B.C.D. May 9	652
Gregory Thaumaturgus, B.C. Nov. 17	846
Guardian Angels. Oct. 2	805

H

Hadrian, M. Sept. 8	781
Hadrian Fortescue, M. July 11	898
Hedda, B.C. July 7	895
Hedwig, W. Oct. 16	821
Helen, E.W. Aug. 18	905
Helerius, M. July 16	900
Henry, E.C. July 15	718
Hermenegild, M. Apr. 13	628
Hermes, M. Aug. 28	772
Hilarion, Ab. Oct. 21	826
Hilary, B.C.D. Jan. 14	564
Hilda, V. Nov. 17	919
Hildelitha and Cuthberga, VV. Sept. 4	908
Hippolytus and Cassian, MM. Aug. 13	754
Honorius, B.C. Sept. 30	910
Hugh, B.C. Nov. 17	918
Hugh Cook, Faringdon, Abb. and Comp., MM. Nov. 14	916
Hugh More, M. Sept. 1	907
Hyacinth, C. Aug. 17	760
Hyginus, Pope, M. Jan. 11	48

I

Ignatius, B.M. Feb. 1	585
Ignatius, C. July 31	736

Alphabetical Index of all Feasts [133]

	PAGE
Illtyd, Ab. Nov. 6	915
Innocents, Holy, MM. Dec. 28	30
Irenaeus, B.M. June 28	698
Isidore, B.C.D. Apr. 4	626

J

	PAGE
James, Ap. July 25	729
James and Philip, App. May 11	655
Jane Frances Fremiot de Chantal, W. Aug. 21	762
Januarius and Comp., MM. Sept. 19	792
Jerome, P.C.D. Sept. 30	804
Jerome Aemiliani, C. July 20	723
Joachim, Father of B.V.M. Aug. 16	759
John, Ap. Ev. Dec. 27	27
John ante Portam Latinam. May 6	649
John Baptist, Beheading of. Aug. 29	773
,, Nativity of. June 24	695
,, Nativity of. Vigil. June 23	693
John I, Pope, M. May 27	667
John Baptist de la Salle, C. May 15	659
John Beche, M. Dec. 1	865
John of Beverley, B.C. May 7	880
,, Oct. 25	880, 913
John Bosco, C. Jan. 31	584
John of Bridlington, C. Oct. 21	912
John Cantius, C. Oct. 20	825
John of Capistrano, C. Mar. 28	622
John Chrysostom, B.C.D. Jan. 27	580
John Cornelius and Comp., MM. July 4	895
John of the Cross, C. Nov. 24	852
John Damascene, C.D. Mar. 27	621
John Eudes, C. Aug. 19	761
John of San Fagondez, C. June 12	682
John Fisher, B. and Thomas More, MM. July 9	896
John of God, Ab. July 12	715
John Haile, M. May 21	884
John Houghton, M. May 12	881
John Larke, M. Mar. 11	873
John Mary Vianney, C., Ab. Aug. 9	749, 904
John Leonardi, C. Oct. 9	813
John of Matha, C. Feb. 8	896
John Ogilvie, M. Mar. 10	925
John Payne, M. Apr. 2, 3	875
John Roberts, M. Dec. 10	867
John Rochester and Comp., MM. May 11	881
John Wall, M. Aug. 26	906
Josaphat, B.M. Nov. 14	843
Joseph, Spouse B.V.M., C. Mar. 19	615
Joseph the Worker. May 1	642
Joseph of Calasanza, C. Aug. 27	770
Joseph of Cupertino, C. Sept. 18	791
Jude and Simon, App. Oct. 28	832
Juliana of Falconieri, V. June 19	688
Julius and Aaron, MM. July 3	895
Justus, B.C. Nov. 10	915
Justin Martyr. Apr. 14	629

K

	PAGE
Kenelm, K.M. July 17	900
Kenneth, Ab. Oct. 12	940
Kentigern, B.C. Jan 14 or 19	868, 923
Keyna, V. Oct. 8	911

L

	PAGE
Lambert, B.M. Sept. 17	920
Lammas Day. Aug. 1	737
Lawrence, M. Aug. 10	753
,, Vigil. Aug. 9	751
Lawrence, B.C. Feb. 3	870
Lawrence Justinian, B.C. Sept. 5	780
Leo I, Pope, C.D. Apr. 11	627
Leo II, Pope, C. July 3	709
Leonard, Ab. Nov. 6	920
Liborius, B.C. July 23	727
Linus, Pope, M. Sept. 23	798
Louis, K.C. Aug. 25	768
Luan, Ab. June 25	934
Lucian, P.M. Jan. 8	920
Lucius I, Pope, M. Mar 4	608
Lucy, V.M. Dec. 13	561
Luke, Ev. Oct. 18	823

M

	PAGE
Maccabees, MM. Aug. 1	737
Machar, B.C. Nov. 12	941
Machutus, B.M. Nov. 15	920
Maglorius (Malo), B.C. Oct. 24	913
Magnus, M. Apr. 16	929
Malrubius, Ab. Apr. 2	930
Marcellinus and Comp., MM. June 2	675
Marcellus I, Pope, M. Jan. 16	567
Marcus and Marcellianus, MM. June 18	687
Margaret, V.M. July 20	723
Margaret Mary Alacoque, V. Oct. 17	821
Margaret, Q.W. June 10	679
Margaret, Q.W. Nov. 16	942
Margaret Pole, M. May 28	887
Marius and Comp., MM. Jan. 19	571
Mark, Ev. Apr. 25	635
Mark, Pope, C. Oct. 7	811
Martha, V. July 29	733
Martin, B.C. Nov. 11	841
,, Translation. July 4	920
Martin I, Pope, M. Nov. 12	842
Martina, V.M. Jan. 30	584
Martyrs of England and Wales. May 4	878
Martyrs, Carthusian. May 12	880
Martyrs of Douai. Oct. 29 or 30	913
Martyrs, University of Oxford. Dec. 1	864
Mary Magdalene, Penitent. July 22	725
Mary Magdalen of Pazzi, V. May 29	670
Matthew, Ap., Ev. Sept. 21	795

Alphabetical Index of all Feasts

	PAGE
Matthias, Ap. Feb. 24 or 25	605
Maughold, B.C. Apr. 27	878
Maurice and Comp., MM. Sept. 22	796
Maurus, Ab. Jan. 15	566
Melchiades, Pope, M. Dec. 10	560
Mellitus, B.C.. Apr. 24	877
Mennas, M. Nov. 11	841
Michael, Archangel. Sept. 29	802
Michael, Appearance of. May 8	651
Milburga, V. Feb. 23	870
Mirin, B.C. Sept. 15	937
Monica, W. May 4	648

N

Nabor and Felix, MM. July 12	715
Nathalan, B.C. Jan. 19	924
Nazarius and Comp. July 28	733
Nereus and Comp., MM. May 12	657
Nicholas, B.C. Dec. 6	555
Nicholas of Tolentino, C. Sept. 10	783
Nicomede, M. June 1	920
Nicomede, M. Sept. 15	787
Ninian, B.C. Sept. 16	909, 938
Norbert, B.C. June 6	678

O

Oliver Plunket, B.M. July 11	898
Osburga, V. Mar. 30	875
Osmund, B.C. Dec. 4	865
Oswald, B.C. Feb. 28	871, 936
Oswald, K.M. Aug. 8, 9 or 11	902

P

Palladius, B.C. July 7	935
Pancras and Comp., MM. May 12	657
Pantaleon, M. July 27	732
Paschal Baylon, C. May 17	661
Patrick, B.C. Mar. 17	613
Patrick, B.C. (Scotland). Mar. 17	927
Paul, Ap., Conversion of. Jan. 25	577
" Commemoration of. June 30	703
Paul of the Cross, C. Apr. 28	638
Paul the First Hermit, C. Jan. 15	566
Paulinus, Bp. of Nola, C. June 22	691
Paulinus, Bp. of York, C. Oct. 10	911
Perpetua, and Felicitas, MM. Mar. 6 or 7	609
Peter and Paul, App. June 29	702
" " Vigil. June 28	700
Peter's Chains. Aug. 1	737
" Chair at Antioch. Feb. 22	602
" Chair at Rome. Jan. 18	569
Peter of Alcantara, C. Oct. 19	824
Peter of Alexandria, B.M. Nov. 26	855
Peter Canisius, C.D. Apr. 27	638
Peter Celestine, Pope, C. May 19	662

	PAGE
Peter Chrysologus, B.C.D. Dec. 4	553
Peter Damian, B.C.D. Feb. 23	604
Peter Martyr. Apr. 29	640
Peter Nolasco, C. Jan. 28	582
Petronilla, V. May 31	672
Philip and James, App. May 11	655
Philip Benizi, C. Aug. 23	765
Philip Neri, C. May 26	665
Pius I, Pope, M. July 11	714
Pius V, Pope, C. May 5	649
Pius X, Pope, C. Sept. 3	778
Placid and Comp., MM. Oct. 5	809
Polycarp, B.M. Jan. 26	579
Pontian, Pope, M. Nov. 19	847
Praxedes, V. July 21	724
Primus and Felician, MM. June 9	678
Prisca, V.M. Jan. 18	569
Processus and Martinian, MM. July 2	708
Protus and Hyacinth, MM. Sept. 11	783
Pudentiana, V. May 19	662

R

Ralph Sherwin, M. Dec. 1	865
Raphael, Archangel. Oct. 24	827
Raymund Nonnatus, C. Aug. 31	776
Raymund of Pennafort, C. Jan. 23	575
Relics, Sacred. Nov. 5	914
Remigius, B.C. Oct. 1	805
Richard, B.C. Apr. 3	875
Richard Gwyn, M. Oct. 16	912
Richard and Comp., MM. Nov. 15	916
Richard Reynolds, M. May 14	882
Richard Whiting and Comp., MM. Dec. 1	863
Robert, Ab. June 7	890
Robert Bellarmine, C.D. May 13	658
Romanus, M. Aug. 9	751
Romuald, Ab. Feb. 7	595
Rose of Lima, V. Aug. 30	774

S

Sabbas, Ab. Dec. 5	555
Sabina, M. Aug. 29	773
Sacred Relics. Nov. 5	914
Samson, B.C. July 28	902
Saturninus, M. Nov. 29	549
Scholastica, V. Feb. 10	598
Sebastian and Fabian, MM. Jan. 20	572
Sebastian Newdigate and Comp., MM. June 19	891
Sebbi, K.C. Sept 1	907
Sennen and Abdon, MM. July 30	735
Seven Brothers and Comp., MM. July 10	713
Seven Founders, CC. Feb. 12	600
Silverius, Pope, M. June 20	690
Silvester, Ab. Nov. 26	854

Alphabetical Index of all Feasts [135]

	PAGE		PAGE
Silvester I, Pope, C. Dec. 31	36	Titus, B.C. Feb. 6	594
Simeon, B.M. Feb. 18	602	Tryphon and Comp., MM. Nov. 10	839
Simon and Jude, App. Oct. 28	832	Twelve Brothers, MM. Sept. 1	776
Simon Stock, C. May 16	883		
Soter and Caius, Popes, MM. Apr. 22	632	**U**	
Stanislas, B.M. May 7	750	Ubald, B.C. May 16	660
Stephen, Proto-martyr. Dec. 26	24	Urban I, Pope, M. May 25	665
„ „ Finding of. Aug. 3	740	Ursula and Comp., VV.MM. Oct. 21	826
Stephen I, Pope, M. Aug. 2	739		
Stephen, K.C. Sept. 2	777	**V**	
Stephen Harding, Ab. Mar. 28, Apr. 17	874, 876	Valentine, P.M. Feb. 14	601
Susanna and Tiburtius, MM. Aug. 11	754	Venantius, M. May 18	661
Swithun, B.C. July 15	898	Vincent Ferrer, C. Apr. 5	626
Symphorosa and Seven Sons, MM. July 18	720	Vincent of Paul, C. July 19	722
		Vincent and Anastasius, MM. Jan. 22	575
		Vitalis, M. Apr. 28	639
T		Vitalis and Agricola, MM. Nov. 4	836
		Vitus and Comp., MM. June 15	686
Teilo, B.C. Feb. 9	870		
Telesphorus, Pope, M. Jan. 5	42	**W**	
Thecla, V.M. Sept. 23	798	*Walburga, V.* Feb. 25	870
Theodore, B.C. Sept. 19 or 26	910	Wenceslas, Duke, M. Sept. 28	801
Theresa, V. Oct. 15	820	*Werbergh, V.* Feb. 3	870
Theresa of the Infant Jesus, V. Oct. 3	806	*Wilfrid, B.C.* Oct. 12	911
Thomas, Ap. Dec. 21	563	William, Ab. June 25	697
Thomas Aquinas, C.D. Mar. 7	609	*William, B.C.* June 8	990
Thomas of Canterbury, B.M. Dec. 29	34	*Willibald, B.C.* June 7	890
„ „ Translation. July 7	895	*Willibrord, B.C.* Nov. 7	915
Thomas of Hereford, B.C. Oct. 3, 5, or 22	910	Winfrid (Boniface), B.M. June 5	677
Thomas More and John Fisher, B., MM. July 9	896	*Winifred, V.M.* Nov. 3	913
Thomas Percy, M. Aug. 26	906	*Wulstan, B.C.* Jan. 19	869
Thomas Plumtree and Comp., MM. Feb. 4	870		
Thomas of Villanova, B.C. Sept. 22	796	**X**	
Tiburtius and Susanna, MM. Aug. 11	754	Xystus II, Pope, and Comp., MM. Aug. 6	745
Tiburtius and Comp., MM. Apr. 14	629		
Timothy, B.M. Jan. 24	576	**Z**	
Timothy and Comp., MM. Aug. 22	764	Zephyrinus, Pope, M. Aug. 26	770

THE COMMON OF SAINTS

Of Supreme Pontiffs	[2]	Of Abbots	[26]
Of One Martyr outside Eastertide	[4]	Of Virgins	[28]
Of Many Martyrs outside Eastertide	[9]	Of those not Virgins	[34]
Of Martyrs in Eastertide	[15]	Of the Dedication of a Church	[38]
Of a Confessor Bishop	[19]	Of Feasts of B.V.M.	[41]
Of Doctors	[22]	Of St. Mary on Saturday	[42]
Of a Confessor not a Bishop	[24]		

VOTIVE MASSES

Of the Most Holy Trinity	[51]	Of all Holy Apostles	[56]
Of the Angels	[52]	Of the Holy Spirit	[58]
Of St. Joseph	[53]	Of the Blessed Sacrament	[59]
Of SS. Peter and Paul, App.	[55]	Of Jesus Christ the Eternal Priest	[61]

Alphabetical Index of all Feasts

	PAGE		PAGE
Of the Holy Cross	[62]	Against the Heathen	[73]
Of the Passion of the Lord	[64]	For the Ending of Schism	[75]
Of St. Mary	[42]	In Time of War	[76]
Of All Saints	835	For Peace	[78]
For the Election of the Chief Bishop	[66]	For Escaping Mortality or in Time of Pestilence	[79]
On the Day of the Creation and Coronation of a Pope	[67]	To ask the Grace of the Holy Spirit	[81]
		For the Remission of Sins	[81]
On the Consecration of a Bishop	[68]	For Travellers or Pilgrims	[82]
On the Anniversary of the Election and Consecration of a Bishop	[68]	For the Sick	[84]
		To ask the Grace of a Good Death	[86]
On Conferring Holy Orders	[69]	For any Necessity	[87]
For Bridegroom and Bride	[69]	For Giving of Thanks	[89]
For the Propagation of the Faith	[72]	Various Prayers	[90]

MASSES OF THE DEAD

Commemoration of All the Faithful Departed	[101]	In daily Masses of the Dead	[110]
On the Day of Death or Burial	[106]	Various Prayers	[112]
On the Third, Seventh, and Thirtieth Day	[106]	Absolution at funerals	[117]
On the Anniversary of the Dead	[108]	Absolution in absence of body	[123]

BLESSINGS

The Blessing of Water	[124]	The Blessing of Sacerdotal Vestments	[128]
,, ,, any Food	[127]	,, ,, Candles	[128]
,, ,, a Lamb at Easter	[127]	,, ,, Corporals	[129]
,, ,, New Fruits	[127]	,, ,, Altar-cloths	[129]
,, ,, Eggs	[127]	,, ,, Tabernacle or Vessel	[129]
,, ,, Bread	[127]